THE VAMPIRE IN FOLKLORE, HISTORY, LITERATURE, FILM AND TELEVISION

THE VAMPIRE IN FOLKLORE, HISTORY, LITERATURE, FILM AND TELEVISION

A Comprehensive Bibliography

Compiled by
J. Gordon Melton *and*
Alysa Hornick

McFarland & Company, Inc., Publishers
Jefferson, North Carolina

LIBRARY OF CONGRESS CATALOGUING-IN-PUBLICATION DATA

The vampire in folklore, history, literature, film and
television : a comprehensive bibliography /
compiled by J. Gordon Melton and Alysa Hornick.
p.   cm.
Includes bibliographical references and index.

ISBN 978-0-7864-9936-6 (softcover : acid free paper) ∞
ISBN 978-1-4766-2083-1 (ebook)

1. Vampires—Bibliography.   2. Vampires in mass media—
Bibliography.   I. Melton, J. Gordon, compiler.
II. Hornick, Alysa, 1981– compiler.

Z5983.V36V36 2015   [GR830.V3]   016.398'45—dc23   2015025779

BRITISH LIBRARY CATALOGUING DATA ARE AVAILABLE

Cover image iStock/Thinkstock

Printed in the United States of America

*McFarland & Company, Inc., Publishers
Box 611, Jefferson, North Carolina 28640
www.mcfarlandpub.com*

To our fellow bibliographers:
Martin Riccardo
Robert Eighteen-Bisang
Massimo Introvigne
Derek Badman
Don Macnaughtan
Roberto Labanti

Table of Contents

Introduction
by J. Gordon Melton

I initiated this bibliography several decades ago as part of an effort to get a handle on a growing personal collection of vampire books and a recognition of the emergence of vampire studies as an academic field of concern through the 1980s. As the centennial of the publication of *Dracula* (1997) approached and as I came to know Robert Eighteen-Bisang and of his effort to construct a comprehensive vampire bibliography, my original more-limited goal of simply managing a growing personal collection became one of assuming responsibility for the development of a comprehensive listing of non-fiction writing about vampires, especially the scholarly books and papers. This effort was given a significant boost by my being asked by the main publisher with whom I had worked in the 1980s, Gale Research, to do a vampire encyclopedia (published in 1994 as *The Vampire Book: The Encyclopedia of the Undead*) and led to two subsequent volumes—*VideoHound's Vampires on Video* (1997) and *The Vampire Gallery: A Who's Who of the Undead* (1998). At the same time, both Eighteen-Bisang and I were continually amazed at the blossoming of vampire studies that occurred through the 1990s, and remained surprised at the exponential increases observed in the new century. Meanwhile, I also worked with my Italian colleague Massimo Introvigne on the production of a comprehensive list of vampire comic books while following *The Vampire Book* with the reference book on vampire movies.

After more than two decades of bibliographic work, it seems that the time has come to bring the project to some culmination, even though the work of the bibliographer seems never to be completed. It is also a peculiar moment when even as the number of titles seems to be exploding, the great change in publishing marked by the transition both to publish-on-demand and digital electronic publishing has reached a tipping point. Almost all books are appearing in digital formats, many with no paper edition at all, and the majority of sales are shifting to the electronic market, though significant sales of paper books remain. This change provided both a disturbing shock to our bibliophile consciousness, but at the same time a welcome relief to those of us who have long since run out of space in our homes for personal libraries. The transition also provides a useful excuse to bring to some closure our lengthy effort to get an overview of the literature.

Thus it was that in 2013 I proposed the idea of a comprehensive listing of books (including dissertations and theses) and articles about vampires and vampire-related topics. Such a bibliography would follow upon the previous bibliographies I had published as well as draw on the work of several colleagues with whom I have previously conspired to create these bibliographies, primarily Robert Eighteen-Bisang and Massimo Introvigne, as well as several scholars who have done more detailed and specialized work, such as *Dark Shadows* scholar Jeff Thompson and especially Alysa Hornick, a Joss Whedon scholar, who graciously agreed to work with me on the *Buffy the Vampire Slayer* and *Angel* material that has come to represent such a large segment of the output of vampire studies in the last decade.

In compiling this bibliography, we have made every effort to personally view each item cited, a task that was made somewhat easier by beginning with my own large personal collection, which contains the majority of material cited, but very much supplemented by the access granted me over the years to the additional significant collections assembled by Eighteen-Bisang and Introvigne, as well as visits to a number of academic libraries, especially those at the University of California—Santa Barbara and Baylor University in Waco, Texas. For any items not seen, we have tried to locate an authoritative source, a process aided by the online publication of most academic library catalogs.

Citations

For each book citation below, we have endeavored to offer a full reference of useful information:

Author. *Title*. Place of publication: publisher, date of publication, number of pages, and format—hardback (hb), paperback (pb), trade paperback (tp). If issued with a dust jacket, that fact is noted (dj). Books that are 8½" × 11" or larger are listed as having been printed in a "Large format." Those smaller than a mass market paperback are listed as "Small format."

We have deviated somewhat in treating dissertations and theses as published monographs and citing them in a similar manner as books, and referring to the school at which the work was done as the publisher.

Author. Title. School location: Names of school, date, number of leaves (pages). Large format.

For journals and other periodicals:

Author. Title. *Name of periodical*. Volume, issue number (date): page numbers.

Where we have found a copy on the internet, we have listed the url. All of the sites were checked just prior to publication and were active at that time.

We have not attempted to annotate every citation, but many items cry out for some comment and some annotations have been made, especially to articles/papers that have been revised and reprinted multiple times.

Studies growing out of the immense attraction to *Buffy the Vampire Slayer* and its spin-off *Angel* have had an immense effect on vampire studies in general, with more than a fourth of all the academic comment on vampire-related subjects being generated by scholars who have focused on Joss Whedon and his artistic creations. The *Buffy* chapter in this work is by far the largest, and comment on *Buffy* now challenges comment on *Dracula* for dominance in the field of vampire studies.

The Scope of This Work: Definitional Questions

As it has evolved, this volume has been designed as an inclusive and comprehensive listing of non-fiction English-language books and articles on the vampire and related subjects. In compiling this listing, I initially had to have a working definition of the topic under consideration. Fortunately, from my previous work on *The Vampire Book*, I had dealt with this issue in an article on what is a vampire, the substance of which appears below:

WHAT IS A VAMPIRE?

The common dictionary definition of a vampire serves as a starting point for inquiry. A vampire is a reanimated corpse that rises from the grave to suck the blood of living people and thus retain a semblance of life. That description certainly fits Dracula, the most famous vampire, but is only a starting point and quickly proves inadequate in approaching the realm of vampire folklore. By no means do all vampires conform to that definition.

For example, while the subject of vampires almost always leads to a discussion of death, all vampires are not resuscitated corpses. Numerous vampires are disembodied demonic spirits. In this vein are the numerous vampires and vampire-like demons of Indian mythology and the *lamiai* of Greece. Vampires can also appear as the disembodied spirit of a dead person that retains a substantial existence; like many reported ghosts, these vampires can be mistaken for a fully embodied living corpse. Likewise, in the modern secular literary context, vampires sometimes emerge as a different species of intelligent life (possibly from outer space or the product of genetic mutation) or to otherwise normal human beings who have an unusual habit (such as blood-drinking) or an odd power (such as the ability to drain people emotionally). Vampire animals, from the traditional bat to the delightful children's characters Bunnicula and Count Duckula, are by no means absent from the literature. These vampires exist in a number of forms, although by far the majority of them are the risen dead.

As commonly understood, the characteristics shared by all of these vampire entities is their need for blood, which they take from living human beings and animals. A multitude of creatures from the world's mythology have been labeled vampires in the popular literature simply because periodic bloodsucking was among their many attributes. When the entire spectrum of vampires is considered, however, that seemingly common definition falls by the wayside, or, at the very least, must be considerably supplemented. Some vampires do not take blood, rather they steal what is considered the life force from their victims. A person attacked by a traditional vampire suffers the loss of blood, which causes a variety of symptoms: fatigue, loss of color in the face, listlessness, depleted motivation, and weakness. For example, left unchecked, tuberculosis is a wasting disease that is similar to the traditional description of the results of a vampire's attack.

Nineteenth century romantic authors and occultists suggested that real vampirism involved the loss of psychic energy to the vampire and wrote of vampiric relationships that had little to do with the exchange of blood. Dracula himself quoted the Bible in noting that "the blood is the life." Thus, it is not necessarily the blood itself that the vampire seeks but the psychic energy or "life force" believed to be carried by it. The metaphor of psychic vampirism can easily be extended to cover various relationships in which one party steals essential life elements from the other, such as when rulers sap the strength of the people they dominate.

On the other extreme, some modern "vampires" are simply blood drinkers. They do not attack and drain their victims, but obtain blood in a variety of legal manners (such as locating a willing donor or a source at a blood bank). In such cases, the consumption of the blood has little to do with any more-or-less ongoing relationship to the source of the blood. It, like food, is merely consumed. Often times, modern vampires even report getting a psychological or sexual high from drinking blood.

Once it is settled that "vampire" covers a wide variety of creatures, a second problem arises. As a whole, the vampires themselves are unavailable for direct examination. With a few minor exceptions, the subject matter of this volume is not vampires per se, but human belief about vampires and vampirism. That being the case, some methodology was needed for considering human belief in entities that objectively do not exist, indeed for understanding my own fascination with a fictional archetype. Not a new problem, the vast literature on vampirism favors one or two basic approaches. The first offers explanations in a social context. That is to say, the existence of vampires provides people with an explanation for otherwise inexplicable events (which in the modern West we tend to explain in scientific terms). The second approach is psychological and explains the vampire as existing in the inner psychic landscape of the individual. The two approaches are not necessarily exclusive of each other.

The worldwide distribution of creatures that can properly be termed "vampires" or have vampire-like characteristics suggests an approach that allows some semblance of order to emerge from the chaos of data. I begin with the obvious. The very different vampire-like creatures around the world function quite differently in their distinct cultures and environments. Thus, the *camazotz* of Central America shares several characteristics with the vampire of Eastern Europe, but each plays a distinct role in its own culture's mythology and is encountered in different situations. While a host of statues and pictures of the *camazotz* survived in Central America, no Eastern European peasant would think of creating such a memorial to the vampire. In each culture, the "vampire" takes on unique characteristics because each must be considered in its indigenous context.

Despite these cultural differences, there are common vampire types that seem to bridge cultural boundaries. For example, the *lamiai*, among the older of the Greek vampire creatures, seems to have arisen in response to the variety of problems surrounding childbirth. The *lamiai* attacked babies and very young children. Thus, otherwise unexplained deaths of a mother giving birth and/or her child could be attributed to vampires. This is similar to the function of the Indonesian *langsuyar* and the Jewish Lilith.

In like measure, vastly different cultures possessed a vampire who primarily attacked young women. Such vampires, which appeared repeatedly in the folklore of Eastern Europe, served a vital role in the process of social control. The stories of these young handsome male vampires warned maidens in their early post-pubescent years not to stray from the counsel of their elders and priests and to avoid glamorous visiting strangers who would only lead to disaster.

Another large group of vampires grew out of encounters with death, especially the sudden unexpected death of a loved one due to suicide, accident, or an unknown illness. People dying unexpectedly left relatives and friends behind with unfinished agendas with the deceased. Strong emotional ties and uncorrected wrongs felt by the recently deceased caused them to leave their resting place and attack family members, lovers, and neighbors against whom they might have had a grievance. If unable to reach a human target, they turned to the victim's food supply (i.e., livestock). Stories of attacks by those recently deceased adult vampires on their relatives and neighbors or their livestock directly underlie the emergence of the modern literary and cinematic vampire.

Leaving folktales behind, the literary vampire of the nineteenth century transformed the ethnic vampire into a cosmopolitan citizen of the modern imagination. The literary vampire interacted in new ways with human society. While the early literary vampires pictured by Goethe, Coleridge, Shelly, Polidori, Byron, and Nodier were basically parasites, possessing few traits to endear them to the people they encountered, nevertheless they performed a vital function by assisting the personification of the darker side possessed by human beings. The romantic poets of the nineteenth century assigned themselves the task, among others, of exploring the dark side of the human consciousness.

In the movement to the stage and screen, the vampire was further transformed. The demonic vampire gained some degree of human feelings, and even as a villain, possessed some admirable traits that brought the likes of Bela Lugosi a large and loyal following. Lugosi brought before the public an erotic vampire that embodied the release of the sexual urges that were so suppressed by Victorian society. In the original stage and screen presentations of Dracula, the vampire's bite substituted for the sexual activity that could not be more directly portrayed. This inherent sexuality of the vampire's attack upon its victims became more literally portrayed in the 1960s, on the one hand through new adult-oriented pornographic vampire movies and on the other in a series of novels and movies that centered upon a sensual seductive vampire. Frank Langella's *Dracula* (1979) and Gary Oldman's *Bram Stoker's Dracula* (1992) were outstanding examples of this latter type of seductive vampire.

The vampire's amazing adaptability accounts for much of its popularity. It served numerous vital functions for different people during previous centuries. For enthusiasts, today's vampire symbolizes important elements of their lives that they feel are being otherwise suppressed by the culture. The most obvious role thrust upon the contemporary vampire has been that of cultural rebel, a symbolic leader advocating outrageous alternative patterns of living in a culture demanding conformity. An extreme example of this new vampire is the vegetarian vampire, such as Bunnicula and Count Duckula, who introduces the vampire to children and who has emerged as an effective tool in teaching children tolerance of other children who are noticeably different.

A psychological approach to the vampire supplements an understanding of its social function. Twentieth-century psychotherapy discovered that modern post–Dracula vampires and vampiric relationships actively distorted their patients' lives. Out of the experiences reported to them, particularly the classic nightmare, many psychologists called attention to the role of specific common human psychological events in the creation and continual reinforcement of vampire beliefs. Psychologist Margaret Shanahan has noted the role of the vampire as a symbol of the widespread experience of inner emptiness she and her colleagues find in their clients. Such inner emptiness leads to a longing for emotional nutrients. Such longing can lead some to become food or inspire envy of those perceived to possess an abundance of nutrients (rich in the life force) and create an accompanying desire to steal that energy. In its most extreme form, such fixation can lead to various forms of blood consumption and even homicidal acts.

The various psychological approaches also explain some popular social pathologies, especially the common practice of scapegoating. Groups can be assigned characteristics of a vampire and treated accordingly with rhetoric that condemns them to the realms outside of social communion. If not checked, such rhetoric can lead to modern forms of staking and decapitation. Throughout the twentieth century, various groups have been singled out and labeled as "vampires." Women became "vamps," and bosses became bloodsuckers. Self-declared victims have branded a wide variety of social groups, rightly or wrongly, as their vampire oppressor.

These two approaches to the vampire seem to account for most of the phenomena of vampirism that I have encountered. Further, they suggest that the vampire (or its structural equivalent) was a universal figure in human culture, which emerged independently at many points in different societies. There is little evidence to suggest that the vampire emerged in one time and place and then diffused around the world from a primal source, a notable exception being the migration of the West African vampire to the Caribbean during the slave era.

The Scope of This Work: Practical Issues

When I began this work, the simple and, in retrospect, somewhat naive objective was to compile all of the non-fiction writing about the vampire, the primary goal being the compilation of a scholarly bibliography which would be useful to the growing number of colleagues who were engaging in vampire and Dracula studies. That simple task was complicated by the need to weed out of the bibliography the growing mass of popular discussions of the vampire that contributed little to our understanding of the vampire's permeation of the popular culture in the West and/or the significance of the rise of the vampire to such an important role in modern life and discourse. It was quite evident that primary interest rested in academically produced literature and the additional material by a variety of non-academic specialists, including local historians, librarians, journalists, and writers who had taken time to master one or more aspects of the vampire's presence in the modern world, and the unique contributions of professionals, from movie directors to novelists, artists, and musicians, who had insightful reflections from their involvement with a variety of vampire-related projects. Thus, the core of the bibliography became a comprehensive list of all the English-language non-fiction books that cover the subject, to which we have added the many scholarly articles published in journals or as chapters in books. Journalists, especially those working for magazines directed to a more popular audience, often cover aspects of vampires and vampirism not yet touched upon by scholars while providing useful commentary and raising questions for future scholarly consideration. Prior to the 1970s, journalism provided much of the content for the understanding of vampires in both the general public and the scholarly community.

Comment upon vampires in English begins in the first half of the nineteenth century but grew very slowly through the next century into the 1960s. Material on the vampire begins to increase significantly in the 1970s, with that increase continuing unabated to the present. Among scholars in the last generation, some periodicals have proved especially important in the emergence of vampire studies, and complete runs of these have been scanned and all of the vampire-related articles included in this bibliography. So included are:

Journal of Dracula Studies
The Bram Stoker Society Journal (1989–2001)
International Vampire
The Journal of Popular Culture
Slayage (online, 2005–present)
Watcher Junior (online, 2005–present)
All Slay

As the bibliography grew, it became necessary to exclude some items from what could easily become a massive and unmanageable list and thus it was decided not to include newspaper articles, most ephemera, and book and movie reviews (realizing that the line between reviews and more substantive scholarly articles commenting on books and movies is vague at best). Juvenile materials have been limited to nonfiction books directed to a juvenile audience, while excluding all juvenile periodical literature.

Of major concern in compiling this bibliography has been the recent large-scale transition from print to digital publication. Concentration has been upon print media, and relative to book-length publications, no special attempt has been made to include those books which were published only as e-books. It is the case that almost all books that have been printed in recent years have also been published in a digital format. It is also the case that an effort, spearheaded by the Gutenberg Project, has been made to create and publish on the internet all of the books that are in the public domain. Where a free copy of a book cited in this bibliography has been located on the Internet, a url for that book has been added to the bibliographical citation.

As with other new fields of inquiry, Internet-based scholarly journals in vampire studies (which have no print edition) have appeared as vital parts of the growth of the field, no more important one than Slayage, which has come to occupy such an important role in studies centered on Joss Whedon and Buffy the Vampire Slayer. Additional Internet-based journals in both vampire studies and related fields (film and television studies, for example) have been reviewed and cited in compiling this bibliography.

The movement of most library catalogues to an electronic format and the publication of the catalogues on the Internet has provided knowledge of and also given access to many doctoral dissertations, master's theses, and even undergraduate honors papers. We have included all known dissertations and theses on vampire and related topics. Increasingly, dissertations and theses are being produced as electronic documents and if we have been able to locate a copy on the Internet available to the general public, that url is cited. Normally, the library of the institution where it was completed retains a copy of all dissertations and theses written by its students. These are listed in the library catalogue, but most are available for electronic assess only to the college or university's local community, or for a fee. Copies must be accessed through more traditional means through the inter-library loan department at one's local library.

In compiling this bibliography, every effort has been made to include all of the relevant scholarly material produced over the last generation, especially the books, published articles, and conference papers. Many scholarly articles originate as papers delivered at a conference, and are later reprinted as a journal article or as an essay in a book or both. Where articles exist in various successive versions, the major citation is to the first print publication of its most recent text. As with books, if a free version of the paper/article is accessible on the Internet, the url of the publication is cited. As with dissertations and theses, almost all articles in recent years have been produced in electronic form, and most academic journals now have some presence online. However, most journal articles remain available only to subscribers or for a fee.

Timeline

This bibliography defined its timeline for inclusion to be 1800 to 2013. That time frame covers the first publications of vampire poetry, prose fiction and drama, the rise of comment on same, the beginnings of what would later be thought of as scholarly vampire literature among folklorists and psychologists, and the development of the vampire as a metaphor to cover various social phenomena. It concludes with the shift of vampire literature from almost exclusively paper publication to the emergence of the new digital formats.

As it evolved, *The Vampire in Folklore, History, Literature, Film and Television* has come to include more than 6,000 citations. Of these the largest number, not unexpectedly, relate to *Dracula* studies (1301 entries) scatted over several chapters concerned with literature and the cinema. The surprise to most of my colleagues has been the large number of works inspired by *Buffy the Vampire Slayer*, the single largest chapter in this work, with some 1283 citations. *Buffy* (including references to the related television show *Angel*) has emerged as the single television show provoking the most scholarly comment, far ahead of such notable shows as *Star Trek* or the *X-Files*.

Vampire Studies:
A Brief Overview

What we now think of as vampire studies begins as a response to a seeming wave of vampire attacks that plagued central Europe beginning in the last half of the 1600s. One case in particular came to the fore, that of Arnold Paul, a Serbian residing in an area recently added to the Austrian Empire. An army veteran, he had retired to his hometown of Medvegia, a small community north of Belgrade, in the spring of 1727, purchased several acres of land, and settled in as a farmer. Engaged to be married, Paul shared a dark secret with his betrothed. During his war days, he had encountered and been attacked by a vampire. Eventually, he had killed the vampire after following it to its grave. He also ate some of the dirt from the vampire's tomb and bathed his wounds in the blood of the vampire to cleanse himself of the effects of the attack. He was, however, still fearful of having been tainted by his encounter. A week after sharing the story of his vampire encounters, Paul was the victim of a fatal accident. Some three weeks after his burial, reports began to circulate of sightings of Paul around his village. When the four people who made the reports died, panic began to spread through the small Serbian community, and the local leaders decided to act to quell the panic. They had Paul's body disinterred to determine if their former neighbor was in fact a vampire. On the 40th day after the burial, the grave was opened. Two military surgeons were among those present as the lid was removed from the coffin. They discovered a body that appeared as if it had just recently died. What seemed to be new skin was present under a layer of dead skin, and the nails had continued to grow. The body was pierced, and blood poured forth. All agreed that Paul was a vampire, and they decided to stake his body to the ground. All heard Paul utter a loud groan as the stake went in. They completed their gruesome task by severing his head and burning his body.

The case could have (and should have) ended there, but it did not. The group moved on to the four other people who had recently died and treated them in a similar manner. No one wanted the deceased to reappear as vampires. Word spread through the countryside of what had occurred. Thus, a few years later when some 17 people died of similar symptoms indicating vampirism over a three-month period, the townspeople remembered the Arnold Paul incident. They were hesitant to act, but then one girl in town complained that one of the recently deceased, a man named Milo, attacked her in the middle of the night.

As the community began to deal with their problem, news of this second wave of vampirism reached Vienna, and the Austrian Emperor ordered an inquiry to be conducted by

Regimental Field Surgeon Johannes Fluckinger. Appointed on December 12, Fluckinger headed for Medvegia and began to gather accounts of what had occurred. Milo's body was disinterred and it was discovered in a state similar to that of Arnold Paul's; the body was then staked and burned.

Fluckinger posed a question: "How was it possible that the vampirism that had been eradicated in 1727 had returned?" The initial investigation determined that Paul had vampirized several cows that the recently dead had fed on. Under Fluckinger's orders, the townspeople then proceeded to dig up the bodies of all who had died in recent months. They disinterred some 40 bodies and found 17 to be in the same preserved state as had Paul's body. They staked and burned the bodies.

Upon his return to Vienna, Fluckinger wrote a full report of his activities that he presented to the Emperor early in 1732. His report was soon published and became a bestseller across Europe. The account of Arnold Paul and the Medvegia vampires appeared in periodicals in France and England. The well-documented nature of the case made it the focus of scholarly rumination on the possible existence of vampires. The stories would prompt a lively debate at the university at Leipzig and lead to the consideration of vampirism in books by Dom Augustin Calmet and Giuseppe Davanzati, two Roman Catholic scholars whose career peaked in the middle of the century. Their largely negative conclusions coincided with the drop-off in the number of reports of incidents of vampirism, at least from the lands of the Austrian Empire. In the early editions of his book covering vampires, however, Calmet, in listing all the alternatives for understanding the reports, presented just the slightest possibility that vampires, in fact, might exist. Thus the first wave of vampire studies, while largely reaching a negative conclusion, had left the door open to further reception of reports of vampirism and certainly to speculations about vampires in the salons of Paris.

Here the matter was left as scholars turned their attention elsewhere. In the meantime, the idea of the vampire entered the English-speaking world, where it was discovered by the Romantics and transformed into a popular topic in poetry, prose fiction, and stage drama. Through the nineteenth century, the literature on vampires received almost no scholarly comment, being considered a rather low form of writing for popular consumption, beneath the level of literature worthy of academic consideration. However, by the end of the century, within one field of inquiry, psychology, recognition of the vampiric nature of some abnormal human behaviors began to prompt comment following the publication of Richard von Krafft-Ebing's pioneering work *Psychopathia Sexualis*. Initially published in 1886, it was translated and published in English in 1903. Krafft-Ebing would become the fountainhead of a sporadically produced set of psychological literature on human pathology that shared multiple characteristics with the vampire. A whole new set of such literature proliferated at the end of the twentieth century.

Closely related to the abnormal psychology literature, within Spiritualist and occult esoteric circles, a new consideration of vampirism arose alongside that of spiritual healing. If healing involved the exchange of spiritual energies, it was reasoned, so a negative form of energy exchange could seemingly occur. Not only could one receive energy for healing, but one's energy could be stolen, thus causing a loss of health. Such energy vampirism became a matter of concern within esoteric communities, and many Spiritualists, theosophists, and ritual magicians felt compelled to comment upon what they considered more than a mere possibility. Their initial comments, in some cases quite extensive, would become the basis of a continuing perspective on vampires and vampirism and underlies both the current proliferation of the literature on "psychic vampirism" and the more pervasive perspective on vampirism within the contemporary community of "real" vampires—the individuals who consider themselves to be vampires.

Prior to the 1970s, little attention was paid to the whole topic of vampires apart from the several very specialized consideration provided by psychologists and occultists. The one exception was the independent (some would say eccentric) scholar Montague Summers. A former Anglican priest, he left the Church of England after accusations of his having sexual relations with some underage boys. He reemerged later as an independent Catholic priest and through much of his life made his living as the author of non-fiction books on such topics as Satanism and witchcraft. He is perhaps best remembered for having translated the medieval witch-hunter's manual, the *Malleus Maleficarum* (aka *The Hammer of Witches*), which so affected the sixteenth- and seventeenth-century European anti-witch crusade.

In the 1920s, Summers turned his attention to vampires and produced two still important books, *The Vampire: His Kith and Kin* (1928) and *The Vampire in Europe* (1929), in which he surveyed the whole field of the interest in vampires including both the folklore and the popular literary and stage vampire of the previous century. Given the pioneering nature of his work, there being little secondary literature on the subject, one continues to be amazed with the comprehensive nature of his survey of the field. For the next half century, Summers was the basic reference book for anyone interested in the topic (and remains required reading for anyone who would consider him/herself an accomplished vampire scholar).

Through the first two-thirds of the twentieth century, vampires and vampirism were topics for the academic fringe. Few and far between were anything resembling a learned treatment of the subject, such as Ernest Jones' psychoanalytical text *On the Nightmare* (1931), which included some substantive commentary on vampirism. Interest in vampires was at best a forbidden pleasure for those addicted to horror novels and movies. That situation would not change until the 1970s.

In 1972, three scholars would offer a new approach to the vampire. From California, literary scholar Leonard Wolf, professor of English at San Francisco State University, published *A Dream of Dracula: In Search of the Living Dead*, which began the process of recovering the novel as an object of academic interest. About the same time, two Boston University historians, Raymond McNally and Radu Florescu, produced the results of their investigation of the real Dracula, Romania's fifteenth-century Prince Vlad the Impaler—*In Search of Dracula*. Their book, recounting their enthusiastic discovery that the literary Count Dracula might have a basis in the career of Vlad did more than any other writing in creating a new field of vampire studies, initially located as an emerging field of interest within Victorian Gothic studies. That emergent interest was initially focused at the International Association for the Fantastic in the Arts and within the Lord Ruthven Assembly (named for the vampire in William Polidori's original vampire novella), a unit within the association for those especially attracted to Dracula and vampires.

The 1970s and 1980s saw the appearance of a host of new vampire scholars, most from college and university English departments including Canadians like Elizabeth Miller, Carol Margaret Davison, and Devendra P. Varma, British scholars like William Hughes and Christopher Frayling, and Americans such as Glennis Byron, Phillis Roth, Carol Senf, and Stephanie Moss. The field was also enlarged by the presence of a number of independent scholars such as Richard Dalby, Bernard Davies, Margaret Carter, David Skal, Clive Leatherdale, Albert Powers, and Leslie Shepard.

The new field of vampire and Dracula studies appeared just as a significant transformation of the vampire occurred. At the end of the 1960s, what are now recognized as two distinctly different forms of the literary vampire were introduced—the good guy vampire and the conflicted vampire. The former, actually introduced as a comic book character, Vampirella, was a traditional hero/heroine who happened to exist on blood but in most ways was to be admired and even loved. The good guy vampire took more substantive form in 1976 with Fred Saberhagen's good guy version of Dracula in his delightful *The Dracula Tape* (1976) and then more notably in the person of the Comte Saint Germain, the main character in a series of novels by Chelsea Quinn Yarbro. Saint Germain initially appeared in *Hotel Transylvania* in 1978. The good guy vampire would become the staple of both paranormal romance novels and young adult fiction. Contemporaneously, the conflicted vampire, a vampire who retains enough humanity to agonize over the ethical issue of having to kill in order to continue its existence, was introduced in the person of Barnabas Collins, the vampire of the daytime television soap opera *Dark Shadows* (1966–1971). The character type was then picked up and developed by Anne Rice in the first of her vampire novels *Interview with the Vampire* (1976).

Prior to the introduction of the good guy vampire and conflicted vampire, the vampire was a rather limited fictional character. A traditional monster, it was either a lone villain, like *Dracula*, or part of an impersonal zombie-like herd, as inhabited Richard Matheson's *I Am Legend*. The traditional vampire had only one destiny—a lonely existence driven by obtaining blood, culminating in violent destruction.[1] Both of the new vampire types, however, were capable of community and the full range of human emotions, and relationships, many of which could be continued over centuries. The possibilities were infinite and writers were quick to mine them. By the end of the 1980s the number of vampire novels produced annually began to increase dramatically and the growth curve has continued through the first decade of the new century to the present. The growing number of worthy pieces of vampire fiction, amid the great mass of very forgettable vampire novels, would coincide with the further development of scholarly interest in both Victorian and Gothic literature, but most importantly with the birth of widespread academic interest in popular culture, especially film and television. During the 1990s, a number of new departments of the visual arts were founded, which coincided with the appearance of a wave of studies on both, amid which interest in horror movies in general and vampire movies in particular was noticeable. The popularity of the vampire led to its becoming a stand-alone specialized topic of interest within a range of other related topics.

The host of new scholars of television studies, of which we became aware from the many books and articles on shows like *Star Trek* and *The X-Files*, were in place as *Buffy the Vampire Slayer* became an unexpected hit at the end of the 1990s. Word of the substantive nature of the show spread quickly within academia, and in 2002, a group of young scholars at the University of East Anglia organized an initial conference, "Blood, Text and Fears: Reading Around *Buffy the Vampire Slayer*," which attracted scholars from across Europe and North America, and from as far away as Australia. By this time, the first of several dozen anthologies of scholarly articles on *Buffy* had been published by Roz Kaveney, *Reading the Vampire Slayer: An Unofficial Critical Companion to* Buffy *and* Angel (2001). The overwhelming response to the East Anglia conference would lead to the first "Slayage Conference on *Buffy the Vampire Slayer*," held in Nashville, Tennessee, in 2004, with some 400 scholars in attendance. Out of the Nashville conference a new sub-field of *Buffy* Studies would be organized with its own journal and regular conference that continues to the present (though the emphasis has evolved into a more general consideration of the entire corpus of the works of *Buffy*-creator Joss Whedon).[2]

The growth of studies of vampires, *Dracula*, and *Buffy* has continued, and while the primary interest remains in English literature, film, and television studies, it now has penetrated most all of the academic disciplines. In the wake of the discontinuance of *Buffy the Vampire Slayer* and *Angel*, interest in the young adult Twilight Saga novels of Stephenie Meyer (the subject of five blockbuster movies), and the Sookie Stackhouse novels of Charlaine Harris (brought to television as *True Blood*) has added considerably to scholarly perspectives on the permeation of the vampire in Western culture, while interest in *Dracula*, the single literary work most often adapted to the screen (more than 40 times), shows no signs of waning. The increasing interest in vampires among young adults, coupled with the manifest fascination of all things vampiric among scholars, suggests that an expanding presence of the vampire in the academic realm is in our future.

Notes

1. While the traditional vampire was somewhat limited, the possibilities for new vampire stories featuring it has remained (a fact amply demonstrated in the writings of Stephen King), and the growth of the good guy and conflicted vampire has not diminished the appearances of the bad guy vampire in the least.

2. On the popularity of *Buffy the Vampire Slayer* among academics writing on popular culture in general and television in particular, see Daniel Lametti, Aisha Harris, Natasha Geiling, and Natalie Matthews-Ramo, "Which Pop Culture Property Do Academics Study the Most? (2012). Posted at: http://www.slate.com/blogs/browbeat/2012/06/11/pop_culture_studies_why_do_academics_study_buffy_the_vampire_slayer_more_than_the_wire_the_matrix_alien_and_the_simpsons_.html. Accessed July 5, 2014.

A Vampire Timeline, with Special Reference to Literature, Stage Drama, the Cinema and Television, 1800–2013

1800

I Vampiri, an opera by Silvestro de Palma, opens in Milan, Italy.

1801

"Thalaba" by Robert Southey is the first poem to mention the vampire in English.

1810

"The Vampyre," an early vampire poem, by John Stagg is published.

1813

Lord Byron's epic poem "The Giaour" includes the hero's encounter with a vampire.

1816

Samuel Taylor Coleridge publishes his still unfinished "Cristabel," written in the 1790s, the first vampire-themed poem in English.

1819

John Polidori's "The Vampyre," the first prose vampire story in English, is published in the April issue of *New Monthly Magazine*.

John Keats composes two vampire-themed poems, "The Lamia," a poem built on ancient Greek legends, and "La Belle Dame sans Merci" (or, "The Beautiful Lady Without Mercy").

1820

Lord Ruthwen ou Les Vampires by Cyprien Berard is published anonymously in Paris.

Le Vampire, the play by Charles Nodier, opens at the Theatre de la Porte Saint-Martin in Paris.

The Vampire; or, The Bride of the Isles, a translation of Nodier's play now reset in Scotland, by James R. Planche, opens in London.

1829

Heinrich Marschner's opera, *Der Vampyr*, based on Nodier's play, opens in Liepzig.

1841

Alexey Tolstoy publishes his short story, "Upyr," while living in Paris. It is the first modern vampire story by a Russian.

1847

"Varney the Vampire" begins its lengthy serialization as a Penny Dreadful novel.

Bram Stoker is born.

1851

Alexandre Dumas' last dramatic work, *Le Vampire*, opens in Paris.

1872

"Carmilla," a novella about a female vampire, is penned by Sheridan Le Fanu.

1888

Emily Gerard's *Land Beyond the Forest* is published. It will become a major source of information about Transylvanian vampire folklore for Bram Stoker's *Dracula*.

1894

H. G. Wells' short story "The Flowering of the Strange Orchid," the story of a blood-sucking plant, and a precursor to science fiction vampire stories.

1897

Dracula, the novel by Bram Stoker, is published in England.

1898

"The Vampire," a poem by Rudyard Kipling, inspired by the painting by Philip Burne-Jones, first exhibited at the new gallery in London in 1897, will in turn inspire the creation of the vamp as a stereotypical character on stage and screen

1913

"Dracula's Guest" by Bram Stoker is published by his widow.

1922

Nosferatu, a German-made silent film produced by Prana Films, is the first attempt to film *Dracula*.

1924

Hamilton Dean's stage version of *Dracula* opens in Derby.

Sherlock Holmes has his only canonical encounter with a vampire in "The Case of the Sussex Vampire."

1927

Hamilton Dean's stage version of *Dracula* debuts at the Little Theatre in London, and shortly thereafter the revised American version, with Bela Lugosi, opens at Fulton Theatre in New York City.

In Hollywood, Tod Browning directs Lon Chaney in *London After Midnight*, no copies of which are known to have survived to the present.

1928

The first edition of Montague Summers's influential work *The Vampire: His Kith and Kin* appears in England.

1929

Montague Summers's second vampire book, *The Vampire in Europe*, is published.

1931

The American film version of *Dracula* with Bela Lugosi, the first vampire talkie, premiers at the Roxy Theatre in New York City.

The Spanish film version of *Dracula* is previewed.

1932

The highly acclaimed movie *Vampyr*, directed by Carl Theodor Dreyer, is released.

1936

Dracula's Daughter is released by Universal Pictures.

1942

A. E. Van Vought's "Asylum" is the first story about an alien vampire.

1943

Son of Dracula (Universal Pictures) stars Lon Chaney, Jr., as Dracula.

1944

John Carradine make his first of many cinema appearances as Dracula in the movie *House of Dracula*.

1953

Drakula Istanbula, a Turkish film adaptation of "Dracula," is released. It identifies Count Dracula with Vlad Tepes.

Eerie no. 8 includes the first comic book adaptation of "Dracula."

1954

The Comics Code banishes vampires from comic books.

I Am Legend by Richard Matheson presents vampirism as a disease that alters the body.

1956

John Carradine plays Dracula in the first television adaptation of the play for *Matinee Theatre*. No copy survives.

Kyuketsuki Ga, the first Japanese vampire film, is released.

1957

The first Italian vampire movie, *I Vampiri*, is released.

American producer Roger Corman makes the first science fiction vampire movie, *Not of This Earth*.

El Vampiro with German Robles is the first of a new wave of Mexican vampire films.

1958

The British company Hammer Films initiates a new wave of interest in vampires with the first of its *Dracula* films, released in the United States as the *Horror of Dracula*.

1959

Plan 9 from Outer Space is Bela Lugosi's last film.

1961

The Bad Flower is the first Korean film adaptation of *Dracula*.

1962

The Count Dracula Society is founded in the United States by Donald Reed.

1964

Parque de Juelos (*Park of Games*) is the first Spanish-made vampire movie.

The Munsters, a horror comedy featuring two vampire characters, begins its two-year run on television.

1965

Jeanne Keyes Youngson founds The Count Dracula Fan Club (now known as the Vampire Empire).

The Munsters, based on the television show of the same name, is the first comic book series featuring a vampire character.

1966

Dark Shadows debuts as an afternoon soap opera on American television.

Paperback Library launchers publication of a series of gothic novels based on *Dark Shadows* written by Canadian author Dan Ross, using the pen name Marilyn Ross. The series, eventually 32 novels, heralds the later development of vampire-themed romance fiction.

1967

In episode 210 of *Dark Shadows*, vampire Barnabas Collins makes his first appearance.

1969

First issue of *Vampirella*, the longest running English-language vampire comic series to date, is released.

Denholm Elliot plays the title role in a BBC television production of *Dracula*.

Does Dracula Really Suck? (aka *Dracula and the Boys*) is released as the first gay vampire movie.

1970

Christopher Lee stars in *El Conde Dracula*, the Spanish film adaptation of *Dracula*.

Sean Manchester founds The Vampire Research Society.

1971

Marvel Comics releases the first copy of a post–Comics Code vampire comic book, *The Tomb of Dracula*. That same year, Morbius, the Living Vampire, becomes the first new vampire character introduced after the revision of the Comics Code allowed the reappearance of vampires in comic books.

1972

In Search of Dracula by Raymond T. McNally and Radu Florescu introduces Vlad the Impaler, the historical Dracula, to the world of contemporary vampire fans in the Western world. *A Dream of Dracula* by Leonard Wolf complements McNally's and Florescu's effort in calling attention to vampire lore.

The Night Stalker with Darrin McGavin becomes the most watched television movie to that point in time. The following year, Richard Matheson receives the Edgar Allan Poe Award from the Mystery Writers of America for his screenplay.

Vampire Kung-Fu is released in Hong Kong as the first of a string of vampire martial arts films.

True Vampires of History by Donald Glut is the first attempt to assemble the stories of all the historical vampire figures.

Stephan Kaplan founds the Vampire Research Centre.

1973

Nancy Garden's *Vampires* launches a wave of juvenile literature for children and youth.

1974

Dan Curtis Productions' version of *Dracula* starring Jack Palance and with a script by Richard Matheson, a made-for-television movie, finally airs after its original slot was pre-empted for a speech by President Richard Nixon. It is the first of the many *Dracula* movies to identify Dracula with Vlad Tepes.

1975

Fred Saberhagen proposes viewing Dracula as a hero rather than a villain in his novel *The Dracula Tape*.

The World of Dark Shadows is founded as the first *Dark Shadows* fanzine.

Stephen King's second novel, *'Salem's Lot*, depicts a monstrous vampire modeled somewhat on Count Orlock who attacks a small town in Maine.

1976

Interview with the Vampire by Anne Rice is published.

Stephen King is nominated for the World Fantasy Award for his vampire novel, *'Salem's Lot*.

Shadowcon, the first national *Dark Shadows* convention, is organized by *Dark Shadows* fans.

Dracula Began by Gail Kimberly is the first novel tying Count Dracula to the historical Vlad Tepes.

1977

A new dramatic version of *Dracula* opens on Broadway starring Frank Langella. It would win two Tony Awards, one for Most Innovative Production of a Revival and one to artist Edward Gorey for Best Costume Design. Frank Langella also receives a nomination for best actor.

Louis Jordan stars in the title role in *Count Dracula*, a three-hour version of Bram Stoker's book on BBC television.

Martin V. Riccardo founds the Vampire Studies Society based in suburban Chicago, Illinois.

1978

Chelsea Quinn Yarbro's book *Hotel Transylvania* joins the volumes of Fred Saberhagen and Anne Rice as the third major effort to begin a reappraisal of the vampire myth during the decade.

Les Daniels issues *The Black Castle*, the first volumes of the Don Sebastian vampire novels.

Eric Held and Dorothy Nixon found the Vampire Information Exchange.

1979

Based on the success of the new Broadway production, Universal Pictures remakes *Dracula*, starring Frank Langella. It joins *Love at First Bite* as one of several outstanding vampire films released during the year.

The band Bauhaus's recording of "Bela Lugosi's Dead" becomes the first hit of the new Gothic rock music movement.

Shadowgram is founded as a *Dark Shadows* fanzine.

1980

Suzy McKee Charnas's *The Vampire Tapestry* will become one of the more heralded vampire novels of the century.

The Bram Stoker Society is founded in Dublin, Ireland.

The World Federation of *Dark Shadows* Clubs (now *Dark Shadows* Official Fan Club) is founded.

1983

Catherine Deneuve, David Bowie, and Susan Sarandon star in *The Hunger*, a cinematic adaptation of the novel by Whitley Strieber. The film featured the song "Bela Lugosi's Dead," performed by Bauhaus.

In the December issue of *Dr. Strange*, Marvel Comics' ace occultist, kills all of the vampires in the world, thus banishing them from Marvel Comics for the next six years.

Dark Shadows Festival is founded to host an annual *Dark Shadows* convention.

1985

The Vampire Lestat, Anne Rice's sequel to *Interview with the Vampire*, is published and reaches the best-seller list.

1987

The Lost Boys opens as the most heralded vampire movie of the year. It will later spawn sequels, but they do not enjoy the original's success.

1988

Ronald Chetwynd-Hayes, who has authored a number of vampire short stories, is awarded the Bram Stoker life-time achievement award. The Bram Stoker Awards were introduced the previous year by the Horror Writers' Association. Vampire books and stories will regularly be nominated, but few will receive an award.

1989

Nancy Collins wins a Bram Stoker Award for her vampire novel *Sunglasses After Dark*, as does Dan Simmons for *Carrion Comfort*.

The Lord Ruthven Society, a vampire-oriented group within the International Association for the Fantastic in the Arts and named for the vampire character in William Polidori's "The Vampyre," begins issuing an annual award for the outstanding work in vampire fiction. The first award goes to Brian Stableford, for his novel *The Empire of Fear*.

1990

Richard Matheson, the author of *I Am Legend* and screenwriter for the television production of *Dracula* starring Jack Palance, receives the Bram Stoker life-time achievement award.

P. N. Elrod releases *Bloodlist*, the first of a dozen *Vampire Files* urban fantasy novels, featuring the private detective and vampire Jack Fleming.

The Lord Ruthven Society's annual fiction award goes to Nancy A. Collins for *Sunglasses After Dark*.

1991

"Vampire: The Masquerade," the most successful of the vampire role-playing games, is released by White Wolf.

1992

Bram Stoker's Dracula, directed by Francis Ford Coppola, opens. It will join the 1931 *Dracula* with Bela Lugosi, the 1958 *Horror of Dracula* with Christopher Lee, and the 1979 version with Frank Langella, as one of the most influential of *Dracula* movies. It will also initiate a series of vampire movies indicative of the vampire's penetration of popular culture by entering the list of highest grossing films of all time.

Fantasy/romance writer Laurell K. Hamilton issues *Guilty Pleasures*, the first of a series of novels featuring vampire hunter *Anita Blake: Vampire Hunter*, described as a professional zombie raiser, vampire executioner, and supernatural consultant for the police. By 2013, she will write more than two dozen Anita Blake books.

The original *Buffy the Vampire Slayer* movie opens to very mixed reviews.

1993

The Lord Ruthven Society's annual fiction award goes to Kim Newman for *Anno Dracula*.

1994

The film version of Anne Rice's *Interview with the Vampire* opens with Tom Cruise as the Vampire Lestat and Brad Pitt as Louis as the next top ten grossing vampire movie of all time. It will be the first vampire movie to gross more than $100,000,000.

Christopher Lee, who has stared in seven movies as Dracula, is awarded the Bram Stoker Life-Time Achievement award.

The Lord Ruthven Society begins issuing an award for best nonfiction book. The first award goes to David J. Skal for *The Monster Show: A Cultural History of Horror*.

1995

Four important vampire movies are released: *Vampire in Brooklyn*, *Dracula: Dead and Loving It*, *Nadja*, and *The Addiction*.

Interview with the Vampire wins multiple Saturn Awards presented by the Academy of Science Fiction, Fantasy & Horror Films, including best horror film.

The Lord Ruthven Society's annual nonfiction award goes to J. Gordon Melton for *The Vampire Book: The Encyclopedia of the Undead*.

1996

From Dusk Till Dawn, written by Quentin Tarantino and starring George Clooney, opens nationwide.

The Lord Ruthven Society's annual fiction award goes to Barbara Hambly for *Traveling with the Dead*, while the nonfiction award goes to Nina Auerbach for *Our Vampires, Ourselves*.

1997

The centennial of the publication of *Dracula* is celebrated with multiple events in England, Ireland, and North America, among which the American and Canadian chapters of the Transylvanian Society of Dracula join with the Count Dracula Fan Club to organize Dracula '97, a large event held in Los Angeles.

Young actors Sarah Michelle Gellar, Nicholas Brendon, Alyson Hannigan, and David Boreanaz join veteran Anthony Stewart Head to star in a new TV series, *Buffy the Vampire Slayer*, which will remake the culture's perception of the vampire myth.

The Lord Ruthven Society's annual fiction award goes to Jonathan Nasaw for *The World on Blood*, while the nonfiction award goes to David J. Skal for *V is for Vampire: An A to Z Guide to Everything Undead*.

1998

Christopher Golden and Nancy Holder collaborate initially on a *Buffy the Vampire Slayer* novel, *Blooded*. Both will go on to do multiple *Buffy*-related books, both fiction and non-fiction, both together and separately.

Blade, starring Wesley Snipes, an adaptation from Marvel's *Tomb of Dracula* comic book, become the vampire blockbuster of the year and joins the top 20 highest grossing vampire movies, all of which have earned more than $40 million.

The Lord Ruthven Society's annual fiction award goes to Chelsea Quinn Yarbro for *Writ in Blood*, while the nonfiction award goes to Carol Margaret Davison and Paul Simpson-Housley for *Bram Stoker's Dracula: Sucking Through the Century*.

1999

Paranormal romance writer Christine Feehan releases *Dark Prince*, the first of more than two dozen vampire novels in her Carpathian series. The Carpathians are pictured as a powerful and ancient race who feed on human blood, but solve the ethical problem by not killing the humans upon whom they feed and among whom they reside.

The growing popularity of *Buffy the Vampire Slayer* leads to a spinoff, *Angel*, built around a good vampire trying to find redemption for the evil of his past. About the same time, the first scholarly reflections on *Buffy* begin to appear.

The Lord Ruthven Society's annual fiction award goes to P. N. Elrod for *The Vampire Files: A Chill in the Blood*, while the nonfiction award goes to Carol A. Senf for *Dracula: Between Tradition to Modernism*.

2000

Steven Katz wins the Bram Stoker Award for the best screenplay for *Shadow of the Vampire*, while Richard Laymon receives the award for the best novel for *Traveling Vampire Show*.

The Shadow of a Vampire opens to critical acclaim, but less success at the box office.

Joss Whedon, the creator and writer for *Buffy the Vampire Slayer*, wins an Emmy Award for Outstanding Writing for a Drama Series.

The Lord Ruthven Society's annual fiction award goes to British fantasy writer Terry Pratchett for his novel *Carpe Jugulum*.

2001

Buffy the Vampire Slayer series is initially recognized by the Horror Writers Association who give the Bram Stoker Award to Yvonne Navarro for a novel directed to young readers called *The Willow Files 2*.

The Lord Ruthven Society's annual fiction award goes to Elaine Bergstrom for her sequel to *Dracula, Blood to Blood: The Dracula Story*, while the nonfiction award goes to Canadian Dracula scholar Elizabeth Miller for *Dracula: Sense and Nonsense*.

2002

Blade II opens, and revenues will out-gross the original *Blade* movie (1998).

The University of East Anglia (UK) hosts "Blood, Text and Fears," the first academic conference devoted to *Buffy the Vampire Slayer*. It will be the first of a number of similar conferences held in the United Kingdom, Australia, and the United States over the next decade.

In recognition of the growing interest in vampire fiction in general and vampire romance novels in particular, the industry periodical *Romantic Times* initiates an annual "best vampire romance" novel award. The first award goes to Sherrilyn Kenyon for *Night Pleasures*.

Anticipating the future success of the series, Charlaine Harris' first Sookie Stackhouse novel, *Dead Until Dark* (released 2001), wins the Anthony Award given to the Best Paperback Mystery of the year.

The Lord Ruthven Society's annual fiction award goes to fantasy–science fiction writer Jean Lorrah for her novel *Blood Will Tell*, while the nonfiction award goes to folklorist Michael Bell for *Food for the Dead: On the Trail of New England's Vampires*.

2003

Anne Rice, author of the multiple volumes of the Vampire Chronicles, receives the Bram Stoker Life-time Achievement Award. Also receiving an award is *Bubba Ho-Tep* by Don Coscarelli (best screenplay).

Underworld, which will eventually spawn three sequels, opens and generates a second successful vampire franchise beside *Blade*.

Heather Graham, the author of multiple romantic vampire novels, receives the Nora Roberts Lifetime Achievement Award from the Romance Writers of America.

The World Horror Association presents Chelsea Quinn Yarbro, the author of the many St. Germain vampire novels, with a Grand Master award.

Susan Sizemore wins a *Romantic Times* Choice Award for the best vampire romance novel of the year for *I Burn for You*.

The Lord Ruthven Society's annual fiction award goes to Charlaine Harris for the second volume in her Sookie Stackhouse/Southern Vampire Mysteries series, *Living Dead in Dallas*. The nonfiction award goes to William Patrick Day for his study of *Vampire Legends in Contemporary American Culture: What Becomes a Legend Most*.

2004

Blade Trinity, the least successful of the three *Blade* movies, opens, but is eclipsed by *Van Helsing*, which becomes the major vampire movie of the year. *Blade Trinity* now ranks sixteenth all-time and van Helsing seventh.

MaryJanice Davidson wins a *Romantic Times* Choice Award for the best vampire romance novel of the year for *Undead and Unemployed*.

The Lord Ruthven Society's annual fiction award goes to Andrew Fox for his tale of New Orleans, *Fat White Vampire Blues*. James B. South wins the nonfiction award for his pioneering *Buffy the Vampire Slayer and Philosophy: Fear and Trembling in Sunnydale*.

2005

Sherrilyn Kenyon again wins a *Romantic Times* Choice Award for the best vampire romance novel of the year for *Seize the Night*.

Richard Dalby and William Hughes share the Lord Ruthven Award for nonfiction for their presentation of *Bram Stoker: A Bibliography*. The award for fiction is received by David Sosnowski for his novel *Vamped*.

2006

Leading romance fiction writer Nora Roberts enters the realm of paranormal fiction with her vampire-oriented Circle Trilogy, *Morrigan's Cross*, *Dance of the Gods*, and *Valley of Silence*.

J. R. Ward wins a *Romantic Times* Choice Award, for the best vampire romance novel of the year for *Lover Awakened*.

The Lord Ruthven Society's annual fiction award goes to Elizabeth Kostova for *The Historian*, while the nonfiction award goes to Jorg Waltje for his study of vampire crime, *Blood Obsession: Vampires, Serial Murder, and the Popular Imagination*.

2007

I Am Legend, the third adaption of the novel by Richard Matheson, opens as the highest-grossing December movie ever. It will join the Twilight Saga movies as the highest grossing vampire movies of all time and the only ones in the top one hundred highest grossing movies of all time.

P. C. Cast and her daughter Kristin Cast issue *Marked*, the first of their successful young adult "House of Night" vampire book series.

Linda Lael Miller, the author of a number of romantic vampire novels, receives the Nora Roberts Lifetime Achievement Award from the Romance Writers of America.

J. R. Ward again wins a *Romantic Times* Choice Award for the best vampire romance novel of the year for *Lover Unbound*. In addition, two vampire-themed novels also win the awards for the best urban fantasy (Jeaniene Frost, *Halfway to the Grave*) and best urban fantasy protagonist (Kim Harrison, *A Few Demons More*) novels.

Bruce A. McClelland wins the Lord Ruthven Award for the best nonfiction vampire book, *Slayers and their Vampires: A Cultural History of Killing the Dead*. The fiction award goes to Barbara Hambly, the first novelist to win the award a second time, for *Renfield, the Slave of Dracula*.

2008

Chelsea Quinn Yarbro, author of the multiple volumes of the Saint Germain series, receives the Bram Stoker Life-time Achievement Award.

True Blood, a television series based on the Sookie Stackhouse *Southern Vampire Mysteries* series of novels by Charlaine Harris, begins on HBO.

Michele Bardsley, author of the Broken Heart novel series, wins the *Romantic Times* Best Vampire Romance Choice Award for her *Because Your Vampire Said So*. Other vampire-themed novels to win in various paranormal romance categories include MaryJanice Davidson's *Undead and Unworthy*, Sherrilyn Kenyon's *Acheron*, and Jeanne C. Stein's *Legacy*.

Stephenie Meyer, author of the best-selling Twilight Saga series of novels, receives the Children's Choice Book Award as the Author of the Year from the Children's Book Council. In addition, the national newspaper *USA Today* also names Meyer as its Author of the Year while *Time* magazine added her to its list of the "100 Most Influential People in 2008."

Twilight, the first movie of the Twilight Saga, opens in theaters.

Spin magazine declares the American rock band Vampire Weekend, which had just released its self-named first album, the Year's Best New Band. The band also receives three nominations from the Q Awards, but does not win.

The Lord Ruthven Society's annual fiction award goes to Joel H. Emerson for *The Undead*, while the nonfiction award goes to David Keyworth for *Troublesome Corpses: Vampires and Revenants from Antiquity to the Present*.

2009

Brian Lumley, author of the multiple volumes of the Necroscope series, receives the Bram Stoker Life-time Achievement Award. Christopher Conlon also receives an award for his edited anthology *He Is Legend: An Anthology Celebrating Richard Matheson*.

The Twilight Saga: New Moon opens to record-breaking audiences, and goes on to become the second-largest grossing vampire movie of all time.

The Vampire Diaries, a television series based on the young adult book series written by L. J. Smith in the 1990s, opens on the CW network. Its success will lead to the republication and revival of the book series, which will lead to a number of new series titles, though most are not written by Smith.

True Blood wins an Emmy Award as the Best Drama Series on television.

Michelle Rowen wins a *Romantic Times* Choice Award for the best vampire romance novel of the year for *Tall, Dark and Fangsome*. Nalini Singh also wins the best urban fantasy protagonist award for her novel *Angel's Blood*.

The Lord Ruthven Society's annual fiction award goes to James Reese for *The Dracula Dossier*, while the nonfiction award goes to Elizabeth Miller (her second award) and Robert Eighteen-Bisang for their editing and comments upon *Bram Stoker's Notes for Dracula: A Facsimile Edition*.

2010

The Twilight Saga: Eclipse breaks opening records set by *New Moon*, and becomes the highest-grossing vampire movie of all time.

Jeaniene Frost wins a *Romantic Times* Choice Award for the best vampire romance novel of the year for *Eternal Kiss of Darkness*.

Siouxsie Sioux, lead singer of Siouxsie and the Banshees, receives a Q Award for her Outstanding Contribution to Music.

A new television series, *The Vampire Diaries*, receives multiple Peoples' Choice and Teen Choice Awards. It would continue to be a favorite show receiving Teen Choice Awards annually.

Guillermo del Toro and Chuck Hogan share the Lord Ruthven Society's annual fiction award for their novel, *The Strain*. The nonfiction award goes to James Reese for *The Dracula Dossier*, while the nonfiction award goes to Mary Y. Hallab for *Vampire God: The Allure of the Undead in Western Culture*.

2011

The Twilight Saga: Breaking Dawn Part 1 opens and continues the success of the Twilight series. It will become the fourth-largest grossing vampire film of all time.

J. R. Ward wins a *Romantic Times* Choice Award for the third time for the best vampire romance novel of the year for *Lover Unleashed*.

Charlaine Harris, author of the Sookie Stackhouse vampire novel series, the basis for the *True Blood* television series, receives the first Straight for Equality Award for her portrayal of gays and lesbians in her work.

The Horror Writers of America joins with the Bram Stoker Family Estate and the Rosenbach Museum & Library to present a one-time only Vampire Novel of the Century Award to Richard Matheson for *I Am Legend*.

The Lord Ruthven Society's annual fiction award goes to S. M. Stirling for *A Taint in the Blood*, while the nonfiction award goes to Edgar Browning and Caroline Joan (Kay) Picart, *Dracula in Visual Media: Film, Television, Comic Book and Electronic Game Appearances, 1921–2010*.

2012

A series of very successful vampire movies during the year, led by *The Twilight Saga: Breaking Dawn Part 2*, the third highest-grossing vampire movies of all time, also includes *Abraham Lincoln Vampire Hunter*, *Underworld: Awakening*, *Dark Shadows*, and *Hotel Transylvania*, a feature-length cartoon.

Jeaniene Frost wins the *Romantic Times* Choice Award for the best vampire romance novel of the year for the second time for *Once Burned*. Jaye Wells' *Blue-Bloodied Vamp* also wins for the best urban fantasy novel.

Charlaine Harris, author of the very successful Sookie Stackhouse series of novels, wins a second Anthony Award for *The Sookie Stackhouse Companion* as the best non-fiction book on mystery fiction.

The Lord Ruthven Society's annual fiction award goes to Glen Duncan for *The Last Werewolf*, in which vampires form part of the context of the story, while the nonfiction award goes to Susannah Clements for *The Vampire Defanged*.

2013

Romance author Kresley Cole wins her third Best Paranormal Romance award from the Romance Writers of America for *Shadow's Claim* (2013). The author of multiple vampire novels, she had previously won awards for *A Hunger Like No Other* (2007) and *Kiss of a Demon King* (2010). Following the receipt of her third award, she was also inducted into the RWA Hall of Fame.

Jeaniene Frost repeats as the winner of the *Romantic Times* Choice Award for the best vampire romance novel of the year for *Twice Tempted*. In addition, Anne Bishop, whose vampire-themed novel *Written in Red*, wins the best urban fantasy award.

Charlaine Harris, author of the popular Sookie Stackhouse series of vampire novels, long identified as primarily a mystery writer, is named the president of the Mystery Writers of America.

Vampire Weekend, a rock band, releases its third album, *Modern Vampires of the City*, which will earn a Grammy Award as the best alternative album. The band will also win the Q Award for the Best Act in the World Today.

The Lord Ruthven Society's annual fiction award goes to Tim Powers, for *Hide Me Among the Graves*, while the nonfiction award goes to Jeffrey Weinstock for *The Vampire Film: Undead Cinema*.

I. Vampires and Vampirism: General Sources

Bibliographies, Libraries and Booklore

This bibliography continues an interest in vampires begun in my teen years that began to manifest bibliographically in the 1980s when I became the editor of a series for Garland Publishing Company, "The Unexplained, the Mysterious and the Supernatural: Series of Topical Bibliographical Guides to Anomalies." The second item for the series was Martin Riccardo's now rare collector's item, *Vampires Unearthed: The Complete Multi-Media Vampire and Dracula Bibliography* (1983). Not the first bibliographical work on vampires (see items by Dalby and Varma below), it was the first to attempt to assemble a list of literature across the whole expanse of what was becoming an emerging field of academic interest.

Since the mid-'80s, a number of bibliographers and librarians have contributed to the effort to keep up with the mountain of vampire literature, and I heartily acknowledge all my colleagues who have toiled to make this effort possible beginning with Robert Eighteen-Bisang, upon whose work I have directly built, and about whom I have spoken at greater length elsewhere. Here I would make note of the work of Derik Badman, Don Macnaughtan, and Alysa Hornick, whose work on *Buffy the Vampire Slayer* and *Angel*, saved me considerable time in having to keep up with the material myself. I also note the work of Melinda Hayes, Jacque Finne and Norbert Spehner, who both alerted me to and did a masterful job of compiling European materials, many of which I would possibly have otherwise missed.

In recent years, a number of bibliographies have appeared on the Internet. Most are quite brief and many items label a bibliography little more than a list of book titles without any bibliographical information. A few, however, make a real contribution to the bibliographical task and are cited below.

Also included below are filmographies, which may also be cited in the introductory section to vampire cinema elsewhere in this work.

1. Altner, Patricia. *Vampire Readings: An Annotated Bibliography*. Lanham, MD: Scarecrow Press, 1998. 161 pp. tp.

2. Arndt, Russell J. *Horror Comics in Black and White: A History and Catalog, 1964–2004.* Jefferson, NC: McFarland & Company, 2013, pp. 300-pb.

3. Arant, Wendi, and Candace R. Benefiel, eds. *The Image and Role of the Librarian.* New York: Haworth Information Press, 2002. 186 pp. hb. The essays in this volume contain numerous references to Rupert Giles, the librarian in the *Buffy the Vampire Slayer* television series and the image of the librarian Anthony Stewart Head, the actor who portrayed Giles, conveyed to the listening audience. This volume was published simultaneously as an issue of *The Reference Librarian* 78 (2002).

4. Badman, Derek A. "Academic Buffy Bibliography." *Slayage: The Online International Journal of Buffy Studies* 2, 3 [7] (December 2002). Posted at: http://www.whedonstudies.tv.

5. Bauer, Druann, Cailey Williams, Merrill Miller, and Samantha LaChey. "*Comprehensive Annotated Bibliography on Vampire Media.*" *New York Review of Science Fiction* (November 2010). This article was the result of a senior research project by the three students at Ohio Northern University.

6. Bleiler, Everett F. *Guide to Supernatural Fiction.* Kent, OH: Kent State University, 1983. 723 pp.

7. Browning, John Edgar, and Caroline Joan (Kay) Picart. *Dracula in Visual Media: Film, Television, Comic Book and Electronic Game Appearances, 1921–2010.* Jefferson, NC: McFarland & Company, 2011. 304 pp. tp. *Dracula in Visual Media: Film, Television, Comic Book and Electronic Game Appearances, 1921–2010* received the 2011 award for the best nonfiction book of the previous year given annually by the Lord Ruthven Society.

8. Carter, Margaret L. *The Vampire in Literature: A Critical Bibliography.* Ann Arbor: UMI Research Press, 1989. 132 pp. hb. dj. This key work in vampire bibliographical research was followed by supplements issued annually by Carter from 1990 through 2009.

9. Cohen, Benjamin S. *Horror Films: A Bibliographic Guide to Horror, Terror and Macabre Cinema.* N.p.: the author, 1995. Posted at: http://filmtv.eserver.org/horror_films.txt.

10. Cotter, Robert Michael "Bobb." *The Great Monster Magazines: A Critical Study of the Black and White Publications of the 1950s, 1960s and 1970s.* Jefferson, NC: McFarland and Company, 2008. 230 pp.

11. Cox, Stephen B. *Blood: A Vampyric Bibliography.* Reading, UK: Coxland Press, 1994. 44 pp.

12. Crawford, Gary W., and Brian J. Showers. *Joseph Sheridan Le Fanu: A Concise Bibliography.* Dublin, Ireland: The Swan River Press, 2011. 44 pp. For an even more extensive bibliography on Le Fanu see Crawford's "J. Sheridan Le Fanu: A Database," posted at http://www.lefanustudies.com/database.html.

13. Cullen, John. "Rupert Giles, the Professional-image Slayer." *American Libraries* 31, 5 (2000): 42.

14. Dalby, Richard. *Bram Stoker: A Bibliography of First Editions, Illustrated.* London: Dracula Press, 1983. 81 pp. tp.

15. _____, and Richard Hughes. *Bram Stoker: A Bibliography.* Westcliff-On-Sea, Essex, UK: Desert Island Books, 2004. 184 pp. tp. *Bram Stoker: a Bibliography* received the 2005 award as the best nonfiction book of the previous year given annually by the Lord Ruthven Society.

16. Davison, Carol Margaret. "The Bloody Bibliography." In Carol Margaret Davison, ed., with Paul Simpson-Housley. *Bram Stoker's Dracula: Sucking through the Century, 1897–1997.* Toronto: Dundurn Press, 1997, pp. 419–32.

17. DeCandido, GraceAnne A. "Bibliographic Good vs. Evil in *Buffy the Vampire Slayer.*" *American Libraries* 30, 8 (Sept. 1999): 44–47. Rpt. as: "Rupert Giles and Search Tools for Wisdom in *Buffy the Vampire Slayer.*" Posted at: http://www.well.com/user/ladyhawk/Giles.html.

18. DeMarco, Joseph. "Vampire Literature: Something Young Adults Can Really Sink Their Teeth Into." *Emergency Librarian* 24 (1997): 26–8.

19. Eighteen-Bisang, Robert. "Hutchinson's Colonial Library Edition of Dracula." *Journal of Dracula Studies* 3 (2001): 53–69. Posted at: http://www.blooferland.com/drc/index.php?title=Journal_of_Dracula_Studies.

20. _____. "The Literate Vampire: A Bibliography." In Rosemary Ellen Guiley, with J. B. Macabre. *The Complete Vampire Companion.* New York: Macmillan, 1994, pp. 197–221.

21. _____. "Sinking Teeth into the Literary Vampire." In Rosemary Ellen Guiley, with J. B. Macabre. *The Complete Vampire Companion.* New York: Macmillan, 1994, pp. 53–66.

22. _____, and J. Gordon Melton. *Dracula: A Century of Editions, Adaptations and Translations. Part One: English Language Editions.* Santa Barbara, CA: Transylvanian Society of Dracula, 1998. 41 pp. pb. Staples.

23. Estill, Adriana. "Going to Hell: Placing the Library in *Buffy the Vampire Slayer.*" In John Buschman and Gloria J. Leckie, eds. *The Library as Place: History, Community, and Culture.* Westport, CT: Libraries Unlimited, 2007, pp. 235–250.

24. Ferraro, S. "Novels You Can Sink Your Teeth Into." *New York Times Magazine* 140, 4838 (October 14, 1990): 26–33.

25. Finné, Jacques. *Bibliographie de Dracula.* Lausanne, Switz.: L'Age d'Homme, 1986. 215 pp. tp.

26. Fonseca, Anthony J., and June Michele Pulliam. "Vampires and Werewolves: Children of the Night." In Anthony J. Fonseca and June Michele Pulliam. *Hooked on Horror: A Guide to Reading Interests in Horror Fiction.* Englewood, CO: Libraries Unlimited, Inc., 1999, pp. 65–98.

27. Frank, Frederick S. *Guide to the Gothic II: an Annotated Bibliography of Criticism, 1983–1993.* Lanham, MD: Scarecrow Press, 1995. 523 pp. See especially the sections on John William Polidori, Joseph Sheridan Le Fanu, Bram Stoker, and Vampirism and Werewolfism.

28. _____. *Montague Summers: A Bibliographical Portrait.* Metuchen, NJ: Scarecrow Press, 1988. 277 pp.

29. Goldstone, Lawrence, and Nancy Goldstone. *Slightly Chipped: Footnotes in Booklore.* New York: St. Martin's Press, 1999. 213 pp. Includes chapter on the *Dracula* notes and the Rosenbach Museum (pp. 103—25).

30. Good, Wendy Van Wyck. "Dracula Collections at the Rosenbach Museum & Library." In Carol Margaret Davison, ed., with Paul Simpson-Housley. *Bram Stoker's Dracula: Sucking through the Century, 1897–1997.* Toronto: Dundurn Press, 1997, pp. 405–09.

31. Harrison, K. C. "Vampire Readings: An Annotated Bibliography." *Reference Reviews* 13, 3 (1999): 29–30.

32. Harvey, Robert J. *Dark Visions: A Price Guide to Collectible Vampire Literature.* Fort Worth TX: the author, 1995. 146 pp. tp.

33. Hayes, Melinda, comp. "Thumbnail Images of Bram Stoker's *Dracula* editions." Posted at: http://www-lib.usc.edu/~melindah/Stoker/dracthum.htm.

34. _____. *Vampiri Europeana, or, A Bibliography of Non-English European Resources on Vampires in Literature, Folklore, and Popular Culture.* 1998. Posted at: http://www-lib.usc.edu/~melindah/eurovamp/vampeuro.html. The most extensive listing of vampire materials in other than English (especially German) currently available.

35. Hernaday, A. M. "Vampires and Vampiresses: A Reading of 62." *Books Abroad* 50 (Summer 1976): 570–76.

36. Hornick, Alysa. "Mapping the Whedonverses: Whedon Studies 1999 and Beyond." In Mary Alice Money for PopMatters.com, ed. *Joss Whedon: The Complete Companion: The TV Series, the Movies, the Comic Books and More.* London: Titan Books, 2012, pp. 457–464.

37. _____. Whedonology: An Academic Whedon Studies Bibliography. Posted at: http://www.whedonstudies.tv/whenology-an-academic-whedon-studies-bibliography.html.

38. Hövelmann, Gerd H. "Wissenschaftliche Vampir-Literatur: Eine bibliographische Heimsuchung [Scientific literature on vampires: A bibliographic visitation]. *Zeitschrift für Anomalistik* 7 (2007): 205–235. Posted at: http://www.anomalistik.de/images/stories/pdf/zfa/zfa2007_3_205_hoevelmann.pdf. The English abstract reads: This bibliography includes more than four hundred scientific references related to "vampires" as a cultural phenomenon. Included are books and papers from anthropology; historical sciences; linguistics; historical philology; history of art, literature, cinema and theatre; sociology; educational science; political science, economics; psychology; psychiatry; medicine and forensic medicine; zoology; biology and biochemistry.

39. Hughes, William. *Bram Stoker: A Bibliography.* Ser.: Victorian Fiction Research Guides, #26. [St. Lucia, Qld, Aust.]: Victorian Fiction Research Unit, Department of English, University of Queensland Press, 1997. 73 pp. tp.

40. Hynes, James. "Literary Sequels, Pastiches, and Adaptations." In Bram Stoker. *Dracula.* New York: Barnes & Noble/Sterling Publishing, 2012, pp. 349–53.

41. Jones, Robert Kenneth. *The Shudder Pulps: A History of the Weird Menace Magazines of the 1930s.* West Linn, OR: FAX Collector's Editions. 1975. 238 pp. tp. Rpt.: N.p.: Wildside Press, 2007. 238 pp. hb. & tp.

42. Kem, Jessica Freya. *Cataloging the Whedonverse: Potential Roles for Librarians in Online Fan Fiction.* Chapel Hill: School of Information and Library Science, University of North Carolina, M.A. thesis, 2005. 57 pp. Posted at: http://dc.lib.unc.edu/cdm/singleitem/collection/s_papers/id/729/rec/12.

43. Loving, Matthew. "Charles Nodier: The Romantic Librarian." *Libraries & Culture* 38, 2 (2003): 166–188.

44. Macnaughtan, Don. *The Buffyverse Catalog: A Complete Guide to* Buffy the Vampire Slayer *and* Angel *in Print, Film, Television, Comics, Games* *and Other Media, 1992–2010.* Jefferson, NC: Mc-Farland & Company, 2011. 318 pp. tp.

45. Madison, Bob. "A Dracula Filmography." In Bob Madison, ed. *Dracula: The First Hundred Years.* Baltimore, MD: Midnight Marquee Press, 1997, pp. 302–321.

46. Marotta, Linda. "Top Ten Vampire Books." In Anthony Timpone, ed. *Fangoria Vampires.* New York: HarperPrism, 1996, pp. 173–81.

47. _____. "The Top 10 Books That Suck." *Fangoria* 116 (September 1992): 46–4.

48. Matthews, Patricia O'Brien. *Fang-tastic Fiction: Twenty-first Century Paranormal Reads.* Chicago: American Library Association Editions, 2010. 242 pp. tp.

49. Mayfield, Sarah, Leigh Lunsford, and Rhonda Brock-Servais. "Romancing the Bite: Statistical Analysis of Young Adult Vampire Novels." *Incite: Journal of Undergraduate Scholarship* (2011). Posted at: http://blogs.longwood.edu/incite/2012/01/30/romancing-the-bite-statistical-analysis-of-young-adult-vampire-novels/.

50. Meloni, Christine, "The Rise of Vampire Literature." *Library Media Connection* (October 2007): 32–33.

51. Melton, J. Gordon. "All Things *Dracula*: A Bibliography of Editions Reprints, Adaptations, and Translations." Posted at: http://www.cesnur.org/2003/dracula/. The largest listing of the many editions of the novel Dracula in its many forms (books, sound recordings, movies, etc.) currently (2013) available. Also included is a listing of a number of the editions in the forty+ languages into which Dracula has been translated.

52. _____. "Images from the Hellmouth: *Buffy the Vampire Slayer* Comic Books 1998–2002." *Slayage: The Online International Journal of Buffy Studies* 2, 2 [6] (September 2002). Posted at: http://www.whedonstudies.tv.

53. _____. "List of Vampire Movies in English (origins—2013)." Posted at: http://www.cesnur.org/2009/vampires_movies.htm. Currently the largest list of vampire movies (some 2400 titles) ever assembled.

54. _____. *The Official Vampirella Collector's Checklist, 1969–1998.* Santa Barbara, CA: Transylvanian Society of Dracula, 1999. 30 pp. pb. Large Format.

55. _____. *The Vampire in the Comic Book.* New York: Count Dracula Fan Club, 1993. 32 pp. pb. Spiral bound.

56. _____. "Words from the Hellmouth: A Bibliography of Books on *Buffy the Vampire Slayer*." *Slayage: The Online International Journal of Buffy Studies* 1, 4 [4] (December 2001) [Revised and Expanded, March 2003]. Posted at: http://www.whedonstudies.tv.

57. _____, and Lee Scott. *The Vampire and the Comic Book.* New York: Dracula Press, 1994. 76 pp. pb. Staples.

58. _____, and Robert Eighteen-Bisang. "Vampire Fiction for Children and Youth, 1960 to the Present." *Transylvanian Journal: Dracula and Vampire Studies* 2, 1 (Spring/Summer 1996): 24–30.

59. Miller, Elizabeth. "Stoker/Dracula: Recommended Reading List." N.d.: 9 pp. Posted at: http://blooferland.com/drc/index.php?title=Main_Page. A very useful introductory guide for those new to the field of the most significant items concerning the novel *Dracula* and its author Bram Stoker.

60. Naschy, Paul. "Filmography." *Videooze* 6/7 (Fall 1994): 20–42.

61. O'Sullivan, Gerald P. "The Montagu Summers Collection of Betty Forbes: A Representative List." In Montague Summers. *The Vampire, His Kith and Kin: A Critical Edition.* Ed. by John Browning. Berkeley, CA: Apocryphile Press, 2011, pp. 399–408.

62. Ramsland, Katherine. "Eloquent Fantasies." *Biblio: Exploring the World of Books* 3, 10 (October 1998): 30–35.

63. Rathbun Mark, and Graeme Flanagan, comps. *Richard Matheson: He Is Legend: An Illustrated Bio-Bibliography.* Chico, CA: Rio Lindo, 1984. 55 pp. hb.

64. Riccardo, Martin V. *Vampires Unearthed: The Complete Multi-Media Vampire and Dracula Bibliography.* New York: Garland Publishing, 1983. 135 pp. hb. Issued as No. 2 of Garland's "The Unexplained, the Mysterious and the Supernatural: Series of Topical Bibliographical Guides to Anomalies," over which J. Gordon Melton served as series editor.

65. Russell, Sharon A., James Craig Holte, and Mary Pharr. "Vampire Fiction and Criticism: A Core Collection." In Leonard Heldreth and Mary Pharr, eds. *The Blood Is the Life: Vampires in Literature.* Bowling Green, KY: Bowling Green State University Press, 1999, pp. 261–66.

66. Ruthner, Clemens. "Forschungsliteratur: Vampirismus. Kommentierte interdisziplinäre Auswahlbibliografie." N.d.: 16 pp. Posted at: http://www.kakanien.ac.at/beitr/materialien/CRuthner 1.pdf. This academically oriented bibliography includes both English and non–English materials.

67. Shepard, Leslie. "The Library of Bram Stoker." *Bram Stoker Society Journal* 4 (1992): 28–34.

68. Showalter, Elaine. "Blood Sells: Vampire Fever and Anxieties for the fin-de-siecle." *Times Literary Supplement* (January 8, 1993): 14.

69. Spehner, Norbert. "Bibliographie internationale des études sur Dracula [Dracula: International Secondary Sources], 1: Littérature: monographies, recueils, thèses [Monographies, dissertations, collections]." Special issue of *Marginalia* 10 (January 2010): 1–32. Posted at: http://www.academia.edu/761469/DRACULA_Part_1.

70. _____. "Bibliographie internationale des études sur Dracula [Dracula: International Secondary Sources], 2: Littérature : articles et extraits [Literature : articles and book chapters]." Special issue of *Marginalia* 11 (January 2010): 1–32. Posted at: http://www.academia.edu/761471/DRACULA_Part_2.

71. _____. "Bibliographie internationale des études sur Dracula [Dracula: International Secondary Sources], 3: Dracula au cinéma [Dracula at the movies]." Special issue of *Marginalia* 12 (January 2010): 1–39. Posted at: http://www.academia.edu/761476/DRACULA_Part_3.

72. _____. *Dracula: Opus 300.* Montreal: Ashem Fictions, 1996. 68 pp. pb.

73. Spratford, Becky Siegel. "Vampires: Books with Bite." In Becky Siegel Spratford. *The Readers' Advisory Guide to Horror.*

74. _____, and Tammy Hennigh Clausen. "Vampires: Dracula Will Never Die." In Becky Siegle Spratford and Tammy Hennigh Clausen. *The Horror Reader's Advisory: The Librarian's Guide to Vampires, Killer Tomatoes, and Haunted Houses.* Chicago: American Library Association, 2004, pp. 39–48.

75. Thompson, Lars, and Becci Hayes. "Teacher's Guide to *Dracula.*" In Lars Thompson and Becci Hayes. *Companions to Literature: Monstermania*, Missisauga, ON: School Book Fairs Limited, 1993.

76. Varma, Devendra P. "The Vampire in Legend, Lore, and Literature." Introduction to: *Varney the Vampire; or, The Feast of Blood.* New York: Arno Press, 1970, vol. 1, pp. xiii–xxx. Rpt. in: Margaret L. Carter, ed. *The Vampire in Literature: a Critical Bibliography.* Ann Arbor: UMI Research Press, 1989, pp. 13–30.

77. Varney, Bertena. "The Rise of Vampire Literature." In Hallie Tibbetts, ed. *Sirens: Collected Papers 2009–2011.* Sedalia, CO: Narrate Conferences, 2012, pp. 135–47.

78. Vellutini, John. "Vampire Filmography." *Oriental Cinema* 15 (n.d. [1997]): 10–23.

79. Viets, Henry R. "The London Editions of Polidori's *The Vampyre.*" *Papers of the Bibliographical Society of America* 63 (1969): 83–103.

80. Willis, Donald C. *Horror and Science Fiction Films: A Checklist.* 3 vols. Metuchen, NJ: The Scarecrow Press, 1972, 1982, 1984.

81. Wilson, Colin. "Dracula (Bram Stoker)" In Kim Newman & Stephen Jones, eds. *Horror: 100 Best Books.* New York, Carroll & Graf Publishers, 1990, pp. 51–52.

Encyclopedias, Dictionaries and Biographical Guides

The creation of reference books is one of the necessary tasks in defining an academic discipline, and beginning in the 1990s, a set of reference works—encyclopedias, biographical dictionaries, and others—joined the bibliographies in recognizing the formation of a genuine sub-discipline of vampire and Dracula studies.

82. Bane, Theresa. *Actual Factual Dracula: A Compendium of Vampires.* Randleman, NC: NeDeo Press, 2007. 446 pp. hb. boards.

83. _____. *Encyclopedia of Vampire Mythology.* Jefferson, NC: McFarland & Company, 2010. 207 pp. hb.

84. Barber, Dolan. *Monsters Who's Who.* New York: Crescent Books, 1974. 120 pp. Includes brief entries on Dracula, Empusae, Lamia, Morbius, Nosferatu, Redcap, and vampires.

85. Branson-Trent, Gregory. *The Undead: An Encyclopedia of Vampires, Mummies, Ghouls, Zombies, and More.* N.p.: the author, 2009. tp.

86. Bunson, Matthew. *The Vampire Encyclopedia.* New York: Crown Trade Paperbacks, 1993. 303 pp. tp. Rpt.: London: Thames and Hudson, 1993. 303 pp. tp. Rpt.: New York: Gramercy Books, 2000. 303 pp. hb. dj.

87. Bush, Laurence C. *Asian Horror Encyclopedia: Asian Horror Culture in Literature, Manga, & Folklore.* San Jose, CA: Writers Club Press, 2001. 227 pp. tp.

88. Cheung, Theresa. *The Element Encyclopedia of Vampires.* London: Harper Element, 2009. 685 pp. hb.

89. Copper, Basil. "Vampires and Werewolves." In Richard Davis, ed. *The Encyclopedia of Horror.* London: Octopus Books, 1981, pp. 88–113.

90. Curran, Bob. *Encyclopedia of the Undead: A Field Guide to the Creatures That Cannot Rest in Peace.* Franklin Lakes, NJ: Clear Lake Books, 2006. 310 pp. tp. Rpt. London: Bounty Books, 2009. 310 pp. tp.

91. Flynn, John L. *Cinematic Vampires: The Living Dead on Film and Television, from The Devil's Castle (1896), to Bram Stoker's Dracula (1992).* Jefferson, NC: McFarland & Company, 1992. 320 pp. hb.

92. Gee, Joshua. *Encyclopedia Horrifica: The Terrifying TRUTH! About Vampires, Ghosts, Monsters, and More.* New York: Scholastic, 2007. 138 pp. hb. Large format A playful reference book directed to children.

93. Guiley, Rosemary Ellen. *The Encyclopedia of Vampires, Werewolves, and Other Monsters.* New York: Checkmark Books, 2004. 352 pp. pb. Large format. 2nd ed.: New York: Checkmark Books, 2011. 430 pp. pb. Large format.

94. Haining, Peter. *A Dictionary of Vampires.* London: Robert Hale, 2001. 288 pp. hb. dj.

95. Hill, Douglas. "Vampire." In Richard Cavendish, ed. *Man, Myth, and Magic: An Illustrated Encyclopedia of the Supernatural.* New York: Marshall Cavendish Corporation, 1970, pp. 2922–28.

96. Jones, Stephen. *The Illustrated Vampire Movie Guide.* London: Titan Books, 1993. 144 pp. pb. Large format.

97. Joshi, S. T. *Encyclopedia of the Vampire: The Living Dead in Myth, Legend, and Popular Culture.* Santa Barbara, CA: Greenwood Press, 2010. 453 pp. hb. boards.

98. Ladouceur, Liisa. *Encyclopedia Gothica.* Toronto, ON: ECW Press, 2011. 313 pp. hb, A guidebook to the Goth subculture.

99. Mayo, Mike. *The Horror Show Guide: The Ultimate Frightfest of Movies.* Detroit, MI: Visible Ink Press, 2013. 477 pp. tp.

100. Melton, J. Gordon. *The Vampire Book: The Encyclopedia of the Undead.* Detroit: Gale Research Company, 1994. 852 pp. hb. Rpt.: Detroit: Visible Ink Press, 1994. 852 pp. tp. Revamped second ed.: Detroit: Visible Ink Press, 1998. 919 pp. tp. Rpt.: Detroit: Visible Ink Press, 1998. 919 pp. hb. Rev. third ed.: Detroit: Visible Ink Press, 2010. 909 pp. tp. Excerpt rpt. in: Angela Cybulski, ed. *Vampires: Fact or Fiction?* Ser.: Opposing Viewpoints. Farmington Hills, MI: Greenhaven Press/Thomson, Gale, 2003. pp. 101–09. Condensed third ed. Detroit: Visible Ink Press, 2013. 478 pp. tp. *The Vampire Book* received the Lord Ruthven Society's award as the best nonfiction book of the year. It would also be named the best nonfiction book on vampires by the Transylvanian Society of Dracula as its Dracula centennial celebration, Dracula '97.

101. _____. *The Vampire Gallery.* Farmington Hill, MI: Visible Ink Press, 1998. 500 pp. tp.

102. _____. *VideoHound's Vampires on Video.* Detroit: Visible Ink Press, 1997. 335 pp. tp.

103. Mercer, Mick. *Music to Die For: The International Guide to Today's Extreme Music Scene.* London: Cherry Red Books, 2009. 609 pp. tp.

104. Middleton, Brad. *Un-Dead TV: The Ultimate Guide to Vampire Television.* Pepperell, MA: By Light Unseen Media, 2012. 512 pp. tp.

105. Monster Encyclopedia: Monsters, Zombies, *Vampires and More*. New York: Parragon Books, 2012. 224 pp. hb. Juvenile.

106. Ramsland, Katherine. *The Vampire Companion: The Official Guide to Anne Rice's The Vampire Chronicles.* New York: Ballantine Books, 1993. 507 pp. hb. dj. Rev. ed.: 1995. 577 pp. tp. Rpt.: London: Little Brown and Company, 1996. 577 pp. tp.

107. Robbins, Rossell Hope. "Vampire." In Rossell Hope Robbins. *The Encyclopedia of Witchcraft and Demonology*. New York: Crown Publishers, 1959, pp. 521–25.

108. Sanguinarius. *The Dictionary of Sanguinese: Terminology and Lingo in the Vampire Community*. N.p.: Sanguinarius.org 2008. 64 pp. tp. Rev. ed. As: *The Dictionary of Vampspeak: Terminology and Lingo in the Vampire Community*. Charleston, SC: Sangunarius.org, 2008. 51 pp. tp. Sanguinarius is the public name of a leader in the real vampire community who has become a prominent figure in the networking of people who consider themselves to be vampires.

109. Spence, Lewis. "Vampire." In Lewis Spence. *An Encyclopedia of Occultism: A Compendium of Information on the occult Sciences, Occult Personalities, Psychic Science, Magic, Demonology, Spiritism and Mysticism*. New York: Dodd, Mead & Company, 1920, pp. 419–21.

110. Varney, Bertena. *Lure of the Vampire: A Pop Culture Reference Book of Lists, Websites and Very Personal Essays*. Bowling Green KY: the author, 2011. 160 pp. tp.

111. *Videohound's Complete Guide to Cult Flicks and Trash Pics*. Detroit, MI: Visible Ink Press, 1996. 439 pp. tp.

112. *Videohound's Worst Nightmares: Vampires, Werewolves & Other Creatures of the Night*. Detroit, MI: Visible Ink Press, 1995. 124 pp. pb. Small format. Staples.

113. Weisser, Thomas. *Asian Cult Cinema*. New York: Boulevard Books, 1997. 317 pp. tp.

114. _____, and Yuko Mihara Weisser. *Japanese Cinema Encyclopedia: The Horror, Fantasy, and Sci Fi Films*. Miami, FL: Vital Books, 1997. 327 pp. tp.

Books, Monographs and Articles

While the vast majority of vampire texts focus on fairly limited aspects of the phenomena, as the field grew in popularity authors have attempted to present overviews of what has become both a large field of interest and an immensely important field of inquiry. At the same time, a basic question concerning the reality of vampires continues to emerge, given the origin of the legends in supernatural folklore. This question has become more complicated with the claims of contemporary "real" vampires and the promotion of vampire images to describe psychological relationships and states of being. Thus books and articles in this section attempt to survey the field of vampires and vampirism and/or attempt to offer some perspective on their reality. Some target vampires while others the realm of belief in vampires and the entertainment they bring in films and literary fiction and still others attempt to analyze the appeal of vampire in the modern world.

The volumes listed below vary immensely in the depth of approaching the phenomenon and while a number have proved of value, those by Day, Frost, Guiley, Haining, Marigny, and Skal have emerged as the most useful. A variety of mostly self-published and publish-on-demand titles have proven to be either extremely expensive and/or difficult to locate and have thus failed to find an audience in the field.

115. Acocella, Joan. "In the Blood: Why Do Vampires Still Thrill?" *The New Yorker* (March 16, 2009): 101–107.

116. Aldiss, Brian. "Vampires—the Ancient Fear." In Joan Gordon and Veronica Hollinger, eds. *Blood Read: The Vampire as Metaphor in Contemporary Culture*. Philadelphia: University of Pennsylvania Press, 1997, pp. ix–xi.

117. Amador, Victoria. "'I am not like other people': Tippi Hedren, Vampires, and Marnie." *Journal of Dracula Studies* 3 (2001): 42–49.

118. _____. "The Post-Feminist Vampire: A Heroine for the Twenty-First Century." *Journal of Dracula Studies* 5 (2003): 16–22.

119. Ashley, Leonard R. N. *The Complete Book of Vampires*. New York: Barricade Books,

1998. 366 pp. tp. Rpt.: London: Souvenir Press, 1998. 366 pp. tp. While surveying the world of vampires, Ashley reprints excerpts from a number of vampire writings, both fiction and nonfiction.

120. Atwater, Cheryl. "Living in Death: The Evolution of Modern Vampirism." *Anthropology of Consciousness* 11, 1–2 (2000): 70–77.

121. Auerbach, Nina "Vampires in the Light." In Bram Stoker. *Dracula*. Ser.: Norton Critical Editions. Ed. by Nina Auerbach and David J. Skal. New York: W. W. Norton & Company, 1998, pp. 389–404.

122. _____. "Vampires in the 1970s: Feminist Oligarchies and Kingly Democracy." In Carol Margaret Davison, ed., with Paul Simpson-Housley. *Bram Stoker's Dracula: Sucking through the Century, 1897–1997*. Toronto: Dundurn Press, 1997, pp. 195–211.

123. Bacon, Simon, and Katarzyna Bronk, eds. *Undead Memory: Vampires and Human Memory in Popular Culture*. Bern, Switz.: Peter Lang International Academic Publishers, 2013. 303 pp. hb. Includes contributions from Christopher Frayling, Leo Ruickbie, Marius Crişan, Naomi Segal, Hadas Elber-Aviram, Katharina Rein, Enrique Ajuria Ibarra, Sorcha Ní Fhlainn, Hannah Priest, Angela Tumini, and Simon Bacon.

124. Baird, Ileana Popa. *Cultural Stereotypes—From Dracula's Myth to Contemporary Diasporic Productions*. Saarbucken, Germany: VDM Verlag Dr. Mueller e.K., 2007. 96 pp. tp.

125. Barbetti, Susan. "The Vampire's Bite." *Sky and Telescope* 109, 4 (2005): 12.

126. Bartelt, Dana Jan. *Vampires: From Folklore to Fiction*. N.p.: the author, 2013. 85 pp. tp.

127. Bartlett, Wayne, and Flavia Idriceanu. *Legends of Blood: The Vampire in History and Myth*. Phoenix Mill, Gloucestershire, UK: Sutton Publishing, 2005. 224 pp. hb. dj. Rpt.: Westport, CT: Praeger Publishers, 2006. 232 pp. hb.

128. Beckley, Timothy Green. "The Real Plan Nine from Outer Space." Timothy Green Buckley. *Round Trip to Hell in a Flying Saucer: UFO Parasites—Alien Soul Suckers—Invaders from Demonic Realms*. New Brunswick, NJ: Conspiracy Journal/Global Communications, 2010. 300 pp. Large Format. An interesting conflation of beliefs in extraterrestrials, conspiracy theories and vampires.

129. Beresford, Matthew. *From Demons to Dracula: The Creation of the Modern Vampire Myth*. London: Reaktion Books, 2008. 240 pp. tp.

130. Berger, Sam. "Do Vampires Exist?" *Fate* 5, 6 (November-December 1951): 79–82.

131. Bixby, Ted M. *American Monsters*. N.p.: the author, 2012. 318 pp. tp.

132. Branson-Trent, Gregory. *Vampires Among Us: The Children of the Night*. N.p.: New Image Productions, 2010. 310 pp. tp.

133. Brodman, Barbara, and James E. Doan, eds. *Images of the Modern Vampire: The Hip and the Atavistic*. Madison. NJ: Fairleigh Dickinson University Press, 2013. 263 pp. hb. Includes contributions by Victoria Williams, Murray Leede, Melissa Olsen, Simon Bacon, Donna Mitchell, Karin Hirmer, Cheyenne Mathews, Ze 'lie Asava, Marie-Luise Loeffler, Alaina Steiner, Ben Murnane, Hope Jennings and Christine Wilson, Sarah Heaton, Batia Stolar, and Burcu Genc.

134. _____. *The Universal Vampire: Origins and Evolution of a Legend*. Madison, NJ: Fairleigh Dickinson University Press, 2013. 249 pp. hb. boards. Includes essays by Matthias Teichert, Paul E. H. Davis, Alexis M. Milmine, Cristina Artenie, Edward O. Keith, Leo Ruickbie, Clemens Ruthner, Nancy Schumann, James E. Doan, Katherine Allocco, Jamieson Ridenhour, Masaya Shimokusu, Tomas Jesus Garza, Adriana Gordillo, and Raul Rodriguez-Herntindez and Claudia Schaefer.

135. Brown, Carolyn. "Figuring the Vampire: death, desire, and the image." In Sue Golding, ed. *The Eight Technologies of Otherness*. London: Routledge, 1997, pp. 117–33.

136. Browning, John Edgar, and Caroline Joan Picart, eds. *Draculas, Vampires, and Other Undead Forms: Essays on Gender, Race, and Culture*. Methuen, NJ: Scarecrow Press, 2009. 338 pp. hb. Includes articles by Gary D. Rhodes, Paul R. Lehman and John Edgar Browning, Caroline Joan (Kay) Picart and Cecil Greek, Lisa Nystrom, Justin Everett, Santiago Lucendo, Jimmie Cain, Paul Newland, Martina G. Lüke, Andrew Hock-Soon Ng, Sean Moreland and Summer Pervez, Dale Hudson, Wayne Stein, and Nicholas Schlegel.

137. Bunch, Charles K. Vampires, Werewolves, and Zombies on Gay Internet Personals: Smash a Few Monsters to Find Love on Dating Sites. Boise, ID: the author, 2012. 127 pp. tp.

138. Burgess, Randy. *Vampires*. Kansas City, MO: Andrews and McMeel, 1996. *Unpaged*. Small format.

139. Bush, Carey Lynn. *The Dead Unveiled*. Warrensburg: Central Missouri State University, M.A. thesis, 1999. 71 pp. Large format.

140. Butler, Erik. *Metamorphoses of the Vampire in Literature and Film: Cultural Transformations in Europe, 1732–1933.* Rochester, NY: Camden House, 2010. 225 pp. hb.

141. _____. *The Rise of the Vampire.* London: Reaktion Books, 2013. 179 pp. hb.

142. Byrne, Deirdre. "The Lure of the Unspeakable: Why Vampires Don't Have Sex." In Hermann Wittenberg and Loes Nas, eds. *AUETSA 96/Southern African Studies. Proc. of the Conf. of the Assn. of University English Teachers of South Africa, University of the Western Cape, 30 June–5 July 1996.* 2 vols. Bellville, South Africa: University of Western Cape Press, 1996.

143. Castro, Adam-Troy. *V Is for Vampire: An Illustrated Alphabet of the Undead.* New York: Harper Voyager, 2011. 64 pp. hb.

144. Chromik-Krzykawska, Anna. "Flowing Subjectivities: Vampires, Femininity and Jouissance." In Elizabeth Nelson with Jillian Burcar & Hannah Priest, eds. *Creating Humanity, Discovering Monstrosity.* Oxford: Inter-Disciplinary Press, 2010, pp. 73–86.

145. Cininas, Jazmina. "Wolfsbane, Fangs and Hirsute Heretics: Tracing the Confluences between Lycanthropy, Witchcraft and Vampirism in the Female Werewolf." In Jonathan A. Allan and Elizabeth E. Nelson, eds. *Inversions of Power and Paradox.* Oxford: Inter-Disciplinary Press, 2011, pp. 3–14. Originally presented as a paper at the 8th annual 'Monsters and the Monstrous' conference held at Oxford University, September 2010.

146. Congdon, James. *It Started with Dracula: The Count, My Mother, and Me.* N.p.: Bettie Youngs Books Publisher, 2011. 323 pp. tp.

147. Copper, Basil. *The Vampire in Legend, Fact and Art.* London: Robert Hale, 1973. 208 pp. hb. dj. Rpt.: Secaucus, NJ: Citadel Press, 1974. 208 pp. hb. dj. Rpt.: London: Corgi, 1975. 222 pp. pb.

148. Crawford, Heide. "Vampires: Myths and Metaphors of Enduring Evil." *Comparative Literature Studies* 44, 4 (2007): 518–521.

149. Curran, Bob. *Biblio Vampiro: A Vampire Handbook.* Hauppauge, NY: Barrons, 2010. 80 pp. hb. boards.

150. _____. *Explore Vampires.* Avebury, Marlborough, UK: Explore Books, 2007. 164 pp. tp. Illus. by Ian Brown.

151. _____. *Vampires: A Field Guide to the Creatures of That Stalk the Night.* Franklin Lakes, NJ: New Page Books, 2005. 222 pp. tp.

152. Day, Peter, ed. *Vampire: Myths and Metaphors of Enduring Evil.* Ser.: At the Interface/Probing the Boundaries 28. Amsterdam: Rodopi, 2006. 257 pp. tp. This volume includes a selection of papers originally delivered at the Vampires: Myths and Metaphors of Enduring Evil Conference held at Budapest, Hungary, May 22–24, 2003, by Elizabeth Miller, Hyun-Jung Lee, Lois Drawmer, Peter Mario Kreuter, Terry Phillips, Phil Bagust, Stacey Abbott, Sharon Sutherland, James Tobias, Elizabeth McCarthy, Mursel Icoz, and Pete Remington. These papers were originally published in Carla T. Kungl's volume of the same name (2003) which collected all of the papers of the same conference. Day also added three additional papers by Darren Oldbridge, Meg Barker, and Fiona Peters not delivered at the original conference.

153. de Laurence, L. W. "Vampirism, Witchcraft and Black Art: Their Dangers and How to Avoid Them." In L. W. de Laurence. *Great Book of Magical Art, Hindu Magic and East Indian Occultism, and the Book of Secret Hindi, Ceremonial, and Talismanic Magic.* Chicago: The de Laurence Company, 1939, pp. 498–532. Posted at: http://www.scribd.com/doc/171779399/Great-Book-of-Magical-Art-L-W-De-Laurence. Rpt.: N.p.: Kessinger Publishing, n.d. 34 pp.

154. Dembeck, Chet. *Real Vampires, Zombies, UFOs & Monster Stories Based on Historical Newspaper Accounts: Plus Bonus Short Stories.* Baltimore, MD: the author, 2009. 82 pp. tp.

155. De Silver, Drago. *Hidden Dimensions, Ancient Magic, Witchcraft, Vampires & Reptilian Masters.* N.p.: the author, 2013. tp.

156. de Vere, Nicholas. *The Dragon Legacy: The Secret History of an Ancient Bloodline.* San Diego, CA: The Book Tree, 2004, 437 pp. tp.

157. Dixon, J. M. *The Weiser Field Guide to Vampires: Legends, Practices, and Encounters Old and New.* San Francisco: Samuel Weiser, 2009. 189 pp. tp.

158. Doniger, Wendy. "Sympathy for the Vampire." *Nation* 261, 17 (Nov. 20, 1995): 608–12.

159. Douglas, Drake. "The Vampire." In Drake Douglas. *Horror!* New York: Macmillan Company, 1966, pp. 17–56. Rpt. as: *Horrors! (The Awful Truth About the Monsters, Vampires, Werewolves, Zombies, Phantoms, Mummies, and Ghouls of Literature—and How They Went to Hollywood).* New York: Overbrook Press, 1991, pp. 17–56.

160. "Dracula: Everything You Always Wanted to Know About Vampires...." Special Issue. *Souvenir Issue* (August 1979). Large format.

161. Draeger, John. "Should Vampires Be Held Accountable for Their Bloodthirsty Behavior?" In Richard Greene and K. Silem Mohammad, eds. *The Undead and Philosophy: Chicken Soup for the Soulless.* La Salle, IL: Open Court, 2006, pp. 119–27. Rpt. in Richard Greene and K. Silem Mohammad, eds. *Zombies, Vampires, and Philosophy: New Life for the Undead.* La Salle, IL: Open Court, 2010, pp. 119–27

162. Dyer, Richard. "Children of the Night: Vampirism as Homosexuality, Homosexuality as Vampirism." In Susannah Radstone, ed. *Sweet Dreams: Sexuality, Gender and Popular Fiction.* London: Lawrence & Wishart, 1988, pp. 47–72.

163. Eaves, A. Osborne. *Modern Vampirism: Its Dangers and How to Avoid Them.* Harrogate, UK: Talisman, 1904. 54 pp. pb. Excerpt rpt. in: Jan Perkowski. *Vampires of the Slavs.* Cambridge, MA: Slavica Publishers, 1976, pp. 196–216.

164. Ebeling, R. M. *The Vampire in Human Form: A Study in Depravity.* London: Royce Bentley, Lyons & Chapman, 1961.

165. Efthimiou, Costas J., and Sohang Gandhi. "Cinema Fiction vs. Physics Reality: Ghosts, Vampires, and Zombies." *Skeptical Inquirer* 31, 4 (August 2007). Posted at http://www.csicop.org/si/show/cinema_fiction_vs._physics_reality/.

166. Elber-Aviram, Hadas. "Constitutional Amnesia and Future Memory: Science Fiction's Posthuman Vampire." In Simon Bacon, and Katarzyna Bronk, eds. *Undead Memory: Vampires and Human Memory in Popular Culture.* Bern, Switz.: Peter Lang International Academic Publishers, 2013, pp. 105–26.

167. Enright, D. J. "Vampires, Werewolves, Zombies and Other Monsters." in D. J. Enright, ed. *The Oxford Book of the Supernatural.* Oxford: Oxford University Press, 1994, pp. 205–39.

168. Enright, Laura L. *Vampires' Most Wanted: The Top 10 Book of Bloodthirsty Biters, Stake-wielding Slayers, and Other Undead Oddities.* Washington, DC: Potomac Books, 2011. 320 pp. tp.

169. _____, and Angus Hall. "The Legend of the Vampire." In Daniel Farson and Angus Hall. *Mysterious Monsters.* London: Bloomsbury Books, 1991, pp. 9–25.

170. Farson, Daniel. "Why Believe in Vampires." In Daniel Farson and Angus Hall. *Mysterious Monsters.* London: Bloomsbury Books, 1991, pp. 26–41.

171. Fellows, Alfred. "The Vampire Legend." *Occult Review* 8 (September 1908): 124ff. Rpt. in: Bernhardt J. Hurwood, ed. *The First Occult Review Reader.* New York: Award Books, 1968, pp. 123–32.

172. Frayling, Christopher. "Foreword" In Simon Bacon, and Katarzyna Bronk, eds. *Undead Memory: Vampires and Human Memory in Popular Culture.* Bern, Switz.: Peter Lang International Academic Publishers, 2013, pp. xiff.

173. _____. *Nightmare: The Birth of Horror.* London: BBC Books, 1996. 224 pp. hb. dj.

174. Frost, Brian J. "Metamorphoses of the Vampire." *Shadow* 3, 4 (August 1974): 16–26.

175. _____. *Monster with a Thousand Faces.* Bowling Green, OH: Bowling Green State University Press, 1989. 152 pp. hb. & tp.

176. Furneaux, Rupert. "The Vampire." In Rupert Furneaux. *Legend and Reality.* London: Allan Wingate, 1959, pp. 9–17.

177. Gelder, Ken. "Vampires in Greece." In Ken Gelder. *The Horror Reader.* New York: Routledge, 2000, pp. 228–41.

178. Gledhill, Eva Hayles. "A Monstrous Aporia: The Redemption of the Vampire as a Metaphor for a Stake in Moral Agency." In Seth Alcorn and Steven A. Nardi, eds. *Twisted Mirrors: Monstrous Reflections of Humanity.* Oxford: Inter-Disciplinary Press, 2012, pp. 181–92.

179. Grace, Angela. *Dark Angels Revealed: From Dark Rogues to Dark Romantics, the Most Mysterious and Mesmerizing Vampires and Fallen Angels from Count Dracula to Edward Cullen Come to Life.* Beverly. MA: Fair Winds Press, 2011. 239 pp. tp.

180. Griffiths, R. J. K. *Vampire's Freaky Fact's and Mad Myth's.* N.p.: lulu.com, 2011. 128 pp. tp.

181. Guiley, Rosemary Ellen, with J. B. Macabre. *The Complete Vampire Companion.* New York: Macmillan, 1994. 258 pp. tp. Large format. Includes contributions by Martin V. Riccardo, John Gilbert, Robert Eighteen-Bisang, Margaret L. Carter, Joanne P. Austin, J. B. Macabre, Les Daniels, Lawrence Greenberg, and Allen G. Gittens.

182. Haining, Peter, ed. *The Dracula Scrapbook.* New York: Bramwell House, 1976. 176 pp. hb. Large format. Includes contributions from Charles Dickens, Emily Gerard, Radu Florescu, Gabriel Ronay, Franz Hartmann, Montague Summers, Tim Stout, Kingsley Amis, Christopher Lee, Peter Cushing, Terry Coleman, Forest J. Ackerman, Boris Karloff, Denis Gifford, Manly Wade Wellman, S. J. Daunders, Ivor J. Brown, Elliott O'Donnell, Daniel Farson, Bernard Davies, Donald A. Reed, Leo Heiman, and Peter Simple.

183. _____. *The Flesh Eaters: True Stories of Cannibals and Blood Drinkers.* London: Boxtree, 1994. 240 pp. pb.

184. _____, ed. *The Midnight People.* London: Leslie Frewin, 1968. 255 pp. hb. dj.Rpt.: New York: Popular Library, n.d. 207 pp. pb.Rpt.: London: Everest Books, 1975. 255 pp. pb. Rpt. as: *Vampires at Midnight.* New York: Grosset & Dunlap, 1970. 255 pp. hb. dj.Rpt.: London: Warner Books, 1993. 255 pp. pb. Along with a variety of fictional pieces, this anthology contains a foreword by Christopher Lee plus additional non-fiction items by Montague Summers and Augustus Hare.

185. _____. "The Terror of the Bloodsucker." In Peter Haining. *The Leprechan's Kingdom.* New York: Harmony Books, 1980, pp. 99–105.

186. Hall, Derek. *The Legend and Romance of the Vampire.* Edison, NJ: Chartwell Books, 2010. 253 pp. tp.

187. Hallab, Mary Y. *Vampire God: The Allure of the Undead in Western Culture.* Albany: State University of New York Press, 2009. 169 pp. hb & tp.

188. Hammer, Karen Oldham. *Vampires: The Dark Fantasy of the 18th and 19th Centuries.* Fayetteville, AR: Fayetteville State University, M.A. thesis, 2005. 43 pp. Large format.

189. Hanson, Ellis. "Undead." In Diana Fuss, ed. *Inside/Outside: Lesbian Theories, Gay Theories.* London: Routledge, 1991, pp. 324–40.

190. Hartmann, Franz. "An Authenticated Vampire Story." *Occult Review* 10 (September 1909): 144ff.

191. _____. "Vampires." *Occult Review* 7 (May 1908): 256ff.

192. Hill, Douglas. *Return from the Dead.* London: McDonald, 1970. 119 pp. pb. Rpt. as: *The History of Ghosts, Vampires, and Werewolves.* Newton Sq., PA: Harrow Books, 1973. 119 pp. pb. Rpt.: Baltimore: Castle Books, 1973. 119 pp. hb. Rpt.: New York: Harper and Row, 1973. pb.

193. _____, **and Pat Williams.** "Here Be Monsters." In Douglas Hill and Pat Williams. *The Supernatural.* New York: New American Library, 1965, pp. 185–210.

194. Hillyer, Vincent. *Vampires.* Los Banos, CA: Loose Change Publications, 1988. 125 pp. pb. Large format.

195. Hinckley, David Jesse. *With Uncanny Aim: Horror Fiction, the Repression of Culture, the Cult of the Repressed.* Riverside: University of California, Ph.D. dissertation, 1999. 277 pp. Large format.

196. Hodder, Reginald. "Vampires." *Occult Review* 19 (April 1914): 225ff.

197. Holte, James Craig. "The Vampire" In Malcolm South, ed. *Mythical and Fabulous Creatures: A Source Book and Research Guide.* New York: Bedrick, 1988, pp. 243–64.

198. Hoyt, Olga. *Lust for Blood: The Consuming Story of Vampires.* Briarcliff Manor, NY: Stein and Day, 1984. 245 pp. hb. dj. Rpt.: Chelsea, UK: Scarborough House, 1984. 245 pp. tp. Rpt.: Latham, MD: Scarborough Books, 1992. 245 pp. tp.

199. Hughes, William. "'The Raw Yolky Taste of Life': Spirituality, Secularity, and the Vampire." *Gothic Studies* 2 (2000): 148–156.

200. _____. "Vampire." In Marie Mulvey-Roberts, ed. *The Handbook to Gothic Literature.* London: Macmillan, 1998, pp. 240–43.

201. Hurwitz, Siegmund. *Lilith the First Eve: Historical and Psychological Aspects of the Dark Feminine.* Einsiedeln, Switz.: Daimon Verlag, 1992. 262 pp. tp. An expanded English edition of the original German edition originally published in 1990.

202. Hurwood, Bernhardt J. *Passport to the Supernatural: An Occult Compendium from All Ages and Many Lands.* New York: Taplinger Publisher Company, 1972. 319 pp. hb. dj. Rpt.: London: Robert Hale & Company, 1972. 319 pp. hb.

203. _____. *Supernatural Wonders from Around the World.* New York: Barnes & Noble, 1972. 319 pp. hb. dj.

204. _____. *Vampires.* New York: Quick Fox, 1981. 129 pp. pb. Large format.

205. _____. "Vampires and Werewolves Today." In Bernhardt J. Hurwood. *Terror by Night.*

New York: Lancer, 1963, pp. 161–172. Rpt. as: *The Monstrous Undead*. New York: Lancer, 1969. Rev. ed. as: *The Vampire Papers*. New York: Pinnacle, 1976.

206. _____. *Vampires, Werewolves, and Ghouls.* New York: Ace Books, 1968. 158 pp.

207. Jackson, Kevin. *Bite: A Vampire Handbook.* London: Portobello Books, 2009. 199 pp. hb.

208. Jackson, Nigel. *The Compleat Vampyre: The Vampyre Shaman, Werewolves, Witchery and the Dark Mythology of the Undead.* Chieveley, Berks, UK: Capall Bann Publishing, 1995. 158 pp. tp.

209. Johnson, Judith E. "Women and Vampires: Nightmare or Utopia?" *Kenyon Review* 15, 1 (Winter 1993): 72–80.

210. Kaplan, Matt. *Medusa's Gaze and Vampire's Bite: The Science of Monsters.* New York: Scribner, 2012. 244 pp. hb. dj.

211. Karg, Barb, Arjean Spaite, and Rick Sutherland. *The Everything Vampire Book.* Avon, MA: Adams Media, 2009. 289 pp. tp.

212. Karp, W. "Dracula Returns; or Vampirism as an Antidote to the Blues." *Horizon* 18 (Autumn 1976): 40–41.

213. Kavaler-Adler, Susan. "Vaginal Core or Vampire Mouth: The Visceral Level of Envy in Women: An Exploration of the Protosymbolic Politics of Object Relations." In Nancy Burke. *Gender & Envy.* New York: Routledge, 1998, pp. 221–38.

214. Kearns, Martha E. "'Vampires' Victims: A Feminist Perspective." A paper presented at the annual conference of the Popular Culture Association, Louisville, KY, March 1992.

215. Keesey, Pam. *Vamps: An Illustrated History of the Femme Fatale.* San Francisco, CA: Cleis Press, 1997. 171 pp. pb. Large format.

216. Kelso, Sylvia. "The Feminist and the Vampire: Constructing Postmodern Bodies." *Journal of the Fantastic in the Arts* 8. 4 (1997): 472–87.

217. Klein, Victor C. *Soul Shadows.* New Orleans, LA: Lycanthrope Press, 1996. 134 pp. tp. This anthology includes both fiction and nonfiction chapters.

218. Konstantinos. *Vampires: The Occult Truth.* St. Paul, MN: Llewellyn Publications, 1996. 194 pp. tp.

219. Kreuter, Peter Mario. "The Name of the Vampire: some reflections on current linguistic theories on the origin of the word vampire." In Carla T. Kungl, ed. *Vampires: Myths and Metaphors of Enduring Evil.* Oxford: Inter-Disciplinary Press, 2003. pp. 63–65. Posted at: http://www.inter-disciplinary.net/publishing/id-press/ebooks/vampires-myths-and-metaphors-of-enduring-evil. Rpt. in: Peter Day, ed. *Vampire: Myths and Metaphors of Enduring Evil.* Amsterdam: Rodopi, 2006, pp. 57–64.

220. Kungl, Carla T. "A New Spin on an Old Tale." In Carla T. Kungl, ed. *Vampires: Myths and Metaphors of Enduring Evil.* Oxford: Inter-Disciplinary Press, 2003, pp. 1–2. Posted at: http://www.inter-disciplinary.net/publishing/id-press/ebooks/vampires-myths-and-metaphors-of-enduring-evil.

221. _____, ed. *Vampires: Myths and Metaphors of Enduring Evil.* Oxford: Inter-Disciplinary Press, 2003. 137 pp. pb. Large format. Posted at: http://www.inter-disciplinary.net/publishing/id-press/ebooks/vampires-myths-and-metaphors-of-enduring-evil. This volume collects all of the papers presented at the Vampires: Myths and Metaphors of Enduring Evil Conference held in Budapest, Hungary, May 22–24 2003. Papers were contributed by Elizabeth Miller, Tomasz Warchol, James Tobias, Benson Saler and Charles A. Ziegler, Lois Drawmer, Kim Hoelzli, Paul Marchbank, David Cole, Phil Bagust, Sally Miller, Hyun-Jung Lee, Peter Mario Kreuter , Nursel Icoz, Elizabeth McCarthy, Terry Phillips, Pete Remington, Sharon Sutherland, Milly Williamson, Carla T. Kungl, Dee Amy-Chinn, Marina Levina, Suzanne Scott, Sarah Lynne Bowman, and Stacey Abbott. A selection of these papers were later made by Peter Day and published in his like-named volume.

222. Ladouceur, Liisa. *How to Kill a Vampire: Fangs in Folklore, Film and Fiction.* Toronto: ECW Press, 2013. 190 pp. tp.

223. Larson, Mia, Maria Lexhagen, and Christine Lundberg. "Thirsting for Vampire Tourism: Developing Pop Culture Destinations." *Journal of Destination Marketing and Management* 2, 2 (2013): 74–84

224. Latham, Robert. Consuming Youth: *Vampires, Cyborgs, and the Culture of Consumption.* Chicago: University of Chicago Press, 2002. 321 pp. tp.

225. Lecouteux, Claude. *The Secret History of Vampires: Their Multiple Forms and Hidden Purposes.* Rochester, VT: Inner Traditions, 2010. 184

pp. tp. A book originally published in French as *Histoire des vampires: Autopsie d'un mythe.*

226. Leigh-Hunt, Shelley. *Everything You Need to Know About Vampires.* New York: Dracula Press, 1989. 8 pp. pb. Staples.

227. Maberry, Jonathan. *Vampire Universe: The Dark World of Supernatural Beings That Haunt Us, Hunt Us, and Hunger for Us.* New York: Citadel Press, 2006. 317 pp. tp.

228. _____, and David F. Kramer. *They Bite: Endless Cravings of Supernatural Predators.* New York: Citadel Press/Kensington Publishing, 2009. 371 pp. tp.

229. Mack, Carol K., and Dinah Mack. *A Field Guide to Demons, Vampires, Fallen Angels and Other Subversive Spirits.* New York: Henry Holt and Company, 2009. 306 pp. tp.

230. Marek, Hillary, and Nicholas Cooper. *Daze and Knights: The Truth Behind Vampires and Zombies.* N.p.: White Rabbit Publications, 2010. 170 pp. tp.

231. Marigny, Jean. *Vampires: The World of the Undead.* London: Thames and Hudson, 1994. 143 pp. pb. Rpt. as: *Vampires: Restless Creatures of the Night.* New York: Abrams, 1994. 143 pp. pb.

232. Marlan, Dawn Alohi. *The Ends of Seduction, or, Libertines, Respectable Folks, Vampires, and Harassers.* Chicago: University of Chicago, Ph.D. dissertation, 2000. 187 pp. Large format.

233. Marsden, Simon. *The Journal of a Ghosthunter.* London: Little, Brown and Company, 1994. 128 pp. hb. dj. Large format.Rpt.: New York: Abbeville Press, 1994. 128 pp. hb. Large format. Rpt.: London: Tiger Books International, 1998. 128 pp. hb. dj. Large format.

234. _____. *Vampires: The Twilight World.* Bath, Somerset, UK: Palazzo Editions, 2011. 192 pp. hb. Large format. An anthology of fiction, nonfiction, and photographs exploring the images and legends of the vampire.

235. Masallo, Robert. "Vampires, Werewolves and Zombies." In Robert Masello. *Fallen Angels...and Spirits of the Dark.* New York: Perigee, 1994, pp. 109–38.

236. Mascetti, Manuela Dunn. *Chronicles of the Vampire.* London: Bloomsbury, 1991. 191 pp. hb. dj. Rev. ed. as: *Vampire: The Complete Guide to the World of the Undead.* New York: Viking Penguin, 1992. 224 pp. tp.Excerpt rpt. in: Angela Cybulski, ed. *Vampires: Fact or Fiction?* Ser.: Opposing

Viewpoints. Farmington Hills, MI: Greenhaven Press/Thomson, Gale, 2003. pp. 33–40.

237. Masters, Anthony. *The Natural History of the Vampire.* London: Rupert Hart-Davis, 1972. 259 pp. hb. dj. Rpt.: New York: G. P. Putnam's Sons, 1972. 259 pp. hb. dj. Rpt.: London: Mayflower, 1974. 258 pp. pb. Rpt.: New York: Berkley Books, 1976. 280 pp. pb. Excerpt rpt. in: Angela Cybulski, ed. *Vampires: Fact or Fiction?* Ser.: Opposing Viewpoints. Farmington Hills, MI: Greenhaven Press/Thomson, Gale, 2003. pp. 50–60.

238. McGrath, J. K. *V Is for Vampire.* N.p.: the author, 2011. 362 pp.

239. McLeod, Judyth A. *Vampires: A Bite-Sized History.* Miller's Point, NSW, Aust./London: Murdoch Books/Pier 9, 2010. 239 pp. hb. boards.

240. McNally, Raymond T. *A Clutch of Vampires.* New York: Bell Publishing Company, 1974. 255 pp. hb. dj. Rpt.: London: New English Library, 1974. 220 pp. pb. Among the nonfiction items included by McNally are folklore and historical observations by Phlegon of Tralles, Philostratus, Jan Jacob Maria de Groot, Walter Map, William of Newburgh, Henry More, Erasmus Franciscus, Augustin Calmet, Augustus Hare, William Seabrook, Montague Summers, Madame Helena P. Blavatsky, and Ion Creanga.

241. Methot, Jeff. *The Vampire Archetype.* N.p.: lulu.com, 2009. 324 pp. tp.

242. Meyer, Robert J. *Vampirism as an Alternate Lifestyle and The Most Complete List Ever Compiled of Vampires Throughout History.* Princeton, NJ: The Vampire Press, n.d. 4 pp. pb. Small format. Folklore.

243. Miller, Genevieve. *Vampire Knits. Projects to Keep You Knitting from Twilight to Dawn.* New York: Potter Craft, 2010. 144 pp. tp.

244. Montague, Charlotte. *Vampires from Dracula to Twilight: The Complete Guide to Vampire Mythology.* Eastbourne, East Sussex, UK: Omnipress/Canary Press, 2010. 192 pp. hb. dj.

245. Montalbano, Margaret. *Dying for Love: The Vampire as Model of Erotic Union.* New York: New York University, Graduate School of Arts and Science, Ph.D. dissertation, 2001. 415 pp. Large format.

246. Mutch, Deborah. *The Modern Vampire and Human Identity.* New York: Palgrave Macmillan, 2012. 220 pp. hb.

247. Necula, Virgil. *Life with Vampires in Country of Dracula.* West Conshohocken, PA: Infinity Publishing, 2008. 189 pp. tp.

248. Nelson, Elizabeth. "Monstrous Desire: Love, Death and the Vampire Marriage." In Elizabeth Nelson with Jillian Burcar & Hannah Priest, eds. *Creating Humanity, Discovering Monstrosity.* Oxford: Inter-Disciplinary Press, 2010, pp. 229–38.

249. Nelson, Jonathan H. "Platonic Critique of the Vampire." In Eoghain Hamilton. *The Gothic: Probing the Boundaries.* Oxford: Inter-Disciplinary Press, 2010, pp. 129–36.

250. Nickell, Joe. *Tracking the Man Beasts: Sasquatch, Vampires, Zombies, and More.* Amherst, NY: Prometheus Books, 2011. 239 pp. tp.

251. Ní Fhlainn, Sorcha. "'Old things, fine things': Of Vampires, Antique Dealers and Timelessness." In Simon Bacon, and Katarzyna Bronk, eds. *Undead Memory: Vampires and Human Memory in Popular Culture.* Bern, Switz.: Peter Lang International Academic Publishers, 2013, pp. 183–210.

252. Orlomoski, Caitlyn. *From Monsters to Victims: Vampires and Their Cultural Evolution from the Nineteenth to the Twenty-First Century.* Storrs: University of Connecticut–Storrs, Honors Scholar thesis, 2011. 51 pp. Large format. Posted at: http://digitalcommons.uconn.edu/srhonors_theses/208.

253. Palmer, Louis H. *Vampires in the New World.* Santa Barbara, CA: Praeger, 2013. 176 pp. hb. dj.

254. Palmer, Paula. "The Vampire: Transgressive Sexuality." In Paula Palmer. *Lesbian Gothic: Transgressive Fictions.* London: Wellington House, 1999, pp. 99–112.

255. Paparesta, Ronald. "The Vampire: Tool of the Devil." *Journal of Vampirism* 1, 4 (Summer 1978): 10–14.

256. Peters, Fiona. "Looking in the Mirror: Vampires, the Symbolic, and the Thing." In Peter Day, ed. *Vampire: Myths and Metaphors of Enduring Evil.* Amsterdam: Rodopi, 2006, pp. 177–88.

257. Petit, Christopher. "Vampires Past and Present." *Elle* 4, 7 (March 1989): 368–73.

258. Phillips-Summers, Diana. *Vampires: A Bloodthirsty History in Art and Literature.* Hod Hosharon, Israel: Astrolog Publishing House, 2003. 144 pp. tp. Illus. by Daniel Ackerman.

259. Pivárcsi, István. *Just a Bite: A Transylvania Vampire Expert's Short History of the Undead.* Trans. by Dorottya Olchváry, Dániel Dányi, and Paul Olchváry. Williamstown, MA: New Europe Books, 2012. 285 pp. tp.

260. Polidoro, Massimo. "In Search of Dracula." *Skeptical Inquirer* 30, 2 (March/April 2006): 23–27.

261. Proctor, David. *The Quotable Vampire.* New York: Kensington Books, 1997. 85 pp. pb. Small format.

262. Prothero, Owen. "Vampires and Vampirism." *Occult Review* 10 (December 1909): 332ff.

263. Reece, Gregory L. *Creature of the Night: In Search of Ghosts, Vampires, Werewolves and Demons.* London: I. B. Tauris, 2012. 208 pp. tp.

264. Riccardo, Martin V. *The Lure of the Vampire.* Chicago: Adams Press, 1983. 67 pp. pb.

265. _____. "Vampires—An Unearthly Reality." *Fate 46*, 2 (February 1993): 61–70.

266. Rickels, Laurence A. *The Vampire Lectures.* Minneapolis: University of Minnesota Press, 1999. 358 pp. hb. & tp.

267. Rydman, Michael. The Enduring Appeal of Vampires." *Grand Valley Review* 5, 2 (1989): 44–48. Posted at: http://scholarworks.gvsu.edu/gvr/vol5/iss2/18.

268. Satu, Aislinn. *The History of Ghosts and Vampires.* San Bernardino, CA: the author, 2013. 25 pp. tp.

269. Saudo, Nathalie. "'Every speck of dust […] a devouring monster in embryo': The Vampire's Effluvia in *Dracula* by Bram Stoker." In John S. Bak, ed. *Post/modern Dracula: From Victorian Themes to Postmodern Praxis.* Cambridge: Cambridge Scholars Publishing, 2007, pp. 45–60.

270. _____. "'I Was Glad to See Her Paleness and Her Illness': la redoutable bonne santé dans *Dracula*." *Études anglaises* 58, 4 (2005): 402–415.

271. Saxon, Kurt. *Classic Ghosts and Vampires.* Eureka, CA: Atlan "A" Dformularies, 1979. 163 pp. pb. Large format.

272. Schopp, Andrew. "Cruising the Alternatives: Homoeroticism and the Contemporary Vampire." *Journal of Popular Culture* 30, 4 (Spring 1997): 231–43.

273. Seabrook, William. "The Vampire and Werewolf." In William Seabrook. *Witchcraft: Its Power in the World Today.* New York: Harcourt Brace & Co., 1940. Rpt.: New York: Lancer Books, 1968, pp. 98–155. Excerpt in: McNally, Raymond T. *A Clutch of Vampires.* New York: Bell Publishing Company, 1974, pp. 169–78.

274. Segura, Allison C. *Perfect Creatures: A Social and Cultural Interpretation of Vampires in Fiction and Film.* Lafayette: University of Louisiana at Lafayette, Ph.D. dissertation, 2008. 134 pp. Large format.

275. Shirley, Ralph. "The Problem of Vampires?" *Occult Review* 40 (November 1924): 244ff. Rpt. as: "Is Belief in Vampires Justifiable? *The Bram Stoker Society Journal* 8 (1996): 18ff. Rpt. in: Leslie Shepard and Albert Power, eds. *Dracula: Celebrating 100 Years.* Dublin: Mentor Press, 1997, pp. 18–21.

276. Simpson, Robert. "Children of the Night: The Truth About Vampires, Werewolves, and Shapeshifters." *Twilight Zone Magazine* 7, 5 (December 1987): 22–25, 84–85.

277. Skal, David J. "Blood-Borne Monster." *Out* (December-January 1993).

278. _____. *The Monster Show: A Cultural History of Horror.* New York: W. W. Norton & Company, 1993. 432 pp. hb. dj. *The Monster Show: A Cultural History of Horror* received the first (1994) award as the best nonfiction book of the previous year given annually by the Lord Ruthven Society.

279. _____. *Romancing the Vampire: From Past to Present.* Atlanta, GA: Whitman Publishing, 2009. 144 pp. hb. slipcase. Large format.

280. _____. *V Is for Vampire: The A–Z Guide to Everything Undead.* New York: Plume/Penguin, 1996. 288 pp. tp. *V Is for Vampire: The A-Z Guide to Everything Undead* received the 1997 award as the best nonfiction book of the previous year given annually by the Lord Ruthven Society.

281. _____, ed. *Vampires: Encounters with the Undead.* New York: Black Dog & Leventhal Publishers, 2001. 604 pp. hb. dj. Large format. This anthology, largely of fictional contributions, also includes non-fiction pieces by Dudley Wright, Augustin Calmet, Helena Petrovna Blavatsky, Agnes Murgoci, Glady Hall, Norine Dresser, and Rosemary Ellen Guiley.

282. Slemen, Tom. *Vampires.* Liverpool, UK: The Bluecoat Press, 2007. 141 pp. tp.

283. Sobol, Gianna. *True Blood: A Field Guide to Vampires: (And Other Creatures of Satan).* San Francisco, CA: Chronicle Books (November 2013. 144 pp. hb. boards.

284. Sorescu, Martin. "Vampires and Vampirology." *Times Literary Supplement* (January 11, 1991).

285. Spence, Lewis. "The Vampire Legend— Its Origin & Nature." *Occult Review* 27 (March 1918): 137ff.Rpt. in: *The Dark Shadows Book of Vampires and Werewolves.* New York: Paperback Library, 1970, pp. 123–35.

286. Stand, Ginger. "A Concise History of Blood-Sucking, Vampyrmania and Voyeurism." *Downtown* 306 (November 18, 1992): 14, 24, 29.

287. Steiger, Brad. "The Horror of Vampires and Ghouls." In Brad Steiger. *Monsters among Us.* Rockport, MA: ParaResearch, 1982. Rpt.: New York: Berkley, 1989, pp. 119–41. Rpt. Lakeville, MN: Galde Press, 2006, pp. 119–41.

288. _____. *Real Vampires, Night Stalkers, and Creatures of the Darkside.* Detroit: Visible Ink, 2009. 287 pp. tp.

289. Stevenson, Jay. *The Complete Idiot's Guide to Vampires.* Indianapolis, IN: Alpha Books, 2002. 314 pp. tp.

290. Stewart, Barbara. *Bloodlines: The Little Book of Vampires.* Vancouver, BC: Arsenal Pulp Press, 1995. 95 pp. pb. Small format.

291. Strumer, Andre Marc. *The Creatures of the Night: Vampires from Books to Films.* Hattiesburg: University of Southern Mississippi, Ph.D. dissertation, 2007. 267 pp. Large format.

292. Suckling, Nigel. *Book of the Vampire.* Illus. by Bruce Pennington. Wisley, Surrey, UK: Facts, Figures & Fun, 2008. 224 pp. hb.

293. _____. *Vampires.* Wisley, Surrey, UK: Facts, Figures & Fun, 2006. 96 pp. hb.

294. Summers, Montague. *The Vampire, His Kith and Kin.* London: Routledge, Kegan Paul, Trench, 1928. 256 pp. hb. Posted at: http://www.sacred-texts.com/goth/vkk/index.htm. Rpt.: New Hyde Park, NY: University Books, 1960. 356 pp. hb. Rpt. as: *The Vampire in Lore and Legend.* New York: Dover, 2001. 356 pp. tp. Rpt. as: *The Vampire: His Kith and Kin, A Critical Edition.* Ed. by John Browning. Berkeley, CA: Apocryphile Press, 2011. 433 pp. tp.

295. _____. *The Vampire in Europe.* London: Routledge, Kegan Paul, Trench, Trübner, & Co., 1929. 329 pp. hb. Posted at: http://www.scribd.com/doc/56466672/Summers-Montague-The-Vampire-in-Europe-1968.Rpt.: New Hyde Park, NY: University Press, 1961. 329 pp. hb. Rpt.: New York: Gramercy Books, 1996. 329 pp. hb. dj. Rpt.: New York: Random House, 1996. 329 pp. hb. Excerpt in: McNally, Raymond T. *A Clutch of Vampires.* New York: Bell Publishing Company, 1974, pp. 179–82. Excerpt rpt. in: Angela Cybulski, ed.

Vampires: Fact or Fiction? Ser.: Opposing Viewpoints. Farmington Hills, MI: Greenhaven Press/Thomson, Gale, 2003. pp. 41–49. Excerpt rpt. as: *The Vampire in Russia, Romania and Bulgaria.* Whitefish, MT: Kessinger Publishing, 2005. 52 pp. pb. Large format.

296. ***A Survivor's Guide to Dracula.*** Bucharesti: Transylvanian Society of Dracula, n.d. [1999]. 16 pp. pb. Large format.

297. Szigethy, Anna, and Anne Graves. *Vampires from Drakul to the Vampire Lestat.* Toronto: Key Porter Books, 2001. 202 pp. tp.

298. Taylor, Joules. *Vampires.* London: Spruce/New York: Octopus Books USA, 2009. 192 pp. tp.

299. Terry, Nicole. *Vampirism & Sadism.* New York: Count Dracula Fan Club, 1987. 6 pp. pb. Staples.

300. Thompson, Dave. *If You Like True Blood...Here Are Over 200 Films, TV Shows and Other Oddities that You Will Love.* Milwaukee, WI: Backbeat Book/Hal Leonard Corporation, 213. 231 pp. tp.

301. Thompson, Leslie M. "The Vampire in an Age of Technology." In Francis Edward Abernathy, ed. *T for Texas.* Dallas: E-Heart Press, 1982, pp. 151–160.

302. Thomson-Smith, Lydia D. *The Revival of Vampires: Twilight Hits Dracula.* Beau-Bassin, Mauritius: FastBook Publishing, 2010. 240 pp.

303. Thorne, Russ. *Gothic Dreams: Vampires: Fantasy Art, Fiction and the Movies.* Illust. by Anne Stokes. London: Flame Tree Publishing, 2013. 128 pp. hb. boards.

304. Thorne, Tony. *Children of the Night: Of Vampires and Vampirism.* London: Victor Gollancz, 1999. 296 pp. hb. dj.

305. Time-Life Books, Editors of. "Vampires." In: The Editors of Time Life Books. *Transformations.* Alexandria, VA: Time-Life Books, 1989, 108–36.

306. Underwood, Peter, ed. *The Vampire's Bedside Companion: The Amazing World of Vampires in Fact and Fiction.* London: Leslie Frewin, 1975. 248 pp. hb. A collection of fiction and nonfiction writing on the vampire. Non-fiction contributors include Devendra P. Varma and Sean Manchester.

307. Varma, Devendra P. "The Genesis of Dracula: A Re-Visit." In Peter Underwood, ed. *The Vampire's Bedside Companion: The Amazing World of Vampires in Fact and Fiction.* London: Leslie Frewin, 1975, pp. 53–68.

308. _____. "The Vampire in Legend, Lore, and Literature." Introduction to: *Varney the Vampire; or, The Feast of Blood.* New York: Arno Press, 1970, vol. 1, pp. xiii–xxx. Rpt. in: Margaret L. Carter, ed. *The Vampire in Literature: a Critical Bibliography.* Ann Arbor: UMI Research Press, 1989, pp. 13–30.

309. Volta, Ornella. *The Vampire.* New York: Award, 1965. 159 pp. pb. Rpt.: London: Tandem, n.d. [1965]. 169 pp. pb. From the original French edition published as *Le Vampire.* Paris: Jean-Jacques Pauvert, 1962. 237 pp. pb.

310. Voltaire. *Philosophical Dictionary.* Trans. by Peter Gay. New York Harcourt, Brace & World, 1967. 664 pp. tp. Frequently reprinted. Posted at: http://history.hanover.edu/texts/voltaire/volindex.html. In his comments, Voltaire, acting as spokesperson for the French phase of the Enlightenment, dismisses the emerging conversation on vampires in the eighteenth century by noting, "After slander, nothing is communicated more promptly than superstition, fanaticism, sorcery, and tales of those raised from the dead."

311. _____. *A Pocket Philosophical Dictionary.* Trans. by John Fletcher. Oxford: Oxford University Press, 2011. 283 pp.

312. _____. *The Works of Voltaire: A Contemporary Version.* Vol. VII. Trans. by William F. Fleming. New York: E. R. DuMont, 1901.

313. Weinstock, Jeffrey Andrew. "Vampires, Vampires, Everywhere!" *Phi Kappa Phi Forum* 90, 3 (2010): 4–5.

314. Wilson, Rowan. *Strange but True Vampires.* New York: Sterling Publishing Co., 1997. 170 pp. pb.

315. Winnubst, Shannon. "Vampires, Anxieties, and Dreams: Race and Sex in the Contemporary United States." *Hypatia* 18, 3 (2003): 1–20.

316. Youngson, Jeanne Keyes. *The Bizarre World of Vampires.* Chicago: Adams Press, 1996. 40 pp. pb. Staples.

317. _____, **and Shelley Leigh Hunt.** *Do Vampires Exist? A Special Report from Dracula World Enterprises.* New York: Dracula Press, 1993. 20 pp. pb. Staples.

318. Žižek, Stephen. "Kant as a Theoretician of Vampirism, 1994." In Gilda Williams, ed. *The Gothic.* Ser.: Whitechapel: Documents of Contemporary Art. Cambridge, MA: The MIT Press, 2007, pp. 139–44.

II. Folklore and History

Folklore and Mythology

Recognition of and study of the vampire begins with the presence of the vampire and vampire-like characters in the world's folklore. The vampire is not present in all of the world's traditional societies, but where absent, other supernatural entities appear who fill in much of the vampire's function. The earliest vampires we encounter are females (such as the lamia and Pontianak) who attack children and provide an explanation for otherwise incomprehensible deaths of infants.

Next come the male vampires who arise after experiencing an unnatural death (that is, a death that occurred from a violent accident, a wasting disease, or away from one's village). In its Eastern European form, this vampire would become the one most familiar to us in the modern world.

In addition to these two main vampire types, there are a number of lesser creatures who have been identified as vampires because of their blood drinking or consumption of a victim's life force, and a set of creatures who have been cited for their acting (at times) like a vampire in some respects, especially the succubus (and incubus), the banshee, the west African witch, the Southeast Asian pontianak, the Mexican weeping woman (La Llorona), and the mara.

Relative to the English-speaking world, the vampire was initially described in the nineteenth century ethnographic, anthropological, and folklore literature that offered some awareness of its global presence and variety, at least within the academic community. More popular awareness of the folklore vampire awaited the publication of Dudley Wright's *Vampires and Vampirism* (which would be frequently reprinted under a variety of titles) and the two books of Montague Summers that attempted to summarize all we know about vampires as the twentieth century began.

The folklore literature holds an ambiguous place in the analysis of the contemporary permeation of the culture by the vampire. The folklore was certainly the source and inspiration of the original vampire poems and stories in the nineteenth century, though once the literary vampire was created, it moved further and further away from its folkloric origins. In the 1890s, Bram Stoker re-injected folklore at a significant level into the developing construct of the literary vampire, and his treatment of the Transylvanian vampire in *Dracula* (derived from the writings of Emily Gerard) would become integral to the tradition to the present.

Most recently, the emergence of both the sympathetic conflicted vampire and especially the "good guy" vampire in the 1970s represents major steps away from both the pre-modern vampire of folklore and the modern vampire of the late-nineteenth century literary tradition. Both older forms of the vampire were entirely negative characters, while the new vampires allowed book readers and moviegoers to openly identify with the bloodsuckers. The new vampires signaled the emergence of new forms of vampiric existence that continues to serve the needs of the contemporary post-modern and urbanized reading public.

319. Abbott, G. F. "Vampire." In: G. F. Abbott. *Macedonian Folklore.* Chicago: Argonaut, Inc., Publishers, 1969, pp. 217–22. Posted at: http://www.archive.org/stream/macedonianfolklo00abborich/macedonianfolklo00abborich_djvu.txt.

320. Afanas'ev, Aleksander. "Poetic Views of the Slavs Regarding Nature." Trans. by Jan Perkowski. In Jan Perkowski, ed. *Vampires of the Slavs.* Cambridge, MA: Slavica Press, 1976, pp. 160–79.

321. _____. "The Vampire." In Aleksander Afanas'ev. *Russian Fairy Tales.* Trans. by Norbert Guterman. New York: Pantheon Books, 1945, pp. 593–98.

322. "**Asema: The Vampires of Surinam.**" *International Vampire* 1, 1 (Fall 1990): 16.

323. Askenasy, Hans. "Werewolves, Witches and Vampires." In Hans Askenasy. *Cannibalism from Sacrifice to Survival.* Amherst, NY: Prometheus Press, 1994, pp. 149–63.

324. Bain, R. Nisbet, trans. "The Vampire and St. Michael." In R. Nisbet Bain, ed. *Cossack Fairy Tales and Folk Tales.* London: George G. Harrap & Co., 1916, pp. 102–17. Posted at: https://archive.org/details/cossackfairytal00baingoog. Rpt. Millwood, NY: Kraus Reprint Co., 1975. Rpt. in: Jan Perkowski, ed. *Vampires of the Slavs.* Cambridge, MA: Slavica Press, 1976, pp. 235–41.

325. Barber, Paul. "Forensic Pathology and the European Vampire." *Journal of Folklore Research* 24, 1 (Jan.-Apr. 1987): 1–32. Rpt. in: Alan Dundas, ed. *The Vampire: A Casebook.* Madison: University of Wisconsin Press, 1998. pp. 109–142.

326. _____. "The Real Vampire." *Natural History* (October 1990): 79–106.

327. _____. "Staking Claims: The Vampires of Folklore and Fiction." *Skeptical Inquirer* 20, 2 (March/April 1996). Posted at: http://www.csicop.org/si/9603/staking.html.

328. _____. *Vampires, Burial, and Death: Folklore and Reality.* New Haven, CT: Yale University Press, 1988. 236 pp. hb & tp. Excerpt rpt. in: Angela Cybulski, ed. *Vampires: Fact or Fiction?* Ser.: Opposing Viewpoints. Farmington Hills, MI: Greenhaven Press/Thomson, Gale, 2003. pp. 91–100.

329. Baring-Gould, Sabine. "A Hungarian Bather in Blood." In Sabine Baring-Gould. *The Book of Werewolves.* London: Smith, Elder & Co., 1865. 139–41 pp. Posted at: http://www.gutenberg.org/ebooks/5324. Rpt.: New York: Causeway Books, 1973, pp. 139–41.

330. Barndon, Elizabeth. "Superstitions in Vermillion Parish." In Moody C. Boatright, Wilson M. Hudson, and Allen Maxwell, eds. *The Golden Log.* Dallas: Southern Methodist University Press, 1962, pp. 108–18.

331. Batty, Judith A,. and Edward Garcia Kraul. *La Llorona: Encounters with the Weeping Woman.* Santa Fe, NM: Word Process, 1988. 108 pp. tp. Rpt.: Santa Fe, NM: Sunstone Press, 2004. 108 pp. tp.

332. Bell, Michael E. *Food for the Dead: On the Trail of New England's Vampires.* New York: Carroll & Graf, 2001. 331 pp. hb. dj. *Food for the Dead: On the Trail of New England's Vampires* received the 2002 award as the best nonfiction book of the previous year given annually by the Lord Ruthven Society.

333. _____. "Vampires and Death in New England, 1784 to 1892." *Agricultural History* 31, 2 (2006): 124–140.

334. _____. "Vampires in Rhode Island?" *Old Rhode Island* 4, 8 (October 1994): 9–12.

335. "**The Blood Drawing Ghosts.**" In. Jeremiah Curtin. *Tales of the Fairies of the Ghost World Collected from Oral Tradition in South-West Munster.* New York: Lemma Publishing Corporation, 1970, pp. 180–91. Rpt. in: Sean Kelly, ed. *Irish Folk & Fairy Tales.* New York: Gallery Press, 1982, pp. 241–48.

336. Blum, Richard, and Eva Blum. *The Dangerous Hour: The Lore of Crisis and Mystery in Rural Greece.* London: Chatto & Windus, 1970. 410 pp.

337. Bogatyrëv, Pëtr. *Vampires in the Carpathians: Magical Acts, Rites and Beliefs in Sub-*

carpathian Rus. New York: East European Monographs, 1998. 188 pp. hb.

338. Brass, Tom. "Nymphs, Shepherds, and Vampires: The Agrarian Myth on Film." *Dialectical Anthropologist* 25 (2000): 205–37. Posted at: http://www.scribd.com/doc/83661783/Nymphs-Shepherds-and-Vampires-The-Agrarian-Myth-on-Film-2000-Dialectical-Anthropology.

339. Brautigam, Rob. "The Vampire of the Rue Serpente." *Coven Journal* 4 (1990): 24.

340. _____. "Vampires in Bulgaria." *International Vampire* 1, 2 (Winter 1991): 16–17.

341. Breene, R. S. "An Irish Vampire" *The Occult Review* 42, 4 (October 1925): 242–45. Rpt. in: Montague Summers. *The Vampire in Europe*. London: Routledge, Kegan Paul, Trench, Trübner, & Co., 1929, pp. 118–22. Posted at: http://www.scribd.com/doc/27257523/The-Vampire-in-Europe. Rpt. in: Donald F. Glut. *True Vampires of History*. New York: HC Publishers, 1971, pp. 170–77. Rpt. in: Anthony Masters. *The Natural History of the Vampire*. New York: G. P. Putnam's Sons, 1972, pp. 136–39. Rpt. in: Basil Copper. *The Vampire in Legend, Fact and Art*. Secaucus, NJ: Citadel Press, 1974, pp. 154–57. Rpt. in: *Bram Stoker Society Journal* 7 (1995): 16–19.

342. Brown, Ivor J. "The Unquiet Grave of the Vampire." *Fate Magazine* (UK) (January 1967). Rpt. in: Peter Haining, ed. *The Dracula Scrapbook*. New York: Bramwell House, 1975, pp. 131–34.

343. Brundage, Burr Cartwright. "The Cultic Uses of Darkness." In Burr Cartwright Brundage. *The Jade Steps: A Ritual Life of the Aztecs*. Salt Lake City: University of Utah Press, 1985, pp. 144–52.

344. _____. "The Goddesses." In Burr Cartwright Brundage. *The Fifth Sun: Aztec Gods, Aztec World*. Austin: University of Texas Press, 1979, pp. 153–75.

345. Burns, Stu. "A Short History of Vampire Folklore." In Elizabeth Miller, ed. *Bram Stoker's Dracula: A Documentary Volume*. Detroit: Thompson/Gale, 2005, pp. 29–35.

346. Burton, Richard. *Vikram the Vampire*. London: Longmans, Green & Co, 1870. 319 pp. hb. Posted at: http://www.fullbooks.com/Vikram-and-the-Vampire1.html. Rpt.: London: Tylston and Edwards, 1893. 243 pp. hb. Limited to 200 copies. Rpt.: New York: Dover Publications, 1969. 243 pp. tp. Rpt.: Rochester, VT: Park Street Press, 1992. 243 pp. tp.

347. Cajkanovic, Vaselin. "The Killing of a Vampire." *The Folklore Forum* 7 (1974): 260–71. Rpt. in: Alan Dundas, ed. *The Vampire: A Casebook*. Madison: University of Wisconsin Press, 1998, pp. 72–84.

348. Calmet, Dom Augustine. *Dissertations upon the Apparitions of Angels, Demons, and Ghosts, and Concerning the Vampires of Hungary, Bohemia, Moravia, and Silesia*. 2 vols. London: M. Cooper, 1759. Rpt. as: *The Phantom World*. 2 vols. London: Richard Bently, 1850. hb. Rpt.: Philadelphia: A. Hart, Late Carey & Hart, 1850. Posted at: http://www.gutenberg.org/catalog/world/readfile?fk_files=1556734. Rpt.: Vol. 2 only as: *Treatise on Vampires and Revenants: The Phantom World*. Brighton, East Sussex, UK: Desert Island Books, 1993. 192 pp. hb. dj. Rpt. as: *The Phantom World*. London: Wordsworth Edition in association with The Folklore Society, 2001. 337 pp. tp. The English edition is a translation of *Dissertations sur les Apparitions des Anges des Démons et des Espits, et sur les revenants et Vampires de Hingrie, de Boheme, de Moravie, et de Silésie* (Paris, 1746). Brief excerpts have also been reprinted by Perkowski in the *Vampires of the Slavs*, by Raymond T. McNally in *A Clutch of Vampires*, and by David Skal in *Vampires: Encounters with the Dead*.

349. Cheng, Sandra. "The Soul, Evil Spirits and the Undead: Vampires, Death and Burial in Jewish Folklore and Law." *Preternature* 1, 2 (2012).

350. Cininas, Jazmina. "Wolfsbane, Fangs and Hirsute Heretics: Tracing the Confluences between Lycanthropy, Witchcraft and Vampirism in the Female Werewolf." In Jonathan A. Allan and Elizabeth E. Nelson, eds. *Inversion of Power and Paradox: Studying Monstrosity*. Oxford, UK: Inter-Disciplinary Press, 2012, pp. 3–14.

351. Citro, Joseph. "The Hungary Dead." In Joseph Citro. *Passing Strange: True Tales of New England Hauntings and Horror*. New York: Houghton Mifflin, 1996, pp. 204–19.

352. _____. "Vampires." In Joseph Citro. *The Vermont Monster Guide*. Lebanon, NH: University Press of New England, 2009, pp. 59–60.

353. _____. "Vampires, Graveyards, and Ghouls." In Joseph Citro. *Green Mountain Ghosts, Ghouls & Unsolved Mysteries*. New York: Houghton Mifflin, 1994, pp. 67–80.

354. Clebert, Jean Paul. *The Gypsies*. Harmondsworth, Middlesex, UK: Penguin Books, 1963. 282 pp.

355. Clive-Ross, F. "The Croglin Vampire." *Tomorrow Magazine* 11, 2 (Spring 1963): 103–09.

356. Codrington, R. H. *The Melanesians.* Oxford: Clarendon Press, 1891. 419 pp. hb. Rpt.: 1969. 419 pp. Posted at: https://archive.org/details/melanesiansstudi00codruoft.

357. Coleman, Marion Moore. *A World Remembered: Tales and Lore of the Polish Land.* Cheshire, CT: Cherry Hill Books, 1965. 299 pp. tp.

358. Colombo, John Robert, ed. *Windingo: An Anthology of Fact and Fantastic Fiction.* Saskatoon, SK: Western Producer Prairie Books, 1982. 208 pp. hb. dj.

359. Connelly, James H. "The Voudou Vampire." *The Word* 2 (1905): 57–63, 117–124.

360. Cooper, Brian. "The Word Vampire: Its Slavonic Form and Origin." *Journal of Slavic Linguistics* 13, 2 (Summer-Fall 2005): 251–70.

361. Coxwell, C. Fillingham. "Concerning Vampires." In C. Fillingham Coxwell. *Siberian and Other Folk-tales.* London: C. W. Daniel Company, 1925, pp. 420–21. Rpt.: New York: AMS Press, n.d., pp. 420–21.

362. Craigie, William A. "Monsters." In William A. Craigie. *Scandinavian Folk-Lore.* London: Alexander Gardner, 1896, pp. 249–74. Rpt.: Detroit: Singing Tree Press, 1970, pp. 249–75.

363. Crooke, William. "The Spirits of the Malevolent Dead, and Demons." In William Crooke. *Religion & Folklore of Northern India.* London: Humphrey Milford/Oxford University Press, 1926, pp. 183–226.

364. Curran, Bob. *Bloody Irish: Celtic Vampire Legends.* Dublin: Merlin Publishing, 2002. 186 pp. tp. Folklore. Rpt.: New York: Fall River Press, 2009. 198 pp. hb. dj.

365. Curtin, Jeremiah. "European Folk-Lore in the U.S." *Journal of American Folklore* 2 (1889): 56–59.

366. D'Agostino, T. "'Rhode Island: The Vampire Capital of America." *Fate* 54, 10 (October 2001): 19–21.

367. Danilou, Alain. "Night Wanderers (raksasa)." In Alain Danilou. *Hindu Polytheism.* New York: Pantheon Books, 1964, pp. 309–310.

368. Day, William Patrick. *Vampire Legends in Contemporary American Culture: What Becomes a Legend Most.* Lexington: University of Kentucky Press, 2002. 256 pp. hb. *Vampire Legends in Contemporary American Culture: What Becomes a Legend Most* received the 2003 award as the best non-fiction book of the previous year given annually by the Lord Ruthven Society.

369. "The Dead and the Living." In: Reimund Kvideland and Henning K. Sehmsdorf, eds. *Scandinavian Folk Belief and Legend.* Minneapolis: University of Minnesota Press, 1988, pp. 87–128.

370. de Aragon, John. *The Legend of La Llorona.* Las Vegas, NM: Pan American Pub. Co., 1980. 94 pp. Rpt.: Santa Fe, NM: Sunstone Press, 2006. 94 pp. tp.

371. de Groot, J. J. M. *The Religious System of China.* Leyden: E. J. Brill, 1892–1910. 928 pp. Posted at: http://www.archive.org/stream/religioussystem00groogoog/religioussystem00groogoog_djvu.txt. Excerpt in: McNally, Raymond T. *A Clutch of Vampires.* New York: Bell Publishing Company, 1974, pp. 33–34.

372. de Visser, M. W. *The Dragon in China and Japan.* Amsterdam: J. Müller, 1913. 242 pp. Rpt.: Weisbaden, Germany: Dr. Martin Sändig oHG, 1969. Posted at: http://www.archive.org/stream/cu31924021444728/cu31924021444728_djvu.txt.

373. De Wit, Augusta. *Java Facts and Fancies.* Singapore: Oxford University Press, 1984. 328 pp. hb.

374. Doan, James E. "The Vampire in Native American and Mesoamerican Lore." In Barbara Brodman and James E. Doan, eds. *The Universal Vampire: Origins and Evolution of a Legend.* Madison, NJ: Fairleigh Dickinson University Press, 2013, pp. 137–47.

375. Dömötör, Tekla. *Hungarian Folk Beliefs.* Bloomington: Indiana University Press, 1982. 323 pp. hb.

376. Dorson, Richard M. *Folk Legends of Japan.* Rutland, VT: Charles E. Tuttle Company, 1962. 256 pp. hb.

377. Drapkin, C. M. "The Vampire of Croglin Grange." *The Skeptic* (September 1992). Rpt.: *Fortean Times* (April-May 1993): 39–41.

378. du Boulay, Juliet. "The Greek Vampire: A Study of Cyclic Symbolism in Marriage and Death." *Man* n.s. 17, 2 (June 1982): 219–238. Rpt. in Alan Dundes. *The Vampire: A Casebook.* Madison: University of Wisconsin Press, 1998, pp. 85–108.

379. Dundas, Alan, ed. *The Vampire: A Casebook.* Madison: University of Wisconsin Press, 1998. 182 pp.

380. _____. "The Vampire as Bloodthirsty Revenant: A Psychoanalytic Postmortem." In Alan Dundas, ed. *The Vampire: A Casebook.* Madison: University of Wisconsin Press, 1998, pp. 159–175. Rpt. In: Alan Dundas. *Bloody Mary in the Mirror: Essays in psychoanalytic folkloristics.* Jackson: University Press of Mississippi, 2002, pp. 16–32.

381. Durham, M. Edith. "Of Magic, Witches and Vampires in the Balkans." *Man* 23 (1923): 189–92.

382. Dyall, Valentino. "Vampire of Croglin Hall." *Fate* 7, 4 (April 1954): 96–104.

383. Endicott, E. M. *An Analysis of Malay Magic.* Singapore: Oxford University Press, 1970. 188 pp. hb.

384. Evans-Wentz, W. Y. *The Tibetan Book of the Dead.* Oxford: Oxford University Press/London: Humphrey Milford, 1927. 248 pp. hb. Posted at: http://www.scribd.com/doc/159573069/eBook-the-Tibetan-Book-of-the-Dead. Rpt.: New York: Causeway Books, 1973.

385. Fine, John V. A., Jr. "In Defense of Vampires." *East European Quarterly* 21 (1987): 15–23. Rpt. in: Alan Dundas, ed. *The Vampire: A Casebook.* Madison: University of Wisconsin Press, 1998, pp. 57–66. Rpt. in: Angela Cybulski, ed. *Vampires: Fact or Fiction?* Ser.: Opposing Viewpoints. Farmington Hills, MI: Greenhaven Press/Thomson, Gale, 2003, pp. 24–32.

386. Flaxton, Holly. ""What Then Is an Asema?" *International Vampire* 2 (n.d.): 15–16.

387. Fontenrose, Joseph. *Python: A Study of Delphic Myth and Its Origins.* Berkeley: University of California Press, 1959. 616 pp. Posted at: http://www.kilibro.com/books/9780520040915-python.

388. Forde, Daryll. "Spirits, Witches, and Sorcerers." In Daryll Forde. *Yakö Studies.* London: Oxford University Press, 1964, pp. 210–233.

389. Frazer, J. G. *Balder the Beautiful: The Fire Festivals of Europe and the Doctrine of the External Soul.* 2 vols. London: Macmillan and Co., 1913. Posted at: http://www.fullbooks.com/Balder-The-Beautiful-Vol-I-1.html.

390. Gallop, Rodney. *Portugal: A Book of Folk-Ways.* Cambridge: Cambridge University Press, 1936. 291 pp.

391. Garza, Thomas J., comp. *The Vampire in Slavic Cultures.* San Diego, CA: Cognella, 2010. 572 pp. pb. Large format. A notable collection of primary and secondary materials on the Slavic vampire.

392. Gelder, Ken. "Vampires in Greece." In Ken Gelder. *The Horror Reader.* New York: Routledge, 2000, pp. 228–41.

393. Georgieva, Ivanichka. *Bulgarian Mythology.* Sofia, Bulgaria: Svyet, 1985. 210 pp.

394. Gerard, Emily. *The Land Beyond the Forest.* 2 vols. London: Will Blackwood & Sons, 1888. Rpt.: New York: Harper and Brothers, 1888. Posted at: https://archive.org/details/cu31924011921420.

395. _____. "Transylvanian Superstitions." *The Nineteenth Century* 18 (1885): 135–50. Rpt. in: Peter Haining, ed. *The Dracula Scrapbook.* New York: Bramwell House, 1975, pp. 40–43. Rpt.: New York: Count Dracula Fan Club, n.d. 3 pp. This article would later be reprinted as a chapter in Gerard's book on Transylvania and more importantly, become the major source consulted by Bram Stoker for information on vampire folklore in his writing of *Dracula.* Transylvania was, of course, part of Hungary at this time. It did not become part of Romania until after World War I.

396. Gerrits, Andre, and Nanci Adler. *Vampires Unstaked: National images, stereotypes and myths in East Central Europe.* Amsterdam: Koninklijke Nederlandse Akademie van Wetenschappen (Royal Netherlands Academy of Arts and Science), 1995. 248 pp. tp.

397. Gibbons, Luke. "The Vampire Strikes Back." In Luke Gibbons. *Gaelic Gothic: Race, Colonization, and Irish Culture.* Galway, Ireland: Arlen House, 2004, 96 pp.

398. Goldin, P. R. "The Cultural and Religious Background of Sexual Vampirism in Ancient China." *Theology and Sexuality* 12, 3 (2006): 285–307.

399. Gooch, Stan. "Incubi and Succubi in Suburbia." In Stan Gooch. *The Origins of Psychic Phenomena: Poltergeists, Incubi, Succubi, and the Unconscious Mind.* Rochester, VT: Inner Traditions, 2007, pp. 6–189.

400. Gottlieb, Richard M. "The European Vampire: Applied Psychoanalysis and Applied Legend." *Folklore Forum* 24, 2 (1991): 39–61.

401. Grady, Frank. "Vampire Culture." In Jeffrey Jerome Cohen, ed. *Monster Theory: Reading Culture.* Minneapolis: University of Minnesota Press, 1996, pp. 225–42.

402. Graham, W. A. "Spirit Worship." In W. A. Graham. *Siam.* London: Alexander Moring,

1924, pp. 280–92. Posted at: https://archive.org/details/siamhandbookofpr00grah.

403. Graves, Robert, and Raphael Patai. *The Hebrew Myths: The Book of Genesis.* Garden City, NY: Doubleday, 1964. 311 pp. tp. Includes a lengthy discussion of the Hebrew vampiric figure Lilith.

404. Groome, Francis Hindes. "Roumanian-Gypsy Stories No. 5.—The Vampire." In Francis Hindes Groome. *Gypsy Folk Tales.* London: Hurst and Blackett, 1899, pp. 14–19. Posted at: http://www.sacred-texts.com/neu/roma/gft/.

405. Gross, Glenn Watson. *The Trail of the Vampire: A Study of the Demonic in Folklore and History.* Austin: Senior Honors Thesis, University of Texas-Austin, 1983. 92 pp. Large format.

406. Haining, Peter. *The Flesh Eaters: True Stories of Cannibals and Blood Drinkers.* London: Boxtree, 1994. 240 pp. pb.

407. _____. *The Leprechaun's Kingdom.* New York: Harmony Books, 1980. 128 pp. pb. Large format. Haining includes a discussion of banshees and vampires in his observations of Irish spirit entities.

408. Hare, Augustus. "The Vampire of Croglin Grange." In: Augustus Hare. *The Story of My Life.* Vol. 4 London: Allen, 1900, pp. 203–08. Posted at: http://www.nwf.org/~/media/PDFs/GABC/The%20Vampire.ashx. Rpt. as: *In My Solitary Life.* London: George Allen & Unwin, 1953, pp. Rpt. as: *Peculiar People: The Story of My Life.* Chicago: Academy Chicago Publishers, 1995, pp. 187–210. Rpt. in: Peter Haining, ed. *The Midnight People.* London: Leslie Frewin, 1968, pp 21–25. Rpt. in: *The Dark Shadows Book of Vampires and Werewolves.* New York: Paperback Library, 1970, pp. 75–79. Rpt. in: Donald F. Glut. *True Vampires of History.* New York: HC Publishers, 1971, pp. 74–84. Rpt.: Anthony Masters. *The Natural History of the Vampire.* New York: G. P. Putnam's Sons, 1972, pp. 132–36. Rpt. in: Basil Copper. *The Vampire in Legend, Fact and Art.* Secaucus, NJ: Citadel Press, 1974, pp. 51–54. Rpt. in: McNally, Raymond T. *A Clutch of Vampires.* New York: Bell Publishing Company, 1974, pp. 155–62.

409. Hartnup, Karen. *On the Beliefs of the Greeks: Leo Allatios and Popular Orthodoxy.* Leiden: Brill, 2004. 370 pp. Hartnup discusses at length all the Greek traditions about vampires up to Allatius (1586–1669).

410. Henningsen, Gustav. "The Witches of Zugarramurdi." *Saioak. Revista de Estudios Vascos* 2 (1978): 182–195. Condensed version in: Gustav Henningsen. *The Witches' Advocate: Basque Witch-craft and the Spanish Inquisition (1609–1614).* Reno: University of Nevada Press, 1980, pp. 27ff.

411. Herskovits, Melville J., and Frances S. Herskovits. "Divination and Magic." In: Melville J. Herskovits and Frances S. Herskovits. *Trinidad Village.* New York: Alfred A. Knopf, 1947, pp. 351 pp. hb. Rpt.: New York: Octagon Books, 1964. 351 pp.

412. _____. "Notes on the Culture of the Paramaribo Negroes." In: Melville J. Herskovits and Frances S. Herskovits. *Suriname Folk-Lore.* New York: Columbia University Press, 1936, pp. 1ff. Posted at http://www.scribd.com/doc/92019069/Surinam-Folk-Lore. Rpt.: New York: AMS Press, 1969. 665 pp.

413. Holder, Geoff. "The Croglin Vampire and the Renwick Cockatrice." In Geoff Holder. *Paranormal Cumbria.* Stroud, UK: The History Press, 2012.

414. Horton, George B. *Home of Nymphs and Vampires: The Islaes of Greece.* Indianapolis: The Bobb-Merrill Company, 1929. 219 pp. hb.

415. Howell, Signe. "Bas" In Signe Howell. *Society and Cosmos: Chewong of Pennisula Malasia.* Singapore: Oxford University Press, 1984, pp. 104–14.

416. Howey, M. Oldfield. *The Encircled Serpent: A Study of Serpent Symbolism in All Countries and Ages.* New York: Arthur Richmond Company, 1955. 411 pp.

417. _____. "Vampire Cats." In M. Oldfield Howey. *The Cat in Magic.* London: Rider & Co., 1930, pp. 173–178. Rpt.: London: Bracken Books, 1993, pp. 173–78.

418. Hrbkova, Sarka B. "Jan Neruda" In Sarka B. Hrbkova. *Czechoslovak Stories.* Lansing: University of Michigan Library, 1920, pp. 71–74. Posted at: http://www.archive.org/stream/czechoslovakstor00hrbk/czechoslovakstor00hrbk_djvu.txt. Rpt.: Freeport, NY: Books for Libraries Press, 1970, pp. 71–74.

419. Hufford, David J. *The Terror That Comes in the Night: An Experience-centered Study of Supernatural Assault Traditions.* Philadelphia: University of Pennsylvania Press, 1989. 278 pp.

420. Hurwitz, Siegmund. *Lilith, the First Eve: Historical and Psychological Aspects of the Dark Feminine.* Trans. by Gela Jacobson. Einsiedeln, Switzerland: Daimon Verlag, 1992. 262 pp. tp.

421. Jarosz, Lucy A. "Agents of Power, Landscapes of Fear: The Vampires and Heart Thieves of Madagascar. *Environment and Planning D-society & Space* 12, 4 (1994): 421–436.

422. Johnson, Patrick. "Count Dracula and the Folkloric Vampire: Thirteen Comparisons." *Journal of Dracula Studies* 3 (2001): 33–41.

423. Jones, Hartford E. *Vampirism in the Philippines: A Brief Description and Survey.* New York: Count Dracula Fan Club Research Division, 1985.

424. Kennedy, Raymond. "Gods, Ghosts, and Spirits." In Raymond Kennesy. *The Ageless Indies.* New York: John Day Company, 1942, pp. 105–11.

425. Kinder, Nancy. "The 'Vampires' of Rhode Island." *Yankee* (October 1970): 114–15, 166–67. Rpt. in: *Mysterious New England.* Dublin, NH: Yankee Publishing, 1971. Rev. ed. 1979, pp. 211–15.

426. King, Alexander D. "Soul Suckers: Vampiric Shamans in Northern Kamchatka, Russia." *Anthropology of Consciousness* 10, 4 (1999): 57–68.

427. Kinsley, David. "Kali." In David Kinsley. *Hindu Goddesses: Visions of the Divine Feminine in the Hindu Religious Tradition.* Berkeley: University of California Press, 1988, pp. 116–31.

428. Kirkley, Bacil F. "Dracula, the Monastic Chronicles and Slavic Folklore." *Midwest Folklore* 6, 3 (1956): 133–39. Rpt. in Margaret L. Carter, ed. *Dracula: The Vampire and the Critics.* Ann Arbor: UMI Research Press, 1988, pp. 11–17.

429. _____. "La Llorona and Related Themes." *Western Folklore* 19 (1960): 155–68.

430. Kligman, Gail. *The Wedding of the Dead: Ritual Poetics and Popular Culture in Transylvania.* Berkeley: University of California Press, 1988. 410 pp.

431. Knowlson, T. Sharper. "Vampires." In T. Sharper Knowlson. *The Origins of Popular Superstitions and Customs.* London: T. Werner Laurie, 1930, pp. 212–19. Posted at: http://www.sacred-texts.com/neu/eng/osc/osc71.htm.

432. Kramer, Kaley. "Madmen in the Middle: Folklore and Science in Bram Stoker's *Dracula.*" In Karen Sayer and Rosemary Mitchell, eds. *Victorian Gothic.* Leeds, UK: Leeds Centre for Victorian Studies, Trinity and All Saints College, University of Leeds, 2003, pp. 69–80.

433. Krauss, Friedrich S. "South Slavic Countermeasures Against Vampires." *Globus* 62

(1892): 203–204. Reprinted in Alan Dundas, ed. *The Vampire: A Casebook.* Madison: University of Wisconsin Press, 1998. pp. 67–71.

434. Kreuter, Peter Mario. "The Role of Women in Southeast European Vampire Belief." In Amila Buturovic and Irvin Cemil Schick, eds. *Women in the Ottoman Balkans: Gender, culture and history.* London: I. B. Tauris, 2007, pp. 231–42.

435. Krys, Svitlana. "Vampire Lore: From the Writings of Jan Louis Perkowski." *Canadian Slavonic Papers* 51, 1 (March 2009).

436. Kula, Ramsey. "The Bomoh and Hantu—Hantu: Malay Myth or Mysticism?" In Ramsey Kula, ed. *Souls: True Ghost Stories.* Book One. Singapore: Knightsbridge Communications, 1991, unpaged.

437. _____. "Hanti Pontianak—Mati Beranak." In Ramsey Kula, ed. *Souls: True Ghost Stories.* Book Two. Singapore: Knightsbridge Communications, 1991, unpaged.

438. Ladouceur, Liisa. *How to Kill a Vampire: Fangs in Folklore, Film and Fiction.* Toronto: ECW Press, 2013. 190 pp. tp.

439. Lavergen, Remi. *A Phonetic Transcription of the Creole Negro's Medical Treatments, Superstitions, and Folklore in the Parish of Pointe Coupée.* Baton Rouge: Louisiana State University, M.A. thesis, 1930. 55 pp. Large format.

440. Lawson, John Cuthbert. *Modern Greek Folklore and Ancient Greek Religion: A Study in Survivals.* New Hyde Park, NY: University Books, 1964. 620 pp.

441. Laycock, Joseph. Tylor, Vampires, and the Anthropology of Religion." *Arc, The Journal of the Faculty of Religious Studies, McGill University* 28 (2010): 115–139.

442. Leake, William Martin. *Travels in Northern Greece.* 4 vols. 1835. Rpt.: Amsterdam: Adolph M. Hakkert, 1967. 667 pp. hb. Posted at: http://www.archive.org/stream/travelsinnorthe08leakgoog/travelsinnorthe08leakgoog_djvu.txt.

443. Lee, Dorothy Demetracopoulou. "Greek Accounts of the Vrykolakas." *Journal of American Folklore* 54 (1941):126–132.

444. Leland, G. C. *Gypsy Sorcery and Fortune Telling.* London: T. Fisher Unwin, [1891]. 260 pp. Posted at: http://www.sacred-texts.com/pag/gsft/gsft00.htm. Rpt. As: *Gypsy Sorcery.* New York: Tower Books, n.d. 267 pp. pb.

445. León, Luis D. *La Llorona's Children: Religion, Life, and Death on the U.S.-Mexican Borderlands.* Berkeley: University of California Press, 320 pp. hb. & tp.

446. Leonard, Arthur Glyn. "The Demonology of the People as Practiced in Witchcraft." In Arthur Glyn Leonard. *The Lower Niger and its Tribes.* London: Macmillan and Co., 1906, pp. 477–501. Posted at: http://www.archive.org/stream/lowernigeritstri00leonrich/lowernigeritstri00leonrich_djvu.txt.

447. Lienhardt, R. G. "Some Notions of Witchcraft among the Dinka." *Africa* 21 (1951): 4, 303–18.

448. Lysaght, Patricia. *The Banshee: The Irish Supernatural Death Messenger.* Dublin, Ireland: The O'Brien Press, 1996 434 pp.

449. Macculloch, J. A. "The Future Life." In J. A. MacCulloch. *The Celtic and Scandinavian Religions.* London: Hutchinson's University Library, [1948], pp. 80–85. Rpt.: London: Constable, 1993. 180 pp. tp.

450. Machal, Jan. "Slavic Mythology." In Jan Perkowski, ed. *Vampires of the Slavs.* Cambridge, MA: Slavica Press, 1976, pp. 23–31.

451. MacKenzie, Andrew. *Dracula Country: Travels and Folk Beliefs in Romania.* London: Arthur Baker, 1977. 176 pp. hb.

452. Mackenzie, Donald A. *Myths of China and Japan.* London: Gresham Publishing Company, 1923. 404 pp. hb. Posted at: http://www.archive.org/stream/mythsofchinajap00mack/mythsofchinajap00mack_djvu.txt.

453. Marinescu, At. M. "Pricolicii." *Familia* 8 (1872).

454. Mayo, Herbert. *Letters on the Truths Contained in Popular Superstitions.* Frankfort, Germany: John David Sauerleander/ Edinburgh: Blackwood, 1894. Rpt. in: Kurt Saxon. *Classic Ghosts and Vampires.* Eureka, CA: Atlan "A" Formularies, 1978, pp. 92–131. These letters, including one on "Vampirism," originally appeared in 1847 in *Blackwood's Magazine.*

455. _____. "Vampirism." *Blackwood's Magazine* 61, 378 (April 1847): 432–440.

456. McClelland, Bruce Alexander. *Sacrifice, Scapegoat, Vampire: The Social and Religious Origins of the Bulgarian Folkloric Vampire.* Charlottesville: University of Virginia, Ph.D. dissertation, 1998. 429 pp. Large format.

457. McClenon, James, and Emily D. Edwards. "The Incubus in Film, Experience, and Folklore." *Southern Folklore* 52, 1 (1996): 3–18. Posted at: http://libres.uncg.edu/ir/uncg/f/E_Edwards_Incubus_1995.pdf.

458. Meregtante, Anthony S. *Good and Evil: Mythology and Folklore.* New York: Harper & Row, 1978. 242 pp.

459. Meyers, William. *Vampires or Gods?* San Francisco, CA: III Publishing, 1993. 192 pp. pb. Large format.

460. Mijativies, Csedomille, trans. "The Three Brothers." In Csedomille Mijativies, ed. *Serbian Folklore.* New York: Benjamin Blom, 1968, pp. 256–94. Rpt. in: Jan Perkowski, ed. *Vampires of the Slavs.* Cambridge, MA: Slavica Press, 1976, pp. 242–47.

461. Morgan, Mogg. *Supernatural Assault in Ancient Egypt: Seth, Evil Sleep & the Egyptian Vampire.* Oxford, UK: Mandrake, 2nd ed., 2010. 194 pp.

462. Moszynski, Kazimierz. "Slavic Folk Culture." Trans. by Jan Perkowski. In Jan Perkowski, ed. *Vampires of the Slavs.* Cambridge, MA: Slavica Press, 1976, pp. 180–87.

463. Murgoci, A. "The Vampire in Rumania." *Folklore* 37, 4 (December 31, 1926): 320–49. Rpt. in: In Alan Dundas, ed. *The Vampire: A Casebook.* Madison: University of Wisconsin Press, 1998. pp. 12–34. Excerpt in David Skal, ed. *Vampires: Encounters with the Undead.* New York: Black Dog & Leventhal Publishers, 2001, pp. 31–34.

464. Narbonne, Steven. "La Llorona, the Weeping Woman." *Fate* 49 2 (February 1996): 50–52.

465. Naylor, Kenneth E. "The Source of the Word Vampir in Slavic." *Southeastern Europe* 10, 1 (1983): 93–98.

466. Nelson, Elizabeth. "Monstrous Desire: Love, Death, and the Vampire Marriage." In Jonathan A. Allan and Elizabeth E. Nelson, eds. *Inversion of Power and Paradox: Studying Monstrosity.* Oxford, UK: Inter-Disciplinary Press, 2012, pp. 229–38.

467. Neruda, Jan. "The Vampire." In Sarka B. Hrbkova, trans. *Czechoslovak Stories.* New York: Duffield and Company, 1920, pp. 75–80. Posted at: http://www.archive.org/stream/czechoslovakstor00hrbk/czechoslovakstor00hrbk_djvu.txt. Rpt.: Freeport, NY: Books for Libraries Press,

1970, pp. 75–80. Rpt. in: Marie Busch and Otto Pick, trans. *Selected Czech Tales*. Oxford, UK: Humphrey Milford, 1925, pp. 90–96.

468. Nicoloff, Assen. *Bulgarian Folklore*. Cleveland, OH: the author, 1975. 133 pp.

469. _____. *Bulgarian Folktales*. Cleveland, OH: the author, 1979. 296 pp.

470. Nutini, Hugo G., and John M. Roberts. *Bloodsucking Witchcraft: An Epistemological Study of Anthropomorphic Supernaturalism in Rural Tlaxcala*. Tucson: University of Arizona Press, 1993. 476 pp.

471. Ocker, J. W. "Vampires. In J. W. Ocker. *The New England Grimpendium*. Woodstock, VT: Countryman Press, 2010, pp. 228–31.

472. O'Donnell, Elliott. *The Banshee*. London: Sands & Company; 1907. 255 pp. hb. Posted at: http://archive.org/stream/thebanshee34263 gut/34263.txt.

473. _____. "Vampires and Some Northcountry Ghosts." In Elliott O'Donnell. *Haunted Britain*. London: Rider & Company, 1948. Rpt.: London: World Distributors, 1963, pp. 122–26.

474. _____. "Werwolves and Vampires and Ghouls." In Eliot O'Donnell. *Werwolves*. London, Methuen. 1912, pp. 56–63. Posted at: http://archive.org/stream/werwolves26629gut/26629.txt. Rpt.: New York: Longvue Press 1965, pp. 62–69.

475. _____. "Vampires, Werewolves, Fox Women, etc." In Elliott O'Donnell. *Byways of Ghostland*. London: William Rider & Son, 1911, pp. 110–131. Posted at: http://www.scribd.com/doc/8016411/Byways-of-Ghostland-Elliot-ODonnell. Rpt. in: Dennis Wheatley, ed. *Satanism and Witches*. Vol. 2 of the Dennis Wheatley Library of the Occult. London: Sphere, 1974, pp. 102–15.

476. Oinas, Felix. "East European Vampires." In Felix J. Oinas. *Essays on Russian Folklore and Mythology*. Columbus, OH: Slavica Publishers, 1984, pp. 433ff.

477. _____. "East European Vampires & Dracula." *Journal of Popular Culture* 16, 1 (1982): 108–16. Rpt. in: Alan Dundas, ed. *The Vampire: A Casebook*. Madison: University of Wisconsin Press, 1998. pp. 47–56.

478. _____. *Essays on Russian Folklore and Mythology*. Columbus, OH: Slavica Publishers, 1985. 183 pp.

479. _____. "Heretics as Vampires and Demons in Russia." *Slavic and East European Journal* 22, 4 (1978): 433–41.

480. Oke, Kristin. *Monsters Among Us— Modern Fears Mirrored in Vampire Tales*. Allendale, MI: Grand Valley State University, Honors Project, 2011. Posted at: http://scholarworks.gvsu.edu/honorsprojects/107.

481. O'Leary, Crystal L. "Transcending Monstrous Flesh: A Revision of the Hero's Mythic Quest." *Journal of the Fantastic in the Arts* 13, 3 [51] (2003): 239–49.

482. Oliphant, Samuel Grant. "The Story of the Strix: Ancient." *Transactions and Proceedings of the American Philological Association* 44 (1913): 133–40.

483. Pashley, Robert. *Travels in Crete*. 2 vols. London: John Murray, 1837. 650 pp. Posted at http://catalog.hathitrust.org/Record/000649866. Includes reflection on various Greek vampires.

484. Patai, Raphael. *The Hebrew Goddess*. 3rd ed. Detroit, MI: Wayne State University Press, 1990. 369 pp. hb. Patai includes an extensive discussion of the vampiric Hebrew "goddess" Lilith.

485. _____. "Lilith." *The Journal of American Folklore* 77, 306 (Oct.-Dec. 1964): 295–314.

486. Penard, A. P., and T. E. Penard. "Surinam Folk-Tales." *Journal of American Folk-Lore* 30, 116 (April-June 1917): 239–43. Posted at: http://www.jstor.org/stable/534344?seq=1.

487. Pereira, Filomena Maria. *Lilith: The Edge of Forever*. Las Colinas, TX: Ide House, 1998. 215 pp.

488. Perez, Domino Renee. "Caminando con La Llorona: Traditional and Contemporary Narratives." In Norma E. Cantu and Olga Najera-Ramirez, eds. *Chicana Traditions: Continuity and Change*. Urbana: University of Illinois Press, 2002, pp. 100–16.

489. _____. "The Politics of Taking: La Llorona in the Cultural Mainstream." *The Journal of Popular Culture* 45, 1 (February 2012): 153–172.

490. _____. *There Was a Woman: La Llorona from Folklore to Popular Culture*. Austin: University of Texas Press, 2008, 272 pp. tp.

491. Perkowski, Jan I. *Cats, Bats, and Vampires*. New York: Dracula Press, 1992. 11 pp.

492. _____. *Daemon Contamination in Balkan Vampire Lore*. New York: Dracula Press, 1992. 14 pp.

493. _____. *The Darkling—A Treatise on Slavic Vampirism*. Columbus, OH: Slavica Publishers Inc., 1989. 169 pp.

494. _____. "On the Origin of the Kasubian Succuba." *Journal of Vampirism* 2, 1 (Fall 1978): 8–12.

495. _____. "A Recent Vampire Death." In Jan Perkowski, ed. *Vampires of the Slavs*. Cambridge, MA: Slavica Press, 1976, pp. 156–59.

496. _____. "The Romanian Folkloric Vampire." *East European Quarterly* 16, 3 (September 1982): 311–22. Rpt. in: Alan Dundas, ed. *The Vampire: A Casebook*. Madison: University of Wisconsin Press, 1998. pp. 35–46.

497. _____. "The Sun, the Slavs, and Vampires." In *Proceedings of the Helios Conference*. Albany: State University Press of New York, 1978.

498. _____. "The Vampire—A Study in Slavic Bi-Culturalism." *Proceedings Pacific Northwest Conference on Foreign Languages* 25, 1 (1974): 252–53. Rpt. in: Jan Perkowski, ed. *Vampires of the Slavs*. Cambridge, MA: Slavica Press, 1976, pp. 136–39.

499. _____. *The Vampire as Revenant*. New York: Dracula Press, 1992. 7 pp.

500. _____. "Vampires, Dwarves, and Witches Among the Ontario Kashubs." *Canadian Centre for Folk Culture Studies*, Mercury series No. 1. Ottawa, ON: National Museum of Man, National Museums of Canada, 1972, pp. 1–9, 21–29, 49–4. Rpt. in Jan Perkowski, ed. *Vampires of the Slavs*. Cambridge, MA: Slavica Press, 1976, pp. 188–200.

501. _____, ed. *Vampires of the Slavs*. Cambridge, MA: Slavica Press, 1976. 294 pp. Posted at: http://www.scribd.com/doc/36617293/Jan-Perkovski-Vampires-of-the-Slavs. Includes excerpts from the writings of Jan Machal, Aleksandr N. Afanas'ev, Kazimierz Moszyinski, T. P. Vukanović, and Raymond L. Ditmars and Arthur M. Greenhall.

502. Petrovitch, Woislav M. "Vampires." In Woislav M. Petrovitch. *Hero Tales and Legends of the Serbians*. London: George G. Harrap & Company, 1914, pp. 21–22. Posted at: http://www.scribd.com/doc/26744859/Hero-Tales-and-Legends-of-the-Serbians-1914-Woislav-M-Petrovitch. Rpt.: New York: Kraus Reprint, 1972, pp. 21–22.

503. Phillips, Charles, et al. *Forests of the Vampire: Slavic Myth*. Ser.: Myth and Mankind. Amsterdam, Netherlands: Time-Life Books, 1999. 143 pp. hb.

504. Prabhu, Gayathri. *Vikram and the Undead*, Lincoln: University of Nebraska–Lincoln. Ph.D. dissertation, 2011. 124 pp. Large format.

505. Qualls, Bethany E. "How to Quiet a Vampire: A Sotie (review)." *Serbian Studies: Journal of The North American Society for Serbian Studies* 1, 1 (2009): 191–194.

506. Ralston, William Ralston Stedden. *Russian Folk-Tales*. London: Smith Elder, 1873. 382 pp. hb. Posted at: http://www.forgottenbooks.org/readbook/Russian_Folk-Tales_1000062370 #7. Rpt.: New York: Arno Press, 1977. 382 pp. hb.

507. _____. *Songs of the Russian People*. London: Ellis & Green, 1872. 447 pp. hb. Posted at: http://www.scribd.com/doc/4335161/Ralston-Songs-of-The-Russian-People-. Rpt.: New York: Haskell House Publishers, 1970. 447 pp. Excerpt in: McNally, Raymond T. *A Clutch of Vampires*. New York: Bell Publishing Company, 1974, pp. 183–84.

508. Ramos, Maximo. "The Aswang Syncrasy in Philippine Folklore." *Western Folklore* 28, 4 (October 1969): 238–48.

509. _____. "Belief in Ghouls in Contemporary Philippine Society." *Western Folklore* 27, 3 (January 1968): 184–90.

510. _____. *Creatures of Philippine Lower Mythology*. Manila: University of the Philippines Press, 1971. 390 pp.

511. Rattray, R. Sutherland. *Ashanti Proverbs*. Oxford: Clarendon Press, 1916. 190 pp. hb. Posted at: https://openlibrary.org/books/OL23279117M/Ashanti_proverbs.

512. Rich, Elihu. "Vampires." In Edward Smedley, W. Cooke Taylor, Henry Thompson, and Elihu Rich. *The Occult Science: Sketches of the Traditions and Superstitions of Past Times, and the Marvels of the Present Day*. London: Richard Griffin and Company, 1855, pp. 66–71.

513. Rogo, Scott. "In-depth Analysis of the Vampire Legend." *Fate* 21, 9 (September 1968): 70–77.

514. _____. "Reviewing the Vampire of Croglin Grange." *Fate* 21, 6 (June 1968): 44–48.

515. Rondina, Christopher. *Vampire Legends of Rhode Island*. North Attleborough, MA: Covered Bridge Press, 1997. 80 pp. tp.

516. _____. *The Vampire Hunter's Guide to New England: True Tales of the Yankee Undead*.

North Attleborough, MA: Covered Bridge Press, 2000. 186 pp. tp.

517. _____. *Vampires of New England.* N.p.: On Cape Publications, 2008. 170 pp. tp.

518. Ruel, Malcolm. "Were-animals and the Introverted Witch Among the Dinka." In Mary Douglas, ed. *Witchcraft Confessions and Accusations.* Abingdon, Oxfordshire, UK: Routledge, 2004, pp. 333–350.

519. "Rumors of Vampires in North Carolina." *Beyond Reality* (February 1981): 62.

520. Santos, Cristina. "'Hell Hath No Fury Like a Woman Scorned': Refigurations of the Legend of La Llorona." In Gabriela Funk, ed. *Estudos sobre Cultura Popular: Homenagem ao Professor Doctor José Almeida Pavão.* Ponta Delgada: Câmara Municipal de Ponta Delgada, 2006, pp. 241–57.

521. _____. "Monstrous Mother or Victim? The Figure of La Llorona." In Jonathan A. Allan and Elizabeth E. Nelson, eds. *Inversions of Power and Paradox.* Oxford: Inter-Disciplinary Press, 2011, pp. 107–14.

522. _____. "Vampires, and Witches, and Werewolves, Oh My!" in Cristina Santos and Adriana Spahr, eds. *Defiant Deviance: The Irreality of Reality of the Cultural Imaginary.* New York: Peter Lang, 2006, pp. 35–52.

523. Saunero-Ward, Verónica H. "Giovanna Rivero's 'Contraluna': Meeting the Monstrous Lilith." In Cristina Santos and Adriana Spahr. *Monstrous Deviations in Literature and the Arts.* Oxford: Inter-Disciplinary Press, 2011.

524. Saxon, Kurt. *Classic Ghosts and Vampires.* Eureka, CA: Atlan "A" Formularies, 1978. 165 pp. pb. Large format. This omnibus collection of old books reprints Herbert Mayo's 1849 volume *Letters on the Truths Contained in Popular Superstitions,* which included a letter on "Vampirism," originally published in the April 1847 issue of *Blackwood's Magazine.*

525. Schierup, Carl-Ulrik. "Why Are Vampires Still Alive? Wallachian Immigrants in Scandinavia." *Ethos* 51, 3–4 (1986): 173–98.

526. Senate, Richard l. "Ojai Vampire tale." In Richard l. Senate. *Ghosts of the California Coast: Ghost Hunting on California's Gold Coast.* Ventura, CA: Pathfinder Publishing, 1986, pp. 16–18.

527. Senn, Harry A. *Were-wolf and Vampire in Romania.* New York: East European Monograph, Columbia University Press, 1982. 148 pp. hb.

528. Shandley, Robert, Tazim Jamal, and Aniela Tanase. "Location Shooting and the Filmic Destination: Transylvanian Myths and the Post-Colonial Tourism Enterprise." *Journal of Tourism and Cultural Change* 4, 3 (December 2006): 137–158.

529. Shortt, Vere D. "The Vampire Superstition." *Occult Review* 22 (December 1915): 354ff.

530. Sinistrari, Ludovico Maria. Demoniality: or, Incubi and Succubi. Paris: Isidore Liseux, 1879. Rpt. N.p.: Moonglow Books, 2009. 104 pp. tp. Sinistrari (1622–1701), an Italian Franciscan priest, originally wrote his influential text on the incubus and succubus in Latin in the 17th century. It was translated into English late in the 19th century.

531. Skeat, Walter William. *Malay Magic: An Introduction to the Folklore and Popular Religion of the Malay Peninsula.* London: Macmillan, 1900. 685 pp. hb. Posted at: https://openlibrary.org/books/OL7077585M/Malay_magic. Rpt.: New York: Barnes & Noble, 1966.

532. _____, **and Charles Otto Blagden.** "Bamboo No. 2." In Walter William Skeat and Charles Otto Blagden. *Pagan Races of the Malay Peninsula.* Vol. 1. London: Macmillan and Company, 1906, pp. 473–77. Posted at: https://archive.org/details/paganracesofmala01skea. Rpt.: New York: Barnes & Noble, 1966, pp. 473–77.

533. Sledzik, Paul S., and Nicholas Bellantoni. "Bioarcheological and Biocultural Evidence for the New England Vampire Folk Belief." *The American Journal of Physical Anthropology* 94, 2 (June 1994): 269–274. Posted at http://www.ceev.net/biocultural.pdf.

534. Smith, Henry G., ed. *Chinese Tales of Vampires, Beasts, Genies and Men.* Burnham-on-Sea, Somerset, UK: Llanerch Press, 2011. 200 pp. tp.

535. Smith, W. Ramsey. *Myths and Legends of the Australian Aboriginals.* New York: Farrar & Rinehart, n.d. 356 pp. hb. Posted at: https://archive.org/details/mythslegendsofau00smit.

536. Snowiss, Mark D. *The Power of Identity: A Study of Romanian Truths and Myths.* Santa Barbara: University of California—Santa Barbara, Honors thesis, 1993. 198 pp. Large Format.

537. Sokolov, Y. *Russian Folklore.* Trans. by Catherine Ruth Smith. New York: Macmillan, 1950. 760 pp. hb. Rpt.: Hatboro, Pa., Folklore Associates, 1966. 760 pp. tp.

538. Spariousu, Mihal I., and Dezsö Benedek. *Ghosts, Vampires, and Werewolves: Eerie Tales from Transylvania.* New York: Orchard Books, 1994. 104 pp. hb. dj.

539. Spence, Lewis. "Ghosts of China (Stories of vampires, spirits, elementals, and demons)." *Occult Review* 66 (July 1939): 197ff.

540. _____. "The Vampire Legend—Its Origin and Nature." *Occult Review* 27 (March 1918): 137–45. Rpt. in: *The Dark Shadows Book of Vampires and Werewolves.* New York: Paperback Library, 1970, pp. 123–36.

541. Spiro, Melford E. "Ghosts and Demons." In Medford E. Spiro. *Burmese Supernaturalism.* Englewood Cliffs, NJ: Prentice-Hall, 1967. Exp. ed.: Philadelphia: Institute for the Study of Human Issues, 1978, pp. 33–39.

542. Starkie, Walter. "On the Road Toward Budapest: Vagabonds and Vampires." In: Walter Starkie. *Raggle Taggle: Adventures with a Fiddle in Hungary and Romania.* London: John Murray, 1934, pp. 27–47.

543. _____. "Vampires in Hungary." *International Vampire* 1, 4 (Summer 1991).

544. _____. *Vampires of the Slavs.* Cambridge, MA: Slavica Publishers, 1976. 294 pp.

545. Stetson, George R. "The Animistic Vampire in New England." *American Anthropologist* 9, 1 (1896): 1–13. Posted at: http://www.ceev.net/animistic.pdf.

546. Stevens, Rockwell. "The Vampire's Heart." In Walter Hard, Jr., and Janet Greene, eds. *Mischief in the Mountains.* Montpelier, VT: Vermont Life Magazine, 1970, pp. 71–80.

547. Sutherland, Gail Hinich. "The Family of Demons." In Gail Hinich Sutherland. *The Disguises of the Demon: The Development of the Yaksa in Hinduism and Buddhism.* Albany: State University of New York Press, 1991, pp. 49–61.

548. Swancutt, Katherine. "The Undead Genealogy: Omnipresence, Spirit Perspectives, and a Case of Mongolian Vampirism." *Journal of the Royal Anthropological Institute.* 14, 4 (December 2008): 843–64.

549. Talbot, P. Amaury. "Ojje or Witchcraft." In P. Amaury Talbot. *In the Shadow of the Bush.* London: William Heinemann, 1912. pp. 191–202. Posted at: http://fax.libs.uga.edu/GN653x T3/#. Rpt.: New York: Negro Universities Press/ Greenwood Publishing Corp., 1969, pp. 190–202.

550. Tannahill, Reay. *Flesh and Blood: A History of the Cannibal Complex.* New York: Stein & Day, 1975. 209 pp. hb. dj. See chapter on "Werewolves and Vampires" pp. 108–36. Rpt.: London: Hamish Hamilton, 1975. 209 pp. hb. Rev. ed.: Boston: Little, Brown, 1997. 320 pp. hb. dj.

551. Taylor, Troy. "Illinois Vampires." In Troy Taylor. *Monsters of Illinois: Mysterious creatures of the Prairie State.* Mechanicsburg, PA: Stackpole Books, 2011, pp. 95–101.

552. Teichert, Matthias. "'Draugula': The Draugr in Old Norse-Icelandic Saga Literature and His Relationship to the Post-Medieval Vampire Myth." In Barbara Brodman and James E. Doan, eds. *The Universal Vampire: Origins and Evolution of a Legend.* Madison, NJ: Fairleigh Dickinson University Press, 2013, pp. 3–16.

553. Teiser, Stephen. "Hungary Ghosts." In Stephen Teiser. *The Ghost Festival in Medieval China.* Princeton, NJ: Princeton University Press, 1996, pp. 124–29.

554. Thundy, Zacharias P. "The Indian Vampire: Nomen et Numen." In Leonard Heldreth and Mary Pharr, eds. *The Blood Is the Life: Vampires in Literature.* Bowling Green, KY: Bowling Green State University Press, 1999, pp. 43–55.

555. Thurston, H. "Broucolaccas: A Study in Medieval Ghost Lore." *The Month* 90 (November 1897): 502–520.

556. Trigg, E. B. *Gypsy Demons & Divinities: The Magical and Supernatural Practices of the Gypsies.* London: Sheldon Press, 1973. 238 pp.

557. Tsaliki, Anastasia. "Vampires Beyond Legend: A Bioarchaeological Approach." In M. La Verghetta and L. Capasso, eds. *Proceedings of the XIII European Meeting of the Paleopathology Association, Chieti, Italy, 18–23 Sept. 2000.* Teramo-Italy: Edigrafital S.P.A., 2000, pp. 295–300.

558. Tyler, Royall. *Japanese Tales.* New York: Pantheon Books, 1987. 341 pp.

559. "The Unquiet Dead." In Lady Gregory. *Visions and Beliefs in the West of Ireland.* Vol. 2 New York: George Putnam's Sons, 1920, pp. 89–106.

560. Ventura, Varla. *Banshees, Werewolves, Vampires, and Other Creatures of the Night: Facts, Fictions, and First-Hand Accounts.* San Francisco, CA: Red Wheel/ Weiser Books, 2013. 238 pp.

561. Vukanović, T. P. "The Vampire." In Jan Perkowski, ed. *Vampires of the Slavs.* Cambridge, MA: Slavica Press, 1976, pp. 274–318.

562. Wachtel, Nathan. *Gods and Vampires: Return to Chipaya.* Chicago: University of Chicago Press, 1994. 153 pp. Trans. by Carol Volk. hb. & tp. Folklore. Original French ed. as: *Dieux et vampires: Retour à Chipaya.* Paris: Editions du Seuil, 1999.

563. Wandycz, Piotr. "Western Images and Stereotypes of Central and Eastern Europe." in André Gerrits and Norman Adler eds., *Vampires Unstaked: National Images, Stereotypes and Myths in East Central Europe.* Amsterdam, Royal Netherlands Academy of Arts and Sciences 1995, pp, 5–23.

564. Williams, Hector. "The Vampire of Lesbos." *Archaeology* (March/April 1994): 22.

565. Willoughby-Meade, G. *Ghost and Vampire Tales of China.* London: East and West, Ltd., 1925. 27 pp. pb. This essay was originally presented as a paper before the China Society on May 28, 1925.

566. Wood, Daniel J. *Realm of the Vampire: History and the Undead.* Lakeville, MN: Galde Press, 2011. 160 pp. tp.

567. _____. "Vampires and Disease: The Bloodsucking Corpse of English Tradition." *Fate* 61, 12 (December 2007): 28–34.

568. _____. "The White Death of New England." *Fate* 62, 1 (January 2008): 27–33.

569. Woodward, Ian. *The Vampire Delusion.* New York: Paddington Press, 1979. 256 pp.

570. Wright, Dudley. "A Living Vampire." *Occult Review* 12 (July 1910): 45ff.

571. _____. *Vampires and Vampirism.* London: William Rider and Sons, 1914. 217 pp. hb. Rpt.: New York: Gordon Press, 1970. 217 pp. hb. Rpt.: Detroit, MI: Gale Research Company, 1973. 217 pp. hb. dj. Rpt. as: *The Book of Vampires.* New York: Causeway, 1974. 217 pp. hb. Rpt.: Hippocene Books, 1987. 217 pp. hb. Rpt.: New York: Dorset, 1987. 217 pp. hb. dj. Rpt.: Detroit: Omnigraphics, 1989. 217 pp. hb. Rpt.: Thornhill, Dumfriesshire, UK: Tynron Press, 1991. 217 pp. hb. dj. Rpt. as: *The History of Vampires.* New York: Dorset, 1993. 217 pp. hb. Excerpt in: David Skal, ed. *Vampires: Encounters with the Undead.* New York: Black Dog & Leventhal Publishers, 2001, pp. 17–22. Frequently reprinted under different names.

Historical Perspective

In 1972, two historians who focused upon Eastern Europe created a whole new phase of vampire studies by suggesting that the novel *Dracula* was based upon an appropriation of Hungarian and Romanian history beginning with the career of a then obscure fifteenth-century Romanian ruler, Vlad Tepes (i.e., Vlad the Impaler). One of the two, Raymond McNally, pushed the hypothesis even further by suggesting that Vlad has consumed some of his enemies' blood and then bringing the Slovakian ruler Elizabeth Bathory into the discussion as a "female Dracula." The work of McNally and his colleague, Radu Florescu, both opened a scholarly discussion of Vlad and other historical figures who exhibited vampire-like characteristics and initiated a generation of debates over the accuracy of their description of Vlad, considered a significant figure in the formation of their country by Romanians.

While most of the McNally-Florescu thesis concerning Bram Stoker's appropriation of Romanian history has been discarded, their work has generated a significant amount of historical work on the development of the contemporary interest in the vampire and the role of those historical figures who drank, or, in the case of Bathory, bathed in blood. As a result, both Vlad Tepes and Elizabeth Bathory have become popular figures in the English-speaking world and are frequently identified as vampires in fictional works. It is also the case that a history of the vampire can now be written, beginning with the origin of the vampire in written accounts, the early modern debates on the reality of vampires, the evolution of the literary vampire, and its contemporary emergence as both a tool for psychologists and an image permeating popular culture in the West.

572. Brodman, Barbara, and James E. Doan, eds. *The Universal Vampire: Origins and Evolution of a Legend.* Madison, NJ: Fairleigh Dickinson University Press, 2013. 249 pp. hb. boards. Includes essays by Matthias Teichert, Paul E. H. Davis, Alexis M. Milmine, Cristina Artenie, Edward O. Keith, Leo Ruickbie, Clemens Ruthner, Nancy Schumann, James E. Doan, Katherine Allocco, Jamieson Ridenhour, Masaya Shimokusu, Tomas Jesus Garza, Adriana Gordillo, and Raul Rodriguez-Herntindez and Claudia Schaefer.

573. Burke, Peter. "Witchcraft and Magic in Renaissance Italy: Gianfrancesco Pico and His Strix." In Sydney Anglo, ed. *The Damned Art: Essays in the Literature of Witchcraft.* London: Routledge & Kegan Paul, 1977, pp. 32–52.

574. Claremont, Chris. "In Search of Dracula: A True History of Dracula and Vampire Legends." *Dracula Lives!* 1, 4 (January 1974): 22–27.

575. Curran, Bob. *American Vampires: Their True Bloody History from New York to California.* Franklin Lakes, NJ: New Page Books, 2012. 251 pp. tp.

576. Daly, Teri. "The Medieval Vampire." *Tournaments Illuminated* 20 (Autumn 1996): 20–23.

577. Davis, K. Octavia. *Geographies of the (M)other: Narratives of Geography and Eugenics in Turn of the Century British Culture.* San Diego: University of California, Ph.D. dissertation, 1998. 262 pp. Large format.

578. Day, William Patrick. *Vampire Legends in Contemporary American Culture: What Becomes a Legend Most.* Lexington: University of Kentucky Press, 2002. 256 pp. hb.

579. Decker, Dwight R. "Transylvania: Vacation Spot of Europe?" *Dracula Lives!* 1, 4 (January 1974): 28.

580. Dittmer, Jason. "Teaching the Social Construction of Regions in Regional Geography Courses; or, Why Do Vampires Come from Eastern Europe?" *Journal of Geography in Higher Education* 30, 1 (2006): 49–61.

581. Dresser, Norine. "Into the Light: Romania Stakes Its Claim to Dracula." *The World & I* (October 1995): 198–207.

582. Gabory, Emile. *Alias Bluebeard: The Life and Death of Gilles De Raiz.* Trans. by Alvah C. Bessie. New York: Brewer & Warren, 1930. 315 pp. hb.

583. Gelder, Ken. "Vampires in Greece." In Ken Gelder. *The Horror Reader.* New York: Routledge, 2000, pp. 228–41.

584. Girard, Monica. "Teaching and Selling *Dracula* in Twenty-first-Century Romania." In John S. Bak, ed. *Post/modern Dracula: From Victorian Themes to Postmodern Praxis.* Cambridge: Cambridge Scholars Publishing, 2007, pp. 75–92.

585. Glover, David. "Travels in Romania: Myths of Origins, Myths of Blood," *Discourse: Journal for Theoretical Studies in Media and Culture* 16, 1 (1994). Posted at: http://digitalcommons. wayne.edu/discourse/vol16/iss1/7. Rpt. in Glennis Byron, ed. *Dracula (Bram Stoker): Contemporary Critical Essays.* London: Macmillan Press, 1999, pp. 197–217.

586. _____. *Vampires, Mummies, and Liberals.* Durham, NC: Duke University Press, 1996. 212 pp. hb. & tp.

587. _____. "Vampires, Mummies, and Liberals: Questions of Character and Modernity." In Jack Lynch, ed. *Dracula.* Ipswich, MA: Salem Press, 2009, pp. 218–251.

588. Glut, Don. *True Vampires of History.* New York: HC Publishers, 1971. 191 pp. hb. Rpt.: Rockville, MD: Sense of Wonder Press, 2004. 107 pp. tp. Rpt.: New York: Castle Books, n.d. 107 pp. hb. dj. Glut made an initial attempt to construct a history of vampirism by compiling accounts of both folkloric vampire appearances and the careers of serial killers who were believed to have consumed blood.

589. Green, Barbara. *Secrets of the Grave.* Brighouse, UK: Palmyra Press, 2001. 120 pp. Green includes a discussion that connects Robin Hood to vampirism.

590. Guiley, Rosemary Ellen. "A New Introduction." In Montague Summers. *The Vampire, His Kith and Kin: A Critical Edition.* Ed. by John Browning. Berkeley, CA: Apocryphile Press, 2011, pp. xix–xxii.

591. Gürçaglar, S. T. "Adding Towards a Nationalist Text: On a Turkish Translation of *Dracula.*" *Target* 13, 1 (2002): 125–148.

592. Halliday, Ron. *Edinburgh After Dark: Vampires, Ghosts and Witches of the Old Town.* Edinburgh, Scotland: Black & White Publishing, 2010. 214 pp.

593. Haraway, Donna J. "Universal Donors in a Vampire Culture: It's All in the Family: Biological Kinship Categories in the Twentieth-Century United States." In William Cronon, ed. *Uncommon Ground: Toward Reinventing Nature.* New York: W. W. Norton & Co., 1995, pp. 321–76.

594. Hartmann, Franz. "An Authenticated Vampire Story." *The Occult Review* 10 (September 1909): 144–49. Rpt. in: Peter Haining, ed. *The Dracula Scrapbook.* New York: Bramwell House, 1976, pp. 72–75.

595. _____. "Vampires." *Borderland* (London) 3, 3 (July 1896). Rpt.: *The Occult Review* 7 (May 1908): 256–58.

596. Huet, Marie-Hélène. "Deadly Fears: Dom Augustin Calmet's Vampires and the Rule over Death." *Eighteenth-Century Life* 21 (1997): 222–32.

597. Imre, Aniko. "Dracu-fictions and Brand Romania." *Flow* (online journal of television and media studies) (February 19, 2010). Posted at: http://flowtv.org/2010/02/dracu-fictions-and-brand-romaniaaniko-imre-and-alice-bardan-university-of-southern-california/.

598. Introvigne, Massimo. "Antoine Faivre: Father of Contemporary Vampire Studies." In Richard Caron, Joscelyn Godwin, Wouter J. Hanegraaff, and Jean Louis Viellard Baron, eds. *Ésotérisme, Gnoses & Imaginaire Symbolique: Mélanges offerts à Antoine Faivre.* Leuven, Belgium: Peeters, 2001, pp. 595–610.

599. _____. "Satanism Scares and Vampirism from the Eighteenth Century to the Present." *Transylvanian Journal: Dracula and Vampire Studies* 2, 1 (Spring/Summer 1996): 31–46.

600. Irdanova, Dina. "Cashing in on Dracula: Eastern Europe's Hard Sells." *Framework: The Journal of Cinema and Media* 48, 1 (Spring 2007): 46–63.

601. Jones, Stephen, and Jo Fletcher, eds. *Secret City: Strange Tales of London.* London: Titan Books, 1997. 142 pp. hb. Large format. Limited to 300 copies on occasion of World Fantasy Convention of 1997.

602. Kast, Sheilah, and Jim Rosapepe. *Dracula Is Dead: How Romanians Survived Communism, Ended It, and Emerged Since 1989 as the New Italy.* Baltimore: Bancroft, 2009. 409 pp. hb. dj.

603. Kenna, Rudolph. "1954/The South Side Vampire." In Rudolph Kenna. *They Belonged to Glasgow: The City from the Bottom Up.* Glasgow: Neil Wilson Publishing, 2011, pp. 107–08.

604. Keyworth, David G. *Troublesome Corpses: Vampires & Revenants, from Antiquity to the Present.* Westcliffe-on-Sea: Desert Island Books, 2007. 320 pp. hb. *Troublesome Corpses: Vampires & Revenants, from Antiquity to the Present* received the 2008 award for the best nonfiction book of the previous year given annually by the Lord Ruthven Society.

605. _____. "Was the Vampire of the Eighteenth Century a Unique Type of Undead Corpse?" *Folklore* 117, 3 (2006): 241–60.

606. Klaniczay, G. "The Decline of Witches and the Rise of Vampires in 18th Century Hapsburg Monarchy." *Ethnologica Europea* 17 (1987): 165–80. Rpt. in: Gábor Klansczay. *The Use of Supernatural Power.* Princeton, NJ: Princeton University Press, 1990, pp. 168–88.

607. Kord, Susanne. "Outbreak: Serbian Vampires Come to Life in Germany (Leipzig and Vienna, 1732–1755)." In Suzanne Kord. *Murderesses in German Writing, 1720–1860: Heroines of Horror.* Cambridge University Press, 2009, pp. 43–51.

608. Lehrer, Milton G. *Transylvania: History and Reality.* Silver Spring, MD: Bartleby Press, 1986. 306 pp. hb. dj.

609. Lewis, D. B. Wyndham. *The Soul of Marshal Gilles de Raiz, with Some Account of His Life and Times, His Abominable Crimes, and His Expiation.* London: Eyre & Spottiswoode, 1952. 209 pp. hb. dj.

610. Linebaugh, Peter. *Ysilanti Vampire May Day.* Ypsilanti, MI: Occupy Ypsilanti, 2012. tp.

611. Loring, F. G. "The Tomb of Sarah." [1900.] In James Dickie, ed. *The Undead: Vampire Masterpieces.* London: Pan Books Ltd., 1973, 92–105.

612. Lucendo, Santiago. "Return Ticket to Transylvania: Relations Between Historical Reality and Vampire Fiction." In John Edgar Browning and Caroline Joan Picart, eds. *Dracula, Vampires, and Other Undead Forms.* Lanham, MD: The Scarecrow Press, 2009, pp. 115–26.

613. Mehtonen, P. M. "The International Vampire Boom and Post-Soviet Gothic Aesthetics." In P. M. Mehtonen. *Gothic Topographies: Language, Nation Building and "Race."* Farnham, UK: Ashgate Publishing Ltd, 2013.

614. Miller, Craig. "The Vampire Prioress of Robin Hood's Grave." *Fate* 50, 7 (July 1997): 42–45.

615. Moench, Doug. "Transylvania on a Budget." *Dracula Lives!* 2, 1 (March 1974): 18–19.

616. _____. "Vampire Killing for Fun and Profit." *Monsters of the Movies* 1, 9 (Summer 1975): 52, 54, 56, 58.

617. Mulvey-Roberts, Marie. "Menstrual Misogyny and Taboo: The Medusa, Vampire, and the Female Stigmatic." In Andrew Shail and Gillian Howie, ed. *Menstruation A Cultural History.* Basingstoke, UK: Palgrave Macmillan, 2005.

618. Newburgh, William of. *Selections from the Historia Rerum Anglicarum of William of Newburgh.* Trans and ed. by C. Johnson. London: S.P.C.K./New York: Macmillan Company, 1920. 63 pp. Posted at: https://archive.org/details/selectionsfromhi00willrich.

619. Nolan, James. "The 12th Century Vampire Fragments of Walter Map and William of Newburgh." 2006. 10 pp. Posted at : http://www.academia.edu/299068/Unearthing_Medieval_Vampire_Stories_In_England_Fragments_From_De_Nugis_Curialium_and_Historia_Rerum_Anglicarum.

620. Oldbridge, Darren. "'Dead man walking': The Historical Context of Vampire Beliefs." In Peter Day, ed. *Vampire: Myths and Metaphors of Enduring Evil.* Amsterdam: Rodopi, 2006, pp. 81–92.

621. Paglia, Camille. *Sexual Personae: Art and Decadence from Nefertiti to Emily Dickinson.* New Haven, CT: Yale University Press, 1990. 718 pp. hb. Rpt.: New York: Vintage Books, 1991. 718 pp. tp.

622. _____. *Vamps and Tramps: New Essays.* New York: Vintage, 1994. 532 pp. tp.

623. Phillips, Lawrence. *London Gothic Place, Space and the Gothic Imagination.* London: Continuum International Publishing, 2010. 204 pp. hb.

624. Richi, Brian. *Vampires through the Ages: Lore and Legends of the World's Most Notorious Blood Drinkers.* Woodbury, MN: Llewellyn Publications, 2012. 215 pp. tp.

625. Ridenhour, James. *In Darkest London: The Gothic Cityscape in Victorian Literature.* Lanham, MD: Jamieson Ridenhour (Author) Scarecrow Press, 2012. 170 pp. hb.

626. Ruickbie, Leo. "Memento (non)mori: Memory, Discourse and Transmission during the Eighteenth-Century Vampire Epidemic and After."

In Simon Bacon, and Katarzyna Bronk, eds. *Undead Memory: Vampires and Human Memory in Popular Culture.* Bern, Switz.: Peter Lang International Academic Publishers, 2013, pp. 21–58.

627. Ruthner, Clemens. "Undead Feedback: Adaptations and Echoes of Johann Fluckinger's Report, Visum et Repertum (1732), until the Millennium." In Barbara Brodman and James E. Doan, eds. *The Universal Vampire: Origins and Evolution of a Legend.* Madison, NJ: Fairleigh Dickinson University Press, 2013, pp. 91–106.

628. Sage, Victor. "*Dracula* and the Codes Victorian of Pornography. In Dominique Sipière, ed., *Dracula: Insémination-dissémination,* Amiens, Presses de l'UFR Clerc, Université de Picardie, 1996, pp. 31–48. Rpt. in Gilles Menegaldo and Dominique Sipière, eds. *Dracula: L'oeuvre de Bram Stokeret le film de Francis F. Coppola.* Paris, Ellipses, 2005, pp. 55–69.

629. _____. "Exchanging Fantasies: Sex and the Serbian Crisis in *The Lady of the Shroud.*" In William Hughes and Andrew Smith, eds. *Bram Stoker: History, Psychoanalysis and the Gothic.* Basingstoke, UK: Macmillan, 1998, pp. 116–??.

630. St. Clair, Stanislas Graham Bower, and Charles Brophy. *Twelve Years Study of the Eastern Question in Bulgaria.* London: Chapman & Hall, 1877. 319 pp. hb. Posted at: http://www.forgottenbooks.com/books/Twelve_Years_Study_of_the_Eastern_Question_1400039321.

631. Schneck, Robert Damon. *President's Vampire: Strange-but-True Tales of the United States of America.* New York: Barnes & Noble Books, 2007. 223 pp. tp.

632. Shandley, Robert, Tazim Jamal, and Aniela Tanase. "Location Shooting and the Filmic Destination: Transylvanian Myths and the Post-Colonial Tourism Enterprise." *Journal of Tourism and Cultural Change* 4, 3 (December 2006): 137–158.

633. Showers, Brian J. *Literary Walking Tours of Gothic Dublin.* Dublin: Nonsuch Ireland, 2006. 130 pp. tp. Illus. by Duane Spurlock.

634. Smith, Eric D. "A Presage of Horror! Cacotopia, the Paris Commune, and Bram Stoker's *Dracula.*" *Criticism* 52, 1 (2010): Posted at: http://digitalcommons.wayne.edu/criticism/vol52/iss1/4.

635. Stamp, Cordelia. *Dracula Discovered.* Whitby, UK: Caedmon, 1981. 17 pp. tp. 2nd. Ed.: Whitby, UK: Abbey Press, 1988. tp.

636. _____. *Whitby: A Brief History*. Whitby, UK: Caedmon of Whitby, 2007. tp.

637. Stuart, Bonnie E. *Haunted New Orleans: Southern Spirits, Garden District Ghosts, and Vampire Venues*. Guilford, CT: Globe Pequot, 2012. 288 pp. tp.

638. Trigo, Benigno. "Anemia and Vampires: Figures to Govern the Colony, Puerto Rico, 1880 to 1904." *Comparative Studies in Society and History* 41, 1 (Jan., 1999): 104–123.

639. Trow, M. J. *A Brief History of Vampires*. London: Robinson, 2010. Rpt.: Philadelphia, PA: Running Press, 2010. 448 pp.

640. Vermeir, Koen. "Vampires as Creatures of the Imagination: Theories of Body, Soul and Imagination in Early Modern Vampire Tracts (1659–1755)." Paris, France: Univ Paris Diderot, Sorbonne Paris Cité, 2010. 34 pp. Posted at: http://hal.archives-ouvertes.fr/docs/00/60/93/87/PDF/Vermeir_-_Vampires_as_creatures_of_the_imagination.pdf. A paper originally presented at the Princeton-Bucharest Seminar in Early Modern Philosophy, July 2009.

641. Wood, Daniel J. *Realm of the Vampire: History and the Undead*. Lakeville, MN: Galde Press, 2011. 160 pp. tp.

Vlad Tepes

Vlad Tepes (aka Vlad the Impaler) (1431–1476?) was a ruler of Wallachia, one of the three areas that constitute modern Romania. His efforts to create a centralized government and curb the powers of the local feudal lords earn him a place in the country's history as a major creator of modern Romania, while his battles against overwhelming forces, the invading Turkish Muslims then attempting to extend their empire up the Danube River, made him somewhat of a hero to the Christian West. His practice of impaling his enemies, both foreign and domestic, made him a hated character by those who opposed him.

Virtually unknown in the west prior to the 1970s, he was lifted out of obscurity when his title "Dracula" (referring to his father's joining a Christian coalition to oppose the Turkish threat, the Order of the Dragon) was linked to Bram Stoker's use of the name for the main character in his novel. This information began to immediately inform novelists and filmmakers. The writer Gail Kimberly introduced Vlad into her novel *Dracula Began*, and Richard Matheson wrote him into his screenplay for the next adaptation of Stoker's novel, the televised version of *Dracula* starring Jack Palance.

The scholarly debate on Vlad made him an object of attention and has led to a number of books and academic papers. It is now obvious that the link between Vlad and the fictional Count Dracula is quite tenuous and whether Vlad's popularity in the popular culture will continue is most questionable.

642. Agniel, Lucien. "Real Dracula Was no Tourist Attraction." *Smithsonian* 5, 11 (February 1975): 108–113.

643. Andreescu, Stefan. *Vlad the Impaler: Dracula*. Trans. by Ioana Voia. Bucharest: Romanian Cultural Foundation Publishing. House, 1999. 298 pp. tp.

644. Andreescu, Stefan, and Raymond T. McNally. "Exactly Where Was Dracula Captured in 1462?" *East European Quarterly* 23, 2 (1989): 269–82.

645. Baddeley, Gavin, and Paul Woods. *Vlad the Impaler: Son of the Devil, Hero of the People*. Chatham, Kent, UK: Ian Allan Publishing, 2010. 335 pp. tp.

646. Beattie, John. "In Search of the Real Dracula." *Mayflair* 23, 4 (undated): 20–22, 94–98.

647. Bentley, Juliette. "Vlad Voivode Dracula." *Supernatural* 2 (1969).

648. Charles River Editors. *The Life and Legacy of Vlad the Impaler*. Ser.: Legends of the

Middle Ages. Cambridge, MA: Charles River Editors, 2012. 43 pp. tp.

649. Cioranescu, George. "Vlad the Impaler—Current Parallels with a Medieval Romanian Prince." *Radio Free Europe Research: Background Report* 23 (January 31, 1977): 1–10.

650. Constantiniu, Florin. "Vlad Tepes." *Romanian Bulletin* (October 1977).

651. Crossen, John F. "The Stake That Spoke: Vlad Dracula and a Medieval Gospel of Violence." In Elizabeth Miller, ed. *Dracula; The Shade and the Shadow.* Westcliff-on-Sea, Essex, UK: Desert Island Books, 1998, pp. 180–91.

652. Czabai, Stephen. "The Real Dracula." *The Hungarian Quarterly* 7 (Autumn 1941): 327–32.

653. Diamantis, Sophie. "An Interview with Raymond T. McNally." *Delirium* 3 (1996): 48–51.

654. *Dracula: A Translation of the 1488 Nürnberg Edition with an Essay by Beverley D. Eddy.* Philadelphia: Rosenbach Museum Library, 1985. 20 pp. pb.

655. Dukes, Paul. "Dracula: Fact, Legend, and Fiction." *History Today* 32 (July 1982): 44–47.

656. Dutu, Alexandru. "Portraits of Vlad Tepes: Literature, Pictures and Images of the Ideal Man." In Kurt W. Treptow. *Dracula: Essays on the Life and Times of Vlad Tepes.* New York: East European Monographs, 1991, pp. 239–45.

657. Eddy, Beverley D. "Introduction." *Dracula: A Translation of the 1488 Nürnberg Edition with and Essay by Beverley D. Eddy.* Philadelphia: Rosenbach Museum & Library, 1985. Unpaged. pb.

658. Ene, Georgeta. "Romanian Folklore About Vlad Tepes." *Revue des études Européennes* nr. 4 (1976): 581–90.

659. Florescu, John. "A Night in Dracula's Castle." *Seventeen* 33 (January 1974): 36.

660. Florescu, Radu. "The Dracula Image in the Works of Ispirescu and Radulescu-Codin." *Cahiers Roumains d'Études Littéraires* 3 (1977): 28–34.

661. ____. "Dracula in Romanian Literature." In Jean Lacroix, ed. *Dracula: Le voïvode et le vampire.* Montpellier, Université Paul Valéry, 1983, pp. 139–149.

662. ____. "Dracula as Hero." *International History Magazine* 8 (August 1973). Rpt. in: Peter Haining, ed. *The Dracula Scrapbook.* New York: Bramwell House, 1975, pp. 57–64.

663. ____. "What's in a Name: Dracula or Vlad the Impaler?" In Elizabeth Miller, ed. *Dracula; The Shade and the Shadow.* Westcliff-on-Sea, Essex, UK: Desert Island Books, 1998, pp. 192–201.

664. ____, **and Raymond T. McNally.** *The Complete Dracula.* Acton, MA: Copley Publishing Group, 1992. 409 pp. Reprints *In Search of Dracula* and *Dracula: A Biography of Vlad the Impaler, 1431–1476.*

665. ____, **and** ____. *Dracula: A Biography of Vlad the Impaler, 1431–1476.* New York: Hawthorn Books, 1973. 239 pp. hb. dj. Rpt.: London: Robert Hale, 1973. 239 pp. tp.

666. ____, **and** ____. *Dracula: Prince of Many Faces.* Boston: Little, Brown and Company, 1989. 261 pp. hb. dj. Rpt.: Boston: Back Bay Books, 1989. 261 pp. tp.

667. Giurescu, Constantin C. *The Life and Deeds of Vlad the Impaler: Dracula.* New York: Romanian Library, 1969.

668. Gruia, Catalin. *What About Dracula? Romania's Scizophrenic Dilemma. Or Vlad and the Vampire: The Double Life of Dracula.* N.p.: 37-Minutes Publishing, 2013. 100 pp. tp.

669. Heiman, Leo. "Meet the Real Count Dracula." *Fate* 21, 3 (March 1968): 53–60. Rpt. in: Peter Haining, ed. *The Dracula Scrapbook.* New York: Bramwell House, 1976, pp. 165–71. Re: Count Alexander Cepesi, a contemporary descendant of Vlad Tepes.

670. Jens, Sir. *In the Shadow of Empires: The Historic Vlad Dracula, the Events He Shaped and the Events That Shaped Him.* N.p.: First Break Publishing, 2012. 174 pp. tp.

671. Leblanc, Benjamin. "Vlad Dracula: An Intriguing Figure in the Fifteenth Century." *Journal of the Dark* 5 (1997). Posted at: http://www.htspweb.co.uk/fandf/romlit/specnew/vlad/archive2/leblanc2.htm.

672. Light, Duncan. "The Status of Vlad Ţepeş in Communist Romania: A Reassessment." *Journal of Dracula Studies* 9 (2007): 9–21. Posted at http://www.blooferland.com/drc/index.php?title=Journal_of_Dracula_Studies.

673. McNally, Raymond T. "Separation Granted, Divorce Denied, Annulment Unlikely." *Journal of Dracula Studies* 1 (1999): 25–27. Posted at http://www.blooferland.com/drc/index.php? title=Journal_of_Dracula_Studies.

674. _____, **and Radu Florescu.** *In Search of Dracula*. New York: Galahad Books, 1972. 223 pp. hb. dj. Rpt.: Greenwich, CT: New York Graphic Society, 1973. 223 pp. hb. dj. Rpt.: New York: Warner Books, 1973. 247 pp. pb. Rpt.: London: New English Library, 1979. 219 pp. pb. Rev. ed. as: *In Search of Dracula: Twenty Years Later*. Boston: Houghton, Mifflin, 1994. 297 pp. tp. Rpt.: London: Robson Books, 1995. 300 pp. tp.

675. _____. "In Search of the Real Dracula." In Anthony Timpone. *Fangoria Vampires*. New York: HarperPrism, 1996, pp. 182–91.

676. Michałowicz, Konstanty. "Concerning the Wallachian Voivode Dracula." In Konstantin Mihailovic. *Memoirs of a Janissary*. Ed. by Svat Soucek. Trans. by Benjamin Stolz. Princeton, NJ: Markus Wiener Publishers, 2011, pp. 65–68.

677. Moench, Doug. "Yes, Virginia, There Is a Real Dracula (Undead and Well in Wallachia)." *Dracula Lives!* 6 (May 1974): 18–25.

678. Nandris, Grigore. "The Historical Dracula: The Theme of His Legend in the Western and in the Eastern Literature of Europe." *Comparative Literature Studies* 3, 4 (1966): 367–96. Rpt. as: "The Historical Dracula." In A. Owen Aldridge, ed. *Comparative Literature: Matter and Method*. Urbana: University of Illinois Press, 1969, pp. 109–43.

679. _____. "A Philological Analysis of Dracula and Rumanian Place Names and Masculine Personal Names in a/ea." *Slavonic and East European Review* 37 (1959): 321–27.

680. Neagoe, Manole. "The Truth About Dracula." *Holidays in Romania* 19 (December 1976): 8–9.

681. R., Sam. "Dracula—Separating Fiction from Reality." In Sam R. *The Complete Insider's Guide to Romania: 2011*. N.p.: the author, 2011, pp. 23–27. This material has been reprinted in new editions subsequently issued annually.

682. Rezachevici, Constantin. "From the Order of the Dragon to Dracula." *Journal of Dracula Studies* 1 (1999): 3–5. Posted at http://www.blooferland.com/drc/index.php?title=Journal_of_Dracula_Studies.

683. _____. "Vlad Tepes and His Use of Punishments." *Journal of Dracula Studies* 8 (2006): 30–36. Posted at http://www.blooferland.com/drc/index.php?title=Journal_of_Dracula_Studies.

684. Ronay, Gabriel. *The Dracula Myth*. London: H. W. Allen, 1972. 180 pp. hb. Rpt.: London: Pan Books, 1975. 190 pp. pb. Rpt. as: *The Truth About Dracula*. New York: Stein and Day, 1974. hb. Rpt.: New York: Day Books, 1979. 180 pp. pb.

685. Stoicescu, Nocolae. *Vlad Tepes: Prince of Wallachia*. Bucharest: Editura Academiei Republichi Socialiste Romania, 1978. 194 pp. hb.

686. Treptow, Kurt W. *Dracula: Essays on the Life and Times of Vlad Tepes*. New York: East European Monographs, 1991. 336 pp. hb.

687. _____. *Vlad III Dracula: The Life and Times of the Historical Dracula*. Iasi, Romania: Center for Romanian Studies, 2000. 240 pp. hb.

688. Trow, M. J. *Vlad the Impaler: In Search of Dracula*. Thrupp, Shroud, Gloucs., UK: Sutton Publishing, 2003. 280 pp. hb. Rpt. Thrupp, Shroud, Gloucs., UK: Sutton Publishing, 2004. 294 pp. tp.

Elizabeth Bathory

Elizabeth Bathory (1560–1614) was a Slovakian countess who was said to have tortured and murdered numerous young women, in whose blood she was said to have bathed. Because of her reputed use of blood to revive her youthful appearance, she has become known as one of the "true" vampires in history.

Bathory lived most of her life at Castle Cachtrice, near the town of Vishine, northeast of present-day Bratislava, where Austria, Hungary, and the Slovak Republic come together. Elizabeth was arrested on December 29, 1610, and placed on trial a few days later. The first trial (rightly characterized as a show trial by Bathory's biographer Raymond T. McNally) was followed by a second trial convened on January 7, 1611. At this trial, a register found in Elizabeth's living quarters was introduced as evidence. It noted the names of 650 "victims," all recorded in her handwriting. She and her accused co-conspirators were subsequently convicted of 80 counts of murder. The accomplices were sentenced to be executed, and Elizabeth was sentenced to life imprisonment in solitary confinement.

In his 1983 book, *Dracula Was a Woman: In Search of the Blood Countess of Transylvania*, McNally made the strongest case for including Bathory in the history of vampirism along with Vlad Tepes. He had taken notice of Bathory from the prior mention by Donald Glut in *True Vampires of History* (1971) and Gabriel Ronay in *The Truth About Dracula* (1972). But McNally then went into great depths to document her vampiric acts, which would set off a debate among the countess' detractors and defenders. In the intervening decades, just as Romanians moved to defend Vlad, so Slovakians took the lead in attempting to distance Bathory from any connection to vampirism. Meanwhile, other historians have also challenged the evidence presented at Bathory's trial as insufficient to back up the charges of wrongdoing brought against her.

While historians have debated her career and fate, stories about her have inspired a host of novels and movies. Not only have both attempted to bring her fabled story to life, but Bathory has appeared as a character in a variety of movies set in the twentieth century. Valentine Penrose's early novel, *Erzsebet Bathory, La Comtesse Sanglante* (1962), translated into English as *The Bloody Countess* (1970), would inspire the first of the major Bathory films, *Countess Dracula* (Hammer, 1970), starring Ingrid Pitt. (Actually, an earlier Bathory movie had been made by Italian director Mario Bava, but his *I Vampiri* [aka *The Devil's Commandment*] had less ripple effects than did the still popular Hammer production.) Bathory has supplied a continuing source for introducing a female into vampire films, which have been dominated by male figures, but has been of far less interest in written media.

689. Blocker, Lynn. *Immortal Legacy: The Story of the "Countess Elizabeth Bathory" and The Legends of the Soul Eaters.* N.p.: the author, 2010. 262 pp. tp.

690. Carroll, Leslie. "Erzsébet (Elizabeth) Bathory, the Blood Countess." In Leslie Carroll. *Royal Pains: A Rogues' Gallery of Brats, Brutes, and Bad Seeds.* New York: NAL Trade, 2011, pp. 161–82.

691. Craft, Kimberly L. *Infamous Lady: The True Story of Countess Erzsébet Báthory.* N.p.: the author, 2009. 331 pp. tp. Craft is also the author of a historical novel about Bathory entitled *Elizabeth Báthory: A Memoire: As Told by Her Court Master, Benedict Deseo.*

692. _____. *The Private Letters of Countess Erzsébet Báthory.* N.p.: the author, 2011. 142 pp. tp.

693. Gibson, Dirk Cameron. "Vampire Serial Killers." In Dirk C. Gibson. *Legends, Monsters, or Serial Murderers? The Real Story Behind an Ancient Crime.* Santa Barbara, CA: Praeger/ABC-

Clio, 2012, pp. 11–32. Covers Elizabeth Bathory and Vincenzo Verzini.

694. Kord, Susanne. "Blood Baths: The Case of Elizabeth Bathory." In Suzanne Kord. *Murderesses in German Writing, 1720–1860: Heroines of Horror.* Cambridge University Press, 2009, pp. 54–70.

695. McNally, Raymond T. *Dracula Was a Woman: In Search of the Blood Countess of Transylvania.* New York: McGraw Hill, 1983. 254 pp. hb. dj. Rpt.: London: Hale, 1984. 238 pp. hb. dj. Rpt.: London: Hamlyn Paperback, 1985. 254 pp. pb.

696. Nicholas, Margaret. "Elizabeth Bathory." In: Margaret Nicholas. *The World's Wickedest Women.* London: Octopus, 1984. Rpt.: New York: Berkley Books, 1988, pp. 152–54.

697. Penrose, Valentine. *The Bloody Countess.* London: Calder & Boyars, 1970. 192 pp. hb. Rpt.: London: Creation Books, 1996. 157 pp. tp. Original French edition as: *Erzsebet Bathory: La Comtesse Sanglante.* Paris: 1962.

698. Robinson, Janet S. "'Your tale merely confirms that women are mad and vain': The Uncanny Rendering of Countess Elizabeth Bathory's Life as Vampire Legend." In Douglas Brode and Leah Deyneka, eds. *Dracula's Daughters: The Female Vampire on Film.* Lanham, MD: Scarecrow Press, 2013, pp. 139–57.

699. Santos, Cristina. "Vampire, Witch, Serial Killer or All of the Above? The Bloody Countess Elizabeth Bathory." In Cristina Santos and Adriana Spahr. *Monstrous Deviations in Literature*

and the Arts. Oxford: Inter-Disciplinary Press, 2011, 187–202.

700. Thorne, Tony. *Countess Dracula: Life and Times of Elisabeth Bathory, the Blood Countess.* London: Bloombury, 1997. 274 pp. hb.

701. Webb, William. "Elizabeth Bathory: The Countess of Blood." In William Webb. *Scary Bitches: 15 of the Scariest Women You'll Ever Meet!* N.p.: Absolute Crime, 2013, pp. 8–13 pp.

Vampire Slayers

Beginning with Abraham Van Helsing, the sworn enemy of vampires in the novel *Dracula* (1897), the vampire hunter, usually self-trained and self-credentialed, has become a vital element in vampire lore, though usually taking second billing to the vampire in the literature through the twentieth century. The situation began to change with the advent of Blade the Vampire Slayer, a character created by comic book writer Marv Wolfman and introduced into the 1970s pioneering Marvel comic book series, *The Tomb of Dracula*. Blade, who initially gathered comment as an early African American hero figure in comic books, slowly gained a following among vampire enthusiasts and finally became the subject of his own movie (1998). The movie proved popular enough to lead to two sequels and a short-lived television series. In the meantime, through the 1990s, Blade was transformed from a somewhat normal-appearing courageous figure into a muscular Marvel superhero character.

Even as he gained space in the Marvel universe, Blade's popularity was eclipsed by Buffy the Vampire Slayer. Originally the subject of a less than spectacular 1992 movie, Buffy became an overnight sensation when introduced to television in 1997. The Buffy phenomenon would not only establish the vampire hunter beside the vampire as an equally important character, but rescue previous vampire hunters, such as the Hammer Studios character Kronos, from relative obscurity. "Van Helsing" has become a generic name for contemporary vampire hunters, with numerous descendants of the original Abraham Van Helsing making appearances in various novels and movies.

Prominent vampire slayers (including more general monster hunters who include vampires prominently among their targets) include Kolchak the Night Stalker, Anita Blake (subject of a set of best-selling novels by Laurel Hamilton), Jack Crow (from the novel *Vampires* by John Steakly, later made into a movie by John Carpenter), Gabriel Van Helsing (hero of the movie *Van Helsing*), Blood Rayne (a character from a popular electronic game who jumped to comic books and the movies), and Alucard (Count Dracula turned vampire slayer in the anime series *Hellsing*). Alucard would, like the vampires Angel and Spike, from the *Buffy* series, turn on his own kind while remaining a vampire himself.

Like Blade, Blood Rayne was a dhampir or half-vampire. In Eastern Europe, a widow who had become pregnant during her time of official mourning often claimed that her child's father was her deceased husband, who had returned as a vampire to impregnate her. The child would subsequently be assigned a status as vampire slayer. In like measure, D, the popular Japanese anime character, is a dhampir.

Another recent addition to the literature are the various groups/organizations that establish themselves as ongoing associations and training schools for vampire hunters. Such organizations have their lineage in the Talamasca, a paranormal research organization that includes vampire hunting in its agenda, introduced in the Anne Rice novels. The most famous vampire-fighting organization is the Watchers Council, which trains and assigns each new slayer in the *Buffy the Vampire Slayer* series. A number of slayers, including both Jack Crow and Alucard, act as agents of the Roman Catholic Church.

Most characters in novels, games, and movies who kill vampires are, of course, not vampire hunters as such, but merely people who have to defend themselves when set upon by vampires.

The British independent bishop Sean Manchester emerged as the primary contemporary exponent of the actual existence of vampires, and he assigned himself the task of killing them wherever they are found. Manchester's fame is related to a reputed vampire killing that took place in Highgate Cemetery in London.

One essential item for modern vampire slayers is the vampire slayer's kit that would contain the elements needed to block a vampire's attack and then dispatch the monster to its final reward. Such kits have circulated among those interested in vampires and have been sold at auction through the twentieth century. All appear to be fakes (made to sell to vampire enthusiasts rather than actually intended for killing vampires), but remain pricey as oddities of vampire lore. The best source of information on such kits is a report found on the Internet: "Regarding Ernst Blomberg: Purveyor of fine Vampire Killing Kits," posted at http://spooky-landcrypt.webs.com/blomberg.html.

The literature commenting upon vampire slayers grades into the pseudo-documentary literature about vampires (see chapter IX), of which multiples pieces purport to be manuals on slaying vampires. See the item by Demetrios Zavavinos below.

702. Ahern, Jerry. "Modern-Day Vampire Hunter." *Saga* 59, 6 (December 1981): 30–33.

703. Cushing, Peter. *An Autobiography.* London: Weidenfelf & Noicolson, 1988. 157 pp. hb. dj.

704. _____. *An Autobiography and Past Forgetting.* Baltimore, MD: Midnight Marquee Press, 1999. 255 pp. tp.

705. _____. "How I Became a Monster Hunter." In Peter Cushing, ed. *Tales of a Monster Hunter.* London: Futura, 1978, pp. 1–13.

706. _____. *"Past Forgetting:" Memoirs of the Hammer Years.* London: Weidenfeld and Nicolson, 1988. 112 pp. hb.

707. _____. *Tales of a Monster Hunter.* London: Arthur Baker, 1977. 208 pp. hb. Rpt.: London: Futura, 1978. 208 pp. pb.

708. Del Vecchio, Deborah. "Farewell to Saint Peter." *Fangoria* 139 (January 1995): 66–69. re: Peter Cushing.

709. _____, **and Tom Johnson.** *Peter Cushing: The Gentle Man of Horror and His 91 Films.* Jefferson, NC: McFarland & Company, 1992. 485 pp. hb.

710. Duda, Heather L. *An Examination of the Contemporary Monster Hunter in Popular Culture: Murderers and Men of God.* Indiana, PA: Indiana University of Pennsylvania, Ph.D. dissertation, 2006. 182 pp. Large format.

711. _____. *The Monster Hunter in Modern Popular Culture.* Jefferson, NC: McFarland & Company, 2008. 185 pp. tp.

712. Krys, Svitlana. "Slayers and Their Vampires: A Cultural History of Killing the Dead."

Canadian Slavonic Papers 52, 3/4 (September-December 2010).

713. Ladouceur, Liisa. *How to Kill a Vampire: Fangs in Folklore, Film and Fiction.* Toronto: ECW Press , 2013. 190 pp. tp.

714. Lyon, Michelle, with Mark C. MacKinnon. *Hellsing.* Guelph, ON: Guardians of Order, 2002. 80 pp. pb. Large format.

715. Maberry, Jonathan, and Janice Gable Bashman. *Wanted Undead or Alive: Vampire Hunters and Other Kick-Ass Enemies of Evil.* New York: Citadel, 2010. 366 pp. tp.

716. MacDougal, Shane. *The Vampire Slayers' Field Guide to the Undead.* Doylestown, PA: Strider Nolan Publishing, 2003. 686 pp. tp.

717. Manchester, Sean. *The Vampire Hunter's Handbook.* London: Gothic Press, 1997. 96pp.

718. McClelland, Bruce. *Slayers and Their Vampires: A Cultural History of Killing the Dead.* Ann Arbor: University of Michigan Press, 2006. 280 pp. tp.

719. Miller, David. *The Peter Cushing Companion.* Richmond, UK: Reynolds & Hearn, 2000. tp. Rev. ed.: 2002. 192 pp. tp. Rev. ed. as: *The Complete Peter Cushing.* Richmond: Reynolds & Hearn, 2005. 208 pp. tp. Rev. ed. as: *Peter Cushing: A Life in Film.* London: Titan Books, 2013. 192 pp.

720. Milne, Rob. *Return of the Vampire Hunter: An Exclusive Interview with Reclusive Vampire Hunter David Farrant.* London: The British Psychic and Occult Society, 2003. 51 pp.

721. Moench, Doug. "Vampire Killing for Fun and Profit." *Monsters of the Movies* 1, 9 (Summer 1975): 52, 54, 56, 58.

722. Penke, Mark Stephen. *The Vampire Survival Bible—Identifying, Avoiding, Repelling, and Destroying the Undead.* Vol. 1. N.p.: lulu.com, 2012. 421 pp.

723. _____. *The Vampire Survival Bible—Identifying, Avoiding, Repelling, and Destroying the Undead.* Vol. 2. N.p.: lulu.com, 2012.

724. Pohl-Weary, Emily. *Girls Who Bite Back: Witches, Mutants, Slayers and Freaks.* Toronto: Sumach Press, 2004. 360 pp. tp.

725. Ramsland, Katherine. "Dr. Blomberg's Anti-Vampire Kit." *Dead of Night* 6 (Summer 1990): 48.

726. Sommers, Steve. *Van Helsing: The Making of the Legend.* Ed. by Linda Sunshine. New York: Newmarket Press, 2004. 160 pp. pb. Large format. Includes the complete screen play for the movie Van Helsing. .

727. Starrs, D. Bruno. "Envisioning and Indulgence: Dracula and Van Helsing." *Traffic: An Interdisciplinary Postgraduate Journal* 5 (2005): 67–76.

728. Van Dover, J. K. "Professor, Psychical Research Agent, Detective: Van Helsing's Role in *Dracula*" In Bram Stoker. *Dracula.* Ser.: Ignatius Critical Editions. San Francisco, CA: Ignatius Press, 2012, pp. 545–556.

729. Zaravinos, Demitrios. *The Modern Day Vampire Hunter's Guidebook of D. Zaravinos.* N.p.: the author, 2010. 190 pp. tp.

III. Literature

Vampire Literature Before Dracula

The vampire makes its initial appearance in British literature in poetry, possibly the earliest mention being "Thalaba" (1801), a poem by Robert Southey, with additional citations soon to follow in the work of John Stagg and Lord Byron. The first work in which the vampire is an essential element in the work is Samuel Taylor Coleridge's lengthy poem "Cristabel," initially published in 1816, though seemingly written over a decade earlier. It was followed by "Lamia," built on ancient Greek legends of the female vampire. Keats will later write one of the more notable Romantic vampire-themed poems, "La Belle Dame sans Merci" ("The Beautiful Lady without Mercy"), published in 1819.

The Romantic era of vampire-themed poetry set the context for the first vampire prose story in English, "The Vampyre" written by Lord Byron's former physician/drug dealer John William Polidori. Originally published in a periodical under Byron's name, the story attained a fame and circulation it might not have otherwise had even as both Polidori and Byron moved to have Byron's name removed from the text. In any case, the story's villain, Lord Ruthven, a character based upon Polidori's former employer, would become the dominant vampire character in English literature for the rest of the century.

"The Vampyre" inspired a number of dramatists, and within a year of its publication a set of plays began to appear in the Parisian theatres, quickly followed by one in London, that allowed the vampire to make its initial permeation of the popular culture. Writers would continually return to it through the remainder of the century. The stage drama and the short story would be the main forms in which the vampire would be embodied, but the first novels would also appear. The initial novel, *Varney the Vampire*, was written as a series of penny dreadfuls, distributed chapter by chapter with no author named, on a weekly basis and later compiled into a book. Over the two years it was composed, it possibly had multiple authors.

Amid the many vampire stories to appear through the century, the high point of writing on the vampire would be reached in 1872, with the appearance of the novella "Carmilla," by Irish writer Sheridan Le Fanu and culminate in 1897 with *The Blood of the Vampire* by Florence Marryat. Almost forgotten today, Marryat was a very popular author in her own time, far more famous than Bram Stoker.

The radical rise in popularity of *Dracula* (1897) in the last decades of the twentieth century, coupled with a parallel increase in interest in Victoriana, has prompted a revival of interest in the previous writings on the vampire through the nineteenth century. With the rediscovery and establishment of the theme of the psychic vampire, which drains the energy of its victims rather than blood, contemporary scholars have found the vampire as a prominent character in such literary notables as Edgar Allan Poe and Emily Brontë, neither of whom ever wrote about any bloodsucker, or barely mention the "vampire." The psychic vampire in literature also resonated with the vampire theme that emerged in Spiritualist and other esoteric literature.

730. Anderson, Matthew Neil. *Predatory Portraiture: Goethe's* Faust *and the Literary Vampire in Gogol's* [P]opmpem *and Wilde's* The Picture of Dorian Gray. Austin: University of Texas, M.A. thesis, 2010. 40 pp. Large format.

731. Andriano, Joseph. *Our Ladies of Darkness: Feminine Daemonology in Male Gothic Fiction.* University Park: Pennsylvania State University Press, 1993, 182 pp.

732. Ash, Russell. "The Vampyre and Its Author, Doctor John William Polidori, 1985–1821." In John William Polidori. *The Vampyre: A Tale.* N.p.: Gubblecote Press, 1974, pp. 1–9. Limited to 2000 copies.

733. Austin, April Laurie. *A Study of the Canine Imagery in the Victorian Novels* Wuthering Heights *and* Dracula. Warrensburg: Central Missouri State University, M.A. thesis, 1999. 66 pp. Large format.

734. Babener, Liahna Klenman. *Predators of the Spirit: The Vampire Theme in Nineteenth-Century Literature.* Los Angeles: University of California at Los Angeles, Ph.D. dissertation, 1975. 490 pp. Large format.

735. Bailey, J. O. "What Happens in 'The Fall of the House of Usher.'" *American Literature* 35 (1964): 445–66.

736. Baldick, Chris. "Dangerous Discoveries and Mad Scientists: Some Late-Victorian Horrors." In Chris Baldick. *Frankenstein's Shadow: Myth, Monstrosity, and Nineteenth-Century Writings.* Oxford: Clarendendon Press, 1987, pp. 141–62.

737. Balmori, Stephanie E. *The Vampire in the Poetry of Delmira Agustini.* Tallahassee: Florida State University, M.A. thesis, 2009. 85 pp. Large format.

738. Behrendt, Patricia Flanagan. "Dangerous Wounds: Vampirism as a Social Metaphor in Zola's *Therese Raquin*." *European Studies Journal* 2, 2 (1985): 32–40.

739. Bhalla, Alok. *Politics of Atrocity and Lust: The Vampire Tale as a Nightmare History of England in the Nineteenth Century.* New Delhi, India: Sterling, 1990. 88 pp. hb.

740. Bleiler, Everett F. "Introduction." In [James Malcolm Rymer]. *Varney the Vampire.* New York: Dover Publications, 1972, pp. v–xv.

741. Bloom, Clive, et al. *Nineteenth Century Suspense: From Poe to Conan Doyle.* New York: St. Martin's Press, 1988. 139 pp. Includes essays on the vampire by Anne Cranny-Francis, Philip Martin, and Anne Cranny-Francis.

742. Blythe, Hal, and Charlie Sweet. "Poe's Satiric Use of Vampirism in 'Bernice.'" *Poe Studies* 14, 1 (June 1981): 23–24.

743. Boone, Troy Monroe. *Unearthing Plots: Vampirism and Victorian Culture.* Rochester, NY: University of Rochester, Ph.D. dissertation, 1994. 298 pp. Large format.

744. Botting, Fred. "Hypocrite, Vampire..." *Gothic Studies* 9 (2007): 16–34.

745. _____. "Vampires." In Fred Botting. *Gothic.* London: Routledge, 1996, pp. 144–54.

746. Brantlinger, Patrick. "Imperial Gothic: Atavism and the Occult in the British Adventure Novel, 1880–1914." *English Language Teaching* 28 (1985): 243–252.

747. Brogan, James. "Vampire Bats and Blake's Spectre." *Blake Newsletter* 37 (Summer 1976): 32–33.

748. Brownell, M. R. "Pope and the Vampires in Germany." *Eighteenth Century Life* 2 (June 1976): 96–97.

749. Bruhm, Steven. "Gothic Sexualities." In Anna Powell and Andrew Smith, eds. *Teaching the Gothic.* Basingstoke, England: Palgrave Macmillan, 2006, pp. 93–106.

750. Burduck, Michael L. "Browning's Use of Vampirism in 'Porphyria's Lovers.'" *Studies in Browning and His Circle* 14 (1986): 63–65.

751. Burns-Davies, Erin. *"And yet God has not said a word!": Robert Browning and the Romantic*

Killer in Literature. Boca Raton: Florida Atlantic University, M.A. thesis, 2004. 49 pp. Large format.

752. Carter, Margaret L. *"Fiend, Spectre, or Delusion?" Narrative Doubt and the Supernatural in Gothic Fiction.* Irvine: University of California—Irvine, Ph.D. dissertation, 1986. 253 pp. Large format.

753. _____. "A Preface: From Polidori to Prest." In [James Malcolm Rymer]. *Varney the Vampire.* New York: Arno Press, 1998, pp. xxxi–xlii.

754. _____. *Specter or Delusion? The Supernatural in Gothic Fiction.* Ann Arbor: UMI Research Press, 1987. 131 pp. hb. & tp. A revision of Carter's Ph.D. dissertation (1986) at the University of California-Irvine.

755. Clapp, Edwin R. "La Belle Dame as Vampire." *Philological Quarterly* 27 (1948): 89–92.

756. Coad, David. "The Other in the *Moonstone* and *Dracula.*" *Annales du monde Anglophone,* Université de Provence, Aix-Marseille, 4, Le courant gothique et ses avatars dans la littérature anglo-saxonne (October 1996): 33–54.

757. Cole, Dave. "Anatomy of a Literary Vampirism." In Carla T. Kungl, ed. *Vampires: Myths and Metaphors of Enduring Evil.* Oxford: Inter-Disciplinary Press, 2003, pp. 39–43.

758. Crawford, Heide. "The Cultural-Historical Origins of the Literary Vampire in Germany." *Journal of Dracula Studies* 7 (2005): 1–7.

759. _____. "Ernst Benjamin Salomo Raupach's Vampire Story "Wake Not the Dead!" *The Journal of Popular Culture* 45, 6 (December 2012): 1189–1205.

760. Dalton, Margaret. *A. K. Tolstoy.* New York: Twayne Publishers, 1972. 171 pp. Russian novelist Count Aleksey Konstantinovich Tolstoy (1817–1875), is remembered for his novella *The Vampire* (1841).

761. Davis, Octavia. "Morbid Mothers: Gothic Heredity in Florence Marryat's *The Blood of the Vampire.* In Ruth Bienstock Anolik, ed. *Horrifying Sex: Essays on Sexual Difference in Gothic Literature.* Jefferson, NC: McFarland & Company, 2007, pp. 40–57.

762. Davis, Paul E. H. *"Dracula* Anticipated: The 'Undead' in Anglo-Irish Literature." In Barbara Brodman and James E. Doan, eds. *The Universal Vampire: Origins and Evolution of a Legend.* Madison, NJ: Fairleigh Dickinson University Press, 2013, pp. 17–31.

763. Davison, Carol Margaret. "The Rise of the Vampiric Wandering Jew: A Sinister German-English Co-Production." In Carol Margaret Davison. *Anti-Semitism and British Gothic Literature.* New York, Palgrave Macmillan, 2004, pp. 87–119.

764. Day, Gary. "The State of Dracula: Bureaucracy and the Vampire." In Alice Jenkins and Juliet John, eds. *Rereading Victorian Fiction.* New York: St. Martin's Press, 2000, pp. 81–95.

765. del Principe, David. "Misbegotten, Unbegotten, Forgotten: Vampires and Monsters in the Works of Ugo Tarchetti, Mary Shelley, Bram Stoker, and the Gothic Tradition." *Forum Italicum* 29, 1 (1995): 3–25.

766. Dennison, Michael James. *Delights of the Night and Pleasures of the Void: Vampirism and Entropy in Nineteenth Century Literature.* New Orleans: Louisiana State University, Ph.D. dissertation, 1997. 268 pp. Large format.

767. _____. *Vampirism: Literary Tropes of Decadence and Entropy.* Ser.: Currents in Comparative Romance Languages and Literature.New York: Peter Lang, 2001. 155 pp. hb. boards.

768. Dewees, Amanda Raye. *Bloodlines: Domestic & Family Anxieties in Nineteenth-Century Vampire Literature.* Athens: University of Georgia, Ph.D. dissertation, 1998. 266 pp. Large format.

769. Dickens, Charles, Jr. "Vampyres and Ghouls." *All Year Round* (May 20, 1871). Rpt. in: Peter Haining, ed. *The Dracula Scrapbook.* New York: Bramwell House, 1975, pp. 13–20.

770. Dijkstra, Bram. *Evil Sisters: The Threat of Female Sexuality and the Cult of Manhood.* New York: Alfred A. Knopf, 1996. 480 pp. hb. dj.

771. Dimic, Milan V. "Vampiromania in the Eighteenth Century: The Other Side of Enlightenment." *Man and Nature/L'Homme et la Nature: Proceedings of the Canadian Society for Eighteenth Century Studies* 3 (1984): 1–22.

772. Doerksen, Teri Ann. "Deadly Kisses: Vampirism, Colonialism, and the Gendering of Horror." In James Craig Holte, ed. *The Fantastic Vampire: Studies in the Children of the Night: Selected Essays from the Eighteenth International Conference on the Fantastic in the Arts.* Vol. 19. Westport, CT: Greenwood Publishing Group, 2002, pp. 137–43.

773. Durot-Boucé, Elizabeth. "'Chew You Up and Spit You Out': Rewriting a Familiar Fixture of the Gothic Novel." *Anglophonia: French Journal of English Studies* 15 (2004): 209–16.

774. Ellis, Markman. "Vampires, Credulity and Reason." In Markman Ellis. *The History of Gothic Fiction*. Edinburgh: Edinburgh University Press, 2000, pp. 161–203.

775. Engelhardt, Carol Marie. *A Vampire in the Bedroom: The Representation of Women in Victorian Fiction and Social Theory*. Washington University, M.A. thesis, 1990. 176 pp. Large format.

776. Fleishhack, Maria. "Vampires and Mummies in Victorian Gothic Fiction." *Inklings: Jahrbuch für Literatur und Ästhetik* 27 (2009): 62–77.

777. Fleissner, Jennifer L. "Henry James's Art of Eating." *English Literary History* 75, 1 (Spring 2008): 27–62.

778. Frayling, Christopher, ed. *The Vampire: Lord Ruthven to Count Dracula*. London: Victor Gollancz, 1978. 336 pp. hb. dj. Rpt. as: *The Vampyre: A Bedside Companion*. New York: Charles Scribner's Sons, 1978. 336 pp. hb. dj. Rev. ed. as: *Vampyres: From Lord Byron to Count Dracula*. London: Faber and Faber, 1991. 429 pp. hb. dj. Rev. ed. as: *Vampyres: From Lord Byron to Count Dracula*. London: Faber and Faber, 1991. 429 pp. tp. Frayling includes a selection of non-fiction observations of the vampire by Joseph Pitton de Tournefort, Dom Augustin Calmet, Alexandre Dumas, Richard van Krafft-Ebing, Ernest Jones, and Maurice Richardson.

779. _____. "Vampires." *London Magazine* 14 (June-July 1974): 94–104.

780. Gardner, Michele Jeanne. *The Vampire in English Literature*. University of Waterloo, M.A. thesis, 1991. 148 pp. Large format.

781. Genc, Burcu. *Masochistic Men and Female Vampires: A New Approach to Rape Fantasy: An Exploration of Rape Fantasy through the Female Vampires of Romantic and Victorian Periods*. Saarbrücken, Germany: LAP/Lambert Academic Publishing, 2011. 60 pp. tp.

782. George, Samantha, and William Hughes, eds. *Open Graves, Open Minds: Representations of Vampires and the Undead from the Enlightenment to the Present Day*. Manchester, UK: Manchester University Press, 2013. 320 pp. hb. dj.

783. Gilbert, John. "The Vampire Poets." In Rosemary Ellen Guiley, with J. B. Macabre. *The Complete Vampire Companion*. New York: Macmillan, 1994, pp. 56–57.

784. Goetsch, Paul. "Monsters in the Victorian Age." In Paul Goetsch. *Monsters in English Literature: From the Romantic Age to the First World War*. Frankfurt am Main, Peter Lang, 2002, pp. 126–56.

785. Granger, John. "Gothic Romance: The Spooky Atmosphere Formula from Transylvania: *Harry Potter* as an Echo of the Brontë Sisters, *Frankenstein, The Strange Case of Dr. Jekyll and Mr. Hyde*, and *Dracula*." In John Granger. *Harry Potter's Bookshelf: The Great Books Behind the Hogwarts Adventures*. New York, Berkley Books, 2009, pp. 65–104.

786. Grixti, Joseph. "Uncanny Vampire Forms and the Growth of Gothic Fictions." In Joseph Grixti. *Terrors of Uncertainty: The Cultural Context of Horror Fiction*. London: Routledge, 1989, pp. 14–22.

787. Guyant, Valerie L. Vixen, *Virgin or Vamp? Female Characters in Vampire Literature Past and Present*. Rockford: Northern Illinois University, Ph.D. dissertation, 2011. 329 pp. Large format.

788. Hackenberg, S. "Vampires and Resurrection Men: The Perils and Pleasures of the Embodied Past in 1840s Sensational Fiction." *Victorian Studies* 52, 1 (2009): 63–75.

789. Haefele-Thomas, Ardel. "'One does things abroad that one would not dream of doing in England': Miscegenation and Queer Female Vampirism in J. Sheridan Le Fanu's 'Carmilla' and Florence Marryat's *The Blood of the Vampire*." In Ardel Haefele-Thomas. *Queer Others in Victorian Gothic: Transgressing Monstrosity*. Cardiff: University of Wales Press, 2012.

790. Halberstam, Judith Marian. *Parasites and Perverts: Anti-Semitism and Sexuality in Nineteenth Century Gothic Fiction*. Minneapolis: University of Minnesota, Ph.D. dissertation, 1991. 196 pp. Large format.

791. Hammack, Brenda Mann. "Florence Marryat's Female Vampire and the Scientizing of Hybridity." *Studies in English Literature* 48, 4 (2008): 885–896.

792. Heiland, Donna. "Uncanny Monsters in the Work of Mary Shelley, John Polidori and James Malcolm Rymer." In Donna Heiland. *Gothic & Gender: An Introduction*. Malden, MA: Blackwell, 2004, pp. 98–113.

793. Heldreth, Leonard, and Mary Pharr, eds. *The Blood Is the Life: Vampires in Literature*. Bowling Green, KY: Bowling Green State University Press, 1999. 275 pp. hb. & tp. The editors have compiled papers by J. P. Telotte, Robert F. Geary, Jean Lorrah, Zacharias P. Thundy, Martin J. Wood, Lloyd Worley, Joe Sanders, Sharon A. Russell, Sondra Ford Swift, Margaret L. Carter, Elizabeth Hardaway, Michael R. Collings, Carol A. Senf, Bernadette Lynn Bosky, Lillian Marks Heldreth, Donald Pharr, and James Craig Holtencis.

794. Hennelly, Mark M., Jr. "'As Well Fill Up the Space Between': A Liminal Reading of *Christabel.*" *Studies in Romanticism* 38 (1999): 203–22.

795. Hines, Richard Davenport. *Gothic: Four Hundred Years of Excess, Horror, Evil and Ruin.* London: Fourth Estate, 1998. 438 pp. hb. dj.

796. Huang, Pin-Ching. "Of Humans and Monsters: Monstrous Representations of Foreigner in *Wuthering Heights.*" In Jonathan A. Allan and Elizabeth E. Nelson, eds. *Inversions of Power and Paradox.* Oxford, UK: Inter-Disciplinary Press, 2011, pp. 209–218.

797. Hughes, Bill. "'Legally Recognised Undead': essence, difference, and assimilation in Daniel Waters's *Generation Dead.*" In Sam George and Bill Hughes, eds. *Open Graves, Open Minds: Representations of Vampires and the Undead from the Enlightenment to the Present Day.* Manchester: Manchester University Press, 2013, pp. 245–63.

798. Hughes, William. "Fictional Vampires." In David Punter, ed. *A Companion to the Gothic,* Oxford: Blackwell, 2000, pp. 143–54. Rpt. in: David Punter ed. *A New Companion to the Gothic.* Malden, MA: Wiley-Blackwell, 2012, pp. 197–210.

799. Jennings, Lee Byron. "An Early German Vampire Tale: Wilhelm Waiblinger's 'Olura.'" *Suevica. Beiträge zur schwäbischen Literatur- und Geistesgeschichte.* 9 (2001/2002): 295–306.

800. Kendall, Lyle, Jr. "The Vampire Motif in 'The Fall of the House of Usher.'" *College English* 24, 6 (March 1963): 450–453.

801. Khan, Slahuddin Joseph. *Vampires, Prostitutes, and Beauteous Beings: Ironic Representations of Revolution in Michelet, Flaubert, and Rimbaud.* Irvine: University of California–Irvine, Ph.D. dissertation, 1999. 236 pp. Large format.

802. Kiessling, Nicolas. "Variations of Vampirism." *Poe Studies* 14, 1 (June 1981): 23–24.

803. _____. "Demonic Dread: The Incubus Figure in British Literature." In G. R. Thompson, G. R. *The Gothic Imagination: Essays in Dark Romanticism.* Pullman: Washington State University Press, 1974, pp. 22–41.

804. Kord, Susanne. "Containment: Female Vampires in Literature from Goethe to the Grimms (1797–1823)." In Suzanne Kord. *Murderesses in German Writing, 1720–1860: Heroines of Horror.* Cambridge University Press, 2009, pp. 71–81.

805. Krishnan, Lakshmi. "'Why Am I So Changed?': Vampiric Selves and Gothic Doubleness in Wuthering Heights." *Journal of Dracula Studies* 9 (2007): 39–49.

806. Lampert-Weissig, Lisa. "The Vampire as Dark and Glorious Necessity in George Sylvester Viereck's *House of the Vampire* and Hanns Heinz Ewers' *Vampir.*" In Sam George and Bill Hughes, eds. *Open Graves, Open Minds: Representations of Vampires and the Undead from the Enlightenment to the Present Day.* Manchester: Manchester University Press, 2013, pp. 79–95.

807. Lewis, Paul. "The Intellectual Functions of Gothic Fiction: Poe's 'Ligeia' and Tieck's 'Wake not the Dead.'" *Comparative Literature Studies* 16 (1979): 207–21.

808. MacFie, Sian. "'They Suck Us Dry': A Study of Late Nineteenth Century Projections of Vampiric Women." In Philip Shaw and Peter Stockwell, eds. *Subjectivity and Literature from the Romantics to the Present.* London: Printer, 1991, pp. 58–67.

809. Malchow, Harold L. "Vampire Gothic and Late-Victorian Identity." In Howard l. Malchow. *Gothic Images of Race in Nineteenth-Century Britain.* Redwood City, CA: Stanford University Press, 1996, pp. 124–66.

810. Massey, Irving. "The Third Self: *Dracula, Strange Case of Dr. Jekyll and Mr. Hyde* and Mérimée's *Lokis.*" *The Bulletin of the Midwestern Language Association* 6, 2 (Autumn 1973): 57–67.

811. McAteer, Michael. "A Troubled Union: Representation of Eastern Europe in Nineteenth-Century Irish Protestant Literature." In Barbara Korte, Eva Ulrike Pirker, and Sissy Helff, eds. *Facing the East in the West: Images of Eastern Europe in British Literature, Film and Culture.* Amsterdam: Rodopi, 2010, pp.205–18.

812. McCann, Andrew. "Rosa Praed and the Vampire-Aesthete." *Victorian Literature and Culture* 35, 1 (March 2007): 175–87.

813. McNally, Raymond T. "In Search of the Lesbian Vampire: Barbara von Cilli, Le Fanu's 'Carmilla' and the Dragon Order." *Journal of Dracula Studies* 3 (2001): 8–14.

814. Metzger, lore. "Modifications of Genre: A Feminist Critique of 'Christabel' and 'Die Braut de Korinth.'" In Margaret A. Higonnet, ed. *Borderwork: Feminist Engagements with Comparative Literature*. Ithaca, NY: Cornell University Press, 1994, pp. 81–99.

815. Michelis, Angelica. "'Dirty Mamma': Horror, Vampires, and the Maternal in Late Nineteenth-Century Gothic Fiction." *Critical Survey* 15, 3 (2003): 5–18.

816. Mighall, Robert. "Making a Case: Vampirism, Sexuality, and Interpretation." In Robert Mighall. *A Geography of Victorian Gothic Fiction: Mapping History's Nightmares*. New York: Oxford University Press, 1999, pp. 210–47.

817. _____. "'A pestilence which walketh in darkness': Diagnosing the Victorian Vampire." In Glennis Byron and David Punter, eds. *Spectral Readings: Towards a Gothic Geography*. Basingstoke, UK: Macmillan/New York: St. Martin's Press, 1999, pp. 108–24.

818. _____. "Sex, History and the Vampire." In William Hughes and Andrew Smith, eds. *Bram Stoker: History, Psychoanalysis and the Gothic*. Basingstoke, UK: Macmillan, 1998, pp. 62ff.

819. Morrison, Robert, and Chris Baldick. "Introduction." In Robert Morrison, and Chris Baldick, eds. *The Vampyre and Other Tales of the Macabre*. Oxford, UK: Oxford University Press, 1997, pp. vii–xxii.

820. Munford, Rebecca. "Dracula's Daughters: Angela Carter and Pierrette Fleutiaux Vampiric Exchanges." In Avril Horner and Sue Zlosnik, eds. *Le Gothic: Influences and Appropriations in Europe and America*. New York, Palgrave Macmillan, 2008, pp. 116–34.

821. Mustafa, Jamil Muhammed. *Mapping the Late Victorian Subject: Psychology, Cartography and the Gothic Novel*. Chicago: University of Chicago, Ph.D. dissertation, 1949. 224 pp. Large format.

822. Mutch, Deborah. "Introduction: 'A swarm of chuffing draculas': The Vampire in English and American Literature." In Deborah Mutch. *The Modern Vampire and Human Identity*. Basingstoke, UK/New York: Palgrave Macmillan, 2013, pp. 1–17.

823. Nadal, Marita. "Variations on the Grotesque: From Poe's 'The Black Cat' to Oates's 'The White Cat.'" *Mississippi Quarterly: The Journal of Southern Cultures* 57, 3 (2004): 455–71.

824. Nadine, Claudia. "Feminine Subject? or, Baudelaire's Disappearing Muse in 'Les Metamophorses du vampire.'" In Carrol F. Coates, ed. *Repression and Expression: Literary and Social Coding in Nineteenth-Century France*. New York: Peter Lang, 1996. From a paper delivered at the 18th Colloquium in Nineteenth-Century French Studies held in 1992 at Binghamton, N.Y.

825. Nethercot, Arthur H. "Coleridge's 'Christabel' and Lefanu's 'Carmilla.'" *Modern Philology* 47, 1 (August 1949): 32–38.

826. _____. *The Road to Tryermaine: A Study of History, Background, and Purposes of Coleridge's "Christabel."* Chicago: University of Chicago Press, 1939. 230 pp. hb. Rpt.: New York: Russell & Russell, 1962. 230 pp. hb. Rpt.: New York: Greenwood Press, 1978. 230 pp. hb.

827. Olorenshaw, Robert. "Narrating the Monster: From Mary Shelley to Bram Stoker." In Stephen Bann, ed. *Frankenstein: Creation and Monstruosity*. London: Reaktion Books, 1994, pp. 158–176.

828. Paolucci, Peter Leonard. *Re-Reading the Vampire from John Polidori to Anne Rice: Structures of Impossibility Among Three Narrative Variations in the Vampire Tradition*. York, UK: York University, Ph.D. dissertation, 2000.

829. Parker, Berlinda Z. *The Narcotic Gaze: Ocular Imagery and the Vampire Motif in Christabel, Carmilla, and Dracula*. Florida Atlantic University, M.A. thesis, 1982. 71 pp. Large format.

830. Paroissien, David. *Henry James and the Use of the Vampire Emblem*. Las Vegas: New Mexico Highlands University, M.A. thesis, 1965. 64 pp. Large format.

831. Phillips, Ivan. "The Vampire in the Machine: Exploring the Undead Interface." In Sam George and Bill Hughes, eds. *Open Graves, Open Minds: Representations of Vampires and the Undead from the Enlightenment to the Present Day*. Manchester: Manchester University Press, 2013, pp. 25–44.

832. Praz, Mario. *The Romantic Agony*. Trans. by Angus Davidson. New York: Oxford University Press, 1951. 506 pp. hb. Rpt.: New York: Meridian, 1956. 502 pp. tp.

833. Reed, Toni. *Demon Lovers and Their Victims in British Fiction*. Lexington: University Press of Kentucky, 1988. 171 pp. hb. dj.

834. Richmond, Lee. "Edgar Allan Poe's 'Morella: Vampire of Volition." *Studies in Short Fiction* 9 (1972): 93–94.

835. Richmond Garza, Elizabeth M. "The Vampire's Gaze: Gothic Performance in Theory and Practice." *Comparatist: Journal of the Southern Comparative Literature Association* 22 (1998): 91–109.

836. Ridenhour, James. *In Darkest London: The Gothic Cityscape in Victorian Literature.* Lanham, MD: Jamieson Ridenhour (Author) Scarecrow Press, 2012. 170 pp. hb.

837. Riffaterre, Hermine. "Love and Death: Gautier's 'Morte Amoureuse.'" In Hermine Riffaterre. *The Occult in Language and Literature.* New York: New York Literary Forum, 1980, pp. 65–74.

838. Roberts, Bette B. "Varney, the Vampire, Or, Rather, Varney, the Victim." *Gothic* New series 2 (1987): 1–5.

839. Roderique, Jennifer L. "Re-contextualizing Martian Vampires: 1890s science fiction in *Cosmopolitan* magazine." *Media History* 6, 1 (2000): 19–32.

840. Rogers, Susan L. "The Eye/I of the Vampire: Lacanian Subjectivity in Théophile Gautier's 'la Morte Amoureuse.'" *Lit-literature Interpretation Theory* 5, 2 (1994): 169–185.

841. Rogers, Susan Leigh. *Vampire Vixens: The Female Undead and the Lacanian Symbolic Order in Tales by Gautier, James, and LeFanu.* Irvine: University of California-Irvine, M.A. thesis, 1993. 193 pp. Large format.

842. Sage, Victor. *Horror Fiction in the Protestant Tradition.* New York: St. Martin's Press, 1988. 262 pp. hb. dj.

843. St. Armand, Barton Levi. "'I Must Have Died at Ten Minutes Past One:' Posthumous Reverie in Harriet Prescott Spofford's 'The Amber Gods.'" In Howard Kerr, John W. Crowley, and Charles L. Crow, eds. *The Haunted Dusk: America Supernatural Fiction, 1820–1920.* Athens: University of Georgia Press, 1983, pp. 101–119.

844. Scoggin, Daniel. "Surveying the Vampire in Nineteenth-Century British Literature." In Diane Long Hoeveler and Tamar Heller, eds. *Approaches to Teaching Gothic Fiction: The British and American Traditions.* New York: Modern Language Association of America, 2003.

845. Scott, Keith. "Blood, Bodies, Books: Kim Newman and the vampire as cultural text." In Deborah Mutch. *The Modern Vampire and Human Identity.* Basingstoke, UK/New York: Palgrave Macmillan, 2013, pp. 18–36.

846. Sedgwick, Marcus. "The Elusive Vampire: Folklore and Fiction—Writing *My Swordhand Is Singing.*" In Sam George and Bill Hughes, eds. *Open Graves, Open Minds: Representations of Vampires and the Undead from the Enlightenment to the Present Day.* Manchester: Manchester University Press, 2013, pp. 264–75.

847. Seed, David. "'A Pestilence That Walketh in Darkness': Diagnosing the Victorian Vampire." In Glennis Byron and David Punter, eds. *Spectral Readings: Towards a Gothic Geography.* New York, Palgrave Macmillan, 1999, pp. 108–24.

848. Senf, Carol A. *Daughter of Lilith: An Analysis of the Vampire Motif in Nineteenth-Century English Literature.* Buffalo: State University of New York at Buffalo, Ph. D. dissertation, 1978. 279 pp. Large format.

849. _____. "Daughters of Lilith: Women Vampires in Popular Literature." In Leonard Heldreth and Mary Pharr, eds. *The Blood Is the Life: Vampires in Literature.* Bowling Green, KY: Bowling Green State University Press, 1999, pp. 199–216.

850. _____. "The Vampire in *Middlemarch* and George Eliot's Quest for Historical Reality." *New Orleans Review* 14, 1 (1987): 87–97.

851. _____. *The Vampire in Nineteenth-Century English Literature.* Bowling Green, OH: Bowling Green State University Popular Press, 1988. 204 pp. hb. dj.

852. Showers, Brian J. *Literary Walking Tours of Gothic Dublin.* Dublin: Nonsuch Ireland, 2006. 130 pp. tp. Illus. by Duane Spurlock.

853. Smith, Janette. *The Physical Vampire in Nineteenth Century English Literature.* Providence, RI: Brown University, M.A. thesis, 1942. 70 pp. Large format.

854. Sutherland, Rebecca Jean. *Dancing with the Devil: The Vampire Motif in Selected Nineteenth Century Literature.* Kirksville: Northeast Missouri State University, M.A. thesis, 1989. 82 pp. Large format.

855. Thierfelder, William R., III. "Zola's *Therese Raquin.*" *Explicator* 41, 3 (1983): 33–34.

856. Thilmany, Julie Ann. *Draining Life Forces: Vampirism in Emily Bronte's* Wuthering

Heights. Ames: Iowa State University, M.A. thesis, 1998. 42 pp. Large format. Posted at: http://lib.dr.iastate.edu/cgi/viewcontent.cgi?article=1166&context=rtd.

857. Thornburg, Thomas R. *The Quester and the Castle: The Gothic Novel as Myth with Special Reference to Bram Stoker's Dracula.* Muncie, IN: Ball State University, D.Ed. dissertation, 1969. 173 pp. Large format.

858. Tracy, Robert. "Loving You All Ways: Vamps, Vampires, Necrophiles and Necrofilles in Nineteenth Century Fiction." In Regina Barreca, ed. *Sex and Death in Victorian Literature.* Bloomington: Indiana University Press, 1990, pp. 32–59.

859. _____. "Undead, Unburied: Anglo-Ireland and the Predatory Past." *Literature, Interpretation, Theory* 10, 1 (1999): 13–33.

860. Tropp, Martin. "*Dracula* and the Liberation of Women." In Martin Tropp. *Images of Fear: How Horror Stories Helped Shape Modern Culture, (1818–1918).* Jefferson, NC: McFarland & Company, 1999, pp. 157–71.

861. Turner, E. S. "Gothic Hangover." In E. S. Turner. *Boy Will Be Boys.* London: Michael Joseph, 1948, pp. 21–36. 2nd ed.: 1957. 3rd ed.: 1975. Rpt.: Harmondsworth, Middlesex, UK: Penguin, 1976, pp. 9–37.

862. Twitchell, James B. "La Belle Dame as Vampire." *College English Association Critic* 37 (1975): 31–33.

863. _____. *Dreadful Pleasures: An Anatomy of Modern Horror.* New York: Oxford University Press, 1985. 353 pp. hb. dj.

864. _____. "Heathcliff as Vampire." *Southern Humanities Review* 11 (1877): 355–362.

865. _____. *The Living Dead: A Study of the Vampire in Romantic Literature.* Durham, NC: Duke University Press, 1981. 219 pp. hb. & tp.

866. _____. "Poe's 'The Oval Portrait' and the Vampire Motif." *Studies in Short Fiction* 14, 4 (Fall 1977): 387–93.

867. _____. "'The Rime of the Ancient Mariner' as Vampire Poem." *College Literature* 4 (1977): 21–39.

868. _____. "The Vampire Myth." *American Imago* 37, 1 (Spring 1980): 83–92. Rpt. in Margaret L. Carter, ed. *Dracula: The Vampire and the Critics.* Ann Arbor: UMI Research Press, 1988, pp. 109–16.

869. Vinci, Robert. *The Vampire in English Romantic Literature.* Queens, NY: St. John's University, M.A. thesis, 1959. 152 pp. Large format.

870. Voloshin, Beverly R. "Explanation in 'Fall of the House of Usher.'" *Studies in Short Fiction* 23, 4 (1986): 419–28.

871. Wallen, Jeffrey. "Alive in the Grave: Walter Pater's Renaissance." *English Literary History* 66, 4 (Winter 1999): 1033–1051.

872. Watkins, Daniel. "History as Demon in Coleridge's 'The Rime of the Ancient Mariner.'" *Papers on Language and Literature: A Journal for Scholars and Critics of Language and Literature* 24, 1 (1988): 23–33.

873. Whitehead, Gwendolyn. "The Vampire in Nineteenth-Century Literature." *The University of Mississippi Studies in English* 8 (1990): 243–48.

874. Wolf, Leonard. *Horror: A Connoisseur's Guide to Literature and Film.* New York: Facts on File, 1989. 262 pp.

875. Woodson, Rita Dale. *Images of the Vampire in the Poetical Works of Samuel Taylor Coleridge.* Rock Hill, SC: Winthrop University, M.A. thesis, 1990. 110 pp. Large format.

876. Zivley, Sherry-Lutz. "The Source of the Vampire and 'Frisco Seal' in Plath's 'Daddy.'" *ANQ: A Quarterly Journal of Short Articles, Notes, and Reviews.* 4, 4 (Oct. 1991): 194.

Lord Byron, William Polidori and "The Vampyre"

The initial appearance of the vampire in prose literature occurs as another product of that same fabled summer (1816, noted for its lack of warm weather due to volcanic ash in the atmosphere), when Lord Byron, Percy Shelley, and Mary Wollstonecraft Godwin (later Mary Shelley), gathered in Geneva, and when Mary Godwin wrote the original chapter of *Frankenstein*. Shortly after that gathering, Lord Byron broke relations with his physician John William Polidori, who had supplied the psychoactive drugs that had set the context for the group's writings, and the now alienated Polidori retaliated on his employer with a story of a vampire, one that strangely resembled Byron in many ways. That story, "The Vampyre," later published in 1819 under Byron's name, would gain fame as the original piece of vampire literary prose, and its main character, Lord Ruthven, would become the most famous vampire through the remainder of the nineteenth century. He would star in a number of vampire stage dramas and at least one opera.

Later overshadowed by *Frankenstein*, also a product of that strange summer, and then more recently by *Dracula*, "The Vampyre" has only begun to be recognized as vampire studies emerged in the late twentieth century for its important role in the development of the vampire as a literary character during the century after its appearance. It has certainly become one of the most reproduced vampire stories in vampire fiction anthologies. Meanwhile, Polidori has been a featured character in a variety of movies about Shelley and Byron, most notably *Gothic* (1986), *Haunted Summer* (1988), and *Rowing in the Wind* (1988).

877. Acosta, Christine O. *The Victorian Aristocracy Exposed: Stoker's Use of John Polidori and Vlad Tepes in* Dracula. Dominguez Hills: California State University, Dominguez Hills, M.A. thesis, 2007. 37 pp. Large format.

878. Adams, Donald K. "Dr. John William Polidori." In: *Vampyre: A Tale Written by Dr. Polidori.* Pasadena: G. Dahlstrom, 1968, pp. vii–xlii.

879. Alliata, Michela Vanon. "The Physician and ⊠is Lordship: John William Polidori's *The Vampyre.*" In Kararzyna Więckowska, ed. *The Gothic: Studies in History, Identity and Space.* Oxford: Interdisciplinary Press, 2012, pp. 13–22.

880. Aquilina, Conrad. "The Deformed Transformed; or, from Bloodsucker to Byronic Hero: Polidori and the Literary Vampire." In Sam George and Bill Hughes, eds. *Open Graves, Open Minds: Representations of Vampires and the Undead from the Enlightenment to the Present Day.* Manchester: Manchester University Press, 2013, pp. 24–38.

881. Astle, Richard Sharp. "Ontological Ambiguity and Historical Pessimism in Polidori's 'The Vampyre.'" *Sphinx* 8 (1977): 8–16.

882. Barbour, Judith. "Dr. John William Polidori, Author of 'The Vampyre.'" In Deidre Coleman and Peter Otto, eds. *Imagining Romanticism: Essays on English and Australian Romanticism.* West Cornwall, CT: Locust Hill Press, 1992, pp. 85–110.

883. Berger, Fred H. "The Haunted Summer." *Propaganda* 20 (Summer 1993): 28–36.

884. Bishop, Franklin Charles. "Introduction." In John William Polidori. *'The Vampyre' and Other Writings.* Manchester: Carcanet, 2005, pp. vii–xix.

885. _____. *Polidori! A Life of Dr. John Polidori.* Chislehurst, UK: The Gothic Society, 1991. 92 pp. tp.

886. Bleiler, Everett F. "John Polidori and the Vampire." In E. F. Bleiler, ed. *Three Gothic Novels.* New York: Dover Publications, 1966, pp. xxxi–xl.

887. Budge, Gavin. "The Vampyre":Romantic Metaphysics and the Aristocratic Other." In Ruth Bienstock Anolik and Douglas L. Howard. *The Gothic Other: Racial and Social Constructions in the Literary Imagination.* Jefferson, NC: McFarland & Company, 2004, pp. 212–35.

888. Carrere, Emmanuel. *Gothic Romance.* Trans. by Lanie Goodman. New York: Charles Scribner's Sons, 1988. 307 pp. Polidori.

889. Coghen, Monika. "Lord Byron and the Metamorphoses of Polidori's Vampyre." *Studia Litteraria Universitatis Iagellonicae Cracoviensis* 6 (2011): 29–40.

890. Dangerfield, Elma. *Byron and the Romantics in Switzerland, 1816.* London: Ascent Books, 1978. 93 pp. hb. dj.

891. Harson, Robert R. *'A Profile of John Polidori,' with a New Edition of "The Vampire."* Athens: Ohio University, Ph.D. dissertation, 1966. 157 pp. Large format.

892. Kamla, Thomas. "E. T. A. Hoffman's Vampirism Tale: Instinctual Perversion." *American Imago* 43, 3 (1985): 235–53.

893. Kristensen, Anne C. *Evolution of the Vampire Genre: From Polidori's* The Vampyre *to* Buffy the Vampire Slayer. Aalborg, Denmark, Aalborg Universitet, M.A. thesis, 2003. 104 pp. Large format.

894. Lewis, Stephanie Elizabeth. *"Congeries of Pleasing Horrors"*: *Fantasmagoriana and the Writings of the Diodati Group*. St. John's: Memorial University of Newfoundland, M.A. thesis, 1995. 149 pp. Large format.

895. Macdonald, D. L. *Poor Polidori: A Critical Biography of the Author of "The Vampire."* Toronto: University of Toronto Press, 1991. 333 pp. hb. dj.

896. ____, and Kathleen Scherf. "Introduction." In D. L. Macdonald and Kathleen Scherf, eds. *The Vampyre and Ernest Berchtold, or The Modern Oedipus: Collected Fiction of John William Polidori*. Toronto: University of Toronto Press, 1994, pp. 1–29.

897. McGinley, Kathryn. "Development of the Byronic Vampire: Byron, Stoker, Rice." In Gary Hoppenstand and Ray B. Browne, eds. *The Gothic World of Anne Rice*. Bowling Green, OH: Bowling Green University Popular Press, 1996, pp. 71–90.

898. Marlowe, Derek. *A Single Summer with L.B.: The Summer of 1816*. London: Cape, 1969. 252 pp. hb. Rpt. New York: Viking Press, 1970. 252 pp. hb.

899. Morrill, David F. "'Twilight Is not Good for Maidens:' Uncle Polidori and the Psychodynamics of Vampirism in Goblin Market." *Victorian Poetry* 28, 1 (Spring 1990): 1–16.

900. O'Connor, Mary Irene. "The Gothic Influences." In Mary Irene O'Connor. *A Study of the Sources of Han d'Islande and the Significance of the Literary Development of Victor Hugo*. Washington: Catholic University of America, 1942, pp. 63–89. A discussion of the role of Polidori's "The Vampyre" on Hugo.

901. O'Malley, Patrick R. "The Blood of the Saints: Vampirism from Polidori to Dracula." In Patrick O'Malley. *Catholicism, Sexual Deviance, and Victorian Gothic Culture*. Cambridge: Cambridge University Press, 2006, pp. 130–64.

902. Paolucci, Peter Leonard. *Re-Reading the Vampire from John Polidori to Anne Rice: Structures of Impossibility among Three Narrative Variations in the Vampire Tradition*. York, UK: York University, Ph.D. dissertation, 2000. 306 pp. Large format.

903. Polidori, John William. *The Diary of John William Polidori, 1816, relating to Byron, Shel-*

ley, etc. Ed. by William Michael Rosetti. London: Elkin Mathews, 1911. 228 pp. hb. Rpt. Ithaca, NY: Cornell University Library, 2009. 228 pp. This reprint is one of several contemporary photo-reprint editions of the 1911 edition of Polidori's *Diary*.

904. Rieger, James. "Dr. Polidori and the Genesis of *Frankenstein*." *Studies in English Literature* 3 (1963): 461–72. Rpt. in: James Rieger. *The Mutiny Within: The Heresies of Percy Bysshe Shelley*. New York: George Braziller, 1967, pp. 237–47.

905. Seed, David. "'The Platitude of Prose:' Byron's Vampire Fragment in the Context of His Verse Narrative." In Bernard Beatty and Vincent Newey, eds. *Byron and the Limits of Fiction*. Liverpool: Liverpool University Press, 1988, 126–47.

906. Senf, Carol A. "Polidori's "The Vampyre": Combining the Gothic with Realism." *North Dakota Quarterly* 56, 1 (Winter 1988): 197–208.

907. Sha, Richard C. "Byron, Polidori and the Epistimology of Romantic Pleasure." In Thomas H. Schmid and Michelle Faubert. *Romanticism and Pleasure*. Basingstoke, UK: Palgrave Macmillan, 2010, pp. 17–38.

908. Skarda, Patricia L. "Vampirism and Plagiarism: Byron's Influence and Polidori's Practice ('The Vampyre: A Tale')." *Studies in Romanticism* 28, 2 (Summer 1989) 249–69.

909. Smiley, Philip. "Polidori the Physician." *Ampleforth Journal* 77, 2 (Summer 1971): 85–87.

910. Stein, Atara. *The Byronic Hero in Film, Fiction, and Television*, Carbondale: Southern Illinois University Press, 2009. 245 pp.

911. Stiles, Anne, Stanley Finger, and John Bulevich. "Somnambulism and Trance States in the Works of John William Polidori, Author of 'The Vampyre.'" *European Romantic Review* 21 (2010): 789–807.

912. Switzer, Richard. "Lord Ruthwen and the Vampires." *The French Review* 29, 2 (December 1955): 107–112.

913. Telotte, J. P. "A Parasitic Perspective: Romantic Participation and Polidori's *The Vampyre*." In Leonard Heldreth and Mary Pharr, eds. *The Blood Is the Life: Vampires in Literature*. Bowling Green, KY: Bowling Green State University Press, 1999, pp. 9–18.

914. Twitchell, James B. "Shelley's Use of Vampirism in The Cenci." *Tennessee Studies in Literature* 24 (1979): 120–33.

915. _____. "The Supernatural Structure of Byron's Manfred." *Studies in English Literature, 1500–1900* 15 (1975): 601–14.

916. Viets, Henry R. "'By the Visitation of God': The Death of John William Polidori, M.D., in 1821." *British Medical Journal* (1961): 1773–75.

917. _____. "John William Polidori, M.D., and Lord Byron—A Brief Interlude in 1816." *New England Journal of Medicine* 264 (1961): 553–57.

918. _____. "The London Editions of Polidori's *The Vampyre*." *Papers of the Bibliographical Society of America* 63 (1969): 83–103.

919. Whitton, Charlotte. "Lord Byron on Vampires." *Queen's Quarterly* 57 (1950): 474–78.

Sheridan Le Fanu and "Carmilla"

Carmilla is the title character in the vampire novella by Irish/British writer Sheridan Le Fanu (1814–1873). She appears in a story that bears her name originally published in a short fiction collection titled *In a Glass Darkly* (1872). The story recounts the vampire Carmilla's encounter with Laura, her female victim, and Laura's family. Most of the vampire's appearances through the nineteenth century occurred in short fiction pieces, and "Carmilla" stands out as one of the most unique and entertaining. It is also notable for its lesbian subtext. It has frequently been reprinted in vampire story anthologies and most recently has appeared in a stand-alone annotated edition.

"Carmilla" would become an influence on Bram Stoker's presentation of the vampire in *Dracula*, especially in his treatment of the female vampires who attack Jonathan Harker early in the novel, though the strongest influence was in the deleted opening chapter later published as the short story "Dracula's Guest."

As interest in Victorian literature and the Gothic grew in the late twentieth century, a focus on Sheridan Le Fanu in general and "Carmilla" in particular emerged. That focus now finds its nexus in a scholarly journal, *Le Fanu Studies*, founded in 2006.

Through the last half of the twentieth century, "Carmilla" has had a major role in the development of the vampire cinema. In 1961 French director Roger Vadim made the first movie directly based on Carmilla, *Et Mourir de Plaisir* (aka *Blood and Roses*) as a vehicle for his wife, actress Annette Vadim. Then at the beginning of the 1970s, in the wake of its other successful vampire movies, Hammer Films made three Carmilla movies: *Lust for a Vampire* (1970), *The Vampire Lovers* (1970), and *Twins of Evil* (1971). The Hammer movies inspired other attempts to bring "Carmilla" to the screen, including *La Hija de Dracula* (aka *The Daughter of Dracula*) and *Vampires vs. Zombies* (2004) (aka *Carmilla the Lesbian Vampire*). Additional movie versions were made for television, the most notable being the 1989 adaptation for the short-lived *Nightmare Classics* series.

920. Andriano, Joseph. "'Our Duel Existence': Archetypes of Love and Death in Le fanu's 'Carmilla.'" In *Contours of the Fantastic: Selected Essays from the Eighth International Conference on the Fantastic in the Arts.* Westport, CT: Greenwood Press, 1990. 49–55.

921. Backus, Margot Gayle. "A Very Strange Agony: Parables of Sexual Subject Formation in *Melmoth the Wanderer, Carmilla* and *Dracula*." In Margot Gayle Backus. *The Gothic Family Romance: Heterosexuality, Child Sacrifice, and the Anglo-Irish Colonial Order.* Durham, NC: Duke University Press, 1999, pp. 109–43.

922. Barclay, Glen St. John. "Vampires and Ladies: Sheridan LeFanu." In Glen St. John Barclay. *Anatomy of Horror: The Masters of Occult Fiction.* London: Weidenfeld and Nicolson, 1978, pp. 22–38.

923. Begnal, Michael H. *Joseph Sheridan Le Fanu.* Lewisburg, PA: Bucknell University Press, 1971. 87 pp.

924. Benson, E. F. "Sheridan Le Fanu." *Studies in Weird Fiction* 2 (1987): 36–7.

925. Boone, Troy Monroe. *Unearthing Plots: Vampirism and Victorian Culture.* Rochester, NY: University of Rochester, Ph.D. dissertation, 1994. 292 pp. Large format.

926. Brock, Marilyn. "The Vamp and the Good English Mother: Female Roles in Le Fanu's Carmilla and Stoker's *Dracula.*" In Marilyn Brock, ed. *From Wollstonecraft to Stoker: Essays on Gothic and Victorian Sensation Fiction.* Jefferson. NC: McFarland & Company, 2009, pp. 120–31.

927. Brown, Joseph. "Ghosts and Ghouls in Le Fanu." *Canadian Journal of Irish Studies* 8 (1982): 5–15.

928. Browne, Nelson. *Sheridan Le Fanu.* New York: Roy Publishers, 1951. 135 pp. hb. dj. Rpt.: London: Arthur Barker, 1951. 135 pp. hb.

929. Buchelt, Lisabeth C. "A 'Ghastly Fancy': The Picturesque and the Gothic in *Carmilla* as a Vampire Aesthetic." In Joseph Sheridan Le Fanu. *Carmilla: A Critical Edition.* Ed. by Kathleen Costello-Sullivan. Syracuse, NY: Syracuse University Press, 2013, pp. 122–37.

930. Campbell, James L., Sr. "Sheridan Le Fanu." In E. F. Bleiler, ed. *Supernatural Fiction Writers.* Vol. I. New York: Charles Scribner's Sons, 1985, pp. 219–31.

931. Cavaliero, Glen. "Victorian Gothic: Sheridan Le Fanu." In Glen Cavaliero. *The Supernatural and English Fiction.* Oxford: Oxford University Press, 1995, pp. 33–44.

932. Costello-Sullivan, Kathleen. "Introduction: Meet Carmilla." In Joseph Sheridan Le Fanu. *Carmilla: A Critical Edition.* Ed. by Kathleen Costello-Sullivan. Syracuse, NY: Syracuse University Press, 2013, pp. xvii–xxvi.

933. Crawford, Gary W. "Sheridan Le Fanu and *In a Glass Darkly.*" *The Romantist* 4–5 (1980–1981): 25–27.

934. _____, Jim Rockhill, and Brian J. Showers, eds. *Reflections in a Glass Darkly: Essays on J. Sheridan Le Fanu.* New York: Hippocampus Press, 2011. 471 pp.

935. _____, and Brian J. Showers. *Joseph Sheridan Le Fanu—A Concise Bibliography.* Dublin, Ireland: The Swan River Press, 2011. 44 pp.

936. Davis, Michael. "Gothic's Enigmatic Signifier: The Case of J. Sheridan le Fanu's 'Carmilla.'" *Gothic Studies* 6, 2 (November 2004): 223–35.

937. Denman, Peter. "Le Fanu and Stoker: A Probable Connection." *Eire-Ireland* 9 (Autumn 1974): 152–158.

938. Fox, Renée. "Carmilla and the Politics of Indistinguishability." In Joseph Sheridan Le Fanu. *Carmilla: A Critical Edition.* Ed. by Kathleen Costello-Sullivan. Syracuse, NY: Syracuse University Press, 2013, pp. 110–21.

939. Gal, Ana Gratiela. "Reinventing Irishness in Sheridan Le Fanu's 'Carmilla.'" *Journal of Dracula Studies* 10 (2008): 19–25.

940. Gallagher, Sharon May. *Three Nineteenth-Century Irish Novelists, Their Gothic Myth, and National Literature: Charles Robert Maturin, Joseph Sheridan Le Fanu, and Bram Stoker.* Philadelphia: University of Pennsylvania, Ph.D. dissertation, 2004. 163 pp. Large format.

941. Geary, Robert F. "'Carmilla' and the Gothic Legacy: Victorian Transformations of Supernatural Horror." In Leonard Heldreth and Mary Pharr, eds. *The Blood Is the Life: Vampires in Literature.* Bowling Green, KY: Bowling Green State University Press, 1999, pp. 19–29.

942. Gibson, Matthew. "Jane Cranstoun, Countess Purgstall: A Possible Inspiration for Le fanu's 'Carmilla.'" *Le Fanu Studies* 2, 2 (2007). Posted at http://www.lefanustudies.com/cranstoun .html.

943. Haslam, Richard. "Theory, Empiricism, and 'Providential Hermeneutics': Reading and Misreading Sheridan Le Fanu's 'Carmilla' and 'Schalken the Painter.'" *Papers on Language and Literature* 47, 4 (Fall 2011): 339–62.

944. Heim, William J. "Joseph Sheridan Le Fanu." In Frank Magill, ed. *Critical Survey of Long Fiction.* Vol. 4. Englewood Cliffs, NJ: Salem Press, 1983, pp. 1620–28.

945. Heller, Tamar. "The Vampire in the House: Hysteria, Female Sexuality, and Female Knowledge in Le Fanu's 'Carmilla' (1872)." In Barbara Leah Harman and Susan Meyer, eds. *The New*

Nineteenth Century: Feminist Readings of Under-read Victorian Fiction. New York: Garland Publishing, 1996, pp. 77–95.

946. Jönsson, Gabriella. "The Second Vampire: *filles fatales* in J. Sheridan Le Fanu's *Carmilla* and Anne Rice's *Interview with the Vampire.*" *Journal of the Fantastic in the Arts* 17. 1 (2006): 33–48.

947. Killeen, Jarlath. "An Irish Carmilla?" In Joseph Sheridan Le Fanu. *Carmilla: A Critical Edition.* Ed. by Kathleen Costello-Sullivan. Syracuse, NY: Syracuse University Press, 2013, pp. 99–109.

948. Kinyon, Leslie. "Ladies of the Darkness: Trows, Rusalki, Vampires, and White Ladies of Literature and Folklore" *Internet Journal of Science Fiction* 2, 2 (March 2005). Posted at: http://www.irosf.com/q/zine/article/10127.

949. LaPerrière, Maureen-Claude. *Unholy Transubstantiation: Christifying the Vampire and Demonizing the Blood.* Montreal, PQ, CA: University of Montreal, Ph.D. dissertation, 2008. 259 pp. Large format.

950. Lapinski, Piya Pal. "Dickens's Miss Wade and J. S. Le Fanu's 'Carmilla': The Female Vampire in Little Dorrit." *Dickens Quarterly* 11, 2 (Aug. 1994): 81–87.

951. Leal, Amy. "Unnameable Desires in Le Fanu's 'Carmilla.'" *Names* 55, 1 (March 2007): 37–52.

952. Lee, Hyun-Jung. "'One for ever': desire, subjectivity and the threat of the abject in Sheridan le Fanu's Carmilla." In Carla T. Kungl, ed. *Vampires: Myths and Metaphors of Enduring Evil.* Oxford: Inter-Disciplinary Press, 2003. pp. 59–62. Rpt. in: Peter Day, ed. *Vampire: Myths and Metaphors of Enduring Evil.* Amsterdam: Rodopi, 2006, pp. 21–38.

953. Le Fanu, Sheridan. *The Annotated Carmilla.* Ed. by D. McDowell Blue. N.p.: Thornkirk Press, 2011. 146 pp. This annotated edition includes a Preface by Andrew M. Boylan and an introduction by David A. Sutton.

954. Major, Adrienne Antrim. "Other Love: Le Fanu's *Carmilla* as Lesbian Gothic." In Ruth Bienstock Anolik, ed. *Horrifying Sex: Essays on Sexual Difference in Gothic Literature.* Jefferson, NC: McFarland & Company, 2007, pp. 151–66.

955. McCormack, W. J. "Irish Gothic and After." In Seamus Deane, ed. *The Field Day Anthology of Irish Writing,* Vol. 2. Dublin, Ireland:: Field Day Publications, 1991, pp. 831–854.

956. _____. "Le Fanu, J. Sheridan." In Marie Mulvey-Roberts, ed. *The Handbook to Gothic Literature.* London: Macmillan, 1998, pp. 145–46.

957. McCorristine, Shane. "Ghost Hands, Hands of Glory, and Manumission in the Fiction of Sheridan Le Fanu." *Irish Studies Review* 17, 3 (August 2009): 275–295.

958. Melada, Ivan. *Sheridan Le Fanu.* Boston: G. K. Hall, 1987. 142 pp. Twayne English Authors Series 438.

959. Michelis, Angelica. "'Dirty Mamma': Horror, Vampires, and the Maternal in Late Nineteenth-Century Gothic Fiction." *Critical Survey* 15, 3 (2003): 5–18.

960. Nethercot, Arthur H. "Coleridge's 'Christabel' and Le Fanu's 'Carmilla.'" *Modern Philology* 47, 1 (August 1949): 32–38.

961. Orel, Harold. "Joseph Sheridan Le Fanu: Developing the Horror Tale." In Harold Orel. *The Victorian Short Story: The Development and Triumph of a Literary Genre.* Cambridge, UK: Cambridge University Press, 1986, pp. 33–55.

962. _____. "'Rigid Adherence to Facts': Le Fanu's *In a Glass Darkly.*" *Erie-Ireland: A Journal of Irish Studies* 20 (1895): 65–88.

963. Parker, Berlinda Z. *The Narcotic Gaze: Ocular Imagery and the Vampire Motif in Christabel, Carmilla, and Dracula.* Florida Atlantic University, M.A. thesis, 1982. 71 pp. Large format.

964. Ridenhour, Jamieson. "'If I Wasn't a Girl, Would You Like Me Anyway?': Le Fanu's *Carmilla* and Alfredson's *Let the Right One In.*" In Barbara Brodman and James E. Doan, eds. *The Universal Vampire: Origins and Evolution of a Legend.* Madison, NJ: Fairleigh Dickinson University Press, 2013, pp. 165–76.

965. _____. "'A Terrible Beauty: 'Carmilla' as Aisling." *Cleave: A Journal of Literary Criticism* 1, 2 (2002): 56–63.

966. Rogers, Susan Leigh. *Vampire Vixens: The Female Undead and the Lacanian Symbolic Order in Tales by Gautier, James, and LeFanu.* Irvine: University of California-Irvine, M.A. thesis, 1993. 193 pp. Large format.

967. Saler, Benson, and Charles A. Ziegler. "Dracula and Carmilla: Mythmaking and the Mind." In Carla T. Kungl, ed. *Vampires: Myths and Metaphors of Enduring Evil.* Oxford: Inter-Disciplinary Press, 2003, pp. 17–20. Rpt. as: "Dracula and Carmilla: Monsters and the Mind." *Philosophy and Literature* 29, 1 (April 2005): 218–227.

968. Senf, Carol A. "Women and Power in *Carmilla*." *Gothic* new series 2 (1987): 25–33.

969. Showers, Brian J. *Literary Walking Tours of Gothic Dublin.* Dublin, Ireland: Nonsuch Publishing, 2006. 160 pp. tp.

970. Signoretti, Elizabeth. "Repossessing the Body: Transgressive Desire in 'Carmilla' and Dracula." *Criticism* 38, 4 (1996): 607–32.

971. Smart, Robert A. "Postcolonial Dread and the Gothic: Refashioning Identity in Sheridan LeFanu's 'Carmilla' and Bram Stoker's *Dracula*." In Tabish. Khair and Johan Hoglund, eds. *Transnational and Postcolonial Vampires: Dark Blood.* Basingstoke, UK: Palgrave Macmillan, 2012, pp. 10–45.

972. Smith, Stephen D. "Carmilla: J. Sheridan Le Fanu and Hammer's Karnstein Trilogy." *Monsterscene* 8 (Summer 1996): 12–18.

973. Stoddart, Helen. "The Precautions of Nervous People Are Infectious: Sheridan Le Fanu's Symptomatic Gothic." *Modern Language Review* 86 (1991): 19–34.

974. Strong, Lauren. "*Blood and Roses* (1960): Realizing the Vision of 'Carmilla.'" In Douglas Brode and Leah Deyneka, eds. *Dracula's Daughters: The Female Vampire on Film.* Lanham, MD: The Scarecrow Press, 2014. pp. 83–93.

975. Sweeney, St. John. "Sheridan Le Fanu, The Irish Poe." *Journal of Irish Literature* 15 (1986): 3–32.

976. Thomas, Ardel. "'One does things abroad that one would not dream of doing in England': miscegenation and queer female vampirism in J. Sheridan Le Fanu's 'Carmilla' and Florence Marryat's *The Blood of the Vampire*." In Ardel Thomas. *Queer Others in Victorian Gothic: Transgressing Monstrosity.* Cardiff: University of Wales Press, 2012.

977. Thomas, Tammis Elise. "Masquerade Liberties and Female Power in Le Fanu's *Carmilla*." In Elton E. Smith and Robert Haas. eds. *The Haunted Mind: The Supernatural in Victorian Literature.* Lanham, MD: Scarecrow, 1999, pp. 30–65.

978. Ulin, Julieann. "Sheridan Le Fanu's Vampires and Ireland's Invited Invasion." In Sam George and Bill Hughes, eds. *Open Graves, Open Minds: Representations of Vampires and the Undead from the Enlightenment to the Present Day.* Manchester: Manchester University Press, 2013, pp. 39–55.

979. Veeder, William. "Carmilla: The Arts of Repression." *Texas Studies in Language and Literature* 22 (1980): 197–223.

980. Wagenknecht, Edward. "Sheridan Le Fanu." In Edward Wagenknecht. *Seven Masters of Supernatural Fiction.* Westport, CT: Greenwood Press, 1991.

981. Wegle, Mark. "Fear Unknowable: Le Fanu's Contribution to the Literary Fantastic." In Steffen Hantke, ed. *Horror.* Vashon Island, WA: Paradoxa, 2002, pp. 32–51.

982. Welter, Nancy. "Women Alone: Le Fanu's 'Carmilla' and Rossetti's 'Goblin Market.'" *Victorian Sensations: Essays on a Scandalous Genre.* Ed. Kimberly Harrison and Richard Fantina. Columbus: Ohio University Press, 2006, pp. 138–48.

983. West, Nancy M. "On Celluloid Carmillas." In Joseph Sheridan Le Fanu. *Carmilla: A Critical Edition.* Ed. by Kathleen Costello-Sullivan. Syracuse, NY: Syracuse University Press, 2013, pp. 138–48.

984. Williams, Lauren E. *Visualizing the Vampire:* Carmilla *(1872) and the Portrayal of Desire.* Cincinnati, OH: University of Cincinnati, M.A. thesis, 2009. 94 pp. Large format.

985. Willis, Martin. "Le Fanu's 'Carmilla,' Ireland, and Diseased Vision." *Essays and Studies* 61 (2008): 111–30.

986. Wolf, Leonard. "Introduction." In Leonard Wolf ed. *Carmilla and 12 Other Classic Tales of Mystery.* New York: Signete, 1996, pp. vii–xviii.

Bram Stoker and Dracula, *the Novel*

Just as Lord Ruthven, the main character in Polidori's novella "The Vampyre," had set the image of the vampire through the nineteenth century, Dracula, the title character in Bram Stoker's 1897 novel, became the dominant image of the "vampire" in the popular culture in the decades after World War I. Stoker took the rather vague and contradictory picture of the vampire from the nineteenth-century literature and earlier times and developed a far more fascinating, satisfying, and powerful character whose vampiric life still dominates the popular mythology. That dominance is often punctuated even as contemporary novelists detail the elements of the deviance of their vampire character from the Dracula norm—though, of course, decade by decade Dracula has himself morphed to fit the evolving needs of stage, screen, and the changing times.

The specialized study of *Dracula* emerged in the 1970s as a concentration within film studies and a subfield among specialists in nineteenth century Victorian and Gothic literature. One important circle of scholars emerged as the Lord Ruthven Assembly, which gathered at the annual conference of the International Association for the Fantastic in the Arts. As a contingent of Dracula specialists emerged into visibility, they focused upon the original novel by Bram Stoker, the early silent film adaptation, *Nosferatu*, and the 1931 original horror with sound, Bela Lugosi's *Dracula*.

As the examination of the novel began, conversation was greatly stimulated by the strong assertion offered by historians Raymond McNally and Radu Florescu that the character Dracula was substantially based on the career of fifteenth-century Romanian ruler Vlad Tepes. Though strongly opposed by Romanian scholars, the theses quickly entered the popular culture and enlivened discussions within scholarly circles for several decades, until largely discarded. While the last-minute adoption of "Dracula" as the title of his novel proved a significant change, it appears to have been based on very little actual knowledge of Vlad Tepes' career.

This chapter includes materials primarily on the novel *Dracula* and the issues that arise from it, its author Bram Stoker, and its main character, the vampire Dracula. Other chapters are devoted to materials reflecting on the *Dracula* stage productions, movies, and television appearances, or books and papers on the historical "Dracula"—Vlad Tepes.

Dracula has proved a substantive novel with material worthy of comment relative to ongoing conversations on, to name a few, the status and role of women, the emergence of the gay and lesbian community, the rise of psychological sciences, and the British Empire and changing international relationships at the end of the nineteenth century.

The novel *Dracula* fully entered the public domain in the 1960s, after which dozens of editions appeared, with several dozen being available at any moment in the decades since. The continued popularity of the novel and existence of so many editions have supported the development of annotated editions with substantive commentary including lengthy introductions and afterwords. Such editions are noted below under the name of the author of such comments.

Above its many adaptations for the stage, *Dracula* has become the single literary work most frequently brought to the screen, with over 40 such adaptations having been produced by the end of 2013.

987. Aciman, Alexander, and Emmett Resin. "*Dracula*, by Bram Stoker." In Alexander Aciman and Emmett Resin. *Twitterature: The World's Greatest Books in Twenty Tweets or Less.* New York: Penguin Books, 2009, pp. 155–56.

988. Acocella, Joan. "Introduction." In Bram Stoker. *Dracula.* New York: Everyman's Library/Alfred A. Knopf, 2010, pp. vii–xviii.

989. Adams, Norman. "Bram Stoker." *Leopard* 2 (June 22, 1976): 8.

990. Aldiss, Brian. "Dracula." In Frank Magill, ed. *Survey of Modern Fantasy Literature.* Vol. 1. Englewood Cliffs, NJ: Salem Press, 1983, pp. 404–409.

991. Alexander, Bryan. "Dracula and the Gothic Imagination of War." *Journal of Dracula*

Studies 2 (2000): 15–23. Posted at: http://www.blooferland.com/drc/index.php?title=Journal_of_Dracula_Studies.

992. Allen, Brooke. Introduction." In Bram Stoker. *Dracula.* New York: Barnes & Noble, 2003, pp. xiii–xxix.

993. Anderson, Mark. "The Shadow of the Modern: Gothic Ghosts in Stoker's *Dracula* and Kafka's *Amerika.*" In Gehrard Richter, ed. *Literary Paternity: Literary Friendship.* Chapel Hill: University of North Carolina Press, 2002, pp. 382–398.

994. Anderson, Richard. "Dracula, Monsters and the Apprehensions of Modernity." In Carol Margaret Davison. *Bram Stoker's Dracula: Sucking Through the Centuries, 1897–1997.* Toronto: Dundurn Press, 1997, pp. 321–30.

995. Andras, Carmen Marta. "The Image of Transylvania in English Literature." *Journal of Dracula Studies* 1 (1999): 38–47. Posted at: http://www.blooferland.com/drc/index.php?title=Journal_of_Dracula_Studies.

996. Anttonen, Ramona. "The Savage and the Gentleman: A Comparative Analysis of Two Vampire Characters in Bram Stoker's *Dracula* and Anne Rice's *The Vampire Lestat.*" Växjö, Sweden: Växjö University, Student thesis, 2000. 24 pp. Posted at: http://www.diva-portal.org/smash/get/diva2:206843/FULLTEXT01.pdf.

997. Arata, Stephen D. "The Occidental Tourist: *Dracula* and the Anxiety of Reverse Colonization." *Victorian Studies* 33, 4 (Summer 1990): 621–645. Rpt. in: Carol A. Senf. *The Critical Response to Bram Stoker.* Westport CT: Greenwood Press, 1993, pp. 84–104. Rpt. in: Bram Stoker. *Dracula.* Ser.: Norton Critical Editions. Ed. by Nina Auerbach and David J. Skal. New York: W. W. Norton & Company, 1998, pp. 462–70. Rpt. in: Glennis Byron, ed. *Dracula (Bram Stoker): Contemporary Critical Essays.* London: Macmillan Press, 1999, pp. 119–44. Excerpt Rpt. in: Ken Gelder. *The Horror Reader.* New York: Routledge, 2000, pp. 161–71.

998. Ardanuy, Jordi, and Luisa Romero. "The Journey of the Damned Coffin." *Journal of Dracula Studies* 5 (2003):40–42. Posted at: http://www.blooferland.com/drc/index.php?title=Journal_of_Dracula_Studies.

999. Aristodemou, Maria. "Casting Light On *Dracula*: Studies in Law and Culture." *Modern Law Review* 56, 5 (September 1993): 760–65.

1000. Armstrong, Nancy. "Feminism, Fiction, and the Utopian Promise of *Dracula.*" In Jack Lynch, ed. *Dracula.* Pasadena, CA: Salem Press, 2009, pp. 252–78.

1001. Arter, Janice. *Feminist Reflections on Stoker's Heroines.* New York: Dracula Unlimited, n.d. 2 pp. pb.

1002. Auerbach, Nina. "Dracula: A Vampire of Our Own." In Glennis Byron, ed. *Dracula (Bram Stoker): Contemporary Critical Essays.* London: Macmillan Press, 1999, pp. 145–72.

1003. _____. "Dracula Keeps Rising from the Grave." In Elizabeth Miller, ed. *Dracula; The Shade and the Shadow.* Westcliff-on-Sea, Essex, UK: Desert Island Books, 1998, pp. 23–27.

1004. Austin, April Laurie. *A Study of the Canine Imagery in the Victorian Novels* Wuthering Heights *and* Dracula. Warrensburg: Central Missouri State University, M.A. thesis, 1999. 66 pp. Large format.

1005. Austin, Joanne P. "Bram Stoker: The Lifeblood of Dracula." In Rosemary Ellen Guiley, with J. B. Macabre. *The Complete Vampire Companion.* New York: Macmillan, 1994, pp. 72–83.

1006. Ayles, Daphne. "The Two Worlds of Bram Stoker." *Dublin Magazine* 9 (Winter-Spring 1971–1972): 62–66.

1007. Azzarello, Robert. "Unnatural Predators: Queer Theory Meets Environmental Studies in Bram Stoker's *Dracula.*" In Noreen Giffney and Myra J. Hird. *Queering the Non/Human.* Aldershot, UK/Burlington, VT: Ashgate, 2008.

1008. Backus, Margot Gayle. "A Very Strange Agony: Parables of Sexual Subject Formation in *Melmoth the Wanderer, Carmilla* and *Dracula.*" In Margot Gayle Backus. *The Gothic Family Romance: Heterosexuality, Child Sacrifice, and the Anglo-Irish Colonial Order.* Durham, NC: Duke University Press, 1999, pp. 109–43.

1009. Bak, John S., ed. *Post/modern Dracula: From Victorian Themes to Postmodern Praxis.* Newcastle, UK: Cambridge Scholars Publishing, 2007. 180 pp. Includes contributions by William Hughes, Ludmilla Kostova, David Punter, Nathalie Saudo, Françoise Dupeyron-Lafay, Monica Girard, Jean Marigny, Jean-Marie Lecomte, and Jacques Coulardeau.

1010. Bankard, Jennifer Sopchockchai. *Testing Reality's Limits: 'Mad' Scientists, Realism, and the Supernatural in Late Victorian Popular Fic-*

tion. Chicago: Northeastern University, Ph.D. dissertation, 2013. 253 pp. Large format. Posted at: http://hdl.handle.net/2047/d20003011.

1011. Banville, John. "Introduction." In Bram Stoker. *Dracula*. London: The Folio Society, 2008, pp. ix–xv.

1012. Barclay, Glen St. John. "Sex and Horror: Bram Stoker." In Glen St. John Barclay. *Anatomy of Horror: The Masters of Occult Fiction*. London: Weidenfeld and Nicolson, 1978, pp. 39–57.

1013. Barrows, Adam. "At the Limits of Imperial Time; or, Dracula Must Die! 'The shortcomings of timetables': Greenwich, Modernism, and the Limits of Modernity." In Adam Barrows. *The Cosmic Time of Empire: Modern Britain and World Literature*. Berkeley: University of California Press, 2011, pp. 75–99.

1014. Barry, Jonathan. "In Search of Dracula." In Leslie Shepard and Albert Power, eds. *Dracula: Celebrating 100 Years*. Dublin: Mentor Press, 1997, pp. 84–95.

1015. Bartel, Elke. "From Archfiend to Angel: Dracula's Political Dimension." *Journal of Popular Culture* 27, 3 (April 2005): 15–25.

1016. Beal, Timothy K. "The Blood Is the Life." In Timothy K. Beal. *Religion and Its Monsters*. New York: Routledge, 2002, pp. 123–40.

1017. Beetz, Kirk H. "Bram Stoker." *Research Guide to Biography & Criticism* 6 (1991): 731ff.

1018. Beizer, Janet L. "Postscript: Speculations on Dracula, Frankenstein, and Rachilde's Monster." In Janet L. Beizer. *Ventriloquized Bodies: Narratives of Hysteria in Nineteenth-Century France*. Ithaca, NY: Cornell University Press, 1994, pp. 261–270.

1019. Belford, Barbara. *Bram Stoker: A Biography of the Author of Dracula*. New York: Alfred A. Knopf, 1996. 381 pp. hb. dj. Rpt.: London: Weidenfeld and Nicolson, 1996. 381 pp. hb. dj.

1020. Bender, John B. "The Novel as Modern Myth: *Robinson Crusoe, Frankenstein, Dracula*." In John Bender. *Ends of Enlightenment*. Stanford, CA: Stanford University Press, 2012, pp. 95–108.

1021. Bentley, C. F. "The Monster in the Bedroom: Sexual Symbolism in Bram Stoker's *Dracula*. *Literature and Psychology* 22, 1 (1972): 27–34. Rpt. in Margaret L. Carter, ed. *Dracula: The Vampire and the Critics*. Ann Arbor: UMI Research Press, 1988, pp. 25–34.

1022. Berthin, Christine. "Secretions and Secretaries: The Secret of *Dracula*." In Christine Berthin. *Gothic Hauntings: Melancholy Crypts and Textual Ghosts*. New York: Palgrave Macmillan, 2010, pp. 111–32.

1023. Best, Don, ed. *Bram Stoker Unearthed*. New York: Dracula Press, 1997. 28 pp. pb. Large format.

1024. Bierman, Joseph S. "A Crucial Stage in the Writing of *Dracula*." In William Hughes and Andrew Smith, eds. *Bram Stoker: History, Psychoanalysis and the Gothic*. Basingstoke, UK: Macmillan, 1998, pp. 151–72.

1025. _____. "*Dracula*: Prolonged Childhood Illness, and the Oral Triad." *American Imago* 29 (1972): 186–98. Rpt. in: Carol A. Senf. *The Critical Response to Bram Stoker*. Westport CT: Greenwood Press, 1993, pp. 46–51.

1026. _____. "The Genesis and Dating of *Dracula* from Bram Stoker's Working Notes." *Notes and Queries* 24 (1977): 39–41. Rpt. in: Margaret L. Carter, ed. *Dracula: The Vampire and the Critics*. Ann Arbor: UMI Research Press, 1988, pp. 51–55.

1027. Bjärstorp, Sara. "The Sensation of Narrative: Strategies of Representation in *The Woman in White* and *Dracula*." In Karin Aijmer and Britta Olinder, eds. *Proceedings from the 8th Nordic Conference on English Studies*. Goteborg: Goteborgs Universitet Acta Univ, 2003, pp. 207–215.

1028. Black, Holly. "Introduction." In Bram Stoker. *Dracula*. London: Puffin, 2009, pp. v–vii.

1029. Blinderman, Charles S. "Vampurella: Darwin and Count Dracula." *The Massachusetts Review* 21, 2 (Summer 1980): 411–28.

1030. Bloom, Harold. "*Dracula* (Bram Stoker)." In Harold Bloom. *The Taboo*. New York: Infobase Publishing, 2010.

1031. Bloom, Harold, ed. *Bram Stoker's Dracula*. Ser.: Bloom's Modern Critical Interpretations. New York: Chelsea House Publications, 2002. 243 pp. hb. boards. Includes articles by Harold Bloom, Phillis A. Roth, Carol A. Senf, Geoffrey Wall, Christopher Craft, John Allen Stevenson, Daniel Pick, Kathleen L. Spencer, Jennifer Wicke, Laura Sagolla Croley, and Nina Auerbach.

1032. Bollen, Katrien, and Raphael Ingelbien. "An Intertext That Counts? *Dracula*, the *Woman in White*, and Victorian Imagination of the Foreign Others." *English Studies* 90, 4 (2009): 403–420.

1033. Bolton, Matthew J. "*Dracula* and Victorian Anxieties." In Jack Lynch, ed. *Dracula*. Pasadena, CA: Salem Press, 2009, pp. 55–71.

1034. Boone, Troy. "'He Is English and Therefore Adventurous': Politics, Decadence, and *Dracula*." *Studies in the Novel* 25 (Spring 1993): 76–91.

1035. Borrell, John. "In Quest of the Vampire Count (Dracula)." *Time* 136, 22 (November 19, 1990): 14, 16.

1036. Botting, Fred. "Dracula, Romance and the Radcliffean Gothic." *Women's Writing* 1, 2 (1994): 181–201.

1037. Boucher, Anthony. "Introduction." In Bram Stoker. *Dracula*. New York: Limited Editions Club, 1965, pp. v–xi. Rpt. in: Bram Stoker. *Dracula*. Norwalk, CT: The Heritage Press, 1965, pp. v–xi.

1038. Boudreau, Brigitte. "Mother Dearest, Mother Deadliest: Object Relations Theory and the Trope of Failed Motherhood in *Dracula*." *Journal of Dracula Studies* 11 (2009): 5–22.

1039. _____. "Sexing the Book: The Paratexts of Bram Stoker's *Dracula*." *Journal of Dracula Studies* 13 (2011): 25–53.

1040. Bratlinger, Patrick. "Imperial Gothic: Atavism and the Occult in the British Adventure Novel, 1880–1914." In Patrick Brantlinger. *Rule of Darkness: British Literature and Imperialism, 1830–1914*. Ithaca, NY: Cornell University Press, 1988, pp. 227–54.

1041. Brennan, Matthew C. "Bram Stoker's Dracula (1897)." In Matthew C. Brennan. *The Gothic Psyche: Disintegration and Growth in Nineteenth-Century English Literature*. Columbia, SC: Camden House, 1997.

1042. _____. "The Novel as Nightmare: Decentering of the Self in Bram Stoker's *Dracula*." *Journal of the Fantastic in the Arts* 7, 4 (1996): 48–59.

1043. _____. "Repression, Knowledge, and Saving Souls: The Role of the 'New Woman' in Stoker's *Dracula* and Murmau's *Nosferatu*." *Studies in the Humanities* 19 (June 1992): 1–10.

1044. Bridges, Meille D. "Tales from the Crypt: Bram Stoker and the Curse of the Egyptian Mummy." *Victorians Institute Journal* 36 (2008): 137ff.

1045. Briefel, Aviva. "Hands of Beauty, Hands of Horror, Fear and Egyptian Art at the Fin de Siè-cle." *Victorian Studies* 50, 2 (Winter 2008): 263–271.

1046. _____. "The Victorian Literature of Fear." *Literature Compass* 4, 2 (March 2007): 508–523.

1047. Brock, Marilyn. "The Vamp and the Good English Mother: Female Roles in Le Fanu's Carmilla and Stoker's *Dracula*." In Marilyn Brock, ed. *From Wollstonecraft to Stoker: Essays on Gothic and Victorian Sensation Fiction*. Jefferson. NC: McFarland & Company, 2009. Pp. 120–131.

1048. Bronfen, Elisabeth. "Hysteric and Obsessional Discourse: Responding to Death in *Dracula*." In Elisabeth Bronfen. *Over Her Dead Body: Death, Femininity and the Aesthetic*. Manchester, UK: Manchester University Press/New York: Routledge, 1992, pp. 313–322. Rpt. in: Glennis Byron, ed. *Dracula (Bram Stoker): Contemporary Critical Essays*. London: Macmillan Press, 1999, pp. 55–67.

1049. Brownell, Eric. "Our Lady of the Telegraph: Mina as Medieval Cyborg in 'Dracula.'" *Journal of Dracula Studies* 12 (2010): 29–51. Posted at: http://www.blooferland.com/drc/index.php?title=Journal_of_Dracula_Studies.

1050. Browning, John Edgar. *Bram Stoker's Dracula, the Critical Feast: An Annotated Reference of Early Interviews and Reactions, 1897–1913*. Berkeley, CA: Apocryphile Press, 2011. 179 pp. tp.

1051. _____. *The Forgotten Writings of Bram Stoker*. Basingstoke, UK: Palgrave Macmillan, 2012. 266 pp. hb.

1052. Buhler, James. "The Beauty of Horror: Kilar, Coppola, and Dracula." In Neil Lerner, ed. *Music in the Horror Film: Listening to Fear*. New York: Routledge, 2010, pp. 187–205.

1053. Burke, Mary. "Eighteenth and Nineteenth Century Sources to Bram Stoker's Gypsies." *ANQ: A Quarterly Journal of Short Articles, Notes and Reviews* 48, 1 (Winter 2005): 54–59.

1054. Burns, Frederick A. *Influences and Innovations: Bram Stoker and the Irish Supernatural Tradition*. Belfast, Ireland: The Queen's University of Belfast, M.A. thesis, 1992.

1055. Butler, Charles E. *The Romance of Dracula*. N.p.: Su asti Publishing, 2011. Unpaged. tp.

1056. Butler, Kristy. "Vampiric Narratives: Constructing Authenticity in Bram Stoker's *Dracula*." *Forum* 12 (n.d). Posted at: http://www.forumjournal.org/site/issue/12/kristy-butler.

1057. Byron, Glennis. "Bram Stoker's Gothic and the Resources of Science." *Critical Survey* 19, 2 (2007): 48–67.

1058. _____, ed. *Dracula (Bram Stoker): Contemporary Critical Essays.* London: Macmillan Press, 1999. 222 pp. hb & tp. Rpt.: New York: St. Martin's Press, 1999. 225 pp. hb. Includes articles by David Punter, Phyllis A. Roth, Franco Moretti, Elizabeth Bronfen, Rebecca A. Pope, Christopher Craft, Stephen D. Arata, Nina Auerbach, Judith Halberstam, and David Glover.

1059. _____. "Introduction." In Bram Stoker. *Dracula.* Ed. by Glennis Byron. Peterborough, ON: Broadview Press, 1998, pp.9–25.

1060. Cain, Jimmie Earl, Jr. *Bram Stoker and Russophobia.* Jefferson, NC: McFarland & Company, 2006. 203 pp. tp. Literature.

1061. _____. "*Dracula*: Righting Old Wrongs and Displacing New Fears." In Jack Lynch, ed. *Dracula.* Pasadena, CA: Salem Press, 2009, pp. 168–217.

1062. _____. "Racism and the Vampire: The Anti-Slavic Premise of Bram Stoker's *Dracula* (1897)." In John Browning, Caroline Joan Picart, and David J. Skal, eds. *Draculas, Vampires, and Other Undead Forms: Essays on Gender, Race and Culture.* Eds. Lanham, MD: Scarecrow, 2009, pp. 127–134.

1063. _____. *Travelogues of Empire: Bram Stoker's* Dracula *and* The Lady of the Shroud. Atlanta: Georgia State University, Ph.D. dissertation, 1996. 203 pp. Large format.

1064. _____. "'With the Unspeakables:' Dracula and Russophobia—Tourism, Racism and Imperialism." In Elizabeth Miller, ed. *Dracula: The Shade and the Shadow.* Westcliff-on-Sea, Essex, UK: Desert Island Books, 1998, pp. 104–115.

1065. Cambra, Walter C. *Selected Commentaries on Bram Stoker's* Dracula. N.p.: The Bram Stoker Circle, n.d. [1996]. An informally published collection of papers on Dracula with each paper individually numbered.

1066. Carlson, M. M. "What Stoker Saw: An Introduction to the History of the Literary Vampire." *Folklore Forum* 10, 2 (1977): 26–32.

1067. Carroll, Siobhan. "Resurrecting Redgauntlet: The Transformation of Walter Scott's Nationalist Revenants in Bram Stoker's *Dracula.*" In Bianca Tredennick, ed. *Victorian Transformations: Genre, Nationalism and Desire in Nineteenth-century Literature.* Farnham, Surrey, UK/Burlington, VT: Ashgate Pub., 2011, pp. 115–32.

1068. Carter, Margaret L., ed. *Dracula: The Vampire and the Critics.* Ann Arbor: UMI Research Press, 1988. 253 pp. hb. Includes articles by Bacil F. Kirtley, Richard Wasson, Christopher Bentley, Carrol L. Fry, Devendra P. Varma, Joseph S. Bierman, Phyllis A. Roth, Judith Weissman, Mark M. Hennelly, Jr., Carol A. Senf, Christopher Gist Raible, James Twitchell, Burton Hatlen, Gail B. Griffin, Thomas B. Byers, Ernest Fontana, Christopher Craft, David Seed, Devendra P. Varma, Gwenyth Hood, and Alan Johnson.

1069. _____. "Revampings of Dracula in Contemporary Fiction." *Journal of Dracula Studies* 3 (2001): 15–19. Posted at: http://www.blooferland.com/drc/index.php?title=Journal_of_Dracula_Studies. Rpt.: Elizabeth Miller, ed. *Bram Stoker's Dracula: A Documentary Volume.* Detroit: Thompson/Gale, 2005, pp. 337–41.

1070. Case, Alison A. "The Documentary Novel: Struggles for Narrative Authority in *The Woman in White* and *Dracula.*" In Alison A. Case. *Plotting Women: Gender and Narration in the Eighteenth- and Nineteenth-Century BritishNovel.* Charlottesville: University Press of Virginia, 1999.

1071. _____. "Tasting the Original Apple: Gender and the Struggle for Narrative Authority in *Dracula.*" *Narrative* 1 (1993): 223–43.

1072. Castle, Gregory. "Ambivalence and Ascendancy in Bran Stoker's *Dracula.*" In Bram Stoker. *Dracula.* Ed. by J. P. Riquelme. Boson: Bedford/St. Martin's Press, 2002, pp. 518–537.

1073. Cavaliero, Glen. "*Dracula* and *The Beetle.*" In Glen Cavaliero. *The Supernatural and English Fiction.* Oxford: Oxford University Press, 1995, pp. 45–51.

1074. Ceccio, Joseph F. "Evil in the Worlds of Bram Stoker's *Dracula* (1897) and Elizabeth Kostova's *The Historian* (2005)." *Popular Culture Review* 19, 2 (2008): 51–50.

1075. Chapman, Paul M. *Birth of a Legend: Count Dracula, Bram Stoker, and Whitby.* York, UK: G. H. Smith, 2007. 268 pp. hb. dj.

1076. Chelminski, Rudy. "The Curse of Count Dracula." *Smithsonian* 34, 1 (2003): 110–115.

1077. Church, John Thomas. *Dracula: The Corpse That Walked by Night.* New York: Eerie Publications, 1976. 66 pp. Cover says, "Dracula Classic."

1078. Clark, Damien. "Preying on the Pervert: The Uses of Homosexual Panic in Bram Stoker's *Dracula*." In Ruth Bienstock Anolik, ed. *Horrifying Sex: Essays on Sexual Difference in Gothic Literature.* Jefferson, NC: McFarland & Company, 2007, pp. 167–176.

1079. Clasen, Mathias. "Attention, Predation, Counterintuition: Why Dracula Won't Die." *Style* 46, 3 (2012): 378.

1080. Claypole, Jonty. "Afterword." In Bram Stoker. *Dracula.* London: Collector's Library, 2003, pp. 518–26.

1081. Clemens, Valdine. "The Reptilian Brain at the fin-de-siècle: *Dracula*." In Valdine Clemens. *The Return of the Repressed: Gothic Horror from* The Castle of Otranto *to* Alien. Albany: State University of New York Press, 1999, pp. 153–84.

1082. Clemens, Valerie. "*Dracula*: The Reptilian Brain at the Fin de Siècle." In Elizabeth Miller, ed. *Dracula: The Shade and the Shadow.* Westcliff-on-Sea, Essex, UK: Desert Island Books, 1998, pp. 205–218.

1083. Coe, Richard M. "It Takes Capital to Defeat Dracula: A New Rhetorical Essay." *College English* 48, 3 (1986): 231–242.

1084. Colatrella, Carol. "Fear of Reproduction and Desire for Replication in *Dracula*." *The Journal of Medical Humanities* 17, 3 (Autumn 1996): 179–189.

1085. Collins, Dick. "The Children of the Night: Stoker's Dreadful Reading and the Plot of *Dracula*." *Journal of Dracula Studies* 8 (2006): 1–13. Posted at: http://www.blooferland.com/drc/index.php?title=Journal_of_Dracula_Studies.

1086. _____. "The Devil and Daniel Farson: How Did Bram Stoker Die?" *Journal of Dracula Studies* 10 (2008): 1–9. Posted at: http://www.blooferland.com/drc/index.php?title=Journal_of_Dracula_Studies.

1087. Cornwell, N. "A Singular Invasion: Revisiting the Postcolonialism of Bram Stoker's *Dracula*." In Andrew Smith & William Hughes, eds. *Empire and Gothic.* London: Palgrave, 2002, pp. 88–102.

1088. Cosgrove, Brian. "Ever Under Some Unnatural Conditions: Bram Stoker and the Colonial Fantastic." In Brain Cosgrove, ed. *Literature and the Supernatural: Essays on the Maynooth Bicentenary.* Blackrock, Co. Dublin, Ireland: Columba Press, 1995.

1089. Cougherty, R. J., Jr. "Voiceless Outsiders: Count Dracula as Bram Stoker." *New Hibernian Review* 4, 1 (Spring 2000): 139–51.

1090. Coundouriotis, Eleni. "*Dracula* and the Idea of Europe." *Connotations: A Journal for Critical Debate* 9, 2 (1999–2000): 143–159. Posted at: http://www.uni-tuebingen.de/connotations/coundour92.htm.

1091. Coursey, Erik Le Roy. *The "New Woman" and the Politics of Gender in Bram Stoker's Dracula.* San Francisco: San Francisco State University, M.A. thesis 1993. 79 pp. Large format.

1092. Cowthorn, James, and Michael Moorcock. "Bram Stoker, *Dracula*." In James Cowthorn and Michael Moorcock. *Fantasy: The 100 Best Books.* New York: Carroll & Graf, 1988, pp. 47–58.

1093. Craft, Christopher Charles. *Another Kind of Love: Sodomy, Inversion, and Male Homosexual Desire in English Discourse, 1850–1897.* Berkeley: University of California, Ph.D. dissertation, 1989. 291 pp. Large format.

1094. _____. "Just Another Kiss: Inversion and Paranoia in Bram Stoker's *Dracula*." In Christopher Craft. *Another Kind of Love: Male Homosexual Desire in English Discourse, 1850–1920.* Berkeley: University of California Press, 1994. Posted at: http://publishing.cdlib.org/ucpressebooks/view?docId=ft1m3nb11d&chunk.id=ch3;doc.view=print.

1095. _____. "'Kiss Me with Those Red Lips': Gender and Inversion in Bram Stoker's *Dracula*." *Representations* 8 (Fall 184): 107–133. Rpt. in: Margaret L. Carter, ed. *Dracula: The Vampire and the Critics.* Ann Arbor: UMI Research Press, 1988, pp. 167–94. Rpt. in: Elaine Showalter, ed. *Speaking of Gender.* New York: Routledge, 1989, pp. 216–42. Rpt. in: Bram Stoker. *Dracula.* Ser.: Norton Critical Edition Ed. by Nina Auerbach and David J. Skal. New York: W. W. Norton & Company, 1998, pp. 444–459. Rpt. in: Glennis Byron, ed. *Dracula (Bram Stoker): Contemporary Critical Essays.* London: Macmillan Press, 1999, pp. 93–118. Rpt. in: Harold Bloom, ed. *Bram Stoker's Dracula.* Ser.: Bloom's Modern Critical Interpretations. New York: Chelsea House Publications, 2002, pp. 39–69.

1096. Cramer, Marc. "The Secret Language of Count Dracula." *Americas* 49 (1997): 58–59.

1097. Cranny-Francis, Anne. "Sexual Politics and Political Repression in Bram Stoker's *Dracula*." In Clive Bloom et al, eds. *Nineteenth Century*

Suspense: From Poe to Conan Doyle. Basingstoke, UK: Macmillan Press, 1988, pp. 64–79.

1098. Creed, Barbara. "Man as Menstrual Monster: Dracula and His Uncanny Brides." In Barbara Creed. *Phallic Panic*. Melbourne, Aust.: Melbourne University Press, 2005, pp. 69–95.

1099. Cribb, Susan M. "'If I Had to Write with a Pen': Readership and Bram Stoker's Diary Narrative." *Journal of the Fantastic in the Arts* 10, 2 (1999): 133–141.

1100. Crişan, Marius. "Bram Stoker's Transylvania: Between Historical and Mythical Readings." *Trans: Internet-Zeitschrift für Kulturwissenschaften* 17 (April 2010). Posted at: http://www.inst.at/trans/17Nr/6–7/6–7_crisan17.htm.

1101. _____. "The Land Between Good and Evil: Stoker's Transylvania." *English Studies 2007*. Torino: Trauben, 2007, pp. 55–78.

1102. _____. "The Models for Castle Dracula in Stoker's Sources on Transylvania." *Journal of Dracula Studies* 10 (2008): 10–18. Posted at: http://www.blooferland.com/drc/index.php?title=Journal_of_Dracula_Studies.

1103. _____. "Transylvania as a Borderland Between the West and the East." *Yearbook of the "Gheorghe Sincai" Institute for Social Sciences and the Humanities of the Romanian Academy* 11 (2008): 57–63.

1104. Croley, Laura Sagolla. "The Rhetoric of Reform in Stoker's *Dracula:* Depravity, Decline, and the *Fin-de-Siècle* 'Residuum.'" *Criticism* 37, 1 (1995): 85–108. Posted at: http://digitalcommons.wayne.edu/criticism/vol37/iss1/4. Rpt. in: Harold Bloom, ed. *Bram Stoker's Dracula*. Ser.: Bloom's Modern Critical Interpretations. New York: Chelsea House Publications, 2002, pp. 169–90.

1105. Curran, Bob. "Was Dracula an Irishman?" *History Ireland* 8, 2 (Summer 2000): 12–15.

1106. Cussick, Edmund. "Stoker's Language of the Supernatural: A Jungian Approach to the Novels." In Victor Sage and Allan Lloyd Smith, eds. *Gothic Origins and Innovations*. Amsterdam: Rodopi, 1994, pp. 140–149.

1107. d'Addario, John. "We're All Suckers for Dracula." *Advocate: The National Gay and Lesbian Newsmagazine* 536 (October 24, 1989): 40–42.

1108. Dalby, Richard. "*The Beetle* and *Dracula*." *Bram Stoker Society Journal* 6 (1994): 35–43. Rpt. in: Leslie Shepard and Albert Power, eds.

Dracula: Celebrating 100 Years. Dublin: Mentor Press, 1997, pp. 71–77.

1109. _____. "The Centenary of a Whitby Shipwreck Remembered." *Whitby Gazette* (November 8, 1985). Rev. as: "The 'Dmitry' from Varna." *Bram Stoker Society Journal* 2 (1990): 22–23.

1110. _____. "Makt Myrkkranna—Power of Darkness." *Bram Stoker Society Journal* 5 (1993): 2–6. (Re: Icelandic translation of *Dracula*).

1111. _____. *To My Dear Friend Hommy Beg: The Great Friendship Between Bram Stoker and Hall Caine*. Dublin: Swan River Press, 2011. 47 pp. pb.

1112. Daly, Nicholas. "*Dracula* and the Rise of Professionalism." *Texas Studies in Literature and Language* 39 (1997): 181–203.

1113. _____. "Incorporated Bodies: Dracula and Professionalism. In Nicholas Daly. *Modernism, Romance, and the Fin de siècle: Popular Fiction and British Culture*. Cambridge: Cambridge University Press, 1999, pp. 30–52. Rpt. in: Harold Bloom, ed. *Edwardian and Georgian Fiction*. Philadelphia: Chelsea House Publishers, 2005, pp. 331–54.

1114. Daniels, Les. "Bram Stoker." In E. F. Bleiler, ed. *Supernatural Fiction Writers*. Vol. I. New York: Charles Scribner's Sons, 1985, pp. 375–81.

1115. D'Arc, James V. "The Mormon as Vampire: A Comparative Study of Winifred Graham's The Love Story of a Mormon, the Film *Trapped by the Mormons*, and Bram Stoker's *Dracula*." *BYU Studies* 46, 2 (2007), 169–179.

1116. Davies, Bernard. "Count Dracula's Consorts." *Transylvanian Journal: Dracula and Vampire Studies* 1, 1 (Fall 1995): 5–10.

1117. _____. "Inspirations, Imitations and In-Jokes in Stoker's *Dracula*." In Elizabeth Miller, ed. *Dracula; The Shade and the Shadow*. Westcliff-on-Sea, Essex, UK: Desert Island Books, 1998, pp. 131–37.

1118. _____. *Whitby Dracula Trail*. Scarborough, No. Yorkshire, UK: Scarborough Borough Council, n.d. 12 pp. pb. Staples.

1119. Davies, David Stuart. "Introduction." In Bram Stoker. *Dracula's Guest & Other Stories*. Ware, Hertfordshire, UK: Wordsworth, 2006, pp. 7–13.

1120. Davies, Gill. "London in *Dracula*; Dracula in London." *Literary London: Interdicipli-*

nary Studies in the Representation of London 2: 1 (March 2004). Posted at: http://www.literary london.org/london-journal/march2004/davies. html.

1121. Davis, Paul E. H. "Bram Stoker: The Eternal Vampire." In Paul E. H. Davis. *From Castle Rackrent to Castle Dracula: Anglo-Irish Agrarian Fiction in the Nineteenth Century*. Buckingham: University of Buckingham Press, 2010, pp. 257–88.

1122. Davison, Carol Margaret. "Blood Brothers: Dracula and Jack the Ripper." In Carol Margaret Davison, ed., with Paul Simpson-Housley. *Bram Stoker's Dracula: Sucking through the Century, 1897–1997*. Toronto: Dundurn Press, 1997, pp. 147–173.

1123. _____. "Britain, Vampire Empire: Fin-de-Siècle Fears and Bram Stoker's Dracula." In Carol Margaret Davison. *Anti-Semitism and British Gothic Literature*. New York, Palgrave Macmillan, 2004, pp. 120–57.

1124. _____, ed., with Paul Simpson-Housley. *Bram Stoker's Dracula: Sucking through the Century, 1897–1997*. Toronto: Dundurn Press, 1997. 432 pp. tp. *Bram Stoker's Dracula: Sucking through the Century, 1897–1997* received the 1998 award as the best nonfiction book of the previous year given annually by the Lord Ruthven Society. It includes articles by Patrick Mcgrath, Gerald Walker and Lorraine Wright, Carol A. Senf, Jan B. Gordon, Stephanie Moss, Carol Margaret Davison, Margaret L. Carter, Nina Auerbach, Veronica Hollinger, Norma Rowen, Jacquelne Leblanc, Jake Brown, Natalie Bartlett and Bradley Bellows, Richard Anderson, Livy Visano, Benjamin H. Leblanc, Jeanne Keyes Youngson, Bernard Da Vies, Leslie Shepard, Dennis Mcintyre, Elizabeth Miller, Lawrence Watt-Evans, and Wendy Van Wyck Good.

1125. Dean, R. L. "Dreaming of Dracula After the First Hundred Years." In Bram Stoker. *Dracula*. Denver: Micawber Fine Editions, 2001, pp. iii–xvi.

1126. Deane, Shamus. "Landlord and Soil: Dracula." in Shamus Deane. *Strange Country: Modernity and Nationhood in Irish Writing Since 1790*. Oxford, UK: Clarendon, 1997, pp. 89–94, 212–215.

1127. Dearinger, Lindsay. "Playing Vampire Games: Rules and Play in *Varney the Vampire* and *Dracula*." *Journal of Dracula Studies* 14 (2012): 53–75. Posted at: http://www.blooferland.com/drc/index.php?title=Journal_of_Dracula_Studies.

1128. Deaville, James. "The Beauty of Horror: Kilar, Coppola, and *Dracula*." In Neil Lerner, ed. *Music in the Horror Film: Listening to Fear*. New York: Routledge, 2010, pp. 187–2o5.

1129. Demetrakapoulous, Stephanis. "Feminism, Sex-Role Exchanges, and Other Subliminal Fantasies in Bram Stoker's *Dracula*." *Frontiers: A Journal of Women's Studies* 2, 3 (1977): 104–13.

1130. Denman, Peter. "Le Fanu and Stoker: A Probable Connection." *Eire-Ireland* 9 (Autumn 1974): 152–158.

1131. Dern, John A. "The Revenant of Vienna: A Critical Comparison of Carol Reed's Film *The Third Man* and Bram Stoker's Novel *Dracula*." *Literature/Film Quarterly* 33, 1 (2005).

1132. Dickens, David. "The German Matrix of Stoker's *Dracula*." In Elizabeth Miller, ed. *Dracula: The Shade and the Shadow*. Westcliff-on-Sea, Essex, UK: Desert Island Books, 1998, pp. 31–40.

1133. _____, and Elizabeth Miller. "Michel Beheim, German Meistergesang, and *Dracula*." *Journal of Dracula Studies* 5 (2003): 27–31. Posted at: http://www.blooferland.com/drc/index.php?title=Journal_of_Dracula_Studies.

1134. Dijkstra, Bram. "Dracula's Antifeminism." In Michael E. Stuprich, ed. *Horror*. San Diego, CA: Greenhaven Press, 2001, pp. 134–142.

1135. _____. "Metamorphoses of the Vampire: Dracula and His Daughters." In Bram Dijkstra. *Idols of Perversity: Fantasies of Feminine Evil in Fin de Siècle Culture*. New York: Oxford University Press, 1986, pp. 333–51. Rpt. as "Dracula's Backlash." In Bram Stoker. *Dracula*. Ser.: Norton Critical Editions. Ed. by Nina Auerbach and David J. Skal. New York: W. W. Norton & Company, 1998, pp. 460–62.

1136. Dingley, R. J. "Count Dracula and the Martians." In Kath Filmer, ed. *The Victorian Fantastists: Essays on Culture, Society and Belief in the Mythopoeic Fiction of the Victorian Age*. New York: St. Martin's Press, 1991, pp. 13–24.

1137. Dittmer, Jason. "Dracula and the Cultural Construction of Europe." *Connotations* 12, 2–3 (2002/2003): 233–48.

1138. Doan, James E., and Barbara Brodman. "Adapting *Dracula* to an Irish Context: Reconfiguring the Universal Vampire." In Barbara Brodman and James E. Doan, eds. *Images of the Modern Vampire: The Hip and the Atavistic*. Madison. NJ: Fairleigh Dickinson, 2013, pp. 219–50.

1139. Docsănescu, N. "With Jonathan Harker in the Birgau Mountains." *Holidays in Romania* 15, 5 (1973): 6–7.

1140. Dominguez-Rué, Emma. "Sins of the Flesh: Anorexia, Eroticism and the Female Vampire in Bram Stoker's *Dracula*." *Journal of Gender Studies* 19, 3 (2010): 297–308.

1141. Doty, Mark. "Insatiable." *Granta* 117 (Autumn 2011): 196–208. A discussion of the relationship between Walt Whitman and Bram Stoker.

1142. Douthat, Ross, and David Hopson. *Dracula/Bram Stoker.* Ser.: Sparknotes. New York: Spark Publishing, 2002. 73 pp. pb.

1143. Dowse, Robert E., and David Palmer. "*Dracula*: The Book of Blood." *The Listener* (March 7, 1963): 428–29.

1144. Drawmer, Lois. "Sex, Death, and Ecstasy: The Art of Transgression." In Carla T. Kungl, ed. *Vampires: Myths and Metaphors of Enduring Evil.* Oxford: Inter-Disciplinary Press, 2003. pp. 21–26. Posted at: http://www.inter-disciplinary. net/publishing/id-press/ebooks/vampires-myths-and-metaphors-of-enduring-evil. Rpt. in: Peter Day, ed. *Vampire: Myths and Metaphors of Enduring Evil.* Amsterdam: Rodopi, 2006, pp. 39–56.

1145. Drummond, James. "Bram Stoker's Cruden Bay." *Scots Magazine* (April 1976): 23–38.

1146. _____. "Dracula's Castle." *Scotsman* (June 26, 1976).

1147. Dupeyron-Lafay, Françoise. "Fragmented, Invisible, and Grotesque Bodies in *Dracula.*" In John S. Bak, ed. *Post/modern Dracula: From Victorian Themes to Postmodern Praxis.* Cambridge: Cambridge Scholars Publishing, 2007, pp. 61–74.

1148. Easterling, Siobhan. *Dracula: Demons, Victims and Heroes: A Discussion of the 21st Century Feminine Reader Response.* Växjö, Sweden: Linnaeus University, Independent thesis 2012. 26 pp. Large format. Posted at: http://www.diva-portal.org/smash/get/diva2:601773/FULLTEXT 01.pdf.

1149. Eighteen-Bisang, Robert. "Dracula, Jack the Ripper and 'A Thirst for Blood.'" *Journal of Dracula Studies* Anniversary Issue (2005): 29–46. Posted at: http://www.blooferland.com/drc/ index.php?title=Journal_of_Dracula_Studies.

1150. _____. "Preface." In Bram Stoker. *Dracula: The Rare Text of 1901.* White Rock, BC: Transylvania Press, 1994, pp. ix.

1151. _____, and Elizabeth Miller. *Bram Stoker's Notes for* Dracula: *A Facsimile Edition.* Jefferson, NC: McFarland & Company, 2008. 331 pp. hb. *Bram Stoker's Notes for* Dracula: *A Facsimile Edition* received the 2009 award for the best nonfiction book of the previous year given annually by the Lord Ruthven Society.

1152. Elbert, Monika. "Frontier Bloodlust in England: American Captivity Narratives and Stoker's *Dracula.*" In Monika Elbert. *Transnational Gothic Literary and Social Exchanges in the Long Nineteenth Century.* Farnham, UK: Ashgate Publishing, 2013, pp. 69–80.

1153. Elfenbein, Andrew. "Introduction." In Bram Stoker. *Dracula.* Ser.: Longman Cultural Editions. Boston: Longman, 2011, pp. xi–xvi. tp.

1154. Elliott, Tara. "The Use of Count Famous in "Buffy vs. Dracula"." *Journal of Dracula Studies* 8 (2006): 14–19. Posted at: http://www. blooferland.com/drc/index.php?title=Journal_ of_Dracula_Studies.

1155. Ellman, Maud. "Introduction." In Bram Stoker. Dracula. New York: Oxford University Press, 1998, pp. vii–xxviii.

1156. Elmessiri, Nur. "Burying Eternal Life in Bram Stoker's *Dracula*: The Sacred in an Age of Reason." *Alif: Journal of Comparative Poetics* 14 (1994): 101–135.

1157. Eltis, Sol. "Corruption of the Blood and Degeneration of the Race: *Dracula* and Policing the Borders of Gender." In Bram Stoker. *Dracula.* Ser: Case Studies in Contemporary Criticism. Ed. by John Paul Riquelme. Boston: Bedford/New York: St. Martin's, 2002, pp. 450–65.

1158. Faig, Kenneth W., Jr. "About Bram." *The Romanticist* 4–5 (1980–1981): 39–40.

1159. Fairweather, Donald. *Dracula: A Romance.* Hamilton, ON: McMaster University, M.A. thesis, 1977. 111 pp. Large format. Posted at: http: //digitalcommons.mcmaster.ca/cgi/viewcontent. cgi?article=1224&context=opendissertations.

1160. Farson, Daniel. *The Man Who Wrote Dracula.* London: Michael Joseph, 1975. 240 pp. hb. dj. Rpt.: New York: St. Martin's Press, 1976. 240 pp. pb. Rpt.: Leicestershire: F. A. Thorpe, 1996. 465 pp. hb. boards. Large print edition.

1161. Feimer, Joel N. "Bram Stoker's *Dracula*: The Challenge of the Occult to Science, Reason, and Psychology." In Michelle K. Langford, ed. *Contours of the Fantastic: Selected Essays from the*

Eighteenth International Conference on the Fantastic in the Arts. Westport, CT: Greenwood Publishing Group, 1990, pp. 165–71.

1162. Feinstein, Sandy. "Dracula and Chloral Chemistry Matters." *Victorian Review* 35, 1 (Spring 2009): 96ff.

1163. Fejes, Nárcisz. "Feared Intrusions: A Comparative Reading of *Borat* and *Dracula*." *The Journal of Popular Culture* 44, 5 (October 2011): 992–1009.

1164. Ferguson, Christine. "Nonstandard Language and the Cultural Stakes of Stoker's *Dracula*." *English Literary History* 71, 1 (Spring 2004): 229–49.

1165. _____. "Standard English at Stake in Stoker's *Dracula*." In Christine Ferguson. *Language, Science, and Popular Fiction in the Victorian fin-de-siècle*. Aldershot, UK/Burlington, VT: Ashgate, 2006, pp. 131–54.

1166. Fernbach, Amamnda. "Dracula's Decadent Flesh." In Elizabeth Miller, ed. *Dracula: The Shade and the Shadow*. Westcliff-on-Sea, Essex, UK: Desert Island Books, 1998, pp. 219–28.

1167. Finn, Anne-Marie. *Sources of a Nightmare: The Genesis of Dracula*. St. John's, NF: Memorial University of Newfoundland, B.A. Honors dissertation, 1995. 52 pp. Large format.

1168. _____. "Stoker's Armchair Vacation: The Research for Dracula." *Transylvanian Journal: Dracula and Vampire Studies* 2, 1 (Spring Summer 1996): 5–13.

1169. Fitzgerald, Mary. "Mina's Disclosure: Bram Stoker's *Dracula*." In Toni O'Brien Johnson and David Cairns, eds. *Gender in Irish Writing*. Buckingham, UK: Open University Press, 1991,.

1170. Fleissner, Jennifer L. "Dictation Anxiety: The Stenographer's Stake in *Dracula*." *Nineteenth Century Contexts* 22, 3 (2000): 417–456. Rpt. in: Leah Price and Pamela Thurswell, eds. *Literary Secretary/Secretarial Culture*. Aldershot, UK/Burlington, VT: Ashgate, 2005, pp. 63–90.

1171. Fleming, Colin. "Digging Up the Truth About Bram Stoker." *The Virginia Quarterly Review* 89, 3 (Summer 2013): 207–10.

1172. Flinn, Paul. "Leaving the West and Entering the East: Refiguring the Alien from Stoker to Coppola." In Deborah Cartmell, et al., eds. *Alien Identities: Exploring Differences in Film and Fiction*. London: Pluto Press, 1999, pp. 31–38.

1173. Foster, Dennis. "'The little children can be bitten': A Hunger for Dracula." In Bram Stoker. *Dracula*. Ed. by John Paul Riquelme. Boston: Bedford/New York: St. Martin's, 2002, pp. 483–99. Case Studies in Contemporary Criticism.

1174. Foster, Jon Wilson. "*Dracula* and Detection." In Jon Wilson Foster. *Irish Novels 1890–1940: New Bearings in Culture and Fiction*. New York/Oxford: Oxford University Press, 2008, pp. 356–83.

1175. Frank, Anne-Mareike. *Bram Stoker: Dracula—The Relationship of Jonathan and Mina Harker*. München, Germany: Grin Verlag, 2005. 15 pp.

1176. Frayling, Christopher. "Preface." In Bram Stoker. *Dracula*. London: Penguin, 2003, pp. vii–xii.

1177. Friberg, Erica. *The Professor and the Typist: Characterisation and Plot Devices in Dracula*. Stockholm, Sweden: Stockholm University, Student thesis, 2011. 22 pp. Large format. Posted at: http://www.diva-portal.org/smash/get/diva2:488014/FULLTEXT01.pdf.

1178. Frost, Robert. "Virgins and Vampires: Bram Stoker's *Dracula* and the Victorian Woman." *English Review* 13, 1 (2002): 27–29.

1179. Fry, Carrol L. "Fictional Conventions and Sexuality in *Dracula*." *The Victorian Newsletter* 42 (Fall 1972): 20–22. Rpt. in: Margaret L. Carter, ed. *Dracula: The Vampire and the Critics*. Ann Arbor: UMI Research Press, 1988, pp. 35–38.

1180. _____, and Carla Edwards. "The New Naturalism: Primal Screams in Abraham Stoker's *Dracula*." *The Midwest Quarterly* 47, 1 (Autumn 2005). Rpt. in: Jack Lynch, ed. *Dracula*. Ipswich, MA: Salem Press, 2009, pp. 138–52.

1181. Gagnier, Nancy. "The Authentic Dracula: Bram Stoker's Hold on Vampiric Genres. " In Lauren M. E. Goddlad and Michael Bibby, eds. *Goth: Undead Subculture*. Durham, NC: Duke University Press, 2007, pp. 293–304.

1182. Gagnier, Regenia. "Evolution and Information: Or, Eroticism and Everyday Life in *Dracula* and Late Victorian Aestheticism." In Regina Barreca, ed. *Sex and Death in Victorian Literature*. Bloomington: Indiana University Press, 1990, pp. 140–57.

1183. Galvan, Jill. "Securing the Line: Automatism and cross-Cultural Encounters in Late-Gothic Fictions." In Jill Galvan. *The Sympathetic*

Medium: Feminine Channeling, the Occult, and Communication Technologies, 1859–1919. Ithaca, NY: Cornell University Press, 2010, pp. 61–98.

1184. Garnett, Rhys. "Dracula and the Beetle: Imperial and Sexual Guilt and Fear in Late Victorian Fantasy." In Rhys Garnett. *Science Fiction Roots and Branches*. New York: St. Martin's Press, 1990, pp. 30–56.

1185. Garrett, Peter K. "Dracula." In Peter K. Garrett. *Gothic Reflections: Narrative Force in Nineteenth-Century Fiction*. Ithaca, NY: Cornell University Press, 2003, pp. 123–38.

1186. Gates, David. "Bram Stoker's *Dracula* and the Gothic Tradition" Hamilton, ON: McMaster University, M.A. thesis, 1976. 112 pp. Large format. Posted at: Http://digitalcommons.mcmaster.ca/opendissertations/4700.

1187. Geary, Robert F. "The Powers of *Dracula*." *Journal of the Fantastic in the Arts* 4, 1 (1991): 81–91.

1188. George, Sam[antha]. "He make in the mirror no reflect': Undead Aesthetics and Mechanical Reproduction—Dorian Gray, *Dracula*, and David Reed's 'Vampiric Painting.'" In Sam George and Bill Hughes, eds. *Open Graves, Open Minds: Representations of Vampires and the Undead from the Enlightenment to the Present Day*. Manchester: Manchester University Press, 2013, pp. 56–78.

1189. Gerard, Emily. *The Land Beyond the Forest*. 2 vols. London: Will Blackwood & Sons, 1888. Rpt.: New York: Harper and Brothers, 1888. Upon close examination, Gerard's work turned out to be a major source used by Bram Stoker for his developing understanding of the vampire's nature and behavior.

1190. _____. "Transylvanian Superstitions." *The Nineteenth Century* 18 (1885): 135–50. Rpt. in: Peter Haining, ed. *The Dracula Scrapbook*. New York: Bramwell House, 1975, pp. 138–41. Rpt.: New York: Count Dracula Fan Club, n.d. 3 pp.

1191. Gerke, Robert S. "The Structure of Horror in *Dracula*." *The Bulletin of the West Virginia Association of College English Teachers* 15 (1993): 9–20.

1192. Gibson, Matthew. "Bram Stoker and the Treaty of Berlin (1878)." *Gothic Studies* 6, 2 (November 2004): 236–251.

1193. _____. *Dracula and the Eastern Question: British and French Vampire Narratives of the Nineteenth-Century Near East*. London: Palgrave Macmillan, 2006. 240 pp. tp.

1194. Gladden, Samuel Lyndon. "*Dracula's* Earnestness: Stoker's Debt to Wilde. *English Language Notes* 42, 4 (2005): 62–74. Rpt. in: Jack Lynch, ed. *Dracula*. Pasadena, CA: Salem Press, 2009, pp. 153–67.

1195. Glassman, Peter. "Afterword." In Bram Stoker. *Dracula*. New York: HarperCollins, 2000, pp. 427–30.

1196. Glendening, John. "What 'modernity cannot kill': Evolution and Primitivism in Stoker's *Dracula*." In John Glendening. *The Evolutionary Imagination in Late-Victorian Novels: An entangled bank*. Aldershot, UK/Burlington, VT: Ashgate, 2007, pp. 174–225.

1197. Glover, David. "Bram Stoker and the Crisis of the Liberal Subject." *New Literary History* 23, 4 (Autumn 1992): 983–1002.

1198. _____. "'Dark enough fur any man': Bram Stoker's Sexual Ethnology and the Question of Irish Nationalism." In Roman de la Campa, E. Ann Kaplan, and Michael Sprinker, eds. *Late Imperial Culture*. London and New York, Verso, 1995, pp. 55–72.

1199. _____. "'Our Enemy is Not Merely Spiritual': Degeneration and Modernity in Bram Stoker's *Dracula*." *Victorian Literature and Culture* 22 (1994): 249–65.

1200. _____. "Why White? On Worms and Skin in Bram Stoker's Later Fiction." *Gothic Studies* 2 (2000): 346–360.

1201. Glut, Don. *The Dracula Book*. Metuchen, NJ: Scarecrow Press, 1975. 388 pp. hb.

1202. Goldsworthy, Vesna. "The Balkan Threat: Vampires, Spies, Murder and the Orient Express: *Dracula* and the Balkan Gothic." In Vesna Goldsworthy. *Inventing Ruritania: The Imperialism of the Imagination*. New Haven, CT: Yale University Press, 1998, pp. 73–111.

1203. Gordon, Jan B. "The 'Transparency' of *Dracula*." In Carol Margaret Davison, ed., with Paul Simpson-Housley. *Bram Stoker's Dracula: Sucking through the Century, 1897–1997*. Toronto: Dundurn Press, 1997, pp. 95–122.

1204. Gough, Noel. "Textual Authority in Bram Stoker's *Dracula*: or, What's Really at Stake in Action Research? *Educational Action Research* 4, 2 (1996): 257–266.

1205. Grant, Marcus. "Dracula." In Marcus Grant. *Horror: A Modern Myth.* London: Heinemann Educational Books, 1974, 47–72.

1206. Green, Andrew. "Voyeurs and Vampires: Sex and Sexuality in Bram Stoker's *Dracula*." *English Review* 14, 1 (2003): 24–27.

1207. Greenway, James. "Unconscious cerebration" and the Happy Ending of *Dracula*." *Journal of Dracula Studies* 4 (2002): 1–9. Posted at: http://www.blooferland.com/drc/index.php?title=Journal_of_Dracula_Studies.

1208. Greenway, John L. "Seward's Folly: *Dracula* as a Critique of 'Normal Science.'" *Stanford Literature Review* 3, 2 (Fall 1986): 213–230. Rpt. in: Carol A. Senf. *The Critical Response to Bram Stoker.* Westport CT: Greenwood Press, 1993, pp. 73–84.

1209. Greenwood, Rex. *Dracula: The Untold Story.* Little Stonegate, York, UK: Noel Richardson & Co., n.d. 20 pp. pb. Staples.

1210. Griffin, Gail B. "'Your Girls That You All Love Are Mine': *Dracula* and the Victorian Male Sexual Imagination." *International Journal of Women's Studies* 3, 5 (September/October 1980): 454–465. Rpt. in: Margaret L. Carter, ed. *Dracula: The Vampire and the Critics.* Ann Arbor: UMI Research Press, 1988, pp. 137–48.

1211. Gross, Sarah. "*Dracula* and the Spectre of Famine." In George Cusack, ed. *Hungry Words: Images of Famine in the Irish Canon.* Dublin: Irish Academic Press, 2006, pp. 77–110.

1212. Gruia, Catalin. *What About Dracula? Romania's Schizophrenic Dilemma.* Np.: the author, 2013. 100 pp. tp.

1213. Gutjahr, Paul. "Stoker's *Dracula*." *The Explicator* 52, 1 (Autumn 1993): 36–38.

1214. Häberlein, Christoph. *Issues of Sexuality in Bram Stoker's* Dracula. München, Germany: Grin Verlag, 2006. 17 pp.

1215. Haining, Peter, ed. *The Dracula Centenary Book.* London: Souvenir, 1987. 160 pp. hb. dj. Rev. ed. as: *The Dracula Scrapbook.* London: Chancellor Press, 1992. 160 pp. hb. boards. Rpt.: Stamford, CT: Longmeadow Press, 1992. 160 pp. hb. dj. Large format.

1216. _____. *The Dracula Scrapbook.* New York: Bramwell House, 1976. 176 pp. hb. Large format.

1217. Haining, Peter, and Peter Tremayne. *The Undead: The Legend of Bram Stoker and Dracula.* London: Constable, 1997. 199 pp. hb. dj.

1218. Halberstam, Judith Marian. "Technologies of Monstrosity: Bram Stoker's *Dracula*." *Victorian Studies* 36, 3 (1993): 333–52. Rpt. in: Judith Halberstam. *Skin Shows: Gothic Horror and the Technology of Monsters.* Durham, NC: Duke University Press, 1995, pp. 86–105. Rpt. in: Sally Ledger and Scott McCracken eds. *Cultural Politics at the fin de siècle.* Cambridge: Cambridge University Press, 1995, pp. 248–66. Rpt. in: Glennis Byron, ed. *Dracula (Bram Stoker): Contemporary Critical Essays.* London: Macmillan Press, 1999, pp. 173–96. Rpt. in: Gilda Williams. *The Gothic.* Ser.: Whitechapel: Documents of Contemporary Art. Cambridge, MA: MIT Press, 2007, pp. 68–74.

1219. Hall, Jasmine Yong. "Solicitor Soliciting: The Dangerous Circulation of Professionalism in *Dracula* (1897)." In Barbara Leah Harman and Susan Meyer, eds. *The New Nineteenth Century: Feminist Readings of Underread Victorian Fiction.* New York: Garland Publishing, 1996, pp. 97–116.

1220. Harris, Jena. "A View from the Classroom: Why *Dracula* No Longer Frightens Us." *Journal of Dracula Studies* 3 (2001): 50–52.

1221. Harse, Katherine Jane. *Horrible Shadow: Otherness in Nineteenth Century Gothic and Speculative Fiction.* Calgary, AB: University of Calgary, M.A. thesis, 1995. 365 pp. Large format.

1222. Harse, Katie. "*Dracula's* Reflection: *The Jewel of the Seven Stars*." In James Craig Holte, ed. *The Fantastic Vampire: Studies in the Children of the Night: Selected Essays from the Eighteenth International Conference on the Fantastic in the Arts.* Vol. 19. Westport, CT: Greenwood Publishing Group, 2002, pp. 23–30.

1223. _____. "High Duty and Savage Delight: The Ambiguous Nature of Violence in *Dracula*." *Journal of the Fantastic in the Arts* 10, 2 (1999): 116–23.

1224. _____. "Power of Combination: *Dracula* and Secret Societies." In David Ketterer, ed. *Flashes of the Fantastic: Selected Essays from the War of the Worlds Centennial, Nineteenth International Conference on the Fantastic in the Arts.* Westport (CT), Greenwood Press, 2005, pp. 195–202.

1225. _____. "'Sick of Count Dracula': Scott, Carter, Rice and the Response to Stoker's Authority." *Journal of the Fantastic in the Arts* 13, 3 (2003): 250–57.

1226. _____. "'Stalwart Manhood:' Failed Masculinity in *Dracula*." In Elizabeth Miller, ed. *Dracula: The Shade and the Shadow.* Westcliff-on-

Sea, Essex, UK: Desert Island Books, 1998, pp. 229–38.

1227. Hatlen, Burton. "The Return of the Repressed/Oppressed in Bram Stoker's *Dracula*." *Minnesota Review* 15 (1980): 80–97. Rpt. in: Margaret L. Carter, ed. *Dracula: The Vampire and the Critics*. Ann Arbor: UMI Research Press, 1988, pp. 117–36.

1228. Havlik, Robert J. "Walt Whitman and Bram Stoker: The Lincoln Connection." *Walt Whitman Quarterly Review* 4 (Spring 1987): 9–16.

1229. Haworth-Maden, Clare. *The Essential Dracula.* London: Bison Books, 1992. 96 pp. hb. dj. Large format. Rpt.: New York: Crescent Books, 1992. 96 pp. hb. dj. Large format. Rpt.: Leicester: Magna books, 1992. 96 pp. hb. dj. Large format.

1230. Hebblethwaite, Kate. "Introduction." Bram Stoker. *Dracula's Guest and Other Weird Tales.* London: Penguin Books, 2006, pp. xi–xxxix.

1231. Heiss, Lokke. "Madame Dracula: The Life of Emily Gerard." *Journal of the Fantastic in the Arts* 10 (1999): 174–86.

1232. Helsabeck, Keith Hinkleman. '*Chasing After Monsters with a Butterfly Net': The Victorian Approach to Vampires in Stoker's* Dracula. Greensboro: University of North Carolina at Greensboro, Ph.D. dissertation, 2008. 54 pp. Large format. Posted at: http://libres.uncg.edu/ir/uncg/f/umi-uncg-1609.pdf.

1233. Hennelly, Mark M., Jr. "Betwixt Sunset and Sunrise: Liminality in Dracula." *Journal of Dracula Studies* 7 (2005): 8–18. Posted at: http://www.blooferland.com/drc/index.php?title=Journal_of_Dracula_Studies.

1234. _____. "*Dracula*: The Gnostic Quest and Victorian Wasteland." *English Literature in Transition: 1880–1920* 20 (1977): 13–26. Rpt. in: Peter Messent, ed. *Literature of the Occult: A Collection of Critical Essays.* Englewood Cliffs, NJ: Prentice-Hall, 1981, pp. 139–55. Rpt. in: Margaret L. Carter, ed. *Dracula: The Vampire and the Critics*. Ann Arbor: UMI Research Press, 1988, pp. 79–92.

1235. _____. "Twice Told Tales of Two Counts." *Wilkie Collins Society Journal* 2 (1982): 15–31.

1236. _____. "The Victorian Book of the Dead: *Dracula*." *Journal of Evolutionary Psychology* 13 (1992): 204–11.

1237. Higgins, Ian. "The Waste Land and *Dracula*." *Notes and Queries* 55, 4 (2008): 499–500.

1238. Hillen, John Sean. *Digging for Dracula*. Dublin: Dracula Transylvanian Club, 1997. 211 pp. tp. In souvenir box.

1239. Hindle, Maurice. "Introduction." In Bram Stoker. *Dracula*. New York, London: Penguin Books, 1993, pp. vii–xxx. Rpt. in: Bram Stoker. *Dracula*. London: Penguin, 2003, pp. xvii–xxxix.

1240. Hindley, Meredith. "When Bram Met Walt." *Humanities* 33, 6 (November/December 2012): 24–27; 50–53.

1241. Hoelzli, Kim. "Exorcising the Beast: The Darwinian Influences on the Narrative of Bram Stoker's *Dracula*." In Carla T. Kungl, ed. *Vampires: Myths and Metaphors of Enduring Evil.* Oxford: Inter-Disciplinary Press, 2003, pp. 27–30. Posted at http://www.inter-disciplinary.net/publishing/id-press/ebooks/vampires-myths-and-metaphors-of-enduring-evil.

1242. Hoeveler, Diane Long. "Objectifying Anxieties: Scientific Ideologies in Bram Stoker's *Dracula* and *The Lair of the White Worm*." *Romanticism on the Net* 44 (November 2006). Posted at: http://www.erudit.org/revue/ron/2006/v/n44/014003ar.html.

1243. Hogle, Jerrold E. "Stoker's Counterfeit Gothic: *Dracula* and Theatricality at the Dawn of Simulation." In William Hughes and Andrew Smith, eds. *Bram Stoker: History, Psychoanalysis and the Gothic.* Basingstoke, UK: Macmillan, 1998, pp. 205ff.

1244. Höglund, Johan. "Catastrophic Transculturation in *Dracula, The Strain* and *The Historian*." *Transnational Literature* 5, 1 (2012): 1–11. Posted at: http://dspace.flinders.edu.au/jspui/bitstream/2328/26432/1/Catastrophic_Transculturation.pdf. A paper originally presented at the conference on the Post/Colonial and Transcultural: Contending Modernities, Presaging Globalisation, sponsored by the Nordic Network for Literary Transculturation Studies.

1245. Holden, Philip. "Castle, Coffin, Stomach: *Dracula* and the Banality of the Occult." *Victorian Literature and Culture* 29, 2 (2001): 469–85.

1246. Holmes, Marjorie. "Introduction." In Bram Stoker. *Dracula*. London: J. M. Dent/Rutland, VT: Charles E. Tuttle, 1995, pp. vii–xiv.

1247. Holte, James Craig. "A Clutch of Vampires: An Examination of Contemporary *Dracula* Texts." *Journal of Dracula Studies* 6 (2004): 9–12. Posted at: http://www.blooferland.com/drc/index.php?title=Journal_of_Dracula_Studies.

1248. Holterhoff, Kate. "Liminality and Power in Bram Stoker's *Jewel of Seven Stars*." In Marilyn Brock, ed. *From Wollstonecraft to Stoker: Essays on Gothic and Victorian Sensation Fiction*. Jefferson, NC: McFarland & Company, 2009, pp. 2000-.

1249. Hood, Gwenyth. "Sauron and Dracula." *Mythlore* 52 (1987): 11–17. Rpt. in: Margaret l. Carter, ed. Dracula: *The Vampire and the Critics*. Ann Arbor: UMI Research Press, 1988, pp. 215–30.

1250. Hopkins, Lisa. *Bram Stoker: A Literary Life*. Ser.: Literary Lives. London: Palgrave Macmillan, 2007. 208 pp. hb.

1251. ____. "Crowning the King, Mourning His Mother: *The Jewel of Seven Stars* and *The Lady of the Shroud*." In William Hughes and Andrew Smith, eds. *Bram Stoker: History, Psychoanalysis and the Gothic*. Basingstoke, UK: Macmillan, 1998, pp. 134ff.

1252. ____. "Fragmenting the Gothic: Jane Eyre and *Dracula*." In Lisa Hopkins. *Screening the Gothic*. Austin: University of Texas Press, 2005, pp. 88–115.

1253. ____. "Monsters and Mothers: Bram Stoker." In Lisa Hopkins. *Giants of the Past: Popular Fictions and the Idea of Evolution*. Lewisburg, PA: Bucknell University Press, 2004.

1254. ____. "Vampires and Snakes: Monstrosity and Motherhood in Bram Stoker." *Irish Studies Review* 5, 19 (June 1997): 5–8.

1255. Hotz, Mary Elizabeth. "Dracula's Last Word." Mary Elizabeth Hotz. *Literary Remains: Representation of Death and Burial in Victorian England*. Albany: State University of New York Press, 2009, pp. 153–68.

1256. Houston, Gail Turley. "Bankerization Panic and the Corporate Personality in *Dracula*." In Gail Turley Houston. *From Dickens to Dracula: Gothic, Economics, and Victorian Fiction*. Cambridge: Cambridge University Press, 2005, pp. 112–31.

1257. ____. *From Dickens to Dracula: Gothic, Economics, and Victorian Fiction*. Ser.: Cambridge Studies in Nineteenth-Century Literature and Culture. Cambridge: Cambridge University Press, 2005. 135 pp. hb.

1258. Hovi, Tuomas. "Dracula Tourism and Romania." In Silvu Miloiu, ed. *Europe as Viewed from the Margins. An East-Central European Perspective from World War I to Present*. Targoviste, Romania: Valahia University Press, 2008, pp. 73–84.

1259. Hovi, Tuomas. "Dracula Tourism as Pilgrimage?" In Tore Ahlback, ed. *Pilgrimages Today*. Abo, Finland: Donner Institute for Research in Religious and Cultural History, 2010, pp. 211–27.

1260. Howes, Marjorie. "The Mediation of the Feminine: Bisexuality, Homoerotic Desire, and Self-Expression in Bram Stoker's *Dracula*." *Texas Studies in Literature and Language* 30, 1 (1988): 104–119.

1261. ____, and Pat Smith. *A Study Guide to Bram Stoker's Dracula*. Los Angeles Audio Books, 1994. 21 pp. pb. Distributed with audio cassette of text narrated by F. Murray Abraham.

1262. Hryhorczuk, Nicholas. "The Dracula Dilemma: Tourism, Identity and the State in Romania." *Journal of Tourism and Cultural Change* 11, 1–2 (June 2013): 147–148.

1263. Hughes, William. *Beyond Dracula: Bram Stoker's Fiction and Its Cultural Context*. London: Macmillan Press, 2000. 216 pp. hb. dj.

1264. ____. "Bram Stoker." In Marie Mulvey-Roberts, ed. *The Handbook to Gothic Literature*. New York: New York University Press, 1998, pp. 223–225.

1265. ____. *Bram Stoker's Dracula*. London: Continuum International Publishing Group, 2009. 150 pp. tp.

1266. ____. "Delusions of Palor; Sanguine Depletions, Eroticism and the Economics of Blood in *Dracula*." In Claude Fierobe, ed. *Dracula: Mythe et metamorphoses*. Villeneuve d'Ascq: Presses Universitaires du Septentrion, 2005.

1267. ____. *Discourse and Culture in the Fiction of Bram Stoker*. Norwich, UK: University of East Anglia, Ph.D. dissertation, 1994.

1268. ____. "'The Fighting Quality': Physiognomy, Masculinity and Degeneration in Bram Stoker's Later Fiction. In Andrew Smith, Diane Mason, and William Hughes, eds. *Fictions of the Unease: The Gothic from Otranto to the X-Files*. Bath, UK: Sulis, 2002, pp. 119–131.

1269. ____. "For the Blood Is Life: The Construction of Purity in Bram Stoker's *Dracula*." In Tracey Hill ed. *Decadence, Writing, History and the Fin de Siècle*. Bath, UK: Sulis Press, 1997.

1270. _____. "Habituation and Incarceration: Mental Physiology and Asylum Abuse in *The Woman in White* and *Dracula*." In Andrew Mangham, ed. *Wilkie Collins Interdisciplinary Essays.* Newcastle, UK: Cambridge Scholars Publishing, 2007, pp. 136–148.

1271. _____. "Introducing Patrick to His New Self: Bram Stoker and the 1907 Dublin Exhibition." *Irish Studies Review* 19 (Summer 1997).

1272. _____. "Introduction." In Bram Stoker, *Dracula.* Ed. by William Hughes and Diane Mason. eds. Bath: Bath Spa University Press, Artswork Books, 2007, pp. 11–31.

1273. _____. "'Militant Instinct': The Perverse Eugenics of Bram Stoker's Fiction." *Bram Stoker Society Newsletter* 6 (1994): 11–19.

1274. _____. "Mixed up with Count Dracula in an Indexy Kind of Way: Fictional Vampires in the Nineteenth and Twentieth Century." In David Punter, ed. *A Companion to the Gothic.* Oxford, Blackwell, 1999, pp. 143–54.

1275. _____. "A Noble Manliness: Chivalry and Masculinity in Bram Stoker's *The Snake's Pass.*" In N. Sammells and A. Marshall, eds. *Irish Encounters: Poetry and Prose 1890 to the Present.* Bath, UK: Sulis Press, 1998.

1276. _____. "On the Sanguine Nature of Life: Blood, Identity, and the Vampire." In John S. Bak, ed. *Post-modern Dracula: From Victorian Themes to Postmodern Praxis.* Newcastle, UK: Cambridge Scholars Publishing, 2007, pp. 3–12.

1277. _____. "Profane Resurrections: Bram Stoker's Self-Censorship in The Jewel of the Seven Stars." In Allan Lloyd Smith and Victor Sage, eds. *Gothick: Origins and Innovations.* Amsterdam: Rodopi, 1994, pp. 132–139.

1278. _____. "The Sanguine Economy: Blood and the Circulation of Meaning in *Bram Stoker's Dracula*." In Dominique Sipière, ed. *Dracula: Insémination-dissémination.* Amiens, Presses de l'UFR Clerc, Université de Picardie, 1996, pp. 49–65. Rpt. in: Gilles Menegaldo and Dominique Sipière, eds. *Dracula: L'oeuvre de Bram Stoker et le film de Francis F. Coppola.* Paris, Ellipses, 2005, pp. 71–82.

1279. _____. "A Singular Invasion: Revisiting the Postcolonialism of Bram Stoker's *Dracula*." In Andrew Smith and William Hughes, eds. *Empire and the Gothic. The Politics of Genre.* New York: Palgrave Macmillan, 2002, pp. 88–102.

1280. _____. "So Unlike the Normal Lunatic: Abnormal Psychology in Bram Stoker's *Dracula*."

University of Mississippi Studies in English 11–12 (1993–1995): 1–10.

1281. _____. "'Terror That I Dare Not Think Of:' Masculinity, Hysteria and Empiricism in Stoker's *Dracula*." In Elizabeth Miller, ed. *Dracula: The Shade and the Shadow.* Westcliff-on-Sea, Essex, UK: Desert Island Books, 1998, pp. 93–103.

1282. _____. "This Mystifying Medley of Ancient Egypt and the Twentieth Century: Bram Stoker and Popular Egyptology." *The Bram Stoker Society Journal* 4 (1992): 37–45.

1283. _____. "'Who Is the Third Who Walks Always Beside You?': Eliot, Stoker, and Stetson in The Waste Land." In Avril Horner and Sue Zlosnik, eds. *Le Gothic: Influences and Appropriations in Europe and America.* New York, Palgrave Macmillan, 2008, pp. 151–165.

1284. _____, **and Andrew Smith, eds.** *Bram Stoker: History, Psychoanalysis and the Gothic.* Basingstoke, UK: Macmillan, 1998. 155 pp. hb. Rpt.: New York: St. Martin's Press, 1998. 229 pp. hb. Includes essays by Alison Milbank, Maggie Kilgour, Robert Mighall, Marie Mulvey Roberts, Robert Edwards, Victor Sage, Lisa Hopkins, David Punter, David Seed, Jerrold E. Hogle, and Joseph S. Bierman.

1285. _____. "Introduction: Bram Stoker, the Gothic, and the Development of Cultural Studies." In William Hughes and Andrew Smith, eds. *Bram Stoker: History, Psychoanalysis and the Gothic.* Basingstoke, UK: Macmillan, 1998, pp. 1ff.

1286. Hurley, Marjorie. "Seduction by Serrogate: Stoker's *Dracula*." *Sequoia* 28, 2 (1984): 24–36.

1287. Hurwood, Bernhardt J. "The Case of the Vampire Count." In Bernhardt J. Hurwood. *Ghosts Ghouls & Other Horrors.* New York: Scholastic Book Services, 1971, pp. 51–53.

1288. Hustis, Harriet. "Black and White and Read All Over: Performative Textuality in Bram Stoker's *Dracula*." *Studies in the Novel* 33, 1 (Spring 2001): 18–33.

1289. Hyles, Vernon. "Stoker, *Frankenstein*, *Dracula*, Sex, Violence, and Incompetence." *Round Table of South Central College English Association* 27 (1986): 7–8.

1290. Hyman, Gwen. "'His Special Pabalum': Thirsting to Connect (Dracula)." In Gwen Hyman. *Making a Man: Gentlemanly Appetites in the Nineteenth-Century British Novel.* Athens: Ohio University Press, 2009, pp. 202–40.

1291. Hynes, James. "Introduction." In Bram Stoker. *Dracula*. New York: Barnes & Noble/Sterling Publishing, 2012, pp. xi–xviii.

1292. Ingelbien, Raphael. "'Gothic Genealogies: Dracula, Bowen's Court, and Anglo-Irish Psychology." *English Literary History* 70 (2003): 1089–1105.

1293. Ionescu, Don. "Who's Afraid of Dracula?" *Romania Situation Report* 6 (May 26, 1986): 19–22.

1294. Iordanova, Dina. "Cashing in on Dracula: Eastern Europe's Hard Sells." *Framework: The Journal of Cinema and Media* 48, 1 (2007): 2000- Posted at: http://digitalcommons.wayne.edu/framework/vol48/iss1/3.

1295. Irvin, Eric. "Dracula's Friends and Forerunners." *Quadrant* 135 (1978): 42–44.

1296. Jamal, Tazim, and Aniela Tanase. "Impacts and Conflicts Surrounding Dracula Park, Romania: The Role of Sustainable Tourism Principles." *Journal of Sustainable Tourism* 13, 5 (September 2005): 440–455.

1297. Jann, Rosemary. "Saved by Science? The Missed Messages of Stoker's *Dracula*." *Texas Studies in Literature and Language* 31 (Summer 1989): 273–87.

1298. Jian, Ying, and Xiao-hong Zhang. "An Analysis on Dracula from Cultural Perspective." *English Language and Literature Studies* 2, 4 (2012): 100ff. Posted at: http://www.ccsenet.org/journal/index.php/ells/article/view/22321.

1299. Johansson, Fredrik. *From Conqueror to Rebel Without a Cause: The Change in the Symbolic Function of Vampires, from Bram Stoker's Imperialistic Dracula to Anne Rice's Anarchistic The Vampire Lestat.* Växjö, Sweden: Växjö University, Student thesis, 2009. 21 pp. Large format. Posted at: http://www.diva-portal.org/smash/get/diva2:206524/FULLTEXT01.pdf.

1300. Johnson, Alan P. "Bent and Broken Necks; Signs of Design in Stoker's *Dracula*." *The Victorian Newsletter* 72 (Fall 1987): 17–19. Rpt. in: Margaret L. Carter, ed. *Dracula: The Vampire and the Critics*. Ann Arbor: UMI Research Press, 1988, pp. 231–45.

1301. _____. "Dual Life: The Status of Women in Stoker's *Dracula*." *Tennessee Studies in Literature* 27 (1984): 20–39. Rpt. in: Don William Cox, ed. *Sexuality and Victorian Literature*. Knoxville: University of Tennessee Press, 1984, pp. 20–39.

1302. Johnson, Allan. "Modernity and Anxiety in Bram Stoker's *Dracula*." In Jack Lynch, ed. *Dracula*. Ipswich, MA: Salem Press, 2009, pp. 72–84.

1303. Johnson, Beth. "Afterword." In Bram Stoker. *Dracula*. West Berlin, NJ: Townsend Press, Inc., 2003, pp. 415–28.

1304. Johnson, Patrick. "Count Dracula and the Folkloric Vampire: Thirteen Comparisons." *Journal of Dracula Studies* 3 (2001): 33–41. Posted at: http://www.blooferland.com/drc/index.php?title=Journal_of_Dracula_Studies.

1305. Johnson, Roger. "The Bloofer Ladies." *Dracula Journals* 1, 4 (1982).

1306. Jones, Stephen, and Jo Fletcher, eds. *Secret City: Strange Tales of London*. London: Titan Books, 1997. 142 pp. hb. Large format. This volume, which served as the 1997 World Fantasy Convention program book, included brief contributions by a number of people including R. Chetwynd-Hayes, Christopher Frayling, Kim Newman, Bram Stoker, Les Daniels, Christopher Lee, and Basil Copper. It had a limited printing of 300 copies.

1307. Jones, Steven Phillip. "Dracula's Guest: The Missing Chapter." In *Dracula: The Lady in the Tomb* [comic book] 1 (January 1991): 27–28.

1308. Kabel, Ans. "Dr. Jekyll, Mr. Hyde, and Count Dracula." In Peter Liebregts and Wim Tigges, eds. *Beauty and the Beast: Christina Rossetti, Walter Pater, R. L. Stevenson and Their Contemporaries*. Ser.: DQR Studies in Literature. Amsterdam: Rodopi, 1996.

1309. Kane, Michael. "Insiders/Outsiders: Conrad's 'The Nigger of the "Narcissus"' and Bram Stoker's 'Dracula.'" *The Modern Language Review* 92, 1 (January 1997). Rpt. in: Michael Kane. *Modern Men: Mapping Masculinity in English and German Literature, 1880–1930*. London: Cassell, 1999, pp. 120–40.

1310. Kaufman, Robert. *Bram Stoker's Dracula*. Ser.: Monarch Notes. New York: Barnes & Noble, 1998. 91 pp. pb.

1311. Kaye, Marvin. "Bram Stoker: The Paradox of a Private Public Man." In Bram Stoker. *Dracula: The Definitive Edition*. New York: Barnes & Noble, 1996, pp. 403–19. Rpt.: New York: Fall River Press, 2009, pp. 403–19.

1312. _____. "Introduction." In Bram Stoker. *Dracula: The Definitive Edition*. New York: Barnes & Noble, 1996, pp. ix–xxi. Rpt.: New York: Fall River Press, 2009, pp. ix–xxi.

1313. Keats, Patrick. "Stoker's *Dracula*." *Explicator* 50, 1 (Autumn 1991): 26–27.

1314. Keridiana, Chez. "You Can't Trust Wolves No More Nor Women ": Canines, Women, and Deceptive Docility in Bram Stoker's *Dracula*." *Victorian Review* 38, 1 (Spring 2012): 77ff.

1315. Khader, Jamil. "Un/Speakability and Radical Otherness: The Ethics of Trauma in Bram Stoker's *Dracula*." *College Literature* 39, 2 (2012): 73–97.

1316. Kiberd, Declan. "Undead in the Nineties: Bram Stoker and *Dracula*." In Declan Kiberd. *Irish Classics*. Cambridge, MA: Harvard University Press, 2001, pp. 379–98. Rpt.: London: Granta 2000, pp. 379–98.

1317. Kilgour, Maggie. "Vampiric Arts: Bram Stoker's Defense of Poetry." In William Hughes and Andrew Smith, eds. *Bram Stoker: History, Psychoanalysis and the Gothic*. Basingstoke, UK: Macmillan, 1998, pp. 47ff.

1318. Kilpatrick, Nancy. "Introduction." In Bram Stoker. *Dracula*. Winnipeg, MB: Coscom Entertainment, 2005, pp. 5–7.

1319. King, Maureen Claire. *From Dracula to the "New Evil": The Social and Sexual Politics of Vampire Fiction*. Regina, SK: University of Regina, M.A. thesis, 1993.

1320. Kittler, Friedrich A. "Dracula's Legacy." *Stanford Humanities Review* 1 (1989): 143–73. Rpt. in: John Johnston, ed. *Literature, Media, Information Systems: Essays*. Amsterdam: G+B Arts International, 1997, pp. 50–84.

1321. Kleberg, Lars. "In Search of Dracula, or the Journey to Eastern Europe." In Inga Brandell, ed. *State Frontiers: Borders and Boundaries in the Middle East*. London: I. B. Taurus, 2006, pp. 187–198. Rpt. as: "In Search of Dracula, or Cultures in Dialogue." *Postcolonial Europe* (January 20, 2010). Posted at: http://www.postcolonial-europe. eu/index.php/en/studies/89-in-search-of-dracula-or-cultures-in-dialogue.

1322. Kline, Salli J. *The Degeneration of Women: Bram Stoker's* Dracula *as Allegorical Criticism of the Fin de Siècle: Mit einer zusammenfassung auf deutsch: Avec un résumé un râesumâe en franðcais*. Rheinbach-Merzbach, Germany: CMZ-Verlag, 1992. 315 pp. Large format.

1323. Klinger, Leslie. "The Context of Dracula." In Leslie Klinger ed. *The New Annotated Dracula*. New York: Norton, 2008, pp. xix–l.

1324. _____. "Dracula After Stoker: Fictional Accounts of the Count." In Leslie Klinger ed. *The New Annotated Dracula*. New York: Norton, 2008, pp. 531–536.

1325. _____. "Dracula's Family Tree." In Leslie Klinger, ed. *The New Annotated Dracula*. New York: Norton, 2008, pp. 569–579.

1326. _____. "Sex, Lies and Blood: Dracula in Academia." In Leslie Klinger ed. *The New Annotated Dracula*. New York: Norton, 2008, pp. 537–546.

1327. Kostova, Elizabeth. "Introduction." In Bram Stoker. *Dracula*. Boston: Back Bay Books/ Little, Brown and Company, 2005, pp. v–xii. Rpt. in: Bram Stoker. *Dracula*. London: Sphere, 2006, pp. v–xii.

1328. Kostova, Ludmilla. "Straining the Limits of Interpretation: Bram Stoker's *Dracula* and Its Eastern European Contexts." In John S. Bak, ed. *Post-modern Dracula: From Victorian Themes to Postmodern Praxis*. Cambridge: Cambridge Scholars Publishing, 2007, pp. 13–30.

1329. Kottmayer, Sophia Vivienne. "Transgressing Gender Roles: Shape-Shifting in Bram Stoker's *Dracula*." In Sophia Vivienne Kottmayer, ed. *Live Evil: Of Magic and Men*. Oxford: Interdisciplinary Press, 2011, pp. 53–62.

1330. Kramer, Kaley. "Madmen in the Middle: Folklore and Science in Bram Stoker's *Dracula*." In Karen Sayer and Rosemary Mitchell, eds. *Victorian Gothic*. Leeds, UK: Leeds Centre for Victorian Studies, Trinity and All Saints College, University of Leeds, 2003, pp. 69–80.

1331. Kreisel, Deanna K. "Demanc and Desire in *Dracula*." In Lana L. Dalley and Jill Rappoport, eds. *Economic Women: Essays on Desire and Dispossession in Nineteenth-Century British Culture*. Athens: Ohio State University Press, 2013, pp. 10–24.

1332. Krieg, Joann P. "Literary Contemporaries." In Donald D. Kummings, ed. *A Companion to Walt Whitman*. Malden, MA: Blackwell, 2006, pp. 392–408.

1333. Krumm, Pascale. "Metamorphosis as Metaphor in Bram Stoker's *Dracula*" *The Victorian Newsletter* 88 (Autumn 1995): 5–10.

1334. Kuzmanovic, Dejan. "Vampiric Seduction and Vicissitudes of Masculine Identity in Bram Stoker's *Dracula*." *Victorian Literature and Culture* 37, 2 (2009): 411–425.

1335. Lancaster, Ashley Craig. "Demonizing the Emerging Woman: Misrepresented Morality in *Dracula* and *God's Little Acre*." *Journal of Dracula Studies* 6 (2004): 27–33. Posted at: http://www.blooferland.com/drc/index.php?title=Journal_of_Dracula_Studies.

1336. Lapidos, Juliet. "The *Paris Review* Perspective." In Jack Lynch, ed. *Dracula*. Pasadena, CA: Salem Press, 2009, pp.18–20.

1337. Laurent, Diane M. "Bram Stoker's *Dracula*: The Ultimate Victorian Novel." *Journal of the Dark* 5 (Winter 1995–1996): 40–42.

1338. Law, Jules David. "Being There: Gothic Violence and Virtuality in *Frankenstein, Dracula,* and *Strange Days*." *English Literary History* 73, 4 (Winter 2006): 975–996.

1339. _____. "Ever-Widening Circulations: *Dracula* and the Fear of Management." In Jules David Law. *The Social Life of Fluids: Blood, Mmilk, and Water in the Victorian Novel*. Ithaca, NY: Cornell University Press, 2010, pp. 146–66.

1340. Leatherdale, Clive. *Dracula: The Novel and the Legend: A Study of Bram Stoker's Gothic Masterpiece*. Wellingborough, Northamptonshire, UK: Aquarian Press, 1985. 256 pp. hb. Rpt.: Wellingborough, Northamptonshire, UK: Aquarian Press, 1985. 256 pp. tp. Rev. ed.: Brighton, East Sussex, UK: Desert Island Books, 1993. 256 pp. hb. dj.

1341. _____. *The Origins of Dracula: The Background to Bram Stoker's Gothic Masterpiece*. London: William Kimber, 1987. 239 pp. hb. Rpt.: Brighton, East Sussex, UK: Desert Island Books, 1995. 239 pp. hb. dj.

1342. _____. "Stoker's Banana Skins: Errors, Illogicalities and Misconceptions in *Dracula*." In Elizabeth Miller, ed. *Dracula: The Shade and the Shadow*. Westcliff-on-Sea, Essex, UK: Desert Island Books, 1998, pp. 138–154.

1343. LeBlanc, Benjamin. "The Death of Dracula: A Darwinian Approach to the Vampire's Evolution." In Carol Margaret Davison, ed., with Paul Simpson-Housley. *Bram Stoker's Dracula: Sucking through the Century, 1897–1997*. Toronto: Dundurn Press, 1997, pp.351–75.

1344. Lecercle, Jean-Jacques. "The Kitten's Nose: Dracula and Witchcraft." *Essays and Studies* 54 (2001): 71–86. Rpt. in: Fred Botting, ed. *The Gothic*. Cambridge, Brewer, 2001, pp. 71–86.

1345. Lecomte, Jean-Marie. "Postmodern Verbal Discourse in Coppola's *Bram Stoker's Dracula*." In John S. Bak, ed. *Post/modern Dracula: From Victorian Themes to Postmodern Praxis*. Cambridge: Cambridge Scholars Publishing, 2007, pp. 107–22.

1346. Levy, Anita. "Fictions of Illicit Reproduction: *The Picture of Dorian Gray* and *Dracula*." In Anita Levy. *Reproductive Urges: Popular Novel Reading, Sexuality and the English Nation*. Philadelphia: University of Pennsylvania Press, 1999, pp. 129–79.

1347. Lewis, Pericles. "*Dracula* and the Epistemology of the Victorian Gothic Novel." In Elizabeth Miller, ed. *Dracula: The Shade and the Shadow*. Westcliff-on-Sea, Essex, UK: Desert Island Books, 1998, pp. 71–81.

1348. Li, Shang-jen. "Ghost, Vampire, and Scientific Naturalism: Observation and Evidence in the Supernatural Fiction of Grant Allen, Bram Stoker and Arthur Conan Doyle." In Mu-chou Poo, ed. *Rethinking Ghosts in World Religions*. Leiden: Brill, 2009.

1349. Light, Duncan. *The Dracula Dilemma: Tourism, Identity and the State in Romania*. Ser. New Directions in Tourism Analysis. Farnham, Surrey, UK: Ashgate Publishing Co., 2012. 196 pp.

1350. _____. "Dracula Tourism in Romania: Cultural Identity and the State." *Annals of Tourism Research* 14, 3 (2007): 746–65.

1351. _____. "Halloween in Transylvania." Hugh O'Donnell, ed. *Treat or Trick? Halloween in a Globalising World*. Newcastle on Tyne, UK: Cambridge Scholars Publishing, 2009, pp. 186–98.

1352. _____. "The People of Bram Stoker's Transylvania." *Journal of Dracula Studies* 7 (2005): 38–44, Posted at: http://www.blooferland.com/drc/index.php?title=Journal_of_Dracula_Studies.

1353. _____. "When was *Dracula* First Translated into Romanian?" *Journal of Dracula Studies* 11 (2009): 42–60. Posted at: http://www.blooferland.com/drc/index.php?title=Journal_of_Dracula_Studies.

1354. Linneman, Laura. "The Fear of Castration and Male Dread of Female Sexuality: The Theme of the 'vagina dentata' in *Dracula*." *Journal of Dracula Studies* 12 (2010): 11–28. Posted at: http://www.blooferland.com/drc/index.php?title=Journal_of_Dracula_Studies.

1355. Lorrah, Jean. "Dracula Meets the New Woman." In Leonard Heldreth and Mary Pharr, eds. *The Blood Is the Life: Vampires in Literature.* Bowling Green, KY: Bowling Green State University Press, 1999, pp. 31–42.

1356. Lörinczi, Marinella. "The Technique of 'Reversal' in *Dracula* and *The Lady of the Shroud.*" In Elizabeth Miller, ed. *Dracula; The Shade and the Shadow.* Westcliff-on-Sea, Essex, UK: Desert Island Books, 1998, pp. 155–161.

1357. Lucendo, Santiago. "Racism and the Vampire: The Anti-Slavic Premise of Bram Stoker's *Dracula.*" In John Edgar Browning and Caroline Joan Picart, eds. *Dracula, Vampires, and Other Undead Forms.* Lanham, MD: The Scarecrow Press, 2009, pp. 127–34.

1358. Ludlam, Harry. *A Biography of Dracula: The Life and Times of Bram Stoker.* London: W. Foulsham & Co., 1962. 200 pp. hb. Rpt.: London: Quality Book Club, 1962. 200 pp. Rpt. as: *A Biography of Bram Stoker: Creator of Dracula.* London: New English Library, 1977. 223 pp. pb.

1359. _____. *My Quest for Bram Stoker.* New York: Dracula Press, 2000.

1360. Lynch, Jack, ed. *Dracula.* Ser. Critical Insights.Ipswich, MA: Salem Press, 2009. 339 pp. hb. boards. Includes contributions by Richard Means, Juliet Lapidos, Bridget M. Marshall, Camille-Yvette Welsch, Matthew J. Bolton, Allan Johnson, Beth E. McDonald, Carrol L. Fry, Carla Edwards, Samuel Lyndon Gladden, Jimmie E. Cain, Jr., David Glover, Nancy Armstrong, and Patricia McKee.

1361. _____. "On Dracula." In Jack Lynch, ed. *Dracula.* Ipswich, MA: Salem Press, 2009, pp. 3–12.

1362. MacDonald, Tara. Teaching Dracula in the Netherlands." *Victorian Review* 38, 1 (Spring 2012): 12ff.

1363. MacGillivray, Royce. "*Dracula*: Bram Stoker's Spoiled Masterpiece." *Queens Quarterly* 79 (1972): 518–27. Rpt. in: Carol A. Senf. *The Critical Response to Bram Stoker.* Westport CT: Greenwood Press, 1993, pp. 61–68.

1364. McAlduff, Paul S. "The Publication of Dracula." *Journal of Dracula Studies* 14 (2012): 37–51. Posted at: http://www.blooferland.com/drc/index.php?title=Journal_of_Dracula_Studies.

1365. Mack, Douglas S. "Dr. Jekyll, Mr. Hyde, and Count Dracula." In Peter Liebregts and Wim Tigges, eds. *Beauty and the Beast: Christina Rossetti, Walter Pater, R. L. Stevenson, and Their Contemporaries.* Amsterdam: Rodopi, 1996, pp. 149–56.

1366. Madison, Bob. "Books of Blood: The Continued Adventures of Dracula." In Bob Madison, ed. *Dracula: The First Hundred Years.* Baltimore, MD: Midnight Marquee Press, 1997, pp. 52–87.

1367. _____, ed. *Dracula: The First Hundred Years.* Baltimore, MD: Midnight Marquee Press, 1997. 322 pp. tp. Includes contributions by David J. Hogan, Tom Johnson, Gregory William Mank, Frank Dello Stritto, Rickey L. Shanklin, Gary J. Svehla, Randy Vest, Steve Verlieb, Tom Weaver, Gary Don Rhodes, and David J. Skal.

1368. Magnum, Teresa. "Interdisciplinary and Cultural Contexts." In Maunder, Andrew, and Jennifer Phegley, eds. *Teaching Nineteenth-Century Fiction.* Basingstoke, UK: Palgrave Macmillan, 2010, pp. 60–74.

1369. Malara, Gina. *"The Insufficient Void"*: The Problem of an Earthly Paradise in *Wuthering Heights* and *Dracula. Lewisburg, PA: Bucknell University, honors thesis, 2011.*

1370. Mallory, Michael. "Frankenstein and Dracula Meet the Critics." *Scarlet Street* 8 (Fall 1992): 30–33.

1371. Mandler, David. "Vambery, Victorian Culture, and Stoker's *Dracula.*" in Steven Totosy de Zepetnek and Louise O. Vasvarieds, eds. *Comparative Hungarian Cultural Studies.* Lafayette, IN: Purdue University Press, 2011, pp. 47–58.

1372. Marchbank, Paul. "*Dracula*: Degeneration, Sexuality and the Jew." In Carla T. Kungl, ed. *Vampires: Myths and Metaphors of Enduring Evil.* Oxford: Inter-Disciplinary Press, 2003, pp. 31–38.

1373. Marigny, Jean. "*Dracula*: Tradition and Postmodernism in Stoker's Novel and Coppola's Film." In John S. Bak, ed. *Post/modern Dracula: From Victorian Themes to Postmodern Praxis.* Cambridge: Cambridge Scholars Publishing, 2007, pp. 95–106.

1374. _____. "The Images of Dracula in Contemporary Fiction." *Transylvanian Journal* 3, 1 (1997): 5–10.

1375. _____. "Secrecy as Strategy in *Dracula.*" *Journal of Dracula Studies* 2 (2000): 3–7. Posted at: http://www.blooferland.com/drc/index.php?title=Journal_of_Dracula_Studies.

1376. Marocchino, Kathryn. "Structural Complexity in Bram Stoker's *Dracula*: Unraveling the 'Mysteries.'" *Bram Stoker Society Journal* 2 (1990): 3–21.

1377. Marshall, Bridget M. "Stoker's *Dracula* and the Vampire's Literary History." In Jack Lynch, ed. *Dracula*. Ipswich, MA: Salem Press, 2009, pp. 23–37.

1378. Martin, Philip. "The Vampire in the Looking Glass: Reflection and Projection in Bram Stoker's *Dracula*." In Clive Bloom et al, eds. *Nineteenth Century Suspense: From Poe to Conan Doyle*. Basingstoke, UK: Macmillan Press, 1988, pp. 80–92.

1379. Mascia, Stacey L. Hearth and Home: A Psycho-Sexual Reading of Procreating the Vampire Race in Dracula by Bram Stoker." *Journal of Literature & Art Studies* 1, 3 (September 2011): 167ff.

1380. Maser, Jack D. "Dracula and the Afterlife: A Psychological Explanation." *Journal of Dracula Studies* 7 (2005): 28–37. Posted at: http://www.blooferland.com/drc/index.php?title=Journal_of_Dracula_Studies.

1381. Massey, Irving. "The Third Self: *Dracula, Strange Case of Dr. Jekyll and Mr. Hyde* and Mérimée's *Lokis*." *The Bulletin of the Midwestern Language Association* 6, 2 (Autumn 1973): 57–67.

1382. Maunder, Andrew. *Bram Stoker*. Tavistock, Devon, UK: Northcote House Publishers, 2004. 128 pp. pb.

1383. McBee, Holly J. "Vampires Do(n't) Exist: Using Past and Present Technologies to Make Dracula Real." *Journal of Dracula Studies* 13 (2011): 7–24. Posted at: http://www.blooferland.com/drc/index.php?title=Journal_of_Dracula_Studies.

1384. McBride, William Thomas. "Dracula and Mephistopheles: Shyster Vampires." *Literature-Film Quarterly* 18, 2 (April 1990): 116.

1385. McCrea, Barry. "Heterosexual Horror: Dracula, the Closet, and the Marriage-Plot." *Novel* 43, 2 (2010): 251–270.

1386. McDonald, Beth E. "Recreating the World: The Sacred and the Profane in Bram Stoker's *Dracula*." In Beth E. McDonald. *The Vampire as Numinous Experience: Spiritual Journeys with the Undead in British and American Literature*, Jefferson, NC: McFarland & Company, 2004, vii, 200 pages. Rpt. in: Lynch, Jack (ed.), *Dracula*: Critical Insights, Pasadena, CA: Salem Press, 2009, pp. 87–137.

1387. _____. "The Vampire as Trickster Figure in Bram Stoker's *Dracula*." *Extrapolation* 33, 2 (1992): 128–44.

1388. McGrath, Patrick. Bram Stoker and His Vampire." In Carol Margaret Davison, ed., with Paul Simpson-Housley. *Bram Stoker's Dracula: Sucking through the Century, 1897–1997*. Toronto: Dundurn Press, 1997, pp. 41–48.

1389. McKee, Patricia. "Racialization, Capitalism, and Aesthetics in Stoker's *Dracula*." *Novel: A Forum of Fiction* 36, 1 (2002): 42–60. Rpt. in: Jack Lynch, ed. *Dracula*. Pasadena, CA: Salem Press, 2009, pp.279–306.

1390. McMillan, Gloria. "Somebody Stole My Gal: Word Cluster Analysis of Exogamy Fears in Stoker's *Dracula*." *Extrapolation* 43, 3 (2002): 330–41.

1391. McNally, Raymond T. "Bram Stoker and Irish Gothic." In James Craig Holte, ed. *The Fantastic Vampire: Studies in the Children of the Night: Selected Essays from the Eighteenth International Conference on the Fantastic in the Arts*. Vol. 19. Westport, CT: Greenwood Publishing Group, 2002, pp. 11–22.

1392. _____. "Introduction." In Bram Stoker. *Dracula: The Rare Text of 1901*. White Rock, BC: Transylvania Press, 1994, pp. xi–xii.

1393. _____. "Separation Granted, Divorce Denied, Annulment Unlikely." *Journal of Dracula Studies* 1 (1999): 25–27. Posted at: http://www.blooferland.com/drc/index.php?title=Journal_of_Dracula_Studies.

1394. _____, **and Radu Florescu, eds.** *The Essential Dracula: A Completely Illustrated & Annotated Edition of Bram Stoker's Classic Novel*. New York: Mayflower, 1979. 320 pp. hb. Large format. An annotated edition of the novel *Dracula*.

1395. McWhir, Ann. "Pollution and Redemption in *Dracula*." *Modern Language Studies* 17, 3 (1987): 31–40.

1396. Means, Richard. "Biography of Bram Stoker." In Jack Lynch, ed. *Dracula*. Pasadena, CA: Salem Press, 2009, pp.13–17.

1397. Merrill, John Nigel. *Walking in Dracula Country*. Matlock: Trail Crest Publications, 1993. 34 pp.

1398. Messent, Peter B. "Dracula." In Peter B. Messent. *Literature of the Occult: A Collection of Critical Essays*. Englewood Cliffs, NJ: Prentice-Hall, 1981.

1399. Mewald, Katharina. "The Emancipation of Mina? The Portrayal of Mina in Stoker's *Dracula* and Coppola's *Bram Stoker's Dracula.*" *Journal of Dracula Studies* 10 (2008): 31–39. Posted at: http://www.blooferland.com/drc/index.php?title=Journal_of_Dracula_Studies.

1400. Meyers, Jeffrey. "Afterword." In Bram Stoker. *Dracula*. New York: Signet Classics, 2007, pp. 381–89.

1401. Mighall, Robert. "Making a Case: Vampirism, Sexuality and Interpretation." In Robert Mighall, *A Geography of Victorian Gothic Fiction: Mapping History's Nightmares*. New York: Oxford University Press, 2003, pp. 210–47.

1402. _____. "Vampires and Victorians: Count Dracula and the Return of the Repressive Hypothesis." In Gary Day, ed. *Varieties of Victorianism: The Uses of the Past*. New York: St. Martin's Press, 1998, pp. 236–249.

1403. Milbank, Alison. "'Powers of Old and New': Stoker's Alliances with Anglo-Irish Gothic." In William Hughes and Andrew Smith, eds. *Bram Stoker: History, Psychoanalysis and the Gothic*. Basingstoke, UK: Macmillan, 1998, pp. 12ff.

1404. Milburn, Diane. "'Denn die Toten reiten schnell': Anglo-German Cross-Currents in Bram Stoker's *Dracula.*" In Susanne Stark, ed. *The Novel in Anglo-German Context: Cultural Cross-Currents and Affinities*. Amsterdam: Rodopi, 2000, pp. Papers from a conference held at the University of Leeds, September 15–17, 1997.

1405. Milburn, Diane. "'For the Dead Travel Fast:' *Dracula* in Anglo-German Context." In Elizabeth Miller, ed. *Dracula: The Shade and the Shadow*. Westcliff-on-Sea, Essex, UK: Desert Island Books, 1998, pp. 41–53.

1406. Millar, Peter. "Dracula Country." *High Life* (April 1993): 88—93.

1407. Miller, C. Brook. "From Blood to Blotter: Anglo-Saxonism, America and Arnoldian Right Reason in Bram Stoker's *Dracula.*" In C. Brook Miller. *Our American Cousin: Anglo-American Cultural Politics and British National Identities (Joseph Conrad, Henry James, Bram Stoker, George Bernard Shaw)*. Bloomington: Indiana University, Ph.D. dissertation 2003. 269 pp. Large format.

1408. Miller, Elizabeth. "Back to the Basics: Re-examining Stoker's Sources for *Dracula.*" *Journal of the Fantastic in the Arts* 10, 2 (1999): 187–96.

1409. _____. "Coffin Nails: Smokers and Non-smokers in *Dracula.*" *Journal of Dracula Studies* 1 (1999): 33–37. Posted at: http://www.blooferland.com/drc/index.php?title=Journal_of_Dracula_Studies.

1410. _____. "Coitus Interruptus: Sex, Bram Stoker, and *Dracula.*" *Romanticism on the Net* 44 (November 2006). Posted at: http://www.erudit.org/revue/ron/2006/v/n44/014002ar.html.

1411. _____. *Dracula*. New York: Parkstone Press, [2001]. 238 pp. hb. dj. Large format.

1412. _____. *A Dracula Handbook*. St. John's, Newfoundland, Canada: Transylvanian Society of Dracula, 2001. 107 pp. pb. Spiral. Rev. ed.: Bucharest, Romania: Editura Gerot, 2003. 180 pp. Rev. ed.: N.p.: Xlibris Corporation, 2005. 200 pp. tp.

1413. _____. *Dracula: Sense & Nonsense*. Westcliffe-on-Sea: Desert Island Books, 2000. 256 pp. hb. dj. *Dracula: Sense & Nonsense* received the 2001 award as the best nonfiction book of the previous year given annually by the Lord Ruthven Society. The volume called attention to a number of errors that had crept into Dracula studies over the last generation.

1414. _____. "Dracula: The Ever Widening Circle." In Elizabeth Miller, ed. *Bram Stoker's Dracula: A Documentary Volume*. Detroit: Thompson/Gale, 2005, pp. 341–49.

1415. _____. "*Dracula*: The Narrative Patchwork." *Udolpho* (September 1994) 27–30.

1416. _____. *Dracula: The Shade and Shadow*. Westcliffe-on-Sea: Desert Island Books, 1998. 256 pp. hb. dj.

1417. _____. *Frankenstein* and *Dracula*: The Question of Influence." In Alienne Becker, ed. *Visions of the Fantastic*. Westport, CT: Greenwood Press, 1996, pp. 123–29.

1418. _____. "The Genesis of Dracula." *Transylvanian Journal: Dracula and Vampire Studies* 1, 1 (Fall 1995): 11–16.

1419. _____. "Getting to Know the Un-Dead: Bram Stoker, Vampires and Dracula." In Carla T. Kungl, ed. *Vampires: Myths and Metaphors of Enduring Evil*. Oxford: Inter-Disciplinary Press, 2003. pp. 3–6. Rpt. in: Peter Day, ed. *Vampire: Myths and Metaphors of Enduring Evil*. Amsterdam: Rodopi, 2006, pp. 3–20.

1420. _____. "The Question of Immortality: Vampires, Count Dracula and Vlad the Impaler." *Journal of Dracula Studies* 4 (2002). Posted at:

http://www.blooferland.com/drc/index.php?title
=Journal_of_Dracula_Studies.

1421. _____. *Reflections on Dracula: Ten Essays*. White Rock, BC: Transylvanian Press, 1997. 226 pp. tp.

1422. _____. "Schizophrenic Dracula: Romania, the Media, and the World Dracula Conference." In Elizabeth Miller, ed. *Bram Stoker's Dracula: A Documentary Volume*. Detroit: Thompson/Gale, 2005, pp. 352–57.

1423. _____. "Shapeshifting *Dracula*: The Abridged Edition of 1901." In James Craig Holte, ed. *The Fantastic Vampire: Studies in the Children of the Night: Selected Essays from the Eighteenth International Conference on the Fantastic in the Arts*. Vol. 19. Westport, CT: Greenwood Publishing Group, 2002, pp. 3–9.

1424. _____, ed. *Blood Offerings for Dracula: Winning Entries for the Count's Creative Writing Contest*. Los Angeles: Transylvanian Society of Dracula, 1997. 46 pp.

1425. _____, ed. *Bram Stoker's Dracula: A Documentary Volume*. Ser.: Dictionary of Literary Biography #304. Detroit: Thompson/Gale, 2005. 480 pp. hb. Large format. Rev. ed. as: *Bram Stoker's Dracula: A Documentary Journey into Vampire Country and the Dracula Phenomena*. New York Pegasus Books, 2009. 391 pp. tp.

1426. _____ and Dacre Stoker. *The Lost Journal of Bram Stoker: The Dublin Years*. London: The Robson Press/Biteback Publishing, 2013. 337 pp. hb. dj.

1427. _____, and Margaret L. Carter. "Filing for Divorce: Count Dracula and Vlad Tepes." In Elizabeth Miller, ed. *Dracula; The Shade and the Shadow*. Westcliff-on-Sea, Essex, UK: Desert Island Books, 1998, pp. 165–179.

1428. Milmine, Alexis M. "Retracing the Shambling Steps of the Undead: The Blended Folkloric Elements of Vampirism in Bram Stoker's *Dracula*." In Barbara Brodman and James E. Doan, eds. *The Universal Vampire: Origins and Evolution of a Legend*. Madison, NJ: Fairleigh Dickinson University Press, 2013, pp. 33–43.

1429. Montalbano, Margaret. "From Bram Stoker's *Dracula* to *Bram Stoker's 'Dracula*.'" In Robert Stam and Alessandra Raengo, eds. *A Companion to Literature and Film*. Malden, MA: Blackwell Publishing, 2004, pp. 385–398.

1430. Morash, Chris. "'Ever Under Some Unnatural Condition': Bram Stoker and the Co-lonial Fantastic." In Brian Cosgrove, ed. *Literature and the Supernatural: Essays for the Maynooth Bicentenary*. Blackrock, County Dublin: Columba Press, 1995.

1431. Moretti, Franco. "A Capital Dracula." In Susan Fischer, David Forgacs, and David Miller, eds. *Signs Taken for Wonders: Essays in the Sociology of Literary Forms*. New York: Varso, 1988. pp. 90–104. Rpt. in: Bram Stoker. *Dracula*. Ser.: Norton Critical Editions. Ed. by Nina Auerbach and David J. Skal. New York: W. W. Norton & Company, 1998, pp. 431–44.

1432. _____. "The Dialectic of Fear: Dracula and Frankenstein." *New Left Review* 136 (November-December 1982): 67–84. Rpt. in: Franco Moretti. *Signs Taken for Wonders: Essays in the Sociology of Literary Forms*. London: Verso, 1983, pp. 83–108.

1433. _____. "*Dracula* and Capitalism." In Glennis Byron, ed. *Dracula (Bram Stoker): Contemporary Critical Essays*. London: Macmillan Press, 1999, pp. 43–54.

1434. Morrison, Daniel D. "My Day with Dracula." *American Way* 23 (1990): 116–20.

1435. Morrison, Ronald D. "Reading Barthes and Reading *Dracula*: Between Work and Text." *Kentucky Philological Review* 9 (1994): 23–28.

1436. Moses, Michael Valdez. "The Irish Vampire: *Dracula*, Parnell, and the Troubled Dreams of Nationhood." *Journal X* 2, 1 (Autumn 1997): 67–111.

1437. Moss, Stephanie. "Bram Stoker." In Darren Harris-Fain, ed. *British Fantasy and Science Fictions Writers Before World War I*. Dictionary of Literary Biography, Vol. 178. Detroit: Gale Research Company, 1997, pp. 229–237.

1438. _____. "Bram Stoker and the Society for Psychical Research." In Elizabeth Miller, ed. *Dracula: The Shade and the Shadow*. Westcliff-on-Sea, Essex, UK: Desert Island Books, 1998, pp. 82–92.

1439. Moxey, John Llewellyn, interviewed by Tom Weaver. "Night Stalking: An Interview with John Llewellyn Moxey." In Bob Madison, ed. *Dracula: The First Hundred Years*. Baltimore, MD: Midnight Marquee Press, 1997, pp. 256–65.

1440. Muirhead, Marion. "Corruption Becomes Itself Corrupt: Entropy in *Dracula*." In Elizabeth Miller, ed. *Dracula: The Shade and the Shadow*. Westcliff-on-Sea, Essex, UK: Desert Island Books, 1998, pp. 239–46.

1441. Mulvey-Roberts, Marie. "Dracula and the Doctors: Bad Blood, Menstrual Taboo and the New Woman." In William Hughes and Andrew Smith, eds. *Bram Stoker: History, Psychoanalysis and the Gothic.* Basingstoke, UK: Macmillan, 1998, pp. 78–95.

1442. Murch, Brianna. *Beyond Maidens, Minxes, and Mothers: The Female Vampire and Gothic Other in* Dracula, Hellsing, *and* Chibi Vampire. Bridgewater, MA: Bridgewater State University, B.A. Honors thesis, 2013. 25 pp. In *BSU Honors Program Theses and Projects.* Item 8. Posted at: http://vc.bridgew.edu/honors_proj/8.

1443. Murphy, Brian. "The Nightmare of the Dark: The Gothic Legacy of Count Dracula." *Odyssey: A Journal of the Humanities* 1, 2 (1976): 9–15.

1444. Murray, Paul. *From the Shadow of Dracula: The Life of Bram Stoker.* London: Jonathan Cape, 2004. 320 pp. hb. dj. Rpt.: London: Pimlico, 2005. 352 pp. tp.

1445. _____. "Lafcadio Hearn and the Irish Tradition." *Irish Studies Review* 4, 15 (June 1996): 2–9.

1446. _____. W. B. Yeats and Bram Stoker." *The Yeats Journal of Korea* 12 (1999).

1447. Muskovits, Eszter. "The Threat of Otherness in Bram Stoker's Dracula." *Trans: Revue de Littérature Générale et Comparée* 10 (2010). Posted at: http://www.doaj.org/doaj?func=search&template=&uiLanguage=en&query=Dracula&filter=media%3A%22article%22.

1448. Myers, Walter Dean. "Introduction." In Bram Stoker. *Dracula.* New York: Scholastic, Inc., 2005, pp. v–vii.

1449. Nandris, Grigore. "The Historical Dracula: The Theme of His Legend in the Western and in the Eastern Literature of Europe." *Comparative Literature Studies* 3, 4 (1966): 367–96. Rpt. as: "The Historical Dracula." In A. Owen Aldridge, ed. *Comparative Literature: Matter and Method.* Urbana: University of Illinois Press, 1969.

1450. Nävsjö, Dana. *From Threat to Thrill: A Comparative Study of Bram Stoker's* Dracula *and Stephenie Meyer's* Twilight. Linköping, Sweden: Linköping University, Student thesis, 2013. 32 pp. Large format. Posted at: http://www.diva-portal.org/smash/get/diva2:615426/FULLTEXT01.pdf.

1451. Nelson, James. "Introduction." In Bram Stoker. *Dracula.* New York, Dodd Mead, 1970, pp. vii–x.

1452. Newcomb, Erin. "Between Reason and Faith: Breaking the Status Quo in Stoker's *Dracula*." *Journal of Dracula Studies* 13 (2011): 83–106. Posted at: http://www.blooferland.com/drc/index.php?title=Journal_of_Dracula_Studies.

1453. Nicholson, Eleanor Bourg. "Introduction." In Bram Stoker. *Dracula.* San Francisco, CA: Ignatius Press, 2012, pp. ix–xxii. Ignatius Critical Editions.

1454. Nicholson, Mervyn. "Bram Stoker and C. S. Lewis: *Dracula* as a Source of *That Hideous Strength*." *Mythlore* 19, 3 (Summer 1993): 16–22.

1455. Ní Fhlainn, Sorcha. "The Eternal Changeling: Dracula's Transformations through the 1970s." In Paul L. Yoder and Peter Mario Kreuter. *The Horrid Looking Glass: Reflections on Monstrosity.* Oxford: Inter-Disciplinary Press, 2011, pp.

1456. _____. "'His Eyes Blazed Redly': Skinning, Satanism and Mephisthophelian Romance: Hannibal Lecter and Bram Stoker's *Dracula* (1992)." In Sorcha Ní Fhlainn. *Our Monstrous (S)kin: Blurring the Boundaries Between Monsters and Humanity.* Oxford: Inter-Disciplinary Press, 2010.

1457. Nyberg, Suzanna. "Men in Love: The Fantasizing of Bram Stoker and Edvard Munch." In James Craig Holte, ed. *The Fantastic Vampire: Studies in the Children of the Night: Selected Essays from the Eighteenth International Conference on the Fantastic in the Arts.* Vol. 19. Westport, CT: Greenwood Publishing Group, 2002, pp. 45–55.

1458. Olsen, Melissa. "Dracula the Anti-Christ: New Resurrection of an Immortal Prejudice." In Barbara Brodman and James E. Doan, eds. *Images of the Modern Vampire: The Hip and the Atavistic.* Madison. NJ: Fairleigh Dickinson, 2013, pp. 29–40.

1459. O'Malley, Patrick R. "The Blood of the Saints: Vampirism from Polidori to *Dracula*." In Patrick O'Malley. *Catholicism, Sexual Deviance, and Victorian Gothic Culture.* Cambridge: Cambridge University Press, 2006, pp. 130–64.

1460. O'Neil, Thomas. "Historic Houses: In the Shadow of Dracula, the Dark Trail Leading to Bran Castle." *Architectural Digest* 41, 4 (April 1984): 176–84.

1461. Osborough, W. N. "The Dublin Castle Career (1866–1878) of Bram Stoker." *Gothic Studies,* 1 (1999): 222–240.

1462. Parrino, Maria. "Food, Blood, Body and Knowledge in *Frankenstein* and *Dracula*." In Eoghain Hamilton. *The Gothic: Probing the Boundaries*. Oxford: Inter-Disciplinary Press, 2010, pp. 145–52.

1463. Paris, Mark M. "From Clinic to Classroom While Uncovering the Evil Dead in *Dracula*: A Psychoanalytic Pedagogy." In James M. Cahalan and David B. Downing, eds. *Practicing Theory in Introductory College Literature Courses*. Urbana, IL: National Council of Teachers of English, 1991, pp. 47–56.

1464. Parker, Berlinda Z. *The Narcotic Gaze: Ocular Imagery and the Vampire Motif in Christabel, Carmilla, and Dracula*. Boca Raton: Florida Atlantic University, M.A. thesis, 1982. 71 pp. Large format.

1465. Parkin-Gounelas, Ruth. "Dracula and the Death Drive." In Ruth Parkin-Gounelas. *Literature and Psychoanalysis: Intertextual Readings*. New York: Palgrave Macmillan, 2001, pp. 199–207.

1466. Parlour, Susan. "Vixens and Virgins in the Nineteenth-Century Anglo-Irish Novel: Representations of the Feminine in Bram Stoker's *Dracula*." *Journal of Dracula Studies* 11 (2009): 61–80. Posted at: http://www.blooferland.com/drc/index.php?title=Journal_of_Dracula_Studies.

1467. Parson, Maria. "Vamping the Woman: Menstrual Pathologies in Bram Stoker's *Dracula*." *The Irish Journal of Gothic and Horror Stores* 1 (October 2006). Posted at: http://irishgothichorrorjournal.homestead.com/mariaprinter.html.

1468. Paul, Jason. "Corporeal Corruption and the Extrapolation of the Soul: An Analysis of Abraham Stoker's *Dracula* and Mary Shelley's *Frankenstein*." In Jason Paul. *Formative Years: A Collection of Literary Critiques*. N.p.: the author, 2012, pp. 64–70.

1469. Pecher, Janine. *Characters in Bram Stoker's* Dracula. München, Germany: Grin Verlag, 2008. 24 pp.

1470. Pedlar, Valerie. "Dracula: Fin-de-Siècle Fantasy." In Dennis Walder, ed. *The Nineteenth-Century Novel: Identities*. London: Routledge, 2001, pp. 196–216.

1471. _____. "The Zoophagus Maniac: Madness and Degeneracy in *Dracula*." In Valerie Pedlar. *The Most Dreadful Visitation: Male Madness in Victorian Fiction*. Liverpool: Liverpool University Press, 2006.

1472. Pencak, William. "'Appalling in Its Gloomy Fascination': Stoker's *Dracula*." In James Craig Holte, ed. *The Fantastic Vampire: Studies in the Children of the Night: Selected Essays from the Eighteenth International Conference on the Fantastic in the Arts*. Vol. 19. Westport, CT: Greenwood Publishing Group, 2002, pp. 31–35.

1473. Perry, Dennis R. "Whitman's Influence on Stoker's *Dracula*." *Walt Whitman Review* 3, 3 (1986): 29–35. Posted at: http://dx.doi.org/10.13008/2153-3695.1860.

1474. Philips, Robert, and Branimir Rieger. "The Agony and the Ecstasy: A Jungian Analysis of Two Vampire Novels, Meredith Ann Pierce's *The Dark Angel* and Bram Stoker's *Dracula*." *West Virginia University Philological Papers* 31 (1986): 10–19.

1475. Pick, Daniel. "'Terrors of the Night': *Dracula* and 'Degeneration' in the Late Nineteenth Century." *Critical Quarterly* 30 (1988): 71–87. Rpt. in: Lyn Pykett, ed. *Reading fin de siècle Fictions*. London and New York, Longman, 1996, pp. 149–165. Rpt. in: Harold Bloom, ed. *Bram Stoker's Dracula*. Ser.: Bloom's Modern Critical Interpretations. New York: Chelsea House Publications, 2002, pp. 93–110. Excerpt rpt. in: Carol A. Senf. *The Critical Response to Bram Stoker*. Westport CT: Greenwood Press, 1993, pp. 130–31.

1476. Picker, John M. "The Victorian Aura of the Recorded Voice." *New Literary History* 32, 3 (Summer 2001): 769–786.

1477. Pikula, Tanya. "Bram Stoker's *Dracula* and Late-Victorian Advertising Tactics: Earnest Men, Virtuous Ladies, and Porn." *English Literature in Transition, 1880–1920* 55, 3 (2012): 283–302.

1478. Pinkerton, Mark. "Why Westenra?" *Bram Stoker Society Journal* 7 (1995): 12–16. Rpt.: In Leslie Shepard and Albert Power, eds. *Dracula: Celebrating 100 Years*. Dublin: Mentor Press, 1997, pp. 43–46.

1479. Pope, Rebecca A. "Writing and Biting in Dracula." *Literature, Interpretation, Theory* 1 (1990): 99–216. Rpt. in: Glennis Byron, ed. *Dracula (Bram Stoker): Contemporary Critical Essays*. London: Macmillan Press, 1999, pp. 68–92.

1480. Power, Albert. "Bram Stoker and the Tradition of Irish Supernatural Literature." *Bram Stoker Society Journal* 3 (1991): 3–21. Rpt. in: Leslie Shepard and Albert Power, eds. *Dracula: Celebrating 100 Years*. Dublin: Mentor Press, 1997, pp. 58–70. Rev. text in: Elizabeth Miller, ed. *Bram Stoker's*

Dracula: A Documentary Volume. Detroit: Thompson/Gale, 2005, pp. 105–11.

1481. _____. "The Ghostly Tale—Must the Author Believe?" In Leslie Shepard and Albert Power, eds. *Dracula: Celebrating 100 Years.* Dublin: Mentor Press, 1997, pp. 22–31.

1482. Prescott, Charles E., and Grace A. Giorgio. "Vampiric Affinities: Mina Harker and the Paradox of Femininity in Bram Stoker's *Dracula.*" *Victorian Literature and Culture* 33, 2 (September 2005): 487–515.

1483. Priest, Hannah. "Monstrous Literature: The Case of Dacre Stoker's *Dracula the Undead.*" In Jonathan A. Allan and Elizabeth E. Nelson, eds. *Inversions of Power and Paradox.* Oxford, UK: Inter-Disciplinary Press, 2011, pp. 163–70. Originally presented as a paper at the 8th annual 'Monsters and the Monstrous' conference held at Oxford University, September 2010.

1484. Punter, David. "Bram Stoker's *Dracula*: Tradition, Technology, Modernity." In John S. Bak, ed. *Post/modern Dracula: From Victorian Themes to Postmodern Praxis.* Newcastle, UK: Cambridge Scholars Publishing, 2007, pp. 31–42.

1485. _____. *"Dracula* and Taboo." In Glennis Byron, ed. *Dracula (Bram Stoker): Contemporary Critical Essays.* London: Macmillan Press, 1999, pp. 22–29.

1486. _____. "Echoes in the Animal House: *The Lair of the White Worm.*" In William Hughes and Andrew Smith, eds. *Bram Stoker: History, Psychoanalysis and the Gothic.* Basingstoke, UK: Macmillan, 1998, pp. 173ff.

1487. Rance, Maxime. "Dracula in the Wasteland." *Notes and Queries* 34 (December 1987): 508–509.

1488. Rance, Nicholas. "Jonathan's Great Knife: Dracula Meets Jack the Ripper." *Victorian Literature and Culture* 30, 2 (2002): 439–454. Rpt. in: Alexandra Warwick and Martin Willis, eds. *Jack the Ripper: Media, Culture, History.* Manchester, UK: Manchester University Press, 2007.

1489. Reese, Katherina. *Deconstructing Dracula: The Reality Behind the Myth.* München, Germany: GRIN Verlag, 2010. 40 pp. pb.

1490. Reeve, Brian, et al. "Bram Stoker's Life." In Bram Stoker. *Dracula.* Richmond, Surrey, UK: One World Classics, 2008, pp. 363–393.

1491. Richards, Jeffrey. "Gender, Race, and Sexuality in Bram Stoker's Other Novels." In

Christopher Parker, ed. *Gender Roles and Sexuality in Victorian Literature.* Aldershot, UK: Scolar Press, 1995, pp. 143–71.

1492. Richards, Leah. "Mass Production and the Spread of Information in *Dracula*: Proof of so Wild a Story." *English Literature in Transition, 1880–1920* 52, 4 (2009): 440–457.

1493. Rieger, Gabriel A. "'Some Longing and at the Same Time Some Deadly Fear': Victorian Masochism and *Dracula.*" *Journal of the Fantastic in the Arts* 17, 1 (2006): 49–59.

1494. Riquelme, John Paul. "Combining Perspectives on *Dracula.*" In Bram Stoker. *Dracula.* Ed. by John Paul Riquelme. Boston: Bedford/New York: St. Martin's, 2002, pp. 573–77.

1495. _____. "A Critical History of *Dracula.*" In Bram Stoker. *Dracula.* Ser.: Case Studies in Contemporary Criticism. Ed. by John Paul Riquelme. Boston: Bedford/New York: St. Martin's, 2002, pp. 409–33. Rev. and updated in: Elizabeth Miller, ed. *Bram Stoker's Dracula: A Documentary Volume.* Detroit: Thompson/Gale, 2005, pp. 358–75.

1496. _____. "Deconstruction and Dracula." In Bram Stoker. *Dracula.* Ser.: Case Studies in Contemporary Criticism. Ed. by John Paul Riquelme. Boston: Bedford/New York: St. Martin's, 2002, pp. 538–59.

1497. _____. "Doubling and Repetition/Realism and Closure in *Dracula.*" In Bram Stoker. *Dracula.* Ser.: Case Studies in Contemporary Criticism. Ed. by John Paul Riquelme. Boston: Bedford/New York: St. Martin's, 2002, pp. 559–72.

1498. _____. "Gender Criticism and *Dracula.*" In Bram Stoker. *Dracula.* Ser.: Case Studies in Contemporary Criticism. Ed. by John Paul Riquelme. Boston: Bedford/New York: St. Martin's, 2002, pp. 434–49.

1499. _____. "Introduction: Biographical and Historical Contexts. In Bram Stoker. *Dracula.* Ser.: Case Studies in Contemporary Criticism. Ed. by John Paul Riquelme. Boston: Bedford/New York: St. Martin's, 2002, pp. 3–21.

1500. _____. "The New Historicism and *Dracula.*" In Bram Stoker. *Dracula.* Ser.: Case Studies in Contemporary Criticism. Ed. by John Paul Riquelme. Boston: Bedford/New York: St. Martin's, 2002, pp. 500–18.

1501. _____. "Psychoanalytic Criticism and *Dracula.*" In Bram Stoker. *Dracula.* Ser.: Case Studies in Contemporary Criticism. Ed. by John Paul

Riquelme. Boston: Bedford/New York: St. Martin's, 2002, pp. 466–83.

1502. _____. "Toward a History of Gothic and Modernism: Dark Modernity from Bram Stoker to Samuel Beckett." *Modern Fiction Studies* 46, 3 (Fall 2000): 585–605.

1503. Robbins, Ruth. "Dracula: (cultural) Capital and (epistemological) Crisis." In Ruth Robbins. *Pater to Foster, 1873–1924*, New York: Palgrave Macmillan, 2003, pp. 149–54.

1504. Roberts, Bette B. "Victorian Values in the Narration of *Dracula*." *Studies in Weird Fiction* 6 (Fall 1989): 10–14.

1505. Rogers, David. "Introduction." In Bram Stoker. *Dracula & Dracula's Guest and Other Stories*. Ware, Hertsfordshire, UK: Wordsworth Editions, [2009], pp. 7–21.

1506. Ronay, Gabriel. *The Dracula Myth.* London: H. W. Allen, 1972. 180 pp. hb. Rpt.: London: Pan Books, 1975. 190 pp. pb. Rpt. as: *The Truth About Dracula.* New York: Stein and Day, 1974. hb. Rpt.: New York: Day Books, 1979. 180 pp. pb.

1507. Rosenberg, Nancy F. "Desire and Loathing in Bram Stoker's *Dracula*." *Journal of Dracula Studies* 2 (2000): 8–14. Posted at: http://www.blooferland.com/drc/index.php?title=Journal_of_Dracula_Studies.

1508. Roth, Phyllis A. *Bram Stoker.* Ser.: Twayne's English Authors (#343). Boston: Twayne Publishing Co., 1982. 167 pp. hb.

1509. _____. "Suddenly Sexual Women in Bram Stoker's *Dracula*." *Literature and Psychology* 27, 3 (1977): 113–121. Rpt. in: Margaret L. Carter, ed. *Dracula: The Vampire and the Critics.* Ann Arbor: UMI Research Press, 1988, pp. 57–67. Rpt. in: Bram Stoker. *Dracula.* Ser.: Norton Critical Editions. Ed. by Nina Auerbach and David J. Skal. New York: W. W. Norton & Company, 1998, pp. 411–21. Rpt. in: Glennis Byron, ed. *Dracula (Bram Stoker): Contemporary Critical Essays.* London: Macmillan Press, 1999, pp. 30–42. Rpt. in: Harold Bloom, ed. *Bram Stoker's Dracula.* Ser.: Bloom's Modern Critical Interpretations. New York: Chelsea House Publications, 2002, pp. 3–14.

1510. Rowen, Norma. "Teaching the Vampire: *Dracula* in the Classroom." In Carol Margaret Davison, ed., with Paul Simpson-Housley. *Bram Stoker's Dracula: Sucking through the Century, 1897–1997.* Toronto: Dundurn Press, 1997, pp. 231–47.

1511. Rusu, Elena Maria. "Feminine 'Roles' in Dracula by Bram Stoker." *Gender Studies* 3 (2004): 168–173.

1512. Ruthner, Clemens. "Bloodsucker with Teutonic Tongues: The German Speaking World and the Origins of *Dracula*." In Elizabeth Miller, ed. *Dracula: The Shade and the Shadow.* Westcliff-on-Sea, Essex, UK: Desert Island Books, 1998, pp. 54–67.

1513. Sage, Victor. "*Dracula* and the Codes Victorian of Pornography. In Dominique Sipière, ed., *Dracula: Insémination-dissémination*, Amiens, Presses de l'UFR Clerc, Université de Picardie, 1996, pp. 31–48. Rpt. in: Gilles Menegaldo and Dominique Sipière, eds. *Dracula: L'oeuvre de Bram Stoker et le film de Francis F. Coppola.* Paris, Ellipses, 2005, pp. 55–70.

1514. _____. "Exchanging Fantasies: Sex and the Serbian Crisis in *The Lady of the Shroud*." In William Hughes and Andrew Smith, eds. *Bram Stoker: History, Psychoanalysis and the Gothic.* Basingstoke, UK: Macmillan, 1998, pp. 116–??.

1515. Saldanha de Gama, Gilza. "Dracula's Heirs." *Journal of Dracula Studies* 2 (2000): 34–37. Posted at: http://www.blooferland.com/drc/index.php?title=Journal_of_Dracula_Studies.

1516. Saler, Benson, and Charles A. Ziegler. "Dracula and Carmilla: Mythmaking and the Mind." In Carla T. Kungl, ed. *Vampires: Myths and Metaphors of Enduring Evil.* Oxford: Inter-Disciplinary Press, 2003, pp. 17–20. Posted at http://www.inter-disciplinary.net/publishing/id-press/ebooks/vampires-myths-and-metaphors-of-enduring-evil. Rpt. as: "*Dracula* and *Carmilla*: Monsters and the Mind." *Philosophy and Literature* 29, 1 (April 2005): 218–227.

1517. Sanders, Thomas E. "Profile: Bram Stoker." *Night Cry* 1 (1986): 72–79.

1518. Sandner, David. "Up-to-date with a Vengeance: Modern Monsters in Bram Stoker's *Dracula* and Margaret Oliphant's 'The Secret Chamber.'" *Journal of the Fantastic in the Arts* 8, 3 (1997): 294–309.

1519. Scandura, Jani. "Deadly Professions: *Dracula*, Undertakers and the Embalmed Corpse." *Victorian Studies* 40 (1996): 1–31.

1520. Schaffer, Talia. "A Wilde Desire Took Me: A Homoerotic History of *Dracula*." *English Literary History* 61, 2 (Summer 1994): 381–425. Rpt. in: Bram Stoker. *Dracula.* Edited by Nina Auerbach and David J. Skal. New York: W. W.

Norton & Company (Norton Critical Edition), 1998, 47–82.

1521. Schaffrath, Stephan. "Order-versus-Chaos Dichotmoy in Bram Stoker's *Dracula*." *Extrapolation: A Journal of Science Fiction and Fantasy* 43, 1 (Spring 2002): 98–112.

1522. Schmid, David. "Is the Pen Mightier Than the Sword? The Contradictory Function of Writing *Dracula*." In Elizabeth Miller, ed. *Dracula; The Shade and the Shadow*. Westcliff-on-Sea, Essex, UK: Desert Island Books, 1998, pp. 119–130.

1523. Schmitt, Cannon. "Mother Dracula: Orientalism, Degeneration, and Anglo-Irish National Subjectivity at the Fin de Siècle." Special issue on *Irishness and (Post) Modernism*. *Bucknell Review* 38 (1994): 25–43. Rpt. in: Cannon Schmitt. *Alien Nation: Nineteenth-century Gothic Fictions and English Nationality*. Philadelphia: University of Pennsylvania Press, 1997, pp. 135–55.

1524. Schneider, Kirk J. "*Dracula*: A Study in Hyperconstriction." In Kirk J. Schneider. *Horror and the Holy: Wisdom Teachings of the Monster Tale*. Chicago: Open Court, 1993, pp. 17–30.

1525. _____. "Wisdom-Horror: Dracula and Frankenstein." In Kirk J. Schneider. *Horror and the Holy: Wisdom-Teachings of the Monster Tale*. Chicago, IL: Open Court, 1993, pp. 13–42.

1526. Schoolfield, George C. "England: Bram Stoker." In George C. Schoolfield. *A Baedecker of Decadence: Charting a Literary Fashion, 1884–1927*. New Haven, CT: Yale University Press, 2003, pp. 215–32.

1527. Scott, Rebecca. *The Bliss of Death: A Demystification of the Late Nineteenth Century "Femme Fatale" in Selected Works of Bram Stoker, Rider Haggard, Joseph Conrad, and Thomas Hardy*. York, UK: University of York, Ph.D. Dissertation, 1989. 462 pp. Large format.

1528. Seed, David. "Eruptions of the Primitive into the Present: *The Jewel of Seven Stars* and *The Lair of the White Worm*." In William Hughes and Andrew Smith, eds. *Bram Stoker: History, Psychoanalysis and the Gothic*. Basingstoke, UK: Macmillan, 1998, pp. 188-??.

1529. _____. "The Narrative Method of *Dracula*." *Nineteenth Century Fiction* 40, 1 (1986): 61–75. Rpt. in: Margaret L. Carter, ed. *Dracula: The Vampire and the Critics*. Ann Arbor: UMI Research Press, 1988, pp. 195–206.

1530. Sellers, Jason. "Dracula's Band of the Hand: Suppressed Male Onanism." *English Language Notes* 43, 2 (2005): 148–158.

1531. Sendrea, Alexander. *The Making of a Vampire: Paracelsus, Rabbi Loew, St. Germain, Dracula*. New York: America Institute for Writing Research, 1982. 167 pp. tp. History.

1532. Senf, Carol A. *Critical Response to Bram Stoker*. Westport, CT: Greenwood Press, 1993. 195 pp. hb. Senf collects, comments upon, and contextualizes a number of critical responses to Dracula and other writings of Bram Stoker.

1533. _____. "*Dracula* and *The Lair of the White Worm*: Bram Stoker's Commentary on Victorian Science." *Gothic Studies* 2 (2000): 218–231.

1534. _____. "Dracula: Another Victorian Femme Fatale?" *Journal of Popular Culture* 2, 2, (1986): 33–43.

1535. _____. *Dracula: Between Tradition and Modernism*. New York: Twayne Publishers, 1998. 132 pp. hb. dj. *Dracula: Between Tradition and Modernism* received the 1999 award as the best nonfiction book of the previous year given annually by the Lord Ruthven Society.

1536. _____. "'Dracula': Stoker's Response to the New Woman." *Victorian Studies* 26, 1 (Autumn 1982): 33–49.

1537. _____. "*Dracula, The Jewel of the Seven Stars*, and Stoker's 'Burden of the Past.'" In Carol Margaret Davison, ed., with Paul Simpson-Housley. *Bram Stoker's Dracula: Sucking through the Century, 1897–1997*. Toronto: Dundurn Press, 1997, pp. 777–94.

1538. _____. "*Dracula*: The Unseen Face in the Mirror." *Journal of Narrative Technique* 9 (1979): 160–70. Rpt. in: Margaret L. Carter, ed. *Dracula: The Vampire and the Critics*. Ann Arbor: UMI Research Press, 1988, pp. 93–103. Rpt. in: Bram Stoker. *Dracula*. Edited by Nina Auerbach and David J. Skal. New York: W. W. Norton & Company (Norton Critical Edition), 1998, pp. 421–421. Rpt. in: Harold Bloom, ed. *Bram Stoker's Dracula*. Ser.: Bloom's Modern Critical Interpretations. New York: Chelsea House Publications, 2002, pp. 15–26.

1539. _____. "*The Lady of the Shroud*: Stoker's Successor to *Dracula*." *Essays and Studies* 19 (1990): 82–96.

1540. _____. "Response to 'Dracula and the Idea of Europe.'" *Connotations* 10, 1 (2000/2001): 47–58.

1541. _____. "Rethinking the New Woman in Stoker's Fiction: Looking at Lady Athlyne." *Journal of Dracula Studies* 9 (2007): 1–8. Posted at: http://www.blooferland.com/drc/index.php?title=Journal_of_Dracula_Studies.

1542. _____. *Science and Social Science in Bram Stoker's Fiction.* Westport, CT: Greenwood Press, 2002. 176 pp. hb.

1543. Shaffer, Talia. "A Wilde Desire Took Me.': The Homoerotioc History of *Dracula*." *English Literary History* 61, 2 (1994): 381–425.

1544. Shang-Jen, Li. "Ghosts, Vampires, and Scientific Naturalism: Observation and Evidence in the Supernatural Fiction of Grant Allen, Bram Stoker and Arthur Conan Doyle." In Mu-chou Poo, ed. *Rethinking Ghosts in World Religions.* Leiden: Brill, 2009.

1545. Shapiro, Stephen. "Transvaal, Transylvania: *Dracula*'s World System and Gothic Periodicity." *Gothic Studies* 10, 1 (2008): 29–47.

1546. Shenkman, Richard. "Dracula." In Richard Shenkman. *Legends, Lies and Cherished Myths of World History.* New York: HarperCollins, 1993. Rpt.: New York: HarperPerennial, 1994, pp. 193–94.

1547. Shepard, Leslie. "Bram Stoker's Dublin." *Bram Stoker Society Journal* 5 (1993): 9–13. Rpt.: In Leslie Shepard and Albert Power, eds. *Dracula: Celebrating 100 Years.* Dublin: Mentor Press, 1997, pp. 181–186.

1548. _____. "The Gothic Novel and Bram Stoker." In Leslie Shepard and Albert Power, eds. *Dracula: Celebrating 100 Years.* Dublin: Mentor Press, 1997, pp. 47–57.

1549. _____. "A Note on the Death Certificate of Bram Stoker." *Bram Stoker Society Journal.* 4 (1992): 34–36. Rpt. in: Carol Margaret Davison, ed., with Paul Simpson-Housley. *Bram Stoker's Dracula: Sucking through the Century, 1897–1997.* Toronto: Dundurn Press, 1997, pp. 411–16. Rpt. in: Leslie Shepard and Albert Power, eds. *Dracula: Celebrating 100 Years.* Dublin: Mentor Press, 1997, pp. 178–80.

1550. _____. "The Writing of Dracula." In Leslie Shepard and Albert Power, eds. *Dracula: Celebrating 100 Years.* Dublin: Mentor Press, 1997, pp. 35–42.

1551. _____, **and Albert Power, eds.** *Dracula: Celebrating 100 Years.* Dublin, Mentor Press, 1997. 192 pp, pb. Includes contributions by Ralph Shirley Mark Pinkerton, Richard Dalby, , Vincent Hillyer, Jonathan Barry, Don Sanroy, Bela Lugosi, Jeanne Keyes Youngson, and John Exshaw.

1552. Showers, Brian J. *Literary Walking Tours of Gothic Dublin.* Dublin: Nonsuch Publishing, 2006. 160 pp. tp.

1553. Shue, Laura Leigh. *Reconstruction and Representation of Gender Roles in Bram Stoker's Dracula.* Warrensburg: Central Missouri State University, M.A. thesis 1994. 88 pp. Large format.

1554. Siegel, Mark. "Dracula as Anti-Quest." In Mark Siegel. *Hugo Gernsback: Father of Modern Science Fiction: With Essays on Frank Herbert and Bram Stoker.* San Bernardino, CA: The Borgo Press, 1988.

1555. Signoretti, Elizabeth. "Repossessing the Body: Transgressive Desire in 'Carmilla' and Dracula." *Criticism* 38, 4 (1996): 607–32.

1556. Silver, Alain, and James Ursini. "The Other Bram Stoker." In Alain Silver and James Ursini. *More Things Than Are Drempt Of: Masterpieces of Supernatural Horror—From Mary Shelley to Stephen King—in Literature and Film.* New York: Limelight Editions, 1994, pp. 31–39.

1557. Simmons, Clare A. "Fables of Continuity: Bram Stoker and Medivalism." In William Hughes and Andrew Smith, eds. *Bram Stoker: History, Psychoanalysis and the Gothic.* Basingstoke, UK: Macmillan, 1998, pp. 29ff.

1558. Simmons, James R. "If America Goes on Breeding Men Like That': *Dracula*'s Quincey Morris Problematized." *Journal of the Fantastic in the Arts* 12, 4 (2002): 425–36.

1559. Skal, David J. "Afterword—Him and Me: A Personal Slice of the Dracula Century." In Bob Madison, ed. *Dracula: The First Hundred Years.* Baltimore, MD: Midnight Marquee Press, 1997, pp. 292–301.

1560. _____. "Happy Birthday, Dracula." *Rage* 1, 12 (July 1997): 57–60.

1561. _____. *Hollywood Gothic: The Tangled Web of Dracula from Novel to Stage to Screen.* New York: W. W. Norton & Company, 1990. 243 pp. hb. dj. Large format. Rpt.: New York: W. W. Norton & Company, 1990. 243 pp. pb. dj. Large format.

1562. Skelton, Philip. "Growing Gold: Antecedent and Empire." In Gilles Menegaldo and Dominique Sipière, eds. *Dracula: L'oeuvre de Bram Stoker et le film de Francis F. Coppola,* Paris, Ellipses, 2005, pp. 71–81.

1563. Smajic, Sradjan. "Dracula and Duty." *Textual Practice* 23, 1 (2009): 49–71.

1564. Smart, Robert A. "Blood and Money in Bram Stoker's *Dracula*: The Struggle Against Monopoly." In John Louis DiGaetani, ed. *Money: Lure, Lore, and Literature.* Westport, CT: Greenwood Press, 1994, pp. 253–260.

1565. _____. "Postcolonial Dread and the Gothic: Refashioning Identity in Sheridan Le-Fanu's 'Carmilla' and Bram Stoker's *Dracula*." In Tabish. Khair and Johan Hoglund, eds. *Transnational and Postcolonial Vampires: Dark Blood.* Basingstoke, UK: Palgrave Macmillan, 2012, pp. 10–45.

1566. Smith, Andrew. "Bringing Bram Stoker Back from the Margins." *Irish Studies Review* 9, 2 (August 2001): 241–246.

1567. _____. "Demonizing the Americans: Bram Stoker's Postcolonial Gothic." *Gothic Studies* 5 (2003): 20–31.

1568. _____. "Displacing Masculinity: Sherlock Holmes, Count Dracula and London." Andrew Smith. *Victorian Demons: Medicine, Masculinity, and the Gothic at the fin-de-siècle.* Manchester, UK: Manchester University Press, 2004.

1569. Smith, Eric D. "A Presage of Horror! Cacotopia, the Paris Commune, and Bram Stoker's *Dracula*." *Criticism* 52, 1 (2010): Posted at: http://digitalcommons.wayne.edu/criticism/vol52/iss1/4.

1570. Smith, Malcolm. "*Dracula* and the Victorian Frame of Mind." *Trivium* 24 (1989): 76–97.

1571. Snyder, Helen Lavinia. *A Comparative Analysis of the Transformation of Myths in Dracula the Novel, Stageplay, and Movie.* San Jose, CA: San Jose State University, M.A. thesis, 1978. 75 pp. Large Format.

1572. Sova, Dawn B. "Dracula (Bram Stoker). In Dawn B. Sova. *Literature Suppressed on Social Grounds.* New York, Facts on File, 2006, pp. 117–19.

1573. Sparks, Tabitha. "Medical Gothic and the Return to the Contagious Disease Acts in Stoker and Machen." *Nineteenth Century Feminism,* 6 (2002): 87–102.

1574. _____. "New Women, Avenging Doctors: Gothic Medicine in Bram Stoker and Arthur Machen." In Tabitha Sparks. The *Doctor in the Victorian Novel: Family Practices.* Franham, UK: Ashgate, 2009.

1575. Spear, Jeffrey L. "Gender and Dis-Ease in *Dracula*." In Lloyd Davis, ed. *Virginal Sexuality and Textuality in Victorian Literature.* Albany: State University of New York Press, 1993, pp. 179–192.

1576. Spencer, Kathleen. "Purity and Danger: *Dracula*, the Urban Gothic, and the Late Victorian Degeneracy Crisis." *English Literary History* 59 (Spring 1992): 197–225. Rpt. in: Harold Bloom, ed. *Bram Stoker's Dracula.* Ser.: Bloom's Modern Critical Interpretations. New York: Chelsea House Publications, 2002, pp. 111–40.

1577. Stade, George. "Dracula's Women." *Partisan Review* 53, 2 (1986): 200–215. Rpt. as "Dracula's Women, and Why Men Love to Hate Them." In Gerald Fogel, Frederick M. Lane, and Robert S. Liebert, eds. *The Psychology of Men: Psychoanalytic Perspectives.* New Haven, CT: Yale University Press, 1996, pp. 25–48. Rpt. as "Dracula's Women, and Why Men Love to Hate Them." In George Stade. *Equipment for Living: Literature, Moderns, Monsters, Popsters and Us.* Grosseto, Italy: Pari Publishing, 2007, pp. 127–152.

1578. _____. "Introduction." In Bram Stoker. *Dracula.* London, Toronto, New York, Sydney: Bantam Books, 1981, pp. v–xiv.

1579. Stamp, Cordelia. *Dracula Discovered.* Whitby, UK: Caedmon, 1981. 17 pp. 2nd. ed.: Whitby, UK: Abbey Press, 1988.

1580. _____. *Whitby: A Brief History.* Whitby, UK: Caedmon of Whitby, 2007.

1581. Starrs, D. Bruno. "Envisioning and Indulgence: Dracula and Van Helsing." *Traffic: An Interdisciplinary Postgraduate Journal* 5 (2005): 67–76.

1582. Stavick, J. ed. "Love at First Beet: Vegetarian Critical Theory Meats *Dracula*." *The Victorian Newsletter* Number 89 (Spring 1996): 23–28.

1583. Steinmeyer, Jim. *Who Was Dracula? Bram Stoker's Trail of Blood.* New York: Jeremy P. Tarcher/Penguin, 2013. 321 pp.

1584. Stevenson, John Allen. "A Vampire in the Mirror: The Sexuality of *Dracula*." *Publications of the Modern Language Association* 103 (1988): 139–49. Rpt. in: Harold Bloom, ed. *Bram Stoker's Dracula.* Ser.: Bloom's Modern Critical Interpretations. New York: Chelsea House Publications, 2002, pp. 71–91.

1585. Stewart, Garrett. "'Count Me In:' Dracula, Hypnotic Participation, and the Late-

Victorian Gothic of Reading." *Literature Interpretation Theory* 5, 1 (June 1994): 1–18.

1586. Stewart-Gordon, James. "Durable *Dracula*—Beloved Fiend of the Horror Circuit." *Reader's Digest* 107 (November 1975): 49–56.

1587. Stiles, Anne. "Bram Stoker's *Dracula* and Cerebral Automatism." In Anne Stiles. *Popular Fiction and Brain Science in the Late Nineteenth Century.* Cambridge, UK/New York: Cambridge University Press, 2012, pp. 50–82.

1588. ____. "Cerebral Automatism, the Brain, and the Soul in Bram Stoker's *Dracula.*" *Journal of the History of the Neurosciences* 15, 2 (July 2006): 131–152.

1589. Stoddard, Jane (Lorna). "Mr. Bram Stoker: A Chat with the Author of *Dracula.*" In Bram Stoker, *Dracula.* Ed. by Glennis Byron. Peterborough, ON: Broadview Press, 1998, pp. 484–88.

1590. Stoker, Bram. *Bram Stoker's Notes for Dracula: A Facsimile Edition.* Annotated and Transcribed by Robert Eighteen-Bisang and Elizabeth Miller. Jefferson, NC: McFarland & Company, 2008. 331 pp. hb.

1591. ____. "Churchill Talks to Stoker: Stoker as a Journalist." In Leslie Shepard and Albert Power, eds. *Dracula: Celebrating 100 Years.* Dublin: Mentor Press, 1997, pp. 99–105. Rpt. From: *The Daily Chronicle* (January 15, 1908).

1592. ____. "Fifty Years on the Stage: An Appreciation of Miss Ellen Terry." *The Graphic.* Rpt.: *Bram Stoker Society Journal* 1 (1989): 24–28.

1593. ____. "Preface to the Icelandic Edition of *Dracula.*" Posted at: http://draculatheun-dead.com/Dracula_the_Un-Dead/Iceland_Preface.html. Rpt. in: *A Bram Stoker Omnibus.* London: Foulsham, 1986. Rpt. as: "Makt Myrkkranna—Power of Darkness." *Bram Stoker Society Journal* 5 (1993): 7–8. Rpt. in: Clive Leatherdale. *Dracula Unearthed.* Westcliff-on-the-Sea, Essex, UK: Desert Island Books, 1998. Rpt. in: *Journal of Dracula Studies* 2 (2000): 46. Posted at: http://www.blooferland.com/drc/index.php?title=Journal_of_Dracula_Studies.

1594. Stoker, Dacre. "Foreword." In Bram Stoker. *Dracula.* New York: Harper, 2009, pp. vii–x.

1595. "Stoker's Whitby—An Exploration." *For the Blood Is the Life* 2, 11 (Winter 1991-92): 20–23.

1596. Storey, Neill. *The Dracula Secrets: Jack the Ripper and the Darkest Sources of Bram Stoker.* Stroud, Gloucestershire, UK: The History Press, 2012. 303 pp. hb. dj.

1597. Stott, Rebecca. "*Dracula*: A Social Purity Crusade." In Rebecca Stott. *The Fabrication of the Late Victorian Femme Fatale: The Kiss of Death.* Basingstoke, UK: Palgrave Macmillan, 1992, pp. 52–87. hb.

1598. ____. *The Kiss of Death: A Demytification of the Late Nineteenth Century 'Femme fatale' in the Selected Work of Bram Stoker, Rider Haggard, Joseph Conrad, and Thomas Hardy.* York, UK: University of York, Ph.D. dissertation, 1990. Large format.

1599. Straub, Peter. "Introduction." In Bram Stoker. *Dracula.* New York: The Modern Library, 2001, pp. xiv–xxvi.

1600. Sutherland, John. "Why Does the Count Come to England?" In John Sutherland. *Is Heathcliff a Murderer? Great Puzzles in Nineteenth-Century Fiction.* Oxford: Oxford University Press, 2002, pp. 233–38. Rpt as: "Afterword: Why Does the Count Come to England?" In Bram Stoker. *Dracula.* London et al: Penguin English Library, 2012, pp. 441–45.

1601. Tague, Gregory F. "Crisis in the Ethics of Self: From *Frankenstein* to *Dracula.*" In Gregory F. Tague, ed. *Origins of English Literary Modernism, 1870–1914.* Palo Alto, CA: Academica Press, 2009.

1602. Thiele, David. "*Dracula* and Whitmania: 'The pass-word primeval.'" *English Literature in Transition 1880–1920* 48, 2 (2005): 188–205.

1603. Thomas, Ronald R. "Specters of the Novel: *Dracula* and the Cinematic Afterlife of the Victorian Novel." *Nineteenth-Century Contexts* 22, 1 (2000): 77–102. Rpt. in: John Kucich and Dianne F. Sadoff, eds. *Victorian Afterlife: Postmodern Culture Rewrites the Nineteenth Century.* Minneapolis: University of Minnesota Press, 2000, pp. 288–310.

1604. Thompson, Ian. *Dracula's Whitby.* Stroud, Gloucestershire, UK: Amberley Publishing, 2012. 125 pp. tp.

1605. Thornburg, Thomas R. *The Quester and the Castle: The Gothic Novel as Myth with Special Reference to Bram Stoker's Dracula.* Muncie, IN: Ball State University, D.Ed. dissertation, 1969. 173 pp. Large format.

1606. Thornton, Sarah. "Bitten or Typewritten: Transmission in Patrick McGrath's *Blood Disease* and in Stoker's *Dracula*." In Dominique Sipière, ed. *Dracula: Insémination-dissémination*. Amiens, Presses del'UFR Clerc, Université de Picardie, 1996, pp. 83–94.

1607. Timpone, Anthony, ed. *Dracula: The Complete Vampire*. New York: Starlog Communications International, 1992. 90 pp. pb. Large format.

1608. Tóibín, Colin. "Introduction." In Bram Stoker. *Dracula*. London: Constable, 2012, pp. ix–xvii.

1609. Tomaszewska, Monika. "Vampirism and the Degeneration of the Imperial Race—Stoker's Dracula as the Invasive Degenerate Other." *Journal of Dracula Studies* 6 (2004): 1–8.

1610. Tremayne, Peter. "Was Dracula an Irishman?" In *History Ireland* 8, 3 (Autumn 2000). Posted at http://www.historyireland.com/18th-19th-century-history/was-dracula-an-irishman-2/.

1611. ____. "Bram Stoker." In Peter Tremayne. *The Irish Masters of Fantasy*. Portmarnock, Dublin: Wolfhound Press, 1979, pp. 151–157.

1612. ____. "The Irish Dracula." *Bram Stoker Society Journal* 1 (1989): 29–31.

1613. Tropp, Martin. "*Dracula* and the Liberation of Women." In Martin Tropp. *Images of Fear: How Horror Stories Helped Shape Modern Culture, (1818–1918)*. Jefferson, NC: McFarland & Company, 1999, pp. 157–71.

1614. Twitchell, James B. "Analyzing Dracula's Enduring Popularity." In Miachel E. Stuprich, ed. *Horror*. San Diego, CA: Greenhaven Press, 2001, pp. 126–133.

1615. Twyning, John. "Dracula and Gothic Tourism." In John Twyning. *Forms of English History in Literature, Landscape, and Architecture*. Basingstoke, UK: Palgrave Macmillan, 2012, pp. 185–220.

1616. Umland, Samuel J. *Dracula Notes*. Lincoln, NB: Cliff Notes, 1983. 77 pp. pb. Ser: Cliff Notes. Literature.

1617. Ungar, Steven P. *In the Footsteps of Dracula: A Personal Journey and Travel Guide*. New York: World Audience/Audience Artist Group, 2010. 253 pp. tp.

1618. Valente, Joseph. "Double Born: Bram Stoker and the Metrocolonial Gothic." *Modern Fiction Studies* 46, 3 (Fall 2000): 632–645.

1619. ____. *Dracula's Crypt: Bram Stoker, Irishness, and the Question of Blood*. Urbana: University of Illinois Press, 2002. 173 pp. hb. dj. Literature.

1620. ____. "Introduction." In Bram Stoker. *Dracula*. New York: Pocket Books, 2003, pp. vii–xxvi.

1621. Vander Ploeg, Scott. "Stoker's *Dracula*: A Neo Gothic Experiment." In James Craig Holte, ed. *The Fantastic Vampire: Studies in the Children of the Night: Selected Essays from the Eighteenth International Conference on the Fantastic in the Arts*. Vol. 19. Westport, CT: Greenwood Publishing Group, 2002, pp. 37–44.

1622. Varma, Devendra P. "Dracula's Voyage: From Pontus to Hellespontus." In Margaret L. Carter, ed. *Dracula: The Vampire and the Critics*. Ann Arbor: UMI Research Press, 1988, pp. 207–13.

1623. ____. "The Genesis of *Dracula*." In Peter Underwood, ed. *The Vampire's Bedside Companion: The Amazing World of Vampires in Fact and Fiction*. London: Leslie Frewin, 1975, pp. 53–68. Rpt. in: Margaret L. Carter, ed. *Dracula: The Vampire and the Critics*. Ann Arbor: UMI Research Press, 1988, pp. 39–50.

1624. ____. "The Message of *Dracula*." In Peter Haining, ed. *The Dracula Scrapbook*. New York: Bramwell House, 1975, p. 158.

1625. Varnado, S. L. "The Daemonic in Dracula." In S. L. Varnado. *Haunted Presence*. Tuscaloosa: Alabama University Press, 1987, pp. 95–114.

1626. Vellela, Tony. "The Passion of Dracula." *HiLife* (April 1979): 35–38, 80–81.

1627. Vest, Randy. "Sex and Eroticism from Dracula and His Breed—A Tooth in Cheek Overview (Or: Are Those Fangs You're Baring or Are You Just Happy to See Me?)" In Bob Madison, ed. *Dracula: The First Hundred Years*. Baltimore, MD: Midnight Marquee Press, 1997, pp. 200–15.

1628. Viragh, Attila. "Can the Vampire Speak? *Dracula* as Discourse on Cultural Extinction." *English Literature in Transition, 1880–1920* 56, 2 (2013): 231–45.

1629. Vorsino, Michael. "The Dragon, the Raven and the Ring." *Journal of Dracula Studies* 5 (2003): 23–26.

1630. Vukadinovic, Jelena. *Dracula and Victorianism: A Conservative or Subversive Novel?* München, Germany: Grin Verlag, 2005. 27 pp.

1631. Walker, Gerald, and Lorraine Wright. "Locating *Dracula:* Contextualizing the Geography of Transylvania." In Carol Margaret Davison, ed., with Paul Simpson-Housley. *Bram Stoker's Dracula: Sucking through the Century, 1897–1997.* Toronto: Dundurn Press, 1997, pp. 49–75.

1632. Walker, Richard J. "The Blood Is Life: Bram Stoker's Infected Capital." In Richard J. Walker. *Labyrinths of Deceit: Culture, Modernity and Identity in the Nineteenth-Century.* Liverpool, UK: Liverpool University Press, 2007, pp. 256–283.

1633. Wall, Geoffrey. "'Different from Writing': *Dracula* in 1897." *Literature and History* 10, 1 (1984): 15–23. Rpt. in: Harold Bloom, ed. *Bram Stoker's Dracula.* Ser.: Bloom's Modern Critical Interpretations. New York: Chelsea House Publications, 2002, pp. 27–37.

1634. Walsh, Thomas P. "*Dracula*: Logos and Myth." *Research Studies* 47 (1979): 229–37.

1635. Warren, Louis. "Buffalo Bill Meets Dracula: William F. Cody, Bram Stoker, and the Frontier of Racial Decay." *American Historical Review* 107, 4 (2002): 1124–57.

1636. Warwick, Alexandra. "Vampires and the Empire: Fears and Fictions of the 1890s." In Sally Ledger and Scott McCracken, eds. *Cultural Politics at the Fin De Siecle.* Cambridge: Cambridge University Press, 1995, pp. 202–20.

1637. Wasson, Richard. "The Politics of *Dracula*." *English Literature in Transition* 9 (1966): 24–27. Rpt. in: Margaret L. Carter, ed. *Dracula: The Vampire and the Critics.* Ann Arbor: UMI Research Press, 1988, pp. 19–23.

1638. Waters, Colin. *Whitby & the Dracula Connection.* Whitby, UK: Whitby Press, n.d. 12 pp. 12 pp. pb. Staples.

1639. Weinstock, Jeffrey. "Circumcising Dracula." *Journal of the Fantastic in the Arts* 12, 1 (2001): 90–102.

1640. Weiss, Kenneth M. "Dracula! A Paradigm Shift in Evolutionary Genetics: Death of a Theory at the Hands of the Undead?" *Evolutionary Anthropology: Issues, News, and Reviews* 21, 5 (September/October 2012): 176–181.

1641. Weissman, Judith. "Bram Stoker: Semidemons and Secretaries." In Judith Weisman. *Half Savage and Hardy and Free: Women and Rural Radicalism in the Nineteenth Century Novel.* Middletown, CT: Wesleyan University Press, 1987, pp. 189–207.

1642. _____. "Women and Vampires: *Dracula* as Victorian Novel." *Midwest Quarterly* 18 (1977): 392–405. Rpt. in: Margaret L. Carter, ed. *Dracula: The Vampire and the Critics.* Ann Arbor: UMI Research Press, 1988, pp. 69–77.

1643. Welsch, Camille-Yvette. "Welsch A Look at the Critical Reception of *Dracula.*" In Jack Lynch, ed. *Dracula.* Ipswich, MA: Salem Press, 2009, pp. 38–54.

1644. Wertsman, Vladimir F. "Who Is Dracula? Over 500 Years of Facts, Fiction and Fascination." *Multicultural Review* 5, 2 (June 1996): 54–57.

1645. Westerbeck, C. L. "Innocent Dracula: Myth Rather Than Melodrama." *Commonweal* 107 (January 18, 1980): 16–18.

1646. Wheatley, Dennis. "Introduction." In Bram Stoker. *Dracula.* London: Sphere Books, 1974, pp. 9–10.

1647. Whedon, Fay. "Bram Stoker: Hello, Thank You, and Goodbye." In *Bram Stoker's Dracula Omnibus.* London: Orion, 1992, pp.vi–xiv.

1648. Whitelaw, Nancy. *Bram Stoker: Author of Dracula.* Greensboro, NC: Morgan Reynolds, 1998. 112 pp. hb.

1649. Wicke, Jennifer. "Vampiric Typewriting: *Dracula* and Its Media." *English Literary History* 59, 2 (1992): 467–93. Rpt. in: Harold Bloom, ed. *Bram Stoker's Dracula.* Ser.: Bloom's Modern Critical Interpretations. New York: Chelsea House Publications, 2002, pp. 141–67. Excerpt rpt. in: Ken Gelder. *The Horror Reader.* New York: Routledge, 2000, pp. 172–85.

1650. Więckowska, Kararzyna. "Reality, or the Illusion of the Secret: Gothic Fictions of Masculinity." In Kararzyna Więckowska, ed. *The Gothic: Studies in History, Identity and Space.* Oxford: Interdisciplinary Press, 2012, pp. 107–17. A discussion of the nature of male gender identity. as presented in the writings of by Robert Louis Stevenson, Bram Stoker, or Joseph Conrad.

1651. Wilkinson, Charles W. *The Unification of Bram Stoker's Dracula and Its Original First Chapter, "Walpurgis Night."* Greenville, NC: East Carolina University, M.A. thesis, 1994. 55 pp. Large format.

1652. Williams, Anne. "*Dracula*: Si(g)ns of the Fathers." *Texas Studies in Literature and Language* 33, 4 (1991): 445–463.

1653. _____. "Why Are Vampires Afraid of Garlic? *Dracula.*" In Anne Williams. *Art of Dark-*

ness: A Poetics of Gothic. Chicago: University of Chicago Press, 1995, pp. 121–34.

1654. Wilson, Andrew Norman. "Introduction." In Bram Stoker. *Dracula*. Oxford: Oxford University Press, 1983, pp. vii–xix.

1655. Wilson, Deborah S. "Technologies of Misogyny: The Transparent Maternal Body and Alternate Reproductions in *Frankenstein, Dracula*, and Some Selected Media Discourses." In Deborah S. Wilson and Christine Monnera Laennec, eds. *Bodily Discursions: Genders, Representations, Technologies*. Albany: State University of New York Press, pp. 105–34.

1656. Winthrop-Young, Geoffrey. "Undead Networks: Information Processing and Media Boundary Conflicts in *Dracula*." In Donald Bruce and Anthony Purdy, eds. *Literature and Science*. Amsterdam: Rodopi, 1994, pp. 107–129.

1657. Wixson, Kellie Donovan. "*Dracula*: An Anglo-Irish Gothic Novel." In Elizabeth Miller, ed. *Dracula; The Shade and the Shadow*. Westcliff-on-Sea, Essex, UK: Desert Island Books, 1998, pp. 247–256.

1658. Wolf, Leonard, ed. *The Annotated Dracula*. New York: C. N. Potter, 1975. 362 pp. hb. dj. Large format. Rpt.: New York: Ballantine Books, 1975. 362 pp. pb. Large format. Rev. ed. as: *The Essential Dracula*. New York: Plume, 1993. 484 pp. tp. Rev. ed.: New York: ibooks/Simon & Schuster, 2004. 484 pp.

1659. _____. *Dracula: The Connoisseur's Guide*. New York: Broadway Books, 1997. 321 pp. tp.

1660. _____. *A Dream of Dracula: In Search of the Living Dead*. Boston, MA: Little, Brown, 1972. 327 pp. hb. Rpt.: London: New English Library, 1976. 326 pp. pb. Rpt.: New York: Popular Library, 1977. 326 pp. pb.

1661. _____. "Introduction." In *The Annotated Dracula*. New York: C. N. Potter, 1975, pp. viii–xviii. Rev. text in: Leonard Wolf ed. *The Essential Dracula*. New York: Plume, 1993, pp. vii–xxiii. Excerpt rpt. in: Bram Stoker. *Dracula*. Philadelphia/London: Courage Books/Running Press, 1995, pp. 515–28.

1662. _____. "Returning to *Dracula*." In Bram Stoker. *Dracula*. New York: Signet Classic, 1992, pp. i–xii. Rpt. in: Bram Stoker. *Dracula*. New York: Signet Classics, 2007, pp. v–xvi.

1663. Wolf, Leonard, and David Skal. "Beyond Dracula: New Age Evil." *Imagi-Movies* 2, 2 (Winter 1994): 24–30, 35–36, 40–41, 61.

1664. Wood, Robin. "Burying the Undead: The Use and Obsolerscence of Count Dracula." In Barry Keith Grant. *The Dread of Difference: Gender and the Horror Film*. Austin: University of Texas Press, 1996, pp. 364–78. The author compares and contrasts the figure of Count Dracula as found in Bram Stoker's original novel, the 1922 movie *Nosferatu* and the 1979 *Dracula* directed by John Badham.

1665. Wright, Julia. "Bram Stoker and Oscar Wilde: All Points East." In Julia Wright. *Ireland, India and Nationalism in Nineteenth-Century Literature*. Cambridge: Cambridge University Press, 2007, pp. 182–210.

1666. Wyman, Leah M., and George N. Dionisopoulos. "Transcending the Virgin/Whore Dichotomy: Telling Mina's Story in *Bram Stoker's Dracula*." *Women's Studies in Communication* 23, 2 (Spring 2000): 209–37.

1667. Wynne, Catherine. "Bram Stoker, Geneviève Ward and *The Lady of the Shroud*: Gothic Weddings and Performing Vampires." *English Literature in Transition (1880–1920)* 49, 3 (2006): 251–71.

1668. Yong Hall, Jasmine. "Solicitors Soliciting: The Dangerous Circulations of Professionalism in *Dracula*." In Barbara Leah Harman and Susan Meyer, eds. *The New Nineteenth Century: Feminist Readings of Underrated Victorian Fiction*. New York, Garland, 1996, pp. 97–117.

1669. Youngson, Jeanne Keyes. *Dracula Made Easy*. New York: Hearthstone Book/Carlton Press, 1978. 32 pp. hb. Literature.

1670. Yu, Erc Kwan-Wai. "Productive Fear: Labor, Sexuality, and Mimicry in Bram Stoker's *Dracula*." *Texas Studies in Literature and Language* 48, 2, (Summer 2006): 145–170.

1671. Zanger, Jules. "A Sympathetic Vibration: Dracula and the Jews." *English Literature in Transition 1880–1920* 34 (1991): 33–44.

1672. Zhanial, Susanne. *Monsters on the Margin—the Abject in Literature: A Study of* The Phantom of the Opera, Dracula *and* She. Saarbrücken, Germany: VDM Verlag, 2009. 188 pp. tp.

1673. Zieger, Susan Marjorie. "Un-Death and Bare Life: Addiction and Eugenics in *Dracula* and *The Blood of the Vampire*." In Susan Marjorie Zieger. *Inventing the Addict: Drugs, Race and Sexuality in Nineteenth-Century British and American Literature*. Amherst: University of Massachusetts Press, 2008, pp. 136–232.

Vampire Literature Since Dracula

During the first half of the twentieth century, the number of vampire-themed novels and short stories increased steadily, though not spectacularly, with many short stories appearing in the growing number of inexpensive literary magazines especially those emphasizing fantasy, science fiction and/or horror. Few pieces of the literature stand out, possibly the most notable being the appearances of the vampire in the writings of authors most known for their literary output otherwise such as mystery writer John Dickson Carr, fantasy writer Robert E. Howard, and the adventure writer Sax Rohmer. This literature, in which the vampire is always a villain, culminates in the science fiction novel of Richard Matheson, *I Am Legend*.

The literary popularity of the vampire would be radically changed toward the end of the 1960s when the vampire villain would be joined by two additional figures, the conflicted vampire and the hero vampire, popularly termed the "good guy" vampire. Conflicted vampires remain the bloodsucking killers presented in nineteenth century vampire novels, but gain the sympathy of the audience with their suffering under the dilemma in which they are found, being forced to kill in order to remain alive. Conflicted vampires retain their humanity and sense of morality and either seek a means to escape or learn to cope with their situation. In either case, vampires were provided with a broad, almost infinite, range of new possibilities as literary characters and their early exemplars—*Dark Shadows'* Barnabas Collins and Anne Rice's protagonists Louis and Lestat quickly became endeared to a host of fans.

The conflicted vampire would be joined by the vampire hero/heroine, the first example being a comic book character, the extraterrestrial Vampirella, who hails from another planet where blood flows like water and is so consumed. Traveling to earth, Vampirella quickly finds a blood substitute on which to survive and can subsequently emerge as a super-hero. The hero vampires, sometimes termed "moral vampires," retain all of their human moral sense, refusing to kill humans in pursuit of their needed nourishment, and ultimately locate an alternative source of blood (from animals, blood banks, or a blood substitute) so they do not have to steal it directly from victims who either die in the encounter or are left physically harmed and feeling personally violated. Such good guy vampires could emerge as leading characters in novels (and later in movies and television shows), and enjoy the same spectrum of roles, choices, and possibilities as any non-vampire character.

The emergence of three basic vampire types—the villain, the conflicted vampire, and the hero vampire—allowed the emergence of a new broad vampire literature which increased spectacularly decade-by-decade beginning in the 1970s. Over half of all the vampire novels ever written have been published in the first decade of the 21st century. Especially notable has been the inclusion of the vampire in romance literature (with over half of all sales in paperback books now being romance novels) and the designation of paranormal romance as a significant subgenre. The vampire paranormal romance novels far outnumber the other paranormal subgenres, each of which feature a different supernatural character—werewolves, fairies, ghosts, witches, etc.

Also, beginning with Daniel Ross, Chelsea Quinn Yarbro, Fred Saberhagen, and Anne Rice, a growing number of authors appeared who did not just write one or two vampire novels, but who dedicated much of their literary career to writing vampire-themed stories, most around a rather limited number of characters whose story is developed in a dozen or more novels—Brian Lumley, Laurel Hamilton, Sherrilyn Kenyon, Charlene Hamilton, Amanda Ashley, Mary Janice Davidson, Christine Feehan, and the list goes on. In the romance field, the idea of writing novels in series has become commonplace and a host of vampire series have appeared, many being planned before the first book rolls off the press.

The success of the paranormal romance writers would be followed by an emerging host of juvenile writers adapting the vampire for encounters for children and youth. The youth-oriented literature almost exclusively focuses on the good guy vampire, though some of the more successful series (*Buffy the Vampire Slayer*, *The Vampire Diaries*, Vampire Academy, and the Twilight Saga) prominently feature conflicts between good and bad vampires. Much of the children's vampire literature is built around characters like Bunnicula, the vampire rabbit, the epitome of the vegetarian vampire.

The contemporary development of vampire literature has, understandably, yet to prompt the amount of attention that has been devoted to *Dracula* and other nineteenth century literature. Much of this literature is viewed as popular storytelling rather than serious literature, and with the exception of the writings of a few (like Laurel Hamilton) prompted little comment. Most who have received comment, like Charlaine Harris and L. J. Smith, have done so after their work was adapted for television or the movies, and most of the comment has gone to the screen versions rather than the novels themselves. It will take another generation to see which of the recent literature will survive and find some lasting resonance with literary scholars and commentators.

1674. Ames, Melissa. "Vamping up Sex: Audience, Age & Portrayals of Sexuality in Vampire Narratives." *Journal of Dracula Studies* 12 (2010): 83–104. Posted at: http://www.blooferland.com/drc/index.php?title=Journal_of_Dracula_Studies.

1675. Anderson, James. "The Necroscope Saga." In Anthony Timpone. *Fangoria Vampires.* New York: HarperPrism, 1996, pp. 215–22.

1676. Antoni, Rita. "A Vampiric Relation to Feminism: The Monstrous-Feminine in Whitley Strieber's and Anne Rice's Gothic Fiction." *Americana: E-Journal of American Studies in Hungary* 4, 1 (Spring 2008). Posted at http://americanaejournal.hu/vol4no1/antoni.

1677. Antosh, Ruth B. "Michel Tremblay and the Fantastic of Violence." In William Coyle, ed. *Aspects of Fantasy: Selected Essays from the Second International Conference on the Fantastic in Literature and Film.* Westport, CT: Greenwood Press, 1986, pp. 17–22.

1678. Ashwood, Sharon. "Death Becomes Her." In Laurell K. Hamilton with Leah Wilson, eds. *Ardeur: 14 Writers on the Anita Blake, Vampire Hunter Series.* Dallas, TX: BenBella Books, 2010, pp. 151–61.

1679. Bailie, Helen T. "Blood Ties: The Vampire Lover in the Popular Romance." *Journal of American Culture* 34, 2 (2011): 141–148.

1680. Bak, John S. "Preface: Bad Blood; or, Victorian Vampires in the Postmodern Age of AIDS." In John S. Bak, ed. *Post/modern Dracula: From Victorian Themes to Postmodern Praxis.* Cambridge: Cambridge Scholars Publishing, 2007, pp. xi–xxiv.

1681. Bak, John S., ed. *Post/modern Dracula: From Victorian Themes to Postmodern Praxis.* Newcastle, UK: Cambridge Scholars Publishing, 2007. 180 pp. Includes contributions by William Hughes, Ludmilla Kostova, David Punter, Nathalie Saudo, Françoise Dupeyron-Lafay, Monica Girard, Jean Marigny, Jean-Marie Lecomte, and Jacques Coulardeau.

1682. Ballesteros-Gonzáles, Antonio. "Count Dracula's Bloody Inheritors: The Postmodern Vampire." In Dominique Sipière, ed. *Dracula: Insémination. Dissémination.* Amiens: Sterne, 1996, pp. 107–19.

1683. Baran, Henryk. "Some Reminiscences in Blok: Vampirism and Its Antecedents." In Walter N. Vickery and Bogdan B. Sagatov, eds. *Aleksandr Blok Centennial Conference.* Columbus, OH: Slavica, 1984, pp. 43–60. Poetry.

1684. Barnes, Jennifer Lynn. "Sweet Caroline." In Red and Vee. *A Visitor's Guide to Mystic Falls.* Dallas, TX: Smart Pop/Benbella Books, 2010, pp. 143–57.

1685. Barr, Marleen S. "Holding Fast to Feminism and Moving Beyond: Suzy McKee Charnas's *The Vampire Tapestry.*" In Tom Staicar, ed. *The Feminine Eye: Science Fiction and the Women Who Write It.* New York: Ungar, 1982, pp. 60–72.

1686. _____. "Suzy McKee Charnas." In Marleen S. Barr, Ruth Salvaggio, and Richard Law. *Suzy McKee Charnas, Octavia Butler, and Joan D. Vigne.* Mercer Island, WA: Starmont House, 1986, pp. 7–52.

1687. Benefiel, Candace R. "Fangs for the Memories: Vampires in the Nineties." *Wilson Library Bulletin* (May 1995): 35–38.

1688. Benefiel, Candace R. *Reading Laurell K. Hamilton.* Santa Barbara, CA: Libraries Unlimited, 2011. 163 pp. hb. boards.

1689. Berka, Sigrid. "'Das bissigste Stück der Saison': The Textual and Sexual Politics of Vampirism in Elfriede Jelinek's *Krankheit oder Moderne Frauen.*" *The German Quarterly* 68, 4 (1995): 372–388.

1690. Beville, Maria. "Gothic Politics and the Mythology of the Vampire: Brendan Kennelly's Postcolonial Inversions in Cromwell: A Poem." In Tabish. Khair and Johan Hoglund, eds. *Transnational and Postcolonial Vampires: Dark Blood.* Basingstoke, UK: Palgrave Macmillan, 2012, pp. 153–72.

1691. Blue, David McDowell. *Your Vampire Story: (And How to Write It).* N.p.: Thornkirk Press, 2012. 64 pp. tp.

1692. Bodart, Joni Richards. "Vampires: The Aristocratic Monster." In Joni Richards Bodart. *They Suck, They Bite, They Eat, They Kill: The Psychological Meaning of Supernatural Monsters in Young Adult Fiction.* Ser.: Scarecrow Studies in Young Adult Literature. Lanham, MD: Scarecrow Press, 2011, pp. 3–73. Includes comments on the works of Curtis Klause, Cynthia Leityich Smith, Melissa de la Cruz, Alexandra Harvey, Heather Brewer, and Beth Fantaskey.

1693. Bosky, Bernadette Lynn. "Making the Implicit, Explicit: Vampire Erotica and Pornography." In Leonard Heldreth and Mary Pharr, eds. *The Blood Is the Life: Vampires in Literature.* Bowling Green, KY: Bowling Green State University Press, 1999, pp. 217–33.

1694. Botting, Fred. "Romance Consumed: Death, Simulation and the Vampire." In Fred Botting. *Gothic Romanced: Consumption, Gender and Technology in Contemporary Fictions.* Abingdon, UK: Routledge, 2008, pp. 60–105.

1695. Boyer, David. Pittsburgh, PA: Whitmore Publishing, 2010. 252 pp. tp. This volume includes interviews with a number of horror writers known for their vampire volumes including Anne Rice, Kim Newman, Laura Bickle, Tamara Thorne, Craig Spector, and John Skipp.

1696. Brinks, Ellen, and Lee Talley. "Unfamiliar Ties: Lesbian Constructions of Home and Family in Jeanette Winterson's *Oranges Are Not the Only Fruit* and Jewelle Gomez's *The Gilda Stories.*" In Catherine Wiley and Fiona R. Barnes, eds. *Homemaking: Women Writers and the Politics of Home.* New York: Garland, 1996, pp. 145–74.

1697. Browning, John Edgar. "The Dangerous Dead." In P. C. Cast, ed. *Nyx in the House of Night: Mythology, Folklore and Religion in the P. C. and Kristin Cast Vampyres Series.* Dallas, TX: Benbella Books, 2011, pp. 13–29.

1698. Brox, Ali. "'Every Age Has the Vampire It Needs': Octavia Butler's Vampiric Vision in *Fledgling.*" *Utopian Studies* 19, 3 (Summer 2008): 391–409.

1699. Burke, Jessica. "Consuming the Other: Cannibals and Vampires in Carmen Boullosa's Fiction." *Romance Notes* 49, 2 (April 2009): 177ff.

1700. Byron, Glennis, and Aspasia Stephanou. "Neo-imperialism and the Apocalyptic Vampire Narrative: Justin Cronin's *The Passage.*" In Tabish. Khair and Johan Hoglund, eds. *Transnational and Postcolonial Vampires: Dark Blood.* Basingstoke, UK: Palgrave Macmillan, 2012, pp. 189–201.

1701. Carter, Margaret L. *Different Blood: The Vampire as Alien.* N.p.: Amber Quill Press, 2004. 158 pp. tp.

1702. _____. "Feminism and the Liberated Vampire." *The Vampire Journal* 8 (Summer 1989): 51–53.

1703. _____. "From Villain to Hero." In Rosemary Ellen Guiley, with J. B. Macabre. *The Complete Vampire Companion.* New York: Macmillan, 1994, pp. 67–72.

1704. _____. "A Gravedigger's Dozen of Outstanding Vampire Tales." *NIEKAS 45: Essays on Dark Fantasy.* Center Harbor, NH: Niekas Publications, 1998, pp. 39–43.

1705. ____. "I, Strahd: Narrative Voice and Variations on a Non-Player Character in TSR's 'Ravenloft' Universe." In James Craig Holte, ed. *The Fantastic Vampire: Studies in the Children of the Night: Selected Essays from the Eighteenth International Conference on the Fantastic in the Arts.* Vol. 19. Westport, CT: Greenwood Publishing Group, 2002, pp. 89–99.

1706. ____. "Interview with Suzy McKee Charnas." *The Vampire's Crypt* 2 (Summer 1990): 3–10.

1707. ____. "Revampings of Dracula in Contemporary Fiction." *Journal of Dracula Studies* 3 (2001): 15–19. Rpt.: Elizabeth Miller, ed. *Bram Stoker's Dracula: A Documentary Volume.* Detroit: Thompson/Gale, 2005, pp. 337–41.

1708. ____. "Share Alike: Dracula and the Sympathetic Vampire in Mid–Twentieth Century Pulp Fiction." In Carol Margaret Davison, ed., with Paul Simpson-Housley. *Bram Stoker's Dracula: Sucking through the Century, 1897–1997.* Toronto: Dundurn Press, 1997, pp. 175–94.

1709. ____. "The Vampire." In S. T. Joshi, ed. *Icons of Horror and the Supernatural: An Encyclopedia of Our Worst Nightmares.* Westport, CT: Greenwood Press, 2007.

1710. ____. "The Vampire as Alien in Contemporary Fiction." In Joan Gordon and Veronica Hollinger, eds. *Blood Read: The Vampire as Metaphor in Contemporary Culture.* Philadelphia: University of Pennsylvania Press, 1997, pp. 27–44.

1711. ____. "Vampire Human Symbiosis in *Fevre Dream* and the *Empire of Fear*." In Leonard Heldreth and Mary Pharr, eds. *The Blood Is the Life: Vampires in Literature.* Bowling Green, KY: Bowling Green State University Press, 1999, pp. 165–76.

1712. ____. *Vampirism in Literature: Shadow of a Shade.* New York: Gordon Press, 1975. 176 pp. hb. dj.

1713. ____. "Xenophobia and Its Subversion in *Darker Than You Think*." *Journal of Dracula Studies* 4 (2002). Posted at http://www.bloofer land.com/drc/index.php?title=Journal_of_ Dracula_Studies.

1714. Case, Alison A. "Tracking the Vampire." *Differences: A Journal of Feminist Cultural Studies* 3 (1991): 1–20. Rpt. in Ken Gelder, ed. *The Horror Reader.* London: Routledge, 2000, pp. 198–209.

1715. Cast, P. C., with Kim Doner. *The Fledgling Handbook 101.* New York: St. Martin's Griffin, 2010. 157 pp. tp.

1716. Cast, P. C. with Leah Wilson. *Nyx in the House of Night: Mythology, Folklore and Religion in the P. C. and Kristin Cast Vampyres Series.* Dallas, TX: Benbella Books, 2011. 219 pp. tp.

1717. Castellana, Christina. "Holding on to Self: The Masculine Drive in 'Investigating Jericho' and *I Am Legend*." *Journal of Dracula Studies* 10 (2008): 26–30. Posted at http://www.bloofer land.com/drc/index.php?title=Journal_of_ Dracula_Studies.

1718. Caudle, Jenifer M. *Queer Blood: The Vampire as Sexually Transgressive Literary Image.* Birmingham: University of Alabama at Birmingham, M.A. thesis, 1993. 68 pp. Large format.

1719. Chambers, Claire, and Sue Chaplin. "Bilqis the Vampire Slayer: Sarwat Chadda's British Muslim Vampire Fiction." In Tabish. Khair and Johan Hoglund, eds. *Transnational and Postcolonial Vampires: Dark Blood.* Basingstoke, UK: Palgrave Macmillan, 2012, pp. 138–52.

1720. Charnas, Suzy McKee. "Meditations in Red: On Writing *The Vampire Tapestry*." In Joan Gordon and Veronica Hollinger, eds. *Blood Read: The Vampire as Metaphor in Contemporary Culture.* Philadelphia: University of Pennsylvania Press, 1997, pp. 59–67.

1721. Cheiro. "The Haunting Horror of the White Bat." In *True Ghost Stories.* London: The London Publishing Company, n.d. [ca. 1929]. 269 pp,.

1722. Cheng, Vincent J. "Stephen Dedalus and the Black Panther Vampire." *James Joyce Quarterly* 24, 2 (Winter 1978): 161–176.

1723. Christensen, Alaina. "New Readings of the Vampire. Blood-Abstinent Vampires & the Women Who Consume Them." In Barbara Brodman and James E. Doan, eds. *Images of the Modern Vampire: The Hip and the Atavistic.* Madison. NJ: Fairleigh Dickinson University Press, 2013, pp. 131–46.

1724. Clamp, Cathy. "Mom! There's Something Dead Sucking on My Neck." In Laurell K. Hamilton with Leah Wilson, eds. *Ardeur: 14 Writers on the Anita Blake, Vampire Hunter Series.* Dallas, TX: BenBella Books, 2010, pp. 71–78.

1725. Clare, Cassandra, and Joshua Lewis. *The Shadowhunter's Codex.* New York: Margaret K. McElderry Books, 2013. 274 pp. hb. slipcase.

1726. Clark, Maureen. "Terror as White Female in Mudrooroo's Vampire Trilogy." *Journal of Commonwealth Literature* 41, 2, (2006): 121–138.

1727. Clasen, Mathias. "Vampire Apocalypse: A Biocultural Critique of Richard Matheson's *I Am Legend.*" *Philosophy and Literature* 34, 2 (2010): 313–328.

1728. Clements, Susannah. The *Vampire Defanged: How the Embodiment of Evil Became a Romantic Hero.* Grand Rapids, MI: Brazos Press, 2011. 197 pp. tp. The *Vampire Defanged: How the Embodiment of Evil Became a Romantic Hero* received the 2012 award for the best nonfiction book of the previous year given annually by the Lord Ruthven Society.

1729. Clemon, Gregory A. *The Vampire Figure in Contemporary Latin American Narrative Fiction.* Gainesville: University of Florida, Ph.D. dissertation, 1996. 331 pp. Large format.

1730. Cleto, Sara. "'Darkness has too much to offer': Revising the Gothic Vampire." *Supernatural Studies* 1, 1 (Summer 2013): 53–64.

1731. Clifton, Jacob. "Showing the Scars." In Laurell K. Hamilton with Leah Wilson, eds. *Ardeur: 14 Writers on the Anita Blake, Vampire Hunter Series.* Dallas, TX: BenBella Books, 2010, pp. 183–96.

1732. Cokal, Susann. "'Hot with rapture and cold with fear': Grotesque, Sublime, and Postmodern Transformations in Patrick Süskind's *Perfume.*" In Thomas Fahy. *The Philosophy of Horror.* Lexington: University Press of Kentucky, 2010, pp. 179–96.

1733. Collings, Michael R. "Vampires in Space: Fantasy and Science Fiction in Colin Wilson's *The Mind Parasites* and *The Space Vampires.*" In Leonard Heldreth and Mary Pharr, eds. *The Blood Is the Life: Vampires in Literature.* Bowling Green, KY: Bowling Green State University Press, 1999, pp. 187–95.

1734. Cook, Dylan, comp. *Beguiled: Enchanted by the Modern Day Vampire.* N.p.: the author, 2011. 229 pp. tp.

1735. Corstorphine, Kevin. "Panic on the Streets of Stockholm: Sub/urban Alienation in the Novels of John Ajvide Lindqvist." In Eoghain Hamilton. *The Gothic: Probing the Boundaries.* Oxford: Inter-Disciplinary Press, 2010, pp. 137–44. Rpt. in Gord Barentsen, ed. *A Language Spoken in Tongues: Essays of the Transcultural Gothic.* Oxford: Inter-Disciplinary Press, 2012, pp.

1736. Cranny-Francis, Anne. "De-Fanging the Vampire: S. M. Charnas's *The Vampire Tapestry* as Subversive Horror Fiction." In Brian Docherty, ed. *American Horror Fiction: From Brockden Brown to Stephen King.* New York: St. Martin's Press, 1900, pp. 155–175.

1737. Crişan, Marius. "Vampire Narratives as Juggling with Romanian History: Dan Simmons's *Children of the Night* and Elizabeth Kostova's *The Historian.*" In Simon Bacon, and Katarzyna Bronk, eds. *Undead Memory: Vampires and Human Memory in Popular Culture.* Bern, Switz.: Peter Lang International Academic Publishers, 2013, pp. 59–84.

1738. Crossen, Carys. "'Would you please stop trying to take your clothes off?': Abstinence and Impotence of Male Vampires in Contemporary Fiction and Television." In Elizabeth Nelson with Jillian Burcar & Hannah Priest, eds. *Creating Humanity, Discovering Monstrosity.* Oxford: Inter-Disciplinary Press, 2010, pp. 251–60.

1739. Crow, Charles L. "Fear, Ambiguity, and Transgression: The Gothic Novel in the United States." In Alfred Bendixen, ed. *A Companion to the American Novel.* Hoboken, NJ: Wiley-Blackwell, 2012, pp. 127–146.

1740. Dane, Jordan. "The Magic of Being Cherokee." In P. C. Cast, ed. *Nyx in the House of Night: Mythology, Folklore and Religion in the P. C. and Kristin Cast Vampyres Series.* Dallas, TX: Benbella Books, 2011, pp. 89–100.

1741. Davis, Kathy Sue. "Beauty in the Beast: The 'Feminization' of Weyland in the *Vampire Tapestry.*" *Extrapolation* 43, 1 (2002): 62–79.

1742. _____. "Re-Vamping the Self: History, Storytelling, and the Vampire Protagonist." A paper presented at The 23rd Annual International Conference on the Fantastic in the Arts. Fort Lauderdale, March 20–24, 2002.

1743. _____. *Sympathy for the Devil: Female Authorship and the Literary Vampire.* Columbus: Ohio State University, Ph.D. dissertation, 1999. 247 pp. Large format.

1744. Day, Robert Adams. "How Stephen Wrote His Vampire Poem." *James Joyce Quarterly* 17 (Winter 1970): 183–97.

1745. Dean, John. "The Immigrant of Darkness: The Vampire in American Fiction." *Foundation: The Review of Science Fiction* 33 (Spring 1985): 19–24.

1746. Dickie, James. "Introduction." In James Dickie, ed. *The Undead: Vampire Masterpieces.* London: Neville Spearman, 1971, pp. 11–25. Rpt.: London, Pan Books, 1973, pp. 11–26.

1747. Edwards, Rachel. "Myth, Allegory and Michael Tournier." *Journal of European Studies* 19, 2 (1989): 99–121.

1748. Ellington, Devon. "Ardeur's Purpose." In Laurell K. Hamilton with Leah Wilson, eds. *Ardeur: 14 Writers on the Anita Blake, Vampire Hunter Series.* Dallas, TX: BenBella Books, 2010, pp. 107–19.

1749. Faegen, Trinity. "The Otherworld Is Greek to Me." In P. C. Cast, ed. *Nyx in the House of Night: Mythology, Folklore and Religion in the P. C. and Kristin Cast Vampyres Series.* Dallas, TX: Benbella Books, 2011, pp. 119–27.

1750. Faxneld, Per. "Feminist Vampires and the Romantic Satanist Tradition of Counter-Readings." In Andrea Ruthven and Gabriela Mádlo, eds. *Women as Angel, Women as Evil: Interrogating the Boundaries.* Oxford: Inter-Disciplinary Press, 2012.

1751. Fenicchia, Lindsey M. *The Modern Vampire as Romantic Hero: Acceptance, Love and Self-Control.* Brockport, NY: The College at Brockport, M.A. thesis, 2012. 64 pp. Large format. Posted at http://digitalcommons.brockport.edu/eng_theses/3/.

1752. Fitzgerald, Gil. "History as Horror: Chelsea Quinn Yarbro." In Darnell Schweitzer, ed. *Discovering Modern Horror Fiction, II.* Mercer Island, WA: Starmont House, 1988, pp. 128–34.

1753. Flanagan, Caitlin. "What Girls Want: A Series of Vampire Novels Illuminates the Complexities of Female Adolescent Desire." *The Atlantic* 302 (December 2008): 108–120.

1754. Flessner, Robert F. "Demian and Omophagia." *Germanic Notes* 17, 2 (1986): 21–23.

1755. Fondren, Natasha. "The Domestication of a Vampire Executioner" In Laurell K. Hamilton with Leah Wilson, eds. *Ardeur: 14 Writers on the Anita Blake, Vampire Hunter Series.* Dallas, TX: BenBella Books, 2010, pp. 91–104.

1756. Foster, Thomas C. "Nice to Eat You: Acts of Vampires." In Thomas C. Foster. *How to Read Literature Like a Professor: A Lively and Entertaining Guide to Reading Between the Lines.* New York: Harper Perennial, 2003, pp. 15–21.

1757. Foust, Ronald. "Rite of Passage: The Vampire Tale as Cosmogonic Myth." In William Coyle, ed. *Aspects of Fantasy: Selected Essays from the Second International Conference on the Fantastic in Literature and Film.* Westport, CT: Greenwood, 1986, pp. 73–84.

1758. Francine, Christina. "A Visit with Chelsea Quinn Yarbro." *Internet Journal of Science Fiction* 2, 5 (June 2005). Posted at: http://www.irosf.com/q/zine/article/10155.

1759. Frisch, Adam J. "Holding Fast to Feminism and Moving Beyond: Suzy McKee Charnas's The Vampire Tapestry." In Thomas Staicar, ed. *The Feminine Eye: Science Fiction and the Women Who Write It.* New York: Ungar Co., 1982, pp. 60–72.

1760. Frost, R. L. "A Race of Devils: Frankenstein, Dracula and Science Fiction." *Journal of Dracula Studies* 5 (2003): 1–10. Posted at: http://www.blooferland.com/drc/index.php?title=Journal_of_Dracula_Studies.

1761. Galenorn, Yasmine. "She Is Goddess." In P. C. Cast, ed. *Nyx in the House of Night: Mythology, Folklore and Religion in the P. C. and Kristin Cast Vampyres Series.* Dallas, TX: Benbella Books, 2011, pp. 153–66.

1762. Gee, James Paul, and Elisabeth R. Hayes. "A Young Girl and Her Vampire Stories: How a Teenager Competes with a Best-Selling Author." In James Paul Gee and Elisabeth R. Hayes. *Women and Gaming: The Sims and 21st Century Learning.* New York: Palgrave Macmillan, 2010, pp. 125–44.

1763. Gelder, Ken, ed. *The Horror Reader.* New York: Routledge, 2000. 414 pp. tp.

1764. _____. *Reading the Vampire.* London: Routledge, 1994. 161 pp. tp.

1765. Gilbert, John. "Wamphyri: Vampires for Modern Times." In Rosemary Ellen Guiley, with J. B. Macabre. *The Complete Vampire Companion.* New York: Macmillan, 1994, pp. 89–92.

1766. Gilpin, Vicky. "Vampires and Female Spiritual Transformation: Laurell K. Hamilton's Anita Blake, Vampire Hunter." In Kim Paffenroth and John W. Morehead, eds. *The Undead and Theology.* Eugene, OR: Pickwick Publications, 2012, pp. 3–18.

1767. Gomez, Jewelle. "Speculative Fiction and Black Lesbians." *Signs: Journal of Women in Culture and Society* 18, 4 (Summer 1993): 948–56.

1768. Gordillo, Adriana. "Dracula Comes to Mexico: Carlos Fuentes's Vlad, Echoes of Origins, and the Return of Colonialism." In Barbara Brodman and James E. Doan, eds. *The Universal Vampire: Origins and Evolution of a Legend.* Madison, NJ: Fairleigh Dickinson University Press, 2013, pp. 209–23.

1769. Gordon, Joan. "Rehabilitating Revenants, or Sympathetic Vampires in Recent Fiction." *Extrapolation: A Journal of Science Fiction and Fantasy* 29, 3 (Fall 1988): 227–34.

1770. Gordon, Joan. "Sharper Than a Serpent's Tooth: The Vampire in Search of Its Mother." In Joan Gordon and Veronica Hollinger, eds. *Blood Read: The Vampire as Metaphor in Contemporary Culture.* Philadelphia: University of Pennsylvania Press, 1997, pp. 45–55.

1771. Gordon, Joan, and Veronica Hollinger, eds. *Blood Read: The Vampire as Metaphor in Contemporary Culture.* Philadelphia: University of Pennsylvania Press, 1997. 264 pp. Contains articles by Brian Aldiss, Joan Gordon and Veronica Hollinger, Nina Auerbach, Jules Zanger, Margaret L. Carter, Joan Gordon, Suzy McKee Charnas, Brian Stableford, Jewelle Gumez, Nicola Nixon, Rob Latham, Miriam Jones, Trevor Holmes, Mari Kotani, and Veronica Hollinger.

1772. Grady, Frank. "Vampire Culture." In Jeffrey Jerome Cohen, ed. *Monster Theory: Reading Culture.* Minneapolis: University of Minnesota Press, 1996, pp. 25–41.

1773. Greenberg, Louis. "Sins of the Blood: Rewriting the Family in Two Postmodern Vampire Novels." *Journal of Literary Studies* 26, 1 (2010): 163–178.

1774. Gresh, Lois H. *The Mortal Instruments Companion: City of Bones, Shadowhunters, and the Sight: The Unauthorized Guide.* New York: St. Martin's Griffin York, 2013. 215 pp. tp.

1775. Gross, Louis S. *Redefining the American Gothic: From Wieland to the Day of the Dead.* Ann Arbor: UMI Research Press, 1989. Cf. pp. 48–52.

1776. Grossman, Gael Elyse. *The Evolution of the Vampire in Adolescent Literature.* East Lansing: Michigan State University, Ph.D. dissertation, 2001. 166 pp. Large format.

1777. Guyant, Valerie L. Vixen, *Virgin or Vamp? Female Characters in Vampire Literature Past and Present.* Rockford: Northern Illinois University, Ph.D. dissertation, 2011. 329 pp. Large format.

1778. Hamilton, Laurell K., ed. *Ardeur: 14 Writers on the Anita Blake Vampire Hunter Series.*

Dallas: BenBella Books, 2010. 196 pp. Includes contributions from Nick Mamatas, Heather Swain, Lilith Saintcrow. L. Jagi Lamplighter, Marella Sands. Cathy Clamp, Alasdair Stuart, Natasha Fondren, Devon Ellington, Melissa L. Tatum, Mihhail Lyubanshy, Sharon Ashwood, Vera Nazarian, and Jacob Clifton.

1779. Hardaway, Elizabeth. "'Ourselves Expanded': The Vampire's Evolution from Bram Stoker to Kim Newman." In Leonard Heldreth and Mary Pharr, eds. *The Blood Is the Life: Vampires in Literature.* Bowling Green, KY: Bowling Green State University Press, 1999, pp. 177–186.

1780. Harrison, Kim. *The Hallows Insider. New Fiction, Facts, Maps, Murders, and More in the World of Rachel Morgan.* New York: Harper Voyager, 2011. 301 pp. hb. dj.

1781. Heldreth, Leonard, and Mary Pharr, eds. *The Blood Is the Life: Vampires in Literature.* Bowling Green, KY: Bowling Green State University Press, 1999. 275 pp. hb. & tp.

1782. Heldreth, Lillian Marks. "Vampire Variations: Tanith Lee's Evolution of the Genre." In Leonard Heldreth and Mary Pharr, eds. *The Blood Is the Life: Vampires in Literature.* Bowling Green, KY: Bowling Green State University Press, 1999, pp. 235–45.

1783. Hendershot, Cyndy. "Vampire and Replicant: The One-Sex Body in a Two-Sex World." *Science Fiction Studies* 22 (1995): 373–98.

1784. Heumann, Michael Douglas. *Ghost in the Machine: Sound and Technology in Twentieth Century Literature.* Riverside: University of California, Ph.D. dissertation, 1998. 226 pp. Large format.

1785. Hillyer, Vincent. "The Enigma of the Count of Saint Germain." In Shepard, Leslie, and Albert Power. *Dracula: Celebrating 100 Years.* Dublin, Ireland: Mentor Press, 1977, pp. 78–83.

1786. Hofman-Howley, Ingrid. "Romancing the Vampire: The Lives and Loves of Two Vampire Slayers–Anita and Buffy." *Refractory: A Journal of Entertainment Media* 8 (2005). Posted at: http://refractory.unimelb.edu.au/2008/08/22/refractory-volume-8–2005/.

1787. Höglund, Johan. "Catastrophic Transculturation in *Dracula, The Strain* and *The Historian.*" *Transnational Literature* 5, 1 (2012): 1–11. Posted at: http://dspace.flinders.edu.au/jspui/bitstream/2328/26432/1/Catastrophic_Transculturation.pdf. A paper originally presented at the conference on the Post/Colonial and Transcultural: Contending Modernities, Presaging Globalisation, sponsored by the the Nordic Network for Literary Transculturation Studies.

1788. Holland-Toll, Linda J. "Harder Than Nails, Harder Than Spade: Anita Blake as "The Tough Guy" Detective." *The Journal of American Culture* 27, 2 (June 2004): 175–189,.

1789. Hollinger, Veronica. "Fantasies of Absence: The Postmodern Vampire." In Joan Gordon and Veronica Hollinger, eds. *Blood Read: The Vampire as Metaphor in Contemporary Culture*. Philadelphia: University of Pennsylvania Press, 1997, pp. 199–212.

1790. _____. "The Vampire and/as the Alien." *Journal of the Fantastic in the Arts* 5, 3 (1993): 5–17.

1791. _____. "The Vampire and the Alien: Gothic Horror and Science Fiction." In Carol Margaret Davison, ed., with Paul Simpson-Housley. *Bram Stoker's Dracula: Sucking through the Century, 1897–1997*. Toronto: Dundurn Press, 1997, pp. 213–230.

1792. _____. "The Vampire and the Alien: Variations on the Outsider." *Science Fiction Studies* 16, 2 (July 1989): 145–60. Posted at: http://www.depauw.edu/sfs/pioneers/hollinger%2048.htm.

1793. Howe, Deborah, and James Howe. *Bunnicula*. Ser.: Troll Book Buzz Teacher Guide. Manwah, NJ: Troll Associates, 1995. 17 pp. pb. Large format.

1794. Hughes, William. "The Taste of Blood Meant the End of Aloneness': Vampires and Gay Men in Poppy Z. Brite's *Lost Souls*." In William Hughes and Andrew Smith. *Queering the Gothic*. Manchester: Manchester University Press, 2009, pp. 142–57.

1795. Jackson, Rosemary. *Fantasy: The Literature of Subversion*. London: Methuen, 1981. 211 pp. hb. & tp.

1796. Jones, Miriam. "The Gilda Stories: Revealing the Monsters at the Margins." In Joan Gordon and Veronica Hollinger, eds. *Blood Read: The Vampire as Metaphor in Contemporary Culture*. Philadelphia: University of Pennsylvania Press, 1997, pp. 151–67.

1797. Jones, Robert Kenneth. *The Shudder Pulps: A History of the Weird Menace Magazines of the 1930s*. West Linn, OR: FAX Collector's Editions. 1975. 238 pp.

1798. Jones, Stephen, and Jo Fletcher, eds. *Secret City: Strange Tales of London*. London: Titan Books, 1997. 142 pp. hb. Large format. Limited to 300 copies on occasion of World Fantasy Convention of 1997.

1799. Jowett, Lorna. "Between the Jaws of the Tender Wolf: Authorship, Adaptation, and Audience." In Sonya Andermahr and Lawrence Phillips, eds. *Angela Carter: New Critical Readings*. London: Bloomsbury Academic, 2012, pp. 33–43.

1800. Judge, Virginia. *Contemporary Literary Treatments of the Vampire*. Winthrop College, M.A. thesis, 1988. 64 pp. Large format.

1801. Kenyon, Sherrilyn, with Althea Kontis. *The Dark-Hunter Companion*. New York: St. Martin's Griffin, 2007. 420 pp. tr.pb.

1802. Ketchum, Jack. "On *I Am Legend*." In Stanley Waiter, Matthew Bradley, and Paul Stuve. *The Twilight and Other Zones: The Dark Worlds of Richard Matheson*. New York: Citadel Press, 2009, pp. 134–42.

1803. Khader, J. "Will the Real Robert Neville Please, Come Out? Vampirism, the Ethics of Queer Monstrosity, and Capitalism in Richard Matheson's *I Am Legend*?" *Journal of Homosexuality* 60, 4 (2013): 532–57.

1804. King, Maureen. "Contemporary Women Writers and the 'New Evil': The Vampires of Anne Rice and Suzy McKee Charnas." *Journal of the Fantastic in the Arts* 5, 3 (1993): 75–84.

1805. Kisner, Adrienne L. *Reading Between the Lines: The Potential of Popular Young Adult Fiction in Adolescent Spiritual Formation*. Boston, MA: Boston University School of Theology, Ph.D. dissertation, 2011. 226 pp. Large format.

1806. Koetting, Christopher. "Vampire Classic: *I Am Legend*." In Anthony Timpone. *Fangoria Vampires*. New York: HarperPrism, 1996, pp. 203–14.

1807. Kokkola, Lydia. "Virtuous Vampires and Voluptuous Vamps: Romance Conventions Reconsidered in Stephenie Meyer's "Twilight" Series." *Children's Literature in Education* 42, 2 (June 2011): 165–79.

1808. Kord, Susanne. "The Plague Vampires." In Susanne Kord. *Murderesses in German Writing, 1720–1860: Heroines of Horror*. Ser.: Cambridge Studies in German. Cambridge, UK: Cambridge University Press, 2009, pp. 43–81.

1809. Kotani, Mari. Techno-Gothic Japan: From Seishi Yokomizo " The Death's-Head Stranger to Mariko Ohara's Ephemera the Vampire." In Joan Gordon and Veronica Hollinger, eds. *Blood Read: The Vampire as Metaphor in Contemporary Culture.* Philadelphia: University of Pennsylvania Press, 1997, pp. 189–98.

1810. Kotker, Joan G. "Roses Are Red (2000)/Violets Are Blue (2001." In Joan G. Kotker. *James Patterson: A Critical Companion.* Ser.: Critical Companions to Popular Contemporary Writers. Westport, CT: Grerenwood Press, 2004, pp. 103–22.

1811. Lampert-Weissig, Lisa. "The Vampire as Dark and Glorious Necessity in George Sylvester Viereck's *House of the Vampire* and Hanns Heinz Ewers' *Vampir.*" In Sam George and Bill Hughes, eds. *Open Graves, Open Minds: Representations of Vampires and the Undead from the Enlightenment to the Present Day.* Manchester: Manchester University Press, 2013, pp. 79–95.

1812. Lamplighter, L. Jagi. "Dating the Monsters." In Laurell K. Hamilton with Leah Wilson, eds. *Ardeur: 14 Writers on the Anita Blake, Vampire Hunter Series.* Dallas, TX: BenBella Books, 2010, pp. 41–55.

1813. Landrum, Crystakl Michelle Collis. *The Hand That Rocks the Cradle: Male Mothering in Nineteenth-Century Literature.* Athens: University of Georgia, Ph.D. dissertation, 1998. 203 pp. Large format.

1814. Lankford, Bryan. "The Elements of Life." In P. C. Cast, ed. *Nyx in the House of Night: Mythology, Folklore and Religion in the P. C. and Kristin Cast Vampyres Series.* Dallas, TX: Benbella Books, 2011, pp. 128–42.

1815. Lawler, Amy C., and Donald l. Lawler. "The St. Germain Series." In Frank N. Magill, ed. *Survey of Modern Fantasy Literature.* Vol. 3. Englewood Cliffs, NJ: Salem Press, 1983, pp. 1343–46.

1816. Lawler, Donald L. "The Dracula Tape Series." In Frank N. Magill, ed. *Survey of Modern Fantasy Literature.* Vol. 1. Englewood Cliffs, NJ: Salem Press, 1983, pp. 410–17.

1817. Leffler, Yvonne. "Chick-Fangs, Power Relations, and Being Human." *The Gothic: Probing the Boundaries,* editor E Hamilton, Oxford: Inter-Disciplinary Press, 2012, pp. 101–107. Rpt. in: Gord Barentsen, ed. *A Language Spoken in Tongues: Essays of the Transcultural Gothic.* Oxford: Inter-Disciplinary Press, 2012.

1818. Leon, Hilary M. "Why We Love the Monsters: How Anita Blake, Vampire Hunter, and

Buffy the Vampire Slayer Wound Up Dating the Enemy. *Slayage* 1 (Jan. 2001). Posted at http://www.whedonstudies.tv.

1819. Lindgren Leavenworth, Maria. *Fanged Fan Fiction: Variations on* Twilight, True Blood, *and* The Vampire Diaries. Jefferson, NC: McFarland & Company, 2013. 236 pp. tp.

1820. Löffler, Marie-Luise. "'Of Vampire Born': Interracial Mothering in Black Women's Speculative Fiction." *Current Objectives of Postgraduate American Studies* 10 (2009). Posted at: http://www-copas.uni-regensburg.de/articles/issue_10/10_02_text_loeffler.php.

1821. ____. "'She Would Be No Man's Property Ever Again': Vampirism, Slavery, and Black Female Heroism in Contemporary African American Women's Fiction." In Barbara Brodman and James E. Doan, eds. *Images of the Modern Vampire: The Hip and the Atavistic.* Madison. NJ: Fairleigh Dickinson University Press, 2013, pp. 113–28.

1822. Lumley, Brian, and Stanley Wiater, eds. *The Brian Lumley Companion.* New York: TOR, 2002. 397 pp. hb. tp. Literature.

1823. Lyubansky, Mihhail. "Are the Fangs Real." In Laurell K. Hamilton with Leah Wilson, eds. *Ardeur: 14 Writers on the Anita Blake, Vampire Hunter Series.* Dallas, TX: BenBella Books, 2010, pp. 137–48.

1824. Maasik, Sonia, and Jack Solomon. "Interpreting Popular Signs: The Vampire." In Sonia Maasik and Jack Solomon. *Signs of Life in the USA: Readings on Popular Culture for Writers.* 7th ed. New York: Bedford/St. Martin's, 2011, pp. 13–17.

1825. Macabre, J. B. "Giving Voice to the Undead; or, Vampire Authors." In Rosemary Ellen Guiley, with J. B. Macabre. *The Complete Vampire Companion.* New York: Macmillan, 1994, pp. 93–102.

1826. Mahoney, Karen. "Night in the House of Good and Evil." In P. C. Cast, ed. *Nyx in the House of Night: Mythology, Folklore and Religion in the P. C. and Kristin Cast Vampyres Series.* Dallas, TX: Benbella Books, 2011, pp. 1–10.

1827. Mamatas, Nick. "Giving the Devil Her Due." In Laurell K. Hamilton with Leah Wilson, eds. *Ardeur: 14 Writers on the Anita Blake, Vampire Hunter Series.* Dallas, TX: BenBella Books, 2010, pp. 1–10.

1828. Mann, William J. "Waiting for the Vampire" In Greg Herren, ed. *Shadows of the*

Night: Queer Tales of the Uncanny and Unusual. New York: Southern Tier Editions/Harrington Park Press, 2004, pp. 127–54.

1829. Marigny, Jean. "The Images of Dracula in Contemporary Fiction." *Transylvanian Journal* 3, 1 (1997): 5–10.

1830. Marshall, Bridget M. "Stoker's *Dracula* and the Vampire's Literary History." In Jack Lynch, ed. *Dracula.* Ipswich, MA: Salem Press, 2009, pp. 23–37.

1831. Martin, Timothy P. "Joyce and Wagner's Pale Vampire." *James Joyce Quarterly* 23, 4 (Summer 1986): 491–96.

1832. Masterson, Lee. "Vampires." In Kim Richard, ed. *The Complete Guide to Writing Paranormal Novels.* Vol. 1. Calgary, AB: Dragon Moon Press, 2011, pp. 211–32.

1833. Matthews, Cheyenne. "Lightening the White Man's Burden': Evolution of the Vampire from the Victorian Racialism of *Dracula* to the New World Order of *I Am Legend.*" In Barbara Brodman and James E. Doan, eds. *Images of the Modern Vampire: The Hip and the Atavistic.* Madison. NJ: Fairleigh Dickinson University Press, 2013, pp. 85–98.

1834. Matthews, Patricia O'Brien. *Fang-tastic Fiction: Twenty-First-Century Paranormal Reads.* Chicago: American Library Association, 2011. 258 pp.

1835. Mayfield, Sarah, Leigh Lunsford, and Rhonda Brock-Servais. "Romancing the Bite: Statistical Analysis of Young Adult Vampire Novels." *Incite: Journal of Undergraduate Scholarship* (2011). Posted at: http://blogs.longwood.edu/incite/2012/01/30/romancing-the-bite-statistical-analysis-of-young-adult-vampire-novels/.

1836. McCombs, Judith. "'Up in the Air So Blue:' Vampire and Victims, Great Mother Myth, and Gothic Allegory in Margaret Atwood's First Unpublished Novel." *The Centennial Review* 33, 3 (Summer 1989): 251–57.

1837. McDonald, Beth E. *Holy Terror: The Vampire as Numinous Experience in British and American Literature.* Norman: University of Oklahoma, Ph.D. dissertation, 2000. 258 pp. Large format.

1838. _____. *The Vampire as Numinous Experience: Spiritual Journeys with the Undead in British and American Literature.* Jefferson, NC: McFarland & Company, 2004. 200 pp. tp. Literature.

1839. McGuire, Karen. "Of Artists, Vampires, and Creativity." *Studies in Weird Fiction* 11 (1992): 2–4.

1840. McGunnigle, Christopher. "Root Canals: The Neutered Vampire and the Metamorphosis of Undead Metaphor." *Journal of Dracula Studies* 4 (2002). Posted at http://www.blooferland.com/drc/index.php?title=Journal_of_Dracula_Studies.

1841. Melton, J. Gordon. "The Vegetarian Vampire: On Introducing Dracula to Children." *Transylvanian Journal: Dracula and Vampire Studies* 2, 1 (Spring/Summer 1996): 15–23.

1842. Merino, Julio Angel Olivares. "Once Upon the Sleeping Canon: Literary Lustre in Cradle of Filth's Wintry Romances." *Journal of Dracula Studies* 3 (2001): 20–26. Posted at http://www.blooferland.com/drc/index.php?title=Journal_of_Dracula_Studies.

1843. Michand, Marilyn. "Modern Gothic." In David Seed, ed. *A Companion to Twentieth-Century United States Fiction.* Hoboken, NJ: Wiley-Blackwell, 2009, pp. 60–71.

1844. Moore, Michelle E. "Kelene: The Face in the Mirror." In James Craig Holte, ed. *The Fantastic Vampire: Studies in the Children of the Night: Selected Essays from the Eighteenth International Conference on the Fantastic in the Arts.* Vol. 19. Westport, CT: Greenwood Publishing Group, 2002, pp. 123–28. Re: *Kelene: The First Bride of Dracula* by Chelsea Quinn Yarbro.

1845. _____. "'The Unsleeping Cabal': Faulkner's Fevered Vampires and the Other South." *The Faulkner Journal* 24, 2 (Spring 2009): 55–76.

1846. Murphy, Warren, and Richard Sapir. *The Assassin's Handbook.* Ed. By Will Murray. New York: Pinnacle Book, 1982. Rev ed. as: *Inside Sinanju.* New York: Pinnacle Books, 1985. 268 pp. pb. The Destroyer Series.

1847. Mutch, Deborah. "Matt Haig's the Radleys: vampires for the neoliberal age." In Deborah Mutch. *The Modern Vampire and Human Identity.* Basingstoke, UK/New York: Palgrave Macmillan, 2013, pp. 177–93.

1848. Nadal, Marita. "Variations on the Grotesque: From Poe's 'The Black Cat' to Oates's 'The White Cat.'" *Mississippi Quarterly: The Journal of Southern Cultures* 57, 3 (2004): 455–71.

1849. Nahrung, Jason. "Vampires in the Sunburnt Country: Australian Explorations of the

Vampire Gothic Landscape." *Studies in Australian Weird Fiction* 2 (2008): 61–95.

1850. Nayar, Pramod K. "Vampirism and Posthumanism in Octavia Butler's *Fledgling.*" *Notes on Contemporary Literature* 41, 2 (March 2011): 6–10.

1851. Nazarian, Vera. "Death's Got Your Back." In Laurell K. Hamilton with Leah Wilson, eds. *Ardeur: 14 Writers on the Anita Blake, Vampire Hunter Series.* Dallas, TX: BenBella Books, 2010, pp. 165–78.

1852. Ndalianis. Angela. "Paranormal Romance: Anita Blake, Sookie Stackhouse and the Monsters who Love Them." In Angela Ndalianis. *The Horror Sensorium: Media and the Senses.* Jefferson, NC: McFarland & Company, 2012, pp. 73–106.

1853. Nelson, Victoria. *Gothicka: Vampire Heroes, Human Gods, and the New Supernaturalism.* Cambridge, MA: Harvard University Press, 2012. 333 pp. hb. dj.

1854. Nordberg, Heidi L. "Blood Spirit/Blood Bodies: The Viral in the Vampire Chronicles of Anne Rice and Chelsea Quinn Yarbro." In James Craig Holte, ed. *The Fantastic Vampire: Studies in the Children of the Night: Selected Essays from the Eighteenth International Conference on the Fantastic in the Arts.* Vol. 19. Westport, CT: Greenwood Publishing Group, 2002, pp. 111–22.

1855. O'Connor, Mimi. The *Official Illustrated Movie Companion. City of Bones: The Mortal Instruments.* New York: Margaret K. McElderry Books, 2013. 122 pp. Large format.

1856. _____. *Shadowhunter's Guide: City of Bones. The Mortal Instruments.* New York: Margaret K. McElderry Books, 2013. 128 pp.

1857. Oliver, Jana. "By the Marks You Shall Know Them." In P. C. Cast, ed. *Nyx in the House of Night: Mythology, Folklore and Religion in the P. C. and Kristin Cast Vampyres Series.* Dallas, TX: Benbella Books, 2011, pp. 31–45.

1858. Olson, Daniel. "Vlad Lives! The Ultimate Gothic Revenge in Elizabeth Kostova's *The Historian.*" In Daniel Olson. *21st-Century Gothic: Great Gothic Novels Since 2000.* Lanham, MD: Scarecrow Press, 2010, pp. 285–301.

1859. Overstreet, Deborah Wilson. *Not Your Mother's Vampire: Vampires in Young Adult Fiction.* Methuen, NJ: Scarecrow Press, 2006. 162 pp. tp.

1860. Özüm, Aytül. "Deconstructed Masculine Evil in Angela Carter's *The Bloody Chamber* Stories." In Laura Torres Zuñiga and Isabel M. Andrés Cuevas, eds. *Constructing Good and Evil.* Oxford: Interdisciplinary Press, 2011, pp. 153–62.

1861. Palmer, Paulina. "Male Gay Fiction Since Stonewall: Ideology, Conflict, and Aesthetics." *Textual Practice* 27, 4 (July 2013): 738–741.

1862. Patterson, Kathy Davis. "Echoes of Dracula: Racial Politics and the Failure of Segregated Spaces in Matheson's *I Am Legend.*" *Journal of Dracula Studies* 7 (2005): 19–27. Posted at: http://www.blooferland.com/drc/index.php?title=Journal_of_Dracula_Studies.

1863. _____. "'Haunting Back': Vampire Subjectivity in the Gilda Stories." *Femspec* 6, 1 (2005): 35–45.

1864. Pearson, Wendy Gay. "'I, the Undying': The Vampire of Subjectivity and the Aboriginal 'I' in Mudrooroo's *The Undying.*" In Annalisa Oboe, ed.: *Mongrel Signatures: Reflections on the Work of Mudrooroo.* Amsterdam, Rodopi, 2003, pp. 185–202.

1865. Pérez, Ann María Losada. "'In Me More Than Myself': The Monstrous as a Site of Fear and Desire in Angela Carter's *The Bloody Chamber* and *The Erl-King.*" In Jonathan A. Allan and Elizabeth E. Nelson, eds. *Inversions of Power and Paradox.* Oxford: Inter-Disciplinary Press, 2011, pp. 173–80.

1866. Pharr, Donald. "Nancy Collin's Vampire Noir: An Overview of the Sonja Blue Series." In Leonard Heldreth and Mary Pharr, eds. *The Blood Is the Life: Vampires in Literature.* Bowling Green, KY: Bowling Green State University Press, 1999, pp. 247–57.

1867. Philips, Robert, and Branimir Rieger. "The Agony and the Ecstasy: A Jungian Analysis of Two Vampire Novels, Meredith Ann Pierce's *The Dark Angel* and Bram Stoker's *Dracula.*" *West Virginia University Philological Papers* 31 (1986): 10–19.

1868. Phillips, Terry. "The Discourse of the Vampire in First World War Writing." In Carla T. Kungl, ed. *Vampires: Myths and Metaphors of Enduring Evil.* Oxford: Inter-Disciplinary Press, 2003. pp. 79–84. Posted at: http://www.inter-disciplinary.net/publishing/id-press/ebooks/vampires-myths-and-metaphors-of-enduring-evil. Rpt. in: Peter Day, ed. *Vampire: Myths and Metaphors of Enduring Evil.* Amsterdam: Rodopi, 2006, pp. 65–80.

1869. Piatti-Farnell, Lorna. *The Vampire in Contemporary Popular Literature.* New York: Routledge, 2014. 234 pp. hb.

1870. Powell, Anna. *Psychoanalysis and Sovereignty in Popular Vampire Fictions.* Lewiston, NY: Edwin Mellen Press, 2003. 296 pp. hb.

1871. Pringle, David. "'Jack of Shadows' by Roger Zelazny." In David Pringle. *Modern Fantasy, The Hundred Best Novels: An English Language Selection, 1946–1987.* London: Grafton Books, 1988, pp. 144–45.

1872. _____. "'The Vampire Tapestry' by Suzy McKee Charnas." In David Pringle. *Modern Fantasy, the Hundred Best Novels: An English Language Selection, 1946–1987.* London: Grafton Books, 1988. Rpt.: New York : Peter Bedrick Books, 1989.

1873. Priest, Hannah. "'Hell! was I becoming a vampyre slut?': Sex, Sexuality and Morality in Young Adult Vampire Fiction." In Deborah Mutch. *The Modern Vampire and Human Identity.* Basingstoke, UK/New York: Palgrave Macmillan, 2013, pp. 55–75.

1874. Ramsland, Katherine. "Drac the Ripper: James Reece's *The Dracula Dossier*: Consciousness, Disorders and Nineteenth-Century Terror." In Daniel Olson. *21st-Century Gothic: Great Gothic Novels Since 2000.* Lanham, MD: Scarecrow Press, 2010, pp. 158–70.

1875. Rath, Mary C. *Vampire in Popular Fiction.* London: University of London, Ph.D. dissertation, 2001. 593 pp. Large format.

1876. Rathbun Mark, and Graeme Flanagan, comps. *Richard Matheson: He Is Legend: An Illustrated Bio-Bibliography.* Chico, CA: Rio Lindo, 1984. 55 pp. hb.

1877. Ready, Robert. "Textula." *Journal of Narrative Theory* 40, 3 (Fall 2010): 275–96.

1878. Rees, David. *What Do Draculas Do? Essays on Contemporary Writers of Fiction for Children and Young Adults.* Metuchen, NJ: Scarecrow Press, 1990. 248 pp.

1879. Riley, Samantha Michele. "Unmasking Mary Shelley's Frankenstein in Patrick Süskind's *Das Parfum*." In Cristina Santos and Adriana Spahr. *Monstrous Deviations in Literature and the Arts.* Oxford: Inter-Disciplinary Press, 2011.

1880. Rivett, Miriam. "*Cirque du Freak.*" *Children's Literature in Education* 33, 2 (June 2002): 97–106.

1881. Rose, Jeane. "'A Girl Like That Will Give Your AIDS!': Vampirism as AIDS Metaphor in *Killing Zoe*." In James Holte Craig, ed. *The Fantastic Vampire: Studies in the Children of the Night: Selected Essays from the Eighteenth International Conference on the Fantastic in the Arts.* Vol. 19. Westport, CT: Greenwood Publishing Group, 2002, pp. 145–50.

1882. Rose, Julie. *Faulkner's Horror and the American Gothic Cultural Imagination (1930–1945).* New York: New York University, Ph.D. dissertation, 1999. 235 pp. Large format.

1883. Rottensteiner, Franz. *The Fantasy Book: An Illustrated History from Dracula to Tolkein.* New York: Collier Books, 1978. 158 pp. pb. Large format.

1884. Rowen, Michelle, and Richelle Mead. *Vampire Academy: The Ultimate Guide.* New York: Razorbill, 2011. 305 pp. tp.

1885. Ruane, Richard T. *Performing Camp, Vamp and Femme Fatale: Revisiting, Reinventing and Retelling the Lives of Post-death, Retro-Gothic Women.* Denton: University of North Texas, M.A. thesis, 1999. 72 pp. Large format. Posted at http://digital.library.unt.edu/ark:/67531/metadc2239/m1/75/.

1886. Russell, Sharon A. "The Construction of the Vampire in Yarbro's *Hotel Transylvania*." In James Craig Holte, ed. *The Fantastic Vampire: Studies in the Children of the Night: Selected Essays from the Eighteenth International Conference on the Fantastic in the Arts.* Vol. 19. Westport, CT: Greenwood Publishing Group, 2002, pp. 129–34.

1887. _____. "Introducing Count Saint-Germain: Chelsea Quinn Yarbro's Heroic Vampire." In Leonard Heldreth and Mary Pharr, eds. *The Blood Is the Life: Vampires in Literature.* Bowling Green, KY: Bowling Green State University Press, 1999, pp. 141–53.

1888. Ruthven, Suzanne. "The Vampyre." In Suzanne Ruthven. *Horror Upon Horror: A Step by Step Guide to Writing a Horror Novel.* Alresford, Hants., UK: Compass Books, 2013, pp. 21–29.

1889. Saintcrow, Lilith. "Ambiguous Anita." In Laurell K. Hamilton with Leah Wilson, eds. *Ardeur: 14 Writers on the Anita Blake, Vampire Hunter Series.* Dallas, TX: BenBella Books, 2010, pp. 25–39.

1890. Samuelsson, Victoria. *What Manner of Man Is This? The Depiction of Vampire Folklore in* Dracula *and* Fangland. Stockholm, Sweden:

Stockholm University, Student thesis, 2012. 21 pp. Large format. Posted at: http://www.diva-portal. org/smash/get/diva2:533934/FULLTEXT03.pdf.

1891. Sanders, Joe. "The Pretense that the World Is Sane: Saberhagen's *Dracula*." In Leonard Heldreth and Mary Pharr, eds. *The Blood Is the Life: Vampires in Literature.* Bowling Green, KY: Bowling Green State University Press, 1999, pp. 105–19.

1892. Sands, Marella. "Bon Rapports."' In Laurell K. Hamilton with Leah Wilson, eds. *Ardeur: 14 Writers on the Anita Blake, Vampire Hunter Series.* Dallas, TX: BenBella Books, 2010, pp. 59–67.

1893. Santos, Cristina. "'I love you to death': Boullosa's Interview with a Vampire in Isabel." In Christine Santos. *Bending the Rules in the Quest for an Authentic Female Identity: Clarice Lispector and Carmen Boullosa.* New York: Peter Lang, 2004.

1894. Saunero-Ward, Verónica H. "Giovanna Rivero's 'Contraluna': Meeting the Monstrous Lilith." In Cristina Santos and Adriana Spahr. *Monstrous Deviations in Literature and the Arts.* Oxford: Inter-Disciplinary Press, 2011.

1895. Scarborough, Dorothy. "Daemonic Spirits—Vampires." In Dorothy Scarborough. *The Supernatural in Modern English Fiction.* New York: G. P. Putnam's Sons, 1917, pp. 158–66.

1896. Sceats, Sarah. "Oral Sex: Vampiric Transgression and the Writing of Angela Carter." *Tulsa Studies in Women's Literature* 20 (2001): 107–21.

1897. Schumann, Nancy. *Take a Bite. Female Vampires in Anglo-American Literature and Folklore.* London: Callio Press Limited, n.d. [2011?], 131 pp. tp.

1898. ____. "Women with Bite: Tracing Vampire Women from Lilith to *Twilight*." In Barbara Brodman and James E. Doan, eds. *The Universal Vampire: Origins and Evolution of a Legend.* Madison, NJ: Fairleigh Dickinson University Press, 2013, pp. 109–20. Rpt.: Seidel, Michael. "Ulysses' Black Panther Vampire." *James Joyce Quarterly* 13 (Summer 1976): 415–27.

1899. Senf, Carol A. "Brides of Dracula: From Novel to Film." *Studies in Popular Culture* 7 (1984): 64–71.

1900. Serrano, Carmen. *Monsters, Vampires and Doppelgängers: Innovation and Transformation*

of *Gothic Forms in Latin American Narratives.* Irvine: University of California, Irvine, Ph.D. dissertation, 2009. 184 pp. Large format.

1901. Shaffer, E. S., ed. *Fantastic Currencies in Comparative Literature: Gothic to Postmodern.* Ser.: Comparative Criticism: Vol. 24. Cambridge: Cambridge University Press, 2003. 366 pp. hb. Includes lengthy section, "Literature and Translation/Jan Potacki and *The Manuscript Found in Saragossa*: Novel and Film." Though not what one would call a work of vampire fiction, Potaki's novels includes vampires in its supernatural world.

1902. Shelton, Melinda L. "From Garden to Jungle." *Lambda Book Report: A Review of Contemporary Gay and Lesbian Literature* 9, 3 (2000): 6–9.

1903. Shore, Amy. *A Guide for Using Bunnicula in the Classroom.* Westminister, CA: Teacher-created Resources, 2004. 48 pp. pb.

1904. Siegel, Carol. "Female Heterosexual Sadism: The Final Feminist Taboo in *Buffy the Vampire Slayer* and the Anita Blake Vampire Hunter Series." In Merri Lisa Johnson, ed. *Third Wave Feminism and Television: Jane Puts It in a Box.* London: I. B. Taurus and Co., 2007, pp. 56–77. A paper originally presented as "Third-Wave Feminist Sadism: Why Buffy's Loss is Anita Blake's Gain" at the 2006 PCA/ACA National Conference, April 12–15, 2006.

1905. Skrip, Jack. "I Drink, Therefore I Am: Introspection in the Contemporary Vampire Novel." *Studies in Weird Fiction* 14 (1994): 3–7.

1906. Smith, Andrew. "Vampirism, Masculinity, and Degeneracy: D. H. Lawrence's Modernist Gothic." In Andrew Smith and Jeff Wallace, eds. *Gothic Modernisms.* Basingstoke, UK: Palgrave Macmillan, 2001, pp. 150–66.

1907. Smith, Elizabeth Hayes, with Adam Kissel. *Perfume: The Story of a Murderer/Patrick Suskind.* N.p: GradeSaver 2010. 91 pp. tp.

1908. Smith, L. J. and Annette Pollert. *Night World: The Ultimate Fan Guide.* New York: Simon Pulse, 2009. 282 pp. pb.

1909. Smith-Ready, Jeri. "Freedom of Choice." In P. C. Cast, ed. *Nyx in the House of Night: Mythology, Folklore and Religion in the P. C. and Kristin Cast Vampyres Series.* Dallas, TX: Benbella Books, 2011, pp. 105–15.

1910. Spencer, Liv. *Navigating the Shadow World: The Unofficial Guide to Cassandra Clare's*

The Mortal Instruments. Toronto: ECW Press, 2013. 301 pp.

1911. Stableford, Brian. "The Many Returns of Dracula." In Brian Stableford. *Slaves of the Death Spiders and Other Essays on Fantastic Literature.* San Bernardino, CA: Borgo Press/Wildside Press, 2007, pp. 121–132.

1912. _____. "*Sang* for Supper: Notes on the Metaphorical Use of Vampires in the *Empire of Fear* and *Young Blood*. In Joan Gordon and Veronica Hollinger, eds. *Blood Read: The Vampire as Metaphor in Contemporary Culture.* Philadelphia: University of Pennsylvania Press, 1997, pp. 69–84.

1913. _____. *Space, Time, and Infinity: Essays on Fantastic Literature.* N.p.: Wildside Press, 2006, 208 pp. See especially chapters 11 and 12, "What We Know About Vampires" (149–158) and "A Brief History of Vampires" (159–170).

1914. Steiber, Ellen. "The Divine Cat." In P. C. Cast, ed. *Nyx in the House of Night: Mythology, Folklore and Religion in the P. C. and Kristin Cast Vampyres Series.* Dallas, TX: Benbella Books, 2011, pp. 47–66.

1915. Stoltzfus, Ben. "Robbe-Grillet's Mythical Biography: Reflections of La Belle Captive in Le Miroir qui revient." *Stanford French Review* 12, 2–3 (Fall-Winter 1988): 387–404.

1916. Stuart, Alasdair. "The Other Side of the Street." In Laurell K. Hamilton with Leah Wilson, eds. *Ardeur: 14 Writers on the Anita Blake, Vampire Hunter Series.* Dallas, TX: BenBella Books, 2010, pp. 81–88.

1917. Sturgis, Amy H. "Reimagining 'Magic City': How the Casts Mythologize Tulsa." In P. C. Cast, ed. *Nyx in the House of Night: Mythology, Folklore and Religion in the P. C. and Kristin Cast Vampyres Series.* Dallas, TX: Benbella Books, 2011, pp. 71–86.

1918. Subramanian, Janani. "In the Shadow of a Metaphor: *The Vampire Diaries* and Southern History." *Flow* (online journal of television and media studies) (July 16, 2010). Posted at: http://flowtv.org/2010/07/the-vampire-diaries-and-southern-history/.

1919. Swain, Heather. "Girls Gone Wild." In Laurell K. Hamilton with Leah Wilson, eds. *Ardeur: 14 Writers on the Anita Blake, Vampire Hunter Series.* Dallas, TX: BenBella Books, 2010, pp. 11–23.

1920. Swift, Sindra Ford. "Toward a Vampire as Savior: Chelsea Quinn Yarbro's *Saint-Germain* Series Compared with Edward Bulwar Lytton's *Zanoni.*" In Leonard Heldreth and Mary Pharr, eds. *The Blood Is the Life: Vampires in Literature.* Bowling Green, KY: Bowling Green State University Press, 1999, pp. 155–64.

1921. Tatum, Melissa L. "Trying the System." In Laurell K. Hamilton with Leah Wilson, eds. *Ardeur: 14 Writers on the Anita Blake, Vampire Hunter Series.* Dallas, TX: BenBella Books, 2010, pp. 123–34.

1922. Thaler, Ingrid. "Traveling through Time: Vampire Fiction and the Black Atlantic in Jewelle Gomez's *The Gilda Stories* (1991)." In Ingrid Thaler. *Black Atlantic Speculative Fictions: Octavia E. Butler, Jewelle Gomez, and Nalo Hopkinson.* New York: Routledge, 2010.

1923. Tolan, Fiona. "Sucking the Blood out of Second Wave Feminism: Postfeminist Vampirism in Margaret Atwood's *The Robber Bride.*" *Gothic* 9, 2 (2007): 45–57.

1924. Tombs, Peter. "Bloodlust." *Redeemer* 1, 1 (December 1992): 8–11.

1925. Torsney, Cheryl B. "The Vampire Motif in Absalom, Absalom!" *Southern Review* 20, 3 (1984): 562–69.

1926. Trapp, Joona Smitherman. "The Image of the Vampire in the Struggle for Societal Power: Dan Simmons's *Children of the Night.*" *Journal of the Fantastic in the Arts* 10, 2 (1999): 155–62.

1927. Turcotte, Gerry. "Re-mastering the Ghosts: Mudrooroo and Gothic Refigurations." In Annalisa Oboe, ed. *Mongrel Signatures. Reflections on the Work of Mudrooroo.* Amsterdam: Rodopi Press, 2003, pp. 129–151.

1928. _____. "Vampiric Decolonization: Fanon, 'Terrorism' and Mudrooroo's Vampire Trilogy." In Alfred J. Lopenz, ed., *Postcolonial Whiteness: A Critical Reader on Race and Empire.* Albany: State University of New York Press, 2005, pp. 103–118.

1929. Tuttleton, James W. "Vitality and Vampirism in *Tender Is the Night.*" In Milton R. Stern, ed. *Critical Essays of F. Scott Fitzgerald's Tender Is the Night.* Boston: G. K. Hall, 1986, pp. 238–46.

1930. Waiter, Stanley, Matthew Bradley, and Paul Stuve. *The Twilight and Other Zones: The Dark Worlds of Richard Matheson.* New York: Citadel Press, 2009. 362 pp.

1931. Ward, J. R. *The Black Dagger Brotherhood: An Insider's Guide.* New York: New American Library 2008. 478 pp. tp.

1932. Wilgus, Neal. "Fred Saberhagen: Berserkers and Vampires." In *Seven by Seven: Interviews with American Science Fiction Writers of the West and Southwest.* San Bernardino, CA: Borgo Press, 1996, pp. 84–92.

1933. ____. "Saberhagen's New Dracula: The Vampire as Hero." In Darrell Schweitzer, ed. *Discovering Modern Horror Fiction 1.* San Bernardino, CA: The Borgo Press, 1987, pp. 92–98.

1934. Winnubst, Shannon. "Vampires, Anxieties, and Dreams: Race and Sex in the Contemporary United States." *Hypatia* 18, 3 (2003): 1–20.

1935. Wisker, Gina. "Celebrating Difference: The Vampire in African-American and Caribbean Women's Writing." In Tabish. Khair, and Johan Hoglund, eds. *Transnational and Postcolonial Vampires: Dark Blood.* Basingstoke, UK: Palgrave Macmillan, 2012, pp. 46–65.

1936. ____. "If Looks Could Kill: Contemporary Women's Vampire Fictions." In Lynne Pearce and Gina Wisker, eds. *Fatal Attractions: Rescripting romance in contemporary literature and film.* London: Pluto Press, 1998.

1937. ____. "Love Bites: Contemporary Women's Vampire Fictions." In David Punter, ed. *A Companion to the Gothic.* Oxford, UK and Malden, MA: Blackwell Publishers, 2000, pp. 167–79. Rpt. in: David Punter, ed. *A New Companion to the Gothic.* Malden, MA: Wiley-Blackwell, 2012, pp. 224–39.

1938. Worley, Lloyd. "Loving Death: The Meaning of Male Impotence in Vampire Literature." *Journal of the Fantastic in the Arts* 2, 1 (1989): 25–36.

1939. Worton, Michael. "Use and Abuse of Metaphor in Tournier's 'Le Vol di vampire.'" *Paragraph: A Journal of Modern Critical Theory* 10 (Oct. 1987): 13–28.

1940. Wu, Yan. "The Virtuous Vampire of YA Romance." In Yan Wu. *(Re)imagining the World: Children's Literature's Response to Changing Times.* Dordrecht: Springer, 2014, pp. 118–19.

1941. Yarbro, Chelsea Quinn. "My Favorite Enigma: The Historical Comte de Saint-Germain." In Chelsea Quinn Yarbro. *The Saint-Germain Chronicles.* New York: Timescape Books/Pocket Books, 1983, pp. 174–81. Posted at: http://www.freevampirebook.net/book2/Yarbro1809/46601.html. Rev. text reprinted in: Chelsea Quinn Yarbro. *Vampire Stories of Chelsea Quinn Yarbro.* White Rock, BC: Transylvania Press; 1994, pp. 303–10.

1942. ____. "Mythical Metamorphosis: Evolution in Horror Literature." *Transylvanian Journal: Dracula and Vampire Studies* 1, 1 (Fall 1995): 27–34.

1943. ____. "Nancy Kilpatrick: An Appreciation." In *The Vampire Stories of Nancy Kilpatrick.* Ontario, Canada and New York: Mosaic Press, 2000, pp. 2–4.

1944. ____, **and Suzy McKee Charnas.** "Beyond Dracula: Advocates." *Imagi-Movies* 2, 2 (Winter 1994): 42–45, 61.

1945. Zschikke, Magdalena. *The Other: From Monster to Vampire: The Figure of the Lesbian in Fiction.* Santa Cruz: University of California, Ph.D. dissertation, 1994. 263 pp. Large format.

Sherlock Holmes' Vampire Encounters

As the novel *Dracula* and the short stories written by Sir Arthur Conan Doyle entered the public domain, and as both became the center of attention by scholars specializing in the Victorian era, interested parties began to speculate on the possibility of the two literary figures meeting and what would be the outcome of such an encounter. Initially, a single novel, *Sherlock Holmes vs. Dracula: The Adventure of the Sanguinary Count,* written by Loren D. Estleman, appeared (1978). It would inspire a few additional titles, and over the next decades some dozen novels would be added to the lineup. In addition, an initial comic book series, *Scarlett in Gaslight,* would be published in 1986. Quite apart from any mention of *Dracula,* Conan Doyle, of course, wrote several "vampire" stories, most notably "The Adventure of the Sussex Vampire," a prominent example of the pseudo-vampire story, as well as "The Parasite," a vampire story without Holmes.

In the last half of the twentieth century, Holmes scholars began to comment substantively on Conan Doyle's vampires and on the post–Conan Doyle Dracula-Holmes novels. The first attempt to bring the "Sussex Vampire" to the screen (1993) further bolstered the interest of vampire-oriented followers of Holmes. Most recently, in their collection of Conan Doyle's vampire stories, editors Robert Eighteen-Bisang and Martin H. Greenberg have called attention to Conan Doyle's more substantive venture into vampire lore. Their compilation includes no less than eight additional vampire stories written by the creator of Sherlock Holmes.

1946. Cottom, Daniel. "Sherlock Holmes Meets Dracula." *English Literary History* 79, 3 (Fall 2012): 537–567.

1947. Cranny-Francis, Anne. "Arthur Conan Doyle's *The Parasite*: The Case of the Anguished Author." In Clive Bloom et al, eds. *Nineteenth Century Suspense: From Poe to Conan Doyle*. Basingstoke, UK: Macmillan Press, 1988, pp. 93–106.

1948. Davies, David Stuart. "On the Set with...The Sussex Vampire." *Scarlet Street* (1992): 44–46.

1949. Detweiller, Arminius Conan. "One Good Reason Why Holmes Did Not Meet Dracula in 1890." *The Baker Street Chronicle* 4, 5 (September-October 1984). Posted at: http://www.sherlockpeoria.net/WeirdSherlock/Dracula Trilogy.html.

1950. Edmonds, Martin. "Introduction." In Arthur Conan Doyle. *The Parasite*. N.p.: Company, 164, 1999, pp. 1–22.

1951. Eighteen-Bisang, Robert. "Introduction." In Arthur Conan Doyle. *Vampire Stories*. Ed. by Robert Eighteen-Bisang and Martin H. Greenberg. New York: Skyhorse Publishing, 2009, pp. vi–ix.

1952. _____. "A Sherlock Holmes Vampire Bibliography." In Arthur Conan Doyle. *Vampire Stories*. Ed. by Robert Eighteen-Bisang and Martin H. Greenberg. New York: Skyhorse Publishing, 2009, pp. 257–71.

1953. Hendershot, Cyndy. "The Restoration of the Angel: Female Vampirism in Doyle's "The Adventure of the Sussex Vampire." *The Victorian Newsletter* 89 (Spring 1996): 10–13.

1954. Jones, Kelvin. *The Carfax Syndrome: Being a Study of Vampirism in the Canon.* New York: Magico Magazine, 1984. 18 pp. pb. Staples.

1955. Katz, Robert S. "John H. Watson, M.D.: Pioneer Neuropathologist." *The Baker Street Journal: An Irregular Quarterly of Sherlockiana* 32, 3 (Sept. 1982): 150–52.

1956. Keefauver, Brad A. "Sherlock Holmes and the Secretly Dead: A Near Fatal Case of Close-Mindedness." *The Baker Street Chronicle* 4, 5 (September-October 1984). Posted at: http://www.sherlockpeoria.net/WeirdSherlock/Dracula Trilogy.html.

1957. Leonard, William. "Re: Vampires." *The Baker Street Journal Christmas Annual*. Rpt. in: Peter Haining, ed. *A Sherlock Holmes Companion*. New York: Barnes & Noble, 1994, pp. 175–80.

1958. Li, Shang-jen. "Ghost, Vampire, and Scientific Naturalism: Observation and Evidence in the Supernatural Fiction of Grant Allen, Bram Stoker and Arthur Conan Doyle." In Mu-chou Poo, ed. *Rethinking Ghosts in World Religions*. Leiden: Brill, 2009, pp. 183–210.

1959. Lilley, Jessie. "Sherlock Holmes as Dracula." *Scarlet Street* 8 (Fall 1992): 23, 100. Re: Jeremy Brett.

1960. Lovisi, Gary. "Sherlock and the Count." *Baker Street Gazette* (Summer 1987). Rpt. in: Gary Lovisi. *Relics of Sherlock Holmes*. Brooklyn, NY: Gryphon Publications, 1989, pp. 33–34.

1961. Ludlow, Peter. "From Sherlock and Buffy to Klingon and Norrathian Platinum Pieces: Pretense, Contextalism, and the Myth of Fiction." *Philosophical Issues* 16, 1 (September 2006): 162–183.

1962. O'Brien, Thomas F. "Re: Vampires, Again." *The Baker Street Journal* new series 37 (September 1987): 154–57.

1963. Redmond, Chris. "Me. Dodd's Client and Mr. D'odd." *The Baker Street Journal: An Irregular Quarterly of Sherlockiana* 35, 2 (June 1985): 99–101.

1964. Roden, Barbara, "Vampyres." *The Journal of the Arthur Conan Doyle Society* 4 (1993): 104–13.

1965. Smith, Andrew. "Displacing Masculinity: Sherlock Holmes, Count Dracula and London." Andrew Smith. *Victorian Demons: Medicine,* *Masculinity, and the Gothic at the fin-de-siècle.* Manchester, UK: Manchester University Press, 2004, pp. 118–49.

The Vampire Chronicles of Anne Rice

Between 1976 and 2003, writer Anne Rice completed ten novels which became known collectively as "The Vampire Chronicles"—*Interview with the Vampire* (1976), *The Vampire Lestat* (1985), *The Queen of the Damned* (1988), *The Tale of the Body Thief* (1992), *Memnoch the Devil* (1995), *The Vampire Armand* (1998), *Merrick* (2000), *Blood and Gold* (2001), *Blackwood Farm* (2002), and *Blood Canticle* (2003). In addition, she also authored two additional related novels—*Pandora* (1998) and *Vittorio the Vampire* (1999)—that were designated the "New Tales of the Vampires."

Following the appearance of *The Vampire Lestat*, Rice emerged as the single most popular writer of vampire novels through the rest of the twentieth century, and inspired other writers to pursue the vampire as a compelling metaphor for a variety of elements in the human condition. She would become the first of the contemporary vampire writers to be taken seriously by literary critics and scholars and spawn multiple books and articles commenting on her work. Though not the first to place the action of her vampire writings in New Orleans, she significantly strengthened that identification and spurred the development of a whole new segment of the local tourist industry catering to vampire fans.

1966. Amador, Victoria. "The Gothic Louisiana of Charlaine Harris and Anne Rice." In Deborah Mutch. *The Modern Vampire and Human Identity.* Basingstoke, UK/New York: Palgrave Macmillan, 2013, pp. 163–76.

1967. Ambrose, Kala. "The Casket Girls of the Old Ursuline Monastery and Other Vampire Lore." In Kala Ambrose. *Spirits of New Orleans: Voodoo Curses, Vampire Legends and Cities of the Dead.* Covington, KY: Clerisy Press, 2012, pp. 96–107.

1968. *Anne Rice: A Reader's Checklist and Reference Guide.* Middletown, CT: CheckerBee. 1999. 72 pp. pb.

1969. Anthony, Patricia. "Anne Rice: From the Popular Vampire to the Popular Christ." *Popular Culture Review* 21, 2 (2010): 37–47.

1970. Antoni, Rita. "A Vampiric Relation to Feminism: The Monstrous-Feminine in Whitley Strieber's and Anne Rice's Gothic Fiction." *Americana: E-Journal of American Studies in Hungary* 4, 1 (Spring 2008). Posted at http://americana ejournal.hu/vol4no1/antoni.

1971. Anttonen, Ramona. "The Savage and the Gentleman: A Comparative Analysis of Two Vampire Characters in Bram Stoker's *Dracula* and Anne Rice's *The Vampire Lestat.*" Växjö, Sweden: Växjö University, Student thesis, 2000. 24 pp. Posted at: http://www.diva-portal.org/smash/get/diva2:206843/FULLTEXT01.pdf.

1972. Austin, Joanne P. "Anne Rice: Giving the Vampire a Conscience." In Rosemary Ellen Guiley, with J. B. Macabre. *The Complete Vampire Companion.* New York: Macmillan, 1994, pp. 84–88.

1973. Ayaz, Sandra Marie. *Contemporary Sanguines: The Metamorphosis of the Vampire Myth as Manifest in the Works of Anne Rice.* Boca Raton: Florida Atlantic University, M.A. thesis, 1992. 97 pp. Large format.

1974. Badley, Linda. "Transfigured Vampires: Anne Rice." In Linda Badley. *Writing Horror and the Body: The Fiction of Stephen King, Clive Barker, and Anne Rice.* Westport, CT: Greenwood Press, 1996, pp. 105–38.

1975. Ballesteros-Gonzáles, Antonio. "Vampirism as Metaphor of Millennial Disease: The Case of Anne Rice's Vampire Chronicles." In Zbigniew Bialas and Wieslaw Krajka, eds. *East Central*

European Traumas and a Millennial Condition. Boulder, CO: East European Monographs, 1999, pp. 165–76.

1976. Bassett, Jonathan F. "It's Hard Out Here for an Immortal: Angst and Ennui in *Interview with the Vampire* and the Television Series *Highlander*." *PSYART, an Online Journal for the Psychological Study of the Arts* (2011). Posted at http://www.psyartjournal.com/article/show/f_bassett-its_hard_out_here_for_an_immortal_angst_.

1977. Beahm, George, ed. *The Anne Rice Companion.* Williamsburg, VA: GB Ink, 1995. 215 pp. hb. Rev. ed. as: *The Unauthorized Anne Rice Companion.* Kansas City, MO: Andrews and McMeel, 1996. 246 pp. hb. Includes contributions by Martha Ann Brett Samuel and Ray Samuel, Ronette King, Coleman Warner, Ronnie Virgets, Sascha Mabus-Vuosper, Colleen Doran, George Beahm, with Britton E. Trice, Katherine Ramsland, Michael R. Collings, Bette B. Roberts, Stanley S. Wiater, Gerri Hirshev, Dale Rice, Merle Ginsberg, Mikal Gilmore, Martha Frankel, and Anthony Lane.

1978. Beebe, John. "He Must Have Wept When He Made You: The Homoerotic *Pothos* in the Movie Version of *Interview with the Vampire*." In Katherine Ramsland, ed. *The Anne Rice Reader.* New York: Ballantine Books, 1997, pp. 196–211.

1979. Bell, James. "Decadence, Dandyism, and Aestheticism in *The Vampire Chronicles*." *Journal of the Fantastic in the Arts* 17, 3 (2006): 284–93.

1980. Benefiel, Candace R. "Blood Relations: The Gothic Perversion of the Nuclear Family in Anne Rice's *Interview with the Vampire*." *Journal of Popular Culture* 38, 2 (2004): 261–273.

1981. Berger, Fred H. "From Lilith to Lestat." *Propaganda* 17 (Fall 1991): 12–15.

1982. Biodrowski, Steve, and Alan Jones. "Interview with the Vampire." *Imagi-Movies* 2, 2 (Winter 1994): 20–23.

1983. _____. "Interview with the Vampire: Production Designer." *Imagi-Movies* 2, 2 (Winter 1994): 23.

1984. Blumreich-Moore, Kathleen M. "Unholy Rapture: Mysticism in Anne Rice's *Interview with the Vampire*." *Grand Valley Review* 5, 2 (1989). Posted at: http://scholarworks.gvsu.edu/gvr/vol5/iss2/19.

1985. Bonacquisti, Dawn. "*The hopeless guise, this helpless form*": Innocence and Monstrosity in *Great Expectations* and *Interview with a Vampire.* Tampa: University of South Florida, M.A. thesis, 1996. 36 pp. Large format.

1986. Bone, Kristin L. "Tragic Monsters and Heroic Villains: Anne Rice's Contribution to the Rise of the Heroic Vampire." In Grace Halden and Gabriela Mádlo, eds. *Concerning Evil.* Oxford: Inter-Disciplinary Press, 2013.

1987. Brooks, Clifford. "Checking in with Anne Rice." *The Scream Factor* 1 (Winter 1988): 20.

1988. Ceccio, Joseph F. "Anne Rice's The Tale of the Body Thief and the Astral Projection Literary Tradition." In Gary Hoppenstand and Ray B. Browne, eds. *The Gothic World of Anne Rice.* Bowling Green, OH: Bowling Green University Popular Press, 1996, pp. 163–71.

1989. Chandler, Anthony M. *Vampires Incorporated: Self-Definition in Anne Rice's Vampire Chronicles.* Montreal, PQ: McGill University, M.A. thesis, 1998. 78 pp. Large format.

1990. Chung Debbie Joyce. "'Such Blood, Such Power': The Lot Complex in Anne Rice's *Interview with the Vampire*." *Hungarian Journal of English and American Studies* 6, 2 (Fall 2000): 173–181.

1991. Collings, Michael R. "Of Vampires and Their Ilk: Traditions, Transformations, and the UnDead." In George Beahm, ed. *The Anne Rice Companion.* Williamsburg, VA: GB Ink, 1995, pp. 92–97. Rpt. as: George Beahm, ed. *The Unauthorized Anne Rice Companion.* Kansas City, MO: Andrews and McMeel, 1996, pp. 101–06.

1992. Conant, Jennet. "Lestat, C'est Moi." *Esquire* 121, 3 (March 1994): 70–75.

1993. Copeland, Dawn. *Anne Rice's Existential Quest: Louis' Search for Meaning.* Murfreesboro: Middle Tennessee State University, M.A. thesis, 1993. 71 pp. Large format.

1994. Cordes, Rebecca, "'The Vampire-Myth Established—Bram Stoker's *Dracula*' and 'The Use of Vampire Mythology in Anne Rice's *Vampire Chronicles*.'" In Rebecca Cordes. *Anne Rice's Vampire Chronicles: Myth and History.* Osnabrück, Germany: Der Andere, 2004, pp. 19–64.

1995. Diamantis, Sophie. "La Commedia del Sangue: The Vampyr Theatre." *Delirium* 3 (1996): 18–20.

1996. _____. "The Gothic Rice." *Propaganda* 21 (Spring 1994): 10–11.

1997. Dickinson, Joy [Joy Dickinson Tipping]. *Haunted City: An Unauthorized Guide to the Magical, Magnificent New Orleans of Anne Rice.* Secaucus, NJ: Carol Publishing/Citadel Press, 1995. 263 pp. tp. Third edition. New York: Citadel Publishing/Kensington Publishing Corp, 2004. 316 pp. tp.

1998. Diehl, Digby. "Anne Rice Interview." *Playboy* (March 1993): 53–54, 56, 58–64. Rpt in: George Beahm, ed. *The Anne Rice Companion.* Williamsburg, VA: GB Ink, 1995, pp. 40–58. Rpt. in: George Beahm. *The Unauthorized Anne Rice Companion.* Kansas City, MO: Andrews and McMeel, 1996, pp. 38–58.

1999. Doane, Janice, and Devon Hodges. "Undoing Feminism: From the Preoedipal to Postfeminism in Anne Rice's Vampire Chronicles." *American Literary History* 2, 3 (Fall 1990): 422–42. Rpt. as: Devon Hodges and Janice l. Doane. "Undoing Feminism in Anne Rice's Vampire Chronicles." In James Naremore and Patrick Brantlinger, eds. *Modernity and Mass Culture.* Bloomington: Indiana University Press, 1991, pp. 158–75.

2000. Fasolino, Greg. "Lestat of the Art—The Dark Gift Discussed." *Reflex: Alternative Music and Culture* 29 (1992): 42–46.

2001. Frankel, Martha. "Interview with the Author of *Interview with the Vampire.*" *Movieline* 5, 5 (January/February 1994): 58–62, 96–97.

2002. Gee, James Paul. "Dracula, the Vampire Lestat and TESOL." *TESOL Quarterly* 22, 2 (June 1988): 201–225.

2003. Gelder, Ken. "The Vampire Writes Back: Anne Rice and the (Re)turn of the Author." In Ken Gelder. *Popular Fiction: The Logics and Practices of a Literary Field.* London: New York: Routledge, 2004, pp. 118–28.

2004. Gilmore, Mikal. "The Devil and Anne Rice." *Rolling Stone* (July 13–17, 1995). Rpt in: George Beahm, ed. *The Anne Rice Companion.* Williamsburg, VA: GB Ink, 1995. 215 pp. 137–46. Rpt. as: George Beahm, ed. *The Unauthorized Anne Rice Companion.* Kansas City, MO: Andrews and McMeel, 1996, pp. 148–58.

2005. Greaves, Tim. "Interview with a Vampire." *Draculina* 22 (March 1995): 14–15, 62–63.

2006. Haas, Lynda, and Robert Haas. "Living with(out) Boundaries: The Novels of Anne Rice." In Tony Magistrale and Michael A. Morrison, eds. *A Dark Night's Dreaming: Contemporary American Horror Fiction.* Columbia: University of South Carolina Press, 1996, pp. 55–67.

2007. Haggerty, George. "Anne Rice and the Queering of Culture." *Novel: A Forum on Fiction* 32 (1998): 5–18. Rpt. in: George Haggerty. *Queer Gothic.* Urbana: University of Illinois Press, 2006, pp. 185–200.

2008. Harse, Katie. "'Sick of Count Dracula': Scott, Carter, Rice and the Response to Stoker's Authority." *Journal of the Fantastic in the Arts* 13, 3 (2003): 250–57.

2009. Hirshey, Gerri. "Flesh for Fantasy." *Rolling Stone* (November 20, 1986). Rpt. in: George Beahm, ed. *The Anne Rice Companion.* Williamsburg, VA: GB Ink, 1995. 215 pp. 117–23. Rpt. as: George Beahm, ed. *The Unauthorized Anne Rice Companion.* Kansas City, MO: Andrews and McMeel, 1996, pp. 128–34.

2010. Hoffman, Eric. "Inner-View with the Vampire!" *Famous Monsters of Filmland* 206 (January/February 1995): 8–23.

2011. Holditch, W. Kenneth. "The Landscape of Childhood Memories: New Orleans in the Life and Work of Anne Rice." In Katherine Ramsland, ed. *The Anne Rice Reader.* New York: Ballantine Books, 1997, pp. 38–54.

2012. Holmes, Trevor. "Becoming-Other: (Dis)Embodiments of Race in Anne Rice's Tale of the Body Thief." *Romanticism on the Net: An Electronic Journal Devoted to Romantic Studies* 44 (2006): 20 paragraphs.

2013. _____. "Coming Out of the Coffin: Gay Males and Queer Goths in Contemporary Vampire Fiction." In Joan Gordon and Veronica Hollinger, eds. *Blood Read: The Vampire as Metaphor in Contemporary Culture.* Philadelphia: University of Pennsylvania Press, 1997, pp. 169–88.

2014. Hoppenstand, Gary, and Ray B. Browne, eds. *The Gothic World of Anne Rice.* Bowling Green, OH: Bowling Green University Popular Press, 1996. 261 pp. hb. boards. Rpt.: Bowling Green, OH: Bowling Green University Popular Press, 1996. 261 pp. tp. Includes contributions by Katherine Ramsland, Frank A. Salamone, Garyn G. Roberts, Kathryn McGinley, Edward J. Ingebretsen, Terri R. Liberman, Diana C. Reep, Joseph F. Ceccio, William A. Francis, Aileen Chris Shafer, Ann Larabee, Ellen M. Tsagaris, Bette B. Roberts, Marte Kinlaw, Cynthia Kasee, and James F. Iaccino.

2015. _____. "Vampires, Witches, Mummies, and Other Charismatic Personalities: Exploring the Anne Rice Phenomenon." In Gary Hoppenstand and Ray B. Browne, eds. *The Gothic World of Anne Rice*. Bowling Green, OH: Bowling Green University Popular Press, 1996, pp. 1–12.

2016. Iaccino, James F. "The World of *Forever Knight*: A Television Tribute to Anne Rice's New Age Vampire." In Gary Hoppenstand and Ray B. Browne, eds. *The Gothic World of Anne Rice*. Bowling Green, OH: Bowling Green University Popular Press, 1996, pp. 231–46.

2017. Ingebretsen, Edward J. "Anne Rice: Raising Holy Hell, Harlequin Style." In Gary Hoppenstand and Ray B. Browne, eds. *The Gothic World of Anne Rice*. Bowling Green, OH: Bowling Green University Popular Press, 1996, pp. 91–108.

2018. "Interview with Anne Rice." *American Fantasy* 2, 3 (Spring 1987): 36–43.

2019. Johansson, Fredrik. *From Conqueror to Rebel Without a Cause: The Change in the Symbolic Function of Vampires, from Bram Stoker's Imperialistic Dracula to Anne Rice's Anarchistic The Vampire Lestat*. Växjö, Sweden: Växjö University, Student thesis, 2009. 21 pp. Large format. Posted at: http://www.diva-portal.org/smash/get/diva2:206524/FULLTEXT01.pdf.

2020. Jönsson, Gabriella. "The Second Vampire: *filles fatales* in J. Sheridan Le Fanu's *Carmilla* and Anne Rice's *Interview with the Vampire*." *Journal of the Fantastic in the Arts* 17. 1 (2006): 33–48.

2021. Jowett, Lorna. "'Mute and Beautiful': The Representation of the Female in Anne Rice's *Interview with the Vampire*." *FEMSPEC: An Interdisciplinary Feminist Journal Dedicated to Critical and Creative Work in the Realms of Science Fiction, Fantasy, Magical Realism, Surrealism, Myth, Folklore, and Other Supernatural Genres* 4, 1 (2002): 59–67.

2022. Keller, James R. *Anne Rice and Sexual Politics: The Early Novels*. Jefferson, NC: McFarland & Company, 2000. 175 pp.

2023. Kemp, Kurt Alan. *Anne Rice's Vampire Aesthetic: Redefining the Vampire Tradition*. Charleston: Eastern Illinois University, M.A. thesis, 1994. 95 pp. Large format. Posted at http://repository.eiu.edu/theses/docs/32211998858840.pdf.

2024. Kemppainen, Tatja. "Your Heart Bleeds for Me: Finding the Essential Human in Anne Rice's *Interview with the Vampire*." *Moderna Språk* 94, 2 (2000): 122–36.

2025. King, Maureen. "Contemporary Women Writers and the 'New Evil': The Vampires of Anne Rice and Suzy McKee Charnas." *Journal of the Fantastic in the Arts* 5, 3 (1993): 75–84.

2026. Kinlaw, Marte and Cynthia Kasee. "Gens de Couleur Libre Ethnic Identity in The Feast of All Saints." In Gary Hoppenstand and Ray B. Browne, eds. *The Gothic World of Anne Rice*, Bowling Green, OH: Bowling Green University Popular Press, 1996, pp. 231–46.

2027. Klamer, Aaron J. *The Pain of an Amputated Limb: Subjective Morality and Existentialism in Anne Rice's Interview with the Vampire*. Kalamazoo: Western Michigan University, honor thesis, 1999. 20 pp. Large format. Posted at: http://scholarworks.wmich.edu/honors_theses/821.

2028. Kutzuba, Kerry. "'Lestat, C'est Moi': Anne Rice's Revelation of Self through The Vampire Chronicles." *Undergraduate Review: A Journal of Undergraduate Student Research* 1 (1997): 37–48. Posted at: http://fisherpub.sjfc.edu/ur/vol1/iss1/6.

2029. Laffite, Michel Pierre. "Gothic Ennui: On the Cultural Relevance of *The Picture of Dorian Gray* (1891), *Vathek* (1786) and *Interview with the Vampire* (1976)." In Kararzyna Więckowska, ed. *The Gothic: Studies in History, Identity and Space*. Oxford: Interdisciplinary Press, 2012, pp. 4–11.

2030. Lana, Victor. *Gothic Feminism in Anne Rice's The Vampire Chronicles*. Jamaica, NY: St John's University, Ph.D. dissertation, 1995. 132 pp. Large format.

2031. Langley, Jason Paul. *Gender Busting: Exploring Masculine and Feminine Roles in the Novels of Anne Rice*. Jonesboro: Arkansas State University, senior honors thesis, 1996. 51 pp. Large format.

2032. LaPerrière, Maureen-Claude. "Triply Filiated: Lestat and the Three Fathers." *Journal of Dracula Studies* 8 (2006): 37–44.

2033. _____. *Unholy Transubstantiation: Christifying the Vampire and Demonizing the Blood*. Montreal, PQ, CA: University of Montreal, Ph.D. dissertation, 2008. 259 pp. Large format.

2034. Liberman, Terri R. "Eroticism as Moral Fulcrum in Rice's Vampire Chronicles." In Gary Hoppenstand and Ray B. Browne, ed. The Gothic World of Anne Rice. Bowling Green, OH: Bowling Green University Popular Press, 1996, pp. 109–21.

2035. Mackay, Kathleen. "A Literary Friendship: Life Is Not a Footrace." In Katherine Ramsland, ed. *The Anne Rice Reader.* New York: Ballantine Books, 1997, pp. 28–37.

2036. Marcus, Jana. *In the Shadows of the Vampire: Reflections from the World of Anne Rice.* New York: Thunder's Mouth Press, 1997. 174 pp. tp.

2037. Marigny, Jean, and Victor Reinking. "The Different Faces of Eros in the Vampire Chronicles of Anne Rice." *Para-Doxa* 1, 3 (1995): 352–62.

2038. Martin, Anya. "A Conversation with Anne Rice." *Cemetary Dance* 3, 3 (Summer 1991): 34–39.

2039. Matthews, Tom, and Lucille Beachy. "Fangs for Nothing: Coppola's Dracula and Rice's Lestat: Cultural Icons for an Age of Enervation." *Newsweek* (November 30, 1992) 74–75.

2040. McDonald, Beth E., "Eros and the Thanatotic Hero: Anne Rice's Vampire Chronicles." In Beth E. Mcdonald. *The Vampire as Numinous Experience: Spiritual Journeys with the Undead in British and American Literature.* Jefferson: McFarland, 2004, pp. 129–168.

2041. McDonnell, David. "*Interview with the Vampire*: Tom Cruise Speaks." In Anthony Timpone. *Fangoria Vampires.* New York: HarperPrism, 1996, pp. 25–32.

2042. _____. "Lestat Speaks!" *Fangoria* 139 (January 1995): 38–39.

2043. McGinley, Kathryn. "Development of the Byronic Vampire: Byron, Stoker, Rice." In Gary Hoppenstand and Ray B. Browne, ed. *The Gothic World of Anne Rice.* Bowling Green, OH: Bowling Green University Popular Press, 1996, pp. 71–90.

2044. Mitchell, Ann Elizabeth. *The Rhetorical Accomplishment of Subversion in Anne Rice's Vampire Chronicles.* Carbondale: Southern Illinois University, M.A. thesis, 1992. 95 pp. Large format.

2045. Mitchell, Donna. "Race, Gender and the Vampire. The Madonna and Child: Re-Evaluating Social Conventions through Anne Rice's Forgotten Females." In Barbara Brodman and James E. Doan, eds. *Images of the Modern Vampire: The Hip and the Atavistic.* Madison. NJ: Fairleigh Dickinson, 2013, pp. 57–70.

2046. Montesano, Anthony P. "Beyond Dracula: In Defense of Cruise." *Imagi-Movies* 2, 2 (Winter 1994): 39.

2047. Mulvey-Roberts, Marie. "Interviewing the Author of *Interview with the Vampire.*" *Gothic Studies* 1 (1999): 169–81.

2048. _____. "Rice, Ann (1941–)." In Marie Mulvey-Roberts, ed. *The Handbook of Gothic Literature.* New York: New York University Press, 1998, pp. 188–89.

2049. Nardone, Laurie Ann. *The Body Shop: The Politics and Poetics of Transformation.* Atlanta, GA: Emory University, Ph.D. dissertation, 1997. 199 pp. Large format.

2050. Nassbaaumer, Janina. *The Vampire in Literature: A Comparison of Bram Stoker's Dracula and Anne Rice's Interview with the Vampire.* Hamburg, Germany: Anchor Academic Publishing (September 6, 2013. 44 pp. pb. Large format.

2051. Newitz, Annalee. "Abuse and Its Pleasures: Compensatory Fantasy in the Popular Fiction of Anne Rice." In Tomoko Kuribayashi and Julie Tharp, eds. *Creating Safe Space: Violence and Women's Writing.* Albany: State University of New York Press, 1998, pp. 179–199.

2052. Ní Fhlainn, Sorcha. "1976: The Duality in Postmodern Vampiric Identity and Evil in George A Romero's *Martin* and Anne Rice's *Interview with the Vampire.*" In Sorcha Ni Fhlainn & William Andrew Myers, eds. *The Wicked Heart: Studies in the Phenomenon of Evil.* Oxford: Inter-Disciplinary Press, 2006, pp. 171–82. Posted at: http://www.academia.edu/413983/The_Wicked_Heart_Studies_in_the_Phenomena_of_Evil.

2053. Noll, Richard. "Lestat: The Vampire as Degenerate Genius." In Katherine Ramsland, ed. *The Anne Rice Reader.* New York: Ballantine Books, 1997, pp. 150–66.

2054. Nordberg, Heidi L. "Blood Spirit/Blood Bodies: The Viral in the Vampire Chronicles of Anne Rice and Chelsea Quinn Yarbro." In James Craig Holte, ed. *The Fantastic Vampire: Studies in the Children of the Night: Selected Essays from the Eighteenth International Conference on the Fantastic in the Arts.* Vol. 19. Westport, CT: Greenwood Publishing Group, 2002, pp. 111–22.

2055. Nußbaumer, Janina. *The Vampire in Literature: A Comparison of Bram Stoker's Dracula and Anne Rice's Interview with the Vampire.* Hamburg, Germany: Anchior Academic Publishing, 2013. 38 pp. pb.

2056. Osap, Sonja. *Queer as Vampires: A Study of Anne Rice's* Interview with the Vampire *through Queer Theory.* Växjö, Sweden: Linnaeus University, Student thesis, 2010. 25 pp. Large format. Posted at: http://www.diva-portal.org/smash/get/diva2:324995/FULLTEXT01.pdf.

2057. Paolucci, Peter Leonard. *Re-Reading the Vampire from John Polidori to Anne Rice: Structures of Impossibility Among Three Narrative Variations in the Vampire Tradition.* Toronto, ON: York University, Ph.D. dissertation, 2000. 306 pp. Large format.

2058. Perry, David. "Do the Rice Thing." *Omni* 12, 1 (October 89): 26–28.

2059. Raileanu, Nicoleta Maria. *The Social and Psychological Relevance of Anne Rice's Queen of the Damned and Pandora in the Context of the Gothic Tradition.* Columbia: University of Missouri, Ph.D. Dissertation, 1998. 229 pp. Large format.

2060. Ramsland, Katherine. "Anne Rice: An Overview." In Katherine Ramsland, ed. *The Anne Rice Reader.* New York: Ballantine Books, 1997, pp. 5–27.

2061. _____. "Anne Rice, Seeking Recognition as a Writer." *The Blood Review* 2 (January 1990): 29–34.

2062. _____. *The Anne Rice Trivia Book.* New York: Ballantine Books, 1994. 244 pp.

2063. _____. "Forced Consent and Voluptuous Captivity: The Paradoxical Psychology Behind Anne Rice's Erotic Imagination." In Katherine Ramsland, ed. *The Anne Rice Reader.* New York: Ballantine Books, 1997, pp. 322–46.

2064. _____. "*Interview with the Vampire*: How the Movie Finally Got Made." In Katherine Ramsland, ed. *The Anne Rice Reader.* New York: Ballantine Books, 1997, pp. 167–95.

2065. _____. "Let the Flesh Instruct the Mind: A Quadrant Interview with Anne Rice." *Quadrant: The Journal of the C. G. Jung Foundation for Analytical Psychology* ?14, 2 (1991). Rpt. in: Katherine Ramsland, ed. *The Anne Rice Reader.* New York: Ballantine Books, 1997, pp. 55–73.

2066. _____. "The Lived World of Anne Rice." In Gary Hoppenstand and Ray B. Browne, eds. *The Gothic World of Anne Rice.* Bowling Green, OH: Bowling Green University Popular Press, 1996, pp. 13–33.

2067. _____. *Prism in the Night: A Biography of Anne Rice.* New York: Dutton, 1991. 385 pp. hb. dj. Rpt.: New York: Plume Books, 1992. 398 pp. tp.

2068. _____. *The Vampire Companion: The Official Guide to Anne Rice's The Vampire Chroni-*cles. New York: Ballantine Books, 1993. 507 pp. hb. dj. Rev. ed.: 1995. 577 pp. tp. Rpt.: London: Little Brown and Company, 1996. 577 pp. tp.

2069. _____, ed. *The Anne Rice Reader.* New York: Ballantine Books, 1997. 359 pp. 359 pp. pb. Above and beyond her own contribution, editor Katherine Ramsland had included contribution of vampire-related material by Kathleen, Mackay, W. Kenneth Holdrich, Gail Abbott Zimmerman, Bette Roberts, Richard Noll, and John Beebe.

2070. Reep, Diana C., Joseph F. Ceccio, and William A. Francis. "Anne Rice's *Interview with the Vampire*: Novel versus Film." In Gary Hoppenstand and Ray B. Browne, ed. *The Gothic World of Anne Rice.* Bowling Green, OH: Bowling Green University Popular Press, 1996, pp. 123–47.

2071. Remington, Pete. "'You're Whining Again Louis': Anne Rice's Vampires as Indices of the Depressive Self." In Peter Day, ed. *Vampires: Myths and Metaphors of Enduring Evil.* Amsterdam, Netherlands: Rodopi, 2006, pp. 227–43.

2072. Rende, Carol Anne. *Anne Rice's Recreation of Mary Shelley's Frankenstein.* West Chester, PA: West Chester University, M.A. thesis, 1994. 43 pp. Large format.

2073. Reynolds, Sandra S. *Through the Eyes of a Vampire: The Efforts of Rhetorical Context in Two of Anne Rice's Vampire Chronicles.* Denton: Texas Woman's University, M.A. thesis, 1996. 652 pp. Large format.

2074. Rice, Anne. *Called Out of Darkness: A Spiritual Confession.* New York: Alfred A. Knopf, 2008. 245 pp. hb. dj.

2075. _____. "Playboy Interview." *Playboy* 40, 3 (March 1993): 53–64. See: Digby Diehl.

2076. Riley, Michael. *Conversations with Anne Rice.* New York: Ballantine Books, 1996. 296 pp. tp. Rpt. as: *Interview with Anne Rice.* London: Chatto & Windus, 1996. 296 pp. tp.

2077. Roberts, Bette B. *Anne Rice.* New York: Twayne Publishers, 1994. 173 pp. hb.

2078. _____. "Anne Rice and the Gothic Tradition." In George Beahm, ed. *The Unauthorized Anne Rice Companion.* Kansas City, MO: Andrews and McMeel, 1996, pp. 107–19. Rpt in: Katherine Ramsland, ed. *The Anne Rice Reader.* New York: Ballantine Books, 1997, pp. 124–149.

2079. _____. "Anne Rice's *Interview with a Vampire.*" *New Mexico Humanities Review* (1979): 48–??.

2080. _____. "Making the Case: Teaching Stephen King and Anne Rice through the Gothic Tradition." In Diane Long Hoeveler and Tamar Heller, ed. *Approaches to Teaching Gothic Fiction: The British and American Traditions.* New York: Modern Language Association of America, 2003, pp. 223–29.

2081. _____. "The Mother Goddess in H. Rider Haggard's *She* and Anne Rice's *Queen of the Damned.*" In James Craig Holte, ed. *The Fantastic Vampire: Studies in the Children of the Night: Selected Essays from the Eighteenth International Conference on the Fantastic in the Arts.* Vol. 19. Westport, CT: Greenwood Publishing Group, 2002, pp. 103–110.

2082. Roberts, Garyn G. "Gothicism, Vampirism, and Seduction: Anne Rice's 'The Master of Rampling Gate.'" In Gary Hoppenstand and Ray B. Browne, eds. *The Gothic World of Anne Rice.* Bowling Green, OH: Bowling Green University Popular Press, 1996, pp. 55–70.

2083. Rout, Kathleen. "Who Do You Love? Anne Rice's Vampires and Their Moral Transition." *The Journal of Popular Culture* 36 (2003): 473–479.

2084. Rowe, Michael Charles. "Anne Rice: Creating the Vampire Chronicles." In Anthony Timpone. *Fangoria Vampires.* New York: HarperPrism, 1996, pp. 41–46.

2085. _____. "Queen of the Fanged." *Fangoria* 116 (September 1992): 18–21.

2086. Salamone, Frank A. "The Anthropological Vision of Anne Rice." In Gary Hoppenstand and Ray B. Browne, eds. The Gothic World of Anne Rice. Bowling Green, OH: Bowling Green University Popular Press, 1996, pp. 35–55.

2087. Salisbury, Mark. "*Interview with the Vampire*: Neil Jordan on Directing." In Anthony Timpone. *Fangoria Vampires.* New York: HarperPrism, 1996, pp. 32–40.

2088. Schumann, Nancy. "Heartbreaking Beauties—Pre-Modern Vampires." In Nancy Schumann. *Take a Bite. Female Vampires in Anglo-American Literature and Folklore.* London: Callio Press Limited, n.d. [2011?], pp. 67–90.

2089. Sessums, Kevin. "Cruise Speed." *Vanity Fair* (October 1994): 188–195, 270–273.

2090. Shafer, Aileen Chris. "Let Us Prey: Religious Codes and Rituals in The Vampire Lestat." In Gary Hoppenstand and Ray B. Browne,

eds. *The Gothic World of Anne Rice.* Bowling Green, OH: Bowling Green University Popular Press, 1996, pp. 149–61.

2091. Smith, Jennifer. *Anne Rice: A Critical Companion.* Ser.: Critical Companions to Popular Contemporary Writers. Westport, CT: Greenwood Press, 1996. 193 pp. hb.

2092. Smith, Kalila Katherina. *New Orleans Ghosts and Vampires: Journey into Darkness...* New Orleans, LA: De Simonin Publications, 2004. 173 pp. tp.

2093. Sonser, Anna M. *A Passion for Consumption: The Gothic Novel in America.* Bowling Green, OH: Bowling Green State University Popular Press, 2001. 162 pp.

2094. _____. *Subversion, Seduction, and the Culture of Consumption: The American Gothic Revisited in the Work of Toni Morrison, Joyce Carol Oates, and Anne Rice.* Toronto: University of Toronto, Ph.D. dissertation, 2000. 225 pp. Large format.

2095. Stärk, Bianca. Interview with the Vampire *and* Wuthering Heights *and the Diabolical Reversal of the Nuclear Family.* Munchen, Germany: GRIN Verlag, 2007. 32 pp. pb.

2096. Stein, Atara. "Conclusion: The Vampire with the Face of an Angel." In Atara Stein. *The Byronic Hero in Film, Fiction, and Television.* Carbondale: Southern Illinois University Press, 2009, pp. 213–218.

2097. _____. "Immortals and Vampires and Ghosts, Oh My! Byronic Heroes in Popular Culture." In Laura Mandell and Michael Eberle-Sinatra, eds. *Romanticism and Contemporary Culture.* Special Issue of *Romantic Circles Praxis Series* (February 2002). Posted at: http://www.rc.umd.edu/praxis/contemporary/stein/stein.html.

2098. That Other Tour, LLC. *Anne Rice's Unauthorized French Quarter Tour: Featuring the Vampire Chronicles and Mayfair Witches.* New Orleans: That Other Tour LLC, 2012. 172 pp. tp.

2099. Tomc, Sandra. "Dieting and Damnation: Anne Rice's *Interview with the Vampire.*" *English Studies in Canada* 22, 4 (1996): 441–60. Rpt.: Joan Gordon and Veronica Hollinger, eds. *Blood Read: The Vampire as Metaphor in Contemporary Culture.* Philadelphia: University of Pennsylvania Press, 1997, pp. 97–113.

2100. Valls De Gomis, Estelle. "Dracula versus Lestat." Spécial Anne Rice issue. *Requiem* (Archivs du vampirisme) 9 (1998–1999): 55–57.

2101. Wasson, Sara. "Coven of the Articulate": Orality and Community in Anne Rice's Vampire Fiction." *The Journal of Popular Culture* 45, 1 (February 2012): 197–213.

2102. Waxman, Barbra Frey. "Postexistentialism in the Neo-Gothic Mode: Anne Rice's *Interview with a Vampire.*" *Mosaic* 25, 3 (Summer 1992): 79–97.

2103. Wiater, Stanley. "Anne Rice, Dark Dreamer: An Interview with the Writer." In George Beahm, ed. *The Anne Rice Companion.* Williamsburg, VA: GB Ink, 1995. 215 pp. 110–16. Rpt. in Bram Stoker. *Dracula.* Ed. by John Paul Riquelme. Ser.: Case Studies in Contemporary Criticism. Boston: Bedford/New York: St. Martin's, 2002, pp. 577–99. Rpt. in: George Beahm, ed. *The Unauthorized Anne Rice Companion.* Kansas City, MO: Andrews and McMeel, 1996, pp. 120–27.

2104. _____. "The Rice Papers." *Fear* 16 (April 1990): 12–15.

2105. Wilbern, David. "Appetites and Anxieties: The Unfathomed, The Undead, the Under Toad: *Jaws, Interview with the Vampire, The World According to Garp.*" In David Wilbern. *The American Popular Novel After World War II: A Study of 25 Best Sellers, 1947–2000.* Jefferson, NC: McFarland & Company, 2013, pp. 65–83.

2106. Wood, Martin J. "New Life for an Old Tradition: Anne Rice and Vampire Literature." In Leonard G. Heldreth and Mary Pharr, eds. *The Blood Is the Life: Vampires in Literature.* Bowling Green, OH: Bowling Green University Popular Press, 1999, pp. 59–78.

2107. Worley, Lloyd. "Anne Rice's Protestant Vampires." In Leonard Heldreth and Mary Pharr, eds. *The Blood Is the Life: Vampires in Literature.* Bowling Green, KY: Bowling Green State University Press, 1999, pp. 79–92.

2108. Zimmerman, Gail Abbott. "The World of the Vampire: Rice's Contribution." In Katherine Ramsland, ed. *The Anne Rice Reader.* New York: Ballantine Books, 1997, pp. 101–23.

Stephen King's Vampires

Relative to vampires, horror writer Stephen King (b. 1947) is best known for his early work, *'Salem's Lot*, but in subsequent years he has produced a number of vampire characters from the extra-terrestrial vampires in *The Tommyknockers* (1987) to the well-traveled "Night Flier" (1988). In addition to these more famous stories, vampires also appear in *Wolves of the Calla, Song of Susannah,* and *The Dark Tower* (the fifth, sixth, and seventh books in *The Dark Tower* series, issued 2003–2005) and in several of his short stories, such as "Graveyard Shift," "Jerusalem's Lot," "One for the Road," "Popsy," and "The Little Sisters of Eluria," many of his more recent vampire items having been somewhat lost amid his vast output of popular horror novels.

Following his graduation from the University of Maine at Orono in 1970, King began his working career as a high school English teacher. His first book, *Carrie*, appeared in 1973 and he resigned his teaching job to become a full-time author. His second novel, *'Salem's Lot*, his classic vampire novel, appeared in 1975. By this time, he had emerged as the best-selling horror writer in the United States. *'Salem's Lot* was nominated for the World Fantasy Award for Best Novel, given by the World Fantasy Convention for the best fantasy fiction published in English during the previous calendar year.

King has produced literally hundreds of books and short stories and his popularity has led to the production of a large body of commentary on his writings. Only a relatively small segment of the commentary on his writings focuses on his vampire stories, and most of the ruminations on his vampires are integrated into considerations of his larger body of work. That being said, *'Salem's Lot* remains one of his most noteworthy novels, the only piece of his writing to be adapted to the screen twice, and the source of a significant body of commentary. King considers the Dark Tower novels *Wolves of the Calla* and *Song of Susannah* as his sequels to *'Salem's Lot.*

In addition to his published writings, in 1992 King also wrote the screenplay for *Sleepwalkers*, a story about a family of shape-shifting psychic vampires. It was the first of his movies to be made from an original script rather than being developed from a previously published novel or short story.

2109. Badley, Linda. *Writing Horror and the Body: The Fiction of Stephen King, Clive Barker, and Anne Rice.* Westport CT: Greenwood, 1996. 183 pp. hb.

2110. Casey, Susan. "Stephen King's *'Salem's Lot*: The Miniseries." In Anthony Timpone. *Fangoria Vampires.* New York: HarperPrism, 1996, pp. 151–57.

2111. Collings, Michael R. *The Films of Steven King.* Mercer Island, WA: Starmont House, 1986. 201 pp.

2112. Eads, Sean. "The Vampire George Middler: Selling the Monstrous in *'Salem's Lot.*" *The Journal of Popular Culture* 43, 1 (February 2010): 78–96.

2113. Furth, Robin. *Stephen King's The Dark Tower: A Concordance.* 2 vols. New York: Charles Scribner's Sons, 2003. Rev. ed. as *Stephen King's The Dark Tower: The Complete Concordance*, Revised and Updated. New York: Charles Scribner's Sons, 2012. 689 pp.

2114. Hicks, James E. "Stephen King's Creation of Horror in 'Salems Lot: A Prolegomena toward a New Hermeneutic of the Gothic Novel." In Gary Hoppenstand and Ray B. Browne, eds. *The Gothic World of Stephen King: Landscape of Nightmares.* Bowling Green, OH: Bowling Green University Press, 1987, pp. 75–83.

2115. Kelley, Bill. "*'Salem's Lot.*" *Cinefantastique* 9, 2 (1979): 9–13.

2116. King, Stephen. *Danse Macabre.* New York: Everest House, 1981. 400 pp. hb. dj. Stephen King discusses vampires in the midst of his larger discussion of the nature of horror in general. See especially chapter 3, "Tales of the Tarot" (pp. 60–88).

2117. Lidston, Robert. "*Dracula* and *'Salem's Lot*: Why the Monsters Won't Die." *West Virginia University Philological Papers* 28 (1982): 70–78.

2118. Magistrale, Tony. *Hollywood's Stephen King.* New York: Palgrave Macmillan, 2003. 233 pp. hb. dj. See subchapters on *The Night Flier* and *'Salem's Lot.*

2119. Mazur, Christine Teresa. *Gothic Fiction, Liminality, and Popular Culture: Stephen King's "Grotesque" Social Commentary in 'Salem's Lot.* Winnipeg: University of Manitoba, M.A. thesis, 1997. 87 pp. Large format.

2120. Pharr, Mary. "Vampiric Appetite in *I Am Legend*, *'Salem's Lot*, and *The Hunger.*" In Leonard Heldreth and Mary Pharr, eds. *The Blood Is the Life: Vampires in Literature.* Bowling Green, KY: Bowling Green State University Press, 1999, pp. 93–103.

2121. Pringle, David. "*'Salem's Lot*'by Stephen King." In David Pringle. *Modern Fantasy, The Hundred Best Novels: An English Language Selection, 194–1987.* London: Grafton Books, 1988, pp. 156–58.

2122. Reino, Joseph. "The Dracula Myth: Shadow and Substance." In Joseph Reino. *Stephen King: The First Decade, Carrie to Pet Sematary.* Boston: Twayne Publishers, 1988, pp. 18–33.

2123. Roberts, Bette B. "Making the Case: Teaching Stephen King and Anne Rice through the Gothic Tradition." In Diane Long Hoeveler and Tamar Heller, ed. *Approaches to Teaching Gothic Fiction: The British and American Traditions.* New York: Modern Language Association of America, 2003. 223–29.

2124. Russell, Sharon A. "'Salem's Lot (1975)." In Sharon A. Russell. *Stephen King: A Critical Companion.* Ser.: Critical Companions to Popular Contemporary Writer. Westport, CT: Greenwood Press, 1996, pp. 27–43.

2125. Sanders, Joe S. "Closure and Power in *'Salem's Lot.*" *Journal of the Fantastic in the Arts* 10, 2 (1999): 142–154. Posted at http://krex.k-state.edu/dspace/handle/2097/15350.

2126. Vincent, Bev. *The Dark Tower Companion: A Guide to Stephen King's Epic Fantasy.* New York: NAL Trade, 2013. 498 pp. tp.

2127. _____. *The Road to The Dark Tower: Exploring Stephen King's Magnum Opus.* New York: NAL Trade, 2004. 350 pp. tp.

2128. Watson, Christine. "*'Salem's Lot*." In Frank N. Magill, ed. *Survey of Modern Fantasy Literature*. Vol. 3. Englewood Cliffs, NJ: Salem Press, 1983. pp. 1350–55.

2129. Wiater, Stanley, Christopher Golden, and Hank Wagner. "'Salem's Lot." In Stanley Wiater, Christopher Golden, and Hank Wagner. *The Stephen King Universe*. Renaissance Books, 2001, pp. 191–209. In the same volume see also the comments on the short story "Jerusalem's Lot" and "The Night Flier," and the novel *The Tommyknockers*.

2130. Winter, Douglas E. "*'Salem's Lot*." In Douglas E. Winter. *Stephen King: The Art of Darkness*. New York: New American Library, 1984, pp. 36–44.

IV. Vampires on Stage and Screen

Stage Drama

Inspired by the original English-language vampire tale, "The Vampyre," which he initially believed to have been written by Lord Byron, French playwright Charles Nordier produced a play featuring Lord Ruthven, the story's villain. The stage production became an instant hit in Paris, and within the year a number of additional vampire plays appeared across the city to feed the popular demand. Meanwhile, James Robinson Planché adapted "The Vampyre" for the London stage. The young Alexandre Dumas arrived in Paris while Nordier's play was still attracting audiences. He would soon begin his own literary career with a vampire play and twice later in life returned to the vampire theme when faced with critical financial problems.

The stage would remain the most prominent tool for introducing the vampire into popular culture through the mid–twentieth century, when it would be eclipsed by the cinema. *Dracula* would be adapted to the stage in the 1920s, the stage play being the direct cause of the making of the *Dracula* movie starring Bela Lugosi, who had earlier appeared in the New York stage production.

In spite of having lost out in popularity to the movies, new vampire stage plays proliferated through the last half of the twentieth century to the present, and numerous stage productions have taken place in recent years, from lavish Broadway productions to the many high school and college-level revampings of the 1920s *Dracula* play, which has been kept in print by its publisher, Samuel French.

From its appearance in the 1820s, the vampire has contributed immensely to the dramatic world, highlighted by Bram Stoker's initial staging of *Dracula* in 1897 as a means of securing his copyrights, the use of the vampire by August Strindberg early in the twentieth century in his attempts to develop new forms of dramatic productions, the effective staging of *Dracula* in the 1920s by Hamilton Dean, and the proliferation of vampire plays in the late twentieth century. The successful revival of the Broadway production of *Dracula* in the late 1970s would lead a young Frank Langella from the stage to the new cinematic adaptation of *Dracula* by Universal Studios in 1979.

2131. Aldridge, A. Owen. "The Vampire Theme: Dumas Père and the English State." *Revue des Langues Vivants* 39 (1973–74): 312–24.

2132. Auerbach, Nina. *Ellen Terry: Player in Her Time.* New York: W. W. Norton, 1987. 504 pp. tp.

2133. _____. "Escaping the Vampire Trap." A paper presented at the Victorian Theatre and Theatrically Conference of the Victorian Committee of the Doctoral Program in English held at the City University of New York, May 8, 1992.

2134. Balkin, Sarah. "Strindberg's Vampiric Narrators." *Genre* 46, 1 (Spring 2013): 1–31. Posted at: http://www.academia.edu/2174671/Strindbergs_Vampiric_Narrators.

2135. Barham, Jeremy. "Dismembering the Musical Voice: Mahler, Melodrama and *Dracula* from Stage to Screen." In Sarah Hibberd, ed. *Melodramatic Voices: Understanding Music Drama.* Farnham, Surrey, UK/Burlington, VT: Ashgate, 2011, pp. 237–62.

2136. Beard, William. "*Dracula: Pages from a Virgin's Diary.*" In William Beard. *Into the Past: The Cinema of Guy Maddin.* Toronto, ON: University of Toronto Press, 2010, pp. 163–91.

2137. Bennett, Cleon Vernon. *James Robinson Planche: Victorian Craftsman.* Madison: University of Wisconsin—Madison, Ph.D. dissertation. 1971. 450 pp. Large format.

2138. Brandon, Clare Therese. *Charles Nodier and Deviant Romanticism.* New York: Fordham University, Ph.D. dissertation, 1980. 170 pp. Large format.

2139. Braun, Anne-Kathrin. "From Page to Stage: Narrative Strategies in Lochhead's *Dracula.*" *Gothic Studies* 3 (2001): 196–210.

2140. Burwick, Frederick. "Vampires in Kilts." In Frederick Burwick. *Romantic Drama: Acting and Reacting.* Cambridge, UK: Cambridge University Press, 2009, pp. 230–57.

2141. Case, Sue-Ellen. "Dracula's Daughters: In-Corporating Avatars in Cyberspace." In Janelle G. Reinelt and Joseph R. Roach, eds. *Critical Theory and Performance.* Ann Arbor: University of Michigan Press, 2007, pp. 547–562. Rpt. in Sue Ellen Case, *Feminist and Queer Performance: Critical Strategies.* Basingstoke, UK: Palgrave Macmillan, 2009, pp. 170–87.

2142. _____. "Tracking the Vampire." *differences* 3, 2 (1991): 1–20. Rpt. in: Katie Conboy, Nadia Medina, and Sarah Stanbury, eds. *Writing on the Body: Female Embodiment and Feminist Theory.* New York: Columbia University Press, 1997, pp. 380–400. Rpt. in: Sue Ellen Case, *Feminist and Queer Performance: Critical Strategies.* Basingstoke, UK: Palgrave Macmillan, 2009, pp. 66–85.

2143. Corwin, Thomas Leonard. *Magic, Trick-Work, and Illusion in the Vampire Plays.* Lubbock: Texas Tech University, Ph.D. dissertation, 1987. 155 pp. Large format. Posted at: http://repositories.tdl.org/ttu-ir/bitstream/handle/2346/15206/31295005242952.pdf?sequence=1.

2144. Desmet, Christy. "Remembering Ophelia: Ellen Terry and the Shakespearizing of *Dracula.*" In Christy Desmet and Anne Williams, ed. *Shakespearean Gothic.* Cardiff: University of Wales Press, 2009, pp. 198–216.

2145. Dircks, P. T. "James Robinson Planche and the English Burletta Tradition." *Theatre Survey* 17 (1976): 68–81.

2146. Dumas, Alexandre. *The Memoirs of Alexandre Dumas.* Trans. by A. F. Davidson. 2 vols. London: W. H. Allen & Co., 1891. Rev. ed. as: *My Memoirs.* Trans. by Craig Bell. Philadelphia, PA: Chilton, 1961. Excerpt rpt. as: "A Visit to the Theatre." In Christopher Frayling. *Vampyres: From Lord Byron to Count Dracula.* London: Faber and Faber, 1991, pp. 131–44. See especially Chapter 18, "An Eventful Night at the Theatre (1821)," pp. 33–56. Dumas describes his arrival in Paris at the height of the interest in vampires by the city's dramatists, most notably Charles Nodier.

2147. Dunn, Denise. "The Vampire from Stage to Screen." *Monsters of the Movies* 1, 7 (June 1975): 8–11.

2148. Dvoskin, Michelle G. *Under Their Spell: How the Musical Episodes of* Xena: Warrior Princess *and* Buffy the Vampire Slayer *Queer the Audience.* Austin: University of Texas, M.A. thesis, 2006.

2149. Elliott, Kenneth. "Crossover Crossdressing: Vampire Lesbians and the Assimilation of Ridiculous Theatre." In Stratos E. Constantinidis, ed. *Text & Presentation, 2005.* Jefferson, NC: McFarland & Company, 2006, pp. 159–68.

2150. Emmet, Alfred. "The Vampire Trap." *Theatre Notebook: A Journal of the History and Technique of the British Theatre* 34, 3 (1980): 128–29.

2151. Finn, Anne-Marie. "Whose Dracula Is It Anyway? Deane, Balderston and the World Famous Vampire Play." *Journal of Dracula Studies* 1 (1999): 8–14.

2152. Fletcher, Kathy. "Planche, Vestris, and the Transvestite Role: Sexuality and Gender in Victorian Popular Theatre." *Nineteenth Century Theatre* 15 (1987): 9–33.

2153. Forbes, Barbara Aileen Martin. *Costumes for the Robber Baron* and *The Passion of Dracula*. Berkeley: University of California., Ph.D. dissertation, 1981. 172 pp. Large format.

2154. Foster, David William. "Jose Gonzalez Castillo's Los invertidos and the Vampire Theory of Homosexuality." *Latin American Theatre Review* 22, 2 (Spring 1989): 19–29.

2155. Garland, Rosie. "Coming Out at Night: Performing as the Lesbian Vampire Rosie Lugosi." In Nina Rapi and Maya Chowdhry, eds. *Acts of Passion: Sexuality, Gender, and Performance.* New York: Harrington Park Press, 1998, pp. 201–08.

2156. Garner, Edward. *Was You Ever in Dovedale? Derbyshire from Dracula to the Derby Run.* Wilmslow, Cheshire, UK: Sigma Leisure, 1995. 150 pp. tp.

2157. Gener, Randy. "Communing with the Vampire." *American Theatre* 25, 3 (2008): 28ff.

2158. Gorman, Herbert. *The Incredible Marquis: Alexandre Dumas.* New York: Farrar & Rinehart, 1929. 466 pp. hb.

2159. Gracia, Jorge J. E. "From Horror to Hero: Film Interpretations of Stoker's Dracula." In William Irwin & Jorge J. E. Gracia, eds. *Philosophy and the Interpretation of Pop Culture.* Lanham (MD), Rowman & Littlefield Publishers, 2007, pp. 187–214.

2160. Gray, Jonathan M. "A Historical Explanation of Vampires in 1820s Paris Boulevard Theater." A paper presented at the annual conference of the Popular Culture Association, Louisville, KY, March 1992.

2161. Harland, Robert. "Melodrama Hath Charms: Planche's Theatrical Domestication of Polidori's 'The Vampyre.'" *Journal of Dracula Studies* 3 (2001), 3–7.

2162. High, Jeffrey L. "From Martyr to Vampire: The Figure of Mary Stuart in Drama from Vondel to Swinburne." In Jeffrey L. High. *Who Is This Schiller Now? Essays on His Reception and Significance.* Woodbridge: Boydell & Brewer, 2011, pp. 321–39.

2163. Hoeveler, Diane Long. "Victorian Gothic Drama," in Andrew Smith and William Hughes, eds. *The Victorian Gothic: An Edinburgh Companion.* Edinburgh: Edinburgh University Press, 2012, pp. 57–71.

2164. Holroyd, Michael. *A Strange Eventful History: The Dramatic Lives of Ellen Terry, Henry Irving, and Their Remarkable Families.* New York: Farrar, Straus and Giroux, 2009. 620 pp. hb. dj.

2165. Holte, James Craig. "Female Film Vampires." *Journal of the Fantastic in the Arts* 10, 2 (September 1999): 163–73.

2166. Homan, Richard L. "Freud's 'Seduction Theory' on Stage: Deane's and Balderston's Dracula." *Literature and Psychology* 38, 1 & 2 (1992): 57–70.

2167. Hopkins, Lisa. "Jane Eyre and Dracula." In Lisa Hopkins. *Screening the Gothic.* Austin: University of Texas Press, 2005, pp. 88–115.

2168. Kabatchnik, Amnon. "*The Adventure of the Sussex Vampire* (1988), Peter Buckley." In Amnon Kabatchnik. *Blood on the Stage, 1975–2000: Milestone Plays of Crime, Mystery and Detection.* Lanham, MD: Scarecrow Press, 2012, pp. 364–67.

2169. _____. "*Count Dracula* (1971) by Ted Tiller." In Amnon Kabatchnik. *Blood on the Stage, 1950–1975: Milestone Plays of Crime, Mystery and Detection.* Lanham, MD: Scarecrow Press, 2011, pp. 66–68.

2170. _____. "*Dracula* (1927) by Hamilton Deane and John Balderston." In Amnon Kabatchnik. *Blood on the Stage, 1925–1950: Milestone Plays of Crime, Mystery and Detection.* Lanham, MD: Scarecrow Press, 2009, pp. 85–92.

2171. _____. "*Dracula* (1973) by Crane Johnson." In Amnon Kabatchnik. *Blood on the Stage, 1950–1975: Milestone Plays of Crime, Mystery and Detection.* Lanham, MD: Scarecrow Press, 2011, pp. 592–94.

2172. _____. "*Dracula* (1980) John Mattera (United States, 1953–)." In Amnon Kabatchnik. *Blood on the Stage, 1975–2000: Milestone Plays of Crime, Mystery and Detection.* Lanham, MD: Scarecrow Press, 2012, pp. 149–53.

2173. _____. "*Dracula* (1995) Steve Dietz (United States, 1958—)." In Amnon Kabatchnik. *Blood on the Stage, 1975–2000: Milestone Plays of Crime, Mystery and Detection.* Lanham, MD: Scarecrow Press, 2012, pp. 462–67.

2174. _____. "*Dracula Baby* (1970) by Bruce Ronald, John Jakes, and Clare Staunch." In Amnon Kabatchnik. *Blood on the Stage, 1950–1975: Milestone Plays of Crime, Mystery and Detection.* Lanham, MD: Scarecrow Press, 2011, pp. 337–42.

2175. Kemp, George P. "Dracula: Eroticism in the Vampire Genre." In Douglas Radcliffe-

Umstead, ed. *Varieties of Film Expression*. Kent, OH: Romance Languages Dept., Kent State University, 1989, pp. 128–134.

2176. Kerrigan, John. "Aeschylus and Dracula." In John Kerrigan. *Revenge Tragedy: Aeschylus to Armageddon*. Oxford/New York: Oxford University Press, 1996, pp. 33–58.

2177. Kessler, Joan C. "Charles Nodier's Demons: Vampirism as Metaphor in Smarra." *French Forum* 16, 1 (January 1991): 51–66.

2178. Lima, Robert. "*Nosferatu*: A Play on the Vampire by Francisco Nieva." *Modern Drama* 44, 2 (Spring 2001): 232–246.

2179. _____. "The Prey of the Vampire': Malign Decadence in Francisco Nieva's *Nosferatu*. In Robert Lima. *Stages of Evil: Occultism in Western Theater and Drama*. Lexington: University of Kentucky Press, 2005, pp. 177–94.

2180. Loving, Matthew. "Charles Nodier: The Romantic Librarian." *Libraries & Culture* 38, 2 (2003): 166–188.

2181. Macabre, J. B. "The Stage Struck Vampire." In Rosemary Ellen Guiley, with J. B. Macabre. *The Complete Vampire Companion*. New York: Macmillan, 1994, pp. 103–08.

2182. MacDonald, Jan. "The Devil Is Beautiful: *Dracula*: Freudian Novel and Feminist Drama." In Peter Reynolds, ed. *Novel Images: Literature in Performance*. London: Routledge, 1993, pp. 80–104.

2183. Majestic, Bill. "Dracula Returns." *Plays* 36 (May 1977): 25–36.

2184. Martini, Emanuela. "The Vampires Ball: An Historico-Cinematic Overview of the Dracula Motif." *Cineforum* 33, 1, (January/February 1993): 16–29.

2185. McBride, William T. "Dracula and Mephistopheles: Shyster Vampires." *Literature/Film Quarterly* 18, 2 (1990): 116–121.

2186. McCarty, John. "Grand Guignol—The Roots of Splatter." In John McCarty. *Splatter Movies*. Albany, NY: FantaCo Enterprises, 1981, pp. 2–26.

2187. McFarland, Ronald. "The Vampire on Stage: A Study in Adaptations." *Comparative Drama* 21, 1 (Spring 1987): 19–32.

2188. McGivering, Ann Isabel. *An Exploration of the Interrelationship of Theatre & Film: A Case Study of* Dracula. Providence, RI: Brown University, M.A. thesis, 1984. 85 pp. Large format.

2189. McGlasson, Michael. "Hamilton Deane and John C. Balderston: The Men Who 'Revamped' Count Dracula." *Journal of Dracula Studies* 9 (2007): 22–28. Posted at: http://www.bloofer land.com/drc/index.php?title=Journal_of_ Dracula_Studies.

2190. McIntosh, Audrey Anne Keith. *The Business Manager at Irving's Lyceum, "an individual who calls himself Bram Stoker, who seems to occupy some anomalous position between secretary and valet," or the Forefather of Theatre Administrators*. Glasgow, Scotland: University of Glasgow, M.Litt. thesis, 1991.

2191. Merritt, Henry. "'Dead Many Times': 'Cathleen ni Houlihan,' Yeats, Two Old Women, and a Vampire." *The Modern Language Review* 96, 3 (July 2001): 644–653.

2192. Mitchell, Michael Washbourne. *Creating the Role of Count Dracula in Hamilton Deane and John L. Balderston's Dracula: The Vampire Play for Public Performance*. Gainesville: University of Florida, Ph.D. dissertation, 1988. 126 pp. Large format.

2193. Moss, Stephanie. "Bram Stoker and the London Stage." *Journal of the Fantastic in the Arts* 10, 2 (1999): 124–32.

2194. Nelson, Hilda. *Charles Nodier*. New York: Twayne Publishers, 1972. 188 pp. hb.

2195. Oliver, A. Richard. *Charles Nodier: Pilot of Romanticism*. Syracuse, NY: Syracuse University Press, 1964. 276 pp. hb. dj.

2196. Riquelme, John Paul. "Toward a History of Gothic and Modernism: Dark Modernity from Bram Stoker to Samuel Beckett." *Modern Fiction Studies* 46, 3 (Fall 2000): 585–605.

2197. Ruane, Richard T. *Performing Camp, Vamp and Femme Fatale Revisiting, Reinventing and Retelling the Lives of Post-death, Retro-Gothic Women*. Denton: University of North Texas, M.A. thesis, 1999. 72 pp. large format. Posted at: http:// digital.library.unt.edu/ark:/67531/metadc2239/ m1/75/.

2198. Schraft, Robin J. "The Vampire Image in Dramatic Literature." *Theatre Southwest* (April 1989): 18–21.

2199. Scott, J. Farham. "The Original Bloodsucking Freak: A History of *Dracula* on Stage." *Toxic Horror* 2 (February 1990): 40–45.

2200. Shepard, Les. "Bram Stoker and the Theatre." *Bram Stoker Society Journal* 1 (1989): 5–

23. Rpt. in: Leslie Shepard and Albert Power, eds. *Dracula: Celebrating 100 Years*. Dublin: Mentor Press, 1997, pp. 159–175.

2201. ____. *Bram Stoker: Irish Theatre Manager and Author*. Dublin: Impact Publications, 1994. 20 pp. pb. Staples.

2202. Skal, David J. "'His Hour Upon the Stage': Theatrical Adaptations of Dracula." In Bram Stoker. *Dracula*. Edited by Nina Auerbach and David J. Skal. Ser.; Norton Critical Editions. New York: W. W. Norton & Company, 1998, pp. 371–380.

2203. ____. *Hollywood Gothic: The Tangled Web of Dracula from Novel to Stage to Screen*. New York: W. W. Norton & Company, 1990. 243 pp. hb. dj. Large format. Rpt.: New York: W. W. Norton & Company, 1990. 243 pp. pb. dj. Large format.

2204. Snyder, Helen Lavinia. *A Comparative Analysis of the Transformation of Myths in Dracula the Novel, Stageplay, and Movie*. San Jose, CA: San Jose State University, M.A. thesis, 1978. 75 pp. Large format.

2205. Sözalan, Ozden. "Liz Lockhead's *Dracula*." *The Staged Encounter: Contemporary Feminism and Women's Drama*. Stuttgart, Germany: ibidem–Verlag, 2004, pp. 128–36.

2206/07. Stoker, Bram. "Fifty Years on the Stage: An Appreciation of Miss Ellen Terry." *The Graphic: An Illustrated Weekly Newspaper* (London) (April 28, 1906): 537. Rpt.: *Bram Stoker Society Journal* 1 (1989): 24–28. Posted at: http://www.bramstoker.org/nonfic/stage.html.

2208. Stuart, Roxana. "The Eroticism of Evil: The Vampire in Nineteenth-Century Melodrama." In James Redmond, ed. *Melodrama*. Cambridge, UK: Cambridge University Press, 1992, pp. 223–44.

2209. ____. *Stage Blood: Vampires of the 19th Century Stage*. Bowling Green, OH: Bowling Green University Popular Press, 1994. 377 pp. hb. & tp.

2210. ____. *The Vampire of Nineteenth Century Melodrama*. New York: City University of New York, Ph.D. dissertation, 1993. 462 pp. Large format.

2211. Tornqvist, Egil. "The Stage Director." In Egil Tornqvist. *Between Stage and Screen: Ingmar Bergman Directs*. Amsterdam: Amsterdam University Press, 2007, pp. 23–92. In his early career, Bergman directed a new version of August Strindberg's trend-breaking drama, *The Ghost Sonata* (aka *The Dream Play*), which includes vampires among its spectrum of supernatural characters.

2212. ____. *Strindberg's The Ghost Sonata*. Amsterdam: Amsterdam University Press, 2004. 270 pp. hb. Tornqvist provides a guide to Swedish dramatist August Strindberg's trend-breaking drama, *The Ghost Sonata* (aka *The Dream Play*), which includes vampires among its spectrum of supernatural characters.

2213. Varty, Anne. "Liz Lockhead and the Gothic." In Anne Varty. *The Edinburgh Companion to Liz Lochhead*. Edinburgh: Edinburgh University Press, 2013, pp. 86–104.

2214. White, Timothy. "Dracula; The Warmblooded Revival of the Debonaire King of the Undead." *Crawdaddy* (June, 1978): 26–33.

2215. Wynne, Catherine, ed. *Bram Stoker and the Stage: Reviews, Reminiscences, Essays and Fiction*. 2 vols. London: Pickering & Chatto, 2012.

2216. ____. *Bram Stoker, Dracula and the Victorian Gothic Stage*. Basingstoke, UK: Palgrave Macmillan, 2013. 195 pp. hb.

Cinematic Vampires: General

In his study *Cinematic Vampires*, John L. Flynn names *The Devil's Castle*, a two-minute silent film created by Georges Méliès, as the first vampire film. The film's storyline has the vampire/demon Mephistopheles changing into a bat and being opposed by a cross-wielding human. However, it would be several other silent era vampire movies, most notably the German *Nosferatu* (1922) and the Hollywood vamp movie *A Fool There Was* (1915), which would finally establish the permanent presence of the vampire theme of the cinematic world.

Universal's *Dracula* (1931) would go on to become the first horror (and vampire) talkie, and its success would inspire a variety of vampire black and white movies through the '30s and '40s. Less recognized is *Dracula*'s role in inspiring vampire movies internationally, though it shares credit with the Spanish version of *Dracula* that was made by Universal concurrently with the Lugosi version. After a brief hiatus in the 1950s, the production of vampire movies would pick up in the 1960s and enjoy some success through the next decades, with the most notable coming from Hammer Studios in England, before falling from favor in the mid–1980s.

Toward the end of the 1980s, vampire movies began to make a comeback and by the mid–1990s, at least one a week was appearing. This rise in the production of independent vampire films coincided with the explosion in independent films generally due to the widespread availability of inexpensive moviemaking equipment and the popularity of horror as a genre favored by new young filmmakers. The number of such films has grown steadily to the present and shows no sign of slowing down. The new characters of the good-guy vampire and the conflicted vampire have greatly expanded the storyline available to screenwriters.

This chapter lists those items that attempt to either survey the whole world of vampire films through the decades, assess the impact and meaning of vampire films in general, or place vampire movies into the wider context of horror films. No attempt has been made to survey the huge biographical literature on all of the Hollywood directors and actors who may have worked on a vampire movie at some point in their career, all of the books that attempt to present the "best" or "most notable" (or "worst") movies through the ages and include brief discussions of various vampire movies, or reviews of individual movies. At the same time, separate sections have been developed on the more prominent vampire movies and eras—the silent era, the Universal era, the postwar era, the Hammer movies, Coppola's *Bram Stoker's Dracula*, the Twilight Saga, and Asian vampires.

For a complete listing of vampire and vampire-themed movies see J. Gordon Melton, "List of Vampire Movies in English (origins—2013)" posted at http://www.cesnur.org/2009/vampires_movies.htm. Some 2,400 such movies have been located, over 2,000 of which are full feature-length films.

2217. Abbott, Stacey. *Celluloid Vampires: Life After Death in the Modern World.* Austin: University of Texas Press, 2007. 266 pp. tp.

2218. _____. "The Undead in the Kingdom of Shadows: The Rise of the Cinematic Vampire." In Sam George and Bill Hughes, eds. *Open Graves, Open Minds: Representations of Vampires and the Undead from the Enlightenment to the Present Day.* Manchester: Manchester University Press, 2013, pp. 96–112.

2219. Ahmad Aalya, and Murray Leeder. "The Sick Rose: *Rabid* and the Female Science Vampire." In Douglas Brode and Leah Deyneka. *Dracula's Daughters: The Female Vampire on Film.* Lanham, MD: The Scarecrow Press, 2014. pp. 235–51.

2220. "All Vampire Issue." Special Issue of *Midnight Marque* 47 (Summer 1995).

2221. Anatol, Giselle Liza. "Narratives of Race and Gender: Black Vampires in U.S. Film." In Douglas Brode and Leah Deyneka. *Dracula's Daughters: The Female Vampire on Film.* Lanham, MD: The Scarecrow Press, 2014. pp. 195–217.

2222. Andrews, Nigel. *Horror Films.* New York: Gallery Books, 1985. 95 pp.

2223. Atwater, Barry. "The Blood Is the Life." *Monsters of the Movies* 1, 3 (October 1974): 64–67.

2224. Backstein, Karen. "(Un)safe Sex: Romancing the Vampire." *Cineaste* 35, 1 (2009): 38–41.

2225. Baddeley, Gavin. *Vampire Lovers: Screen's Seductive Creatures of the Night: A Book of Undead Pin-Ups.* London: Plexus, 2010. 192 pp. tp.

2226. Bauer, Rachel Noël. "Hearing Dracula: Sound as Sign in Film." *RLA: Romance Languages Annual* 11 (1999): 138–143.

2227. Beal, Timothy K. "Screening Monsters." In Timothy K. Beal. *Religion and Its Monsters.* New York: Routledge, 2002, pp. 141–58.

2228. Bean, Robin. "Dracula and the Mad Monk." *Films and Filming* (August 1965): 55ff.

2229. Bearden, Keith. "Pretty Bloody Funny." *Fangoria* 149 (January 1996): 56–62, 82.

2230. Beck, Calvin Thomas. *Scream Queens: Heroines of the Horrors.* New York: Collier Books, 1978. 343 pp. tp. Includes chapters on Vampira, Barbara Steele, and Stephanie Rothman.

2231. Benshoff, Harry M. *Monsters in the Closet: Homosexuality and the Horror Film.* Manchester, UK: Manchester University Press, 1997. 328 pp. hb.

2232. Bignell, Jonathan. "Dracula Goes to the Movies: Cinematic Spectacle and Gothic Literature." In Dominique Sipière, ed. *Dracula: Insémination Dissemination.* Amiens, Presses de l'UFRClerc, Université de Picardie, 1996, pp. 133–142.

2233. _____. "A Taste of the Gothic: Film and Television Versions of *Dracula.* In Robert Giddings & Erica Sheen, eds. *The Classic Novel: From Page to Screen.* New York: St. Martin's Press, 2000, pp. 114–130.

2234. Biodrowski, Steve, and Dennis Fischer. "100 Years of Dracula." *Cinefantastique* 29, 4/5 (October 1997): 100–109, 126.

2235. Borst, Ronald V. "The Vampire in the Cinema." *Photon* 18 (1969): 18–45.

2236. Brederoo, N. J. "Dracula in Film." In Valeria Tinkler-Villani and Peter Davidson, eds., with Jane Stevenson. *Exhibited by Candlelight: Sources and Developments in the Gothic Tradition.* Amsterdam: Rodopi, 1995, pp 271–82.

2237. Brode, Douglas. "Introduction: "Lamia and Lilith live!" (or at least are un-dead)." In Douglas Brode and Leah Deyneka. *Dracula's Daughters: The Female Vampire on Film.* Lanham, MD: The Scarecrow Press, 2014. pp. 1–19.

2238. _____, **and Leah Deyneka.** *Dracula's Daughters: The Female Vampire on Film.* Lanham, MD: The Scarecrow Press, 2014. 310 pp. hb. boards. Includes contributions by Douglas Brode, Andrea Weiss, Jeffrey Andrew Weinstock, Paige A. Willson, Melissa Ursula Dawn Goldsmith and Anthony J. Fonseca, Lindsay Hallam, Lauren Strong, Jack W. Shear, Janet S. Robinson, Alexis Finnerty, Carol A. Senf, Giselle Liza Anatol, Brigid Cherry, Aalya Ahmad and Murray Leeder, Kendall R. Phillips, Cynthia J. Miller, and Victoria Amador.

2239. Broom, Michael Burnham. *The Literary Monster on Film: Five Nineteenth Century British Novels and Their Cinematic Adaptations.* Jefferson, NC: McFarland & Company, 2010. 218 pp. tp. Includes a discussion of Dracula.

2240. Brown, Jake. "Draculafilm: 'High' and 'Low' Until the End of the World" In Carol Margaret Davison, ed., with Paul Simpson-Housley. *Bram Stoker's Dracula: Sucking through the Century, 1897–1997.* Toronto: Dundurn Press, 1997, pp. 269–82.

2241. Brown, Tom. "Out of the Darkness." *Film Threat Video* 9 (1993): 38–44.

2242. Browning, John Edgar, and Caroline Joan (Kay) Picart. *Dracula in Visual Media: Film, Television, Comic Book and Electronic Game Appearances, 1921–2010.* Jefferson, NC: McFarland & Company, 2011. 304 pp. tp. *Dracula in Visual Media: Film, Television, Comic Book and Electronic Game Appearances, 1921–2010* received the 2011 award for the best nonfiction book of the previous year given annually by the Lord Ruthven Society.

2243. Carducci, Mark. "This Vampire Draws More Than Blood! *Famous Monsters of Filmland* 206 (January/February 1995): 24–28.

2244. Caws, Mary Ann. "What to Wear in a Vampire Film." In Adrienne Munich, ed. *Fashion in Film.* Bloomington: Indiana University Press, 2011, pp. 49–53.

2245. Clarens, Carlos. *An Illustrated History of the Horror Film.* New York: G. P. Putnam's Sons, 1967. 256 pp. Rpt.: Toronto: Longmans Green, 1968. 256 pp. Rev. ed. as: *Horror Movies: An Illustrated Survey.* London: Secker & Warburg, 1968. 264 pp.

2246. Clark, Mark. *Smirk, Sneer and Scream: Great Acting in Horror Cinema.* Jefferson, NC: McFarland & Company, 2004. 257 pp. hb. & tp.

2247. Cook, Pam. "Dracula." In José Arroyo, ed. *Action/Spectacle Cinema: A Sight and Sound Reader.* London, British Film Institute, 2008, pp. 221–24.

2248. Daniels, Stephen. "Vampires, Zombies, and Mummies." In Stephen Daniels. *Movie Monsters.* Mahwah, NJ: Watermill Press, 1980, pp. 27–47.

2249. Davidson, Robert K. *Great Monsters of the Movies.* New York: Pyramid Books, 1977. 128 pp. pb.

2250. Desmarais, James Joseph. *An Historical and Descriptive Study of the Cinematic Vampire from 1922 through 1974.* Fullerton: California State University, M.A. thesis, 1975. 132 pp. Large format. Copy at USC.

2251. Dika, Vera. "From Dracula with Love." In Barry Keith Grant, ed. *The Dread of Difference: Gender and the Horror Film.* Austin: University Press of Texas Press, 1996, pp. 388–400.

2252. Donald, James. "The Fantastic, the Sublime and the Popular; or, What's at Stake in Vampire Films?" In James Donald, ed. *Fantasy and the Cinema.* London: BFI [British Film Institute] Publishing, 1989, pp. 233–51. Rpt. as: "What's at Stake in Vampire Films? The Pedegogy of Monsters." In James Donald. *Sentimental Education: Schooling, Popular Culture and the Regulation of Liberty.* London: Verso, 1992, pp. 99–121.

2253. Duncan, Andrew. "I Would Never Dream of Watching a Horror Film." *Radio Times* (London) (August 6–12, 1994): 28–31.

2254. Dunn, Denise. "The House that Horror Built." *Monsters of the Movies* 1, 7 (June 1975): 4–7.

2255. _____. "The Vampire from Stage to Screen." *Monsters of the Movies* 1, 7 (June 1975): 8–11.

2256. Duvoli, John R. "Invasion of the 1960s' Non-Traditional Vampire Movie." *Midnight Marquee* 47 (Summer 1995): 23–28.

2257. Dyer, Richard. "Dracula and Desire." *Sight and Sound* 3 (1993): 8–12. Rpt. in: Ginette Vincendeau, ed. *Film/Literature/Heritage: A Sight and Sound Reader.* London: British Film Institute, 2001, pp. 91–97.

2258. Edelson, Edward. *Great Monsters of the Movies.* Garden City, NY: Doubleday & Company, 1973. 101 pp. hb. Rpt.: New York: Pocketbooks, 1974. 119 pp. pb.

2259. Ekstedt, Richard A. "Enticed by the Dark...Clutching the 'Hand of Night.'" *Midnight Marquee* 40 (Spring 1990): 28–30.

2260. England, Nancy Faye Rosenberg. *Establishing a Dracula Film Genre: Key Texts, Antecedents, and Offspring.* Arlington: University of Texas at Arlington, Ph.D. dissertation, 2009.

2261. Evans, Walter. "Monster Movies: A Sexual Theory." *Journal of Popular Film* 4, 2 (1975). Rpt. in: Jack Nachbar and Kevin Lause, eds. *Popular Culture: An Introductory Text.* Bowling Green, OH: Bowling Green State University Popular Press, 1992, pp. 463–75.

2262. Everson, William K. "Vampires." In William K. Everson. *Classics of the Horror Film.* New York: Citadel, 1974, pp. 191–202.

2263. Finnerty, Alexis. "The Dangers of Innocence: An Analysis of Film Representations of Female Vampire Children." In Douglas Brode and Leah Deyneka. *Dracula's Daughters: The Female Vampire on Film.* Lanham, MD: The Scarecrow Press, 2014, pp. 159–71.

2264. Flynn, John L. *Cinematic Vampires: The Living Dead on Film and Television, from* The Devil's Castle *(1896), to* Bram Stoker's Dracula *(1992).* Jefferson, NC: McFarland & Company, 1992. 320 pp. hb.

2265. Frank, Alan. *Monsters and Vampires.* Secaucus, NJ: Derbibooks, 1972. 160 pp. hb. dj. Large format. Rpt. London: Octopus Books, 1976. 160 pp. hb. Rpt. as: *The Movie Treasury: Monsters and Vampires.* London: Cathay Books, 1976. 160 pp.

2266. Freeland, Cynthia A. *The Naked and the Undead: Evil and the Appeal of Horror.* Boulder, CO: Westview Press, 2000. 320 pp. hb. dj.

2267. Garcia, Jorge J. E. "From Horror to Hero: Film Interpretations of Stoker's *Dracula*." In William Irwin and Jorge J.E. Gracia, eds. *Philosophy and the Interpretation of Pop Culture.* Latham, MD: Rowman & Littlefield, 2006, pp. 187–214.

2268. Gelder, Ken. "Citational Vampires: Transnational Techniques of Circulation in *Irma Vep, Blood: The Last Vampire* and *Thirst*." In Tabish Khair and Johan Hoglund, eds. *Transnational and Postcolonial Vampires: Dark Blood.* Basingstoke, UK: Palgrave Macmillan, 2012, pp. 81–104.

2269. _____. *New Vampire Cinema.* Basingstoke, UK: Palgrave Macmillan, 2012. 155 pp. tp.

2270. Gifford, Denis. "The Vampire." In Dennis Gifford. *Movie Monsters.* London: Littlehampton Book Services, 1969.

2271. Glut, Don. "Variations on a Vampire Theme." *Monsters of the Movies* 1, 3 (October 1974): 48–33.

2272. Hallenbeck, Bruce G., ed. "Sexuality in the Vampire Film: From *Dracula* to *Spermula*." *Bits & Pieces* 9 (Fall 1994): 4–8.

2273. Halliwell, Leslie. "The Baron, the Count, and Their Ghoul Friends." *Films and Filming* (June 1969): 12–16 (July 1969): 13–16.

2274. _____. *The Dead That Walk: Dracula, Frankenstein, the Mummy and Other Favorite Movie Monsters.* New York: Continuum, 1988. 262 pp. hb.

2275. _____. "The Dread of Dracula." In Leslie Halliwell. *The Dead That Walk: Dracula, Frankenstein, the Mummy, and Other Favorite Movie Monsters.* New York: Continuum, 1988, pp. 14–98.

2276. Harbin, Leigh Joyce. "A Dangerous Woman and a Man's Brain: Mina Harker, Clarice Starling and the Empowerment of the Gothic Heroine in Novel and Film." *West Virginia University Philological Papers* (Fall 2002).

2277. Harmon, Jim. "The Life Story of Dracula." *Monsters of the Movies* 1, 3 (October 1974): 69–74.

2278. Heldreth, Leonard G. "Vampires in Film and Television: Introduction." *Journal of Popular Film and Television* 27, 2 (1999): 2–3.

2279. Hogan, David J. *Dark Romance: Sexuality in the Horror Film.* Jefferson, NC: McFarland & Company, 1986. 334 pp. hb & tp.

2280. Holte, James Craig. "A Century of Draculas." *Journal of the Fantastic in the Arts* 10, 2 (1999): 109–15.

2281. _____. "Imitations of Immortality: Shadow of the Vampire." *Journal of Dracula Studies* 4 (2002). Posted at: http://www.blooferland.com/drc/index.php?title=Journal_of_Dracula_Studies.

2282. _____. "Not All Fangs Are Phallic: Female Film Vampires." *Journal of the Fantastic in the Arts* 10, 2 (1999): 163–73.

2283. Hudson, Dale M. *Border Crossings and Multicultural Whiteness: Nationalism in the Global Production and U.S. Reception of Vampire Films.* Amherst: University of Massachusetts–Amherst, Ph.D. dissertation, 2004. 531 pp. Large format.

2284. Iacob, Mihai. "The (Re)Construction of Transylvania in Vampire Films." In Prieto-Arranz, José Igor, Patricia Bastida-Rodríguez, Caterina Calafat-Ripoll, and Christina Suárez-Gómez, eds. *De-Centring Cultural Studies: Past, Present and Future of Popular Culture.* Newcastle upon Tyme, UK: Cambridge Scholars Publishing, 2013, pp. 293–304.

2285. Jenkins, Henry. "Reception Theory and Audience Research: The Mystery of the Vampire's Kiss." In Christine Glenhill and Linda Williams, eds. *Reinventing Film Studies.* New York: Bloomsbury USA, 2000, pp. 165–82.

2286. Jones, Alan. "Gothic." *Cinefantastique* 17, 1 (January 1987): 4–5, 61.

2287. Jones, Darryl I. "Vampires: Children of the Night." In Darryl I. Jones. *Horror: A Thematic History in Fiction and Film.* London, Hodder Arnold Publication, 2002, pp. 70–122.

2288. Jones, E. Michaels. "Dracula and Sin." In E. Michaels Jones. *Monsters from the Id: The Rise of Horror in Fiction and Film.* Dallas, TX: Spence Pub Co., 2000, pp. 101–132.

2289. Jones, Stephen. *The Illustrated Vampire Movie Guide.* London: Titan Books, 1993. 144 pp. pb. Large format.

2290. Joslin, Lyndon W. *Count Dracula Goes to the Movies: Stoker's Novel Adapted, 1922–1995.* Jefferson, NC: McFarland & Company, 1999. 237 pp. hb. boards. 2nd ed. as: *Count Dracula Goes to the Movies: Stoker's Novel Adapted, 1922–2003.* Jefferson, NC: McFarland & Company, 2nd edition, 2006. 264 pp. hb.

2291. Kane, Tim. *Changing Vampire of Film and Television: A Critical Study of the Growth of a Genre.* Jefferson, NC: McFarland & Company, 2006. 232 pp. tp.

2292. Keesey, Pam. *Vamps: An Illustrated History of the Femme Fatale.* San Francisco, CA: Cleis Press, 1997. 171 pp. pb. Large format.

2293. Kemp, George P. "Dracula: Eroticism in the Vampire Genre." In Douglas Umstead-Radcliffe, ed. *Varieties of Filmic Expression.* Kent, OH: Romance Langs. Dept., Kent State University, 1989, pp. 128–34.

2294. Kendrick, Walter. *The Thrill of Fear: 250 Years of Scary Entertainment.* New York: Grove Weidenfeld, 1991. 292 pp.

2295. Kreitzer, L. Joseph. "*Dracula*: 'The Blood is the Life!.'" In Larry J. Kreitzer. *Pauline Images in Fiction and Film: On Reversing the Hermeneutical Flow.* Sheffield, UK: Sheffield Academic, 1999, pp. 113–42.

2296. Ladouceur, Liisa. *How to Kill a Vampire: Fangs in Folklore, Film and Fiction.* Toronto: ECW Press, 2013. 190 pp. tp.

2297. Latman, Audrey I. *Rotten Blood: Vampire Film as a Metaphor for AIDS.* Waltham, MA:

Brandeis University, Senior Honor thesis 1994. 126 pp. Large format.

2298. London, Rose. *Zombie: The Living Dead.* New York: Bounty Books, 1976. 111 pp.

2299. Loughlin, Gerard. "Want of Family." In Gerard Loughlin. *Alien Sex: The Body and Desire in Cinema and Theology.* Hoboken, NJ: Wiley-Blackwell, 2004, pp. 201–26.

2300. Macabre, J. B. "Blood and Celluloid: The Vampire Legend as Recorded by the Silver Screen." In Rosemary Ellen Guiley, with J. B. Macabre. *The Complete Vampire Companion.* New York: Macmillan, 1994, pp. 222–30.

2301. ____. "Staked by Silver: Vampires and the Silver Screen." In Rosemary Ellen Guiley, with J. B. Macabre. *The Complete Vampire Companion.* New York: Macmillan, 1994, pp. 109–23.

2302. ____. "Those Who Direct the Undead: Conversations with Vampire Filmmakers." In Rosemary Ellen Guiley, with J. B. Macabre. *The Complete Vampire Companion.* New York: Macmillan, 1994, pp. 124–133.

2303. Mander, Gabrielle. *Bite.* London: Bounty Books, 2012. 160 pp. hb. dj.

2304. Marrero, Robert. *Dracula: The Vampire Legend on Film.* Key West, FL: Fantasma Books, 1992. 120 pp. tp. Rev. ed as: *Vampire Movies.* Key West, FL: Fantasma Books, 1994. 176 pp. pb. Large format.

2305. McClenon, James, and Emily D. Edwards. "The Incubus in Film, Experience, and Folklore." *Southern Folklore* 52, 1 (1996): 3–18. Posted at: http://libres.uncg.edu/ir/uncg/f/E_Edwards_Incubus_1995.pdf.

2306. McDonald, Jan. "The Devil Is Beautiful: Dracula, Freudian Novel and Feminist Drama." In Peter Reynolds, ed. *Novel Images: Literature in Performance.* London, Routledge, 1993, pp. 80–104.

2307. McGivering, Ann Isabel. *An Exploration of the Interrelationship of Theatre & Film: A Case Study of Dracula.* Providence, RI: Brown University, M.A. thesis, 1984. 85 pp. Large format.

2308. Melton, J. Gordon. *VideoHound's Vampires on Video.* Detroit: Visible Ink Press, 1997. 335 pp. tp.

2309. Mennel, Barbara. *Queer Cinema: Schoolgirls, Vampires, and Gay Cowboys.* New York: Wallflower Press, 2012. 224 pp. tp.

2310. Merskin, Debra L. "Homosexuality and Horror: The Lesbian Vampire Film." In Debra L. Merskin. *Media, Minorities, and Meaning: A Critical Introduction.* New York: Peter Lang, 2011, pp. 282–308.

2311. Miller, Cynthia, and A. Bowdoin van Van Riper, eds. *Undead in the West: Vampires, Zombies, Mummies, and Ghosts on the Cinematic Frontier.* Lanham, MD: Scarecrow Press, 2012. 344 pp. hb.

2312. ____. *Undead in the West II: They Just Keep Coming.* Lanham, MD: Scarecrow Press, 2012. 352 pp. hb.

2313. Muir, John Kenneth. *Horror Movies FAQ: All That's Left to Know About Slashers, Vampires, Zombies, Aliens and More.* New York: Applause Theatre & Cinema Books, 2013. 386 pp. tp.

2314. Murphy, Michael J. *The Celluloid Vampires: A History and Filmography, 1897–1979.* Ann Arbor, MI: Pierian Press, 1979. 351 pp. hb.

2315. Nance, Scott. *Bloodsuckers: Vampires at the Movies.* Las Vegas, NV: Pioneer Books, 1992. 149 pp. pb. Large format.

2316. Neale, Stephen. "The Fantastic, the Sublime, and the Popular; or at Stake in Vampire Films?" In James Donald, ed. *Fantasy and the Cinema.* London: BFI Publishing, 1989.

2317. Newman, Kim. *Nightmare Movies: A Critical History of the Horror Film, 1968–88.* London: Bloomsbury, 1988. 255 pp. Rpt. as: *Nightmare Movies: A Critical Guide to Contemporary Horror Films.* New York: Harmony Books, 1989. 255 pp.

2318. Odell, Colin, and Michelle LeBlanc. *Vampire Films.* Halpenden, Herts., UK: Pocket Essentials, 2000. 96 pp. pb. Rev. ed.: Halpenden, Herts., UK: Pocket Essentials, 2008. 160 pp. pb.

2319. Pate, Janet. "Count Dracula." In Janet Pate. *The Black Book of Villains.* London: David & Charles, 1975, pp. 34–37. Rpt. as: *The Great Villains.* Indianapolis, IN: Bobbs-Merrill, 1975, pp. 34–37.

2320. Pattison, Barrie. *The Seal of Dracula.* New York: Bounty Books, 1975. 136 pp. hb. Rpt.: London: Lorrimer Publishing, 1975. 136 pp. tp.

2321. Pippin, Tina. "Of Gods and Demons: Blood Sacrifice and Eternal Life in *Dracula* and the Apocalypse of John." In George Aichele & Richard Walsh, eds. *Screening Scripture: Intertextual Connections Between Scripture and Film.* Harrisburg, PA: Trinity Press International, 2002, pp. 24–41.

2322. Pirie, David. *The Vampire Cinema.* London: Hamlyn, 1977. 175 pp. hb. dj. Large format. Rpt. as: *The Complete Vampire Cinema.* New York: Crescent Books, 1977. 176 pp. pb. Large format. Rpt.: London: Gallery Books, 1984. 176 pp. hb. dj. Large format.

2323. Powers, Tim. "Dracula." In Tim Powers. *Horror Movies.* Minneapolis, MN: Lerner Publications Company, 1989, pp. 11–20.

2324. Reed, Donald. *The Vampire on the Screen.* Inglewood, CA: Wagon & Star Publishers, 1965. 28 pp. pb. Staples. Cinema.

2325. Reeder, Steven. "Dracula as a Tragic Hero: The Illumination of Film on a Text." *Nineteenth Century Literature in English* 10.2 (2006): 243–271.

2326. Reijinders, Stijn. "Dracula." In Stijn Reijinders. *Places of the Imagination: Media, Tourism, Culture.* Farnham, Surrey, UK: Ashgate, 2011, pp. 81–114.

2327. Robinson, Janet S. "'Your tale merely confirms that women are mad and vain': The Uncanny Rendering of Countess Elizabeth Ba'thory's Life as Vampire Legend." In Douglas Brode and Leah Deyneka. *Dracula's Daughters: The Female Vampire on Film.* Lanham, MD: The Scarecrow Press, 2014. pp. 139–57.

2328. Roof, Judith. "Unauthorized Reproduction; Vampires' Uncanny Metonymy." In Judith Roof. *Reproductions of Reproduction: Imaging Symbolic Change.* New York: Routledge, 1996, pp. 139–70.

2329. Roth, Lane. *The Vampire Film: Intrinsic and Extrinsic Analysis of Three Archetypes.* Tallahassee: Florida State University, M.A. thesis, 1974. 95 pp. pb. Large format.

2330. Russell, Sharon A. "The Influence of *Dracula* on the Lesbian Vampire Film." *Journal of Dracula Studies* 1 (1999): 28–32.

2331. _____. "The Transformed Woman: Female Clothing in the Vampire Film." In Donald Palumbo, ed. *Spectrum of the Fantastic.* Westport, CT: Greenwood Press, 1988, pp. 209–17.

2332. Sadoff, Dianne F. "Reproducing Monsters, Vampires, and Cyborgs." In Dianne F. Sadoff. *Victorian Vogue: British Novels on Screen.* Minneapolis: University of Minnesota Press, 2010, pp. 101–48.

2333. Salisbury, Mark. "The Full-Blooded Approach." *Fangoria Horror Spectacular* 10 (1994): 39–43.

2334. Schweitzer, Darrel. "Count Dracula and his Adapters." In Darrel Schweitzer. *Windows of the Imagination; Essays on Fantasy Literature.* San Bernardino, CA: The Borgo Press, 1997, pp. 129–142.

2335. Segura, Allison C. *Perfect Creatures: A Social and Cultural Interpretation of Vampires in Fiction and Film.* Lafayette: University of Louisiana at Lafayette, Ph.D. dissertation, 2008. 133 pp. Large format.

2336. Senf, Carol A. "The Women of Dracula Films: Brides, Daughters, and Fierce Opponents." In Douglas Brode and Leah Deyneka. *Dracula's Daughters: The Female Vampire on Film.* Lanham, MD: The Scarecrow Press, 2014. pp. 173–93.

2337. _____, ed. "Brides of Dracula: From Novel to Film." *Studies in Popular Culture* 7 (1984): 64–71.

2338. Senn, Bryan, and John Johnson. *Fantastic Cinema Subject Guide.* Jefferson, NC: McFarland & Company, 1992, pp. 524 62.

2339. Shepard, Leslie. "Bram Stoker and the Cinema." *Bram Stoker Society Journal* 7 (1995): 2–12. Rpt.: In Leslie Shepard and Albert Power, eds. *Dracula: Celebrating 100 Years.* Dublin: Mentor Press, 1997, pp. 106–16.

2340. Silver, Alain, and James Ursini. "The Other Bram Stoker." In Alain Silver and James Ursini. *More Things Than Are Drempt Of: Masterpieces of Supernatural Horror—From Mary Shelley to Stephen King—in Literature and Film.* New York: Limelight Editions, 1994, pp. 31–39.

2341. _____. "Vampire Redux: Critical Studies of the Vampire Film." *Midnight Marque* 47 (Summer 1995): 58–61.

2342. Smith, Angela. "Eugenic Reproduction: Chimeras in *Dracula* and *Frankenstein*." In Angela Smith. *Hideous Progeny: Disability, Eugenics, and Classic Horror Cinema.* New York: Columbia University Press, 2012, pp. 33–82.

2343. Smith, Sarah J. *Children, Cinema and Censorship: From Dracula to Dead End.* London: I. B. Tauris, 2005. 237 pp. tp.

2344. Stanley, John. *Creature Features Movie Guide.* Pacifica, CA: Creatures at Large, 1981. 208 pp. 4th edition as: *Creature Features Movie Guide Strikes Again.* Pacifica, CA: Creatures at Large Press, 1994. 454 pp. hb. Slipcase. Cinema.

2345. Steiger, Brad. "The Vampires." In Brad Steiger. *Monsters, Maidens, and Mayhem: A Picto-*

rial History of Hollywood Film Monsters. New York: Merit Books, 1965, pp. 35–48.

2346. Stewart, Garrett. "Film's Victorian Retrofit." *Victorian Studies* 38, 2 (Winter 1995): 153–198.

2347. Stout, Tim. "The Vampire in Films." In Peter Haining. *The Dracula Scrapbook.* New York: Bramwell House, 1976, pp. 77–93.

2348. Strumer, Andre Marc. *The Creatures of the Night: Vampires from Books to Films.* Hattiesburg: University of Southern Mississippi, Ph.D. dissertation, 2007. 267 pp. Large format.

2349. Svehla, Gary J. "Forgotten Vampires of the Cinema." *The Monster Times* (October 1973): 3–5, 29.

2350. _____, and Susan Svehla, eds. *Bitches, Bimbos, and Virgins: Women in the Horror Film.* Baltimore, MD: Midnight Marquee Press, 1996, 287 pp. tp.

2351. Thomas, Ronald R., "Specters of the Novels: Dracula and the Cinematic Afterlife of the Victorian Novel." *Nineteenth Century Contexts* 22, 1 (2000): 77–102. Rpt. in John Kucich & Dianne F. Sadoff, eds. *Victorian Afterlife: Postmodern Culture Rewrites the Nineteenth Century.* Minneapolis: University of Minnesota Press, 2000, pp. 288–310.

2352. Thompson, Dave. *If You Like True Blood...Here Are Over 200 Films, TV Shows and Other Oddities That You Will Love.* Milwaukee, WI: Backbeat Book/Hal Leonard Corporation, 213. 231 pp. tp.

2353. Timpone, Anthony, ed. *Fangoria Vampires.* New York: HarperPrism, 1996. 222 pp. pb.

2354. Toufic, Jalal Omram. *Vampires.* Evanston, IL: Northwestern University, Ph.D. dissertation, 1992. 244 pp. Large format.

2355. _____. *Vampires: An Uneasy Essay on the Undead in Film.* Barrytown, NY: Station Hill Press, 1993. 235 pp. tp.

2356. Trotter, Jack. "The Cinematic Dracula: From Nosferatu to Bram Stoker's *Dracula*" In Bram Stoker. *Dracula.* Ignatius Critical Editions. San Francisco, CA: Ignatius Press, 2012, pp. 529–43.

2357. Ursini, James, and Alain Silver. *The Vampire Film.* South Brunswick, NJ: A. S. Barnes and Company, 1975. 238 pp. tp. Rev. ed. as: Alain Silver and James Ursini. *The Vampire Film: From Nosferatu to Bram Stoker's Dracula.* New York: Limelight Editions, 1993. 273 pp. tp. Rev. ed. as: *The Vampire Film: From Nosferatu to Bram Stoker's Dracula.* New York: Limelight Editions, 2004. 342 pp. tp. 4th rev, ed. as: *The Vampire Film: From Nosferatu to True Blood.* Milwaukee, WI: Hal Leonard Corporation, 2011. 488 pp. tp.

2358. *Videohound's Complete Guide to Cult Flicks and Trash Pics.* Detroit, MI: Visible Ink Press, 1996. 439 pp. tp.

2359. *Videohound's Worst Nightmares: Vampires, Werewolves & Other Creatures of the Night.* Detroit, MI: Visible Ink Press, 1995. 124 pp. pb. Small format. Staples.

2360. Waller, Gregory A. *The Living and the Undead: From Stoker's Dracula to Romero's Dawn of the Dead.* Urbana: University of Illinois Press, 1986. 376 pp. hb. dj. Rev. ed. as: *The Living and the Undead: Slaying Vampires, Exterminating Zombies.* Urbana: University of Illinois Press, 2010. 376 pp. tp.

2361. Walton, Patricia L. "I Want to Bite Your Neck." In Patricia L. Walton. *Our Cannibals, Ourselves.* Urbana: University of Illinois Press, 2004, pp. 64–84.

2362. Weaver, Tom. "Cinema Dracula." In *Dracula: The Complete Vampire.* New York: Starlog Communications, 1992, pp. 4–20.

2363. Weinstock, Jeffrey. *The Vampire Film: Undead Cinema.* New York: Wallflower Press, 2012. 144 pp. tp. *The Vampire Film: Undead Cinema* received the 2013 award for the best nonfiction book of the previous year given annually by the Lord Ruthven **Society.**

2364. Weiss, Andrea. "The Lesbian Vampire Film: A Subgenre of Horror." In Douglas Brode and Leah Deyneka. *Dracula's Daughters: The Female Vampire on Film.* Lanham, MD: The Scarecrow Press, 2014. pp. 21–35.

2365. _____. *Vampires and Violets: Lesbianism in the Cinema.* London: Pandora Press, 1991. 184 pp. tp.

2366. Weller, Lea Cassandra. *The Evolution of the Vampire in Film and Television: From Beast to Beauty.* Derby, UK: the author, 2013. 123 pp. tp.

2367. Welsch, Jim, and John Tibbetts. "Vision of Dracula." *American Classic Screen* 5, 1 (1980): 12–16.

2368. Welsh, Paul. *The Spine Chillers: Chaney jun., Cushing, Lee & Price.* Ilfracombe, Devon, UK: Arthur H. Stockwell, 1975. 68 pp. pb.

2369. Whalen, Tom. "Romancing Film: Images of Dracula." *Literature/Film Quarterly* 23, 2 (1995): 99–101.

2370. Wolf, Leonard. *A Dream of Dracula: In Search of the Living Dead.* Boston, MA: Little, Brown, 1972. 327 pp. hb. Rpt.: London: New English Library, 1976. 326 pp. pb. Rpt.: New York: Popular Library, 1977. 326 pp. pb.

2371. _____. *Horror: A Connoisseur's Guide to Literature and Film.* New York: Facts on File, 1989. 262 pp. tp.

2372. Wood, Robin. "Burying the Undead: The Use and Obsolescence of Count Dracula." *Mosaic* 16, 1–2 (Winter-Spring 1983): 175–87. Rpt. in Barry Keith Grant, ed. *The Dread of Difference: Gender and the Horror Film.* Austin: University of Texas Press, 1996, pp. 364–78.

2373. _____. "Return of the Repressed." *Film Comment* 14, 4 (July-August 1978): 25–32.

2374. Wooley, John. "Comic Screams." In *Dracula: The Complete Vampire.* #6 of *Starlog Movie Magazine Presents.* New York: Starlog Communications International, 1992.

2375. Wright, Gene. "Vampires." In Gene Wright. *Horror Shows—The A to Z of Horror in Film, TV, Radio and Theater.* New York: Facts on File, 1986, pp. 168–202.

2376. Zimmerman, Bonnie. "Daughters of Darkness: The Lesbian Vampire on Film." In Barry Keith Grant, ed. *Planks of Reason.* Metuchen, NJ: Scarecrow Press, 1984, pp. 153–63. Rpt. in: Barry Keith Grant and Christopher Sharrett, eds. *Planks of Reason: Essays on the Horror Film.* Lanham, MD: Scarecrow Press, 2004, pp. 98–110.

2377. _____. "Daughters of Darkness: Lesbian Vampires." *Jump-Cut* 24–25 (1981): 23–24. Rpt. in Barry Keith Grant, ed. *The Dread of Difference: Gender and the Horror Film.* Austin: University of Texas Press, 1996, pp. 379–87.

Cinematic Vampires: The Silent Era

This section covers material developed to analyze (and simultaneously praise) a very small but important set of movies made prior to the 1931 *Dracula* starring Bela Lugosi, the first talkie vampire movie. These movies include *Nosferatu* (1922), *London After Midnight* (1927), and *Vampyr* (1932). Of these, *Nosferatu* would be remade as a technicolor movie in 1979 and (the now lost) *London After Midnight* as a black and white talkie, *Mark of the Vampire* (1935).

Additionally notable in the silent era is Theda Bara's *A Fool There Was* (1915), a film developed from Porter Emerson Browne's 1909 Broadway play and partially inspired by Rudyard Kipling's poem "The Vampire," which stands as the fountainhead of the "vamp" tradition of femme fatales.

Nosferatu is generally considered the first vampire film, but two films possibly preceded it. The first, a 1920 Russian film, was long believed lost. Recently, what now appears to be this lost film was found in the Serbian archives, and a segment of it showing Jonathan Harker's early interaction with Count Dracula has been published online. Another film, *Drakula halála*, was released in Hungary in 1921. No known copy has survived, but some stills remain. The story line follows a woman on a visit to an insane asylum where she encounters a real vampire.

2378. Abbott, Stacey. "Spectral Vampires: *Nosferatu* in the light of new technology." In Steffen Hantke, ed. *Horror Film: Creating and Marketing Fear.* Jackson: University Press of Mississippi, 2004, pp. 3–20.

2379. Asbjorn, Jon. A. "From *Nosferatu* to Von Carstein: Shifts in the Portrayal of Vampires." *Australian Folklore* 16 (2001):97–106.

2380. Ashbury, Roy. *Nosferatu.* London: York Press, 2001. 86 pp. tp.

2381. Badley, Linda. "The Shadow and the Author: Herzog's Kinski, Kinski's Nosferatu, and Myths of Autorship." In Steffen Hantke, ed. *Caligari's Heirs: The German Cinema of Fear After 1945.* Lanham, MD: Scarecrow Press, 2007, pp. 57–70.

2382. Byrne, Richard B. *Films of Tyranny; Shot Analyses of* The Cabinet of Dr. Caligari, The Golem, *and* Nosferatu. Madison, WI: College Print. & Typing Co., 1966. 152 pp.

2383. Calhoon, Kenneth S. "F. W. Murnau, C. D. Friedrich, and the Conceit of the Absent Spectator." *Modern Language Notes* 120, 3 (2005): 633–53. Posted at: http://pages.uoregon.edu/gerscan/faculty/profiles/kcalhoon/pdf/absent_spectator.pdf.

2384. _____. "Werner Herzog's View of Delft: Or, *Nosferatu* and the Still Life." In Brad Prager, *A Companion to Werner Herzog.* Malden, MA: Wiley-Blackwell, 2012, pp. 101–26.

2385. Cardullo, Bert. "Expressionism and Nosferatu." *San Jose Studies* 11, 3 (1985): 25–33.

2386. Carney, Raymond. *Speaking the Language of Desire: The Films of Carl Dreyer.* Cambridge: Cambridge University Press, 1989. 363 pp. hb.

2387. Casper, Kent Casper, and Susan Linville. "Romantic Inversions in Herzog's *Nosferatu,*" *The German Quarterly* 64, 1 (1991): 17–24.

2388. Catania, Saviour. "Absent Presences in Liminal Places: Murnau's *Nosferatu* and the Otherworld of Stoker's *Dracula.*" *Literature/Film Quarterly* 32, 3 (2004): 229–236.

2389. Coates, Paul. "The Sleep of Reason: Monstrosity and Disavowal." In Paul Coates. *The Gorgon's Gaze: German Cinema, Expressionism, and the Image of Horror.* Cambridge, UK: Cambridge University Press, 1991, pp. 74–107.

2390. Coolidge-Rust, Marie. *London After Midnight.* New York: Grosset and Dunlap, 1928. 261 pp. hb. dj. Rpt.: London: The Readers Library Publishing Company, 1929. 250 pp. hb. Rev. ed.: *London After Midnight.* Couch Pumpkin Classics. Ed. by Neils W. Erickson. N.p.: Couch Pumpkin Press, 2010.242 pp. pb. & hb. The last known print of *London After Midnight,* directed by Tod Browning, who later directed *Dracula* with Bela Lugosi, was destroyed in a fire in 1967. What remains is the novel derived from the movie.

2391. Crane, Jonathan Lake. "Nosferatu." In *Terror and Everyday Life: Singular Moments in the History of the Horror Film.* Thousand Oaks, CA: SAGE Publications, 1994, pp. 46–70.

2392. _____. *Terror and Everyday Life: A History of Horror.* Urbana: University of Illinois, Ph.D. dissertation, 1991, 297 pp. Large format.

2393. Cutts, John. "Vampyr." *Films and Filming* (December 1960): 17ff.

2394. Eisner, Lotte H. *The Haunted Screen: Expressionism in the German Cinema and the Influence of Max Reinhardt.* Berkeley: University of California Press, 1969. 354 pp. hb. 2nd. Rev. ed.: 2008. 360 pp.

2395. _____. "M." In Lotte Eisner. *Fritz Lang.* Oxford, UK: Oxford University Press; 1977, pp. 111–28.

2396. _____. *Murnau.* London, Secker & Warburg, 1973. 287 pp. hb. Rpt.: Berkeley: University of California Press, 1973. 287 pp. tp.

2397. Elsaesser, Thomas. "No End to Nosferatu (1922)." In Noah Isenberg, ed. *Weimar Cinema: An Essential Guide to Classic Films of the Era.* New York: Columbia University Press, 2009, pp. 79–94.

2398. _____. "Nosferatu, Tartuffe and Faust: Secret Affinities in Friedrich Wilhelm Murnau." In Thomas Elsässer. *Weimar Cinema and After: Germany's Historical Imaginary.* London: Routledge, 2000, pp. 195–222.

2399. Everson, William K. "Mark of the Vampire/London After Midnight." In William K. Everson. *Classics of the Horror Film.* New York: Citadel, 1974, pp. 125–29.

2400. _____. "Vampyr." In William K. Everson. *Classics of the Horror Film.* New York: Citadel, 1974, pp. 62–69.

2401. Gelder, Ken. "Citational Vampires: Transnational Techniques of Circulation in *Irma Vep, Blood: The Last Vampire* and *Thirst.*" In Tabish. Khair and Johan Hoglund, eds. *Transnational and Postcolonial Vampires: Dark Blood.* Basingstoke, UK: Palgrave Macmillan, 2012, pp. 81–104.

2402. Ginini, Ronald. *Theda Bara: A Biography of the Silent Screen Vamp, with a Filmography.* Jefferson, NC: McFarland & Company, 2012. 168 pp. tp.

2403. Golden, Eve. *Vamp: The Rise and Fall of Theda Bara.* Vestal, NY: Empire Publishing, 1996. 274 pp. hb. dj.

2404. Granlycke, Jenny. "Freidrich Wilhelm Murnau (F. W. Plumpe)." *For the Blood Is the Life* 2, 7 (Winter 1990–91): 16–18.

2405. Guillermo, Gilberto Perez. "F. W. Murnau, an Introduction." *Film Comment* 7, 2 (Summer 1971): 13–15.

2406. _____. "Shadow and Substance: Murnau's *Nosferatu*." *Sight & Sound* 36, 3 (Summer 1967): 150–53, 159.

2407. Haberman, Steve. *Silent Screams.* Ser.: Chronicles of Terror: Baltimore, MD: Luminary Press, 2003. 240 pp. hb.

2408/09. Hanke, Ken. "The Tod Browning-Lon Chaney Films." In Ken Hanke. *A Critical Guide to Horror Film Series.* New York: Garland Publishing, 1991, pp. 3–12.

2410. Hensley, Wayne E. "The Contribution of F.W. Murnau's *Nosferatu* to the Evolution of *Dracula*." *Literature/Film Quarterly* 30, 1 (2002): 59–64.

2411. Herzog, Todd. "Fritz Lang's *M*." In Noah Isenberg, ed. *Weimar Cinema: An Essential Guide to Classic Films of the Era.* New York: Columbia University Press, 2009, pp. 291–310.

2412. Higashi, Sumiko. "The Vampire." In Sumiko Higashi. *Virgins, Vamps, and Flappers: The American Silent Movie Heroine.* Montreal: Eden Press Women's Publications, 1978, pp. 55–78.

2413. Jackson, Kevin. *Nosferatu (1922): Eine Symphonie Des Grauens.* Ser.: BFI Film Classics. London: BFI Publishing, 2013. 126 pp. tp.

2414. Jameux, Charles. *Murnau.* Paris: Editions Universities, 1965. 188 pp.

2415. Jensen, Lisa. *The Horror Film—Analysis of "Nosferatu" from 1922 and 1979.* Munchen: GRIN Verlag, 2011. 36 pp. pb.

2416. Jensen, Paul M. *The Cinema of Fritz Lang.* New York/London: A.S. Barnes & Co./A. Zwemmer Ltd., 1969. 224 pp. tp.

2417. Johnson, Timothy W. "Nosferatu." In Frank N. Magill, ed. *Magill's Survey of Cinema.* Vol. 2. Englewood, NJ: Salem Press, 1982, pp. 806–09.

2418. Kaes, Anton. "Dracula Revisited." In Anton Kaes. *Shell Shock Cinema: Weimar Culture and the Wounds of War.* Princeton, NJ: Princeton University Press, 2009, pp. 98–107.

2419. Kawin, Brace. "Nosferatu." *Film Quarterly* 33 (Spring 1980): 45–47.

2420. Kerouac, Jack. "Nosferatu." In Jack Kerouac. *Film and the Liberal Arts.* New York, Holt, Rinehart, Winston, 1970, pp. 354–357.

2421. Kinnard, Roy. *Horror in Silent Films: A Filmography, 1896–1929.* Jefferson, NC: McFarland & Company, 1995. 278 pp. Includes entries on a number of the classic vampire films.

2422. Kracauer, Siegfried. *From Caligari to Hitler: A Psychological History of the German Film.* Princeton, NJ: Princeton University Press, 1947. 361 pp. hb. Rev. expanded ed.: 2004.

2423. Kreimeier, Klaus. "From Vampire to Vamp: On the Background of a Cinematic Myth." In Rolf Aurich, Wolfgang Jacobsen, and Gabriele Jatho, eds. *Artificial Humans: Manic Machines Controlled Bodies.* Berlin: Jovis Verlagsbüro: 2000, pp. 77–96.

2424. Lehman, Peter, and William Luhr. "Film and the Other Arts: *Dr. Jekyll & Mr. Hyde* and *Nosferatu*." In Peter Lehman and William Luhr. *Thinking About Movies: Watching, Questioning, Enjoying.* Malden, MA/Oxford, UK: Blackwell, 2003, pp. 191–219.

2425. Lengeman, William. "Before Bela and Boris: Early Stages and Screen Adaptations of *Dracula* and *Frankenstein*." *Internet Review of Science Fiction* 2, 10 (November 2005) Posted at: http://www.irosf.com/q/zine/article/10206.

2426. "London After Midnight: Revelations in Black." *Ghastly* 2 (1992): 9–12.

2427. Luhr, William. "*Nosferatu* and the Postwar German Film." *Michigan Academician* 14: 4 (Spring 1982): 453–58.

2428. Luke, Martina G. "Nosferatu the Vampyre (1979) as a Legacy of Romanticism." In John Edgar Browning and Caroline Joan Picart, eds. *Dracula, Vampires, and Other Undead Forms.* Lanham, MD: The Scarecrow Press, 2009, pp. 153–64.

2429. Manvell, Roger. "Introduction." In *Masterworks of the German Cinema: The Golem—Nosferatu—M—The Threepenny Opera.* New York: Harper & Row, 1973, pp. 7–17.

2430. Mayne, Judith. "Dracula in the Twilight: Murnau's *Nosferatu* (1922)." In Eric Rentschler, ed. *German Film & Literature: Adaptations and Transformations.* London: Methuen, 1986, pp. 25–39. Rpt. New York: Routledge, 1986.

2431. _____. "Herzog, Murnau and the Vampire." In Timothy Corrigan, ed. *The Films of Werner*

Herzog: Between Mirage and History. New York: Methuen, 2013. pp. 119–32.

2432. Michaels, Lloyd. "Nosferatu, or the Phantom of the Cinema." In Andrew Horton and Stuart Y. McDougal, eds. *Play It Again Sam: Retakes on Remakes.* Berkeley: University of California Press, 1998, pp. 238–49.

2433. ____. "Reviving the Undead: Herzog's Remake of *Nosferatu.*" In Lloyd Michaels. *The Phantom of the Cinema: Character in Modern Film.* New York: New York State University Press, 1998, pp. 67–82,.

2434. Nosferatu: *History, Criticism & Interpretation.* Lakewood, CO: Centipede Press, 2005. 448 pp. hb. Limited to 540 copies. This volume collects essays by a number of scholars and film critics, including Lotte H. Eisner, Siegfried Kracuaer, Lane Roth, David J. Skal, and Robin Wood, speaking about *Nosferatu* (1922).

2435. Peirse, Alison. "*Vampyr* and the European Avant-Garde." In Alison Peirse. *After Dracula: The 1930s Horror Film.* London: I. B. Tauris, 2013, pp. 81–100.

2436. Pflaum, Hans Günther. "Nosferatu, A Symphony of Terror. " In Hans Günther Pflaum. *German Silent Movie Classics.* Wiesbafen: Friedrich-Murnau-Stiftung and Transit Film, en collaboration avec Goethe-Institut Inter Nations, 2002.

2437. Powell, Anna. "The Movement Image: Horror Cinematography and *Mise-en-scène.*" In Anna Powell. *Deleuze and Horror Film.* Edinburgh: Edinburgh University Press, 2005, pp. 109–53.

2438. Prager, Brad. *The Cinema of Werner Herzog: Aesthetic Ecstasy and Truth.* London: Wallflower Press, 2007. 178 pp. pb.

2439. Prawer, S. S. "Books into Film II: Dreyer's Vampyr." In S. S. Prawer. *Caligari's Children: The Film as Tale of Terror.* Oxford: Oxford University Press, 1980, pp. 138–63.

2440. ____. *Nosferatu: Phantom der Nacht.* Ser.: BFI Film Classics. London: British Film Institute, 2004. 87 pp. tp.

2441. Riley, Philip J., ed. *Dracula Starring Lon Chaney—An Alternate History for Classic Film Monsters.* Duncan, OK: BearManor Media, 2010. 175 pp.

2442. ____. *London After Midnight.* New York: Cornwall Books, 1985. 178 pp. hb. Large format. Rpt. as: *London After Midnight—A Recon-*struction. Duncan, OK: BearManor Media, 2011. 178 pp. pb. Large format.

2443. Romer, Richard Ira. *The Cinematic Treatment of Protagonists in Murnau's* Nosferatu, Browning's Dracula *and Whale's* Frankenstein. New York: Columbia University, Ed.D. thesis, 1984. 149 pp. Large format.

2444. Roth, Lane. "Dracula Meets the Zeitgeist: *Nosferatu* (1922) as Film Adaptation." *Literature/Film Quarterly* 7, 4 (1979): 309–13.

2445. ____. "Film, Society and Ideas: *Nosferatu* and *Horror of Dracula.*" In Barry Keith Grant. *Planks of Reason: Essays on the Horror Film.* Metuchen, NJ: Scarecrow Press, 1984, pp. 245–54.

2446. Rudkin, David. *Vampyr.* London: British Film Institute, 2008. 79 pp. tp.

2447. Segal, Naomi. "André Gide, *Nosferatu* and the Hydraulics of Youth and Age." In Simon Bacon, and Katarzyna Bronk, eds. *Undead Memory: Vampires and Human Memory in Popular Culture.* Bern, Switz.: Peter Lang International Academic Publishers, 2013, pp. 85–104.

2448. Senn, Bryan. "The Enigma of Vampyr." *Midnight Marque* 47 (Summer 1995): 5–10.

2449. Smith, Evans Lansing. "Framing the Underworld: Threshold Imagery in Murnau, Cocteau and Bergman." *Literature/Film Quarterly* 24, 3 (1996): 241–254.

2450. Todd, Janet M. "The Class-ic Vampire." In Michael Klein and Gillian Parker, eds. *The English Novel and the Movies.* New York: Frederick Ungar Publishing Co., 1981, pp. 197–210.

2451. Tumini, Angela. "Vampiresse: Embodiment of Sensuality and Erotic Horror in Carl Th. Dreyer's *Vampyr* and Mario Bava's *The Mask of Satan.*" In Barbara Brodman and James E. Doan, eds. *The Universal Vampire: Origins and Evolution of a Legend.* Madison, NJ: Fairleigh Dickinson University Press, 2013, pp. 121–35.

2452. Unrau, Rona. "Eine Symphonie des Grauens, or The Terror of Music: Murnau's *Nosferatu.*" *Literature/Film Quarterly* 24, 3 (1996): 234–240.

2453. Vampyr: A Film by Carl Dreyer. [Criterion Collection: New York, 2008] 43 pp. pb. Included in Criterion Collection boxed DVD set of *Vampyr.*

2454. Walker, Beverly. "Werner Herzog's *Nosferatu.*" *Sight and Sound* 47, 4 (Autumn 1978): 202–05.

2455. Weinstock, Jeffrey Andrew. "Sans Fangs: Theda Bara, *A Fool There Was*, and the cinematic vamp." In Douglas Brode and Leah Deyneka. *Dracula's Daughters: The Female Vampire on Film*. Lanham, MD: The Scarecrow Press, 2014. pp. 37–43.

2456. Williams, Andrew P. "The Silent Threat: A (Re)Viewing of the Sexual 'Other' in *The Phantom of the Opera* and *Nosferatu*." *The Midwest Quarterly* 38, 1 (1996): 90–101.

2457. Wood, Robin. "Burying the Undead: The Use and Obsolescence of Count Dracula." In Barry Keith Grant. *The Dread of Difference: Gender and the Horror Film*. Austin: University of Texas Press, 1996, pp. 364–78. The author compares and contrasts the figure of Count Dracula as found in Bram Stoker's original novel, the 1922 movie *Nosferatu* and the 1979 *Dracula* directed by John Badham.

2458. _____. "The Dark Mirror: Murnau's *Nosferatu*." *Film Comment* 7 (Summer 1971). Rpt: Robin Wood and Richard Lippe, eds. *The American Nightmare: Essays on the Horror Film*. Toronto: Festival of Festivals, 1979, pp. 43–49.

2459. _____. "F. W. Murmau." *Film Comment* 12, 3 (May-June 1976): 4–19.

Cinematic Vampires: The Universal Era

Beginning with *Dracula*, Universal Studios began to issue a set of horror movies that included the first vampire talkies and inspired a set of vampire movies by other studios. The Universal horror films, the last of which appeared in 1948, span the era of black and white filmmaking and presage the movement into Technicolor that meaningfully begins with the Hammer films in the 1950s.

At the fountainhead of the new vampire films is *Dracula*, a film adapted from the Broadway play, and often credited with saving Universal from the effects of the Great Depression. The film is noteworthy both for its quality, which made it a financial success, and its being made simultaneously with a Spanish version that utilized the same sets and a translation of the script, but a different director, crew, and cast. Thought lost for many years, the Spanish version was rediscovered and again made available in the 1990s.

The English version with Bela Lugosi has reached a certain iconic status and its success certainly spawned a variety of responses from other studios, many of which turned out to be pseudo-vampire movies. Universal saw *Dracula* as one among a spectrum of horror movies and was initially slow to develop additional vampire sequels, but finally did a half dozen, the last one (1948) being a comedy reflection upon the films of the previous two decades starring the team of Bud Abbott and Lou Costello. Vampire movies would subsequently disappear for a decade until revived by Hammer Studios in England in 1958.

Dracula and its star Bela Lugosi have been the focus of some of the most significant comment upon horror movies in general and vampire movies in particular.

2460. [Ackerman, Forrest J]. "Bram Stoker's *Dracula* with Bela Lugosi." *Famous Monsters of Filmland* 5, 1 (April 1963): 52–67.

2461. Barnett, Buddy. "A Hollywood Tour of Bela Lugosi." *Videosonic Arts* 1 (1990): 64–79.

2462. Barrenechea, Antonio. "Hemispheric Horrors: Celluloid Vampires from the 'Good Neighbor' Era" *Comparative American Studies* 7, 3 (2009): 225–237. Posted at: http://www.utm.utoronto.ca/~w3his490/A-Barrenechea-GNP.horror.films.pdf.

2463. Benlloch, Inés. *1931 Dracula: Ethnic Identity in Hollywood's Spanish-Language Films*. Austin: University of Texas at Austin, M.A. thesis, 2004. 53 pp. Large format.

2464. Bennett, Rod. "Grim Fairy Tales." *Wonder* 7 (1993): 13–21. Re: Universal horror films.

2465. Bernard, Mark. "'A Foreign Man in a Fog': Robert Siodmak, Lon Chaney, Jr., and Son of Dracula." *Journal of Dracula Studies* 14 (2012): 77–99.

2466. Bloom, Abigail Burnham. "Vampire and Victim." In Abigail Burnham Bloom. *The Literary Monster on Film: Five Nineteenth Century British Novels and Their Cinematic Adaptations.* Jefferson, NC: McFarland & Company, 2010, pp. 146–88.

2467. Bojarski, Richard. *The Films of Bela Lugosi.* Secaucus, NJ: Citadel Press, 1980. 256 pp. pb. Large format. Cinema. Rpt. as: *The Complete Films of Bela Lugosi.* Secaucus, NJ: Citadel Press, 1992. 256 pp. pb. Large format.

2468. Brederoo, Nico J. "Dracula in Film." *In* Valeria Tinkler Viviani, Peter Davidson, and Jane Stevenson, eds. *Exhibited by Candlelight: Sources and Developments in the Gothic Tradition.* Amsterdam: Rodopi, 1995, pp. 171–81.

2469. Bronfen, Elisabeth. "Speaking with Eyes: Tod Browning's *Dracula* and Its Phantom Camera." In Bernd Herzogenrath, ed. *The Films of Tod Browning.* London: Black Dog Publishing, 2006, pp. 151–71.

2470. Brosnan, John. *The Horror People.* New York: St. Martin's Press, 1976. 304 pp. hb. dj. Rpt.: New York: New American Library, 1977. 306 pp. pb. Contains biographical chapters on Bela Lugosi, Tod Browning, Christopher Lee, and Peter Cushing, and chapters on the films produced by Hammer and by Roger Corman. The appendix contains a number of brief biographical statements about a variety of people associated with vampire movies.

2471. Brunas, Michael John, and Tom Weaver. *Universal Horrors: The Studios Classic Films, 1931–1946.* Jefferson, NC: McFarland & Company, 1990. 616 pp. hb.

2472. Burns, Bonnie. "Dracula's Daughter: Cinema, Hypnosis, and the Erotics of Lesbianism." In Karla Jay, ed. *Lesbian Erotics.* New York: New York University Press, 1995, pp. 196–211.

2473. Butler, Charles E. *Vampires Everywhere: The Rise of the Movie UnDead.* N.p.: Su asti Publishing, 2012. 98 pp. tp.

2474. Butler, Erik. *Metamorphoses of the Vampire in Literature and Film: Cultural Transformations in Europe, 1732–1933.* Rochester, NY: Camden House, 2010. 225 pp. hb.

2475. Butler, Ivan. "Dracula and Frankenstein." In Ivan Butler. *The Horror Film.* New York: A. S. Barnes & Co., 1967. Rev. ed.: 1970. Rpt. as: *Horror in the Cinema.* New York: Paperback Library, 1971, pp. 39–58.

2476. Clarens, Carlos. "Children of the Night: Hollywood, 1928–1947." In Carlos Clarens. *An Illustrated History of Horror and Science-fiction Films.* New York: J. P. Putnam's Sons, 1967, pp. 59–104. Rpt.: Cambridge, MA: Da Capo Press, 1997, pp. 59–104.

2477. Copner, Mike. "Lugosi-Then and Now." *Videosonic Arts* 1 (1990): 11–24.

2478. _____. "Man of Mystery." *Videosonic Arts* 1 (1990): 25–47.

2479. _____. "Manly Hall Story." *Videosonic Arts* 1 (1990): 48–51.

2480. Coughlin, Jim. "The Supporting Cast of Universal's *Dracula:* Herbert Bunston, Frances Dade, Charles Gerrard." *Midnight Marque* 47 (Summer 1995): 63–70.

2481. Creed, Barbara. "Man as Menstrual Monster: Dracula and his Uncanny Brides." In Barbara Creed. *Phallic Panic.* Melbourne, Aust.: Melbourne University Press, 2005, pp. 69–95.

2482. Cremer, Robert. *Lugosi: The Man Behind the Cape.* Chicago: Henry Regnery Company, 1976. 307 pp. hb. dj.

2483. Del Valle, David. "Beyond Bela: John Carradine on Filling Lugosi's Dracula Cape." *Imagi-Movies* 2, 2 (Winter 1994): 58–59.

2484. Doherty, Thomas Patrick. "Rugged Individualism: *Dracula* (1931), *Frankenstein* (1931) and Their Progeny." In Thomas Patrick Doherty. *Pre-Code Hollywood: Sex, Immorality, and Insurrection in American Cinema 1930–1934.* New York: Columbia University Press, 1999, pp. 299–307.

2485. Dunbar, Brian. *Dracula and Bram Stoker's Dracula.* Ser.: York Film Notes. London: York Press, 2000. 91 pp. tp.

2486. Edwards, Larry. *Bela Lugosi: Master of the MacAbre.* Bradenton, FL: McGuinn & McGuire Publishing, 1997. 214 pp. tp.

2487. Everson, William K. "The Last Days of Lugosi." *Castle of Frankenstein* 2, 4 (1966): 18–25.

2488. Gelino, Mike, and David Harlan. "The Return of the Vampire: Studio History, Cast & Credits." *Hollywood Horror Classics* 2 (1994): 16–23.

2489. Gifford, Denis. "Karloff and Lugosi, the Universal Monsters." In *A Pictorial History of Horror Movies.* London: Hamlyn, 1973, 78–99.

2490. Gordon, Richard. "An Appreciation of Bela Lugosi." In Gary J. Svehla and Susan Svehla, eds. *Bela Lugosi.* Baltimore, MD: Midnight Marquee Press, 2007, pp. 258–71.

2491. Hall, Gladys. "'When She Was Fed': Bela Lugosi's Real-Life Vampire Romance." In David Skal, ed. *Vampires: Encounters with the Undead.* New York: Black Dog & Leventhal Publishers, 2001, pp. 353–56.

2492. Hanke, Ken. "Bela Lugosi and the Monogram Nine." *Filmfax* 44 (April/May 1994): 57–63, 94.

2493. _____. "The Universal Dracula Films." In Ken Hanke. *A Critical Guide to Horror Film Series.* New York: Garland Publishing, 1991, pp. 23–32.

2494. Harland, Robert. "Quiero chupar tu sangre: A Comparison of the Spanish- and English-Language Versions of Universal Studio's *Dracula.*" *Journal of Dracula Studies* 9 (2007): 29–38.

2495. Hatfield, Hurd. "Personal Recollections of Acting from Oscar Wilde's *The Picture of Dorian Gray* to Bram Stoker's *Dracula.*" *Bram Stoker Society Journal* 7 (1995): 34–40.

2496. Haydock, Ron. "Bela Lugosi: His Life and Undeath." *Monsters of the Movies* 1, 3 (October 1974): 4–11.

2497. _____. "Beware the Bat People." *Monsters of the Movies* 4 (December 1974): 32–35.

2498. Hensley, Wayne E. "Stoker's *Dracula.*" *The Explicator* 58, 2 (Winter 2000): 89–90.

2499. Herzogenrath, Bernd, ed. *The Films of Tod Browning.* London: Black Dog Publishing, 2006. 239 pp. tp.

2500. Hoffman, Eric. "Mighty Bela Steps Up to Bat!" *Famous Monsters of Filmland* 211 (February/March 1996): 50–53.

2501. Hogan, David J. "Abbott and Costello Meet Frankenstein." In Gary J. Svehla and Susan Svehla, eds. *Bela Lugosi.* Baltimore, MD: Midnight Marquee Press, 2007, pp. 204–15.

2502. _____. "Lugosi, Lee, and the Vampire Lovers." In David J. Hogan. *Dark Romance: Sexuality in the Horror Film.* Jefferson, NC: McFarland & Company, 1986, pp. 138–63.

2503. Humphries, Reynold. "Mark of the Vampire: Seeing Is Believing." In Bernd Herzogenrath, ed. *The Cinema of Tod Browning: Essays on the Macabre and the Grotesque.* Jefferson NC: McFarland & Company, 2008.

2504. Jankovich, Mark, and Shane Brown. "'The Screen's Number One and Number Two Bogeymen': The Critical Reception of Boris Karloff and Bela Lugosi in the 1930s and 1940s." In Kate Egan and Sarah Thomas. *Cult Film Stardom: Offbeat Attractions and Processes of Cultification.* Basingstoke, UK: Palgrave Macmillan, 2012, pp. 243–58.

2505. Johnson, Tom. "Dracula: The Strangest Passion the World Has Ever Known." Tom Johnson. *Censored Screams: The British Ban on Hollywood Horror in the Thirties.* Jefferson, NC: McFarland & Company, 1997.

2506. Kaes, Anton. "Dracula Revisited." In Anrton, Kaes. "Shell Shock Cinema: Weimar Culture and the Wounds of War." Princeton, NJ: Princeton University Press, 2009, pp. 98–107.

2507. Kelly, Kevin E. "Lugosi in Hollywood: A Hungarian Actor's Rise and Fall as a Movie Star." *Hungarian Studies Review* 11, 1 (1996: 115–135.

2508. Kovári, Orsolya. "Mr Dracula–On Béla Lugosi." *Hungarian Review* 3 (2013): 95–103.

2509. Lafond, Frank. "Tod Browning vs George Melford: Dracula's Doppelgänger." In Bernd Herzogenrath, ed. *The Cinema of Tod Browning: Essays on the Macabre and the Grotesque.* Jefferson, NC:, McFarland & Company, 2008.

2510. Leifert, Don. "Return of the Vampire." In Gary J. Svehla and Susan Svehla, eds. *Bela Lugosi.* Baltimore, MD: Midnight Marquee Press, 2007, pp. 183–89.

2511. Lennig, Arthur. *The Count: The Life and Films of Bela "Dracula" Lugosi.* New York: G. P. Putnam's Sons, 1974. 347 pp. hb. dj. Rev. ed. as: *The Immortal Count: The Life and Films of Bela Lugosi.* Lexington: University of Kentucky Press, 2003. 548 pp. hb. dj.

2512. Lugosi, Bela. "I Like Playing Dracula." *Wonder* 7 (1993): 44–45. Rpt. in: Leslie Shepard and Albert Power, eds. *Dracula: Celebrating 100 Years.* Dublin: Mentor Press, 1997, pp. 117–19.

2513. Mallory, Michael. *Universal Studios Monsters: A Legacy of Horror.* New York: Universe Publishing, 2002. 252 pp. hb & pb.

2514. Mank, Gregory William. "Carroll Borland." In Carroll Borland. *Countess Dracula.*

Absecon, NJ: Magic-Image Filmbooks, 1994, pp. 18–39.

2515. _____. "Clash of the Draculas: Bela Lugosi vs. John Carradine." In Bob Madison, ed. *Dracula: The First Hundred Years*. Baltimore, MD: Midnight Marquee Press, 1997, pp. 126–142.

2516. _____. "Dracula's Last Bride." In Bob Madison, ed. *Dracula: The First Hundred Years*. Baltimore, MD: Midnight Marquee Press, 1997, pp. 108–125.

2517. _____. "Elizabeth Allan: The True 'Vamp' of *Mark of the Vampire*." *Monsters from the Vault* 2 (Winter 1996): 4–11.

2518. _____. "John Carradine." In Gregory William Mank. *The Hollywood Hissables*. Metuchen, NJ: Scarecrow Press, 1989, pp. 55–130.

2519. _____. "The Mark of the Vampire." In Gregory William Mank. *Hollywood Cauldron: Thirteen Horror Films from the Genre's Golden Age*. Jefferson, NC: McFarland & Company, 1994, pp. 89–120.

2520. "The Mark of the Vampire." *Famous Monsters of Filmland* Pt. 1. 61 (January 1970): 22–28; Pt. 2. 62 (February 1970):.

2521. Matthews, Melvin E. "The Horror Cycle Begins: *Dracula* and *Frankenstein* (1931)." In Melvin E. Matthews. *Fear Itself: Horror on the Screen and in Reality During the Depression and World War II*. Jefferson, NC: McFarland & Company, 2009, pp. 5–36.

2522. Mcfaden, Brian. "The Vampire's Ghost." In Brian McFadden. *Republic Horrors: The Serial Studio's Chillers*. N.p.: Kohner, Madison & Danforth; 1 edition (January 30, 2013. Pp. 79–98.

2523. Miller, Jeffrey S. "Abbott and Costello Meet Frankenstein." In Jeffrey S. Miller. *Horror Spoofs of Abbott and Costello: A Critical Assessment of the Comedy Team's Monster Films*. Jefferson, NC: McFarland & Company, 2013, pp. 29–64.

2524. Mitchell, Lisa. "Bela Lugosi at the Midnite Delicatessen." *Famous Monsters of Filmland*. (1976). Rpt.: *Videosonic Arts* 1 (1990): 52–60.

2525. Moench, Doug. "Bela Lugosi: Dracula of Stage and Screen & Coffin." *Dracula Lives* 3 (October 1973): 26–31.

2526. Nowak, Lars. "Cinematic Torture Machines: Tod Browning and Masochism," in Bernd Herzogenrath, ed. *The Cinema of Tod Browning: Essays on the Macabre and Grotesque*. London: Black Dog Publishing, 2006. 239 pp. pp. 50–69.

2527. Oates, Joyce Carol. "Dracula." In David Rosenberg, ed. *The Movie That Changed My Life*. New York: Viking Press, 1991, pp. 60–75. Rpt. as: "The Vampire's Secret: (Re)Viewing Tod Browning's *Dracula* after Forty Years." In Joyce Carol Oates. *Uncensored: Views and (Re)Views*. New York, Ecco, 2005, pp. 327–38.

2528. _____. "Dracula (Tod Browning, 1931): The Vampire's Secret." *Southwest Review* 76, 4 (Autumn 1991): 498–510.

2529. O'Bannon, Dan, and Matt Lohr. "*Dracula* (1931)." In Dan Obannon and Matt Lohr. *Dan O'Bannon's Guide to Screenplay Structure*. Studio City, CA: Michael Wiese Productions, 2013, pp. 104–10.

2530. Parnum, John, and Gregory Mank. "House of Carradine: Why Isn't Lugosi in the House?" *Midnight Marque* 47 (Summer 1995): 18–22.

2531. Peary, Danny. "Plan 9 from Outer Space." In Danny Peary. *Cult Movies: The Classic, the Sleepers, the Weird, and the Wonderful*. New York: Delta, 1989, pp. 266–70.

2532. Phillips, Jack R. "Dracula's Daughter: The Balderston Version." *Scarlet Street* 8 (Fall 1992): 54–56.

2533. Phillips, Kendall R. "Dracula (1931)." In Kendall R. Phillips. *Projected Fears: Horror Films and American Culture*. Westport, CT: Praeger, 2005, pp. 11–34.

2534. "Public Vampire No. 1: The Story of Bela Lugosi, Ambassador from Transylvania." *Monsterama* 1 (Spring 1991): 53–61.

2535/36. Rhodes, Gary Don. "*Dracula* (1931): Addenda to the Children of the Night." *Cult Movies* 13 (1995): 35–39.

2537. _____. *Lugosi: His Life in Films, on Stage, and in the Hearts of Horror Lovers*. Jefferson, NC: McFarland & Company, 1997. 414 pp. tp. Rev. ed.: Jefferson, NC: McFarland & Company, 2006. 430 pp. tp.

2538. _____. "Manly P. Hall, Dracula (1931), and the Complexities of the Classic Horror Film Sequel." In John Edgar Browning and Caroline Joan Picart, eds. *Dracula, Vampires, and Other Undead Forms*. Lanham, MD: The Scarecrow Press, 2009, pp. 3–18.

2539. _____, **and Bill Kaffenberger.** *No Traveler Returns: The Lost Years of Bela Lugosi.* Fort Worth, TX: BearManor Media, 2012. 343 pp. tp.

2540. _____, **and John Parris Springer.** "They Give Us That 'Weird Feeling': Vampire Women in Films of the Thirties." In Gary Svelha and Susan Svelha, eds. *Bitches, Bimbos, and Virgins: Women in the Horror Film.* Baltimore, MD: Midnight Marquee Press, 1996, pp. 25–81.

2541. _____, **with Richard Sheffield.** *Bela Lugosi—Dreams and Nightmares.* Narbeth, PA: Collectables Press, 2007. 352 pp. hb.

2542. Riley, Philip J., ed. *Abbott and Costello Meet Frankenstein.* Abescon, NJ: Magicimage Filmbooks; 1990. 103 pp. pb. Large format.

2543. _____. *Dracula's Daughter—An Alternate History for Classic Film Monsters.* Duncan, OK: BearManor Media, 2009. 173 pp. pb. Large format.

2544. _____, **ed.** *House of Dracula (Original Shooting Script).* Abescon, NJ: MagicImage Filmbooks, 1993. 104 pp. pb. Large format.

2545. _____. *House of Frankenstein (Original Shooting Script).* Abescon, NJ: MagicImage Filmbooks, 1991. 119 pp. pb. Large format.

2546. _____. *The Wolf Man vs. Dracula: An Alternate History for Classic Film Monsters.* Duncan, OK: BearManor Media, 2010. 136 pp. pb. Large format.

2547. _____, **ed.** *MagicImage Filmbooks Presents Dracula (The Original 1931 Shooting Script).* Atlantic City, NJ: MagicImage Filmbooks, 1990. 81 pp. pb. Large format.

2548. Romer, Richard Ira. *The Cinematic Treatment of the Protagonists in Murnau's* Nosferatu, *Browning's* Dracula *and Whale's* Frankenstein. New York: Columbia University Teachers College, Ph.D. dissertation, 1984. 149 pp. Large format.

2549. Roth, Lane. "*Dracula/Dracula*: Some Thoughts About the Hammer and Universal Versions." *Photon* 27 (1977): 40–41.

2550. Sadoff, Dianne F. "Reproducing Monsters, Vampires, and Cyborgs." In Diane F. Sadoff. *Victorian Vogue: British Novels on Screen.* Minneapolis: University of Minnesota Press, 2009, pp. 101–48.

2551. Sanders, Clinton R. "The Armadillso in Dracula's Foyer: Conventions and Innovation in Horror Cinema." In Paul Loukides & Linda K.

Fuller. *Beyond the Stars II: Plot Conventions in American Popular Film.* Bowling Green, OH: Bowling Green State University Popular Press, 1991, pp. 143–60.

2552. Scrivani, Richard. "Dracula's Daughter: The Film." *Scarlet Street* 8 (Fall 1992): 57–59, 100.

2553. Senn, Bryan. *Golden Horrors: An Illustrated Critical Filmography of Terror Cinema, 1931–1939.* Jefferson, NC: McFarland & Company, 2006. 518 pp. hb.

2554. _____. "Horror Cinema's First Family: Dracula, Daughter, and Son." *Monsterscene* 7 (Spring 1996): 8–25.

2555. Sevastakis, Michael. "*Dracula*: The Amorous Death." In Michael Sevastakis. *Songs of Love and Death: The Classical American Horror Film of the 1930s.* Westport, CT: Greenwood Press, 1993, pp. 3–24.

2556. _____. *Dracula's Daughter*: Vampirism as Psychosis." In Michael Sevastakis. *Songs of Love and Death: The Classical American Horror Film of the 1930s.* Westport, CT: Greenwood Press, 1993, pp. 163–80.

2557. Skal, David J. *Dark Carnival: The Secret World of Tod Browning, Hollywood's Master of the Macabre.* New York: Doubleday and Company, 1995. 359 pp.

2558. _____. "Dracula Unseen." In Anthony Timpone. *Fangoria Vampires.* New York: HarperPrism, 1996, pp. 193–202.

2559. _____. *Hollywood Gothic: The Tangled Web of Dracula from Novel to Stage to Screen.* New York: W. W. Norton & Company, 1990. 243 pp. hb. dj. Large format. Rpt.: New York: W. W. Norton & Company, 1990. 243 pp. pb. Large format.

2560. _____, **and Elias Savada.** "Malibu after Midnight: The Final Days of Tod Browning." *Monsterscene* 6 (Fall 1995): 10–27.

2561. Smith, Angela Marie. "Chimeras in *Dracula* and *Frankenstein*." In Angela Smith. *Hideous Progeny: Disability, Eugenics, and Classic Horror Cinema.* New York: Columbia University Press, 2012, pp. 33–82.

2562. _____. "Monsters in the Bed: The Horror-film Eugenics of *Dracula* and *Frankenstein*." In Susan Currell and Christina Cogdell, eds. *Popular Eugenics: National Efficiency and American Mass Culture in the 1930s.* Athens: Ohio University Press, 2006, pp. 332–58.

2563. Smith, Don G. "*Son of Dracula* and Other Nonseries Universal Films (1941–1946)" In Don G. Smith. *Lon Chaney Jr: Horror Film Star, 1906–1973.* Jefferson, NC: McFarland & Company, 1996, pp. 81–97.

2564. Snyder, Helen Lavinia. *A Comparative Analysis of the Transformation of Myths in Dracula the Novel, Stageplay, and Movie.* San Jose, CA: San Jose State University, M.A. thesis, 1978. 75 pp. Large format.

2565. Soister, John. "Mother Riley Meets the Vampire." In Gary J. Svehla and Susan Svehla, eds. *Bela Lugosi.* Baltimore, MD: Midnight Marquee Press, 2007, pp. 230–43.

2566. Spadoni, Robert. *Uncanny Bodies: The Coming of Sound Film and the Origins of the Horror Genre.* Berkeley: University of California Press, 2007. 190 pp. tp.

2567. Stritto, Frank J. Dello. "At Long Last Lugosi! Film History's Evolving View of Bela Lugosi." *Cult Movies* 13 (1995): 26–34.

2568. _____. *A Quaint & Curious Volume of Forgotten Lore: The History & Mythology of Classic Horror Films.* Los Angles: Cult Movies Press, 2003. 380 pp. hb. dj.

2569. _____. "The Vampire Strikes Back!" In Bob Madison, ed. *Dracula: The First Hundred Years.* Baltimore, MD: Midnight Marquee Press, 1997, pp. 142–67.

2570/71. _____, and Andi Brooks. *Vampire over London: Bela Lugosi in Britain.* Los Angeles: Cult Movies Press, 2001. 363 pp. hb.

2572. Svehla, Gary J. "Mark of the Vampire." In Gary J. Svehla and Susan Svehla, eds. *Bela Lugosi.* Baltimore, MD: Midnight Marquee Press, 2007, pp. 110–13.

2573. _____, and Susan Svehla. "Harlots, Hedonists and Heroines; the Women of Hammer Films." In Gary Svehla and Susan Svehla, eds. *Bitches, Bimbos and Virgins: Women of the Horror Film.* Baltimore, MD: Midnight Marquee Press, 2011, pp. 26–42.

2574. _____, and Susan Svehla, eds. *Bela Lugosi.* Ser.: Midnight Marquee Actors. Baltimore, MD: Midnight Marquee Press, 1995. 312 pp. tp. Rev. ed.: Baltimore, MD: Midnight Marquee Press, 2007. 298 pp. tp. This volume pays homage to Lugosi by collecting articles by a number of critics on each of his movies, including his vampire-related titles.

2575. Sweeney, Matthew. "The Mark of the Vampire." In Bernd Herzogenrath, ed. *The Films of Tod Browning.* London: Black Dog Publishing, 2006, pp. 201–07.

2576. Uddin, Shahab. *Masculinity, Feminity and Other Curiosities in Tod Browning* Freaks *and* Dracula. München, Germany: Grin Verlag, 2008. 20 pp.

2577. Vieira, Mark. "Dracula's Daughter." In Mark Vieira. *Hollywood Horror: From Gothic to Cosmic.* New York, Harry N. Abrams, 2003.

2578. _____. "Tod Browning's Dracula." In Mark Vieira. *Hollywood Horror: From Gothic to Cosmic.* New York, Harry N. Abrams, 2003.

2579. Weaver, Tom. *Poverty Row Horrors! Monogram, PRG and Republic Horror Films of the Forties.* Jefferson, NC: McFarland & Company, 1993. 392 pp. Contains entries on *The Devil Bat* (PRG, 1940) (pp. 14–25); *Spooks Run Wild* (Monogram, 1941) (pp. 45–52); *The Vampire's Ghosts* (Republic, 1945) (pp. 211–18); and *Devil Bat's Daughter* (PRG, 1946) (pp. 246–52).

2580. Willson, Paige A., Melissa Ursula Dawn Goldsmith, and Anthony J. Fonseca. "Alienation, Essentialism, and Existentialism through Technique: An Analysis of Set Design, Lighting, Costume, and Music in *Dracula's Daughter* and *Nadja.*" In Douglas Brode and Leah Deyneka, eds. *Dracula's Daughters: The Female Vampire on Film.* Lanham, MD: Scarecrow Press, 2013, pp. 45–67.

2581. Wood, Bret. "Dracula." In Gary J. Svehla and Susan Svehla, eds. *Bela Lugosi.* Baltimore, MD: Midnight Marquee Press, 2007, pp. 10–24.

Cinematic Vampires: World War II

The end of the Universal Era (1948) provides an appropriate break point in the story of vampire films. For the next decade, the movie industry worldwide begins to revive from the effects of World War II and around the world a few vampire movies will be made, most notably in Europe and Southeast Asia. Mario Bava, whose work will dominate Italian horror films for the next generation, will direct *I vampiri*, the first Italian horror movie and the first of several notable vampire movies for which he will be responsible.

In the late 1950s, studios will begin the transition to color, a transition led by Hammer movies in England beginning in 1958 with a new version of *Dracula*, though black and white horror movies will continue to be made through the mid–1960s. By the end of the 1960s, color is the norm everywhere and Hammer will dominate the vampire subgenre until the studio's collapse in the mid–1970s. After a brief hiatus, in the mid–1980s vampire films will become part of a steadily rising industry both reflecting and stimulating the increasing permeation of Western culture with vampire mythology. *Bram Stoker's Dracula*, directed by Francis Ford Coppola (1992), followed by *Interview with the Vampire* (1994), would initiate a new era of blockbuster vampire flicks that two decades later would see the Twilight Saga movies join the list of the most lucrative movies of all time.

The post-war development and expansion of the movie industry would coincide with the development of new departments of film studies in Western universities and a new interest in vampire related movies and television in college and university English departments that would in turn stimulate the academic study of horror movies in general and vampire movies in particular. While most academic consideration would be given to the rather limited number of films released to theatres, horror and vampire movies became very popular among independent filmmakers, who have turned out hundreds of movies for the home video and successor DVD market.

Since the development of sound movies and the original production of *Dracula* to the present day, over 2,000 feature-length vampire movies have been released the great majority by independent filmmakers and most never receiving a theatre screening nor a showing on either network or cable television. While the internet has made most of these films accessible for the indy movie fan, a substantial number of these films have become quite rare and difficult to obtain (or even occasionally view) for the average vampire fan. Also, it should be noted that between five percent and ten percent of vampire movies are adult movies and are known to and circulate only among those who regularly consume sexually explicit films.

2582. Abbott, Stacey. "Embracing the Metropolis: Urban Vampires in American Cinema of the 1980s and 90s." In Carla T. Kungl, ed. *Vampires: Myths and Metaphors of Enduring Evil*. Oxford: Inter-Disciplinary Press, 2003. pp. 133–37. Posted at: http://www.inter-disciplinary.net/publishing/id-press/ebooks/vampires-myths-and-metaphors-of-enduring-evil. Rpt. in: Peter Day, ed. *Vampire: Myths and Metaphors of Enduring Evil*. Amsterdam: Rodopi, 2006, pp. 125–42.

2583. Abery, James. "The Vampyr Chronicles." *Shivers* 14 (January 1995): 4–5, 32–35.

2584. Abramowitz, Rachel. "Young Blood." *Premiere* 8, 3 (November 1994): 62–72, 116.

2585. Allen, Thomas. "Yeh, But Did He Die?" *The Long Island Catholic* (July 26, 1979). Re: *Dracula* (1979).

2586. Allocco, Katherine. "Subspecies Vamp: Denice Duff." *Femme Fatales* 2, 4 (Spring 1994): 8–13, 60.

2587. Altman, Mark A. "Beaming Aboard Subspecies." *Femme Fatales* 2, 4 (Spring 1994): 14–17, 60. Re: Melanie Shatner.

2588. Amador, Victoria. "Dracula's Postfeminist Daughters in the Twenty-first Century." In Douglas Brode and Leah Deyneka. *Dracula's Daughters: The Female Vampire on Film*. Lanham, MD: The Scarecrow Press, 2014. pp. 285–97.

2589. Ambrisco, Alan, and Lance Svehla. "'The coin of our realm': Blood and Images in *Dracula 2000*." *Journal of Dracula Studies* 8 (2006): 20–29.

2590. Ambrogio, Anthony. "Children of the Night: Dracula's Progeny." *Midnight Marquee* 55 (Fall 1997): 40–55.

2591. _____. "Dracula Schmacula! Misinformation Never Dies." *Video Watchdog* 19 (1993): 32–47.

2592. Annandale, David. "Guerrilla Vamping: *Vampyros Lesbos*, the Becoming-Woman of Women and the Unravelling of the Male Gaze." *Paradoxa* 17 (2002): 257–70. Rpt. in: Steffen Hantke, ed. *Horror.* Vashon Island, WA: Paradoxa, 2002. Pp. 257–70.

2593. Armstrong, Michael. "Some Like It Chilled. Part 3. The Undead." *Films and Filming* (April 1971) 31ff.

2594. Austin, Guy. "Vampirism, Gender Wars and the 'Final Girl': French Fantasy Film in the Early Seventies." *French Cultural Studies* 7, 21 (1996): 321–331.

2595. Bacal, Simon. "Vampire on Campus." *Shivers* 13 (December 1994): 32–35. Re: *Vampires Embrace: The Nosferatu Diaries.*

2596. Bacon, Simon. "The Breast Bites Back: How the Projected 'Bad' Object of the Female Vampire Achieves Autonomy in L. Wiseman's *Underworld Evolution*." In Andrea Ruthven & Gabriela Mádlo, eds. *Illuminating the Dark Side: Evil. Women. The Feminine.* Oxford: Inter-disciplinary Press, 2010.

2597. _____. "The Inescapable Moment: The Vampire as Individual and Collective Trauma in *Let Me In* by Matt Reeves." In Simon Bacon, and Katarzyna Bronk, eds. *Undead Memory: Vampires and Human Memory in Popular Culture.* Bern, Switz.: Peter Lang International Academic Publishers, 2013, pp. 263–88.

2598. _____. "*The Lost Boys*?! Monstrous Youth of the Cinematic Teenage Vampire." In Janice Zehentbauer and Eva Gledhill, eds. *Beyond the Monstrous: Reading from the Cultural Imaginary.* Oxford: Inter-Disciplinary Press, 2013.

2599. _____. "Trauma and the Vampire: The Violence of the Inescapable Moment in *Let Me In* (2010) by Matt Reeves." In Jessica Aliaga Lavrijsen and Michael Bick, eds. *Is This a Culture of Trauma?* Oxford: Inter-Disciplinary Press, 2013.

2600. Badham, John, interviewed by Tom Weaver. "The Vampire's Return: John Badham on the Making of *Dracula*." In Bob Madison, ed. *Dracula: The First Hundred Years.* Baltimore, MD: Midnight Marquee Press, 1997, pp. 241–55. Re: *Dracula* (1979).

2601. Baker, David. "Seduced and Abandoned: Lesbian Vampires on Screen 1968–74.": *Continuum* 26, 4 (August 2012): 553–563.

2602. Balbo, Lucas, Peter Blumenstock, and Christian Kessler. *Obsession: The Films of Jess Franco.* Berlin: Graf Haufen & Frank Trebbin, 1993. 255 pp. hb. dj. Large format.

2603. Barrenechea, Antonio. "Hemispheric Horrors: Celluloid Vampires from the 'Good Neighbor' Era" *Comparative American Studies* 7, 3 (2009): 225–237.

2604. Beard, William. "*Dracula: Pages from a Virgin's Diary*." In William Beard. *Into the Past: The Cinema of Guy Maddin.* Toronto, ON: University of Toronto Press, 2010, pp. 163–91.

2605. Berg, Tina Desireé. "Vampires and the Loss of Innocence." *Femme Fatales* 3, 4 (Spring 1995): 12–15.

2606. Bernstein, Abbie. "*Fright Night*: On-set Diary." In Anthony Timpone, ed. *Fangoria Vampires.* New York: HarperPrism, 1996, pp. 88–98.

2607. Beugnet, Martine. "Figures of Vampirism: French Cinema in the Era of Global Transylvania." *Modern & Contemporary France* 15, 1 (2007): 77–88.

2608. Bignell, Jonathan. "Dracula Goes to the Movies: Cinematic Spectacle and Gothic Literature." In D. Sipière, ed. *Dracula: Insemination-Dissemination.* Amiens: University of Picardie Press, 1996, pp. 133–43.

2609. _____. "A Taste of the Gothic: Film and Television Versions of *Dracula*." In Robert Giddings and Erica Sheen, eds. *The Classic Novel: From Page to Screen.* Manchester: Manchester University Press, 2000, pp. 114–30.

2610. Billson, Anne. *Let the Right One In.* Ser.: Devil's Advocates. Leighton Buzzard, UK: Auteur, 2011. 112 pp. tp.

2611. Biodrowski, Steve. "Barbara Steele: Queen of Horror." *Imagi-Movies* Pt. 1. 1, 2 (Winter 1993/94): 34–43; Pt. 2.

2612. _____. "Beyond Dracula: Bonfire of the Vampires." *Imagi-Movies* 2, 2 (Winter 1994): 36–38.

2613. _____. "Beyond Dracula: The Vampire Connection." *Imagi-Movies* 2, 2 (Winter 1994): 26–27.

2614. _____. "Beyond Dracula: Vampire Glamour (and Gore)." *Imagi-Movies* 2, 2 (Winter 1994): 30–35.

2615. _____. "Cronos." *Imagi-Movies* 2, 2 (Winter 1994): 52–53.

2616. ____. "Dracula. The Oft-Told-Story." *Cinefantastique* 23, 4 (December 1992): 27–30.

2617. Black, Andy. Le Frison des Vampires." In *Necronomicon Book Three*. Hereford, UK: Noir Publishing, 1999, pp. 126–30.

2618. Blumenstock, Peter. "Fangs Over France: The Two Vampire Orphans." In Anthony Timpone, ed. *Fangoria Vampires*. New York: Harper Prism, 1996, pp. 142–50.

2619. ____. "Jean Rollin Has Risen from the Grave." *Video Watchdog* 31 (1996): 36–57.

2620. ____. "Orphans of Gore." *Fangoria* 149 (January 1996): 13–18.

2621. ____, **and Tim Lucas.** "Versions and Vampires: Jean Rollin on Homevideo." *Video Watchdog* 31 (1996): 28–57.

2622. Brass, Tom. "Nymphs, Shepherds, and Vampires: The Agrarian Myth on Film." *Dialectical Anthropology* 25 (2000): 205–237. Posted at: http://www.scribd.com/doc/83661783/Nymphs-Shepherds-and-Vampires-The-Agrarian-Myth-on-Film-2000-Dialectical-Anthropology.

2623. Bridges, Bill. *"Jugular Wine*: A Vampire Odyssey." *White Wolf Inphobia* 52 (February 1995): 62–64.

2624. Burel, Marcel. "The Naked and the Dead: Monster Meets Jean Rollin." *Monster! International* 2, 4 (1994): 6–12.

2625. Cherry, Brigid. *"Daughters of Darkness*: Vampire Aesthetics and Gothic Beauty." In Douglas Brode and Leah Deyneka. *Dracula's Daughters: The Female Vampire on Film*. Lanham, MD: The Scarecrow Press, 2014. pp. 219–33.

2626. Clavir, Judith. "Black Spookery: Blacula, Dracula A. D. 1972." In Arthur Asa Berger, ed. *Film in Society*. New Brunswick, NJ: Transaction Books, 1980, pp. 115–120.

2627. Coleman, Lindsay Krishna. "The Whore with the Vampire Heart: Frontier Romanticism in *John Carpenter's Vampires*." In Cynthia Miller and A. Bowdoin van Van Riper, eds. *Undead in the West: Vampires, Zombies, Mummies, and Ghosts on the Cinematic Frontier*. Lanham, MD: Scarecrow Press, 2012, pp. 33–44.

2628. Coleman, Robin R. Means. "Scream, Whitey, Scream—Retribution, Enduring Women, and Carnality: 1970s." In Robin R. Means Coleman. *Horror Noire: Blacks in American Horror Films from the 1890s to Present*. New York: Routledge, 2011, pp. 118–44.

2629. Collins, Kevin. "Lina Romay: Magical Moments Frozen in Time." *Draculina* 27 (1996): 16–21, 55.

2630. Constandinides, Costas. "Film Remake or Film Adaptation: New Media Hollywood and the Digitalization of Monsters in *Van Helsing*." In Scott A. Lukas and John Marmysz, eds. *Fear, Cultural Anxiety, and Transformation: Horror, Science Fiction and Fantasy Films Remade*. Lanham, MD: Lexington Books, 2009, pp. 243–64.

2631. Corman, Roger, with Jim Jerome. *How I Made a Hundred Movies in Hollywood and Never Lost a Dime*. New York: Delta, 1990. 237 pp.

2632. Crawley, Tony. "Barbara Steele." In Bill George, ed. *Eroticism in the Fantasy Cinema*. Pittsburgh, PA: Imagine, 1984, pp. 99–103.

2633. ____. "Woman as Vampire: *The Hunger*." In Barbara Creed. *The Monstrous—Feminine: Film, Feminism, Psychoanalysis*. London: Routledge, 1993, pp. 59–72.

2634. Crick, Robert Alan. "Black and White and Red All Over: Newsprint, Vampires, and Jeff Rice's *The Night Stalker*." *Midnight Marquee* 47 (Summer 1995): 49–51.

2635. Crisafulli, Chuck. "Makeover for a Vampire." *Fangoria* 139 (January 1995): 34–37, 81.

2636. Dapena, Gerard. "Reveries of Blood and Sand: The Cinema of Jean Rollin." In Robert G. Weiner and John Cline, eds. *Cinema Inferno: Celluloid Explosions from the Cultural Margins*. Lanham, MD: Scarecrow Press, 2010, pp. 226–43.

2637. Davies, David Stuart. "On the Set with...The Sussex Vampire." *Scarlet Street* (1992): 44–46.

2638. de Coulteray, George. "Sexual Assassins and Vampires." In George de Coulteray. *Sadism in the Movies*. New York: Medical Press, 1965, pp. 123–34.

2639. DeGiglio-Bellemare, Mario. "Vampires Reading Feuerbach: Catholic Orthodoxy and Lines of Flight in Abel Ferrara." *Golem: Journal of Religion and Monsters* 3, 1 (Spring 2009). Posted at: http://lomibao.net/golem/current.php.

2640. del Campo, Edgar Martín. "The Global Making of a Mexican Vampire: Mesoamerican, European, African, and Twentieth-Century Media Influences on the Teyollohcuani." *History of Religions* 49, 2 (2009): 107–140.

2641. Del Valle, David. "Barbara Steele." *Chiller Theatre Magazine* 1 (Winter 1994–95): 11–15.

2642. Dougherty, Margot. "The Vampire Strikes Back." *Entertainment Weekly* (January 18, 1991): 30–35.

2643. Edwards, Justin D. "Canada, Quebec and David Cronenberg's Terrorist-Vampires," In Tabish. Khair and Johan Hoglund, eds. *Transnational and Postcolonial Vampires: Dark Blood.* Basingstoke, UK: Palgrave Macmillan, 2012, pp. 66–80.

2644. Epps, Brad. "The Space of the Vampire: Materiality and Disappearance in the Films of Iván Zuletta." In Jo Labanyi and Tatjana Pavlovic, eds. *A Companion to the Spanish Cinema.* Malden, MA: Wiley-Blackwell, 2012, pp. 581–96.

2645. Exshaw, John. "Jess Franco: or the Misfortunes of Virtue." *The Irish Journal of Gothic and Horror Studies* 1 (October 2006). Online journal posted at http://irishgothichorrorjournal.home stead.com/john.html.

2646. "Fangs for the Memory." *Scarlet Street* 8 (Fall 1992): 68–87.

2647. Farmer, Donald. "The Making of Red Lips." *Draculina* 20 (Summer 1994): 22–24. Rpt.: *Scream Queens Illustrated* 7 (1995): 18–28.

2648. Fellner, Chris. "The Merchants of Menace." *Scary Monsters Magazine* 17 (December 1995): 55–63.

2649. Felsher, Michael. *Near Dark: Pray for Daylight.* Troy, MI: Anchor Bay Entertainment, 2002. 16pp. Booklet distributed in DVD of *Near Dark.* Cinema.

2650. Fentome, Steve. "Mexi-Monster Meltdown." *Monster! International* 2 (1992): 4–13.

2651. Ferrante, Anthony C. "The Bad Boys of Horror." *Fangoria* 149 (Janaury 1996): 32–37, 76.

2652. _____. "*From Dusk to Dawn*: An Interview with Quentin Tarantino and Robert Rodriguez." In Anthony Timpone, ed. *Fangoria Vampires.* New York: HarperPrism, 1996, pp. 16–24.

2653. _____. "*From Dusk to Dawn*: Reservoir Dead." *Fangoria* 148 (November 1995): 40–46, 81.

2654. _____. "On-set with *From Dusk to Dawn.*" In Anthony Timpone, ed. *Fangoria Vampires.* New York: HarperPrism, 1996, pp. 4–15.

2655. Flinn, Paul. "Leaving the West and Entering the East: Refiguring the Alien from Stoker to Coppola." In Deborah Cartmell, et al., eds. *Alien Identities: Exploring Differences in Film and Fiction.* London: Pluto Press, 1999, pp. 31–38.

2656. Fox, Michael D., and Mark Burchett. "The Making of Vamps." *Draculina* 26 (1996): 9–12.

2657. Fry, Carrol L., and **John Robert Craig.** "'Unfit for Earth, Undoomed for Heaven': The Genesis of Coppola's Byronic Dracula." *Literature/Film Quarterly* 30, 4 (2002): 271–78.

2658. Gagne, Paul R. "The Hunger." *Cinnefantastique* 1, 4 (April/May 1983): 16–22.

2659. _____. "Martin." In Paul R. Gagne. *The Zombie That Ate Pittsburgh: The Films of George A. Romero.* New York: Dodd, Mead & Company, 1987. 71–82.

2660. Gallagher, Hugh. "*Vampire Conspiracy*: Interview with Director Geoffrey." *Draculina* 25 (1996): 4–12.

2661. Garfinkel, Gary. "Blonde Heaven." *Femme Fatales* 2, 4 (Spring 1994): 54–55.

2662. Gayles, Jonathan. "Black Macho and the Myth of the Superwoman Redux: Masculinity and Misogyny in *Blade.*" *The Journal of Popular Culture* 45, 2 (April 2012): 284–300.

2663. González, Jose Luis, and **Michael Secula.** "Interview: Paul Naschy." *Videooze* 6/7 (Fall 1994): 9–18.

2664. Grahl, Till. *Gothicism and Interpersonal Relationships in Recent Hollywood Films: Monsters & Maniacs, Vampires & Vamps.* Saarbrucken, Germany: VDM Verlag Dr. Muller, 2007. 123 pp. tp. Rpt.: Saarbrucken, Germany: AV Akademikerverlag, 2012. 132 pp. pb.

2665. Gray, Beverly. *Roger Corman: Blood-Sucking Vampires, Flesh-Eating Cockroaches, and Driller Killers.* Los Angeles: Renaissance Books, 2000. 302 pp. tp. Rev. ed.: New York: Thunder's Mouth Press, 2004. 318 pp. tp. 3rd. ed.: Santa Monica, CA: AZ Ferris Publications, 2013. 226 pp. tp.

2666. Greaves, Tim. *Vampyres.* Eastleigh, Hants, UK: 1-Shot Publications, 1996. 85 pp. tp. Rpt.: Glen Carbon, IL: Draculina Publishing, 1996. 85 pp. tp.

2667. _____. "Vampyros Lesbos." *Necronomicon* 3 (n.d.): 33–35.

2668. Greene, Doyle. *Mexploitation Cinema: A Critical History of Mexican Vampire, Wrestler, Ape-man And Similar Films, 1957–1977.* Jefferson, NC: McFarland & Company, 2005. 202 pp. tp.

2669. Gregory, Christopher. "Vampire Lesbianism." In Christopher Gregory. *Behind the*

Screams: The Truth About Horror Films. N.p.: the author, 2012, pp. 81–84. tp.

2670. Grenier, Cynthia. "Dracula Sucks." *Oui* 2, 11 (November 1973): 51–52, 122–23.

2671. Gross, Ed. "Chris Sarandon, Vampire." In Anthony Timpone, ed. *Fangoria Vampires.* New York: HarperPrism, 1996, pp.99–104.

2672. Gross, Edward, and Marc Shapiro. *The Vampire Interview Book: Conversations with the Undead.* East Meadow, NY: Image Publishing, 1991. 134 pp. pb. Large format.

2673. Guariento, Steve. "Bava Fever!" *Samhain* Pt. 1. 37 (March/April 1993): 22–26; Pt. 2. 38 (May/June 1993): 23–26; Pt. 3. 40 (September/October 1993): 22–26.

2674. Gunn, Bill. "Ganja and Hess." In Phyllis Rauch Klotman, ed. *Screenplays of the African American Experience.* Bloomington: Indiana University Press, 1991, pp. 13–90.

2675. Hadleigh, Boze. "Vamps: *The Hunger*." In Boze Hadleigh. *The Lavender Screen. The Gay and Lesbian Films: Their Stars, Makers, Characters, and Critics.* New York: Citadel Press, 1993, pp. 207–11.

2676. Hakola, Outi J. "Blood on the Border: The Mexican Frontier in *Vampires* (1998) and *Vampires: Los Muertos* (2002)." In Cynthia Miller and A. Bowdoin van Van Riper, eds. *Undead in the West: Vampires, Zombies, Mummies, and Ghosts on the Cinematic Frontier.* Lanham, MD: Scarecrow Press, 2012, pp. 113–32.

2677. Halberstam, Judith Marian. "On Vampires, Lesbians, and Coppola's *Dracula*." *Brightlights* 11 (Fall 1993): 7–9.

2678. Hallam, Lindsay. "A Beautiful Life of Evil and Hate: The Vampire-Witch in Mario Bava's *Black Sunday*." In Douglas Brode and Leah Deyneka. *Dracula's Daughters: The Female Vampire on Film.* Lanham, MD: The Scarecrow Press, 2014. pp. 69–81.

2679. Hanaham, James. "Bela Lugosi Is Dead and I Don't Feel So Good Either." In James Hanahan. *Gothic: Transmutations of Horror in Late Twentieth-Century Art.* Cambridge, MA: MIT Press, 1997, pp. 118–192.

2680. Hanson, Ellis. "Lesbians Who Bite." In Ellis Hanson. *Out Takes: Essays on Queer Theory and Film.* Durham, NC: Duke University Press Books, 1999, pp. 183–222.

2681. Hatcher, Lint. "The Monster Squad: An Apologetic." *Wonder* 7 (1993): 33–34.

2682. Hoffman, Eric. "Case File: Blacula." *Monsters of the Movies* 1, 3 (October 1974): 54–57.

2683. _____. "Count Yorga—The Vampire for Here and Now." *Monsters of the Movies* 2 (August 74): 62–66.

2684. Hogan, David J. "The High Priestess of Horror: Barbara Steele." In David J. Hogan. *Dark Romance: Sexuality in the Horror Film.* Jefferson, NC: McFarland & Company, 1986, pp. 164–80.

2685. Holte, James Craig. "*Blade*: A Return to Revisionism." *Journal of Dracula Studies* 3 (2001): 27–32.

2686. _____. *Dracula in the Dark: The Dracula Film Adaptations.* Westport, CT: Greenwood Press, 1997. 161 pp. hb.

2687. _____, ed. *The Fantastic Vampire: Studies in the Children of the Night: Selected Essays from the Eighteenth International Conference on the Fantastic in the Arts.* Vol. 19. Westport, CT: Greenwood Publishing Group, 2002. 178 pp. hb. boards. Includes contributions by Elizabeth Miller, Raymond T. McNally, Katie Harse, William Pencak, Scott Vander Ploeg, Suzanna Nyberg, Tony Fonseca, Leslie Tannenbaum, Margaret Carter, Bette Roberts, Heidi L. Nordberg, Stephanie Moss, Sharon A. Russell, Teri Ann Doerksen, and Jeane Rose.

2688. Howarth, Tony. *The Haunted World of Mario Bava.* Godalming, Surrey, UK: FAB Press, 2003. 352 pp. hb. & tp.

2689. Hunter, Jack. *Psychedelic Sex Vampires: Jean Rollin Cinema.* London: Glitter Books, 2012. 96 pp. tp.

2690. Hurley, Kelly. "Reading Like an Alien: Posthuman Identity in Ridley Scott's *Alien* and David Cronenberg's *Rabid*." In Judith Halberstam and Ira Livingston, eds. *Posthuman Bodies (Unnatural Acts).* Bloomington: Indiana University Press, 1995, pp. 203–24.

2691. Hutchinson, Tom, and Roy Pickard. "Dracula: Aristocrat of Blood." In Tom Hutchinson and Roy Pickard. *Horror: A History of Horror Movies.* London: Royce Publications, 1983, pp. 6–31.

2692. Hutson, Shawn. *Horror Film Quiz Book.* London: Sphere Books, 1991. 232 pp. pb.

2693. Hutton, Peter. "Creatures of the Night." *Critical Quarterly* 33, 4 (December 1991): 118–120.

2694. Ibarra, Enrique Ajuria. "Vampire Echoes and Cannibal Rituals: Undead Memory, Monstrosity and Genre in J. M. Grau's *We Are What We Are.*" In Simon Bacon, and Katarzyna Bronk, eds. *Undead Memory: Vampires and Human Memory in Popular Culture.* Bern, Switz.: Peter Lang International Academic Publishers, 2013, pp. 157–82.

2695. "Interview with a Vampire: Frank Langella on Dracula." *Fantastic Films* 2, 6 (November 1979): 40–45, 62.

2696. Irdanova, Dina. "Cashing in on Dracula: Eastern Europe's Hard Sells." *Framework: The Journal of Cinema and Media* 48, 1 (Spring 2007): 46–63.

2697. Jones, Alan. "Dario Argento's *Dracula 3-D.*" In Alan Jones. *Dario Argento: The Man, the Myths & the Magic.* FAB Press, 2012, pp. 384–99.

2698. _____. "Transylvania 6-5000." *Cinefantastique* 15, 5 (January 1986): 10, 53.

2699. _____, and Mark Kermode. "Steele and Lace." *The Dark Side* (August 1991): 38–43.

2700. Jongeward, Steven. "Fright Night 2." *Cinefantastique* Part 1. 18, 4 (May 1988): 18, 57; Part 2. 18, 5 (July 1988): 15, 59.

2701. Jonker, Leif. "Low Budget Production Hell or, the Making of Leif Jonker's *Darkness*, the Ultimate in Vampire Horror." *Alternative Cinema* 2 (Summer 1994): 39–43.

2702. Jordan, John J. "Vampire Cyborgs Scientific Imperialism: A Reading of the Science-Mysticism Polemic in *Blade.*" *Journal of Popular Film and Television* 27, 2 (1999): 4–15.

2703. Kahan, Saul. "Transylvania—Polanski Style." *Cinema* 3, 3 (December 1966): 7ff.

2704. Kelley, Bill. "What Dracula Is Up To." *Imagi-Movies* 1, 2 (Winter 1993–94): 46–48.

2705. Kim, Kyu Kyun. "Park Chan-wook's Thirst: Body, Guilt and Exsanguination." In Alison Peirse and Daniel Martin, eds. *Korean Horror Cinema.* Edinburgh: Edinburgh University Press, 2013, pp. 199–206.

2706. Kirkland, Ewan. "Whiteness and the Contemporary Vampire in Film and Television." In Deborah Mutch. *The Modern Vampire and Human Identity.* Houndmills, Basingstoke, Hampshire, UK/New York: Palgrave Macmillan, 2013, pp. 93–110.

2707. Knee, Adam. "The Compound Genre Film: *Billy the Kid versus Dracula* Meets *The Harvey Girls.*" In Elaine D. Cancalon and Antoine Spacagna, eds. *Intertextuality in Literature and Film: Selected Papers from the Thirteenth Annual Florida State University Conference on Literature and Film.* Gainesville: University Press of Florida, 1994.

2708. Knight, Christ. "The Vampire with the Golden Gun." *Cinefantastique* 4, 1 (1975).

2709. Konigsberg, Ira. "How Many Draculas Does It Take to Change a Lightbulb?" In Andrew Horton and Stuart Y. McDougal, eds. *Play It Again Sam: Retakes on Remakes.* Berkeley: University of California Press, 1998, pp. 250–76.

2710. Kotter, Michael. "*Shadow of the Vampire.*" *Senses of Cinema* 15 (April 2001). Posted at: http://sensesofcinema.com/2001/13/vampire/.

2711. Kuhn, Annette, with Susannah Radstone, eds. *The Women's Companion to International Film.* London: Virago, 1990. 464 pp. Rpt. as: *Women in Film: An International Guide.* New York: Fawcett Columbine, 1991. 500 pp.

2712. Labanyi, Jo, and Tatjana Pavlovic. "The Space of the Vampire: Materiality and Disappearance in the Films of Iván Zulueta." In Jo Labanyi and Tatjana Pavlovic, eds. *A Companion to Spanish Cinema.* Oxford: Blackwell Publishing, 2012, pp. 581–596.

2713. Latham, Rob. "Consuming Youth: The Lost Boys Cruise Mallworld." In Joan Gordon and Veronica Hollinger, eds. *Blood Read: The Vampire as Metaphor in Contemporary Culture.* Philadelphia: University of Pennsylvania Press, 1997, pp. 129–147.

2714. Laycock, Joseph. "Crossing the Spiritual Wasteland in *Priest.*" In Kim Paffenroth and John W. Morehead, eds. *The Undead and Theology.* Eugene, OR: Pickwick Publications, 2012, pp. 19–33.

2715. Le Cain, Maximillan. "The Frontiers of Genre and Trance: Five Films by Jess Franco." *Senses of Cinema* 27 (July 2003). Posted at: http://sensesofcinema.com/2003/feature-articles/jess_franco/.

2716. Lee, Michael. "Unmasking Patriarchy's Savior: Gender Politics in *Samson versus the Vampire Women.*" In Gary D. Rhodes, ed. *Horror at the Drive-in: Essays in Popular Americana.* Jefferson, NC: McFarland & Company, 2003, pp. 187–98.

2717. Leeder, Murray. Forget Peter Vincent: Nostalgia, Self-Reflexivity and the Genre Past of Fright Night." *Journal of Popular Film and Television* 36, 4 (2009): 190–99. Posted at: http://www.academia.edu/1531463/_Forget_Peter_Vincent_Nostalgia_Self-Reflexivity_and_the_Genre_Past_in_Fright_Night_.

2718. _____. "'A Species of One': The Atavistic Vampire from Dracula to *The Wisdom of Crocodiles*." In Barbara Brodman and James E. Doan, eds. *Images of the Modern Vampire: The Hip and the Atavistic.* Madison. NJ: Fairleigh Dickinson University Press, 2013, pp. 15–28.

2719. Lehman, Paul R., and John Edgar Browning. "The Dracula and the Blacula (1972) Cultural Revolution." In John Edgar Browning and Caroline Joan Picart, eds. *Dracula, Vampires, and Other Undead Forms.* Lanham, MD: The Scarecrow Press, 2009, pp. 19–36.

2720. Lilley, Jessie. "I was a Teenage Vampyre." *Scarlet Street* 10 (Spring 1993): 50–52. Interview with Richard Dempsey.

2721. Losano, Wayne A. "The Vampire Rises Again in the Films of the 70's." *The Film Journal* 2, 2 (1973): 60–62.

2722. Lucas, Tim. *Mario Bava: All the Colors of the Dark.* Cincinnati, OH: Video Watchdog, 2007. 125 pp. hb.

2723. _____. "Versions & Vampires: Jean Rollin on Home Video." *Video Watchdog* 31 (1996): 28–35.

2724. "Lust at First Bite." *The Dark Side* (July 1992): 5–10. Interview with Jean Rollin.

2725. Macabre, J. B. "Innocent Blood." *World of Fandom* 2, 17 (Winter 1993): 36–37.

2726. _____. "Sleep with a Vampire." *World of Fandom* 2, 17 (Winter 1993): 78–79.

2727. _____. "Vampires & Other Stereotypes." *World of Fandom* 2, 17 (Fall 1993):56–57. An interview with indy filmmaker Kevin Lindenmuth.

2728. Madison, Bob. "*Dracula: Dead and Loving It*: Dracula in the 1990s." In Bob Madison, ed. *Dracula: The First Hundred Years.* Baltimore, MD: Midnight Marquee Press, 1997, pp. 282–91.

2729. Magid, Ron. "The Fang Club." *Cinescape* 1, 4 (January 1995): 40–46.

2730. Marshall, Lorne. "Unhallowed Grounds: Vampire Films of the Seventies." *Midnight Marquee* 45 (Summer 1993): 6–19.

2731. Martin, John. "Cinecitta of the Living Dead." *The Dark Side* (February 1993): 54–58.

2732. Matturro, Keith. "Making of *Depraved*." *Draculina* 18 (Winter 1994): 32–37.

2733. McCarty, John. "Grand Guignol—the Roots of Splatter." In John McCarty. *Splatter Movies.* Albany, NY: FantaCo Enterprises, 1981, pp. 2–26.

2734. _____. *The Modern Horror Film.* New York: Citadel Press/Carol Publishing Group, 1990. 244 pp. Includes comments on the *Horror of Dracula* (1958), *The Brides of Dracula* (1960), *The Fearless Vampire Killers* (1967), *Blood of Dracula* (1974), *Captain Kronos Vampire Hunter* (1974), and *Gothic* (1986).

2735. McCormick, Patricia. "Barbara Steele's Ephemeral Skin: Feminism, Fetishism and Film." *Senses of Cinema* 22 (2002). Posted at: http://sensesofcinema.com/issue/22/.

2736. Mendik, Xavier, and Graham Harper. "For Your Viewing Pleasure: The Sadean Aesthetics of *From Dusk Till Dawn*." In *Necronomicon Book Three.* Hereford, UK: Noir Publishing, 1999, pp. 105–25.

2737. Michaels, Lloyd. "*Nosferatu*, or the Phantom of the Cinema. In Andrew Horton and Stuart Y. McDougal, eds. *Play It Again Sam: Retakes on Remakes.* Berkeley: University of California Press, 1998, pp. 238–49.

2738. Mikul, Chris. "Lesbian Vampire." In Chris Mikul. *Bizarrism: Strange Lives, Cults, Celebrated Lunacy.* Manchester, UK: Critical Vision, 2000, pp. 30–36.

2739. Miller, Cynthia J. "Liberating the Vampire, but Not the Woman: Kathryn Bigelow's *Near Dark* (1987)." In Douglas Brode and Leah Deyneka. *Dracula's Daughters: The Female Vampire on Film.* Lanham, MD: The Scarecrow Press, 2014. pp. 267–83.

2740. Miller, Mark A. "The Diva of Dark Drama: Barbara Steele." *Filmfax* 19 (March 1990); 63–71, 94.

2741. Milne, Tom. "*Communion* and *Martin*." *Sight and Sound* 47, 1 (Winter 1977/78): 55–56.

2742. Moir, Patricia. "Beyond Dracula: The Adaptable Vampire." *Imagi-Movies* 2, 2 (Winter 1994): 46–49.

2743. Moore, Anne. "Sex & Blood: *Embrace of the Vampire*." In Anthony Timpone, ed. *Fangoria*

Vampires. New York: HarperPrism, 1996, pp. 135–141.

2744. Moran, Brian. "Samson vs. the Vampire Women." *Scary Monsters Magazine* 14 (March 1995): 36–38.

2745. Moss, Stephanie. "Dracula and The Blair Witch Project." In Sarah L. Highley and Jeffrey Andrew Weinstock ,eds. *Nothing That Is: Millennial Cinema and the Blair Witch Controversies.* Detroit, MI: Wayne State University Press, 2004.

2746. Naschy, Paul. "Filmography." *Videooze* 6/7 (Fall 1994): 20–42.

2747. Newland, Paul. "The Greateful Undead: Count Dracula and the Transnational Counterculture in *Dracula A.D. 1972* (1972)." In John Edgar Browning and Caroline Joan Picart, eds. *Dracula, Vampires, and Other Undead Forms.* Lanham, MD: The Scarecrow Press, 2009, pp. 135–52.

2748. Newman, Kim. "Vampires and Other Stereotypes." In Kim Newman. *Nightmare Movies: Horror on Screen Since the 1960s.* New York: Bloomsbury USA, 2011, pp. 333–78.

2749. Nicholls, Stan. "Out for the Count." *The Dark Side* (February 1993): 21–23.

2750. Ní Fhlainn, Sorcha. "'It's Morning in America': The Rhetoric of Religion in the Music of the *Lost Boys*, and the Deserved Death of the 1980's Vampire." In Niall Scott. The Role of the Monster: Myths and Metaphors of Enduring Evil. Oxford: inter–Disciplinary Press, 2009, pp. 147–56. Posted at: http://www.scribd.com/doc/61699474/The-Role-of-the-Monster-Myths-and-Metaphors-of-Enduring-Evil.

2751. _____. "1976: The Duality in Postmodern Vampiric Identity and Evil in George A Romero's *Martin* and Anne Rice's *Interview with the Vampire*." *In* Sorcha Ni Fhlainn & William Andrew Myers, eds. *The Wicked Heart: Studies in the Phenomenon of Evil.* Oxford: Inter-Disciplinary Press, 2006, pp. 171–82. Posted at: http://www.academia.edu/413983/The_Wicked_Heart_Studies_in_the_Phenomena_of_Evil.

2752. Nixon, Nicola. "When Hollywood Sucks, or, Hungry Girls, Lost Boys and Vampirism in the Age of Reagan." In Joan Gordon and Veronica Hollinger, eds. *Blood Read: The Vampire as Metaphor in Contemporary Culture.* Philadelphia: University of Pennsylvania Press, 1997, pp. 115–28.

2753. "No, but I Saw the Movie." *The Times Literary Supplement* (December 8, 1966): 1148.

2754. Noel, Gerard. *Barbara Steele: An Angel for Satan.* Introduction by Alan Upchurch. Ser.: Horror Picture Collection. 2 vols. Cahors, France: Gerard Noel Faneditions, 1991. Bilingual text (English and French).

2755. O'Brien, Brad. "Fucanelli as a Vampiric Frankenstein and Jesus as His Vampiric Monster: The Frankenstein and Dracula Myth in Guillermo del Toro's *Cronos*." In Richard J. Hand and Jay McRoy, eds. *Monstrous Adaptations: Generic and Thematic Mutations in Horror Film.* Manchester, UK: Manchester University Press, 2007, pp. 172–180.

2756. O'Connor, Mimi. *The Mortal Instruments. City of Bones: The Official Illustrated Movie Companion.* New York: Margaret K. McElderry Books, 2013. 122 pp. Large format.

2757. O'Flinn, Paul. "Leaving the West and Entering the East: Refiguring the Alien from Stoker to Coppola." In Deborah Cartmell, I. Q. Hunter, Heidi Kaye, and Imelda Whelehan, eds. eds. *Alien Identities: Exploring Differences in Film and Fiction.* London: Pluto Press, 1999, pp. 31–38.

2758. Page, Edwin. "From Dusk to Dawn." In Edwin Page. *Quintessential Tarantino: The Films of Quentin Tarantino.* London: Marion Boyars Publishers, 2005, pp. 161–82.

2759. Page, Rachel E., Robert G. Weiner, and Cynthia J. Miller. "Billy the Kid vs. Dracula: The Old World Meets the Old West." In Cynthia Miller and A. Bowdoin van Van Riper, eds. *Undead in the West: Vampires, Zombies, Mummies, and Ghosts on the Cinematic Frontier.* Lanham, MD: Scarecrow Press, 2012, pp. 45–64.

2760. Palmer, Randy. "The Day Dracula Died." *Imagi-Movies* 1, 2 (Winter 1993/94): 44–48.

2761. _____. "Dracula Without the Crepe." *Famous Monsters* 133 (1977).

2762. Parker, John. *Polanski.* London: Victor Gollancz, 1993. 287 pp. hb. Includes substantive reflection on *Fearless Vampire Killers.*

2763. Parnum, John. "High Midnight: The Vampire Goes West." *Midnight Marque* 47 (Summer 1995): 40–48.

2764. Paul, Louis. "Erotic Sex/Horror Part II: The Franco Years." *Draculina* 11 (February 1991): 16–17, 42.

2765. Paul, William. *Laughing Screaming: Modern Hollywood Horror and Comedy.* New York: Columbia University Press, 1994. 510 pp.

2766. Paxton, Timothy, with David To-darello. "Kiss Me Monster: The Creature Features of Jesus Franco." *Monster! International* 2 (1992): 14–19.

2767. Peary, Danny. "The Little Shop of Horrors." In Danny Peary. *Cult Movies: The Classic, the Sleepers, the Weird, and the Wonderful.* New York: Delta, 1989, pp. 203–05.

2768. Peary, Dennis. "Stephanie Rothman: R-Rated Feminist." In Karyn Kay and Gerald Peary, eds. *Women in the Cinema.* New York: E. P. Dutton, 1977, pp. 179–92.

2769. Petersen, Anne Helen. "That Teenage Feeling." *Feminist Media Studies* 12, 1 (2012): 51–67.

2770. Philip, Richard. "Dracupuncture, Transylvanian Style." *After Dark* 10, 11 (March 1978): 62–67.

2771. Phillips, Kendall R. "Romero's Mythic Bodies: *Martin* and *Knightriders*." In Kendall R. Phillips. *Dark Directions: Romero, Craven, Carpenter, and the Modern Horror Film.* Carbondale: Southern Illinois University Press, 201, pp. 59–72.

2772. _____. "'You said forever': postmodern temporality in Tony Scott's *The Hunger*." In Douglas Brode and Leah Deyneka. *Dracula's Daughters: The Female Vampire on Film.* Lanham, MD: The Scarecrow Press, 2014. pp. 253–65.

2773. Piccirilli, Tom, and T. Ranstill. "Addicted to Murder." *Draculina* 23 (July 1995): 20–27.

2774. Pirie, David. "New Blood." *Sight and Sound* (Spring 1971): 73ff.

2775. "Play It Again, Bram!" *Famous Monsters of Filmland* 211 (February/March 1996): 8–18.

2776. Power, Jenny. "Klaus Kinski—An Appreciation." *For the Blood Is the Life* 2, 11 (Winter 1991–92): 11.

2777. Pribisic, Milan. "Guy Maddin's *Dracula*: Virgins, Vampires, and the Theatre Film.'" In David Church, ed. *Playing with Memories: Essays on Guy Maddin.* Winnipeg, MB: University of Manitoba Press, 2009, pp. 159–70.

2778. Rabkin, William. "Making *The Lost Boys*." In Anthony Timpone, ed. *Fangoria Vampires.* New York: HarperPrism, 1996, pp. 105–110.

2779. Rae, Graham. "An Exercise in Scottish Celluloid Psychosis: Blood Junkies." *Film Threat Video Guide* 9 (1993): 62–65.

2780. Randolph, Bill. "The Making of *Bloodscent*." *Draculina* 22 (March 1995): 16–21.

2781. "Requiem for a Vampire." *Necronomicon* 3 (n.d.): 28–29.

2782. Rhodes, Gary Don. "The Vampire's Kiss: Echoes of Bram Stoker in the Vampire Film of the 1980s." In Bob Madison, ed. *Dracula: The First Hundred Years.* Baltimore, MD: Midnight Marquee Press, 1997, pp. 266–82.

2783. Ripoll, Juan Julia. "Interview: Paul Naschy." *Draculina* 10 (Feb. 1990): 12–15. Rpt.: *Draculina Fear Book* 3 (1995): 24–26.

2784. Rodriguez-Herntindez, Raul, and Claudia Schaefer. "Sublime Horror: Transparency, Melodrama, and the *Mise-en-Scene* of Two Mexican Vampire Films." In Barbara Brodman and James E. Doan, eds. *The Universal Vampire: Origins and Evolution of a Legend.* Madison, NJ: Fairleigh Dickinson University Press, 2013, pp. 225–38.

2785. Rolfe, Lee. "David Cronenberg on Rabid." *Cinefantastique* 6, 3 (Winter 1977): 26.

2786. Rollin, Jean. *Virgins and Vampires.* Ed. by Peter Blumenstock. Schwenningen, Germany: Crippled Dick Hot Wax, 1997. 156 pp. pb. Large format.

2787. Ronan, Margaret. "Drac Is Back!" *Weird World* 3 (1979): 2–5. Re: *Dracula* (1979).

2788. Ryan, Al. "First Lady of the Silver Scream." *Chiller Theatre Magazine* 1 (Winter 1994-95): 21–26.

2789. Sanderson, Peter. "The Dead Yet Move: Toei's Animated *Tomb of Dracula* Movie." *Comics Feature* 13/13 (Sept./Oct. 1981): 58.

2790. Sands, Julian. "Julian Sands-Vampire!" *Shivers* 2 (August 1992): 8–11.

2791. Sargeant, Jack. "From Dusk Till Dawn." In Jack Hunter, ed. *Harvey Keitel: Movie Top Ten.* London: Creation Books, 1999, pp. 137–46.

2792. Satian, Al, and Don Glut. "Count Yorga Speaks." *Monsters of the Movies* 2 (August 1974): 67–74.

2793. Scahill, Andrew. "Defanged: The Curious Case of the Family-Friendly Vampire." *Flow* (online journal of television and media studies) (November 5, 2012). Posted at: http://flowtv.org/

2012/11/defanged-the-curious-case-of-the-family-friendly-vampire/.

2794. Schulte-Sasse, Linda. "Courtier, Vampire, or Vermin? Jew Suss's Contradictory Effort to Render the 'Jew' Other." In Linda Schulte-Sasse. *Entertaining the Third Reich: Illusions of Wholeness in Nazi Cinema.* Durham, NC: Duke University Press, 1996, pp. 47–92. Rpt. in: Terri Ginsberg and Kirsten Moana Thompson, eds. *Perspectives on German Cinema.* New York: G.K. Hall/London: Prentice Hall International, 1996, pp. 184–220.

2795. Segal, Jeff. "Vampire Love Stories: Locating the Jugular of Et Mourir de Plaisir." *Monster International* 1 (1992): 19–21.

2796. Senn, Bryan, Richard Sheffield and Jim Clatterbaugh. "El Vampiro Speaks! An Interview with Mexican Horror Star Germán Robles." *Monsters from the Vault* 13, 24 (2008): 16–22.

2797. Shapiro, Marc. "Brothers in Blood." *Fangoria* 149 (January 1996): 20–25.

2798. _____. "*To Sleep with a Vampire*: Bloodsuckers on a Budget." In Anthony Timpone, ed. *Fangoria Vampires.* New York: HarperPrism, 1996, pp. 127–34.

2799. _____. "Vampire in Brooklyn Is No Laughing Matter." *Fangoria* 148 (November 1995): 34–39, 81.

2800. _____. "Who Dares to Sleep with a Vampire?" *Fangoria* 116 (September 1992): 40–43, 68.

2801. Sharrett, Christopher. "The Horror Film in Neoconservative Culture." *Journal of Popular Film & Television* 21, 3 (Fall 1993): 100–10.

2802. Shear, Jack W. "Soft Focus, Sharp Knives: The Projection of Vampiric Fantasy in Jess Franco's *Succubus*." In Douglas Brode and Leah Deyneka. *Dracula's Daughters: The Female Vampire on Film.* Lanham, MD: The Scarecrow Press, 2014. pp. 95–113.

2803. Sheehan, Henry. "Trust the Teller: Henry Sheehan Talks with James V. Hart about Dracula." *Film/Literature/Heritage: A Sight and Sound Reader.* Ed. Ginette Vincendeau. London: British Film Institute, 2001. 271–274.

2804. Shipka, Danny. *Perverse Titillation: The Exploitation Cinema of Italy, Spain and France, 1960–1980.* Jefferson, NC: McFarland & Company, 2011. 246 pp. tp.

2805. Showers, Brian J. "Sex, Succubae, and Surrealism." *Draculina* 8 (August 1988), Rpt.: *Draculina Fear Book* 2 (1993): 36–41.

2806. Shuter, Michael. "Sex Among the Coffins or, *Lust at First Bite* with William Margold." *Draculina* 17 (December 1993): 32–34.

2807. Snider, Brandon T. *Vampire Academy: The Official Illustrated Movie Companion.* New York: Razorbill, 2013. 142 pp. pb. Large format.

2808. Snyder, Andrew, and Dolores Tierney." Importation/Mexploitation, or, How a Crime-Fighting Vampire-Slaying Mexican Wrestler almost Found Himself in an Italian Sword and Sandals Epic." In Steven Jay Schneider and Tony Williams, eds. *Horror International.* Detroit, MI: Wayne State University Press, 2005, pp. 33–55.

2809. Sobcheck, Vivian. "Revenge of *The Leech Woman*: On the Dread of Aging in the Low-budget Horror Film." In Ken Gelder. *The Horror Reader.* New York: Routledge, 2000, pp. 336–47.

2810. Sommers, Steve. *Van Helsing: The Making of the Legend.* Ed. by Linda Sunshine. New York: Newmarket Press, 2004. 160 pp. pb. Large format. Includes the complete screen play for the movie Van Helsing.

2811. Strick, Philip. "Nosferatu—The Vampyre." *Sight and Sound* 48, 2 (1979): 127–128.

2812. Strong, Lauren. "*Blood and Roses* (1960): Realizing the Vision of 'Carmilla.'" In Douglas Brode and Leah Deyneka. *Dracula's Daughters: The Female Vampire on Film.* Lanham, MD: The Scarecrow Press, 2014. pp. 83–93.

2813. Strong, Simon. "*Sous la páve, le pláge*! Lesbian Vampires Vs the Situationist International." *Senses of Cinema* 31 (April 2004). Posted at: http://sensesofcinema.com/2004/feature-articles/lesbian_vampires_vs_situationist_international/.

2814. Suttle, Bill. "1–800-Vampire." *Scream Queens Illustrated* 1, 1 (Fall 1993): 47–51.

2815. Tannenbaum, Leslie. "Policing Eddie Murphy: The Unstable Black Body in *Vampire in Brooklyn*." In James Holte Craig, ed. *The Fantastic Vampire: Studies in the Children of the Night: Selected Essays from the Eighteenth International Conference on the Fantastic in the Arts.* Vol. 19. Westport, CT: Greenwood Publishing Group, 2002, pp. 69–75.

2816. Testa, James. "The Erotic Mystique of Dracula." *Adam Film World* 7, 9 (March 1980): 18–23, 72.

2817. Tohill, Cathal, and Peter Tombs. *Immortal Tales: Sex and Horror Cinema in Europe,*

1956–1984. London: Primitive Press, 1994. 272 pp. pb. Large format. Rpt.: London: Titan Press, 1995. 171 pp. pb. Large format. Rpt: New York: St. Martin's Press, 1995. 272 pp. pb. Large format.

2818. Tumini, Angela. "Death and the City: Repressed Memory and Unconscious Anxiety in Michael Almereyda's *Nadja*." In Simon Bacon, and Katarzyna Bronk, eds. *Undead Memory: Vampires and Human Memory in Popular Culture.* Bern, Switz.: Peter Lang International Academic Publishers, 2013, pp. 239–62.

2819. _____. "Vampiresse: Embodiment of Sensuality and Erotic Horror in Carl Th. Dreyer's *Vampyr* and Mario Bava's *The Mask of Satan*." In Barbara Brodman and James E. Doan, eds. *The Universal Vampire: Origins and Evolution of a Legend.* Madison, NJ: Fairleigh Dickinson University Press, 2013, pp. 121–35.

2820. Turner, George. "The Two Faces of Dracula." *American Cinematographer* 69, 5 (May 1988): 34–42.

2821. Tyree, J. M. "Warm-Blooded: True Blood and Let the Right One In." *Film Quarterly* 63, 2 (2009): 31–37.

2822. "Vampire Centerfolds." *Draculina* 26 (1996): 24–28.

2823. "La Vampire Nue." *NecronomicoN* 4 (n.d.): 57–58.

2824. Van Riper, A. Bowdoin. "Savage, Scoundrel, Seducer: The Moral Order Under Siege in the *From Dusk Till Dawn* Trilogy." In Cynthia Miller and A. Bowdoin van Van Riper, eds. *Undead in the West: Vampires, Zombies, Mummies, and Ghosts on the Cinematic Frontier.* Lanham, MD: Scarecrow Press, 2012, pp. 97–112.

2825. Vellutini, John. "Return of the Leaping Dead." *Oriental Cinema* 15 9n.d. [1997]): 5–10.

2826. _____. "Vampire Filmography." *Oriental Cinema* 15 (n.d. [1997]): 10–23.

2827. Vertlieb, Steve. "Dracula in the 1970s: Prints of Darkness." In Bob Madison, ed. *Dracula: The First Hundred Years.* Baltimore, MD: Midnight Marquee Press, 1997, pp. 216–39.

2828. Waltje, Jörg. "Filming *Dracula*; Vampires, Genre, and Cinematography." *Journal of Dracula Studies* 2 (2000): 24–33.

2829. _____. *Vampires, Genre, and the Compulsion to Repeat.* Boulder: University of Colorado, Ph.D. dissertation, 1998. 222 pp. Large format.

2830. Warren, Bill. "Behind the Screams: *Innocent Blood*." In Anthony Timpone, ed. *Fangoria Vampires.* New York: HarperPrism, 1996, pp. 111–119.

2831. _____. "Directing *Children of the Night*." In Anthony Timpone, ed. *Fangoria Vampires.* New York: HarperPrism, 1996, pp. 120–126.

2832. _____. "Dracula: Clown Prince of Darkness." *Fangoria* 149 (January 1996): 26–30.

2833. _____. Seduction of the *Innocent Blood*." *Fangoria* 116 (September 1992): 34–38, 62.

2834. Watt, Tony "Tex." "Lee Gordon Demarbre's *Jesus Christ Vampire Hunter*." In Tony "Tex" Watt. *TonyWatt.com Presents Kount Kracula's Twisted Sinema! Obscure 21st Century Underground Horror/Sci-Fi/Fantasy/Thriller Movies & Shorts #1.* N.p.: the author, 2012, pp. 65–84.

2835. Weisser, Thomas. *Asian Cult Cinema.* New York: Boulevard Books, 1997. 317 pp. tp.

2836. _____. *Asian Trash Cinema: The Book.* Houston, TX: Asian Trash Cinema/European Trash Cinema Publications, 1994. 187 pp. rp.

2837. _____, **and Yuko Mihara Weisser.** *Japanese Cinema Encyclopedia: The Horror, Fantasy, and Sci Fi Films.* Miami, FL: Vital Books, 1997. 327 pp. tp.

2838. Weitzner, Roy. "Fright Night II." *Slaughter House Magazine* 1, 1 (1988): 20–23.

2839. Welsh, Jim, and John Tibbetts. "Visions of Dracula." *American Classic Screen* 5, 1 (November/December 1980): 12–16.

2840. White, Timothy. "Dracula: The Warm-blooded Revival of the Debonair King of the Undead." *Crawdaddy* (June 1978): 16–33. Re: *Dracula* (1979).

2841. Willard, David. "The New Breed: Cinema's Quest to Build a Better Vampire." *Midnight Marque* 47 (Summer 1995): 53–57.

2842. Williams, Victoria. "The Vampire in Modern Film. Reflecting Dracula: The Un-dead in Alfred Hitchcock's *Shadow of a Doubt*." In Barbara Brodman and James E. Doan, eds. *Images of the Modern Vampire: The Hip and the Atavistic.* Madison. NJ: Fairleigh Dickinson University Press, 2013, pp. 1–14.

2843. Willson, Paige A., Melissa Ursula Dawn Goldsmith, and Anthony J. Fonseca. "Alienation, Essentialism, and Existentialism through Technique: An Analysis of Set Design, Lighting,

Costume, and Music in *Dracula's Daughter* and *Nadja.*" In Douglas Brode and Leah Deyneka. *Dracula's Daughters: The Female Vampire on Film.* Lanham, MD: The Scarecrow Press, 2014. pp. 45–67.

2844. Wilt, David. "Los Vampiros." *Imagi-Movies* 2, 2 (Winter 1994): 50–52.

2845. Wolter, Charolotte. "Fright Night." *Cinefantastique* 15, 5 (January 1986): 7.

2846. Wood, Robin. "Burying the Undead: The Use and Obsolerscence of Count Dracula." In Barry Keith Grant. *The Dread of Difference: Gender and the Horror Film.* Austin: University of

Texas Press, 1996, pp. 364–78. The author compares and contrasts the figure of Count Dracula as found in Bram Stoker's original novel, the 1922 movie *Nosferatu* and the 1979 *Dracula* directed by John Badham.

2847. Zimmerman, Bonnie. "*Daughters of Darkness*: The Lesbian Vampire on Film." In Barry Keith Grant. *The Dread of Difference: Gender and the Horror Film.* Austin: University of Texas Press, 1996, pp. 379–87.

2848. Zulich, Mária. "The Creation of the Video Vampire." *Cinemacabre* 3 (Summer 1980): 26–33.

Cinematic Vampires: Hammer Movies

Hammer Films, the film studio whose horror movies in the 1960s brought a new dimension to the vampire myth, became the most successful British film company in the generation after World War II. Hammer burst upon the scene after the film industry had neglected the horror genre for several decades. Universal Pictures, which owned the motion picture rights to both *Frankenstein* and *Dracula* at that time, had backed away from producing further horror movies, and thus Hammer's owners were able to work out a deal by which Universal sold them the rights to *Dracula* and *Frankenstein.*

In creating the new horror features, Hammer emphasized the use of full color. Blood flowed freely and monstrous acts would be fully portrayed on screen—not merely implied for the audience to imagine. Hammer also assembled a very capable team that included director Terence Fisher, screenwriter Jimmy Sangster, and actors Christopher Lee and Peter Cushing. After their first picture, *The Curse of Frankenstein*, the team plunged immediately into the production of *Dracula*, now best known by its American title, *The Horror of Dracula* (1958). Sangster and Fisher dropped Universal's screenplay and had no problem deviating from Bram Stoker's story in adapting the lengthy novel and its complicated plot to the screen. Vampiric sexuality also was more overt, with the biting understood as a metaphor for the sex act. *The Horror of Dracula* made Christopher Lee an international star.

As Hammer moved ahead with its next horror movies, it increasingly encountered problems from censors. It actually cancelled plans to film *I Am Legend,* the renowned science fiction vampire book, after the censor's office let it be known that the movie would be banned in England. Hammer also moved away from vampire storylines altogether for a short period. Its second vampire movie, *The Brides of Dracula,* appeared in 1960, to be followed by *Kiss of the Vampire* two years later. Lee returned to his Dracula role in *Dracula*, *Prince of Darkness* (1965), which emphasized its continuity with the earlier film by beginning with a scene from the *Horror of Dracula*. Subsequent films developed a series of creative ways to resurrect the count, who would always be killed at the end of each film. Lee would go on to portray the Count in *Dracula Has Risen from the Grave* (1968), *Taste the Blood of Dracula* (1970), and *Scars of Dracula* (1971).

Hammer paid intense attention to vampirism from 1970 to 1972, during which time it ventured far beyond the *Dracula* story. It drew on Sheridan Le Fanu's story, "Carmilla," for *The Vampire Lovers* (1970), with Ingrid Pitt in the starring role. Her success led to her being cast as the vampiric countess Elizabeth Bathory in *Countess Dracula*. Simultaneously, the Carmilla theme would be continued in *Lust for a Vampire* (1971), in which Carmilla is played by Yutte Stengaard. 1971 also saw the appearance of an interestingly different film, *Vampire Circus*. Finally, in 1972, Hammer tried to bring Dracula into the modern age in *Dracula A.D. 1972*, with Lee and his perennial co-star, Peter Cushing, who had become almost as famous as Lee for his portrayal of Abraham Van Helsing. In *Dracula A.D. 1972*, Cushing played a descendent of the Victorian vampire hunter but again tracked Dracula to his death.

The year 1972 also saw the appearance of *Twins of Evil*, the third of the Carmilla-inspired films, and *Captain Kronos, Vampire Hunter*. Lee made his last appearance as the Hammer Dracula in *The Satanic Rites of Dracula* (aka *Count Dracula and His Vampire Bride*, 1973). It continued both the Count's adventures in 1970s England and the ever-present pursuit by Van Helsing.

The vampire world created by Hammer climaxed with a cooperative project between Hammer and the Shaw Brothers, a massive movie production company in Hong Kong. Roy Ward Baker would direct *The Legend of the Seven Golden Vampires* (aka *The Seven Brothers Meet Dracula*, 1974). The story has Van Helsing (portrayed by Peter Cushing) traveling to China in search of an elusive Dracula who had disappeared from Europe. Once in China, Van Helsing teams up with his Chinese counterpart, Hsu Tien-an, the local vampire hunter, who uses his martial arts skills to defeat the vampires. The film, unfortunately, proved a commercial failure, and Hammer Films, already in financial trouble, moved into bankruptcy in 1975. An era of vampire movies was over, though the body of material it produced continued to inspire movie makers worldwide. Attempts would be made to revive Hammer, but with only marginal success, though the memory of what it accomplished has been kept alive by a new generation of fans and students of film history who have turned out a host of books celebrating the Hammer accomplishments.

2849. Adams, Steve. "Christopher Lee: 'I've Made My Last Horror Film.'" *Quasimodo's Monster Magazine* 1, 3 (1975).

2850. Ambrogio, Anthony. *Peter Cushing.* Baltimore, MD: Luminary Press, 2004. 281 pp. tp.

2851. Amis, Kingsley. "Dracula, Frankenstein, Sons and Co." In *What Became of Jane Austen? And Other Questions.* New York: Harcourt, Brace, Jovanich, 1970, pp 125–35.

2852. Barbano, Nicolas. "Yutte Stengaard: A Collage." *Little Shop of Horrors* 12 (April 1994): 1997.

2853. Barnes, Alan. "Gothic." *Hammer Horror* 1 (March 1995): 16–18.

2854. Borst, Ronald V. "Horror of Dracula: An Analysis of the Hammer Film Classic." *Photon* 27 (1977): 23–35.

2855. _____. "Meet Mr. Christopher Lee in an Exclusive Monster Times Interview." *The Monster Times* 1, 8 (1972).

2856. Brode, Douglas. "Heritage of Hammer: Carmilla Karnstein and the Sisterhood of Satan." In Douglas Brode and Leah Deyneka. *Dracula's Daughters: The Female Vampire on Film.* Lanham, MD: The Scarecrow Press, 2014. pp. 115–37.

2857. Brosnan, John. *The Horror People.* New York: St. Martin's Press, 1976. 304 pp. Rpt.: New York: New American Library, 1977. 306 pp. pb. Contains biographical chapters on Christopher Lee, and Peter Cushing, and chapters on the films produced by Hammer.

2858. Butler, Charles E. *Vampires: Under the Hammer.* N.p.: Su asti Publishing, 2013. 182 pp.

2859. Büttner, Roland. *The Role of Sexuality in the British Vampire Films by Hammer.* München, Germany: GRIN Verlag, 2008. 56 pp.

2860. "Christopher Lee: Dracula." *Movie Monsters* 1, 1 (December 1974): 26–33.

2861. "Christopher Lee Enters the House of Hammer." *Scarlet Street* 8 (Fall 1992): 43–47.

2862. "Christopher Lee—The Art of Playing Dracula." *Souvenir Issue-Dracula* 17 (1979).

2863. "Christopher Lee—The Man Behind the Monster." *House of Hammer* 1, 1 (1976).

2864. "Christopher Lee Times Three." *Famous Monsters* 117 (1975).

2865. Collins, Kevin, and Kelli Coughlin. "They Were the Monster Makers! A Horrific Look at the House of Hammer." *Drive-In Cinema* 1 (1996): 8–18.

2866. Cotter, Robert Michael "Bobb." *Ingrid Pitt: Queen of Horror: The Complete Career.* Jefferson, NC: McFarland & Company, 2010. 230 pp.

2867. _____. *The Women of Hammer Horror: A Biographical Dictionary and Filmography.* Jefferson, NC: McFarland & Company, 2013. 248 pp. hb.

2868. Cushing, Peter. *An Autobiography.* London: Weidenfelf & Noicolson, 1988. 157 pp. hb. dj.

2869. _____. *An Autobiography and Past Forgetting.* Baltimore, MD: Midnight Marquee Press, 1999. 255 pp. tp.

2870. _____. "How I Became a Monster Hunter." In Peter Cushing, ed. *Tales of a Monster Hunter.* London: Futura, 1978, pp. 1–13.

2871. _____. *"Past Forgetting:" Memoirs of the Hammer Years.* London: Weidenfeld and Nicolson, 1988. 112 pp.

2872. _____. *Tales of a Monster Hunter.* London: Arthur Baker, 1977. 208 pp. hb. Rpt.: London: Futura, 1978. 208 pp. pb.

2873. Del Valle, David. "A Conversation with Ingrid Pitt." *Chiller Theatre Magazine* 1 (Winter 1994–95): 34–40.

2874. Del Vecchio, Carl. "I Met David Peel." *Little Shop of Horrors* 12 (April 1994): 77–81.

2875. Del Vecchio, Deborah. "Farewell to Saint Peter." *Fangoria* 139 (January 1995): 66–69. re: Peter Cushing.

2876. _____, **and Tom Johnson.** *Peter Cushing: The Gentle Man of Horror and His 91 Films.* Jefferson, NC: McFarland & Company, 1992. 485 pp. hb.

2877. Dixon, Wheeler Winston. *The Charm of Evil: The Life and Films of Terence Fisher.* Ser.: Filmmakers #26. Metuchen, NJ: Scarecrow Press, 1991. 574 pp. hb.

2878. Dobson, David C. "Horror of Dracula." In Arthur Lennig, ed. *Classics of the Film.* Madison: Wisconsin Film Society Press, 1965, pp. 232–36.

2879. "Dracula Prince of Darkness." *Hammer Horror* 2 (April 1995): 21–32.

2880. Earnshaw, Tony. "Interview with the Director." *Hammer Horror* 2 (April 1995): 6–9.

2881. Egan, Kate. "A Real Horror Star: Articulating the Extreme Authenticity of Ingrid Pitt." In Kate Egan and Sarah Thomas. *Cult Film Stardom: Offbeat Attractions and Processes of Cultification.* Basingstoke, UK: Palgrave Macmillan, 2012, pp. 212–25.

2882. Exshaw, John. "Christopher Lee on Dracula." *Bram Stoker Society Journal* 6 (1994): 7–10.

2883. _____. "Interviews with Peter Cushing and Christopher Lee." In Leslie Shepard and Albert Power, eds. *Dracula: Celebrating 100 Years.* Dublin: Mentor Press, 1997, pp. 127–33.

2884. Eyles, Allen, Elbert Adkinson, Nicolas Fry, eds. *The House of Horror: The Story of Hammer Films.* London: Lorrimer Publishing Ltd., 1973. 127 pp. Rpt.: New York: Third Press, 1974. tp. Rev. and exp. ed. as: *The House of Horror: The Complete Story of Hammer Films.* London: Lorrimer Publishing, 1981. 144 pp. tp. Rpt.: 1984. 144 pp. tp. Rpt.: New York: Lorrimer Publishing, 1984. 144 pp. tp. Rev. and exp. ed. as: *The House of Horror: The Complete Hammer Films Story.* London: Creation Books, 1994. 175 pp. tp.

2885. Fearney, Donald. *Peter Cushing.* London: the author, 1996. 106 pp. pb. Large format.

2886. Fischer, Dennis. "Christopher Lee Interview: Horror After Hammer." *Midnight Marquee* 45 (Summer 1993): 30–36.

2887. _____. "Hammer's Hunt for a New Vein of Vampire Film: Three Semi-Classics from the Seventies." *Midnight Marque* 47 (Summer 1995): 29–35.

2888. Fisher, Terence. "Horror Is My Business." In Alain Silver & James Ursini, eds. *The Horror Film Reader*. New York, Limelight Editions, 2004, pp. 67–74.

2889. Frayling, Christopher. "Hammer's Dracula." In Bernice M. Murphy, Elizabeth McCarthy, and Darryl Jones, eds. *It Came from the 1950s! Popular Culture, Popular Anxieties*. Basingstoke, UK: Palgrave Macmillan, 2011, pp. 108–34.

2890. George, Bill. "'Anna, More Coffee!' The Allure of Hammer." In Bill George. *Eroticism in the Fantasy Cinema*. Pittsburgh, PA: Imagine, 1984. pp. 89–98.

2891. Greaves, Tim. *Linda Hayden: Dracula and Beyond*. Eastleigh, Hamp., UK: 1 Shot Publications, [1995]. 51 pp. pb. Staples.

2892. _____. *Luan Peters: Homage to a Seraph*. Eastleigh, Hamp., UK: 1 Shot Publications, [1994]. 35 pp. pb. Staples.

2893. _____. *Veronica Carlson: An Illustrated Memento*. Eastleigh, Hamp., UK: 1 Shot Publications, [1993]. 51 pp. pb. Staples.

2894. _____. *Yutte Stensgaard: Memoirs of a Vampire*. Eastleigh, Hamp., UK: 1 Shot Publications [1992]. 43 pp. pb. Staples.

2895. _____, **and Kevin Collins.** *Daughter of the Night: Carmilla on the Screen*. Eastleigh, Hamp., UK: 1 Shot Publications, [1993]. 67 pp. pb.

2896. Grifford, Denis. "The Best of British Blood." In *A Pictorial History of Horror Movies*. London: Hamlyn, 1973, pp. 192–209.

2897. Gullo, Christopher. *In All Sincerity, Peter Cushing*. N.p.: Xlibris Corporation, 2004. 420 pp. tp.

2898. Hallenbeck, Bruce G. *British Cult Cinema: The Hammer Vampire*. Bristol, UK: Hemlock Books, 2010. 239 pp. tp.

2899. _____. "Countess Dracula." *Femme Fatale* 1, 3 (Winter 1992/1993): 52–55.

2900. _____. "Veronica Carlson: 'Dracula's Most Beautiful Victim' Remembers the House of Hammer." *Femme Fatales* 1, 1 (Summer 1992): 46–48.

2901. _____. "Veronica Has Risen from the Grave." *Scarlet Street* 9 (Winter 1993): 64–68.

2902. Hanke, Ken. "The Hammer Dracula Films." In Ken Hanke. *A Critical Guide to Horror Film Series*. New York: Garland Publishing, 1991, pp. 195–206.

2903. Hannan, Michael. "Sound and Music in Hammer's Vampire Films." In Philip Hayward, ed. *Terror Tracks: Music, Sound and Horror Cinema*. London: Equinox, 2009, pp. 60–74.

2904. Harmon, Jim, and Eric Hoffman. "The Hammer Films of Cushing-Lee." *Monsters of the Movies* 1, 8 (August 1975): 30–39.

2905. Harner, Gary W. "Hammer Studios' Karnstein Trilogy: The Lesbian Vampire and the Desiring Female." *Midnight Marque* 47 (Summer 1994): 38–48.

2906. Hearn, Marcus. *Hammer Glamour*. London: Titan Books, 2009. 160 pp. hb.

2907. _____, **and Alan Barnes.** *The Hammer Story*. London: Titan Books, 1997. 191 pp. hb.

2908. Hewetson, Alan. "An Exclusive Interview with Christopher 'Dracula' Lee." *Nightmare* 17 (1974).

2909. Hilliard, Richard. "Hammer Horror." *Chiller Theatre Magazine* 1 (Winter 1994-95): 27–33.

2910. Hoffman, Eric. "Christopher Lee—Master of Horror and Villiany." *Science Fiction, Horror and Fantasy* 1, 1 & 2 (1977).

2911. _____. "Legend of the Seven Golden Vampires." *Monsters of the Movies* 1, 7 (June 1975): 46–48.

2912. Hogan, David J. "Lugosi, Lee, and the Vampire Lovers." In David J. Hogan. *Dark Romance: Sexuality in the Horror Film*. Jefferson, NC: McFarland & Company, 1986, pp. 138–63.

2913. Holte, James Craig. *Dracula in the Dark: The Dracula Film Adaptations*. Westport, CT: Greenwood Press, 1997. 161 pp. hb.

2914. _____. "Resurrection in Britain: Christopher Lee and Hammer *Draculas*. In James Holte Craig, ed. *The Fantastic Vampire: Studies in the Children of the Night: Selected Essays from the Eighteenth International Conference on the Fantastic in the Arts*. Vol. 19. Westport, CT: Greenwood Publishing Group, 2002, pp. 77–87.

2915. Huckvale, David. *Hammer Film Scores and the Musical Avant-Garde*. Jefferson, NC: McFarland & Company, 2008. 235 pp. tp.

2916. Hunter, Jack. *Eyes of Blood: The Hammer Films*. London: Glitter Books, 2012. 112 pp. pb.

2917. Hutchings, Peter. *Dracula: A British Film Guide.* London: I. B. Tauris, 2003. 128 pp. tp.

2918. _____. *Hammer and Beyond: The British Horror Film.* Manchester: Manchester University Press, 1993. 193 pp. tp. Cinema.

2919. _____. *Terence Fisher.* Manchester: Manchester University Press, 2002. 224 pp. hb. boards.

2920. "Ingrid Pitt: A Profile." *For the Blood Is the Life* 2, 10 (Autumn 1991): 17.

2921. Jensen, Paul M. "Terence Fisher." In Paul Jensen. *The Men Who Made the Monsters.* Ser.: Twayne's Filmmakers. New York: Twayne Publishers, 1996.

2922. Jewel, John. *Lips of Blood: An Illustrated Guide to Hammer's Dracula Movies Starring Christopher Lee.* London: Glitter Books, 2002. 136 pp. tp.

2923. Johnson, Tom. "Brides of Dracula: Hammer Horror's Second Vampire Classic." *Midnight Marque* 47 (Summer 1995): 36–39.

2924. _____. "Hammer Goes Back to Back." *Monsters from the Vault* 2 (Winter 1996): 12–16.

2925. _____, **and Deborah Del Vecchio.** *Hammer Films: An Exhaustive Filmography.* Jefferson, NC: McFarland and Company, 1996. 410 pp. hb. boards. Cinema.

2926. _____, **and Mark A. Millar.** *The Christopher Lee Filmography: All Theatrical Releases, 1948–20.* Jefferson, NC: McFarland & Company, 2009. 480 pp. tp.

2927. Kelley, Bill. "Christopher Lee: King of the Courts." In *Dracula: The Complete Vampire.* Special issue of *Starlog Movie Magazine Presents* No. 6. New York: Starlog Communications, 1992, pp. 44–53.

2928. _____. "Christopher Lee: The Enduring Count." In Anthony Timpone, ed. *Fangoria Vampires.* New York: HarperPrism, 1996, pp. 74–87.

2929. Kermode, Mark. "Tale of a Vampire: The British Bloodsucker." *Fangoria* 116 (September 1992): 29–32.

2930. Killick, Jane. "Christopher Lee." *Shivers* 13 (December 1994): 8–13.

2931. Kinsey, Wayne. "Don't Dare See It Alone!": The Fifties Hammer Invasion." In Bernice M. Murphy, Elizabeth McCarthy, and Darryl Jones, eds. *It Came from the 1950s! Popular Culture,*

Popular Anxieties. Basingstoke, UK: Palgrave Macmillan, 2011, pp. 72–89.

2932. _____. *Hammer Films—A Life In Pictures: The Visual Story of Hammer Films.* Sheffield, UK: Tomahawk Press, 2009. 224 pp. tp.

2933. _____. *Hammer Films: The Bray Studio Years.* Richmond, UK: Reynolds & Hearn, 2002. 356 pp. tp.

2934. Larson, Randall D. *Music from the House of Hammer.* Methuen, NJ: Scarecrow Press 1996. 224 pp. hb.

2935. Laws, Stephen. "Peter Cushing O.B.E.— A Tribute." *Hammer Horror* 1 (March 1995): 11.

2936. Lee, Christopher. "Are Movie Monsters Human?" *Famous Monsters of Filmland* 29 (1964).

2937. _____. "Christopher Lee Speaks Out." *Hammer's Halls of Horror* 2, 9 (1978).

2938. _____. "Dracula." *Monsters of the Movies* 1, 7 (June 1975): 12–13.

2939. _____. "Dracula and I." In Peter Haining, ed. *The Dracula Scrapbook.* New York: Bramwell House, 1976. 176 pp.

2940. _____. *Tall, Dark, and Gruesome.* London: W. H. Allen, 1977. 284 pp. hb. dj. Rpt. London: Granada Publishing, 1978. 286 pp. pb. Rev. ed.: London: Victor Gollancz, 1997. 320 pp. hb. dj. Rpt.: London: Vista, 1998. 448 pp. pb. Rpt. Baltimore, MD: Midnight Marquee Press, 1999. 319 pp. tp. Rev. ed. as: *Lord of Misrule: The Autobiography of Christopher Lee.* London: Orion, 2003. 354 pp. hb. dj.

2941. Leggett, Paul. "The Filmed Fantasies of Terence Fisher." *Christianity Today* 25 (January 1981): 32–33.

2942. _____. *Terence Fisher: Horror, Myth and Religion.* Jefferson, NC: McFarland and Company, 2002. 208 pp. tp.

2943. Leider, R. Allen. "A Candid Conversation with Christopher Lee...The End of the Count?" *The Monster Times* 1, 27 (1973).

2944. Marrero, Robert. *Dracula: The Vampire Legend on Film.* Key West, FL: Fantasma Books, 1992. 120 pp. tp. Rev. ed. as: *Vampire Movies.* Key West FL: Fantasma Books, 1994. 176 pp. tp.

2945. _____. *Horrors of Hammer.* Key West, FL: RGM Publications, 1984. 131 pp. tp.

2946. _____. *Vampires Hammer Style.* Key West, FL: RGM Publications, 1974. 98 pp. tp.

2947. Maxford, Howard. *Hammer, House of Horror: Behind the Screams.* London: B. T. Batsford, 1996. 192 pp. tp. Rpt.: Woodstock, NY: Overlook Press, 1996. 192 pp. hb. dj.

2948. McCarty, John. *Hammer Films.* Harpenden, Herts., UK: Pocket Essentials, 2002. 95 pp. pb.

2949. _____. "Hammer Horror." In John McCarty. *Splatter Movies.* Albany, NY: FantaCo Enterprises, 1981, pp. 35–52.

2950. McDonald, T. Liam. "The Horrors of Hammer: The House That Blood Built." In Christopher Golden, ed. *Cut! Horror Writers on Horror Film.* New York: Berkley Books, 1992, pp. 151–60.

2951. McGlasson, Michael. "It's All in the Blood: The Bram Stoker/Peter Cushing Alliance." *Journal of Dracula Studies* 5 (2003): 11–15.

2952. _____. *The Unknown Peter Cushing.* Duncan, OK: Bear Manor Media, 2011. 132 pp. tp.

2953. McKay, Sinclair. *A Thing of Unspeakable Horror: The History of Hammer Films.* London: Aurum, 2008. 288 pp. tp.

2954. Meikle, Denis. *A History of Hammer: The Rise and Fall of the House of Hammer, 1949–1979.* Metuchen, NJ: Scarecrow Press, 1996. 420 pp. hb. Rpt.: Lanham, MD: Scarecrow Press, 2001. 420 pp. tp. Rev. ed.: Lanham, MD: Scarecrow Press, 2008. 312 pp. hb.

2955. Miller, David. *The Peter Cushing Companion.* Richmond, UK: Reynolds & Hearn, 2000. tp. Rev. ed.: 2002. 192 pp. tp. Rev. ed. as: *The Complete Peter Cushing.* Richmond: Reynolds & Hearn, 2005. 208 pp. tp. Rev. ed. as: *Peter Cushing: A Life in Film.* London: Titan Books, 2013. 192 pp.

2956. Miller, Mark A. *Christopher Lee and Peter Cushing and Horror Cinema: A Filmography of Their 22 Collaborations.* Jefferson, NC: McFarland and Company, 1995. 437 pp. tp.

2957. Moench, Doug. "Christopher Lee—Hammer's Hero of Horror." *Dracula Lives* 1, 12 (1975): 42–45, 62–65.

2958. Naha, Ed. "Christopher Lee." *Starlog* 6, 70 (1983).

2959. Nazzaro, Joe. "Dressed to Kill." *Hammer Horror* 2 April 1995): 12–14. Re: Michele Burke, make-up artist.

2960. Noel, Gerard. *Christopher Lee: One More Time.* Ser.: Horror Picture Collection. Cahors, France: Gerard Noel Faneditions, 1991. 39 pp. pb. Staples. Introduction by Robert Belardinelli. Text in both English and French.

2961. _____. *Christopher Lee Part 2: One More Time.* Ser.: Horror Picture Collection. France: Gerard Noel Faneditions, 1991. 39 pp. pb. Staples. Introduction by Robert Belardinelli. Text in both English and French.

2962. _____. *Christopher Lee: Prince of Darkness.* Ser.: Horror Picture Collection. Cahors, France: Collection Horror Pictures, 1991. 38 pp. pb. Staples. Text in both English and French.

2963. Owen, Dean, and Philip J. Riley. *The Brides of Dracula.* Duncan, OK: BearManor Media, 2011. 154 pp.

2964. Parrish, James Robert, and Michael R. Pitts. "Christopher Lee." *Cinefantastique* 3, 1 (Fall 1973) 4–23.

2965. Parry, Michael. "The Return of Christopher Lee." *Castle of Frankenstein* 2, 6 (1965).

2966. Parsons, Maria. "Vamping the Woman: Mental Pathologies in Bram Stoker's Dracula." *Irish Journal of Gothic and Horror Studies* 1 (October 2006). Online journal posted at: http://irishgothichorrorjournal.homestead.com/maria.html.

2967. "Peter Cushing—The Hammer Years." *Hammer Horror* 1 (March 1995): 5–10.

2968. Pirie, David. *Hammer: A Cinema Case Study.* London: British Film Institute, 1980. 64 pp. hb.

2969. _____. *Heritage of Horror: The English Gothic Cinema, 1946–1972.* London: Gordon Fraser, 1973. 192 pp. hb. Rev. ed. as: *A New Heritage of Horror: The English Gothic Cinema.* London: I. B. Tauris, 2008, 254 pp. hb & tp.

2970. Pitt, Ingrid. *The Ingrid Pitt Bedside Companion for Vampire Lovers.* London: BT Batsford, 1998. 192 pp. tp.

2971. _____. *Life's a Scream: The Autobiography of Ingrid Pitt.* London: William Heinemann, 1999. 292 pp. Exp. ed. as: *Ingrid Pitt: Darkness Before Dawn.* Baltimore, MD: Luminary Press, 2004. 232 pp. tp.

2972. _____. "Pitt of Horror: Metamorphosis." *Chiller Theatre Magazine* 1 (Winter 1994–95): 41–44.

2973. Pohle, Robert W., Jr., and Douglas C. Hart. *The Films of Christopher Lee.* Metuchen, NJ: Scarecrow Press, 1983. 227 pp.

2974. Potts, John. "What I Owe to Hammer Horror." *Senses of Cinema* 47 (May 2008). Posted at: http://sensesofcinema.com/2008/feature-articles/hammer-horror/.

2975. Powell, Anna. "The Perverse World of Hammer Horror." Anna Powell. *Psychonanalysis and Sovereignty in Popular Vampire Fictions.* Lewiston, NY: Edwin Mellen Press, 2003.

2976. Rigby, Jonathan. *Christopher Lee: The Authorized Screen History.* London: Richards & Hearn, 2001. 256 pp. hb. dj. Second ed.: 2003. 272 pp. hb. dj. Third ed.: 2007. 304 pp. pb.

2977. Ringel, Harry. "Hammer Horror: The World of Terence Fisher." In Thomas R. Adkins, ed. *Graphic Violence on the Screen.* New York: Monarch Press, 1976, pp. 35–45.

2978. _____. "The Horrible Hammer Films of Terence Fisher." *Take One* 3, 9 (January/February 1972): 8–12.

2979. _____. "Terence Fisher: The Human Side." *Cinefantastique* 4, 3 (Fall 1975): 5–16.

2980. _____. "Terence Fisher Underlining." *Cinefantastique* 4, 3 (Fall 1976): 19–26.

2981. Roth, Lane. "*Dracula/Dracula*: Some Thoughts About the Hammer and Universal Versions." *Photon* 27 (1977): 40–41.

2982. _____. "Film, Society and Ideas: *Nosferatu* and *Horror of Dracula*." In Barry Keith Grant. *Planks of Reason: Essays on the Horror Film.* Metuchen, NJ: Scarecrow Press, 1984, pp. 245–54.

2983. Sangster, Jimmy, with Russ Jones. "Horror of Dracula." *Monsters of the Movies* 1, 7 (June 1975): 14–66.

2984. Schulman, Stephen." "Hammer Films: Count Dracula and Baron Frankenstein." *Fright and Fantasy* 3 (Spring-Summer 1973): 14–26.

2985. Searle, Joshua. *The Fluctuating Popularity of Hammer's Gothic Horror Films, 1957–1976.* Portsmouth, UK: University of Portsmouth, BA dissertation, 2013.

2986. Shinnick, Kevin G. "Saint Peter." *Chiller Theatre Magazine* 1 (Winter 1994-95): 6–10.

2987. Smith, Stephen D. "Carmilla: J. Sheridan Le Fanu and Hammer's Karnstein Trilogy." *Monsterscene* 8 (Summer 1996): 12–18.

2988. Soren, David. "Hammer and the Threat of Television." In David Soren. *The Rise and Fall of the Horror Film: An Art Historical Approach to Fantasy Cinema.* Columbia, MO: Lucas Bros. Publishers, 1977, pp. 83–87. Rpt. Baltimore, MD: Midnight Marquee Press, 2002.

2989. Svehla, Gary J. "Hammer Films and the Resurrection of Dracula." in Bob Madison, ed. *Dracula: The First Hundred Years.* Baltimore, MD: Midnight Marquee Press, 1997, pp. 186–99.

2990. _____, and Susan Svehla. "Women Take a Bite Out of Classic Horror: *Dracula's Daughter* and the *Mark of the Vampire*." In Gary Svehla and Susan Svehla, eds. *Bitches, Bimbos and Virgins: Women of the Horror Film.* Baltimore, MD: Midnight Marquee Press, 2011, pp. 104–26.

2991. _____, and Susan Svehla, eds. Hammer Films. Baltimore, MD: Midnight Marquee Press, 2011. 273 pp. tp.

2992. _____, and Susan Svehla, eds. *Memories of Hammer.* Baltimore: Luminary Press, 2002. 256 pp. hb. boards.

2993. Swires, Steve. "Butcher, Baker, Vampire Film Maker." *Fangoria* 116 (September 1992): 54–59. Re: Roy Ward Baker.

2994. Toefsfer, Susan. "Christopher Lee—A Candid Conversation." *The Monster Times* 1, 46 (1976).

2995. "A Tribute to Hammer Films." Special Issue of *Midnight Marquee* 47 (Summer 1994).

2996. Valley, Richard. "Interview with an Ex-Vampire." *Scarlet Street* 4 (Fall 1991): 40–44. Re: Christopher Lee.

2997. _____. "Mornings with Peter Cushing." *Scarlet Street* Pt. 1. 8 (Fall 1992): 34–38, 101; Pt. 2. 9 (Winter 1993): 58–63.

2998. "Vampire Circus." *Necronomicon* 7 (n.d.): 26–28.

2999. Walden, Victoria. *Studying Hammer Horror.* Leighton Buzzard, UK: Auteur, 2010.

3000. Welsh, Paul. *The Spine Chillers: Chaney jun., Cushing, Lee & Price.* Elms Court, Ilfracombe, Devon, UK: Arthur H. Stockwell, 1975. 68 pp.

Cinematic Vampires: Francis Ford Coppola and Bram Stoker's Dracula

For vampire fans, the early 1990s was marked by the new version of the novel *Dracula* brought to the screen by director Francis Ford Coppola, who had become attracted to the project by reading the screenplay authored by James V. Hart. Coppola assembled an all-star cast that included Gary Oldman (Dracula), Keanu Reeves (Jonathan Harker), Winona Ryder (Mina Murray), and Anthony Hopkins (Abraham Van Helsing). He also asserted that he would make a version of the novel that was true to the storyline and included all of the major characters including Quincey Morris (portrayed by Billy Campbell), the American character who was most often the first to disappear from the cast whenever *Dracula* was brought to the stage or screen.

The film became controversial from the beginning, with many critics complaining that there was no call to create another version of *Dracula* (the single literary piece that has most frequently been adapted to film). Coppola also made a number of production decisions to give the film a unique quality and to make sure it was completed on time. *Dracula* fans were quick to point out that the claim of faithfulness to the book did not align with the inclusion of the opening scenes concerning Vlad Tepes, even if current scholarship concerned itself with the debate over the use made of facts about Vlad by Bram Stoker.

In the end, Coppola continued the transformation of Dracula into a sensual lover/ seducer of the two principle female characters—Lucy Westener (portrayed by Sadie Frost) and Mina Murray—with Oldman following a trend started by Frank Langella in his 1979 performance in Universal's *Dracula*.

The final result was a notable cinematic success, with Columbia Pictures enjoying record-breaking box office results and Coppola presenting what would become one of the most commented-upon motion pictures of the decade. Of the more than 40 film adaptations of the novel, *Bram Stoker's Dracula* joined the 1931 version starring Bela Lugosi, the 1958 Hammer version starring Christopher Lee, and the 1979 Frank Langella version as one among the small circle of truly notable adaptations. It won three Academy Awards for its technical expertise.

The hoped-for success of the movie also prompted the development of a significant merchandizing campaign that saw the production of a comic book series, trading cards, toys, games, a soundtrack CD, clothing, jewelry, and a variety of additional items associated with the movie that were available when the movie opened in the fall of 1992. Science fiction writer Fred Saberhagen, who had written a successful series of novels on *Dracula*, authored the novelization of Hart's screenplay.

3001. Abramowitz, Rachel. "Neck Vampire." *Premiere* 6, 4 (December 1992): 48–58.

3002. Austin, Thomas. "*Bram Stoker's Dracula*: Gone with the Wind + Fangs." In Thomas Austin. *Hollywood, Hype and Audiences: Selling and Watching Popular Film in the 1990s.* Manchester, UK: Manchester University Press, 2002, pp. 114–152.

3003. _____. "'Gone with the Wind Plus Fangs': Genre, Taste and Distinction in the Assembly, Marketing and Reception of *Bram Stoker's Dracula*." In Steve Neale, ed. *Genre and Contemporary Hollywood.* London: British Film Institute, 2002.

3004. Bacal, Simon. "Transylvania, Dracula, His Castle...Matte World." *Starburst* 15, 4 (172) (December 1992): 24–29.

3005. Bassan, Raphaël. "Francis Ford Coppola's *Dracula* and the Tradition of Vampire in Films." *Europe* 71, 765 (Jan./Feb. 1993): 192–196.

3006. Bartle, Louise A. "Hart of Darkness." *Fanta Zone/Superstar Facts and Pics* 27 (1992): 33–37.

3007. Bignell, Jonathan. "Spectacle and the Postmodern in the Contemporary American Cinema." *La Licorne* 36 (1996): 163–80.

3008. Biodrowski, Steve. "The Brides of 'Bram Stoker's Dracula.'" *Femme Fatales* 1, 3 (Winter 1992/1993): 16–19.

3009. _____. "Coppola's *Dracula. Cinefantastique* 23, 4 (December 1992): 24–26, 31, 35, 39, 43, 47, 51, 55. One of a set of articles on the Coppola film in this issue of *Cinefantastique.*

3010. _____. "'*Dracula*': Vampire Effects." *Cinefantastique* 23, 4 (December 1992): 40–42.

3011. Brett, Anwar. "The Drac Pack." *Samhain* 37 (March/April 1993): 6–9.

3012. Coppola, Francis Ford, and Eiko Ishioka. *Coppola and Eiko on Bram Stoker's Dracula.* San Francisco: Collins Publishers, 1992. 96 pp. pb. Large format. Ed. by Susan Dworkin. Photographs by David Seidner.

3013. Coppola, Francis Ford, and James V. Hart. *Bram Stoker's Dracula: The Film and the Legend.* New York: Newmarket Press, 1992. 172 pp. pb. Large format. Rpt.: London: Pan Books, 1992. 172 pp. pb. Large format.

3014. Corbin, Carol, and Robert A. Campbell. "Postmodern Iconography and Perspective in Coppola's *Bram Stoker's Dracula*," *Journal of Popular Film and Television* 27, 2 (Summer 1999): 40–48.

3015. Coulardeau, Jacques. "The Vision of Religion in Francis Ford Coppola's *Bram Stoker's Dracula.*" In John S. Bak, ed. *Post/modern Dracula: From Victorian Themes to Postmodern Praxis.* Cambridge: Cambridge Scholars Publishing, 2007, pp. 123–40.

3016. Crowley, Cornelius. "Is There an Irish Dimension in *Dracula* ?" In Gilles Menegaldo and Dominique Sipière, eds. *Dracula: L'oeuvre de Bram Stoker et le film de Francis F. Coppola.* Paris, Ellipses, 2005, pp. 149–58.

3017. Deaville, James. "The Beauty of Horror: Kilar, Coppola, and Dracula." In Neil Lerner, ed. *Music in the Horror Film: Listening to Fear.* New York: Routledge, 2010, pp. 187–205.

3018. Devine, Alexandre. "*Bram Stoker's Dracula.*" *Annals Australia: Journal of Catholic Culture* 104, 1 (January 1993).

3019. Devine, Scott. "A Vampire He Couldn't Refuse." *Fanta Zone/Superstar Facts and Pics* 27 ((1992): 25–31.

3020. Dika, Vera. "From Dracula—with Love." In Barry Keith Grant. *The Dread of Difference: Gender and the Horror Film.* Austin: University of Texas Press, 1996, pp. 388–400.

3021. Dunbar, Brian. *Dracula and Bram Stoker's Dracula.* Ser.: York Film Notes. London: York Press, 2000. 91 pp. tp.

3022. Duperray, Max, and Dominique Sipière. *Dracula: Bram Stoker et Francis Ford Coppola.* Paris: Armand-Colin, 2005. 170 pp. tp. A collection of essays by the authors on Coppola's *Bram Stoker's Dracula,* half in French and half in English.

3023. Dyer, Richard. "Dracula and Desire." *Sight and Sound* 3 (1993): 8–12. Rpt. in: Ginette Vincendeau, ed. *Film/Literature/Heritage: A Sight and Sound Reader.* London: British Film Institute, 2001, pp. 91–97.

3024. Eberle-Sinatra, Michael. "Exploring Gothic Sexuality." *Gothic Studies* 7, 2 (November 2005): 123–126.

3025. Ehrenstein, David. "One from the Art." *Film Comment* 29, 1 (January-February, 1993): 27–30.

3026. Elsaesser, Thomas. "The Love That Never Dies: Francis Ford Coppola and *Bram Stoker's Dracula.*" In Thomas Elsaesser. *The Persistence of Hollywood.* New York: Routledge, 2012, pp. 257–70.

3027. _____. "Specularity and Engulfment: Francis Ford Coppola and *Bram Stoker's Dracula.*" In Steve Neale and Murray Smith, eds. *Contemporary Hollywood Cinema.* New York: Routledge, 1998, pp. 191–206.

3028. "Fang Warfare." *The Dark Side* (February 1993): 5–8. Interview with Coppola.

3029. Fry, Carrol, and John Robert Craig. "'Unfit for Earth, Undoomed for Heaven': The Genesis of Coppola's Byronic *Dracula.*" *Literature/Film Quarterly* 30 (2002): 271–78.

3030. Halberstam, Judith, and J. McElhaney. "On Vampires, Lesbians, and Coppola's *Dracula/Bram Stoker's Dracula* by Francis Ford Coppola." *Bright Lights* 11 (Fall 1993); 7–9, 45–46.

3031. Harbin, Leigh Joyce. "A Dangerous Woman and a Man's Brain: Mina Harker, Clarice Starling and the Empowerment of the Gothic Heroine in Novel and Film." *West Virginia University Philological Papers* 49 (2002–2003):30–37.

3032. Himpele, Jeff D. "The Travels and Transfigurations of *Dracula.* In Jeff D. Himpele. *Circuits of Culture: Media, Politics, and Indigenous Identity in the Andes.* Minneapolis: University of Minnesota Press, 2007, 41–46.

3033. Hinson, Hal. "*Bram Stoker's Dracula.*" In Peter Keough, ed. *Flesh and Blood: The National Society of Film Critics on Sex, Violence, and Censorship.* San Francisco, CA: Mercury House, 1995, pp. 167–69.

3034. Hirschorn, Michael W. "Winona Among the Grown-ups." *Esquire* 118, 5 (November 1992): 114–117, 182.

3035. Hogan, David J. "*Bram Stoker's Dracula*: The Coffin Opens." In Bob Madison, ed. *Dracula: The First Hundred Years.* Baltimore, MD: Midnight Marquee Press, 1997, pp. 20–41.

3036. Hughes, William. "The Sanguine Economy: Blood and the Circulation of Meaning in *Bram Stoker's Dracula.*" In Dominique Sipière, ed. *Dracula: Insémination-dissémination.* Amiens, Presses del'UFR Clerc, Université de Picardie, 1996, pp. 49–65. Rpt. in: Gilles Menegaldo and Dominique Sipière, eds. *Dracula: L'oeuvre de Bram Stoker et le film de Francis F. Coppola.* Paris, Ellipses, 2005, pp. 71–82.

3037. Jones, Alan. "Interview with the Producer." *Shivers* 14 (January 1995): 24–27.

3038. Julien, Nathalie. *From Dracula to Bram Stoker's Dracula: The Transcription of Novelistic Narration to the Screen.* Lyon, France: Université Lumière, Lyon, 1999, 76 pp.

3039. Jurkiewicz, Kenneth. "Francis Coppola's Secret Gardens: Bram Stoker's 'Dracula' and the Auteur as Decadent Visionary." In Allienne R. Becker, ed. *Visions of the Fantastic: Selected Essays from the Fifteenth International Conference on the Fantastic in the Arts.* Ser.: Contributions to the study of science fiction and fantasy; no. 68. Westport, CT: Greenwood Press, 1996, pp. 167–71.

3040. Kline, Michael. "The Vampire as Pathogen: Bram Stoker's *Dracula* and Francis Ford Coppola's *Bram Stoker's Dracula.*" West Virginia University Philological Papers 42–43 (1997–1998): 36–44.

3041. Lanone, Catherine. "Bram Stoker's *Dracula* or Femininity as a Forsaken Fairy Tale." In Gilles Menegaldo and Dominique Sipière, eds. *Dracula: L'oeuvre de Bram Stoker et le film de Francis F. Coppola.* Paris, Ellipses, 2005, pp. 199–206.

3042. Lapolla, Franco. "Dracula." *Cineforum* 33, 1 (January/February 1993): 6–15.

3043. LeBlanc, Jacqueline. "'It is not good to note this down': *Dracula* and Erotic Technologies of Censorship." In Carol Margaret Davison, ed., with Paul Simpson-Housley. *Bram Stoker's Dracula: Sucking through the Century, 1897–1997.* Toronto: Dundurn Press, 1997, pp. 249–68.

3044. Lecomte, Jean-Marie. "Postmodern Verbal Discourse in Coppola's *Bram Stoker's Dracula.*" in John S. Bak, ed. *Post/Modern Dracula: From Victorian Theme to Postmodern Praxis.* Newcastle, UK: Cambridge Scholars Press, 2007, pp. 107–122.

3045. Macabre, J. B. "Dracula." *World of Fandom* 2, 17 ((Winter 1993): 14–17.

3046. Magid, Ron. "Effects Add Bite to Bram Stoker's Dracula." *American Cinematographer* 73, 12 (December 1992): 5–60, 62, 64.

3047. Magistrale, Tony. "Vampiric Terrors." In Tony Magistrale. *Abject Terrors: Surveying the Modern and Postmodern Horror Film.* New York: Peter Lang, 2005.

3048. Marigny, Jean. "Tradition and Postmodernism in Stoker's Novel and Coppola's Film." In John S. Bak, ed. *Post/Modern Dracula: From Victorian Theme to Postmodern Praxis.* Newcastle, UK: Cambridge Scholars Publishing, 2007, pp. 97–106.

3049. Marshall, Erik. "Defanging Dracula: The Disappearing Other in Coppola's *Bram Stoker's Dracula.*" In Ruth Bienstock Anolik and Douglas L. Howard. *The Gothic Other: Racial and Social Constructions in the Literary Imagination.* Jefferson, NC: McFarland & Company, 2004, pp. 289–302.

3050. Mathews, Tom. "Fangs for Nothing; Coppola's Dracula and Rice's Lestat: Cultural Icons for an Age of Enervation." *Newsweek* 120, 22 (Nov. 30, 1992): 74.

3051. McConnell, Frank. "Rough Beast Slouching: A Note on Horror Movies." *Kenyon Review* 32 (1970): 109–120.

3052. McGunnigle, Christopher. "My Own Vampire: The Metamorphosis of the Queer Monster in Francis Ford Coppola's *Bram Stoker's Drac-*

ula." *Gothic Studies* 7, 2 (November 2005): 172–84.

3053. Menegaldo, Giles, and Dominique Sipière, eds. *Dracula: L'oeuvre de Bram Stoker et le film de Francis F. Coppola.* Paris, Ellipses, 2005. 379 pp. A collection of essays, half in French and half in English. Included are English-language essays by Victor Sage, Philip Skelton, William Hughes, Cornelius Crowley, Catherine Lanone, Raphaëlle Costa de Beauregard, and Eithne O'Neill,.

3054. Mewald, Katharina. "The Emancipation of Mina? The Portrayal of Mina in Stoker's *Dracula* and Coppola's *Bram Stoker's Dracula*." *Journal of Dracula Studies* 10 (2008): 31–39.

3055. Montalbano, Margaret. "From Bram Stoker's *Dracula* to *Bram Stoker's Dracula*." In Robert Stam and Alessandra Raengo, eds. *A Companion to Literature and Film.* Malden, MA: Blackwell Publishing, 2004, pp. 385–398.

3056. Nystrom, Lisa. "Blood, Lust, and the Fe/Male Narrative in Bram Stoker's Dracula (1992) and the Novel (1897)." In John Edgar Browning and Caroline Joan Picart, eds. *Dracula, Vampires, and Other Undead Forms.* Lanham, MD: The Scarecrow Press, 2009, pp. 63–76.

3057. O'Brien, Edward W. "Bram Stoker's Dracula: Eros or Agape?" *Fantasy Commentator* 8, 1/2 [45–46] (Winter 1993–1994): 75–79.

3058. O'Neill, Eithne. "The Exoticism of Evil: The Spectatoras Vampire: Francis Ford Coppola's Bram Stoker's Dracula." In Gilles Menegaldo and Dominique Sipière, eds. *Dracula: L'oeuvre de Bram Stokeret le film de Francis F. Coppola.* Paris, Ellipses, 2005, pp. 287–95.

3059. Phillips, Gene D. "Fright Night: Bram Stoker's Dracula." In Gene D. Phillips. *Godfather: The Intimate Francis Ford Coppola.* Lexington: The University Press of Kentucky, 2004, pp. 283–99.

3060. Poole, Francis. "*Bram Stoker's Dracula.*" *McGill Cinema Annual 1993.* Pasadena, CA: Salem Press, 1994, pp. 77–81.

3061. Reed, Thomas L. "'Belle et le vampire': Focus and Fidelity in *Bram Stoker's Dracula*." *Literature-Film Quarterly* 38, 4 (2010): 289–310.

3062. Rohrer, Trish Deitch. "Coppola's Bloody Valentine." *Entertainment Weekly* 145 (November 20, 1992): 23–31. Re: *Bram Stoker's Dracula* (1992).

3063. _____. "Gary Oldman." *Entertainment Weekly* 145 (November 20, 1992): 32–34.

3064. Sage, Victor. "*Dracula* and the Codes Victorian of Pornography. In Dominique Sipière, ed., *Dracula: Insémination-dissémination*, Amiens, Presses de l'UFR Clerc, Université de Picardie, 1996, pp.31–48. Rpt. in: Gilles Menegaldo and Dominique Sipière, eds. *Dracula: L'oeuvre de Bram Stokeret le film de Francis F. Coppola.* Paris, Ellipses, 2005, pp. 55–70.

3065. Schmidhammer, Gabriele. *Literature in Film:* Bram Stoker's Dracula. Innsbruck, Aust.: Innsbrück Universität, student mémoire, 1997, 108 pp.

3066. Scott, Lindsey. "Crossing Oceans of Time: Stoker, Coppola and the 'new vampire' film." In Sam George and Bill Hughes, eds. *Open Graves, Open Minds: Representations of Vampires and the Undead from the Enlightenment to the Present Day.* Manchester: Manchester University Press, 2013, pp. 113–30.

3067. Sheehan, Henry. "Trust the Teller: Henry Sheehan Talks with James V. Hart About *Dracula*." In Ginette Vincendeau, ed. *Film/literature/heritage.* London: British Film Institute, 2001, pp: 271–74.

3068. Sinclair, T. "Invasion of the Blood." In Ginette Vincendeau, ed. *Film/literature/heritage.* London: British Film Institute, 2001, pp: 101–04.

3069. Spelling, Ian. "*Bram Stoker's Dracula*: Gary Oldman." In Anthony Timpone, ed. *Fangoria Vampires.* New York: HarperPrism, 1996, pp. 54–60.

3070. _____. "*Bram Stoker's Dracula*: Winona Ryder." In Anthony Timpone, ed. *Fangoria Vampires.* New York: HarperPrism, 1996, pp. 68–73.

3071. Steranko, Jim. "Collaborating with Francis Ford Coppola on the Ultimate Horror Thriller...Dracula." *Preview* 2 49 (November/February 1993): 18–39, 59.

3072. Stevenson, Jay. "The Day Dracula Morphed." *Imagi-Movies* 1, 2 (Winter 1992/94): 49.

3073. Taussig, Victor. "*Bram Stoker's Dracula.*" *Film Analyst* 10 (1992): 1–9.

3074. Turner, George. "*Bram Stoker's Dracula*: A Happening Vampire." *American Cinematographer* 73, 11 (November 1992): 36–45.

3075. _____. "Dracula Meets the Son of Coppola." *American Cinematographer* 73, 11 (November 1992): 46–52.

3076. Verhoeven, Deb. "Coppola's Dracula: Biting Off More Than You Can Eschew." *Scripsi* 8, 3 (1993): 197–204. Posted at: http://www.academia.edu/720056/Coppolas_Dracula_Biting_Off_More_than_You_Can_Possibly_Eschew.

3077. Vetlieb, Steve. "The Awakening Spectre in Bram Stoker's *Dracula*." *Cinemacabre* 1 (Winter/Spring 1978/79): 4–12.

3078. Warchol, Tomasz. "How Coppola Killed Dracula." In Carla T. Kungl, ed. *Vampires: Myths and Metaphors of Enduring Evil*. Oxford: Inter-Disciplinary Press, 2003, pp. 7–10.

3079. Warren, Bill. "*Bram Stoker's Dracula*: Anthony Hopkins." In Anthony Timpone, ed. *Fangoria Vampires*. New York: HarperPrism, 1996, pp. 61–67.

3080. _____ . "*Bram Stoker's Dracula*: James V. Hart, Screenwriter." In Anthony Timpone, ed. *Fangoria Vampires*. New York: HarperPrism, 1996, pp. 47–54.

3081. Welsh, James M. "Sucking Dracula: Mythic Biography into Fiction into Film, or Why Francis Ford Coppola's *Dracula* Is Not Really Bram Stoker's *Dracula* or Wallachia's *Dracula*." In James M. Welsh, Peter Lev, eds. *The Literature/Film Reader: Issues of Adaptation*. Lanham, MD: Scarecrow Press, 2007, pp. 165–74.

3082. Whalen, Tom. "Romancing Film: Coppola's *Dracula*." *Literature/Film Quarterly* 23, 2 (1995): 99–101.

3083. Worland, Rick. "Demon Lover: *Bram Stoker's Dracula*." In Rick Worland. *The Horror Film: An Introduction*. Malden, MA: Blackwell Publications, 2007, pp 253–65.

3084. Wyman, Leah M., and George N. Dionisopoulos. "Primal Urges and Civilized Sensibilities: The Rhetoric of Gendered Archetypes, Seduction, and Resistance in *Bram Stoker's Dracula*." *Journal of Popular Film and Television* 27.2 (1999): 32–39.

3085. _____ . "Transcending the Virgin/Whore Dichotomy: Telling Mina's Story in *Bram Stoker's Dracula*." *Women's Studies in Communication* 23, 2 (Spring 2000): 209–37.

Cinematic Vampires: The Twilight *Saga*

The name *Twilight* Saga refers to four vampire novels written by Stephenie Meyer and directed to a young teenage audience—*Twilight* (2005), *New Moon* (2006), *Eclipse* (2007), and *Breaking Dawn* (2008). These bestselling novels were then transformed into five very successful movies, with the storyline of *Breaking Dawn* being divided into two movies. The novels follow a teenage romance between 17-year-old human girl Isabella (or Bella) Swan and her vampire boyfriend, Edward Cullen. The initial chapters of a potential fifth novel, *Midnight Sun*, were leaked on the Internet. It was never completed, though the twelve chapters that were penned now rest on Meyer's personal website www.StephenieMeyer.com.

The *Twilight* Saga experienced spectacular success in book form, and was translated into some 20 languages. The movies shared an analogous success, the five movies together being the ninth highest grossing film series of all time (as of the end of 2013), just ahead of *Spiderman*, which ranked 10th. The five *Twilight* movies are five of the six highest grossing vampire movies of all time, the only challenge coming from *I Am Legend*, which ranks third. The *Twilight* Saga also led to the development of a spectrum of related merchandise—clothing, jewelry, cosmetics, trading cards, comic books, dolls, and toys.

While clearly fitting into the vampire genre, *Twilight* posited some unique variations relative to *Dracula* and other pre–1970 vampire literature. Meyer's vampires, a variation on the "good guy" vampire, are immune to the harmful effects of crosses, wooden stakes, holy water, garlic, and sunlight, while walking into the sunlight causes their skin to glitter like diamonds. *Twilight's* vampires have mirror reflections but do not have fangs. Their skin is pale and icy cold to the touch. They do not need sleep. They have extremely quick reflexes and can run fast and leap high, but they don't shape shift into bats or fly. While Stoker's Dracula has bad breath, Edward's is sweet. But Meyer's vampires are sustained by blood alone, which lightens their eyes and flushes their skin slightly. They are immensely strong (especially during the first year of their vampire life), and their transformation makes them physically stunning and beautiful. Like good guy vampires in general, they avoid human blood, and largely feed off animals.

The *Twilight* vampires fit clearly into the tradition of good guy vampires that began with Vampirella and Chelsea Quinn Yarbro's Saint Germain. Edward's family, the Cullens, refer to themselves as "vegetarians," by which they mean that they obtain blood from animals and refrain from killing humans. This allows them to remain within the human moral world.

Stephanie Meyer is a member of the Church of Jesus Christ of Latter-day Saints (the Mormons), and much has been made of the books as a reflection of both Mormon beliefs and morality. Edward Cullen falls deeply in love with Bella, but for a variety of reasons abstains from all sexual relations until marriage.

The *Twilight* Saga also includes werewolves as essential characters and the relationship between vampires and werewolves constitutes a major additional story line. The werewolves are all members of the Quileute nation of Native Americans who are given the ability to shift into their wolf persona by Meyer. The werewolf presence in the novels appears to reflect the longstanding relation developed between the Mormons and Native Americans.

Following the opening provided by the development of scholarly comment on *Buffy the Vampire Slayer*, once the *Twilight* movies began to appear, academic articles and books soon followed. The first books appeared in 2008, with more than a dozen being published in 2010 alone. Additionally, numerous fan books about the actors who starred in the movies were also published (a sample of which is included in the juvenile texts in a separate section in this work).

3086. Abele, Robert. *The Twilight Saga: The Complete Film Archive: Memories, Mementos, and Other Treasures from the Creative Team Behind the Beloved Motion Pictures.* Boston: Little, Brown Books for Young Readers, 2012. 151 pp. hb.

3087. Aleiss, Angela. "Mormon Influence, Imagery Runs Deep through Twilight." *Religious Herald* (July 07, 2010). Posted at: http://www.religiousherald.org/index.php?option=com_content&task=view&id=4368&Itemid=53.

3088. Ames, Melissa. "Twilight Follows Tradition: Analyzing Biting Critiques of Vampire Narratives for Their Portrayals of Gender and Sexuality." In Melissa Click, Jennifer Stevens Aubrey, and Elizabeth Behm-Morawitz, eds. *Bitten by Twilight: Youth Culture, Media, & the Vampire Franchise.* New York: Peter Lang Publishing, 2010, pp. 37–53.

3089. Anatol, Giselle Liza. *Bringing Light to Twilight: Perspectives on a Pop Culture Phenomenon.* New York: Palgrave Macmillan, 2011. 248 pp. hb.

Includes contributions by Margaret Kramar, Kristina Deffenbacher and Mikayla Zagoria-Moffet, Kim Allen Gleed, Maria Lindgren Leavenworth, Meredith Wallis, Tammy Dietz, Rhonda Nicol, Merinne Whitton, Tracy L. Bealer, Joseph Michael Sommers and Amy L. Hume, Michael J. Goebel, Angie Chau, Joo Ok Kim and Giselle Liza Anatol, Brianna Burke, and Tara K. Parmiter.

3090. Arnaudin, Edwin. *Mormon Vampires: The Twilight Saga and Religious History.* Chapel Hill: University of North Carolina, M.A. thesis, 2008. 102 pp. Large format. Posted at: http://dc.lib.unc.edu/cdm/ref/collection/s_papers/id/1009.

3091. Ashcraft, Donna M. *Deconstructing Twilight: Psychological and Feminist Perspectives on the Series.* New York: Peter Lang Publishing, 2012. 247 pp. tp.

3092. Aubrey, Jennifer Stevens, Scott Walus, and Melissa A. Click. "Twilight and the Production of the 21st Century Teen Idol." In

Melissa Click, Jennifer Stevens Aubrey, and Elizabeth Behm-Morawitz, eds. *Bitten by Twilight: Youth Culture, Media, & the Vampire Franchise.* New York: Peter Lang Publishing, 2010, pp. 225–39.

3093. Babu, Aiswarya S. "Stephenie Meyer's Twilight: A Vampire Tale?" *The IUP Journal of American Literature* 4, 2 (May 2011): 37–45.

3094. Baelo-Allué, Sobia. "From *Twilight* to *Fifty Shades of Grey*: Fan Fiction, Commercial Culture, and Grassroots Creativity." In Claudia Bucciferro, ed. *The Twilight Saga: Exploring the Global Phenomenon.* Lanham, MD: Scarecrow Press, 2013, pp. 227–40.

3095. Bardola, Nicola. *The Twilight Phenomenon: The Unofficial Companion to the Bestselling Vampire Series.* Trans. by Solveig Emerson. London: Piccadilly, 2009. 211 pp. tp.

3096. Beahm, George, with the Forks Chamber of Commerce. *Twilight Tours: An Illuminated Guide to the Real Forks.* Nevada City, CA: Underwood Books, 2009. 112 pp. hb. boards.

3097. Bealer, Tracy L. "Of Monsters and Men: Toxic Masculinity and the TwentyFirst Century Vampire in the *Twilight* Saga." In Giselle Liza Anatol. *Bringing Light to Twilight: Perspectives on a Pop Culture Phenomenon.* New York: Palgrave Macmillan, 2011, pp. 139–52.

3098. Beck, Bernard. "Fearless Vampire Kissers: Bloodsuckers We Love in *Twilight, True Blood* and Others." *Multicultural Perspectives* 13, 2 (2011): 90–92.

3099. Bedoya, Paola A. *Team Edward or Team Jacob? The Portrayal of Two Versions of the "Ideal" Male Romantic Partner in the Twilight Film Series.* Atlanta: Georgia State University, M.A. thesis, 2011. 100 pp. Large format. *Posted at:* http://digitalarchive.gsu.edu/communication_theses/85.

3100. Behm-Morawitz, Elizabeth, Melissa A. Click, and Jennifer Stevens Aubrey. "Relating to Twilight: Fans' Responses to Love and Romance in the Vampire Franchise." In Melissa Click, Jennifer Stevens Aubrey, Elizabeth Behm-Morawitz, eds. *Bitten by Twilight: Youth Culture, Media, & the Vampire Franchise.* New York: Peter Lang Publishing, 2010, pp. 137–54.

3101. Berg, Erica. "Team Jacob." In E. David Klonsky and Alexis Black, eds. *The Psychology of Twilight.* Dallas, TX: Smart Pop/Benbella Books, 2011, pp. 23–34.

3102. Bernard, Michelle. . "I Know What You Are": A Philosophical Look at Race, Identity, and Mixed-Blood in the *Twilight* Universe." In Claudia Bucciferro, ed. *The Twilight Saga: Exploring the Global Phenomenon.* Lanham, MD: Scarecrow Press, 2013, pp. 181–94.

3103. Blasingame, James. "Interview with Stephenie Meyer." *Journal of Adolescent & Adult Literacy* 49, 7 (April 2006): 630–33.

3104. Bliss, Ann V. "Abstinence, American-Style." In Amy M. Clarke and Marijane Osborn, eds. *The* Twilight *Mystique: Critical Essays on the Novels and Films.* Jefferson, NC: McFarland & Company, 2010, pp. 107–20.

3105. Bloom, Clive. "After Midnight: Goth Culture, Vampire Games and the Irresistible Rise of Twilight." In Clive Bloom. *Gothic Histories: The Taste for Terror, 1764 to the Present.* London: Continuum International Publishing, 2010, pp. 179–90.

3106. Bore, Inger-Lise Kalviknes, and Rebecca Williams. "Transnational Twilighters: A Twilight Fan Community in Norway." In Melissa Click, Jennifer Stevens Aubrey, Elizabeth Behm-Morawitz, eds. *Bitten by Twilight: Youth Culture, Media, & the Vampire Franchise.* New York: Peter Lang Publishing, 2010, pp. 189–205.

3107. Borgia, Danielle N. "Twilight: The Glamorization of Abuse, Codependency, and White Privilege." *The Journal of Popular Culture* (2011). Posted at: http://onlinelibrary.wiley.com/doi/10.1111/j.1540–5931.2011.00872.x/full.

3108. Branch, Lori. "Carlisle's Cross: Locating the Post-Secular Gothic." In Amy M. Clarke and Marijane Osborn, eds. *The* Twilight *Mystique: Critical Essays on the Novels and Films.* Jefferson, NC: McFarland & Company, 2010, pp. 60–79.

3109. Brande, Robin." Edward, Heathcliff, and Our Other Secret Boyfriends." In Ellen Hopkins with Leah Wilson, eds. *A New Dawn: Your Favorite Authors on Stephenie Meyer's Twilight Series.* Dallas TX: BenBella Books, 2008, pp. 141–53.

3110. Brugger, Eveline. "'Where Do the Cullens Fit In?': Vampires in European Folklore, Science, and Fiction." In Nancy R. Reagin. *Twilight and History.* New York: John Wiley & Sons, 2010, pp. 227–44.

3111. Bruner, Kurt, and Olivia Bruner. *The Twilight Phenomenon: Forbidden Fruit or Thirst Quenching.* Shippensburg, PA: Destiny Image,

2009. 173 pp. A Christian attempt at responding to the Twilight Saga.

3112. Bucciferro, Claudia, ed. *The Twilight Saga: Exploring the Global Phenomenon*. Lanham, MD: Scarecrow Press, 2013. 260 pp. hb.

3113. Burke, Brianna. "The Great American Love Affair: Indians in the *Twilight* Saga." In Giselle Liza Anatol. *Bringing Light to Twilight: Perspectives on a Pop Culture Phenomenon*. New York: Palgrave Macmillan, 2011, pp. 207–20.

3114. Burkhart, Kat. "Getting Younger Every Decade: Being a Teen Vampire During the Twentieth Century." In Nancy R. Reagin. *Twilight and History*. New York: John Wiley & Sons, 2010, pp. 245–62.

3115. Burkley, Melissa. "Team Edward vs Team Jacob: Prejudice in Twilight." In E. David Klonsky and Alexis Black, eds. *The Psychology of Twilight*. Dallas, TX: Smart Pop/Benbella Books, 2011, pp.

3116. Buskirk, Byrnn R. "Chastity, Power, and Delayed Gratification: The Lure of Sex in the *Twilight* Saga." In Claudia Bucciferro, ed. *The Twilight Saga: Exploring the Global Phenomenon*. Lanham, MD: Scarecrow Press, 2013, pp. 155–68.

3117. _____. *Why Is Everyone Hatin' on Bella? Choice Feminism and Free Agency in the Twilight Saga*. Bethlehem, PA: Lehigh University, M.A, thesis, 2012. 51 pp. Large format. Posted at: http://preserve.lehigh.edu/etd/1058.

3118. Buttsworth, Sara. "CinderBella: Twilight, Fairy Tales, and the Twenty-First-Century American Dream." In Nancy R. Reagin. *Twilight and History*. New York: John Wiley & Sons, 2010, pp. 47–69.

3119. Caine, Rachel. "The Great Debate." In Ellen Hopkins with Leah Wilson, eds. *A New Dawn: Your Favorite Authors on Stephenie Meyer's Twilight Series*. Dallas TX: BenBella Books, 2008, pp. 169–86.

3120. Carnell, Susan. "The Case for Edward Cullen." In E. David Klonsky and Alexis Black, eds. *The Psychology of Twilight*. Dallas, TX: Smart Pop/Benbella Books, 2011, pp. 35–52.

3121. Catalán-Morseby, Elizabeth. *Vampires in* The Twilight Saga: *The Reinvention and Humanization of the Vampire Myth*. Växjö, Sweden: Linnaeus University, Student thesis, 2010. 30 pp. Large format.

3122. Chadwick, Tyler. "Why Twilight Is Good for You: How the Uncanny Can Make Us More Christ-like." *Sunstone* 157 (December 2009): 46–50.

3123. Chambers, Barbara, and Robert Peaslee. Reading *Twilight*: Fandom, Romance, and Gender in the Age of Bella." In Claudia Bucciferro, ed. *The Twilight Saga: Exploring the Global Phenomenon*. Lanham, MD: Scarecrow Press, 2013, pp. 47–62.

3124. Chau, Angie. "Fashion Sucks...Blood: Clothes and Covens in *Twilight* and Hollywood Culture." In Giselle Liza Anatol. *Bringing Light to Twilight: Perspectives on a Pop Culture Phenomenon*. New York: Palgrave Macmillan, 2011, pp. 179–90.

3125. Cherry, M. [penname of Michelle Cherry Sampson]. *Twi-What? A Guide to the 'Twilight' Phenomenon (Origin to August 2011)*. Ed. by Stephanie Ezell. Columbia, TN: VOSS/Organizer, 2011. 270 pp. tp.

3126. Christensen, Alaina. "New Readings of the Vampire. Blood-Abstinent Vampires & the Women Who Consume Them." In Barbara Brodman and James E. Doan, eds. *Images of the Modern Vampire: The Hip and the Atavistic*. Madison. NJ: Fairleigh Dickinson University Press, 2013, pp. 131–46.

3127. Claasen, Sophie-Charlotte. *"Freed from Desire": The Concept of Romantic Love and the Desexualisation of the Vampire in Stephenie Meyer's* Twilight *Novels*. München, Germany: GRIN Verlag, 2013. 40 pp. pb.

3128. Clare, Cassandra. "Dear Aunt Charlotte." In Ellen Hopkins with Leah Wilson, eds. *A New Dawn: Your Favorite Authors on Stephenie Meyer's Twilight Series*. Dallas TX: BenBella Books, 2008, pp. 117–28.

3129. Clarke, Amy M. "Introduction: Approaching Twilight." In Amy M. Clarke and Marijane Osborn, eds. *The Twilight Mystique: Critical Essays on the Novels and Films*. Jefferson, NC: McFarland & Company, 2010, pp. 3–14.

3130. _____, **and Marijane Osborn, eds.** *The Twilight Mystique: Critical Essays on the Novels and Films*. Jefferson, NC: McFarland & Company, 2010, 237 pp. tp. Includes contributions by Marijane Osborn, Yvette Kisor, Lori Branch, James Mc Elroy and Emma Catherine Mc Elroy, Kristian Jensen, Ann V. Bliss, Sarah Schwartzman, Susan Jeffers, Keri Wolf, Janice Hawes, Stephanie L. Dowdle, Christine M. Mitchell, and Pamela H. Demory.

3131. Clasen, Tricia. "Taking a Bite Out of Love: The Myth of Romantic Love in the Twilight

Series." In Melissa Click, Jennifer Stevens Aubrey, Elizabeth Behm-Morawitz, eds. *Bitten by Twilight: Youth Culture, Media, & the Vampire Franchise*. New York: Peter Lang Publishing, 2010, pp. 119–34.

3132. Clement-Moore, Rosemary. "Romeo, Ripley, and Bella Swan." In Ellen Hopkins with Leah Wilson, eds. *A New Dawn: Your Favorite Authors on Stephenie Meyer's Twilight Series*. Dallas TX: BenBella Books, 2008, pp. 25–38.

3133. Click, Melissa. "Rabid," "obsessed," and "frenzied": Understanding *Twilight* Fangirls and the Gendered Politics of Fandom." *Flow* (online journal of television and media studies) (December 18, 2009). Posted at: http://flowtv.org/2009/12/rabid-obsessed-and-frenzied-understanding-twilight-fangirls-and-the-gendered-politics-of-fandom-melissa-click-university-of-missouri/.

3134. _____, Jennifer Stevens Aubrey, and Elizabeth Behm-Morawitz, eds. *Bitten by Twilight: Youth Culture, Media, & the Vampire Franchise*. New York: Peter Lang Publishing, 2010. 302 pp. Includes contributions by Margaret M. Toscano, Melissa Ames, Natalie Wilson, Carrie Anne Platt, Danielle Dick McGeough, Kathryn Kane, Tricia Clasen, Elizabeth Behm-Morawitz, Melissa A. Click, Jennifer Stevens Aubrey, Cathy Leogrande, Juli Parrish, Inger-Lise Kalviknes Bore and Rebecca Williams, Jessica Sheffield and Elyse Merlo, Scott Walus, Marianne Martens, Cyntha Willis-Chun, and Elana Levine.

3135. Clyman, Jeremy. "Self-Regulating: The Secret to Success in Twilight." In E. David Klonsky and Alexis Black, eds. *The Psychology of Twilight*. Dallas, TX: Smart Pop/Benbella Books, 2011, pp. 133–50.

3136. Cochran, Kate. "'An Old-Fashioned Gentleman'? Edward's Imaginary History." In Nancy R. Reagin. *Twilight and History*. New York: John Wiley & Sons, 2010, pp. 7–25.

3137. Coker, Catherine. "Courting Edward Cullen: Courtship Rituals and Marital Expectations in Edward's Youth." In Nancy R. Reagin. *Twilight and History*. New York: John Wiley & Sons, 2010, pp. 70–85.

3138. _____. "That Girl: Bella, Buffy, and the Feminist Ethics of Choice in *Twilight* and *Buffy the Vampire Slayer*." *Slayage: The Journal of the Whedon Studies Association* 8, 4 [32] (Winter 2011). Posted at whedonstudies.tv.

3139. Cook, Chris. *Twilight Territory: A Fan's Guide to Forks & LaPush*. Forks, WA: Fork Forum/Olympic View Publishing Book, 2009. 89 pp. tp.

3140. Cremer, Andrea Robertson. "A Subtle and Dangerous Gift: Jasper Hale and the Specter of the American Civil War." In Nancy R. Reagin. *Twilight and History*. New York: John Wiley & Sons, 2010, pp. 163–81.

3141. Crosby, Amy R. *Romanticized Images of Sexual Victimization in Young Adult Literature: The 'Twilight' Series*." Macomb: Western Illinois University, M.L.A.S. thesis, 2011. 65 pp. Large format.

3142. Deacon, Louise. *Twilight, True Love and You: Seven Secret Steps to Finding Your Edward or Jacob*. Chichester, West Sussex, UK: Summersdale, 2012. 303 pp. tp.

3143. de Bruin-Molé, Megen. *The Horror of Dracula: Twilight and the 21st-Century Vampire*. Amsterdam: University of Amsterdam, Bachelor's thesis, 2010. 28 pp. Large format. Posted at: http://www.academia.edu/616708/The_Horror_of_Dracula_Twilight_and_the_21st-Century_Vampire.

3144. Deffenbacher, Kristina, and Mikayla Zagoria-Moffet. "Textual Vampirism in the *Twilight* Saga: Drawing Feminist Life from Jane Eyre and Teen Fantasy Fiction." In Giselle Liza Anatol. *Bringing Light to Twilight: Perspectives on a Pop Culture Phenomenon*. New York: Palgrave Macmillan, 2011, pp. 31–42.

3145. Demory, Pamela H. "The Pleasures of Adapting: Reading, Viewing, Logging On." In Amy M. Clarke and Marijane Osborn, eds. *The Twilight Mystique: Critical Essays on the Novels and Films*. Jefferson, NC: McFarland & Company, 2010, pp. 202–16.

3146. Dimming, Jessica. *"Would you understand what I meant if I said I was only human?": The Image of the Vampire in Stephenie Meyer's* Twilight *and Charlaine Harris's* Dead Until Dark. Karlstad, Sweden: Karlstad University, Student thesis, 2013. 32 pp. Large format. Posted at http://www.diva-portal.org/smash/get/diva2:601773/FULLTEXT01.pdf.

3147. Dinella, Lisa, and Gary Lewandowski. "It's All in the Family." In E. David Klonsky and Alexis Black, eds. *The Psychology of Twilight*. Dallas, TX: Smart Pop/Benbella Books, 2011, pp. 169–201.

3148. Dorsey-Elson, Laura K. "Twilight Moms" and the "Female Midlife Crisis": Life Transitions, Fantasy, and Fandom." In Claudia Bucciferro, ed. *The Twilight Saga: Exploring the Global Phenomenon*. Lanham, MD: Scarecrow Press, 2013, pp. 65–78.

3149. Dowdle, Stephanie L. "Why We Like Our Vampires Sexy." In Amy M. Clarke and Marijane Osborn, eds. *The* Twilight *Mystique: Critical Essays on the Novels and Films*. Jefferson, NC: McFarland & Company, 2010, pp. 179–88.

3150. Drangholt, Janne Stigen. "Managing the Self: A Study of *katabasis* in *Twilight*." In Mariah Larsson and Ann Steiner, eds. *Interdisciplinary Approaches to Twilight Studies in Fiction, Media and a Contemporary Cultural Experience*. Lund, Sweden: Nordic Academic Press, 2011, pp. 97–108.

3151. Dufault, Monica. "Mirror, Mirror on the Wall: Youth, Age and the Monstrosity of Beauty in The Twilight Saga." In Janice Zehentbauer and Eva Gledhill, eds. *Beyond the Monstrous: Reading from the Cultural Imaginary*. Oxford: Inter-Disciplinary Press, 2013.

3152. Edwards, Kim. "Good Looks and Sex Symbols: The power of the Gaze and the Displacement of the Erotic in Twilight." *Screen Education* 53 (2009): 26–32.

3153. Erzen, Tanya. *Fanpire: The Twilight Saga and the Women Who Love It*. Boston, MA: Beacon Press, 2012. 158 pp. hb. dj.

3154. Esquirol-Salom, Meritxell. "The Twilight Saga: Gender, Consumerism, and Cultural Franchises." In Prieto-Arranz, José Igor, Patricia Bastida-Rodríguez, Caterina Calafat-Ripoll, and Christina Suárez-Gómez, eds. *De-Centering Cultural Studies: Past, Present and Future of Popular Culture*. Newcastle upon Tyme, UK: Cambridge Scholars Publishing, 2013, pp. 247–64.

3155. Fäller, Kathrin. *"And It's All There"— Intertextual Structures, Themes, and Characters in Stephenie Meyer's "Twilight" Series*. Munich, Germany: GRIN Verlag, 2011. 126 pp. pb. Large format.

3156. Farnsworth, H. Davis. "Vampire Families Are Forever." *Sunstone* 157 (December 2009): 31–37.

3157. Fosl, Peter S., and Eli Fosl. "Vampire-Diimmerung: What Can Twilight Tell Us About God?" In Rebecca Housel and J. Jeremy Wisnewski. *Twilight and Philosophy: Vampires, Vegetarians, and the Pursuit of Immortality*. New York: John Wiley & Sons, 2009, pp. 63–77.

3158. Frankel, Valerie Estelle. "Two Boy Heroes (and a Sparkly Vampire) Teach the SAT." In Valerie Estelle Frankel, ed. *Teaching with Harry Potter: Essays on Classroom Wizardry from Elementary School to College*. Jefferson, NC: McFarland & Company, 2013, pp. 70–80.

3159. Frederick, David A., et al. "Bella and the Psychobiology of Love and Attraction." In E. David Klonsky and Alexis Black, eds. *The Psychology of Twilight*. Dallas, TX: Smart Pop/Benbella Books, 2011, pp. 1–22.

3160. Gerber, Linda. "Dancing with Wolves." In Ellen Hopkins with Leah Wilson, eds. *A New Dawn: Your Favorite Authors on Stephenie Meyer's Twilight Series*. Dallas TX: BenBella Books, 2008, pp. 55–67.

3161. Gleed, Kim Allen. "*Twilight*, Translated." In Giselle Liza Anatol. *Bringing Light to Twilight: Perspectives on a Pop Culture Phenomenon*. New York: Palgrave Macmillan, 2011, pp. 59–68.

3162. Glenn, Catherine. "Motorcycles, and Strangers, and Cliff Diving! Oh, My!" In E. David Klonsky and Alexis Black, eds. *The Psychology of Twilight*. Dallas, TX: Smart Pop/Benbella Books, 2011, pp. 151–68.

3163. Gobrecht, Cindy Biondi. *Confessions of a Christian Twi-hard: My Life Lessons and the Twilight Saga*. Bloomington, IN: WestBow Press, 2012. 90 pp. tp.

3164. Godwin, Victoria. *Twilight* Anti-fans: "Real" Fans and "Real" Vampires." In Claudia Bucciferro, ed. *The Twilight Saga: Exploring the Global Phenomenon*. Lanham, MD: Scarecrow Press, 2013, pp. 93–196.

3165. Goebel, Michael J. "'Embraced' by Consumption: *Twilight* and the Modern Construction of Gender." In Giselle Liza Anatol. *Bringing Light to Twilight: Perspectives on a Pop Culture Phenomenon*. New York: Palgrave Macmillan, 2011, pp. 169–78.

3166. Gomez-Galisteo, M. Carmen. "Vampire Meets Girl: Gender Roles and the Vampire's Side of The Story in *Twilight, Midnight Sun* and *The Vampire Diaries*." *Neoamericanist* 5, 2 (2011): 1–6.

3167. Goodall, Janet, and Emyr Williams. "Paradigmatic Brilliance: Or, So Sparkly, It's Broken." *Journal of Dracula Studies* 14 (2012): 7–16.

3168. Grace, Angela. *Dark Angels Revealed: From Dark Rogues to Dark Romantics, the Most*

Mysterious and Mesmerizing Vampires and Fallen Angels from Count Dracula to Edward Cullen Come to Life. Beverly. MA: Fair Winds Press, 2011. 239 pp. tp.

3169. Granger, John. *Spotlight: A Close-up Look at the Artistry and Meaning of Stephanie Meyer's Twilight Saga,* Allentown, PA: Zossima Press: Allentown, PA, 2010. 271 pp. tp.

3170. Grant, A. J. "Focus on the Family: Good and Evil Vampires in the Twilight Saga." In Jamey Heit, ed. *Vader, Voldemort and Other Villains: Essays on Evil in Popular Media.* Jefferson, NC: McFarland & Company 2011, pp. 64–79.

3171. Gravatt, Sandra. *From Twilight to Breaking Dawn: Religious Themes in the Twilight Saga.* Atlanta, GA: Chalice Press, 2010. 118 pp. tp.

3172. Green, Jonathan. "When Your Eternal Companion Has Fangs." *Dialogue: A Journal of Mormon Thought* 421, 2 (Summer 2009): 141–43.

3173. Greenburg, Tamara. "Transcendence and Twilight." In E. David Klonsky and Alexis Black, eds. *The Psychology of Twilight.* Dallas, TX: Smart Pop/Benbella Books, 2011, pp. 201–14.

3174. Gresh, Lois H. *The Twilight Companion: The Unauthorized Guide to the Series.* New York: St. Martin's Grifiin, 2008. 242 pp. tp.

3175. Groover, Michelle. *Twilight* and Twitter: An Ethnographic Study." In Claudia Bucciferro, ed. *The Twilight Saga: Exploring the Global Phenomenon.* Lanham, MD: Scarecrow Press, 2013, pp. 79–92.

3176. Guillard, Julianne. *The 'Twilight' of Our Years: Text, Identity, and Reader Subjectivity.* University Park: Pennsylvania State University, Ph.D. dissertation, 2011. 168 pp. Large format.

3177. Haastrup, Helle Kannik. "Living Life Her Way: The Multifunctionality of the Film-star Interview." In Mariah Larsson and Ann Steiner, eds. *Interdisciplinary Approaches to Twilight Studies in Fiction, Media and a Contemporary Cultural Experience.* Lund, Sweden: Nordic Academic Press, 2011, pp. 177–94.

3178. Hanks, Maxine. "Do Mormon Moms Dream of Monstrous Gods? Stephanie Meyer's Twilight Myth as Mormon Heroine's Journey." *Sunstone* 157 (December 2009): 26–30.

3179. Hanser, Gaïane. "Isabella Swan: A Twenty-First Century Victorian Heroine?" In Claudia Bucciferro, ed. *The Twilight Saga: Exploring the Global Phenomenon.* Lanham, MD: Scarecrow Press, 2013, pp. 123–38.

3180. Happel, Alison, and Jennifer Esposito. "Vampires, Vixens, and Feminists: An Analysis of Twilight. *Educational Studies: A Journal of The American Education Studies Association* 46, 5 (2010): 524–531.

3181. Hardwicke, Catherine. *Twilight: Director's Notebook: The Story of How We Made the Movie Based on the Novel by Stephenie Meyer.* New York: Little, Brown Young Readers, 2009. 163 pp. hb. boards.

3182. Hardy, Elizabeth Baird. "Jasper Hale, the Oldest Living Confederate Veteran." In Nancy R. Reagin. *Twilight and History.* New York: John Wiley & Sons, 2010, pp. 89–105.

3183. _____. "Smoky Mountain Twilight: The Appalachian Roots of Emmett McCarty Cullen and His Family." In Nancy R. Reagin. *Twilight and History.* New York: John Wiley & Sons, 2010, pp. 106–26.

3184. Hawes, Janice. "Sleeping Beauty and the Idealized Undead: Avoiding Adolescence." In Amy M. Clarke and Marijane Osborn, eds. *The* Twilight *Mystique: Critical Essays on the Novels and Films.* Jefferson, NC: McFarland & Company, 2010, pp. 163–78.

3185. Heath, Elaine A. *The Gospel According to Twilight: Women, Sex, and God.* Louisville, KY: Westminster John Knox Press, 2011. 184 pp. tp.

3186. Heaton, Sarah. "Consuming Clothes and Dressing Desire in the Twilight Series." In Deborah Mutch. *The Modern Vampire and Human Identity.* Basingstoke, UK/New York: Palgrave Macmillan, 2013, pp. 76–92.

3187. _____. "Vampire Vogue and Female Fashion: Dressing Skin and Dressing-up in the Sookie Stackhouse and Twilight Series." In Barbara Brodman and James E. Doan, eds. *Images of the Modern Vampire: The Hip and the Atavistic.* Madison. NJ: Fairleigh Dickinson University Press, 2013, pp. 175–90.

3188. Herrera, Silvia E. *The New Woman Persona in 'Dracula' and the Twilight' Series: An Elliptical Struggle of Social Order.* Edinburg: University of Texas–Pan American, M.A. thesis, 2011.

3189. Hewitt, B. L. *The Twilight Effect.* N.p.: the author, 2011. 183 pp. tp.

3190. Hofstätter, Birgit. *How to Pull A Vampire's Tooth: Heterosexual Norm in Stephenie Meyer's "The Twilight Saga" and Its Pedagogical Implications.* Saarbrücken, Germany: Akademikerverlag, 2012. 92 pp. tp.

3191. Hopkins, Ellen. "To Twilight or Not to Twilight." In Ellen Hopkins with Leah Wilson, eds. *A New Dawn: Your Favorite Authors on Stephenie Meyer's Twilight Series.* Dallas TX: BenBella Books, 2008, pp. vii–x.

3192. Hopkins, Ellen, ed. *A New Dawn: Your Favorite Authors on Stephenie Meyer's Twilight Saga: Completely Unauthorized.* Dallas: Benbella Books, 2009. 186 pp. tp. Includes contributions by Susan Vaught, Megan McCafferty, Rosemary Clement-Moore, Anne Ursu, Linda Gerber, Ellen Steiber, K. A. Nuzum, Cara Lochwood, Cassandra Clare, James A. Owen, Robin Brande, Janette Rallison, and Rachel Caine.

3193. Horvath, Heidi. "Bella and the Beast: A Transformative Tale." In Seth Alcorn and Steven A. Nardi, eds. *Twisted Mirrors: Monstrous Reflections of Humanity.* Oxford: Inter-Disciplinary Press, 2012, pp. 171–80.

3194. Housel, Rebecca. "The 'Real' Danger: Fact vs. Fiction for the Girl Audience." In Rebecca Housel and J. Jeremy Wisnewski. *Twilight and Philosophy: Vampires, Vegetarians, and the Pursuit of Immortality.* New York: John Wiley & Sons, 2009, pp. 177–90.

3195. _____. "The Tao of Jacob." In Rebecca Housel and J. Jeremy Wisnewski. *Twilight and Philosophy: Vampires, Vegetarians, and the Pursuit of Immortality.* New York: John Wiley & Sons, 2009, pp. 237–46.

3196. Housel, Rebecca, and J. Jeremy Wisnewski, eds. *Twilight and Philosophy: Vampires, Vegetarians, and the Pursuit of Immortality.* New York: John Wiley & Sons, 2009. 259 pp. tp. Includes essays by George A. Dunn, Jean Kazez, Nicolas Michaud, Andrew Terjesen and Jenny Terjesen, Peter S. Fosl and Eli Fosl, Brendan Shea, Eric Silverman, Sara Worley, Naomi Zack, Bonnie Mann, Abigail E. Myers, Leah McClimans and J. Jeremy Wisnewski, Rebecca Housel, Jennifer L. McMahon, Dennis Knepp, Philip Puszcalowski, and Marc E. Shaw.

3197. Isaksson, Malin, and Maria Lindgren Leavenworth. "Gazing, Initiating, Desiring: Alternative Constrictions of Agency and Sex in Twifics." In Mariah Larsson and Ann Steiner, eds. *Interdisciplinary Approaches to Twilight Studies in Fiction, Media and a Contemporary Cultural Experience.* Lund, Sweden: Nordic Academic Press, 2011, pp. 127–76.

3198. Jeffers, Susan. "Bella and the Choice Made in Eden." In Amy M. Clarke and Marijane Osborn, eds. *The Twilight Mystique: Critical Essays on the Novels and Films.* Jefferson, NC: McFarland & Company, 2010, pp. 137–52.

3199. Jennings, Hope, and Christine Wilson. "Disciplinary Lessons: Myth, Female Desire, and the Monstrous Maternal in Stephenie Meyer's Twilight Series." In Barbara Brodman and James E. Doan, eds. *Images of the Modern Vampire: The Hip and the Atavistic.* Madison. NJ: Fairleigh Dickinson University Press, 2013, pp. 161–74.

3200. Jensen, Kristian. "Noble Werewolves or Native Shape-Shifters?" In Amy M. Clarke and Marijane Osborn, eds. *The Twilight Mystique: Critical Essays on the Novels and Films.* Jefferson, NC: McFarland & Company, 2010, pp. 92–106.

3201. Jepson, Eric W. "Saturday's Werewolf: The Doctrine That Makes Stephanie Meyer's Lycanthropes Golden Investigators." *Sunstone* 157 (December 2009): 21–25.

3202. Jones, Bethan. "Buffy vs. Bella: Gender, Relationships and the Modern Vampire." In Deborah Mutch. *The Modern Vampire and Human Identity.* Houndmills, Basingstoke, Hampshire, UK/New York: Palgrave Macmillan, 2013, pp. 37–54.

3203. Kane, Kathryn. "A Very Queer Refusal: The Chilling Effect of the Cullens' Heteronormative Embrace." In Melissa Click, Jennifer Stevens Aubrey, and Elizabeth Behm-Morawitz, eds. *Bitten by Twilight: Youth Culture, Media, & the Vampire Franchise.* New York: Peter Lang Publishing, 2010, pp. 103–18.

3204. Kärrholm, Sara. "Loving You Is Like Loving the Dead: Eroticization of the Dead Body." In Mariah Larsson and Ann Steiner, eds. *Interdisciplinary Approaches to Twilight Studies in Fiction, Media and a Contemporary Cultural Experience.* Lund, Sweden: Nordic Academic Press, 2011, pp. 47–80.

3205. Kazez, Jean. "Dying to Eat: The Vegetarian Ethics of Twilight." In Rebecca Housel and J. Jeremy Wisnewski. *Twilight and Philosophy: Vampires, Vegetarians, and the Pursuit of Immortality.* New York: John Wiley & Sons, 2009, pp. 25–37.

3206. Kellner, Douglas. "Teens and Vampires: From *Buffy the Vampire Slayer* to *Twilight's* Vampire Lovers." In Shirley R. Steinberg, ed. *Kinderculture: The Corporate Construction of Childhood.* 3nd ed. Boulder, CO: Westview Press, 2011, pp. 55–72.

3207. Kidd, Katherine. *Experience Twilight: The Ultimate Twilight Fan Travel Guide.* Illust. by Sabrina Kent. N.p.: Experience Twilight, 2009. 48 pp. tp.

3208. Kim, Joo Ok, and Giselle Liza Anatol. "Trailing in Jonathan Harker's Shadow: Bella as Modern-Day Ethnographer in Meyer's *Twilight* novels." In Giselle Liza Anatol. *Bringing Light to Twilight: Perspectives on a Pop Culture Phenomenon.* New York: Palgrave Macmillan, 2011, pp. 191–206.

3209. Kirk, Robert G. W., and Neil Pemberton. *Leech.* London: Reaktion Books, 2013. 208 pp. tp.

3210. Kisor, Yvette. "Narrative Layering and 'High-Culture' Romance." In Amy M. Clarke and Marijane Osborn, eds. *The Twilight Mystique: Critical Essays on the Novels and Films.* Jefferson, NC: McFarland & Company, 2010, pp. 35–59.

3211. Klonsky, E. David, and Alexis Black, eds. *The Psychology of Twilight.* Dallas, TX: Smart Pop/BenBella Books, 2011. 256 pp. tp. Includes contributions by Berg, Erica, Susan Carnell, David A. Frederick, Melissa Burkley, Jeremy Clyman, Robin Rosenberg, Tamara Greenburg, Catherine Glenn, Lisa Dinella and Gary Lewandowski, Mikhail Lyubanksy, Melissa Burkley, Peter Stromberg, and Pamela Rutledge.

3212. Knepp, Dennis. "Bella's Vampire Semiotics." In Rebecca Housel and J. Jeremy Wisnewski. *Twilight and Philosophy: Vampires, Vegetarians, and The Pursuit of Immortality.* New York: John Wiley & Sons, 2009, pp. 209–17.

3213. Kokkola, Lydia. "Virtuous Vampires and Voluptuous Vamps: Romance Conventions Reconsidered in Stephenie Meyer's 'Twilight' Series." *Children's Literature in Education* 42, 2 (June 1, 2011): 165–79.

3214. Kramer, Margaret. "The Wolf in the Woods: Fepresentations of "Little Red Riding Hood" in *Twilight.*" In Giselle Liza Anatol. *Bringing Light to Twilight: Perspectives on a Pop Culture Phenomenon.* New York: Palgrave Macmillan, 2011, pp. 15–30.

3215. Lamb, Tracie. "Twilighting." *Sunstone* 157 (December 2009): 38–39.

3216. Lampert-Weissig, Lisa. "A Latter Day Eve: Reading *Twilight* Through *Paradise Lost.*" *Journal of Religion and Popular Culture* 23, 3 (November 1, 2011): 330–341.

3217. _____. "Mormon Female Gothic: Blood, Birth, and the Twilight Saga." *Journal of Dracula Studies* 13 (2011): 55–81.

3218. Landers, Jessica Marie. *The Modern Vampire Phenomenon Paradox: Simultaneous Contradictions and Unlimited Limits.* New Brunswick: Rutgers The State University of New Jersey, M.A. thesis, 2011. 86 pp. Large format. Posted at: http://rucore.libraries.rutgers.edu/rutgers-lib/31111/.

3219. Larsson, Mariah. "I Know What I Saw: The Female Gaze and the Male Object of Desire." In Mariah Larsson and Ann Steiner, eds. *Interdisciplinary Approaches to Twilight Studies in Fiction, Media and a Contemporary Cultural Experience.* Lund, Sweden: Nordic Academic Press, 2011, pp. 63–80.

3220. _____, and Ann Steiner. "Introduction." In Mariah Larsson and Ann Steiner, eds. *Interdisciplinary Approaches to Twilight Studies in Fiction, Media and a Contemporary Cultural Experience.* Kund, Sweden: Nordic Academic Press, 2011. 305 pp. 9–23.

3221. _____, eds. *Interdisciplinary Approaches to Twilight Studies in Fiction, Media and a Contemporary Cultural Experience.* Lund, Sweden: Nordic Academic Press, 2011. 305 pp. tp. Includes contributions by Karin Nykvist, Sara Kärrholm, Mariah Larsson, Karin Lövgren, Janne Stigen Drangsholt, Yvonne Leffler, Malin Isaksson, Maria Lindgren Leavenworth, Annbritt Palo and Lena Manderstedt. Christina Olin-Scheller, Helle Kannik Haastrup, Ann Steiner, Maria Verena Siebert, Pamela Schultz Nybacka, Györgyi Vajdovich, Taliah Pollack, and Pierre Wiktorin.

3222. Leaf, Brian. *Defining Breaking Dawn: Vocabulary Workbook for Unlocking the SAT, ACT, GED, and SSAT.* Lincoln, NB: Cliffs Notes, 2010. 183 pp. tp.

3223. _____. *Defining Eclipse: Vocabulary Workbook for Unlocking the SAT, ACT, GED, and SSAT.* Lincoln, NB: Cliffs Notes, 2010. 183 pp. tp.

3224. _____. *Defining New Moon: Vocabulary Workbook for Unlocking the SAT, ACT, GED, and SSAT.* Lincoln, NB: Cliffs Notes, 2009. 183 pp. tp.

3225. _____. *Defining Twilight: Vocabulary Workbook for Unlocking the SAT, ACT, GED, and SSAT.* Lincoln, NB: Cliffs Notes, 2009, 183 pp. tp.

3226. Leffler, Yvonne. "Reading for Plot Character and Pleasure." In Mariah Larsson and Ann Steiner, eds. *Interdisciplinary Approaches to Twilight Studies in Fiction, Media and a Contemporary Cultural Experience.* Lund, Sweden: Nordic Academic Press, 2011, pp. 111–26.

3227. Leggatt, Judith, and Kristin Burnett. "Biting Bella: Treaty Negotiation, Quileute History, and Why "Team Jacob" Is Doomed to Lose." In Nancy R. Reagin. *Twilight and History.* New York: John Wiley & Sons, 2010, pp. 26–46.

3228. Leogrande, Cathy. "My Mother, Myself: Mother-Daughter Bonding via the Twilight Saga." In Melissa Click, Jennifer Stevens Aubrey, and Elizabeth Behm-Morawitz, eds. *Bitten by Twilight: Youth Culture, Media, & the Vampire Franchise.* New York: Peter Lang Publishing, 2010, pp. 155–71.

3229. Levine, Elana. "Afterword." In Melissa Click, Jennifer Stevens Aubrey, and Elizabeth Behm-Morawitz, eds. *Bitten by Twilight: Youth Culture, Media, & the Vampire Franchise.* New York: Peter Lang Publishing, 2010, pp. 281–86.

3230. Lexhagen, Maria, and Christine Lundberg. "The Popular Culture Tourism Service System: The Case of *Twilight.*" *Impresa Ambiente Management* 3, 2 (2010).

3231. Liedl, Janice. "Carlisle Cullen and the Witch Hunts of Puritan London." In Nancy R. Reagin. *Twilight and History.* New York: John Wiley & Sons, 2010, pp. 145–62.

3232. Lindgren Leavenworth, Maria. "Variations, Subversions, and Endless Love: fan fiction and the *Twilight* saga." In Giselle Liza Anatol. *Bringing Light to Twilight: Perspectives on a Pop Culture Phenomenon.* New York: Palgrave Macmillan, 2011, pp. 69–82.

3233. _____, and Malin Isaksson. *Fanged Fan Fiction: Variations on* Twilight, True Blood *and* The Vampire Diaries. Jefferson, NC: McFarland & Co., 2013. 228 pp. tp.

3234. Lochwood, Cara. "Destination: Forks, Washington." In Ellen Hopkins with Leah Wilson, eds. *A New Dawn: Your Favorite Authors on Stephenie Meyer's Twilight Series.* Dallas TX: BenBella Books, 2008, pp. 105–15.

3235. Loiacono, Grace, and Laura Loiacono. "Better Turned Than 'Cured'? Alice and the Asylum." In Nancy R. Reagin. *Twilight and History.* New York: John Wiley & Sons, 2010, pp. 127–44.

3236. Lovgrin, Karin. "Fear of Aging: Negotiating Age." In Mariah Larsson and Ann Steiner, eds. *Interdisciplinary Approaches to Twilight Studies in Fiction, Media and a Contemporary Cultural Experience.* Lund, Sweden: Nordic Academic Press, 2011, pp. 81–96.

3237. Lucas, Paul. "Alice, Bella, and Economics: Financial Security and Class Mobility in *Twilight.*" In Claudia Bucciferro, ed. *The Twilight Saga: Exploring the Global Phenomenon.* Lanham, MD: Scarecrow Press, 2013, pp. 169–90.

3238. Lundberg, Christine, and Maria Lexhagen. "Bitten by the *Twilight Saga*: From Pop Culture Consumer to Pop Culture Tourist." In Richard Sharpley and Philip Stone, eds. *The Contemporary Tourist Experience: Concepts and Consequences.* Abingdon, UK: Routledge, 2112, pp. 147–164.

3239. Lyubansky, Mihhail. "The Gestalt of Twilight." In E. David Klonsky and Alexis Black, eds. *The Psychology of Twilight.* Dallas, TX: Smart Pop/Benbella Books, 2011, pp. 93–114.

3240. Maloney-Mangold, Michelle. "Manifest Destiny Forever: The *Twilight* Saga, History, and a Vampire's American Dream." In Claudia Bucciferro, ed. *The Twilight Saga: Exploring the Global Phenomenon.* Lanham, MD: Scarecrow Press, 2013, pp. 33–46.

3241. Mann, Bonnie. "Vampire Love: The Second Sex Negotiates the Twenty-first Century." In Rebecca Housel and J. Jeremy Wisnewski. *Twilight and Philosophy: Vampires, Vegetarians, and the Pursuit of Immortality.* New York: John Wiley & Sons, 2009, pp. 131–45. Rpt. in William Irwin and David Kyle Johnson, eds. *Introducing Philosophy through Pop Culture: From Socrates to South Park, Hume to House.* Chichester, UK/Malden, MA: Wiley-Blackwell, 2010, pp. 228–37.

3242. Martens, Marianne. "Consumed by Twilight: The Commodification of Young Adult Literature." In Melissa Click, Jennifer Stevens Aubrey, and Elizabeth Behm-Morawitz, eds. *Bitten by Twilight: Youth Culture, Media, & the Vampire Franchise.* New York: Peter Lang Publishing, 2010, pp. 243–60.

3243. Maurer, Yael. "Transcending the Massacre: Vampire Mormons in the Twilight Series." In Deborah Mutch. *The Modern Vampire and Human Identity.* Basingstoke, UK/New York: Palgrave Macmillan, 2013, pp. 146–62.

3244. Mayfield, Sarah, Leigh Lunsford, and Rhonda Brock-Servais. "Romancing the Bite: Statistical Analysis of Young Adult Vampire Novels." *Incite: Journal of Undergraduate Scholarship* (2011). Posted at: http://blogs.longwood.edu/incite/2012/01/30/romancing-the-bite-statistical-analysis-of-young-adult-vampire-novels/.

3245. McCafferty, Megan. "The Good Girl Always Goes for the Bad Boy." In Ellen Hopkins with Leah Wilson, eds. *A New Dawn: Your Favorite Authors on Stephenie Meyer's Twilight Series*. Dallas TX: BenBella Books, 2008, pp. 15–24.

3246. McClimans, Leah, and J. Jeremy Wisnewski. "Undead Patriarchy and the Possibility of Love." In Rebecca Housel and J. Jeremy Wisnewski. *Twilight and Philosophy: Vampires, Vegetarians, and the Pursuit of Immortality*. New York: John Wiley & Sons, 2009, pp. 163–75.

3247. McConnell, Kathleen (aka Kathy Mac). "The First Three Quarters of Bella Swan's Quartet." In Hallie Tibbetts, ed. *Sirens: Collected Papers 2009–2011*. Sedalia, CO: Narrate Conferences, 2012, pp. 148–64.

3248. _____. "The Twilight Quartet: Romance, Porn, Pain and Complicity." In Kathleen McConnell. Pain, *Porn and Complicity: Women heroes from* Pygmalion *to* Twilight. Hamilton, ON: Wolsak and Wynn Pub., 2012, pp. 121–72.

3249. McElroy, James, and Emma Catherine McElroy. "Eco-Gothics for the Twenty-First Century." In Amy M. Clarke and Marijane Osborn, eds. *The* Twilight *Mystique: Critical Essays on the Novels and Films*. Jefferson, NC: McFarland & Company, 2010, pp. 80–91.

3250. McGeough, Danielle Dick. "Twilight and Transformations of Flesh: Reading the Body in Contemporary Youth Culture." In Melissa Click, Jennifer Stevens Aubrey, and Elizabeth Behm-Morawitz, eds. *Bitten by Twilight: Youth Culture, Media, & the Vampire Franchise*. New York: Peter Lang Publishing, 2010, pp. 87–102.

3251. McLennan, Rachel. "Bela's Promises: Adolescence and (Re)capitulation in Stephenie Meyer's Twilight Series." In Justin Edwards, Agnieszka Soltysik Monnet, eds. *The Gothic in Contemporary Literature and Popular Culture: Pop Goth*. New York: Routledge, 2012, pp. 84–95.

3252. McMahon, Jennifer L. "Twilight of an Idol: Our Fatal Attraction to Vampires." In Rebecca Housel and J. Jeremy Wisnewski. *Twilight and Philosophy: Vampires, Vegetarians, and the Pursuit of Immortality*. New York: John Wiley & Sons, 2009, pp. 193–208.

3253. Mendoza, Stephanie. "From Dawn to Twilight: The Byronic Vampire." *Theocrit: Journal of Undergraduate Theory and Criticism* 1, 1 (Spring 2009): 9–24.

3254. Mercer, Joyce. "Vampires, Desire, Girls and God: *Twilight* and the Spiritualities of Adolescent Girls." *Pastoral Psychology* 60, 2 (April 1, 2011): 263–278.

3255. Meyer, Stephenie. *The Twilight Saga: The Official Illustrated Guide*. Boston, MA: Little, Brown Books for Young Readers, 2013. 543 pp. hb dj.

3256. Meyers, Gina. *Bite at Twilight: Vampires, Forks, and Knives Cookbook*. Fresno, CA: Serendipity Press, 2009. 94 pp. pb. Large format. In addition to the several *Twilight*-themed cook books published as paperback books, Meyer has also compiled additional titles which were published as e-books.

3257. _____. *Love at First Bite in Color*. Fresno, CA: Serendipity Press, 2011. 65 pp. tp.

3258. _____. *Love at First Bite: The Unofficial Twilight Cookbook*. New York: iUniverse, 2010. 198 pp. tp.

3259. _____. *The Unofficial Twilight Trivia Book*. Fresno, CA: Serendipity Press, 2010. 94 pp. tp.

3260. Michaud, Nicolas. "Can a Vampire Be a Person?" In Rebecca Housel and J. Jeremy Wisnewski. *Twilight and Philosophy: Vampires, Vegetarians, and the Pursuit of Immortality*. New York: John Wiley & Sons, 2009, pp. 39–47.

3261. Miller, Catriona. "Twilight: Discourse Theory and Jung." In Christopher Hauke and Luke Hockley, eds. *Jung and Film II: The Return: Further Post-Jungian Takes on the Moving Image*. New York: Routledge, 2011, 185–205.

3262. Morey, Anne. *Genre, Reception, and Adaptation in the "Twilight" Series*. Ser.: Ashgate Studies in Childhood, 1700 to the Present. Farnham, Surrey, UK: Ashgate, 2012. 236 pp. hb.

3263. Murname, Ben. "'Exactly My Brand of Heroin': Contexts and the Creation of the Twilight Phenomenon." In Barbara Brodman and James E. Doan, eds. *Images of the Modern Vampire: The Hip and the Atavistic*. Madison. NJ: Fairleigh Dickinson University Press, 2013, pp. 147–60.

3264. Mutch, Deborah. 2011. "Coming Out of the Coffin: The Vampire and Transnationalism in the *Twilight* and Sookie Stackhouse Series." *Critical Survey* 23, 2 (2011): 75–90.

3265. Myers, Abigail E. "Edward Cullen and Bella Swan: Byronic and Feminist Heroes...or Not." In Rebecca Housel and J. Jeremy Wisnewski. *Twilight and Philosophy: Vampires, Vegetarians, and the Pursuit of Immortality*. New York: John Wiley & Sons, 2009, pp. 147–62.

3266. Natoli, Joseph. "The Twittering of Twilight." *The Journal of Popular Culture* 43, 4, (August 2010): 671–680.

3267. Nävsjö, Dana. *From Threat to Thrill: A Comparative Study of Bram Stoker's* Dracula *and Stephenie Meyer's* Twilight. Linköping, Sweden: Linköping University, Student thesis, 2013. 32 pp. Large format. Posted at: http://www.diva-portal.org/smash/get/diva2:615426/FULLTEXT01.pdf.

3268. Nayar, Pramod. "How to Domesticate a Vampire: Gender, Blood Relations and Sexuality in Stephenie Meyer's *Twilight*." *Nebula* 7, 3 (September 2010): 60–76. Posted at http://nobleworld.biz/images/Nayar3.pdf.

3269. Nelson, Elizabeth. "Monstrous Desire: Love, Death, and the Vampire Marriage." In Jonathan A. Allan and Elizabeth E. Nelson, eds. *Inversion of Power and Paradox: Studying Monstrosity.* Oxford, UK: Inter-Disciplinary Press, 2012, pp. 229–38.

3270. Nevárez, Lisa. "Renesmee as (R)omantic Child: A Glimpse into Bella and Edward's Fairy Tale Cottage." In Claudia Bucciferro, ed. *The Twilight Saga: Exploring the Global Phenomenon.* Lanham, MD: Scarecrow Press, 2013, pp. 109–22.

3271. Nicol, Rhonda. "'When you kiss me, I want to die': Arrested Feminism in *Buffy the Vampire Slayer* and the *Twilight* Series." In Giselle Liza Anatol. *Bringing Light to Twilight: Perspectives on a Pop Culture Phenomenon.* New York: Palgrave Macmillan, 2011, pp. 113–24.

3272. Nuzum, K. A. "As Time Goes By." In Ellen Hopkins with Leah Wilson, eds. *A New Dawn: Your Favorite Authors on Stephenie Meyer's Twilight Series.* Dallas TX: BenBella Books, 2008, pp. 91–103.

3273. Nybacka, Pamela Schultz. "Selling, Giving, Sharing: Stephenie Meyer's Logic of Authorship in Literary Market Success." In Mariah Larsson and Ann Steiner, eds. *Interdisciplinary Approaches to Twilight Studies in Fiction, Media and a Contemporary Cultural Experience.* Lund, Sweden: Nordic Academic Press, 2011, pp. 229–44.

3274. Nykvist, Karin. "The Body Project." In Mariah Larsson and Ann Steiner, eds. *Interdisciplinary Approaches to Twilight Studies in Fiction, Media and a Contemporary Cultural Experience.* Lund, Sweden: Nordic Academic Press, 2011, pp. 29–46.

3275. O'Claire, Alana. *Vampire Bites: Delicious Twilight-Inspired Recipes to Sink Your Teeth Into.* N.p.: Tebbo, 2010. 110 pp. tp.

3276. O'Grady, Stephanie. *Thirst for Fullness: An Application of John Paul II's Theology of the Body to the Twilight Saga.* Center Valley, PA: DeSales University, Senior Honors thesis, 2011. 58 pp. Large format.

3277. Olin-Scheller, Christina. "'I want Twilight information to grow in my head': Convergence Culture from a Fan Perspective." In Mariah Larsson and Ann Steiner, eds. *Interdisciplinary Approaches to Twilight Studies in Fiction, Media and a Contemporary Cultural Experience.* Lund, Sweden: Nordic Academic Press, 2011, pp. 159–74.

3278. Oliver, Ashley. *Queer Sex Gods or Patriarchs with Fangs? Gender and Sexuality in Modern Vampire Narratives* Buffy the Vampire Slayer, True Blood, *and* Twilight. Waterville, ME: Colby College, BA Honors thesis, 2012.

3279. Osborn, Marijane. "Luminous and Liminal: Why Edward Shines." In Amy M. Clarke and Marijane Osborn, eds. *The Twilight Mystique: Critical Essays on the Novels and Films.* Jefferson, NC: McFarland & Company, 2010, pp. 15–34.

3280. Owen, James A. "A Moon...A Girl... Romance!" In Ellen Hopkins with Leah Wilson, eds. *A New Dawn: Your Favorite Authors on Stephenie Meyer's Twilight Series.* Dallas TX: BenBella Books, 2008, pp. 129–39.

3281. Palo, Annbritt, and Lena Manderstedt. "Negotiating Norms of Gender and Sexuality Online." In Mariah Larsson and Ann Steiner, eds. *Interdisciplinary Approaches to Twilight Studies in Fiction, Media and a Contemporary Cultural Experience.* Lund, Sweden: Nordic Academic Press, 2011, pp. 143–58.

3282. Parke, Maggie, and Natalie Wilson, ed. *Theorizing Twilight: Critical Essays on What's at Stake in a Post-Vampire World.* Jefferson, NC: McFarland & Company, 2011. 246 pp. tp. Includes contributions by Tanya Erzen, Maggie Parke, Heather Anastasiu, Colette Murphy, Ananya Mukherjea, Ashley Benning, Angela Tenga, Sarah Wakefield, Jessica Groper, Hila Shachar, Melissa Miller, Ashley Donnelly, Natalie Wilson, Anne Torkelson, and Lindsey Issow Averill.

3283. Parmiter, Tara K. "Green is the New Black: Ecophobia and the Gothic Landscape in the *Twilight* Series." In Giselle Liza Anatol. *Bringing Light to Twilight: Perspectives on a Pop Culture Phenomenon.* New York: Palgrave Macmillan, 2011, pp. 221–34.

3284. Parrish, Juli. "Back to the Woods: Narrative Revisions in New Moon Fan Fiction at Twilighted." In Melissa Click, Jennifer Stevens Aubrey, and Elizabeth Behm-Morawitz, eds. *Bitten by Twi-*

light: Youth Culture, Media, & the Vampire Franchise. New York: Peter Lang Publishing, 2010, pp. 173–88.

3285. Pearlman, Julia Rose. *Happily (For)ever After: Constructing Conservative Youth Ideology in the Twilight Series.* Middleton, CT: Wesleyan University, Honors Theses, 2010. 99 pp. Large format. Posted at: http://wesscholar.wesleyan.edu/etd_hon_theses/584.

3286. Pearson, Jennifer. *Representations of Native American Characters in Stephenie Meyer's 'Twilight' Saga.* Greenville, NC: East Carolina University, M.A. thesis, 2011. 83 pp. Large format. Posted at: http://thescholarship.ecu.edu/bitstream/handle/10342/3539/Pearson_ecu_0600M_10416.pdf?sequence=1.

3287. Platt, Carrie Anne. "Cullen Family Values: Gender and Sexual Politics in the Twilight Series." In Melissa Click, Jennifer Stevens Aubrey, and Elizabeth Behm-Morawitz, eds. *Bitten by Twilight: Youth Culture, Media, & the Vampire Franchise.* New York: Peter Lang Publishing, 2010, pp. 71–86.

3288. Pollack, Taliah. "Damnation or Salvation? Vampire Ethics, Edward Cullen, and the Byronic Hero." In Mariah Larsson and Ann Steiner, eds. *Interdisciplinary Approaches to Twilight Studies in Fiction, Media and a Contemporary Cultural Experience.* Lund, Sweden: Nordic Academic Press, 2011, pp. 263–78.

3289. Priest, Hannah. "'Hell! was I becoming a vampyre slut?': Sex, Sexuality and Morality in Young Adult Vampire Fiction." In Deborah Mutch. *The Modern Vampire and Human Identity.* Basingstoke, UK/New York: Palgrave Macmillan, 2013, pp. 55–75.

3290. ____. "Pack versus Coven: Guardianship of Tribal Memory in Vampire versus Werewolf Narratives." In Simon Bacon, and Katarzyna Bronk, eds. *Undead Memory: Vampires and Human Memory in Popular Culture.* Bern, Switz.: Peter Lang International Academic Publishers, 2013, pp. 213–38.

3291. Pulliam, June. "Gothic, Romantic, or Just Sadomasochistic? Gender and Manipulation in Stephenie Meyer's Twilight Saga." In Daniel Olson. *21st-Century Gothic: Great Gothic Novels since 2000.* Lanham, MD: Scarecrow Press, 2010, pp. 573–83.

3292. Puszczalowski, Philip. "Space, Time, and Vampire Ontology." In Rebecca Housel and J. Jeremy Wisnewski. *Twilight and Philosophy: Vam-*pires, Vegetarians, and the Pursuit of Immortality.* New York: John Wiley & Sons, 2009, pp. 219–26.

3293. Rallison, Janette. "To Bite, or Not to Bite; That Is the Question." In Ellen Hopkins with Leah Wilson, eds. *A New Dawn: Your Favorite Authors on Stephenie Meyer's Twilight Series.* Dallas TX: BenBella Books, 2008, pp. 155–67.

3294. Reagin, Nancy R. "Introduction: Frozen in Time." In Nancy R. Reagin. *Twilight and History.* New York: John Wiley & Sons, 2010, pp. 1–3.

3295. ____, ed. *Twilight & History.* New York: John Wiley & Sons, 2010.274 pp. tp. Includes essays by Nancy R. Reagin, Kate Cochran, Judith Leggatt and Kristin Burnett, Sara Buttsworth, Catherine Coker, Elizabeth Baird Hardy, Grace Loiacono and Laura Loiacono, Janice Liedl, Andrea Robertson Cremer, Kyra Glass von der Osten, Birgit Wiedl, Eveline Brugger, and Kat Burkhart.

3296. Reed, Clara. "Vampires and Gentiles: Jews, Mormons and Embracing the Other." In Deborah Mutch. *The Modern Vampire and Human Identity.* Basingstoke, UK/New York: Palgrave Macmillan, 2013, pp. 128–45.

3297. Reklis, Kathryn. "The Lure of Mormon Romance." *The Christian Century* 129, 23 (November 14, 2012). Posted at http://www.questia.com/library/1G1–312402071/the-lure-of-mormon-romance.

3298. Riess, Jana. "Book of Mormon Stories That Steph Meyer Tells to Me: LDS Themes in the Twilight Saga and *The Host.*" *BYU Studies* 48, 3 (2009): 141–47.

3299. Roback, Diane. "Stephenie Meyer Is the New Queen in Children's Succeeding Rowling." *Publishers Weekly* 256, 12 (March 23, 2009): 30.

3300. Roberts, Dave. *The Twilight Gospel: The Spiritual Roots of the Stephenie Meyer Vampire Saga.* Oxford, UK: Monarch Books, 2009. 160 pp. tp.

3301. Rocha, Lauren. "Bite Me: *Twilight* Stakes Feminism." *Undergraduate Review* 7 (2011): 148–153.

3302. Rosenberg, Robin. "Vegetarian Vamps." In E. David Klonsky and Alexis Black, eds. *The Psychology of Twilight.* Dallas, TX: Smart Pop/Benbella Books, 2011, pp. 115–32.

3303. Rutledge, Pamela. "The Twilight Convergence." In E. David Klonsky and Alexis Black, eds. *The Psychology of Twilight.* Dallas, TX: Smart Pop/Benbella Books, 2011, pp. 233–54.

3304. Sanders, Autumn H. M. *Teaching to the Canon or the Students: The Use of Popular Literature in ELA Classrooms.* Brockport, NY: The College of Brockport, M.A. thesis, 2012. 114 pp. Large format. Posted at: http://digitalcommons.brockport.edu/cgi/viewcontent.cgi?article=1024&context=eng_theses.

3305. Schau, Hope Jensen, and Margo Buchanan-Oliver. "The Creation of Inspired Lives: Female Fan Engagement with the Twilight Saga." In Cele C. Otnes and Linda Tuncay Zayer, eds. *Gender, Culture, and Consumer Behavior.* New York: Routledge, 2012, pp. 33–60.

3306. Schuck, Emily. "Re-masculating the Vampire: Conceptions of Sexuality and the Undead from Rossetti's Proserpine to Meyer's Cullen," *LUX: A Journal of Transdisciplinary Writing and Research from Claremont Graduate University* 2, 1 (2013): 1–7. Posted at: http://scholarship.claremont.edu/lux/vol2/iss1/26.

3307. Schumann, Nancy. "The Vamp Next Door: Present Day Vampires." In Nancy Schumann. *Take a Bite. Female Vampires in Anglo-American Literature and Folklore.* London: Callio Press Limited, n.d. [2011?], pp. 91–110.

3308. _____. "Women with Bite: Tracing Vampire Women from Lilith to Twilight." In Barbara Brodman and James E. Doan, eds. *The Universal Vampire: Origins and Evolution of a Legend.* Madison, NJ: Fairleigh Dickinson University Press, 2013, pp. 109–20.

3309. Schwartzman, Sarah. "Is Twilight Mormon?" In Amy M. Clarke and Marijane Osborn, eds. *The Twilight Mystique: Critical Essays on the Novels and Films.* Jefferson, NC: McFarland & Company, 2010, pp. 121–36.

3310. Shapiro, Marc. *Stephenie Meyer: The Unauthorized Biography of the Creator of the Twilight Saga.* New York: St. Martin's Griffin, 2009. 211 pp. tp.

3311. Shaw, Marc E. "For the Strength of Bella? Meyer, Vampires, and Mormonism." In Rebecca Housel and J. Jeremy Wisnewski. *Twilight and Philosophy: Vampires, Vegetarians, and The Pursuit of Immortality.* New York: John Wiley & Sons, 2009, pp. 227–36.

3312. Shea, Brendan. "To Bite or Not to Bite: Twilight, Immortality, and the Meaning of Life." In Rebecca Housel and J. Jeremy Wisnewski.

Twilight and Philosophy: Vampires, Vegetarians, and the Pursuit of Immortality. New York: John Wiley & Sons, 2009, pp. 79–92.

3313. Sheffield, Jessica, and Elyse Merlo. "Biting Back: Twilight Anti-Fandom and the Rhetoric of Superiority." In Melissa Click, Jennifer Stevens Aubrey, and Elizabeth Behm-Morawitz, eds. *Bitten by Twilight: Youth Culture, Media, & the Vampire Franchise.* New York: Peter Lang Publishing, 2010, pp. 207–22.

3314. Shipley, Marisa. *Dressing the Part: How Twilight Fans Self-Identify through Dress at an Official Twilight Convention.* San Antonio, TX: Trinity University, honors thesis, 2010. 51 pp. Large format. Posted at: http://digitalcommons.trinity.edu/comm_honors/3.

3315. Siebert, Maria Verena. "Kidult Readers: The Cross-Generational Appeal of *Harry Potter* and *Twilight.*" In Mariah Larsson and Ann Steiner, eds. *Interdisciplinary Approaches to Twilight Studies in Fiction, Media and a Contemporary Cultural Experience.* Lund, Sweden: Nordic Academic Press, 2011, pp. 213–226.

3316. Silverman, Eric. "Mind Reading and Morality: The Moral Hazards of Being Edward." In Rebecca Housel and J. Jeremy Wisnewski. *Twilight and Philosophy: Vampires, Vegetarians, and the Pursuit of Immortality.* New York: John Wiley & Sons, 2009, pp. 93–105.

3317. Smith, Cindy. "*Twilight* and the Half-Dead Infant Monster." In Elizabeth Nelson with Jillian Burcar & Hannah Priest, eds. *Creating Humanity, Discovering Monstrosity.* Oxford: Inter-Disciplinary Press, 2010, pp. 261–70.

3318. Smyth, Karen Elizabeth. "'*What's a Nice Mormon Girl Like You Doing Writing About Vampires?': Stephenie Meyer's Twilight Saga and the Church of Jesus Christ of Latter-day Saints?* Williamsburg, VA: College of William and Mary, M.A. thesis, 2011. 59 pp, Large format.

3319. Snider, Zoë. "Vampires, Werewolves, and Oppression: Twilight and Female Gender Stereotypes." *Young Scholars in Writing: Undergraduate Research in Writing and Rhetoric* 9 (2012): 128–36.

3320. Sommers, Joseph Michael, and Amy L. Hume. "The Other Edward: *Twilight*'s Queer Construction of the Vampire as an Idealized Teenage Boyfriend." In Giselle Liza Anatol. *Bringing Light to Twilight: Perspectives on a Pop Culture Phenomenon.* New York: Palgrave Macmillan, 2011, pp. 153–66.

3321. Somogyi, Emma, and Mark David Ryan. "Mainstream Monsters: The Otherness of Humans in *Twilight*, *The Vampire Diaries*, and *True Blood*." In Claudia Bucciferro, ed. *The Twilight Saga: Exploring the Global Phenomenon.* Lanham, MD: Scarecrow Press, 2013, pp. 197–212.

3322. Spencer, Liv. *Love Bites: The Unofficial Saga of Twilight.* Toronto: ecw Press, 2010. 203 pp. tp.

3323. Spooner, Catherine. "'Gothic Charm School; or, How Vampires Learned to Sparkle.'" In Sam George and Bill Hughes, eds. *Open Graves, Open Minds: Representations of Vampires and the Undead from the Enlightenment to the Present Day.* Manchester: Manchester University Press, 2013, pp. 146–64.

3324. Stasiewicz-Bieńkowska, Agnieszka. "Monstrosising Infertility: Supernatural Barren Females in the *Twilight* Series by Stephenie Meyer." In Agnieszka Stasiewicz-Bieńkowska and Karen Graham, eds. *Monstrous Manifestations: Reality and Imaginings of the Monster.* Oxford: Inter-Disciplinary Press, 2013, pp. 151–60.

3325. Steiber, Ellen. "Tall, Dark, and... Thirsty?" In Ellen Hopkins with Leah Wilson, eds. *A New Dawn: Your Favorite Authors on Stephenie Meyer's Twilight Series.* Dallas TX: BenBella Books, 2008, pp. 69–89.

3326. Steiner, Ann. "Gendered Readings: Bella's Books and Literary Consumer Culture." In Mariah Larsson and Ann Steiner, eds. *Interdisciplinary Approaches to Twilight Studies in Fiction, Media and a Contemporary Cultural Experience.* Lund, Sweden: Nordic Academic Press, 2011, pp. 195–212.

3327. Stevens, Kirsten. "Meet the Cullens: Family, Romance, and Female Agency in *Buffy the Vampire Slayer* and *Twilight*." *Slayage: The Journal of the Whedon Studies Association* 8, 1 [29] (Spring 2010). Posted at whedonstudies.tv.

3328. Stiolar, Detie. "The Politics of Reproduction in Stephenie Meyer's Twilight Saga." In Barbara Brodman and James E. Doan, eds. *Images of the Modern Vampire: The Hip and the Atavistic.* Madison. NJ: Fairleigh Dickinson University Press, 2013, pp. 191–208.

3329. Stromberg, Peter. "The Emotional Pleasures of Reading Twilight." In E. David Klonsky and Alexis Black, eds. *The Psychology of Twilight.* Dallas, TX: Smart Pop/Benbella Books, 2011, pp. 215–32.

3330. Sturhan, Nicole L. *Twilight Travels 2011. Book Locations.* Tacoma. WA: Nicole Sturhan & Lora Fox, 2013. 39 pp. tp.

3331. _____. *Twilight Travels 2011. Movie Locations.* Tacoma. WA: Nicole Sturhan & Lora Fox, 2013. 56 pp. tp.

3332. Summers, Sarah. "'Twilight is so anti-feminist that I want to cry': Twilight Fans Finding and Defining Feminism on the World Wide Web." *Computers and Composition* 27 (2010): 315–323.

3333. Sutton, Travis, and Harry M. Benshoff. "'Forever family' values: Twilight and the Modern Mormon Vampire." In Aviva Briefel and Sam J. Miller, eds. *Horror After 9/11: World of Fear, Cinema of Terror.* Austin: University of Texas Press, 2011, pp. 200–219.

3334. Sykley, Julie-Anne. *The Twilight Mind: Twilight Saga Psychology Skills.* John Hunt Publishing, 2012. 228 pp. tp.

3335. Thurber, Ann. *Bite Me: Desire and the Female Spectator in* Twilight, *The* Vampire Diaries, *and* True Blood. Atlanta, GA: Emory University, M.A. thesis, 2011. 100 pp. Large format.

3336. Toscano, Margaret M. "Mormon Morality and Immortality in Stephenie Meyer's Twilight Series." In Melissa Click, Jennifer Stevens Aubrey, and Elizabeth Behm-Morawitz, eds. *Bitten by Twilight: Youth Culture, Media, & the Vampire Franchise.* New York: Peter Lang Publishing, 2010, pp. 21–36.

3337. Ursu, Anne. "My Boyfriend Sparkles." In Ellen Hopkins with Leah Wilson, eds. *A New Dawn: Your Favorite Authors on Stephenie Meyer's Twilight Series.* Dallas TX: BenBella Books, 2008, pp. 39–53.

3338. Vajdovich, Györgyi. "'I'm with the vampires, of course': Twilight Novels and Films as Vampire Stories." In Mariah Larsson and Ann Steiner, eds. *Interdisciplinary Approaches to Twilight Studies in Fiction, Media and a Contemporary Cultural Experience.* Lund, Sweden: Nordic Academic Press, 2011, pp. 247–62.

3339. Vaught, Susan. "A Very Dangerous Boy." In Ellen Hopkins with Leah Wilson, eds. *A New Dawn: Your Favorite Authors on Stephenie Meyer's Twilight Series.* Dallas TX: BenBella Books, 2008, pp. 1–13.

3340. Vaz, Mark Cotta. *Twilight: The Complete Illustrated Movie Companion.* New York, Boston: Little, Brown and Company, 2008. 142 pp. pb. Large format.

3341. _____. *The Twilight Saga Breaking Dawn Part 1: The Official Illustrated Movie Companion*. New York, Boston: Little, Brown and Company, 2011. 142 pp. pb. Large format.

3342. _____. *The Twilight Saga: Eclipse: The Official Illustrated Movie Companion*. Boston: Little Brown and Company, 2010. 142 pp. pb. large format.

3343. _____. *The Twilight Saga: Moon Light: The Official Illustrated Movie Companion*. New York, Boston: Little, Brown and Company, 2009. 142 pp. pb. Large format.

3344. Veldman-Genz, Carole. "Serial Experiments in Popular Culture: The Resignification of Gothic Symbology in Anita Blake Vampire Hunter and the *Twilight* Series." In Giselle Liza Anatol. *Bringing Light to Twilight: Perspectives on a Pop Culture Phenomenon*. New York: Palgrave Macmillan, 2011, pp. 43–58.

3345. Vicary, Amamda M., and Jennifer L. Rosner. "Vampires and Werewolves Aren't So Different After All." In E. David Klonsky and Alexis Black, eds. *The Psychology of Twilight*. Dallas, TX: Smart Pop/Benbella Books, 2011, pp. 75–92.

3346. Vogel, Kathrin. *Literary Tradition and Symbolism of the Female Vampire and Its Adaptation in Stephenie Meyer's Twilight Saga*. München, Germany: GRIN Verlag, 2013. 60 pp. pb.

3347. von der Osten, Kyra Glass. "Like Other American Families, Only Not: The Cullens and the 'Ideal' Family in American History." In Nancy R. Reagin. *Twilight and History*. New York: John Wiley & Sons, 2010, pp. 182–203.

3348. Wallis, Meredith. "True Blood Waits: The Romance of Law And Literature." In Giselle Liza Anatol. *Bringing Light to Twilight: Perspectives on a Pop Culture Phenomenon*. New York: Palgrave Macmillan, 2011, pp. 83–96.

3349. Wasson, Sara, and Sarah Artt. "The Twilight Saga and the Pleasures of Spectatorship: The Broken Body and the Shining Body." In Sam George and Bill Hughes, eds. *Open Graves, Open Minds: Representations of Vampires and the Undead from the Enlightenment to the Present Day*. Manchester: Manchester University Press, 2013, pp. 181–91.

3350. Weckerle, Lisa. "Individuality and Collectivity in *The Hunger Games, Harry Potter*, and *Twilight*." In Claudia Bucciferro, ed. *The Twilight Saga: Exploring the Global Phenomenon*. Lanham, MD: Scarecrow Press, 2013, pp. 213–26.

3351. Weisner, Karen S. "Case Study 1: Young Adult/Children's." In Karen S. Weisner. *Writing the Fiction Series: The Complete Guide for Novels and Novellas*. Blue Ash, OH: Writers Digest, 2013, pp. 225–28.

3352. Whitton, Merinne. "'One is not born a vampire, but becomes one': Motherhood and Masochism in *Twilight*." In Giselle Liza Anatol. *Bringing Light to Twilight: Perspectives on a Pop Culture Phenomenon*. New York: Palgrave Macmillan, 2011, pp. 125–38.

3353. Wiedl, Birgit. "The Sort of People Who Hired Michelangelo as Their Decorator: The Volturi as Renaissance Rulers." In Nancy R. Reagin. *Twilight and History*. New York: John Wiley & Sons, 2010, pp. 207–26.

3354. Wiktorin, Pierre. "The Vampire as a Religious Phenomenon." In Mariah Larsson and Ann Steiner, eds. *Interdisciplinary Approaches to Twilight Studies in Fiction, Media and a Contemporary Cultural Experience*. Lund, Sweden: Nordic Academic Press, 2011, pp. 279–96.

3355. Williams, Jennifer H. "A Vampire Heaven: The Economics of Salvation in *Dracula* and *Twilight*." In Sam George and Bill Hughes, eds. *Open Graves, Open Minds: Representations of Vampires and the Undead from the Enlightenment to the Present Day*. Manchester: Manchester University Press, 2013, pp. 165–80.

3356. Willis-Chun, Cynthia. "Touring the Twilight Zone: Cultural Tourism and Commodification on the Olympic Peninsula." In Melissa Click, Jennifer Stevens Aubrey, Elizabeth Behm-Morawitz, eds. *Bitten by Twilight: Youth Culture, Media, & the Vampire Franchise*. New York: Peter Lang Publishing, 2010, pp. 261–79.

3357. Willms, Nicole. "'Doesn't He Own a Shirt?': Rivalry and Masculine Embodiment in *Twilight*." In Claudia Bucciferro, ed. *The Twilight Saga: Exploring the Global Phenomenon*. Lanham, MD: Scarecrow Press, 2013, pp. 139–52.

3358. Wilson, Natalie. "Civilized Vampires versus Savage Werewolves: Race and Ethnicity in the Twilight Series." In Melissa Click, Jennifer Stevens Aubrey, and Elizabeth Behm-Morawitz, eds. *Bitten by Twilight: Youth Culture, Media, & the Vampire Franchise*. New York: Peter Lang Publishing, 2010, pp. 55–70.

3359. Wilson, Natalie. *Seduced by* Twilight: *The Allure and Contradictory Messages of the Popular Saga*. Jefferson, NC: McFarland & Company, 2011. 242 pp. tp.

3360. Wolberg, Steve. *The Trouble with Twilight: Why Today's Vampire Craze Is Hazardous to Your Health.* Shippensburg, PA: Destiny Image Publishers, 2010. 189 pp. pb.

3361. Wolf, Keri. "Bella and Boundaries, Crossed and Redeployed." In Amy M. Clarke and Marijane Osborn, eds. *The Twilight* Mystique: *Critical Essays on the Novels and Films.* Jefferson, NC: McFarland & Company, 2010, pp. 152–62.

3362. Worley, Sara. "Love and Authority Among Wolves." In Rebecca Housel and J. Jeremy Wisnewski. *Twilight and Philosophy: Vampires, Vegetarians, and the Pursuit of Immortality.* New York: John Wiley & Sons, 2009, pp. 107–18.

3363. Zack, Naomi. "Bella Swan and Sarah Palin: All the Old Myths Are Not True." In Rebecca Housel and J. Jeremy Wisnewski. *Twilight and Philosophy: Vampires, Vegetarians, and the Pursuit of Immortality.* New York: John Wiley & Sons, 2009, pp. 121–29.

Cinematic Vampires from Asia

While the majority of concern with the modern vampire has been generated simultaneously with the permeation of images of the Eastern European vampire throughout the West and more recently into the rest of the world, Asia had its own vampires and vampire-like mythical beings such as the Pontianak, a lamia-like figure found in various Southeast Asian countries. After World War II, however, the Asian movie industry emerged in force, and Malaysia, Hong Kong, and Japan began to produce vampire movies in the 1950s. They were later joined by Korea and Indonesia.

Japan has emerged as possibly the Asian country in which the vampire has proved most popular. Along with the many vampire movies that have originated there, Japan has been the source of a rich comic book culture in which the vampire has been a significant theme. Growing from the graphic arts world (termed manga in Japan), vampires have moved to television, especially in the form of cartoons (termed anime).

In this section, books and articles related to all aspects of Asian vampire folklore, movies, television, and graphic arts have been assembled.

3364. Amano, Yoshitaka. *The Art of Vampire Hunter D.* Milwaukie, OR: DH Press, 2007. 200 pp. pb.

3365. _____. *The Art of Vampire Hunter D: Bloodlust.* Screenplay by Yoshiaki Kawajiri. San Diego: IDW Publishing, July 2006. unpaged. hb.

3366. _____. *Coffin: The Art of Vampire Hunter D.* Milwaukie, OR: DH Press, 2007. 200 pp. pb. Slipcase.

3367. _____. *Worlds of Amano.* Text by Jean Wacquet. Trans. by Samantha Robertson. Milwaukie, OR: DH Press, 2007. 156 pp. hb. Large format.

3368. _____. *Yoshitaka Amano.* Japan, 1996. 104 pp. tp. Text in Japanese. slipcase.

3369. Baker, Neal. "The US–Japan Security Alliance and *Blood: The Last Vampire*." *Journal of the Fantastic in the Arts* 13, 2 (2002): 143–52.

3370. Bucklin, R. P. "My Soul Is Slashed." *Asian Trash Video* 1, 5 (1994): 38–40.

3371. Bush, Laurence C. *Asian Horror Encyclopedia: Asian Horror Culture in Literature, Manga, & Folklore.* San Jose, CA: Writers Club Press, 2001. 227 pp. tp.

3372. Chan, Tommy. "Vampire." In Pugalenthi Sr, ed. *Black Powers 3.* Singapore: Asuras, 1995, pp. 108–118.

3373. Danilou, Alain. "Night Wanderers (raksasa)." In Alain Danilou. *Hindu Polytheism.* New York: Pantheon Books, 1964, pp. 309–310.

3374. de Groot, J. J. M. *The Religious System of China.* Leyden: E. J. Brill, 1892–1910. 928 pp. Posted at: http://www.archive.org/stream/religious system00groogoog/religioussystem00groogoog_ djvu.txt. Excerpt in: McNally, Raymond T. *A*

Clutch of Vampires. New York: Bell Publishing Company, 1974, pp. 33–34.

3375. de Visser, M. W. *The Dragon in China and Japan*. Amsterdam: J. Müller, 1913. 242 pp. Rpt.: Weisbaden, Germany: Dr. Martin Sändig oHG, 1969. Posted at: http://www.archive.org/stream/cu31924021444728/cu31924021444728_djvu.txt.

3376. De Wit, Augusta. *Java Facts and Fancies*. The Hague, W.P. van Stockum, 1900. 266 pp. Rpt.: Singapore: Oxford University Press, 1984. 321 pp.

3377. Dorson, Richard M. *Folk Legends of Japan*. Rutland, VT: Charles E. Tuttle Company, 1962. 256 pp.

3378. Galbraith, Stuart W. *Japanese Science Fiction, Fantasy, and Horror Films: A Critical Analysis of 103 Features Released in the United States, 1950–1992*. Jefferson, C: McFarland & Company, 1994. 424 pp. tp. Contains entries on *The Vampire Doll* (1970) (pp. 194–96); *Lake of Dracula* (1971) (pp. 204–07); and *Evils of Dracula* (1975) (pp. 225–27).

3379. Gelder, Ken. "Citational Vampires: Transnational Techniques of Circulation in *Irma Vep, Blood: The Last Vampire* and *Thirst*." In Tabish. Khair and Johan Hoglund, eds. *Transnational and Postcolonial Vampires: Dark Blood*. Basingstoke, UK: Palgrave Macmillan, 2012, pp. 81–104.

3380. Genc, Burcu. "The Vampire from an Evolutionary Perspective in Japanese Animation: Blood+." In Barbara Brodman and James E. Doan, eds. *Images of the Modern Vampire: The Hip and the Atavistic*. Madison. NJ: Fairleigh Dickinson, 2013, pp. 209–18.

3381. Ghosh, Tapan K. *Bollywood Baddies: Villains, Vamps and Henchmen in Hindi Cinema*. Thousand Oaks, CA: SAGE Publications, 2013. 232 pp. tp.

3382. Goldin, P. R. "The Cultural and Religious Background of Sexual Vampirism in Ancient China." *Theology and Sexuality* 12, 3 (2006): 285–307.

3383. Hammond, Stefan, and Mike Wilkins. *Sex and Zen & a Bullet in the Head: The Essential Guide to Hong Kong's Mind-Bending Films*. New York: Fireside, 1996. 272 pp. tp.

3384. Hart, Christopher. *Manga for the Beginner Midnight Monsters: How to Draw Zombies, Vampires, and Other Delightfully Devious Charac-*

ters of Japanese Comics. New York: Watson-Guptill, 2013. 176 pp. tp.

3385. Hino, Matsuri. *The Art of Vampire Knight: Matsuri Hino Illustrations*. San Francisco, CA: VIZ Media LLC, 2011. 96 pp. hb. Large format.

3386. Hudson, Dale. "Modernity as Crisis: Goeng Si and Vampires in Hong Kong Cinema." In John Edgar Browning and Caroline Joan Picart, eds. *Dracula, Vampires, and Other Undead Forms*. Lanham, MD: The Scarecrow Press, 2009, pp. 203–34.

3387. Kawajiri, Yoshiaki. *The Art of Vampire Hunter D Bloodlust*. Vol. 2. San Diego, CA: Idea & Design Works, 2007. 48 pp. hb.

3388. Lam, Stephanie. "Hop on Pop: Jiangshi Films in a Transnational Context." *CineAction* 78 (2009): 46–51.

3389. Lee, Russell. *Russell Lee's Celebrity Ghost Stories. Vol. 4, True Singapore Ghost Stories*. Singaore: Native Cokmunications, 1993. 150 pp. pb.

3390. Lee, Russell, & a Team of Ghost Writers. *The Almost Complete Collection of True Singapore Ghost Stories 5*. Singapore: Angsana Books, 1995. 170 pp. pb. See especially Part II, "Russell Lee Investigates Vampires." (pp. 53–58).

3391. Lim, Danny. *The Malaysian Book of the Undead*. Petaling Jaya, Malaysia: Matahari Books, 2008. 115 pp. tp.

3392. Logan, Bey. *Hong Kong Action Cinema*. Woodstock, NY: Overlook Press, 1995. 191 pp. pb. Large format.

3393. Mackenzie, Donald A. *Myths of China and Japan*. London: Gresham Publishing Company, 1923. 404 pp. hb.

3394. Maizurah. "My Mother Saw a Pontianak." In Russell Lee. *Celebrity Ghost Stories*. Singapore: Native Communications, 1993, pp. 82–85.

3395. Moore, Khadijah. "The Vampire in the Mango Tree." In Khadijah Moore. *Haunting Stories*. Singapore: Planet Press, 1995, pp. 45–50.

3396. Moreland, Sean, and Summer Pervez. "Becoming-Death: The Lollywood Gothic of Khwaja Sarfraz's *Zinda Laash* (Dracula in Pakistan [US title], 1967). In John Edgar Browning and Caroline Joan Picart, eds. *Dracula, Vampires, and Other Undead Forms*. Lanham, MD: The Scarecrow Press, 2009, pp. 187–202.

3397. Nambai. *Pontianak with Survival Guide.* Kuala Lumpur, Malaysia: Al-Ameen Serve Holdings, 2007. 186 pp. pb.

3398. Ng, Hock-Soon. "'Death and the Maiden': The Pontianak as Excess in Malay Popular Culture." In John Edgar Browning and Caroline Joan Picart, eds. *Dracula, Vampires, and Other Undead Forms.* Lanham, MD: The Scarecrow Press, 2009, pp. 167–86.

3399. O'Brien, Daniel. *Spooky Encounters: A Gwailo's Guide to Hong Kong Horror.* Manchester, UK: Headpress/Critical Vision, 2003. 191 pp. tp.

3400. Pereira, Mervyn. "Vampires and Witches Keep Malaysia Lively." *Pioneer Press* (IL) (February 19, 1967).

3401. Pugalenthi, ed. *Pontianak.* Singapore: Asuras/ VJ Times International, 1996. 142 pp.

3402. _____. *Pontianak—Nightmares.* Singapore: Asuras/ VJ Times International, 2000. 134 pp.

3403. _____. *School Nightmares: True Ghost Stories of Schools.* Singapore: Asuras/ VJ Times International, 1996. 135 pp.

3404. _____. *Vampires—Nightmares.* Singapore: Asuras/VJ Times International, 2000. 124 pp.

3405. Richards, Andy. *Asian Horror.* Harpenden, Herts., UK: Kamera Books, 2010. 159 pp. pb.

3406. Schlegel, Nicholas. "Identity Crisis: Imperialist Vampires in Japan? In John Edgar Browning and Caroline Joan Picart, eds. *Dracula, Vampires, and Other Undead Forms.* Lanham, MD: The Scarecrow Press, 2009, pp. 261–78.

3407. See, Ng Pei. "Vampire Scare," in Jopzita Omar, ed. *Shaitan.* Singapore: Asuras, 1996, pp. 53–63.

3408. Shimokusu, Masaya." A Cultural Dynasty of Beautiful Vampires: Japan's Acceptance, Modifications, and Adaptations of Vampires." In Barbara Brodman and James E. Doan, eds. *The Universal Vampire: Origins and Evolution of a Legend.* Madison, NJ: Fairleigh Dickinson University Press, 2013, pp. 179–94.

3409. Skeat, Walter William. *Malay Magic: An Introduction to the Folklore and Popular Religion of the Malay Peninsula.* [London]: Macmillan, 1900. 685 pp. hb. Posted at: http://www.scribd.com/doc/60226479/Malay-Magic. Rpt.: New York: Barnes & Noble, 1966. 685 pp. hb. Rpt.: New York, Dover Publications, [1967]. 685 pp.

3410. Smith, Henry G., ed. *Chinese Tales of Vampires, Beasts, Genies and Men.* Burnham-on-Sea, Somerset, UK: Llanerch Press, 2011. 200 pp. tp.

3411. Spence, Lewis. "Ghosts of China (Stories of vampires, spirits, elementals, and demons)." *Occult Review* 66 (July 1939): 197ff.

3412. _____, and Charles Otto Blagden. "Bamboo No. 2." In Walter William Skeat and Charles Otto Blagden. *Pagan Races of the Malay Peninsula.* Vol. 1. London: Macmillan and Company, 1906, pp. 473–77. Posted at: https://openlibrary.org/books/OL6982670M/Pagan_races_of_the_Malay_Peninsula. Rpt.: New York: Barnes & Noble, 1966, pp. 473–77.

3413. Stein, Wayne. "Enter the Dracula: The Silent Screams and Cultural Crossroads of Japanese and Hong Kong Cinema." In John Edgar Browning and Caroline Joan Picart, eds. *Dracula, Vampires, and Other Undead Forms.* Lanham, MD: The Scarecrow Press, 2009, pp. 235–60.

3414. _____, and John Edgar Browning. "Western Eastern: Decoding Hybridity and Cyberzen Gothic in *Vampire Hunter D* (1985)." In Andrew Hock Soon Ng, ed. *Asian Gothic: Essays on Literature, Film and Anime.* Jefferson, NC: McFarland & Company, 2008, pp. 210–23. Rpt. in: John Edgar Browning and Caroline Joan Picart, eds. *Dracula, Vampires, and Other Undead Forms.* Lanham, MD: The Scarecrow Press, 2009, pp. 279–95.

3415. Stokes, Lisa Odham. "At the Hong Kong Hop: *Mr. Vampire* Spawns Bloodsucking Genre." In Steffen Hantke, ed. *Horror.* Vashon Island, WA: Paradoxa, 2002.

3416. Teiser, Stephen. "Hungary Ghosts." In Stephen Teiser. *The Ghost Festival in Medieval China.* Princeton, NJ: Princeton University Press, 1996, pp. 124–29.

3417. *There Are Ghosts Everywhere in Singapore.* Vol. One. Singapore: The Publishing Consultant, 1998. 128 pp. pb.

3418. Tyler, Royall. *Japanese Tales.* New York: Pantheon Books, 1987. 341 pp.

3419. *Vampire Hunter D Art Book.* San Diego, CA: IDW Publishing, 2006. 56 pp. hb. ??.

3420. Vellutini, John. "Return of the Leaping Dead." *Oriental Cinema* 15 9n.d. [1997]): 5–10.

3421. _____. "Vampire Filmography." *Oriental Cinema* 15 (n.d. [1997?]): 10–23.

3422. Weisser, Thomas. *Asian Cult Cinema.* New York: Boulevard Books, 1997. 317 pp. tp.

3423. _____. *Asian Trash Cinema: The Book.* Houston, TX: Asian Trash Cinema/European Trash Cinema Publications, 1994. 187 pp. rp.

3424. _____, **and Yuko Mihara Weisser.** *Japanese Cinema Encyclopedia: The Horror, Fantasy, and Sci Fi Films.* Miami, FL: Vital Books, 1997. 327 pp. tp.

3425. Willis, Donald C. "The Fantasy Asian Video Invasion: Hopping Vampires, Annoying Aliens, and Atomic Cats." *Marque Marquee* 43 (Winter 1992): 4–11.

V. Vampires on Television

General Sources

The earliest appearances of the vampire on television occur in several televised stage productions of *Dracula*, the first of which occurred in 1956, with John Carradine taking the starring role as the Count for a *Matinee Theatre* production. Unfortunately, no copy of this show has survived, only a few pictures of Carradine in costume. The first series to feature continuing vampire characters, in this case two, Lily (portrayed by Yvonne De Carlo) and Grandpa Dracula (Al Lewis), was *The Munsters*, a comedic series which ran from 1964 to 1966. It would be followed by *Dark Shadows*, a daytime soap opera, which introduced the vampire Barnabas Collins (portrayed by Jonathan Frid) in 1969. Through the next quarter of a century, at least in the West, vampires would come and go until 1997, when *Buffy the Vampire Slayer* became an international success, first through the English-speaking world and then in the French, Italian and German-speaking lands and more recently, the world. Through the years of the twenty-first century, multiple vampire series have run concurrently on television.

Interestingly, the longest running vampire character on television is Count von Count, the Dracula-like vampire featured on the children's series *Sesame Street*, where he fulfills his task of teaching its youthful audience basic counting from one to ten.

Meanwhile, in Japan, a vital vampire presence developed among younger viewers as the vampire became a popular character in the world of anime (animated film) which developed from manga (comic books). *Vampire Princess Miyu*, which originally appeared in a four-episode mini-series in 1988, was the first international success. It would be followed by dozens of series in succeeding decades as Japanese anime developed an international following.

In the wake of *Buffy the Vampire Slayer*, the vampire has had a continuous presence on American television with the *Vampire Diaries* (adapted from the young adult novels of L. J. Smith; *True Blood*, adapted from the vampire mystery romance novels of Charlaine Harris; and the Canadian series *Being Human*, developed from the equally successful British series of the same name. Meanwhile, the children's books of Sonja Holleyman would be adapted for the delightful children's series, *Mona the Vampire*.

3426. Anchors, William E., Jr. "The Munsters." *Epi-log* 37 (December): 36–43, 63.

3427. Bassom, David. "A Knight to Remember?" *Shivers* 14 (January 1995): 40–43.

3428. Bignell, Jonathan. "A Taste of the Gothic: Film and Television Versions of *Dracula*. In Robert Giddings & Erica Sheen, eds. *The Classic Novel: From Page to Screen*. New York: St. Martin's Press, 2000, pp. 114–130.

3429. Blake, Linnie. "Vampires, Mad Scientists and the Unquiet Dead: Gothic Ubiquity in the Post–9/11 US Television." In Justin Edwards and Agnieszka Soltysik Monnet, eds. *The Gothic in Contemporary Literature and Popular Culture: Pop Goth.* New York: Routledge, 2012, pp. 39–56.

3430. Borsellino, Mary. "Damon Salvatore: Vampire Hunter." In Red and Vee. *A Visitor's Guide to Mystic Falls.* Dallas, TX: Smart Pop/Benbella Books, 2010, pp. 129–42.

3431. Brennan, Sarah Rees. "Women Who Love Vampires Who Eat Women." In Red and Vee. *A Visitor's Guide to Mystic Falls.* Dallas, TX: Smart Pop/Benbella Books, 2010, pp. 1–19.

3432. Bridgeman, Mary. "Forged in Love and Death: Problematic Subjects in *The Vampire Diaries.*" *The Journal of Popular Culture* 46, 1 (February 2013): 3–19.

3433. Broderick, James F. "Vampirism." In James F. Broderick. *The Literary Galaxy of Star Trek: An Analysis of References and Themes in the Television Series and Films.* Jefferson, NC: McFarland & Company, 2006, pp. 109–117.

3434. Burns, Kevin. "Al Lewis: Famous Munster of Filmland." *Famous Monsters of Filmland* 209 (August/September 1995): 8–16.

3435. Calhoun, Crissey. *Love You to Death: The Unofficial Companion to the Vampire Diaries.* Toronto: ECW Press, 2010. 222 pp. tp.

3436. _____. *Love You to Death: The Unofficial Companion to The Vampire Diaries, Season 2.* Toronto: ECW Press, 2011. 288 pp. tp.

3437. _____. *Love You to Death: The Unofficial Companion to The Vampire Diaries, Season 3.* Toronto: ECW Press, 2012. 225 pp. tp.

3438. _____. *Love You to Death: The Unofficial Companion to The Vampire Diaries, Season 4.* Toronto: ECW Press, 2013. 261 pp. tp.

3439. Cawiezel, Marc. "My Monster Memory of Elvira." *Scary Monsters Magazine* 6 (March 1993): 8–11.

3440. Cox, Stephen Cox. *The Addams Chronicles: Everything You Ever Wanted to Know About the Addams Family.* New York: HarperPerennial, 1991. 205 pp. tp. Rpt.: New York: HarperCollins, 1991. 256 pp. pb.

3441. _____. *The Munsters: A Trip Down Mockingbird Lane.* Back Stage Books, 2006. 207 pp. tp. Large format.

3442. _____. *The Munsters: Television's First Family of Fright.* Chicago: Contemporary Books, 1989. 174 pp. pb. Large format. Rpt.: London: Plexus, 1990. 174 pp. pb.

3443. Crossen, Carys. "'Would you please stop trying to take your clothes off?' Abstinence and Impotence of Male Vampires in Contemporary Fiction and Television." In Elizabeth Nelson with Jillian Burcar & Hannah Priest, eds. *Creating Humanity, Discovering Monstrosity.* Oxford: Inter-Disciplinary Press, 2010, pp. 251–60.

3444. Darras, Helen. *Eddie Munster aka Butch Patrick.* East Setauket, NY: the author, 2008. hb.

3445. Davis, Michael. *Street Gang: The Complete History of Sesame Street.* New York: Viking, 2008. 379 pp. hb. dj. Include the story of Count von Count, the show's vampiric character.

3446. Dawidziak, Mark. *The Night Stalker Companion: A 25th Anniversary Tribute.* Beverly Hills, CA: Pomegranate Press, 1997. 206 pp.

3447. de Giacomo, Jacqueline. "Tell-Tale Deaths and Monstrous Quests: *Being Human* and Visions of Death in Millennial Gothic Fictions." In Eoghain Hamilton. *The Gothic: Probing the Boundaries.* Oxford: Inter-Disciplinary Press, 2010, pp. 179–86.

3448. de Ville, Venalla. "Elvira: Mistress of the Dark." *Femme Fatales* 4, 4 (December 1995): 32–41, 60.

3449. Despain, Bree. "Bonnie Bennett: A New Kind of Best Friend." In Red and Vee. *A Visitor's Guide to Mystic Falls.* Dallas, TX: Smart Pop/Benbella Books, 2010, pp. 21–33.

3450. "Elvira: Mistress of Merchandise." *Scary Monsters Magazine* 6 (March 1993): 16–18.

3451. Everett, Justin. "The Borg as Vampire in Star Trek: The Next Generation (1987–1994) and Start Trek: First Contact (1996): An Uncanny Reflection/" In John Edgar Browning and Caroline Joan Picart, eds. *Dracula, Vampires, and Other Undead Forms.* Lanham, MD: The Scarecrow Press, 2009, pp. 77–92.

3452. Ferrante, Anthony C. "The Campaign for *Addams Family Values.*" *Fangoria* 129 (December 1993): 46–52.

3453. Gray, Claudia. "The War Between the States." In Red and Vee. *A Visitor's Guide to Mystic Falls.* Dallas, TX: Smart Pop/Benbella Books, 2010, pp. 35–49.

3454. Harvey, Alyxandra. "In Which Our Intrepid Heroines Discuss the Merits of the Bad Boy Versus the Reformed Bad Boy." In Red and Vee. *A Visitor's Guide to Mystic Falls.* Dallas, TX: Smart Pop/Benbella Books, 2010, pp. 67–84.

3455. Heldreth, Leonard G. "Vampires in Film and Television: Introduction." *Journal of Popular Film and Television* 27, 2 (1999): 2–3.

3456. "Here Come the Munsters...Again!" *Monsterscene* 6 (Fall 1995): 29–33.

3457. Higgins, Jenny. "Interview with a Vampire: Geraint Wyn Davies." *Playgirl* (November 1995): 8–9, 97.

3458. Iaccino, James F. "The World of *Forever Knight*: A Television Tribute to Anne Rice's New Age Vampire." In Gary Hoppenstand and Ray B. Browne, eds. *The Gothic World of Anne Rice.* Bowling Green, OH: Bowling Green University Popular Press, 1996, pp. 231–46.

3459. Jowett, Lorna, and Stacey Abbott. *TV Horror: Investigating the Dark Side of the Small Screen.* London: I. B. Tauris, 2013. 207 pp. tp.

3460. Kane, Tim. *Changing Vampire of Film and Television: A Critical Study of the Growth of a Genre.* Jefferson, NC: McFarland & Company, 2006. 232 pp. tp.

3461. Kaszubski, Michael. "Count Gore DeVol." *Scary Monsters Magazine* 11 (June 1994): 17–19.

3462. Kirkland, Ewan. "Whiteness and the Contemporary Vampire in Film and Television." In Deborah Mutch. *The Modern Vampire and Human Identity.* Basingstoke, UK/New York: Palgrave Macmillan, 2013, pp. 93–110.

3463. Kling, Heidi R. "Case Notes: Salvatore, Stefan and Salvatore, Damon." In Red and Vee. *A Visitor's Guide to Mystic Falls.* Dallas, TX: Smart Pop/Benbella Books, 2010, pp. 117–28.

3464. Lindgren Leavenworth, Maria, and Malin Isaksson. *Fanged Fan Fiction: Variations on* Twilight, True Blood, *and* The Vampire Diaries. Jefferson, NC: McFarland & Co., 2013. 228 pp. tp.

3465. Lyon, Michelle, with Mark C. MacKinnon. *Hellsing.* Guelph, ON: Guardians of Order, 2002. 80 pp. pb. Large format.

3466. Macabre, J. B. "Don't Touch That Dial: Vampires on the Tube." In Rosemary Ellen Guiley, with J. B. Macabre. *The Complete Vampire Companion.* New York: Macmillan, 1994, pp. 134–44.

3467. Mahoney, Karen. "Dear Diary..." In Red and Vee. *A Visitor's Guide to Mystic Falls.* Dallas, TX: Smart Pop/Benbella Books, 2010, pp. 159–74.

3468. "Making the Munsters TV Movie." *Famous Monsters of Filmland* 211 (February/March 1996): 42–48.

3469. McMahon-Coleman, Kimberley. "'Myriad Mirrors: Doppelgängers and Doubling in *The Vampire Diaries*.'" In Sam George and Bill Hughes, eds. *Open Graves, Open Minds: Representations of Vampires and the Undead from the Enlightenment to the Present Day.* Manchester: Manchester University Press, 2013, pp. 210–24.

3470. Middleton, Brad. *Un-Dead TV: The Ultimate Guide to Vampire Television.* Pepperell, MA: By Light Unseen Media, 2012. 512 pp. tp.

3471. Muir, John Kenneth. "Cliffhangers: The Curse of Dracula." In John Kenneth Muir. *Terror Television: American Series, 1970–1999.* Jefferson, NC: McFarland & Company, 2001, pp. 91–95.

3472. _____. "Dracula: The Series (1990–1991)." In John Kenneth Muir. *Terror Television: American Series, 1970–1999.* Jefferson, NC: McFarland & Company, 2001, pp. 91–95.

3473. Nazarian, Vera. "You're My Obsession." In Red and Vee. *A Visitor's Guide to Mystic Falls.* Dallas, TX: Smart Pop/Benbella Books, 2010, pp. 85–101.

3474. *The Official Addams Family Magazine.* New York: Starlog Communications International, 1991. 66 pp. pb. Large format.

3475. Parker, Evie. *100% the Vampire Diaries: The Unofficial Guide.* New York: Bantam, 2010. 60 pp. pb.

3476. Peel, John. *The Addams Family and Munsters Program Guide.* London: Virgin, 1996. 294 pp. pb.

3477. Red and Vee. "Introduction: A Visitor's Guide to Mystic Falls." In Red and Vee of VampireDiaries.net, with Leah Wilson. *A Visitor's Guide to Mystic Falls.* Dallas, TX: Smart Pop/Benbella Books, 2010, pp. ix–xiii.

3478. Red and Vee of Vampire-Diaries.net, with Leah Wilson. *A Visitor's Guide to Mystic Falls: Your Favorite Authors on* The Vampire Diaries. Dallas, TX: Smart Pop/Benbella, 2010. 190 pp. tp.

3479. Rees, Robert R. "Friends on the Fringe: Vampira Speaks." *Draculina* 27 (1996): 6–8, 55.

3480. Rowe, Michael Charles. "Nick Knight, Vampire Cop." In Anthony Timpone. *Fangoria Vampires*. New York: HarperPrism, 1996, pp. 166–72.

3481. Satian, Al, and Heather Johnson. "The Night Stalker in His Lair." *Monsters of the Movies* 1, 3 (October 1974): 59–63.

3482. Sharkey, Jack. *The Addams Family*. New York: Pyramid Books, 1965. 175 pp. pb.

3483. Skerchock, John. *Vampira Unauthorized*. Kearny, NJ: Michael Eniches, 2010. 100 pp. Large format.

3484. Skovron, Jon. "Ladies of the Night, Unite!" In Red and Vee. *A Visitor's Guide to Mystic Falls*. Dallas, TX: Smart Pop/Benbella Books, 2010, pp. 51–65.

3485. Smith, L. J., and Annette Pollert. *Night World: The Ultimate Fan Guide*. New York: Simon Pulse, 2009. 282 pp. pb. Re: *The Vampire Dairies*.

3486. Story, David. *America of the Rerun: TV Shows That Never Die*. Secaucus, NJ: Carol Pub. Group, 1993. 239 pp. Includes reflections on *The Addams Family*, *The Munsters*, and *Dark Shadows*.

3487. Strauss, Jon. "Forever Knight." *Epi-Log* 36 (November 1993): 4–11; 37 (December 1993): 29–35, 62.

3488. Thompson, Dave. *If You Like True Blood...Here Are Over 200 Films, TV Shows and Other Oddities That You Will Love*. Milwaukee, WI: Backbeat Book/Hal Leonard Corporation, 213. 231 pp. tp.

3489. Van Hise, James. *Addams Family Revealed: An Unauthorized Look at America's Spookiest Family*. Las Vegas, NV: Pioneer Books, 1991. 157 pp. pb. Large format.

3490. Watson, Elena M. *Television Horror Movie Hosts: 68 Vampires, Mad Scientists and Other Denizens of the Late-Night Airwaves Examined and Interviewed*. Jefferson, NC: McFarland & Company, 1991. 242 pp. tp.

3491. Weller, Lea Cassandra. *The Evolution of the Vampire in Film and Television: From Beast to Beauty*. Derby, UK: the author, 2013. 123 pp. tp.

3492. Wheatley, Helen. *Gothic Television*. Manchester, UK: Manchester University Press, 2007. 256 pp. tp. This volume originally appeared as the author's Ph.D. dissertation (2002) completed at the University of Warwick (UK).

3493. White, Kiersten. "Don't Be Fooled by That Noble Chin: Stefan Sucks." In Red and Vee. *A Visitor's Guide to Mystic Falls*. Dallas, TX: Smart Pop/Benbella Books, 2010, pp. 103–16.

Dark Shadows

The first episodes of *Dark Shadows,* an American television soap opera with a Gothic setting, originally aired in 1966. It ran five days a week in the late afternoon. Facing likely cancellation from low ratings, producer Dan Curtis made a variety of changes, the most important of which was the introduction of a vampire character, Barnabas Collins, portrayed by Jonathan Frid. Subsequently the ratings soared, and *Dark Shadows* went on to become the first successful television show to feature a vampire storyline. It ran for four years, being discontinued in 1971, but built a large loyal fan base that continues to keep the show alive. Curtis also produced two movies directly inspired by the show, and in a creative partnership with writer Richard Matheson, produced several additional vampire themed productions, including a made-for-television *Dracula* movie starring Jack Palance.

In the wake of its success, a set of *Dark Shadows* novels and comic books were written, and a variety of games, puzzles, trading cards, toys, jewelry, and clothing items appeared. The fan base organized clubs and produced a wealth of newsletters, fanzines, fan fiction, and, most important for this bibliography, commentaries on the show and its stars.

Given the continued interest in the show by the fan base, in 1991 Curtis moved to revive

Dark Shadows as a prime time weekly series that starred Ben Cross as Barnabas Collins, but it fell victim to the live televised coverage of the first Gulf War. A 2004 pilot for a new series was produced, but the series was never picked up by one of the television networks. Finally, director Tim Burton did a movie based on the series, but even though it starred the immensely popular Johnny Depp, the movie (2012) failed to capture a significant audience in the United States, though it did quite well worldwide.

Over the years since the original show ended, Katherine Leigh Scott, one of its stars, launched Pomegranate Press, which has produce a set of high quality books about the show. More recently, a new set of *Dark Shadows* novels have appeared, including several by Lara Parker, another of the show's stars. Over the years the complete *Dark Shadows* TV series (as well as the 1991 series) was released on VHS video and subsequently on DVD.

The major fan gathering, which in recent years has attracted as many as 1,500 attendees, is hosted by Dark Shadows Festivals, formed in 1983. The annual summer gathering alternates between Southern California and New York, and has regularly featured members of the cast who have been unusually generous in making themselves available to the fans.

Dark Shadows had its major run prior to the designation of instructors of television studies and the formation of the departments that study television now located in many universities, hence comment on the show has, unfortunately, been far less than some of the more recent vampire-oriented series such as *Buffy the Vampire Slayer*, *Angel*, *True Blood*, or *Vampire Diaries*.

3494. Abbott, Stacey. "Dark Shadows." In Stacey Abbott, ed. *The Cult TV Book.* New York: I. B. Tauris, 2010, pp. 205–07.

3495. Benshoff, Harry M. *Dark Shadows.* Ser.: TV Milestones. Detroit, MI: Wayne State University Press, 2011. 130 pp. tp.

3496. _____. "Secrets, Closets, and Corridors through Time: Negotiating Sexuality and Gender Through *Dark Shadows.*" in Cheryl Harris and Alison Alexander, eds. *Theorizing Fandom: Fans, Subculture and Identity,* Cresskill, NJ: Hampton Press, 1988, pp. 199–218.

3497. Borzellieri, Frank. *The Physics of Dark Shadows: Time Travel, ESP, and the Laboratory.* New York: Cultural Studies Press, 2008. 90 pp. tp.

3498. Burton, Tim. "Introduction." In Mark Salisbury. *Dark Shadows: The Visual Companion.* Ed. by Leah Gallo. London: Titan Books, 2012, pp. 6–7.

3499. Clark, Dale. *Dark Shadows Questions and Answers.* 6 vols. Dallas: Old House Publishing, undated [1990–94].

3500. Clark, Melody, and Beth Klapper. *A Gift of Memory: The Grayson Hall Memorial Collection.* Lancaster, CA: Synchronistic Press, 1987. 72 pp.

3501. Clark, Melody, Kathleen Resch, and Marcy Robin. "The *Dark Shadows* History." In Kathryn Leigh Scott, ed. *The Dark Shadows Companion: 25th Anniversary Collection.* Los Angeles: Pomegranate Press, 1990, pp. 42–48.

3502. Cobert, Robert. *Dark Shadows Music Book: Original Music from the Classic TV Series and Films.* Los Angeles: Pomegranate Press, 1996. 112 pp. tp.

3503. Culhane, Michael. "Barnabas and I." In Kathryn Leigh Scott and Jim Pierson. *Dark Shadows Almanac: Thirtieth Anniversary Tribute.* Los Angeles: Pomegranate Press, 1995, pp. 172–73.

3504. *Dark Shadows Festival Memory Book, 1983–1993.* Maplewood, NJ: *Dark Shadows* Festival, 1993. 143 pp. pb. Large format.

3505. *Dark Shadows: The Introduction of Barnabas.* Maplewood, NJ: Dark Shadows Festival, 1988. 144 pp. pb. Large format.

3506. Dawidziak, Mark. "Dark Shadows." *Cinefantastique* 21, 3 (December 1990): 24–33.

3507. DeCenzo, George. "My Days in the Shadows." In Kathryn Leigh Scott and Jim Pierson. *Dark Shadows Almanac: Thirtieth Anniversary Tribute.* Los Angeles: Pomegranate Press, 1995, pp. 29–34.

3508. Dwyer, Jessica. "*Dark Shadows*: A *Horror Hound* Retrospective." *Horror Hound* 34 (March-April 2012): 26–33.

3509. Frid, Jonathan, comp. *Barnabas Collins: A Personal Picture Album.* New York: Paperback Library, 1969. 128 pp. pb.

3510. _____. "A Foreword." In Kathryn Leigh Scott, ed. *The Dark Shadows Companion: 25th Anniversary Collection.* Los Angeles: Pomegranate Press, 1990, pp. 12–13.

3511. Gerani, Gary. "The Many Horrors of Dan Curtis." *Weird Tales of the Macabre* 1 (January 1975): 24–30.

3512. Glut, Don. "Barnabas: Dark Shadows in the Bright Afternoon." *Monsters of the Movies* 1, 3 (October 1974): 12–17.

3513. Goodman, Stuart. "Shooting Shadows." In Kathryn Leigh Scott and Jim Pierson, eds. *The Dark Shadows Almanac: Millennium Edition.* Los Angeles: Pomegranate Press, 2000, pp. 25–27.

3514. Graham, Jean. *Music from Dark Shadows.* San Diego, CA: Peacock Press, n.d. 22 pp. pb. Large format.

3515. Gross, Darren. "Closed Rooms in the *House of Dark Shadows*." *Video Watchdog* 40 (1997): 26–31.

3516. _____. "Illuminating *Night of Dark Shadows*." *Video Watchdog* 40 (1997): 32–45.

3517. _____. "Shedding Light on *Night of Dark shadows*." In Kathryn Leigh Scott and Jim Pierson, eds. *The Dark Shadows Almanac: Millennium Edition.* Los Angeles: Pomegranate Press, 2000, pp. 157–83.

3518. Gross, Edward. *Dark Shadows Files: The Secret of Barnabas.* Canoga Park, CA: Psi Fi Movie Press, 1986. 57 pp. pb. Large format.

3519. _____. *Dark Shadows Files: The Terror Begins.* Canoga Park, CA: Psi Fi Movie Press, 1986. 57 pp. pb. Large format.

3520. _____. *Dark Shadows Files: A 20th Anniversary Tribute.* Canoga Park, CA: Psi Fi Movie Press, 1986. 57 pp. pb. Large format.

3521. _____. *The Dark Shadows Interviews.* Las Vegas, NV: Schuster & Schuster, 1988. 101 pp. pb. Large format.

3522. _____. *Dark Shadows Special: Return to Collinwood.* Canoga Park, CA: Psi Fi Movie Press, 1986. 47 pp. pb. Large format.

3523. _____, **and James Van Hise.** *Dark Shadows Tribute.* Las Vegas, NV: Pioneer Books, 1990. 144 pp. pb. Large format.

3524. Gross, Mark J. "Vampires Fly to Sign Autographs." *Autograph Magazine* (October 30, 2010).

3525. Hall, Matthew. "*Dark Shadows* and Me." In Kathryn Leigh Scott, ed. *The Dark Shadows Companion: 25th Anniversary Collection.* Los Angeles: Pomegranate Press, 1990, pp. 23–38.

3526. Hall, Sam. "A Word from Me." In Kathryn Leigh Scott, ed. *The Dark Shadows Companion: 25th Anniversary Collection.* Los Angeles: Pomegranate Press, 1990, pp. 39–41.

3527. Hamrick, Craig. *Barnabas & Company: The Cast of the TV Classic Dark Shadows.* Lincoln, NB: iUniverse, Inc., 2003. 276 pp. tp.

3528. _____. *The Dark Shadows Collectibles Book.* Los Angeles: Pomegranate Press, 1998. 104 pp. pb.

3529. _____. *The Dark Shadows Collector's Guide.* Manhattan, KS: Clique Publishing, Inc., 1991. 136 pp. pb.

3530. _____. *The Dark Shadows Collector's Guide Update, #3.* Manhattan, KS: Clique Publishing, Inc., 1994. 47 pp. pb.

3531. Henesy, David. "A Conversation with David Henesy." In Kathryn Leigh Scott, ed. *35th Anniversary Dark Shadows Memories.* Los Angeles: Pomegranate Press, 2001, pp. 81–89.

3532. Hyatt, Wesley. "Dark Shadows." In Wesley Hyatt. *The Encyclopedia of Daytime Television.* New York: Billboard Books, 1997, pp. 108–11.

3533. Isles, Alexandra Moltke. "Foreword." In Kathryn Leigh Scott, ed. *35th Anniversary Dark Shadows Memories.* Los Angeles: Pomegranate Press, 2001, pp. xi–xiv.

3534. Jamison, R. J. *Grayson Hall: A Hard Act to Follow.* Lincoln, NE: iUniverse, Inc., 2006. 224 pp. tp.

3535. Jarvis, Sharon. "Dark Shadows." In Sharon Jarvis. *True Tales of the Unknown: The Uninvited.* New York: Bantam Books, 1989, pp. 20–36. Vampire researcher Stephen Kaplan visit a *Dark Shadows* convention as the guest lecturer.

3536. Johnson, Nina, and O. Crock. *Dark Shadows: The First Year.* Los Angeles: Blue Whale Books, 2006. 265 pp. pb. Large format.

3537. Kurta, Jeff. "House of Dark Shadows." *Scary Monsters Magazine* 16 (September 1995): 75–79.

3538. Lampley, Jonathan Malcolm. "Dark Shadows. In David Lavery, ed. *The Essential Cult Television Reader*. Lexington: University Press of Kentucky, 2010, pp. 84–89.

3539. Laurie, Simon. "Who's A-Frid of the Big Bad Vampire?" *Famous Monsters of Filmland* 59 (November 1969): 40–46.

3540. Levantino, Richard. "Studio Kid." In Kathryn Leigh Scott and Jim Pierson, eds. *The Dark Shadows Almanac: Millennium Edition*. Los Angeles: Pomegranate Press, 2000, pp. 233–35.

3541. Malis, Jody Cameron, ed. *The Dark Shadows Cookbook*. New York: Ace, 1970. 175 pp. pb.

3542. Manning, Stuart. "Shadows Over Britain." In Kathryn Leigh Scott and Jim Pierson, eds. *The Dark Shadows Almanac: Millennium Edition*. Los Angeles: Pomegranate Press, 2000, pp. 124–25.

3543. McKinley-Haas, Mary. "Designing Shadows." In Kathryn Leigh Scott and Jim Pierson. *Dark Shadows Almanac: Thirtieth Anniversary Tribute*. Los Angeles: Pomegranate Press, 1995, pp. 51–52.

3544. Miller, Walter, Jr. "Studio Days." In Kathryn Leigh Scott and Jim Pierson. *Dark Shadows Almanac: Thirtieth Anniversary Tribute*. Los Angeles: Pomegranate Press, 1995, pp. 43–46.

3545. Morrissey, K. J. "Monster Memories of *Dark Shadows*." *Scary Monsters Magazine* 16 (September 1995): 10–12.

3546. Nahmod, David-Elijah. "Ladies of the Shadows." *Famous Monsters of Filmland* 261 (May-June 2012): 56–61.

3547. Nickerson, Denise. "Child of the Shadows." In Kathryn Leigh Scott and Jim Pierson, eds. *The Dark Shadows Almanac: Millennium Edition*. Los Angeles: Pomegranate Press, 2000, pp. 237–38.

3548. Parker, Lara. "Fans." In Kathryn Leigh Scott and Jim Pierson. *Dark Shadows Almanac: Thirtieth Anniversary Tribute*. Los Angeles: Pomegranate Press, 1995, pp. 39–42.

3549. _____. "Lara's Descent into Gothic Romance." In Kathryn Leigh Scott and Jim Pierson, eds. *The Dark Shadows Almanac: Millennium Edition*. Los Angeles: Pomegranate Press, 2000, pp. 13–20.

3550. _____. "Out of Angelique's Shadow." In Kathryn Leigh Scott, ed. *The Dark Shadows Companion: 25th Anniversary Collection*. Los Angeles: Pomegranate Press, 1990, pp. 14–21.

3551. Patrick, Dennis. "Laughter in the Shadows." In Kathryn Leigh Scott and Jim Pierson. *Dark Shadows Almanac: Thirtieth Anniversary Tribute*. Los Angeles: Pomegranate Press, 1995, pp. 175.

3552. Pegg, Robert. "Battling Barnabases." *Fangoia* 116 (September 1992): 50–53, 68.

3553. _____. "Illuminating *Dark Shadows*." In Anthony Timpone. *Fangoria Vampires*. New York: HarperPrism, 1996, pp. 158–65.

3554. Pennock, Chris. "My Shadowy Past." In Kathryn Leigh Scott and Jim Pierson, eds. *The Dark Shadows Almanac: Millennium Edition*. Los Angeles: Pomegranate Press, 2000, pp. 23–24.

3555. Pierson, Jim, ed. *Dark Shadows Celebrity Cookbook*. Maplewood, NJ: Dark Shadows Festival Publications, 1989. 130 pp. pb.

3556. _____. *Dark Shadows Resurrected*. Las Vegas, NV: Pomegranate Press, 1992. 175 pp. tp.

3557. _____. "Episode Guide." In Kathryn Leigh Scott, ed. *The Dark Shadows Companion: 25th Anniversary Collection*. Los Angeles: Pomegranate Press, 1990, pp. 175–200.

3558. _____, ed. *The History of Dark Shadows, 1966–1967*. Fort Worth, TX: Dark Shadows Festival Publications, 1987. pb. Large format.

3559. _____. "The Legend of *Dark Shadows*." In Kathryn Leigh Scott, ed. *35th Anniversary Dark Shadows Memories*. Los Angeles: Pomegranate Press, 2001, pp. 189–91.

3560. _____, and Robert Finocchio, ed. *The Dark Shadows Actors Directory*. Dark Shadows Festival Publications, 1990.

3561. PopTopics Media, editors of. *Dark Shadows*. London: PopTopics Media, 2012. pb. Large format.

3562. Resch, Kathleen, ed. *The Dark Shadows Concordance 1795*. Temple City, CA: Pentagram Publications, 1989. 206 pp. pb. Large format.

3563. _____. *The Dark Shadows Concordance 1897*. Santa Clara, CA: Pentagram Publications, 1981. 132 pp. pb. Large format.

3564. _____. *The Dark Shadows Concordance 1840.* Temple City, CA: Pentagram Publications, 1987. 288 pp. pb. Large format.

3565. _____. *The Dark Shadows Concordance 1968.* 2 vols. Temple City, CA: Pentagram Publications, 1989, 1990. pb. Large format.

3566. _____. *The Dark Shadows Concordance 1970 Parallel Time.* Temple City, CA: Pentagram Publication, 1990. 140 pp. pb. Large format.

3567. _____. "The *Dark Shadows* Story." In Kathryn Leigh Scott, ed. *35th Anniversary Dark Shadows Memories.* Los Angeles: Pomegranate Press, 2001, pp. 81–151.

3568. _____. *Shadows in the 90's: The Dark Shadows Concordance 1991.* Temple City, CA: Pentagram Publications, 1992. 224 pp. pb. Large format.

3569. _____, **and Marcy Robin, eds.** *Dark Shadows in the Afternoon.* East Meadow, NY: Image Publishing, 1991. 112 pp. pb. Large format.

3570. Robin, Marcy. "Afternoon Class: Joan Bennett on Dark Shadows." *Scarlet Street* 9 (Winter 1993): 46.

3571. _____. "Dark Shadows on Videotape." *Scarlet Street* 8 (Fall 1992): 51–52.

3572. Salisbury, Mark. *Dark Shadows: The Visual Companion.* Ed. by Leah Gallo. London: Titan Books, 2012. 192 pp. hb. Large format. This large picture book includes an introduction by the 2012 film by director Tim Burton and an afterword by Richard D. Zanuck.

3573. Samaras, Helen. *Fangs for the Memory: Memoirs of Dark Shadows Fans and Cast Members.* West Hempstead, NY: Evil Twin Publishing, 1994. 140 pp. pb. Large format.

3574. scifiGate [pseudonym of Sandy VanDensen and Lori DeGiacomo]. *The Dark Shadows Internet Guide.* Port Orchard, WA: Lightning Rod Ltd., 2000.

3575. Scott, Katheryn Leigh. "And They Said It Would Never Last..." In Kathryn Leigh Scott and Jim Pierson. *Dark Shadows Almanac: Thirtieth Anniversary Tribute.* Los Angeles: Pomegranate Press, 1995, pp. 11–14.

3576. _____, **ed.** *The Dark Shadows Companion: 25th Anniversary Collection.* Los Angeles: Pomegranate Press, 1990. 208 pp. tp.

3577. _____. "Maggie Comes Home." In Kathryn Leigh Scott and Jim Pierson, eds. *The Dark Shadows Almanac: Millennium Edition.* Los Angeles: Pomegranate Press, 2000, pp. 1–3.

3578. _____. "My Memories of *Dark Shadows.*" In Kathryn Leigh Scott, ed. *35th Anniversary Dark Shadows Memories.* Los Angeles: Pomegranate Press, 2001, pp. 1–79.

3579. _____. *My Scrapbook Memories of Dark Shadows.* Los Angeles: Pomegranate Press, 1986. 152 pp. tp.

3580. _____. *35th Anniversary Dark Shadows Memories.* Los Angeles: Pomegranate Press, 2001. 302 pp. tp.

3581. _____, **and Jim Pierson.** *Dark Shadows Almanac: Thirtieth Anniversary Tribute.* Los Angeles: Pomegranate Press, 1995. 176 pp. tp.

3582. _____, **and Jim Pierson, eds.** *The Dark Shadows Movie Book.* Los Angeles: Pomegranate Press, 1988. 312 pp. tp. Television.

3583. Scott, Katheryn Leigh, Jim Pierson, and David Selby. *The Dark Shadows Almanac: Millennium Edition.* Los Angeles: Pomegranate Press, 2000. 271 pp. tp.

3584. Selby, David. "Foreword." In Kathryn Leigh Scott and Jim Pierson, eds. *The Dark Shadows Almanac: Millennium Edition.* Los Angeles: Pomegranate Press, 2000, pp. ix–xi.

3585. _____. "Foreword." In Kathryn Leigh Scott and Jim Pierson. *Dark Shadows Almanac: Thirtieth Anniversary Tribute.* Los Angeles: Pomegranate Press, 1995, pp. vii–viii.

3586. Smith, Debbie. "The Creative Genius Behind *Dark Shadows.*" In Kathryn Leigh Scott and Jim Pierson. *Dark Shadows Almanac: Thirtieth Anniversary Tribute.* Los Angeles: Pomegranate Press, 1995, pp. 35–38.

3587. Smith, Dick. "The Aging of Barnabas." In Kathryn Leigh Scott and Jim Pierson. *Dark Shadows Almanac: Thirtieth Anniversary Tribute.* Los Angeles: Pomegranate Press, 1995, p. 171.

3588. Stockel, Shirley, and Victoria Weidner. *A Guide to Collecting "Dark Shadows" Memorabilia.* Florissant, MO: *Collinwood Chronicle*, 1992. 107 pp.

3589. Story, David. "Dark Shadows." In David Story, *America of the Rerun: TV Shows That Never Die.* Secaucus, NJ: Carol Pub. Group, 1993, pp. 224–39.

3590. Thompson, Jeff. "Barnabas, Quintin, and the Prolific Author: The *Dark Shadows* Novels of Dan 'Marilyn' Ross." *Paperback Parade* 43 (August 1995): 80–91.

3591. ____. *Dark Dreamer: Dan Curtis and Television Horror, 1966–2006.* Nashville: Middle Tennessee State University, Ph.D. dissertation, 2007. 317 pp. Jeff Thompson is an associate professor of English at Tennessee State University in Nashville.

3592. ____. *The* Dark Shadows *Comic Books.* Los Angeles: Joseph Collins Publications, 1984, Rev. ed. 1988. 115 pp.

3593. ____. "*Dark Shadows* Fandom, Then and Now." In Jonathan Lampley and Kris Barton, eds. *Fan CULTure: An Examination of Participatory Fandom in the 21st Century.* Jefferson, NC: McFarland & Company, 2013, pp. 23–35.

3594. ____. *The Effective Use of Actual Persons and Events in the Historical Novels of Dan Ross.* Nashville: Tennessee State University, M.A. thesis, 1991. 206 pp. Large format.

3595. ____. "A History of the East Coast Dark Shadows Festivals: 1983–1991." Unpublished paper, 1991. 12 pp.

3596. ____. *House of Dan Curtis: The Television Mysteries of the* Dark Shadows *Auteur.* Nashville: Westview, 2010. 197 pp. hb. With a Foreword by *Dark Shadows* star John Karlen.

3597. ____. "Introduction: The Best of *Dark Shadows.*" *Dark Shadows: The Best of the Original Series.* Neshannock, PA: Hermes Press, 2012. The original *Dark Shadows* comic books were published by Gold Key Comics, with art work by Joe Certa and George Wilson, and writing by Donald J. Arneson and Arnold Drake. Reprints the Gold Key *Dark Shadows* comic books #1, 4, 6, 8, 11, 14, 17, 18, 24, 31, 32, and 33.

3598. ____. "Introduction: *Dark Shadows* and the Comics." *Dark Shadows: The Complete Original Series,* vol. 1. Neshannock, PA: Hermes Press, 2010. Reprints the Gold Key *Dark Shadows* comic books #1–7.

3599. ____. "Introduction: A Final Look at the Comics." *Dark Shadows: The Complete Original Series,* vol. 5. Neshannock, PA: Hermes Press, 2012, pp. 5–11. Reprints the Gold Key *Dark Shadows* comic books #29–35.

3600. ____. "Introduction: A Look at the Comics." *Dark Shadows: The Complete Original Series,* vol. 2. Neshannock, PA: Hermes Press, 2011. Reprints the Gold Key *Dark Shadows* comic books #8–14.

3601. ____. "Introduction: A Look at the Comics." *Dark Shadows: The Complete Original Series,* vol. 3. Neshannock, PA: Hermes Press, 2011. Reprints the Gold Key *Dark Shadows* comic books #15–21.

3602. ____. "Introduction: A Look at the Comics." *Dark Shadows: The Complete Original Series,* vol. 4. Ed. Daniel Herman. Neshannock, PA: Hermes Press, 2012. Reprints the Gold Key *Dark Shadows* comic books #22–28.

3603. ____. "Introduction: The Story Digest." *Dark Shadows: The Original Series Story Digest.* Ed. Daniel Herman. Neshannock, PA: Hermes Press, 2011. Reprints the Gold Key *Dark Shadows Story Digest Magazine* #1 (June 1970).

3604. ____. *The Television Horrors of Dan Curtis:* Dark Shadows, The Night Stalker, *and Other Productions, 1966–2006.* Jefferson, NC: McFarland, 2009. 200 pp. Rondo Award nominee for Best Book.

3605. Tomashoff, Sy. "Building Shadows." In Kathryn Leigh Scott and Jim Pierson. *Dark Shadows Almanac: Thirtieth Anniversary Tribute.* Los Angeles: Pomegranate Press, 1995, pp. 19–28. Rpt. in: Kathryn Leigh Scott and Jim Pierson, eds. *The Dark Shadows Almanac: Millennium Edition.* Los Angeles: Pomegranate Press, 2000, pp. 221–31.

3606. Van Hise, James. *Dark Shadows Handbook.* Granada Hills, CA: Pop Cult, Inc., 1988. 57 pp. pb. Large format.

3607. Wallace, Art. *Shadows on the Wall.* N.p. [Los Angeles]: Dan Curtis Productions, n.d. 91 pp. pb.

3608. Wallace, Marie. "Beyond Shadows." In Kathryn Leigh Scott and Jim Pierson. *Dark Shadows Almanac: Thirtieth Anniversary Tribute.* Los Angeles: Pomegranate Press, 1995, p. 47.

3609. ____. *On Stage & In Shadows: A Career Memoir.* New York: iUniverse, 2095. 183 pp. tp.

3610. Wandrey, Donna. "The Shadows Cult." In Kathryn Leigh Scott and Jim Pierson. *Dark Shadows Almanac: Thirtieth Anniversary Tribute.* Los Angeles: Pomegranate Press, 1995, pp. 48–50.

3611. Williamson, Milly. "Television, Vampires and the Body: Somatic Pathos." *Intensities: The Journal of Cult Media* 4 (2007).

3612. Wilson, Ann. *Dark Shadows Program Guide.* Los Angeles: Pomegranate Press, 2000. Unpaged. tp.

3613. _____. "Episode Guide." In Kathryn Leigh Scott, ed. *35th Anniversary Dark Shadows Memories.* Los Angeles: Pomegranate Press, 2001, pp. 213–302.

3614. Zanuck, Richard D. "Afterword." In Mark Salisbury. *Dark Shadows: The Visual Companion.* Ed. by Leah Gallo. London: Titan Books, 2012, pp. 182–89.

Buffy the Vampire Slayer/Angel

The year 1997 was a busy year for vampire studies as scholars gathered for several conferences commemorating the centennial of the publication of *Dracula* culminating in Dracula '97, a weekend for scholars and fans alike in Los Angeles. There was also some apprehension as many expected the increasing interest in vampires shown through the decade to decline sharply after the centennial passed. None placed any hope in a new television show based on a so-so movie that appeared in the spring of 1997 on a relatively small American television network. However, vampire fans across the nation joined the young adult audience already assembled by the WB channel for the opening episode of *Buffy the Vampire Slayer* only to be immediately taken by the new series. Here was a new take on the vampire, integrating the traditional lore with the Cthulhu Mythos of H. P. Lovecraft and giving the focus to the vampire slayers, a small group of high school kids and their older librarian mentor. As they realized the creative writing behind the multilayered show and the teen audience identified with the plot lines focused on Sunnydale (a fictional presentation of Santa Barbara, California), the audience increased weekly. *Buffy* became a teen phenomena and then garnered an adult audience as the word spread that the show was something special.

Not since Bela Lugosi's *Dracula* had the vampire character been offered so successfully to the popular culture. Its sophisticated presentation of a variant vampire myth demanded the attention of the small cadre of vampire and *Dracula* scholars (who initially divided over its worth and significance), but more importantly began to attract a new large audience of scholars, most of whom had previously not given the vampire any attention at all. That is, they were attracted to the show, not necessarily to the idea of a vampire or vampire slayer, but to the quality of the production, beginning with its writing by Buffy's originator, Joss Whedon. Devotees of the show came not only from the field of literature, the traditional home of those interested in vampires, but from a variety of new emerging fields focused on television and pop culture, and then reached out to include psychologists interested in fan behavior, philosophers interested in the show's metaphysics and ethics, feminists who became aware of the show's female hero, and linguists concerned with the ever-changing fluctuations in language. Even librarians were delighted that one of their own had been included among the superheroes of vampire fighters.

Just as the second season completed its successful run, the first scholarly articles began to appear and within a few years a variety of articles demonstrated the broad possibilities for understanding the complex storyline and the insightful writing behind it. In 2000, two English professors, David Lavery, from Middle Tennessee State University, and Rhonda Wilcox, from Gordon College in Georgia, started work on an anthology of *Buffy* articles. They received so many worthy submissions to their call for papers that they not only produced a watershed volume, *Fighting the Forces: What's at Stake in* Buffy the Vampire Slayer (2002), but launched a new online refereed journal to publish the overflow. *Slayage* continued as the primary focus of *Buffy* studies as the new interdisciplinary field expanded. That expansion was then further marked by the holding of a first international conference on *Buffy*—Blood, Text and Fears: Reading Around *Buffy the Vampire Slayer*—held at the University of East Anglia, October 19–20, 2002.

The East Anglia conference would lead to the monumental Slayage Conference on *Buffy the Vampire Slayer*, held in Nashville, Tennessee, in May of 2004, which attracted over 300 scholars for three days of papers. The conference became vivid testimony that *Buffy* studies were far more than a passing fad. Slowly, students of vampire lore, literature, and cinema began to realize that attention to *Buffy* had become a major item on their agenda. While a few scholars feared the possibility that *Buffy* would draw attention away from *Dracula* and even the more contemporary writings of Anne Rice, by the middle of the first decade of the new century, scholars attracted to the show were producing fully half of all the vampire-related academic writing that appeared annually with no signs of letting up. Indeed, as the *Buffy* show evolved, following its third season, it spun off a new series featuring the object of Buffy's star-crossed love, the vampire Angel.

As scholarship on *Buffy the Vampire Slayer* developed, some efforts to get a handle on the spreading literature were initiated by Derek A. Badman, David Lavery, and J. Gordon Melton, and like much of the *Buffy* scholarship in general, appeared online. These initial efforts were then continued by Don Macnaughtan and Alysa Hornick, and reached a new plateau with Macnaughton's *The Buffyverse Catalog: A Complete Guide to* Buffy the Vampire Slayer *and* Angel *in Print, Film, Television, Comics, Games and Other Media, 1992–2010* (2011).

Meanwhile, the ending of the *Buffy* television series after seven seasons followed a year later by that of *Angel* created a minor crisis for *Buffy* studies, a crisis quickly alleviated by a slight refocus and expansion of scholarly attention from *Buffy* and *Angel* to the whole body of Joss Whedon's writing and television/cinema productions. That has led to only a slight decrease in the attention given *Buffy* which by all projections will remain a significant element of scholarly attention to various related themes for the foreseeable future. With the founding of the Whedon Studies Association, the original academic *Buffy* bibliography initially compiled by Badman, which in 2005 passed to the oversight of Alysa Hornick, has re-emerged as *Whedonology: An Academic Whedon Studies Bibliography* (posted at: http://www.whedonstudies.tv/whedonology-an-academic-whedon-studies-bibliography.html). *Buffy the Vampire Slayer* has become and remains (2014) as the single television show that has attracted the most academic comment.

What appears below as an exclusively *Buffy the Vampire Slayer* and *Angel* bibliography has been developed from the *Whedonology* site. It is both more limited in that it centers on *Buffy* and *Angel*, and somewhat more expanded in that it plainly includes additional non-academic non-fictional materials generated by journalists and learned lay writers which have contributed to pushing the discussion of Buffy (and her friends and fellow slayers) and Angel (and his cohort) forward. We have also opted to include only those items written in English.

Included elsewhere in this volume are *Buffy* and *Angel*–related non-fictional materials written for children and youth (including fan material tracking the careers of the stars such as Sarah Michelle Geller and David Boreanaz). The listing includes all articles published in the peer-reviewed *Slayage: The Online International Journal of Buffy Studies* between its founding in 2001 and 2009, at which time it underwent a change in title and scope to become *Slayage: The Journal of the Whedon Studies Association*—a name which reflects its inclusion of writings on the larger body of Joss Whedon's productions, i.e., the Whedonverses. Since 2009, therefore, only *Slayage* articles on *Buffy* and *Angel* are included. In both of its incarnations, *Slayage* has been co-edited by David Lavery and Rhonda V. Wilcox, with occasional guest editors. All articles may be accessed online at http://www.whedonstudies.tv/.

In addition, the Whedon Studies Association hosts an archive site for a selection of papers delivered in 2004 at the first of what would become the biennial Slayage conferences. This 2004 conference was but one of more than a dozen academic conferences that have been held on *Buffy the Vampire Slayer* and *Angel* and the larger body of this archive may be accessed through the *Slayage* site at http:www.whedonstudies.tv/scbtvs-2004.html. Above and beyond the 2004 Slayage conference, papers from other conferences have also been published online, and the URLs for as many conference papers as have been found are included in the citations below.

With *Slayage* providing the major outlet for graduate and professional scholarship in Whedon Studies, and given the growing body of worthy scholarship at the undergraduate and graduate levels, especially in film and media studies, a second outlet, *Watcher Junior*, a peer-reviewed online journal, was founded in 2005. Originally co-edited by Lynne Edwards and Katy Stevens, *Watcher Junior* was edited by David Kociemba after 2009. Its articles on *Buffy* and *Angel* are listed below and all may now also be accessed at the Whedon Studies site, http://www.whedonstudies.tv/. Prior to launching *Watcher Junior*, Katy Stevens also published three issues of a fanzine *All Slay* (2003–04), which contained scholarly essays on *Buffy*. Articles from *All Slay* are cited below, but they are unfortunately not available online.

Due to length and scope constraints, we must also by necessity exclude a number of worthy writings that have appeared online on fan sites, blogs, and both niche and mainstream media outlets. The fact that there have been, and continue to be, so many such writings is a testament to *Buffy*'s continued popularity and influence.

All web links are to free, full-text articles, that were accessible at the time of writing.

3615. Abbott, Stacey. *Angel*. Detroit: Wayne State University Press, 2009. 136 pp. tp.

3616. _____. "Case Study: *Buffy the Vampire Slayer*." In Stacey Abbott, ed. *The Cult TV Book*. New York: I. B. Tauris, 2010, pp. 100–102.

3617. _____. "From Madman in the Basement to Self-Sacrificing Champion: The Multiple Faces of Spike." In Dee Amy-Chinn and Milly Williamson, eds. *The Vampire Spike in Text and Fandom: Unsettling Oppositions in* Buffy the Vampire Slayer. Special Issue of *European Journal of Cultural Studies* 8, 3 (August 2005): 329–344.

3618. _____. "Introduction: A Seminal Show Canceled by the Idiot Networks." In Stacey Abbot. *Angel*. Detroit: Wayne State University Press, 2009, pp. 1–8.

3619. _____. "It (Re-)Started with a Girl: The Creative Interplay Between TV and Comics in

Angel: After the Fall." In AmiJo Comeford and Tamy L. Burnett, eds. *The Literary* Angel: *Essays on Influences and Traditions Reflected in the Joss Whedon Series*. Jefferson, NC: McFarland, 2010, pp. 221–232.

3620. _____. "Joss Whedon 101: *Angel*." In Mary Alice Money for PopMatters.com, ed. *Joss Whedon: The Complete Companion: The TV Series, the Movies, the Comic Books and More*. London: Titan Books, 2012, pp. 161–167. An earlier version appeared as part of PopMatters.com's *Spotlight: Joss Whedon*, originally posted on March 15, 2011.

3621. _____. "Kicking Ass and Singing 'Mandy': A Vampire in L.A." In Stacey Abbott, ed. *Reading* Angel: *The TV Spin-off with a Soul*. New York: I. B. Tauris, 2005, pp. 1–13.

3622. _____. "A Little Less Ritual and a Little More Fun: The Modern Vampire in *Buffy the Vam-*

pire Slayer." *Slayage: The Online International Journal of Buffy Studies* 1, 3 (June 2001). Posted at: http://www.whedonstudies.tv/.

3623. _____. "'Nobody Scream...or Touch My Arms': The Comic Stylings of Wesley Wyndham-Pryce." In Stacey Abbott, ed. *Reading* Angel*: The TV Spin-off with a Soul.* New York: I. B. Tauris, 2005, pp. 189–202. A paper originally presented as "The Comic Stylings of Wesley Wyndham-Pryce" at the Slayage Conference on *Buffy the Vampire Slayer,* Nashville, TN, May 27–30 2004.

3624. _____. "Walking the Fine Line Between Angel and Angelus." *Slayage: The Online International Journal of Buffy Studies* 3, 1 (August 2003). Posted at: http://www.whedonstudies.tv/. A paper originally presented at Blood, Text and Fears: Reading Around *Buffy the Vampire Slayer,* University of East Anglia, October 19–20, 2002.

3625. _____. "'We'll Follow Angel to Hell... or Another Network: The Fan Response to the End of *Angel.*" In Stacey Abbott, ed. *Reading* Angel*: The TV Spin-off with a Soul.* New York: I. B. Tauris, 2005, pp. 230–233.

3626. _____, ed. *Reading Angel: The TV Spin-off with a Soul.* London: I. B. Tauris, 2005. 265 pp. tp. Includes contributions by Phil Colvin, Matthew Mills, Roz Kaveney, Tammy A Kinsey, Ben Jacob, Stan Beeler, Sara Upstone, Janet K. Halfyard, Matt Hills and Rebecca Williams, Michaela D.E. Meyer, Jennifer Stoy, Janine R. Harrison, Sharon Sutherland and Sarah Swan, Ann Simonds, and David Lavery and Rhonda Wilcox.

3627. Abbott, Stacey, and Lorna Jowett. "Buffy Hereafter: From the Whedonverse to the Whedonesque; October 17–19, 2007, Istanbul: Conference Report." In Rhonda V. Wilcox and Tanya R. Cochran, eds. *Special Issue on* Firefly *and* Serenity. *Slayage: The Online International Journal of Buffy Studies* 7, 1 [25] (Winter 2008). Posted at: http://www.whedonstudies.tv/.

3628. Aberdein, Andrew. "Balderdash and Chicanery: Science and Beyond in *Buffy the Vampire Slayer.*" In James B. South, ed. Buffy *and Philosophy: Fear and Trembling in Sunnydale.* Chicago: Open Court, 2003, pp. 79–90. A paper originally presented at Blood, Text and Fears: Reading Around *Buffy the Vampire Slayer,* University of East Anglia, October 19–20, 2002.

3629. Abu-Remaileh, Razan. "Vampires, Race and Citizenship in *Buffy the Vampire Slayer.*" *Ignite: Undergraduate Journal of the Institute for Gender, Race, Sexuality and Social Justice* 5.1

(2013): 6–12. Posted at: http://ojs.library.ubc.ca/index.php/ignite/article/view/184337/184042.

3630. Adams, Bonnie Jett. "Caleb, the First Evil, and 'That most precious invention of all mankind: the notion of goodness.'" In U. Melissa Anyiwo and Karoline Szatek-Tudor, eds. Buffy *Conquers the Academy: Conference Papers from the 2009/2010 Popular Culture/American Culture Associations.* Newcastle upon Tyne, UK: Cambridge Scholars Publishing, 2013, pp. 105–119. A paper originally presented as "'Crazy Preacher Man Spoutin' Off at the Mouth about the Whore of Babylon or Some-such': *Buffy the Vampire Slayer*'s Caleb, Christianity, and Comedy Gold" at the PCA/ACA National Conference, New Orleans, LA, April 8–11, 2009.

3631. Adams, Michael. "*Buffy* and the Death of Style." In Lynne Y. Edwards, Elizabeth L. Rambo, and James B. South, eds. Buffy *Goes Dark: Essays on the Final Two Seasons of* Buffy the Vampire Slayer *on Television.* Eds. Jefferson, NC: McFarland, 2009, pp. 83–94. A paper originally presented as "'Don't Give Me Songs/Give Me Something to Sing About': *Buffy the Vampire Slayer* and the Death of Style," at the Slayage Conference on *Buffy the Vampire Slayer,* Nashville, TN, May 27–30, 2004.

3632. _____. "Introduction: Beyond Slayer Slang: Pragmatics, Discourse, and Style in *Buffy the Vampire Slayer.*" In Michael Adams, ed. *Beyond Slayer Slang: Pragmatics, Discourse, and Style in* Buffy the Vampire Slayer. Special Issue of *Slayage: The Online International Journal of Buffy Studies* 5, 4 [20] (May 2006). Posted at: http://www.whedonstudies.tv/.

3633. _____. "Meaningful Infixing: A Nonexpletive Form." *American Speech* 79, 1 (Spring 2004): 110–12.

3634. _____. "Meaningful Interposing: A Countervalent Form." *American Speech* 80, 4 (Winter 2005): 437–41.

3635. _____. "Negotiating with Slang." In Michael Adams. *Slang: The People's Poetry.* Oxford: Oxford University Press, 2009, pp. 93–104.

3636. _____. "Slayer Slang." In Erin McKean, ed. *Verbatim: From the Bawdy to the Sublime, the Best Writing on Language for Word Lovers, Grammar Mavens, and Armchair Linguists.* San Diego: Harcourt, 2001, pp. 134–141.

3637. _____. "Slayer Slang (Part 1)." *Verbatim: The Language Quarterly* 24, 3 (1999): 1–4. Posted at: http://www.verbatimmag.com/summer99.html#slayer1.

3638. _____. "Slayer Slang (Part 2)." *Verbatim: The Language Quarterly* 24, 4 (1999): 1–7. Posted at: http://www.verbatimmag.com/online_issues.html.

3639. _____. *Slayer Slang: A Buffy the Vampire Slayer Lexicon.* Oxford: Oxford University Press, 2003. 308 pp. hb. dj.

3640. _____, ed. *Beyond Slayer Slang: Pragmatics, Discourse, and Style in* Buffy the Vampire Slayer. Special Issue of *Slayage: The Online International Journal of Buffy Studies* 5, 4 [20] (May 2006). Posted at: http://www.whedonstudies.tv/.

3641. Adams, Wendy A. "'I Made a Promise to a Lady': Critical Legal Pluralism as Improvised Law in *Buffy the Vampire Slayer.*" *Critical Studies in Improvisation* 6, 1 (June 2010): 1–14. Posted at: http://www.criticalimprov.com/article/view/1083/1707.

3642/43. Adler, Anthony Curtis. *The Afterlife of Genre: Remnants of the Trauerspiel in* Buffy the Vampire Slayer. Brooklyn, NY: Punctum, 2014. 76 pp. Posted at: http://punctumbooks.com/titles/afterlife-genre/.

3644. Agee, Richard S. *"Hot Chicks with Superpowers": Feminist Empowerment in* Buffy the Vampire Slayer. Mt Pleasant: Central Michigan University, M.A. thesis, 2013. 194 pp. Posted at: http://condor.cmich.edu/cdm/ref/collection/p1610-01coll1/id/3767.

3645. Aichele, George. "The Politics of Sacrifice." *Bible and Critical Theory* 1, 2 (April 2005): 6–10.

3646. _____. "Simulating Jesus." In George Aichele. *The Phantom Messiah: Postmodern Fantasy and the Gospel of Mark.* New York: T & T Clark International, 2006, pp. 203–221.

3647. Albright, Richard S. "'[B]reakaway pop hit or...book number?': 'Once More, with Feeling' and Genre." *Slayage: The Online International Journal of Buffy Studies* 5, 1 [17] (June 2005). Posted at: http://www.whedonstudies.tv/. A paper originally presented at the Slayage Conference on *Buffy the Vampire Slayer,* Nashville, TN, May 27–30, 2004.

3648. Alderman, Naomi. "'Those whom the powers wish to destroy, they must first make mad': Gods, Prophecy and Death: The Classical Roots of Madness in *Buffy the Vampire Slayer.*" A paper originally presented at the Slayage Conference on *Buffy the Vampire Slayer,* Nashville, TN, May 27–30, 2004.

3649. _____, **and Annette Seidel-Arpaci.** "Imaginary Para-Sites of the Soul: Vampires and Representations of 'Blackness' and 'Jewishness' in the Buffy/Angelverse." *Slayage: The Online International Journal of Buffy Studies* 3, 2 [10] (November 2003). Posted at: http://www.whedonstudies.tv/. A paper originally presented at Blood, Text and Fears: Reading Around *Buffy the Vampire Slayer,* University of East Anglia, October 19–20, 2002.

3650. Alessio, Dominic. "'Things are Different Now?': A Postcolonial Analysis of *Buffy the Vampire Slayer.*" *The European Legacy* 6, 6 (2001): 731–40.

3651. Alexander, Amanda. "Sex, Crime and the 'Liberated Woman' in *The Virgin Bride* and *Buffy the Vampire Slayer.*" *Australian Feminist Law Journal* 18 (2003): 77–92.

3652. Alexander, Brooks. "Witchcraft in Popular Entertainment: *The Craft, Buffy,* and Beyond." In Brooks Alexander. *Witchcraft Goes Mainstream: Uncovering Its Alarming Impact on You and Your Family.* Eugene, OR: Harvest House Publishers, 2004, pp. 91–120.

3653. Alexander, Jenny. "A Vampire Is Being Beaten: De Sade through the Looking Glass in *Buffy* and *Angel.*" *Slayage: The Online International Journal of Buffy Studies* 4, 3 [15] (December 2004). Posted at: http://www.whedonstudies.tv/. A paper originally presented at the Slayage Conference on *Buffy the Vampire Slayer,* Nashville, TN, May 27–30, 2004.

3654. Ali, Asim. "Community, Language, and Postmodernism at the Mouth of Hell." In Mary Kirby-Diaz, ed. *Buffy and Angel Conquer the Internet: Essays on Online Fandom.* Jefferson, NC: McFarland, 2009, pp. 107–125. A paper originally presented as "Community from Hell" at the Slayage Conference on *Buffy the Vampire Slayer,* Nashville, TN, May 27–30, 2004. Posted at: http://terpconnect.umd.edu/~aali/buffnog.html.

3655. _____. "'In the World, But Not of It': An Ethnographic Analysis of an Online *Buffy the Vampire Slayer* Fan Community." In Mary Kirby-Diaz, ed. *Buffy and Angel Conquer the Internet: Essays on Online Fandom.* Jefferson, NC: McFarland, 2009, pp. 87–106.

3656. _____. *Subjacent Culture, Orthogonal Community: An Ethnographic Analysis of an On-Line* Buffy the Vampire Slayer *Fan Community.* College Park: University of Maryland, Ph.D. dissertation, 2013.

3657. Allrath, Gaby. "Life in Doppelgangland: Innovative Character Conception and Alternate Worlds in *Buffy the Vampire Slayer* and *Angel*." In Gaby Allrath and Marion Gymnich, eds *Narrative Strategies in Television Series*. New York: Palgrave Macmillan, 2005, pp. 132–150.

3658. Alnwick, Marie. *Translating the Buffyverse: Examining French Fan Response to Buffy* contre les vampires. Ottawa, ON, CA: University of Ottawa, M.A. thesis, 2007. 174 pp. Large format.

3659. Aloi, Peg. "Skin Pale as Apple Blossom." In Glenn Yeffeth, ed. *Seven Seasons of* Buffy: *Science Fiction and Fantasy Writers Discuss Their Favorite Television Show*. Dallas, TX: BenBella Books, 2003, pp. 41–47.

3660. Alsford, Mike. "The Outsider: Heroes and Otherness." In Mike Alsford, ed. *Heroes and Villains*. Waco, TX: Baylor University Press, 2006, pp. 23–61.

3661. Althans, Katrin. "Playing the Buffyverse, Playing the Gothic: Genre, Gender and Cross-Media Interactivity in *Buffy the Vampire Slayer: Chaos Bleeds*." In Gretchen Papazian and Joseph M. Sommers, eds. *Game On, Hollywood! Essays on the Intersection of Video Games and Cinema*. Jefferson, NC: McFarland, 2013, pp. 20–34.

3662. Amy-Chinn, Dee. "Good Vampires Don't Suck: Sex, Celibacy and the Body of Angel." In Carla T. Kungl, ed. *Vampires: Myths and Metaphors of Enduring Evil*. Oxford: Inter-Disciplinary Press, 2003, pp. 115–120. A paper originally presented at Vampires: Myths and Metaphors of Enduring Evil, Budapest, Hungary, May 22–24, 2003.

3663. _____. "Queering the Bitch: Spike, Transgression and Erotic Empowerment." In Dee Amy-Chinn and Milly Williamson, eds. *The Vampire Spike in Text and Fandom: Unsettling Oppositions in* Buffy the Vampire Slayer. Special issue of *European Journal of Cultural Studies* 8, 3 (August 2005): 313–328. A paper originally presented at Blood, Text and Fears: Reading Around *Buffy the Vampire Slayer*, University of East Anglia, October 19–20, 2002.

3664. _____ **and Milly Williamson.** "Introduction." In Dee Amy-Chinn and Milly Williamson, eds. *The Vampire Spike in Text and Fandom: Unsettling Oppositions in* Buffy the Vampire Slayer. Special issue of *European Journal of Cultural Studies* 8, 3 (August 2005): 275–288.

3665. _____ **and Milly Williamson, eds.** *The Vampire Spike in Text and Fandom: Unsettling Oppositions in* Buffy the Vampire Slayer. Special

Issue of *European Journal of Cultural Studies* 8, 3 (August 2005): 275–399. Includes contributions by Dee Amy-Chinn and Milly Williamson, Stacey Abbott, Matt Hills and Rebecca Williams, Sue Turnbull, and Vivien Burr.

3666. Anderson, Angel. "Doyle as 'The Passing Figure' and Nella Larson's *Passing*." In AmiJo Comeford and Tamy L. Burnett, eds. *The Literary Angel: Essays on Influences and Traditions Reflected in the Joss Whedon Series*. Jefferson, NC: McFarland & Company, 2010, pp. 30–40.

3667. Anderson, Kristen Julia. "Seeing Green: Willow and Tara Forever." In Jennifer Kate Stuller, ed. *Fan Phenomena:* Buffy the Vampire Slayer. Chicago: Intellect, 2013, pp. 102–111.

3668. Anderson, Wendy Love. "Prophecy Girl and the Powers That Be: The Philosophy of Religion in the Buffyverse." In James B. South, ed. Buffy *and Philosophy: Fear and Trembling in Sunnydale*. Ed. Chicago: Open Court, 2003, pp. 212–226.

3669. _____. "What Would Buffy Do?" *Christian Century* 120, 10 (2003): 43.

3670. Andrade, Jessica. *The Gender Politics of Female Action Heroes in Television and Films*. Seattle: University of Washington, M.A. thesis, 2005. 70 pp. Large format. Posted at: https://digital.lib.washington.edu/researchworks/handle/1773/2099.

3671. Anyiwo, U. Melissa. "Introduction." In U. Melissa Anyiwo and Karoline Szatek-Tudor, eds. Buffy *Conquers the Academy: Conference Papers from the 2009/2010 Popular Culture/American Culture Associations*. Newcastle upon Tyne, UK: Cambridge Scholars Publishing, 2013, pp. 1–5.

3672. _____. "More Than Just a Spin-Off: The Enduring Allure of *Angel*." In U. Melissa Anyiwo and Karoline Szatek-Tudor, eds. Buffy *Conquers the Academy: Conference Papers from the 2009/2010 Popular Culture/American Culture Associations*. Newcastle upon Tyne, UK: Cambridge Scholars Publishing, 2013, pp. 149–161.

3673. _____, **and Karoline Szatek-Tudor, eds.** Buffy *Conquers the Academy: Conference Papers from the 2009/2010 Popular Culture/American Culture Associations*. Newcastle upon Tyne, UK: Cambridge Scholars Publishing, 2013. 278 pp. hb & tp. Includes contributions by Amanda Hobson, U. Melissa Anyiwo, Dev Kumar Bose and Esther Liberman-Cuenca, Nadine Farghaly, Mona Rocha, Cassie Hemstrom, Heather M. Porter, Lisa M. Vetere, Birte W. Horn, Bonnie Jett Adams, Ruth

Caillouet, Michael Aaron Perry, and U. Melissa Anyiwo.

3674. Aoun, Steven. "Idiot's Box: R.I.P. Buffy—Shadow Boxer Slash Serial Killer 1997–2003." *Metro Magazine: Media & Education Magazine* 138 (Fall 2003): 146–149. Posted at: http://search.informit.com.au/documentSummary;dn=832582147667789.

3675. Atchley, Clinton P. E. *"King Lear, Buffy,* and Apocalyptic Revisionism." In Kevin K. Durand, ed. Buffy *Meets the Academy: Essays on the Episodes and Scripts as Texts.* Jefferson, NC: McFarland, 2009, pp. 81–90. A paper originally presented as "'Is This the Promis'd End': *King Lear, Buffy,* and Apocalyptic Revisionism," at SC3: The Slayage Conference on the Whedonverses, Henderson State College, Arkadelphia, AR, June 5–8, 2008.

3676. Attinello, Paul G. "Rock, Television, Paper, Musicals, Scissors: *Buffy, The Simpsons,* and Parody." In Paul Attinello, Janet K. Halfyard, and Vanessa Knights, eds. *Music, Sound, and Silence in* Buffy the Vampire Slayer. Farnham, Surrey, UK: Ashgate Publishing, 2010, pp. 235–247.

3677. _____, Janet K. Halfyard, and Vanessa Knights, eds. *Music, Sound, and Silence in* Buffy the Vampire Slayer. Farnham, Surrey, UK: Ashgate Publishing, 2010. 332 pp. tp. Includes contributions by Keith Negus, John C. King and Christophe Beck, Vanessa Knights, Janet K. Halfyard, Louis Niebur, Rob Haskins, Arnie Cox and Rebecca Fülöp, Katy Stevens, Gerry Bloustien, Catherine Driscoll, Rob Cover, Renée T. Coulombe, Kathryn Hill, Diana Sandars and Rhonda V. Wilcox, Amy Bauer, Paul Attinello, and Anahid Kassabian.

3678. B., Matthew. "Relating Success to Gender in the *Angel*verse." *All Slay* 3 (2004).

3679. Bach, Jacqueline. "Not Just Another Love Song: *Buffy*'s Music as Representation of Emerging Adulthood." In Emily Dial-Driver, Sally Emmons-Featherston, Jim Ford, and Carolyn Anne Taylor, eds. *The Truth of* Buffy: *Essays on Fiction Illuminating Reality.* Jefferson, NC: McFarland & Company, 2008, pp. 38–54.

3680. _____. "Welcome to the Hellmouth: *Buffy*'s Music Arc." In Kendra Preston Leonard, ed. Buffy, *Ballads, and Bad Guys Who Sing: Music in the Worlds of Joss Whedon.* Lanham, MD: Scarecrow Press, 2011, pp. 7–28. A paper originally presented at the Southwest Popular Culture Association Conference, 2003.

3681. _____, Jessica Broussard, and Melanie K. Hundley. "Buffy Versus Bella: Teaching About Place and Gender." In Emily Dial-Driver, Sally Emmons, and Jim Ford. eds. *Fantasy Media in the Classroom: Essays on Teaching with Film, Television, Literature, Graphic Novels, and Video Games.* Jefferson, NC: McFarland & Company, 2012, pp. 182–202.

3682. Bacon-Smith, Camille. "Foreword: The Color of the Dark in Buffy the Vampire Slayer." In Rhonda V. Wilcox and David Lavery, eds. *Fighting the Forces: What's at Stake in* Buffy the Vampire Slayer. Lanham, MD: Rowman & Littlefield Publishers, 2002, pp. xi–xiii. Rev. as "The Color of the Dark." *Slayage: The Online International Journal of Buffy Studies* 2, 4 [8] (March 2003). Posted at: http://www.whedonstudies.tv/.

3683. Badman, Derek A. "Academic Buffy Bibliography." *Slayage: The Online International Journal of Buffy Studies* 2.3 [7] (December 2002). Posted at: http://www.whedonstudies.tv/.

3684. Bailey, Mike. "Personal Identity in Joss Whedon's Shows." PopMatters.com's *Spotlight: Joss Whedon* (March 30, 2011). Posted at: http://www.popmatters.com/feature/138881-personal-identity-in-joss-whedon/.

3685. Baker, Amanda M. *Joss Whedon: Finding Religious Themes in a Science Fiction Universe.* Lynchburg, VA: Liberty University, BA honors thesis, 2009. Large format. 30 pp. Posted at: http://digitalcommons.liberty.edu/cgi/viewcontent.cgi?article=1105&context=honors.

3686. Baker, Djoymi. "Contested Spaces: The Internet Ate My TV, the TV Company Ate My Internet Site." *Refractory: A Journal of Entertainment Media* 1 (2002). Posted at: http://refractory.unimelb.edu.au/2002/08/06/contested-spaces-the-internet-ate-my-tv-the-tv-company-ate-my-internet-site-djoymi-baker/.

3687. Bandy, Elizabeth A. *Growing Up with* Buffy: *How Adolescent Female Fans Use the Program in Their Everyday Lives.* Stanford, CA: Stanford University, Ph.D. dissertation, 2007. 194 pp. Large format.

3688. Barbaccia, Holly G. "Buffy in the 'Terrible House.'" *Slayage: The Online International Journal of Buffy Studies* 1, 4 [4] (December 2001). Posted at: http://www.whedonstudies.tv/.

3689. Bardi, C. Albert, and Sherry Hamby. "Existentialism Meets Feminism in Buffy the Vampire Slayer." In Joy Davidson with Leah Wilson, eds. *The Psychology of Joss Whedon: An Unautho-*

rized Exploration of Buffy, Angel, *and* Firefly. Dallas, TX: BenBella Books, 2007, pp. 105–117.

3690. Bar-Lev, Jennifer. "*Buffy the Vampire Slayer* and the Israeli-Palestinian Conflict." A paper presented at SC4: The Slayage Conference on the Whedonverses, Flagler College, St. Augustine, FL, June 3–6, 2010. 12 pp. Posted at: http://jeniferbarlev.files.wordpress.com/2010/08/buffy-online-lecture.pdf.

3691. Barnes, Elizabeth. "The New Hero: Women, Humanism and Violence in *Alias* and *Buffy the Vampire Slayer*." In Stacey Abbott and Simon Brown, eds. *Investigating* Alias: *Secrets and Spies*. New York: I. B. Tauris, 2007, pp. 57–72.

3692. Bartel, Hope K. and Timothy E. G. Bartel. "The Harrowing of Hell: 'Anne' and the Greek Paschal Tradition in Conversation." In Anthony R. Mills, John W. Morehead, and J. Ryan Parker, eds. *Joss Whedon and Religion: Essays on an Angry Atheist's Explorations of the Sacred*. Jefferson, NC: McFarland & Company, 2013, pp. 28–38.

3693. Bartlem, Edwina. "Coming Out on a Hell Mouth." *Special Issue on* Buffy the Vampire Slayer. Eds. Angela Ndalianis and Felicity Colman. *Refractory: A Journal of Entertainment Media* 2 (2003). Posted at: http://refractory.unimelb.edu.au/2003/03/06/coming-out-on-a-hell-mouth-edwina-bartlem/. A paper originally presented at The Buffyverse: A Symposium on *Buffy the Vampire Slayer*, Melbourne, Australia: University of Melbourne, November 21, 2002.

3694. Barton, Kristin M. "TV's Grim Reaper: Why Joss Whedon Continually Kills the Characters We Love." In Mary Alice Money for PopMatters.com, ed. *Joss Whedon: The Complete Companion: The TV Series, the Movies, the Comic Books and More*. London: Titan Books, 2012, pp. 153–158. An earlier version appeared as part of PopMatters.com's *Spotlight: Joss Whedon*, originally posted on April 5, 2011.

3695. Bates, Margaret, Emily M. Gustafson, Bryan C. Porterfield, and **Lawrence B. Rosenfeld.** "'When Did Your Sister Get Unbelievably Scary?': Outsider Status and Dawn and Spike's Relationship." *Slayage: The Online International Journal of Buffy Studies* 4, 4 [16] (March 2005). Posted at: http://www.whedonstudies.tv/.

3696. Battis, Jes. *Blood Relations: Chosen Families in* Buffy the Vampire Slayer *and* Angel. Jefferson, NC: McFarland & Company, 2005. 200 pp. tp.

3697. _____. *Queer Spellings: Magic and Melancholy in Fantasy-Fiction*. Burnaby, BC, CA:

Simon Fraser University, Ph.D. dissertation, 2007. 277 pp. Large format. Posted at: http://summit.sfu.ca/system/files/intems1/8288/etd3176.pdf.

3698. Bauer, Amy. "'Give Me Something to Sing About': Intertextuality and the Audience in 'Once More, with Feeling.'" In Paul Attinello, Janet K. Halfyard, and Vanessa Knights, eds. *Music, Sound, and Silence in* Buffy the Vampire Slayer. Farnham, Surrey, UK: Ashgate Publishing, 2010, pp. 209–234.

3699. Bavidge, Jenny. "Chosen Ones: Reading the Contemporary Teen Heroine." In Glyn Davis and Kay Dickinson, eds. *Teen TV: Genre, Consumption, Identity*. London, British Film Institute [BFI], 2004, pp. 41–53.

3700. Bayles, Jaq. *Drop-Dead Monstrous: The Funcion of Female Perversity in* Buffy the Vampire Slayer. Brighton, UK: University of Sussex, M.A. thesis, 2001.

3701. Beagle, Peter S. "The Good Vampire: Spike and Angel." In Glenn Yeffeth, ed. *Five Seasons of* Angel: *Science Fiction and Fantasy Writers Disccuss Their Favorite Vampire*. Dallas, TX: Benbella Books, 2004, pp. 115–124.

3702. Bear, Elizabeth. "We're Here to Save You." In Lynne M. Thomas and Deborah Stanish, eds. *Whedonistas! A Celebration of the Worlds of Joss Whedon by the Women Who Love Them*. Des Moines, IA: Mad Norwegian Press, 2011, pp. 83–85.

3703. Beddows, Emma. "Buffy the Transmedia Hero." *Colloquy: Text Theory Critique* 24 (2012): 143–158. Posted at: http://artsonline.monash.edu.au/colloquy/download/colloquy_issue_twenty-four_/beddows.pdf.

3704. Beeler, Karin. "Cheerleader/Seer: The Hybrid Visions of Cordelia Chase in *Buffy the Vampire Slayer* and *Angel*. In Karin Beeler. *Seers, Witches and Psychics on Screen: An Analysis of Women Visionary Characters in Recent Television and Film*. Jefferson, NC: McFarland & Company, 2008, pp. 25–37.

3705. Beeler, Stan. "Outing Lorne: Performance for the Performers." In Stacey Abbott, ed. *Reading* Angel: *The TV Spin-off with a Soul*. New York: I. B. Tauris, 2005, pp. 88–100.

3706. Behm, Elizabeth A. *Where's the Power in Girl Power? Images of Femininity and Feminism on Network Television*. Los Angeles: University of Southern California, M.A. thesis, 2003. 89 pp. Large format.

3707. Beirne, Rebecca. "Queering the Slayer-text: Reading Possibilities in *Buffy the Vampire Slayer*." *Refractory: A Journal of Entertainment Media* 5 (2004). Posted at: http://refractory.unimelb.edu.au/2004/02/03/queering-the-slayer-text-reading-possibilities-in-buffy-the-vampire-slayer-rebecca-beirne/. A paper originally presented at Staking a Claim: Exploring the Global Reach of *Buffy*, University of South Australia, Adelaide, Australia, July 22. 2003.

3708. Berger, Laura. *'Cup of tea, cup of tea, almost got shagged': Being a Man in a Feminist Coming of Age Story: Giles in* Buffy the Vampire Slayer. St. Catharines, ON, CA: Brock University, M.A. thesis, 2011. A paper originally presented as "'Cup of Tea, Cup of Tea, Almost Got Shagged': The Late-Life Bildungsroman of Rupert Giles in *Buffy the Vampire Slayer*" at SCW5: The Slayage Conference on the Whedonverses, University of British Columbia, Vancouver, British Columbia, July 12–15, 2012.

3709. _____. "Joss Whedon 101: *Buffy the Vampire Slayer* (The Movie)." In Mary Alice Money for PopMatters.com, ed. *Joss Whedon: The Complete Companion: The TV Series, the Movies, the Comic Books and More*. London: Titan Books, 2012, pp. 429–431. An earlier version appeared as part of PopMatters.com's *Spotlight: Joss Whedon*, originally posted on March 3, 2011.

3710. _____, and Keri Ferencz. "Returning to the Basement: Excavating the Unconscious in *Buffy*'s 'Restless.'" In Mary Alice Money for PopMatters.com, ed. *Joss Whedon: The Complete Companion: The TV Series, the Movies, the Comic Books and More*. London: Titan Books, 2012, pp. 112–125. An earlier version appeared as part of PopMatters.com's *Spotlight: Joss Whedon*, originally posted on March 13, 2011.

3711. Berger, Rose Marie. "Damnation Will Not Be Televised." *Sojourners: Faith in Action for Social Justice* 32.6 (November-December 2003): 11. Posted a: http://sojo.net/magazine/2003/11/damnation-will-not-be-televised.

3712. Berner, Amy. "The Path of Wesley Wyndam-Price." In Glenn Yeffeth, ed. *Five Seasons of* Angel: *Science Fiction and Fantasy Writers Discuss Their Favorite Vampire*. Dallas, TX: Benbella Books, 2004, pp. 145–151.

3713. Bernstein, Abbie. "It's Not Easy Being Green and Nonjudgmental." In Glenn Yeffeth, ed. *Five Seasons of* Angel: *Science Fiction and Fantasy Writers Discuss Their Favorite Vampire*. Dallas, TX: Benbella Books, 2004, pp. 65–77.

3714. Berridge, Susan. "Teen Heroine TV: Narrative Complexity and Sexual Violence in Female-Fronted Teen Drama Series." *New Review of Film and Television Studies* 11, 4 (2013): 477–496.

3715. Betancourt, Michael. "Educating Buffy: The Role of Education in *Buffy the Vampire Slayer*." *Transylvanian Journal: Dracula and Vampire Studies* 3, 2 (1998): 1–10. Posted at: http://www.michaelbetancourt.com/pdf/TJ_buffy.pdf. A paper originally presented at the International Conference on the Fantastic in the Arts, Ft. Lauderdale, FL, 1998.

3716. Bianchi, Diana. "Taming Teen-Language: The Adaptation of 'Buffyspeak' into Italian." In Delia Chiaro, Chiara Bucaria, and Christine Heiss, eds. *Between Text and Image: Updating Research in Screen Translation*. Amsterdam: John Benjamins, 2008, pp. 185–198.

3717. Bieszk, Patricia. "Vampire Hip: Style as Subcultural Expression in *Buffy the Vampire Slayer*." *Refractory: A Journal of Entertainment Media*'s *State of Play*. (February 4, 2005). Posted at: http://refractory.unimelb.edu.au/2005/02/04/vampire-hip-style-as-subcultural-expression-in-buffy-the-vampire-slayer-patricia-bieszk/. A paper originally presented at What Lies Beneath: Postgraduate Conference, AHCCA, University of Melbourne, Melbourne, Australia, November 6, 2003.

3718. Billson, Anne. *Buffy the Vampire Slayer*. Ser.: BFI TV Classics. London: British Film Institute [BFI], 2005. 154 pp. tp.

3719. Birrer, Doryjane. "A New Species of Humanities: The Marvelous Progeny of Humanism and Postmodern Theory." *Journal of Narrative Theory* 37, 2 (Summer 2007): 217–245.

3720. Bishop, Kyle. "Technophobia and the Cyborg Menace: Buffy Summers as Neo-Human Avatar." *Journal of the Fantastic in the Arts* 19, 3 (Fall 2009): 349–363.

3721. Biskup, Kristina. *(Dis)Continuities of Gender: Femininity in* Buffy the Vampire Slayer. Berlin, Germany: Freie Universität Berlin, M.A. thesis, 2006. Large format.

3722. Blackburn, Kasey. *Women of Color Consuming Prime Time Television: A Qualitative Study*. Madison: University of Wisconsin, Ph.D. dissertation, 2002. 272 pp. Large format.

3723. Blakely, David. "Signs, Signs, Everywhere Signs: Brechtian Techniques in *Buffy*." In

Emily Dial-Driver, Sally Emmons-Featherston, Jim Ford, and Carolyn Anne Taylor, eds. *The Truth of Buffy: Essays on Fiction Illuminating Reality*. Jefferson, NC: McFarland & Company, 2008, pp. 107–119.

3724. Blanco, Thèrése A. "'You're Beneath Me': The Stigma of Vampirism in the Buffyverse." A paper presented at the Slayage Conference on *Buffy the Vampire Slayer*, Nashville, TN, May 27–30, 2004.

3725. Blasingame, Katrina. "'I Can't Believe I'm Saying This Twice in the Same Century...But Duh...': The Evolution of *Buffy the Vampire Slayer* Sub-Culture Language through the Medium of Fanfiction." In Michael Adams, ed. *Beyond Slayer Slang: Pragmatics, Discourse, and Style in* Buffy the Vampire Slayer. Special Issue of *Slayage: The Online International Journal of Buffy Studies* 5.4 (20), May 2006. Posted at: http://www.whedonstudies.tv/. A paper originally presented at the Slayage Conference on *Buffy the Vampire Slayer*, Nashville, TN, May 27–30, 2004.

3726. Bley, Rebecca. "RL on LJ: Fandom and the Presentation of Self in Online Life." In Mary Kirby-Diaz, ed. *Buffy and Angel Conquer the Internet: Essays on Online Fandom*. Jefferson, NC: McFarland & Company, 2009, pp. 43–61.

3727. Bloustien, Geraldine. "'And the rest is silence': Silence and Death as Motifs in *Buffy the Vampire Slayer*." In Paul Attinello, Janet K. Halfyard, and Vanessa Knights, eds. *Music, Sound, and Silence in* Buffy the Vampire Slayer. Farnham, Surrey, UK: Ashgate Publishing, 2010, pp. 91–108.

3728. _____. "*Buffy* Night at the Seven Stars: A 'Subcultural' Happening at the 'Glocal' Level." In Andy Bennett and Keith Kahn-Harris, eds. *After Subculture: Critical Studies in Contemporary Youth Culture*. New York: Palgrave Macmillan, 2004, pp. 148–160. A paper originally presented as "*Buffy* Night at the Seven Stars" at Blood, Text and Fears: Reading Around *Buffy the Vampire Slayer*, University of East Anglia, October 19–20, 2002.

3729. _____. "Carpe Diem or 'Fish of the Day?' Time as Leitmotif in *Buffy the Vampire Slayer*." Featured lecture at the Slayage Conference on *Buffy the Vampire Slayer*, Nashville, TN, May 27–30, 2004. 12 pp. Posted at: http://www.slayageonline.com/SCBtVS_Archive/Talks/Bloustien.pdf.

3730. _____. "Fans with a Lot at Stake: Serious Play & Mimetic Excess in *Buffy the Vampire Slayer*." *European Journal of Cultural Studies* 5, 4 (2002): 427–49.

3731. Bobbitt, Rebecca. "Wesley as Tragic Hero." In Kevin K. Durand, ed. Buffy *Meets the Academy: Essays on the Episodes and Scripts as Texts*. Jefferson, NC: McFarland & Company, 2009, pp. 169–175. A paper originally presented as "'Not All of Us Have Muscle to Fall Back On': Wesley Wyndam-Price as Tragic Hero" at SC2: The Slayage Conference on the Whedonverses, Gordon College, Barnesville, GA, May 25–28, 2006.

3732. Bodger, Gwyneth. "Buffy the Feminist Slayer? Constructions of Femininity in *Buffy the Vampire Slayer*." In Angela Ndalianis and Felicity Colman, eds. *Special Issue on* Buffy the Vampire Slayer. *Refractory: A Journal of Entertainment Media* 2 (2003). Posted at: http://refractory.unimelb.edu.au/2003/03/06/buffy-the-feminist-slayer-constructions-of-femininity-in-buffy-the-vampire-slayer-gwyneth-bodger/.

3733. Booker, M. Keith. "*Buffy* Keeps It Cool." In M. Keith Bodger. *Red, White, and Spooked: The Supernatural in American Culture*. Westport, CT: Praeger, 2009, pp. 89–101.

3734. _____. "Hard-Boiled Magic: The Vampire Detective." In M. Keith Bodger. *Red, White, and Spooked: The Supernatural in American Culture*. Westport, CT: Praeger, 2009, pp. 67–82.

3735. Boreliz, Caitlin. "Kaylee Frye: Slaying the Angel in the House." *Watcher Junior: The Undergraduate Journal of Whedon Studies* 6, 1 [7] (July 2012). A paper originally presented at the 33rd Annual Southwest/Texas PCA/ACA Conference, Albuquerque, NM, February 8–11, 2012. Posted at: http://www.whedonstudies.tv/.

3736. Bose, Dev Kumar and Esther Liberman-Cuenca. "*Buffy, Angel*, and the Complications of the Soul: A Collaborative Perspective on the Origin Episodes." In U. Melissa Anyiwo and Karoline Szatek-Tudor, es. *Buffy Conquers the Academy: Conference Papers from the 2009/2010 Popular Culture/American Culture Associations* Newcastle upon Tyne, UK: Cambridge Scholars Publishing, 2013, pp. 6–18. A paper originally presented as "*Buffy, Angel*, and Complications of the Soul: Observations on Lineage, Colonial Identity, and Gender Roles" at the 2009 PCA/ACA National Conference, New Orleans, LA, April 8–11, 2009.

3737. Bosseaux, Charlotte. "Bloody hell. Sodding, blimey, shagging, knickers, bollocks. Oh God, I'm English: Translating Spike." In Sam George and Bill Hughes, eds. *Open Graves, Open Minds: Vampires and the Undead in Modern Culture*. Special Issue of *Gothic Studies* 15, 1 (May

2013): 21–32. A paper originally presented at the conference on Open Graves, Open Minds: Vampires and the Undead in Modern Culture, University of Hertfordshire, Hatfield, UK, April 16–17, 2010.

3738. _____. "*Buffy the Vampire Slayer*: Characterization in the Musical Episode of the TV Series." *The Translator: Studies in Intercultural Communication* 14, 2 (2008): 343–372.

3739. _____. "Translating Britishness in the French Versions of *Buffy the Vampire Slayer*." *Quaderns de Filologia* 13 (2008): 85–103.

3740. Bowers, Cynthia. "Generation Lapse: The Problematic Parenting of Joyce Summers and Rupert Giles." *Slayage: The Online International Journal of Buffy Studies* 2 (2001). Posted at: http://www.whedonstudies.tv/.

3741. Bowman, James. "Childish Wish-Fulfullment." *New Criterion* 18, 3 (November 1999): 54–59.

3742. Bowman, Laurel. "Whedon Meets Sophocles: Prophecy and *Angel*. In AmiJo Comeford and Tamy L. Burnett, ed. *The Literary Angel: Essays on Influences and Traditions Reflected in the Joss Whedon Series*. Jefferson, NC: McFarland & Company, 2010, pp. 191–205.

3743. Boyette, Michele. "The Comic Anti-hero in *Buffy the Vampire Slayer*, or Silly Villain: Spike is for Kicks." *Slayage: The Online International Journal of Buffy Studies* 1, 4 [4] (December 2001).

3744. Boyle, Karen. "The Days of Whose Lives? Violence, (Post-)Feminism and Television." *Media and Violence: Gendering the Debates*. London: Sage, 2005. 187–193. Also accepted (but not presented) in earlier form as "Male Violence, (Post-)Feminist Television Criticism and Buffy the Vampire Slayer" for the Slayage Conference on *Buffy the Vampire Slayer*, Nashville, TN, May 27–30, 2004.

3745. Brace, Patricia. "Fashioning Feminism: Whedon, Women, and Wardrobe." In Dean A. Kowalski and S. Evan Kreider, eds. *The Philosophy of Joss Whedon*. Lexington: University Press of Kentucky, 2011, pp. 117–32.

3746. Bradney, Anthony. "The Case of *Buffy the Vampire Slayer* and the Politics of Legal Education." In Steven Greenfield and Guy Osborn, eds. *Readings in Law and Popular Culture*. New York: Routledge, 2006, pp. 15–30.

3747. _____. "Choosing Laws, Choosing Families: Images of Law, Love and Authority in *Buffy the Vampire Slayer*." *Web Journal of Current Legal Issues* 2 Web JCLI (2003). Posted at: http://webjcli.ncl.ac.uk/2003/issue2/bradney2.html. A paper originally presented at Blood, Text and Fears: Reading Around *Buffy the Vampire Slayer*, University of East Anglia, October 19–20, 2002.

3748. _____. "For and Against the Law: *Buffy the Vampire Slayer*, *Angel* and the Academy." *Entertainment and Sports Law Journal* 9, 1 (2011). Posted at: http://www2.warwick.ac.uk/fac/soc/law/elj/eslj/issues/volume9/bradney.

3749. _____. "'I Made a Promise to a Lady': Law and Love in *Buffy the Vampire Slayer*." *Slayage: The Online International Journal of Buffy Studies* 3, 2 [10] (November 2003).

3750. _____. "Images of Law in *Buffy the Vampire Slayer*." Paper presented at the Slayage Conference on *Buffy the Vampire Slayer*, Nashville, TN, May 27–30, 2004. Posated at: http://www.slayageonline.com/SCBtVS_Archive/Talks/Bradney.pdf.

3751. _____. "'It's About Power': Law in the Fictional Setting of a Quaker Meeting and in the Everyday Reality of *Buffy the Vampire Slayer*." *Issues in Legal Scholarship* 6, 1 (January 2006).

3752. _____. "'The Morally Ambiguous Crowd': The Image of a Large Law Firm in *Angel*." *Northern Ireland Legal Quarterly* 56 (2005): 21–37.

3753. _____. "The Politics and Ethics of Researching the Buffyverse." *Slayage: The Online International Journal of Buffy Studies* 5, 3 [19] (February 2006). A paper originally presented as "The Politics and Ethics of writing about the Buffyverse" at Bring Your Own Subtext: Social Life, Human Experience and the Works of Joss Whedon, Conference, University of Huddersfield, Huddersfield, UK, June 29-July 1, 2005.

3754. Brannon, Julie Sloan. "'It's About Power': *Buffy*, Foucault, and the Quest for Self." *Slayage: The Online International Journal of Buffy Studies* 6, 4 [24] (Summer 2007). A paper originally presented at the 2003 PCAS/ACAS Annual Conference, Atlantic Beach, FL, October 2–4, 2003.

3755. Branston, Gill, and Roy Stafford. "Case Study: *Buffy the Vampire Slayer*." In Gill Branston and Roy Stafford. *The Media Student's Book*. 3rd ed. New York: Routledge, 2003, pp. 82–89.

3756. Braun, Beth. "*The X-files* and *Buffy the Vampire Slayer*: The Ambiguity of Evil in Supernatural Representations." *Journal of Popular Film & Television* 28, 2 (2000): 88–94. Posted at: http://www.slayageonline.com/EBS/buffy_studies/scholars_critics/a_e/braun.htm.

3757. Breton, Rob, and Lindsey McMaster. "Dissing the Age of Moo: Initiatives, Alternatives, and Rationality in *Buffy the Vampire Slayer*." *Slayage: The Online International Journal of Buffy Studies* 1, 1 [1] (January 2001). Posted at: http://www.whedonstudies.tv/.

3758. Bridges, Elizabeth. "Grimm Realities: *Buffy* and the Uses of Folklore." In Kevin K. Durand, ed. Buffy *Meets the Academy: Essays on the Episodes and Scripts as Texts*. Jefferson, NC: McFarland & Company, 2009, pp. 91–103. A paper originally presented as "*Buffy* and Old World Folklore" at SC3: The Slayage Conference on the Whedonverses, Henderson State College, Arkadelphia, AR, June 5–8, 2008.

3759. Bridwell, Nick. "Joss Whedon 101: *Buffy the Vampire Slayer* Season Eight." In Mary Alice Money for PopMatters.com, ed. *Joss Whedon: The Complete Companion: The TV Series, the Movies, the Comic Books and More*. London: Titan Books, 2012, pp. 337–340. An earlier version appeared as part of PopMatters.com's *Spotlight: Joss Whedon*, originally posted on March 22, 2011.

3760. _____. "Wesley Wyndam-Pryce: Joss Whedon's True Tragic Hero." PopMatters.com's *Spotlight: Joss Whedon* (March 15, 2011). Posted at: http://www.popmatters.com/feature/138257-wesley-wyndam-pryce-joss-whedons-true-tragic-hero/.

3761. Brin, David. "Buffy vs. the Old-fashioned 'Hero.'" In Glenn Yeffeth, ed. *Seven Seasons of* Buffy: *Science Fiction and Fantasy Writers Discuss Their Favorite Television Show*. Dallas, TX: Benbella Books, 2003, pp. 1–4.

3762. Brown, Glenn. "Consequence and Change in the Works of Joss Whedon, and Why It Matters." PopMatters.com's *Spotlight: Joss Whedon* (March 28, 2011). Posted at: http://www.popmatters.com/feature/138725-consequence-and-change-in-the-works-of-joss-whedon-and-why-it-matter/.

3763. Brown, Jeffrey A. "Kinky Vampires and Action Heroines." In Jeffrey A. Brown. *Dangerous Curves: Action Heroines, Gender, Fetishism, and Popular Culture*. Jackson: University Press of Mississippi, 2011, pp. 185–207.

3764. Browne, Daniel. "One Man's Myth: How Joss Whedon Showed Me the Crack in the Invisible Wall." *New Orleans Review* 38, 2 (Fall 2012). Posted at: http://www.neworleansreview.org/one-mans-myth-how-joss-whedon-showed-me-the-crack-in-the-invisible-wall/.

3765. Bruggink, Heidi J. *Taking Back the Night:* Buffy the Vampire Slayer *and Girl Power Feminism*. Cambridge, MA: Harvard University, BA honors thesis, 2005. 53 pp. Large format.

3766. Bryce, Devon Elizabeth. *Surviving the Change: The Domestication of the Vampire in Literature, Film, and Television*. Edmonton, AL, CA: University of Alberta, M.A. thesis, 2009. 129 pp.

3767. Buchanan, Ginjer. "The Journey of Jonathan Levenson: From Scenery to Sacrifice." In Paul Ruditis, ed. Buffy the Vampire Slayer: *The Watcher's Guide*. Vol. 3. New York: Simon, 2004, pp. 241–248.

3768. Buckman, Alyson R. "Triangulated Desire in *Angel* and *Buffy*." In Erin B. Waggoner, ed. *Sexual Rhetoric in the Works of Joss Whedon: New Essays*. Jefferson, NC: McFarland & Company, 2010, pp. 48–92. A paper originally presented as "'Is there anyone here that hasn't slept together?': Triangulated Desire in *Buffy* and *Angel*" at the 31st Annual Southwest/Texas PCA/ACA Conference, Albuquerque, NM, February 10–13, 2010.

3769. *Buffy the Vampire Slayer! The Best Websites and Factoids: An Unofficial Independent Guide*. Port Orchard, WA: Lightning Rod Ltd., 2002. 52 pp. tp.

3770. Buinicki, Martin and Anthony Enns. "Buffy the Vampire Disciplinarian: Institutional Excess, Spiritual Technologies, and the New Economy of Power." *Slayage: The Online International Journal of Buffy Studies* 1, 4 [4] (December 2001). Posted at: http://www.whedonstudies.tv/.

3771. Bundgaard, Andra. *The Female Heroine and the New Vampires on Television: A Comparison of* Buffy the Vampire Slayer, True Blood *and* The Vampire Diaries. Dublin: Dublin City University, M.A. thesis, 2012. This thesis was originally presented in shortened form at TV Fangdom: A Conference on Television Vampires, University of Northampton, Northampton, UK, June 7–8, 2013.

3772. Burdolski, Lauren. "Reflections of Society in the Buffyverse." Paper presented at the Slayage Conference on *Buffy the Vampire Slayer*, Nashville, TN, May 27–30, 2004. Posted at: http://www.whedonstudies.tv/.

3773. Burkhead, Cynthea. "Case Study: *Buffy the Vampire Slayer*." In Cynthia Burkhead. *Dreams in American Television Narratives from Dallas to Buffy*. London: Bloomsbury, 2013, pp. 83–90 pp. This paper originally appeared as a chapter in Burkhead's Ph.D. dissertation. *Dancing Dwarfs and Talking Fish: The Narrative Functions of Television Dreams* (2010. Pp. 121–135).

3774. _____. *Dancing Dwarfs and Talking Fish: The Narrative Functions of Television Dreams*. Murfreesboro: Middle Tennessee State University, Ph.D. dissertation, 2010. 218 pp.

3775. _____. *Joss Whedon: Conversations*. Ser.: Television Conversations. Oxford: University Press of Mississippi, 2011.

3776. _____**, Ian G. Klein, and David Kociemba.** "Whedon and His Players: A Report on New Scholarship at SC4." In Cynthea Masson and Rhonda V. Wilcox, eds. *Fantasy Is Not Their Purpose: Joss Whedon's* Dollhouse. Special Issue of *Slayage: The Journal of the Whedon Studies Association* 8, 2–3 [30–31] (Summer/Fall 2010). Posted at: http://www.whedonstudies.tv/.

3777. Burnett, Tamy L. "Anya as Feminist Model of Positive Female Sexuality." In Erin B. Waggoner, ed. *Sexual Rhetoric in the Works of Joss Whedon: New Essays*. Jefferson, NC: McFarland & Company, 2010, pp. 117–145.

3778. _____. "Fred's Captivity Narrative: American Contexts for (Re)Writing Community Identity from Mary Rowlandson to *Angel*." In AmiJo Comeford and Tamy L. Burnett, ed. *The Literary* Angel: *Essays on Influences and Traditions Reflected in the Joss Whedon Series*. Jefferson, NC: McFarland & Company, 2010, pp. 69–84. A paper originally presented as "'A Stunning Revelation of My True Path in Life': The American Captivity Narrative from Mary Rowlandson to Fred Burkle" at SC4: The Slayage Conference on the Whedonverses, Flagler College, St. Augustine, FL, June 3–6, 2010.

3779. _____. *"Just a Girl": The Community-Centered Cult Television Heroine, 1995–2007*. Lincoln: University of Nebraska, Ph.D. dissertation, 2010. 208 pp. Large format. Posted at: http://digitalcommons.unl.edu/cgi/viewcontent.cgi?article=1030&context=englishdiss.

3780. Burns, Angie. "Passion, Pain and 'Bad Kissing Decisions': Learning About Intimate Relationships from *Buffy* Season Six." *Slayage: The Online International Journal of Buffy Studies* 6, 1 [21] (Fall 2006). Posted at: http://www.whedon

studies.tv/. A paper originally presented as "Monstrous Love and Muscular Sex: Learning About Intimate Relationships from *Buffy the Vampire Slayer*" at the International Conference Critical Psychology: Contesting Conflict, Challenging Consensus, University of Bath, UK, August 2003, and subsequently presented at Bring Your Own Subtext: Social Life, Human Experience and the Works of Joss Whedon, Conference, University of Huddersfield, Huddersfield, UK, June 29-July 1, 2005.

3781. Burr, Vivien. "Ambiguity and Sexuality in Buffy the Vampire Slayer: A Sartrean Analysis." *Sexualities* 6, 3 (August 2003): 343–60.

3782. _____. "Bad Girls Like It Rough (And Good Girls Don't?): Representations of BDSM in *Buffy the Vampire Slayer*." *Phoebe: Gender and Cultural Critiques* 18, 1 (2006): 45–57. A paper originally presented as "Bad Girls Like It Rough…And Good Girls Don't? Representations of Sexuality in *Buffy the Vampire Slayer*" at the Pleasure & Danger Revisited conference, Cardiff University, Cardiff Wales, UK, July 2004.

3783. _____. "Bringing Your Own Subtext: Individual Differences in Viewers' Responses to *Buffy*." Paper presented at the Slayage Conference on *Buffy the Vampire Slayer*, Nashville, TN, May 27–30, 2004. Posted at: http://www.slayageonline.com/SCBtVS_Archive/.

3784. _____. "*Buffy* vs. the BBC: Moral Questions and How to Avoid Them." *Slayage: The Online International Journal of Buffy Studies* 2, 4 [8] (March 2003). Posted at: http://www.whedonstudies.tv/.

3785. _____. "'It All Seems So Real': Intertextuality in the Buffyverse." In Angela Ndalianis and Felicity Colman, eds. *Special Issue on* Buffy the Vampire Slayer. *Refractory: A Journal of Entertainment Media* 2 (2003). Posted at: http://refractory.unimelb.edu.au/2003/03/18/vol2/.

3786. _____. "'Oh Spike, you're covered in sexy wounds!': The Erotic Significance of Wounding and Torture in *Buffy the Vampire Slayer*." In Vivien Burr and Jeff Hearn, ed. *Sex, Violence, and the Body: The Erotics of Wounding*. New York: Palgrave Macmillan, 2009, pp. 137–156.

3787. _____. "Performing the Imaginative Variation: Using *Buffy* to Teach Sartre." A paper presented at the Slayage Conference on *Buffy the Vampire Slayer*, Nashville, TN, May 27–30, 2004. Posted at: http://www.slayageonline.com/SCBtVS_Archive/Talks/Burr.pdf.

3788. ____. "Scholar/'shippers and Spikea-holics: Academic and Fan Identities at the Slayage Conference on *Buffy the Vampire Slayer*." In Dee Amy-Chinn and Milly Williamson, eds. *The Vampire Spike in Text and Fandom: Unsettling Oppositions in* Buffy the Vampire Slayer. Special Issue of *European Journal of Cultural Studies* 8.3, August 2005, pp. 375–383. A paper originally presented at Bring Your Own Subtext: Social Life, Human Experience and the Works of Joss Whedon, Conference, University of Huddersfield, Huddersfield, UK, June 29-July 1, 2005.

3789. ____. "Sex and Censorship: The Case of *Buffy the Vampire Slayer*." *Young: Nordic Journal of Youth Research* 13, 3 (2005).

3790. ____, and Christine Jarvis. "'Friends are the family we choose for ourselves': Young People and Families in the TV Series *Buffy the Vampire Slayer*." *Young: Nordic Journal of Youth Research* 13, 3 (2005). A paper originally presented as "'Friends are the family we choose for ourselves': Young People and Families in *Buffy the Vampire Slayer*" at the Slayage Conference on *Buffy the Vampire Slayer*, Nashville, TN, May 27–30, 2004. Posted at: http://www.slayageonline.com/SCBtVS_Archive/.

3791. ____, and Christine Jarvis. "Imagining the Family: Representations of Alternative Lifestyles in *Buffy the Vampire Slayer*." *Qualitative Social Work* 6, 3 (September 2007): 263–280.

3792. ____, and Christine Jarvis. "The Transformative Potential of Popular Television: The Case of *Buffy the Vampire Slayer*." *Journal of Transformative Education* 9, 3 (July 2011): 165–182.

3793. Bushman, David and Arthur Smith. "Unlimited Potentials: Reflections of the Slayer." In Jennifer Kate Stuller, ed. *Fan Phenomena:* Buffy the Vampire Slayer. Chicago: Intellect, 2013, pp. 150–159.

3794. Busse, Kristina. "Crossing the Final Taboo: Family, Sexuality, and Incest in Buffyverse Fan Fiction." In Rhonda V. Wilcox and David Lavery, ed. *Fighting the Forces: What's at Stake in* Buffy the Vampire Slayer. Lanham, MD: Rowman & Littlefield, 2002, pp. 207–217. A paper originally presented as "Buffyverse Beyond Slash: Crossing the Final Taboo in Fan Fiction" at the Computers and Writing Conference, Fort Worth, TX, May 2000.

3795. Bussolini, Jeffrey. "Blood, Vamps and Christianity." A paper originally presented at Blood, Text and Fears: Reading Around *Buffy the Vampire Slayer*, University of East Anglia, October 19–20, 2002. This paper was later published in Italian translation as "Sangue, Vampiri e Cristianità." In Barbara Maio, ed. Buffy the Vampire Slayer: *Legittimare la Cacciatrice*. Rome: Bulzoni Editore, 2007, pp. 65–78.

3796. ____. "Los Alamos Is the Hellmouth." *Slayage: The Online International Journal of Buffy Studies* 5, 2 [18]] (September 2005). Posted at: http://www.whedonstudies.tv/. A paper originally presented at the Slayage Conference on *Buffy the Vampire Slayer*, Nashville, TN, May 27–30, 2004.

3797. ____. "Television Intertextuality After *Buffy*: Intertextuality of Casting and Constitutive Intertextuality." *Slayage: The Journal of the Whedon Studies Association* 10, 1 [35] (Winter 2013). Posted at: http://www.whedonstudies.tv/. A paper originally presented as "Television Intertextuality After *Buffy*" at SC3: The Slayage Conference on the Whedonverses, Henderson State College, Arkadelphia, AR, June 5–8, 2008, and subsequently at the 2010 PCAS/ACAS Annual Conference, Savannah, GA, October 7–9, 2010.

3798. Butler, Lori M. "'The Ants Go Marching': Effective Lyrics in *Buffy* Episodes." *The Truth of* Buffy: *Essays on Fiction Illuminating Reality*. Eds. Emily Dial-Driver, Sally Emmons-Featherston, Jim Ford and Carolyn Anne Taylor. Jefferson, NC: McFarland & Company, 2008, pp.120–130.

3799. Buttsworth, Sara. "'Bite Me': Buffy and the Penetration of the Gendered Warrior-hero." *Continuum: Journal of Media & Cultural Studies* 16, 2 (2002): 185–99.

3800. ____. Body Count: The Politics of Representing the Gendered Body in Combat in Australia and the United States. Crawley, Western Australia: University of Western Australia, Ph.D. dissertation, 2003. 394 pp. Large format.

3801. ____. "Who's Afraid of Jessica Lynch? Or, One Girl in All the World? Gendered Heroism and the Iraq War." *Australasian Journal of American Studies* 24, 2 (December 2005): 42–62. Posted at: http://www.anzasa.arts.usyd.edu.au/a.j.a.s/Articles/2_05/Buttsworth.pdf. Revised from material presented in *Body Count*.

3802. Buus, Stephanie. "Hell on Earth." *Cooperation and Conflict* 44, 4 (2009): 400–419.

3803. Byers, Michele. *Buffy the Vampire Slayer: The Insurgence of Television as a Performance Text*. Toronto: University of Toronto, Ph.D. dissertation, 2000. 432 pp. Large format. Posted at: http://www.collectionscanada.gc.ca/obj/s4/f2/dsk2/ftp03/NQ53861.pdf.

3804. _____. "*Buffy the Vampire Slayer*: The Next Generation of Television." In Rory Dicker and Alison M. Piepmeier, eds. *Catching a Wave: Reclaiming Feminism for the 21st Century*. Boston, MA: Northeastern University Press, 2003, pp. 171–187.

3805. Caelsto, Mary. *The Fool's Journey through Sunnydale: The Archetypes of the Major Arcana as Seen on* Buffy the Vampire Slayer. Grimes, IA: Jupiter Garden Press, 2010. 176 pp. tp.

3806. Caillouet, Ruth. "I Date Dead People: Buffy, Bella, Sookie, and the Lure of the Dead Boyfriend." In U. Melissa Anyiwo and Karoline Szatek-Tudor, eds. Buffy *Conquers the Academy: Conference Papers from the 2009/2010 Popular Culture/American Culture Associations*. Newcastle upon Tyne, UK: Cambridge Scholars Publishing, 2013, pp. 120–135. A paper originally presented in earlier form at the 2009 PCA/ACA National Conference, New Orleans, LA, April 8–11, 2009, and as "Dating Dead Boyfriends: Buffy, Bella, Sookie, and the Love of Vampires" at the 2012 PCA/ACA National Conference, Boston, MA, April 11–14, 2012.

3807. Call, Lewis. "Slaying the Heteronormative: Representations of Alternative Sexuality in *Buffy* Season Eight Comics." In Erin B. Waggoner, ed. *Sexual Rhetoric in the Works of Joss Whedon: New Essays*. Jefferson, NC: McFarland & Company, 2010, pp. 106–116. A paper originally presented at the 30th Annual Southwest/Texas PCA/ACA Conference, Albuquerque, NM, February 25–28, 2009.

3808. _____. "'Sounds Like Kinky Business to Me': Subtextual and Textual Representations of Erotic Power in the Buffyverse." *Slayage: The Online International Journal of Buffy Studies* 6, 4 [24] (Summer 2007 Posted at: http://www.whedon studies.tv/. Rev. as: "Sounds like kinky business to me": BDSM on *Buffy* and *Angel*." In Lewis Call. *BDSM in American Science Fiction and Fantasy*. Basingstoke, UK: Palgrave Macmillan, 2012, pp. 147–82.

3809. Callander, Michelle. "Bram Stoker's Buffy: Traditional Gothic and Contemporary Culture." *Slayage: The Online International Journal of Buffy Studies* 1, 3 [3] (June 2001). Posted at: http://www.whedonstudies.tv/.

3810. Calvert, Bronwen. "Going Through the Motions: Robots in *Buffy the Vampire Slayer*." *Slayage: The Online International Journal of Buffy Studies* 4, 3 [15] (December 2004). Posted at: http://www.whedonstudies.tv/. A paper originally presented at the Slayage Conference on *Buffy the Vampire Slayer*, Nashville, TN, May 27–30, 2004.

3811. _____. "'The Shell I'm In': Illyria and Monstrous Embodiment." In Mary Alice Money for PopMatters.com, ed. *Joss Whedon: The Complete Companion: The TV Series, the Movies, the Comic Books and More*. London: Titan Books, 2012, pp. 181–190. A paper originally presented as "'The Shell I'm In': Monstrous Embodiment and the Case of Illyria in *Angel*" at *Buffy* Hereafter: From the Whedonverse to the Whedonesque: An Interdisciplinary Conference on the Work of Joss Whedon and its Aftereffects, Istanbul, Turkey, October 17–19, 2007.

3812. Campbell, Richard and Caitlin Campbell. "Demons, Aliens, Teens and Television." *Television Quarterly* 34, 1 (2001). Rpt. in *Slayage: The Online International Journal of Buffy Studies* 2 (2001). Posted at: http://www.whedon studies.tv/.

3813. Camron, Marc. "The Importance of Being the Zeppo: Xander, Gender Identity and Hybridity in *Buffy the Vampire Slayer*." *Slayage: The Online International Journal of Buffy Studies* 6, 3 [23] (Spring 2007). Posted at: http://www.whedon studies.tv/.

3814. Canavan, Gerry. "Zombies, Reavers, Butchers, and Actuals in Joss Whedon's Work." In Mary Alice Money for PopMatters.com, ed. *Joss Whedon: The Complete Companion: The TV Series, the Movies, the Comic Books and More*. London: Titan Books, 2012, pp. 285–297. An earlier version appeared as part of PopMatters.com's *Spotlight: Joss Whedon*, originally posted on April 3, 2011.

3815. Cantwell, Marianne. "Collapsing the Extra/Textual: Passions and Intensities of Knowledge in *Buffy the Vampire Slayer* Online Fan Communities." *Refractory: A Journal of Entertainment Media* 5 (2004). Posted at: http://refractory.uni melb.edu.au/2004/02/03/vol5/.

3816. Cardow, Andrew. "Everyman with Fangs: The Acceptance of the Modern Vampire." *Business Research Working Paper Series* 6 (2007). Auckland, NZ: Department of Management and International Business, Massey University, 2007. 12 pp. Posted at: http://muir.massey.ac.nz/handle/10179/651?show=full.

3817. Carroll, Shiloh R. *Fantasy and Pedagogy: The Use of Fantasy in College Classrooms*. Radford, VA: Radford University, M.A. thesis, 2008. 98 pp. Large format. Posted at: http://www.academia.edu/246055/FANTASY_AND_PEDAGOGY_THE_USE_OF_FANTASY_IN_COLLEGE_CLASSROOMS.

3818. _____. "Psychology of a 'Superstar': A Pyschological Analysis of Jonathan Levinson." *Slayage: The Online International Journal of Buffy Studies* 7, 4 [28] (Summer 2009). Posted at: http://www.whedonstudies.tv/.

3819. **Carroll, Valerie A.** *Re-Presenting and Representing on Girl Power TV: Examining Portrayals of Resistance and Domination from* Dark Angel, Charmed, *and* Buffy the Vampire Slayer. St. Louis, MO: Saint Louis University, Ph.D. dissertation, 2005. 195 pp. Large format.

3820. **Carson, Tom.** "So-Called Vampires: Buffy Battles Teendom's Demons." *Village Voice* 10 (June 1997): 51.

3821. **Carter, Margaret L.** "A World without Shrimp." In Glenn Yeffeth, ed. *Seven Seasons of Buffy: Science Fiction and Fantasy Writers Discuss Their Favorite Television Show.* Dallas, TX: Benbella Books, 2003, pp. 176–187.

3822. **Casey, Erin.** "The Dystopian Future in Joss Whedon's Work." In Mary Alice Money for PopMatters.com, ed. *Joss Whedon: The Complete Companion: The TV Series, the Movies, the Comic Books and More.* London: Titan Books, 2012, pp. 398–400. An earlier version appeared as part of PopMatters.com's *Spotlight: Joss Whedon,* originally posted on April 10, 2011.

3823. **Chaffey, Lucian.** *Teleodyssey.* Melbourne, Aust.: University of Melbourne, Ph.D. dissertation, 2007. 379 pp. Large format.

3824. **Chambers, Samuel A.** "The Meaning of 'Family.'" In Samuel A. Chambers. *The Queer Politics of Television.* New York: I. B. Tauris, 2009, pp. 131–170.

3825. _____, **and Daniel Williford.** "Anti-Imperialism in the Buffyverse: Challenging the Mythos of Bush as Vampire Slayer." *Poroi: An Interdisciplinary Journal of Rhetorical Analysis and Intervention* 3, 2 (2004): 109–29. Posted at: http://ir.uiowa.edu/cgi/viewcontent.cgi?article=1040&context=poroi&sei-redir=1&referer=http%3A%2F%2Fsearch.yahoo.com%2Fsearch%3B_ylt%3DAqZj8jdFO4rDB0JV.fB8Sr2bvZx4%3Fp%3DWilliford.%2B%2522Anti-Imperialism%2Bin%2Bthe%2BBuffyverse%26toggle%3D1%26cop%3Dmss%26ei%3DUTF-8%26fr%3Dyfp-t-180-17#search=%22Williford.%20Anti-Imperialism%20Buffyverse%22.

3826. **Chandler, Holly.** "Slaying the Patriarchy: Transfusions of the Vampire Metaphor in *Buffy the Vampire Slayer.*" *Slayage: The Online International Journal of Buffy Studies* 3, 1 [9] (August 2003). Posted at: http://www.whedonstudies.tv/.

3827. **Chang, Lisa.** "'Like Other Girls': Reinforcive Gender Roles in *Buffy the Vampire Slayer.*" *Comm-Entary: The Undergraduate Journal of Communication* (Spring 2003): 21–36. Posted at: http://unhcommentary.files.wordpress.com/2012/01/spring03.pdf.

3828. **Chess, Shira.** *(En)Gendering the Boob Tube: Technology, Agency, and the Action TV Femme.* Boston, MA, Emerson College, M.A. thesis, 2003. 79 pp. Large format.

3829. **Chiat, Kevin.** "Giant Dawn and Mutant Superheroes: Joss Whedon in Comics." In Mary Alice Money for PopMatters.com, ed. *Joss Whedon: The Complete Companion: The TV Series, the Movies, the Comic Books and More.* London: Titan Books, 2012, pp. 341–352.

3830. **Chin, Vivian.** "Buffy? She's Like Me, She's Not Like Me—She's Rad." In Frances Early and Kathleen Kennedy, eds. *Athena's Daughters: Television's New Women Warriors.* Syracuse, NY: Syracuse University Press, 2003, pp. 92–102.

3831. **Ciencin, Scott and Denise Ciencin.** "I Know You Are, but Who Am I? Dawn." In Paul Ruditis, ed. Buffy the Vampire Slayer: *The Watcher's Guide.* Vol. 3. New York: Simon, 2004, pp. 277–282.

3832. **Clark, Daniel A., and P. Andrew Miller.** "Buffy, the Scooby Gang, and Monstrous Authority: *Buffy the Vampire Slayer* and the Subversion of Authority." *Slayage: The Online International Journal of Buffy Studies* 1, 3 [3] (June 2001). Posted at: http://www.whedonstudies.tv/.

3833. **Clark, Lynn Schofield.** "Touched by a Vampire Named Angel: The Supernatural in Contemporary Teen Popular Culture." In Lynn Schofield Clark. *From Angels to Aliens. Teenagers, the Media and the Supernatural.* New York: Oxford University Press, 2003, pp. 46–74, 261–265. A paper originally presented as "Touched by a (Vampire Named) Angel: Or, Is Buffy a Celebration of the Occult?" at Console-ing Passions: International Conference on Television, Audio, Video, New Media and Feminism, New Orleans, LA, May 30–June 2, 2004.

3834. **Clark, Myf.** "'Oh, hello there gentle viewers': The Fan Community and *Buffy the Vampire Slayer.*" *Watcher Junior: The Journal of Undergraduate Research in Buffy Studies* 1, 1 [1] (July 2005). Posted at: http://www.watcherjunior.tv/.

3835. **Clarke, Ann E.** *"Sexual Tension You Could Cut with a Knife": Sexuality on* Buffy the Vampire Slayer. Adelaide, Aust.: Flinders University of South Australia, BA honors thesis, 2004. 49 pp. Large format.

3836. Clarke, Jamie. "Affective Entertainment in 'Once More with Feeling': A Manifesto for Fandom." In Angela Ndalianis and Felicity Colman, eds. *Special Issue on* Buffy the Vampire Slayer. *Refractory: A Journal of Entertainment Media* 2 (2003). Posted at: http://refractory.unimelb.edu.au/2003/03/18/vol2/.

3837. Clayton, Amy E. "The Future of Feminism Is Slayed: Tomboyism in Joss Whedon's *Fray*." *Red Feather: An International Journal of Children's Visual Culture* 1, 1 (Spring 2010): 26–38. Posted at: http://www.redfeatherjournal.org/uploads/fray.pdf.

3838. Clements, Susannah. "*Buffy the Vampire Slayer*: Sin and Sacrifice, Postmodern Style." Susannah Clements. *The Vampire Defanged: How the Embodiment of Evil Became a Romantic Hero.* Grand Rapids, MI: Brazos, 2011, pp. 57–80.

3839. Clemons, Leigh A. "Genre and the Impact on Storytelling in *Season Eight*." In Kevin K. Durand, ed. Buffy *Meets the Academy: Essays on the Episodes and Scripts as Texts.* Jefferson, NC: McFarland & Company, 2009, pp. 25–31. A paper originally presented as "The Liminal Season Eight: Genre Change and Its Impact on Character/Story in *Buffy the Vampire Slayer, Season Eight*" at SC3: The Slayage Conference on the Whedonverses, Henderson State College, Arkadelphia, AR, June 5–8, 2008.

3840. _____. "Real Vampires Don't Wear Shorts: The Aesthetics of Fashion in *Buffy the Vampire Slayer*." In Matthew Pateman, ed. Buffy *and Aesthetics.* Special Issue of *Slayage: The Online International Journal of Buffy Studies* 6, 2 [22] (Winter 2006). Posted at: http://www.whedonstudies.tv/.

3841. Clendinning, Elizabeth. "Spike Ensouled: The Sonic Transformations of a Champion." In Kendra Preston Leonard, ed. Buffy*, Ballads, and Bad Guys Who Sing: Music in the Worlds of Joss Whedon.* Lanham, MD: Scarecrow Press, 2011, pp. 75–98. A paper originally presented in earlier form as "Seeking Spike's Soul: A Musical, Personal Journey" at the 2010 PCA/ACA National Conference, St. Louis, MO, March 31–April 3, 2010.

3842. Cocca, Carolyn E. "First Word 'Jail,' Second Word 'Bait': Adolescent Sexuality, Feminist Theories, and *Buffy the Vampire Slayer*." *Slayage: The Online International Journal of Buffy*

Studies 3, 2 [10] (November 2003). Posted at: http://www.whedonstudies.tv/.

3843. Cochran, Tanya R. "And the Myth Becomes Flesh." In Jodie A. Kreider and Meghan K. Winchell, eds. Buffy *in the Classroom: Essays on Teaching with the Vampire Slayer.* Jefferson, NC: McFarland & Company, 2010, pp. 35–45.

3844. _____. "Complicating the Open Closet: The Visual Rhetoric of *Buffy the Vampire Slayer*'s Sapphic Lovers." In Rebecca Beirne, ed. *Televising Queer Women: A Reader.* New York: Palgrave Macmillan, 2008, pp. 49–63. A paper originally presented as "Complicating the Open Closet: Vito Russo and the Visual Rhetoric of *Buffy the Vampire Slayer*'s Sapphic Lovers" at the 36th Annual Northeast Modern Language Association (NEMLA) Convention, Boston, MA, March 31-April 3, 2005.

3845. _____. "Fan-Scholars and Scholar-Fans: Life in the Shadowlands" in Tanya R. Cochran. *Toward a Rhetoric of Scholar-Fandom*, Atlanta: Georgia State University, Ph.D. dissertation, 2009. pp. 110–141. A paper originally presented as "Whedon Fan-Scholars and Scholar-Fans: Life in the Shadowlands." It was a Featured lecture at SC4: The Slayage Conference on the Whedonverses, Flagler College, St. Augustine, FL, June 3–6, 2010.

3846. _____. "'Let's Watch a Girl': Whedon, Buffy, and Fans in Action." In Jennifer Kate Stuller, ed. *Fan Phenomena:* Buffy the Vampire Slayer. Chicago: Intellect, 2013, pp. 28–37.

3847. _____. "'Past the brink of tacit support': Fan Activism and the Whedonverses." *Transformative Works and Cultures* 10 (2012). A paper originally presented as "'Past the Brink of Tacit Support': Joss Whedon and the Rhetoric of Fan Activism" at the 2010 PCAS/ACAS Annual Conference, Savannah, GA, October 7–9, 2010. Posted at: http://journal.transformativeworks.com/index.php/twc/article/view/331.

3848. _____. "Slaying Pupils, Siring Students: Composition Befriends *Buffy the Vampire Slayer*" in Tanya R. Cochran. *Toward a Rhetoric of Scholar-Fandom.* Atlanta: Georgia State University, Ph.D. dissertation, 2009. pp. 21–46. Originally presented as "Slaying Pupils, Siring Students: *Buffy the Vampire Slayer* in the Composition Classroom," a paper for the Interdisciplinary Conference for Teachers of Undergraduates, Gordon College, Barnesville, GA, March 2004.

3849. _____. *Toward a Rhetoric of Scholar-Fandom.* Atlanta: Georgia State University, Ph.D. dissertation, 2009. 257 pp. Large format. Posted at: http://scholarworks.gsu.edu/english_diss/51/.

3850. _____, and Jason A. Edwards. "*Buffy the Vampire Slayer* and the Quest Story: Revising the Hero, Reshaping the Myth." In David Whitt and John Perlich, eds. *Sith, Slayers, Stargates & Cyborgs: Modern Mythology in the New Millennium.* New York: Peter Lang, 2008, pp. 145–169.

3851. _____, and Rhonda V. Wilcox. "A New Frontier: Whedon Studies and *Firefly/Serenity.*" In Rhonda V. Wilcox and Tanya R. Cochran, eds. *Special Issue on* Firefly *and* Serenity. *Slayage: The Online International Journal of Buffy Studies* 7, 1 [25] (Winter 2008). Posted at: http://www.whedonstudies.tv/.

3852. Cogan, Brian. "'Can't Even Shout, Can't Even Cry' but You Can Learn! Non-Verbal Communication in 'Hush.'" In Jodie A. Kreider and Meghan K. Winchell, eds. Buffy *in the Classroom: Essays on Teaching with the Vampire Slayer.* Jefferson, NC: McFarland & Company, 2010, pp. 114–125.

3853. Coker, Catherine [Cait]. "That Girl: Bella, Buffy, and the Feminist Ethics of Choice in *Twilight* and *Buffy the Vampire Slayer.*" *Slayage: The Journal of the Whedon Studies Association* 8, 4 [32] (Winter 2011). Posted at: http://www.whedonstudies.tv/.

3854. Cole, C. L. "Suburban Icons/Communist Pasts." *Journal of Sport and Social Issues* 26, 3 (2002): 231–234.

3855. Cole, Kelly. *From Homeboys to Girl Power: Media Mergers, Emerging Networks, and 1990s Television.* Madison: University of Wisconsin, Ph.D. dissertation, 2005. 380 pp. Large format.

3856. Cole, Phillip. "Rousseau and the Vampires: Toward a Political Philosophy of the Undead." In Richard Greene and K. Silem Mohammad, eds. The Undead and Philosophy: Chicken Soup for the Soul. LaSalle IL: Opebn Court, 2006, pp. 186–96. Rev. ed. as: *Zombies, Vampires, and Philosophy: New Life for the Undead.* Chicago: Open Court, 2010, pp. 183–96.

3857. Collier, Noelle R., Christine A. Lumadue, and H. Ray Wooten. "*Buffy the Vampire Slayer* and *Xena: Warrior Princess*: Reception of the Texts by a Sample of Lesbian Fans and Web Site Users." *Journal of Homosexuality* 56, 5 (2009): 575–609.

3858. Colman, Felicity. "The Sight of Your God Disturbs Me: Questioning the Post-Christian Bodies of Buffy, Lain, and George." *Refractory: A Journal of Entertainment Media* 3 (2003). Posted at: http://refractory.unimelb.edu.au/2003/06/26/vol3/.

3859. Colvin, Phil. "Angel: Redefinition and Justification through Faith." In Stacey Abbott, ed. *Reading* Angel: *The TV Spin-off with a Soul.* New York: I. B. Tauris, 2005, pp. 17–30.

3860. Comeford, AmiJo. "Cordelia Chase as Failed Feminist Gesture." In Kevin K. Durand, ed. Buffy *Meets the Academy: Essays on the Episodes and Scripts as Texts.* Jefferson, NC: McFarland & Company, 2009, pp. 150–160.

3861. _____. "Helping the Helpless: Medieval Romance in *Angel.*" In AmiJo Comeford and Tamy L. Burnett, eds. The Literary Angel: *Essays on Influences and Traditions Reflected in the Joss Whedon Series.* Jefferson, NC: McFarland & Company, 2010, pp. 175–190. A paper originally presented in earlier form as "Knights, Dragons, and Maidens vs. Champions, Demons, and the Helpless: Medieval Romance and Chivalry in *Angel*" at the 30th Annual Southwest/Texas PCA/ACA Conference, Albuquerque, NM, February 25–28, 2009.

3862. _____. "Structural Identity, or Saussure Visits *Buffy/Angel*'s World: An Oppositional View of *Angel.*" Paper presented at the Slayage Conference on *Buffy the Vampire Slayer*, Nashville, TN, May 27–30, 2004. Posted at: http://www.slayageonline.com/SCBtVS_Archive/Talks/Comeford.pdf.

3863. _____, Ian G. Klein, and Elizabeth Rambo. "Academics Assemble: A Report on New Scholarship at SC5." *Slayage: The Journal of the Whedon Studies Association* 9, 2 [34] (Fall 2012). Posted at: http://www.whedonstudies.tv/.

3864. Comeford, AmiJo, and Tamy L. Burnett. "Introduction: Los Angeles, City of Story." In AmiJo Comeford and Tamy L. Burnett, eds. *The Literary* Angel: *Essays on Influences and Traditions Reflected in the Joss Whedon Series.* Jefferson, NC: McFarland & Company, 2010, pp. 1–13.

3865. _____ and Tamy L. Burnett, eds. *The Literary* Angel: *Essays on Influences and Traditions Reflected in the Joss Whedon Series.* Jefferson, NC: McFarland & Company, 2010. 264 pp. tp. Includes contributions by Lorna Jowett, Angel Anderson, Jennifer Hamilton, Sharon Sutherland and Sarah Swan, Anika Stafford, Victoria Pettersen Lantz, Mary Ellen Iatropoulos, Katia McClain, K. Shannon Howard, Cynthea Masson, Laurel Bowman, Alison Jaquet, and Stacey Abbott.

3866. Conaton, Chris. "Cinderella in the High School Hallways: The Place of Smart Girls on Teen Television." *The Mid-Atlantic Almanack* 13 (2004). Posted at: http://www.academia.edu/794511/Cinderella_in_the_High_School_Hallways_The_Place_of_Smart_Girls_on_Teen_Television.

3867. _____. *Girls Who (Don't) Wear Glasses: The Performativity of Smart Girls on Teen Television*. Bowling Green, OH: Bowling Green State University, Ph.D. dissertation, 2007. 289 pp. Large format.

3868. _____. "Joss Whedon: Pioneer of the Body Count." PopMatters.com's *Spotlight: Joss Whedon* (April 12, 2011). Posted at: http://www.popmatters.com/feature/139152-joss-whedon-grim-reaper/.

3869. Connolly, Jane. *The Representation of Homosexuality in the Television Series* Buffy the Vampire Slayer. Dublin, Ireland: Trinity College, Ph.D. dissertation, 2007.

3870. Connor, James. "Cultural Loyalty: Loyalty and *Buffy the Vampire Slayer*." In James Connor. *The Sociology of Loyalty*. New York: Springer, 2007, pp. 117–127.

3871. Cooper, L. Andrew. "Judith Halberstam's *Skin Shows* and Joss Whedon's *Buffy the Vampire Slayer*." In L. Andrew Cooper. *Gothic Realities: The Impact of Horror Fiction on Modern Culture*. Jefferson, NC: McFarland & Company, 2010, pp. 86–93.

3872. Cordesman, Anthony. "Biological Warfare and the 'Buffy' Paradigm." *CSIS: Center for Strategic and International Studies* (September 29, 2001). Posted at: https://csis.org/files/media/csis/pubs/buffy012902%5B1%5D.pdf and at http://www.whedonstudies.tv/essays/Cordesman_Buffy.pdf.

3873. Costa, Allie. "Part of Something: Or, *Buffy the Vampire Slayer*: My First Long-Term Relationship." In Paul Ruditis, ed. Buffy the Vampire Slayer: *The Watcher's Guide*. Vol. 3. New York: Simon, 2004, pp. 271–276.

3874. Coulombe, Renée T. "'I Had It All Wrong': New Vampires, Grrrl Heroes and the Third Wave Body in *Buffy the Vampire Slayer*." In Isabella van Elferen, ed. *Nostalgia or Perversion? Gothic Rewriting from the Eighteenth Century Until the Present Day*. Newcastle: Cambridge Scholars Publishing, 2007, pp. 206–222.

3875. _____. "'You're just a girl!' Punk Rock Feminism and the New Hero in *Buffy the Vampire Slayer*." In Paul Attinello, Janet K. Halfyard, and Vanessa Knights, eds. *Music, Sound, and Silence in* Buffy the Vampire Slayer. Farnham, Surrey, UK: Ashgate Publishing, 2010, pp. 149–163.

3876. Cover, Rob. "Bliss and Time: Death, Drugs, and Posthumanism in *Buffy the Vampire Slayer*." *Slayage: The Journal of the Whedon Studies Association* 8, 4 [32] (Winter 2011). Posted at: http://www.whedonstudies.tv/.

3877. _____. "From Butler to Buffy: Notes Towards a Strategy for Identity Analysis in Contemporary Television Narrative." *Reconstruction: Studies in Contemporary Culture* 4, 2 (Spring 2004). Posted at: http://reconstruction.eserver.org/042/cover.htm.

3878. _____. "'More Than a Watcher': *Buffy* Fans, Amateur Music Videos, Romantic Slash and Intermedia." In Paul Attinello, Janet K. Halfyard, and Vanessa Knights, eds. *Music, Sound, and Silence in* Buffy the Vampire Slayer. Farnham, Surrey, UK: Ashgate Publishing, 2010, pp. 131–148.

3879. _____. "'Not to be toyed with': Drug Addiction, Bullying and Self-empowerment in *Buffy the Vampire Slayer*." *Continuum: Journal of Media & Cultural Studies* 19, 1 (March 2005): 85–101.

3880. _____. "(Re)Cognising the Body: Performativity, Embodiment and Abject Selves in *Buffy the Vampire Slayer*." *Aesthethika: International Journal on Culture, Subjectivity and Aesthetics* 2, 1 (Fall 2005): 68–83.

3881. Cox, Arnie, and Rebecca Fülöp. "'What rhymes with lungs?': When Music Speaks Louder Than Words." In Paul Attinello, Janet K. Halfyard, and Vanessa Knights, eds. *Music, Sound, and Silence in* Buffy the Vampire Slayer. Farnham, Surrey, UK: Ashgate Publishing, 2010, pp. 61–78.

3882. Cox, J. Renée. "Got Myself a Soul? The Puzzling Treatment of the Soul in *Buffy*." In Emily Dial-Driver, Sally Emmons-Featherston, Jim Ford, and Carolyn Anne Taylor, eds. *The Truth of Buffy: Essays on Fiction Illuminating Reality*. Jefferson, NC: McFarland & Company, 2008, pp. 24–37.

3883. Craig, Jamie [Pepper Espinoza and Vivien Dean]. "Older and Far Away." In Lynne M. Thomas and Deborah Stanish, eds. *Whedonistas! A Celebration of the Worlds of Joss Whedon by the Women Who Love Them*. Des Moines, IA: Mad Norwegian Press, 2011, pp. 165–170.

3884. Craigo-Snell, Shannon. "What Would Buffy do? Feminist Ethics and Epistemic Violence." *Jump Cut: A Review of Contemporary Media* 48 (2006). Posted at: http://www.ejumpcut.org/archive/jc48.2006/BuffyEthics/index.html.

3885. Crosby, Sara. "The Cruelest Season: Female Heroes Snapped into Sacrificial Heroines." In Sherrie A. Inness, ed. *Action Chicks: New Images of Tough Women in Popular Culture.* New York: Palgrave Macmillan, 2004, pp. 153–178.

3886. Crusie, Jennifer. "The Assassination of Cordelia Chase." In Glenn Yeffeth, ed. *Five Seasons of* Angel: *Science Fiction and Fantasy Writers Discuss Their Favorite Vampire.* Dallas, TX: Benbella Books, 2004, pp. 187–197.

3887. _____. "Dating Death." In Glenn Yeffeth, ed. *Seven Seasons of* Buffy: *Science Fiction and Fantasy Writers Discuss Their Favorite Television Show.* Dallas, TX: Benbella Books, 2003, pp. 85–96. Rpt as: "Dating Death: Love and Sex in Buffy the Vampire Slayer." Posted at: http://www.jennycrusie.com/for-writers/essays/dating-death/.

3888. Cullen, John. "Rupert Giles, the Professional-image Slayer." *American Libraries* 31, 5 (2000): 42.

3889. Culp, Christopher M. "'But...you're just a girl': The Feminine Mystique of Season Five." *Watcher Junior: The Journal of Undergraduate Research in Buffy Studies* 2, 1 [2] (July 2006). Posted at: http://www.watcherjunior.tv/.

3890. _____. "'What does it take to strike a spark?': Nietzsche's Apollonian/Dionysian Balance in *Buffy.*" *Watcher Junior: The Journal of Undergraduate Research in Buffy Studies* 1, 1 [1] (July 2005). Posted at: http://www.watcherjunior.tv/.

3891. Curry, Agnes B. "Is Joss Becoming a Thomist?" *Slayage: The Online International Journal of Buffy Studies* 4, 4 [16] (March 2005). Posted at: http://www.whedonstudies.tv/. A paper originally presented as "Gosh, is Joss a Thomist!?" at the Slayage Conference on *Buffy the Vampire Slayer*, Nashville, TN, May 27–30, 2004.

3892. _____, and Josef Velazquez. "'Just a Family Legend': The Hidden Logic of *Buffy*'s 'Chosen Family.'" In Lynne Y. Edwards, Elizabeth L. Rambo, and James B. South, eds. *Buffy Goes Dark: Essays on the Final Two Seasons of* Buffy the Vampire Slayer *on Television.* Jefferson, NC: McFarland & Company, 2009, pp. 143–166.

3893. Daniel, Leith. "Weeding Out the Offensive Material: Beauty, Beasts, 'Gingerbread,' Television, Literature and Censorship." In Jodie A. Kreider and Meghan K. Winchell, eds. Buffy *in the Classroom: Essays on Teaching with the Vampire Slayer.* Jefferson, NC: McFarland & Company, 2010, pp. 146–157.

3894. Daniels, Susanne, and Cynthia Littleton. "Welcome to Sunnydale." In Susanne Daniels and Cynthia Littleton. *Season Finale: The Unexpected Rise and Fall of the WB and UPN.* New York: Harper, 2007, pp. 102–134.

3895. _____. "Vampires and Vertical Integration." In Susanne Daniels and Cynthia Littleton. *Season Finale: The Unexpected Rise and Fall of the WB and UPN.* New York: Harper, 2007, pp. 248–276.

3896. Da Ros, Giada. "When, Where, and How Much Is *Buffy the Vampire Slayer* a Soap Opera?" *Slayage: The Online International Journal of Buffy Studies* 4, 1–2 [13–14] (October 2004). Posted at: http://www.whedonstudies.tv/.

3897. Daspit, Toby A. "Buffy Goes to College, Adam 'Murder(s) to Dissect': Education and Knowledge in a Postmodern World." In James B. South, ed. Buffy *and Philosophy: Fear and Trembling in Sunnydale.* Chicago: Open Court, 2003, pp. 117–130. A paper originally presented at the JCT Conference on Curriculum Theory and Classroom Practice, Dayton, Ohio, October 2002.

3898. Daugherty, Anne Millard. "Just a Girl: Buffy as Icon." In Roz Kaveney, ed. *Reading the Vampire Slayer: An Unofficial Critical Companion to* Buffy *and* Angel. 1st ed. New York: I. B. Tauris, 2001, pp. 148–165.

3899. Davidson, Joy. "Introduction." In Joy Davidson with Leah Wilson, eds. *The Psychology of Joss Whedon: An Unauthorized Exploration of* Buffy, Angel, *and* Firefly. Dallas, TX: Benbella Books, 2007, pp. 1–5.

3900. _____. "'There's My Boy...'" In Glenn Yeffeth, ed. *Five Seasons of* Angel: *Science Fiction and Fantasy Writers Discuss Their Favorite Vampire.* Dallas, TX: Benbella Books, 2004, pp. 199–216. Rpt. in: Joy Davidson with Leah Wilson, ed. *The Psychology of Joss Whedon: An Unauthorized Exploration of* Buffy, Angel, *and* Firefly. Dallas, TX: Benbella Books, 2007, pp. 197–215.

3901. _____, with Leah Wilson, eds. *The Psychology of Joss Whedon: An Unauthorized Exploration of* Buffy, Angel, *and* Firefly. Dallas, TX: Benbella Books, 2007. 224 pp. tp. Includes contributions by Robert Kurzban, Carol Poole, Thomas Flamson, Nicholas R. Eaton and Robert F. Krueger, Nancy S. Weinfield, Brian Rabian and Michael Wolff, Wind Goodfriend, C. Albert Bardi and

Sherry Hamby, Misty K. Hook, Bradley J. Daniels, Siamak Tundra Naficy and Karthik Panchanathan, Stephanie R. Deluse, Mikhail Lyubansky, and Ed Connor.

3902. Davies, Matt. "'You Can't Charge People for Saving Their Lives!' Work in *Buffy the Vampire Slayer*." *International Political Sociology* 4, 2 (June 2010): 178–195. A paper originally presented in earlier form at the International Studies Association 48th Annual Convention, Chicago, IL, February 2007.

3903. Davis, Elizabeth Anne. *Monstress: [Re]Flexions through the Virtual Looking Glass on the Hyperglyphics of Fairy Tales and the Network of the Text.* Tuscaloosa: University of Alabama, Ph.D. dissertation, 2005. 58 pp. Large format.

3904. Davis, Robert A. "*Buffy the Vampire Slayer* and the Pedagogy of Fear." *Slayage: The On-line International Journal of Buffy Studies* 1, 3 [3] (June 2001). Posted at: http://www.whedonstudies.tv/.

3905. Day, William Patrick. "Return of the Slayer." In William Patrick Day. *Vampire Legends in Contemporary American Culture: What Becomes a Legend Most.* Lexington: University Press of Kentucky, 2002, pp. 129–166.

3906. DeBrandt, Don. "Angelus Populi." In Glenn Yeffeth, ed. *Five Seasons of* Angel: *Science Fiction and Fantasy Writers Discuss Their Favorite Vampire.* Dallas, TX: Benbella Books, 2004, pp. 1–13.

3907. DeCandido, GraceAnne A. "Bibliographic Good vs. Evil in *Buffy the Vampire Slayer*." *American Libraries* 30, 8 (1999): 44–7. Rpt. as "Rupert Giles and Search Tools for Wisdom in *Buffy the Vampire Slayer*." Posted at: http://www.well.com/user/ladyhawk/Giles.html.

3908. Dechert, S. Renée. "'My Boyfriend's in the Band': *Buffy* and the Rhetoric of Music." In Rhonda V. Wilcox and David Lavery, eds. *Fighting the Forces: What's at Stake in* Buffy the Vampire Slayer. Lanham, MD: Rowman & Littlefield, 2002, pp. 218–226.

3909. Dehnert, Carmen. "'I'm Under Your Spell': Willow & Tara: The Vanishing of the Other and the Utopia of Love." A paper presented at *Buffy* Hereafter: From the Whedonverse to the Whedonesque: An Interdisciplinary Conference on the Work of Joss Whedon and its Aftereffects, Istanbul, Turkey, October 17–19, 2007. This paper was later translated into German and reprinted as "'I'm Under Your Spell': Lesbische Liebe, Narziss-

mus und die Utopie in *Buffy the Vampire Slayer*." In Annika Beckmann, et al, eds. *Horror als Alltag: Texte zu* Buffy the Vampire Slayer. Berlin: Vebrecher, 2010, pp. 125–138.

3910. ____, and Lars Quadfasel. "On Souls, Chips and the Surplus of Desire: Castration and the Oedipal Vampire." A paper presented at *Buffy* Hereafter: From the Whedonverse to the Whedonesque: An Interdisciplinary Conference on the Work of Joss Whedon and Its Aftereffects, Istanbul, Turkey, October 17–19, 2007. This paper was later translated into German and reprinted as "Der Chip, die Seele und das Surplus des Begehrens: Der Kastrationskomplex des ödipalen Vampirs." In Annika Beckmann, et al, eds. *Horror als Alltag: Texte zu* Buffy the Vampire Slayer. Berlin: Vebrecher, 2010, pp. 139–156.

3911. DeKelb-Rittenhouse, Diane. "Sex and the Single Vampire: The Evolution of the Vampire Lothario and Its Representation in *Buffy*." In Rhonda V. Wilcox and David Lavery, eds. *Fighting the Forces: What's at Stake in* Buffy the Vampire Slayer. Lanham, MD: Rowman & Littlefield, 2002, pp. 143–152.

3912. de Lint, Charles. "Why I Like *Buffy*." In Paul Ruditis, ed. Buffy the Vampire Slayer: *The Watcher's Guide.* Vol. 3. New York: Simon, 2004, pp. 283–286.

3913. DeLusé, Stephanie R. "More Than Entertainment: Notes on a Spiritual Recovery and What Jossverse Gave Me that Religion and Therapy Didn't." In Joy Davidson with Leah Wilson, eds. *The Psychology of Joss Whedon: An Unauthorized Exploration of* Buffy, Angel, *and* Firefly. Dallas, TX: Benbella Books, 2007, pp. 155–170.

3914. Dempsey-Richardson, Caleb R. *'It's like we were being watched...like there were only 3 walls, and not a fourth wall': Manifestations of Metafiction in* Buffy the Vampire Slayer. Richmond: Eastern Kentucky University, M.A. thesis, 2013. 81 pp.

3915. Dentzien, Nicole. "The Fisher Queen: *Buffy the Vampire Slayer*, Death and Mythology." *Literatur in Wissenschaft und Unterricht* 36, 1 (2004): 51–8.

3916. Destefano, Rashi F. N. *Who Are We? A Moral and Visual Analysis of* Buffy the Vampire Slayer. Amherst, MA: Amherst College, BA honors thesis, 2004. 92 pp. Large format.

3917. Dethlefsen, Alta E. *A Feminist Named Buffy? Women in Horror Films of the 1990s.* Columbia: University of South Carolina, M.A. thesis, 1995. 69 pp. Large format.

3918. Dial-Driver, Emily. "The Fantastic Classroom: Teaching *Buffy the Vampire Slayer*." In Emily Dial-Driver, Sally Emmons, and Jim Ford, eds. *Fantasy Media in the Classroom: Essays on Teaching with Film, Television, Literature, Graphic Novels, and Video Games*. Jefferson, NC: McFarland & Company, 2012, pp. 171–181.

3919. _____. "Preface." In Emily Dial-Driver, Sally Emmons-Featherston, Jim Ford, and Carolyn Anne Taylor, eds. *The Truth of* Buffy: *Essays on Fiction Illuminating Reality*. Jefferson, NC: McFarland & Company, 2008, pp. 1–3.

3920. _____. "What's It All About, *Buffy* ?" In Emily Dial-Driver, Sally Emmons-Featherston, Jim Ford, and Carolyn Anne Taylor, eds. *The Truth of* Buffy: *Essays on Fiction Illuminating Reality*. Jefferson, NC: McFarland & Company, 2008, pp. 9–23.

3921. _____, and **Jesse Stallings.** "Texting *Buffy*: Allusions of Many Kinds." In Emily Dial-Driver, Sally Emmons-Featherston, Jim Ford, and Carolyn Anne Taylor, eds. *The Truth of* Buffy: *Essays on Fiction Illuminating Reality*. Jefferson, NC: McFarland & Company, 2008, pp. 142–157.

3922. Dial-Driver, Emily, Sally Emmons-Featherston, Jim Ford, and Carolyn Anne Taylor, eds. *The Truth of* Buffy: *Essays on Fiction Illuminating Reality*. Jefferson, NC: McFarland & Company, 2008. 242 pp. tp. Includes contributions by J. Renée Cox, Jacqueline Bach, Kenneth S. Hicks, Frances E. Morris, Gary Moeller, David Blakely, Lori M. Butler, J. Michael McKeon, Jesse Stallings, Gregory J. Thompson, Juliet Evusa, and Kenneth S. Hicks.

3923. Dias Branco, Sérgio. "Being Her/She in 'Who Are You?'." A paper presented at Its the End of the World...Again: Why Buffy Still Matters: A *Buffy the Vampire Slayer* Mini-Conference, University of North Carolina, Greensboro, NC (March 16, 2007). Posted at: https://www.academia.edu/5100168/Being_Her_She_in_Who_Are_You_.

3924. Diehl, Laura. "Why Drusilla's More Interesting Than Buffy." *Slayage: The Online International Journal of Buffy Studies* 4, 1–2 [13–14] (October 2004). Posted at: http://www.whedonstudies.tv/. A paper originally presented as "Why Drusilla Is More Interesting Than Buffy" at the Slayage Conference on *Buffy the Vampire Slayer*, Nashville, TN, May 27–30, 2004.

3925. Di Gregorio, Luciano. "*Buffy the Vampire Slayer*: Using a Popular Culture Post-modern Text in the Classroom." *Australian Screen Education* 42 (Autumn 2006): 90–93.

3926. Dobson, Nichola. "The Regeneration of *Doctor Who*: The Ninth Doctor and the Influence of the Slayer." *Flow TV: A Critical Forum on Television and Media Culture* 4, 4 (April 2006). Posted at: http://flowtv.org/2006/04/doctor-who-buffy-the-vampire-slayer-british-tv/.

3927. Donaruma, William. "Once More with Feeling: The Hellmouth in Postmodern Heaven." A paper presented at the Slayage Conference on *Buffy the Vampire Slayer*, Nashville, TN, May 27–30, 2004. Posted at: http://www.slayageonline.com/SCBtVS_Archive/Talks/Donaruma.pdf.

3928. Donovan, Ryan P. "*Buffy the Vampire Slayer* Season 8." In Bart H. Beaty and Stephen Weiner, eds. *Critical Survey of Graphic Novels: Heroes & Superheroes*. Ipswich, MA: Salem Press, 2012, pp. 150–155.

3929. Doran, Selina. "The 'Faith Goes Dark' Storyline and Viewers: Interpretation of Gendered Roles." *Slayage: The Journal of the Whedon Studies Association* 9, 2 [34] (Fall 2012). Posted at: http://www.whedonstudies.tv/.

3930. Doty, Alexander. "Afterword." *Making Things Perfectly Queer: Interpreting Mass Culture*. Minneapolis: University of Minnesota Press, 1993, pp. 97–104. A brief treatment of the *Buffy the Vampire Slayer* movie.

3931. Double, Krystalle. *Female Roles and Fan Fiction in* Charmed, Supernatural, *and* Buffy the Vampire Slayer. Kalamazoo: Western Michigan University, BA honors thesis, 2013. Posted at: http://scholarworks.wmich.edu/honors_theses/2221.

3932. Douglas, Susan J. "Warrior Women in Thongs." In Susan J. Douglas. *Enlightened Sexism: The Seductive Message That Feminism's Work Is Done*. New York: Times Books, 2010, pp. 76–100.

3933. Dowling, Jennifer. "'We Are Not Demons': Homogenizing the Heroes in *Buffy the Vampire Slayer* and *Angel*." In Angela Ndalianis and Felicity Colman, eds. *Special Issue on* Buffy the Vampire Slayer. *Refractory: A Journal of Entertainment Media* 2 (2003): Posted at: http://refractory.unimelb.edu.au/2003/03/18/vol2/. A paper originally presented at The Buffyverse: A Symposium on *Buffy the Vampire Slayer*, University of Melbourne, Melbourne, Australia, November 21, 2002.

3934. Downey, Rebecca Ann. *"Because It's Superman's Book, You Moron": Geeks, Metafiction and Feminism in* Buffy the Vampire Slayer. Carlisle,

PA, Dickinson College, BA honors thesis, 2003. 53 pp. Large format.

3935. Drewniok, Malgorzata. "'I feel strong. I feel different': Transformations, Vampires and Language in *Buffy the Vampire Slayer*." In Sam George and Bill Hughes, eds. *Open Graves, Open Minds: Representations of Vampires and the Undead from the Enlightenment to the Present Day*. Manchester: Manchester University Press, 2013, pp. 131–45. A paper originally presented at SC4: The Slayage Conference on the Whedonverses, Flagler College, St. Augustine, FL, 3–6 June 2010. Also presented at Open Graves, Open Minds: Vampires and the Undead in Modern Culture, University of Hertfordshire, Hatfield, UK, 16–17 April 2010, and as "Changing Identity on the Small Screen: Transformations, Vampires and Language in *Buffy the Vampire Slayer*" at TV Fangdom: A Conference on Television Vampires, University of Northampton, Northampton, UK, 7–8 June 2013.

3936. _____. "'You're Strong. I'm Stronger': Vampires, Masculinity & Language in *Buffy*." In Mary Alice Money for PopMatters.com, ed. *Joss Whedon: The Complete Companion: The TV Series, the Movies, the Comic Books and More*. London: Titan Books, 2012, pp. 49–56. A paper originally presented as "'You're strong. I'm stronger. You have no idea what you're dealing with': Vampires, Masculinity and Language in *Buffy the Vampire Slayer*," for the Fractured Images/Broken Words conference, Lancaster University, UK, June 12, 2010, and subsequently appeared as part of PopMatters.com's *Spotlight: Joss Whedon*, posted on March 9, 2011.

3937. Driscoll, Catherine. "Bronze Things; Things of Bronze: Popular Music Cultures in *Buffy the Vampire Slayer*." In Paul Attinello, Janet K. Halfyard, and Vanessa Knights, eds. *Music, Sound, and Silence in* Buffy the Vampire Slayer. Farnham, Surrey, UK: Ashgate Publishing, 2010, pp. 111–130.

3938. _____. "The Metaphore of Adolescense: Akira and Buffy." In Catherine Driscoll. Teen Film: A Critical Introduction. London: Bloomsbury Academic, 2011, pp. 95–100.

3939. Driver, Martha W., and Sid Ray, eds. *The Medieval Hero on Screen: Representations from Beowulf to Buffy*. Jefferson, NC: McFarland & Company, 2004. 268 pp. tp.

3940. Driver, Susan. "Willow's Queer Transformations on *Buffy the Vampire Slayer*: Coming of Age, Coming Out, Becoming Powerful." In Suan Driver. *Queer Girls and Popular Culture: Reading, Resisting, and Creating Media*. New York: Peter Lang, 2007, pp. 57–90.

3941. Dryburgh, Monika. "*Buffy the Vampire Slayer* and Popular Children's Nursery Rhymes." *All Slay* 2 (2004).

3942. _____. "'It's Like a Whole Big Sucking Thing': Queer as the Norm on *Buffy the Vampire Slayer*." *All Slay* 3 (2004).

3943. Duda, Heather L. *An Examination of the Contemporary Monster Hunter in Popular Culture: Murderers and Men of God*. Indiana: Indiana University of Pennsylvania, Ph.D. dissertation, 2006. 182 pp. Large format.

3944. _____. *The Monster Hunter in Modern Popular Culture*. Jefferson, NC: McFarland and Company, 2008. 192 pp. tp.

3945. Dudley, Rebecca. Lesbians and Buffy the Vampire Slayer: *Popular Culture, the Internet and the Creation of Community*." Philadelphia: University of Pennsylvania, M.A. thesis, 2001. 44 pp. Large format.

3946. Dunn, George A. and Brian McDonald. "'A Very Strong Urge to Hit You': Mimetic Rivalry and Scapegoating in *Buffy the Vampire Slayer*." *Slayage: The Online International Journal of Buffy Studies* 7, 2 [26] (Spring 2008). Posted at: http://www.whedonstudies.tv/. A paper originally presented at the Slayage Conference on *Buffy the Vampire Slayer*, Nashville, TN, May 27–30, 2004.

3947. Dunne, Michael. "How About a Nice Musical?" In Michael Dunn. *American Film Musical Themes and Forms*. Jefferson, NC: McFarland & Company, 2004, pp. 179–180.

3948. Dupuy, Coralline. "Is Giles Simply Another Dr. Van Helsing? Continuity and Innovation in the Figure of the Watcher in *Buffy the Vampire Slayer*." In Angela Ndalianis and Felicity Colman, eds. *Special Issue on* Buffy the Vampire Slayer. *Refractory: A Journal of Entertainment Media* 2 (2003). Posted at: http://refractory.unimelb.edu.au/2003/03/18/vol2/.

3949. Durand, Kevin K. "'Are You Ready to Finish This?': The Battle Against the Patriarchal Forces of Darkness" in *Slayage: The Online International Journal of Buffy Studies* 7, 4 [28] (Summer 2009). Posted at: http://www.whedonstudies.tv/. Rev. as: "The Battle Against the Patriarchal Forces of Darkness." In Kevin K. Durand, ed. Buffy *Meets the Academy: Essays on the Episodes and Scripts as Texts*. Jefferson, NC: McFarland & Company, 2009, pp. 176–184. A paper originally presented as "Let's Finish This: The First, Caleb, the Watcher's Council, and the Fight Against the Patriarchal Forces of Darkness" at SC2: The Slayage Conference on the Whedonverses, Gordon College, Barnesville, GA, May 25–28, 2006.

3950. ____. *"Buffy's* Insight into Wollstonecraft and Mill." In Kevin K. Durand, ed. Buffy *Meets the Academy: Essays on the Episodes and Scripts as Texts.* Jefferson, NC: McFarland & Company, 2009, pp. 115–121.

3951. ____. "Canon Fodder: Assembling the Text." In Kevin K. Durand, ed. Buffy *Meets the Academy: Essays on the Episodes and Scripts as Texts.* Jefferson, NC: McFarland & Company, 2009, pp. 9–16.

3952. ____. "Introduction: Pop Culture Meets the Academy." In Kevin K. Durand, ed. Buffy *Meets the Academy: Essays on the Episodes and Scripts as Texts.* Jefferson, NC: McFarland & Company, 2009, pp. 1–5.

3953. ____. "It's All About Power." In Kevin K. Durand, ed. Buffy *Meets the Academy: Essays on the Episodes and Scripts as Texts.* Jefferson, NC: McFarland & Company, 2009, pp. 45–56.

3954. ____, **ed.** Buffy *Meets the Academy: Essays on the Episodes and Scripts as Texts.* Jefferson, NC: McFarland & Company, 2009. 230 pp. tp. Along with several essays he authored himself, the editor has included contributions by Brent Linsley, Leigh Clemons, David Fritts, Susan Payne-Mulliken and Valerie Renegar, Clinton P.E. Atchley, Elizabeth Bridges, Denise Tischler Millstein, Melanie Wilson, AmiJo Comeford, Rebecca Bobbitt, Lauren Schultz, Keith Fudge, and Tamara Wilson.

3955. Durant, Amy. *"In every generation there is a chosen one": Choice, Family and Motherhood in* Buffy the Vampire Slayer *and* Twilight. Manchester, UK: University of Manchester, BA honors thesis, 2011. 29 pp.

3956. Duricy, Michael P. "Marian Symbols in the *Buffy the Vampire Slayer* Television Series on the WB." Paper presented at the Slayage Conference on *Buffy the Vampire Slayer,* Nashville, TN, May 27–30 2004. Posted at: http://www.slayage online.com/SCBtVS_Archive/Talks/Duricy.pdf and at http://campus.udayton.edu/mary/mar.htm.

3957. Dvoskin, Michelle G. *Under Their Spell: How the Musical Episodes of* Xena: Warrior Princess *and* Buffy the Vampire Slayer *Queer the Audience.* Austin: University of Texas, M.A. thesis, 2006.

3958. Early, Frances H. "The Female Just Warrior Reimagined: From Boudicca to Buffy." In Frances Early and Kathleen Kennedy, eds. *Athena's Daughters: Television's New Women Warriors.* Syracuse, NY: Syracuse University Press, 2003, pp. 55–65.

3959. ____. "Staking Her Claim: Buffy the Vampire Slayer as Transgressive Woman Warrior." *Journal of Popular Culture* 35, 3 (2001): 11–28. Rpt. in *Slayage: The Online International Journal of Buffy Studies* 2, 2 [6] (September 2002). Posted at: http://www.whedonstudies.tv/.

3960. Edelson, Cheryl D. *Siting Horror: Place and Space in American Gothic Fiction.* Riverside: University of California–Riverside, Ph.D. dissertation, 2007. 188 pp. Large format.

3961. Edwards, Lynne Y. "Slaying in Black and White: Kendra as Tragic Mulatto in *Buffy the Vampire Slayer.*" In Rhonda V. Wilcox and David Lavery, eds. *Fighting the Forces: What's at Stake in* Buffy the Vampire Slayer. Lanham, MD: Rowman & Littlefield, 2002, pp. 85–97.

3962. ____, **and Carly Haines.** "Reality Bites: *Buffy* in the UPN Years." In Eds. Lynne Y. Edwards, Elizabeth L. Rambo, and James B. South, eds. *Buffy Goes Dark: Essays on the Final Two Seasons of* Buffy the Vampire Slayer *on Television.* Jefferson, NC: McFarland & Company, 2009, pp. 130–142.

3963. Edwards, Lynne Y., Elizabeth L. Rambo, and James B. South, eds. *Buffy Goes Dark: Essays on the Final Two Seasons of* Buffy the Vampire Slayer *on Television.* Jefferson, NC: McFarland & Company, 2009. 232 pp. tp. Along with essays they authored themselves, the editors have included contributions by David Lavery, David Perry, David Kociemba, Alissa Wilts, Brandy Ryan, Ira Shull and Anne Shull, Michael Adams, Rhonda V. Wilcox, Gregory Erickson and Jennifer Lemberg, Carly Haines, Agnes B. Curry and Josef Velazquez, and Paul Hawkins.

3964. Edwards, Ted. *Buffy X-posed.* Rocklin, Ca: Prima Publishing, 1998. 208 pp. tp. Oversize format.

3965. Elden, Gro. *The Buffyverse and Its Inhabitants: A Study of Fans of* Buffy the Vampire Slayer. Amsterdam, Netherlands, International School for Humanities and Social Sciences, Universiteit van Amsterdam, M.A. thesis, 2002.

3966. Elliott, Tara. "The Use of Count Famous in 'Buffy vs. Dracula.'" *Journal of Dracula Studies* 8 (2006): 14–19. Posted at: http://www.blooferland.com/drc/index.php?title=Journal_of_Dracula_Studies.

3967. Ellwood, Taylor. "Invoking Buffy: How to Use Pop Culture Icons as God-Forms." In Fiona Horne, ed. *Pop! Goes the Witch: The Disinformation Guide to 21st Century Witchcraft*. New York: The Disinformation Company, 2004, pp. 184–187.

3968. Emmons-Featherston, Sally. "Is That Stereotype Dead? Working with and Against 'Western' Stereotypes in *Buffy*." In Emily Dial-Driver, Sally Emmons-Featherston, Jim Ford, and Carolyn Anne Taylor, eds. *The Truth of* Buffy: *Essays on Fiction Illuminating Reality*. Jefferson, NC: McFarland & Company, 2008, pp. 55–66. A paper originally presented as "Slaying the Stereotypes: Working with and Against 'Western' Stereotypes in *Buffy*" at the 28th Annual Southwest/Texas PCA/ACA Conference, Albuquerque, NM, February 14–17, 2007.

3969. England, Marcia. *Who's Afraid of the Dark? Not Buffy! A Feminist Examination of the Paradoxical Representations of Public and Private Space in* Buffy the Vampire Slayer. Seattle: University of Washington, M.A. thesis, 2002. 82 pp. Large format.

3970. Epps, Garrett. "Can Buffy's Brilliance Last?" *The American Prospect* 13, 2 (2002): 28–31. Posted at: http://prospect.org/article/can-buffys-brilliance-last.

3971. Erickson, Gregory T. "'Religion Freaky' or a 'Bunch of Men Who Died?': The (A)theology of *Buffy*." *Slayage: The Online International Journal of Buffy Studies* 4, 1–2 [13–14] October (2004). Posted at: http://www.whedonstudies.tv/. A paper originally presented as "Revisiting *Buffy*'s (A)Theology: Religion 'Freaky' or Just 'A Bunch of Men Who Died'" at the Slayage Conference on *Buffy the Vampire Slayer*, Nashville, TN, May 27–30, 2004.

3972. _____. "'Sometimes You Need a Story': American Christianity, Vampires, and *Buffy*." In Rhonda V. Wilcox and David Lavery, eds. *Fighting the Forces: What's at Stake in* Buffy the Vampire Slayer. Lanham, MD: Rowman & Littlefield, 2002, pp. 108–119.

3973. _____, and Jennifer Lemberg. "Bodies and Narrative in Crisis: Figures of Rupture and Chaos in Seasons Six and Seven." In Lynne Y. Edwards, Elizabeth L. Rambo, and James B. South, eds. *Buffy Goes Dark: Essays on the Final Two Seasons of* Buffy the Vampire Slayer *on Television*. Jefferson, NC: McFarland & Company, 2009, pp. 114–129.

3974. _____, and Richard W. Santana. "Television Drama, Fan Communities, and Theology: God as 'Nothing Solid.'" In Gregory T. Erickson. *Religion and Popular Culture: Rescripting the Sacred*. Jefferson, NC: McFarland & Company, 2008, pp. 113–137.

3975. Espenson, Jane. "Introduction." In Michael Adams. *Slayer Slang: A* Buffy the Vampire Slayer *Lexicon*. New York: Oxford University Press, 2003, pp vii–x.

3976. Estill, Adriana. "Going to Hell: Placing the Library in *Buffy the Vampire Slayer*." In John Buschman and Gloria J. Leckie, eds. *The Library as Place: History, Community, and Culture*. Westport, CT: Libraries Unlimited, 2007, pp. 235–250.

3977. Everingham, Mark, Josef Sivic, and Andrew Zisserman. "'Hello! My name is...Buffy': Automatic Naming of Characters in TV Video." A paper presented at the 17th Annual British Machine Vision Conference, Edinburgh, September 2006. Posted at: http://www.comp.leeds.ac.uk/me/Publications/bmvc06.pdf.

3978. _____, Josef Sivic, and Andrew Zisserman. "'Who Are You?': Learning Person Specific Classifiers from Video." *Proceedings of the IEEE Conference on Computer Vision and Pattern Recognition, June 2009*. 1145–1152. Posted at: http://citeseerx.ist.psu.edu/viewdoc/summary?doi=10.1.1.167.3731. A paper originally presented at the IEEE Conference on Computer Vision and Pattern Recognition, Miami, Fl, June 2009.

3979. Evusa, Juliet. "Witchy Women: Witchcraft in *Buffy* and in Contemporary African Culture." In Emily Dial-Driver, Sally Emmons-Featherston, Jim Ford, and Carolyn Anne Taylor, eds. *The Truth of* Buffy: *Essays on Fiction Illuminating Reality*. Jefferson, NC: McFarland & Company, 2008, pp. 173–184.

3980. Fard, Cyrus. "Everything Is for Sale: The Merchandising of 'Buffy.'" *PopMatters.com* (August 31, 2009). Posted at: http://www.popmatters.com/feature/109964-everything-is-for-sale/.

3981. Farghaly, Nadine. *Patriarchy Strikes Back: Power and Perception in* Buffy the Vampire Slayer. Bowling Green, OH: Bowling Green State University, M.A, thesis, 2009. 79 pp. Large format. This thesis was originally presented in shortened form as "Buffy the Matriarch: Giving Birth to a New World Order" at the 2009 PCA/ACA National Conference, New Orleans, LA, April 8–11, 2009, and then accepted (but not presented) at the

30th Annual Southwest/Texas PCA/ACA Conference, Albuquerque, NM, February 25–28 2009. It would later be published in this condensed form in U. Melissa Anyiwo and Karoline Szatek-Tudor, eds. Buffy *Conquers the Academy: Conference Papers from the 2009/2010 Popular Culture/American Culture Associations*. Newcastle upon Tyne, UK: Cambridge Scholars Publishing, 2013, pp. 19–31.

3982. Feasey, Rebecca. "Investigating Angel: The Hair, the Car and the Wardrobe." *Intensities: The Journal of Cult Media* 4 (December 2007): 97–111. Posted at: http://intensitiescultmedia.files.wordpress.com/2012/12/feasey-investigating-angel.pdf. A paper originally presented at the 26th Annual Southwest/Texas PCA/ACA Conference, Albuquerque, NM, February 9–12, 2005.

3983. Ferrante, Anthony C. "The Changing Faces of Buffy the Vampire Slayer." *Fangoria* 116 (September 1992): 22–24.

3984. Field, Mark. *Buffy the Vampire Slayer: Myth, Metaphor & Morality*. N.p.: the author, 2013. e-book. This book originally appeared in an earlier form as posts on author's website.

3985. Fifarek, Aimee. "'Mind and Heart with Spirit Joined': The Buffyverse as an Information System." *Slayage: The Online International Journal of Buffy Studies* 1, 3 [3] (June 2001). Posted at: http://www.whedonstudies.tv/.

3986. Fingeroth, Danny. "Amazon Grace: Wonder Woman Xena, and Buffy." In Danny Fingeroth, *Superman on the Couch: What Superheroes Really Tell Us About Ourselves and Our Society*. New York: Continuum, 2004, pp. 79–95.

3987. Fisher, Roy, Ann Harris, and Christine Jarvis. *Education in Popular Culture: Telling Tales on Teachers and Learners*. New York: Routledge, 2008. 207 pp. Not a book specifically about *Buffy the Vampire Slayer*, but the authors refer to the show throughout the text.

3988. Flamson, Thomas. "Free Will in a Deterministic Whedonverse." In Joy Davidson with Leah Wilson, eds. *The Psychology of Joss Whedon: An Unauthorized Exploration of Buffy, Angel, and Firefly*. Dallas, TX: Benbella Books, 2007, pp. 35–49.

3989. Fletcher, Lawson. "'Is She Cold?': Telaesthetic Horror and Embodied Textuality in 'The Body.'" *Slayage: The Journal of the Whedon Studies Association* 9, 1 [33] (Spring 2011). Posted at: http://www.whedonstudies.tv/.

3990. Flor, Chris, and Philipp Kneis. "'Normal Again': *Buffy the Vampire Slayer* as Psychotic Narration." In Antje Dallmann, Reinhard Isensee, and Philipp Kneis, eds. *Picturing America: Trauma, Realism, Politics, and Identity in American Visual Culture*. New York: Peter Lang, 2007, pp. 65–77. A paper originally presented in earlier form, by Chris Flor, as "Psychotic Narration and Institutionalization in 'Normal Again'" at the Slayage Conference on *Buffy the Vampire Slayer*, Nashville, TN, May 27–30, 2004.

3991. Foley, Timothy Michael. *Double Coded Feminist TV: Overlooked Contradictions Within* Buffy the Vampire Slayer. Tacoma: University of Washington, M.A. thesis, 2013. 25 pp. Posted at: https://digital.lib.washington.edu/researchworks/handle/1773/22457.

3992. Ford, Jessica. "Coming Out of the Broom Closet: Willow's Sexuality and Empowerment in *Buffy*." In Mary Alice Money for PopMatters.com, ed. *Joss Whedon: The Complete Companion: The TV Series, the Movies, the Comic Books and More*. London: Titan Books, 2012, pp. 94–102. An earlier version appeared as part of PopMatters.com's *Spotlight: Joss Whedon*, originally posted on March 9, 2011.

3993. Ford, Jim. "Introduction." In Emily Dial-Driver, Sally Emmons-Featherston, Jim Ford, and Carolyn Anne Taylor, eds. *The Truth of* Buffy: *Essays on Fiction Illuminating Reality*. Jefferson, NC: McFarland & Company, 2008, pp. 5–8.

3994. _____. "A Life Well-Lived: *Buffy* and the Pursuit of Happiness." In Emily Dial-Driver, Sally Emmons-Featherston, Jim Ford, and Carolyn Anne Taylor, eds. *The Truth of* Buffy: *Essays on Fiction Illuminating Reality*. Jefferson, NC: McFarland & Company, 2008, pp. 201–210.

3995. Forry, Joan Grassbaugh. "'Powerful, Beautiful, and Without Regret': Femininity, Masculinity, and the Vampire Aesthetic." In Richard Greene and K. Silem Mohammad, eds. *Zombies, Vampires, and Philosophy: New Life for the Undead*. Chicago: Open Court, 2010, pp. 237–247.

3996. Forster, Greg. "Faith and Plato: 'You're Nothing! Disgusting, Murderous Bitch!'" In James B. South, ed. Buffy *and Philosophy: Fear and Trembling in Sunnydale*. Chicago: Open Court, 2003, pp. 7–19.

3997. Fossey, Claire. "Never Hurt the Feelings of a Brutal Killer: Spike and the Underground Man." *Slayage: The Online International Journal of Buffy Studies* 2, 4 [8] (March 2003). Posted at: http://www.whedonstudies.tv/.

3998. Foster, Susanne E., and James B. South. "'Look What Free Will Has Gotten You':

Isolation, Individuality, and Choice in *Angel*." In Dean A. Kowalski and S. Evan Kreider, eds. *The Philosophy of Joss Whedon*. Lexington: University Press of Kentucky, 2011, pp. 168–81.

3999. _____. "'There's no place I can be': Whedon, Augustine, and the Earthly City." In Anthony R. Mills, John W. Morehead, and J. Ryan Parker, eds. *Joss Whedon and Religion: Essays on an Angry Atheist's Explorations of the Sacred*. Jefferson, NC: McFarland & Company, 2013, pp. 152–164.

4000. Foy, Joseph J., and Dean A. Kowalski. "Seeking Authenticity in the Whedonverse." In Dean A. Kowalski and S. Evan Kreider, eds. *The Philosophy of Joss Whedon*. Lexington: University Press of Kentucky, 2011, pp. 151–67.

4001. Francis, James, Jr. "'Selfless': Locating Female Identity in Anya/Anyanka through Prostitution." Paper presented at the Slayage Conference on *Buffy the Vampire Slayer*, Nashville, TN, May 27–30, 2004. Posted at: http://www.slayageonline.com/SCBtVS_Archive/Talks/Francis.pdf.

4002. Francis, Rob. "London Calling: *Buffy* from a British Perspective." In Paul Ruditis, ed. Buffy the Vampire Slayer: *The Watcher's Guide*. Vol. 3. New York: Simon, 2004, pp. 255–264.

4003. Frankel, Valerie Estelle. *Buffy and the Heroine's Journey: Vampire Slayer as Feminine Chosen One*. Jefferson, NC: McFarland & Company, 2012. 226 pp. tp.

4004. Free, Anna. "Re-Vamping the Gothic in *Buffy the Vampire Slayer*." *Screen Education* 46 (2007): 138–144.

4005. Freedman, Eric. "Television, Horror and Everyday Life in *Buffy the Vampire Slayer*." In Michael Hammond and Lucy Mazdon, eds. *The Contemporary Television Series*. Edinburgh: Edinburgh University Press, 2005, pp. 159–180.

4006. Fritts, David. "*Buffy*'s Seven-Season Initiation." In Kevin K. Durand, ed. Buffy *Meets the Academy: Essays on the Episodes and Scripts as Texts*. Jefferson, NC: McFarland & Company, 2009, pp. 32–44. A paper originally presented as "From Beneath You It Empowers: *Buffy*'s Seven-Season Initiation" at SC2: The Slayage Conference on the Whedonverses, Gordon College, Barnesville, GA, May 25–28, 2006.

4007. _____. "Warrior Heroes: Buffy the Vampire Slayer and Beowulf." *Slayage: The Online International Journal of Buffy Studies* 5, 1 [17] (June 2005). Posted at: http://www.whedonstudies.tv/. A paper originally presented at the Slayage Conference on *Buffy the Vampire Slayer*, Nashville, TN, May 27–30, 2004. Posted at: http://www.slayageonline.com/essays/slayage17/Fritts.htm.

4008. Frohard-Dourlent, Hélène. "'Lezfaux' Representations: How *Buffy* Season Eight Navigates the Politics of Female Heteroflexibility." In Erin B. Waggoner, ed. *Sexual Rhetoric in the Works of Joss Whedon: New Essays*. Jefferson, NC: McFarland & Company, 2010, pp. 31–47. A paper originally presented as "'Tomorrow I'm gonna blush, then I'm gonna smile...but I'm not sure if it goes any further than that': Heteroflexibility and Buffy's Dabble Outside of Heterosexuality" at the 30th Annual Southwest/Texas PCA/ACA Conference, Albuquerque, NM, February 25–28, 2009.

4009. _____. "When the Heterosexual Script Goes Flexible: Public Reactions to Female Heteroflexibility in the *Buffy the Vampire Slayer* Comic Books." *Sexualities* 15, 5–6 (September 2012): 718–738.

4010. Fuchs, Cynthia. "'Did Anyone Ever Explain to You What "Secret Identity" Means?': Race and Displacement in *Buffy* and *Dark Angel*." In Elana Levine and Lisa Parks, eds. *Undead TV: Essays on* Buffy the Vampire Slayer. Durham, NC: Duke University Press, 2007, pp. 96–115. Rpt. in *Slayage: The Online International Journal of Buffy Studies* 6, 4 [24] (Summer 2007). Posted at: http://www.whedonstudies.tv/.

4011. Fudge, Keith. "Ethics Homework from the Hellmouth: Buffy Stakes Her Claim in the First-Year Composition Classroom." In Jodie A. Kreider and Meghan K. Winchell, eds. Buffy *in the Classroom: Essays on Teaching with the Vampire Slayer*. Jefferson, NC: McFarland & Company, 2010, pp. 94–102. A paper originally presented as "Homework from the Hellmouth: Buffy the Vampire Slayer Stakes Her Claim in the Composition Classroom" at the 2012 PCA/ACA National Conference, Boston, MA, April 11–14, 2012.

4012. _____. "The High School Education of Buffy Summers." In Kevin K. Durand, ed. Buffy *Meets the Academy: Essays on the Episodes and Scripts as Texts*. Jefferson, NC: McFarland & Company, 2009, pp. 203–210. A paper originally presented in earlier form as "No Slayer Left Behind: *Buffy* in the Classroom and Public School Education in *Buffy the Vampire Slayer*" at SC3: The Slayage Conference on the Whedonverses, Henderson State College, Arkadelphia, AR, June 5–8, 2008.

4013. Fudge, Rachel. "The Buffy Effect or, a Tale of Cleavage and Marketing." *Bitch* 4, 1 (1999):

18–21. Posted at: http://bitchmagazine.org/article/buffy-effect.

4014. Fuller, Nikki Faith [pseud. of Nicole de la Rosa]. "The Art of *Buffy* Crafts." In Jennifer Kate Stuller, ed. *Fan Phenomena:* Buffy the Vampire Slayer. Chicago: Intellect, 2013, pp. 112–119.

4015. _____. *The Hero's Journey Revamped in* Buffy the Vampire Slayer. Riverside: California Baptist University, M.A. thesis, 2007. 174 pp. Large format.

4016. _____. "'Touch Me and Die, Vermin!' The Psychoanalysis of Illyria." In Mary Alice Money for PopMatters.com, ed. *Joss Whedon: The Complete Companion: The TV Series, the Movies, the Comic Books and More.* London: Titan Books, 2012, pp. 199–205. An earlier version appeared as part of PopMatters.com's *Spotlight: Joss Whedon*, originally posted on March 16, 2011.

4017. Garret, Kyle. "Failure of the Everyman: The Lost Character That Was Xander Harris." In Mary Alice Money for PopMatters.com, ed. *Joss Whedon: The Complete Companion: The TV Series, the Movies, the Comic Books and More.* London: Titan Books, 2012, pp. 56–60. An earlier version appeared as part of PopMatters.com's *Spotlight: Joss Whedon*, originally posted on March 8, 2011.

4018. _____. "In the Buff: Sexual Conservatism in the Works of Whedon." PopMatters.com's *Spotlight: Joss Whedon* (March 23, 2011). Posted at: http://www.popmatters.com/feature/138586-in-the-buff-sexual-conservatism-in-the-works-of-whedon/.

4019. Gatson, Sarah N., and Amanda Zweerink. "Choosing Community: Rejecting Anonymity in Cyberspace." In Danesh A. Chekki, ed. *Community Structure and Dynamics at the Dawn of the New Millennium.* Stamford, CT: JAI Press, 2000, pp. 105–137.

4020. _____. *Interpersonal Culture on the Internet: Television, the Internet, and the Making of a Community.* Lewiston, NY: Edwin Mellen Press, 2004. 288 pp. hb.

4021. _____. "www.Buffy.com: Cliques, Boundaries, and Hierarchies in an Internet Community." In Rhonda V. Wilcox and David Lavery, eds. *Fighting the Forces: What's at Stake in* Buffy the Vampire Slayer. Lanham, MD: Rowman & Littlefield, 2002, pp. 239–249.

4022. Gelder, Ken. "*Buffy the Vampire Slayer.*" In Ken Gelder. *New Vampire Cinema.* London: Palgrave Macmillan, 2012, pp. 15–19.

4023. Geller, Len. "'Normal Again' and 'The Harvest': The Subversion and Triumph of Realism in *Buffy.*" *Slayage: The Journal of the Whedon Studies Association* 8, 4 [32] (Winter 2011). Posted at: http://www.whedonstudies.tv/.

4024. Genge, N. E. *The Buffy Chronicles: The Unofficial Companion to Buffy the Vampire Slayer.* New York: Three Rivers Press, 1998. 255 pp. tp.

4025. Genz, Stéphanie. "Fighting It: The Supergirl." In Stephanie Genz. *Postfemininities in Popular Culture.* New York: Palgrave Macmillan, 2009, pp. 152–169.

4026. Georgis, Dina. "Moving Past Ressentiment: War and the State of Feminist Freedom." *TOPIA: Canadian Journal of Cultural Studies* 20 (Fall 2008): 109–127. Posted at: https://pi.library.yorku.ca/ojs/index.php/topia/article/viewFile/22881/22455.

4027. Gerlach, David. "Blood, Sex and Education: Teenage Problems and Fears as Presented in *Buffy the Vampire Slayer.*" A seminar paper presented at Philipps-Universität Marburg, Institut für Anglistik und Amerikanistik, Maburg, Germany, 2004. 21 pp.

4028. Gerrits, Jeroen. "When Horror Becomes Human: Living Conditions in *Buffy the Vampire Slayer.*" *MLN: Modern Language Notes* 127, 5 (December 2012): 1059–1070.

4029. Gibson-James, Jessica N. *The Aud One Out in the Final Battle: An Anya-Centered Feminist Analysis of* Buffy the Vampire Slayer. Dayton, OH: University of Dayton, M.A. thesis, 2006. 51 pp. Large format.

4030. Gill, Candra K. "Cuz the Black Chick Always Gets It First: Dynamics of Race in *Buffy the Vampire Slayer.*" In Emily Pohl-Weary, ed. *Girls Who Bite Back: Witches, Mutants, Slayers and Freaks.* Toronto: Sumach Press, 2004, pp. 39–55.

4031. Gill, Pat. "Making a Killing in the Marketplace: Incorporation as a Monstrous Process." In Caroline Joan (Kay) Picart and Cecil Greek, eds. *Monsters in and Among Us: Toward a Gothic Criminology.* Madison, NJ: Fairleigh Dickinson University Press, 2007, pp. 142–163.

4032. Gilman, Laura Anne. "True Shanshu: Redemption through Compassion, and the Journey of Cordelia Chase." In Glenn Yeffeth, ed. *Five Seasons of* Angel: Science Fiction and Fantasy Writers Discuss Their Favorite Vampire. Dallas, TX: Benbella Books, 2004, pp. 179–185.

4033. Gilstrap, Andrew. "Death and the Single Girl: Buffy Grows Up." PopMatters.com (June 10, 2002). Posted at: http://www.popmatters.com/review/buffy-the-vampire-slayer3/.

4034. Ginn, Sherry. *Power and Control in the Television Worlds of Joss Whedon.* Jefferson, NC: McFarland & Company, 2012. 186 pp. tp.

4035. Gleason, Tracy R., and Nancy S. Weinfield. "An Analysis of Slayer Longevity: Relationships on the Hellmouth." In Joy Davidson with Leah Wilson, eds. *The Psychology of Joss Whedon: An Unauthorized Exploration of* Buffy, Angel, *and* Firefly. Dallas, TX: Benbella Books, 2007, pp. 65–77.

4036. Glynn, Kevin. "Challenging Disenchantment: The Discreet Charm of Occult TV." *Comparative American Studies* 1, 4 (December 2003): 421–447.

4037. Gobatto, Nancy. "'Ready to Be Strong?': Buffy, Angelina and Me." In Emily Pohl-Weary, ed. *Girls Who Bite Back: Witches, Mutants, Slayers and Freaks.* Toronto: Sumach Press, 2004, pp. 119–131.

4038. Goile, Joanne E. *Fascinations of Fiction: An Examination of Devices Used Within the Television Programme* Buffy the Vampire Slayer *That Succeed in Blurring the Boundaries Between Viewers and the Fictional Diegesis of the Show.* Auckland, NZ: Auckland University of Technology, M.A. thesis, 2003. 67 pp. Large format. A paper originally presented in earlier form as "Fascinations of Fiction" at Staking a Claim: Exploring the Global Reach of *Buffy*, University of South Australia, Adelaide, Australia, July 22, 2003.

4039. Golden, Christie. "Where's the Religion in Willow's Wicca?" In Glenn Yeffeth, ed. *Seven Seasons of* Buffy: *Science Fiction and Fantasy Writers Discuss Their Favorite Television Show.* Dallas, TX: Benbella Books, 2003, pp. 159–166.

4040. Golden, Christopher, and Nancy Holder. *Buffy the Vampire Slayer: The Watcher's Guide.* New York: Pocket Books, 1998. 298 pp. tp.

4041. Golden, Christopher, Stephen R. Bissette, and Thomas E. Sniegoski. *Buffy the Vampire Slayer: The Monster Book.* New York: Pocket Books, 2000. 370 pp. hb. & tp.

4042. Gölz, Peter. "Fear and Laughing in Sunnydale: Buffy vs Dracula." *Journal of Dracula Studies* 11 (2009): 23–41. Posted at: http://www.blooferland.com/drc/index.php?title=Journal_of_Dracula_Studies.

4043. Goodwill, Jo-Anne S. *The Action Hero Revisioned: An Analysis of Female 'Masculinity' in the New Female Hero in Recent Filmic Texts.* Pretoria: University of South Africa, M.A. thesis, 2009. 149 pp. Large format. Posted at: http://uir.unisa.ac.za/handle/10500/2641.

4044. Graeber, David. "Rebel Without a God: *Buffy the Vampire Slayer* is Gleefully Anti-authoritarian—and Popular." *In These Times* 23, 2 (December 1998). Posted at: http://mikeholt.tripod.com/buffy.html.

4045. Graham, Brita Marie. Buffy *at Play: Tricksters, Deconstruction, and Chaos at Work in the Whedonverse.* Bozeman: Montana State University, M.A. thesis, 2007. 94 pp. Large format. Originally presented as "Buffy at Play: The Deconstructing Trickster at Work in the Whedonverse," a paper for the 27th Annual Southwest/Texas PCA/ACA Conference, Albuquerque, NM, February 8–11, 2006. Posted at: http://etd.lib.montana.edu/etd/2007/graham/GrahamB0507.pdf.

4046. _____. "'Needing to Know the Plural of Apocalypse': *Buffy*'s Lessons in Creating Meaning." Paper presented at the 28th Annual Southwest/Texas PCA/ACA Conference, Albuquerque, NM, February 14–17, 2007. Rpt. as "'Needing to Know the Plural of Apocalypse': *Buffy*'s Lessons in Dismantling Meaning" in Brita Marie. Buffy *at Play: Tricksters, Deconstruction, and Chaos at Work in the Whedonverse.* Bozeman: Montana State University, M.A. thesis, 2007, pp. 29–47.

4047. Graham, Helen. "Post-Pleasure: Representations, Ideologies and Affects of a Newly-Post 9/11 'Feminist' Icon." *Feminist Media Studies* 7, 1 (March 2007): 1–15.

4048. Graham, Paula. "Buffy Wars: The Next Generation." *Rhizomes: Cultural Studies in Emerging Knowledge* 4 (2002) Posted at: http://www.rhizomes.net/issue4/graham.html.

4049. Grant, Julia L. "Slaying Shakespeare in High School: Buffy Battles *The Merchant of Venice* and *Othello.*" In Jodie A. Kreider and Meghan K. Winchell, ed. Buffy *in the Classroom: Essays on Teaching with the Vampire Slayer.* Jefferson, NC: McFarland & Company, 2010, pp. 202–212.

4050. Gray, Jonathan. "Coming Soon! Hype, Intros, and Textual Beginnings." *Show Sold Separately: Promos, Spoilers, and Other Media Paratexts.* New York: New York University Press, 2010, pp. 76–78.

4051. Greenberg, Raz. "*Alien Resurrection,* the Script That Shaped Joss Whedon's Career." In

Mary Alice Money for PopMatters.com, ed. *Joss Whedon: The Complete Companion: The TV Series, the Movies, the Comic Books and More.* London: Titan Books, 2012, pp. 431–440. An earlier version titled "'Alien Resurrection,' the Unproduced Script That Shaped Joss Whedon's Career" appeared as part of PopMatters.com's *Spotlight: Joss Whedon,* originally posted on March 6, 2011.

4052. Greene, Richard, and Wayne Yuen. "Morality on Television: The Case of *Buffy the Vampire Slayer.*" In James B. South, ed. Buffy *and Philosophy: Fear and Trembling in Sunnydale.* Chicago: Open Court, 2003, pp. 271–281.

4053. _____. "Why Can't We Spike Spike? Moral Themes in *Buffy the Vampire Slayer.*" *Slayage: The Online International Journal of Buffy Studies* 1, 2 [2] (March 2001). Posted at: http://www.whedonstudies.tv/.

4054. Greenwald, Sarah J., and Jill E. Thomley. "Mathematically Talented Women in Film and Television: A Summary of the Last Five Years." *Association for Women in Mathematics Newsletter* 38, 1 (January-February 2009): 8–11.

4055. _____. "Mathematically Talented Women in Hollywood: Fred in *Angel.*" *PRIMUS: Problems, Resources, and Issues in Mathematics Undergraduate Studies* 17, 1 (2007): 103–16.

4056. Griffiths, Estelle L. *Talk About Television: The Uses of* Buffy *in Identity Formation and Self-Understanding.* Burnie, Aust.: University of Tasmania, BA honors thesis, 2000. 49 pp. Large format.

4057. Grinnell, Jason D. "Aristotle, Kant, Spike, and Jayne: Ethics and Character in the Whedonverse." In Dean A. Kowalski and S. Evan Kreider, eds. *The Philosophy of Joss Whedon.* Lexington: University Press of Kentucky, 2011, pp. 88–102.

4058. Grossman, Jacob. "Spike, the Initiative, and the Substitution of the Technological for the Metaphysical." A paper presented at the Slayage Conference on *Buffy the Vampire Slayer,* Nashville, TN, May 27–30, 2004. Posted at: http://www.slayageonline.com/SCBtVS_Archive/Talks/Grossman.pdf.

4059. Grzanka, Patrick R. "Buffy the Black Feminist? Intersectionality and Pedagogy." In Jodie A. Kreider and Meghan K. Winchell, eds. Buffy *in the Classroom: Essays on Teaching with the Vampire Slayer.* Jefferson, NC: McFarland & Company, 2010, pp. 186–201.

4060. Guffey, Ensley. "'We Just Declared War': Buffy as General." *Watcher Junior: The Un-*dergraduate Journal of Whedon Studies 5, 1 [6] (July 2011). Posted at: http://www.watcherjunior.tv/. A paper originally presented at SC4: The Slayage Conference on the Whedonverses, Flagler College, St. Augustine, FL, June 3–6, 2010.

4061. Hahn, Kelsie. "Lady Killer: Death of the Feminized Body in the Whedonverse." *Slayage: The Journal of the Whedon Studies Association* 10, 1 [35] (Winter 2013). Posted at: http://www.whedonstudies.tv/. A paper originally presented at the 33rd Annual Southwest/Texas PCA/ACA Conference, Albuquerque, NM, February 8–11, 2012.

4062. Hale, Kelly. "My European Vacation: A Love Letter/Confession." In Lynne M. Thomas and Deborah Stanish, eds. *Whedonistas! A Celebration of the Worlds of Joss Whedon by the Women Who Love Them.* Des Moines, IA: Mad Norwegian Press, 2011, pp. 93–99.

4063. Halfyard, Janet K. "The Dark Avenger: Angel and the Cinematic Superhero." In Stacey Abbott, ed. *Reading* Angel: *The TV Spin-off with a Soul.* New York: I. B. Tauris, 2005, pp. 149–162.

4064. _____. "The Greatest Love of All: Cordelia's Journey of Self-Discovery." Paper presented at the Slayage Conference on *Buffy the Vampire Slayer,* Nashville, TN, May 27–30, 2004. Posted at: http://www.whedonstudies.tv/.

4065. _____. "Love, Death, Curses and Reverses (in F minor): Music, Gender, and Identity in *Buffy the Vampire Slayer* and *Angel.*" *Slayage: The Online International Journal of Buffy Studies* 1, 4 [4] (December 2001 Posted at: http://www.whedonstudies.tv/. Rpt. as "Love, Death, Curses, and Reverses (in E minor): Music, Gender and Identity in *Buffy the Vampire Slayer* and *Angel.*" In Paul Attinello, Janet K. Halfyard, and Vanessa Knights, eds. *Music, Sound, and Silence in* Buffy the Vampire Slayer. Farnham, Surrey, UK: Ashgate Publishing, 2010, pp. 15–31.

4066. _____. "Singing Their Hearts Out: The Problem of Performance in *Buffy the Vampire Slayer* and *Angel.*" *Slayage: The Online International Journal of Buffy Studies* 5, 1 [17] (June 2005). Posted at: http://www.whedonstudies.tv/. Rpt. in Kendra Preston Leonard. Buffy*, Ballads, and Bad Guys Who Sing: Music in the Worlds of Joss Whedon.* Lanham, MD: Scarecrow Press, 2011, pp. 155–171. A paper originally presented as "Singing Their Hearts Out: Performance, Sincerity and Musical Diegesis in *Buffy the Vampire Slayer* and *Angel*" at Blood, Text and Fears: Reading Around *Buffy the Vampire Slayer,* University of East Anglia, October 19–20, 2002.

4067. Hall, Jasmine. "Im/Material Girl: Abjection, Penetration, and the Postmodern Body on *Buffy the Vampire Slayer*." Paper presented at the Slayage Conference on *Buffy the Vampire Slayer*, Nashville, TN, May 27–30, 2004. Posted at: http://www.slayageonline.com/SCBtVS_Archive/Talks/Hall.pdf.

4068. Hallab, Mary Y. "Alternative Lives: *Buffy* and *Angel*." In Mary Y. Hallab. *Vampire God: The Allure of the Undead in Western Culture*. Albany: SUNY [State University of New York] Press, 2009, pp. 122–128.

4069. Hamilton, Jennifer. "Pylean Idol: L.A.'s De(con)struction of a Postmodern Bard." In AmiJo Comeford and Tamy L. Burnett, eds. *The Literary Angel: Essays on Influences and Traditions Reflected in the Joss Whedon Series*. Jefferson, NC: McFarland & Company, 2010, pp. 41–53.

4070. Hammond, Mary. "Monsters and Metaphors: *Buffy the Vampire Slayer* and the Old World." In Sara Gwenllian-Jones and Roberta E. Pearson, eds. *Cult Television*. Minneapolis: University of Minnesota Press, 2004, pp. 147–64.

4071. Hampton, Howard. "American Daemons: *Buffy the Vampire Slayer* and *Studies in Classic American Literature*." In Howard Hampton. *Born in Flames: Termite Dreams, Dialectical Fairy Tales, and Pop Apocalypses*. Cambridge, MA: Harvard University Press, 2007, pp. 372–377.

4072. _____. "American Demons: *Buffy* Amok in D. H. Lawrence's World." *Village Voice Literary Supplement* (May 20, 2003).

4073. _____. "Wrecked in El Dorado: *Angel*." In Howard Hampton. *Born in Flames: Termite Dreams, Dialectical Fairy Tales, and Pop Apocalypses*. Cambridge, MA: Harvard University Press, 2007, pp. 378–386.

4074. Harbin, Leigh. "'You Know You Wanna Dance': *Buffy the Vampire Slayer* as Contemporary Gothic Heroine." *Studies in the Humanities* 32, 1 (June 2005): 22–37.

4075. Harper, Steven. "Dark Fears: Madness in Gothic and Supernatural Drama." In Stephen Harper. *Madness, Power and the Media Class, Gender and Race in Popular Representations of Mental Distress*. New York: Palgrave Macmillan, 2009, pp. 115–116.

4076. _____. "Jasmine: Scariest Villain Ever." In Glenn Yeffeth, ed. *Five Seasons of* Angel: *Science Fiction and Fantasy Writers Discuss Their Favorite Vampire*. Dallas, TX: Benbella Books, 2004, pp. 49–55.

4077. Harris, Charlaine. "A Reflection on Ugliness." In Glenn Yeffeth, ed. *Seven Seasons of* Buffy: *Science Fiction and Fantasy Writers Discuss Their Favorite Television Show*. Dallas, TX: Benbella Books, 2003, pp. 116–120.

4078. Harris, Howard. "*Buffy the Vampire Slayer* in the Business Ethics Classroom." *Slayage: The Online International Journal of Buffy Studies* 7, 3 [27] (Winter 2009). Posted at: http://www.whedonstudies.tv/. A paper originally presented in earlier form as "Using *Buffy* in the Teaching of Business Ethics" at Staking a Claim: Exploring the Global Reach of *Buffy*, University of South Australia, Adelaide, Australia, July 22, 2003.

4079. Harris, Nathan P. *Watch* Buffy *Much? Definitions of Cult Television in Relation to Character Identification*. Adelaide, Aust.: Flinders University of South Australia, BA honors thesis, 2002. 63 pp. Large format.

4080. Harrison, Janine R. "Gender Politics in *Angel*: Traditional vs. Non-Traditional Corporate Climates." In Stacey Abbott, ed. *Reading* Angel: *The TV Spin-off with a Soul*. New York: I. B. Tauris, 2005, pp. 117–131.

4081. Hart, Maryelizabeth. "Slaying the Big Lies: Love Conquers All and Other Monstrous Myths." In Paul Ruditis, ed. Buffy the Vampire Slayer: *The Watcher's Guide*. Vol. 3. New York: Simon, 2004, pp. 265–270.

4082. Harts, Kate. "Deconstructing Buffy: *Buffy the Vampire Slayer*'s Contribution to the Discourse on Gender Construction." *Popular Culture Review* 12, 1 (2001): 79–98.

4083. Haskins, Rob. "Variations on Themes for Geeks and Heroes: Leitmotif, Style, and the Musico-dramatic Moment." *Music, Sound, and Silence in* Buffy the Vampire Slayer. Eds. Paul Attinello, Janet K. Halfyard, and Vanessa Knights. Farnham, Surrey, UK: Ashgate Publishing, 2010. 45–60.

4084. Haslem, Wendy. "'Every Home Should Have One of You': The Serial Killer Disguised as the Perfect Husband." *Special Issue on* Buffy the Vampire Slayer. Eds. Angela Ndalianis and Felicity Colman. *Refractory: A Journal of Entertainment Media* 2 (2003). Posted at: http://refractory.unimelb.edu.au/2003/03/18/vol2/. A paper originally presented at The Buffyverse: A Symposium on *Buffy the Vampire Slayer* held at the University of Melbourne, Melbourne, Australia, November 21, 2002.

4085. Hastie, Amelie. "The Epistemological Stakes of *Buffy the Vampire Slayer*: Television Criticism and Marketing Demands." In Elana Levine and Lisa Parks, eds. *Undead TV: Essays on* Buffy the Vampire Slayer. Durham, NC: Duke University Press, 2007, pp. 74–95.

4086. Hautsch, Jessica. "Staking Her Colonial Claim: Colonial Discourses, Assimilation, Soul-making, and Ass-kicking in *Buffy the Vampire Slayer*." *Slayage: The Journal of the Whedon Studies Association* 9, 1 [33] (Spring 2011). Posted at: http://www.whedonstudies.tv/.

4087. Havelka, Emily Suzanne. *'The painful noun-ing process': The Arduous Journey of Masculinity in* Buffy the Vampire Slayer. Alma, MI: Alma College, BA honors thesis, 2012.

4088. Havens, Candace. *Joss Whedon: The Genius Behind Buffy*. Dallas, TX: Benbella Books, 2003. 171 pp. tp.

4089. _____. "To All the Girls He Loved, Maimed and Banged Before." In Glenn Yeffeth, ed. *Five Seasons of* Angel: Science Fiction and Fantasy Writers Discuss Their Favorite Vampire. Dallas, TX: Benbella Books, 2004. 125–132.

4090. Hawkins, Paul. "Season Six and the Supreme Ordeal." In Lynne Y. Edwards, Elizabeth L. Rambo and James B. South, eds. *Buffy Goes Dark: Essays on the Final Two Seasons of* Buffy the Vampire Slayer *on Television*. Jefferson, NC: McFarland & Company, 2009. 183–197.

4091. Hay, Genevieve. *Vampires and Identity Violence from* The Vampyre *to* Buffy the Vampire Slayer. St. Louis, MO: Washington University, BA honors thesis, 2013.

4092. Hayes, K. [Karen] Stoddard. "Where Have All the Good Guys Gone?" In Glenn Yeffeth, ed. *Five Seasons of* Angel: Science Fiction and Fantasy Writers Discuss Their Favorite Vampire. Dallas, TX: Benbella Books, 2004, pp. 139–144.

4093. Heba, Gary with Robin Murphy. "Heroes and Villains: Morality, the Will to Power, and the Overman in the Work of Joss Whedon." In Dean A. Kowalski and S. Evan Kreider, eds. *The Philosophy of Joss Whedon*. Lexington: University Press of Kentucky, 2011, pp. 133–147.

4094. Heinecken, Dawn M. "*Buffy the Vampire Slayer* and the Body in Relation." In Dawn M. Heinecken. *The Warrior Women of Television: A Feminist Cultural Analysis of the New Female Body in Popular Media*. New York: Peter Lang, 2003, pp. 91–132.

4095. _____. "Fan Readings of Sex and Violence on *Buffy the Vampire Slayer*." *Slayage: The Online International Journal of Buffy Studies* 3, 3–4 [11–12] (April 2004). Posted at: http://www.whedonstudies.tv/. A paper originally presented at Blood, Text and Fears: Reading Around *Buffy the Vampire Slayer*, University of East Anglia, October 19–20, 2002.

4096. _____. "'I Wasn't Planning on Hurting You—Much': Sadomasochism, Melodrama and *Buffy the Vampire Slayer* Fan Fiction." *Spectator* 25, 1 (Spring 2005): 48–60.

4097. _____. *The Women Warriors of Television: A Feminist Cultural Analysis of the New Female Body in Popular Media*, Bowling Green, OH: Bowling Green State University, Ph.D. dissertation, 1999. 208 pp. Large format.

4098. Held, Jacob. "Justifying the Means: Punishment in the Buffyverse." In James B. South, ed. Buffy *and Philosophy: Fear and Trembling in Sunnydale*. Chicago: Open Court, 2003, pp. 227–238.

4099. _____. "The Stuff We're Made Of." Paper presented at the Slayage Conference on *Buffy the Vampire Slayer*, Nashville, TN, May 27–30, 2004. Posted at: http://www.slayageonline.com/SCBtVS_Archive/Talks/Held.pdf.

4100. Helford, Elyce Rae. "'My Emotions Give Me Power': The Containment of Girls' Anger in *Buffy*." In Rhonda V. Wilcox and David Lavery, eds. *Fighting the Forces: What's at Stake in* Buffy the Vampire Slayer. Lanham, MD: Rowman & Littlefield, 2002, pp. 18–34.

4101. Helfrich, Ronald. "'Note to Self, Religion Freaky': When Buffy Met Biblical Studies." In Mary Alice Money for PopMatters.com, ed. *Joss Whedon: The Complete Companion: The TV Series, the Movies, the Comic Books and More*. London: Titan Books, 2012, pp. 37–48. A paper originally presented at Get to the Point: Issues at Stake in *Buffy the Vampire Slayer*, SUNY College at Oneonta, November 2009, and subsequently appeared as part of PopMatters.com's *Spotlight: Joss Whedon*, posted on March 6, 2011.

4102. Helms, Bari L. *Reel Librarians: The Stereotype and Technology*. Chapel Hill: University of North Carolina, M.A. thesis, 2006. 46 pp. Large format. Posted at: https://cdr.lib.unc.edu/record;jsessionid=B0F253A96B0BDFFD4DF5C2DBEADDD7F5?id=uuid%3Abe6a349a-f8aa-42c1-8f11-39550c3b1759.

4103. *Hemery High School Yearbook 1992*.

Los Angeles: Twentieth Century–Fox, 1992. 28 pp. pb. Large format. Actually a press book for the 1992 *Buffy the Vampire Slayer* movie.

4104. Hemmingson, Margaret L. *Sex, Family, and the Home: Portrayals of Gender in the Domestic Sphere in* Buffy the Vampire Slayer *and* Supernatural. Elon, NC: Elon University, BA honors thesis, 2011. 82 pp. Large format. Posted at: http:// elonuniversity.contentdm.oclc.org/cdm/single item/collection/p15446coll7/id/82/rec/6.

4105. Hemstrom, Cassie. "What's at Stake? The Use of Simulacra to (Re)Construct Identity in *Buffy the Vampire Slayer*." In U. Melissa Anyiwo and Karoline Szatek-Tudor, ed. Buffy *Conquers the Academy: Conference Papers from the 2009/2010 Popular Culture/American Culture Associations.* Newcastle upon Tyne, UK: Cambridge Scholars Publishing, 2013. 48–59. A paper originally presented in earlier form as "What's at Stake: Creating a Simulacrum in *Buffy the Vampire Slayer*" at the 2009 PCA/ACA National Conference, New Orleans, LA, April 8–11, 2009.

4106. Hendershot, Heather. "The Good, the Bad, and the Ugly: From *Buffy the Vampire Slayer* to *Dr. 90210*." *Camera Obscura* 21, 1/61 (January 2006): 46–51.

4107. Herman, Caroline. "*Buffy the Vampire Slayer* and Dichotomy of Self: A Study in the Shadow Selves of Buffy and Spike." *Watcher Junior: The Journal of Undergraduate Research in Buffy Studies* 1, 1 [1] (July 2005). Posted at: http://www. whedonstudies.tv/.

4108. Herrmann, Andrew F. "'C-can we rest now?' Foucault and the Multiple Discursive Subjectivities of Spike." *Slayage: The Journal of the Whedon Studies Association* 10, 1 [35] (Winter 2013). Posted at: http://www.whedonstudies.tv/.

4109. _____. "The Scoobies, the Council, the Whirlwind, the Initiative: Portrayals of Organizing in *Buffy the Vampire Slayer*." A paper presented at the Central States Communication Association Convention, Kansas City, MO, April 2–7, 2013. Posted at: http://www.academia.edu/3267039/ The_Scoobies_The_Council_The_Whirlwind_ The_Initiative_Portrayals_of_Organizing_in_ Buffy_the_Vampire_Slayer.

4110. Hertz, Todd. "Don't Let Your Kids Watch *Buffy the Vampire Slayer*: But You Can Tape It and Watch After They Go to Bed." *Christianity Today* (September 18, 2002). Posted at: http:// www.christianitytoday.com/ct/2002/september web-only/9-16-31.0.html?start=2.

4111. Hibbs, Thomas. "*Buffy the Vampire*

Slayer as Feminist Noir." In James B. South, ed. Buffy *and Philosophy: Fear and Trembling in Sunnydale.* Chicago: Open Court, 2003, pp. 49–60.

4112. Hicks, Kenneth S. "Lord Acton Is Alive and Well in Sunnydale: Politics and Power in *Buffy*." In Emily Dial-Driver, Sally Emmons-Featherston, Jim Ford, and Carolyn Anne Taylor, eds. *The Truth of* Buffy: *Essays on Fiction Illuminating Reality.* Jefferson, NC: McFarland & Company, 2008, pp. 67–82.

4113. _____, and Carolyn Anne Taylor. "'I'm Cookie Dough': Exploring *Buffy* Iconography." In Emily Dial-Driver, Sally Emmons-Featherston, Jim Ford, and Carolyn Anne Taylor, eds. *The Truth of* Buffy: *Essays on Fiction Illuminating Reality.* Jefferson, NC: McFarland & Company, 2008, pp. 185–200.

4114. Hill, Annette and Ian Calcutt. "Vampire Hunters: The Scheduling and Reception of *Buffy the Vampire Slayer* and *Angel* in the United Kingdom." *Intensities: The Journal of Cult Media* 1 (2001). Rev. text in: Elana Levine and Lisa Parks, eds. *Undead TV: Essays on* Buffy the Vampire Slayer. Durham, NC: Duke University Press, 2007, pp. 56–73.

4115. Hill, Kathryn. "Buffy's Voice: *Buffy the Vampire Slayer*'s Popular Music Soundtrack and Contemporary Feminism." *Feminist Media Studies iFirst* (February 3, 2012). A paper originally presented in earlier form as "Buffy's Voice: The Power of Popular Music as Feminine/Feminist Narrative" at Staking a Claim: Exploring the Global Reach of *Buffy*, University of South Australia, Adelaide, Australia, July 22, 2003.

4116. _____. "'Easy to Associate Angsty Lyrics with Buffy': An Introduction to a Participatory Fan Culture: *Buffy the Vampire Slayer* Vidders, Popular Music and the Internet." In Mary Kirby-Diaz, ed. *Buffy and Angel Conquer the Internet: Essays on Online Fandom.* Jefferson, NC: McFarland & Company, 2009, pp. 172–196.

4117. _____. "'It's All My Interpretation': Reading Spike through the Subcultural Celebrity of James Marsters." In Dee Amy-Chinn and Milly Williamson, eds. *The Vampire Spike in Text and Fandom: Unsettling Oppositions in* Buffy the Vampire Slayer. Special Issue of *European Journal of Cultural Studies* 8, 3 (August 2005): 345–365.

4118. _____. "Music, Subtexts and Foreshadowings: Contextual Roles of Popular Music in *Buffy the Vampire Slayer*, 1997–2003." Paper presented at the Slayage Conference on *Buffy the Vam-*

pire Slayer, Nashville, TN, May 27–30, 2004. Posted at: http://www.slayageonline.com/SCBtVS_Archive/Talks/KHill.pdf.

4119. _____. "Punks, Geeks and Goths: *Buffy the Vampire Slayer* as a Study of Popular Music Demographics on American Commercial Television." In Paul Attinello, Janet K. Halfyard, and Vanessa Knights, ed. *Music, Sound, and Silence in* Buffy the Vampire Slayer. Farnham, Surrey, UK: Ashgate Publishing, 2010. 165–186.

4120. _____. "S/He's a Rebel: The James Dean Trope in *Buffy the Vampire Slayer*." *Continuum: Journal of Media & Cultural Studies* 27, 1 (February 2013): 124–140.

4121. Hills, Matt, and Rebecca Williams. "*Angel*'s Monstrous Mothers and Vampires with Souls: Investigating the Abject in 'Television Horror.'" In Stacey Abbott, ed. *Reading* Angel: *The TV Spin-off with a Soul*. New York: I. B. Tauris, 2005, pp. 203–217.

4122. Hindle, Michael. "'Jimmy Olsen jokes are pretty much gonna be lost on you': The Importance of Xander in *Buffy the Vampire Slayer*." *Watcher Junior: The Undergraduate Journal of Whedon Studies* 6, 2 [8] (September 2012). Posted at: http://www.watcherjunior.tv/.

4123. Hinojosa, Manuel M. *Teaching Outré Literature Rhetorically in First-Year Composition.* Tucson: University of Arizona, Ph.D. dissertation, 2005. 244 pp. Large format.

4124. Hirji, Faiza. "Embodied Power: The Physicality and Strength of *Buffy the Vampire Slayer*." In Will Wright and Steven Kaplan, eds. *The Image of Power in Literature, Media, and Society: Selected Papers, 2006 Conference, Society for the Interdisciplinary Study of Social Imagery*. Pueblo: Colorado State University, 2006, pp. 25–32. A paper originally presented at the 2006 Conference of the Society for the Interdisciplinary Study of Social Imagery, March 2006, Colorado Springs, CO.

4125. Hirmer, Karin. "Female Empowerment: Buffy and Her Heiresses in Control." In Barbara Brodman and James E. Doan, eds. *Images of the Modern Vampire: The Hip and the Atavistic*. Madison. NJ: Fairleigh Dickinson University Press, 2013, pp. 71–84.

4126. Hixson-Vulpe, Jack. "Lesbian Passage: The Representation of the Lesbian from Pulp to *Buffy*." *Subversions: The Journal of Gender and Sexuality* 3 (Spring 2007): 23–25.

4127. Hobson, Amanda. "Foreword: Why Does *Buffy* Matter?" In U. Melissa Anyiwo and Karoline Szatek-Tudor, eds. Buffy *Conquers the Academy: Conference Papers from the 2009/2010 Popular Culture/American Culture Associations*. Newcastle upon Tyne, UK: Cambridge Scholars Publishing, 2013, pp. ix–xii.

4128. Hodges, Amanda L. and Laurel P. Richmond. "Taking a Bite Out of 'Buffy': Carnivalesque Play and Resistance in Fan Fiction." *Transformative Works and Cultures* 7 (2011). Posted at: http://journal.transformativeworks.org/index.php/twc/article/view/265/231.

4129. Hoffmann, Christine. "Happiness is a Warm Scythe: The Evolution of Villainy and Weaponry in the Buffyverse." *Slayage: The Online International Journal of Buffy Studies* 7, 3 [27] (Winter 2009). Posted at: http://www.slayageonline.com/.

4130. Hofman-Howley, Ingrid. "Romancing the Vampire: The Lives and Loves of Two Vampire Slayers—Anita and Buffy." *Refractory: A Journal of Entertainment Media* 8 (2005). Posted at: http://refractory.unimelb.edu.au/2008/08/22/refractory-volume-8-2005/. A paper originally presented as "Supernatural Superheroes: War and Love in the Lives of Two Vampire Slayers—Anita and Buffy" at Holy Men in Tights: A Superheroes Conference, University of Melbourne, Melbourne, Australia, June 2005.

4131. Holba, Annette M. "Occultic Rhetoric in the Buffyverse: Apocalypse Revisited." In Kylo-Patrick R. Hart and Annette M. Holba, eds. *Media and the Apocalypse*. New York: Peter Lang, 2009, pp. 77–96.

4132. Holder, Nancy. *Buffy: The Making of a Slayer: The Complete Guide*. Seattle, WA: 24North, 2012. 176 pp. hb. boards. Slipcase. Large format. Rpt.: London, Titan Books, 2012. 176 pp. hb. Large format. Published at the end of 2012, The Making of a Slayer arrived just in time to celebrate the 15th anniversary of *Buffy the Vampire Slayer*. Included in the American edition, inside the cover of the slipcase, is an envelope with 13 removable sheets of what is termed "Slayer Lore: Texts and Magicks for the Battle." These papers replicate the ancient spells and prophecies used on-screen to defeat the vampires and other monsters that came at Buffy and her cohorts.

4133. _____. "Death Becomes Him: Blondie Bear 5.0." In Glenn Yeffeth, ed. *Five Seasons of* Angel: *Science Fiction and Fantasy Writers Discuss Their Favorite Vampire*. Dallas, TX: Benbella Books, 2004, pp. 153–166.

4134. _____. "I Want Your Sex: Gender and Power in Joss Whedon's Dystopian Future World." In Jane Espenson with Glenn Yeffeth, ed. *Finding Serenity: Anti-Heroes, Lost Shepherds and Space Hookers in Joss Whedon's* Firefly. Dallas, TX: Benbella Books, 2005, pp. 139–153.

4135. _____. "Learning on the Job." In Lee Goldberg, ed. *Tied In: The Business, History and Craft of Media Tie-In Writing.* New York: International Association of Media Tie-In Writers, 2010, pp. 173–182.

4136. _____. "Ramping Up for a Decade with Joss Whedon." In Lynne M. Thomas and Deborah Stanish, eds. *Whedonistas! A Celebration of the Worlds of Joss Whedon by the Women Who Love Them.* Des Moines, IA: Mad Norwegian Press, 2011, pp. 19–24.

4137. _____. "Slayers of the Last Arc." In Glenn Yeffeth, ed. *Seven Seasons of* Buffy: *Science Fiction and Fantasy Writers Discuss Their Favorite Television Show.* Dallas, TX: Benbella Books, 2003, pp. 195–205.

4138. _____. "Writing Tie-Ins." In Stacey Abbott, ed. *The Cult TV Book.* New York: I. B. Tauris, 2010, pp. 191–197.

4139. _____, with Jeff Mariotte and Maryelizabeth Hart. *Angel: The Casefiles.* Vol. 1. New York: Simon Pulse, 2002. 405 pp. tp.

4140. _____. *Buffy the Vampire Slayer: The Watcher's Guide.* Vol. 2. New York: Pocket Books, 2000. 472 pp. tp.

4141. _____. "Creating *Buffy*: The Production Process." In Nancy Holder, with Jeff Mariotte, and Maryelizabeth Hart, eds. Buffy the Vampire Slayer: *The Watcher's Guide.* Vol. 2. New York: Simon, 2000, pp. 319–452.

4142. _____. "The Pain." In Nancy Holder, with Jeff Mariotte, and Maryelizabeth Hart. Buffy the Vampire Slayer: *The Watcher's Guide.* Vol. 2. New York: Simon, 2000, pp. 111–137.

4143. Holliday, Frederick A. *The Long View: Three Levels of Narration in* Buffy the Vampire Slayer. Lawrence: University of Kansas, Ph.D. dissertation, 2005. 253 pp. Large format.

4144. Hollis, Erin. "Gorgonzola Sandwiches and Yellow Crayons: James Joyce, *Buffy the Vampire Slayer*, and the Aesthetic of Minutiae." In Matthew Pateman, ed. Buffy *and Aesthetics.* Special Issue of *Slayage: The Online International Journal of Buffy Studies* 6, 2 [22] (Winter 2006). Posted at: http://www.whedonstudies.tv/.

4145. _____. "'It's the Perfect Story, So They Say': Viewer Participation and the Works of Joss Whedon." In Miguel Angel Pérez Gómez, ed. *Previously On: Estudios interdisciplinarios sobre la ficción televisiva en la Tercera Edad de Oro de la Televisión.* Seville, Spain: Biblioteca de la Facultad de Comunicación de la Universidad de Sevilla, 2011, pp. 291–305. A paper originally presented in earlier form as "'It's the Perfect Story, So They Say': Heroes, Villains, Ethics, and the Media in *Dr. Horrible's Sing-Along Blog*" at the 30th Annual Southwest/Texas PCA/ACA Conference, Albuquerque, NM, February, 25–28, 2009. Posted at: http://fama2.us.es/fco/previouslyon/18.pdf.

4146. _____. "Revisiting the Gothic: *Buffy the Vampire Slayer* and *Angel* as Contemporary Gothic." In Margaret Sönser Breen. *Good & Evil.* Ser,: Critical Insights. Ipswich, MA: Salem Press, 2012, pp. 238–252.

4147. Hook, Misty K. "Dealing with the F-Word: Joss Whedon and Radical Feminism." In Joy Davidson with Leah Wilson. eds. *The Psychology of Joss Whedon: An Unauthorized Exploration of* Buffy, Angel, *and* Firefly. Dallas, TX: Benbella Books, 2007, pp. 119–129.

4148. Horn, Birte W. "'We're your arch-nemesises... ses'—*Buffy* and 'The Trio': The Americanization of a Mythological Motif." In U. Melissa Anyiwo and Karoline Szatek-Tudor, eds. Buffy *Conquers the Academy: Conference Papers from the 2009/2010 Popular Culture/American Culture Associations.* Newcastle upon Tyne, UK: Cambridge Scholars Publishing, 2013, pp. 89–104. A paper originally presented in earlier form as "'We're your arch-nemesises... ses': The Americanization of Myth in *Buffy the Vampire Slayer*" at the 2009 PCA/ACA National Conference, New Orleans, LA, April 8–11, 2009.

4149. Hornick, Alysa. "Mapping the Whedonverses: Whedon Studies 1999 and Beyond." In Mary Alice Money for PopMatters.com, ed. *Joss Whedon: The Complete Companion: The TV Series, the Movies, the Comic Books and More.* London: Titan Books, 2012, pp. 457–464.

4150. _____. "There Is No Cure for That: Illyria, Dr. Saunders, and the Gendered Body in *Angel* and *Dollhouse*." A paper presented at SC4: The Slayage Conference on the Whedonverses, Flagler College, St. Augustine, FL, June 3–6, 2010. Posted at: http://www.alysa316.com/SC4_Hornick Paper/.

4151. Horrocks, Adrian. "The First Horror Soap: The Innovative Genre Mix of *Buffy the Vam-*

pire Slayer." *Necronomicon: The Journal of Erotic and Horror Cinema* 5 (2007): 7–20.

4152. Horton, Gemma. *Willow as Hybrid: The Transitions of Her Character through Stereotypes Associated to Women in Sci-Fi.* Huddersfield, UK: University of Huddersfield, BA honors thesis, 2006.

4153. Howard, K. Shannon. "Charles Gunn, Wolfram & Hart, and Baudrillard's Theory of the Simulacrum." In AmiJo Comeford and Tamy L. Burnett, ed. *The Literary* Angel: *Essays on Influences and Traditions Reflected in the Joss Whedon Series.* Jefferson, NC: McFarland & Company, 2010, pp. 147–158.

4154. Howell, Amanda. "'If we hear any inspirational power chords?': Rock Music, Rock Culture on *Buffy the Vampire Slayer."* *Continuum: Journal of Media & Cultural Studies* 18, 3 (2004): 406–422.

4155. ____. "More Than Just a Rock'n'Roll Reversal: Tracking Gender on *Buffy the Vampire Slayer."* In Kendra Preston Leonard, ed. Buffy, *Ballads, and Bad Guys Who Sing: Music in the Worlds of Joss Whedon.* Lanham, MD: Scarecrow Press, 2011, pp. 99–117.

4156. Hoyt, Heather. Buffy the Vampire Slayer: *A Hero's Journey.* Carpinteria, CA: Pacifica Graduate Institute, M.A. thesis, 2007. 65 pp. Large format.

4157. Hudson, Jennifer A. "'She's Unpredictable': Illyria and the Liberating Potential of Chaotic Postmodern Identity." *Magazine Americana: The American Popular Culture Magazine* (March 2005). Posted at: http://www.american popularculture.com/archive/tv/shes_unpredictable. htm. A paper originally presented at the 27th Annual Southwest/Texas PCA/ACA Conference, Albuquerque, NM, February 8–11, 2006.

4158. Huehner, Mariah. "Imperfectly Perfect: Why I Really Love Buffy for Being a Pill Sometimes." In Lynne M. Thomas and Deborah Stanish, eds. *Whedonistas! A Celebration of the Worlds of Joss Whedon by the Women Who Love Them.* Des Moines, IA: Mad Norwegian Press, 2011, pp. 86–92.

4159. Hulst, V. van. *Buffy, the Story Teller: A Study into the Way in Which the Popular Television Series* Buffy, the Vampire Slayer *Provides Usable Stories for Its Viewers.* Utrecht, Netherlands: Universiteit Utrecht, Ph.D. dissertation, 2007. 68 pp. Large format. Posted at: http://dspace.library.uu. nl/handle/1874/23266.

4160. Iatropoulos, Mary Ellen. "'Look Where Free Will Has Gotten You': *Brave New World* and *Angel*'s Body Jasmine." A paper presented at the 31st Annual Southwest/Texas PCA/ ACA Conference, Albuquerque, New Mexico, February 10–13, 2010. Posted at: http://www. whedon.info/Look-Where-Free-Will-Has-Gotten. html.

4161. ____. "(Re)Negotiating the Dystopian Dilemma: Huxley, Orwell and *Angel."* In AmiJo Comeford and Tamy L. Burnett, eds. *The Literary* Angel: *Essays on Influences and Traditions Reflected in the Joss Whedon Series.* Jefferson, NC: McFarland & Company, 2010, pp. 115–129. A paper originally presented as "Orwell and *Angel*: (Re)Negotiating the Dystopian Dilemma" at SC4: The Slayage Conference on the Whedonverses, Flagler College, St. Augustine, FL, June 3–6, 2010.

4162. Innocenti, Veronica. *"Buffy the Vampire Slayer* and the Serialization of the Series." A paper presented at Bring Your Own Subtext: Social Life, Human Experience and the Works of Joss Whedon, Conference, University of Huddersfield, Huddersfield, UK, June 29–July 1, 2005. This paper was later published in Italian as "La 'serializzazione' della serie." In Ed. Barbara Maio, ed. Buffy the Vampire Slayer: *Legittimare la Cacciatrice.* Rome: Bulzoni Editore, 2007, pp. 33–44.

4163. Introvigne, Massimo. "Brainwashing the Working Class: Vampire Comics and Criticism from Dr. Occult to *Buffy."* *Slayage: The Online International Journal of Buffy Studies* 2, 3 [7] (December 2002). Posted at: http://www.whedonstudies. tv/. A paper originally presented at Blood, Text and Fears: Reading Around *Buffy the Vampire Slayer,* University of East Anglia, October 19–20, 2002.

4164. ____. "God, New Religious Movements and *Buffy the Vampire Slayer."* Posted at: http://www.cesnur.org/2001/buffy_march01. htm. The website of CESNUR (the Center for Studies on New Religions), March 2001. A paper originally presented as "'There Will Be No Thomas Aquinas at This Table': Notions of God in the New Religious Consciousness" at the Expanding Concepts of God symposium, sponsored by the American Academy of Arts and Sciences, Harvard University, Cambridge, MA, April 7–9, 2000.

4165. ____. "'Modernity Will Not Save Her': Faith, Science, and *Buffy the Vampire Slayer* in the Italian *Dracula Opera Rock."* A paper posted on the website of CESNUR (Center for Studies on New Religions) http://www.cesnur.org/2006/dracula_ rock_eng.htm. [2006].

4166. _____. "Strange Wars: Evangelical Counter-Cultists vs *Buffy the Vampire Slayer*." Posted at: the website of CESNUR (Center for Studies on New Religions) http://www.cesnur.org/testi/Buffy.htm. October 30, 1999.

4167. Isaksson, Malin. "Buffy/Faith Adult Femslash: Queer Porn with a Plot." *Slayage: The Online International Journal of Buffy Studies* 7, 4 [28] (Summer 2009). Posted at: http://www.whedonstudies.tv/. A paper originally presented as "Buffy/Faith Adult Femslash: Porn by Women for Women?" at Codex and Code: Aesthetics, Language and Politics in an Age of Digital Media, Stockholm, Sweden, August 2009.

4168. _____. "The Erotics of Pain: BDSM Femslash Fan Fiction." In Jane Fernandez, ed. *Making Sense of Pain: Critical and Interdisciplinary Perspectives.* Oxford: Inter-Disciplinary Press, 2010, pp. 203–210. Posted at: http://www.inter-disciplinary.net/wp-content/uploads/2010/10/pain2010ever11007102.pdf. A paper originally presented at the 1st Global Conference Making Sense of Pain, Sydney, New South Wales, Australia, February 17–19, 2010.

4169. _____. "Pain as Pleasure: Tough Girls' Love in Fan Fiction." In Hans T. Sternudd and Angela Tumini, eds. *How Does It Feel? Making Sense of Pain.* Oxford: Inter-Disciplinary Press, 2011, pp. 99–116. Posted at: http://www.diva-portal.org/smash/get/diva2:441253/FULLTEXT01.pdf.

4170. Jacob, Benjamin. "Los Angelus: The City of Angel." In Stacey Abbott, ed. *Reading Angel: The TV Spin-off with a Soul.* New York: I. B. Tauris, 2005, pp. 75–87. A paper originally presented at Blood, Text and Fears: Reading Around *Buffy the Vampire Slayer*, University of East Anglia, October 19–20, 2002.

4171. Jagodzinski, Jan. "The Buffyverse Soteriology: Youth's *Garden of Earthly Delights*." In Jan Jagodzinski. *Television and Youth Culture: Televised Paranoia.* New York: Palgrave Macmillan, 2008, pp. 133–149.

4172. _____. "The Death Drive's at Stake: *Buffy the Vampire Slayer*." In Jan Jagodzinski. *Television and Youth Culture: Televised Paranoia.* New York: Palgrave Macmillan, 2008, pp. 111–132.

4173. James, Gareth. "Masquerade and Automation: The Unstable Female Body in *Buffy the Vampire Slayer* and *Alias*." *Watcher Junior: The Journal of Undergraduate Research in Buffy Studies* 3, 1 [3] (September 2007). Posted at: http://www.watcherjunior.tv/.

4174. James, Paula. "Crossing Classical Thresholds: Gods, Monsters and Hell Dimensions in the Whedon Universe." In Dunstan Lowe and Kim Shahabudin, eds. *Classics for All: Reworking Antiquity in Mass Culture.* Newcastle upon Tyne, UK: Cambridge Scholars Publishing, 2009, pp. 237–260. A paper originally presented in earlier for as "Gate-Crashing Gods, and 'Coming Back Wrong': Crossing Classical Thresholds in *Buffy the Vampire Slayer*" at Greeks and Romans in the Buffyverse: Classical Threads in Fantasy and Science Fiction on Contemporary Television, Open University, Milton Keynes, UK, January 7–8, 2004.

4175. Jamison, Anne, Jen Zern [and Bethan Jones]. "*The X-Files*, *Buffy* and the Rise of Internet Fic Fandoms.'" In Anne Jamison. *Fic: Why Fanfiction Is Taking Over the World.* Dallas, TX: Benbella Books, 2013, pp. 111–149. This section of Jamison's book can be broken down further into the following relevant sections: Jamison's untitled introductory passage (pp. 112–117) and "The Bronze Age: *Buffy* Meets the Internet" (pp. 131–138), and Jen Zern's "Fic U: Higher Education through Fanfiction" (pp.139–148). Remaining sections, including Bethan Jones' contribution (pp. 122–129), are limited to *The X-Files.*

4176. Jaquet, Alison. "Detective Fiction/Fictionality from Asmodeus to *Angel*." In AmiJo Comeford and Tamy L. Burnett, eds. *The Literary Angel: Essays on Influences and Traditions Reflected in the Joss Whedon Series.* Jefferson, NC: McFarland & Company, 2010, pp. 206–220.

4177. Jarvis, Christine. "'I run to Death': Renaissance Sensibilities in *Buffy the Vampire Slayer*." *Slayage: The Online International Journal of Buffy Studies* 7, 3 [27] (Winter 2009 Posted at: http://www.whedonstudies.tv/.

4178. _____. "Real Stakeholder Education? Lifelong Learning in the Buffyverse." *Studies in the Education of Adults*, 37, 1 (Spring 2005): 31–46.

4179. _____. "School Is Hell: Gendered Fears in Teenage Horror." *Educational Studies* 27, 3 (2001): 257–67.

4180. _____, and Don Adams. "Dressed to Kill: Fashion and Leadership in *Buffy the Vampire Slayer*." *Slayage: The Online International Journal of Buffy Studies* 6, 1 [21] (Fall 2006). Posted at: http://www.whedonstudies.tv/. A paper originally presented at Bring Your Own Subtext: Social Life, Human Experience and the Works of Joss Whedon, Conference, University of Huddersfield, Huddersfield, UK, June 29-July 1, 2005.

4181. Jarvis, Matt. *"Buffy the Vampire Slayer* and Psychoanalysis." *Psychology Review* 10 (September 2003): 2–5.

4182. Javaid, Hanan. *Getting Slayed by* Buffy: *An Analysis of Meaning in* Buffy the Vampire Slayer. Durham, NC: Duke University, BA honors thesis, 2000. 112 pp. Large format.

4183. Jeney, Cynthia. "If the Apocalypse Comes...Email Me: Or, All I Need to Know About Online Distance Ed, I Learned from *Buffy the Vampire Slayer.*" *Kairos: A Journal for Teachers of Writing and Webbed Environments* 7, 3 (2002). Posted at: http://www.technorhetoric.net/7.3/features/jeney.htm.

4184. _____. "Online Distance Education and the '*Buffy* Paradigm': Welcome to the Hell Mouth." In Jonathan Alexander and Marcia Dickson, eds. *Role Play: Distance Learning and the Teaching of Writing.* Cresskill, NJ: Hampton Press, 2006, pp. 163–189.

4185. Jenkins, Alice, and Susan Stuart. "Extending Your Mind: Nonstandard Perlocutionary Acts in 'Hush.'" *Slayage: The Online International Journal of Buffy Studies* 3, 1 [9] (August 2003). Posted at: http://www.whedonstudies.tv/. A paper originally presented at Blood, Text and Fears: Reading Around *Buffy the Vampire Slayer*, University of East Anglia, October 19–20, 2002.

4186. Jenkins, Henry, with Henry G. Jenkins IV. "'The Monsters Next Door': A Father-Son Dialogue about *Buffy*, Moral Panic, and Generational Differences." In Henry Jenkins, with Henry G. Jenkins IV. *Fans, Bloggers, and Gamers: Media Consumers in a Digital Age.* New York: New York University Press, 2006, pp. 226–248.

4187. Jobbling, J'annine. "The Good and the Monstrous: *Buffy the Vampire Slayer*: 'From Beneath You, It Devours.'" In J'annine Jobbling. *Fantastic Spiritualities: Monsters, Heroes, and the Contemporary Religious Imagination.* London: T. & T. Clark, 2007, pp. 168–188.

4188. Johansen, Vibeke. *'The Divine Exists in Cyberspace Same as Out Here': Academics and the Internet Fan-Scholars of* Buffy the Vampire Slayer. Nathan, Aust.: Griffith University, BA honors thesis, 2004.

4189. _____. "'I Laugh in the Face of Danger. Then I Hide Until It Goes Away': The Transgressive and Problematic Gender Roles of Buffy and Xander." *All Slay* 3 (2004).

4190. _____. "The Importance of *Buffy the Vampire Slayer*'s Lesbians in Today's Gay-Starved Media World." *All Slay* 2 (2004).

4191. Johnson, Catherine. "Quality/Cult Television: *The X-Files* and *Buffy the Vampire Slayer* in 1990s US Television." In Catherine Johnson. *Telefantasy.* London: British Film Institute [BFI], 2005, pp.181 pp. pb.

4192. Johnson, Melissa C. "Appetite and Destruction: Issues of Consumption and Containment in Seasons 2 and 3 of *Buffy the Vampire Slayer.*" A paper presented at SC2: The Slayage Conference on the Whedonverses, Gordon College, Barnesville, GA, May 25–28, 2006. Posted at: http://www.whedonstudies.tv/SCW_Archive/MJohnson.pdf.

4193. _____. "College Isn't Just Job Training and Parties: Stimulating Critical Thinking with 'The Freshman.'" In Jodie A. Kreider and Meghan K. Winchell, eds. Buffy *in the Classroom: Essays on Teaching with the Vampire Slayer.* Jefferson, NC: McFarland & Company, 2010, pp. 103–113.

4194. Jones, Bethan. "Buffy vs. Bella: Gender, Relationships, and the Modern Vampire." In Deborah Mutch, ed. *The Modern Vampire and Human Identity.* New York: Palgrave Macmillan, 2013, pp. 38–54. A paper originally presented at Vegetarians, VILFs and Fang-Bangers: Modern Vampire Romance in Print and On Screen, De Montfort University, Leicester, UK, November 24, 2010.

4195. Jones, Caroline E. "Unpleasant Consequences: First Sex in *Buffy the Vampire Slayer, Veronica Mars,* and *Gilmore Girls.*" *Jeunesse: Young People, Texts, Cultures* 5, 1 (2013). Posted at: http://www.jeunessejournal.ca/index.php/yptc/article/view/157.

4196. Jones, Gerard. "Vampire Slayers." *Killing Monsters: Why Children Need Fantasy, Super Heroes, and Make-Believe Violence.* New York: Basic, 2002. 149–164.

4197. Jones, Kelli. *Getting Acquainted with the Inner Moppet: The Vampire as a Reflection/Catalyst in* The Traveling Vampire Show *and* Buffy the Vampire Slayer. Glenside, PA: Arcadia University, BA honors thesis, 2005.

4198. Joplin, Benjamin. *New Breed, Old Blood: Gothic Horror in Contemporary Fiction and Film.* Buffalo: State University of New York—Buffalo, Ph.D. dissertation, 2006. 260 pp. Large format.

4199. Jowett, Lorna. "Biting Humor: Harmony, Parody, and the Female Vampire." In AmiJo Comeford and Tamy L. Burnett, eds. *The Literary Angel: Essays on Influences and Traditions Reflected in the Joss Whedon Series*. Jefferson, NC: McFarland & Company, 2010, pp. 17–29.

4200. _____. "*Buffy*, Dark Romance and Female Horror Fans." In Jennifer Kate Stuller, ed. *Fan Phenomena:* Buffy the Vampire Slayer. Chicago: Intellect, 2013, pp. 90–101.

4201. _____. "Case Study: *Angel*." In Stacey Abbott, ed. *The Cult TV Book*. New York: I. B. Tauris, 2010, pp. 114–116.

4202. _____. "Helping the Hopeless: *Angel* as Critical Dystopia." *Critical Studies in Television: Scholarly Studies of Small Screen Fictions* 2, 1 (Spring 2007): 74–89. A paper originally presented at Bring Your Own Subtext: Social Life, Human Experience and the Works of Joss Whedon, Conference, University of Huddersfield, Huddersfield, UK, June–1 July 2005. Posted at: http://www.academia.edu/3699184/Helping_the_Hopeless_Angel_as_Critical_Dystopia.

4203. _____. "Lindsey and Angel: Reflecting Masculinity." In Mary Alice Money for PopMatters.com, ed. *Joss Whedon: The Complete Companion: The TV Series, the Movies, the Comic Books and More*. London: Titan Books, 2012, pp. 168–181. A paper originally presented in earlier form as "Self-Made Man: Lindsey McDonald, 'the Cain to Angel's Abel'" at SC3: The Slayage Conference on the Whedonverses, Henderson State College, Arkadelphia, AR, June 5–8, 2008.

4204. _____. "Masculinity, Monstrosity, and Behaviour Modification in *Buffy the Vampire Slayer*." *Foundation: The International Review of Science Fiction* 31, 84 (2002): 59–73.

4205. _____. "'Not Like Other Men?': The Vampire Body in Joss Whedon's *Angel*." *Studies in Popular Culture* 32, 1 (Fall 2009): 37–51. Poste at: http://pcasacas.org/SiPC/32.1/Jowett.pdf.

4206. _____. "Plastic Fantastic? Genre and Science/Technology/Magic in *Angel*." In Lincoln Geraghty, ed. *Channeling the Future: Essays on Science Fiction and Fantasy Television*. Lanham, MD: Scarecrow Press, 2009, pp. 167–182.

4207. _____. "The Problem of Romance and the Representation of Gender in *Buffy* and *Angel*." A paper presented at the Slayage Conference on *Buffy the Vampire Slayer*, Nashville, TN, May 27–30, 2004. Posted at: http://www.slayageonline.com/SCBtVS_Archive/Talks/Jowett.pdf.

4208. _____. *Sex and the Slayer: A Gender Studies Primer for the* Buffy *Fan*. Middletown, CT: Wesleyan University Press, 2005. 254 pp. tp.

4209. _____. "The Summers' House as Domestic Space in Buffy the Vampire Slayer." *Slayage: The Online International Journal of Buffy Studies* 5, 2 [18] (September 2005). Posted at: http://www.whedonstudies.tv/.

4210. _____, **and Stacey Abbott.** *TV Horror: Investigating the Dark Side of the Small Screen*. London: I. B. Taurus, 2013. 270 pp. tp.

4211. Jusino, Teresa. "Why Joss is More Important Than His 'Verse." In Lynne M. Thomas and Deborah Stanish, eds. *Whedonistas! A Celebration of the Worlds of Joss Whedon by the Women Who Love Them*. Des Moines, IA: Mad Norwegian Press, 2011, pp. 171–177.

4212. Kane, Tim. "The Sympathetic Cycle (1987-): *Buffy the Vampire Slayer*." In Tim Kane. *The Changing Vampire of Film and Television: A Critical Study of the Growth of a Genre*. Jefferson, NC: McFarland & Company, 2006, pp. 112–116.

4213. Karras, Irene. "The Third Wave's Final Girl: *Buffy the Vampire Slayer*." *Thirdspace* 1, 2 (2002). Posted at: http://www.thirdspace.ca/journal/article/viewArticle/karras/50.

4214. Kassabian, Anahid. "Afterword." In Eds. Paul Attinello, Janet K. Halfyard, and Vanessa Knights, eds. *Music, Sound, and Silence in* Buffy the Vampire Slayer. Farnham, Surrey, UK: Ashgate Publishing, 2010, pp. 249–250.

4215. Katz, Alyssa. "Buffy the Vampire Slayer." *Nation* (April 6, 1998): 35–36.

4216. Kaveney, Roz. "Gifted and Dangerous: Joss Whedon's Superhero Obsession." In Roz Kaveney. *Superheroes! Capes and Crusaders in Comics and Films*. New York: I. B. Tauris, 2008, pp. 201–225. A paper originally presented as keynote address at SC2: The Slayage Conference on the Whedonverses, Gordon College, Barnesville, GA, May 25–28, 2006.

4217. _____. "The Heirs of Heather: Cordelia, Nicole, and Other Mean Girls." In Roz Kaveney. *Teen Dreams: Reading Teen Film from Heathers to Veronica Mars*. New York: I. B. Tauris, 2006, pp. 85–108.

4218. _____. "A Sense of the Ending: Schrödinger's *Angel*." *Slayage: The Online International Journal of Buffy Studies* 4, 4 [16] (March 2005) Posted at: http://www.whedonstudies.tv/. Rpt. in

Stacey Abbott, ed. *Reading* Angel*: The TV Spin-off with a Soul*. New York: I. B. Tauris, 2005, pp. 57–72.

4219. _____. "'She Saved the World. A Lot': An Introduction to the Themes and Structures of *Buffy* and *Angel*." In Roz Kaveney, ed. *Reading the Vampire Slayer: An Unofficial Critical Companion to* Buffy *and* Angel. New York: I. B. Tauris, 2001, pp. 1–36. Expanded version in: *Reading the Vampire Slayer: An Unofficial Critical Companion to* Buffy *and* Angel. Rev. ed. New York: I/B. Tauris, 2004. 1–82.

4220. _____, ed. *Reading the Vampire Slayer: An Unofficial Critical Companion to* Buffy *and* Angel. London: Tauris Parke Publishing, 2001. 271 pp. tp. Rev. ed.: 2004. 322 pp. tp. In the first edition, editor Kaveney includes essays by Boyd Tonkin, Brian Wall and Michael Zryd, Steve Wilson, Karen Sayer, Zoe-Jane Playden, Anne Millard Daugherty, Dave West, Esther Saxey, Ian Shuttleworth, The second edition adds essays by Jennifer Stoy and Justine Larbalestier, along with interviews of two scriptwriters from the show, Jane Espenson and Steven DeKnight.

4221. Kaveny, Cathleen. "What Women Want: *Buffy*, the Pope, and the New Feminists." *Commonweal: A review of religion, politics, and culture* 130, 19 (2003): 18–24.

4222. Kawal, Jason. "Should We Do What Buffy Would Do?" In James B. South, ed. Buffy *and Philosophy: Fear and Trembling in Sunnydale*. Chicago: Open Court, 2003, pp. 149–159.

4223. Kaye, Sharon M. and Melissa M. Milavec. "Buffy in the Buff: A Slayer's Solution to Aristotle's Love Paradox." In James B. South, ed. Buffy *and Philosophy: Fear and Trembling in Sunnydale*. Chicago: Open Court, 2003. 173–184.

4224. Kearney, Mary Celeste. "The Changing Face of Teen Television, or Why We All Love *Buffy*." In Elana Levine and Lisa Parks, eds. *Undead TV: Essays on* Buffy the Vampire Slayer. Durham, NC: Duke University Press, 2007, pp. 17–41.

4225. Keft-Kennedy, Virginia. "Fantasising Masculinity in Buffyverse Slash Fiction: Sexuality, Violence, and the Vampire." *NJES: Nordic Journal of English Studies* 7, 1 (2008): 49–80.

4226. Keller, Donald. "Spirit Guides and Shadow Selves: From the Dream Life of Buffy (and Faith)." In Rhonda V. Wilcox and David Lavery, eds. *Fighting the Forces: What's at Stake in* Buffy the Vampire Slayer. Lanham, MD: Rowman & Littlefield, 2002, pp. 165–177.

4227. Kellner, Douglas. "*Buffy the Vampire Slayer* as Spectacular Allegory: A Diagnostic Critique." In Shirley R. Steinberg and Joe L. Kincheloe, eds. *Kinderculture: The Corporate Construction of Childhood*. 2nd ed. Boulder, CO: Westview Press, 2004, pp. 49–71. A paper originally presented at the Cultural Studies conference, Melbourne, Australia, 2003. Posted at: http://pages.gseis.ucla.edu/faculty/kellner/essays/buffy.pdf.

4228. _____. "Teens and Vampires: From *Buffy the Vampire Slayer* to *Twilight*'s Vampire Lovers." In Shirley R. Steinberg, ed. *Kinderculture: The Corporate Construction of Childhood*. 3nd ed. Boulder, CO: Westview Press, 2011, pp. 55–72.

4229. Kem, Jessica Freya. *Cataloging the Whedonverse: Potential Roles for Librarians in Online Fan Fiction*. Chapel Hill, NC: School of Information and Library Science, University of North Carolina, M.A. thesis, 2005. 57 pp. Posted at: http://dc.lib.unc.edu/cdm/singleitem/collection/s_papers/id/729/rec/12.

4230. Kenyon, Sherrilyn. "Parting Gifts." In Glenn Yeffeth, ed. *Five Seasons of* Angel: *Science Fiction and Fantasy Writers Discuss Their Favorite Vampire*. Dallas, TX: Benbella Books, 2004, pp. 87–91.

4231. _____. "The Search for Spike's Balls." *Seven Seasons of* Buffy: *Science Fiction and Fantasy Writers Discuss Their Favorite Television Show*. Ed. Glenn Yeffeth. Dallas, TX: Benbella Books, 2003. 25–29.

4232. Keough, Sarah. *The Slayer Goes to College: Teaching* Buffy the Vampire Slayer *in the University*. Milwaukee: University of Wisconsin-Milwaukee, BA honors thesis, 2009. 114 pp. Large format.

4233. Kerns, Dan. "*Angel* by the Numbers." In Glenn Yeffeth, ed. *Five Seasons of* Angel: *Science Fiction and Fantasy Writers Discuss Their Favorite Vampire*. Dallas, TX: Benbella Books, 2004, pp. 23–31.

4234. Kessenich, Laura. "'I'm beginning to understand this now': 'Restless.'" *Watcher Junior: The Undergraduate Journal of Whedon Studies* 4, 2 [5] (June 2010). Posted at: http://www.watcherjunior.tv/.

4235. _____. "'Wait Till You Have an Evil Twin': Jane Espenson's Contributions to *Buffy the Vampire Slayer*." *Watcher Junior: The Journal of Undergraduate Research in Buffy Studies* 3, 1 [3] (September 2007). Posted at: http://www.watcherjunior.tv/.

4236. Kessler, Jackie. "Going Dark." In Lynne M. Thomas and Deborah Stanish, eds. *Whedonistas! A Celebration of the Worlds of Joss Whedon by the Women Who Love Them.* Des Moines, IA: Mad Norwegian Press, 2011, pp. 116–123.

4237. Ketskarova, Violeta Rumyanova. *From* Beowulf *to* Buffy: *Or, Why Do We Keep Chasing Evil Dragons and Glorifying Virtuous Heroes?* Portland, OR, Reed College, BA honors thesis, 2008. 67 pp. Large format.

4238. Kilpatrick, Nancy. "Sex and the Single Slayer." In Glenn Yeffeth, ed. *Seven Seasons of* Buffy: *Science Fiction and Fantasy Writers Discuss Their Favorite Television Show.* Dallas, TX: Benbella Books, 2003, pp. 19–24.

4239. Kim, Janna L., C. Lynn Sorsoli, Katherine Collines, Bonnie A. Zylbergold, Deborah Schooler, and Deborah L. Tolman. "From Sex to Sexuality: Exposing the Heterosexual Script on Primetime Network Television." *Journal of Sex Research* 44, 2 (May 2007): 145–57. Posted at: http://www.academia.edu/252770/From_Sex_to_Sexuality_Exposing_the_heterosexual_script_in_primetime_television_shows.

4240. Kind, Amy. "The Vampire with a Soul: *Angel* and the Quest for Identity." In Thomas Fahy, ed. *The Philosophy of Horror.* Lexington: University Press of Kentucky, 2010, pp. 86–101.

4241. King, John C., and Christophe Beck. "Preface." In Paul Attinello, Janet K. Halfyard, and Vanessa Knights, ed. *Music, Sound, and Silence in* Buffy the Vampire Slayer. Farnham, Surrey, UK: Ashgate Publishing, 2010, pp. xxi–xxiii.

4242. King, Neal. "Brown Skirts: Fascism, Christianity, and the Eternal Demon." In James B. South, ed. Buffy *and Philosophy: Fear and Trembling in Sunnydale.* Chicago: Open Court, 2003, pp. 197–211.

4243. Kinsey, Tammy A. "Transitions and Time: The Cinematic Language of *Angel.*" In Stacey Abbott, ed. *Reading* Angel: *The TV Spin-Off with a Soul.* New York: I. B. Tauris, 2005, pp. 44–56.

4244. Kirby-Diaz, Mary. "*Buffy, Angel,* and the Creation of Virtual Communities." In Mary Kirby-Diaz, ed. Buffy *and* Angel *Conquer the Internet: Essays on Online Fandom.* Jefferson, NC: McFarland & Company, 2009, pp. 18–41. A paper originally presented at the Slayage Conference on *Buffy the Vampire Slayer,* Nashville, TN, May 27–30, 2004, and as "Virtual Communities in the Buffyverse" at the 25th Annual Southwest/Texas PCA/ACA Conference, San Antonio, TX, April 7–10, 2004.

4245. _____. "The Fandom Project: What Makes a Fandom Run? Ships, Fics, Plot Devices, Favorite Characters, and Fancons." *International Journal of the Humanities* 3, 4 (2006): 256–265. A paper originally presented in shortened form, as "The Fandom Project: What Keeps a Fandom Afloat? Report Two: Ships" at SC2: The Slayage Conference on the Whedonverses, Gordon College, Barnesville, GA, May 25–28, 2006, an subsequently presented at the NEPCA 2006 Conference, Rivier College, Nashua, New Hampshire, October 27–28, 2006.

4246. _____. "Ficcers and Shippers: A Love Story." In Jennifer Kate Stuller, ed. *Fan Phenomena:* Buffy the Vampire Slayer. Chicago: Intellect, 2013, pp. 38–51.

4247. _____. "Introduction: Hey, Professor... You Watch *Buffy,* and *Angel?*" In Mary Kirby-Diaz, ed. Buffy *and* Angel *Conquer the Internet: Essays on Online Fandom.* Jefferson, NC: McFarland & Company, 2009, pp. 1–6.

4248. _____. "So, What's the Story? Story-Oriented and Series-Oriented Fans: A Complex of Behaviors." In Mary Kirby-Diaz, ed. Buffy *and* Angel *Conquer the Internet: Essays on Online Fandom.* Jefferson, NC: McFarland & Company, 2009, pp. 62–86.

4249. _____, ed. Buffy *and* Angel *Conquer the Internet: Essays on Online Fandom.* Jefferson, NC: McFarland & Company, 2009. 219 pp. tp. The editor has also included essays by Elizabeth L. Rambo, Rebecca Bley, Asim Ali, David Kociemba, Claudia Rebaza, and Kathryn Hill.

4250. Kirchner, Jesse Saba. "'And in Some Language That's English?': Slayer Slang and Artificial Computer Generation." In Michael Adams, ed. *Beyond Slayer Slang: Pragmatics, Discourse, and Style in* Buffy the Vampire Slayer. Special Issue of *Slayage: The Online International Journal of Buffy Studies* 5, 4 [20] (May 2006). Posted at: http://www.whedonstudies.tv/.

4251. Kirkland, Ewan. "The Caucasian Persuasion of *Buffy the Vampire Slayer.*" *Slayage: The Online International Journal of Buffy Studies* 5, 1 [17] (June 2005). Posted at: http://www.whedonstudies.tv/. A paper originally presented at Bring Your Own Subtext: Social Life, Human Experience and the Works of Joss Whedon, Conference, University of Huddersfield, Huddersfield, UK, June 29-July 1, 2005, and with alternate title "*Buffy the Vampire Slayer* and Constructions of Whiteness" at the Slayage Conference on *Buffy the Vampire Slayer,* Nashville, TN, May 27–30, 2004.

4252. _____. "A Conference Report on Bring Your Own Subtext: Social Life, Human Experience and the Works of Joss Whedon (University of Huddersfield, Summer 2005)." *Slayage: The Online International Journal of Buffy Studies* 5, 2 [18] (September 2005). Posted at: http://www.whedonstudies.tv/.

4253. Kirkpatrick, Kim. "Re-Appropriating Female Identity: Taking Back the Buffybot and Other Bionic Females." *Phoebe: Gender and Cultural Critiques* 18, 1 (2006): 59–73.

4254. _____. "Scoobies and Potentials: The Slayer Community as Hero in *Buffy the Vampire Slayer*." *MP: An Online Feminist Journal* 1, 4 (May 2006). Posted at: http://academinist.org/wp-content/uploads/2010/06/kirkpatrick.pdf.

4255. Klein, Ian G. *'New lines': The Fan and Textual Poaching in the Work of Joss Whedon.* Seattle: University of Washington, BA honors thesis, 2008. A paper originally presented in shortened form at SC3: The Slayage Conference on the Whedonverses, Henderson State College, Arkadelphia, AR, June 5–8, 2008.

4256. Knapp, Raymond. "'Once More, with Feeling' (Television 2001)." In Raymond Knapp. *The American Musical and the Performance of Personal Identity.* Princeton, NJ: Princeton University Press, 2006, pp. 196–204.

4257. Kneale, Ruth. "Rupert Giles." In Ruth Kneale. *You Don't Look Like a Librarian: Shattering Stereotypes and Creating Positive New Images in the Internet Age.* Medford, NJ: Information Today, 2009, p. 61.

4258. Kneen, Bonnie. "'Add it up, it all spells "duh"': The Language of *Buffy, the Vampire Slayer*." *Oxford Dictionaries Online.* Posted August 17, 2012, at: http://blog.oxforddictionaries.com/2012/08/buffy-the-vampire-slayer/.

4259. Knight, Gladys. "Buffy the Vampire Slayer." In Gladys Knight. *Female Action Heroes: A Guide to Women in Comics, Video Games, Film, and Television.* Santa Barbara, CA: Greenwood Press, 2010, pp. 15–28.

4260. Knights, Vanessa. "Introduction: 'Bay City Rollers. Now That's Music': Music as Cultural Code in *Buffy the Vampire Slayer*." In Paul Attinello, Janet K. Halfyard, and Vanessa Knights, eds. *Music, Sound, and Silence in* Buffy the Vampire Slayer. Farnham, Surrey, UK: Ashgate Publishing, 2010, pp. 1–12. A paper originally presented as "'Bay City Rollers. Now That's Music': Coolness, Crassness and Characterisation on *Buffy the Vampire Slayer*" at Sonic Synergies: Creative Cultures, University of South Australia, Adelaide, Australia, July 17–20, 2003. Posted at: http://www.ncl.ac.uk/sacs/POP/papers/sonicvkpop.pdf.

4261. Knoblauch, A. Abby. "From Burke to *Buffy* and Back Again: Intersections of Rhetoric, Magic, and Identification in *Buffy the Vampire Slayer*." *Slayage: The Journal of the Whedon Studies Association* 8, 1 [29] (Spring 2010). Posted at: http://www.whedonstudies.tv/. A paper originally presented as "From Burke to *Buffy*: Explorations of Rhetoric, Writing, and Magic" at the 2009 PCA/ACA National Conference, New Orleans, LA, April 8–11, 2009.

4262. Knowles, Claire. "Sensibility Gone Mad: Or, Drusilla, Buffy and the (D)evolution of the Heroine of Sensibility." In Benjamin A. Brabon and Stephanie Genz, eds. *Postfeminist Gothic: Critical Interventions in Contemporary Culture.* New York: Palgrave Macmillan, 2007, pp. 140–53. A paper originally presented at Removing the Boundaries seminar, School of English, Journalism and European Languages, University of Tasmania, March 24, 2006, and as "Sensibility Gone Mad: or, Drusilla, Buffy and the (D)evolution of the Gothic Heroine" at Staking a Claim: Exploring the Global Reach of *Buffy*, University of South Australia, Adelaide, Australia, July 22, 2003.

4263. Kociemba, David. "'Actually, it explains a lot': Reading the Opening Title Sequences of *Buffy the Vampire Slayer*." In Matthew Pateman, ed. Buffy *and Aesthetics.* Special Issue of *Slayage: The Online International Journal of Buffy Studies* 6, 2 [22] (Winter 2006). Posted at: http://www.whedonstudies.tv/.

4264. _____. "'Fake It Till You Make It': Understanding Media Addiction and *Buffy the Vampire Slayer*." In Mary Kirby-Diaz, ed. *Buffy and Angel Conquer the Internet: Essays on Online Fandom.* Jefferson, NC: McFarland & Company, 2009, pp. 127–146. A paper originally presented as "Fake It to Make It: Media Addiction in *Buffy the Vampire Slayer*" at the 2006 PCA/ACA National Conference, Atlanta, GA, April 12–15, 2006, and at SC2: The Slayage Conference on the Whedonverses, Gordon College, Barnesville, GA, May 25–28, 2006.

4265. _____. "'Over-identify much?': Passion, 'Passion,' and the Author-Audience Feedback Loop in *Buffy the Vampire Slayer*." *Slayage: The Online International Journal of Buffy Studies* 5, 3 [19] (February 2006). Posted at: http://www.whedonstudies.tv/.

4266. _____. "To Spoil or Not to Spoil: Teaching Television's Narrative Complexity." In Jodie A. Kreider and Meghan K. Winchell, eds. Buffy *in the Classroom: Essays on Teaching with the Vampire Slayer.* Jefferson, NC: McFarland & Company, 2010, pp. 7–21. A paper originally presented as "The Spoiler Virgin Project: Teaching Television's Narrative Complexity" at SC3: The Slayage Conference on the Whedonverses, Henderson State College, Arkadelphia, AR, June 5–8, 2008.

4267. _____. "Understanding the Espensode." In Lynne Y. Edwards, Elizabeth L. Rambo, and James B. South, ed. *Buffy Goes Dark: Essays on the Final Two Seasons of* Buffy the Vampire Slayer *on Television.* Jefferson, NC: McFarland & Company, 2009, pp. 23–39.

4268. _____. "'Where's the Fun?': The Comic Apocalypse in 'The Wish.'" *Slayage: The Online International Journal of Buffy Studies* 6, 3 [23] (Spring 2007). Posted at: http://www.whedonstudies.tv/.

4269. _____. "Why Xander Matters: The Extraordinary Ordinary in *Buffy the Vampire Slayer.*" In Jes Battis, ed. *Supernatural Youth: The Rise of the Teen Hero in Literature and Popular Culture.* Lanham, MD: Lexington Books, 2011, pp. 80–101.

4270. Koehler, Julia. "Realism Featured in Fantasy Series: The Portrayal of Death: An Analysis of *Buffy the Vampire Slayer* Season 5, Episode 16." A paper presented at the "Framing Reality": The Hollywood Representation of Broadcast News Journalism Seminar at the John F. Kennedy Institute for North American Studies, Free University of Berlin, Berlin, Germany, Summer 2007.

4271. Koontz [Guffey], K. Dale. *Faith and Choice in the Works of Joss Whedon.* Jefferson, NC: McFarland & Company, 2008. 231 pp. tp.

4272. _____. "Foreword." In Anthony R. Mills, John W. Morehead, and J. Ryan Parker, eds. *Joss Whedon and Religion: Essays on an Angry Atheist's Explorations of the Sacred.* Jefferson, NC: McFarland & Company, 2013, pp. 1–4.

4273. _____. "Heroism on the Hellmouth: Teaching Morality Through *Buffy.*" In Jodie A. Kreider and Meghan K. Winchell, eds. Buffy *in the Classroom: Essays on Teaching with the Vampire Slayer.* Jefferson, NC: McFarland & Company, 2010, pp. 61–72.

4274. Kord, Susanne, and Elisabeth Krimmer. "Vamp(ires)s and Those Who Kill Them: Buffy the Vampire Slayer and Dana Scully." In Susanne Kord and Elisabeth Krimmer. *Hollywood Divas, Indie Queens, and TV Heroines: Contemporary Screen Images of Women.* Lanham, MD: Rowman & Littlefield, 2005, pp. 141–160.

4275. Korsmeyer, Carolyn. "Passion and Action: In and Out of Control." On James B. South, ed. Buffy *and Philosophy: Fear and Trembling in Sunnydale.* Chicago: Open Court, 2003, pp. 160–172.

4276. Köver, Christina. "*Buffy the Vampire Slayer*, Polysemy and the Quest for Feminist Agency." A paper presented at Bring Your Own Subtext: Social Life, Human Experience and the Works of Joss Whedon, Conference, University of Huddersfield, Huddersfield, UK, June 29–July 1, 2005. Posted at: http://chriskoever.glizz.net/docs/Buffy_Huddersfield01.pdf.

4277. Kowalski, Dean A. "Plato, Aristotle and Joss on Being Horrible." In Dean A. Kowalski and S. Evan Kreider, ed. *The Philosophy of Joss Whedon.* Lexington: University Press of Kentucky, 2011, pp. 71–87.

4278. _____. "'You're Welcome on My Boat, God Ain't': Ethical Foundations in the Whedonverse." In Anthony R. Mills, John W. Morehead, and J. Ryan Parker, eds. *Joss Whedon and Religion: Essays on an Angry Atheist's Explorations of the Sacred.* Jefferson, NC: McFarland & Company, 2013, pp. 102–122.

4279. _____, **and S. Evan Kreider.** "Introduction." In Dean A. Kowalski and S. Evan Kreider, eds. *The Philosophy of Joss Whedon.* Lexington: University Press of Kentucky, 2011, pp. 1–5.

4280. _____, **and S. Evan Kreider, eds.** *The Philosophy of Joss Whedon.* Lexington: University Press of Kentucky, 2011. 231 pp. hb. Includes articles by David Baggett, Amy H. Sturgis, Joseph J. Foy, S. Evan Kreider, Dean A. Kowalski, Jason D. Grinnell, Tait Szabo, Patricia Brace, Gary Heba with Robin Murphy, Joseph J. Foy and Dean A. Kowalski, Susanne E. Foster and James B. South, Lisa Hager, and Roger P. Ebertz.

4281. Krátká, Jana, and Patrik Vacek. "Popular Culture Monsters Go to Education: The Czech Republic *Buffy* Case." A paper presented at Monsters and the Monstrous: Myths and Metaphors of Enduring Evil: 6th Global Conference, Mansfield College, Oxford [University], September 2008. 8 pp. Posted at: http://inter-disciplinary.net/ati/Monsters/M6/Kratka%20&%20Vacek%20paper.pdf.

4282. Krause, Marguerite. "It's a Stupid Curse." In Glenn Yeffeth, ed. *Five Seasons of* Angel:

Science Fiction and Fantasy Writers Discuss Their Favorite Vampire. Dallas, TX: Benbella Books, 2004, pp. 103–113.

4283. _____. "The Meaning of *Buffy.*" In Glenn Yeffeth, ed. *Seven Seasons of* Buffy: *Science Fiction and Fantasy Writers Discuss Their Favorite Television Show.* Dallas, TX: Benbella Books, 2003, pp. 97–108.

4284. Krawczyk, Marian. *"She Kicks Ass...in Heels": Negotiating Representations of Femininity in* Buffy the Vampire Slayer. Burnaby, BC, CA: Simon Fraser University, M.A. thesis, 2006. 274 pp. Large format.

4285. Kreider, Jodie A. "'Best Damn Field Trip I Ever Took!': Historical Encounters In and Out of the Classroom." In Jodie A. Kreider and Meghan K. Winchell, eds. Buffy *in the Classroom: Essays on Teaching with the Vampire Slayer.* Jefferson, NC: McFarland & Company, 2010, pp. 158–168.

4286. _____, **and Meghan K. Winchell.** "Introduction: 'Let's Have a Lesson Then,'" In Jodie A. Kreider and Meghan K. Winchell, eds. Buffy *in the Classroom: Essays on Teaching with the Vampire Slayer.* Jefferson, NC: McFarland & Company, 2010, pp. 1–6.

4287. _____, **and Meghan K. Winchell, eds.** Buffy *in the Classroom: Essays on Teaching with the Vampire Slayer.* Jefferson, NC: McFarland & Company, 2010. 231 pp. tp. Includes essays by David Kociemba, Jason Lawton Winslade, Tanya R. Cochran, Barry Morris, K. Dale Koontz, Meghan K. Winchell, Rod Romesburg, Keith Fudge, Melissa C. Johnson, Brian Cogan, Jane Martin, Rosie White, Leith Daniel, Jodie A. Kreider, Kristopher Karl Woofter, Patrick R. Grzanka, and Julia L. Grant.

4288. Krimmer, Elisabeth, and Shilpa Raval. "'Digging the Undead': Death and Desire in *Buffy.*" In Rhonda V. Wilcox and David Lavery, eds. *Fighting the Forces: What's at Stake in* Buffy the Vampire Slayer. Lanham, MD: Rowman & Littlefield, 2002, pp. 153–164.

4289. Kristensen, Anne C. *Evolution of the Vampire Genre: From Polidori's* The Vampyre *to* Buffy the Vampire Slayer. Aalborg, Denmark, Aalborg Universitet, M.A. thesis, 2003. 104 pp. Large format.

4290. Kromer, Kelly. "Silence as Symptom: A Psychoanalytic Reading of 'Hush.'" *Slayage: The Online International Journal of Buffy Studies* 5, 3 [19] (February 2006). Posted at: http://www.whedonstudies.tv/.

4291. Krzywinska, Tanya. "Arachne Challenges Minerva: The Spinning-Out of Long Narrative in *World of Warcraft* and *Buffy the Vampire Slayer.*" Paper presented at the Cine-Excess: An International Conference on Global Cult Film Traditions, London, May 2007. Posted at: http://bura.brunel.ac.uk/bitstream/2438/1058/1/Arachne%20challenges%20Minerva.pdf. A paper originally presented at Working Paper, School of Arts Research Papers, Brunel University West London, 2007, and at the Computer Games: Learning, Meaning and Method Seminar, London Knowledge Lab, London, January 26, 2007.

4292. _____. "Demon Power Girl: Regimes of Form and Force in Videogames *Buffy the Vampire Slayer* and *Primal.*" In Jim Terkeurst and Inga Paterson, eds. *Women in Games Conference Proceedings 2005.* Dundee, UK: University of Abertay Press, 2006, pp. 36–45. A paper originally presented at several conferences including: Power Up: Computer Games, Ideology and Play, University of the West of England, Bristol, 2003; the Slayage Conference on *Buffy the Vampire Slayer*, Nashville, TN, May 27–30, 2004; Active Heroines Study Day, John Moores University, Liverpool UK, 2004; Consuming New Femininities, University of East London, UK, 2005; Woman in Games, University of Aberty, Dundee, UK, 2005; Artful Gaming Forum, Science Museum's Dana Centre, London, UK, 2006; and (as keynote address) at Bring Your Own Subtext: Social Life, Human Experience and the Works of Joss Whedon, Conference, University of Huddersfield, Huddersfield, UK, June 29-July 1, 2005. It was also previously published in (now defunct) e-journal *Intersections* (Autumn 2005). Slightly different versions of this paper have been Posted at: http://bura.brunel.ac.uk/bitstream/2438/1244/1/Demon%20Girl%20Power%20post%20proof%20for%20dundee.pdf and at http://www.slayageonline.com/SCBtVS_Archive/Talks/Krzywinska.pdf.

4293. _____. "Hubble-Bubble, Herbs and Grimoires: Magic, Manichaeanism, and Witchcraft in *Buffy.*" In Rhonda V. Wilcox and David Lavery, ed. *Fighting the Forces: What's at Stake in* Buffy the Vampire Slayer. Lanham, MD: Rowman & Littlefield, 2002, pp. 178–194.

4294. _____. "Playing Buffy: Remediation, Occulted Meta-game-Physics and the Dynamics of Agency in the Videogame Version of *Buffy the Vampire Slayer.*" *Slayage: The Online International Journal of Buffy Studies* 2, 4 [8] (March 2003). Posted at: http://www.whedonstudies.tv/. A paper originally presented at Blood, Text and Fears:

Reading Around *Buffy the Vampire Slayer*, University of East Anglia, October 19–20, 2002.

4295. Kuepker, Tina Marie, comp. *The Unofficial Buffy the Vampire Slayer Internet Guide.* Full Spectrum Information Library Series. Port Orchard, WA: Lightning Rod Publishers, 1999. 40 pp.

4296. Kungl, Carla T. "Fears and Femininity at the Fin-de-siecle: of Vampires and Vampire Slayers." In Carla T. Kungl, ed. *Vampires: Myths and Metaphors of Enduring Evil.* Oxford: Inter-Disciplinary Press, 2003, pp. 109–114. Posted at: http://www.inter-disciplinary.net/publishing/id-press/ebooks/vampires-myths-and-metaphors-of-enduring-evil. A paper originally presented at Vampires: Myths and Metaphors of Enduring Evil, Budapest, Hungary, May 22–24, 2003.

4297. _____, ed. *Vampires: Myths and Metaphors of Enduring Evil.* Oxford: Inter-Disciplinary Press, 2003. 137 pp. Posted at: http://www.inter-disciplinary.net/publishing/id-press/ebooks/vampires-myths-and-metaphors-of-enduring-evil. This volume collects the papers presented at the Vampires: Myths and Metaphors of Enduring Evil Conference held in Budapest, Hungary, May 22–24, 2003. The two sessions on Buffy included papers by Milly Williamson, Carla T. Kungl, Dee Amy-Chinn, Marina Levina, and Suzanne Scott.

4298. LaBennett, Oneka. "Reading *Buffy* and 'Looking Proper': Race, Gender, and Consumption Among West Indian Girls in Brooklyn." In Kamari M. Clarke and Deborah A. Thomas, ed. *Globalization and Race: Transformations in the Cultural Production of Blackness.* Durham, NC: Duke University Press, 2006, pp. 279–298.

4299. Labre, Magdala Peixoto, and Lisa Duke. "'Nothing Like a Brisk Walk and a Spot of Demon Slaughter to Make a Girl's Night': The Construction of the Female Hero in the Buffy Video Game." *The Journal of Communication Inquiry* 28, 2 (2004): 138–56.

4300. Ladouceur, Liisa. "In Praise of the Slayer." In Liisa Ladouceur. *How to Kill a Vampire: Fangs in Folklore, Film and Fiction.* Toronto: ecw Press, 2013, pp. 139–168.

4301. Lady Aeryn. "'Handbook? What handbook?': Mentoring the Chosen One in *Star Wars* and *Buffy the Vampire Slayer.*" *Saga Journal: An Academic Star Wars Fan Journal* 2, 5 (May 2006).

4302. Lamb, Brett. "Whedonesque Women: One Man's Quest for Positive Gender Representations." *Screen Education* 61 (2011): 104–11.

4303. Landers, Jessica Marie. *The Modern Vampire Phenomenon Paradox: Simultaneous Contradictions and Unlimited Limits.* New Brunswick: Rutgers The State University of New Jersey, M.A. thesis, 2011. 86 pp. Large format. Posted at: http://rucore.libraries.rutgers.edu/rutgers-lib/31111/.

4304. Lange, Heidi C. "Those Capitalist Demons! Anti-Market Bias in *Buffy the Vampire Slayer.*" *Journey of Liberty and Society* 1 (2009): 6–13. Posted at: https://studentsforliberty.org/wp-content/uploads/2009/05/journal-of-liberty-and-society_volume–1.pdf.

4305. Lantz, Victoria Pettersen. "Numero Cinco, Border Narratives, and Mexican Cultural Performance in *Angel.*" In AmiJo Comeford and Tamy L. Burnett, eds. *The Literary Angel: Essays on Influences and Traditions Reflected in the Joss Whedon Series.* Jefferson, NC: McFarland & Company, 2010, pp. 98–111.

4306. Larbalestier, Justine. "A *Buffy* Confession." In Glenn Yeffeth, ed. *Seven Seasons of* Buffy: *Science Fiction and Fantasy Writers Discuss Their Favorite Television Show.* Dallas, TX: Benbella Books, 2003, pp. 72–84.

4307. _____. "*Buffy*'s Mary Sue Is Jonathan: *Buffy the Vampire Slayer* Acknowledges the Fans." In Rhonda V. Wilcox and David Lavery, ed. *Fighting the Forces: What's at Stake in* Buffy the Vampire Slayer. Lanham, MD: Rowman & Littlefield, 2002, pp. 227–238.

4308. _____. "The Only Thing Better Than Killing a Slayer: Heterosexuality and Sex in *Buffy the Vampire Slayer.*" In Roz Kavenry, ed. *Reading the Vampire Slayer: An Unofficial Critical Companion to* Buffy *and* Angel. 2nd ed. New York: I. B. Tauris, 2004, pp. 195–219.

4309. Latham, Jo. "'[I]s it dangerous?' Alternative Readings of 'Drugs' and Addiction' in *Buffy the Vampire Slayer.*" *Watcher Junior: The Undergraduate Journal of Whedon Studies* 4, 2 [5] (June 2010). Posted at: http://www.watcherjunior.tv/.

4310. Lavery, David. "Afterword: The Genius of Joss Whedon." In Rhonda V. Wilcox and David Lavery, eds. *Fighting the Forces: What's at Stake in* Buffy the Vampire Slayer. Lanham, MD: Rowman & Littlefield, 2002, pp. 251–256.

4311. _____. "Afterword: *My So-Called Life* Meets *The X-Files*: Winnie Holzman's Influence on Joss Whedon." In Michele Byers and David Lavery, eds. *Dear Angela: Remembering* My So-Called Life. Lanham, MD: Lexington Books, 2007, pp. 211–217.

4312. _____. "Apocalyptic Apocalypses: The Narrative Eschatology of *Buffy the Vampire Slayer*." *Slayage: The Online International Journal of Buffy Studies* 3, 1 [9] (August 2003). Posted at: http://www.whedonstudies.tv/.

4313. _____. "*Buffy the Vampire Slayer*." In Glen Creeber, ed. *50 Key Television Programmes*. London: Arnold, 2004, pp. 31–35.

4314. _____. "'Emotional Resonance and Rocket Launchers': Joss Whedon's Commentaries on the "*Buffy the Vampire Slayer* DVDs." *Slayage: The Online International Journal of Buffy Studies* 2, 2 [6] (September 2002). Posted at: http://www.whedonstudies.tv/.

4315. _____. "Fatal Environment: *Buffy the Vampire Slayer* and American Culture." A paper presented at Staking a Claim: Exploring the Global Reach of *Buffy*, University of South Australia, Adelaide, Australia, July 22, 2003. Posted at: http://davidlavery.net/writings/television/fatal_environment.pdf.

4316. _____. "'I Wrote My Thesis on You': Buffy Studies as an Academic Cult." *Slayage: The Online International Journal of Buffy Studies* 4, 1–2 [13–14] (October 2004). Posted at: http://www.whedonstudies.tv/. A paper originally presented as keynote address at Sonic Synergies: Creative Cultures, University of South Australia, Adelaide, Australia, July 17–20, 2003, and as a featured lecture at the Slayage Conference on *Buffy the Vampire Slayer*, Nashville, TN, May 27–30, 2004.

4317. _____. *Joss Whedon, A Creative Portrait: From* Buffy the Vampire Slayer *to* Marvel's The Avengers. New York: I. B. Tauris, 2013.

4318. _____. "A Religion in Narrative: Joss Whedon and Television Creativity." *Slayage: The Online International Journal of Buffy Studies* 2, 3 [7] (December 2002). Posted at: http://www.whedonstudies.tv/. A paper originally presented at the 2002 PCAS/ACAS Annual Conference, Charlotte, NC, October 3–5, 2002, and subsequently presented at Blood, Text and Fears: Reading Around *Buffy the Vampire Slayer*, University of East Anglia, October 19–20, 2002.

4319. _____, and Cynthea Burkhead, eds. *Joss Whedon: Conversations*. Jackson: University Press of Mississippi, 2011. 198 pp. hb. & tp. This volume compiles some 18 meaty interviews of the creator of Buffy the Vampire Slayer and Angel done by a spectrum of interviewers, arranged chronologically, from the years 2000 to 2009.

4320. Lavigne, Carlen. "Forces of the Universe: Intuition and the Lesbian Witch in *Buffy the Vampire Slayer*." In Jennifer Fisher, ed. *Technologies of Intuition*. Toronto: YYZ Books, 2006, pp. 189–199.

4321. Lavoie, Erin. "'Sex, Love and Sadomasochism: Buffy/Spike as a Queer Relationship." *Watcher Junior: The Undergraduate Journal of Whedon Studies* 6, 2 [8] (September 2012). Posted at: http://www.watcherjunior.tv/. A paper originally presented at NCUR: National Conference on Undergraduate Research, Ithaca College, Ithaca, NY, March 31–April 2, 2011, at Pippi to Ripley: Heroines of Fantasy and Science Fiction, Ithaca College, Ithaca, NY, April 23, 2011, and at the English and Communication Department Colloquium, SUNY Potsdam, Potsdam, NY, May 9, 2011.

4322. Lawler, James. "Between Heaven and Hells: Multidimensional Cosmology in Kant and *Buffy the Vampire Slayer*." In James B. South, ed. Buffy *and Philosophy: Fear and Trembling in Sunnydale*. Chicago: Open Court, 2003, pp. 103–116.

4323. _____. "The Multidimensional Universe of *Buffy the Vampire Slayer*." *The God Tube: Uncovering the Hidden Spiritual Message in Pop Culture*. Chicago: Open Court, 2009. 60–86.

4324. Lecoq, Frédérique. "Play, Identity, and Aesthetics in 'Restless.'" *Slayage: The Journal of the Whedon Studies Association* 9, 2 [34] (Fall 2012 Posted at: http://www.whedonstudies.tv/.

4325. Lee, Keon-Woong. *Sacrificial Cain in the Modern Workplace*. Hong Kong, University of Hong Kong, M. Phil. thesis, 2005. 82 pp. Large format. Posted at: http://hub.hku.hk/bitstream/10722/40959/6/FullText.pdf?accept=1.

4326. Lee, Tiffany Kristin. "The Justice Systems of Slayers and Vengeance Demons: Prosecutorial Discretion in *Buffy the Vampire Slayer*." *Slayage: The Journal of the Whedon Studies Association* 10, 1 [35] (Winter 2013). Posted at: http://www.whedonstudies.tv/.

4327. Lehmann, Joanna. "The Bully Within and Without: Facing Intimidation in *Buffy*." A paper presented at the Slayage Conference on *Buffy the Vampire Slayer*, Nashville, TN, May 27–30, 2004. Posted at: http://www.slayageonline.com/SCBtVS_Archive/Talks/Lehmann.pdf.

4328. Leland, Jennie. *The Phoenix Always Rises: The Evolution of Superheroines in Feminist Culture*. Orono: University of Maine, M.A. thesis, 2007. 123 pp. Large format.

4329. Leon, Hilary M. "Why We Love the Monsters: How Anita Blake, Vampire Hunter, and

Buffy the Vampire Slayer Wound Up Dating the Enemy." *Slayage: The Online International Journal of Buffy Studies* 1, 1 [1] (January 2001). Posted at: http://www.whedonstudies.tv/.

4330. Leonard, Kendra Preston, ed. *Buffy, Ballads, and Bad Guys Who Sing: Music in the Worlds of Joss Whedon.* Lanham, MD: Scarecrow Press, 2011. 308 pp. Includes contributions by Rhonda V. Wilcox, Jacqueline Bach, Elizabeth A. Clendinning, Steve Halfyard, Amanda Howell, Eric Hung, Linda Jencson, Cynthea Masson, Jeffrey Middents, Matthew Mills, Stanley C. Pelkey II, and Christopher Wiley.

4331. Levina, Marina. "How the Vampire Got Neutered: Boundary Surveillance and Techno-scientific Discourse on *Buffy the Vampire Slayer.*" In Carla T. Kungl. *Vampires: Myths and Metaphors of Enduring Evil.* Oxford: Inter-Disciplinary Press, 2003, pp. 121–123. Posted at: http://www.inter-disciplinary.net/publishing/id-press/ebooks/vampires-myths-and-metaphors-of-enduring-evil. A paper originally presented at the Vampires: Myths and Metaphors of Enduring Evil Conference held in Budapest, Hungary, May 22–24, 2003.

4332. Levine, Elana. "*Buffy* and the 'New Girl Order': Defining Feminism and Femininity." In Elana Levine and Lisa Parks, eds. *Undead TV: Essays on* Buffy the Vampire Slayer. Durham, NC: Duke University Press, 2007, pp. 168–189. A paper originally presented in earlier form at National Communication Association Conference, Chicago IL, November 2004, and as an invited lecture, "Buffy and the 'New Girl Order': Two Waves of Television and Feminism," at the Media and Cultural Studies colloquium, Department of Communication Arts, University of Wisconsin—Madison, Spring 2002.

4333. _____, **and Lisa Parks.** "Introduction." *Undead TV: Essays on* Buffy the Vampire Slayer. Eds. Elana Levine and Lisa Parks. Durham, NC: Duke University Press, 2007. 1–15.

4334. _____, **and Lisa Parks, eds.** *Undead TV: Essays on* Buffy the Vampire Slayer. Durham, NC: Duke University Press, 2007. 209 pp. tp. Includes contributions by Mary Celeste Kearney, Susan Murray, Annette Hill and Ian Calcutt, Amelie Hastie, Cynthia Fuchs, Allison McCracken, Jason Middleton, and Elana Levine.

4335. Levine, Michael P., and Steven Jay Schneider. "Feeling for Buffy: The Girl Next Door." In James B. South, ed. Buffy *and Philosophy: Fear and Trembling in Sunnydale.* Chicago: Open Court, 2003, pp. 294–308.

4336. Levy, Sophie. "'You Still My Girl?' Adolescent Femininity as Resistance in *Buffy the Vampire Slayer.*" *Reconstruction: Studies in Contemporary Culture* 3, 1 (2003). Posted at: http://reconstruction.eserver.org/031/levy.htm.

4337. Lichtenberg, Jacqueline. "Power of Becoming." In Glenn Yeffeth, ed. *Seven Seasons of* Buffy: *Science Fiction and Fantasy Writers Discuss Their Favorite Television Show.* Dallas, TX: Benbella Books, 2003, pp. 121–136.

4338. _____. "Victime Triumphant." In Glenn Yeffeth, ed. *Five Seasons of* Angel: *Science Fiction and Fantasy Writers Discuss Their Favorite Vampire.* Dallas, TX: Benella, 2004, pp. 133–138.

4339. Lima, Maria. "I Am Joss Whedon's Bitch." In Lynne M. Thomas and Deborah Stanish, eds. *Whedonistas! A Celebration of the Worlds of Joss Whedon by the Women Who Love Them.* Des Moines, IA: Mad Norwegian Press, 2011, pp. 112–115.

4340. Linsley, Brent. "Canon Fodder Revisited: *Buffy* Meets the Bard." In Kevin K. Durand, ed. Buffy *Meets the Academy: Essays on the Episodes and Scripts as Texts.* Jefferson, NC: McFarland & Company, 2009, pp. 17–24.

4341. _____. "Complexes My Mother Left Me: Spike Meets Robin Wood." In Kevin K. Durand, ed. Buffy *Meets the Academy: Essays on the Episodes and Scripts as Texts.* Jefferson, NC: McFarland & Company, 2009, pp. 131–136.

4342. Lipsett, Joseph. Opposing Buffy: *Power, Responsibility and the Narrative Function of the Big Bad in* Buffy the Vampire Slayer. Ottawa, ON, CA: Carleton University, M.A. thesis, 2006. 212 pp. Large format.

4343. Little, Tracy. "High School Is Hell: Metaphor Made Literal." In James B. South, ed. Buffy *and Philosophy: Fear and Trembling in Sunnydale.* Chicago: Open Court, 2003, pp. 282–293.

4344. Livingston, James. "Apocalypse Now?" In James Livingston. *The World Turned Inside Out: American Thought and Culture at the End of the 20th Century.* Lanham, MD: Rowman & Littlefield, 2010, pp. 89–91.

4345. Locklin, Reid B. "*Buffy the Vampire Slayer* and the Domestic Church: Revisioning Family and the Common Good." *Slayage: The Online International Journal of Buffy Studies* 2, 2 [6] (September 2002). Posted at: http://www.whedonstudies.tv/.

4346. Lodge, Mary Jo. "Beyond 'Jumping the Shark': The New Television Musical." *Studies in Musical Theatre* 1, 3 (December 2007): 293–305.

4347. Loftis, J. Robert. "Moral Complexity in the Buffyverse." *Slayage: The Online International Journal of Buffy Studies* 7, 3 [27] (Winter 2009). Posted at: http://www.whedonstudies.tv/.

4348. Longbons, Jarrod. "Vampires Are People, Too: Personalism in the Buffyverse." In Kim Paffenroth and John W. Morehead, eds. *The Undead and Theology.* Eugene, OR: Pickwick Publications, 2012, pp. 34–53.

4349. Longstreet-Conrad, Roxanne. "Is That Your Final Answer...?" In Glenn Yeffeth, ed. *Seven Seasons of* Buffy: *Science Fiction and Fantasy Writers Discuss Their Favorite Television Show.* Dallas, TX: Benbella Books, 2003, pp. 5–18.

4350. _____. "Mirror/Mirror: A Parody." In Jane Espenson with Glenn Yeffeth, eds. *Finding Serenity: Anti-Heroes, Lost Shepherds and Space Hookers in Joss Whedon's* Firefly. Dallas, TX: Benbella Books, 2005, pp. 169–182.

4351. _____. "Welcome to Wolfram & Hart: The Semi-Complete Guide to Evil." In Glenn Yeffeth, ed. *Five Seasons of* Angel: *Science Fiction and Fantasy Writers Discuss Their Favorite Vampire.* Dallas, TX: Benbella Books, 2004, pp. 33–47.

4352. Lorrah, Jean. "Love Saves the World." In Glenn Yeffeth, ed. *Seven Seasons of* Buffy: *Science Fiction and Fantasy Writers Discuss Their Favorite Television Show.* Dallas, TX: Benbella Books, 2003, pp. 167–175.

4353. _____. "A World Without Love: The Failure of Family in *Angel.*" In Glenn Yeffeth, ed. *Five Seasons of* Angel: *Science Fiction and Fantasy Writers Discuss Their Favorite Vampire.* Dallas, TX: Benbella Books, 2004, pp. 57–63.

4354. Lotz, Amanda D. "Fighting for Families and Femininity: The Hybrid Narratives of the Action Drama." In Amanda D. Lotz. *Redesigning Women: Television After the Network Era.* Urbana: University of Illinois Press, 2006, pp. 68–83.

4355. _____. "Love, Trust and Friendship in *Buffy the Vampire Slayer.*" In Amanda D. Lotz. *Redesigning Women: Television After the Network Era.* Urbana: University of Illinois Press, 2006, pp. 85–86.

4356. Lowe, Donna. "The Last Spike: Jungian Individuation in *Buffy the Vampire Slayer.*" *Watcher Junior: The Journal of Undergraduate Research in Buffy Studies* 2, 1 [2] (July 2006). Posted at: http://www.watcherjunior.tv/.

4357. Ludlow, Peter. "From Sherlock and *Buffy* to Klingon and Norrathian Platinum Pieces: Pretense, Contextualism, and the Myth of Fiction." *Philosophical Issues* 16, 1 (2006): 162–183. Posted at: http://philpapers.org/rec/LUDFSA.

4358. Luria, Rachel. "Nothing Left but Skin and Cartilage: The Body and Toxic Masculinity." In Erin B. Waggoner, ed. *Sexual Rhetoric in the Works of Joss Whedon: New Essays.* Jefferson, NC: McFarland & Company, 2010, pp. 185–193. A paper originally presented at SC3: The Slayage Conference on the Whedonverses, Henderson State College, Arkadelphia, AR, June 5–8, 2008.

4359. Lyn, Liang-Chih. *Blondes and the Horror Genre: The Subversion of Gender and Genre in* Buffy the Vampire Slayer *and* Angel. Zhongli City, Taiwan, National Central University, M.A. thesis, 2006. 66 pp. Large format. Posted at: http://thesis.lib.ncu.edu.tw/ETD-db/ETD-search-c/view_etd?URN=92122003.

4360. Lyubansky, Mikhail. "Buffy's Search for Meaning." In Joy Davidson with Leah Wilson, eds. *The Psychology of Joss Whedon: An Unauthorized Exploration of* Buffy, Angel, *and* Firefly. Dallas, TX: Benbella Books, 2007, pp. 171–183.

4361. MacDonald, Deneka C. "Iconic Eye Candy: *Buffy the Vampire Slayer* and Designer Peer Pressure for Teens." In Rikke Schubart and Anne Gjelsvik, eds. *Femme Fatalities: Representations of Strong Women in the Media.* [Gothenburg, Sweden] Scandinavia: Nordicom Publishing, 2004, pp. 111–26. A paper originally presented at Crossroads in Cultural Studies: Fourth International Conference, Tampere, Finland.

4362. Macnaughtan, Don. *The Buffyverse Catalog: A Complete Guide to* Buffy the Vampire Slayer *and* Angel *in Print, Film, Television, Comics, Games and Other Media, 1992–2010.* Jefferson, NC: McFarland & Company, 2011. 318 pp. tp.

4363. MacNeil, William P. "You Slay Me! *Buffy* as Jurisprude of Desire." *Cardozo Law Review* 24, 6 (2003): 2421–2440. A paper originally presented at Staking a Claim: Exploring the Global Reach of *Buffy*, University of South Australia, Adelaide, Australia, July 22, 2003.

4364. Maddox, Margaret J. *Keeping Her in Her Place: The Perpetual Imprisonment of Joan of Arc.* Fayetteville: University of Arkansas, Ph.D. dissertation, 2004. 285 pp. Large format.

4365. Magistrale, Tony. "Vampiric Terrors: *Dracula, The Hunger, Interview with the Vampire, Bram Stoker's Dracula, Buffy the Vampire Slayer.*" In Tony Magistrale. *Abject Terrors: Surveying the Modern and Postmodern Horror Film.* New York: Peter Lang, 2005, pp. 37–56.

4366. Magnusson, Gert. "Are Vampires Evil? Categorizations of Vampires, and Angelus and Spike as the Immoral and the Amoral." *Slayage: The Journal of the Whedon Studies Association* 9, 2 [34] (Fall 2012). Posted at: http://www.whedon studies.tv/.

4367. ____. "Being a Vampire Sucks: Regarding the Anonymous Vampires in *Buffy the Vampire Slayer.*" *Slayage: The Journal of the Whedon Studies Association* 9, 1 [33] (Spring 2011). Posted at: http://www.whedonstudies.tv/.

4368. ____. "Harmony: The Lonely Life of a Modern Woman." *Slayage: The Journal of the Whedon Studies Association* 9, 2 [34] (Fall 2012). Posted at: http://www.whedonstudies.tv/.

4369. Magoulick, Mary. "Frustrating Female Heroism: Mixed Messages in *Xena, Nikita,* and *Buffy.*" *The Journal of Popular Culture* 39, 5 (Oct 2006): 729–755. Also accepted (but not presented) for the Slayage Conference on *Buffy the Vampire Slayer,* Nashville, TN, May 27–30, 2004.

4370. Mahoney, Melissa. "A Slayer's Death Denial: The Struggle for Authenticity in 'Graduation Day: Part One and Two.'" *Slayage: The Journal of the Whedon Studies Association* 9, 2 [34] (Fall 2012). Posted at: http://www.whedonstudies.tv/.

4371. Mai, Emily. *Writing the Vampire: Constitutions of Gender in* Carmilla, Dracula, *and* Buffy the Vampire Slayer. Nashville, TN: Vanderbilt University, BA honors thesis, 2009. 77 pp. Large format. Posted at: http://discoverarchive. vanderbilt.edu/bitstream/handle/1803/2976/ FINAL%20DRAFT.pdf?sequence=1.

4372. Mainon, Dominique, and James Ursini. "*Buffy the Vampire Slayer.*" In Dominique Mainon and James Ursini. *Modern Amazons: Warrior Women on Screen.* Pompton Plains, NJ: Limelight Editions, 2006, pp. 81–85.

4373. Mains, Christine. "'Dreams Teach': (Im)Possible Worlds in Science Fiction Television." In J. P. Telotte, ed. *The Essential Science Fiction Television Reader.* Lexington: University Press of Kentucky, 2008, pp. 143–158.

4374. Maio, Barbara. "Between Past and Future: Hybrid Design Style in *Firefly* and *Serenity.*" In Rhonda V. Wilcox and Tanya R. Cochran, eds. *Investigating* Firefly and Serenity: *Science Fiction on the Frontier.* New York: I. B. Tauris, 2008, pp. 201–211.

4375. ____. "Girl Power and Magic in the Service of a Cult." English translation by Jeffrey Bussolini. *Slayage: The Online International Journal of Buffy Studies* 6, 3 [23] (Spring 2007). Posted at: http://www.whedonstudies.tv/.

4376. ____. "Watching the Watcher: Analysing the Character of Rupert Giles." A paper presented at SC2: The Slayage Conference on the Whedonverses, Gordon College, Barnesville, GA, May 25–28, 2006. Posted at: http://www.whedon studies.tv/SCW_Archive/Maio.pdf.

4377. Makishima, Keiko. "'You're not the source of me': Adoptive Identity and Child-Heroes in *Buffy the Vampire Slayer.*" *Watcher Junior: The Undergraduate Journal of Whedon Studies* 6, 1 [7] (July 2012). Posted at: http://www.watcherjunior. tv/.

4378. Mallan, Kerry. "Hitting Below the Belt: Action Femininity and Representations of Female Subjectivity." In Kerry Mallan and Sharyn Pearce, eds. *Youth Cultures: Texts, Images, and Identities.* Westport, CT: Praeger, 2003, pp. 139–153.

4379. Maltese, Racheline. "Late to the Party: What *Buffy* Never Taught Me About Being a Girl." In Lynne M. Thomas and Deborah Stanish, eds. *Whedonistas! A Celebration of the Worlds of Joss Whedon by the Women Who Love Them.* Des Moines, IA: Mad Norwegian Press, 2011, pp. 150–155.

4380. Mandala, Susan. "Solidarity and the Scoobies: An analysis of the -y suffix in the television series *Buffy the Vampire Slayer.*" *Language and Literature* 16, 1 (February 2007): 53–73. A paper originally presented at Bring Your Own Subtext: Social Life, Human Experience and the Works of Joss Whedon, Conference, University of Huddersfield, Huddersfield, UK, June 29-July 1, 2005.

4381. Mann, Peter. *The Slayer Files.* Harpenden, Herts: Pocket Essentials, 1999. 95 pp. pb.

4382. Marano, Michael. "River Tam and the Weaponized Women of the Whedonverse." In Jane Espenson with Leah Wilson, eds. *Serenity Found: More Unauthorized Essays on Joss Whedon's* Firefly *Universe.* Dallas, TX: Benbella Books, 2007, pp. 37–48.

4383. Marinov, Monica. "Traveling Between Mediums: *Buffy's* Ascent into Television." *Watcher*

Junior: The Journal of Undergraduate Research in Buffy Studies 2, 1 [2] (July 2006). Posted at: http://www.watcherjunior.tv/.

4384. Marinucci, Mimi. "Feminism and the Ethics of Violence: Why Buffy Kicks Ass." In James B. South, ed. *Buffy and Philosophy: Fear and Trembling in Sunnydale.* Chicago: Open Court, 2003, pp. 61–75.

4385. Marks, Rick Brian. *Targeting Families and Teens: Television Violence on the WB.* Las Vegas: University of Nevada–Las Vegas, M.A. thesis, 2000. 60 pp. Large format.

4386. Markson, Alison Warren. *Definitions of Femininity: Social and Media Influences on Late Adolescent Girls.* Boston, MA: Massachusetts School of Professional Psychology, Ph.D. dissertation, 2004. 217 pp. Large format.

4387. Marshall, C. W. "Aeneas the Vampire Slayer: A Roman Model for Why Giles Kills Ben." *Slayage: The Online International Journal of Buffy Studies* 9 (August 2003): Posted at: http://www.whedonstudies.tv/.

4388. Marshall, Jerilyn. "What Would Buffy Do? The Use of Popular Culture Examples in Undergraduate Library Instruction." A paper presented at the Annual Meeting of the PCA/ACA, Toronto, Ontario, Canada, March 13–16, 2002.

4389. Martens, John W. "The Apocalyptic Vision in Film and Television: Traditional Apocalyptic Films." In John W. Martens. *The End of the World: The Apocalyptic Imagination in Film & Television.* Winnipeg: Shillingford, 2003, pp. 130–137.

4390. Martin, Andrew. "Popular Culture and Narratives of Insecurity." In Patrice Petro and Andrew Martin, eds. *Rethinking Global Security: Media, Popular Culture, and the 'War on Terror'.* New Brunswick: Rutgers University Press, 2006, pp. 104–116.

4391. Martin, Jane. "'Show, Don't Tell': Teaching the Elements of Film Production." In Jodie A. Kreider and Meghan K. Winchell, eds. *Buffy in the Classroom: Essays on Teaching with the Vampire Slayer.* Jefferson, NC: McFarland & Company, 2010, pp. 126–135.

4392. Masson, Cynthea. "Concealing Truths: Rhetorical Questions in 'Once More, with Feeling.'" In Kendra Preston Leonard, ed. *Buffy, Ballads, and Bad Guys Who Sing: Music in the Worlds of Joss Whedon.* Lanham, MD: Scarecrow Press, 2011, pp. 133–153. A paper originally presented in earlier form as "'What Did You Sing About?': Acts of Questioning in 'Once More with Feeling'" at SC2: The Slayage Conference on the Whedonverses, Gordon College, Barnesville, GA, May 25–28, 2006. Posted at: http://www.whedonstudies.tv/SCW_Archive/Masson.pdf.

4393. _____. "'Evil's Spreading Sir...and It's Not Just Over There': Nazism in *Buffy* and *Angel*." In Sara Buttsworth and Maartje Abbenhuis, ed. *Monsters in the Mirror: Representations of Nazism in Post-War Popular Culture.* Westport, CT: Praeger, 2010, pp. 179–99.

4394. _____. "'Is That Just a Comforting Way of Not Answering the Question?': Willow, Questions, and Affective Respose in *Buffy the Vampire Slayer*." In Michael Adams, ed. *Beyond Slayer Slang: Pragmatics, Discourse, and Style in* Buffy the Vampire Slayer. Special Issue of *Slayage: The Online International Journal of Buffy Studies* 5, 4 [20] (May 2006). Posted at: http://www.whedonstudies. tv/. Rev. text as "'Can You Just Be Kissing Me Now?': The Question(s) of Willow in *Buffy the Vampire Slayer*." In Rebecca Beirne, ed. *Televising Queer Women: A Reader.* New York: Palgrave Macmillan, 2008, pp. 65–81.

4395. _____. "'It's a play on perspective': A Reading of Whedon's Illyria through Sartre's *Nausea*." In AmiJo Comeford and Tamy L. Burnett, eds. *The Literary* Angel: *Essays on Influences and Traditions Reflected in the Joss Whedon Series.* Jefferson, NC: McFarland & Company, 2010, pp. 159–172.

4396. _____. "'It's a Thing We Do': Crying with Buffy and Angel." In Michele Byers and David Lavery, ed. *On the Verge of Tears: Why the Movies, Television, Music, Art, Popular Culture, Literature, and the Real World Make Us Cry.* Newcastle upon Tyne, UK: Cambridge Scholars Publishing, 2010, pp. 114–24.

4397. _____, and Marni Stanley. "Queer Eye of that Vampire Guy: Spike and the Aesthetics of Camp." In Matthew Pateman, ed. *Buffy and Aesthetics.* Special Issue of *Slayage: The Online International Journal of Buffy Studies* 6, 2 [22] (Winter 2006). Posted at: http://www.whedonstudies.tv/.

4398. Mastracci, Sharon H. "Public Service Motivation in *Buffy the Vampire Slayer*." *Public Voices* 12, 1 (2011): 67–85. Posted at: http://www.whedonstudies.tv/essays/slayage33/Mastracci.pdf.

4399. Mathers, Ian. "'The Strength and Conviction to Lose So Relentlessly': Heroism in *Angel*." In Mary Alice Money for PopMatters.com, ed. *Joss Whedon: The Complete Companion: The TV Series,* the Movies, the Comic Books and More. London: Titan Books, 2012, pp. 213–219.

4400. Mattessi, Peter. "*Buffy* and the Serialization of the Series." *Metro Magazine* 137 (Summer 2003): 76–77.

4401. Mattson, Kathleen. *The Gentleviewer's Obsessive Guide to Buffy the Vampire Slayer.* N.p.: Paisley Publications, 2012. 174 pp. tp.

4402. Mayer, Sophia R. *Script Girls and Automatic Women: A Feminist Film Poetics.* Toronto: University of Toronto, Ph.D. dissertation, 2006. 300 pp. Large format.

4403. Mayhew, Valerie. "Mary and Buffy Walk into a Bar: The Virgin Deity and *Buffy the Vampire Slayer.*" In Anthony R. Mills, John W. Morehead, and J. Ryan Parker, eds. *Joss Whedon and Religion: Essays on an Angry Atheist's Explorations of the Sacred.* Jefferson, NC: McFarland & Company, 2013, pp. 39–50.

4404. Mayo, Andrea E. "Cops, Teachers, and Vampire Slayers: Buffy as Street-Level Bureaucrat." *Administrative Theory & Praxis* 33, 4 (December 2011): 599–603.

4405. McAvan, Em. "'I Think I'm Kinda Gay': Willow Rosenberg and the Absent/Present Bisexual in *Buffy the Vampire Slayer.*" *Slayage: The Online International Journal of Buffy Studies* 6, 4 [24] (Summer 2007). Posted at: http://www.whedonstudies.tv/.

4406. McClain, Katia. "Angel vs. the Grand Inquisitor: Joss Whedon Re-imagines Dostoevsky." In AmiJo Comeford and Tamy L. Burnett, eds. *The Literary Angel: Essays on Influences and Traditions Reflected in the Joss Whedon Series.* Jefferson, NC: McFarland & Company, 2010, pp. 130–146. A paper originally presented as "Freedom from Suffering or Freedom to Suffer: Joss Whedon Reimagines Dostoevsky" at SC3: The Slayage Conference on the Whedonverses, Henderson State College, Arkadelphia, AR, June 5–8, 2008.

4407. McClelland, Bruce. "By Whose Authority? The Magical Tradition, Violence, and the Legitimation of the Vampire Slayer." *Slayage: The Online International Journal of Buffy Studies* 1, 1 [1] (January 2001). Posted at: http://www.whedonstudies.tv/.

4408. _____. "The Slayer Generation." In Bruce McClelland. *Slayers and Their Vampires: A Cultural History of Killing the Dead.* Ann Arbor: University of Michigan Press, 2006. 168–186.

4409. McConnell, Kathleen. "Chaos at the Mouth of Hell. Why the Columbine High School Massacre had Repercussions for *Buffy the Vampire Slayer.*" *Gothic Studies* 2, 1 (April 2000): 119–135.

4410. McCracken, Allison. "At Stake: Angel's Body, Fantasy Masculinity, and Queer Desire in Teen Television." In Elana Levine and Lisa Parks, eds. *Undead TV: Essays on* Buffy the Vampire Slayer. Durham, NC: Duke University Press, 2007, pp. 116–144.

4411. McDonald, Kathleen. "The More Things Change: Buffy and Angel Enact a Modern-Day Sentimental Novel." In Kathleen McDonald, ed. *Americanization of History: Conflation of Time and Culture in Film and Television.* Newcastle upon Tyne, UK: Cambridge Scholars Publishing, 2010, pp. 108–132.

4412. McDonald, Neil. "*Buffy*: Prime Time Passion Play." *Quadrant* 44, 4 (April 2000): 63–67.

4413. McGrath, Meredith. "How an Atheist and His Demons Created a Shepherd." In Lynne M. Thomas and Deborah Stanish, eds. Whedonistas! A Celebration of the Worlds of Joss Whedon by the Women Who Love Them. Des Moines, IA: Mad Norwegian Press, 2011, pp. 156–164.

4414. McGuire, Seanan. "The Girls Next Door: Learning to Live with the Living Dead and Never Even Break a Nail." In Lynne M. Thomas and Deborah Stanish, eds. Whedonistas! A Celebration of the Worlds of Joss Whedon by the Women Who Love Them. Des Moines, IA: Mad Norwegian Press, 2011, pp. 13–18. Posted at: http://www.tor.com/stories/2010/11/excerpt-whedonistas-a-celebration-of-the-worlds-of-joss-whedon-by-the-women-who-love-them.

4415. McKee, Alan. "*Buffy the Vampire Slayer.*" In Toby Miller, ed. *Television Studies.* London: British Film Institute [BFI], 2002, pp. 69.

4416. McKenzie, Keira. *A Tale Not Told (Novel): Consorting with Devils, Dancing with Angels.* Crawley, Western Australia: University of Western Australia, M.A. thesis, 2003. 282 pp. Large format.

4417. McKeon, J. Michael. "'Love the One You're With': Developing Xander." In Emily Dial-Driver, Sally Emmons-Featherston, Jim Ford, and Carolyn Anne Taylor, eds. *The Truth of* Buffy*: Essays on Fiction Illuminating Reality.* Jefferson, NC: McFarland & Company, 2008, pp. 131–141.

4418. McLaren, Scott. "The Evolution of Joss Whedon's Vampire Mythology and the Ontology of the Soul." *Slayage: The Online International Journal of Buffy Studies* 5, 2 [18] (September 2005). Posted at: http://www.whedonstudies.tv/.

4419. McMillan, Tracie, and Oscar Owen. "The *Buffy* Files." *The Activist* (Winter/Spring 1999). Also published as "Teen Socialist Idols" in *Harper's* (July 1999): 35–36.

4420. McNeilly, Kevin, Susan R. Fisher, and Christina Sylka. "Kiss the Librarian, But Close the Hellmouth: 'It's Like a Whole Big Sucking Thing.'" *Slayage: The Online International Journal of Buffy Studies* 1, 2 [2] (March 2001). Posted at: http://www.whedonstudies.tv/.

4421. McRae, Leanne Helen. *Questions of Popular Cult(ure).* Perth, Western Australia: Media Communication & Culture School, Arts Division, Murdoch University, Ph.D. dissertation, 2003. 282 pp. Large format.

4422. McTee, Sasha Rene. *"But, You're Just a Girl": The Female Hero in Modern Science Fiction and Fantasy.* New Orleans: University of New Orleans, M.A. thesis, 2013. 61 pp. Large format. Posted at: http://scholarworks.uno.edu/td/1655/.

4423. Meaney, Geraldine. "Dead, White, Male: Irishness in *Buffy the Vampire Slayer* and *Angel.*" In Diane Negra, ed. *The Irish in Us: Irishness, Performativity, and Popular Culture.* Durham, NC: Duke University Press, 2006, pp. 254–281.

4424. Medendorp, Liz. "*Buffy*speak: The Internal and External Impact of Slayer Slang." In Jennifer Kate Stuller, ed. *Fan Phenomena: Buffy the Vampire Slayer.* Chicago: Intellect, 2013, pp. 64–73.

4425. Melton, J. Gordon. "Images from the Hellmouth: *Buffy the Vampire Slayer* Comic Books 1998–2002." *Slayage: The Online International Journal of Buffy Studies* 2, 2 [6] (September 2002). Posted at: http://www.whedonstudies.tv/.

4426. _____. "Words from the Hellmouth: A Bibliography of Books on *Buffy the Vampire Slayer.*" *Slayage: The Online International Journal of Buffy Studies* 1, 4 [4] (December 2001) [Revised and Expanded, March 2003]. Posted at: http://www.whedonstudies.tv/.

4427. Mendelsohn, Farah. "Surpassing the Love of Vampires; or Why (and How) a Queer Reading of Buffy/Willow is Denied." In Rhonda V. Wilcox and David Lavery, eds. *Fighting the Forces: What's at Stake in* Buffy the Vampire Slayer. Lanham, MD: Rowman & Littlefield, 2002, pp. 45–60.

4428. Mendick, Heather. "Hippy Chix and Geek Chic: What do Positive Images of Women Mathematicians Look Like?" *Proceedings of the British Society for Research into Learning Mathematics* 25, 2 (June 2005): 55–60. Posted at: http://www.bsrlm.org.uk/IPs/ip25–2/BSRLM-IP-25-2-Full.pdf.

4429. Merrick, Robin M. Buffy *Can Be Stuffy: The Rhetoric of Pop Culture and Post-Feminist Ideology with Composition Applications in* Buffy the Vampire Slayer. Tahlequah, OK: Northeastern State University, M.A. thesis, 2003. 50 pp. Large format.

4430. Messina, Justin. "The Legacy of the Slayer: How *Buffy* Lives On in *Chaos Bleeds.*" *Watcher Junior: The Undergraduate Journal of Whedon Studies* 6, 2 [8] (September 2012). Posted at: http://www.watcherjunior.tv/.

4431. Mestre, Robert. *The Big Book of Buffy Bites 2008.* Morrisville, NC: LULU Enterprises, 2008. 275 pp. pb. Large format.

4432. Meyer, Jenna. *"You're a Vampire...Was That an Offensive Term? Should I Say 'Undead American'?" The Evolution of the Vampire in Popular Culture.* Buffalo: State University of New York—Buffalo, M.A. thesis, 2010. 60 pp. Large format.

4433. Meyer, Michaela D. E. "From Rogue in the 'Hood to Suave in a Suit: Black Masculinity and the Transformation of Charles Gunn." In Stacey Abbott, ed. *Reading* Angel: *The TV Spin-off with a Soul.* New York: I. B. Tauris, 2005, pp. 176–188.

4434. Middents, Jeffery R. "A Sweet Vamp: Critiquing the Treatment of Race in *Buffy* and the American Musical Once More (with Feeling)." *Slayage: The Online International Journal of Buffy Studies* 17 (2005). Posted at: http://www.whedonstudies.tv/. Rpt. in Kendra Preston Leonard, ed. Buffy, *Ballads, and Bad Guys Who Sing: Music in the Worlds of Joss Whedon.* Lanham, MD: Scarecrow Press, 2011, pp. 119–132. A paper originally presented at the Slayage Conference on *Buffy the Vampire Slayer*, Nashville, TN, May 27–30, 2004.

4435. Middleton, Jason. "Buffy as *Femme Fatale*: The Cult Heroine and the Male Spectator." In Elana Levine and Lisa Parks, eds. *Undead TV: Essays on* Buffy the Vampire Slayer. Durham, NC: Duke University Press, 2007, pp. 145–167.

4436. Mikosz, Philip, and Dana Och. "Previously on *Buffy the Vampire Slayer*..." *Slayage: The Online International Journal of Buffy Studies* 2, 1

[5] (May 2002). Posted at: http://www.whedon studies.tv/.

4437. Miles, Lawrence, Lars Pearson, and Christa Dickson. *Dusted: The Unauthorized Guide to Buffy the Vampire Slayer.* New Orleans, LA: Mad Norwegian Press, 2003. 336 pp. tp.

4438. Miller, Jessica Prata. "'The I in Team': Buffy and Feminist Ethics." In James B. South, ed. Buffy *and Philosophy: Fear and Trembling in Sunnydale.* Chicago: Open Court, 2003, pp. 35–48.

4439. Mills, Anthony R. "*Buffy*verse Fandom as Religion." In Jennifer Kate Stuller, ed. *Fan Phenomena:* Buffy the Vampire Slayer. Chicago: Intellect, 2013, pp. 134–143.

4440. _____. "Introduction." In Anthony R. Mills, John W. Morehead, and J. Ryan Parker, eds. *Joss Whedon and Religion: Essays on an Angry Atheist's Explorations of the Sacred.* Jefferson, NC: McFarland & Company, 2013, pp. 7–10.

4441. _____. "Preface." In Anthony R. Mills, John W. Morehead, and J. Ryan Parker, eds. *Joss Whedon and Religion: Essays on an Angry Atheist's Explorations of the Sacred.* Jefferson, NC: McFarland & Company, 2013, pp. 5–6.

4442. _____, John W. Morehead, and J. Ryan Parker, eds. *Joss Whedon and Religion: Essays on an Angry Atheist's Explorations of the Sacred.* Jefferson, NC: McFarland & Company, 2013. 232 pp.

4443. Mills, Matthew. "*Angel's* Narrative Score." In Kendra Preston Leonard, ed. Buffy, *Ballads, and Bad Guys Who Sing: Music in the Worlds of Joss Whedon.* Lanham, MD: Scarecrow Press, 2011, pp. 173–208.

4444. _____. "*Ubi Caritas*? Music as Narrative Agent in *Angel.*" In Stacey Abbott, ed. *Reading* Angel: *The TV Spin-off with a Soul.* New York: I. B. Tauris, 2005, pp. 31–43.

4445. Milner, Andrew. "Postmodern Gothic: Buffy, the X-Files and the Clinton Presidency." *Continuum: Journal of Media & Cultural Studies* 19, 1 (2005): 103–116.

4446. _____. "Texts and Contexts: From *Rossums's Universal Robots* to *Buffy the Vampire Slayer.*" In Andrew Milner. *Literature, Culture and Society.* 2nd ed. New York: Routledge, 2005, pp. 239–294.

4447. Milson, Jack. "The Power of Fandom in the Whedonverse." In Mary Alice Money for PopMatters.com, ed. *Joss Whedon: The Complete* Companion: *The TV Series, the Movies, the Comic Books and More.* London: Titan Books, 2012, pp. 270–284. An earlier version appeared as part of PopMatters.com's *Spotlight: Joss Whedon,* originally posted on April 11, 2011.

4448. Minear, Tim. "Foreword." In Dean A. Kowalski and S. Evan Kreider, eds. *The Philosophy of Joss Whedon.* Lexington: University Press of Kentucky, 2011, pp. vii–ix.

4449. Moeller, Gary. "Is It Art? The Artful 'Hush' of St. Francis and the Gentlemen Blue Meanies." In Emily Dial-Driver, Sally Emmons-Featherston, Jim Ford, and Carolyn Anne Taylor, ed. *The Truth of* Buffy: *Essays on Fiction Illuminating Reality.* Jefferson, NC: McFarland & Company, 2008, pp. 96–106.

4450. Moldovano, Pnina. "Virtually a Femme Fatale: The Case of *Buffy's* Faith." In Erin B. Waggoner, ed. *Sexual Rhetoric in the Works of Joss Whedon: New Essays.* Jefferson, NC: McFarland & Company, 2010, pp. 194–214.

4451. Molloy, Patricia. "Demon Diasporas: Confronting the Other and the Other Worldly in *Buffy the Vampire Slayer* and *Angel.*" In Jutta Weldes, ed. *To Seek Out New Worlds: Science Fiction and World Politics.* New York: Palgrave Macmillan, 2003, pp. 99–122.

4452. Monette, Sarah. "The Kindness of Monsters." In Lynne M. Thomas and Deborah Stanish, ed. *Whedonistas! A Celebration of the Worlds of Joss Whedon by the Women Who Love Them.* Des Moines, IA: Mad Norwegian Press, 2011, pp. 131–134.

4453. Money, Mary Alice. "The Undemonization of Supporting Characters in *Buffy.*" In Rhonda V. Wilcox and David Lavery, eds. *Fighting the Forces: What's at Stake in* Buffy the Vampire Slayer. Lanham, MD: Rowman & Littlefield, 2002, pp. 98–107.

4454. _____, for PopMatters.com, ed. *Joss Whedon: The Complete Companion: The TV Series, the Movies, the Comic Books and More.* London: Titan Books, 2012. 485 pp. This comprehensive volume originated as a collection of articles published online in 2011 at "Popmatters.com," an expansive British media/pop culture site that covered the rise of Joss Whedon through the first decade of the 21st century. The original articles, many written by *Buffy* scholars, were assembled under the general guidance of Robert Moore and appeared under the collected title "Spotlight Joss Whedon." The original articles remained on the

Popmatters.com site until the publication of the book. Following the decision to create a book version of the website, PopMatters.com designated Mary Alice Money as the editor. She was assisted in her task by PopMatters' Senior Editor Karen Zarker and Alysa Hornick, who prepared the bibliographic essay. While most of the book covers *Buffy* and *Angel*, it is not limited to those two television shows, but also covers other (non-vampire) projects initiated by Whedon such as *Firefly* and *Serenity*. It also covers the *Buffy* and *Angel* comic books from Dark Horse and IDW. Contributors to the book version with entries relative to *Buffy* and/or *Angel* include Robert Moore, Tanya R. Cockran. Romand Helfrich, Malgorzata Drewnick, Kyle Garrett, Nathan Pensky, Michale Curtis Nelson, Nandini Ramachandran, Fay Murray and Holly Golding, Jessica Ford, Rhonda V. Wilcox, Laura Berger and Karl Ferencz, Lily Rothman, Dr. Shirly Q, Kristin Barton, Stacey Abbott, Lorna Jowett, Bronwen Calvert, Don Tresca, Nikki Faith Fuller, Ian Mathers, Patrick Shad, Sesar R. Bustamonte, Kevin Chiat, Jack Milson, Nick Bridwell, Angela Zhang, and Alysa Hornick. d. After the book was published, the essays included in the book were largely removed from the internet, and only brief excerpts remained. Some essays, those not included in the book, continue to appear on the original "Spotlight Joss Whedon" site, at http://www.popmatters.com/special/section/spotlight-joss-whedon/.

4455. Montgomery, Carla. "Innocence." In Glenn Yeffeth, ed. *Seven Seasons of* Buffy: *Science Fiction and Fantasy Writers Discuss Their Favorite Television Show*. Dallas, TX: Benbella Books, 2003, pp. 152–158.

4456. Montz, Amy L. "'Size Doesn't Matter?': The Disembodied Miniature in *Buffy the Vampire Slayer*." A paper presented at the Slayage Conference on *Buffy the Vampire Slayer*, Nashville, TN, May 27–30, 2004. Posted at: http://www.slayageonline.com/SCBtVS_Archive/Talks/Montz.pdf.

4457. Moore, James. "Monsters Made to Order." In Paul Ruditis, ed. Buffy the Vampire Slayer: *The Watcher's Guide*, Vol. 3. New York: Simon, 2004, pp. 287–292.

4458. Moore, Robert. "How *Buffy* Changed Television." In Mary Alice Money for PopMatters.com, ed. *Joss Whedon: The Complete Companion: The TV Series, the Movies, the Comic Books and More*. London: Titan Books, 2012, pp. 140–153.

4459. _____. "Introduction: Why Cast a Spotlight on Joss Whedon?" In Mary Alice Money for

PopMatters.com, ed. *Joss Whedon: The Complete Companion: The TV Series, the Movies, the Comic Books and More*. London: Titan Books, 2012, pp. 11–21. An earlier version titled "Why Cast a Spotlight on Joss Whedon?" appeared as part of PopMatters.com's *Spotlight: Joss Whedon*, originally posted on March 3, 2011.

4460. _____. "Joss Whedon 101: *Buffy the Vampire Slayer*." In Mary Alice Money for PopMatters.com, ed. *Joss Whedon: The Complete Companion: The TV Series, the Movies, the Comic Books and More*. London: Titan Books, 2012, pp. 25–28. An earlier version appeared as part of PopMatters.com's *Spotlight: Joss Whedon*, originally posted on March 7, 2011.

4461. Moorman, Jennifer. "'Kinda Gay': Queer Cult Fandom and Willow's (Bi)Sexuality in *Buffy the Vampire Slayer*." In Jes Battis, ed. *Supernatural Youth: The Rise of the Teen Hero in Literature and Popular Culture*. Lanham, MD: Lexington Books, 2011, pp. 102–115.

4462. Morehouse, Lyda. "Romancing the Vampire and Other Shiny Bits." In Lynne M. Thomas and Deborah Stanish, eds. *Whedonistas! A Celebration of the Worlds of Joss Whedon by the Women Who Love Them*. Des Moines, IA: Mad Norwegian Press, 2011, pp. 100–106.

4463. Morris, Barry. "Round Up the Usable Suspects: Archetypal Characters in the Study of Popular Culture." In Jodie A. Kreider and Meghan K. Winchell, eds. Buffy *in the Classroom: Essays on Teaching with the Vampire Slayer*. Jefferson, NC: McFarland & Company, 2010, pp. 46–60.

4464. Morris, Frances E. "Willow's Electric Arcs: Moral Choices Sparked by Connections." In Emily Dial-Driver, Sally Emmons-Featherston, Jim Ford, and Carolyn Anne Taylor, ed. *The Truth of* Buffy: *Essays on Fiction Illuminating Reality*. Jefferson, NC: McFarland & Company, 2008, pp. 83–95. A paper originally presented as "Electric Arcs: Character Development in *Buffy*" at the 28th Annual Southwest/Texas PCA/ACA Conference, Albuquerque, NM, February 14–17, 2007.

4465. Morse, Joan. "Dawn as Ophelia: The Conflicting Femininities of *Buffy the Vampire Slayer*." *Watcher Junior: The Journal of Undergraduate Research in Buffy Studies* 4, 1 [4] (November 2009). Posted at: http://www.whedonstudies.tv/.

4466. Moss, Gabrielle. "From the Valley to the Hellmouth: Buffy's Transition from Film to Television." *Slayage: The Online International Journal of Buffy Studies* 1, 2 [2] (March 2001 Posted at: http://www.whedonstudies.tv/.

4467. Muir, John Kenneth. "Once More, with Feeling." In John Kenneth Muir. *Singing a New Tune: The Rebirth of the Modern Film Musical, from* Evita *to* De-Lovely *and Beyond.* New York: Applause, 2005, pp. 276–282.

4468. Mukherjea, Ananya. "'When you kiss me, I want to die': Gothic Relationships and Identity *Buffy the Vampire Slayer.*" *Slayage: The Online International Journal of Buffy Studies* 7, 2 [26] (Spring 2008). Posted at: http://www.whedon studies.tv/. A paper originally presented as "'When you kiss me, I want to die': Gothic Relationships and Social Taboos on *Buffy the Vampire Slayer*" at SC3: The Slayage Conference on the Whedon-verses, Henderson State College, Arkadelphia, AR, June 5–8, 2008.

4469. Muntersbjorn, Madeline M. "Pluralism, Pragmatism, and Pals: The Slayer Subverts the Science Wars." In James B. South, ed. Buffy *and Philosophy: Fear and Trembling in Sunnydale.* Chicago: Open Court, 2003, pp. 91–102.

4470. Murphy, Bernice M. "'Ah, but Underneath...': *Buffy the Vampire Slayer* and *Desperate Housewives.*" In Bernice M. Murphy. *The Suburban Gothic in American Popular Culture.* New York: Palgrave MacMillan, 2009, pp. 166–192.

4471. Murphy, Kevin Andrew. "Unseen Horrors & Shadowy Manipulations." In Glenn Yeffeth, ed. *Seven Seasons of* Buffy: *Science Fiction and Fantasy Writers Discuss Their Favorite Television Show.* Dallas, TX: Benbella Books, 2003, pp. 137–151.

4472. Murphy, Kylie. "Choosing Cordelia: Re-Vamping Feminism: The Third Wave of the Small Screen." In Kylie Murphy. *Bitch: The Politics of Angry Women.* Perth, Western Australia: Murdoch University, Ph.D. dissertation, 2002. pp. 60–100.

4473. Murray, Faye, and Holly Golding. "Women Who Hate Women: Female Competition in *Buffy the Vampire Slayer.*" In Mary Alice Money for PopMatters.com, ed. *Joss Whedon: The Complete Companion: The TV Series, the Movies, the Comic Books and More.* London: Titan Books, 2012, pp. 83–94. An earlier version appeared as part of Pop-Matters.com's *Spotlight: Joss Whedon,* originally posted on March 9, 2011.

4474. Murray, Susan. "I Know What You Did Last Summer: Sarah Michelle Gellar and Cross-Over Teen Stardom." In Elana Levine and Lisa Parks, eds. *Undead TV: Essays on* Buffy the Vampire Slayer. Durham, NC: Duke University Press, 2007, pp. 42–55.

4475. Musgrove, Kristie L. *Lilith Rising: American Gothic Fiction and the Evolution of the Female Hero in Sarah Wood's* Julia and the Illuminated Baron, *E.D.E.N. Southworth's* The Hidden Hand, *and Joss Whedon's* Buffy the Vampire Slayer. Arlington: University of Texas at Arlington, M.A. thesis, 2008. 71 pp. Large format. Posted at: http://dspace.uta.edu/bitstream/handle/10106/1096/umi-uta-2210.pdf?sequence=1.

4476. Myers, Brian. *An Exploration of Female Superheroes in Television.* Tallahassee: Florida State University, BA honors thesis, 2006. 77 pp. Large format. Posted at: http://digitool.fcla.edu///exlibris/dtl/d3_1/apache_media/L2V4bGlic mlzL2R0bC9kM18xL2FwYWNoZV9tZWRp YS8xNjA4MjQ=.pdf.

4477. Naficy, Siamak Tundra, and Karthik Panchanathan. "Buffy the Vampire Dater." In Joy Davidson with Leah Wilson, eds. *The Psychology of Joss Whedon: An Unauthorized Exploration of Buffy, Angel, and* Firefly. Dallas, TX: Benbella Books, 2007, pp. 141–153.

4478. Negus, Keith. "Foreword." In Paul Attinello, Janet K. Halfyard, and Vanessa Knights, eds. *Music, Sound, and Silence in* Buffy the Vampire Slayer. Farnham, Surrey, UK: Ashgate Publishing, 2010, pp. xv–xviii.

4479. Nel, David. "'Does the Phrase 'Vampire Slayer' Mean Anything to You?': The Discursive Construction of the Just Woman Warrior Trope in Joss Whedon's *Buffy the Vampire Slayer* TV Series." In Jes Battis, ed. *Supernatural Youth: The Rise of the Teen Hero in Literature and Popular Culture.* Lanham, MD: Lexington Books, 2011, pp. 65–79.

4480. Nelson, Michael Curtis. "Pedagogy of the Possessed: Teaching and Learning in *Buffy.*" In Mary Alice Money for PopMatters.com, ed. *Joss Whedon: The Complete Companion: The TV Series, the Movies, the Comic Books and More.* London: Titan Books, 2012, pp. 69–75. An earlier version appeared as part of PopMatters.com's *Spotlight: Joss Whedon,* originally posted on March 13, 2011.

4481. Nevitt, Lucy, and Andy William Smith. "'Family Blood Is Always the Sweetest': The Gothic Transgressions of Angel/Angelus." In Angela Ndalianis and Felicity Colman, ed. *Special Issue on* Buffy the Vampire Slayer. *Refractory: A Journal of Entertainment Media* 2 (2003). Posted at: http://refractory.unimelb.edu.au/2003/03/18/vol2/.

4482. Newsom, Victoria A. *Girls of Power: "Girl Power" in* Buffy the Vampire Slayer, *Sailor*

Moon, *and Queen Amidala from* Star Wars Episode One: The Phantom Menace. Bowling Green, OH: Bowling Green State University, M.A. thesis, 2000. 75 pp. Large format.

4483. Nichols, Tamara J. *Hero Unveiled: Transformation of Myth through* Buffy the Vampire Slayer. Carpinteria, CA: Pacifica Graduate Institute, Ph.D. dissertation, 2008. 172 pp. Large format.

4484. Nicol, Rhonda. "'When you kiss me, I want to die': Arrested Feminism in *Buffy the Vampire Slayer* and the *Twilight* Series." In Giselle Liza Anatol. *Bringing Light to* Twilight: *Perspectives on a Pop Culture Phenomenon*. New York: Palgrave Macmillan, 2011, pp. 113–24.

4485. Niebur, Louis. "'What's my melody?' Music and the Deployment of Genre in *Buffy the Vampire Slayer*." In Paul Attinello, Janet K. Halfyard, and Vanessa Knights, eds. *Music, Sound, and Silence in* Buffy the Vampire Slayer. Farnham, Surrey, UK: Ashgate Publishing, 2010, pp. 33–44.

4486. Noble, Julia F. *Slaying for Keeps: Gender, Genre, and Saving the World in* Buffy the Vampire Slayer. Tuscaloosa: University of Alabama, M.A. thesis, 2000. 80 pp. Large format.

4487. Norris, Gregory. *The Q Guide to Buffy* the *Vampire Slayer: Stuff You Didn't Even Know You Wanted to Know...About Buffy, Angel, the Big Bads, and the Show That Wouldn't Die*. New York: Allyson Books, 2008. 188 pp. tp.

4488. Nuzum, Eric. "I May Be Dead, but I'm Still Pretty." In Eric Nuzum. *The Dead Travel Fast: Stalking Vampires from Nosferatu to Count Chocula*. New York: Thomas Dunne Books, 2007, pp. 186–216.

4489. Nylin, Sören. "Mad, Bad Scientists and Cute, Curious Magicians: The Quest for Knowledge in *Buffy* and the Whedonverse." *Slayage: The Online International Journal of Buffy Studies* 7, 4 [28] (Summer 2009). Posted at: http://www. whedonstudies.tv/.

4490. O'Connor, Tom. "'It's Rather Poetic': *Buffy the Vampire Slayer* & Deleuze's Becoming-Art." In Tom O'Connor. *Poetic Acts and New Media*. Lanham, MD: University Press of America, 2007, pp. 107–144.

4491. Oliver, Ashley. *Queer Sex Gods or Patriarchs with Fangs? Gender and Sexuality in Modern Vampire Narratives* Buffy the Vampire Slayer, True Blood, *and* Twilight. Waterville, ME: Colby College, BA honors thesis, 2012.

4492. Olson, Wendy. "Enlightenment Rhetoric in *Buffy the Vampire Slayer*: The Ideological Implications of Worldviews in the Buffyverse." *Slayage: The Online International Journal of Buffy Studies* 7, 2 [26] (Spring 2008). Posted at: http:// www.whedonstudies.tv/.

4493. O'Malley, Cynthia Ryan. "Bringing the Power Together: Willow's Four Personalities." Unpublished paper written for undergraduate course, Middle Tennessee State University, Murfreesboro, TN, 2004.

4494. _____. *'These things are Shadow-casters. You put them in motion and they tell you a story': An exploration of Jungian Shadow work in* Buffy the Vampire Slayer. Murfreesboro: Middle Tennessee State University, M.A. thesis, 2007. 130 pp. Large format.

4495. Onciul-Omelus, Jamie. Buffy the Vampire Slayer *as Shero: Re-Defining the Mythological Hero*. Prince George, BC, CA: University of Northern British Columbia, M.A. thesis, 2005. 97 pp. Large format.

4496. O'Neill, William L. "Interlude: *Buffy the Vampire Slayer*." In William L. O'Neill. *A Bubble in Time: America During the Interwar Years, 1989–2001*. Chicago: Ivan R. Dee, 2009, pp. 235–242.

4497. Ono, Kent A. "To Be a Vampire on *Buffy the Vampire Slayer*: Race and ('Other') Socially Marginalizing Positions on Horror TV." In Elyce Rae Helford, ed. *Fantasy Girls: Gender in the New Universe of Science Fiction and Fantasy Television*. Lanham, MD: Rowman & Littlefield, 2000, pp. 163–186.

4498. O'Reilly, Julie Dianne. *Bewitched Again: Supernaturally Powerful Women on Television, 1996–2011*. Jefferson, NC: McFarland & Company, 2013. 248 pp. tp. Not a book specifically about *Buffy the Vampire Slayer*, but the author refers to the show throughout the text.

4499. _____. *Power versus Empowerment: A Textual Analysis of Television's Superpowered Women, 1996–2005*. Bowling Green, OH: Bowling Green State University, Ph.D. dissertation, 2005. 245 pp. Large format.

4500. _____. "The Wonder Woman Precedent: Female (Super)Heroism on Trial." *Journal of American Culture* 28, 3 (September 2005): 273–283. Posted at: http://cuwhist.files.wordpress. com/2012/03/the-wonder-woman-precedent-female-superheroism-on-trial.pdf.

4501. Orth, Cameron. "'Joss Whedon' as Cult *Auteur*: A Case Study in Convergent Production." Unpublished paper written for film course, Dartmouth College, Hanover, NH, 2012. 15 pp. Posted at: http://www.academia.edu/3464642/ Joss_Whedon_as_Cult_Auteur.

4502. _____. "Postmodern Television: Finding Noir TV in Unexpected Places." Unpublished paper written for film course, Dartmouth College, Hanover, NH, [2012(?)]. 14 pp. Posted at: http://www.academia.edu/3464662/Postmodern_ Television_finding_noir_tv_in_unexpected_places.

4503. Ostow, Micol. "'Chosen': A Postmodern Postmortem on *Buffy* as Contemporary Icon." In Paul Ruditis, ed. Buffy the Vampire Slayer: *The Watcher's Guide,* Vol. 3. New York: Simon, 2004, pp. 351–356.

4504. _____. "Why I Love *Buffy.*" *Sojourner: The Women's Forum* 24, 3 (1998): 20–35.

4505. Ouellette, Jennifer. *The Physics of the Buffyverse.* New York: Penguin, 2006. 325 pp. tp.

4506. Overbey, Karen Eileen, and Lahney Preston-Matto. "Staking in Tongues: Speech Act as Weapon in *Buffy.*" In Rhonda V. Wilcox and David Lavery, eds. *Fighting the Forces: What's at Stake in* Buffy the Vampire Slayer. Lanham, MD: Rowman & Littlefield, 2002, pp. 73–84.

4507. Overstreet, Deborah Wilson. "Welcome to the Buffyverse: Vampires, High School, and the Hellmouth." In Deborah Wilson Overstreet. *Not Your Mother's Vampire: Vampires in Young Adult Fiction.* Lanham, MD: Scarecrow Press, 2006, pp. 109–25.

4508. Oviedo, Marilda. *A Qualitative Study of Typology in* Buffy the Vampire Slayer *Fanfiction.* Lubbock: Texas Tech University, M.A. thesis, 2007. 99 pp. Large format. Posted at: http://repositories. tdl.org/ttu-ir/bitstream/handle/2346/14528/ Oviedo_Marilda_Thesis.pdf?sequence=1.

4509. Owen, A. Susan. "*Buffy the Vampire Slayer*: Vampires, Postmodernity, and Postfeminism." *Journal of Popular Film & Television* 27, 2 (1999): 24–31.

4510. P, Kathryne. "The Nature and Role of Camp in *Buffy the Vampire Slayer* and *Angel.*" *All Slay* 3 (2004).

4511. Palmer, Lorrie. "Ruby Red and Emerald Green: The Queer Demon Diva of My Dreams." *Camera Obscura* 23 (2008): 194–199.

4512. Palmer, Louis H. "Buffy Rules." In Louis H. Palmer. *Vampires in the New World.* Santa Barbara, CA: Praeger, 2013, pp. 99–105.

4513. Parke, Faith. "'I Hope Evil Takes MasterCard': Faith the Vampire Slayer and the Image of the Bad Girl in Society." *Watcher Junior: The Undergraduate Journal of Whedon Studies* 5, 1 [6] (July 2011). Posted at: http://www.watcherjunior. tv/.

4514. Parks, Lisa. "Brave New Buffy: Rethinking 'TV Violence.'" In Mark Jancovich and James Lyons, ed. *Quality Popular Television: Cult TV, the Industry and Fans.* London: British Film Institute [BFI], 2003, pp. 118–133. A paper originally presented as "Brave New Buffy: Rethinking TV Violence and Sexuality" at Console-ing Passions: Television, Video and Feminism Conference, University of Notre Dame, South Bend, IN, May 11–14, 2000.

4515. Parks, Todd P. "Unthinkable Relationships: Vampire/Slayer and HIV Positive/Negative." In Erin B. Waggoner, ed. *Sexual Rhetoric in the Works of Joss Whedon: New Essays.* Jefferson, NC: McFarland & Company, 2010, pp. 18–30. A paper originally presented at the 30th Annual Southwest/Texas PCA/ACA Conference, Albuquerque, NM, February 25–28, 2009.

4516. Parnell, Will. "Reconstruction: Meltdown in the Midst of Beauty." In Will Parnell, ed. *Early Childhood Education and Phenomenology.* Special issue of *The Indo-Pacific Journal of Phenomenology* (May 2012). Posted at: http://www.ipjp. org/index.php?option=com_jdownloads&Ite mid=318&view=viewdownload&catid=4&cid= 195.

4517. Parpart, Lee. "'Action, Chicks, Everything': On-Line Interviews with Male Fans of *Buffy the Vampire Slayer.*" In Frances Early and Kathleen Kennedy, eds. *Athena's Daughters: Television's New Women Warriors.* Syracuse, NY: Syracuse University Press, 2003, pp. 78–91.

4518. Parrish, Juli J. *Inventing a Universe: Reading and Writing Internet Fan Fiction.* Pittsburgh, PA: University of Pittsburgh, Ph.D. dissertation, 2007. 196 pp. Large format.

4519. Pasley, Jeffrey L. "Old Familiar Vampires: Radicalism and Liberalism in the Politics of the Buffyverse." In James B. South, ed. Buffy *and Philosophy: Fear and Trembling in Sunnydale.* Chicago: Open Court, 2003, pp. 254–267. This paper is a condensed version of a longer paper, "You Can't Pin a Good Slayer Down: The Politics,

If Any, of *Buffy the Vampire Slayer.*" 2003. It has been Posted at: the author's website, http://www.pasleybrothers.com/jeff/writings/buffy.htm.

4520. Pateman, Matthew. *The Aesthetics of Culture in* Buffy the Vampire Slayer. Jefferson, NC: McFarland & Company, 2006. 288 pp. tp.

4521. _____. "Introduction." In Matthew Pateman, ed. Buffy *and Aesthetics.* Special Issue of *Slayage: The Online International Journal of Buffy Studies* 6, 2 [22] (Winter 2006). Posted at: http://www.whedonstudies.tv/.

4522. _____. "Restless Readings: Involution, Aesthetics, and *Buffy.*" *Slayage: The Online International Journal of Buffy Studies* 5, 3 [19] (February 2006). Posted at: http://www.whedonstudies.tv/. An excerpt from *The Aesthetics of Culture in* Buffy the Vampire Slayer.

4523. _____. "'That Was Nifty': Willow Rosenberg Saves the World in *Buffy the Vampire Slayer.*" *Shofar: An Interdisciplinary Journal of Jewish Studies* 25, 4 (Summer 2007): 64–77.

4524. _____. "'You say tomato': Englishness in *Buffy the Vampire Slayer.*" *Cercles: Revue Pluridisciplinaire du Monde Anglophone* 8 (2003): 103–113. Posted at: http://www.cercles.com/n8/pateman.pdf.

4525. Paule, Michele. "Buffy's Special Gift to Girls." *The Times Educational Supplement* no. 4578 (April 9, 2004): 17.

4526. _____. "You're on My Campus Buddy! Sovereign and Disciplinary Power at Sunnydale High." *Slayage: The Online International Journal of Buffy Studies* 4, 3 [15]] (December 2004). Posted at: http://www.whedonstudies.tv/. A paper originally presented at the Slayage Conference on *Buffy the Vampire Slayer*, Nashville, TN, May 27–30, 2004.

4527. _____, **and Laura Davison.** "Superheroes and Superlearning: Enriching the Lower School Curriculum with *Buffy the Vampire Slayer.*" *A Project from the Westminster Institute of Education, Oxford Brookes University* website (undated). Posted at: http://cs3.brookes.ac.uk/schools/education/rescon/Buffy%20Brookes.pdf.

4528. Payne-Mulliken, Susan Marie. *The Power of Metaphor: The Construction of Feminism in* Buffy the Vampire Slayer*'s Final Season.* San Diego, CA, San Diego State University, M.A. thesis, 2004. 108 pp. Large format.

4529. _____, **and Valerie Renegar.** "Buffy Never Goes It Alone: The Rhetorical Construc-

tion of Sisterhood in the Final Season." In Kevin K. Durand, ed. Buffy *Meets the Academy: Essays on the Episodes and Scripts as Texts.* Jefferson, NC: McFarland & Company, 2009, pp. 57–77. A paper originally presented by Susan Marie Payne-Mulliken as "Buffy Never Goes It Alone: The Rhetorical Construction of Feminism in *Buffy the Vampire Slayer's* Final Season" at SC2: The Slayage Conference on the Whedonverses, Gordon College, Barnesville, GA, May 25–28, 2006.

4530. Pearl, Michael S. *"All That We Become": Renegotiating Vampire/Performative Masculinity in* Buffy the Vampire Slayer *and* Angel. Gainesville: University of Florida, M.A. thesis, 2004. 60 pp. Large format. Posted at: http://etd.fcla.edu/UF/UFE0004891/pearl_m.pdf.

4531. Pearson, Lars, and Christa Dickson. *Redeemed: The Unauthorized Guide to Angel.* Des Moines, IA: Mad Norwegian Press, 2006. 361 pp. tp.

4532. Peeling, Caitlin, and Meaghan Scanlon. "'What's More Real? A Sick Girl in an Institution...or Some Kind of Supergirl?' The Question of Madness in 'Normal Again,' a Feminist Reading." A paper presented at the Slayage Conference on *Buffy the Vampire Slayer*, Nashville, TN, May 27–30, 2004. Posted at: http://www.slayageonline.com/SCBtVS_Archive/.

4533. Peloff, Amy, and David Boarder Giles. "'Welcome to the Hellmouth': Harnessing the Power of Fandom in the Classroom." In Jennifer Kate Stuller, ed. *Fan Phenomena:* Buffy the Vampire Slayer. Chicago: Intellect, 2013, pp. 74–83.

4534. Pelucir, Talis, comp. *The Unofficial* Buffy the Vampire Slayer *Internet Guide 1999.* Port Orchard, WA: Lightning Rod Unlimited, 1999. 27 pp. pb. Stables. Rev. ed. as: *The Unofficial Buffy the Vampire Slayer New and Improved Guide.* Port Orchard, WA: Lightning Rod Unlimited, 1999. 33 pp. Staples. Note. This publish-on-demand book was updated after every 100 copies sold.

4535. Pender, Patricia. "Andrew and the Homoerotics of Evil." In Erin B. Waggoner, ed. *Sexual Rhetoric in the Works of Joss Whedon: New Essays.* Jefferson, NC: McFarland & Company, 2010, pp. 93–105.

4536. _____. "'I'm Buffy and You're...History': The Postmodern Politics of *Buffy the Vampire Slayer.*" In Rhonda V. Wilcox and David Lavery, eds. *Fighting the Forces: What's at Stake in* Buffy the Vampire Slayer. Lanham, MD: Rowman & Littlefield, 2002, pp. 35–44.

4537. _____. "'Kicking Ass Is Comfort Food': Buffy as Third Wave Feminist Icon." In Stacy Gillis, Gillian Howie, and Rebecca Munford, eds. *Third Wave Feminism: A Critical Exploration.* New York: Palgrave-McMillan, 2004, pp. 164–174. A paper originally presented at Staking a Claim: Exploring the Global Reach of *Buffy*, University of South Australia, Adelaide, Australia, July 22, 2003.

4538. _____. "'Where do we go from here?' *Buffy* Studies and *Slayage* 2006." *Slayage: The Online International Journal of Buffy Studies* 6, 1 [21] (Fall 2006). Posted at: http://www.whedonstudies. tv/.

4539. _____. "Whose Revolution Has Been Televised? *Buffy*'s Transnational Sisterhood of Slayers." A paper presented at the Slayage Conference on *Buffy the Vampire Slayer*, Nashville, TN, May 27–30, 2004. Posted at: http://www.slayage online.com/SCBtVS_Archive/.

4540. Pensky, Nathan. "*Buffy the Vampire Slayer* in the Fantasy Canon." In Mary Alice Money for PopMatters.com, ed. *Joss Whedon: The Complete Companion: The TV Series, the Movies, the Comic Books and More.* London: Titan Books, 2012, pp. 60–69. An earlier version appeared as part of PopMatters.com's *Spotlight: Joss Whedon*, originally posted on March 8, 2011.

4541. _____. "Trickster-Heroes in 'Buffy' and 'Sir Gawain and the Green Knight.'" PopMatters. com (September 8, 2011). Posted at: http://www. popmatters.com/column/147073-trickster-heroes-in-buffy-and-sir-gawain-and-the-green-knight/.

4542. Perdigao, Lisa K. "'I hear it's best to play along': The Poststructuralist Turn in *Buffy the Vampire Slayer.*" *Slayage: The Journal of the Whedon Studies Association* 8, 4 [32] (Winter 2011). Posted at: http://www.whedonstudies.tv/.

4543. _____. "'This one's broken': Rebuilding Whedonbots and Reprogramming the Whedonverse." In Cynthea Masson and Rhonda V. Wilcox, eds. *Fantasy Is Not Their Purpose: Joss Whedon's Dollhouse.* Special Issue of *Slayage: The Journal of the Whedon Studies Association* 8, 2–3 [30–31] (Summer/Fall 2010). Posted at: http://www.whedon studies.tv/. A paper originally presented as "'This one's broken': Rebuilding Really Real Bots in the Whedonverse" at SC4: The Slayage Conference on the Whedonverses, Flagler College, St. Augustine, FL, June 3–6, 2010.

4544. Peristere, Loni. "Mutant Enemy U." In Jane Espenson with Leah Wilson, ed. *Serenity Found: More Unauthorized Essays on Joss Whedon's*

Firefly Universe. Dallas, TX: Benbella Books, 2007, pp. 117–129.

4545. Perry, David. "Marti Noxon: Buffy's Other Genius." In Lynne Y. Edwards, Elizabeth L. Rambo, and James B. South, eds. *Buffy Goes Dark: Essays on the Final Two Seasons of Buffy the Vampire Slayer on Television.* Jefferson, NC: McFarland & Company, 2009, pp. 13–22. A paper originally presented at the Slayage Conference on *Buffy the Vampire Slayer*, Nashville, TN, May 27–30, 2004.

4546. Perry, Michael Aaron. "My First Time: Theological Diversity, the Rhetoric of Conversion, and *Buffy the Vampire Slayer.*" In U. Melissa Anyiwo and Karoline Szatek-Tudor, eds. Buffy *Conquers the Academy: Conference Papers from the 2009/2010 Popular Culture/American Culture Associations.* Newcastle upon Tyne, UK: Cambridge Scholars Publishing, 2013, pp. 136–148. A paper originally presented in earlier form as "My First Time: Social Media, a Theology of Diversity, and the Rhetoric of Conversation in *Buffy the Vampire Slayer*" at the 2009 PCA/ACA National Conference, New Orleans, LA, April 8–11, 2009.

4547. Peters, Mark. "Getting a Wiggins and Being a Bitca: How Two Items of Slayer Slang Survive on the *Television Without Pity* Message Boards." In Michael Adams, ed. *Beyond Slayer Slang: Pragmatics, Discourse, and Style in* Buffy the Vampire Slayer. Special Issue of *Slayage: The Online International Journal of Buffy Studies* 5, 4 [20] (May 2006). Posted at: http://www.slayageonline.com/.

4548. Petrova, Erma. "'I'm declaring an emergency': Leadership and the State of Exception in *Buffy the Vampire Slayer.*" *Slayage: The Journal of the Whedon Studies Association* 10, 1 [35] (Winter 2013). Posted at: http://www.whedonstudies.tv/. A paper originally presented at SCW5: The Slayage Conference on the Whedonverses, University of British Columbia, Vancouver, British Columbia, July 12–15, 2012.

4549. _____. "'You Cannot Run from Your Darkness.' / 'Who Says I'm Running?': Buffy and the Ownership of Evil." In Angela Ndalianis and Felicity Colman, eds. *Special Issue on* Buffy the Vampire Slayer. *Refractory: A Journal of Entertainment Media* 2 (2003). Posted at: http://refractory. unimelb.edu.au/2003/03/18/vol2/.

4550. Phillips, Maxine. "The 'Buffy Paradigm' Revisited: A Superhero and the War on Terror." *Dissent Magazine* 50, 2 (Spring 2003): 81.

4551. _____. "Standing With or Standing By." *Dissent Magazine* 57, 4 (Fall 2010): 112.

4552. Pia, Kristina. *Ghostly Bodies of Knowledge: Authorship, History Writing and Visual Language in* Buffy the Vampire Slayer. Taipei, Taiwan: National Central University, M.A. thesis, 2010. 78 pp. Large format. Posted at: http://thesis.lib.ncu. edu.tw/ETD-db/ETD-search/view_etd?URN= 951202601.

4553. Pierce, Sarah E. *From Demon to Daimon: A Mythic and Depth Psychological Analysis of the American Hero Vampire.* Carpinteria, CA: Pacifica Graduate Institute, PhD. dissertation, 2011 . 238 pp. Posted at: http://gradworks.umi.com/ 3528240.pdf.

4554. Pittis, Patrick. *Staking Our Gender: A Poststructuralist Analysis of Gender Roles and Identity in* Buffy the Vampire Slayer. Orono: University of Maine, BA honors thesis, 2013. 183 pp. Large format. Posted at: http://digitalcommons.library. umaine.edu/cgi/viewcontent.cgi?article=1104& context=honors.

4555. Playdon, Zoe-Jane. "'The Outsiders' Society': Religious Imagery in *Buffy the Vampire Slayer.*" *Slayage: The Online International Journal of Buffy Studies* 2, 1 [5] (May 2002). Posted at: http://www.whedonstudies.tv/.

4556. _____. "'What You Are, What's to Come': Feminisms, Citizenship and the Divine." In Roz Kaveney, ed.. *Reading the Vampire Slayer: An Unofficial Critical Companion to* Buffy *and* Angel. New York: I. B. Tauris, 2001, pp. 120–147. Rpt. in exp. ed.: New York: I. B. Tauris, 2004, pp. 156–194.

4557. Pomeroy, Arthur J. "Hymns to the Ancient Words in (the) Buffyverse." In Arthur J. Pomeroy. *"Then It Was Destroyed by the Volcano": The Ancient World in Film and on Television.* London: Duckworth, 2008, pp. 13–28.

4558. _____. "It's a Man's, Man's, Man's World—Except for Xena and Buffy." In Arthur J. Pomeroy. *'Then It Was Destroyed by the Volcano': The Ancient World in Film and on Television.* London: Duckworth, 2008, pp. 113–14.

4559. Poole, Carol. "'Darn Your Sinister Attraction!': Narcissism in Buffy's Affair with Spike." In Joy Davidson with Leah Wilson, ed. *The Psychology of Joss Whedon: An Unauthorized Exploration of* Buffy, Angel, *and* Firefly. Dallas, TX: Benbella Books, 2007, pp. 21–34.

4560. Porter, Heather M. "Brains vs. Brawn: An Examination of the Use of Intelligence and Violence by Villains in *Buffy the Vampire Slayer.*" In U. Melissa Anyiwo and Karoline Szatek-Tudor, eds.

Buffy *Conquers the Academy: Conference Papers from the 2009/2010 Popular Culture/American Culture Associations.* Newcastle upon Tyne, UK: Cambridge Scholars Publishing, 2013, pp. 60–75. A paper originally presented in earlier form at the 2009 PCA/ACA National Conference, New Orleans, LA, April 8–11, 2009.

4561. _____. "Watching *Buffy*: An Angian Examination of *Buffy* Watchers." A paper presented as "Buffy Lives: An Angian Examination of *Buffy* Watchers" at the Slayage Conference on *Buffy the Vampire Slayer*, Nashville, TN, May 27–30, 2004. Posted at: http://www.slayageonline.com/ SCBtVS_Archive/.

4562. Porter, Lynnette. "Nathan Fillion Misbehaves All Across the Whedonverse." In Mary Alice Money for PopMatters.com, ed. *Joss Whedon: The Complete Companion: The TV Series, the Movies, the Comic Books and More.* London: Titan Books, 2012, pp. 298–303. An earlier version appeared as part of PopMatters.com's *Spotlight: Joss Whedon*, originally posted on March 31, 2011.

4563. _____. "The World of Joss Whedon." In Lynnette Porter. *Tarnished Heroes, Charming Villains and Modern Monsters: Science Fiction in Shades of Gray on 21st Century Television.* Jefferson, NC: McFarland & Company, 2010, pp. 133–150.

4564. Porter, Nicole. *In Search of the Slayer: Audience Negotiation of* Buffy the Vampire Slayer. Portland, OR: Concordia University, M.A. thesis, 2004. 123 pp. Large format.

4565. Porter, Patrick J. "Buffy vs. Dracula: Intertextuality, Carnival and Cult." *Refractory: A Journal of Entertainment Media* 9 (2006). Posted at: http://refractory.unimelb.edu.au/2006/07/ 04/refractory-volume-9-2006/.

4566. _____. *Stories from the Buffyverse: Intertextuality, Temporality and the Cult Fandom of* Buffy the Vampire Slayer. Melbourne, Aust.: University of Melbourne, M.A.thesis, 2007. 131 pp. Large format.

4567. _____. "The Uncomfortable Cult: How Novelty and Subverted Expectations Generate a Cult Following in Contemporary Fantastic Television." *Refractory: A Journal of Entertainment Media* 1 (2002). Posted at: http://refractory. unimelb.edu.au/2002/08/06/vol1/.

4568. Postrel, Virginia. "Why *Buffy* Kicked Ass: The Deep Meaning of TV's Favorite Vampire Slayer." *Reason Online: Free Minds and Free Markets.* (August-September 2003). Posted at: http:// reason.com/archives/2003/08/01/why-buffy-kicked-ass.

4569. Potts, Donna. "Convents, Claddagh Rings, and Even the Book of Kells: Representing the Irish in *Buffy the Vampire Slayer.*" *Studies in Media & Information Literacy Education (SIMILE)* 3, 2 (2003). Posted at: http://utpjournals.metapress.com/content/x591886k8263t988/.

4570. Powroz, Jennifer. *The Hero's Quest of Spike in* Buffy the Vampire Slayer: *An Analysis of Hybridized Gender and the Jungian Shadow.* Ottawa, ON, CA: University of Ottawa, M.A. thesis, 2008.

4571. Price, Jessica. "The Role of Masculinity in *Buffy the Vampire Slayer.*" In Erin B. Waggoner, ed. *Sexual Rhetoric in the Works of Joss Whedon: New Essays.* Jefferson, NC: McFarland & Company, 2010, pp. 215–225.

4572. Q, Shathley. "Chronological Bibliography of Print Comics Written by Joss Whedon." In Mary Alice Money for PopMatters.com, ed. *Joss Whedon: The Complete Companion: The TV Series, the Movies, the Comic Books and More.* London: Titan Books, 2012, pp. 359–360.

4573. Quadfasel, Lars. "Frankfurt School at Sunnydale High: *Buffy the Vampire Slayer* and the Critique of Culture Industry." A paper presented at *Buffy* Hereafter: From the Whedonverse to the Whedonesque: An Interdisciplinary Conference on the Work of Joss Whedon and its Aftereffects, Istanbul, Turkey, October 17–19, 2007. This paper was late published in German as "Frankfurt School, Sunnydale High: Allegorisierung der Kulturindustrie in *Buffy the Vampire Slayer.*" *Horror als Alltag: Texte zu* Buffy the Vampire Slayer. Ed. Annika Beckmann, et al. Berlin: Vebrecher, 2010. 55–84.

4574. R., Skippy [pseudonym of John Rutledge]. "The Door Theologian of the Year." *The Door Magazine* 183 (2002).

4575. Rabian, Brian, and Michael Wolff. "How Buffy Learned to Confront Her Fears...and Lived to Tell About It." In Joy Davidson with Leah Wilson, ed. *The Psychology of Joss Whedon: An Unauthorized Exploration of* Buffy, Angel, *and* Firefly. Dallas, TX: Benbella Books, 2007, pp. 79–90.

4576. Raha, Maria. "Angels, Aliens, and Ass-Kicking." In Maria Raha, *Hellions: Pop Culture's Women Rebels.* Berkeley: Seal Press, 2008, pp. 214–216.

4577. Ramachandran, Nandini. "The Big Bad Universe: Good and Evil According to Joss Whedon." In Mary Alice Money for PopMatters.com, ed. *Joss Whedon: The Complete Companion:*

The TV Series, the Movies, the Comic Books and More. London: Titan Books, 2012, pp. 75–82. An earlier version appeared as part of PopMatters.com's *Spotlight: Joss Whedon*, originally posted on April 7, 2011.

4578. Rambo, Elizabeth L. "I've Got a Little List, or, 'You Guys Wanna Team Up and Take Over Sunnydale U?'" In Mary Kirby-Diaz, ed. *Buffy and Angel Conquer the Internet: Essays on Online Fandom.* Jefferson, NC: McFarland & Company, 2009, pp. 7–17. A paper originally presented at the Slayage Conference on *Buffy the Vampire Slayer*, Nashville, TN, May 27–30, 2004.

4579. _____. "'Lessons' for Season Seven of *Buffy the Vampire Slayer.*" *Slayage: The Online International Journal of Buffy Studies* 3, 3–4 [11–12] (April 2004). Posted at: http://www.whedonstudies.tv/.

4580. _____. "'Queen C' in Boys' Town: Killing the Angel in Angel's House." *Slayage: The Online International Journal of Buffy Studies* 6, 3 [23] (Spring 2007). Posted at: http://www.whedonstudies.tv/. A paper originally presented as "'Queen C' Goes to Boys' Town, or, Killing the Angel in Angel's House" at SC2: The Slayage Conference on the Whedonverses, Gordon College, Barnesville, GA, May 25–28, 2006.

4581. _____. "Yeats' Entropic Gyre and Season Six." In Lynne Y. Edwards, Elizabeth L. Rambo, and James B. South, eds. *Buffy Goes Dark: Essays on the Final Two Seasons of* Buffy the Vampire Slayer *on Television.* Jefferson, NC: McFarland & Company, 2009, pp. 167–182. A paper originally presented at Blood, Text and Fears: Reading Around *Buffy the Vampire Slayer*, University of East Anglia, October 19–20, 2002.

4582. Ramlow, Todd R. "'I Killed Tara': Desire and Death on *Buffy.*" PopMatters.com (June 4, 2002). Posted at: http://www.popmatters.com/review/buffy-the-vampire-slayer2/.

4583. Ramsland, Katherine M. "Body Count." In Katerine M. Ramsland. *The Science of Vampires.* New York: Berkley Boulevard, 2002, pp. 154–174.

4584. _____. "Everything You Even Wanted to Know About Vampire Sex but Were Afraid to Ask." In Kateriene M. Ramsland. *The Science of Vampires.* New York: Berkley Boulevard, 2002, pp. 222–246.

4585. Randell-Moon, Holly. "Being a Nerd and Negotiating Intelligence in *Buffy the Vampire Slayer.*" In Lisa Holderman, ed. *Common Sense: In-*

telligence as Presented on Popular Television. Lanham, MD: Lexington Books, 2008, pp. 173–186.

4586. _____. *"Occasionally, I'm Called Callous and Strange": Famine Nobilis and the Feminine as Hero in* Buffy the Vampire Slayer. Macquarie Park, Aust.: Macquarie University, M.A. thesis, 2004.

4587. Rauch, Stephen. "When 'Until the End of the World' Really Means It: Friendship, Love, and Spiritual Warfare in the Buffyverse and in Garth Ennis' and Steve Dillon's *Preacher.*" A paper presented at the Slayage Conference on *Buffy the Vampire Slayer*, Nashville, TN, May 27–30, 2004. Posted at: http://www.slayageonline.com/SCBtVS_Archive/.

4588. Rayner, Philip, Peter Wall, and Stephen Kruger. "Buffy and Her Fans." In Philip Rayner, Peter Wall, and Stephen Kruger. *Media Studies: The Essential Resources.* New York: Routledge, 2004, pp. 146–157.

4589. Rebaza, Claudia. "The Problematic Definition of 'Fan': A Survey of Fannish Involvement in the Buffyverse." In Mary Kirby-Diaz, ed. *Buffy and Angel Conquer the Internet: Essays on Online Fandom.* Jefferson, NC: McFarland & Company, 2009, pp. 147–171.

4590. Reed, Eric. "The Case for Faith: The Rogue Vampire Slayer's Search for Identity." *Watcher Junior: The Journal of Undergraduate Research in Buffy Studies* 3, 1 [3] (September 2007). Posted at: http://www.whedonstudies.tv/.

4591. Reed, Joseph W. "For a Newer Rite is Here: *Buffy the Vampire Slayer.*" In Angela Ndalianis and Felicity Colman, eds. *Special Issue on* Buffy the Vampire Slayer. *Refractory: A Journal of Entertainment Media* 2 (2003). Posted at: http://refractory.unimelb.edu.au/2003/03/18/vol2/.

4592. Reese, Jenn. "Something to Sing About." In Lynne M. Thomas and Deborah Stanish, ed. *Whedonistas! A Celebration of the Worlds of Joss Whedon by the Women Who Love Them.* Des Moines, IA: Mad Norwegian Press, 2011, pp. 182–189.

4593. Rein, Katharina. "Archives of Horror: Carriers of Memory in *Buffy the Vampire Slayer.*" In Simon Bacon and Katarzyna Bronk, eds. *Undead Memory: Vampires and Human Memory in Popular Culture.* Bern, Switz.: Peter Lang International Academic Publishers, 2013, pp. 130–56.

4594. Resnick, Laura. "The Good, the Bad, and the Ambivalent." In Glenn Yeffeth, ed. *Seven Seasons of* Buffy: *Science Fiction and Fantasy Writers*

Discuss Their Favorite Television Show. Dallas, TX: Benbella Books, 2003, pp. 54–64.

4595. _____. "That Angel Doesn't Live Here Anymore." In Glenn Yeffeth, ed. *Five Seasons of* Angel: *Science Fiction and Fantasy Writers Discuss Their Favorite Vampire.* Dallas, TX: Benbella Books, 2004, pp. 15–22.

4596. Reynolds, Kimberly. "Introduction: *Buffy*: Icon and Antidote." In Geraldine Brennan, Kevin McCarron, and Kimberly Reynolds. *Frightening Fiction.* London: Continuum, 2001, pp. 14–17.

4597. Richards, Chris. "Dead White People: Another Look at *Buffy the Vampire Slayer.*" In Chris Reynolds. *Forever Young: Essays on Young Adult Fictions.* New York: Peter Lang, 2008, pp. 97–112.

4598. _____. "What Are We? Adolescence, Sex, and Intimacy in *Buffy the Vampire Slayer.*" *Continuum: Journal of Media & Cultural Studies* 18.1 (March 2004): 121–137. Rpt. in Chris Reynolds. *Forever Young: Essays on Young Adult Fictions.* New York: Peter Lang, 2008, pp. 65–82. A paper originally presented as "What Are We? Adolescent Transformations in *Buffy the Vampire Slayer*" at the Annual Meeting of the American Education Research Association, New Orleans, April 2002.

4599. Richardson, J. Michael, and J. Douglas Rabb. *The Existential Joss Whedon: Evil and Human Freedom in* Buffy the Vampire Slayer, Angel, Firefly *and* Serenity. Jefferson, NC: McFarland & Company, 2007. 224 pp. tp.

4600/01. _____. "Myth, Metaphor, Morality and Monsters: The Espenson Factor and Cognitive Science in Joss Whedon's Narrative Love Ethic." *Slayage: The Online International Journal of Buffy Studies* 7, 4 [28] (Summer 2009). Posted at: http://www.whedonstudies.tv/. A paper originally presented in earlier form as "Cognitive Science in *Buffy the Vampire Slayer, Angel, Firefly* and *Serenity*: The Espenson Factor" at the 2008 PCA/ACA National Conference, San Francisco, CA, March 19–22, 2008.

4602. Rickels, Laurence A. "*Buffy the Vampire Slayer.*" In Laurence Rickels. *The Vampire Lectures.* Minneapolis: University of Minnesota Press, 1999, pp. 261–263.

4603. Ricketts, Jeremy R. "Varieties of Conversion: Spiritual Transformation in the Buffyverse." In Anthony R. Mills, John W. Morehead, and J. Ryan Parker, eds. *Joss Whedon and Religion:*

Essays on an Angry Atheist's Explorations of the Sacred. Jefferson, NC: McFarland & Company, 2013. 11–27.

4604. Riess, Jana. *What Would Buffy Do? The Vampire Slayer as Spiritual Guide.* San Francisco: Jossey-Bass, 2004. 182 pp. tp.

4605. Riley, Brendan. "From Sherlock to Angel: The Twenty-First Century Detective." *Journal of Popular Culture* 42, 5 (October 2009): 908–922.

4606. Rilstone, Andrew. "14 June." In Andrew Rilstone. *The Viewer's Tale.* N.p.: the author, 2010, pp. 134–138.

4607. Robinson, Jaala. "Joss Giveth." In Lynne M. Thomas and Deborah Stanish, ed. *Whedonistas! A Celebration of the Worlds of Joss Whedon by the Women Who Love Them.* Des Moines, IA: Mad Norwegian Press, 2011, pp. 124–130.

4608. Rocha, Mona. "A Layered Message of Resistance: *Buffy*, Violence, and the Double Bind." In U. Melissa Anyiwo and Karoline Szatek-Tudor, eds. Buffy *Conquers the Academy: Conference Papers from the 2009/2010 Popular Culture/American Culture Associations.* Newcastle upon Tyne, UK: Cambridge Scholars Publishing, 2013, pp. 32–47. A paper originally presented in earlier form at the 32nd Annual Southwest/Texas PCA/ACA Conference, San Antonio, TX, April 20–23, 2011, and at the 2011 PCAS/ACAS Annual Conference, New Orleans, LA, October 6–8, 2011.

4609. Rock, Allison Susan. "Transforming Terrains: Staging the Supernatural in *North by Northwest* and *Buffy the Vampire Slayer.*" *Marvelous Traces in Mundane Spaces: Finding Fantasy in Theater, Film, and Television.* Middletown, CT: Wesleyan University, BA honors thesis, 2010, pp. 23–55. Posted at: http://wesscholar.wesleyan.edu/cgi/viewcontent.cgi?article=1411&context=etd_hon_theses.

4610. Rodeheffer, Marielle D. *A Study of Cult Television,* Buffy the Vampire Slayer, *and the Uses of Gratifications Theory.* Muncie, IN: Ball State University, M.A. thesis, 2007. 80 pp. Large format.

4611. Rogers, Brett M. "The Whedonverses and the Sociology of Academe, or A Report on SC2: The Slayage Conference on the Whedonverses, Gordon College, May 26–28, 2006." *Slayage: The Online International Journal of Buffy Studies* 6, 1 [21] (Fall 2006). Posted at: http://www.whedonstudies.tv/.

4612. _____, and Walter Scheidel. "Driving Stakes, Driving Cars: California Car Culture, Sex, and Identity in *Buffy the Vampire Slayer.*" *Slayage: The Online International Journal of Buffy Studies* 4, 1–2 [13–14] (October 2004). Posted at: http://www.slayageonline.com/.

4613. Romanelli, Kristen. "'It Seems Familiar Somehow': *Buffy the Vampire Slayer.*" *Film Score Monthly Online* 17, 4 (April 2012).

4614. Romesburg, Rod. "Buffy Goes to College: Identity and the Series-Based Seminar Course." In Jodie A. Kreider and Meghan K. Winchell, eds. Buffy *in the Classroom: Essays on Teaching with the Vampire Slayer.* Jefferson, NC: McFarland & Company, 2010, pp. 83–93.

4615. _____. "Regeneration through Vampirism: *Buffy the Vampire Slayer*'s New Frontier." *Slayage: The Online International Journal of Buffy Studies* 5, 3 [19] (February 2006). Posted at: http://www.whedonstudies.tv/.

4616. Rose, Anita. "Of Creatures and Creators: *Buffy* Does *Frankenstein.*" In Rhonda V. Wilcox and David Lavery, eds. *Fighting the Forces: What's at Stake in* Buffy the Vampire Slayer. Lanham, MD: Rowman & Littlefield, 2002, pp. 133–142.

4617. Rose, Jared S. "'You Know, I'm Extremely Youthful. And Peppy!': Buffy, Playing Girl, and Popular Culture Representation of Sex-Worker Feminism." *Watcher Junior: The Undergraduate Journal of Whedon Studies* 5, 1 [6] (July 2011). Posted at: http://www.whedonstudies.tv/.

4618. Rosenfeld, Lawrence B. "Interpersonal Relationships in the Buffyverse: The Connection with Everyday Life." A paper presented at the Slayage Conference on *Buffy the Vampire Slayer,* Nashville, TN, May 27–30, 2004. Posted at: http://www.slayageonline.com/SCBtVS_Archive/.

4619. _____, and Scarlet L. Wynns. "Perceived Values and Social Support in *Buffy the Vampire Slayer.*" *Slayage: The Online International Journal of Buffy Studies* 3, 2 [10] (November 2003). Posted at: http://www.whedonstudies.tv/.

4620. Ross, Sharon M. "Dangerous Demons: Fan Responses to Girls' Power, Girls' Bodies, and Girls' Beauty in *Buffy the Vampire Slayer.*" *Femspec* 5, 2 (2004): 82–100.

4621. _____. "Introduction: Watching Teen TV." In Sharon M. Ross and Louisa Ellen Stein, eds. *Teen Television: Essays on Programming and Fandom.* Jefferson, NC: McFarland & Company, 2008, pp. 3–26.

4622. _____. *Super(natural) Women: Female Heroes, Their Friends, and Their Fans.* Austin: University of Texas, Ph.D. dissertation, 2002.

4623. _____. "Tough Enough: Female Friendship and Heroism in *Xena* and *Buffy*." In Sherrie A. Inness, ed. *Action Chicks: New Images of Tough Women in Popular Culture.* New York: Palgrave Macmillan, 2004, pp. 231–56.

4624. Rothman, Lily. "'I'd Very Still': Anthropology of a Lapsed Fan." In Mary Alice Money for PopMatters.com, ed. *Joss Whedon: The Complete Companion: The TV Series, the Movies, the Comic Books and More.* London: Titan Books, 2012, pp. 126–134. An earlier version appeared as part of PopMatters.com's *Spotlight: Joss Whedon*, originally posted on April 14, 2011.

4625. Rowe, Maddie. "Up Against the Buffers." *English Review* 15, 4 (April 2005): 18–20.

4626. Rowland, Susan. "Puer and Hellmouth: *Buffy the Vampire Slayer* and American Myth." In Sally Porterfield, Keith Polette, and Tita French Baumlin, eds. *Perpetual Adolescence: Jungian Analyses of American Media, Literature, and Pop Culture.* Albany: SUNY [State University of New York] Press, 2009, pp. 31–46.

4627. Rowlands, Mark. "*Buffy the Vampire Slayer*: What Are Obligations? And Why Do We Have Them?" In Mark Rowlands, *Everything I Know I Learned from TV: Philosophy for the Unrepentant Couch Potato.* London: Ebury, 2005, pp. 27–62.

4628. Rowley, Christina, and Jutta Weldes. "The Evolution of International Security Studies and the Everyday: Suggestions from the Buffyverse." Working Paper No. 11–12. Bristol, UK: School of Sociology, Politics and International Studies (SPAIS), University of Bristol, 2012. Posted at: http://www.bris.ac.uk/spais/research/workingpapers/wpspaisfiles/rowley-weldes-11–12.pdf.

4629. _____. "'I Choose to Feel Threatened': Representations of In/Security in *Buffy the Vampire Slayer*." A paper presented at the 2008 PCA/ACA National Conference, San Francisco, CA, March 19–22, 2008. A paper originally presented at the Popular Culture & (World) Politics Conference, University of Bristol, UK, September 11–12, 2008. Posted at: http://citation.allacademic.com/meta/p_mla_apa_research_citation/2/5/2/8/0/pages252804/p252804–1.php.

4630. Ruddell, Caroline. "'I am the Law,' I am the Magics': Speech, Power and the Split Identity of Willow in *Buffy the Vampire Slayer*." In Michael Adams, ed. *Beyond Slayer Slang: Pragmatics, Discourse, and Style in* Buffy the Vampire Slayer. Special Issue of *Slayage: The Online International Journal of Buffy Studies* 5, 4 [20] (May 2006). Posted at: http://www.whedonstudies.tv/. A paper originally presented as "'I am the Law,' I am the Magics': Split Characters, Speech and Power in *Buffy the Vampire Slayer*" at the Slayage Conference on *Buffy the Vampire Slayer*, and subsequently as "'I am the Magics': The Fragile Identity of Willow in *Buffy the Vampire Slayer*" at Charming & Crafty: Witchcraft & Paganism in Contemporary Media, Colloquium, Harvard University, Cambridge, MA, May 2006.

4631. Ruditis, Paul. *Buffy the Vampire Slayer: The Watcher's Guide. Volume 3.* New York: Simon Spotlight, 2004. 359 pp. tp.

4632. _____, and Diana G. Gallagher. *Angel: The Casefiles.* New York: Simon Spotlight Entertainment, 20004. 295 pp. tp.

4633. Rust, Linda. "Welcome to the House of Fun: *Buffy* Fanfiction as a Hall of Mirrors." In Angela Ndalianis and Felicity Colman, eds. Special Issue on *Buffy the Vampire Slayer*. *Refractory: A Journal of Entertainment Media* 2 (2003). Posted at: http://refractory.unimelb.edu.au/2003/03/18/vol2/. A paper originally presented at The Buffyverse: A Symposium on *Buffy the Vampire Slayer*, University of Melbourne, Melbourne, Australia, November 21, 2002.

4634. Rutkowski, Alice. "Why Chicks Dig Vampires: Sex, Blood, and Buffy." *Iris: A Journal About Women* 45 (Fall 2002): 12–20.

4635. Ryan, Brandy. "'It's Complicated...Because of Tara': History, Identity Politics, and the Straight White Male Author." In Lynne Y. Edwards, Elizabeth L. Rambo and James B. South, eds. *Buffy Goes Dark: Essays on the Final Two Seasons of* Buffy the Vampire Slayer *on Television.* Jefferson, NC: McFarland & Company, 2009, pp. 57–74. A paper originally presented as "'It's Complicated...Because of Tara': History, Identity Politics, and the Straight White Male Author of *Buffy the Vampire Slayer*," at the Slayage Conference on *Buffy the Vampire Slayer*, Nashville, TN, May 27–30, 2004. Posted at: http://www.slayageonline.com/SCBtVS_Archive/.

4636. Sainato, Susan B. "Not Your Typical Knight: The Emerging On-Screen Defender." In Martha W. Driver and Sid Ray, eds. *The Medieval Hero on Screen: Representations from* Beowulf *to* Buffy. Jefferson, NC: McFarland & Company, 2004, pp. 138–146.

4637. St. Louis, Renée, and Miriam Riggs. "'And Yet': The Limits of *Buffy* Feminism." *Slayage: The Journal of the Whedon Studies Association* 8, 1 [29] (Spring 2010). Posted at: http://www.whedonstudies.tv/. A paper originally presented as "'... and Yet': The Limitations of Buffy's Feminism" at SC3: The Slayage Conference on the Whedonverses, Henderson State College, Arkadelphia, AR, June 5–8, 2008.

4638. Sakal, Gregory J. "No Big Win: Themes of Sacrifice, Salvation, and Redemption." In James B. South, ed. Buffy *and Philosophy: Fear and Trembling in Sunnydale.* Chicago: Open Court, 2003, pp. 239–253.

4639. Sandars, Diana, and Rhonda V. Wilcox. "Not 'The Same Arrangement': Breaking Utopian Promises in the *Buffy* Musical." In Paul Attinello, Janet K. Halfyard, and Vanessa Knights, eds. *Music, Sound, and Silence in* Buffy the Vampire Slayer. Farnham, Surrey, UK: Ashgate Publishing, 2010, pp. 189–208.

4640. Sanders, Hannah. "*Buffy* and Beyond: Language and Resistance in Contemporary Teenage Witchcraft." *Journal for the Academic Study of Magic* 3 (2005): 25–60.

4641. Santos, Jennifer Marie. *Anxieties of Audience: A Study of Gendered Gothic Reception.* Tempe: Arizona State University, Ph.D. dissertation, 2008. 211 pp. Large format.

4642. Saulnier, Katie. "From Virtuous Virgins to Vampire Slayers: The Evolution of the Gothic Heroine from the Early Gothic to Modern Horror." *Watcher Junior: The Journal of Undergraduate Research in Buffy Studies* 4, 1 [4] (November 2009). Posted at: http://www.whedonstudies.tv/.

4643. Savile, Steve. "*Angel* (1999–2004)." In Steve Savile. *Fantastic TV: 50 Years of Cult Fantasy and Science Fiction.* London: Plexus, 2010, pp. 224–232.

4644. _____. "*Buffy the Vampire Slayer* (1997–2003)." In Steve Savile. *Fantastic TV: 50 Years of Cult Fantasy and Science Fiction.* London: Plexus, 2010, pp. 210–218.

4645. Saxey, Esther. "Staking a Claim: The Series and its Slash Fan-Fiction." In Roz Kaveney, ed. *Reading the Vampire Slayer: An Unofficial Critical Companion to* Buffy *and* Angel. New York: I. B. Tauris, 2001, pp. 187–210.

4646. Sayer, Karen. "'It Wasn't Our World Anymore. They Made It Theirs': Reading Space and Place." In Roz Kaveney, ed. *Reading the Vampire Slayer: An Unofficial Critical Companion to* Buffy *and* Angel. New York: I. B. Tauris, 2001, pp. 98–119. Rpt. in exp. ed.: New York: I. B. Tauris, 2004. 132–155.

4647. Scherf, Manuela. *Character Formation in Fan Fiction Based on Popular TV Series.* Vienna, Austria: Universität Wien [University of Vienna], M.A. thesis, 2008. 155 pp. Large format. Posted at: http://othes.univie.ac.at/3061/1/2008-11-30_0204277.pdf.

4648. Schiff, Len. "Joss Whedon: Absolute Admiration for Sondheim." *Sondheim Review* 11, 4 (2005): 34–35.

4649. Schiffren, Mara. "On Spinning Gyres and Escherian Symmetries: Interpreting the Spatial Architecture of *Angel.*" A paper presented as "On Escherian Dualism and the Metaphysics of the Middle Way: Interpreting the Spatial Architecture of *Angel the Series*" at the Slayage Conference on *Buffy the Vampire Slayer*, Nashville, TN, May 27–30, 2004. Posted at: http://www.teaattheford.net/conversation.php?id=1501.

4650. Schill, Karin. *Femininity & Masculinity: A Reception Study About the Construction of Gender in Four Relationships on the TV Series* Buffy *& Angel.* Örebro, Sweden: Örebro Universitet, BA honors thesis, 2008. 81 pp. Large format. Posted at: http://oru.diva-portal.org/smash/record.jsf?pid=diva2:136108.

4651. Schlozman, Steven C. "Vampires and Those Who Slay Them: Using the Television Program *Buffy the Vampire Slayer* in Adolescent Therapy and Psychodynamic Education." *Academic Psychology* 24, 1 (2000): 49–54. Posted at: http://ap.psychiatryonline.org/article.aspx?articleid=47229.

4652. Schudt, Karl. "Also Sprach Faith: The Problem of the Happy Rogue Vampire Slayer." In James B. South, ed. Buffy *and Philosophy: Fear and Trembling in Sunnydale.* Chicago: Open Court, 2003, pp. 20–34.

4653. Schultz, Lauren Alise. "Concepts of Identity When *Nancy Drew* Meets *Buffy.*" In Kevin K. Durand, ed. Buffy *Meets the Academy: Essays on the Episodes and Scripts as Texts.* Jefferson, NC: McFarland & Company, 2009, pp. 187–202. A paper originally presented in earlier form as "Nancy Drew and Buffy Summers: The Development of the Strong Female Role Model in Adolescent Literature" at SC3: The Slayage Conference on the Whedonverses, Henderson State College, Arkadelphia, AR, June 5–8, 2008.

4654. _____. *Not Just a 'Rather Nasty Experience': Loss and Longing in Modern Young Adult Fantasy*. Washington, DC: American University, M.A. thesis, 2009. 69 pp. Large format.

4655. Schumacher, Lauren. "The Many Faces of Buffy: An Analysis of the Disharmonious Visual Representations of Buffy Summers in Primary and Secondary Texts." *Watcher Junior: The Undergraduate Journal of Whedon Studies* 4, 2 [5] (June 2010). Posted at: http://www.whedonstudies.tv/.

4656. Scott, Suzanne. "All Bark and No Bite: Siring the Neutered Vampire on *Buffy the Vampire Slayer*." In Carla T. Kungl, ed. *Vampires: Myths and Metaphors of Enduring Evil*. Oxford: Inter-Disciplinary Press, 2003, pp. 125–128. Posted at: http://www.inter-disciplinary.net/publishing/id-press/ebooks/vampires-myths-and-metaphors-of-enduring-evil. A paper originally presented at Vampires: Myths and Metaphors of Enduring Evil, Budapest, Hungary, May 22–24, 2003.

4657. Segura, Allison. *Perfect Creatures: A Social and Cultural Interpretation of Vampires in Fiction and Film*. Lafayette: University of Louisiana, Ph.D. dissertation, 2008. 133 pp. Large format.

4658. Sepinwall, Alan. "She saved the world. A lot...*Buffy the Vampire Slayer* gives teen angst some fangs." *The Revolution Was Televised: The Cops, Crooks, Slingers and Slayers Who Changed TV Drama Forever*. New York: Touchstone/Simon & Schuster, 2013, pp. 191–217. Reprinted from earlier edition; N.p.: the author, 2012. e-book.

4659. Shade, Pat. "Screaming to Be Heard: Reminders and Insights on Community and Communication in 'Hush.'" *Slayage: The Online International Journal of Buffy Studies* 6, 1 [21] (Fall 2006). Posted at: http://www.slayageonline.com/. A paper originally presented at the Slayage Conference on *Buffy the Vampire Slayer*, Nashville, TN, May 27–30, 2004.

4660. Shand, Patrick. "IDW Retrospective: A Look Back at IDW's *Angel* with Brian Lynch and Scott Tipton." In Mary Alice Money for PopMatters.com, ed. *Joss Whedon: The Complete Companion: The TV Series, the Movies, the Comic Books and More*. London: Titan Books, 2012, pp. 329–334.

4661. _____. "Joss Whedon 101: *Angel: After the Fall*." In Mary Alice Money for PopMatters.com, ed. *Joss Whedon: The Complete Companion: The TV Series, the Movies, the Comic Books and More*. London: Titan Books, 2012, pp. 324–328.

An earlier version appeared as part of PopMatters.com's *Spotlight: Joss Whedon*, originally posted on April 4, 2011.

4662. _____. "Joss Whedon 101: *Fray*." In Mary Alice Money for PopMatters.com, ed. *Joss Whedon: The Complete Companion: The TV Series, the Movies, the Comic Books and More*. London: Titan Books, 2012, pp. 307–309. An earlier version appeared as part of PopMatters.com's *Spotlight: Joss Whedon*, originally posted on March 13, 2011.

4663. _____. "Much with the Moral Ambiguity: An Examination of the Fallen Heroes and Redeemed Villains in *Buffy the Vampire Slayer Season Eight* and *Angel: After the Fall*." In Mary Alice Money for PopMatters.com, ed. *Joss Whedon: The Complete Companion: The TV Series, the Movies, the Comic Books and More*. London: Titan Books, 2012, pp. 361–367.

4664. Shapiro, NancyKay. "Transgressing with Spike and Buffy." In Lynne M. Thomas and Deborah Stanish, eds. *Whedonistas! A Celebration of the Worlds of Joss Whedon by the Women Who Love Them*. Des Moines, IA: Mad Norwegian Press, 2011, pp. 69–73.

4665. Shapiro, Paul D. "Someone to Sink Your Teeth Into: Gendered Biting Patterns on *Buffy the Vampire Slayer*: A Quantitative Analysis." *Slayage: The Online International Journal of Buffy Studies* 7, 2 [26] (Spring 2008). Posted at: http://www.whedonstudies.tv/. A paper originally presented at It's the End of the World...Again: Why Buffy Still Matters: A *Buffy the Vampire Slayer* Mini-Conference," University of North Carolina, Greensboro, NC, March 16, 2007.

4666. Sharp, Molly Louise. *Gender, Feminism, and Heroism in Joss Whedon and John Cassaday's* Astonishing X-Men *Comics*. Austin: University of Texas, M.A. thesis, 2011. 129 pp. Large format. Posted at: http://repositories.lib.utexas.edu/bitstream/handle/2152/11903/SHARP-THESIS.pdf.

4667. Sharpe, Matthew. "Is Buffy (a) Lacanian? Sunnydale, Or: What Is Enlightenment?" In Angela Ndalianis and Felicity Colman, eds. Special Issue on *Buffy the Vampire Slayer*. *Refractory: A Journal of Entertainment Media* 2 (2003). Posted at: http://refractory.unimelb.edu.au/2003/03/18/vol2/. A paper originally presented at The Buffyverse: A Symposium on *Buffy the Vampire Slayer*, University of Melbourne, Melbourne, Australia, November 2002.

4668. Shaw, Heather. "A Couch Potato's Guide to Demon Slaying: Turning Strangers into

Family, *Buffy*-Style." In Lynne M. Thomas and Deborah Stanish, ed. *Whedonistas! A Celebration of the Worlds of Joss Whedon by the Women Who Love Them*. Des Moines, IA: Mad Norwegian Press, 2011, pp. 49–56.

4669. Shefield, Rebecka. "Smelly Knowledge: An Informal Audit of the Sunnydale High Library in *Buffy the Vampire Slayer*." *University of Toronto Faculty of Information Quarterly* 2, 1 (2009). Posted at: http://fiq.ischool.utoronto.ca/index.php/fiq/article/view/15433.

4670. Sheperd, Dawn Renée. *Marketing Subjectivity:* Buffy the Vampire Slayer *and Construction of the Problematic Female Television Audience*. Raleigh: North Carolina State University, M.A. thesis, 2004. 72 pp. Large format. Posted at: http://repository.lib.ncsu.edu/ir/bitstream/1840.16/2420/1/etd.pdf.

4671. Shepherd, Laura J. *Gender, Violence and Popular Culture: Telling Stories*. New York: Routledge, 2012. 154 pp. See especially chapters 2 and 3, "Morality, legality and gender violence in *Angel*" (p. 13–24) and "Policing the boundaries of desire in *Buffy the Vampire Slayer*" (pp. 25–41).

4672. _____. "Morality, Legality and Gender Violence in *Angel*." *Journal of Gender Studies* 18, 3 (2009): 245–259. Rpt. in Laura J. Shepherd. *Gender, Violence and Popular Culture: Telling Stories*. New York: Routledge, 2012, pp. 13–24.

4673. Sherman, Josepha. "*Angel* or Devil: Playing with Mythology and Folflore in the Angelverse." In Glenn Yeffeth, ed. *Five Seasons of* Angel: *Science Fiction and Fantasy Writers Discuss Their Favorite Vampire*. Dallas, TX: Benbella Books, 2004, pp. 167–177.

4674. Sherman, Yael. "Tracing the Carnival Spirit in *Buffy the Vampire Slayer*: Feminist Reworkings of the Grotesque." *Thirdspace* 3, 2 (2004): 89–107. Posted at: http://www.thirdspace.ca/journal/article/viewArticle/sherman.

4675. Short, Sue. "*Buffy the Vampire Slayer*: Beauty and the 'Big Bad.'" In Sue Short. *Cult Telefantasy Series: A Critical Analysis of* The Prisoner, Twin Peaks, The X-Files, Buffy the Vampire Slayer, Lost, Heroes, Doctor Who, *and* Star Trek. Jefferson, NC: McFarland & Company, 2011, pp. 84–107.

4676. _____. "Fighting Demons: Buffy, Faith, Willow, and the Forces of Good and Evil." In Sue Short. *Misfit Sisters: Screen Horror as Female Rites of Passage*. New York: Palgrave Macmillan, 2007, pp. 111–131.

4677. Showalter, Dennis. "Buffy Goes to War: Military Themes and Images in *Buffy the Vampire Slayer*." A paper presented at the Slayage Conference on *Buffy the Vampire Slayer*, Nashville, TN, May 27–30, 2004. Posted at: http://www.slayageonline.com/SCBtVS_Archive/.

4678. Shull, Ira, and Anne Shull. "The Candide of Sunnydale: Andrew Wells as Satire of Pop Culture and Marketing Trends." In Lynne Y. Edwards, Elizabeth L. Rambo, and James B. South, ed. *Buffy Goes Dark: Essays on the Final Two Seasons of* Buffy the Vampire Slayer *on Television*. Jefferson, NC: McFarland & Company, 2009, pp. 75–82. A paper originally presented as "The Candide of Sunnydale: Andrew as Satire of Pop Culture and Marketing Trends in *Buffy the Vampire Slayer*" at Slayage Conference on *Buffy the Vampire Slayer*, Nashville, TN, May 27–30, 2004.

4679. Shuttleworth, Ian. "'They Always Mistake Me for the Character I Play!': Transformation, Identity and Role-playing in the Buffyverse (and a Defence of Fine Acting)." In Roz Kaveney, ed. *Reading the Vampire Slayer: An Unofficial Critical Companion to* Buffy *and* Angel. New York: I. B. Tauris, 2001. 211–236. Rpt. in exp. ed.: New York: I. B. Tauris, 2004, pp. 233–276.

4680. Sibielski, Rosalind. *From Girl Power to Empowered Girls? Reading Gender, Power, and Adolescent Female Identity through Representations of Girl Power in Contemporary Culture*. Providence, RI: Rhode Island College, M.A. thesis, 2004. 180 pp. Large format.

4681. Siegel, Carol. "Female Heterosexual Sadism: The Final Feminist Taboo in *Buffy the Vampire Slayer* and the *Anita Blake, Vampire Hunter* Series." In Merri Lisa Johnson, ed. *Third Wave Feminism and Television: Jane Puts It in a Box*. New York: I. B. Tauris, 2007, pp. 56–90. A paper originally presented as "Third-Wave Feminist Sadism: Why Buffy's Loss is Anita Blake's Gain" at the 2006 PCA/ACA National Conference, April 12–15, 2006.

4682. Siemann, Catherine. "Darkness Falls on the Endless Summer: Buffy as Gidget for the Fin de Siècle." In Rhonda V. Wilcox and David Lavery, eds. *Fighting the Forces: What's at Stake in* Buffy the Vampire Slayer. Lanham, MD: Rowman & Littlefield, 2002, pp. 120–129.

4683. Simkin, Stevie. "'Who died and made you John Wayne?' Anxious Masculinity in *Buffy the Vampire Slayer*." *Slayage: The Online International Journal of Buffy Studies* 3, 3–4 [11–12] (April 2004). Posted at: http://www.whedonstudies.tv/.

4684. _____. "'You hold your gun like a sissy girl': Firearms and Anxious Masculinity in *Buffy the Vampire Slayer.*" *Slayage: The Online International Journal of Buffy Studies* 3, 3–4 [11–12] (April 2004). Posted at: http://www.whedonstudies.tv/. A paper originally presented at Blood, Text and Fears: Reading Around *Buffy the Vampire Slayer*, University of East Anglia, October 19–20, 2002.

4685. Simmons, Victoria Gay. *Tricksterism in Popular Traditions.* Los Angeles: University of California–Los Angeles, M.A. thesis, 2005. 269 pp. Large format.

4686. Simpson, Craig S. "Myth Versus Faux Myth." *The Chronicle of Higher Education* 47, 37 (May 2001): B15-B16. Posted at: http://chronicle.com/article/Myth-Versus-Faux-Myth/2054.

4687. Sinclair, Katrina. *High School Is Hell: An Analysis of the Cultural Importance of Television and Its Significance in Adolescent Culture through the Television Series* Buffy the Vampire Slayer. North Dunedin, NZ: University of Otago, BA honors thesis, 2003.

4688. Sippola, Lorrie K., Jaime Paget, and Carie M. Buchanan. "Praising Cordelia: Social Aggression and Social Dominance among Adolescent Girls." In Patricia H. Hawley, Todd D. Little, and Philip C. Rodkin, ed. *Aggression and Adaptation: The Bright Side to Bad Behavior.* Mahwah, NJ: Lawrence Erlbaum Associates, Publishers, 2007, pp. 157–183.

4689. Skwire, Sarah E. "'Whose Side Are You On, Anyway?': Children, Adults, and the Use of Fairy Tales in *Buffy.*" In Rhonda V. Wilcox and David Lavery, ed. *Fighting the Forces: What's at Stake in* Buffy the Vampire Slayer. Lanham, MD: Rowman & Littlefield, 2002, pp. 195–204.

4690. Smith, Ashley Lorrain. "Melodrama and Girlculture: *Buffy the Vampire Slayer.*" In Ashley Lorrain Smith. *Girl Power: Feminism, Girlculture and the Popular Media.* Denton: University of North Texas, Ph.D. dissertation, 1999. pp. 81–114. Posted at: http://digital.library.unt.edu/ark:/67531/metadc2200/m1/1/.

4691. South, James B. "'All Torment, Trouble, Wonder, and Amazement Inhabits Here': The Vicissitudes of Technology in *Buffy the Vampire Slayer.*" *Journal of American and Comparative Cultures* 24, 1/2 (2001): 93–102. A paper originally presented at Marquette University PGSA Conference: Technology in the 21st Century, Milwaukee, WI, 2001.

4692. _____, **ed.** Buffy *and Philosophy: Fear and Trembling in Sunnydale.* La Salle, IL: Open Court, 2003. 335 pp. tp. Buffy *and Philosophy: Fear and Trembling in Sunnydale* received the 2004 award as the best nonfiction book of the previous year given annually by the Lord Ruthven Society. It includes contributions by Greg Foster, Karl Schudt, Jessica Prata Miller, Thomas Hibbs, Mimi Marinucci, Andrew Aberdein, Madeline M. Muntersbjorn, James lawler, Toby Daspit, Jason Kawal, Carolyn Korsmeyer, Melissa M. Milavec and Sharon M. Kaye, Scott R. Stroud, Neal King, Wendy Love Anderson, Jacob M. Held, Gregory J. Sakal, Jeffrey L. Pasley, Richard Greene and Wayne Yuen, Tracy little, and Michael Levine and Steven Jay Schneider.

4693. _____. "Kiss Kiss, Stake Stake: Storytelling and the Philosophical Pleasures of Season Seven." In Lynne Y. Edwards, Elizabeth L. Rambo, and James B. South, eds. *Buffy Goes Dark: Essays on the Final Two Seasons of* Buffy the Vampire Slayer *on Television.* Jefferson, NC: McFarland & Company, 2009, pp. 198–210.

4694. _____. "'My God, It's Like a Greek Tragedy': Willow Rosenberg and Human Irrationality." In James B. South, ed. Buffy *and Philosophy: Fear and Trembling in Sunnydale.* Chicago: Open Court, 2003. 131–145.

4695. _____. "On the Philosophical Consistency of Season 7: or, 'It's not about right, not about wrong...'" *Slayage: The Online International Journal of Buffy Studies* 4, 1–2 [13–14] (October 2004). Posted at: http://www.slayageonline.com/. A paper originally presented as "On the Philosophical Consistency of Season 7" at the Slayage Conference on *Buffy the Vampire Slayer*, Nashville, TN, May 27–30, 2004.

4696. Spah, Victoria. "Ain't Love Grand: Spike & Courtly Love." *Slayage: The Online International Journal of Buffy Studies* 2, 1 [5] (May 2002). Posted at: http://www.slayageonline.com/.

4697. Spaise, Terry L. "Necrophilia and SM: The Deviant Side of *Buffy the Vampire Slayer.*" *The Journal of Popular Culture* 38, 4 (2005): 744–762.

4698. Spicer, Arwen. "'It's Bloody Brilliant!': The Undermining of Metanarrative Feminism in the Season Seven Arc Narrative of *Buffy.*" *Slayage: The Online International Journal of Buffy Studies* 4, 3 [15] (December 2004). Posted at: http://www.whedonstudies.tv/. A paper originally presented at the Slayage Conference on *Buffy the Vampire Slayer*, Nashville, TN, May 27–30, 2004.

4699. _____. "'Love's Bitch but Man Enough to Admit It': Spike's Hybridized Gender." *Slayage:*

The Online International Journal of Buffy Studies 2, 3 [7] (December 2002). Posted at: http://www.whedonstudies.tv/.

4700. Spooner, Catherine. "Teen Demons." In Catherone Spooner. *Contemporary Gothic.* London: Reaktion, 2006, pp. 87–123.

4701. Stadler, Jane. "Becoming the Other: Multiculturalism in Joss Whedon's *Angel.*" *Flow TV: A Critical Forum on Television and Media Culture* 7, 4 (April 2007). Posted at: http://flowtv.org/2007/12/becoming-the-other-multiculturalism-in-joss-whedon's-angel/.

4702. Stafford, Anika. "Feminist Abuse Survivor Narratives in *Angel* and Sarah Daniels's *Beside Herself.*" In AmiJo Comeford and Tamy L. Burnett, ed. *The Literary* Angel: *Essays on Influences and Traditions Reflected in the Joss Whedon Series.* Jefferson, NC: McFarland & Company, 2010. 85–97. Originally a paper, "Memory and Madness: *Angel* Finds a Place in Feminist Abuse Survivor Narratives," which was accepted but not p[resented at the 31st Annual Southwest/Texas PCA/ACA Conference, Albuquerque, NM, February 10–13, 2010.

4703. Stafford, Nikki. *Bite Me! Sarah Michelle Gellar and Buffy the Vampire Slayer.* Toronto: ECW Press, 1998. 196 pp. tp. Rev. ed. as: *Bite Me! An Unofficial Guide to the World of Buffy the Vampire Slayer.* Toronto: ECW Press, 2002. 425 pp. tp. Rev. ed. as: *Bite Me! The Unofficial Guide to Buffy the Vampire Slayer.* Toronto: ECW Press, 2007. 397 pp. tp.

4704. _____. *Once Bitten: An Unofficial Guide to the World of Angel.* Toronto: ECW Press, 2004. 438 pp. tp.

4705. Stahl, Madeline. "The Dead Poet's Society." *Watcher Junior: The Journal of Undergraduate Research in Buffy Studies* 2, 1 [2] (July 2006). Posted at: http://www.whedonstudies.tv/.

4706. Stasiak, Lauren. "'When You Kiss Me, I Want To Die': *Buffy the Vampire Slayer* and Gothic Family Values." In Lauren M. E. Goodlad and Michael Bibby. *Goth: Undead Subculture.* Durham, NC: Duke University Press, 2007, pp 307–315.

4707. Stein, Atara. "Conclusion: The Vampire with the Face of an Angel." In Atara Stein. *The Byronic Hero in Film, Fiction, and Television.* Carbondale: Southern Illinois University Press, 2009, pp. 213–218.

4708. _____. "Immortals and Vampires and Ghosts, Oh My! Byronic Heroes in Popular Culture." In Laura Mandell and Michael Eberle-Sinatra, eds. *Romanticism and Contemporary Culture.* Special Issue of *Romantic Circles Praxis Series* (February 2002). Posted at: http://www.rc.umd.edu/praxis/contemporary/stein/stein.html.

4709. Stein, Jeanne C. "My (Fantasy) Encounter with Joss Whedon (and What I've Learned from the Master)." In Lynne M. Thomas and Deborah Stanish, ed. *Whedonistas! A Celebration of the Worlds of Joss Whedon by the Women Who Love Them.* Des Moines, IA: Mad Norwegian Press, 2011, pp. 37–41.

4710. Stein, Louisa Ellen. *"A Transcending-Genre Kind of Thing": Teen/Fantasy TV and Online Audience Culture.* New York: New York University, Ph.D. dissertation, 2006. 349 pp. Large format.

4711. Stengel, Wendy A. F. G. "Synergy and Smut: The Brand in Official and Unofficial *Buffy the Vampire Slayer* Communities of Interest." *Slayage: The Online International Journal of Buffy Studies* 1, 4 [4] (December 2001). Posted at: http://www.whedonstudies.tv/.

4712. Stenger, Josh. "The Clothes Make the Fan: Fashion and Online Fandom When *Buffy the Vampire Slayer* Goes to eBay." *Cinema Journal* 45, 4 (Summer 2006): 26–44.

4713. Stephenson, Sophie. "The Fans Who Never Lost Faith: Slaying 1970s Subculture Theory." *Watcher Junior: The Undergraduate Journal of Whedon Studies* 6, 1 [7] (July 2012). Posted at: http://www.whedonstudies.tv/.

4714. Stevens, Katy. "Battling the Buzz: Contesting Sonic Codes in *Buffy the Vampire Slayer.*" In Paul Attinello, Janet K. Halfyard, and Vanessa Knights, eds. *Music, Sound, and Silence in Buffy the Vampire Slayer.* Farnham, Surrey, UK: Ashgate Publishing, 2010, pp. 79–89.

4715. _____. "Buffy's Spectatorial Dilemma: Time Anomalies in 'Life Serial.'" *All Slay* 1 (2003): 4–6.

4716. _____. "Defending Season Six (Part One)." *All Slay* 1 (2003): 14–15.

4717. _____. "Defending Season Six (Part Two)." *All Slay* 2 (2004).

4718. _____. "Investigating *Angel.*" *All Slay* 2 (2004).

4719. _____. "Moans, Thuds and Power Chords: Sounding Sex in *Buffy.*" *All Slay* 3 (2004).

4720. _____. "Musical Narration Across *Magnolia* and 'Sleeper.'" *All Slay* 1 (2003): 16–17.

4721. _____. "Spike as Spectacle: Liminality and Visual Pleasure." *All Slay* 1 (2003): 7–12. A paper originally presented as "Sex, Spectatorship and the Surface of the Body: Spike as Buffy's 'Dolly'" at the Buffy Down Under Convention, Melbourne, Australia, May 2–4. 2003, and at Staking a Claim: Exploring the Global Reach of *Buffy*, University of South Australia, Adelaide, Australia, July 22, 2003.

4722. **Stevens, Kirsten.** "Meet the Cullens: Family, Romance, and Female Agency in *Buffy the Vampire Slayer* and *Twilight*." *Slayage: The Journal of the Whedon Studies Association* 8, 1 [29] (Spring 2010). Posted at: http://www.whedonstudies.tv/.

4723. **Stevenson, Gregory.** *Televised Morality: The Case of* Buffy the Vampire Slayer. New York: Hamilton, 2003. 299 pp. tp.

4724. **Stokes, Jennifer.** "'Who died and made you John Wayne?' or, Why Riley Finn Could Never be a Scooby." Paper presented at the Slayage Conference on *Buffy the Vampire Slayer*, Nashville, TN, May 27–30, 2004. Posted at: http://www.slayage online.com/SCBtVS_Archive/.

4725. **Stommel, Jesse James.** "I'm Not a Dead Body; I Just Play One on TV: *Buffy the Vampire Slayer* and the Performativity of the Corpse." *Slayage: The Journal of the Whedon Studies Association* 8, 1 [29] (Spring 2010). Posted at: http://www.whedonstudies.tv/. Rpt. in Jesse James Stommel. *Pity Poor Flesh*. Boulder: University of Colorado, Ph.D. dissertation, 2010. pp. 69–82.

4726. **Stoy, Jennifer.** "'And Her Tears Flowed Like Wine': Wesley/Lilah and the Complicated (?) Role of the Female Agent on *Angel*." In Stacey Abbott, ed. *Reading* Angel: *The TV Spin-off with a Soul*. New York: I. B. Tauris, 2005, pp. 163–175.

4727. _____. "Blood and Choice: The Theory and Practice of Family in *Angel*." In Roz Kaveney, ed. *Reading the Vampire Slayer: An Unofficial Critical Companion to* Buffy *and* Angel. 2nd ed. New York: I. B. Tauris, 2004, pp. 220–232.

4728. **Stratton, Jon.** "Buffy Failed: *True Blood* and the Accommodation of Vampires." *Flow* (online journal of television and media studies) (March 26, 2010). Posted at: http://flowtv.org/2010/03/buffy-failed-true-blood-and-the-accommodation-of-vampires-jon-stratton-curtin-university-of-technology/.

4729. **Stratton, Jon.** "*Buffy the Vampire Slayer*: What Being Jewish Has to Do with It." *Television & New Media* 6, 2 (May 2005): 176–199.

4730. **Straub, Kristina.** "Love at the Hellmouth." In Suzanne R. Pucci and James Thompson, ed. *Jane Austen and Co.: Remaking the Past in Contemporary Culture*. Albany: SUNY [State University of New York] Press, 2003, pp. 53–71.

4731. **Stroud, Scott R.** "A Kantian Analysis of Moral Judgment in *Buffy the Vampire Slayer*." Buffy *and Philosophy: Fear and Trembling in Sunnydale*. Ed. James B. South. Chicago: Open Court, 2003. 185–194.

4732. **Stuart, Susan.** "When Ontologies Collide: The Essential Confusion of Existence in the Buffyverse." A paper presented at the Slayage Conference on *Buffy the Vampire Slayer*, Nashville, TN, May 27–30, 2004. Posted at: http://www.slayage online.com/SCBtVS_Archive/.

4733. **Stuller, Jennifer Kate.** "The Best, Worst, Known, and Not-So-Known, Popular Culture Influences on the *Buffy*verse (Or, Joss Whedon's Fandom: 101)." In Jennifer Kate Stuller, ed. *Fan Phenomena:* Buffy the Vampire Slayer. Chicago: Intellect, 2013, pp. 10–27. A paper originally presented as "The Ink-Stained Amazon Presents: A Brief History of the Best, Worst, Known, and Not So Known Pop Culture Influences on the Buffyverse, Mostly" at SC4: The Slayage Conference on the Whedonverses, Flagler College, St. Augustine, FL, June 3–6, 2010. Posted at: http://ink-stainedamazon.com/pdf/JKStuller_Slayage2010_lite.pdf.

4734. _____. "Introduction." In Jennifer Kate Stuller, ed. *Fan Phenomena:* Buffy the Vampire Slayer. Chicago: Intellect, 2013, pp. 4–9.

4735. _____. "One Girl in All the World." In Jennifer Kate Stuller. *Ink-Stained Amazons and Cinematic Warriors: Superwomen in Modern Mythology*. New York: I. B. Tauris, 2010, pp. 73–78.

4736. _____, ed. *Fan Phenomena:* Buffy the Vampire Slayer. Bristol, UK: Intellect Press, 2013. 164 pp. tp. Rpt.: Chicago: Intellect, 2013. 164 pp. tp. Along with essays she authored herself, the editor has included contributions by Tanya R. Cochran, Mary Kirby-Diaz, Liz Medendorp, Amy Peloff and David Boarder Giles, Lorna Jowett, Kristen Julia Anderson, Nikki Faith Fuller, Anthony R, Mills, and David Bushman and Arthur Smith, with interviews of Nikki Stafford, Rhonda Wilcox, Clinton McClung, and Scott Allie.

4737. **Suisted, Laura.** "Breaking Conventions to Build the Buffyverse." *Watcher Junior: The Journal of Undergraduate Research in Buffy Studies* 1, 1 [1] (July 2005). Posted at: http://www.whedon studies.tv/.

4738. Sutherland, Sharon. "Piercing the Corporate Veil with a Stake? Vampire Imagery and the Law." In Carla T. Kungl, ed. *Vampires: Myths and Metaphors of Enduring Evil*. Oxford: Inter-Disciplinary Press, 2003. pp. 95–99. Rpt. in: Peter Day, ed. *Vampire: Myths and Metaphors of Enduring Evil*. Amsterdam: Rodopi, 2006, pp. 143–58. A paper originally presented at Vampires: Myths and Metaphors of Enduring Evil Conference held in Budapest, Hungary, May 22–24, 2003. Posted at: http://papers.ssrn.com/sol3/papers.cfm?abstract_id=796826.

4739. _____, and Sarah Swann. "If a Vampire Bites a Lawyer, is it Cannibalism? The Demonization of Lawyers in *Angel*." A paper originally presented at the *Slayage* Conference on Buffy the Vampire Slayer," Nashville, TN, May 28, 2004. 21 pp. Posted at: http://ssrn.com/abstract=802324, and at http://dx.doi.org/10.2139/ssrn.802324.

4740. _____, and Sarah Swann. "Lilah Morgan: Whedon's Legal Femme Fatale." In AmiJo Comeford and Tamy L. Burnett, ed. *The Literary Angel: Essays on Influences and Traditions Reflected in the Joss Whedon Series*. Jefferson, NC: McFarland & Company, 2010, pp. 54–65.

4741. _____, and Sarah Swann. "The Rule of Prophecy: Source of Law in the City of *Angel*." In Stacey Abbott, ed. *Reading* Angel: *The TV Spin-off with a Soul*. New York: I. B. Tauris, 2005, pp. 132–145.

4742. Swain, Sara. "Losing It: The Construction of Virginity in *Buffy the Vampire Slayer*." In Erin B. Waggoner, ed. *Sexual Rhetoric in the Works of Joss Whedon: New Essays*. Jefferson, NC: McFarland & Company, 2010, pp. 173–184.

4743. Sweeney, Kathleen. "Supernatural Girls: Witches, Warriors, and Anime." In Kathleen Sweeney. *Maiden USA: Girl Icons Come of Age*. New York: Peter Lang, 2008, pp. 155–174.

4744. Switaj, Elizabeth Kate. "Orchestrated Conflict & Real Resistance: The Revolutionary Nature of Buffy the Vampire Slayer's Community." A paper presented at Popular Politics and Vampire Stories: The Appropriation of Vampires in the 21st Century, Symposium, Association for Research in Popular Fiction, July 2007. Posted at: http://www.elizabethkateswitaj.net/BuffyCommunity.pdf.

4745. Symcox, Caroline. "Teething Troubles and Growing Up." In Lynne M. Thomas and Deborah Stanish, ed. *Whedonistas! A Celebration of the Worlds of Joss Whedon by the Women Who Love Them*. Des Moines, IA: Mad Norwegian Press, 2011, pp. 62–68.

4746. Symonds, Gwyn. "'Bollocks!' Spike Fans and Reception of *Buffy the Vampire Slayer*." In Angela Ndalianis and Felicity Colman, eds. *Special Issue on* Buffy the Vampire Slayer. *Refractory: A Journal of Entertainment Media* 2 (2003). Posted at: http://refractory.unimelb.edu.au/2003/03/18/vol2/. A paper originally presented at The Buffyverse: A Symposium on *Buffy the Vampire Slayer*, University of Melbourne, Melbourne, Australia, November 21, 2002.

4747. _____. "'A Little More Soul Than Is Written': James Marsters' Performance of Spike and the Ambiguity of Evil in Sunnydale." *Slayage: The Online International Journal of Buffy Studies* 4, 4 [16] (March 2005). Posted at: http://www.whedonstudies.tv/. A paper originally presented as "'A Little More Soul Than Is Written': Acting Spike and the Ambiguity of Evil in Sunnydale" at the Slayage Conference on *Buffy the Vampire Slayer*, Nashville, TN, May 27–30, 2004.

4748. _____. "'Solving Problems with Sharp Objects': Female Empowerment, Sex, and Violence in *Buffy the Vampire Slayer*." *Slayage: The Online International Journal of Buffy Studies* 3, 3–4 [11–12] (April 2004). Posted at: http://www.whedonstudies.tv/. Rev. text in Gwyn Symonds. *The Aesthetics of Violence in Contemporary Media*. New York: Continuum, 2008, pp. 126–149.

4749. _____. "The Superhero Versus the Troubled Teen: Parenting Connor, and the Fragility of 'Family' in *Angel*." In Wesley Haslem, Angela Ndalianis, and Chris Mackie, eds. *Super/Heroes: From Hercules to Superman*. Washington, DC: New Academia, 2007, pp. 155–165. A paper originally presented at Holy Men in Tights: A Superheroes Conference, University of Melbourne, Melbourne, Australia, June 2005.

4750. _____. "You Can Take the Fan Out of the Academic but Should You? Musings on Methodology." *Philament* 1 (September 2003). Posted at: http://sydney.edu.au/arts/publications/philament/issue1_pdf/GwynSymonds.pdf.

4751. Tabron, Judith. "Girl on Girl Politics: Willow/Tara and New Approaches to Media Fandom." *Slayage: The Online International Journal of Buffy Studies* 4, 1–2 [13–14] (October 2004). Posted at: http://www.whedonstudies.tv/.

4752. Talty, Julie. *Enabling Cult Television: A Modern Expression of an Ancient Phenomenon*. Queensland, Aust.: Griffith University, School of Film, Media and Cultural Studies, BA honors thesis, 2004.

4753. Tassone, Janelle. "Buffy: The Evolution of a Valley Girl." In Angela Ndalianis and Felicity Colman, eds. *Special Issue on* Buffy the Vampire Slayer. *Refractory: A Journal of Entertainment Media* 2 (2003). Posted at: http://refractory.unimelb.edu.au/2003/03/18/vol2/. A paper originally presented at The Buffyverse: A Symposium on *Buffy the Vampire Slayer*, University of Melbourne, Melbourne, Australia, November 21, 2002.

4754. Thomas, Deborah. "*Reading* Buffy." In John Gibbs and Douglas Pye, eds. *Close-up 01: Filmmakers' Choices, The Pop Song in Narrative Film, Reading Buffy*. New York: Wallflower Press, 2006, pp 167–241.

4755. Thomas, Laura. "The *Buffy* Factor: Educators Can Learn a Lot from *Buffy the Vampire Slayer*." *Education Week* (June 11, 2003): 25–27.

4756. Thomas, Lynne M., and Deborah Stanish. "Introduction." In Lynne M. Thomas and Deborah Stanish, eds. *Whedonistas! A Celebration of the Worlds of Joss Whedon by the Women Who Love Them*. Des Moines, IA: Mad Norwegian Press, 2011, pp. 9–12.

4757. _____, eds. *Whedonistas! A Celebration of the Worlds of Joss Whedon by the Women Who Love Them*. Des Moines, IA: Mad Norwegian Press, 2011. 198 pp. tp.

4758. Thomas, Susan Kay. *Slaying Throughout the Ages: The Importance of the Warrior Woman to the Female Readership*. Fargo: North Dakota State University, M.A. thesis, 2004. 65 pp. Large format.

4759. Thompson, Florence. *Female Punishment in* Buffy the Vampire Slayer. Portsmouth, UK: University of Portsmouth, BA honors thesis, 2008.

4760. Thompson, Gregory J., and Sally Emmons-Featherston. "'What Shall Cordelia Say?' *Buffy* as Morality Play for the Twenty-First Century's Therapeutic Ethos." In Emily Dial-Driver, Sally Emmons-Featherston, Jim Ford, and Carolyn Anne Taylor, eds. *The Truth of* Buffy: *Essays on Fiction Illuminating Reality*. Jefferson, NC: McFarland & Company, 2008, pp. 158–172.

4761. Thompson, Jim. "'Just a Girl': Feminism, Postmodernism and *Buffy the Vampire Slayer*." *Special Issue on* Buffy the Vampire Slayer. Eds. Angela Ndalianis and Felicity Colman. *Refractory: A Journal of Entertainment Media* 2 (2003). Posted at: http://refractory.unimelb.edu.au/2003/03/18/vol2/.

4762. Thompson, Kristin. "The Dispersal of Narrative: Adaptations, Sequels, Serials, Spin-offs, and Sagas." *Storytelling in Film and Television*. Cambridge, MA: Harvard University Press, 2003, pp. 74–105.

4763. Thompson, Matthew Ryan. *'Do You Mind, Buffy? I'm Trying to Repress!':* The Monk, Dracula, Buffy the Vampire Slayer *and the Unleashing of the New One-Sex World*. Cambridge, MA: Harvard University, BA honors thesis, 2002. 76 pp. Large format.

4764. Thompson, Micheal. *Dialogues of the Hero in Crisis: A Dialogical Analysis of the Buffy/Faith Relationship in Season Three of* Buffy the Vampire Slayer. Portales: Eastern New Mexico University, M.A. thesis, 2005. 163 pp. Large format.

4765. Thompson, Rachel. "Staking It to the Man." *Herizons* 16, 1 (Summer 2003): 22–25.

4766. Thornbury, Kathy A. *The Conceptualization of Mind: A Corpus Study of a* Buffy the Vampire Slayer *Blog*. Muncie, IN: Ball State University, M.A. thesis, 2007. 132 pp. Large format.

4767. Tischler Millstein, Denise. "The Failed Quest for 'Anti-Self-Consciousness'." In Kevin K. Durand, ed. Buffy *Meets the Academy: Essays on the Episodes and Scripts as Texts*. Jefferson, NC: McFarland & Company, 2009, pp. 104–114.

4768. Tjardes, Sue. "'If You're Not Enjoying It, You're Doing Something Wrong': Textual and Viewer Constructions of Faith, the Vampire Slayer." In Frances Early and Kathleen Kennedy, eds. *Athena's Daughters: Television's New Women Warriors*. Syracuse, NY: Syracuse University Press, 2003, pp. 66–77.

4769. Tomlinson, Martin. "A Question of Faith: Responsibility, Murder and Redemption in *Buffy the Vampire Slayer*." *Chrestomathy: Annual Review of Undergraduate Research at the College of Charleston* 3 (2004): 205–228. Posted at: http://chrestomathy.cofc.edu/documents/vol3/tomlinson.pdf.

4770. Tonkin, Boyd. "Entropy as Demon: Buffy in Southern California." In Roz Kaveney, ed. *Reading the Vampire Slayer: An Unofficial Critical Companion to* Buffy *and* Angel. 1st ed. New York: I. B. Tauris, 2001, pp. 37–52. Rpt in exp. ed: New York: I. B. Tauris, 2004, pp. 83–99.

4771. Topping, Keith. *The Complete Slayer: An Unofficial and Unauthorised Guide to Every Episode of "Buffy the Vampire Slayer"* London: Virgin, 2004. 704 pp. pb.

4772. _____. *Hollywood Vampire: The Apocalypse. The Unofficial and Unauthorized Guide to the Final Season of Angel*. London: Virgin, 2005. 228 pp.

4773. _____. *Hollywood Vampire: A Revised and Updated Unofficial and Unauthorized Guide to Angel*. London: Virgin, 2001. 280 pp. pb. Rev. ed.: 2004. 456 pp. pb.

4774. _____. *Hollywood Vampire: The Unofficial Guide to Angel*. London: Virgin, 2000. 213 pp. pb.

4775. _____. *Slayer: An Expanded and Updated Unofficial and unauthorized Guide to Buffy the Vampire Slayer*. London: Virgin, 2002. 488 pp. pb.

4776. _____. *Slayer: The Last Days of Sunnydale. An Unofficial and Unauthorised Guide to the Final Season of "Buffy the Vampire Slayer."* London: Virgin, 2004. 224 pp. pb.

4777. _____. *Slayer: The Revised and Updated Unofficial Guide to Buffy the Vampire Slayer*. London: Virgin, 2000. 420 pp. pb.

4778. _____. *Slayer: A Totally Awesome Collection of Buffy Trivia*. London: Virgin Publishing, 2004. 226 pp. pb.

4779. _____. *Slayer: The Totally Cool Unofficial Guide to Buffy*. London: Virgin, 1999. 280 pp. pb.

4780. _____. *Slayer: An Unofficial and Unauthorized Guide to Season Six of Buffy the Vampire Slayer*. London: Virgin, 2003. 230 pp. pb.

4781. **Tracy, Kathleen.** *The Girl's Got Bite: The Original Unauthorized Guide to Buffy's World*. New York: St. Martins Griffin, 2003. 342 pp. tp.

4782. _____. *The Girl's Got Bite: The Unofficial Guide to Buffy's World*. Los Angeles: Renaissance Books, 1998. 246 pp. tp.

4783. **Tresca, Don.** "Images of Paraphilia in the Whedonverse." In Erin B. Waggoner, ed. *Sexual Rhetoric in the Works of Joss Whedon: New Essays*. Jefferson, NC: McFarland & Company, 2010, pp. 146–172.

4784. _____. "The Three Faces of Anne: Identity Formation in *Buffy the Vampire Slayer* and *Angel*." In Mary Alice Money for PopMatters.com, ed. *Joss Whedon: The Complete Companion: The TV Series, the Movies, the Comic Books and More*. London: Titan Books, 2012, pp. 191–198. An earlier version appeared as part of PopMatters.com's

Spotlight: Joss Whedon, originally posted on March 14, 2011.

4785. **Tropiano, Stephen.** "*Buffy*'s Willow Rosenberg." In Stephen Tropiano. *The Prime Time Closet: A History of Gays and Lesbians on TV*. New York: Applause, 2002, pp. 181–184.

4786. **Trump, Anne L.** *Identity, Affect and Agency:* Buffy the Vampire Slayer *and the Contemporary Audience*. Fort Collins: Colorado State University, M.A. thesis, 2001.

4787. **Turnbull, Sue.** "Moments of Inspiration: Performing Spike." In Dee Amy-Chinn and Milly Williamson, eds. *The Vampire Spike in Text and Fandom: Unsettling Oppositions in* Buffy the Vampire Slayer. Special Issue of *European Journal of Cultural Studies* 8, 3 (August 2005): 367–373.

4788. _____. "'Not Just Another *Buffy* Paper': Towards an Aesthetics of Television." *Slayage: The Online International Journal of Buffy Studies* 4, 1–2 [13–14] (October 2004). Posted at: http://www.whedonstudies.tv/. This paper was also the keynote address at the Slayage Conference on *Buffy the Vampire Slayer*, Nashville, TN, May 27–30, 2004.

4789. _____. "Teaching *Buffy*: The Curriculum and the Text in Media Studies." *Continuum: Journal of Media & Cultural Studies* 17, 1 (2003): 19–31.

4790. _____. "'Who am I? Who are you?': On the Narrative Imperative of Not Knowing Who You Are in *Buffy the Vampire Slayer*." *Metro Magazine* 137 (2003). A paper originally presented at The Buffyverse: A Symposium on *Buffy the Vampire Slayer*, University of Melbourne, Melbourne, Australia, November 21, 2002.

4791. _____, **and Vyvyan Stranieri.** *Bite Me: Narrative Structures &* "Buffy the Vampire Slayer." Melbourne: Australian Centre for the Moving Image (ACMI), 2003. 80 pp.

4792. **Turner, Amanda.** "'Because It's Wrong': Limitations of Female Empowerment in *Buffy the Vampire Slayer*." *Watcher Junior: The Journal of Undergraduate Research in Buffy Studies* 4, 1 [4] (November 2009). Posted at: http://www.whedonstudies.tv/.

4793. **Upstone, Sara.** "'LA's Got It All': Hybridity and Otherness in *Angel*'s Postmodern City." In Stacey Abbott, ed. *Reading* Angel: *The TV Spinoff with a Soul*. New York: I. B. Tauris, 2005, pp. 101–113.

4794. Valente, Catherynne M. "Let's Go to Work." In Lynne M. Thomas and Deborah Stanish, eds. *Whedonistas! A Celebration of the Worlds of Joss Whedon by the Women Who Love Them.* Des Moines, IA: Mad Norwegian Press, 2011. 178–181.

4795. Van Dyke, Trudi. "'At Midnight Drain the Stream of Life': Vampires and the New Woman." A paper presented at the Slayage Conference on *Buffy the Vampire Slayer*, Nashville, TN, May 27–30, 2004. Posted at: http://www.slayageonline.com/SCBtVS_Archive/.

4796. Van Gameren, Sophia. "'That Boy Is Our Last Hope': Andrew, *Star Wars*, and the Figure of the Jedi in *Buffy the Vampire Slayer*." A paper presented at the Slayage Conference on *Buffy the Vampire Slayer*, Nashville, TN, May 27–30, 2004. Posted at: http://www.slayageonline.com/SCBtVS_Archive/.

4797. Ventura, Michael. "Warrior Women: The Popularity among Teenagers of TV Shows Like La Femme Nikita, Xena: Warrior Princess and Buffy the Vampire Slayer." *Psychology Today* 31, 6 (November-December 1998): 58–61.

4798. Verstelle, Rowan. *From Dracula to Buffy: A Study on the Original Vampire and His Descendants.* Utrecht, Netherlands: Universiteit Utrecht, BA honors thesis, 2013.

4799. Vetere, Lisa M. "The Rage of Willow: Malefic Witchcraft Fantasy in *Buffy the Vampire Slayer*." In U. Melissa Anyiwo and Karoline Szatek-Tudor, eds. Buffy *Conquers the Academy: Conference Papers from the 2009/2010 Popular Culture/American Culture Associations.* Newcastle upon Tyne, UK: Cambridge Scholars Publishing, 2013, pp. 76–88. A paper originally presented in earlier form as "The Rage of Willow: Witchcraft Fantasy in *Buffy the Vampire Slayer*" at the 2009 PCA/ACA National Conference, New Orleans, LA, April 8–11, 2009, and accepted (but not presented) as "The Rage of Willow: A Kleinian Perspective on Witchcraft Performances" for SC3: The Slayage Conference on the Whedonverses, Henderson State College, Arkadelphia, AR, June 5–8, 2008.

4800. Vint, Sherryl. "The Culture Wars from Genesis to *Buffy*." *Science-Fiction Studies* 33, 3 (November 2006): 533–6.

4801. _____. "'Killing Us Softly?': A Feminist Search for the 'Real' Buffy." *Slayage: The Online International Journal of Buffy Studies* 2, 1 [5] (May 2002). Posted at: http://www.slayageonline.com/.

4802. Vlahos, Maria. "Love Hurts, or, Why Buffy Couldn't Find Love." PopMatters.com's *Spotlight: Joss Whedon* (April 4, 2011). Posted at: http://www.popmatters.com/feature/139130-love-hurts-or-why-buffy-couldnt-find-love/.

4803. Voshel, Erick R. "The Strange and Incredible Saga of Willow and Tara on *Buffy the Vampire Slayer*." Article in 4 parts (August 23, 2006). Posted at: http://www.whedon.info/article.php3?id_article=17567.

4804. Vowell, Sarah. "The Nerd Voice." In Sarah Vowell. *The Partly Cloudy Patriot.* New York: Simon & Schuster, 2002, pp. 87–117.

4805. Wright, Steve. "Slaying Sex on the Hellmouth." *All Slay* 3 (2004).

4806. Waggoner, Erin B. "Preface." In Erin B. Waggoner, ed. *Sexual Rhetoric in the Works of Joss Whedon: New Essays.* Jefferson, NC: McFarland & Company, 2010, pp. 1–5.

4807. _____. "The Symbolic Gun in Willow's Love Life." In Erin B. Waggoner, ed. *Sexual Rhetoric in the Works of Joss Whedon: New Essays.* Jefferson, NC: McFarland & Company, 2010, pp. 7–17. A paper originally presented as "Happiness is a Warm Gun: The Symbolic Gun in Willow's Love Life" at the 30th Annual Southwest/Texas PCA/ACA Conference, Albuquerque, NM, February 25–28, 2009.

4808. _____, ed. *Sexual Rhetoric in the Works of Joss Whedon: New Essays.* Jefferson, NC: McFarland & Company, 2010. 278 pp. tp.

4809. Wagner, Hank. "The Family Hour." In Paul Ruditis, ed. Buffy the Vampire Slayer: *The Watcher's Guide.* Vol. 3. New York: Simon, 2004, pp. 249–254.

4810. Walker, Cynthia W., and Amy H. Sturgis. "Joss Whedon and the Evolved Nerd." In Lisa Holderman, ed. *Common Sense: Intelligence as Presented on Popular Television.* Lanham, MD: Lexington Books, 2008, pp. 210–212.

4811. Wall, Brian, and Michael Zryd. "Vampire Dialectics: Knowledge, Institutions and Labour." In Roz Kaveney, ed. *Reading the Vampire Slayer: An Unofficial Critical Companion to* Buffy *and* Angel. 1st ed. New York: I. B. Tauris, 2001, pp. 53–77.

4812. Wallis, Keziah. "Buffy and the Postmodern Vampire." *Not a Film Student* website. (March 2012). Posted at: http://notafilmstudent.wordpress.com/2012/03/02/buffy-and-the-postmodern-vampire/.

4813. Wandless, William. "Undead Letters: Searches and Researches in *Buffy the Vampire*

Slayer." Slayage: The Online International Journal of Buffy Studies 1, 1 [1] (January 2001). Posted at: http://www.whedonstudies.tv/.

4814. Ward, Ashleigh. *"Redemption Is Hard": Television Narrative Structure and the Story of Redemption in* Buffy the Vampire Slayer. Adelaide, Aust.: University of Adelaide, BA honors thesis, 2005. 72 pp. Large format.

4815. Warner, Matthew. "Addictive Plotting as Taught by *Buffy the Vampire Slayer."* In Matthew Warner. *Horror Isn't a 4-Letter Word: Essays on Writing & Appreciating the Genre.* Hyattsville, MD: Guide Dog Books, 2008, pp. 33–38.

4816. Watt, Mike. "Urge to Kill Rising: A Farewell to *Buffy."* *The Incomplete Works of Mike Watt: A Massive Tome of Ego, Balls and Vanity, Volume 1.* N.p.: Happy Cloud Publishing, 2009. pp. 155–165. Originally appeared on FilmThreat.com (July 2, 2003).

4817. Watt-Evans, Lawrence. "Matchmaking on the Hellmouth." In Glenn Yeffeth, ed. *Seven Seasons of* Buffy: *Science Fiction and Fantasy Writers Discuss Their Favorite Television Show.* Dallas, TX: Benbella Books, 2003, pp. 188–194.

4818. Weaver, Roslyn. "Apocalypse Now and Again: The Apocalyptic Paradigm and the Meaning of Life and (Un)Death in *Buffy the Vampire Slayer."* In Anthony R. Mills, John W. Morehead, and J. Ryan Parker, eds. *Joss Whedon and Religion: Essays on an Angry Atheist's Explorations of the Sacred.* Jefferson, NC: McFarland & Company, 2013, pp. 67–82.

4819. Weber, Kathryn. "Exploding Sexual Binaries in *Buffy* and *Angel."* In Erin B. Waggoner, ed. *Sexual Rhetoric in the Works of Joss Whedon: New Essays.* Jefferson, NC: McFarland & Company, 2010, pp. 248–261.

4820. Wee, Valerie. "Teen Television and the WB Television Network." In Sharon Marie Ross and Louisa Ellen Stein, eds. *Teen Television: Essays on Programming and Fandom.* Jefferson, NC: McFarland & Company, 2008, pp. 43–60.

4821. Wegner, Phillip E. "We're Family: Monstrous Kinships, Fidelity, and the Event in *Buffy the Vampire Slayer* and Octavia Butler's *Parable* Novels." In Philip E. Wegner. *Life between Two Deaths, 1989–2001: U.S. Culture in the Long Nineties.* Durham, NC: Duke University Press, 2009, pp. 195–217.

4822. Weis, Suzie. "Here Endeth the Lesson: The Relationship of Buffy and Spike." *Refractory:*

A Journal of Entertainment Media 11 (2007). Posted at: http://refractory.unimelb.edu.au/2007/09/04/refractory-volume-11-2007/.

4823. Wells, Kimberly Ann. "The 'Girl Power Bit': *Buffy the Vampire Slayer's* Witches Change the World." *Screaming, Flying, and Laughing: Magical Feminism's Witches in Contemporary Film, Television, and Novels.* College Station: Texas A&M University, Ph.D. dissertation, 2007. pp. 166–228. Posted at: http://repository.tamu.edu/handle/1969.1/6007.

4824. West, Candace E. "Heroic Humanism and Humanistic Heroism in Joss Whedon's Shows." In Mary Alice Money for PopMatters.com, ed. *Joss Whedon: The Complete Companion: The TV Series, the Movies, the Comic Books and More.* London: Titan Books, 2012, pp. 264–269. An earlier version titled "Heroic Humanism and Humanistic Heroism in Shows of Joss Whedon" appeared as part of PopMatters.com's *Spotlight: Joss Whedon,* originally posted on March 22, 2011.

4825. West, David. "'Concentrate on the Kicking Movie': *Buffy* and East Asian Cinema." In Roz Kaveney, ed. *Reading the Vampire Slayer: An Unofficial Critical Companion to* Buffy *and* Angel. 1st ed. New York: I. B. Tauris, 2001, pp. 166–186.

4826. West, Michelle Sagara. "For the Love of Riley." In Glenn Yeffeth, ed. *Seven Seasons of* Buffy: *Science Fiction and Fantasy Writers Discuss Their Favorite Television Show.* Dallas, TX: Benbella Books, 2003, pp. 65–71.

4827. _____. "Why We Love Lindsey." In Glenn Yeffeth, ed. *Five Seasons of* Angel: *Science Fiction and Fantasy Writers Discuss Their Favorite Vampire.* Dallas, TX: Benbella Books, 2004, pp. 93–101.

4828. Westerfield, Scott. "A Slayer Comes to Town." In Glenn Yeffeth, ed. *Seven Seasons of* Buffy: *Science Fiction and Fantasy Writers Discuss Their Favorite Television Show.* Dallas, TX: Benbella Books, 2003, pp. 30–40.

4829. Whedon, Joss, and Paul Ruditis. "'Restless': A Path to Premonitions." In Paul Ruditis, ed. Buffy the Vampire Slayer: *The Watcher's Guide,* Vol. 3. New York: Simon, 2004, pp. 293–350.

4830. White, Rosemary [Rosie]. "Buffy Incorporated: *Buffy the Vampire Slayer,* Authenticity and the American Teen." *The American Studies Journal* 47 (Summer 2001): 23–29.

4831. _____. "Feminist Icon? Buffy the Vampire Slayer and Postfeminist Television." In Carolyn Brina, Carolyn Britton, and Allison Assiter, eds. *Millennial Visions: Feminisms into the 21st Century*. Cardiff, Wales, UK: Cardiff Academic Press, 2001, pp. 145–160. A paper originally presented at Millennial Visions: Women in the 21st Century, Conference of the Women's Studies Network Association, Bristol, UK, July 2000.

4832. _____. "Television, Violence and Demons: Discussing Media Effects with the Vampire Slayer." In Jodie A. Kreider and Meghan K. Winchell, eds. Buffy *in the Classroom: Essays on Teaching with the Vampire Slayer*. Jefferson, NC: McFarland & Company, 2010, pp. 136–145.

4833. Whitman, Douglas Glen. "The Political Economy of Non-Coercive Vampire Lifestyles." In Richard Greene and K. Silem Mohammad, ed. *Zombies, Vampires, and Philosophy: New Life for the Undead*. Chicago: Open Court, 2010, pp. 169–182.

4834. Whitney, Sarah Elizabeth. *Concrete Angels: Reading the Tough Woman in Contemporary Television*. Charlottesville: University of Virginia, Ph. D. dissertation, 2007. 335 pp. Large format.

4835. Wilcox, Rhonda V. "The Aesthetics of Cult Television." In Stacey Abbott, ed. *The Cult TV Book*. New York: I. B. Tauris, 2010, pp. 31–39.

4836. _____. "The Darkness of 'Passion': Visuals and Voiceovers, Sound and Shadow." In Mary Alice Money for PopMatters.com, ed. *Joss Whedon: The Complete Companion: The TV Series, the Movies, the Comic Books and More*. London: Titan Books, 2012, pp. 102–112. An earlier version appeared as part of PopMatters.com's *Spotlight: Joss Whedon*, originally posted on March 10, 2011.

4837. _____. "Every Night I Save You: Buffy, Spike, Sex, and Redemption." *Slayage: The Online International Journal of Buffy Studies* 2, 1 [5] (May 2002). Posted at: http://www.whedonstudies.tv/. Rev, text in Rhonda V. Wilcox. *Why Buffy Matters: The Art of* Buffy the Vampire Slayer. London: I. B. Tauris, 2005. 79–89. A paper originally presented at the Popular Culture Association Conference, Toronto, Canada, March 2002. http://slayageonline.com/PDF/wilcox2.pdf.

4838. _____. "Foreword: Music in the Key of Whedon." In Kendra Preston Leonard, ed. *Buffy, Ballads, and Bad Guys Who Sing: Music in the Worlds of Joss Whedon*. Lanham, MD: Scarecrow Press, 2011, pp. v–x.

4839. _____. "'I Do Not Hold to That': Joss Whedon and Original Sin." In Rhonda V. Wilcox and Tanya R. Cochran, eds. *Investigating* Firefly

and Serenity: *Science Fiction on the Frontier*. New York: I. B. Tauris, 2008, pp. 155–166. A paper originally presented as a featured lecture at SC2: The Slayage Conference on the Whedonverses, Gordon College, Barnesville, GA, May 25–28, 2006.

4840. _____. "In 'the Demon Section of the Card Catalog': Buffy Studies and Television Studies." *Slayage: The Online International Journal of Buffy Studies* 6, 1 [21] (Fall 2006). Posted at: http://www.whedonstudies.tv/. A joint publication with *Critical Studies in Television: Scholarly Studies of Small Screen Fictions* 1, 1 (Spring 2006): 37–48.

4841. _____. "'Let It Simmer': Tone in 'Pangs.'" *Slayage: The Journal of the Whedon Studies Association* 9, 1 [33] (Spring 2011).). Posted at: http://www.whedonstudies.tv/. A paper originally presented in earlier form as "'Let It Simmer': Tonal Shift in 'Pangs'" at SC4: The Slayage Conference on the Whedonverses, Flagler College, St. Augustine, FL, June 3–6, 2010.

4842. _____. "Poetry: T.S. Eliot Comes to Television: Buffy's 'Restless.'" *Slayage: The Online International Journal of Buffy Studies* 2, 3 [7] (December 2002). Posted at: http://www.whedonstudies.tv/. Rev. text in Rhonda V. Wilcox. *Why Buffy Matters: The Art of* Buffy the Vampire Slayer. London: I. B. Tauris, 2005. 162–173. A paper originally presented in earlier form at the 2002 PCAS/ACAS Annual Conference, Charlotte, NC, October 3–5, 2002.

4843. _____. "Set on This Earth Like a Bubble: Word as Flesh in the Dark Seasons." In Lynne Y. Edwards, Elizabeth L. Rambo. and James B. South, ed. *Buffy Goes Dark: Essays on the Final Two Seasons of* Buffy the Vampire Slayer *on Television*. Jefferson, NC: McFarland & Company, 2009. 95–113. A paper originally presented at Monstrous Bodies in Science, Fiction, and Culture, Georgia Institute of Technology, Atlanta, March 2005.

4844. _____. "'There Will Never Be a 'Very Special' Buffy': Symbol and Language." In Rhonda V. Wilcox. *Why Buffy Matters: The Art of* Buffy the Vampire Slayer. London: I. B. Tauris, 2005. 17–29. Also published in earlier form as "'There Will Never Be a 'Very Special' Buffy': Buffy and the Monsters of Teen Life" in *Journal of Popular Film & Television* 27, 2 (Summer 1999): 16–23; and in *Slayage: The Online International Journal of Buffy Studies* 1, 2 [2] (March 2001). Posted at: http://www.whedonstudies.tv/.

4845. _____. "Unreal TV." In Gary R. Edgerton and Brian G. Rose, ed. *Thinking Outside the Box: A Contemporary Television Genre Reader*. Lexington: University Press of Kentucky, 2005, pp. 201–225.

4846. _____. "Whedon and Company: Worlds Await." PopMatters.com's *Spotlight: Joss Whedon* (April 14, 2011). Posted at: http://www.popmatters.com/feature/139272-whedon-and-company-worlds-await/.

4847. _____. "'Who Died and Made Her the Boss?': Patterns of Mortality in *Buffy the Vampire Slayer.*" In Rhonda V. Wilcox and David Lavery, ed. *Fighting the Forces: What's at Stake in* Buffy the Vampire Slayer. Lanham, MD: Rowman & Littlefield, 2002, pp. 3–17.

4848. _____. *Why Buffy Matters: The Art of* Buffy the Vampire Slayer. London: I. B. Tauris, 2005. 246 pp. tp.

4849. _____, and David Lavery. "Afterword: The Depths of *Angel* and the Birth of *Angel* Studies." In Stacey Abbott, ed. *Reading* Angel: *The TV Spin-off with a Soul.* New York: I. B. Tauris, 2005, pp. 221–229.

4850. _____, and David Lavery. "Introduction." In Rhonda V. Wilcox and David Lavery, eds. *Fighting the Forces: What's at Stake in* Buffy the Vampire Slayer. Lanham, MD: Rowman & Littlefield, 2002, pp. xvii–xxix.

4851. _____, and David Lavery. "*Slayage* at Ten: The Danger of Birthdays." *Slayage: The Journal of the Whedon Studies Association* 8, 4 [32] (Winter 2011). Posted at: http://www.whedonstudies.tv/.

4852. _____, and David Lavery, eds. *Fighting the Forces: What's at Stake in* Buffy the Vampire Slayer. Lanham, MD: Rowman & Littlefield, 2002. 290 pp. tp. Along with essays they authored themselves, the editors have included contributions by Camille Bacon-Smith, Kristina Busse, S. Renee Dechert, Diane DeKalb-Rittenhouse, Lynne Edwards, Gregory Erickson, , Sarah N. Gatson, Elyce Rae Helford, Donald Keller, Elizabeth Krimmer, Tanya Krzywinska, Justine Larbalestier, Farah Mendolsohn, Mary Alice Money, Karen Eileen Overbey, Patricia Pender, Lahney Preston-Matto, Shilpa Ravel, Anita Rose, Catherine Sieman, Sarah E. Skwire, J. P. Williams, and Amanda Zweerink.

4853. Wiley, Christopher. "Theorizing Television Music as Serial Art: *Buffy the Vampire Slayer* and the Narratology of the Thematic Score." In Kendra Preston Leonard, ed. Buffy, *Ballads, and Bad Guys Who Sing: Music in the Worlds of Joss Whedon.* Lanham, MD: Scarecrow Press, 2011, pp. 29–73. Also presented in earlier forms as "'I Believe the Subtext Here Is Rapidly Becoming Text': Music, Gender and Fantasy in *Buffy the Vampire Slayer*" at Blood, Text and Fears: Reading Around *Buffy the Vampire Slayer*, University of East Anglia, 19–20 October 2002, and as "Reading Television (Under)score: The Music of *Buffy the Vampire Slayer*" at Keele University, 18 March 2005, and City University London, 4 May 2005.

4854. Williams, J. P. "Choosing Your Own Mother: Mother-Daughter Conflicts in *Buffy.*" In Rhonda V. Wilcox and David Lavery, ed. *Fighting the Forces: What's at Stake in* Buffy the Vampire Slayer. Lanham, MD: Rowman & Littlefield, 2002, pp. 61–72.

4855. Williams, Rebecca Sian. "'It's About Power!': Executive Fans, Spoiler Whores and Capital in the *Buffy the Vampire Slayer* On-Line Fan Community." *Slayage: The Online International Journal of Buffy Studies* 3, 3–4 [11–12] (April 2004). Posted at: http://www.whedonstudies.tv/.

4856. _____. *A Radical Interpretation of the Text: DeCerteau, (Sub)textual Poaching and Queer Readings in Interpretive Communities.* Cardiff, Wales, UK: Cardiff University, M.A. thesis, 2004. 162 pp. Large format.

4857. _____. *Spoiler Whores and Shipper Wars: Hierarchy and Power in the On-Line* Buffy the Vampire Slayer *Fan Community.* Cardiff, Wales, UK: Cardiff University, BA honors thesis, 2003.

4858. Williams, Todd. "The Threat to the Subject in 'Once More, with Feeling.'" Paper presented at the Slayage Conference on *Buffy the Vampire Slayer*, Nashville, TN, May 27–30, 2004. Posted at: http://www.slayageonline.com/SCBtVS_Archive/.

4859. Williamson, Milly. "*Buffy the Vampire Slayer.*" In David Lavery, ed. *The Essential Cult Television Reader.* Lexington: University Press of Kentucky, 2010, pp. 60–67.

4860. _____. *The Lure of the Vampire: Gender, Fiction and Fandom from Bram Stoker to Buffy the Vampire Slayer.* London: Wallflower Press, 2005. 224 pp. tp.

4861. _____. "Spike, Sex and Subtext: Intertextual Portrayals of the Sympathetic Vampire on Cult Television." In Dee Amy-Chinn and Milly Williamson, ed. *The Vampire Spike in Text and Fandom: Unsettling Oppositions in* Buffy the Vampire Slayer. Special Issue of *European Journal of Cultural Studies* 8, 3 (August 2005): 289–311.

4862. ____. "Vampire Transformations: from Gothic Demon to Domestication?" In Carla T. Kungl, ed. *Vampires: Myths and Metaphors of Enduring Evil.* Oxford: Inter-Disciplinary Press, 2003, pp. 101–107. Posted at: http://www.interdisciplinary.net/publishing/id-press/ebooks/vampires-myths-and-metaphors-of-enduring-evil. A paper originally presented at the Vampires: Myths and Metaphors of Enduring Evil Conference held in Budapest, Hungary, May 22–24, 2003.

4863. Wilson, Diane E. "Buffy vs. Bakhtin: Carnival and Dialogism in the Buffyverse." A paper presented at SC2: The Slayage Conference on the Whedonverses, Gordon College, Barnesville, GA, May 25–28, 2006. Posted at: http://dianewilson.us/buffy/sc2.paper.pdf.

4864. Wilson, Dominique Beth. "Willow and Which Craft? The Portrayal of Witchcraft in Joss Whedon's *Buffy: The Vampire Slayer.*" In Carole M. Cusack, Frances Di Lauro, and Christopher Hartney, eds. *The Buddha of Suburbia: Proceedings of the Eighth Australian and International Religion, Literature and the Arts Conference 2004.* Sydney: RLA Press, 2005, pp. 146–158. A paper originally presented at the Eighth Australian and International Religion, Literature and the Arts Conference, Sydney, Australia, October 1–3, 2004.

4865. Wilson, Melanie. "Buffy's Dream in *Surprise.*" In Kevin K. Durand, ed. *Buffy Meets the Academy: Essays on the Episodes and Scripts as Texts.* Jefferson, NC: McFarland & Company, 2009, pp. 125–130.

4866. ____. "She Believes in Me: Angel, Spike, and Redemption." In Kevin K. Durand, ed. *Buffy Meets the Academy: Essays on the Episodes and Scripts as Texts.* Jefferson, NC: McFarland & Company, 2009, pp. 137–149. A paper originally presented as "'She believes in me': The Method and Mechanics of Redemption in the Buffyverse" at SC3: The Slayage Conference on the Whedonverses, Henderson State College, Arkadelphia, AR, June 5–8, 2008.

4867. ____. "Why the Cheese Man Is an Integral Part of *Restless.*" In Kevin K. Durand, ed. *Buffy Meets the Academy: Essays on the Episodes and Scripts as Texts.* Jefferson, NC: McFarland & Company, 2009, pp. 161–168.

4868. Wilson, Steve. "Laugh, Spawn of Hell, Laugh." In Roz Kaveney, ed. *Reading the Vampire Slayer: An Unofficial Critical Companion to Buffy and Angel.* 1st ed. New York: I. B. Tauris, 2001, pp. 78–97.

4869. Wilson, Tamara. "Keeping *Buffy* in the Classroom." In Kevin K. Durand, ed. *Buffy Meets the Academy: Essays on the Episodes and Scripts as Texts.* Jefferson, NC: McFarland & Company, 2009, pp. 211–218. A paper originally presented as "Keeping *Buffy* in the Classroom: Well, at Least It Isn't High School" at SC3: The Slayage Conference on the Whedonverses, Henderson State College, Arkadelphia, AR, June 5–8, 2008.

4870. Wilts, Alissa. "Evil, Skanky, and Kinda Gay: Lesbian Images and Issues." In Lynne Y. Edwards, Elizabeth L. Rambo, and James B. South, eds. *Buffy Goes Dark: Essays on the Final Two Seasons of* Buffy the Vampire Slayer *on Television.* Jefferson, NC: McFarland & Company, 2009, pp. 41–56.

4871. ____. "Lesbian-Type Lovers: Heterosexual Writer Bias and the Evil/Dead Lesbian Cliché in the Representation of the Willow/Tara Relationship." A paper presented at the Slayage Conference on *Buffy the Vampire Slayer*, Nashville, TN, May 27–30, 2004. Posted at: http://www.slayageonline.com/SCBtVS_Archive/.

4872. Winchell, Meghan K. "Whedon Takes 'the Scary' Out of Feminism." In Jodie A. Kreider and Meghan K. Winchell, eds. *Buffy in the Classroom: Essays on Teaching with the Vampire Slayer.* Jefferson, NC: McFarland & Company, 2010, pp. 73–82.

4873. Winslade, Jason Lawton. "'Have You Tried Not Being a Slayer?': Performing *Buffy* Fandom in the Classroom." In Jodie A. Kreider and Meghan K. Winchell, eds. *Buffy in the Classroom: Essays on Teaching with the Vampire Slayer.* Jefferson, NC: McFarland & Company, 2010. pp. 22–34.

4874. ____. "'Oh...My...Goddess': Witchcraft, Magick, and Thealogy in *Buffy the Vampire Slayer.*" In Anthony R. Mills, John W. Morehead, and J. Ryan Parker, eds. *Joss Whedon and Religion: Essays on an Angry Atheist's Explorations of the Sacred.* Jefferson, NC: McFarland & Company, 2013, pp. 51–66.

4875. ____. "Teen Witches, Wiccans, and 'Wanna-Blessed-Be's': Pop-Culture Magic in *Buffy the Vampire Slayer.*" *Slayage: The Online International Journal of Buffy Studies* 1, 1 [1] (January 2001). Posted at: http://www.whedonstudies.tv/.

4876. Wisker, Gina. "Vampires and School Girls: High School Highjinks on the Hellmouth in *Buffy the Vampire Slayer.*" *Slayage: The Online International Journal of Buffy Studies* 1, 2 [2]

(March 2001). Posted at: http://www.whedon studies.tv/.

4877. Woofter, Kristopher Karl. "Little Red Riding...Buffy? 'Buffy vs. Dracula' in Explorations of Intertextuality in Introduction to College English." In Jodie A. Kreider and Meghan K. Winchell, ed. Buffy *in the Classroom: Essays on Teaching with the Vampire Slayer.* Jefferson, NC: McFarland & Company, 2010, pp. 169–185.

4878. Wright, Susan Ashley. *The Discourse of Fan Fiction.* Louisville, KY: University of Louisville, Ph.D. dissertation, 2009. 209 pp. Large format.

4879. Wurl, Jody. "Shelve Under Television, Young Adult." In Lynne M. Thomas and Deborah Stanish, eds. *Whedonistas! A Celebration of the Worlds of Joss Whedon by the Women Who Love Them.* Des Moines, IA: Mad Norwegian Press, 2011, pp. 135–141.

4880. Yarbro, Chelsea Quinn. "*Angel*: An Identity Crisis." In Glenn Yeffeth, ed. *Five Seasons of* Angel: *Science Fiction and Fantasy Writers Discuss Their Favorite Vampire.* Dallas, TX: Benbella Books, 2004, pp. 79–86.

4881. _____. "Lions, Gazelles and Buffy." In Glenn Yeffeth, ed. *Seven Seasons of* Buffy: *Science Fiction and Fantasy Writers Discuss Their Favorite Television Show.* Dallas, TX: Benbella Books, 2003, pp. 48–53.

4882. Yatron, Cassandra A. *A Second Chance for Women: Sex and Gender in* Buffy the Vampire Slayer. University Park: Pennsylvania State University, BA honors thesis, 2012. 43 pp. Large format. Posted at: https://honors.libraries.psu.edu/paper/13821/.

4883. Yeffeth, Glenn, ed. *Five Seasons of* Angel: *Science Fiction and Fantasy Writers Discuss*

Their Favorite Vampire. Dallas, TX: Benbella Books, 2004. 216 pp. tp.

4884. _____. *Seven Seasons of Buffy: Science Fiction and Fantasy Writers Discuss Their Favorite Television Show.* Dallas, TX: Benbella Books, 2003. 205 pp. tp.

4885. Yerima, Adam Kem. *From Demigods to Slayers: Contemporary Mythology and Gender Economies in* Buffy the Vampire Slayer. San Bernardino: California State University–San Bernardino, M.A. thesis, 2009. 106 pp. Large format.

4886. Zacharek, Stephanie. "Modern and Mythical Sexuality in *Buffy the Vampire Slayer.*" Salonwww, Nov 2002. Posted at: http://www.salon.com/2002/11/09/buffy_paper/. A paper originally presented at Blood, Text and Fears: Reading Around *Buffy the Vampire Slayer*, University of East Anglia, October 19–20, 2002.

4887. Zettel, Sarah. "When Did the Scoobies Become Insiders?" In Glenn Yeffeth, ed. Dallas, *Seven Seasons of* Buffy: *Science Fiction and Fantasy Writers Discuss Their Favorite Television Show.* TX: Benbella Books, 2003, pp. 109–115.

4888. Zhang, Angela. "*Buffy* and *Dollhouse*: Visions of Female Empowerment and Disempowerment." In Mary Alice Money for PopMatters. com, ed. *Joss Whedon: The Complete Companion: The TV Series, the Movies, the Comic Books and More.* London: Titan Books, 2012, pp. 401–406. An earlier version appeared as part of PopMatters. com's *Spotlight: Joss Whedon*, originally posted on April 6, 2011.

4889. Zubiller, Cora. *Philosophical Potential in "Buffy the Vampire Slayer."* München, Germany: GRIN Verlag, 2010. 28 pp.

True Blood

HBO's *True Blood*, loosely based on The Southern Vampire Mysteries series of novels by mystery-writer Charlaine Harris, quickly challenged *Buffy the Vampire Slayer* in terms of popularity and cultural impact. The show was unique in being directed at an adult audience and placing sexual themes in the forefront of its storylines. Unlike *Buffy*, which originated as a mildly successful movie and then was embodied in a television script, *True Blood* had originated as a successful and award-winning series of novels that had found a large audience both among mystery fans and paranormal romance fans. While several dozen novels had been produced as *Buffy* became a successful television phenomenon, none of the *Buffy* novels approached the success of Harris' novels.

The premise of *True Blood* is that after the creation of synthetic blood, vampires are now "out of the coffin" and live freely and openly among humans. One such vampire, the 173-year-old Bill Compton (Stephen Moyer), soon finds himself in the company of telepathic barmaid Sookie Stackhouse (Anna Paquin), and they become romantically involved as the series progresses. The storyline centers on Bon Temps, a town in rural Louisiana, but occasionally ventured to the urban world of New Orleans and Dallas.

The show became a runaway hit for HBO. While continuing to focus on vampires and conflicts within the vampire community, which became a more or less subtle metaphor for homosexuality, as the seasons progressed, an emphasis on shapeshifters/werewolves and fairies also supplied key sub-plots. The LGBT concerns, nevertheless, predominated with issues of the acceptance of vampires by the larger community, the permanency of vampire relationships, and the personal tragedies of living as a minority in a hostile environment running from season to season. A religious opponent to the vampires appeared in the form of the Fellowship of the Sun.

Like *Buffy*, *True Blood* ran for seven seasons, completing its run in 2014. Meanwhile, Harris completed 13 novels in the Sookie Stackhouse series, with the last official novel, *Dead Ever After*, appearing in 2013. It was followed, however, by a fourteenth novel, *After Dead: What Came Next in the World of Sookie Stackhouse*, which detailed the future of the characters. She also penned an additional volume of series-related short stories and one volume, *The Sookie Stackhouse Companion*, which reflected on the series. Along the way, a number of related short stories, many eventually emerging as chapters in the novels, were also published in a variety of venues.

4890. Abbott, Stacey. "TV Love Fangs: The Televisuality of HBO Horror." In Brigid Cherry, ed. *True Blood: Investigating Vampires and Southern Gothic*. London: I. B. Tauris, 2013, pp. 25–38.

4891. Aloi, Peg. "Night Is the Color of Blood." In Leah Wilson, ed. *A Taste of True Blood: The Fangbanger's Guide*. Dallas, TX: Benbella Books, 2010, pp. 177–93.

4892. Amador, Victoria. "Blacks and Whites, Trash and Good Country People in *True Blood*." In Brigid Cherry, ed. *True Blood: Investigating Vampires and Southern Gothic*. London: I. B. Tauris, 2013, pp. 122–38.

4893. _____. "The Gothic Louisiana of Charlaine Harris and Anne Rice." In Deborah Mutch. *The Modern Vampire and Human Identity*. Basingstoke, UK/New York: Palgrave Macmillan, 2013, pp. 163–76.

4894. Anyiwo, U. Melissa. "It's Not Television, It's Transmedia Storytelling: Marketing the 'Real' World of *True Blood*." In Brigid Cherry, ed. *True Blood: Investigating Vampires and Southern Gothic*. London: I. B. Tauris, 2013, pp. 157–71.

4895. Ballantine, Phillipa. "What a Strange Love." In Leah Wilson, ed. *A Taste of True Blood:* *The Fangbanger's Guide*. Dallas, TX: Benbella Books, 2010, pp. 137–43.

4896. Barkman, Adam. "Does God Hate Fangs?" In George A. Dunn and Rebecca Housel, ed. *True Blood and Philosophy: We Wanna Think Bad Things with You*. New York: John Wiley & Sons, 2010, pp. 175–83.

4897. Batillo, Beverley. "From Mystery to Mayhem: The Works of Charlaine Harris." In Charlaine Harris, ed. *The Sookie Stackhouse Companion*. New York: Ace Hardcover, 2011, pp. 289–93.

4898. _____. "Recollections Around the Duckpond: The Fans of Charlaine Harris." In Charlaine Harris, ed. *The Sookie Stackhouse Companion*. New York: Ace Hardcover, 2011, pp. 295–300.

4899. _____, and Victoria Koski. "Sookie Stackhouse Trivia: How Much of a Sookie Fan Are You?" In Charlaine Harris, ed. *The Sookie Stackhouse Companion*. New York: Ace Hardcover, 2011, pp. 226–44.

4900. Beck, Bernard. "Fearless Vampire Kissers: Bloodsuckers We Love in Twilight, True Blood and Others." *Multicultural Perspectives* 13, 2 (2011): 90–92.

4901. Bethke, Bruce, and Karen Bethke. "From Castle Dracula to Merlotte's Bar & Grill." In Leah Wilson, ed. *A Taste of True Blood: The Fangbanger's Guide.* Dallas, TX: Benbella Books, 2010, pp. 223–39.

4902. Blayde, Ariadne, and George A. Dunn. "Pets, Cattle, and Higher Life Forms on True Blood." In George A. Dunn and Rebecca Housel, ed. *True Blood and Philosophy: We Wanna Think Bad Things with You.* New York: John Wiley & Sons, 2010, pp. 33–47.

4903. Brace, Patricia, and Robert Arp. "Coming Out of the Coffin and Coming Out of the Closet." In George A. Dunn and Rebecca Housel, ed. *True Blood and Philosophy: We Wanna Think Bad Things with You.* New York: John Wiley & Sons, 2010, pp. 93–108.

4904. Brick, Emily. "*True Blood* and Online Fan Culture." In Basil Glynn, James Aston, and Beth Johnson, eds. *Television, Sex and Society: Analyzing Contemporary Representations.* New York/London: Bloomsbury Academic, 2012, pp. 47–62.

4905. Buchanan, Ginjer. "Adapt-or Die!" In Leah Wilson, ed. *A Taste of True Blood: The Fangbanger's Guide.* Dallas, TX: Benbella Books, 2010, pp. 211–21.

4906. Bundgaard, Andra. *The Female Heroine and the New Vampires on Television: A Comparison of* Buffy the Vampire Slayer, True Blood *and* The Vampire Diaries. Dublin, Ireland: Dublin City University, M.A. thesis, 2012. 76 pp. Large format.

4907. Cherry, Brigid. "Before the Night Is Through: *True Blood* as Cult TV." In Brigid Cherry, ed. *True Blood: Investigating Vampires and Southern Gothic.* London: I. B. Tauris, 2013, pp. 3–21.

4908. _____, ed. *True Blood: Investigating Vampires and Southern Gothic.* London: I. B. Tauris, 2013. 213 pp. tp.

4909. Choyke, Kelly Lynn. *Domesticating the Vampire: An LGBTQ Audience Reception Study of* True Blood. Carbondale: Southern Illinois University, M.A. thesis, 2012. 109 pp. Large format.

4910. Clifton, Jacob. "A Few Blown Fuses Before the Night Is Over." In Leah Wilson, ed. *A Taste of True Blood: The Fangbanger's Guide.* Dallas, TX: Benbella Books, 2010, pp. 147–62.

4911. Conway, Paula. *Throw a True Blood Party: An Unofficial Guide to Partying with Your Favorite Vamps.* Riverdale, NY: Riverdale Avenue Books, 2013. tp.

4912. Corn, Kevin J., and George A. Dunn. "Let the Bon Temps Roll: Sacrifice, Scapegoats, and Good Times." In George A. Dunn and Rebecca Housel, ed. *True Blood and Philosophy: We Wanna Think Bad Things with You.* New York: John Wiley & Sons, 2010, pp. 139–55.

4913. Craton, Lillian E., and Kathryn E. Jonell. "'I Am Sookie, Hear Me Roar!': Sookie Stackhouse and Feminist Ambivalence." In George A. Dunn and Rebecca Housel, ed. *True Blood and Philosophy: We Wanna Think Bad Things with You.* New York: John Wiley & Sons, 2010, pp. 109–21.

4914. Culver, Jennifer. "Dressing Up and Playing Human: Vampire Assimilation in the Human Playground." In George A. Dunn and Rebecca Housel, ed. *True Blood and Philosophy: We Wanna Think Bad Things with You.* New York: John Wiley & Sons, 2010, pp. 19–31.

4915. Curry, Fred. "Keeping Secrets from Sookie." In George A. Dunn and Rebecca Housel, ed. *True Blood and Philosophy: We Wanna Think Bad Things with You.* New York: John Wiley & Sons, 2010, pp. 203–14.

4916. Curtis, William M. "Honey, If We Can't Kill People, What's the Point of Being a Vampire?" In George A. Dunn and Rebecca Housel, ed. *True Blood and Philosophy: We Wanna Think Bad Things with You.* New York: John Wiley & Sons, 2010, pp. 65–78.

4917. Dimming, Jessica. *"Would you understand what I meant if I said I was only human?": The Image of the Vampire in Stephenie Meyer's* Twilight *and Charlaine Harris's* Dead Until Dark. Karlstad, Sweden: Karlstad University, Student thesis, 2013. 32 pp. Large format. Posted at http://www.diva-portal.org/smash/get/diva2:601773/FULLTEXT01.pdf.

4918. Dunn, George A. "You Look Good Enough to Eat: Love, Madness, and the Food Analogy." In Rebecca Housel and J. Jeremy Wisnewski. *Twilight and Philosophy: Vampires, Vegetarians, and the Pursuit of Immortality.* New York: John Wiley & Sons, 2009, pp. 7–24.

4919. Dunn, George A., and Rebecca Housel, eds. *Trueblood and Philosophy: We Wanna Think Bad Things with You.* New York: John Wiley & Sons, 2010. 246 pp. tp. Includes articles by Christophe l' Robichaud, Jennifer Culver, Ariadne Blayde and George A. Dunn, Joseph J. Foy, Patricia Brace and Robert Arp, Lillian E. Craton and Kothryn E. Janell, Ron Hirschbein, Kevin J. Corn and George A. Dunn, Andrew Terjesen and Jenny

Terjesen, Adam Barkman, and Fred Curry, and Sarah Grubb.

4920. Elliott-Smith, Darren. "The Homosexual Vampire as a Metaphor For...the Homosexual Vampire? *True Blood*, Homonormativity, and Assimilation." In Brigid Cherry, ed. *True Blood: Investigating Vampires and Southern Gothic.* London: I. B. Tauris, 2013, pp. 139–54.

4921. Erickson, Gregory. "Drink in Remembrance of Me: Blood, Bodies and Divine Absence in *True Blood.*" In Brigid Cherry, ed. *True Blood: Investigating Vampires and Southern Gothic.* London: I. B. Tauris, 2013, pp. 74–89.

4922. Foy, Joseph J. "Signed in Blood: Rights and the Vampire-Human Social Contract." In George A. Dunn and Rebecca Housel, ed. *True Blood and Philosophy: We Wanna Think Bad Things with You.* New York: John Wiley & Sons, 2010, pp. 51–64.

4923. Frankel, Valerie Estelle. *Bloodsuckers of the Bayou. The Myths, Symbols and Tales Behind HBO's* True Blood. N.p.: LitCrit Press, 2013. 183 pp. tp.

4924. Grigoriadis, Vanessa. "The Joy of Vampire Sex: The Schlocky, Sensual Secrets behind the Success of *True Blood.*" *Rolling Stone* (September 2, 2010): 54–59.

4925. Gross, Terry. "Fresh Air interview with Alan Ball: True Blood and Towelhead." In Thomas Fahy, ed. *Alan Ball Conversations.* Jackson: University Press of Mississippi, 2013, pp. 84ff.

4926. Grubb, Sarah. "Vampires, Werewolves, and Shapeshifters: The More They Change, the More They Stay the Same." In George A. Dunn and Rebecca Housel, ed. *True Blood and Philosophy: We Wanna Think Bad Things with You.* New York: John Wiley & Sons, 2010, pp. 215–27.

4927. Harris, Charlaine. "The Sookie Short Stories and Related Material." In Charlaine Harris, ed. *The Sookie Stackhouse Companion.* New York: Ace Hardcover, 2011, pp. 211–25.

4928. _____, ed. *The Sookie Stackhouse Companion.* New York: Ace Hardcover, 2011. 461 pp. hb. dj. Rpt. New York: Ace, 2012. 461 pp. tp. While most of this volume was written by the editor, it also includes multiple contributions by Beverly Battillo and Victoria Koski.

4929. Heaton, Sarah. "Vampire Vogue and Female Fashion: Dressing Skin and Dressing-up in the Sookie Stackhouse and Twilight Series." In Barbara Brodman and James E. Doan, eds. *Images of the Modern Vampire: The Hip and the Atavistic.* Madison. NJ: Fairleigh Dickinson University Press, 2013, pp. 175–90.

4930. Hirschbein, Ron. "Sookie, Sigmund, and the Edible Complex." In George A. Dunn and Rebecca Housel, ed. *True Blood and Philosophy: We Wanna Think Bad Things with You.* New York: John Wiley & Sons, 2010, pp. 123–35.

4931. Hollis, Erin. "'Oh Great! Now I Have to Deal with Witches?!': Exploring the 'Archontic' Fan Fiction of *True Blood.*" In Brigid Cherry, ed. *True Blood: Investigating Vampires and Southern Gothic.* London: I. B. Tauris, 2013, pp. 186–200.

4932. Kawanishi, Mana. "Queering Intimacy in *True Blood*: Eric Northman's Desexualized Intimacy." In Seth Alcorn and Steven A. Nardi, eds. *Twisted Mirrors: Monstrous Reflections of Humanity.* Oxford: Inter-Disciplinary Press, 2012, pp. 193–200.

4933. King, Lisa. "The Monstrosity of Vampires and Queers: The Normalizing Force of Charlaine Harris." In Hallie Tibbetts, ed. *Sirens: Collected Papers 2009–2011.* Sedalia, CO: Narrate Conferences, 2012, pp. 179–200.

4934. Koski, Victoria. "A Guide to the World of Sookie Stackhouse." In Charlaine Harris, ed. *The Sookie Stackhouse Companion.* New York: Ace Hardcover, 2011, pp. 313–461.

4935. Koven, Mikel J. "'I'm a Fairy? How Fucking Lame!': *True Blood* as Fairytale. "In Brigid Cherry, ed. *True Blood: Investigating Vampires and Southern Gothic.* London: I. B. Tauris, 2013, pp. 59–73.

4936. Kusnierz, Lauren. "I Prefer My Beefcakes with Fangs: Sexploitation in HBO's *True Blood.*" *Flow* (online journal of television and media studies) (July 15, 2013). Posted at: http://flowtv.org/2013/07/i-prefer-my-beefcakes-with-fangs/.

4937. Kwitney, Alisa, "Blue-Collar Bacchanalia." In Leah Wilson, ed. *A Taste of True Blood: The Fangbanger's Guide.* Dallas, TX: Benbella Books, 2010, pp. 165–75.

4938. Lima, Maria. "Home Is Where the Bar Is." In Leah Wilson, ed. *A Taste of True Blood: The Fangbanger's Guide.* Dallas, TX: Benbella Books, 2010, pp. 33–43.

4939. Lindgren Leavenworth, Maria. *Fanged Fan Fiction: Variations on* Twilight, True Blood, *and* The Vampire Diaries. Jefferson, NC: McFarland & Company, 2013. 236 pp. tp.

4940. _____. "'What are you?': Fear, Desire, and Disgust in the Southern Vampire Mysteries and True Blood." *Nordic Journal of English Studies* 11, 3 (2012): 36–54. Posted at: http://www.diva-portal.org/smash/get/diva2:580220/FULLTEXT03.pdf.

4941. Lloyd, Peter B. "Communion of Blood." In Leah Wilson, ed. *A Taste of True Blood: The Fangbanger's Guide*. Dallas, TX: Benbella Books, 2010, pp. 89–99.

4942. Mamatas, Nick. "Working Class Heroes." In Leah Wilson, ed. *A Taste of True Blood: The Fangbanger's Guide*. Dallas, TX: Benbella Books, 2010, pp. 61–73.

4943. McCabe, Joseph. "Pure Blood." In Leah Wilson, ed. *A Taste of True Blood: The Fangbanger's Guide*. Dallas, TX: Benbella Books, 2010, pp. 101–10.

4944. McClelland, Bruce. "Un-True Blood: The Politics of Artificiality." In George A. Dunn and Rebecca Housel, ed. *True Blood and Philosophy: We Wanna Think Bad Things with You*. New York: John Wiley & Sons, 2010, pp. 79–90.

4945. Mellins, Maria. "The Fangtasia Experience: *True Blood* Fans, Commodification, and Lifestyle." In Brigid Cherry, ed. *True Blood: Investigating Vampires and Southern Gothic*. London: I. B. Tauris, 2013, pp. 172–85.

4946. Mukherjea, Ananya. "Mad, Bad and Delectable to Know: *True Blood's* Paranormal Men and Gothic Romance." In Brigid Cherry, ed. *True Blood: Investigating Vampires and Southern Gothic*. London: I. B. Tauris, 2013, pp. 109–21.

4947. _____. "My Vampire Boyfriend: Post-feminism, 'Perfect' Masculinity, and the Contemporary Appeal of Paranormal Romance." *Studies in Popular Culture* 33, 2 (2011): 1–20.

4948. Mutch, Deborah. 2011. "Coming Out of the Coffin: The Vampire and Transnationalism in the *Twilight* and Sookie Stackhouse Series." *Critical Survey* 23, 2 (2011): 75–90.

4949. Nazarian, Vera. "A Kinder, Gentler Vampire." In Leah Wilson, ed. *A Taste of True Blood: The Fangbanger's Guide*. Dallas, TX: Benbella Books, 2010, pp. 123–36.

4950. Ndalianis. Angela. "Paranormal Romance: Anita Blake, Sookie Stackhouse and the Monsters who Love Them." In Angela Ndalianis.

The Horror Sensorium: Media and the Senses. Jefferson, NC: McFarland & Company, 2012, pp. 73–106.

4951. Peppers-Bates, Susan, and Joshua Rust. "A Vampire's Heat Has Its Reasons That Scientific Naturalism Can't Understand." In George A. Dunn and Rebecca Housel, eds. *True Blood and Philosophy: We Wanna Think Bad Things with You*. New York: John Wiley & Sons, 2010, pp. 187–201.

4952. Peterson, Michael, Laurie Beth Clark, and Lisa Nakamura. "Vampire Politics." *Flow* (online journal of television and media studies) (December 4, 2009). Posted at: http://flowtv.org/2009/12/vampire-politicslisa-nakamura-laurie-beth-clark-michael-peterson/.

4953. Poole, Carol. "The Ego, the Id, and Sookie Stackhouse." In Leah Wilson, ed. *A Taste of True Blood: The Fangbanger's Guide*. Dallas, TX: Benbella Books, 2010, pp. 75–88.

4954. Primiano, Leonard Norman. "'I Wanna Do Bad Things with You': Fantasia on Themes of American Religion from the Title Sequence of HBO's True Blood." In Eric Michael Mazur and Kate McCarthy, eds. *God in the Details: American Religion in Popular Culture*. 2nd ed.: New York: Routledge, 2011, pp. 41–62.

4955. Rabin, Nicole. "True Blood: The Vampire as a Multiracial Critique on Post-Race Ideology." *Journal of Dracula Studies* 12 (2010): 65–81.

4956. Robichaud, Christopher. "To Turn or Not to Turn: The Ethics of Making Vampires." In George A. Dunn and Rebecca Housel, ed. *True Blood and Philosophy: We Wanna Think Bad Things with You*. New York: John Wiley & Sons, 2010, pp. 7–17.

4957. Robison, Rachel. "True and Untrue Blood." In Richard Greene and K. Silem Mohammad, eds. *Zombies, Vampires, and Philosophy: New Life for the Undead*. La Salle, IL: Open Court, 2010, pp. 249–57.

4958. Rogers, Paula. "To Live and Live in Dixie." In Leah Wilson, ed. *A Taste of True Blood: The Fangbanger's Guide*. Dallas, TX: Benbella Books, 2010, pp. 45–59.

4959. Rosenbaum, Bev Katz. "I Love You, I Just Don't Want to Know You (So Much)." In Leah Wilson, ed. *A Taste of True Blood: The Fangbanger's Guide*. Dallas, TX: Benbella Books, 2010, pp. 203–09.

4960. Rothermel, Dennis. "Minoritarian Romantic Fables in HBO's *True Blood*." In Brigid Cherry, ed. *True Blood: Investigating Vampires and*

Southern Gothic. London: I. B. Tauris, 2013, pp. 90–106.

4961. Rubin, Jonna. "SOOKEH! Bee-ill! and the Downfall of William T. Compton." In Leah Wilson, ed. *A Taste of True Blood: The Fangbanger's Guide.* Dallas, TX: Benbella Books, 2010, pp. 19–32.

4962. Russell, Caroline, and Brigid Cherry. "More Than Cold and Heartless: The Southern Gothic Milieu of *True Blood.*" In Brigid Cherry, ed. *True Blood: Investigating Vampires and Southern Gothic.* London: I. B. Tauris, 2013, pp. 39–55.

4963. Schumann, Nancy. "The Vamp Next Door: Present Day Vampires." In Nancy Schumann. *Take a Bite. Female Vampires in Anglo-American Literature and Folklore.* London: Callio Press Limited, n.d. [2011?], pp. 91–110.

4964. Smith, Michelle. "The Postmodern Vampire in 'Post-race' America: HBO's *True Blood,*" In Sam George and Bill Hughes, eds. *Open Graves, Open Minds: Representations of Vampires and the Undead from the Enlightenment to the Present Day.* Manchester: Manchester University Press, 2013, pp. 192–209.

4965. Sobol, Gianna. *Steve Newlin's Field Guide to Vampires: (And Other Creatures of Satan).* San Francisco, CA: Chronicle Books, 2013. 144 pp. hb. boards. A survey of the supernatural creatures (vampires and werewolves) in the *True Blood* universe written as if a dossier compiled by the leader of the anti-vampire Fellowship of the Sun.

4966. _____, Alan Ball, and Benjamin Hayes. *True Blood Drinks & Bites.* San Francisco, CA: Chronicle Books, 2013. 128 pp. hb. boards.

4967. _____, Alan Ball, with Karen Sommer Shalett and Marcelle Beinvenu. *True Blood: Eats, Drinks, and Bites from Bon Temps.* San Francisco: Chronicle Books, 2012. 224 pp. hb. boards.

4968. Stratton, Jon. "Buffy Failed: *True Blood* and the Accommodation of Vampires." *Flow* (online journal of television and media studies) (March 26, 2010). Posted at: http://flowtv.org/2010/03/buffy-failed-true-blood-and-the-accommodation-of-vampires-jon-stratton-curtin-university-of-technology/.

4969. Terjesen, Andrew, and Jenny Terjesen. "Are Vampires Unnatural?" In George A. Dunn and Rebecca Housel, ed. *True Blood and Philosophy: We Wanna Think Bad Things with You.* New York: John Wiley & Sons, 2010, pp. 157–73.

4970. _____. "Carlisle: More Compassionate Than a Speeding Bullet?" In Rebecca Housel and J. Jeremy Wisnewski. *Twilight and Philosophy: Vampires, Vegetarians, and the Pursuit of Immortality.* New York: John Wiley & Sons, 2009, pp. 49–60.

4971. Thurber, Ann. *Bite Me: Desire and the Female Spectator in* Twilight, The Vampire Diaries, *and* True Blood. Atlanta, GA: Emory University, M.A. thesis, 2011. 100 pp. Large format.

4972. Tyree, J. M. "Warm-Blooded: True Blood and Let the Right One In." *Film Quarterly* 63, 2 (2009): 31–37.

4973. Walker, Kirsty. "True Stud." In Leah Wilson, ed. *A Taste of True Blood: The Fangbanger's Guide.* Dallas, TX: Benbella Books, 2010, pp. 111–22.

4974. Waters, Melanie. "Fangbanging: Sexing the Vampire in Alan Ball's *True Blood.*" In Basil Glynn, James Aston, and Beth Johnson, eds. *Television, Sex and Society: Analyzing Contemporary Representations.* New York/London: Bloomsbury Academic, 2012, pp. 33–46.

4975. Wilcott, Becca Wilcott. *Truly, Madly, Deadly: The Unofficial* True Blood *Companion.* Toronto: ECW Press, 2010. 272 pp. tp.

4976. Wilkinson, Jules. "Fangs and Fame." In Leah Wilson, ed. *A Taste of True Blood: The Fangbanger's Guide.* Dallas, TX: Benbella Books, 2010, pp. 195–202.

4977. Wilson, Leah, ed. *A Taste of True Blood: The Fang Banger's Guide.* Dallas, TX: Benbella Books, 2010. 262 pp. tp. Includes contributions by Daniel M. Kimmel, William T. Compton, Jonna Rubin, Maria Lima, Paula Rogers, Nick Mamatas, Carol Poole, Peter B. Lloyd, Joseph McCabe, Kirsty Walker, Vera Nazarian, Phillipa Ballantine, Jacob Clifton, Alisa Kwitney, Peg Aloi, Jules Wilkinson, Bev Katz Rosenbaum, Ginjer Buchanan, Bruce and Karen Bethke.

VI. Vampire Music and Art

Music

While *Dracula*, the original talkie horror film, was done without musical accompaniment, film directors and producers soon became aware of music's ability to build tension and provoke and/or intensify fear, terror, and related feelings, now so integral to the horror cinematic experience. Thus it was natural, as the scholarly community turned its attention to the vampire, that the associated music would finally be granted some attention. Music, however, remains an understudied field.

Musically, the vampire enjoyed a period in the spotlight in the 1980s with the emergence of Gothic rock, a variant of punk rock, whose performers and audience attempted to recreate a gothic environment. Bands such as The Cure, Siouxsie and the Banshees, and the Sisters of Mercy repeatedly featured the vampire in their songs. In her third vampire novel, *The Queen of the Damned*, Anne Rice presents her most popular vampire character, Lestat, as a rock star. His rock career would lead to a Broadway stage production, *Lestat: The Musical*, for which Elton John and Bernie Taupin contributed the score.

Meanwhile, in the wake of the vampire's popularity, a variety of operas, stage musicals, and even ballet performances would be produced. Included was a revival of *Der Vampyr,* an opera in two acts originally written by Heinrich Marschner in 1828 and based on Polidori's "The Vampyre." The new revised version of Marchner's opera appeared in 1992 as *The Vampyr: A Soap Opera*, which included new lyrics by Charles Hart.

The new wave of interest in vampires began to produce its own music among the fans of *Dark Shadows*, who, taking their cue from fans of science fiction, began to develop their own set of "filksongs," songs drawing on the folksong tradition and celebrating *Dark Shadows*. Filksongs had developed originally in the science fiction conventions.

A host of articles have been written about the music used in *Buffy the Vampire Slayer* (1997–2003), especially the single episode from season six, "Once More with Feeling," which was in itself a musical. Most of these articles were collected in one of two volumes, *Music, Sound, and Silence in* Buffy the Vampire Slayer, edited by Paul G. Attinello, Janet K. Halfyard, and Vanessa Knights, and *Buffy, Ballads, and Bad Guys Who Sing: Music in the Worlds of Joss Whedon* edited by Kendra Preston Leonard. Both volumes are cited below, while all of the individual papers from these two volumes are listed in the *Buffy* chapter in this bibliography.

4978. **Anderson, Don.** "A Discography of Goth Rock Artists." In Carol Siegal. *Goth's Dark Empire.* Bloomington: Indiana University Press, 2005, pp. 157–83.

4979. **Attinello, Paul G., Janet K. Halfyard and Vanessa Knights, eds.** *Music, Sound, and Silence in* Buffy the Vampire Slayer. Farnham, Surrey, UK: Ashgate Publishing, 2010. 332 pp. tp. Includes papers by Keith Negus, John C. King and Christophe Beck, Vanessa Knights, Janet K. Halfyard, Louis Niebur, Rob Haskins, Arnie Cox and Rebecca Fülöp, Katy Stevens, Gerry Bloustien, Catherine Driscoll, Rob Cover, Renée T. Coulombe, Kathryn Hill, Diana Sandars and Rhonda V. Wilcox, Amy Bauer, Paul Attinello, and Anahid Kassabian.

4980. **Barham, Jeremy.** "Dismembering the Musical Voice: Mahler, Melodrama and *Dracula* from Stage to Screen." In Sarah Hibberd, ed. *Melodramatic Voices: Understanding Music Drama.* Farnham, Surrey, UK/Burlington, VT: Ashgate, 2011, pp. 237–62.

4981. **Christy, Jo Ann, and Marcy Robin,** eds. *Filksongs for All Eternity.* Temple City, CA: Old Collinwood Publishing House, 1979. 32 pp. pb. Large format.

4982. _____. *Filksongs That God Bump in the Night.* Temple City, CA: Old Collinwood Publishing House, 1983. 38 pp. pb. Large format.

4983. **Christy, Jo Ann, Pat Lammerts, and Marcy Robin, eds.** *Curses! Filked Again!* Temple City, CA: Old Collinwood Publishing House, 1980. 27 pp. pb. Large format.

4984. **Cobert, Robert.** *Dark Shadows Music Book: Original Music from the Classic TV Series and Films.* Los Angeles: Pomegranate Press, 1996. 112 pp. tp.

4985. **Cooper, B. Lee.** "Terror Translated into Comedy: The Popular Music Metamorphosis of Film and Television Horror, 1956–1991." *Journal of American Culture* 20, 3 (Fall 1997): 31–42.

4986. **Deaville, James.** "The Beauty of Horror: Kilar, Coppola, and Dracula." In Neil Lerner, ed. *Music in the Horror Film: Listening to Fear.* New York: Routledge, 2010, pp. 187–205.

4987. **Dechert, S. Renee.** "'My Boyfriend's in the Band!' *Buffy* and the Rhetoric of Music." In Rhonda V. Wilcox and David Lavery, eds. *Fighting the Forces: What's at Stake in Buffy the Vampire Slayer.* Lanham, MD: Rowman & Littlefield Publishers, 2002, pp. 218–26.

4988. **Del Tredici, David, and Alfred Corn.** *Dracula: For Soprano and Thirteen Instruments.* [New York]: Boosey & Hawkes, 1999. 156 pp. Printed version of musical score.

4989. **Dvoskin, Michelle G.** *Under Their Spell: How the Musical Episodes of* Xena: Warrior Princess *and* Buffy the Vampire Slayer *Queer the Audience.* Austin: University of Texas, M.A. thesis, 2006. Large format.

4990. **Fasolino, Greg.** "Lestat of the Art— The Dark Gift Discussed." *Reflex: Alternative Music and Culture* 29 (1992): 42–46.

4991. **Fonseca, [Anthony J.] Tony.** "Bela Lugosi's Dead, but Vampire Music Stalks the Airwaves." In James Craig Holte, ed. *The Fantastic Vampire: Studies in the Children of the Night: Selected Essays from the Eighteenth International Conference on the Fantastic in the Arts.* Vol. 19. Westport, CT: Greenwood Publishing Group, 2002, pp. 59–67.

4992. **Graham, Jean.** *Music from Dark Shadows.* San Diego, CA: Peacock Press, n.d. 22 pp.

4993. **Greenberg, Lawrence.** "The Music of the Vampire." In Rosemary Ellen Guiley, with J. B. Macabre. *The Complete Vampire Companion.* New York: Macmillan, 1994, pp. 157–71.

4994. **Halfyard, Janet K.** "Music of the Night: Scoring the Vampire in Contemporary Film." In Philip Hayward, ed. *Terror Tracks: Music, Sound and Horror Cinema.* London: Equinox, 2009, pp. 171–85.

4995. **Hallett, David, and Robin Martin.** "Overlooked Pearls: The Blue Oyster Cult and the Vampire in Popular Music." *Journal of Dracula Studies* 1 (1999): 15–24. Posted at: http://true legends.info/paranormal/oyster.htm.

4996. **Hannaham, James.** "Bela Lugosi's Dead and I Don't Feel So Good Either." In Karen Kelly and Evelyn McDonnell, eds. *Stars Don't Stand Still in the Sky: Music and Myth.* New York University Press, 1999, pp. 78–87.

4997. **Hannan, Michael.** "Sound and Music in Hammer's Vampire Films." In Philip Hayward, ed. *Terror Tracks: Music, sound and horror cinema.* London: Equinox, 2009, pp. 60–74.

4998. **Hill, Kathryn.** "Buffy's Voice: *Buffy the Vampire Slayer's* Popular Music Soundtrack and Contemporary Feminism." *Feminist Media Studies iFirst* (February 3, 2012). A paper originally presented in earlier form as "Buffy's Voice: The Power of Popular Music as Feminine/Feminist Narrative" at Staking a Claim: Exploring the Global Reach of *Buffy*, University of South Australia, Adelaide, Australia, July 22, 2003.

4999. _____. "'Easy to Associate Angsty Lyrics with Buffy': An Introduction to a Participatory Fan Culture: *Buffy the Vampire Slayer* Vidders, Popular Music and the Internet." In Mary Kirby-Diaz, ed. *Buffy and Angel Conquer the Internet: Essays on Online Fandom*. Jefferson, NC: McFarland & Company, 2009, pp. 172–196.

5000. _____. "Music, Subtexts and Foreshadowings: Contextual Roles of Popular Music in *Buffy the Vampire Slayer*, 1997–2003." Paper presented at the Slayage Conference on *Buffy the Vampire Slayer*, Nashville, TN, May 27–30, 2004. Posted at: http://www.slayageonline.com/SCBtVS_Archive/Talks/KHill.pdf.

5001. _____. "Punks, Geeks and Goths: *Buffy the Vampire Slayer* as a Study of Popular Music Demographics on American Commercial Television." In Paul Attinello, Janet K. Halfyard, and Vanessa Knights, ed. *Music, Sound, and Silence in* Buffy the Vampire Slayer. Farnham, Surrey, UK: Ashgate Publishing, 2010. 165–186.

5002. _____. "S/He's a Rebel: The James Dean Trope in *Buffy the Vampire Slayer*." *Continuum: Journal of Media & Cultural Studies* 27, 1 (February 2013): 124–140.

5003. Huckvale, David. *Hammer Film Scores and the Musical Avant-Garde*. Jefferson, NC: McFarland & Company, 2008. 235 pp. tp.

5004. _____. *James Bernard, Composer to Count Dracula: A Critical Biography*. Jefferson, NC: McFarland & Company, 2006. 311 pp. hb.

5005. Jay, David. *For Bauhaus Lovers*. Tokyo: P I E Books, 2004. 100 pp. Large format.

5006. Jones, Brian. *Entranced: The Siouxsie & the Banshees Story*. Ed. by Chris Charlesworth. London: Omnibus Press, 1989. 96 pp.

5007. Ladouceur, Liisa. *Encyclopedia Gothica*. Toronto, ON: ECW Press, 2011. 313 pp. hb.

5008. Larson, Randall D. *Music from the House of Hammer*. Methuen, NJ: Scarecrow Press, 1996. 224 pp. hb.

5009. _____. *Musique Fantastique: A Survey of Film Music in the Fantastic Cinema*. Methuen, NJ: Scarecrow Press, 1984. 592 pp. hb.

5010. Leonard, Kendra Preston, eds. *Buffy, Ballads, and Bad Guys Who Sing: Music in the Worlds of Joss Whedon*. Lanham, MD: Scarecrow Press, 2010. 308 pp. hb.

5011. Mathur, Paul. *Siouxsie and the Banshees: The Authorised Biography*. London: Sanctuary Publishing, 2003. 277 pp. tp.

5012. Mercer, Mick. *Gothic Rock: All You Need to Know About...but Were Too Gormless to Ask*. Cambridge, UK: Pegasus Publishing, 1991. 178 pp. pb. Large format. Reissued as: *Gothic Rock*. Los Angeles: Cleopatra Records, 1993. pb. Large format.

5013. _____. *Gothic Rock Black Book*. London: Omnibus Press, 1988. 95 pp. pb. Large format.

5014. _____. *Hex Files: The Goth Bible*. Woodstock, NY: Overlook, 1997. 6000 pp.

5015. _____. *Music to Die For: The International Guide to Today's Extreme Music Scene*. London: Cherry Red Books, 2009. 609 pp. tp.

5016. Mills, Matthew. "*Angel*'s Narrative Score." In Kendra Preston, Leonard, ed. *Buffy, Ballads, and Bad Guys Who Sing: Music in the Worlds of Joss Whedon*. Lanham, MD: Scarecrow Press, 2011, pp. 173–208.

5017. _____. "*Ubi Caritas*? Music as Narrative Agent in *Angel*." In Stacey Abbott, ed. *Reading Angel: The TV Spin-off with a Soul*. New York: I. B. Tauris, 2005, pp. 31–43.

5018. Park, Jennifer. "Melancholy and the Macabre: Gothic Rock and Fashion." In Valerie Steele and Jennifer Park. *Gothic: Dark Glamour*. New Haven, CT: Yale University Press, 2008, pp. 115–65.

5019. Pinnell, Andrew. *Heartland: The Sisters of Mercy Biography*. Trowbridge, UK: Heartland Publishing; 1992. 96 pp. tp.

5020. Remington, Pete. "Monster Mash: Pioneers of the Gothic Elements in Rock and Roll." In Niall Scott. The Role of the Monster: Myths and Metaphors of Enduring Evil. Oxford: Inter-Disciplinary Press, 2009, pp. 167–80. Posted at: http://www.scribd.com/doc/61699474/The-Role-of-the-Monster-Myths-and-Metaphors-of-Enduring-Evil.

5021. Reynolds, Simon. "Dark Things and Glory Boys: The Return of Rock with Goth and the New Psychedelia." *Rip It Up and Start Again: Postpunk 1978–1984*. London: Faber and Faber, 2005, pp. 352–69.

5022. Shirley, Ian. *Dark Entries: Bauhaus and Beyond*. Wembly, UK: SAF Publishing, 1994. 191 pp. tp.

5023. Stableford, Brian. "What Music They Make..." *Other Dimensions: The Journal of Multimedia Horror* 3 (Winter 1996).

5024. Stokes, Samuel H. *'Dracula': A Musical Analysis (Richard Herman, Samuel Stokes).* Warrensburg: University of Central Missouri, M.A. thesis, 2005. 151 pp. Large format.

5025. Thompson, Dave. *The Dark Reign of Gothic Rock: In the Reptile House with the Sisters of Mercy, Bauhaus and the Cure.* London: Helter Skelter Publishing, 2002. 288 pp. tp.

5026. ____, and Jo-Ann Greene. *The Cure: A Visual Documentary.* London: Omnibus Press, 1988. 96 pp. pb. Large format.

5027. Voltaire. *What Is Goth? Music, Makeup, Attitude, Apparel, Dance, and General Skullduggery.* Boston: Weiser Books, 2004. 96 pp. hb. boards.

5028. White, Pamela C. "Two Vampires of 1828." *Opera Quarterly* 5, 1 (1987): 22–57.

Art

The popularity of the vampire in the twentieth century has been highly visual, an aspect initially brought to the fore with the changing image of the vampire accompanying its adaptation to the stage and the realization of the evolving cinema vampire's sexual appeal. In the late twentieth century, visual art featuring the vampire initially became popular in the graphic arts realm in the 1970s with the reintroduction of vampires into comic books, not just as occasional guest villains, but as lead characters in their own continuing series. By the end of the century, graphic artists such as John Bolton (England) and Yoshitaka Amano (Japan) emerged and chose the vampire as one of their key subjects, and for which they would become well known.

The popularity of the vampire among graphic artists would manifest in the publication of a number of manuals offering instruction on how to draw vampires.

The more recent interest in vampires would focus attention on the few classical representations of the vampire and succubus by noted artists from William Blake to Francisco Goya and Edvard Munch. In 1897, painter Philip Burne-Jones first displayed his now famous painting "The Vampire," which would lead to the development of the vamp as the stock character of the predatory woman who would take all a man offered without returning his feelings and in the end leave him spent and broken.

5029. Amano, Yoshitaka. *The Art of Vampire Hunter D.* Milwaukie, OR: DH Press, 2007. 200 pp. pb.

5030. ____. *The Art of Vampire Hunter D: Bloodlust.* Screenplay by Yoshiaki Kawajiri. San Diego: IDW Publishing, July 2006. unpaged. hb.

5031. ____. *Coffin: The Art of Vampire Hunter D.* Milwaukie, OR: DH Press, 2007. 200 pp. pb. Slipcase.

5032. ____. *Worlds of Amano.* Text by Jean Wacquet. Trans. by Samantha Robertson. Milwaukie, OR: DH Press, 2007. 156 pp. hb. Large format.

5033. ____. *Yoshitaka Amano.* Japan, 1996. 104 pp. tp. Text in Japanese. slipcase.

5034. Ames, Lee J. *Draw 50 Monsters, Creeps, Superheroes, Demons, Dragons, Nerds, Dirts, Ghouls, Giants, Vampires, Zombies and Other Curiosa...* New York: Trumpet Club, 1983. Unpaged. Pb. Large format. Juvenile.

5035. Beckett-Griffith, Jasmine, and Matthew David Beckett. *Vampire Art Now.* Zurich, Switz.: Edition Olms, 2011. 192 pp. hb. dj. Rpt.: New York: Harper Design, 2011. 192 pp. hb. dj.

5036. Bekmambetov, Timur, et al. *The Art of Abraham Lincoln: Vampire Hunter.* Culver City, CA: Aspen MLT, Inc., 2012. 120 pp. hb. boards.

5037. Bergin, Mark. *How to Draw Vampires, Zombies, and Other Monsters.* New York: Powerkids Press, 2011. 32 pp. pb. Large format. Rpt.: Brighton, UK: Book House, 2011. 32 pp. pb.

5038. Briefel, Aviva. "Hands of Beauty, Hands of Horror, Fear and Egyptian Art at the Fin de Siècle." *Victorian Studies* 50, 2 (Winter 2008): 263–271.

5039. Brown, Carolyn. "Figuring the Vampire: Death, Desire, and the Image." Sue Golding, ed. *The Eight Technologies of Otherness.* London: Routledge, 1997, pp. 117–34.

5040. Butkus, Michael, and Merrie Destefano. *How to Draw Vampires: Discover the Secrets to Drawing, Painting, and Illustrating Immortals of the Night.* Osceola, WI: Walter Foster, 2010. 128 pp. pb.

5041. Caine, Eugene. *Learn to Draw Like the Masters: Vampires: Collected Manuscripts Detailing the Masters' Secrets for Studying, Drawing, and Painting Vampires.* Irvine, CA: Walter Foster Publishing, 2010. 96 pp. hb. boards. Large format.

5042. Daniels, Ian. *How to Draw & Paint Vampires: A Complete Art Course Built Around This Legendary World.* Hauppauge, NY Barron's, 2010. 128 pp. pb. Large format.

5043. Davies, Paul Bryn. *How to Draw Vampires in Simple Steps.* Tunbridge Wells, Kent, UK: Search Press, 2010. 32 pp. pb. Large Format. Art.

5044. Dunn, Ben, et al. *How to Draw Vampires.* San Antonio. TX: Antarctic Press, 2010. 128 pp. Supersize tp. Large format. Rpt. San Antonio. TX: Antarctic Press, 2010. 128 pp. Pocket Manga pb.

5045. Ellis, Steve. *Scream: Draw Classic Vampires, Werewolves, Zombies, Monsters and More.* Cincinnati, OH: Impact Books, 2009. 128 pp. pb. Art. Large format. Extract as: *How to Draw and Paint Vampires: Project Book.* [Osceola, WI]: Metro Books, 2009. 32 pp. pb. Distributed in coffin-shaped kit entitled, "How to Draw and Paint Vampires.."

5046. Faxneld, Per. "Blood, Sperm and Astral Energy-Suckers: Edvard Munch's Vampire." In: Mai Britt Guleng, ed. *eMunch.no—Text and Image.* Oslo: Munch Museum, 2011. pp. 187–198.

5047. Fishel, Emma. *How to Draw Ghost, Vampires & Haunted Houses.* London: Usborne, 1988. 32 pp. pb. Ed. by Janet Cook and Anita Ganeri. Illust. by Victor Ambus, Kim Blundell, Rob McCraig, Mike Pringle, and Graham Round. Rpt.: New York: Scholastic, 1988. 32 pp. pb.

5048. Fisher, Jean. *Vampire in the Text: Narratives of Contemporary Art.* London: Institute of International Visual Arts, 2003. 288 pp. tp.

5049. Frances, Victoria, et al. *Vampires: The World of Shadows Illustrated.* Easthampton, MA: Heavy Metal, 2011. 64 pp. hb. large format.

5050. Gary and Al [Gary Brodsky, Al Occhino]. *How to Draw Sexy Witches Wenches Vampires.* New York: Solson Books, 1998.

5051. Hart, Christopher. *Drawing Vampires: Gothic Creatures of the Night.* New York: Hart Books, 2009. 144 pp. pb. Large format, Art.

5052. _____. *Manga for the Beginner Midnight Monsters: How to Draw Zombies, Vampires, and Other Delightfully Devious Characters of Japanese Comics.* New York: Watson-Guptill, 2013. 176 pp. tp.

5053. Hino, Matsuri. *The Art of Vampire Knight: Matsuri Hino Illustrations.* San Francisco, CA: VIZ Media LLC, 2011. 96 pp. hb. Large format.

5054. Iorilla, Joseph. "Vampires." In Joseph Iorilla. *Born of the Night: The Gothic Fantasy Artwork of Joseph Vargo.* Cleveland, OH: Monolith Graphics, 2005, pp. 27–63.

5055. Irish, Lora S. *The Official Vampire Artist's Handbook: How to Create Your Own Patterns and Illustrations of the Undead.* East Petersburg, PA: Fox Chapel Publishing, 2012. 111 pp. pb. Large format.

5056. Kawajiri, Yoshiaki. *The Art of Vampire Hunter D: Bloodlust.* Vol. 2. San Diego, CA: Idea & Design Works, 2007. 48 pp. hb.

5057. _____. *Vampire Hunter D Art Book.* San Diego, CA: IDW Publishing, 2006. 56 pp. hb.

5058. Kember, Sarah. "'The blood is the life': Cybersubjects and the Myth of the Vampire." In Sarah Kember. *Virtual Anxiety: Photography, New Technologies and Subjectivity.* Manchester, UK: Manchester University Press, 1998, pp. 2100–29.

5059. Kittler, Friedrich. "Dracula's Legacy." In John Johnston, ed. *Literature, Media, Information Systems: Critical Voices in Art, Theory and Culture.* Amsterdam: G + B Arts International, 1997, pp. 50–84.

5060. Kreimeier, Klaus. "From Vampire to Vamp: On the Background of a Cinematic Myth." In Rolf Aurich, Wolfgang Jacobsen, and Gabriele Jatho, eds. *Artificial Humans: Manic Machines*

Controlled Bodies. Berlin: Jovis Verlagsbüro, 2000, pp. 77–96.

5061. Luca, Gherasim. *The Passive Vampire.* Trans. by Krzysztof Fijalkowski. Prague, Czech Republic: Twisted Spoon Press, 2009. 140 pp. tp.

5062. Phillips-Summers, Diana. *Vampires: A Bloodthirsty History in Art and Literature.* Hod Hosharon, Israel: Astrolog Publishing House, 2003. 144 pp. tp. Illus. by Daniel Ackerman.

5063. Roza, Greg. *Drawing Dracula.* New York: Windmill Books, 2011. 24 pp. hb. boards.

5064. Schaffer, Robert S. "The Art of P/ Craig Russell." *Media Showcase* 7 (July 1981): 25–43.

5065. Skal, David. "Fatal Image: The Artist, the Actress, and "The Vampire." In David Skal, ed. *Vampires: Encounters with the Undead.* New York: Black Dog & Leventhal Publishers, 2001, pp. 223–257.

5066. Spurlock, J. David. *How to Draw Chiller Monsters, Werewolves, Vampires, and Zombies.* New York: Watson-Guptill, 2011. 144 pp. pb. Large format.

5067. Thorne, Russ. *Gothic Dreams: Vampires: Fantasy Art, Fiction and the Movies.* Illust. by Anne Stokes. London: Flame Tee Publishing, 2013. 128 pp. hb. boards.

5068. Wall, Jeff. "Interview with Arielle Pelenc on *The Vampires' Picnic.*" In Gilda Williams, ed. *The Gothic.* Ser.: Whitechapel: Documents of Contemporary Art. Cambridge, MA: The MIT Press, 2007, pp. 146–53.

5069. Žižek, Stephen. "Kant as a Theoretician of Vampirism, 1994." In Gilda Williams, ed. *The Gothic.* Ser.: Whitechapel: Documents of Contemporary Art Cambridge, MA: The MIT Press, 2007, pp. 139–44.

Graphic Arts, Comic Books

Comic books emerged as a distinct form of popular literature in the 1930s, and the vampire quickly made its presence known. The first known vampire appeared in the early comic book titled, *More Fun* #7 amid the continuing stories of Dr. Occult, a detective who fought various supernatural villains. Dr. Occult's first major case pitted him against a creature called the "Vampire Master." The story ran for three issues, each installment being one large page, and took on added significance when its creators, Jerry Siegel and Joe Shuster, later created Superman. At the end of the decade (1939), Batman encountered a Transylvanian vampire, the Monk, in issues 31 and 32 of *Detective Comics*.

The origins of the graphic arts vampire as the villain in superhero stories failed to anticipate the initial wave of popularity of bloodsuckers as staple characters in the wave of horror comics that began to appear following World War II. In 1948 the American Comics Group issued the first, and eventually one of the most successful, horror comics, *Adventures into the Unknown*. Then, two years later, William Grimes and artist Al Feldman of EC Comics began the *Crypt of Terror* (later *Tales from the Crypt*) which was quickly joined by the *Vault of Horror* and *Haunt of Fear*. The famous EC titles would inspire over 100 horror comic book titles over the next few years. Avon's *Eerie* #8 (August 1953) became the first of many to adapt Bram Stoker's novel *Dracula* to comic book format.

As horror comics multiplied, however, they came under attack. Psychologist Frederic Wertham (1895–1981) tied them to the spread of juvenile delinquency, and the Comic Magazine Association of America (CMAA), a professional organization created by the comic book publishers, concluded that some form of self-regulation was necessary to the survival of their industry. Attempting to head off congressional action and the arbitrary content of any anti-comic book laws, in 1954 the CMAA promulgated a Comics Code, which regulated the content of comics, especially horror comics. A similar code went into effect in England the following year. Among its many provisions, the Comics Code called for the discontinuance of the words "horror" or "terror" in the title of comic books and forbade the picturing of scenes of depravity, sadism, or excessive gruesomeness. It further banned scenes that included the walking dead, torture, *vampires and vampirism*, ghouls, cannibalism, and werewolves. In the years after the adoption of the code, the only major appearances of a vampire came in Dell Comics, a company that did not formally subscribe to the code. In 1962, a single October/December issue of a new title, *Dracula*, appeared. It centered upon an encounter between several Americans and Count Dracula in Transylvania. The second issue was never published.

In 1958, a new type of magazine, the horror movie fan magazine, arrived on the newsstands. The first, *Famous Monsters of Filmland*, was developed by James Warren and Forrest J Ackerman and published by the Warren Publishing Company. Projected as a movie fanzine, it was not subject to the regulations of the Comics Code, even though it began to include black and white horror comics interspersed with movie stills and feature stories. In 1964 Warren risked the publication of a new black and white horror comic, featuring the very characters and scenes specifically banned by the Comics Code, in a new larger (8½" × 11") magazine format. Because of its larger page size and lack of color, technically, *Creepy* was not a comic book, though it targeted the same youthful audience. Success led to the appearance of a second title, *Eerie*. Meanwhile, vampires reappeared in comic books (full color in a standard comic format) when *The Munsters*, based upon the popular television comedy series, was launched, though with an absence of any visible bloodsucking.

In 1969, amid rising pressure to revamp the Comics Code and provide some liberalization in its enforcement, Gold Key issued the first new comic books to feature a vampire as the leading character. Like *The Munsters*, also by Gold Key, *Dark Shadows* was based on a popular television series. It was joined later that year by Warren's new graphic magazine *Vampirella*, featuring a sexy female vampire from outer space. This extraterrestrial vampire, who quickly found a blood substitute for her sustenance, emerged as the first "good guy" vampire, and her magazine went on to become the most popular and long-lived vampire comic book in the history of the medium.

Finally, in 1970, feeling the competition from the black and white comic magazines, the CMAA issued a revised Comics Code, destined to become effective on January 1, 1971. That important sentence that included vampires was rewritten to read, "Vampires, ghouls, and werewolves shall be permitted to be used when handled in the classic tradition such as *Frankenstein*, *Dracula*, and other high caliber literary works written by Edgar Allan Poe, Saki (H. H. Munro), Conan Doyle, and other respected authors whose works are read in schools throughout the world."

The revision found general acceptance and Marvel Comics moved quickly. It launched a line of new horror titles and in 1972 led in the real return of the vampire to the comic book world with its highly successful *The Tomb of Dracula*, which offered new adventures for Dracula in the modern world.

Marvel also introduced a new vampire, Morbius, who continued, like Dracula, to appear in various titles through the decade. By the end of the 1970s, however, the enthusiasm for horror in general and the vampire in particular waned in favor of superheroes. With two exceptions, no comic book in which a vampire was the leading character was issued through the early and mid–1980s. For Marvel, a definitive encounter occurred in *Dr. Strange* (No. 62,

December 1983), when the mystic Dr. Stephen Strange performed a magical ritual, the Montesi Formula, which had the effect of killing all of the vampires in the Marvel Universe.

The situation in the comic book world paralleled that in the movie and publishing industry in general. The mid–1980s was a dry time for production of new vampire cinema and novels. However, the low point was followed by a massive vampire revival which has continued largely unabated to the present. Year by year, new comic book titles appeared and the number of vampire appearances increased steadily. The first of the new vampire comics, *Blood of the Innocent*, was released at the beginning of 1986. It ran four issues and was followed by *Blood of Dracula* and Marvel's rather unconventional vampire title *Blood* (four issues, 1987–1988). In 1990, Innovation launched a 12-issue adaptation of Anne Rice's best-selling novel *The Vampire Lestat*. These titles heralded the spectacular expansion of vampire comic book publishing, widely visible by the mid–1990s. Ten new vampire titles appeared in 1990, 23 titles in 1991, and 34 in 1992 and 1993. Marvel moved to reverse its destruction of its vampires and reintroduced them into their titles, in a sub-universe, the Midnight Sons. One of the characters, Blade the Vampire Slayer, would rise to the top and, even as Marvel again abandoned the horror field, transform into a superhero of sorts and lead the way for Marvel to enter the movie industry in force.

A significant event in comic book publishing occurred in 1994 with the emergence of the "Bad Girls," female superheroes who were both feminine and deadly. Brian Pulido at Chaos! Comics is generally given the credit for producing the first successful bad girl, Lady Death, but she was soon joined by Shi and the revamped Vampirella, at this point the property of Harris Comics. Chaos! Comics soon expanded into the vampire field with its characters Purgatori and Chastity. Collectively the Bad Girl titles moved into the top of the comics sales lists. Simultaneously, the number of new vampire titles continued to multiply year-by-year through the 1990s.

At the end of the 1990s, amid numerous predictions of the vampire's demise across the board as a topic of comic books, cinema, and narrative fiction, the vampire not only survived but thrived in unprecedented fashion—including a new invasion of primetime television. Leading the way, of course, was *Buffy the Vampire Slayer*. As the TV series attracted its youthful audience, Dark Horse began to issue (1998) a comic title, which included both new stories and comic adaptations of selected episodes. The *Buffy* series would go on to become the third longest–running vampire comic book series in the English-speaking world (after *Vampirella* and the *Tomb of Dracula*), and like them was reprinted in the major European languages. A second series, which appeared after Dark Horse discontinued the original comic series, now carries the story line of the television series forward. IDW Comics also publishes the comic developed from the *Buffy* spin-off series *Angel*.

The comic book has proved a natural venue for vampires and seems to have settled in as the second main type of character (next to the superhero) in comics. Literally hundreds of new titles featuring vampires appeared in the decade after the *Dracula* centennial in 1997. *Dracula* remained a popular source book, and over the years more than three dozen adaptations of the novel have appeared as well as recent new editions of the novel with illustrations by prominent graphic artists such as Jae Lee and Ben Templesmith (the original artist used to bring novelist Steve Niles' vampire titles [*30 Days of Night*] to life).

The largest collection of English-language vampire comic books (2014) is located at the office of the Center for Studies on Popular Culture in Torino, Italy. CESPOC is hosted by CESNUR, the Center for Studies of New Religions, both organizations being headed by Dr. Massimo Introvigne. CESPOC may be contacted through its website at http://www.popularculture.it/. In the United States, the largest publicly accessible collection of vampire comics, though there are several large private collections, including that of J. Gordon Melton, is located at the library of Michigan State University in East Lansing. For access, contact the Special Collections Department through its website at http://www.lib.msu.edu/spc/index/.

5070. Alli, Scott. "Interview." In Jennifer K. Stuller, ed. *Fan Phenomena: Buffy the Vampire Slayer.* Bristol, UK: Intellect Press, 2013, pp. 144–49.

5071. Allocco, Katherine. "Vampiric Viragoes: Villainizing and Sexualizing Arthurian Women in *Dracula vs. King Arthur* (2005)." In Barbara Brodman and James E. Doan, eds. *The Universal Vampire: Origins and Evolution of a Legend.* Madison, NJ: Fairleigh Dickinson University Press, 2013, pp. 149–64.

5072. Bacon, Simon. "Prequel, Sequel or Equal: The Transmedia Vampire and the Graphic Novel." In Natalie Krikowa and Shawn Edrei, eds. *Crossing Channels, Crossing Realms.* Oxford: Inter-Disciplinary Press, 2013. Rpt. in: Jonathan C. Evans and Thomas Giddens, eds. *Cultural Excavation and Formal Expression in the Graphic Novel.* Oxford: Inter-Disciplinary Press, 2013.

5073. Barker, Martin. *A Haunt of Fears: The Strange History of the British Horror Comics Campaign.* London: Pluto Press, 1984. 227 pp.

5074. Benton, Mike. *Horror Comics: The Illustrated History.* Dallas, TX: Taylor Publishing, 1991. 144 pp. hb. Large format.

5075. Bissette, Stephen R. "The Premature Burial: Monster Magazines and the Rebirth of Horror Comics." *Gore Shriek* 4 (1988): 16–31.

5076. Brady, Matt. "Bad Girls Profiles." In *Wizard Bad Girls Special.* New York: Gareb Shamus Enterprises, 1996, pp. 31–110.

5077. Busiek, Kurt. "What Do You Do with...a Vampire? *Comics Feature* 13/13 (Sept./Oct. 1981): 59—64.

5078. Butterworth, Jack. "Warren Comics in the 1970's: The Run of the EC Roses." *Gore Shriek* 6 (1989): 2–12.

5079. Carson, Catherine. "Barbara Leigh: Vampirella." *Femme Fatales* 4, 3 (October 1995): 24–31, 61.

5080. Cziraky, Dan. "Barbara Leigh: The Reel Vampirella." *Chiller Theatre* 1, 2 (1995): 25–30.

5081. Daniels, Les. "It Seems to Be Our Friend Again: The Undead in Comic Books." In Rosemary Ellen Guiley, with J. B. Macabre. *The Complete Vampire Companion.* New York: Macmillan, 1994, pp. 145–56.

5082. Dean, Michael. "The Vampirella Wars: The Untold Story of James Warren's Custody Battle with Harris Comics." *The Comics Journal* 253 (June 2003). Excerpt Posted at: http://www.webcitation.org/5swey7SYy.

5083. Donovan, Ryan P. "*Buffy the Vampire Slayer* Season 8." In Bart H. Beaty and Stephen Weiner, eds. *Critical Survey of Graphic Novels: Heroes & Superheroes.* Ipswich, MA: Salem Press, 2012, pp. 150–155.

5084. Frising, Fritz. "25 years of Vampirella Collectibles." *Scary Monsters Magazine* 12 (September 1994): 56–60.

5085. Gaiman, Neil. "Interview with Alan Moore." *American Fantasy* 2, 2 (Winter 1987): 30–35, 64.

5086. *Ghost Rider and the Midnight Sons Magazine* 1, 1 (December 1993): 1–48.

5087. Gifford, Denis. "The Day the Comics Went Bats." In Peter Haining. *The Dracula Scrapbook.* New York: Bramwell House, 1976, pp. 111–20.

5088. Glut, Donald R. *The Dracula Book.* Metuchen, NJ: Scarecrow Press, 1975. 388 pp.

5089. Goodwin, Archie. "The Warren Empire: A Personal View." *Gore Shriek* 5 (1988).

5090. Goulart, Ron. *The Encyclopedia of American Comics.* New York: Facts on File, 1990. 408 pp.

5091. Hajdu, David. *The Ten-Cent Plague: The Great Comic-Book Scare and How It Changed*

America. New York: Farrar, Straus and Giroux, 2008. 434 pp. hb. dj.

5092. Hayes, Melinda, comp. "Vampirella Comics." Posted at: http://isd.usc.edu/~shoaf/vampirella/.

5093. Hino, Matsuri. *The Art of Vampire Knight: Matsuri Hino Illustrations.* San Francisco: VIZ Media LLC, 2011. 96 pp. hb.

5094. Horn, Maurice, ed. *The World Encyclopedia of Comics.* New York: Chelsea House Publishers, 1976. 785 pp.

5095. Introvigne, Massimo. "English-Language Vampire Comics, 1935–2000: A List and a Catalogue of the Holdings of CESPOC Library." Posted at: http://www.cesnur.org/2007/vampire_comics.htm. The Center for Studies on Popular Culture (CESPOC), based in Torino (Turin), Italy, has assembled the largest collection of vampire-themed comic books know to exist, and its director, Massimo Introvigne, worked with J. Gordon Melton in the production of a listing of both the holdings of the collection (more than 8,000 titles) and a more comprehensive listing of those comic books known to exist (some 10,000 titles). Access to the collection is available, and contact with the CESPOC staff may be made through the website.

5096. Kikuchi, Hideyuki, and Yoshitaka Amano. *Vampire Hunter D: Reader's Guide.* Trans. by Kevin Leahy. Milwaukie, OR: Dark Horse Books, 2010. 255 pp. tp.

5097. Lake, Michael. "Dracula in the Comics." *Journal of Dracula Studies* 5 (2003): 35–39.

5098. Madeley, June M. "Transnational Transformations: A Gender Analysis of Japanese Manga Featuring Unexpected Bodily Transformations." *The Journal of Popular Culture* 45, 4 (August 2012): 789–806,.

5099. "Marv Wolfman's Trial." *The Comics Journal.* Part 1: 236 (August 2001): 22–84. Part 2: 239 (Nov. 2001): 68–112. Includes transcript with comments and sidebars of trial in which Marv Wolfman unsuccessfully challenged ownership of the characters he created for *The Tomb of Dracula.*

5100. Melton, J. Gordon. "Images from the Hellmouth: *Buffy the Vampire Slayer* Comic Books 1998–2002." *Slayage: The Online International Journal of Buffy Studies* 2, 2 [6] (September 2002). Posted at: http://www.whedonstudies.tv/.

5101. ____. *The Official Vampirella Collector's Checklist, 1969–1998.* Santa Barbara, CA: Transyl-vanian Society of Dracula, 1999. 30 pp. pb. Large Format.

5102. ____. "The Vampire in the Comic Book." In *Partial Proceedings of the 8th Annual Comic Arts Conference,* San Diego, California, July 20–22, 2000.

5103. ____. *The Vampire in the Comic Book.* New York: Count Dracula Fan Club, 1993. 32 pp. pb. Spiral bound.

5104. ____, **and Lee Scott.** *The Vampire and the Comic Book.* New York: Dracula Press, 1994. 76 pp. pb. Staples.

5105. Murch, Brianna. (2013). Beyond Maidens, Minxes, and Mothers: The Female Vampire and Gothic Other in *Dracula, Hellsing,* and *Chibi Vampire.* Bridgewater, MA: Bridgewater State University, 2013. In *BSU Honors Program Theses and Projects.* Item 8. Available at: http://vc.bridgew.edu/honors_proj/8.

5106. Nixon, Dorothy. "Comic Book Art, Engineering Principles, and the Highgate Vampire" *Journal of Vampirism* 2, 1 (Fall 1978): 16–17.

5107. Nixon, Elizabeth. "A Multicultural Comic Book Toolbox. 'It ain't John Shaft': Marvel gets multicultural in *The Tomb of Dracula.*" In Frederick Luis Aldama. *Multicultural Comics: From Zap to Blue Beetle.* Austin: University of Texas Press, 2010, pp. 149–56.

5108. Palumbo, Donald. "Marvel's *Tomb of Dracula*: Case Study in a Scorned Medium." In Detore Johnson and Lydia Schurman, eds. *Scorned Literature: Essays on the History and Criticism of Popular Mass-Produced Fiction in America.* Westport, CT: Praeger, 2002, pp. 51–68.

5109. Roach, David A. "Shadows & the Darkness." *Comic Book Artist* 13 (May 2001): 14–17. First article in a special issue on "The "Marvel Horrorshow," focusing on *The Tomb of Dracula* and other Marvel horror titles in the 1970s.

5110. ____, **and Jon B. Cooke, eds.** *The Warren Companion.* Raleigh, NC: Twomorrows Publishing, 2001. 269 pp.

5111. Rosenkranz, Patrick. *Rebel Visions: The Underground Comix Revolution, 1963–1975.* Seattle, WA: Fantagraphic Books, 2002. 292 pp. hb. dj. Large format.

5112. Ryan, John. *Panel by Panel: An Illustrated History of Australian Comics.* Stanmore, NSW, Aust.: Cassell Australia, 1979. 223 pp. hb. dj. Large format.

5113. Sample, Ed. "Down for the Count and Ripped to Shreds." *Amazing Heroes* 80 (October 1985): 22–34.

5114. Sanderson, Peter. "Comic Feature Interviews Marv Wolfman." *Comics Feature* 13/13 (Sept./Oct. 1981): 34–57.

5115. _____. "The Dead Yet Move: Toei's Animated *Tomb of Dracula* Movie." *Comics Feature* 13/13 (Sept./Oct. 1981): 58.

5116. Scott, Lee. "Dracula and Vampires in Comics." *Vampire Information Exchange Network Newsletter.* Part 1: 63 (July 1993): 9–10, 13–16. Part 2: 64 (September 1993): 7–15.

5117. "Sexy Vampire Issue." *Lacunae.* No. 4. Clifton, NY: Lacunae, 1995.

5118. Shanklin, Rickey. "Fangs for the Funny Books; or, Dracula in the Comics." In Bob Madison, ed. *Dracula: The First Hundred Years.* Baltimore, MD: Midnight Marquee Press, 1997, pp. 168–85.

5119. Sharp, Molly Louise. *Gender, Feminism, and Heroism in Joss Whedon and John Cassaday's* Astonishing X-Men *Comics.* Austin: University of Texas, M.A. thesis, 2011. 129 pp. Large format. Posted at: http://repositories.lib.utexas.edu/bitstream/handle/2152/11903/SHARP-THESIS.pdf.

5120. Stine, Scott Aaron. "The Trash Collector: The Blood-soaked History of Eerie Publications." *Gick! Magazine* 1, 4 (Fall/Winter 2000): 32–40, 42.

5121. Suarez, George, ed. *Tales to Terrible to Tell.* Nos. 1–11. Quincy, MA: New England Comics Press, 1991–93. Nos. 10 and 11 appeared under the title *Terrology.*

5122. Teampau, Gelu. "Faces of the Vampire in Comic Books." *Echinox Journal* 21 (2011): 302–317.

5123. Thomas, Ron C. "The Dark Beautiful World of Jon Muth." *Four Color Magazine* 1, 1 (Nov.-Dec. 1986).

5124. Thompson, Jeff. *The* Dark Shadows *Comic Books.* Los Angeles: Joseph Collins Publications, 1984. Rev. ed.: 1988. 115 pp.

5125. _____. "Introduction: The Best of *Dark Shadows.*" *Dark Shadows: The Best of the Original Series.* Neshannock, PA: Hermes Press, 2012. The original Dark Shadows comic books were published by Gold Key Comics, with art work by Joe

Certa and George Wilson, and writing by Donald J. Arneson and Arnold Drake. Reprints the Gold Key *Dark Shadows* comic books #1, 4, 6, 8, 11, 14, 17, 18, 24, 31, 32, and 33.

5126. _____. "Introduction: *Dark Shadows* and the Comics." *Dark Shadows: The Complete Original Series,* vol. 1. Neshannock, PA: Hermes Press, 2010. Reprints the Gold Key *Dark Shadows* comic books #1–7.

5127. _____. "Introduction: A Final Look at the Comics." *Dark Shadows: The Complete Original Series,* vol. 5. Neshannock, PA: Hermes Press, 2012, pp. 5–11. Reprints the Gold Key *Dark Shadows* comic books #29–35.

5128. _____. "Introduction: A Look at the Comics." *Dark Shadows: The Complete Original Series,* vol. 2. Neshannock, PA: Hermes Press, 2011. Reprints the Gold Key *Dark Shadows* comic books #8–14.

5129. _____. "Introduction: A Look at the Comics." *Dark Shadows: The Complete Original Series,* vol. 3. Neshannock, PA: Hermes Press, 2011. Reprints the Gold Key *Dark Shadows* comic books #15–21.

5130. _____. "Introduction: A Look at the Comics." *Dark Shadows: The Complete Original Series,* vol. 4. Ed. Daniel Herman. Neshannock, PA: Hermes Press, 2012. Reprints the Gold Key *Dark Shadows* comic books #22–28.

5131. _____. "Introduction: The Story Digest." *Dark Shadows: The Original Series Story Digest.* Ed. Daniel Herman. Neshannock, PA: Hermes Press, 2011. Reprints the Gold Key *Dark Shadows Story Digest Magazine* #1 (June 1970).

5132. Von Bernewitz, Fred, and Grant Geissman. *Tales of Terror.* Timonium, MD: Gemstone Publishing/Seattle, WA: Fantagraphics, 2000. 296 pp. pb. Large format.

5133. Warren, James. "The Most Famous Monster of All." Interview conducted by Dave Baumuller. *Horror Biz* 4 (1999): 16–31.

5134. _____. "Original Vampirella." *Horror Biz* 4 (1999): 26–27.

5135. _____. "Someone Has to Make It Happen." Interview conducted by Jon B. Cooke. *Comic Book Artist* 4 (Spring 1999): 14–43. One article in a special issue devoted to Warren Publications.

5136. Wasserman, Jeffrey H. "Vampires in the Comics." *The Monster Times* 1, 15 (September 6, 1972): 6–9.

5137. Wolfman, Marv. "What Can Your Say About a Five-Hundred-Year-Old Vampire Who Refuses to Die?" *Dracula Lives! 1* (1973): 46–52.

5138. _____. "Yes, Marv Wolfman Is His Real Name!" *Dracula Lives!* 1, 4 (January 1974): 49.

5139. Wolk, Douglas. "*Tomb of Dracula*: The Cheap, Strong Stuff." In Douglas Wolk. *Reading Comics: How Graphic Novels Work and What They Mean.* Cambridge, MA: Da Capo Press, 2007, pp. 317–28.

VII. The Metaphorical Vampire

Vampires as Social Science Metaphors

Among the most popular functions of the vampire among contemporary commentators is its utilization as a metaphor of unequal power relationships in various social contexts. Such a use seems to have originated with Socialist philosopher Frederick Engels. In his early work *The Condition of the Working Class in England*, he identifies the "vampire property-holding class" as the real source of Europe's social problems. The more famous use, however, occurs some twenty years later when Engels' colleague Karl Marx returns to the vampire metaphor in *Capital*, the first volume of which was published in 1867 (English edition, 1887). In chapter 10, he observes, "Capital is dead labour, that, vampire-like, only lives by sucking living labour, and lives the more, the more labour it sucks. The time during which the labourer works, is the time during which the capitalist consumes the labour-power he has purchased of him."

In recent decades, the use of the vampire as a metaphor for autocratic rulers, dictatorial governments, owners of corporations, and anyone in entrenched authority who exploits a segment of the population has multiplied many times over. The bibliography following represents only a sampling of such literature, with particular attention paid to books that note their use of the vampire metaphor in their title. Since the Nixon administration, it has become common for the president of the United States to be pictured as a vampire relative to one or more aspects of his policies.

From its nineteenth century use in political writing, the vampire has permeated all areas of both the popular and academic culture as a metaphor for a variety of medical, legal, scientific, and especially psychological situations and objects. These additional appearances of the vampire are explored in additional separate chapters on psychology, medicine, religion, the law and crime, and biology later in this section.

5140. Allen, William. *Al Smith's Tammany Hall: Champion Political Vampire.* New York: Institute for Public Service, 1928. 338 pp. hb.

5141. Anderson, Donald Travis. *The Female Vampire and the Politics of Gender.* Edmonton, AB: University of Alberta, M.A. thesis, 1992. 119 pp. Large format.

5142. Atanasoski, Neda. "Dracula as Ethnic Conflict: Representing US Humanitarianism in the Former Yugoslavia." In Niall Scott. *The Role of the Monster: Myths and Metaphors of Enduring Evil.* Oxford: inter–Disciplinary Press, 2009, pp. 77–86. Posted at: http://www.scribd.com/doc/61699474/The-Role-of-the-Monster-Myths-and-Metaphors-of-Enduring-Evil.

5143. Blackburn, Richard Janes. *The Vampire of Reason: An Essay in the Philosophy of History.* London/New York: Verso, 1990. 222 pp. tp.

5144. Blofeld, John. "Manchus, Lute and Vampire-Fox." In John Blofeld. *City of Lingering Splendor: A Frank Account of Old Peking's Exotic Pleasures.* Boston: Shambhala, 1989, pp. 71–90.

5145. Brown, William Montgomery. *The War Vampire and the Churches.* Galion, OH: Bradford-Brown Educational. 1935. 50 pp. pb.

5146. Clark, Gracia. "Gender and Profiteering: Ghana's Market Women as Devoted Mothers And 'Human Vampire Bats.'" In Dorothy L. Hodgson and Sheryl A. McCurdy, eds. *"Wicked" Women and the Reconfiguration of Gender in Africa.* Portsmouth, NH: Heinemann, 2001, pp. 293–311.

5147. Clark, Maureen. "Postcolonial Vampires in the Indigenous Imagination: Philip McLaren and Drew Hayden Taylor." In Tabish Khair and Johan Höglund, eds. *Transnational and Postcolonial Vampires: Dark Blood.* Basingstoke, UK: Palgrave Macmillan, 2012, pp. 121–137.

5148. Cole, Phillip. "Rousseau and the Vampires: Toward a Political Philosophy of the Undead." In Richard Greene and K. Silem Mohammad, eds. *The Undead and Philosophy: Chicken Soup for the Soulless.* La Salle, IL: Open Court, 2006, pp. 183–96. Rpt. in: Richard Greene and K. Silem Mohammad, eds. *Zombies, Vampires, and Philosophy: New Life for the Undead.* La Salle, IL: Open Court, 2010, pp. 183–96.

5149. Engels, Frederick. *The Condition of the Working Class in England.* Trans. by Florence Kelley Wischnewetzky. London: George Allen & Unwin, [1892]. 298 pp. hb. Frequently reprinted. Posted at: http://www.gutenberg.org/ebooks/17306. Rev. ed.: Trans. by W. O. Henderson and W. H. Chaloner. Stanford, CA: Stanford University Press, 1968. 386 pp. hb. Rev. ed.: Oxford, UK: Oxford University Press, 1999. 368 pp. tp.

5150. Fekete, John. "Vampire Value, Infinitive Art, and Literary Theory." In John Fekete, ed. *Life After Postmodernism: Essays in Value and Culture.* New York: St. Martin's Press. 1988, pp. 64–85. Rpt.: Basingstoke, UK: Macmillan Education, 1988. A revised and expanded version of a paper originally presented at the Modern Language Association meeting in New York in 1983.

5151. Frayling, Christopher, and Robert Wokler. "From the Orangu-Tan to the Vampire: Towards an Anthropology of Rousseau." In R. A. Leigh, ed. *Rousseau After Two Hundred Years: Proceedings of the Cambridge University Colloquium.* Cambridge: Cambridge University Press, 1982, pp. 109–29.

5152. Frimpong-Ansah, Jonathan H. *The Vampire State in Africa: The Political Economy of Decline in Ghana.* London: James Curry, 1991. 205 pp. tp. Rpt.: Trenton, NJ: Africa World Press, 1992. 205 pp. tp.

5153. Gibbons, Luke. "The Mirror & the Vamp: Reflections on the Act of Union." In Bruce Stewart, ed. *Hearts and Minds: Irish Culture and Society Under the Act of Union.* Gerrards Cross: Colin Smythe, 2001, pp. 21–39.

5154. Harmon, Harry. *Economic Vampires, Parasites and Cannibals: What You Are Not Supposed to Know About Economics and Politics.* N.p.: the author, 2009. 88 pp. tp.

5155. Hartl, R. F., A. Mehlmann, and A. Novak. "Cycles of Fear: Periodic Bloodsucking Rates for Vampires." *Journal of Optimization Theory and Application* 75, 3 (December 1992): 559–68. Posted at: http://prolog.univie.ac.at/research/publications/downloads/Vampir/vampirli.html.

5156. Höglund, Johan. "Militarizing the Vampire: Underworld and the Desire of the Military Entertainment Complex." In Tabish Khair and Johan Höglund, eds. *Transnational and Postcolonial Vampires: Dark Blood.* Basingstoke, UK: Palgrave Macmillan, 2012, pp. 173–88.

5157. _____, and Tabish Khair. "Introduction: Transnational and Postcolonial Vampires." In Tabish Khair and Johan Höglund, eds. *Transnational and Postcolonial Vampires: Dark Blood.* Basingstoke, UK: Palgrave Macmillan, 2012, pp. 1–9.

5158. Homewood, Chris. "The Return of "undead" History: The West German terrorist as vampire and the problem of "normalizing" the past in Margarethe von Trotta's *Die bleierne Zeit* (1981) and Christian Petzold's *Die innere Sicherheit* (2001)." In Stuart Taberner and Paul Cooke, eds. *German Culture, Politics, and Literature into the Twenty-first Century: Beyond normalization.* Rochester, NY: Camden House, 2006, pp. 121–36.

5159. Kast, Sheilah, and Jim Rosape. *Dracula Is Dead.* Baltimore: Bancroft Press, 2009. 409 pp. hb. dj.

5160. Khair, Tabish. "The Man-Eating Tiger and the Vampire in South Asia." In Tabish Khair and Johan Höglund, eds. *Transnational and Postcolonial Vampires: Dark Blood.* Basingstoke, UK: Palgrave Macmillan, 2012, pp. 105–20.

5161. Khair, Tabish, and Johan Höglund, eds. *Transnational and Postcolonial Vampires: Dark*

Blood. Basingstoke, UK: Palgrave Macmillan, 2012. 248 pp. hb.

5162. Kingston, Geoffrey. "Dracula in Charge of the Blood Bank." *The Economic and Labour Relations Review* 22, 3 (November 2011): 29–44.

5163. Kingston, Uncle Ñoño. *An Economic Proposal: Fact Becoming Reality (MENE MENE TEKEL UPHARSIN): A Token Society That Stabs Vampire Industries in the Heart.* Vol. 1. Lancaster, CA: World citizen SIT Ministries, 2012. 348 pp. tp.

5164. Kurti, Lazzlo. "Transylvania, Land Beyond Reason: Toward an Anthropological Analysis of a Contested Terrain." *Dialectical Anthropology* 14, 1 (1989): 21–52.

5165. London, Herbert, and Edwin S. Rubenstein. *From the Empire State to the Vampire State: New York in a Downward Transition.* Lanham, MD: University Press of America, 1994. 186 pp. tp.

5166. Longinovic, Tomislav Z. *Vampire Nation: Violence as Cultural Imaginary.* Durham, NC: Duke University Press Books, 2011. 212 pp. hb. & tp.

5167. _____. *Vampires Like Us: Writing Down "the Serbs."* Belgrade, Serbia: Belgrade Circle, 2005. 229 pp. tp.

5168. McNally, David. *Monsters of the Market: Zombies, Vampires, and Global Capitalism.* Leiden: Brill, 2011. 296 pp. hb.

5169. Mann, Gregory. "An Africanist's Apostasy: On Luise White's Speaking with Vampires." *The International Journal of African Historical Studies* 41, 1 (2008): 117–21.

5170. Margetts, Emma. *From Cannibal to Consumer: The Shifting Poetic Metaphor of the Vampire.* Perth, Western Australia: Edith Cowan University, M.A. thesis, 2007. Large format. Attached to the thesis is a cd copy of a performance of "The Gothic Opera: A Symphony in Terror."

5171. Martin, Álvaro García. "Haunted Communities: The Greek Vampire or the Uncanny at the Core of Nation Construction." In Agnieszka Stasiewicz-Bieńkowska and Karen Graham, eds. *Monstrous Manifestations: Reality and Imaginings of the Monster.* Oxford: Inter-Disciplinary Press, 2013, pp. 53–64.

5172. Marx, Karl. *Capital: A Critique of Political Economy.* 3 vols. Chicago: Charles H. Kerr,

1906–09. hb. Posted at: http://libcom.org/library/capital-karl-marx. The first complete English edition, has been frequently reprinted. The famous use of the vampire metaphor occurs initially in chapter 10.

5173. Modan, Gabriella Gahlia. "La Loca vs. The Cultural Vampires." In Gabriella Gahlia Modan. *Turf Wars: Discourse, Diversity, and the Politics of Place.* Hoboken, NJ: Wiley-Blackwell, 2008, pp. 170–201.

5174. Nelson, John S. "Cowboys or Vampire Killers? The Bush Gang Rides Again, or American Figures in Foreign Affairs." *Poroi* 2, 2 (2003): 104–117. Posted at: http://dx.doi.org/10.13008/2151-2957.1052.

5175. *Operation Vampire Killer 2000: American Police Action Plan for Stopping the Program for World Government Rule.* Phoenix, AZ: Police Against the New World Order, 1992. 73 pp. tp.

5176. Phillips, Joseph. *Vampire Management: Why Your Job Sucks.* N.p.: the author, 2011. 126 pp. tp.

5177. Ratigan, Dylan. *Greedy Bastards: How We Can Stop Corporate Communists, Banksters, and Other Vampires from Sucking America Dry.* New York: Simon & Schuster, 2012. 245 pp. hb. dj.

5178. Reimann, Günter. *The Vampire Economy: Doing Business Under Fascism.* Auburn, AL: Ludwig von Mises Institute, 1939, 2007. 350 pp. tp.

5179. Robinson, Sara Libby. *Blood Will Tell: Vampires as Political Metaphors Before World War I.* Brighton, MA: Academic Studies Press, 2011. 250 pp. hb.

5180. Rodgers, Walter C. "The Network Correspondent as Historian, Diplomat, Student, and Vampire." In Joe S. Foote, ed. *Live from the Trenches: The Changing Role of the Television News Correspondent.* Carbondale: Southern Illinois University Press, 1998, pp. 30–40.

5181. Rouse, Joseph. "Vampires: Social Constructivism, Realism, and Other Philosophical Undead." *History and Theory* 41, 1 (21002): 60–78.

5182. Rushkoff, Douglas. "Playing Undead." *Swing* 1, 5 (April 1995): 34–43.

5183. Ruthner, Clemens. "Undead Feedback: Adaptations and Echoes of Johann Fluckinger's Report, Visum et Repertum (1732), until the Millennium." In Barbara Brodman and James E. Doan, eds. *The Universal Vampire: Origins and*

Evolution of a Legend. Madison, NJ: Fairleigh Dickinson University Press, 2013, pp. 91–106.

5184. _____. "Vampirism as Political Theory: Voltaire to Alfred Rosenberg and Elfried Jelinek." In Allienne R. Becker, ed. *Visions of the Fantastic: Selected Essays from the Fifteenth International Conference on the Fantastic in the Arts*. Westport, CT: Greenwood Press, 1996, pp. 3–12.

5185. Schneider, Eric C. *Vampires, Dragons, and Egyptian Kings: Youth Gangs in Postwar New York*. Princeton, NJ: Princeton University Press, 2001. 360 pp. tp.

5186. Seligman, Amanda Irene. "'Apologies to Dracula, Werewolf, Frankenstein': White Homeowners and Blockbusters in Chicago." *Journal of the Illinois State Historical Society* (Spring 2001): 70–95. An article from a special issue of the journal on race and housing in post–World War II Chicago.

5187. Smith, Andrew. "Reading Wealth in Nigeria: Occult Capitalism and Marx's Vampires." *Historical Materialism-Research in Critical Marxist Theory* 9, 1 (2001): 39–59.

5188. Smith, Eric D. "A Presage of Horror! Cacotopia, the Paris Commune, and Bram Stoker's *Dracula*." *Criticism* 52, 1 (2010): Posted at: http://digitalcommons.wayne.edu/criticism/vol52/iss1/4.

5189. Steel, Jayne. "Vampira: Representations of the Irish Female Terrorist." *Irish Studies Review* 6, 3 (December 1998): 273–284.

5190. Stojanova, Christina. "Beyond Dracula and Ceausescu: Phenomenology of Horror in Romanian Cinema." In Steven Jay Schneider and Tony Williams, eds. *Horror International*. Detroit, MI: Wayne State University Press, 2005, pp. 200–234.

5191. Stone, Allucquère Rosanne. "The Gaze of the Vampire." In Allucquère Rosanne Stone. *The War of Desire and Technology at the Close of the Mechanical Age*. Cambridge, MA: MIT Press, 1995, pp. 165–84.

5192. _____. "In the Language of Vampire Speak: Overhearing Our Own Voices." In Sue Golding, ed. *The Eight Technologies of Otherness*. London: Routledge, 1997, pp. 58–66.

5193. Taibbi, Matt. *Griftopia: Bubble Machines, Vampire Squids, and the Long Con That Is Breaking America*. New York: Spiegel & Grau, 2010. 252 pp. tp.

5194. Vrbančić, Mario. "Globalisation, Empire, and the Vampire." *CLCWeb: Comparative Literature and Culture* 9, 2 (2007). Posted at: http://dx.doi.org/10.7771/1481-4374.1218.

5195. Warner, A. C. "The Living Dead in Colonial and Neo-Colonial Worlds: Fanon's Mass Attack on the Ego in Cliff, Kincaid and Aidoo." *Human Architecture: Journal of the Sociology of Self-Knowledge*. 5, 3 (2007): 239–50. Posted at: http://scholarworks.umb.edu/humanarchitecture/vol5/iss3/22.

5196. Warwick, Alexandra. "Vampires and the Empire: Fears and Fictions of the 1890s." In Sally Ledger and Scott McCracken eds. *Cultural Politics at the fin de siècle*. Cambridge: Cambridge University Press, 1995, pp. 202–20.

5197. Welkins, Emily. *Till the Last Drop!* N.p.: the author, 2011. 107 pp. pb.

5198. White, Luise. "Cars Out of Place: Vampires, Technology, and Labor in East and Central Africa." *Representations* 43, 1 (1993): 27–50.

5199. _____. *Speaking with Vampires: Rumor and History in Colonial Africa*. Berkeley: University of California Press, 2002. 368 pp. hb. Rpt.: Berkeley: University of California Press, 2002. 368 pp. tp.

5200. _____. "Vampire Priests of Central Africa: African Debates About Labor and Religion in Colonial Northern Zambia." *Comparative Studies in Society and History* 35 (1993): 746–72.

5201. Winnubst, Shannon. "Vampires, Anxieties, and Dreams: Race and Sex in the Contemporary United States." *Hypatia* 18, 3 (Autumn 2003): 1–20.

5202. Zanger, Jules. "Metaphor into Metonymy: The Vampire Next Door.". In Joan Gordon and Veronica Hollinger, eds. *Blood Read: The Vampire as Metaphor in Contemporary Culture*. Philadelphia: University of Pennsylvania Press, 1997, pp. 17–26.

5203. zu Reventlow, Count Ernst. *The Vampire of the Continent*. New York: Jackson Press, 1916. 225 pp. hb. boards. Rpt.: 1917.

Psychological Perspectives on Vampirism

The term psychic vampire has entered the popular culture as psychologists have been caught up in the contemporary vampire culture. The idea of a vampire sucking up energy instead of blood came to the fore originally in Spiritualist circles in the nineteenth century as vampirism was posed as the negative mirror of spiritual healing, seen as the positive transfer of cosmic energy from the spirit realm from one person (the healer) to another (the patient). Vampirism was the stealing of life force from a living human by another (i.e., the spirit of the deceased). Some biblical justification for psychic vampirism was found in Leviticus 17: 17, in the statement, "the life of all flesh is the blood..."

In the contemporary setting, a significant minority within the contemporary vampire community, including many who would never consider actually drinking blood, define themselves as vampires by observing that they need to draw life energy from others to survive. Overwhelmingly, the present "real" vampire community consists of such psychic vampires. Meanwhile, mainstream psychology, which has lost much of its belief in the transfer of cosmic energies (as proposed by nineteenth-century Mesmerists and ceremonial magicians), nevertheless believes strongly in the transfer of emotional energies caused by unbalanced relationships among friends and family. The exploration of such imbalances has led to a new set of pop psychology texts utilizing the vampire metaphor.

The vampire has also found a presence among the relatively small community of practitioners of real ceremonial magic, usually spelled "magick," to distinguish it from stage illusions. Aleister Crowley introduced the vampire into his writings, and it has been passed along to his magical students, and at least two vampire-based religious groups have emerged.

The spread of the vampire metaphor has led to the production of a large literature exploring its psychological implications by both practitioners and observers, while the literary scholar Nina Auerbach, who uses psychological metaphors as a basic tool in her analysis of the lore, has authored one of the most popular academic texts on vampires. Meanwhile, the pop psychology literature, which utilizes the vampire as a metaphor for understanding relationships, grades into the pseudo-documentary literature (see separate section), a set of fictional books that offer, in a somewhat humorous vein, advice on dating, relating to, and loving any attractive vampires one might encounter.

5204/05. Ableman, Paul. *The Mouth and Oral Sex.* London: Christopher Kypreos/Running Man Press, 1969, 200 pp. hb. Rpt.: London: Sphere, 1972. 188 pp. pb. Rpt. as: *The Sensuous Mouth.* New York: Ace, 1969. 264 pp. pb. See especially the discussion of vampirism in chapter 15, "Aphrodisiacs and Erotocentric Magic."

5206. Almond, Barbara R., "Monstrous Infant and Vampiric Mothers in Bram Stoker's *Dracula.*" *International Journal of Psychoanalysis* 88, 1 (2007): 219–235.

5207. Andriano, Joseph. "The Unholy Circle: A Jungian Reading of *Dracula.*" In C. W. Sullivan, III, ed. *The Dark Fantastic.* Westport, CT: Greenwood Press, 1997, pp. 49–55.

5208. Appleby, Robin S. "Dracula and Dora: The Diagnosis and Treatment of Alternative Narrative." *Literature and Psychology* 39, 3 (1993): 16–37.

5209. Astle, Richard. "Dracula as Totemic Monster: Lacan, Freud, Oedipus and History." *Sub-stance* 25 (1980): 98–105.

5210. Auerbach, Nina. "My Vampire, My Friend: The Intimacy Dracula Destroyed." In Joan Gordon and Veronica Hollinger, eds. *Blood Read: The Vampire as Metaphor in Contemporary Culture.* Philadelphia: University of Pennsylvania Press, 1997, pp. 11–16.

5211. _____. *Our Vampires, Ourselves.* Chicago: University of Chicago Press, 1995. 231 pp.

hb. dj. Excerpt rpt. as: "Dracula: A Vampire of Our Own." In Harold Bloom, ed. *Bram Stoker's Dracula*. Ser.: Bloom's Modern Critical Interpretations. Philadelphia: Chelsea House Publications, 2002, pp. 191–228. *Our Vampires, Ourselves* received the 1996 award as the best nonfiction book of the previous year given annually by the Lord Ruthven Society.

5212. Bacon, Simon. "The Vampiric Diaspora: The Complications of Victimhood and Post-Memory as Configured in the Jewish Migrant Vampire." In Deborah Mutch. *The Modern Vampire and Human Identity*. Basingstoke, UK/New York: Palgrave Macmillan, 2013, pp. 111–27. Rpt. in: Barbara Braid and Julitta Rydlewska, eds. *Unity in Diversity: Cultural Paradigm and Personal Identity*. Cambridge: Cambridge Scholars Publishing, 2013, pp. 27–43.

5213. _____. "Zero to Hero: The Transitional Vampire and Human Becoming." *University of Bucharest Review: A Journal of Literary and Cultural Studies* 1 (2011): 5–19.

5214. Belanger, Michelle A. *Psychic Vampire Codex: Manual of Magick & Energy Work*. Weiser Books: York Beach, ME, 2004. 284 pp. tp.

5215. _____. *Sacred Hunger*. Fort Wayne, IN: Dark Moon Press, 2005. 142 pp. tp.

5216. Benezech, M., M. Bourgeois, D. Boukhabza, and J. Yesavage. "Cannibalism and Vampirism in Paranoid Schizophrenia." *The Journal of Clinical Psychiatry* 42, 7 (1981): 290ff. Rpt. in: Richard Noll, ed. *Vampires, Werewolves, and Demons: Twentieth Century Reports in the Psychiatric Literature*. New York: Brunner Mazel, 1992, pp. 57–73.

5217. Bentley, C. F. "The Monster in the Bedroom: Sexual Symbolism in Bram Stoker's *Dracula*." *Literature and Psychology* 22, 1 (1972): 27–34. Rpt. in Margaret L. Carter, ed. *Dracula: The Vampire and the Critics*. Ann Arbor: UMI Research Press, 1988, pp. 25–34 .

5218. Bernstein, Albert J. *Emotional Vampires: Dealing with People Who Drain You Dry*. New York: McGraw-Hill, 2001. 242 pp. tp. Rev. ed.: New York: McGraw-Hill, 2012. 258 pp. tp.

5219. _____. *Emotional Vampires at Work: Dealing with Bosses and Coworkers Who Drain You Dry*. New York: McGraw-Hill, 2013. 256 pp. tp.

5220. Birge, Barbara. "Dracula: The Quest for Female Potency in Transgressive Relationships." *Psychological Perspectives: A Quarterly Journal of Jungian Thought* 29, 1 (1994): 22–36.

5221/22. Blavatsky, Helena P. "Vampirism—It's Phenomena Explained." In Helena P. Blavatsky. *Isis Unveiled*. Vol. I. Science. Wheaton, IL: Theosophical Publishing House, 1877, 1972, pp. 449–57. Posted at: http://www.blavatsky.net/blavatsky/isis_unveiled/isis_unveiled.htm. Excerpt in: McNally, Raymond T. *A Clutch of Vampires*. New York: Bell Publishing Company, 1974, pp. 185–88. Excerpt in: David Skal, ed. *Vampires: Encounters with the Undead*. New York: Black Dog & Leventhal Publishers, 2001, pp.

5223. Bourguignon, André. "Vampirism and Autovampirism," *Annales Médico-Psychologiques* 1 (1972): 181–96. Rpt. in: L. B. Schlesinger and E. Revitch, eds. *Sexual Dynamics of Anti-Social Behavior*. Springfield, IL: Charles C. Thomas, 1983. Rev. ed. 1997, pp. 271–93.

5224. Brady, Christine. *Memoirs of an Astral Vampire*. Culver City, CA: Unquiet Grave Press, 1989. 15 pp. pb. Staples.

5225. Bütz, Michael R. "The Vampire as a Metaphor for Working with Childhood Abuse." *American Journal of Orthopsychiatry* 63, 3 (1993): 426–431.

5226. Byers, Thomas B. "Good Men and Monsters: The Defenses of *Dracula*." *Literature and Psychology* 3, 4 (1981): 24–31. Rpt. in Margaret L. Carter, ed. *Dracula: The Vampire and the Critics*. Ann Arbor: UMI Research Press, 1988, pp. 149–58.

5227. Carlin, Emily. *Defense Against the Dark: A Field Guide to Protecting Yourself from Predatory Spirits, Energy Vampires and Malevolent Magic*. Pompton Plains, NJ: New Page Books, 2011. 224 pp. tp.

5228. Cascio, Toni, and Janice Gasker. "The Vampire's Seduction: Using Bram Stoker's *Dracula* as a Metaphor in Treating Parasitic Relationships." *Journal of Poetry Therapy* 15, 1 (Fall 2001): 19–28.

5229. Chazan, Saralea E. "Symbols of Terror: The Witch/Vampire, the Spider, and the Shark." *Psychoanalytic Psychology* 6, 3 (1989): 325–341.

5230. Chen, Sophie. "Bloodlust." *Psychology Today* 42, 6 (2009): 18.

5231. Chew, Carolyn Roblin. *The Vampire Within, the Mother Without: The Repression of the Feminine as Soul Guide*. Carpinteria, CA: Pacifica Graduate Institute, M.A. thesis, 1993. 103 pp. Large format.

5232. Coats, Daryl R. "Bram Stoker and the Ambiguity of Identity." *Publications of the Mississippi Philological Association* (1984): 88–105.

5233. _____. "Jung and the Irish Vampires." *Journal of Vampirology* 2, 4 (1986): 20–27.

5234. Collins, Carla. *Angels, Vampires & Douche Bags.* Toronto: Burman Books, 2009. 135 pp. tp.

5235. Copjec, Joan. "Vampires, Breast-Feeding, and Anxiety." *October* 58 (1991): 25–43.

5236. Crowley, Aleister. *Magick Without Tears.* Hampton, NJ: Thelema Publishing Company, 1954. Posted at: http://hermetic.com/crowley/magick-without-tears/. Rpt.: Ed. by Israel Regardie. St. Paul, MN: Llewellyn Publications, 1973. hb. & tp. Rpt. Phoenix, AZ: Falcon Press, 1987. 528 pp. tp. Rpt.: Tempe, AZ: New Falcon Publications, 1991. 528 pp. tp. Crowley, the most notable ritual magician of the twentieth century, speaks of vampirism in the esoteric context in a number of his writings such as *De Arte Magica* and *Magick: Book Four.* His most substantive remarks from chapter 66 of *Magick Without Tears.*

5237. Cudney, Kiersten. *Of Monsters and Men: A Fascination with Monsters in Popular Culture and Their Psychological Appeal.* Allendale, MI: Grand Valley State University, Honors Project, 2013. Posted at: http://scholarworks.gvsu.edu/honorsprojects/237.

5238. Cunningham, Claudia. *Biting Back: A No-Nonsense, {No-Garlic} Guide to Facing the Personal Vampires in Your Life.* Woodbury, MN: Llewellyn Publications, 2010. 215 pp. tp.

5239. D'Assier, Adolphe. *Posthumous Humanity: A Study of Phantoms.* Trans. by Henry Steel Olcott. London: G. Redway, 1887. hb. 360 pp. Posted at: http://www.archive.org/stream/cu31924028954596/cu31924028954596_djvu.txt. Rpt.: San Diego: Wizards Bookshelf, 1981. hb. 360 pp.

5240. Davis, Colin. "Vampires, Death Drives, and Silent Film." In Colin Davis. *Haunted Subjects: Deconstruction, Psychoanalysis and the Return of the Dead.* Basingstoke, UK: Palgrave Macmillan, 2007, pp. 20–42.

5241. Deacon, Louise. *Twilight, True Love and You: Seven Secret Steps to Finding Your Edward or Jacob.* Chichester, West Sussex, UK: Summersdale, 2012. 303 pp. tp.

5242. de Laurence, L. W. *Vampirism, Witchcraft and Black Art: Their Dangers and How to Avoid Them.* [Whitefish, MT]: Kessinger Publishing, n.d. [2008]. 38pp. pb. Large format. Reprinted chapter [pp. 498–532] from L. W. de Laurence. *Great Book of Magical Art, Hindu Magic and East Indian Occultism and the Book of East Indian Hindi Occultism, and Talismanic Magic.* Chicago: De Laurence Company, 1915. 635 pp. hb. boards.

5243. Dundas, Alan. "The Vampire as Bloodthirsty Revenant: A Psychoanalytic Postmortem." In Alan Dundas, ed. *The Vampire: A Casebook.* Madison: University of Wisconsin Press, 1998. pp. 159–175. Rpt. in: Alan Dundas. *Bloody Mary in the Mirror: Essays in Psychoanalytic Folkloristics.* Jackson: University Press of Mississippi, 2002, pp. 16–32.

5244. Edwards, Robert. "The Alien and the Familiar in *The Jewel of the Seven Stars* and *Dracula*." In William Hughes and Andrew Smith, eds. *Bram Stoker: History, Psychoanalysis and the Gothic.* Basingstoke, UK: Macmillan, 1998, pp. 96ff.

5245. Eaves, A. Osborne. *Modern Vampirism: Its Dangers and How to Avoid Them.* Harrogate, UK: Talisman, 1904. 54 pp. pb. Rpt. in: Jan Perkowski. *Vampires of the Slavs.* Cambridge, MA: Slavica Publishers, 1976. 294 pp. tp.

5246. Enoch, M. David., and William. H. Trethowan. *Uncommon Psychiatric Syndromes,* 2nd ed. Bristol, UK: John Wright and Sons, Ltd., 1967. 102 pp. hb. Rev. ed.: London: Butterworth/Heinemann, 1991. 269 pp. pb.

5247. Feimer, Joel N. "Bram Stoker's *Dracula*: The Challenge of the Occult to Science, Reason, and Psychology." In Michelle K. Langford, ed. *Contours of the Fantastic: Selected Essays from the Eighteenth International Conference on the Fantastic in the Arts.* Westport, CT: Greenwood Publishing Group, 1990, pp. 165–71.

5248. Fortune, Dion [pseudonym of Violet Mary Firth]. *Psychic Self-Defense.* London: Aquarian Press, 1952. 212 pp. hb. Posted at: http://cdn.preterhuman.net/texts/religion.occult.new_age/Dion%20Fortune%20-%20Psychic%20Self%20Defense.pdf. Rev. ed.: York Beach, ME: Samuel Weiser, 2001. 238 pp. tp. Rpt.: San Francisco, CA: Red Wheel/Weister, 2011. 238 pp. tp.

5249. Gabriel, S., and A. F. Young. "Becoming a Vampire Without Being Bitten: The Narrative Collective-Assimilation Hypothesis." *Psychological Science* 22, 8 (August 2011): 990–4.

5250. Gooch, Stan. "Incubi and Succubi in Suurbia. In Stan Gooch. *The Origins of Psychic Phenomena: Poltergeists, Incubi, Succubi, and the*

Unconscious Mind. Rochester, VT: Inner Traditions, 2007, pp. 6–18.

5251. Gottlieb, Richard M. "The European Vampire: Applied Psychoanalysis and Applied Legend." *Folklore Forum* 24, 2 (1991): 39–61.

5252. ____. "The Legend of the European Vampire: Object Loss and Corporeal Preservation." *Psychoanalytic Study of the Child* 49 (1991): 465–80.

5253. Greenburg, Tamara. "Transcendence and Twilight." In E. David Klonsky and Alexis Black, eds. *The Psychology of Twilight.* Dallas, TX: Smart Pop/Benbella Books, 2011, pp. 201–14.

5254. Harbour, Dorothy. *Energy Vampires: A Practical Guide for Psychic Self-Protection.* Rochester, VT: Destiny Books, 2002. 182 pp. tp.

5255. Harris, Helaine Z. *Are You in Love with a Vampire? Healing the Relationship Drain Game.* Encino, CA: An Awakening Publishing Company, 1997. 244 pp. tp.

5256. ____. "V Is for Vampire: Who's Stealing Your Energy." *Whole Life Times* 202 (February 1999): 31.

5257. Hemphill, R. E., and E. Zabow. "Clinical Vampirism: A Presentation of Three Cases and a Reevaluation of Haigh, the 'Acid-Bath Murder.'" *South African Medical Journal* 63 (1983): 278–281. Rpt. in: Richard Noll, ed. *Vampires, Werewolves, and Demons: Twentieth Century Reports in the Psychiatric Literature.* New York: Brunner Mazel, 1992, pp. 61–73. Rpt. in: Angela Cybulski, ed. *Vampires: Fact or Fiction?* Ser.: Opposing Viewpoints. Farmington Hills, MI: Greenhaven Press/Thomson, Gale, 2003. pp. 125–35.

5258. Henderson, D. James. "Exorcism, Possession, and the Dracula Cult: A Synopsis of Object-Relations Psychology." *Bulletin of the Menninger Clinic* 40, 6 (November 1976): 603–628.

5259. Hennelly, Mark M., Jr. "'As Well Fill Up the Space Between': A Liminal Reading of *Christabel.*" *Studies in Romanticism* 38 (1999): 203–22.

5260. ____. "Betwixt Sunset and Sunrise: Liminality in Dracula." *Journal of Dracula Studies* 7 (2005): 8–18.

5261. ____. "The Victorian Book of the Dead: *Dracula.*" *Journal of Evolutionary Psychology* 13 (1992): 204–11.

5262. Homan, Richard L. "Freud's 'Seduction Theory' on Stage: Deane's and Balderston's

Dracula." *Literature and Psychology* 38, 1 & 2 (1992): 57–70.

5263. Horn, Patrice. "The Vampire Next Door." *Psychology Today* (August 1972): 89–92.

5264. Hort, Barbara E. *Unholy Hungers: Encountering the Psychic Vampire in Ourselves & Others.* Boston: Shambhala, 1996. 264 pp. tp.

5265. Hughes, William. "So Unlike the Normal Lunatic: Abnormal Psychology in Bram Stoker's Dracula." *University of Mississippi Studies in English* 11–12 (1993–1995): 1–10.

5266. ____, **and Andrew Smith, eds.** *Bram Stoker: History, Psychoanalysis and the Gothic.* Basingstoke, UK: Macmillan, 1998. 155 pp. hb. Rpt.: New York: St. Martin's Press, 1998. 229 pp. hb. Includes contributions by Alison Milbank, Clare A. Simmons, Maggie Kilgour, Robert Mighall, Marie Mulvey-Roberts, Robert Edwards, Victor Sage< Lisa Hopkins, Joseph S. Bierman, David Punter, David Seed, and Jerrold E. Hogle.

5267. ____. "Introduction: Bram Stoker, the Gothic, and the Development of Cultural Studies." In William Hughes and Andrew Smith, eds. *Bram Stoker: History, Psychoanalysis and the Gothic.* Basinstoke, UK: Macmillan, 1998, pp. 1- 11.

5268. Hurwitz, Siegmund. *Lilith the First Eve: Historical and Psychological Aspects of the Dark Feminine.* Einsiedeln, Switz.: Daimon Verlag, 1992. 262 pp. tp. An expanded edition of the original German edition published in 1990.

5269. Iaccino, James F. "Vampires: Lonely Children of the Night." In James Iaccino. *Psychological Reflections on Cinematic Terror: Jungian Archetypes in Horror Films.* Westport, CT: Praeger, 1994, pp. 61–74.

5270. Ingelbien, Raphaël. "Gothic Genealogies: Dracula, Bowen's Court, and Anglo-Irish Psychology." *English Literary History* 70, 4 (Winter 2003): 1089–1105.

5271. Jaffe, P. D., and F. DiCataldo. "Clinical Vampirism: Blending Myth and Reality." *Bulletin of the American Academy of Psychiatry and Law* 22, 4 (1994): 533–544.

5272. Jarvis, Matt. "*Buffy the Vampire Slayer* and Psychoanalysis." *Psychology Review* 10 (September 2003): 2–5.

5273. Jenkins, Paul H. *The Vampire as Image and Metaphor: The Modern Hungers of Dionysos.* Carpinteria, CA: Pacifica Graduate Institute, M.A. thesis, 1994. 83 pp. Large format.

5274. Jensen, Hans Mørch, and Henrik Day Poulsen. "Auto-vampirism in Schizophrenia." *Nordic Journal of Psychiatry* 56, 1 (2002): 47–48.

5275. Jones, Ernest. *On the Nightmare.* London: Hogarth Press, 1931. 374 pp. hb. See chapter on "The Vampire." Rpt.: New York: Norton & Co. 1931. 374 pp. hb. Posted at: http://www.scribd.com/doc/3289909/On-The-nightmare-Jones-Ernest-1931-. Rpt.: London: Hogarth Press and the Institute of Psycho-Analysis, 1949. 374 pp. hb. Rpt.: New York: Grove Press 1959. 374 pp. tp. Rev. ed.: New York: Liveright Publishing Corporation, 1971. 374 pp. pb. Excerpt rpt. in: Christopher Frayling, ed. *Vampyres: From Lord Byron to Count Dracula.* London: Faber and Faber, 1991, pp. 398–417. Excerpt rpt. in: Angela Cybulski, ed. *Vampires: Fact or Fiction?* Ser.: Opposing Viewpoints. Farmington Hills, MI: Greenhaven Press/Thomson, Gale, 2003. pp. 110–19.

5276. Karagiannis, K. "'Psychic Vampires.'" *Fate* 39, 5 (May 1996): 40–3.

5277. Katz, Robert S. "John H. Watson, M.D.: Pioneer Neuropathologist." *The Baker Street Journal: An Irregular Quarterly of Sherlockiana* 32, 3 (Sept. 1982): 150–52.

5278. Kayton, Lawrence. "The Relation of the Vampire Legend to Schizophrenia." *Journal of Youth and Adolescence* 1, 4 (1972): 303–14.

5279. Kilgour, Maggie. "Vampiric Arts: Bram Stoker's Defense of Poetry." In William Hughes and Andrew Smith, eds. *Bram Stoker: History, Psychoanalysis and the Gothic.* Basinstoke, UK: Macmillan, 1998, pp. 47–61.

5280. Klonsky, E. David, and Alexis Black, eds. *The Psychology of Twilight.* Dallas, TX: Smart Pop/BenBella Books, 2011. 255 pp. tp. Includes contributions by Berg, Erica, Susan Carnell, David A. Frederick, Melissa Burkley, Jeremy Clyman, Robin Rosenberg, Tamara Greenburg, Catherine Glenn, Lisa Dinella and Gary Lewandowski, Mikhail Lyubansky, Melissa Burkley, Peter Stromberg, and Pamela Rutledge.

5281. Kracauer, Siegfried. *From Caligari to Hitler: A Psychological History of the German Film.* Princeton, NJ: Princeton University Press, 1947. 361 pp. hb. Rev. exp. ed.: 2004. 348 pp.

5282. Krafft-Ebing, R. von (Richard). *Psychopathia Sexualis: With Especial Reference to the Antipathic Sexual Instinct: A Medico-Forensic Study.* Trans by Charles Gilbert Chaddock. Philadelphia and London: F. A. Davis, 1899. 436 pp. hb. Posted at: https://archive.org/details/psychopathiasexualis00kraf. Rev. ed. Trans. by F. J. Rebman. New York: Rebman Company; 1906. 617 pp. hb. Rpt.: New York: Physicians and Surgeons Book Co., 1924. 617pp. hb. Rev. ed. Trans. by Franklin S. Klaf. New York: Stein and Day, 1965. 434 pp. Rpt.: New York: Bell Publishing Co.1965. 434 pp. hb. Except rpt. in: Christopher Frayling. *Vampyres: From Lord Byron to Count Dracula.* London: Faber and Faber, 1991, pp. 390–97. The text of Kraft-Ebing's classic study of variations of sexual behavior treated a number of cases that included vampirism. Richard Noll, in his important study *Vampires, Werewolves, & Demons. Twentieth Century Reports in the Psychiatric Literature,* opens a tantalizing possibility, by noting, "It is quite conceivable that Bram Stoker came into contact with the 1892 English translation of *Psychopathia Sexualis.*" There is, however, no direct evidence of Stoker using Kraft-Ebing during his research or writing for the novel.

5283. Kryn, Randall. "Psychic Vampires." *Journal of Vampirism* 1, 3 (Spring 1978): 3–5.

5284. Lansdale, Edward Geary. "Psychological Action." In Edward Geary Lansdale. *In the Midst of Wars.* New York: Harper & Row, 1972, pp. 69–84.

5285. Lapin, Daniel. *The Vampire, Dracula and Incest.* San Francisco: Gargoyle Publishers, 1995. 197 pp. tp.

5286. Laurence, Diana. *How to Catch and Keep a Vampire: A Step-By-Step Guide to Loving the Bad and the Beautiful.* Portland, ME: Sellers Publishing Inc. (August 28, 2009. 160 pp. tp.

5287. LaVey, Anton Szandor. "Not All Vampires Suck Blood." In Anton Szandor LaVey. *The Satanic Bible.* New York: Avon Books, 1969., pp. 75–80.

5288. Laycock, Joseph. "From Parasite to Symbiote: The Genealogy of the Psychic Vampire," *Proteus: A Journal of Ideas* 26, 2 (2009): 25–31.

5289. Leadbeater, Charles W. *The Astral Plane: Its Scenery, Inhabitants, and Phenomena.* London: Theosophical Publishing House, 1915. 183 pp. hb. Posted at: http://www.onread.com/book/The-Astral-Plane-8541/.

5290. Leslie-Sullivan, Cheryl. *Dracula's Gnostic Quest: Through the Wasteland: Failures of the Flesh, Fracture, and Silence.* Carpinteria, CA: Pacifica Graduate Institute, Ph.D. dissertation, 2005. 442 pp. Large format.

5291. Lindquist, Debra, and Joyce Knudsen. *I'm Sorry, You Didn't Tell Me You Were a Vampire.* N.p.: Color Profiles, Ltd., The imagemaker, 2002. 152 pp. tp. Illus. by Chris Wynkoop.

5292. Lorgen, Eve. *The Dark Side of Cupid: Love Affairs, the Supernatural, and Energy Vampirism.* Rochester, NY: Keyhole Publishing, 2012. 249 pp. tp.

5293. _____. *The Love Bite: Alien Interference in Human Love Relationships.* Bonsall, GA: ELogos & HHC Press, 2000. 249 pp. tp,.

5294. Mac Suibhne, Seamus, and Brendan D. Kelly. "Vampirism as Mental Illness: Myth, Madness and the Loss of Meaning in Psychiatry." *Social History of Medicine* 24 2 (2010): 445–460.

5295. Markman, Ronald, and Dominick Bosco. "The Vampire of Sacramento." In Ronald Markman and Dominick Bosco. *Alone with the Devil: Famous Cases of a Courtroom Psychiatrist.* New York: Doubleday, 1989, pp. 159–93. Rpt.: New York: Warner Books, 1992, pp. 159–93. Rpt. as: *Alone with the Devil: Psychopathic Killings That Shocked the World.* London: Judy Piatkus, 1990. Rpt.: London: Futura, 1991.

5296. Maser, Jack D. "Dracula and the Afterlife: A Psychological Explanation." *Journal of Dracula Studies* 7 (2005): 28–37.

5297. McAfee, Julia. "The Vampire Archetype and Vampiric Relationships." Evanston, IL: The C.G. Jung Institute of Chicago, 1991.

5298. McCully, Robert S. "Vampirism: Historical Perspective and Underlying Process in Relation to a Case of Auto-Vampirism." *Journal of Nervous and Mental Disease* 139, 5 (November 1964): 440–52. Rpt. in: Richard Noll, ed. *Vampires, Werewolves, and Demons: Twentieth Century Reports in the Psychiatric Literature.* New York: Brunner Mazel, 1992, pp. 37–56.

5299. McDonald, Jan. "The Devil Is Beautiful: Dracula, Freudian Novel and Feminist Drama." In Peter Reynolds, ed. *Novel Images: Literature in Performance.* London, Routledge, 1993, pp. 80–104.

5300. McIvor, Elaine Kennedy. *The Cheer-Leaders and Vampires in Your Life: Inspiring People to Inspire Themselves.* N.p.: lulu.com, 2010. 126 pp. tp.

5301. Michelis, Angelica. "'Dirty Mamma': Horror, Vampires, and the Maternal in Late Nineteenth-Century Gothic Fiction." *Critical Survey* 15, 3 (2003): 5–18.

5302. Miller, Catriona. "Twilight: Discourse Theory and Jung." In Christopher Hauke and Luke Hockley, eds. *Jung and Film II: The Return: Further Post-Jungian Takes on the Moving Image.* New York: Routledge, 2011, 185–205.

5303. Miller, Sally. "'Nursery fears made flesh and sinew': Vampires, the Body and Eating Disorders: A Psychoanalytic Approach." In Carla T. Kungl, ed. *Vampires: Myths and Metaphors of Enduring Evil.* Oxford: Inter-Disciplinary Press, 2003, pp. 53–58. Posted at: http://www.inter-disciplinary.net/publishing/id-press/ebooks/vampires-myths-and-metaphors-of-enduring-evil.

5304. Miller, Thomas W., Robert F. Kraus, and Tag Heister. "An Adolescent Vampire Cult in Rural America: Clinical Issues and Case Study." *Child Psychiatry & Human Development* 29, 3 (1999): 209–219.

5305. Morse, Donald R. "The Stressful Kiss: A Biopsychosocial Evaluation of the Origins, Evolution, and Societal Significance of Vampirism." *Stress Medicine* 9, 3 (July 1993): 181–199.

5306. Mustafa, Jamil Muhammed. *Mapping the Late Victorian Subject: Psychology, Cartography and the Gothic Novel.* Chicago: University of Chicago, Ph.D. dissertation, 1949. 224 pp. Large format.

5307. Nelson, Elizabeth. "Abstinence vs. Indulgence: How the New Ethical Vampire Reflects Our Monstrous Appetites." *Journal of Jungian Scholarly Studies* 6, 2 (2010): 1–13.

5308. Noll, Richard. *Bizarre Diseases of the Mind.* New York: Berkley, 1990. 260 pp. pb.

5309. _____. "Lestat: The Vampire as Degenerate Genius." In Katherine Ramsland, ed. *The Anne Rice Reader.* New York: Ballantine Books, 1997, pp. 150–66.

5310. _____. *Vampires, Werewolves, and Demons: Twentieth Century Reports in the Psychiatric Literature.* New York: Brunner Mazel, 1992. 293 pp. tp.

5311. O'Connor, Dan. *Energy Vampire Slaying: 101: How to Combat Negativity and Toxic Attitudes in Your Office, In Your Home, and in Yourself.* [Fargo, ND]: the author, 2011. 110 pp. tp.

5312. Olcott, Henry Steel. "The Vampire." *The Theosophist* 12, 112 (1891). Posted at: http://www.theosophical.ca/adyar_pamphlets/Adyar Pamphlet_No112.pdf. Rpt. as: *The Vampire.* Adyar Pamphlets No. 112. Adyar, Madras, India: Theosophical Publishing House, 1920. 19 pp. pb. Staples. In discussing vampirism, Olcott offers an additional "argument in favour of cremation—if any were needed by thoughtful persons—that there are no vampires save in countries where the dead are buried."

5313. Olry, Regis; Duane E. Haines. "Renfield's Syndrome: A Psychiatric Illness Drawn from Bram Stoker's *Dracula*." *Journal of the History of the Neurosciences* 20 (2011): 368–371.

5314. O'Neill, Jennifer. *Energy Vampires: How to Deal with Negative People.* Kailua, HI: Limitless Publishing, 2013. 139 pp. tp.

5315. Orloff, Judith. "Combatting Emotional Vampires: How to Understand and Protect Your Sensitivity." In Judith Orloff. *Emotional Freedom: Liberate Yourself from Negative Emotions and Transform Your Life.* New York, Harmony Books, 2009, pp. 119–42.

5316. _____. "The Ninth Prescription: Protect Yourself from Psychic Vampires." In Judith Orloff. *Positive Energy: 10 Extraordinary Prescriptions for Transforming Fatigue, Stress, and Fear into Vibrance, Strength, and Love.* New York, Harmony Books, 2005, pp. 288–320.

5317. Ornelas, Steve. *Energy Vampires: Managing Stress & Negative Thoughts in Your Personal & Professional Life.* Pheonix, AZ: GabSum Productions, 2007. 58 pp. tp. Psychology.

5318. Osborne, C. A. "Are You Feeding the Energy Vampire?" *Journal of the American Animal Hospital Association* 36, 2 (March-April 2000): 103–5.

5319. Paris, Mark M. "From Clinic to Classroom While Uncovering the Evil Dead in *Dracula: A Psychoanalytic Pedagogy*." In James M. Cahalan and David B. Downing, eds. *Practicing Theory in Introductory College Literature Courses.* Urbana, IL: National Council of Teachers of English, 1991, pp. 47–56.

5320. Parkin-Gounelas, Ruth. "Dracula and the Death Drive." In Ruth Parkin-Gounelas. *Literature and Psychoanalysis: Intertextual Readings.* New York: Palgrave Macmillan, 2001, pp. 199–207.

5321. Parsons, Maria. "Vamping the Woman: Mental Pathologies in Bram Stoker's Dracula." *Irish Journal of Gothic and Horror Studies* 1 (October 2006). Online journal posted at: http://irishgothichorrorjournal.homestead.com/maria.html.

5322. Paviour, Maria. *Changing Vampires into Angels.* Hadlow Downs, East Sussex, UK: Isiliver Books, 2002. 202 pp. tp. Psychology.

5323. Perlman, Mike. "Dracula: Our Cultural Demon." *Psychological Perspectives: A Quarterly Journal of Jungian Thought* 12, 1 (1981): 88–105.

5324. Philips, Robert, and Branimir Rieger. "The Agony and the Ecstasy: A Jungian Analysis of Two Vampire Novels, Meredith Ann Pierce's *The Dark Angel* and Bram Stoker's *Dracula*." *West Virginia University Philological Papers* 31 (1986): 10–19.

5325. Pierce, Sarah E. *From Demon to Daimon: A Mythic and Depth Psychological Analysis of the American Hero Vampire.* Carpinteria, CA: Pacifica Graduate Institute, Ph.D. dissertation, 2011. 238 pp. Large format.

5326. Pinto, Christopher, and Christobal della Volare. *How to Kill Vampires: Because They Are Unnatural Jerks.* Fort Lauderdale, FL: StarDust Mysteries Publishing, 2013. 120 pp. tp.

5327. Pittaway, Kim. "Emotional Vampires." *Modern Woman* 2, 9 (1994); 45–48.

5328. Powell, Anna. *Psychoanalysis and Sovereignty in Popular Vampire Fictions.* Lewiston, NY: Edwin Mellen Press, 2003. 296 pp. hb.

5329. Powell, Arthur E. *The Astral Body and Other Astral Phenomena.* London: Theosophical Publishing House, 1927, 1973. 265 pp. hb. Posted at: http://www.scribd.com/doc/6464273/The-Astral-Body-Arthur-Powell.

5330. Powers, Kimberly. *Escaping the Vampire: Desperate for the Immortal Hero.* Colorado Springs, CO: David C. Cook, 2009. 190 pp. tp.

5331. Priester, Paul E. "The Metaphorical Use of Vampire Films in Counseling." *Journal of Creativity in Mental Health* 3, 1 (2008): 68–77.

5332. Prins, Herschel. "Vampirism: A Clinical Condition." *British Journal of Psychiatry* 146 (1985): 666–68. Rpt. in: Richard Noll, ed. *Vampires, Werewolves, and Demons: Twentieth Century Reports in the Psychiatric Literature.* New York: Brunner Mazel, 1992, pp. 74–80.

5333. _____. "Vampirism—Legendary or Clinical Phenomenon?" *Medicine, Science, and the Law* 24 (1984): 283–93.

5334. Proud, Louis. *Dark Intrusions: An Investigation into the Paranormal Nature of Sleep*

Paralysis Experiences. San Antonio, TX: Anomalist Books, 2009. 280 pp. tp.

5335. Raines, J. M., L. C. Raines, and M. Singer. "Dracula: Disorders of the Self and Borderline Personality Organization." *The Psychiatric Clinics of North America* 17, 4 (1994): 811–826,.

5336. Ramsland, Katherine. "Hunger for the Marvelous: The Vampire Craze in the Computer Age." *Psychology Today* (November 1989): 31–35.

5337. _____. "Vampire Personality Disorder". *Psychology Today* (November 21, 2012).

5338. Raphael, Marty. *Spiritual Vampires.* Santa Fe, NM: The Message Company, 1995. 255 pp. tp.

5339. Ravensdale, Tom, and James Morgan. *The Psychology of Witchcraft.* New York: Arco Publishing Company, 1974. 200 pp. See chapter "The Vampire.".

5340. Rhodes, Daniel, and Kathleen Rhodes. *Vampires: Emotional Predators Who Want to Suck the Life Out of You.* Amherst, NY: Prometheus Books, 1998. 197 pp. hb.

5341. Riccardo, Martin V. *Liquid Dreams of Vampires.* St. Paul, MN: Llewellyn Publications, 1996. 252 pp. tp.

5342. _____. "Living Vampires, Magic, and Psychic Attacks." In Rosemary Ellen Guiley, with J. B. Macabre. *The Complete Vampire Companion.* New York: Macmillan, 1994, pp. 183–89.

5343. _____. "The Vampire as a Psychic Archetype." *TAT Journal* 2, 3 (Summer 1979): 16–23.

5344. _____. *Vampires as Sleepwalkers.* New York: Dracula Unlimited, n.d., 3 pp. pb. Staples. A Count Dracula Fan Club Monograph.

5345. Richardson, Maurice. "The Psychoanalysis of Ghost Stories." *The Twentieth Century* 166 (1959): 419–31. Excerpt rpt. as: "The Psychology of Dracula." In Christopher Frayling, ed. *Vampyres: From Lord Byron to Count Dracula.* London: Faber and Faber, 1991, pp. 418–22.

5346. Riquelme, John Paul. "Psychoanalytic Criticism and *Dracula*." In Bram Stoker. *Dracula.* Ed. by John Paul Riquelme. Ser.: Case Studies in Contemporary Criticism. Boston: Bedford/New York: St. Martin's, 2002, pp. 466–83.

5347. Sakarya Direne, C. Gunes, E. Ozturk, and V. Sar. "'Vampirism' in a case of dissociative identity disorder and post-traumatic stress disorder." *Psychotherapy and Psychosomatics* 81, 5 (2012): 322–323.

5348. Schlozman, Steven C. "Vampires and Those Who Slay Them: Using the Television Program *Buffy the Vampire Slayer* in Adolescent Therapy and Psychodynamic Education." *Academic Psychiatry* 24 (Mar. 200):49–54. Posted at *Psychiatry on Line:* http://ap.psychiatryonline.org/cgi/content/full/24/1/49?maxtoshow=&HITS=10&hits=10&RESULTFORMAT=&author1=schlozman&searchid=980335745890_545&stored_search=&FIRSTINDEX=&journalcode=ap.

5349. Shuster, Seymour. "*Dracula* and Surgically Induced Trauma in Children." *British Journal of Medical Psychology* 46 (1973): 259–70.

5350. Shuttle, Penelope, and Peter Redgrove. *The Wise Wound: Eve's Curse and Everywoman.* New York: Richard Marek, 1978. 335 pp. hb. Rev. ed. *as: The Wise Wound: Myths, Realities, and Meanings of Menstruation.* New York: Grove, 1988. 358 pp. hb. dj. Rev. ed. as: *The Wise Wound: Menstruation and Everywoman.* London: Marion Boyars Publishers, 2005. 365 pp. tp.

5351. Simon, A. "Emotional Stability Pertaining to the Game *Vampire: The Masquerade.*" *Psychological Reports* 83, 2 (October 1998): 732–4.

5352. Slate, Joe H. *Psychic Vampires.* St. Paul, MN: Llewellyn Publications, 2002. 243 pp. tp. Excerpt rpt. in: Angela Cybulski, ed. *Vampires: Fact or Fiction?* Ser.: Opposing Viewpoints. Farmington Hills, MI: Greenhaven Press/Thomson, Gale, 2003. pp. 69–78.

5353. Smedley, Edward, W. Cook Taylor, Henry Thompson, and Elihu Rich. *The Occult Sciences.* London: Richard Griffin and Company, 1855. 396 pp. hb. Posted at: https://archive.org/details/occultsciencessk00smed. Rpt.: Boston, MA: Adamant Media Corporation, 2005. 396 pp. tp.

5354. Stiles, A. Cerebral Automatism, the Brain, and the Soul in Bram Stoker's *Dracula.*" *Journal of the History of Neuroscience* 15, 2 (June 2006): 131–52.

5355. Sumida, Amy. *The Vampire-Werewolf Complex: How Paranormal Romance Can Help Your Relationship.* N.p.: the author, 2013. 90 pp. tp.

5356. Tancheva, Kornelia. "Vampires Are Them, Vampires Are Us." In Susan Castillo, ed. *In-*

gendering Identities, Porto, Portugal: Universidade Fernando Pessoa, 1996, pp. 81–91.

5357. Thurmond, Dana Brook. *The Influence of Carl Jung's Archetype of the Shadow on Early 20th Century Literature*. Winter Park, FL: Rollins College, Masters of Liberal Studies Thesis, 2012. 75 pp. Large format. Posted at: http://scholarship.rollins.edu/mls/32.

5358. Underwood, Peter. "Psycho-Analyzing the Vampire." In Peter Underwood. *The Vampire's Bedside Companion: The Amazing World of Vampires in Fact and Fiction*. London: Leslie Frewin, 1975, pp. 43–52.

5359. Vanden Bergh, Richard L., and John F. Kelley. "Vampirism—A Review with New Observations." *Archives of General Psychiatry* 2 (1964): 543–547. Rpt. in: Richard Noll, ed. *Vampires, Werewolves, and Demons: Twentieth Century Reports in the Psychiatric Literature*. New York: Brunner Mazel, 1992, pp. 27–36.

5360. Vermeir, Koen. "Vampires as Creatures of the Imagination: Theories of Body, Soul, and Imagination in Early Modern Vampire Tracts (1659–1755)." In Yasmin Haskell, ed. *Diseases of the Imagination and Imaginary Disease in the Early Modern Period*. Turnhout: Brepols, 2011.

5361. Vespertilio, Lono Fructus. *The Psychic Vampires Guide: To Subtle Body Language and Psionics*. Fort Wayne, IN: Dark Moon Press, 2006. 240 pp. tp.

5362. Walters, Sarah Christina. *Exploring the Myth of Demeter and Persephone: Mothers, Daughters, Vampires, Land, and Hope*. Carpinteria, CA: Pacifica Graduate Institute, Ph.D. dissertation, 2000. 291 pp. Large format.

5363. Wells, David. *Your Astrological Moon Sign: Werewolf, Angel, Vampire, Saint Discover Your Hidden Inner Self*. London: Hay House, 2012. 304 pp. tp.

5364. White, Megan, and Hatim A. Omar. "Vampirism, Vampire Cults and the Teenager of Today." *International Journal of Adolescent Medicine and Health* 22, 2 (2010): 189–195.

5365. Wilkes, Brian. *Dracula Diary: Reawakening Your Inner Vlad*. N.p.: Tuscany Global, 2013. 100 pp. tp.

5366. Wilson, N. "A Psychoanalytic Contribution to Psychic Vampirism: A Case Vignette." *American Journal of Psychoanalysis* 60, 2 (June 2000): 177–86.

5367. Winnubst, Shannon. "Vampires, Anxieties, and Dreams: Race and Sex in Contemporary United States." *Hypatia* 18, 3 (2003): 1–20.

5368. Winter, Elizabeth. "All in the Family: A Retrospective Diagnosis of R. M. Renfield in *Dracula*." *Journal of Dracula Studies* 12 (2010): 53–61.

5369. Yeomans, Patricia Ann. *The Vampire as a Psychological Metaphor*. Yellow Springs, OH: Antioch University, M.A. thesis, 1986. 113 pp. Large format.

5370. Zinck, K. Charles, and Myrna Zinck. *Psychological Studies in the Increase of Lycanthropy and Vampirism in America, 1930–1941*. New Orleans, LA: Zachary Ken, 1952. Note: The existence of this title is unverified.

Medical Treatments of Vampirism

Since *Dracula* introduced several physicians into the vampire storyline—most notably by having blood transfusions used in the attempt to save Lucy—doctors have played various roles in vampire stories. Among the more notable were Dr. Julia Hoffman (originally portrayed by Grayson Hall), who attempts to use her medical skill to return *Dark Shadows* vampire Barnabas Collins to his human state—whose effort would be repeated by Natalie Lambert (portrayed by Catherine Disher), the medical examiner in *Forever Knight*, and Sarah Roberts (Susan Sarandon) in *The Hunger*.

More recently, a series of articles by medical researchers and historians have attempted (albeit with relatively little success) to ascribe the belief in vampires to various medical conditions, from psychedelic drugs to porphyria, anemia, and rabies. More interesting has been the metaphorical use of vampirism in the assessment of various psychological disorders (see the chapter on psychological perspectives).

On a number of occasions, beginning with the good vampire Vampirella, artificial blood substitutes that relieve vampires of the necessity of attacking, biting, and/or killing humans have been introduced into fictional vampire storylines. Such artificial blood forms a key element in the plot of the *True Blood* television series based on the novels written by Charlaine Harris.

The medical literature that actually mentions vampires is but a small percentage of a vast body of literature treating subjects related to vampire concerns such as artificial blood substitutes, blood-related research, diseases that have symptoms suggestive of vampires, diseases carried by vampire bats, etc. Only a small selective probing of the literature that searched for actual mentions of vampires, vampirism, and/or Dracula, appears below. The literature on vampire bats, for example, is quite large, as the creature has become a very real problem in Mexico and Central America for its attacks on livestock and its role in spreading disease.

5371. Bak, John S. "Preface: Bad Blood; or, Victorian Vampires in the Postmodern Age of AIDS." In John S. Bak, ed. *Post/modern Dracula: From Victorian Themes to Postmodern Praxis.* Cambridge: Cambridge Scholars Publishing, 2007, pp. xi–xxiv.

5372. Bierman, Joseph S. "*Dracula*: Prolonged Childhood Illness, and the Oral Triad." *American Imago* 29 (1972): 186–98. Rpt. in: Carol A. Senf. *The Critical Response to Bram Stoker.* Westport CT: Greenwood Press, 1993, pp. 46–51.

5373. Bräunlein, P. J. "The Frightening Borderlands of Enlightenment: The Vampire Problem." *Studies in History and Philosophy of Biological and Biomedical Sciences* 43, 3 (September 2012): 710–9.

5374. Burnum, John F. "Medical Vampires." *New England Journal of Medicine* 314, 19 (1986): 1250–1251.

5375. Byrne, Katherine. "Consumption and the Count: The Pathological Origins of Vampirism and Bram Stoker's *Dracula*." In Katherine Byrne. *Tuberculosis and the Victorian Literary Imagination.* Cambridge, UK/New York: Cambridge University Press, 2011, pp. 124–49.

5376. Castel, O., A. Bourry, S. Thévenot, and C. Burucoa. "Bacteria and Vampirism in Cinema." *Médecine et Maladies Infectieuses* 43, 9 (September 2012): 363–7.

5377. Cox, A. M. "Porphyria and Vampirism: Another Myth in the Making." *Postgraduate Medical Journal* 71, 841 (1995): 643–644.

5378. Dunn, Denise. "The Vampire as Addict." *Journal of Vampirism* 2, 3 (Fall 1979): 10–13.

5379. Evans, Tammy. *Porphyria: The Woman Who Has the Vampire Disease.* New Horizon Press, 1997. 288 pp. hb. dj.

5380. Flood, David H. "Blood and Transfusion in Bram Stoker's *Dracula*." *University of Mississippi Studies in English* 7 (1989)" 180–192.

5381. Fricker, Janet. "Artificial Blood—Bad News for Vampires?" *Lancet* 347, 9011 (1996): 1322.

5382. Gomez-Alonso, Juan. "Rabies: A Possible Explanation for the Vampire Legend." *Neurology* 51 (September 1998): 856–59.

5383. Heick, Alex. "Prince Dracula, Rabies and the Vampiric Legend." *Annals of Internal Medicine* 117, 2 (July 1992): 172–73.

5384. Hieb, Lee. "Medicine and the Vampire Economy." *Journal of American Physicians and Surgeons* 17, 4 (Winter 2012): 120–22. Posted at: http://www.jpands.org/vol17no4/hieb.pdf.

5385. Hyman, Rebecca. "Vampire of the Body: The Politics of Chronic Fatigue Syndrome." *Women & Performance: A Journal of Feminist Theory* 11, 1 (1999): 187–201.

5386. Keith, Edward O. "Biomedical Origins of Vampirism." In Barbara Brodman and James E. Doan, eds. *The Universal Vampire: Origins and Evolution of a Legend.* Madison, NJ: Fairleigh Dickinson University Press, 2013, pp. 61-73.

5387. Kline, Michael. "The Vampire as Pathogen: Bram Stoker's *Dracula* and Francis Ford Coppola's *Bram Stoker's Dracula*." *West Virginia University Philological Papers* 42–43 (1997–98): 36–44.

5388. Lavergen, Remi. *A Phonetic Transcription of the Creole Negro's Medical Treatments, Superstitions, and Folklore in the Parish of Pointe Coupée.* Baton Rouge: Louisiana State University, M.A. thesis 1930. 55 pp. Large format.

5389. Lavigne, Carlen. "Sex, Blood and (Un)Death: The Queer Vampire and HIV." *Journal of Dracula Studies* 6 (2004): 19–28.

5390. Marmorstein, Jerome. "Vampires, Werewolves, and Porphyria: Confronting Media Irresponsibility." *Medical Tribune* 25 (September 1985): 45.

5391. Miles, Jennifer. "Healing or Horrifying? Portrayals of Victorian Medicine in Dracula." *Journal of Dracula Studies* 14 (2012): 17–35.

5392. Morse, Donald R. "The Stressful Kiss: A Biopsychosocial Evaluation of the Origins, Evolution, and Societal Significance of Vampirism." *Stress Medicine* 9, 3 (July 1993): 181–199.

5393. Mulvey-Roberts, Marie. "Dracula and the Doctors: Bad Blood, Menstrual Taboo and the New Woman." In William Hughes and Andrew Smith, eds. *Bram Stoker: History, Psychoanalysis and the Gothic.* Basinstoke, UK: Macmillan, 1998, pp. 78–95.

5394. Robertson, Geoffrey. *Does Dracula Have AIDS? and Other Hypotheticals.* Sydney: ABC Books, 1987. 265 pp. pb.

5395. Rose, Jeane. "'A Girl Like That Will Give Your AIDS!': Vampirism as AIDS Metaphor in *Killing Zoe.*" In James Holte Craig, ed. *The Fantastic Vampire: Studies in the Children of the Night: Selected Essays from the Eighteenth International Conference on the Fantastic in the Arts.* Vol. 19. Westport, CT: Greenwood Publishing Group, 2002, pp. 145–50.

5396. Ruickbie, Leo. "Evidence for the Undead: The Role of Medical Investigation in the 18th-Century Vampire Epidemic." In Barbara Brodman and James E. Doan, eds. *The Universal Vampire: Origins and Evolution of a Legend.* Madison, NJ: Fairleigh Dickinson University Press, 2013, pp. 75–89.

5397. Shuster, Seymour. "*Dracula* and Surgically Induced Trauma in Children." *British Journal of Medical Psychology* 46 (1973): 259–70.

5398. Silver, Anna Krugovy. "Vampirism and the Anorexic Paradigm." In Anna Krugovy Silver. *Victorian Literature and the Anorexic Body.* Cambridge: Cambridge University Press, 2002, pp. 116–35.

5399. Sparks, Tabitha. "Medical Gothic and the Return to the Contagious Disease Acts in Stoker and Machen." *Nineteenth Century Feminism*, 6 (2002): 87–102.

5400. _____. "New Women, Avenging Doctors: Gothic Medicine in Bram Stoker and Arthur Machen." In Tabitha Sparks. The *Doctor in the Victorian Novel: Family Practices.* Franham, UK: Ashgate, 2009, pp. 111–32.

5401. Spear, Jeffrey L. "Gender and Dis-Ease in *Dracula.*" In Lloyd Davis, ed. *Virginal Sexuality and Textuality in Victorian Literature.* Albany: State University of New York Press, 1993, pp. 179–192.

5402. Sugg, Richard. *Mummies, Cannibals and Vampires: The History of Corpse Medicine from the Renaissance to the Victorians.* New York: Routledge, 2011. 374 pp.

5403. Szalay, Eva Ludwiga. "Of Gender and the Gaze: Constructing the Disease(d) in Elfriede Jelinek's *Krankheit oder Moderne Frauen.*" *The German Quarterly* 74, 3 (2010): 237–258.

5404. Thornton, Sarah. "Bitten or Typewritten: Transmission in Patrick McGrath's *Blood Disease* and in Stoker's *Dracula.*" In Dominique Sipière, ed. *Dracula: Insémination-dissémination.* Amiens, Presses del'UFR Clerc, Université de Picardie, 1996, pp. 83–94.

5405. Vrettos, Athena. "Physical Immunity and Racial Destiny: Stoker and Haggard." In Athena Vrettos. *Somatic Fictions: Imagining Illness in Victorian Culture.* Stanford, CA: Stanford University Press, 1995, pp. 154–76.

5406. White, M., and H. Omar. "Vampirism, Vampire Cults and the Teenager of Today." *International Journal of Adolescent Medical Health* 22, 2 (April-June 2010): 189–95.

5407. Willis, Martin. "Dracula, Miasma and Germ." *Studies in the Novel* 39, 3 (Fall 2007): 301–25.

5408. _____. "The Invisible Giant, Dracula, and Disease." *Studies in the Novel* 39, 3 (2007): 301–325.

5409. _____. "Le Fanu's 'Carmilla,' Ireland, and Diseased Vision." *Essays and Studies* 61 (2008): 111–30.

Vampires, Religion and Theology

The vampire emerged in European folklore in an essentially religious context, its very existence being a challenge to Christian reflections on the nature of the afterlife, and the early exploration and discussion of vampires highlighted the differences in Roman Catholic and Eastern orthodox funeral practices and care of the body of the deceased. Even earlier, vampires were connected to witches and anti-witchcraft folklore applied to ridding communities of any wayward bloodsuckers. Garlic was, for example, a deterrent to witches before it would be relied upon to drive off any vampires. The novel *Dracula* added to the discussion with Stoker's connecting the vampire's origin to Satan's activity.

Religion has occasionally played a role in vampire literature, especially with evolving opinions on the effectiveness of religious artifacts like the cross to repel vampires. Writers like Anne Rice have discarded religious paraphernalia, while writers such as Laurel Hamilton and Charlene Harris have pictured churches either welcoming or dedicated to fighting vampires. Meanwhile, John Steakey's *Vampires* described vampire hunters in the employ of the Vatican.

More recent religious writings about vampires, emerging in a culture that really does not believe that vampires exist, are more concerned with the popularity of the vampire in the culture, especially as the literature has transformed the one evil monster into an object of sympathy and even adulation. More conservative writers have placed the vampire among a variety of concerns associated with the New Age movement of the 1980s and the esoteric beliefs it espoused. Spokespersons have denounced any attachment to what they see as "occult" reality and struggle with the idea of vampire as hero. At issue for them is the existence of a supernatural world, and the assumption that its more evil side is easier to demonstrate to unbelievers than its good side.

At the same time, some theologians and church spokespersons have attempted to struggle with the vampire's recent popularity and tried to understand it as a culturally significant phenomenon given the high level of secularity in which it operates. Much of this more serious discussion originated in attempts to analyze the religious themes in *Buffy the Vampire Slayer*.

Among the most interesting religious discussion around vampires has grown out of the *Twilight* Saga of Stephenie Meyer. Meyer, a practicing Latter-day Saint, appears to have more or less consciously embodied her Mormon beliefs in her fiction, a fact that has provided for lively debate on what her reading audience has picked up and accepted.

5410. Anderson, Wendy Love. "Prophecy Girl and the Powers That Be: The Philosophy of Religion in the Buffyverse." In James B. South, ed. *Buffy and Philosophy: Fear and Trembling in Sunnydale*. Chicago: Open Court, 2003, pp. 212–226.

5411. Arnold, James W. "Dracula: Another Day at the Blood Bank." *The Catholic Herald Citizen* (August 4, 1979). Re: *Dracula* (1979).

5412. Bartel, Hope K., and Timothy E. G. Bartel. "The Harrowing of Hell: 'Anne' and the Greek Paschal Tradition in Conversation." In Anthony R. Mills, John W. Morehead, and J. Ryan Parker, eds. *Joss Whedon and Religion: Essays on an Angry Atheist's Explorations of the Sacred*. Jefferson, NC: McFarland, 2013, pp. 28–38.

5413. Beal, Timothy K. *Religion and Its Monsters*. New York: Routledge, 2002. 238 pp. hb. & tp.

5414. Belanger, Michelle A. *House Kheperu Archives: The Outer Teachings of House Kheperu*. Brunswick, OH: Emerald Tablet Press, 2011. 314 pp.

5415. _____. *Psychic Vampire Codex: Manual of Magick & Energy Work.* Weiser Books: York Beach, ME, 2004. 284 pp. tp.

5416. _____. *Scared Hunger.* Fort Wayne, IN: Dark Moon Press, 2005. 142 pp..tp.

5417. _____. *The Vampire Ritual Book.* N.p.: the author, 2007. 162 pp. tp.

5418. _____. *Vampires in Their Own Words: An Anthology of Vampire Voices.* York Beach, ME: Weiser Books: 2007. 245 pp. tp.

5419. _____. *Walking the Twilight Path: A Gothic Book of the Dead.* Woodbury, MN: Llewellyn Publications, 2008. 307 pp. tp.

5420. Blumberg, Arnold T. "When You're Undead, the Whole World Is Jewish." In Kim Paffenroth and John W. Morehead, eds. *The Undead and Theology.* Eugene, OR: Pickwick Publications, 2012, pp. 195–208.

5421. Bonewits, Isaac. "Dracula, the Black Christ." *Gnostic* 4, 7 (March 1975): 1, 29–29.

5422. Bucher, John K., Jr. *There Is Power in the Blood: Faith and the Rising Vampire in Popular Culture.* Los Angeles, CA: Gray Matter Books, 2011. 150 pp. tp.

5423. Coulardeau, Jacques. "The Vision of Religion in Francis Ford Coppola's *Bram Stoker's Dracula.*" In John S. Bak, ed. *Post/modern Dracula: From Victorian Themes to Postmodern Praxis.* Cambridge: Cambridge Scholars Publishing, 2007, pp. 123–40.

5424. Dan, Peter. "How Vampires Became Jewish." *Studia Hebraica* 9–10 (2009–2010): 417–429.

5425. D'Arc, James V. "The Mormon as Vampire: A Comparative Study of Winifred Graham's The Love Story of a Mormon, the Film *Trapped by the Mormons,* and Bram Stoker's *Dracula.*" *BYU Studies* 46, 2 (2007), 169–179. Literature.

5426. DeGiglio-Bellemare, Mario. "Vampires Reading Feuerbach: Catholic Orthodoxy and Lines of Flight in Abel Ferrara." *Golem: Journal of Religion and Monsters* 3, 1 (Spring 2009). Posted at: http://lomibao.net/golem/current.php.

5427. DeLusé, Stephanie R. "More Than Entertainment: Notes on a Spiritual Recovery and What Jossverse Gave Me That Religion and Therapy Didn't." In Joy Davidson with Leah Wilson, eds. *The Psychology of Joss Whedon: An Unauthorized Exploration of* Buffy, Angel, *and* Firefly. Dallas, TX: Benbella Books, 2007, pp. 155–170.

5428. Dick, Dan R. "Vampire Christianity." In Dan R. Dick. *Bursting the Bubble: Rethinking Conventional Wisdom About Church Leadership.* Nashville, TN: Abingdon Press, 2008, pp. 85–92.

5429. Duricy, Michael P. "Marian Symbols in the *Buffy the Vampire Slayer* Television Series on the WB." Paper presented at the Slayage Conference on *Buffy the Vampire Slayer,* Nashville, TN, May 27–30 2004. Posted at: http://www.slayage online.com/SCBtVS_Archive/Talks/Duricy.pdf and at http://campus.udayton.edu/mary/mar.htm.

5430. Erickson, Gregory T. "'Religion Freaky' or a 'Bunch of Men Who Died?' The (A)theology of *Buffy.*" *Slayage: The Online International Journal of Buffy Studies* 4, 1–2 [13–14] October (2004). Posted at http://www.whedonstudies.tv/. A paper originally presented as "Revisiting *Buffy*'s (A)Theology: Religion 'Freaky' or just 'A Bunch of Men Who Died'" at the Slayage Conference on *Buffy the Vampire Slayer,* Nashville, TN, May 27–30, 2004.

5431. _____. "'Sometimes You Need a Story': American Christianity, Vampires, and *Buffy.*" In Rhonda V. Wilcox and David Lavery, eds. *Fighting the Forces: What's at Stake in* Buffy the Vampire Slayer. Lanham, MD: Rowman & Littlefield, 2002, pp. 108–119.

5432. _____, **and Richard W. Santana.** "Television Drama, Fan Communities, and Theology: God as 'Nothing Solid.'" In Gregory T. Erickson. *Religion and Popular Culture: Rescripting the Sacred.* Jefferson, NC: McFarland & Company, 2008, pp. 113–137.

5433. Foster, Susanne E., and James B. South. "'There's no place I can be': Whedon, Augustine, and the Earthly City." In Anthony R. Mills, John W. Morehead, and J. Ryan Parker, eds. *Joss Whedon and Religion: Essays on an Angry Atheist's Explorations of the Sacred.* Jefferson, NC: McFarland & Company, 2013, pp. 152–164.

5434. Gardenour, Brenda. "The Biology of Blood-Lust: Medieval Medicine, Theology, and the Vampire Jew." *Film & History* 41, 2 (Fall 2011).

5435. Gilpin, Vicky. "Vampires and Female Spiritual Transformation: Laurell K. Hamilton's Anita Blake, Vampire Hunter." In Kim Paffenroth and John W. Morehead, eds. *The Undead and Theology.* Eugene, OR: Pickwick Publications, 2012, pp. 3–18.

5436. Golden, Christie. "Where's the Religion in Willow's Wicca?" In Glenn Yeffeth, ed. *Seven Seasons of* Buffy: *Science Fiction and Fantasy*

Writers Discuss Their Favorite Television Show. Dallas, TX: Benbella Books, 2003, pp. 159–166.

5437. Gravatt, Sandra. *From Twilight to Breaking Dawn: Religious Themes in the Twilight Saga.* Atlanta, GA: Chalice Press, 2010. 118 pp.

5438. Guilinger, Amando. "Religion and Superstition in Bram Stoker's *Dracula*" In Bram Stoker. *Dracula.* Ser.: Ignatius Critical Editions. San Francisco, CA: Ignatius Press, 2012, pp. 523–27.

5439. Heath, Elaine A. *The Gospel According to Twilight: Women, Sex, and God.* Louisville, KY: Westminster John Knox Press, 2011. 184 pp. tp.

5440. Helfrich, Ronald. "'Note to Self, Religion Freaky': When Buffy Met Biblical Studies." In Mary Alice Money for PopMatters.com, ed. *Joss Whedon: The Complete Companion: The TV Series, the Movies, the Comic Books and More.* London: Titan Books, 2012, pp. 37–48. A paper originally presented at Get to the Point: Issues at Stake in *Buffy the Vampire Slayer,* SUNY College at Oneonta, November 2009, and later posted on Pop Matters.com's *Spotlight: Joss Whedon,* 7 March 2011.

5441. Herbert, Christopher. "Vampire Religion." *Representations* 79, 1 (2002): 100–121.

5442. Herbert, Steven G. "Dracula as Metaphor for Human Evil." *Journal of Religion and Psychical Research* 27, 2 (2004): 62–71.

5443. Hjelm, Titus. "Celluloid Vampires, Technology, and the Decline of Religion." In Christopher Partridge and Eric Christianson, eds. *The Lure of the Dark Side: Satan and Western Demonology in Popular Culture.* London; Oakville, CT: Equinox, 2009, pp. 105–21.

5444. Introvigne, Massimo. "Antoine Faivre: Father of Contemporary Vampire Studies." In Richard Caron, Joscelyn Godwin, Wouter J. Hanegraaff, and Jean Louis Viellard Baron, eds. *Ésotérisme, Gnoses & Imaginaire Symbolique: Mélanges offerts à Antoine Faivre.* Leuven, Belgium: Peeters, 2001, pp. 595–610.

5445. _____. "God, New Religious Movements and *Buffy the Vampire Slayer.*" Posted at http://www.cesnur.org/2001/buffy_march01.htm. The website of CESNUR (the Center for Studies on New Religions), March 2001. A paper originally presented as "'There Will Be No Thomas Aquinas at This Table': Notions of God in the New Religious Consciousness" at the Expanding Concepts of God symposium, sponsored by the American Academy of Arts and Sciences, Harvard University, Cambridge, MA, April 7–9, 2000.

5446. _____. "'Modernity Will Not Save Her': Faith, Science, and *Buffy the Vampire Slayer* in the Italian *Dracula Opera Rock.*" A paper posted on the website of CESNUR (Center for Studies on New Religions) http://www.cesnur.org/2006/dracula_rock_eng.htm. [2006].

5447. _____. "Satanism Scares and Vampirism from the Eighteenth Century to the Present." *Transylvanian Journal: Dracula and Vampire Studies* 2, 1 (Spring/Summer 1996): 31–46.

5448. _____. "Strange Wars: Evangelical Counter-Cultists vs *Buffy the Vampire Slayer.*" Posted at the website of CESNUR (Center for Studies on New Religions) http://www.cesnur.org/testi/Buffy.htm. October 30, 1999.

5449. James, Paula. "Crossing Classical Thresholds: Gods, Monsters and Hell Dimensions in the Whedon Universe." In Dunstan Lowe and Kim Shahabudin, eds. *Classics for All: Reworking Antiquity in Mass Culture.* Newcastle upon Tyne, UK: Cambridge Scholars Publishing, 2009, pp. 237–260. A paper originally presented in earlier form as "Gate-Crashing Gods, and 'Coming Back Wrong': Crossing Classical Thresholds in *Buffy the Vampire Slayer*" at Greeks and Romans in the Buffyverse: Classical Threads in Fantasy and Science Fiction on Contemporary Television, Open University, Milton Keynes, UK, January 7–8, 2004.

5450. Jobbling, J'annine. "The Good and the Monstrous: *Buffy the Vampire Slayer*: 'From Beneath You, It Devours.'" In J'annine Jobbling. *Fantastic Spiritualities: Monsters, Heroes, and the Contemporary Religious Imagination.* London: T. & T. Clark, 2007, pp. 168–88.

5451. _____. "Transforming Worlds: *Buffy the Vampire Slayer*: 'Bite Me.'" In J'annine Jobbling. *Fantastic Spiritualities: Monsters, Heroes, and the Contemporary Religious Imagination.* London: T. & T. Clark, 2007, pp. 103–27.

5452. Kaldera, Raven. *The Ethical Psychical Vampire.* N.p.: Xlibris, 2005. 156 pp. tp. 2nd ed.: Hubbardston, MA: Elkhorn Press, 2008. 150 pp. tp.

5453. Kaveny, Cathleen. "What Women Want: *Buffy,* the Pope, and the New Feminists." *Commonweal: A Review of Religion, Politics, and Culture* 130, 19 (2003): 18–24. Posted at: http://www.whedon.info/What-Women-Want-Buffy-the-pope-the.html.

5454. Keenan, Catlyn. "Fangs and Crosses: What the Vampire Tells Us About American Christianity." A paper presented at the annual meeting of the American Association of Religion, 2011. 25 pages.

5455. Keyworth, David. "The Aetiology of Vampires and Revenants: Theological Debate and Popular Belief: The Aetiology of Vampires and Undead-Corpses." *Journal of Religious History* 34, 2 (2010): 158–73.

5456. _____. "The Socio-Religious Beliefs and Nature of the Contemporary Vampire Subculture." *Journal of Contemporary Religion* 17, 3 (2002): 355–370.

5457. Kisner, Adrienne L. *Reading Between the Lines: The Potential of Popular Young Adult Fiction in Adolescent Spiritual Formation.* Boston, MA: Boston University School of Theology, Ph.D. dissertation, 2011. 226 pp. Large format.

5458. Koontz, K. Dale. *Faith and Choice in the Works of Joss Whedon.* Jefferson, NC: McFarland & Company, 2008. 231 pp. tp.

5459. _____. "Foreword." In Anthony R. Mills, John W. Morehead, and J. Ryan Parker, eds. *Joss Whedon and Religion: Essays on an Angry Atheist's Explorations of the Sacred.* Jefferson, NC: McFarland & Company, 2013, pp. 1–4.

5460. Kreitzer, L. Joseph. "Dracula: 'The Blood Is the Life!'" In Larry J. Kreitzer. *Pauline Images in Fiction and Film: On Reversing the Hermeneutical Flow.* Sheffield, UK: Sheffield Academic, 1999, pp. 113–39.

5461. Krings, Matthias. "Muslim Martyrs and Pagan Vampires: Popular Video Films and the Propagation of Religion in Northern Nigeria." *Postscripts: The Journal of Sacred Texts and Contemporary Worlds* 1, 2–3 (2007): 183–205.

5462. Ladd, Catlyn (now Catlyn Keenan). From *Demon to Saint: The Vampire as Religious Archetype.* Bounder: University of Colorado, M.A. thesis, 2001. 93 pp. Large format.

5463. LaPerrière, Maureen-Claude. *Unholy Transubstantiation: Christifying the Vampire and Demonizing the Blood.* Montreal, PQ, CA: University of Montreal, Ph.D. dissertation, 2008. 259 pp. Large format.

5464. _____. "Real Vampires as an Identity Group: Analysing Causes and Effects of an Introspective Survey by the Vampire Community." In Adam Possamai, ed. *Handbook of Hyper-real Religions.* Ser.: Brill Handbooks on Contemporary Religion. Leiden: Brill, 2012, pp. 141–63.

5465. Lavery, David. "A Religion in Narrative: Joss Whedon and Television Creativity." *Slay-*

age: The Online International Journal of Buffy Studies 2, 3 [7] (December 2002). Posted at http://www.whedonstudies.tv/. A paper originally presented at the 2002 PCAS/ACAS Annual Conference, Charlotte, NC, October 3–5, 2002, and subsequently presented at Blood, Text and Fears: Reading Around *Buffy the Vampire Slayer*, University of East Anglia, October 19–20, 2002.

5466. Lawler, James. "Between Heaven and Hells: Multidimensional Cosmology in Kant and *Buffy the Vampire Slayer.*" In James B. South, ed. Buffy *and Philosophy: Fear and Trembling in Sunnydale.* Chicago: Open Court, 2003, pp. 103–116.

5467. _____. "The Multidimensional Universe of *Buffy the Vampire Slayer.*" *The God Tube: Uncovering the Hidden Spiritual Message in Pop Culture.* Chicago: Open Court, 2009. 60–86.

5468. Laycock, Joseph. "Crossing the Spiritual Wasteland in *Priest.*" In Kim Paffenroth and John W. Morehead, eds. *The Undead and Theology.* Eugene, OR: Pickwick Publications, 2012, pp. 19–33.

5469. Leggett, Paul. "The Filmed Fantasies of Terence Fisher." *Christianity Today* 25 (January 1981): 32–33.

5470. León, Luis D. *La Llorona's Children: Religion, Life, and Death on the U.S.–Mexican Borderlands.* Berkeley: University of California Press, 320 pp. hb & tp.

5471. Loughlin, Gerard. "Want of Family." In Gerard Loughlin. *Alien Sex: The Body and Desire in Cinema and Theology.* Hoboken, NJ: Wiley-Blackwell, 2004, pp. 201–26.

5472. MacCulloch, J. A. "Vampire." In James Hastings, ed. *Encyclopedia of Religion and Ethics.* Vol. XII. Edinburgh: T & T Clark, 1922. pp. 589–91. Posted at http://upload.wikimedia.org/wikipedia/commons/1/16/Encyclopedia_of_Religion_and_Ethics_Volume_12.pdf.

5473. Mayhew, Valerie. "Mary and Buffy Walk into a Bar: The Virgin Deity and *Buffy the Vampire Slayer.*" In Anthony R. Mills, John W. Morehead, and J. Ryan Parker, eds. *Joss Whedon and Religion: Essays on an Angry Atheist's Explorations of the Sacred.* Jefferson, NC: McFarland & Company, 2013, pp. 39–50.

5474. McAvan, Emily. "Buffy and Xena: Polytheisms on Screen." In Emily McAvan. *The Postmodern Sacred: Popular Culture Spirituality in the Science Fiction, Fantasy and Urban Fantasy Genres.* Jefferson, NC: McFarland & Company, 2012, pp. 80–97.

5475. Mills, Anthony R. "*Buffy*verse Fandom as Religion." In Jennifer Kate Stuller, ed. *Fan Phenomena:* Buffy the Vampire Slayer. Chicago: Intellect, 2013, pp. 134–143.

5476. _____. "Introduction." In Anthony R. Mills, John W. Morehead, and J. Ryan Parker, eds. *Joss Whedon and Religion: Essays on an Angry Atheist's Explorations of the Sacred*. Jefferson, NC: McFarland & Company, 2013, pp. 7–10.

5477. _____. "Preface." In Anthony R. Mills, John W. Morehead, and J. Ryan Parker, eds. *Joss Whedon and Religion: Essays on an Angry Atheist's Explorations of the Sacred*. Jefferson, NC: McFarland & Company, 2013, pp. 5–6.

5478. _____, **John W. Morehead, and J. Ryan Parker, eds.** *Joss Whedon and Religion: Essays on an Angry Atheist's Explorations of the Sacred*. Jefferson, NC: McFarland & Company, 2013. 232 pp.

5479. Montgomery, John Hardwick. "Dracula or Jesus?" *New Oxford Review* 61, 2 (April 1994).

5480. Morgan, Clay. *Undead: Revived, Resuscitated, Reborn*. Nashville, TN: Abingdon, 2012. 191 pp. tp.

5481. Nicholes, Elisabeth. "Reading the Book of Stoker as Sacred Text." *Journal of Religion and Popular Culture* 25, 1 (Spring 2013): 7000–.

5482. Ní Fhlainn, Sorcha. "'It's Morning in America': The Rhetoric of Religion in the Music of the *Lost Boys*, and the Deserved Death of the 1980's Vampire." In Niall Scott. The Role of the Monster: Myths and Metaphors of Enduring Evil. Oxford: inter–Disciplinary Press, 2009, pp. 147–56. Posted at: http://www.scribd.com/doc/616 99474/The-Role-of-the-Monster-Myths-and-Metaphors-of-Enduring-Evil.

5483. O'Grady, Stephanie. *Thirst for Fullness: An Application of John Paul II's Theology of the Body to the Twilight Saga*. Center Valley, PA: DeSales University, Senior Honors thesis, 2011. 58 pp. Large format.

5484. O'Malley, Patrick Robert Thomas. *Skeletons in the Cloister: Catholicism, Sexual Deviance, and the Haunting of English National Identity*. Cambridge, MA: Ph.D. dissertation, 1999. 356 pp. Large format.

5485. Paffenroth, Kim, and John W. Morehead, eds. *The Undead and Theology*. Eugene, OR: Pickwick Publications, 2012. 276 pp. Includes vampire articles by Vicky Gilpin, Joseph Laycock, Jarrod Longbons, W Scott Poole, Arnold T. Blumberg, Beth Stovell, and Andrea Subissati.

5486. Partridge, Christopher. "Supernatural Horror: Vampire Novels." In Christopher Partridge. *The Re-Enchantment of the West*. Vol. 1. *Alternative Spiritualities, Sacralization, Popular Culture, and Occulture*. London: Bloomsbury/T&T Clark, 2005, pp. 126–31.

5487. Phillips, Alan G., Jr. "Vampires, Werewolves, and Other Assorted Creatures: The Apocryphal Bestiary of Chick Publications." *Journal of Religion and Popular Culture* 24, 2 (Summer 2012): 277–95.

5488. Pippin, Tina. "Of Gods and Demons: Blood Sacrifice and Eternal Life in *Dracula* and the Apocalypse of John." In George Aichele and Richard Walsh eds. *Screening Scripture: Intertextual Connections Between Scripture and Film*. Harrisburg, PA: Trinity Press International, 2002, pp. 24–41.

5489. Poole, W. Scott. "The Vampire That Haunts Highgate: Theological Evil, Hammer Horror, and the Highgate Vampire Panic in Britain, 1963–1974." In Kim Paffenroth and John W. Morehead, eds. *The Undead and Theology*. Eugene, OR: Pickwick Publications, 2012, pp. 54–76.

5490. Primiano, Leonard Norman. "'I Wanna Do Bad Things with You': Fantasia on Themes of American Religion from the Title Sequence of HBO's True Blood." In Eric Michael Mazur and Kate McCarthy., eds. *God in the Details: American Religion in Popular Culture*. New York: Routledge, 2011, pp. 41–61.

5491. Raible, Christopher Gist. "Dracula: Christian Heretic." *The Christian Century* 96, 4 (January 31, 1979): 103. Rpt. in Margaret L. Carter, ed. *Dracula: The Vampire and the Critics*. Ann Arbor: UMI Research Press, 1988, pp. 105–08.

5492. Rarignac, Noel Montague-Etienne. *The Theology of Dracula: Reading the Book of Stoker as Sacred Text*. Jefferson, NC: McFarland & Company, 2012. 234 pp.

5493. Rath, Tina. "Words, Love and Death." *Redeemer* 1, 1 (December 1992): 16–17.

5494. Reed, Clara. "Vampires and Gentiles: Jews, Mormons and Embracing the Other." In Deborah Mutch. *The Modern Vampire and Human Identity*. Basingstoke, UK/New York: Palgrave Macmillan, 2013, pp. 128–45.

5495. Rice, Anne. *Called Out of Darkness: A Spiritual Confession.* New York: Alfred A. Knopf, 2008. 245 pp. hb. dj.

5496. Roberts, Dave. *The Twilight Gospel: The Spiritual Roots of the Stephenie Meyer Vampire Saga.* Monarch Books, 2009. 160 pp. tp.

5497. Robinson, Sara Libby. "Blood Will Tell: Anti-Semitism and Vampires in British Culture, 1875–1914." *Golem: Journal of Religion and Monsters* 3, 1 (Spring 2009). Posted at: http://lomibao.net/golem/current.php.

5498. Schnoebelen, William. *Romancing Death: A True Story of Vampirism, Death, the Occult, and Deliverance.* Shippensburg, PA: Destiny Image Publishers, 2012. 285 pp. tp.

5499. Schöll, Thomas. *Social and Religious Aspects in Bram Stoker's* Dracula. München, Germany: Grin Verlag, 1995, 12 pp.

5500. Shang-Jen, Li. "Ghosts, Vampires, and Scientific Naturalism: Observation and Evidence in the Supernatural Fiction of Grant Allen, Bram Stoker and Arthur Conan Doyle." In Mu-chou Poo, ed. *Rethinking Ghosts in World Religions.* Leiden: Brill, 2009, pp. 183–210.

5501. Spivey, Mark Thomas. *The Postmodern Vampire Archetype: A Pastoral Perspective for Healing the Wounded in Generation X.* Lincoln, NB: Lincoln Christian Seminary, M.A. thesis, 1996. 122 pp. Large format.

5502. Starrs, D. Bruno. "Keeping the Faith: Catholicism in *Dracula* and Its Adaptations." *Journal of Dracula Studies* 6 (2004): 13–18.

5503. Stovell, Beth. "'Eat of My Body and Drink of My Blood': Johannine Metaphor, Gothic Subculture, and the Undead." In Kim Paffenroth and John W. Morehead, eds. *The Undead and Theology.* Eugene, OR: Pickwick Publications, 2012, pp. 209–26.

5504. Subissati, Andrea. "Fire, Brimstone and PVC: Clive Barker's Cenobites as Agents of Hell." In Kim Paffenroth and John W. Morehead, eds. *The Undead and Theology.* Eugene, OR: Pickwick Publications, 2012, pp. 227–39.

5505. *The Theological Vampire Exposed in a Series of Lectures, Etc.* London: John Brooks, 1883. xiii, 160 pp.

5506. Watt, Tony "Tex." "Lee Gordon Demarbre's *Jesus Christ Vampire Hunter.*" In Tony "Tex" Watt. *TonyWatt.com Presents Kount Kracula's Twisted Sinema! Obscure 21st Century Underground Horror/Sci-Fi/Fantasy/Thriller Movies & Shorts #1.* N.p.: the author, 2012, pp. 65–84.

5507. Watters, John. "Religion and Superstition in Dracula." In Claude Fierobe ed. *Dracula: Mythe et métamorphoses.* Villeneuve d'Ascq, Presses Universitaires du Septentrion, 2005.

5508. Weidner, Eric. *The Image of Religion and Its Function in M.G. Lewis'* The Monk *and Bram Stoker's* Dracula. München, Germany: Grin Verlag, 2006, 21 pp.

5509. Westerbeck, C.L. "Innocent Dracula: Myth Rather Than Melodrama." *Commonweal* 107 (January 18, 1980): 16–18.

5510. Wiktorin, Pierre. "The Vampire as a Religious Phenomenon." In Mariah Larsson and Ann Steiner, eds. *Interdisciplinary Approaches to Twilight Studies in Fiction, Media and a Contemporary Cultural Experience.* Lund, Sweden: Nordic Academic Press, 2011, pp. 279–96.

5511. Wolberg, Steve. *The Trouble with Twilight: Why Today's Vampire Craze Is Hazardous to Your Health.* Shippennsburg, PA: Destiny Image Publishers, 2010. 189 pp. tp.

5512. Wotherspoon, Dorothy I. *The Vampire Myth and Christianity.* Winter Park, FL: Rollins College, Masters of Liberal Studies thesis, 2010. 70 pp. Posted at: http://scholarship.rollins.edu/mls/16.

Vampires and the Law

Comic writer/artist Batton Lash has made a career out of producing stories that illustrate the principle that in the modern world even monsters, including vampires, need a lawyer. Moving from a humorous to far more serious setting, that idea would become an integral part of the storyline in the television series *Angel.* But even in the face of such roles for lawyers amid vampires, one could seriously ask about the need for legal literature relative to vampires. They seem on cursory examination an unimportant aspect of vampire life and lore, though the legal aspects of Dracula's acquiring property in England is a key part of the plot line in Stoker's novel.

The legal aspect of vampire lore comes when one considers the vampire a real creature, one of human origin, and attempts to define its place (or lack thereof) in human society. If the vampire actually exists, he/she/it must gain some legal status in order to survive even incognito, especially so in the modern world, where government authorities, financial institutions, and even retail businesses regularly call an individual's status into question by asking for repeated verifications of one's citizenship and identity. At the same time, real vampires would at least occasionally run into conflicts that could land them in court as the participants in civil proceedings. Thus, the existence of the vampire creates an environment in which speculation of its legal status is more than relevant.

Meanwhile, the legal status of the writings about vampires have become part of the ongoing discussions as authors have complained about colleagues who appear to have stolen both ideas and text from them, the concern of more than one lawsuit, some of which probe the very nature of genre writing. One writer, Marv Wolfman, also went to court attempting (unsuccessfully as it turned out) to break a contract on his early contributions to Marvel's *Tomb of Dracula* series, which a quarter of a century later enjoyed a new success when it became the basis of a movie trilogy. Wolfman was denied any additional recompense as a character he created, Blade the Vampire Slayer, was featured in a set of movies starring Wesley Snipes.

5513. Bartow, Ann. "Bloodsucking Copyrights." *Maryland Law Review* 70, 1 (2010): 62–86. Posted at: http://digitalcommons.law.umaryland.edu/mlr/vol70/iss1/4.

5514. Bradney, Anthony. "The Case of *Buffy the Vampire Slayer* and the Politics of Legal Education." In Steven Greenfield and Guy Osborn, eds. *Readings in Law and Popular Culture.* New York: Routledge, 2006, pp. 15–30.

5515. _____. "Choosing Laws, Choosing Families: Images of Law, Love and Authority in *Buffy the Vampire Slayer*." *Web Journal of Current Legal Issues* 2 Web JCLI (2003). Posted at: http://webjcli.ncl.ac.uk/2003/issue2/bradney2.html. A paper originally presented at Blood, Text and Fears: Reading Around *Buffy the Vampire Slayer*, University of East Anglia, October 19–20, 2002.

5516. _____. "For and Against the Law: *Buffy the Vampire Slayer, Angel* and the Academy." *Entertainment and Sports Law Journal* 9, 1 (2011). Posted at http://www2.warwick.ac.uk/fac/soc/law/elj/eslj/issues/volume9/bradney.

5517. _____. "'I Made a Promise to a Lady': Law and Love in *Buffy the Vampire Slayer*." *Slayage: The Online International Journal of Buffy Studies* 3, 2 [10] (November 2003). Posted at: http://www.slayageonline.com/previously_on.html.

5518. _____. "Images of Law in *Buffy the Vampire Slayer*." Paper presented at the Slayage Conference on *Buffy the Vampire Slayer*, Nashville, TN, May 27–30, 2004. Posted at: http://www.slayageonline.com/SCBtVS_Archive/.

5519. _____. "'It's About Power': Law in the Fictional Setting of a Quaker Meeting and in the Everyday Reality of *Buffy the Vampire Slayer*." *Issues in Legal Scholarship* 8 (January 2006).

5520. _____. "'The Morally Ambiguous Crowd': The Image of a Large Law Firm in *Angel*." *Northern Ireland Legal Quarterly* 56 (2005): 21–37.

5521. _____. "The Politics and Ethics of Researching the Buffyverse." *Slayage: The Online International Journal of Buffy Studies* 5, 3 [19] (February 2006). Posted at: http://www.slayageonline.com/previously_on.html. A paper originally presented as "The Politics and Ethics of Writing About the Buffyverse" at Bring Your Own Subtext: Social Life, Human Experience and the Works of Joss Whedon, Conference, University of Huddersfield, Huddersfield, UK, June 29-July 1, 2005.

5522. Breuninger, Wendy Kae. *Count Dracula in the Courts.* Middletown, CT: Wesleyan University, M.A. thesis, 1981, 78 pp. Large format.

5523. Dean, Michael. "The Vampirella Wars: The Untold Story of James Warren's Custody Battle with Harris Comics." *The Comics Journal* 253 (June 2003). Excerpt posted at http://www.web citation.org/5swey7SYy.

5524. Kamir, Orit. *Stalking: Culture, History and Law.* Lansing: University of Michigan, Law School, Ph.D. dissertation, 1996. 510 pp. Large format.

5525. Ledwon, Lenora Pauline. *Legal Fictions: Constructions of the Female Legal Subject in Nineteenth-Century Law and Literature.* University of Notre Dame, Ph.D. dissertation, 1992. 198 pp. Large format. *Dracula* is one of four novels compared.

5526. Lipton, Jacqueline D. "Copyright's Twilight Zone: Digital Copyright Lessons from the Vampire Blogosphere." *Maryland Law Review* 70, 1 (2010): 1–61. Available at: http://digital commons.law.umaryland.edu/mlr/vol70/iss1/3.

5527. MacNeil, William P. "You Slay Me! *Buffy* as Jurisprude of Desire." *Cardozo Law Review* 24, 6 (2003): 2421–40. A paper originally presented at Staking a Claim: Exploring the Global Reach of *Buffy*, University of South Australia, Adelaide, Australia, 22 July 2003.

5528. "Marv Wolfman's Trial." *The Comics Journal.* Part 1: 236 (August 2001): 22–84. Part 2: 239 (Nov. 2001): 68–112. Transcript with comments and sidebars of trial in which Marv Wolfman challenged ownership of the characters he created for *The Tomb of Dracula.*

5529. McGillivray, Anne. "He Would Have Made a Wonderful Solicitor': Law, Modernity and Professionalism in Bram Stoker's *Dracula*." In David Sugarman and Wesley Pue, eds. *Lawyers and Vampires: Cultural Histories of Legal Professions.* Oxford, Portland: Hart Publishing, 2003, pp. 225–68.

5530. _____. "What Sort of Grim Adventure Was It on Which I Had Embarked?' Lawyers, Vampires, and the Melancholy of Law." *Gothic Studies* 4 (2002): 116–132.

5531. Pickering, Michael. "Attitudes Toward the Destruction of Vampire Bodies in the Habsburg Empire." In Shubhankar Dam & Jonathan Hall, eds. *Inside and Outside the Law.* Oxford: Inter-disciplinary Press, 2009, pp. 119–32. Posted at: http://www.inter-disciplinary.net/wp-content/uploads/2009/09/iol16revc.pdf. Rpt. as: "Sie Mußten ins Feuer': Changing Policies Within the Habsburg Monarchy on the Destruction of Vampire Bodies." In Kiran Sarma and Ben Livings, eds. *Evil and the State: Interdiciplinary Perspectives.* Oxford: Inter-disciplinary Press, 2013.

5532. Rutledge, Thomas E. "Vampires and the Law of Business Organizations: The Fruitless Search for Authenticity." *Journal of Passthrough Entities* (November-December 2011): 63–68. Posted at: http://papers.ssrn.com/sol3/papers.cfm?abstract_id=1970262.

5533. Sugarman, David, and Wesley Pue, eds. *Lawyers and Vampires: Cultural Histories of Legal Professions.* Oxford, UK: Hart Publishing, 2003. 399 pp. hb. & tp.

5534. Sutherland, Sharon. "Piercing the Corporate Veil with a Stake? Vampire Imagery and the Law." In Carla T. Kungl, ed. *Vampires: Myths and Metaphors of Enduring Evil.* Oxford: Inter-Disciplinary Press, 2003. pp. 95–99. Posted at http://www.inter-disciplinary.net/publishing/id-press/ebooks/vampires-myths-and-metaphors-of-enduring-evil. Rpt. in: Peter Day, ed. *Vampire: Myths and Metaphors of Enduring Evil.* Amsterdam: Rodopi, 2006, pp. 143–58. A paper originally presented at Vampires: Myths and Metaphors of Enduring Evil Conference held in Budapest, Hungary, May 22–24, 2003. Posted at: http://papers.ssrn.com/sol3/papers.cfm?abstract_id=796826.

5535. _____, and Sarah Swann. "If a Vampire Bites a Lawyer, is it Cannibalism? The Demonization of Lawyers in *Angel*." A paper originally presented at the *Slayage* Conference on Buffy the Vampire Slayer," Nashville, TN, May 28, 2004. 21 pp. Posted at http://ssrn.com/abstract=802324, and at http://dx.doi.org/10.2139/ssrn.802324.

5536. _____. "Lilah Morgan: Whedon's Legal Femme Fatale." In AmiJo Comeford and Tamy L. Burnett, ed. *The Literary* Angel: *Essays on Influences and Traditions Reflected in the Joss Whedon Series.* Jefferson, NC: McFarland & Company, 2010, pp. 54–65.

5537. _____. "The Rule of Prophecy: Source of Law in the City of *Angel*." In Stacey Abbott, ed. *Reading* Angel: *The TV Spin-off with a Soul.* New York: I. B. Tauris, 2005, pp. 132–145.

5538. Williams, Robert A., Jr. "Vampires Anonymous and Critical Race Practice." *Michigan Law Review* 95 (1997): 741–65. Posted at http://papers.ssrn.com/sol3/papers.cfm?abstract_id=1485065. Originally issued as *Arizona Legal Studies,* Discussion Paper No. 09–32 (October 2009).

Vampirism, Crime and Criminology

Even as vampire studies emerged and matured, police departments were identifying a new priority target, the serial killer, some of whom would through the twentieth century be additionally identified as vampires, the latter identification due to their possessing one or more of a set of characteristics associated with their murders, primarily having to do with their taking and/or consuming the blood of their victims. Some, following their arrest and trials, became the subject of massive media coverage and frequent mention in popular true crime literature. The vampire murderers include Elizabeth Bathory (covered in a separate sub-chapter in this work), Gilles de Rais, John George Haigh, Peter Kürten, Vincenzo Verzini, Bela Kiss, Fritz Haarmann, Richard Chase, and Rod Ferrell. Even the famous Black Dahlia case in Los Angeles, a singular case with a large literature, has been linked to vampirism due to the simple observation that when discovered by the authorities, the victim's body was completely void of blood.

The literature on vampire related crime grades into the literature on the contemporary vampire community, as crime expresses one way, albeit a very minor way, that vampirism manifested in the late twentieth century. A crime that has vampire overtones, if only superficially, makes for good headlines.

It is also noteworthy that the novel *Dracula* appeared only a few years after the Jack the Ripper murders, the Ripper being one of the first cases treated for its serial killer nature. More recently, the idea that the Jack the Ripper killings played into Stoker's development of the *Dracula* plot has found some favor among students of the novel. Thus, the growing number of reflections on the possible connection of *Dracula* and Jack the Ripper are included in this chapter.

The permeation of vampire images in contemporary culture has paralleled the realization of the existence of serial killers, the arrest and prosecution of dozens of individuals accused of multiple homicides, the dedicated study of serial homicide, and the production of a vast literature (both fact-based and fictionalized) on serial killers for popular consumption. In the process, a number of cases have appeared in which the serial killer consumed blood from his/her victims, an action that would lead to their designation as vampire killers. Several who have looked at both serial homicide and vampirism have concluded that vampires are serial killers who attempt to justify their actions by claiming that it is necessary for their own survival.

Among the murderers popularly designated as vampire killers are Bela Kiss (Hungary), Peter Kürten (Germany), Fritz Haarmann (Germany) Martin Dumollard (France), Joseph Vacher (France), Vincenzo Verzenia (Italy), Eusebius Pieydagnelle (Italy), Florencio Roque Fernandez (Argentina), Stanislav Modzieliewski (Poland), Juan Koltrun Poland), Rantao Antonio Cirillo (Italy), John Crutchley (United States), Andrei Chikatilo (Soviet Union), Marcello de Andrade (Brazil), Mauricio Lopez (Mexico), John George Haigh (United Kingdom), Magdalena Solis (Mexico), Tsutomu Miyazaki (Japan), Philip Oyancha (Kenya), Nico Claux (France), Daniel and Manuela Ruda (Germany), Richard Trenton Chase (United States), James Riva (United States), Roderick Ferrell (United States), Joshua Rudiger (United States), and Allan Menzies (Scotland). Among the very few females who were identified as vampires is Enriqueta Marti (Spain).

No systematic attempt has been made to scan the vast literature on true crime, serial killers, or bizarre murders, and hence the items cited below represent only a sampling of the literature covering the more famous cases and criminals linked to vampirism, though an intensive search has been made to locate that portion of the literature that attempts any discussion of the overlapping realm between vampirism and crime. This literature grades into the psychological literature as most of the people accused of being vampire serial killers have also been subject to psychological evaluations due to their out-of-the-ordinary behavior and most have been judged to possess some form of psychological pathology.

A number of the vampire serial killers have been the subject of television documentaries, and a few of feature-length movies, most notably Peter Kurten (*M*, 1931, 1951), Bela Kiss (*Bela Kiss: Prologue*, 2013), Fritz Haarmann (*Tenderness of Wolves*, 1973), Richard Chase (*Rampage*, 1987), and Rod Ferrell (*Vampire Clan*, 2002).

5539. Barber, Paul. "Forensic Pathology and the European Vampire." *Journal of Folklore Research* 24, 1 (Jan.–Apr. 1987): 1–32. Rpt. in: Alan Dundas, ed. *The Vampire: A Casebook*. Madison: University of Wisconsin Press, 1998. pp. 109–142.

5540. Benson, John. "A Vampire Drank His Victim's Blood." In Rose G. Maldelsberg, ed. *Bizarre Murderers*. New York: Pinnacle Books/Windsor Publishing Corp., 1991, pp. 143–72.

5541. Berg, Karl. *The Sadist, an Account of the Crimes of Peter Kurten*. London: Acorn Press, 1935. Rpt.: London: Heinemann, 1945. Rpt. in: *Monsters of Weimar. Comprising the Classic Case Histories: Haarmann—the Story of a Werewolf/Kürten—the Vampire of Düsseldorf*. London: Nemesis, 1993. 306 pp.

5542. Berry-Dee, Christopher. *Cannibal Serial Killers: Profiles of Depraved Flesh-Eating Murderers*. Berkeley, CA: Ulysses Press, 2011. 320 pp. tp. Includes chapters on "The Brooklyn Vampire" Hamilton Howard "Albert" Fish (155–74), "The Vampire of Dusseldorf" Peter Kurten 175–93), "The Vampire of Hanover" Friedrich "Fritz" Heinrich Karl Haarmann 209–27), and "The Vampire Killers" Tracey Avril Wigginton and Lisa M. Ptaschinski (265–82).

5543. Biondi, Ray, and Walt Hecox. *The Dracula Killer*. New York: Pocket Books, 1992. 212 pp. pb. Re: Richard Chase, the serial killer from Sacramento, California.

5544. Borrini, M. "An Exorcism Against a Vampire in Venice: Anthropological and Forensic Study on an Archeological Burial of XVIth Century." *Bulletins et Mémoires de la Société D'anthropologie de Paris* n.s. 20 (2008).

5545. _____, and E. Nuzzolese. "Forensic Approach to an Archaeological Casework of 'Vampire' Skeletal Remains in Venice: Odontological and Anthropological Prospectus." *Journal of Forensic Sciences* 55 (2010): 1634–1637,.

5546. _____, O. Rickards, and C. Martinez Labarga. "The Vampire of Venice: A Real Ancient Ancestor of *Twilight* Investigated by Modern Forensic Sciences." In: *Proceedings of the American Academy of Forensic Sciences*. Chicago, February 21–26, 2011. Vol. 17, Colorado Springs: American Academy of Forensic Sciences, 2011.

5547. Branson-Trent, Gregory. *Abnormal World: Vampires, Jack the Ripper, Psychotic Killers, and More*. N.p.: New Image Productions, 2011. tp.

5548. Bravin, Jess. "The Vampire Killers." In Jess Bravin. *The Terror Courts: Rough Justice at Guantanamo Bay*. New Haven, CT: Yale University Press, 2013, pp. 285–308.

5549. Brickman, Peggy. "The Case of the Druid Dracula." *Journal of College Science Teaching* 36, 2, October 2006. Posted at http://sciencecases.lib.buffalo.edu/cs/files/druid_dracula.pdf.

5550. Clarkson, Wensley. "The Lesbian Vampire Killers." In Wensley Clarkson. *Hell Hath No Fury Like a Woman Scorned: True Stories of Women Who Kill*. London: John Blake, 2003, pp. 1–24.

5551. Constantine, Peter. "The Modern Vampire." In Peter Constantine. *A History of Cannibalism: From Ancient Cultures to Survival Stories and Modern Psychopaths*. Edison, NJ: Chartwell Books, 2009, pp. 154–58.

5552. Davis, Carol Anne. "Can't Get It Out of My Head: Rod Ferrell." In Carol Anne Davis. *Children Who Kill: Profiles of Pre-Teen and Teenage Killers*. London: Allison & Busby, 2004, pp. 155–73.

5553. Davison, Carol Margaret. "Blood Brothers: Dracula and Jack the Ripper." In Carol Margaret Davidson, ed., with Paul Simpson-Housley. *Bram Stoker's Dracula: Sucking through the Century, 1897–1997.* Toronto: Dundurn Press, 1997, pp. 147–173.

5554. Dunboyne, Lord. *The Trial of John George Haigh.* Ser.: Notable Trial Series #78. London: William Hodge, 1953. 271 pp. hb.

5555. Dunning, John. "Mentally Disadvantaged Vampire." In John Dunning. *Mystical Murders.* London: Arrow Books, 1989, pp. 68–82.

5556. Durham, Meenakshi Gigi. "Blood, Lust and Love: Interrogating Gender Violence in the Twilight." *Journal of Children and Media* 6, 3 (2012): 281–299.

5557. Edwards, Wallace. *The Lonely Hearts Vampire: The Bizarre and Horrifying True Account of Serial Killer Bela Kiss.* N.p.: Absolute Crime, 2013. 74 pp. pb.

5558. Eighteen-Bisang, Robert. "Dracula, Jack the Ripper and 'A Thirst for Blood.'" *Journal of Dracula Studies* Anniversary Issue (2005): 29–46.

5559. Ellroy, James. *The Black Dahlia.* New York: Mysterious Press, 1987. 325 pp. hb. dj. Rpt. New York: Warner Books, 1988. 371 pp. pb.

5560. Everitt, David. *Human Monsters: An Illustrated Encyclopedia of the World's Most Vicious Murders.* Chicago: Contemporary Books, 1993. 272 pp. tp.

5561. Fontana, Ernest. "Lambroso's Criminal Man and Stoker's *Dracula.*" *The Victorian Newsletter* 66 (Fall 1984): 25–27. Rpt. in Margaret L. Carter, ed. *Dracula: The Vampire and the Critics.* Ann Arbor: UMI Research Press, 1988, pp. 159–66.

5562. Gibson, Dirk Cameron. "Vampire Serial Killers." In Dirk C. Gibson. *Legends, Monsters, or Serial Murderers? The Real Story Behind an Ancient Crime.* Santa Barbara, CA: Praeger/ABC-Clio, 2012, pp. 11–32. This chapter covers the crimes of Elizabeth Bathory and Vincenzo Verzini.

5563. Gilmore, John. *Severed: The True Story of the Black Dahlia Murder.* Los Angeles: Amok Books, 1998. 230 pp. tp. Rev. ed. 2006. 238 pp. tp.

5564. Godwin, George. *Peter Kurten: A Study in Sadism.* London: Heineman Medical Books, 1938, 1945. 58 pp. Rpt. in: *Monsters of Weimar. Comprising the Classic Case Histories: Haarmann—the Story of a Werewolf/Kürten—the Vampire of Düsseldorf.* London: Nemesis, 1993. 306 pp. tp.

5565. Hemphill, R. E., and E. Zabow. "Clinical Vampirism: A Presentation of Three Cases and a Reevaluation of Haigh, the 'Acid-Bath Murder.'" *South African Medical Journal* 63 (1983): 278–281. Rpt. in: Richard Noll, ed. *Vampires, Werewolves, and Demons: Twentieth Century Reports in the Psychiatric Literature.* New York: Brunner Mazel, 1992, pp. 61–73. Rpt. in: Angela Cybulski, ed. *Vampires: Fact or Fiction?* Ser.: Opposing Viewpoints. Farmington Hills, MI: Greenhaven Press/Thomson, Gale, 2003. pp. 125–35.

5566. Hicks, Ron. *The Vampire Killer: A Journey into the Mind of Tracey Wigginton.* Sydney, Aust.: Bantam, 1972. 343 pp. pb. Rev. ed.: N.p.: Huon Enterprises, 2009. 366 pp. tp.

5567. Hodel, Steve. *Black Dahlia Avenger: The True Story.* New York: Arcade Publishing, 2003. 481 pp. hb.

5568. Honeycomb, Gordon. "John Haigh: The Murder of Mrs. Durand-Deacon, 1949." In Gordon Honeycomb. *The Murders of the Black Museum, 1870–1970.* London: Hutchinson, 1982. Rev. ed. London: Arrow, 1984, pp. 421–37.

5569. Hurwood, Bernhardt J. "Peter Kürten—the Monster of Dusseldorf." In Bernard J. Hurwood. *Monsters Galore.* Greenwich, CT: Fawcett/Gold Medal Books, 1965, pp. 146–64.

5570. Jackson, Stanley. *John George Haigh.* Ser.: Famous Criminal Trials. London: Oldhams, 1953. 127 pp. pb.

5571. Jaffe, P. D., and F. DiCataldo. "Clinical Vampirism: Blending Myth and Reality." *Bulletin of the American Academy of Psychiatry and Law* 22, 4 (1994): 533–544.

5572. Jenkins, Mark Collins. *Vampire Forensics: Uncovering the Origins of an Enduring Legend.* Washington, DC: National Geographic, 2010. 303 pp. hb. dj.

5573. Jones, Aphrodite. *The Embrace.* New York: Pocket Books, 1999. 384 pp. hb. dj.

5574. La Bern, A. *Haigh: The Mind of a Murderer.* London: W. H. Allen, 1973. 187 pp. pb. Rpt.: London: Star Books, 1974. 187 pp. pb.

5575. Lane, Brian. "John George Haigh." In Brian Lane. *An Encyclopedia of Occult and Supernatural Murder.* London: Headline, 1995. 242 pp. Rpt.: London: Brockhampton Press, 1997. 242 pp. hb. dj.

5576. ____, **and Wilfred Gregg.** *An Encyclopedia of Serial Killers.* London: Headline Book Publishing, 1992. 310 pp. hb. dj. Rpt.: New York: Diamondis Communications, 1994. Rpt.: New York: Berkley Books, 1995. 408 pp.

5577. Lasseter, Don. "The Caped 'Count' and the Sexy Teen." In Rose G. Mandelberg, ed. *Bizarre Murderers II.* New York: Pinnacle Books/ Windsor Publishing Corp., 1993, pp. 350–65.

5578. Lefebure, Molly. *Murder with a Difference—The Case of Haigh and Christie.* London: Heineman, 1958. 251 pp. hb. dj.

5579. Lessing, Theodor. *Haarmann—the Story of a Werewolf.* Trans. by Mo Croasdale. In *Monsters of Weimar. Comprising the Classic Case Histories: Haarmann—The Story of a Werewolf/ Kürten—The Vampire of Düsseldorf.* London: Nemesis, 1993. 306 pp. tp. A translation from the 1925 original German edition, *Haarmann—Di geshchite eines Werwolfs.*

5580. Linedecker, Clifford L. *Awful Horror Stories: True Tales of Witches, Ghouls, Cannibals, Crazed Killers, Vampires & Other Creatures of the Night.* Lantana, FL: MicroMags, 1999. 72 pp. pb. Small format.

5581. ____. *The Vampire Killers.* New York: St. Martin's Paperbacks, 1998. 275 pp. pb.

5582. London, Sondra. *True Vampires: Blood-Sucking Killers Past and Present.* Los Angeles: Feral House, 2003. 380 pp. tp. Illus. by Nicolas Claux.

5583. MacDougal, Douglas. "Vampire Rapist Stalks Oklahoma." *True Police* 43, 2 (April 1993): 34–39.

5584. Markman, Ronald, and Dominick Bosco. "The Vampire of Sacramento." In Ronald Markman and Dominick Bosco. *Alone with the Devil: Famous Cases of a Courtroom Psychiatrist.* New York: Doubleday, 1989, pp. 159–93. Rpt.: New York: Warner Books, 1992, pp. 159–93. Rpt. as: *Alone with the Devil: Psychopathic Killings That Shocked the World.* London: Judy Piatkus, 1990. pp. 159–93. Rpt.: London: Futura, 1991.

5585. Martin, Timothy P. "The Kiss of the Vampire." In Moira Martingale. *Cannibal Killers: The History of Impossible Murders.* New York: Carroll & Graf Publisher, 1993, pp. 60–74.

5586. Monaco, Richard, with Bill Burt. *The Dracula Syndrome.* New York: Avon Books, 1993. 167 pp. pb.

5587. Morrissey, Belinda. "Cultural Anxiety and Vampiric Voracity: Tracey Wigginton's 'Hun-ger.'" In Belinda Morrissey. *When Women Kill: Questions of Agency and Subjectivity.* Abingdon, UK: Routledge, 2003, pp. 103–33.

5588. Nelson, Mark, and Sarah Hudson Bayliss. *Exquisite Corpse: Surrealism and the Black Dahlia Murder.* York: Bulfinch Press, 2006. 191 pp. hb. dj.

5589. Oringderff, David L. "Case Study of a Vampire Cult." In David L. Oringderff. *Cults and Criminals: Unraveling the Myths.* Butler, MO: HDB Press, 2013, pp. 165–71. The discussion of vampirism by the author occurs in the midst of a larger discussion of crimes that have a religious, ritualized, and/or occult element associated with them.

5590. Perlmutter, Dawn. "Vampirism." In Dawn Perlmutter. *Investigating Religious Terrorism and Ritualistic Crimes.* Boca Raton, FL: CRC Press, 2003, pp. 145–80.

5591. Phillips, Conrad. *Murderer's Moon-Being Studies of Heath, Haigh, Christie, and Cherney.* Westport, CT: Associated Booksellers, 1956. 238 pp. hb. dj.

5592. Picart, Caroline Joan, and Cecil Greek. "The Compulsions of Real/Reel Serial Killers and Vampires: Toward a Gothic Criminology." In John Edgar Browning and Caroline Joan Picart, eds. *Dracula, Vampires, and Other Undead Forms.* Lanham, MD: The Scarecrow Press, 2009, pp. 37–62.

5593. ____. "When Women Kill: Undead Imagery in the Cinematic Portrait of Aileen Wuornos Caroline." In John Edgar Browning and Caroline Joan Picart, eds. *Dracula, Vampires, and Other Undead Forms.* Lanham, MD: The Scarecrow Press, 2009, pp. 93–112.

5594. Radner, Henry. "Shocking 'Vampire Murder' in Virginia." *Startling Detective* 78, 4 (July 1988): 6–7, 53, 55, 57,-58, 60,-61. Rpt. as: "Weird Case of the Virginia Vampire." *True Police Yearbook* 1, 39 (1990): 6, 57–61.

5595. Ramsland, Katherine. "C.S.I. "Justice Served." In Katherine Ramsland. *True Stories of CSI: The Real Crimes Behind the Best Episodes of the Popular TV Show.* New York: Berkley Trade, 2008, pp. 87–96. tp.

5596. ____. *Piercing the Darkness: Undercover with the Vampires in America Today.* New York: HarperPrism, 1998. 371 pp. hb. dj. Rpt. New York: Harper, 1999. 546 pp. pb.

5597. ____. *The Science of Vampires.* New York: Berkley Boulevard Books, 2002. 276 pp. tp.

5598. _____. "Vampire Crime." *Journal of Dracula Studies* 2 (2000): 34–45.

5599. Rance, Nicholas. "Jonathan's Great Knife: Dracula Meets Jack the Ripper." *Victorian Literature and Culture* 30, 2 (2002): 439–454. Rpt. in Alexandra Warwick and Martin Wills, eds. *Jack the Ripper: Media, Culture, History*. Manchester, UK: Manchester University Press, 2007, pp. 124ff.

5600. Ressler, Robert K., and Thomas Schachtman. "The Vampire Killer." In Robert K. Ressler and Thomas Schachtman. *Whoever Fights Monsters: My Twenty Years Tracking Serial Killers for the FBI*. New York: St. Martin's Paperbacks, 1993, pp. 1–22.

5601. Revitch, Eugene, and Louis B. Schlesinger. "Cannibalism and Vampirism." In Eugene Revitch and Louis B. Schlesinger. *Sex Murder and Sex Aggression: Phenomenology, Psychopathology, Psychodynamics and Prognosis*. Springfield, IL: Charles C Thomas Publisher, 1989, pp. 60–63.

5602. Ronin, Zrami. "Human Vampire Attacks Six-Year-Old Girl." *Beyond* (April 1969): 43–53.

5603. Root, Neil. *Frenzy!: Heath, Haigh and Christie: The First Great Tabloid Murderers*. London: Preface Publishing, 2012. 320 pp. tp. Rpt. as: *Frenzy! Heath, Haigh & Christie: How the Tabloid Press Turned Three Evil Serial Killers into Celebrities*. London: Arrow Books, 2012.

5604. Schwarz, Ted. "Richard Chase: Real Life Dracula." *Chic* 5, 12 (October 1981): 56–60, 70–82, 86.

5605. *Serial Killers and Murderers*. Lincolnwood, IL: Publications International, 1991. See un-numbered chapter on "The Vampire of Düsseldorf."

5606. Sommerfield, Stafford. *The Story of John George Haigh*. Manchester, UK: Hood Pearson, 1950. 127 pp. pb.

5607. Storey, Neill. *The Dracula Secrets: Jack the Ripper and the Darkest Sources of Bram Stoker*. Stroud, Gloucestershire, UK: The History Press, 2012. 304 pp. hb.

5608. Summers, Montague. "Fritz Haarman—The Hanover Vampire." In: Haining, Peter, ed. *The Midnight People*. London: Leslie Frewin, 1968, pp. 15–20. Rpt. as: *Vampires at Midnight*. New York: Grosset & Dunlap, 1970, pp. 15–20. Rpt. in: Ashley, Leonard R. N. *The Complete Book of Vampires*. New York: Barricade Books, 1998, pp. 109–115. This account of Haarmann was lifted by Haining from the text of Summers' *The Vampire: His Kith and Kin* (1928).

5609. Wagner, Margaret Seaton. *The Monster of Dusseldorf: The Life and Trial of Peter Kurten*. London: Faber & Faber, 1932. 248 pp.

5610. Waltje, Jörg. *Blood Obsession: Vampires, Serial Murder, and the Popular Imagination*. New York: Peter Lang, 2005. 157 pp. tp. *Blood Obsession: Vampires, Serial Murder, and the Popular Imagination* received the 2006 award as the best nonfiction book of the previous year given annually by the Lord Ruthven Society.

5611. Webb, William. "The Vampire of Barcelona: Enriquita Martí, the Murderous Witch." In William Webb. *More Scary Bitches! 15 More of the Scariest Women You'll Ever Meet!* N.p.: Absolute Crime Books, 2013, pp. 66–71.

5612. Weston, Terry. *Britain's Bloodiest Serial Killers: From the Vampire Killer to the Crossbow Cannibal*. N.p.: Swordworks, 2010. 90 pp. tp.

Vampire Animals and Plants

Quincey Morris, one of the major characters in Bram Stoker's novel *Dracula*, begins the process of connecting the vampire Dracula to the so-called "vampire" bats of Central and South America, as he relates his memory of the bats' effect on a favorite horse: "I have not seen anything pulled down so quick since I was on the Pampas and had a mare that I was fond of go to grass all in a night. One of those big bats that they call vampires had got at her in the night, and what with his gorge and the vein left open, there wasn't enough blood in her to let her stand up, and I had to put a bullet through her as she lay" (*Dracula*, chapter 12). Since the introduction of the blood-consuming bats of South America, the bat has become one of the principal images associated with the vampire. Simultaneously, whether a vampire can transform into a bat (or other animal, most often a wolf) has been a continuing topic in vampire literature and cinema, which led several producers to develop movies that featured vampire animals other than bats, most notably the canine vampires of *Zoltan, Hound of Dracula* (aka *Dracula's Dog*, 1978), *I Am Legend* (2007), and *Vampire Dog* (2012).

Far more important that the fictional vampire animals are the many species of animals and even a few plants that consume blood, above and beyond the several species of the vampire bat. Biologists and botanists have been quick to use the vampire metaphor in naming and describing a spectrum of animals around the world, even as Charles Darwin made his observations of the vampire finch of the Galapagos Islands a significant element in his development of the theory of evolution.

There is a huge scientific literature on the vampire-like animals, most of a technical nature, and no attempt has been made to list even a large selection of it, only enough to indicate the spectrum of animals to which the term vampire has been attached. In this regard, Bill Schutt's book, *Dark Banquet*, emerges as a helpful survey of the main vampire-like species. Interestingly, the majority of books (as opposed to articles) that cover vampire animals are texts directed to children and youth that attempt to introduce and refute negative stereotypes of bats, especially the vampire bat.

In the 1990s, vampirism entered the world of cryptozoology, the study of hypothesized animals for which biologists seek proof of their existence, through the modern myth of the chupacabra (or goatsucker), a goat-like animal that has been blamed for causing havoc across the Caribbean and Central America. The chupacabra has spawned a variety of books and articles that repeat encounter stories, ruminate on the possibility of the animal's existence, and/or attempt to debunk the myth.

While not as well-known as the vampire animals, there are a variety of plants that have been seen as vampires, possibly the most notable being the parasitic dodder plant that will attach itself to a nearby host plant and suck its vital fluids. The most famous vampire plant is certainly Audrey, the plant featured in the stage and film versions of *Little Shop of Horrors*.

5613. Allen, Glover Morrill. *Bats.* Cambridge, MA: Harvard University Press, 1939. 368 pp. Rpt.: New York: Dover Publications, 2004. 368 pp.

5614. Bagust, Phil. "Vampire Dogs and Marsupia Hyenas: Fear, Myth, and the Tasmanian Tiger's Extinction." In Carla T. Kungl, ed. *Vampires: Myths and Metaphors of Enduring Evil.* Oxford: Inter-Disciplinary Press, 2003. pp. 45–51. Posted at: http://www.inter-disciplinary.net/publishing/id-press/ebooks/vampires-myths-and-metaphors-of-enduring-evil. Rpt. in: Peter Day, ed. *Vampire: Myths and Metaphors of Enduring Evil.* Amsterdam: Rodopi, 2006, pp. 93–106.

5615. Bartholomew, Robert E., and Benjamin Radford. "The Great Puerto Rican Chupacabra Panic." In Robert E. Bartholomew and Benjamin Radford. *The Martians Have Landed! A History of Media-Driven Panics and Hoaxes.* Jefferson, NC: McFarland & Company, 2012, pp. 182–86.

5616. Bhatnagar, Kunwar P. "Ultrastructure of the Pineal Body of the Common Vampire Bat, *Desmodus rotundus.*" *American Journal of Anatomy* 181, 2 (February 1988): 163–178.

5617. Brown, David E. *Vampiro: Vampire Bat in Fact & Fantasy.* Salt Lake City: University of Utah Press, 1999. 146 pp. tp.

5618. Corrales, Scott. *Chupacabras and Other Mysteries.* Murfreesboro, TN: Greenleaf Publications, 1997. 71 pp.

5619. ____. *Chupacabras Diaries: An Unofficial Chronicle of Puerto Rico's Paranormal Predator.* Derrick City, PA: Samizdat Press, 1996. 248 pp.

5620. ____. "How Many Goats Can a Goatsucker Suck?" *Rage* 12 (July 1997): 32–35.

5621. Denault, Lisa K., and Donald A. Mc-Farlane. "Reciprocal Altruism Between Male Vampire Bats, *Desmodus rotundus*." *Animal Behaviour* 49, 3 (March 1995): 855–856.

5622. Ditmars, Raymond L., and Arthur M. Greenhall. "The Vampire Bat: A Presentation of Undescribed Habits and Review of Its History." *Annual Report Smithsonian Institution* (1936): 27–96. Rpt.: *Zoologica* 19, 2 (April 3, 1935): 53–76. Rpt. in: Jan Perkowski, ed. *Vampires of the Slavs.* Cambridge, MA: Slavica Press, 1976, pp. 368–91.

5623. Fiedler, Joachim, and Fachbereich Biologie. "Prey Catching with and Without Echolocation in the Indian False Vampire (*Megaderma lyra*)." *Behavioral Ecology and Sociobiology* 6, 2 (1979): 155–160.

5624. Greenhall, Arthur M. "The Biting and Feeding Habits of the Vampire Bat, *Desmodus rotundus*." *Journal of Zoology* 168, 4 (2009): 451–461.

5625. _____. *Natural History of Vampire Bats.* Boca Ratón, FL: CRC Press, 1988. 246 pp.

5626. Grzymkowski, Eric. *Attack of the Killer Facts! 1,001 Terrifying Truths About the Little Green Men, Government Mind-Control, Flesh-Eating Bacteria, and Goat-Sucking Vampires.* Avon, MA: Adams Media, 2011. 313 pp. tp.

5627. Hairr, John. "Santer, Vampire Beasts and Other Mystery Mammals." In John Hairr. *Monsters of North Carolina: Mysterious Creatures in the Tar Heel State.* Mechanicsburg, PA: Stackpole Books, 2013, pp. 41–62. Includes a discussion of the vampire-like Beast of Bladenboro, North Carolina.

5628. Hopf, Alice L. *Bats.* New York: Dodd, Mead and Company, 1985. 64 pp.

5629. Luer, Carlyle A. *Systematics of Dracula.* [Saint Louis, Mo.]: Missouri Botanical Garden, 1993. 244 pp.

5630. McMillan, Dennis Wayne. *El Chupacabra.* [Branson, MO]: the author, 2007. 7000-pp. tp.

5631. Meinesz, Alexandre. "The Vampire Slug of the Killer Alga." In Alexandre Meinesz. *How Life Began: Evolution's Three Geneses.* Trans. by Daniel Simberloff. Chicago: University of Chicago Press, 2008, pp. 66–95.

5632. Newton, Michael. *Hidden Animals: A Field Guide to Batsquatch, Chupacabra, and Other Elusive Creatures.* Santa Barbara, CA: Greenwood Press, 2009. 200 pp. hb.

5633. Nickell, Joe. "Chupacabras!" in Joe Nickell. *Tracking the Man Beasts: Sasquatch, Vampires, Zombies, and More.* Amherst, NY: Prometheus Books, 2011, pp. 1241–46.

5634. _____. "The Goatsucker Attack." In Joe Nickell. *The Mystery Chronicles: More Real-Life X-Files.* Lexington: The University Press of Kentucky, 2004, pp. 28–30.

5635. Prokop, Pavol, Jana Fancovicová, and Milan Kubiatko. "Vampires Are Still Alive: Slovakian Students' Attitudes Toward Bats." *Anthrozoos* 22, 1 (2009): 19–30.

5636. Radford, Benjamin. "Slaying the Vampire: Solving the Chupacabra Mystery." *Skeptical Inquirer* 35, 3 (May/June 2011): 45–48.

5637. _____. *Tracking the Chupacabra: The Vampire Beast in Fact, Fiction, and Folklore.* Albuquerque: University of New Mexico Press, 2011. 202 pp. tp.

5638. Rajan, K. E., and G. Marimuthu. "Localization of Prey by the Indian False Vampire Bat *Megaderma lyra*." *Mammalia* 63, 2 (1999): 149–158.

5639. Rice, Barry A. *Growing Carnivorous Plants.* Portland, OR: Timber Press, 2006. 224 pp. hb.

5640. Roosevelt, Theodore. "Vampire Bats and the Highlands of Brazil (1914)." In Zachary Michael Jack, ed. *The Green Roosevelt: Theodore Roosevelt in Appreciation of Wilderness, Wildlife, and Wild Places.* Amherst, NY: Cambria Press, 2010. For this article Jack extracts material from chapter six of Theodore Roosevelt's travel log *Through the Brazilian Wilderness* (New York: Charles Scribner's Sons, 1914).

5641. Schmidt, U., and A. M. Greenhall. "Preliminary Studies of the Interactions Between Feeding Vampire Bats, *Desmodus Rotundus*, Under Natural and Laboratory Conditions." *Mammalia* 36, 2 (1972): 241–246.

5642. Schutt, Bill. *Dark Banquet: Blood and the Curious Lives of Blood-Feeding Creatures.* New York: Harmony Books, 2008. 325 pp. hb. dj. Illust. by Patricia J. Wynne.

5643. Seibel, Brad A., Fabienne Chausson, Francois H. Lallier, Franck Zal, and James J. Childress. "Vampire Blood: Respiratory Physiology of the Vampire Squid (*Cephalopoda: Vampyromorpha*) in relation to the oxygen minimum layer." *Experimental Biology Online* 4, 1 (1999): 1–10.

5644. Steele, Philip. *Vampire Bats and Other Creatures of the Night.* New York: Kingfisher, 1995. 40 pp. pb. Large format. Juvenile.

5645. Tandler, Bernard, and Carleton J. Phillips. "Ultrastructure of the Submandibular Gland of the Rare White-Winged Vampire Bat, Diaemus youngi." *European Journal of Morphology* 40, 4 (2002): 253–256.

5646. Taylor, C. B. "Vampire Plants?" *Plant Cell* 10, 7 (1998): 1071–1074.

5647. Thompson, Ben. "El Chupacabra." In *Badass: The Birth of a Legend: Spine-Crushing Tales of the Most Merciless Gods, Monsters, Heroes, Villains, and Mythical Creatures Ever Envisioned.* New York: HarperPaperbacks, 2011, pp. 341–48.

5648. Turner, Dennis. *The Vampire Bat: A Field Study in Behavior and Ecology.* Baltimore, MD: Johns Hopkins University Press, 1975. 145 pp. hb. dj.

5649. Wilkinson, Gerald S. "Food Sharing in Vampire Bats." *Scientific American* 262, 2 (1990): 76–82.

5650. _____. "Reciprocal Food Sharing in the Vampire Bat." *Nature* 308, 5955 (1984): 181–184.

VIII. The Contemporary Vampire Subculture

The Contemporary Vampire

The contemporary interest in all things vampiric is built around the millions of fans of vampire novels, movies, and games, and the members of the academy who have been interested in understanding how vampires have grown to hold such a place in the popular imagination and culture. The fantastic realm created by novelists, dramatists, musicians and those who make the vampire movies and television shows begs fans to act out their interest, which they do by dressing up as their favorite vampire character (at least for Halloween), spending millions on vampire-oriented merchandise, writing fan fiction, wearing fangs, and participating in a spectrum of fan organizations. The most visible fan gatherings are oriented around either the television series *Dark Shadows*, the multifaceted presence of Dracula, the television series *Buffy the Vampire Slayer*, and the books and movies of the *Twilight* Saga—each of which is treated more fully in its own chapter elsewhere in this volume.

Some fans take their interest to greater extremes. They might, for example, participate in time-consuming vampire role-playing games, the most notable being *Vampire: The Masquerade*. They might adopt what is considered a nocturnal vampire life-style that includes sleeping during the day, making their living at night, and vocalizing their desire to be a vampire. There now exists a large community of people (many of whom found their first outlet in the gaming world) who think of themselves as real vampires and who live their life around their vampire existence. As most "real" vampires see themselves as consumers of life energy rather than blood, the literature they produce flows almost imperceptivity into the psychic vampirism considered in the section on "Psychological Perspectives." While most "real" psychic vampires merely attempt to exchange psychic energy with donors, a few actually drink blood.

A singular controversial incident, involving hunter-of-real-vampires Sean Manchester and claims of the killing of a vampire, occurred at Highgate cemetery in London, and has provoked considerable comment. While most did not take the incident seriously, it had legal ramifications and provided evidence for critics of the modern interest in vampires that such interest leads to psychological problems and even crime. The primary criminal incident centered on vampire gamer Rod Ferrell, who allowed his vampire fantasies to lead to multiple murders.

The contemporary vampire community now also includes hundreds of scholars who have made the study of vampires a major segment of their academic career. The great majority of these scholars are found in either literature departments where they specialize in one phase or the other of nineteenth or twentieth century English literature, or film and television departments as specialists in horror cinema or popular culture. However, the academic vampire community now stretches across the many disciplines from psychology and medicine to religion, sociology, and political science. The vast literature generated, of course, provides a mountain of material to lure librarians and bibliographers to the spectacle.

The existence of real vampires was first announced by parapsychologist Stephen Kaplan, who attempted a first census in the early 1980s. That initial effort has now been taken over by a new generation of observers of the real vampire community, which keeps somewhat of a low profile on the edge of the more visible vampire fan community.

5651. Ali, Asim. *Subjacent Culture, Orthogonal Community: An Ethnographic Analysis of an On-Line* Buffy the Vampire Slayer *Fan Community.* College Park: University of Maryland, Ph.D. dissertation, 2013. Large format.

5652. Allman, Kevin. "Modern-day Vampires." *Farout* 1, 2 (Winter 1992): 52–54.

5653. Amy-Chinn, Dee, and Milly Williamson, eds. *The Vampire Spike in Text and Fandom: Unsettling Oppositions in* Buffy the Vampire Slayer. Special Issue of *European Journal of Cultural Studies* 8, 3 (August 2005).

5654. Arnold, Neil. *Paranormal London.* Stroud, UK: The History Press, 2011, 96 pp. tp. See especially, chapter three, "The Highgate Vampire.."

5655. Arthen, Inanna. "Real Vampires." *FireHeart* 2 (1989). Posted at http://www.earthspirit.com/fireheart/fhvampire.html.

5656. Ashantison, Belfazaar. *Beneath the Sheltering Oak.* Fort Wayne, IN: Dark Moon Press, 2013. The author founded the House of Mystic Echoes, a vampiric house operating out of a magical and/or mystical tradition, and a founding member of the New Orleans Vampire Association.

5657. Ashjorn, Jon A. "The Psychic Vampire and Vampyre Subculture." *Australian Folklore* 12 (2002): 143–48.

5658. Baddeley, Gavin. *Goth: Vamps and Dandies.* London: Plexus Publishing, 2010. 159 pp. tp.

5659. _____. *Goth Chic: A Gothic Guide to Dark Culture.* London: Plexus, 2002. 288 pp. tp.

5660. Bandy, Elizabeth A. *Growing up with* Buffy: *How Adolescent Female Fans Use the Program in Their Everyday Lives.* Stanford, CA: Stanford University, Ph.D. dissertation, 2007. 194 pp. Large format.

5661. Barker, Meg. "Vampires for the Modern Mind: Vampire Subcultures. In Peter Day, ed. *Vampire: Myths and Metaphors of Enduring Evil.* Amsterdam: Rodopi, 2006, pp. 109–24.

5662. Barlow, M. "Bloodlust in the 90's" *Blue Blood* 1 (1992): 15.

5663. Belanger, Michelle A. *House Kheperu Archives: The Outer Teachings of House Kheperu.* Brunswick, OH: Emerald Tablet Press, 2011. 314 pp. tp.

5664. _____. *Psychic Vampire Codex: Manual of Magick & Energy Work.* Weiser Books: York Beach, ME, 2004. 284 pp. tp.

5665. _____. *Sacred Hunger.* Fort Wayne, IN: Dark Moon Press, 2005. 142 pp. tp.

5666. _____. *The Vampire Ritual Book.* North N.p.: the author, 2007. 162 pp. tp.

5667. _____. *Vampires in Their Own Words: An Anthology of Vampire Voices.* Weiser Books: York Beach, ME, 2007. 245 pp. tp.

5668. _____. *Walking the Twilight Path: A Gothic Book of the Dead.* Woodbury, MN: Llewellyn Publications, 2008. 307 pp. tp.

5669. Bibeau, Paul. *Sundays with Vlad: From Pennsylvania to Transylvania, One Man's Quest to Live in the World of the Undead.* New York: Three Rivers Press, 2007. 292 pp. tp.

5670. Bjorling, Joel. "Vampires Among Us: A Walk on the Dark Side." *Fate* 49, 2 (February 1996): 44–47.

5671. Blair, Briana. *We Are the Undead, or Are We? Companion: A Collection of Vampire Articles.* N.p.: the author, 2012. tp.

5672. _____. *We Are the Undead, or Are We? Unraveling Your Favorite Vampire Myths and Mysteries.* N.p.: the author, 2011. tp.

5673. Bowman, Sarah Lynne. "'We Only Come Out at Night': An Overview of Vampire Role-Playing." In Carla T. Kungl, ed. *Vampires: Myths and Metaphors of Enduring Evil.* Oxford: Inter-Disciplinary Press, 2003, pp. 129–32. Posted at http://www.inter-disciplinary.net/publishing/id-press/ebooks/vampires-myths-and-metaphors-of-enduring-evil.

5674. Bucher, John K., Jr. *There Is Power in the Blood: Faith and the Rising Vampire in Popular Culture.* Los Angeles, CA : Gray Matter Books, 2011. 150 pp. tp.

5675. Campbell, Ramsey. "The Strange Case of Sean Manchester." In In Stefan Jaworzyn, ed. *Shock Xpress, 1.* London: Titan, 1991. Rev. text in: Ramsey Campbell. *Ramsey Campbell Probably: On Horror and Sundry Fantasies.* Ed. by S. T. Joshi. Hornsea, East Yorkshire, UK: PS Publishing, 2002, pp. 139–50.

5676. CG, Lady. *Practical Vampyrism for Modern Vampyres.* N.p.: Lulu.com, 2005. 168 pp. tp.

5677. Cochran, Tanya R. *Toward a Rhetoric of Scholar-Fandom.* Atlanta: Georgia State University, Ph.D. dissertation, 2009. 246 pp. Large format. Posted at: http://digitalarchive.gsu.edu/english_diss/51.

5678. *The Count Dracula Fan Club Handbook.* New York: Count Dracula Fan Club, n.d. 20pp. pb. Staples.

5679. Crossen, John F. "Funny Draculas & Lady Draculas." *Autograph Times* 4, 10 (November/December 1997): 32–37.

5680. _____. "Happy Birthday, Mr. Dracula!" *Autograph Times* 4, 10 (November/December 1997): 39–43.

5681. _____. "The Toughest Top Five Collecting Dracula." *Autograph Times* 4, 11 (January 1998): 16–19.

5682. _____. "Your Friend, Dracula: A Century of the Count's Autographs." *Autograph Times* 4, 9 (October 1977) 14–19.

5683. Diamantis, Sophie. "Dr. Jeanne Keyes Youngson and the Count Dracula Fan Club Museum." *Delirium* 3 (1996): 38–40.

5684. Donovan, Dale A. "My Dad's Vlad." *Dragon* 15, 5 (162) (October 1990).

5685. Double, Krystalle. *Female Roles and Fan Fiction in* Charmed, Supernatural, *and* Buffy the Vampire Slayer. Kalamazoo: Western Michigan University, BA honors thesis, 2013. 46 pp. Large format. Posted at: http://scholarworks.wmich.edu/honors_theses/2221.

5686. Dresser, Norine. *American Vampires: Fans, Victims, Practitioners.* New York: W. W. Norton & Company, 1989. 255 pp. hb. dj. Rpt.: New York: Vintage Books, 1990. 255 pp. tp. Excerpt rpt. in: Angela Cybulski, ed. *Vampires: Fact or Fiction?* Ser.: Opposing Viewpoints. Farmington Hills, MI: Greenhaven Press/Thomson, Gale, 2003. pp. 61–68, 136–45. Excerpt rpt. in: David Skal, ed. *Vampires: Encounters with the Undead.* New York: Black Dog & Leventhal Publishers, 2001, pp. 495–514.

5687. Elden, Gro. *The Buffyverse and Its Inhabitants: A Study of Fans of* Buffy the Vampire Slayer. Amsterdam, Netherlands, International School for Humanities and Social Sciences, Universiteit van Amsterdam, M.A. thesis, 2002.

5688. Ellis, Bill. "The Highgate Cemetery Vampire Hunt: The Anglo-American Connection in Satanic Cult Lore." *Folklore* 104 (1993): 13–39. Posted at http://www.jstor.org/stable/pdfplus/1260794.pdf?acceptTC=true&jpdConfirm=true. Rpt. in: Bill Ellis. *Raising the Devil: Satanism, New Religions, and the Media.* Lexington: University Press of Kentucky, 2000, pp. 202–39.

5689. Erzen, Tanya. *Fanpire: The Twilight Saga and the Women Who Love It.* Boston, MA: Beacon Press, 2012. 158 pp. tp.

5690. Farrant, David. *Beyond the Highgate Vampire.* London: British Psychic and Occult Society, 1991. pb. Second rev, ed.: London: British Psychic and Occult Society, 1992. 43 pp. pb. Staples. Third rev. ed.: London: British Psychic and Occult Society, 1997. 43 pp. pb. Staples. Third rev. ed.: London: British Psychic and Occult Society, 2002. 63 pp. pb. Staples.

5691. _____. *David Farrant: Out of the Shadows. An Autobiography*, Volume II. London: The British Psychic and Occult Society, 2011. 231 pp. tp.

5692. _____. *The Vampire Syndrome: The Truth Behind the Highgate Vampire Legend.* London: Mutiny! Press, 2000. 65 pp. pb. Staples.

5693. Ford, Michael. *Akhkharu—Vampyre Magick.* N.p.: Lulu.com, 2008. 300 pp. tp.

5694. _____. *Book of the Witch Moon: Chaos, Vampiric & Luciferian Sorcery.* Salt Lake City, UT: Succubus Publishing, 2006. 456 pp. tp.

5695. _____. *Shadows of Azathoth: Horrific Tales of Vampiric Darkness.* Houston, TX: Succubus Productions, 2011. 115 pp. tp.

5696. Garza, Thomas Jesus. "From Russia with Blood: Imagining the Vampire in Contemporary Russian Popular Culture." In Barbara Brodman and James E. Doan, eds. *The Universal Vampire: Origins and Evolution of a Legend.* Madison, NJ: Fairleigh Dickinson University Press, 2013, pp. 195–207.

5697. Gittens, Allen J. "On the Perils of Running The Vampyre Society." In Rosemary Ellen Guiley, with J. B. Macabre. *The Complete Vampire Companion.* New York: Macmillan, 1994, pp. 180–81.

5698. Goddard, Lauren M. E., and Michael Bibby, eds. *Goth: Undead Subculture.* Durham, NC: Duke University Press, 2007. 442 pp. tp.

5699. Goddu, Teresa A. "Vampire Gothic." *American Literary History* 11 (1999): 125–141.

5700. Grady, Fred. "Vampire Culture." In Jeffrey Jerome Cohen, ed. *Monster Theory: Reading Culture.* Minneapolis: University of Minnesota Press, 1996, pp. 225–41.

5701. Grant, Kenneth. *Gamaliel: The Diary of a Vampire, and Dance, Doll, Dance!* London: Starfire Publishing 2003. 158 pp. hb. dj. Limited to 1000 copies.

5702. Grubb, Jeff. "Big Drak Attack." *Dragon* 12, 5 (128) (October 1987).

5703. Guiley, Rosemary Ellen. *Vampires Among Us.* New York: Pocket Books, 1991. 270 pp. pb. Excerpt rpt. in: David Skal, ed. *Vampires: Encounters with the Undead.* New York: Black Dog & Leventhal Publishers, 2001, pp. 523–40.

5704. Guinn, Jeff, with Andy Grieser. *Something in the Blood: The Underground World of Today's Vampires.* Arlington, TX: The Summit Publishing Group, 1996. 204 pp. hb. pb.

5705. Habjan, R. Monk. *Revelations: An Interview with Vampyyri Adrian.* Reading UK: Coxland Press, 1994. 78 pp.

5706. Hallab, Mary Y. *Vampire God: The Allure of the Undead in Western Culture.* Albany: State University Press of New York, 2009. 169 pp. tp. *Vampire God: The Allure of the Undead in Western Culture* received the 2010 award for the best nonfiction book of the previous year given annually by the Lord Ruthven Society.

5707/08. Heiman, Leo. "Meet the Real Count Dracula." *Fate* 21, 3 (March 1968): 53–60. Rpt. in: Peter Haining, ed. *The Dracula Scrapbook.* New York: Bramwell House, 1976, pp. 165–71. Re: Count Alexander Cepesi, a contemporary descendant of Vlad Tepes.

5709. Icke, David. *The Biggest Secret.* Scottsdale, AZ: Bridges of Love, 1999. 517 pp. tp.

5710. _____. *Children of the Matrix: How an Interdimensional Race Has Controlled the World for Thousands of Years—and Still Does.* Ryde, Isle of Wight, UK: David Icke Books, 2001. 501 pp. tp.

5711. Icoz, Mursel. "The Un-Dead: To Be Feared or/and Pitied." In Carla T. Kungl, ed. *Vampires: Myths and Metaphors of Enduring Evil.* Oxford: Inter-Disciplinary Press, 2003. pp. 67–72. Posted at http://www.inter-disciplinary.net/publishing/id-press/ebooks/vampires-myths-and-metaphors-of-enduring-evil. Rpt. in: Peter Day, ed. *Vampire: Myths and Metaphors of Enduring Evil.* Amsterdam: Rodopi, 2006, pp. 209–26.

5712. In Highgate Cemetery. London: Friends of Highgate Cemetery, 1992. 20 pp. pb. Staples.

5713. Issitt, Micah L. *Goths: A Guide to an American Subculture.* Santa Barbara. CA: Greenwood Press, 2011. 159 pp. hb.

5714. Jarvis, Sharon. "Dark Shadows." In Sharon Jarvis. *True Tales of the Unknown: The Uninvited.* New York: Bantam Books, 1989, pp. 20–36. Vampire researcher Stephen Kaplan visit a *Dark Shadows* convention as the guest lecturer.

5715. Jefferson, Darnell. *Vampire 101: The Complete Guide to Becoming a Vampire.* Parker. CO: Outskirts Press, 2010. 178 pp. tp.

5716. Jenkins, Henry, with Henry G. Jenkins IV. "'The Monsters Next Door': A Father-Son Dialogue About *Buffy*, Moral Panic, and Generational Differences." In Henry Jenkins, with Henry G. Jenkins IV. *Fans, Bloggers, and Gamers: Media Consumers in a Digital Age.* New York: New York University Press, 2006, pp. 226–248.

5717. Johansen, Vibeke. *'The Divine Exists in Cyberspace Same as Out Here': Academics and the Internet Fan-Scholars of* Buffy the Vampire Slayer. Nathan, Aust.: Griffith University, BA honors thesis, 2004.

5718. Johnson, V. M. *Dhampir: Child of the Blood.* Fairfield, CT: Mystic Rose Books, 1996. 139 pp. tp.

5719. Kaldera, Raven. *The Ethical Psychic Vampire.* N.p.: Xlibris, 2005. 2nd ed.: Hubbardston, MA: Elkhorn Press, 2008. 150 pp. tp.

5720. Kaplan, Stephen. "On the Vampire Scene. *Journal of Vampirism* 1, 3 (Spring 1978): 9–12.

5721. _____. *Pursuit of Premature Gods and Contemporary Vampires*. South Setauket, Long Island, NY: Vampire Research Center of America, 1976. 261 pp. tp.

5722. _____. *Vampires Are*. Palm Springs, CA: ETC Publications, 1984. 191 pp. tp.

5723. Keyworth, David. "The Socio-Religious Beliefs and Nature of the Contemporary Vampire Subculture." *Journal of Contemporary Religion* 17, 3 (2002): 355–370.

5724. Kilpatrick, Nancy. *The Goth Bible: A Compendium for the Darkly Inclined*. New York: St. Martin's Griffin, 2004. 281 pp. tp. Rpt. London: Medford, NJ: Plexus Publishing, 2005. 281 pp. tp.

5725. King, Marie. "A Real Vampire: A Talk on the Wild Side" *True News* 1, 2 (December 1992): 23–26.

5726. Kirby, Danielle. *Fantasy and Belief: Alternative Religions, Popular Narratives and Digital Cultures*. Durham, UK: Acumen Publishing, 2013. 224 pp. hb. Kirby places vampires within the context of the Otherkin, a loosely related community of individuals who believe themselves to be in some way non-human.

5727. Kirby-Diaz, Mary, ed. *Buffy and Angel Conquer the Internet: Essays on Online Fandom*. Jefferson, NC: McFarland & Company, 2009. 219 pp. tp. The editor has also included essays by Elizabeth L. Rambo, Rebecca Bley, Asim Ali, David Kociemba, Claudia Rebaza, and Kathryn Hill.

5728. Klein, Ian G. *"New lines": The Fan and Textual Poaching in the Work of Joss Whedon*. Seattle: University of Washington, BA honors thesis, 2008. A paper originally presented in shortened form at SC3: The Slayage Conference on the Whedonverses, Henderson State College, Arkadelphia, AR, June 5–8, 2008.

5729. Konstantinos. *Vampires: The Occult Truth*. St. Paul, MN: Llewellyn Publications, 1996. 194 pp. tp.

5730. Kovattana, Amanda. "Confessions of a Lesbian Vampire." In Karla Jay, ed. *Dyke Life: From Growing Up to Growing Old, a Celebration of the Lesbian Experience*. New York: Basic Books, 1995, pp. 207–11.

5731. Landers, Jessica Marie. *The Modern Vampire Phenomenon Paradox: Simultaneous Contradictions and Unlimited Limits*. New Brunswick: Rutgers, The State University of New Jersey, M.A. thesis, 2011. 86 pp. Large format. Posted at: http://rucore.libraries.rutgers.edu/rutgers-lib/31111/.

5732. Langley, Patsy. *The Highgate Vampire Casebook: 1*. London: British Psychic & Occult Society, 2010. 56 pp. pb.

5733. Latham, Robert. *Consuming Youth: Vampires, Cyborgs, and the Culture of Consumption*. Chicago: University of Chicago Press, 2002. 321 pp. hb. & tp.

5734. Laycock, Joseph. "Real Vampires as an Identity Group: Analysing Causes and Effects of an Introspective Survey by the Vampire Community." *Nova Religio—The Journal of Alternative and Emergent Religions* 14, 1 (August 2010): 4–23. Rpt. in: Adam Possamai, ed. *Handbook of Hyper-real Religions*. Ser.: Brill Handbooks on Contemporary Religion. Leiden: Brill, 2012, pp. 141–63.

5735. _____. *Vampires Today: The Truth About Modern Vampirism*. Westport. CT: Praeger, 2009. 200 pp. hb. dj.

5736. Lera, Thomas. "Dracula, Prince of Many Faces." *The American Philatelist* 114, 10 (October 2000): 914–919.

5737. Lilley, Jessie. "I was a Teenage Vampyre." *Scarlet Street* 10 (Spring 1993): 50–52. Interview with Richard Dempsey.

5738. Lindgren Leavenworth, Maria, and Malin Isaksson. *Fanged Fan Fiction: Variations on Twilight, True Blood and The Vampire Diaries*. Jefferson, NC: McFarland & Co., 2013. 228 pp.

5739. Lyon, Michelle, with Mark C. MacKinnon. *Hellsing*. Guelph, ON: Guardians of Order, 2002. 80 pp. pb. Large format. Gaming.

5740. Maasik, Sonia, and Jack Solomon. "Interpreting Popular Signs: The Modern Vampire." In Sonia Maasik and Jack Solomon. *Signs of Life in the USA: Readings on Popular Culture for Writers*. Boston, MA: Bedford/St. Martin's, 2011, pp. 13–18.

5741. Manchester, Sean. "The Highgate Vampire." In Underwood, Peter, ed. *The Vampire's Bedside Companion: The Amazing World of Vampires in Fact and Fiction*. London: Leslie Frewin, 1975, pp. 81–121.

5742. _____. *The Highgate Vampire: The Infernal World of the Undead Unearthed at London's Highgate Cemetery and Environs*. London: Gnostic Press, 1985. 172 pp. Rev. ed.: London: The Gothic Press, 1991. 188 pp. hb. dj.

5743. _____. *The Vampire Hunter's Handbook.* London: Gothic Press, 1997. 96pp.

5744. McCarthy, Elizabeth. "'Death to vampires!': The Vampire Body and the Meaning of Mutilation." In Carla T. Kungl, ed. *Vampires: Myths and Metaphors of Enduring Evil.* Oxford: Inter-Disciplinary Press, 2003. pp. 78–77. Posted at http://www.inter-disciplinary.net/publishing/id-press/ebooks/vampires-myths-and-metaphors-of-enduring-evil. Rpt. in: Peter Day, ed. *Vampire: Myths and Metaphors of Enduring Evil.* Amsterdam: Rodopi, 2006, pp. 189–208.

5745. Medway, Gareth J. *In Search of the Truth.* London: British Psychic and Occult Society, 2002. 8pp. pb. Staples. Includes cd.

5746. Mellins, Maria. "Fashioning a Morbid Identity: Female Vampire Fans and Subcultural Style." In Brigid Cherry, Peter Howell, and Caroline Ruddell. *Twenty-first–century Gothic.* Newcastle on Tyne, UK: Cambridge Scholars Publishing, 2010, pp. 127–48.

5747. _____. "The Female Vampire Community and Online Social Networks: Virtual Celebrity and Mini Communities: Initial Thoughts." *International Journal of Media and Cultural Politics* 4, 2 (2008): 254–258.

5748. _____. *Vampire Culture (Dress, Body, Culture).* London: Bloomsbury Academic, 2013. 160 pp. hb. & tp.

5749. Meyer, Robert J. *Vampirism as an Alternate Lifestyle and the Most Complete List Ever Compiled of Vampires Throughout History.* Princeton, NJ: The Vampire Press, n.d. 4 pp. pb. Small format.

5750. Milne, Rob. *Return of the Vampire Hunter: An Exclusive Interview with Reclusive Vampire Hunter David Farrant.* London: The British Psychic and Occult Society, 2003. 51 pp.

5751. Milspaw, Yvonne J., and Wesley K. Evans. "Variations on Vampires: Live Action Role Playing, Fantasy and the Revival of Traditional Beliefs." *Western Folklore* 69, 2 (Spring 2010): 211ff.

5752. Myhre, Brian Lawrence. *Virtual Societies, a Journey of Powertrips & Personalities. A Dramaturgical and Ethnographic Study of Winnipeg's Original Live-Action Vampire the Masquerade Roleplaying Game Community.* Winnipeg, University of Manitoba, M.A. thesis, 1998. 353 pp. Large format.

5753. Nixon, Dorothy. "Comic Book Art, Engineering Principles, and the Highgate Vampire" *Journal of Vampirism* 2, 1 (Fall 1978): 16–17.

5754. Nocturnum, Corvis [pseudonym of E. R. Vernor]. *Allure of the Vampire: Our Sexual Attraction to the Undead.* Fort Wayne, IN: Dark Moon Press, 2009. 284 pp. tp.

5755. _____. *Embracing the Darkness; Understanding Dark Subcultures.* Fort Wayne, IN: Dark Moon Press, 2005. 234 pp. tp.

5756. _____. *Goth Girls, Vampire Vixen's, and Satan's Sirens.* Fort Wayne, IN: Dark Moon Press/ Old Nick Magazine, 2012. 198 pp. tp.

5757. Nuzum, Eric. *The Dead Travel Fast: Stalking Vampires from Nosferatu to Count Chocula.* New York: Thomas Dunne Press/St. Martin's Press, 2007. 242 pp. hb. dj.

5758. Nyarlathotep, Frater, and Jesse Lindsay, with Alexandria Martinez. *Ardeth: The Made Vampire.* Morrisville, NC: Lulu Enterprises, 2006. 221 pp. tp.

5759. Nyght, Mickal. *Teachings of the Immortals.* N.p.: Immortalis-Animus.com/Eye Scry Publications, 2010. Rev. ed.: 2013. 224 pp. tp.

5760. O'Donnell, Elliott. "The Vampire Society." In Peter Haining, ed . *The Dracula Scrapbook.* New York: Bramwell House, 1976, pp. 135–39. O'Donnell claims to have been initiated into a vampire cult early in the twentieth century.

5761. Oviedo, Marilda. *A Qualitative Study of Typology in* Buffy the Vampire Slayer *Fanfiction.* Lubbock: Texas Tech University, M.A. thesis, 2007. 99 pp. Large format. Posted at: http://repositories.tdl.org/ttu-ir/bitstream/handle/2346/14528/Oviedo_Marilda_Thesis.pdf?sequence=1.

5762. Page, Carol. *Bloodlust: Conversations with Real Vampires.* New York: HarperCollins, 1991. 192 pp. hb. dj. Rpt.: New York: Dell, 1991. 214 pp. pb. Rpt.: London: Warner Books, 1993. 232 pp. pb.

5763. Paglia, Camille. *Sexual Personae: Art and Decadence from Nefertiti to Emily Dickinson.* New Haven, CT: Yale University Press, 1990. 718 pp. hb. Rpt.: New York: Vintage Books, 1991. 718 pp. tp.

5764. _____. *Vamps and Tramps: New Essays.* New York: Vintage, 1994. 532 pp. tp.

5765. Palmer, Paulina. *Lesbian Gothic: Transgressive Fictions.* London: Cassell, 1999. 168 pp. See especially chapter 4, "The Vampire: Transgressive Sexuality," pp. 99–127.

5766. Partridge, Christopher. "Contemporary Vampire Culture." In Christopher Partridge

The Re-Enchantment of the West. Vol 2: Alternative Spiritualities, Sacralization, Popular Culture and Occulture. London: Bloomsbury T&T Clark, 2006, pp. 230–38.

5767. Peterson, Eric, as told to Roberta H. Greenbaum. *I Was a Transvestite Vampire.* Princeton, NJ: The Vampire Press, 1990. 16 pp. pb. Staples.

5768. Poole, Jamie. *Vampires in Our Midst: A Look at Vampires in Our Culture.* London: Janus Publishing Company, 2006. 85 pp. pb.

5769. Poole, W. Scott. "The Vampire That Haunts Highgate: Theological Evil, Hammer Horror, and the Highgate Vampire Panic in Britain, 1963–1979." In Kim Paffenroth and John W. Morehead, eds. *The Undead and Theology.* Eugene, OR: Pickwick Publications, 2012, pp. 54–76.

5770. Porter, Patrick J. *Stories from the Buffyverse: Intertextuality, Temporality and the Cult Fandom of* Buffy the Vampire Slayer. Melbourne, Aust.: University of Melbourne, M.A. thesis, 2007. 131 pp. Large format.

5771. Power, Albert. "A Concise History of the Bram Stoker Society." Dublin: Bram Stoker Society, 2006. 22 pp. A paper published on the cd collecting the 13 annual issues of the *Bram Stoker Society Journal.*

5772. PVN, Frater. *Vampires and the Aristocracy of Blood: Being an Esoteric Legacy of the Holy Grail.* Ser.: Alchemical Notes West Danby, NY: Boleskine House, 1983. 54 pp. tp.

5773. Ramsland, Katherine. "Hunger for the Marvelous: The Vampire Craze in the Computer Age." *Psychology Today* (November 1989): 32–5.

5774. _____. *Piercing the Darkness: Undercover with the Vampires in America Today.* New York: HarperPrism, 1998. 371 pp. hb. dj. Rpt. New York: Harper, 1999. 546 pp. pb.

5775. _____. *The Science of Vampires.* New York: Berkley Boulevard Books, 2002. 276 pp. tp.

5776. Riccardo, Martin V. "Vampire Reports in Modern History." *Anomaly Research Bulletin* (Special Non-Lenear Issue) (1978): 14–20.

5777. Robinson, J. M. *C.R.A.V.E.S. (Cloned Reptilian Alien Vampire Engineered Species).* Baltimore, MD: PublishAmerica, 2004. tp.

5778. Rodriquez Y Gibson, Siôn. *Vampire the Masquerade Redemption: Official Strategy Guide.* Indianapolis, IN: Brady Publishing, 2000. 239 pp. tp.

5779. Ross, Sharon M. *Super(natural) Women: Female Heroes, Their Friends, and Their Fans.* Austin: University of Texas, Ph.D. dissertation, 2002. Large format.

5780. Ruane, Richard T. *Performing "Camp, Vamp and Femme Fatale": Revisiting, Reinventing and Retelling the Lives of Post-Death, Retro-Gothic Women.* Denton: University of North Texas, M.A. thesis, 1999. 72 pp. Large format. Posted at http://digital.library.unt.edu/ark:/67531/metadc2239/m1/1/.

5781. Russo, Arlene. *Vampire Nation.* London: John Blake Publishing, 2005. 277 pp. tp. Rpt. as: *The Real Twilight: True Stories of Modern Day Vampires.* London: John Blake Publishing, 2010. 277 pp. tp.

5782. Sanguinarius. *The Dictionary of Sanguinese: Terminology and Lingo in the Vampire Community.* N.p.: Sanguinarius.org 2008. 64 pp. tp. Rev. ed. as *The Dictionary of Vampspeak: Terminology and Lingo in the Vampire Community.* Charleston, SC: Sangunarius.org, 2008. 51 pp. tp.

5783. _____. *What Do You Think Vampires Are Like? Vampire Poll Responses.* Topeka, KS: Sanguinarius.org, 2009. 120 pp. tp.

5784. Schau, Hope Jensen, and Margo Buchanan-Oliver. "The Creation of Inspired Lives: Female Fan Engagement with the Twilight Saga." In Cele C. Otnes and Linda Tuncay Zayer, eds. *Gender, Culture, and Consumer Behavior.* New York: Routledge, 2012, pp. 33–60.

5785. Scherf, Manuela. *Character Formation in Fan Fiction Based on Popular TV Series.* Vienna, Austria: Universität Wien [University of Vienna], M.A. thesis, 2008. 155 pp. Large format. Posted at http://othes.univie.ac.at/3061/1/2008-11-30_0204277.pdf.

5786. Schnoebelen, William. *Romancing Death: A True Story of Vampirism, Death, the Occult, and Deliverance.* Shippensburg, PA: Destiny Image Publishers, 2012. 285 pp. tp.

5787. _____, and Sharon Schnoebelen. *Lucifer Dethroned.* Chino, CA: Chick Publications, 1993. 349 pp. tp. See especially chapter 18, "Speaking from the Inferno.."

5788. Schoot, Gareth, and Kirstine Moffat. *Fanpires: Audience Consumption of the Modern Vampire.* Washington, DC: New Academia Publishing, 2011. 354 pp. tp.

5789. Schopp, Andrew. "Cruising the Alternatives: Homoeroticism and the Contemporary Vampire." *Journal of Popular Culture* 30, 4 (Spring 1997); 231–43.

5790. Sebastian, Father. *The Sabertook Clan Book.* N.p.: Sabertooth Press, 2010. 148 pp. tp. Limited to 1,000 copies.

5791. _____. *Vampyre Almanac 2000.* New York: The Sanguinarian, 2000. 144 pp. pb.

5792. _____. *Vampyre Almanac 2006.* New York: Rakasha Books, 2006. 203 pp. tp.

5793. _____. *Vampyre Virtues: The Red Veils.* N.p.: Sabertooth Press, 2011. 148 pp. tp.

5794. _____, **and Katherine Ramsland.** *Vampire Almanac: 1998–1999 Edition.* New York: Endless Night, 1998. 180 pp. pb.

5795. _____, **with Konstantinos.** *Vampire Sanguinomicon: The Lexicon of the Living Vampire.* San Francisco, CA: Red Wheel/Weiser, 2010. 286 pp. tp.

5796. _____, **and Michael W. Ford.** *Vampyre Magick: The Grimoire of the Living Vampire.* San Francisco: Weiser Books, 2012. 208 pp.

5797. Shipp, Josh. "Vampires." In Josh Shipp. *The Teen's Guide to World Domination: Advice on Life, Liberty, and the Pursuit of Awesomeness.* New York: St. Martin's Griffin, 2010, pp. 82–91.

5798. Siebert, Maria Verena. "Kidult Readers: The cross-generational appeal of *Harry Potter* and *Twilight.* In Mariah Larsson and Ann Steiner, eds. *Interdisciplinary Approaches to Twilight Studies in Fiction, Media and a Contemporary Cultural Experience.* Lund, Sweden: Nordic Academic Press, 2011, pp. 213–226.

5799. Siegel, Carol. "Identity Hunter D: Asian American Goths and New Masculinities." In Carol Siegal. *Goth's Dark Empire.* Bloomington: Indiana University Press, 2005, pp. 137–56.

5800. Skal, David. "An Interview with a 'Vampire.'" In David Skal, ed. *Vampires: Encounters with the Undead.* New York: Black Dog & Leventhal Publishers, 2001, pp. 215–22.

5801. Smith, Kalila Katherina. *New Orleans Ghosts and Vampires: Journey into Darkness...* New Orleans, LA: De Simonin Publications, 2004. 178 pp. tp.

5802. Snyder, Stephen T. *Dracula's Cohort.* New York: Vampire Research Foundation, n.d. 4 pp. pb. Staples.

5803. Steiger, Brad. "The Horror of Vampires and Ghouls." In Brad Steiger. *Monsters Among Us.* Rockport, MA: ParaResearch, 1982. Rpt.: New York: Berkley, 1989, pp. 119–41. Rpt. Lakeville, MN: Galde Press, 2006, pp. 119–41.

5804. _____. *Real Vampires, Night Stalkers, and Creatures of the Darkside.* Detroit: Visible Ink, 2009. 287 pp. tp.

5805. Stinehill, Paul. "An Interview with Russian Vampires." *Fate* 47, 2 (February 1996): 47.

5806. Stuller, Jennifer Kate, ed. *Fan Phenomena:* Buffy the Vampire Slayer. Bristol, UK: Intellect Press, 2013. 164 pp. tp. Rpt.: Chicago: Intellect, 2013. 164 pp. tp. Includes contributions by Tanya R. Cockran, Mary Kirby-Diaz, Nikki Stafford, Liz Medendorp, Amy Peloff and David Broader Giles, Rhonda Wilcox, Lorna Jowett, Kristen Julia Anderson, Nikki Faith Fuller, Anthony R, Mills, Scott Allie, and David Bushman and Arthur Smith, with an interview of Clinton McClung.

5807. Tobias, James. "The Vampire and the Cyborg Embrace: Affect Beyond Fantasy in Virtual Materialism." In Carla T. Kungl, ed. *Vampires: Myths and Metaphors of Enduring Evil.* Oxford: Inter-Disciplinary Press, 2003. pp. 11–15. Posted at: http://www.inter-disciplinary.net/publishing/id-press/ebooks/vampires-myths-and-metaphors-of-enduring-evil. Rpt. in: Peter Day, ed. *Vampire: Myths and Metaphors of Enduring Evil.* Amsterdam: Rodopi, 2006, pp. 159–76.

5808. Underwood, Peter. "Vampires and Highgate Cemetery." In Peter Enderwood. *The Vampire's Bedside Companion: The Amazing World of Vampires in Fact and Fiction.* London: Leslie Frewin, 1975, pp. 75–80.

5809. *The Vampire Directory.* Metarie, LA: Realm of the Vampire, [1994]. Unpaged. pb. Staples.

5810. *The Vampire Empire Handbook.* New York: Dracula Press, 2003. 22p. pb. Staples.

5811. Vampire Regeneration Movement. *Initiation into the Vampiric Arts.* N.p.: 2008. 109 pp. tp.

5812. *The Vampire's Bible.* Lacey, WA: Temple of the Vampire, 2009. 46 pp. tp.

5813. Vanir, Father J. P. "ChrstVampyr." *TempleUVUP Vampyrian Bible: Vampyr Spirituality.* N.p.: Lulu.com, 2010. 256 pp. tp.

5814. Varney, Bertena. *Lure of the Vampire: A Pop Culture Reference Book of Lists, Websites and*

Very Personal Essays. Bowling Green KY: the author, 2011. 160 pp. tp.

5815. Venters, Jillian. *Gothic Charm School: An Essential Guide for Goths and Those Who Love Them.* New York: Harper, 2009. 236 pp. tp.

5816. Voltaire. *What Is Goth? Music, Makeup, Attitude, Apparel, Dance, and General Skullduggery.* Boston: Weiser Books, 2004. 96 pp. hb. boards.

5817. Williams, DJ. "Contemporary Vampires and (Blood-Red) Leisure: Should We Be Afraid of the Dark?" *Leisure/loisir* 32, 2 (2008): 513–539.

5818. Williams, Emyr, Mandy Robbins, and Laura Picton. "Adolescent Television Viewing and Belief in Vampires." *Journal of Beliefs & Values—Studies in Religion & Education* 27, 2 (2006): 227–229.

5819. Williams, Rebecca. *Spoiler Whores and Shipper Wars: Hierarchy and Power in the On-Line* Buffy the Vampire Slayer *Fan Community.* Cardiff, Wales, UK: Cardiff University, M.A. thesis, 2003. Large format.

5820. Williamson, Milly. *The Lure of the Vampire: Gender, Fiction and Fandom from Bram Stoker to Buffy the Vampire Slayer.* London: Wallflower Press, 2005. 224 pp. tp.

5821. Winslade, J. Lawton. "Teen Witches, Wiccans, and 'Wanna-Blessed-Be's': Pop-Culture Magic in *Buffy the Vampire Slayer.*" *Slayage* 1 (Jan. 2001). Posted at http://www.whedonstudies.tv/.

5822. Woerner, Meredith. *Vampire Taxonomy: Identifying and Interacting with the Modern-day Bloodsucker.* New York: Perigee, 2009. 190 pp. tp.

5823. Wolf, Sappho. *The Hybrid Vampire Handbook.* [Philadelphia]: Vampgeist Press, 2008. 49 pp. pb. Staples.

5824. Wright, Susan Ashley. *The Discourse of Fan Fiction.* Louisville, KY: University of Louisville, Ph.D. dissertation, 2009. 209 pp. Large format.

5825. X, Madeline. *How to Become a Vampire in Six Easy Lessons.* Chicago: Adams Press, 1985. 12 pp. pb. Staples.

5826. Young, Tricia Henry. "Dancing on Bela Lugosi's Grave: The Politics and Aesthetics of Gothic Club Dancing." *Dance Research: The Journal of the Society for Dance Research* 17, 1 (Summer 1999): 75–97.

5827. Youngson, Jeanne Keyes, ed. *Private Files of a Vampirologist: Case Histories & Letters.* Chicago: Adams Press, 1997. 53 pp. pb.

Cookbooks and Cuisine

The emergence of the vampire has provided a context for widespread speculation based upon the real existence of vampires. Many have given thought to what vampires might consume, if they became bored with their rather limited diet of blood. This speculation on a vampire's possible cuisine has given rise to a variety of cookbooks which range from the very serious to the quite humorous.

Along with the cookbooks, a small number of "vampire restaurants" have appeared over the last generation.

5828. Alex, Alicia. *The Vampire Cookbook.* N.p.: the author, 2009. 48 pp. pb.

5829. Artenie, Cristina. "Dracula's Kitchen: A Glossary of Transylvanian Cuisine, Language, and Ethnography." In Barbara Brodman and James E. Doan, eds. *The Universal Vampire: Origins and Evolution of a Legend.* Madison, NJ: Fairleigh Dickinson University Press, 2013, pp. 45–57.

5830. Bacon, Simon. "Eat Me! The Morality of Hunger in Vampiric Cuisine." In Barbara Brodman and James E. Doan, eds. *Images of the Modern Vampire: The Hip and the Atavistic.* Madison. NJ: Fairleigh Dickinson, 2013, pp. 41–54.

5831. Barrows, Leah. *The Vampyre Cookbook.* Seattle, WA: PIRAAS, 2009. 64 pp. tp.

5832. Conway, Paula. *Throw a True Blood Party: An Unofficial Guide to Partying with Your Favorite Vamps.* Riverdale, NY: Riverdale Avenue Books, 2013. 272 pp. pb.

5833. Daily, Kilmore. *The Vampire Cookbook.* New York: Citadel Press, 1965, 64 pp. pb.

5834. *Garlic Dishes Even Dracula Would Love.* New York: Dracula Press, 2000. 19 pp. pb. Staples.

5835. Kelly, Michele Roy, and Andrea Norville. *Love at First Bite: The Complete Vampire Lover's Cookbook.* Avon, MA: Adams Media, 2010. 292 pp. tp.

5836. Malis, Jody Cameron, ed. *The Dark Shadows Cookbook.* New York: Ace, 1970. 180 pp. pb.

5837. Manderino, Tammy. *A Vampire Cooks: 40 Recipes to Sink Your Teeth Into.* N.p.: the author, 2012. 78 pp. tp.

5838. Meyers, Gina. *Bite at Twilight: Vampires, Forks, and Knives Cookbook.* Fresno, CA: Serendipity Press, 2009. 94 pp. pb. Large format.

5839. _____. *Love at First Bite in Color.* Fresno, CA: Serendipity Press, 2011. 65 pp. tp.

5840. _____. *Love at First Bite: The Unofficial Twilight Cookbook.* New York: iUniverse, 2010. 198 pp. tp.

5841. O'Claire, Alana. *Vampire Bites: Delicious Twilight-inspired recipes to sink your teeth into.* N.p.: Tebbo, 2010. 110 pp. tp.

5842. Polway, Marina. *The Dracula Cookbook.* New York: Chelsea House, 1978. 253 pp. hb. dj. Rpt.: New York: Gramercy Books, 2000. 253 pp. hb. dj.

5843. Price, Ardin C., and Trishna Leszczye. *The Dracula Cookbook of Blood.* Huntsville, AL: Mugwort Soup Publications, 1993. 149 pp. tp.

5844. St. Pierre, Todd-Michael. *Thinner You with a Vampire: New Orleans Irresistible Cuisine on a Diet!.* New Orleans, LA: Pontchartrain Press, 2011. 141 pp. tp.

5845. _____. *True Blood Cuisine: The Vampire Cookbook.* New Orleans, LA: Pontchartrain Press, 2011.

5846. Smith-Burton, C. W. [Cynthia Wright]. *The Vampire's Guide to Good Cooking.* Bloomington, IN: AuthorHouse, 2008. 100 pp. tp.

5847. Sobol, Gianna, Alan Ball, and Benjamin Hayes. *True Blood Drinks & Bites.* San Francisco, CA: Chronicle Books, 2013. 127 pp. hb. Boards.

5848. _____, **Alan Ball, with Karen Sommer Shalett and Marcelle Beinvenu.** *True Blood: Eats, Drinks, and Bites from Bon Temps.* San Francisco: Chronicle Books, 2012. 224 pp. hb. boards.

5849. *Twilight—Bella's Family Cookbook—Inspired by Twilight—Featuring Forks Vampire & Werewolf Cuisine.* N.p.: Concerned Citizens, 2009. Spiral bound.

5850. Youngson, Jeanne Keyes. *The Count Dracula Chicken Cookbook.* New York: Count Dracula Fan Club Limited Edition, 1970. 60 pp. pb.

IX. Juvenilia

Children's Books

Since the 1970s a variety of non-fiction books on vampire-related topics have been published for children and youth. Such books range from fact-oriented texts that attempt to interpret the findings of vampire and Dracula studies for a younger audience, to the myth-breaking literature on bats, to the host of fan material related to cinema and television stars of vampire movies and TV shows (most notably *Buffy, Twilight, and The Vampire Diaries*).

No attempt has been made to keep up with the vast fan material related to the numerous stars created by vampire movies and shows, especially in their post-vampire careers, nor to mine the popular newsstand fan magazines produced in response to the dedicated followers of the stars of *Buffy the Vampire Slayer, Angel*, and *Twilight*. Only a sampling of such fan publications appears below.

Also not included in this list are a large number of juvenile texts on monsters, Halloween, and horror, a large percentage of which deal with vampires but only in passing as one among many topics.

5851. Abdullah, Sarin. *Bookworm Mysteris*. Singapore: Bookworm Publishing House, 1993, pp. 67–71.

5852. _____. *Bookworm Mysteris 5*. Singapore: Bookworm Publishing House, 1996.

5853. Abele, Robert. *The Twilight Saga: The Complete Film Archive: Memories, Mementos, and Other Treasures from the Creative Team Behind the Beloved Motion Pictures*. Boston: Little, Brown Books for Young Readers, 2012.152 pp. hb. boards. Large format.

5854. Adams, Isabelle. *Robert Pattinson: Eternally Yours*. New York: HarperCollins, 2008. 192 pp. tp.

5855. Anderson, Marilyn D. *Sarah Michelle Gellar*. Ser.: Galaxy of Superstars. Philadelphia: Chelsea House Pub., 2001. 64 pp. hb. boards.

5856. Arneson, D. J. *Bats: A Nature-Fact Book*. Chicago: Kidsbooks, 1992. 28 pp. pb.

5857. Aylesworth, Thomas G. *Monsters of the Movies*. Philadelphia: J. P. Lippencott Company, 1972. 160 pp. pb.

5858. _____. *The Story of Vampires*. Middletown, CT: Weekly Reader Books, 1982. 85 pp. pb. Rpt.: Middletown CT: Xerox Education Publications, 1982. 85 pp. pb.

5859. _____. *Vampires and Other Ghosts*. Reading, MA: Addison-Wesley, 1972. 127 pp. hb. boards.

5860. Baumann, Elwood D. *Vampires*. New York: Franklin Watts, 1982. 87 pp. hb. dj.

5861. Bennett, Adelaide. *Ancient Werewolves and Vampires: The Roots of the Teeth*. Ser.: Making of a Monster: Vampires & Werewolves. Broomall, PA: Mason Crest Publishers, 2010. 63 pp. hb & pb.

5862. _____. *Global Legends & Lore: Vampires & Werewolves Around the World*. Ser.: Making of a Monster: Vampires & Werewolves. Broomall, PA: Mason Crest Publishers, 2010. 63 pp. hb. & pb.

5863. Bergin, Mark. *How to Draw Vampires, Zombies, and Other Monsters.* New York: Power-Kids Press/Rosen Publishing Group, 2012. 32 pp. hb. boards. Large format.

5864. Besel, Jennifer M. *Vampires.* North Mankato, MN: Capstone Press, 2006. 32 pp. hb.

5865. Bingham, Jane. *Vampires & Werewolves.* Ser.: Solving Mysteries with Science. Basingstoke, UK: Raintree, 2013. 48 pp. hb. & pb.

5866. Boris, Cynthia. *Buffy the Vampire Slayer Pop Quiz.* New York: Pocket Books, 1999. 160 pp. pb.

5867. Branzei, Sylvia. *History of Vampires and Other Real Blood Drinkers.* Illus. by Jack Keely. New York: Grosset & Dunlap, 2009. 48 pp. pb..

5868. Brett, Bernard, and Dorothy D. Ward. *Vampires.* London: Marshall Cavendish Children's, 1980. 128 pp. pb.

5869. Bringle, Jennifer. *Vampires in Film and Television.* New York: Rosen Central, 2011. 64 pp. pb.

5870. Carpenter, Amy. *The Taylor Lautner Album.* Medford, NJ: Plexus Publishing, 2009. 96 pp. pb.

5871. Cohen, Daniel. *Everything You Need to Know About Monsters and Still Be Able to Get to Sleep.* Garden City, NY: Doubleday & Company, 1981. 118 pp. hb. dj.

5872. _____. *Masters of Horror.* New York: Clarion Books, 1984. 119 pp. hb. dj.

5873. _____. *Real Vampires.* New York: Cobblehill Books/E. P. Dutton, 1995. 98 pp. hb. Rpt.: New York: Scholastic, 1995. 114 pp. pb.

5874. _____. *Supermonsters.* New York: Dodd Mead and Company, 1982. 128 pp. hb.

5875. Cohen, Robert Z. *Transylvania: Birthplace of Vampires.* New York: Rosen Central, 2011. 64 pp. hb. & pb.

5876. Cybulski, Angela, ed. *Vampires: Fact or Fiction?* Ser.: Opposing Viewpoints. Farmington Hills, MI: Greenhaven Press/Thomson, Gale, 2003. 175 pp. hb. boards. Includes material taken from the writings of John V. A. Fine, Jr., Manuela Dunn Mascetti, Montague Summers, Anthony Masters, Joe H. Slate, Daniel Farson, Paul Barber, J. Gordon Melton, Ernest Jones, Jill Burcum, R. E. Hemphill and T. Zabow, and Norine Dresser.

5877. Danby, Mary. *Madabout Monsters.* London: Piccolo Books, 1991. 96 pp. pb.

5878. Dreary, Terry. *True Monster Stories.* London: Hippo Books, 1992. 112 pp. pb.

5879. *The Essential Angel.* New York: Pocket Books, 1999. 36p. pb. Large format.

5880. Etingoff, Kim. *Howling at the Moon: Vampires & Werewolves in the New World.* Ser.: Making of a Monster: Vampires & Werewolves. Broomall, PA: Mason Crest Publishers, 2010. 63 pp. pb.

5881. _____. *The Science of the Beast: The Facts Behind the Fangs.* Ser.: Making of a Monster: Vampires & Werewolves. Broomall, PA: Mason Crest Publishers, 2010. 63 pp. pb.

5882. Farson, Daniel. *Vampires, Zombies and Monster Men.* Ser.: The Supernatural. London: Aldus, 1975. 144 pp. hb. Large format. Rpt. Ser.: New Library of the Supernatural. Garden City, NY: Doubleday & Company, 1981. 144 pp. pb. Rpt.: London: Danbury Books, 1975. 144 pp. Excerpt rpt. in: Angela Cybulski, ed. *Vampires: Fact or Fiction?* Ser.: Opposing Viewpoints. Farmington Hills, MI: Greenhaven Press/Thomson, Gale, 2003. pp. 91–100.

5883. Fishel, Emma. *How to Draw Ghost, Vampires & Haunted Houses.* Ed. by Janet Cook and Anita Ganeri. London: Usborne, 1988. 32 pp. pb. Illust. by Victor Ambus, Kim Blundell, Rob McCraig, Mike Pringle, and Graham Round. Rpt.: New York: Scholastic, 1988. 32 pp. pb.

5884. Furman, Elina, and Leah Furman. *Seth Green.* New York: St. Martin's Press, 2000. 152 pp. pb.

5885. Gabriel, Jan. *Meet the Stars of Buffy the Vampire Slayer.* New York: Scholastic, 1998. 165 pp. pb.

5886. Ganeri, Anita. *Vampires and the Undead.* Ser.: The Dark Side. Wayland/Hachette Children's Books, 2010. 32 pp. hb.

5887. Garden, Nancy. *Vampires.* Philadelphia: J. B. Lippencott Company, 1973. 127 pp. pb.

5888. Gee, Joshua. *Encyclopedia Horrifica: The Terrifying Truth! About Vampires, Ghosts, Monsters, and More.* New York: Scholastic, 2007. 138 pp. hb. boards.

5889. Gelman, Rita Golden, and Nancy Lamb. *Vampires and Other Creatures of the Night.* New York: Scholastic, Inc., 1991. 74 pp. pb.

5890. Goldberg, Enid, and Norman Itzkowitz. *Vlad the Impaler: The Real Count Dracula.*

New York: Franklin Watts, 2007. 128 pp. hb. boards.

5891. Gray, Susan Heinrichs. *Bats.* Chicago: Children's Press, 1994. 48 pp. pb.

5892. Gregorich, Barbara. *Vocabulary Vampire.* Santa Barbara, CA: Learning Works, 1982. 48 pp.

5893. Guiley, Rosemary Ellen. *Vampires.* Ser.: Mysteries, Legends, and Unexplained Phenomena. New York: Chelsea House Books, 2008. 126 pp. hb. Rpt.: New York: Checkmark Books, 2008. 126 pp. pb.

5894. Guillain, Charlotte. *Vampires.* Ser.: Mythical Creatures. Basingstoke, UK: Raintree, 2011. 32 pp. hb. & pb. Large format.

5895. Hamilton, John. *Vampires.* Ser.: World of Horror. Edina, MN: ABDO & Daughters, 2007. 32 pp. hb.

5896. Heos, Bridget. *Vampires in Literature.* New York: Rosen Central, 2012. 64 pp. hb. boards.

5897. Higgins, Sydney. *Vampires, Werewolves, Ghosts & UFOs.* Ser.: Fun Reads 5. Lexington, KY: the author, 2013. 98 pp. tp.

5898. Hinkley, James W. *The Book of Vampires.* New York: Franklin Watts, 1979. 48 pp. hb. boards. Illus. by Michael Deas.

5899. Hofer, Charles. *Meet Dracula.* New York: Rosen Publishing Group, 2005. 48 pp. hb. boards.

5900. Howden, Martin. *Blood Rivals: Vampire vs. Werewolf: Robert Pattinson and Taylor Lautner: The Biography.* John Blake, 2010. 263 pp. pb.

5901. _____. *Vampires v. Werewolves: Whose Side Are You On?* London: John Blake, 2010. 165 pp. Double book bound with *Werewolves v Vampires: Whose Side Are You On?* London: John Blake, 2010. 119 pp. pb.

5902. Hurley, Jo. *Kristen Stewart: Bella of the Ball!* New York: Scholastic, 2009. 192 pp. pb.

5903. Indovino, Saina C. *Dracula and Beyond: Famous Vampires & Werewolves in Literature and Film.* Ser.: Making of a Monster: Vampires & Werewolves. Broomall, PA: Mason Crest Publishers, 2010. 63 pp. pb.

5904. _____. *Transylvania and Beyond: Vampires & Werewolves in Old Europe.* Ser.: Making of a Monster: Vampires & Werewolves. Broomall, PA: Mason Crest Publishers, 2010. 63 pp. pb.

5905. Jeffrey, Gary. *Vampires.* Ser.: Graphic Mythical Creatures. New York: Gareth Stevens Publishing, 2012. 24 pp. hb.

5906. Jenkins, Martin. *Informania Vampires.* Cambridge, MA: Candlewick Press, 1998. 92 pp. hb. Rpt.: Cambridge, MA: Candlewick Press, 1998. 92 pp. tp.

5907. Johns, Michael-Anne. *Guys of Twilight.* New York: Scholastic Inc., 2009. 48 pp. pb. Large format.

5908. _____. *Sarah Michelle Gellar.* Kansas City, MO: Andrews McMeel Publishing, 1999. Unpaged. hb. dj. Small format.

5909. _____. *David Boreanaz.* Kansas City, MO: Andrews McMeel Publishing, 1999. Unpaged. hb. dj. Small format.

5910. Kallen, Stuart A. *Vampires.* San Diego, CA: Referencepoint Press, 2008. 108 pp. hb. boards.

5911. _____. *Vampires, Werewolves, and Zombies.* Edina MN: Abdo Pub. Co. 1991. 32 pp. hb.

5912. Kaplan, Arie. *Dracula: The Life of Vlad the Impaler.* New York: Rosen Central, 2011. 64 pp. pb.

5913. Kespert, Deborah. *Vampires.* Ser.: 3-D Chillers. London: Arcturus Publishing, 2011. 16 pp. pb. Large format.

5914. _____. *Vampires, Zombies, and Werewolves.* Ser.: 3-D Chillers. London: Scholastic Paperbacks, 2012. 48 pp. pb. Large format.

5915. Kidd, Katherine. *Experience Twilight: The Ultimate Twilight Fan Travel Guide.* N.p.: the author, 2009. 40 pp. tp. Illust. by Sabrina Kent.

5916. Knox, Barbara, and Stephen F. Brown. *Castle Dracula: Romania's Vampire Home.* Ser.: Castles, Palaces, and Tombs. New York: Bearport, 2005. 32 pp. hb. boards. Large format.

5917. Krensky, Stephen. *Vampires.* Ser. Monster Chronicles. Minneapolis, MN: Lerner Publications Company, 2007. 48 pp. hb. pb.

5918. Kudalis, Eric. *Dracula and Other Vampire Stories.* Minneapolis, MN: Capstone Press, 1994. 48 pp. hb. boards.

5919. Laslo, Cynthia. *Sarah Michelle Gellar.* Chicago: Children's Press, 2000. 48 pp. hb. & pb.

5920. MacDonald, Elizabeth. *Sarah Michelle Gellar.* London: Carlton Books, 2002. 48 pp. pb. Large format.

5921. Malam, John. *Vampires.* Ser.: Monster Mania. London: QED Publishing, 2011. 32 pp. pb.

5922. Maple, Eric. *Monsters.* London: Nutmeg Press, 1981. 32 pp. pb.

5923. Marcovitz, Hal. *Teens and the Supernatural and Paranormal.* Ser.: Gallup Youth Survey: Major Issues and Trends. Broomall PA: Mason Crest Publishers, 2005. 104 pp. hb. boards.

5924. Martin, Dawn. *Vampires.* Series: Hammond Undercover. Long Island City, NY: Hammond World Atlas, 2009. 72 pp. pb. Large format.

5925. Martin, Nicholas. *Fighting the Fangs: A Guide to Vampires and Werewolves.* Ser.: Making of a Monster: Vampires & Werewolves. Broomall, PA: Mason Crest Publishers, 2010. 63 pp. pb.

5926. _____, and Emily Sanna. *Pop Monsters: The Modern-Day Craze for Vampires and Werewolves.* Ser.: Making of a Monster: Vampires & Werewolves. Broomall, PA: Mason Crest Publishers, 2010. 63 pp. pb.

5927. Mason, Paul. *Sarah Michelle Gellar.* Ser.: Star Files. Oxford, UK: Raintree, 2005. 48 pp. hb. boards.

5928. McHargue, Georgess. *Meet the Vampire.* Philadelphia: J. B. Lippencott Company, 1981. 80 pp. hb. Rpt.: New York: Laurel Leaf Books, 1983. 106 pp. pb.

5929. McCracken, Kristine. *Seth Green.* Chicago: Children's Press, 2001. 48 pp. pb.

5930. McMeans, Bonnie. *Vampires.* Detroit, MI: KidHaven, 2006. 48 pp. hb. boards.

5931. Melvin, Matt. *Dracula Is a Racist: A Totally Factual Guide to Vampires.* New York: Rebel Base Books, 2010. 190 pp. tp.

5932. Merrick, Patrick. *Vampire Bats.* Chanhassen, MN: Child's World, 2001. 32 pp. hb.

5933. Miller, Raymond H. *Vampires.* Ser.: Monsters. KidHaven Press, 2004. 48 pp. hb.

5934. Moorey, Teresa. *Vampires: A Beginner's Guide.* London: Hodder & Stoughton, 2000. 84 pp. pb. Rev. ed. as: *Encounters with Vampires.* London: Hodder Education 1, 2011. 88 pp. pb.

5935. Myring, Lynn. *Vampires, Werewolves and Demons.* London: Usborne Publishing, 1979. 64 pp. pb. Rpt. Burlington, ON: Hayes Publishing, 1979. 64 pp. pb. Rpt. London: Usborne Publishing, 1990. 64 pp. pb.

5936. Newquist, Harvey P. *The Book of Blood: From Legends and Leeches to Vampires and Veins.* Boston: Houghton Mifflin Books for Children, 2012. 152 pp. hb. Large format.

5937. Nickson, Chris. *David Boreanaz.* New York: St. Martin's Paperbacks, 1999. 147 pp. pb.

5938. Nobleman, Marc Tyler. *Vampires.* London: Heinemann-Raintree, 2007. 32 pp. hb.

5939. Orme, David. *Vampires.* Winchester, Hampshire, UK: Ransom Publishing, 2009, 32 pp. hb. boards.

5940. Orr, Tamra. *Kristen Stewart.* Ser.: Blue Banner Biographies. Mitchell Lane Publishers, 2009. 32 pp. hb.

5941. Otfinoski, Steven. *Bram Stoker: The Man Who Wrote Dracula.* Ser. Great Life Stories. New York: Franklin Watts/Scholastic, 2005. 112 pp. hb.

5942. Oxlade, Chris. *The Mystery of Vampires and Werewolves.* Ser. Can Science Solve...? London: Heinemann Library, 2002. 32 pp. pb. Large format.

5943. Pan, Michelle, and the fans at Bella AndEdward.com. *Bella Should Have Dumped Edward: Controversial Views & Debates on the Twilight Series.* Berkeley, CA: Ulysses Press, 2010. 199 pp. tp.

5944. Parker, Evie. *100% the Vampire Diaries: The Unofficial Guide.* New York: Bantam, 2010. 62 pp. pb.

5945. Perry, Jan. *Vampires.* New York: Gareth Stevens Publishing, 1999. 24 pp. hb.

5946. Pipe, Jim. *In the Footsteps of Dracula.* Brookfield, CT: Copper Beach Books, 1995. 40 pp. pb.

5947. Poole, Jamie. *Vampires in Our Midst: A Look at Vampires in Our Culture.* London: Janus Publishing Company, 2006. 85 pp. pb.

5948. Powell, Phelan, and Rose Mary Powell. *Sarah Michelle Gellar.* Ser.: Real Life Reader Biographies: Young Entertainers. Bear, DE: Mitchell Lane Publishers, 2000. 32 pp. hb.

5949. Regan, Lisa. *Bloodsucking Beasts.* Ser.: Monsters & Myths. New York: Gareth Stevens Publishing, 2011. 48 pp. pb.

5950. _____. *Vampires, Werewolves & Zombies.* New York: Tangerine Press/Scholastic, 2010. 96 pp. pb.

5951. Regan, Sally. *The Vampire Book.* London: Dorling Kindersley, 2009. 128 pp. pb. Large format.

5952. Reisfeld, Randi. *Sarah Michelle Gellar: She Is the Slayer.* New York: Scholastic, 1998. 128 pp. tp.

5953. Rickman, Amy. *Blood Brothers: The Biography of the Vampire Diaries Paul Wesley.* London: John Blake, 2011. 109 pp. tp. Bound with *The Biography of the Vampire Diaries Ian Somerhalder.* 119 pp. tp.

5954. _____. *Vampire Files: Heartthrobs and Bloodsuckers.* London: John Blake, 2011. 62 pp. hb. boards.

5955. Roberts, Russell. *Vampires.* Ser.: The Mystery Library. San Diego, CA: Lucent Books, 2001. 96 pp. hb. boards.

5956. Ronan, Margaret. *The Dynamite Monster Hall of Fame.* New York: Scholastic Book Services, 1983. 83 pp. pb.

5957. _____. *House of Evil and Other Strange Unsolved Mysteries.* New York: Scholastic Book Services, 1982. 156 pp. pb. Includes chapter on the Vampire of Croglin Grange.

5958. _____, **and Eve Ronan.** *Curse of the Vampires.* New York: Scholastic Book Services. 1979. 89 pp. pb.

5959. Robshaw, Brandon. *Vampires.* Ser.: Lifewire investigates. London: Hodder, 2006. 32 pp. pb. Large format.

5960. Rotruck, A. R. *How to Trap a Zombie, Track a Vampire, and Other Hands-On Activities for Monster Hunters: A Young Wizards Handbook.* Renton, WA: Mirrorstone/Wizards of the Coast, 2010. 80 pp. hb.

5961. Rusher, Josie. *Robert Pattinson Annual 2010: Beyond Twilight.* London: Orion, 2009. 64 pp. hb. Large format.

5962. _____. *Robert Pattinson: True Love Never Dies.* London: Orion, 2009. 64 pp. hb.

5963. _____. *Kristen Stewart: Infinite Romance: Star of the Blockbuster Films Twilight and New Moon.* London: Orion, 2009. 64 pp. hb.

5964. _____. *Taylor Lautner: Me & You: The Star of Twilight and New Moon.* London Orion, 2009. 64 pp. hb.

5965. Ryals, Lexi. *Taylor Lautner: An Unauthorized Biography.* Ser.: Get the Scoop. New York: Price Stern Sloan, 2009. 127 pp. pb.

5966. Sanford, William, and Karl Green. *Dracula's Daughter.* Mankato, MN: Crestwood, 1985. 48 pp. hb.

5967. Sansevere, John R., and Erica Farber. *Go Fango: How to Be a Vampire.* Racine, WI: Wave Book/Western Publishing Company, 1993. 32 pp. hb.

5968. Scavone, Daniel C. *Vampires.* Ser.: Opposing Viewpoints. San Diego, CA: Greenhaven Press, 1990. 80 pp. hb. boards.

5969. Shore, Amy. *A Guide for Using Bunnicula in the Classroom.* Westminster, CA: Teacher Created Materials, 1995. 48 pp. pb. Large format.

5970/71. Smith, Donna. *Vampires.* New York: Scholastic, 1993. 44 pp. Mini-book.

5972. Steele, Philip. *Vampire Bats and Other Creatures of the Night.* Ser.: Young Observer. New York: Kingfisher, 1995. 40 pp. pb. Large format.

5973. Stenning, Paul. *The Robert Pattinson Album.* Plexus Publishing, 2009. 96 pp. pb.

5974. Stewart, Sheila. *The Psychology of Our Dark Side: Humans' Love Affair with Vampires & Werewolves.* Ser.: Making of a Monster: Vampires & Werewolves. Broomall, PA: Mason Crest Publishers, 2010. 63 pp. pb.

5975. Streissguth, Tom. *Legends of Dracula.* Minneapolis: Lerner Publications Company, 1999. 128 pp. hb. boards.

5976. Thorne, Ian. *Dracula.* Mankato, MN: Crestwood, 1982. 47 pp. pb.

5977. Verdick, Mary, ed. *The Blood Suckers and Other True Animal Stories.* Middletown, CT: Xerox Education Corporation, 1981. 96 pp. pb.

5978. *Vlad the Impaler: The Real Dracula.* Minneapolis, MN: Filiquarian Publishing/ Biographiq, 2008. 52 pp. pb.

5979. Vorgard, Treval [pseudonym of Lisa Trutkoff Trumbauer], comp. *A Practical Guide to Vampires.* Renton, WA: Mirrorstone/Wizards of the Coast, 2009. 83 pp. hb. boards. Large format.

5980. Ward, Dorothy *see* Brett, Bernard and Dorothy Ward.

5981. Welch, R. C. *Vampire Almanac.* New York: Random House, 1995. 64 pp. pb.

5982. Williams, Mel. *Robert Pattinson: Fated for Fame.* New York: Simon Pulse, 2009. 48 pp. pb.

5983. _____. *Taylor Lautner: Overnight Sizzlin' Sensation.* New York: Simon Pulse, 2009. 48 pp. pb.

5984. Wilson, Lionel. *The Mystery of Dracula: Fact or Fiction.* New York: Contemporary Perspectives, 1979. 48 pp. hb.

5985. Wolf, Leonard. *Monsters: Twenty Terrible and Wonderful Beasts from the Classic Dragon and Colossal Minotaur to King Kong and the Great Godzilla.* San Francisco, CA: Straight Arrow, 1974. 127 pp. pb.

5986. Woog, Adam. *Vampires in the Movies.* San Diego, CA: ReferencePoint Press, 2010. 80 pp. hb. boards.

Pseudo-Documentaries

Existing in the space between fiction and non-fiction writing is a relatively new set of books that assume the reality of vampires and offer to guide the reader on how to find them and either dispose of the hated blood (energy) sucker or, more positively, develop a permanent, even loving, relationship with the presumably sexy creature. These works of fiction, which largely have grown out of the 1970s' rise of the "good guy" vampire, give the superficial appearance of a non-fiction book, but in fact invite the reader (usually a teenager) into a fantasy world in which vampires exist. While most of these volumes aim at a teenage audience, some of the more interesting examples are the several oversize volumes directed at pre-teen children.

These books grade into the non-fictional psychological literature that posits the existence of strong emotional relationships characterized by power imbalances and uses vampirism as a metaphor to describe the harm that most often results from such imbalance. The boundary between such psychological literature and the pseudo-documentaries is often blurred due to their similar titles and misplacement on bookstore shelves.

5987. Amin, Ibrahim. *The Monster Hunter's Handbook: The Ultimate Guide to Saving Mankind from Vampires, Zombies, Hellhounds, and Other Mythical Beasts.* New York: Bloomsbury USA, 2007. 212 pp. hb.

5988. Ballion, Luc Richard, and Scott Bowen. *Vampire Seduction Handbook: Have the Most Thrilling Love of Your Life.* New York: Skyhorse Publishing, 2009. 243 pp. tp.

5989. Barrial, Elizabeth, and D. H. Altair. *Vampires Don't Sleep Alone: Your Guide to Meeting, Dating, and Seducing a Vampire.* Berkeley, CA: Ulysses Press, 2010. 224 pp. tp.

5990. Bowen, Scott. *The Vampire Survival Guide: How to Fight, and Win, Against the Undead.* New York: Skyhorse Publishing, 2008. 250 pp. hb. boards.

5991. Brookes, Arthur. *Vampireology: The True History of the Fallen Ones.* Somerville, MA: Candlewick Press, 2010. 28 pp. hb. Large format.

5992. Collins, Sophie. *How to Date a Vampire.* London: Spruce/Octopus Publishing Company, 2009. 128 pp. hb.

5993. Dimes, John. *The White Corpse Hustle: A Guide for the Fledgling Vampire.* Baltimore, MD: PublishAmerica, 2004. 85 pp. tp.

5994. Fantaskey, Beth. *Jessica's Guide to Dating on the Dark Side.* New York: Houghton, Miffin, Harcourt Publishing Company, 2009. 354 pp. hb. dj.

5995. Glenday, Craig. *The Vampire Watcher's Handbook: A Guide for Slayers.* New York: St. Martin's Griffin, 2003. 160 pp. hb.

5996. Grey, Amy. *Fangs: Everything the Modern Vampire Needs to Know.* San Francisco: Weldon Owen, 2012. 144 pp. pb.

5997. _____. *How to Be a Vampire.* Sommerville, MA: Candlewick Press, 2009. 144 pp. hb. boards.

5998. Jefferson, Darnell. *Vampire 101: The Complete Guide to Becoming a Vampire.* Parker, CO: Outskirts Press, 2010. 176 pp. tp.

5999. Karg, Barb. *The Girl's Guide to Vampires: All You Need to Know About the Original Bad Boys.* Avon, MA: Adams Media, 2009. 180 pp. pb.

6000. Knight, Mary Jane. *Vampyre: The Terrifying Found Journal of Dr. Cornelius Van Helsing and Gustav de Wolff, His Trusted Companion.* New York: Harper Collins Children's Books, 2007. 30 pp. hb. Large format.

6001. Kupfer, Allen C. *The Journal of Prof. Abraham Van Helsing.* New York: Forge Books, 2004. 208 pp. hb.

6002. Lafont, Evel. *The Vampire Relationship Guide. Vol. One: Meeting & Mating.* 4. Vols. Seattle, WA: the author, 2011. tp.

6003. Laurence, Diana. *How to Catch and Keep a Vampire: A Step by Step Guide to Loving the Bad and the Beautiful.* [Portland, ME]: Sellers Publishers, [2009]. 160 pp. tp.

6004. Ma, Roger. *The Vampire Combat Manual: A Guide to Fighting the Bloodthirsty Undead.* New York: Berkley Trade, 2012. 301 pp. tp.

6005. Mezrich, Vlad. *The Vampire Is Just Not That Much into You.* Scholastic: New York, 2009. 181 pp. pb.

6006. Olson, Kiki. *How to Get a Date with a Vampire (And What to Do with Him Once You've Got Him).* Chicago: Contemporary Books, 1992. 120 pp. tp.

6007. Pemberton Smythe, Julius. *Vampires and Other Monstrous Creatures: As Carried by the Famous Dr. Cornelius Van Helsing on His Fateful Journey to Transylvania.* London: HarperCollins Children's Book, 2007. 80 pp. hb. boards.

6008. Penke, Stephen Mark. *The Vampire Survival Bible—Identifying, Avoiding, Repelling, and Destroying the Undead.* Vol. 1. lulu.com, 2012. 421 pp. pb.

6009. Proctor, Miles, ed. *The New Vampire's Handbook: A Guide for the Recently Turned Creature of the Night.* Villard Trade Paperbacks: New York, 2009. 216 pp. tp.

6010. Raven, Ovelia. *The Truth About Vampires—"How to" Vampire Guide. The Facts You Should Know.* N.p.: Emereo Pty Ltd., 2009. 320 pp. tp.

6011. Rotruck, A. R. *Young Wizards Handbook: How to Trap a Zombie, Track a Vampire, and Other Hands-On Activities for Monster Hunters: A Young Wizards Handbook.* Renton, WA: Mirrorstone/Wizards of the Coast, 2010. 79 pp. hb.

6012. Schwalb, Suzanne, and Margaret Rubiano. *Vampires/Werewolves/Zombies: Compendium Monstrum: From the Pages of Herr Doktor Max Sturm & Baron Ludwig Von Drang.* White Plains, NY: Peter Pauper Press, 2010. 167 pp. hb.

6013. Slonaker, Eric. *The Vampire Hunter's Handbook.* New York: Price Stern Sloan, 2001. 87 pp. pb.

6014. _____. *The Vampire Hunter's Handbook: A Field Guide to the Paranormal.* London: Penguin Books, 2001. 87 pp. pb.

6015. Sobol, Gianna. *Steve Newlin's Field Guide to Vampires: (And Other Creatures of Satan).* San Francisco, CA: Chronicle Books, 2013. 144 pp. hb. boards. A survey of the supernatural creatures (vampires and werewolves) in the *True Blood* universe written as if a dossier compiled by the leader of the anti-vampire Fellowship of the Sun.

6016. Van Helsing, Raphael [pseudonym of Martin Howard]. *The Vampire Hunter's Handbook.* London: Pavilion Books, 2007. 32p. hb. Large format. Rpt. New York: Barnes & Noble, 2007. 32 pp. hb. Large format.

6017. Woerner, Meredith. *Vampire Taxonomy: Identifying and Interacting with the Modern-day Bloodsucker.* New York: Perigee, 2009. 190 pp. tp.

6018. Zaravinos, Demitrios. *The Modern Day Vampire Hunter's Guidebook of D. Zaravinos.* N.p.: the author, 2010. 190 pp. tp.

Appendix A:
Top Grossing Vampire Movies

1. *The Twilight Saga: Eclipse* (2010)	$301,000,000
2. *The Twilight Saga: New Moon* (2009)	$297,000,000
3. *The Twilight Saga: Breaking Dawn Part 2* (2012)	$292,000,000
4. *The Twilight Saga: Breaking Dawn Part 1* (2011)	$281,000,000
5. *I Am Legend* (2007)	$256,000,000
6. *Twilight* (2008)	$193,000,000
7. *Hotel Transylvania* (2012)	$148,000,000
8. *Van Helsing* (2004)	$120,000,000
9. *Interview with the Vampire* (1994)	$105,000,000
10. *Bram Stoker's Dracula* (1992)	$83,000,000
11. *Blade II* (2002)	$82,000,000
12. *Dark Shadows* (2012)	$80,000,000
13. *Blade* (1998)	$70,000,000
14. *Underworld Awakening* (2012)	$62,000,000
15. *Underworld: Evolution* (2006)	$62,000,000
16. *Dracula Untold* (2014)	$56,000,000
17. *Blade: Trinity* (2004)	$52,000,000
18. *Underworld* (2013)	$52,000,000
19. *Underworld: Rise of the Lycans* (2009)	$46,000,000
20. *Love at First Bite* (1979)	$44,000,000
21. *30 Days of Night* (2007)	$40,000,000
22. *Abraham Lincoln: Vampire Hunter* (2012)	$38,000,000
23. *Vampires Suck* (2010)	$37,000,000
24. *Dracula 2000* (2000)	$33,000,000
25. *The Lost Boys* (1987)	$32,000,000

Note: Dollars rounded off to nearest million in total gross as of January 1, 2015.

Appendix B:
Vampire Series on Television

Year	USA/Canada	Europe	Japan/Hong Kong
1960			
	The Munsters (1964–1966)		
1965			
	Dark Shadows[1] (1967–71)		
	Wacky Races (1968–70)		
1970			
	The Hilarious House of Frightenstein (1971–1997)[2]		
	Sesame Street[2] (1972–present)		
1975			
	Monster Squad (1976)		
	Quacula (1979–80)		
1980	Drack Pack (1980)		
1985		The Little Vampire (1985)	
		Ernest Le Vampire (1988–89)	
		Count Duckula (1988–93)	
1990	Groovie Goolies (1990)		
	Dracula: The Series (1990)		
	Gravedale High (1990–91)		
	Little Dracula (1991)		
	Forever Knight (1992–95)		
1995	DarkStalkers (1995)		Vampire Expert (1995–96)
	Kindred: The Embraced (1996)		
	Van-Pires (1997)		
	Buffy the Vampire Slayer (1997–2003)		Master of Mosquiton the Vampire (1997–98)
	The Hunger: Vampires (1997)		The Vampire Princess Miyu (1997–98)
		Ultraviolet (1998)	My Date with a Vampire (1998)
	Angel (1999–2004)		
	Little Dracula (rerun, 1999)		
	Mona the Vampire (1999–2003)		
2000		Monster Mash (2000)	NightWalker (2000)
	The Baskervilles (2000–01)		
	Vampire High (2001–02)		My Date with a Vampire II (2001)
			Descendants of Darkness (2001)
	Greg the Bunny (USA 2002)		Hellsing (2002)
			Vampire Syndrome: Hatu (2002)
			Vampiyan Kids (2002–03)
	My Date with a Vampire III (2003)		
		Petit Vampire (2004, France)	Lunar Legend Tsukihime (2003)

(Year)	(USA/Canada)	(Europe)	(Japan/Hong Kong)
			Bloodhound: Vampire Gigilo (2004)
			Vampire Host (Japan 2004)
			Moon Phase (2004–05)
2005			*Karin* (Japan 2005)
			Trinity Blood (Japan 2005)
			Blood+ (2005–06)
	Blade (2006)	*Young Dracula* (2006)	
			Nigema!? (2006–07)
			Black Blood Brothers (2006–08)
	Blood Ties (2007)	*The Last Van Helsing* (UK 2008)	
	The Lair (2007–08)		
	Moonlight (2007–08)		
	True Blood (2008–14)	*Being Human* (UK 2008–2013)	*Rosario + Vampire* (2008)
	Sanctuary (2008–11)		*Vampire Knight* (2008)
	The Vampire Dairies (2009–)		
	Valemont (2009)		
2010	*The Gates* (2010)		*Dance in the Vampire Bund* (2010)
	Lost Girl (2010–)		
	Being Human (2011–2014)		*Blood-C* (2011)
	The Originals (2013–)		*Blade* (2011)
	Dracula (2013)		
	Hemlock Grove (2013)		
	From Dusk to Dawn (2014–)		
	The Strain (2014–)		

Notes

1. *Dark Shadows* began airing in 1966 but did not add Barnabas Collins, its initial and main vampire character until 1967.

2. *Sesame Street* debuted in 1969 but added its famous vampire character Count von Count during the 1972-73 season.

Appendix C:
Buffy the Vampire Slayer
Conferences (2002–2014)

Blood, Text and Fears: Reading Around *Buffy the Vampire Slayer*, University of East Anglia, October 19–20, 2002.

The Buffyverse: A Symposium on *Buffy the Vampire Slayer*, University of Melbourne, Melbourne, Australia, 21 November 2002.

Staking a Claim: Exploring the Global Reach of *Buffy*, University of South Australia, Adelaide, Australia, 22 July 2003.

Spectacle, Rhythm, and Eschatology, University of Melbourne, Adelaide, Australia, July 24, 2003.

Greeks and Romans in the Buffyverse: Classical Threads in Fantasy and Science Fiction on Contemporary Television, Open University, Milton Keynes, UK, January 7–8, 2004.

Slayage Conference on *Buffy the Vampire Slayer*, Nashville, TN, May 27–30, 2004.

Bring Your Own Subtext: Social Life, Human Experience and the Works of Joss Whedon, Conference, University of Huddersfield, Huddersfield, UK, 29 June 29–July 1, 2005.

SC2: The Slayage Conference on the Whedonverses, Gordon College, Barnesville, GA, May 25–28, 2006.

It's the End of the World...Again: Why Buffy Still Matters: A *Buffy the Vampire Slayer* Mini-Conference," University of North Carolina, Greensboro, NC, March 16, 2007.

Buffy Hereafter: From the Whedonverse to the Whedonesque, Istanbul, Turkey, October 17–19, 2007.

SC3: the Slayage Conference on the Whedonverses, Henderson State College, Arkadelphia, AR, June 5–8, 2008.

Buffy Tueuse de Vampires, Cité Internationale Universitaire de Paris, Paris, France, June 26, 2009.

SC4: the Slayage Conference on the Whedonverses, Flagler College, St. Augustine, FL, June 3–6, 2010.

SCW5: the Slayage Conference on the Whedonverses, University of British Columbia, Vancouver, British Columbia, July 12–15, 2012.

Much Ado About Whedon. The 6th Biennial *Slayage* Conference on the Whedonverses, California State University-Sacramento, 19–22 June 19–22, 2014.

Conferences Focused More Generally on Vampires

Dracula '97, Los Angeles August 1997.

Vampires: Myths and Metaphors of Enduring Evil, Budapest, Hungary, May 22–24, 2003.

Open Graves, Open Minds: Vampires and the Undead in Modern Culture, University of Hertfordshire, Hatfield, UK, April 16–17, 2010.

Vegetarians, VILFs and Fang-Bangers: Modern Vampire Romance in Print and On Screen, De Montfort University, Leicester, UK, November 24, 2010.

Index

References are to entry numbers

www.ingramcontent.com/pod-product-compliance
Lightning Source LLC
Chambersburg PA
CBHW080547270326
41929CB00019B/3227